THE CAMBRIDGE HISTORY OF ENGLISH LITERATURE

VOLUME XV

GENERAL INDEX

CAMBRIDGE
AT THE UNIVERSITY PRESS
1953

PUBLISHED BY
THE SYNDICS OF THE CAMBRIDGE UNIVERSITY PRESS

London Office: Bentley House, N.W. 1
American Branch: New York
Agents for Canada, India, and Pakistan: Macmillan

First edition	1927
Cheap edition	1932
Reprinted	1934
”	1953

First printed in Great Britain at the University Press, Cambridge
Reprinted by Blackie & Son, Ltd, Glasgow

PREFATORY NOTE

The Cambridge History of English Literature was first published between the years 1907 and 1916. The General Index Volume was issued in 1927.

In the preface to Volume I the general editors explained their intentions. They proposed to give a connected account of the successive movements of English literature, to describe the work of writers both of primary and of secondary importance, and to discuss the interaction between English and foreign literatures. They included certain allied subjects such as oratory, scholarship, journalism and typography, and they did not neglect the literature of America and the British Dominions. The History was to unfold itself, "unfettered by any preconceived notions of artificial eras or controlling dates," and its judgments were not to be regarded as final.

This reprint of the text and general index of the *History* is issued in the hope that its low price may make it easily available to a wider circle of students and other readers who wish to have on their shelves the full story of English literature.

Entries in the General Index to pages beyond the following are references to the Bibliographies of the original edition, which are not included in the present reprint of the text:

Volume	I	*page* 418
,,	II	429
,,	III	465
,,	IV	434
,,	V	380
,,	VI	409
,,	VII	397
,,	VIII	390
,,	IX	414
,,	X	410
,,	XI	387
,,	XII	371
,,	XIII	463
,,	XIV	463

CAMBRIDGE
1932

PREFATORY NOTE

The *Cambridge History of English Literature* was first published between the years 1907 and 1916. The General Index Volume was issued in 1927.

In the preface to Volume I the general editors explained their intentions. They proposed to give a connected account of the successive movements of English literature, to describe the work of writers both of primary and of secondary importance, and to discuss the interaction between English and foreign literatures. They included certain allied subjects such as oratory, scholarship, journalism and typography, and they did not neglect the literature of America and the British Dominions. The History was to unfold itself 'unfettered by any preconceived notions of artificial eras or controlling dates', and its judgments were not to be regarded as final.

This reprint of the text and general index of the *History* is issued in the hope that its low price may make it easily available to a wider circle of students and other readers who wish to have on their shelves the full story of English literature.

Entries in the General Index to pages beyond the following are references to the Bibliographies of the original edition, which are not included in the present reprint of the text.

Volume	Page
I	[illegible]
II	[illegible]
III	[illegible]
IV	[illegible]
V	[illegible]
VI	[illegible]
VII	397
VIII	[illegible]
IX	[illegible]
X	[illegible]
XI	[illegible]
XII	[illegible]
XIII	[illegible]
XIV	[illegible]

[illegible]

CONTENTS

Prefatory note . . . . *page* v

A List of Contents of the *Cambridge History of English Literature* ix

General Index 1

A LIST OF CONTENTS

OF THE

CAMBRIDGE HISTORY OF ENGLISH LITERATURE

VOLUME I

Chap. 1	The Beginnings	A. R. Waller
2	Runes and MSS.	Miss A. C. Paues
3	Early National Poetry	H. M. Chadwick
4	Old English Christian Poetry	Miss M. Bentinck Smith
5	Latin Writings in England to the Time of Alfred	M. R. James
6	Alfred and the Old English Prose of his Reign	P. G. Thomas
7	From Alfred to the Conquest	J. S. Westlake
8	The Norman Conquest	A. R. Waller
9	Latin Chroniclers from the Eleventh to the Thirteenth Centuries	W. Lewis Jones
10	English Scholars of Paris and Franciscans of Oxford	Sir J. E. Sandys
11	Early Transition English	J. W. H. Atkins
12	The Arthurian Legend	W. Lewis Jones
13	Metrical Romances, 1200–1500. I	W. P. Ker
14	Metrical Romances, 1200–1500. II	J. W. H. Atkins
15	Pearl, Cleanness, Patience and Sir Gawayne	Sir I. Gollancz
16	Later Transition English: I. Legendaries and Chroniclers	Miss C. L. Thomson
17	Later Transition English: II. Secular Lyrics. Tales. Social Satire	A. R. Waller
18	The Prosody of Old and Middle English	G. Saintsbury
19	Changes in the Language to the Days of Chaucer	Henry Bradley
20	The Anglo-French Law Language	F. W. Maitland

VOLUME II

Chap. 1	Piers the Plowman and its Sequence	J. M. Manly
2	Religious Movements in the Fourteenth Century	J. P. Whitney
3	The Beginnings of English Prose	Miss A. D. Greenwood
4	The Scottish Language	G. Gregory Smith
5	The Earliest Scottish Literature	P. Giles
6	John Gower	G. C. Macaulay
7	Chaucer	G. Saintsbury
8	The English Chaucerians	G. Saintsbury
9	Stephen Hawes	W. Murison

10	The Scottish Chaucerians	G. Gregory Smith
11	The Middle Scots Anthologies: Anonymous Verse and Early Prose	G. Gregory Smith
12	English Prose in the Fifteenth Century: I. Pecock. Fortescue. The Paston Letters	Miss A. D. Greenwood
13	The Introduction of Printing into England and the Early Work of the Press	E. Gordon Duff
14	English Prose in the Fifteenth Century: II. Caxton. Malory. Berners	Miss A. D. Greenwood
15	English and Scottish Education. Universities and Public Schools to the Time of Colet	T. A. Walker
16	Transition English Song Collections	F. M. Padelford
17	Ballads	F. B. Gummere
18	Political and Religious Verse to the Close of the Fifteenth Century—Final Words	A. R. Waller

VOLUME III

Chap. 1	Englishmen and the Classical Renascence	T. M. Lindsay
2	Reformation Literature in England	J. P. Whitney
3	The Dissolution of the Religious Houses	R. H. Benson
4	Barclay and Skelton	A. Koelbing
5	Progress of Social Literature in Tudor Times	H. V. Routh
6	Sir David Lyndsay and the Later Scottish 'Makaris'	T F. Henderson
7	Reformation and Renascence in Scotland	P. Hume Brown
8	The New English Poetry	H. H. Child
9	A Mirror for Magistrates	J. W. Cunliffe
10	George Gascoigne	J. W. Cunliffe
11	The Poetry of Spenser	W. J. Courthope
12	The Elizabethan Sonnet	Sir Sidney Lee
13	Prosody from Chaucer to Spenser	G. Saintsbury
14	Elizabethan Criticism	G. Saintsbury
15	Chroniclers and Antiquaries	C. Whibley
16	Elizabethan Prose Fiction	J. W. H. Atkins
17	The Marprelate Controversy	J. Dover Wilson
18	Of the Laws of Ecclesiastical Polity	F. J. Foakes-Jackson
19	English Universities, Schools and Scholarship in the Sixteenth Century	W. H. Woodward
20	The Language from Chaucer to Shakespeare	J. W. H. Atkins

VOLUME IV

Chap. 1	Translators	C. Whibley
2	The Authorised Version and its Influence	A. S. Cook
3	Sir Walter Ralegh	Mrs L. Creighton
4	The Literature of the Sea	C. N. Robinson

5 Seafaring and Travel — C. N. Robinson
6 The Song-Books and Miscellanies — H. H. Child
7 Robert Southwell. Samuel Daniel — H. H. Child
8 Thomas Campion — S. P. Vivian
9 The Successors of Spenser — H. de Sélincourt
10 Michael Drayton — H. H. Child
11 John Donne — H. J. C. Grierson
12 The English Pulpit from Fisher to Donne — F. E. Hutchinson
13 Robert Burton, John Barclay and John Owen — E. Bensly
14 The Beginnings of English Philosophy — W. R. Sorley
15 Early Writings on Politics and Economics — W. Cunningham
16 London and the Development of Popular Literature — H. V. Routh
17 Writers on Country Pursuits and Pastimes — H. G. Aldis
18 The Book-Trade, 1557–1625 — H. G. Aldis
19 The Foundation of Libraries — J. B. Mullinger

VOLUME V

Chap. 1 The Origins of English Drama — Sir A. W. Ward
2 Secular Influences on the Early English Drama — H. H. Child
3 The Early Religious Drama — W. Creizenach
4 Early English Tragedy — J. W. Cunliffe
5 Early English Comedy — F. S. Boas
6 The Plays of the University Wits — G. P. Baker
7 Marlowe and Kyd — G. Gregory Smith
8 Shakespeare: Life and Plays — G. Saintsbury
9 Shakespeare: Poems — G. Saintsbury
10 Plays of Uncertain Authorship attributed to Shakespeare — F. W. Moorman
11 The Text of Shakespeare — E. Walder
12 Shakespeare on the Continent — J. G. Robertson
13 Lesser Elizabethan Dramatists — Ronald Bayne
14 Some Political and Social Aspects of the Later Elizabethan and Earlier Stewart Period — Sir A. W. Ward

VOLUME VI

Chap. 1 Ben Jonson — A. H. Thorndike
2 Chapman. Marston. Dekker — W. Macneile Dixon
3 Middleton and Rowley — Arthur Symons
4 Thomas Heywood — Sir A. W. Ward
5 Beaumont and Fletcher — G. C. Macaulay
6 Philip Massinger — Emil Koeppel
7 Tourneur and Webster — C. E. Vaughan
8 Ford and Shirley — W. A. Neilson
9 Lesser Jacobean and Caroline Dramatists — Ronald Bayne

10 The Elizabethan Theatre — H. H. Child
11 The Children of the Chapel Royal and their Masters — J. M. Manly
12 University Plays — F. S. Boas
13 Masque and Pastoral — Ronald Bayne
14 The Puritan Attack upon the Stage — J. Dover Wilson

VOLUME VII

Chap. 1 Cavalier Lyrists — F. W. Moorman
2 The Sacred Poets — F. E. Hutchinson
3 Writers of the Couplet — A. H. Thompson
4 Lesser Caroline Poets — G. Saintsbury
5 Milton — G. Saintsbury
6 Caroline Divines — W. H. Hutton
7 John Bunyan. Andrew Marvell — John Brown
8 Historical and Political Writings: I. State Papers and Letters — Sir A. W. Ward
9 Historical and Political Writings: II. Histories and Memoirs — Sir A. W. Ward
10 Antiquaries — G. Saintsbury
11 Jacobean and Caroline Criticism — J. E. Spingarn
12 Hobbes and Contemporary Philosophy — W. R. Sorley
13 Scholars and Scholarship, 1600–1660 — Foster Watson
14 English Grammar Schools — J. B. Mullinger
15 Beginnings of English Journalism — J. B. Williams
16 The Advent of Modern Thought in Popular Literature — H. V. Routh

VOLUME VIII

Chap. 1 Dryden — Sir A. W. Ward
2 Samuel Butler — W. F. Smith
3 Political and Ecclesiastical Satire — C. W. Previté-Orton
4 The Early Quakers — Edward Grubb
5 The Restoration Drama. I — F. E. Schelling
6 The Restoration Drama. II — C. Whibley
7 The Restoration Drama. III — A. T. Bartholomew
8 The Court Poets — C. Whibley
9 The Prosody of the Seventeenth Century — G. Saintsbury
10 Memoir and Letter Writers. I and II *a* — H. B. Wheatley
Memoir and Letter Writers. II *b* — Sir A. W. Ward
11 Platonists and Latitudinarians — J. B. Mullinger
12 Divines of the Church of England, 1600–1700 — W. H. Hutton
13 Legal Literature. I — F. J. C. Hearnshaw
Legal Literature. II — Sir A. W. Ward
14 John Locke — W. R. Sorley
15 The Progress of Science — Sir A. E. Shipley
16 The Essay and the Beginning of Modern English Prose — A. A. Tilley

VOLUME IX

Chap. 1	Defoe—The Newspaper and the Novel	W. P. Trent
2	Steele and Addison	H. V. Routh
3	Pope	E. Bensly
4	Swift	G. A. Aitken
5	Arbuthnot and Lesser Prose Writers	G. A. Aitken
6	Lesser Verse-Writers. I	T. Seccombe
	Lesser Verse-Writers. II	G. Saintsbury
7	Historical and Political Writers: I. Burnet	Sir A. W. Ward
8	Historical and Political Writers: II. Bolingbroke	Sir A. W. Ward
9	Memoir-Writers, 1715–1760	T. Seccombe
10	Writers of Burlesque and Translators	C. Whibley
11	Berkeley and Contemporary Philosophy	W. R. Sorley
12	William Law and the Mystics	Miss C. F. E. Spurgeon
13	Scholars and Antiquaries. I. Bentley, etc.	J. D. Duff
	Scholars and Antiquaries. II. Antiquaries	H. G. Aldis
14	Scottish Popular Poetry before Burns	T. F. Henderson
15	Education	J. W. Adamson

VOLUME X

Chap. 1	Richardson	L. Cazamian
2	Fielding and Smollett	H. H. Child
3	Sterne, and the Novel of his Times	C. E. Vaughan
4	The Drama and the Stage	G. H. Nettleton
5	Thomson and Natural Description in Poetry	A. H. Thompson
6	Gray	D. C. Tovey
7	Young, Collins and Lesser Poets of the Age of Johnson	G. Saintsbury
8	Johnson and Boswell	D. N. Smith
9	Oliver Goldsmith	H. A. Dobson
10	The Literary Influence of the Middle Ages	W. P. Ker
11	Letter-Writers. I	H. B. Wheatley
	Letter-Writers. II. Warwickshire Coterie	W. H. Hutton
12	Historians. I. Hume and Modern Historians	W. Hunt
13	Historians. II. Gibbon	Sir A. W. Ward
14	Philosophers: I. David Hume. II. Adam Smith. III. Other Philosophical Writers	W. R. Sorley
15	Divines	W. H. Hutton
16	The Literature of Dissent, 1660–1760	W. A. Shaw
17	Political Literature, 1755–1775	C. W. Previté-Orton

VOLUME XI

Chap. 1	Edmund Burke	H. J. C. Grierson
2	Political Writers and Speakers	C. W. Previté-Orton
3	Bentham and the Early Utilitarians	W. R. Sorley

4	William Cowper	H. H. Child
5	William Wordsworth	Emile Legouis
6	Coleridge	C. E. Vaughan
7	George Crabbe	H. H. Child
8	Southey. Lesser Poets of the Later Eighteenth Century	G. Saintsbury
9	Blake	J. P. R. Wallis
10	Burns. Lesser Scottish Verse	T. F. Henderson
11	The Prosody of the Eighteenth Century	G. Saintsbury
12	The Georgian Drama	H. V. Routh
13	The Growth of the Later Novel	G. Saintsbury
14	Book Production and Distribution, 1625–1800	H. G. Aldis
15	The Bluestockings	Mrs H. G. Aldis
16	Children's Books	F. J. H. Darton

VOLUME XII

Chap. 1	Sir Walter Scott	T. F. Henderson
2	Byron	F. W. Moorman
3	Shelley	C. H. Herford
4	Keats	C. H. Herford
5	Lesser Poets, 1790–1837	G. Saintsbury
6	Reviews and Magazines in the Early Years of the Nineteenth Century	Hon. A. R. D. Elliot
7	Hazlitt	W. D. Howe
8	Lamb	A. H. Thompson
9	The Landors. Leigh Hunt. De Quincey	G. Saintsbury
10	Jane Austen	H. H. Child
11	Lesser Novelists	H. H. Child
12	The Oxford Movement	W. H. Hutton
13	The Growth of Liberal Theology	F. E. Hutchinson
14	Historians	Sir A. W. Ward
15	Scholars, Antiquaries and Bibliographers	Sir J. E. Sandys

VOLUME XIII

Chap. 1	Carlyle	J. G. Robertson
2	The Tennysons	H. J. C. Grierson
3	Robert Browning and Elizabeth Barrett Browning	Sir Henry Jones
4	Matthew Arnold. Arthur Hugh Clough. James Thomson	W. Lewis Jones
5	The Rossettis. William Morris. Swinburne and others	A. H. Thompson
6	Lesser Poets of the Middle and Later Nineteenth Century	G. Saintsbury
7	The Prosody of the Nineteenth Century	G. Saintsbury
8	Nineteenth-Century Drama	H. H. Child
9	Thackeray	A. H. Thompson
10	Dickens	G. Saintsbury

11	The Political and Social Novel	Sir A. W. Ward
12	The Brontës	A. A. Jack
13	Lesser Novelists	W. T. Young
14	George Meredith. Samuel Butler. George Gissing	W. T. Young

VOLUME XIV

Chap. 1	Philosophers	W. R. Sorley
2	Historians, Biographers and Political Orators	Sir A. W. Ward
3	Critical and Miscellaneous Prose	Hugh Walker
4	The Growth of Journalism	J. S. R. Phillips
5	University Journalism	V. H. Rendall
6	Caricature and the Literature of Sport	H. H. Child
7	The Literature of Travel, 1700–1900	F. A. Kirkpatrick
8	The Literature of Science:	
	(*a*) Physics and Mathematics	W. W. Rouse Ball
	(*b*) Chemistry	M. M. P. Muir
	(*c*) Biology	Sir A. E. Shipley
9	Anglo-Irish Literature	A. P. Graves
10	Anglo-Indian Literature	E. F. Oaten
11	English-Canadian Literature	Pelham Edgar
12	The Literature of Australia and New Zealand	H. H. Child
13	South African Poetry	Sir T. H. Warren
14	Education	J. W. Adamson
15	Changes in the Language since Shakespeare's Time	W. Murison

CAMBRIDGE HISTORY OF ENGLISH LITERATURE

GENERAL INDEX

'A,' v. 480
'A. B.' IV. 117
A., *The Passionate Morrice*, v. 480
'A. W.' IV. 117, 124, 125; 'Thine eyes so bright,' IV. 125; *The Tomb of the Dead*, IV. 125
A Apple Pie, XI. 386, 487
A' the Blue Bonnets are over the Border, XIV. 377
'A was an Apple-pie,' XI. 368
A was an Archer, XI. 370
Aachen, II. 74
Aaron, in *Titus Andronicus*, v. 147, 179
Abacuk, in *The Palice of Honour*, II. 261
Abbey and Overton, *English Church in the 18th century*, IX. 326; XIV. 101, 496
Abbey, Charles John, IX. 326; XIV. 101, 496
Abbey Mill farm, in Jane Austen's *Emma*, XII. 240
Abbey of the Holy Ghost, II. 308, 438
Abbo of Fleury, I. 120, 121, 131
Abbot, Charles, 1st lord Colchester (1757–1829), XIV. 501, 502
Abbot, George (1562–1633), archbishop of Canterbury, IV. 63, 265, 424; VII. 187, 316
Abbot, John (*fl.* 1623), VII. 406
Abbotsford, II. 284; XII. 6, 20, 28, 154, 372, 378 ff., 430; XIV. 278, 375
Abbotsford club, XII. 358, 377
Abbott, Edwin Abbott, XIII. 511; *Philomythus*, XII. 460; *A Shakespearian Grammar*, XIII. 248; XIV. 445
Abbott, Evelyn (1843–1901), XII. 479, 482, 486; XIV. 503
Abbott, Jacob (1803–1879), XI. 492
Abbreochy, diocese of Moray, II. 115
Abdalrahman, caliph, X. 298
Abdullah, the peasant, XIV. 248
À Beckett, Arthur William, XIV. 238, 548
À Beckett, Gilbert Abbott (1811–1856), XIV. 235 ff., 541, 548; *Comic Blackstone, The*, XIV. 237; *Comic History of England, The*, XIV. 237; *Comic History of Rome, The*, XIV. 237
À Beckett, Gilbert Arthur (1837–1891), XIV. 238
Abeken, Caspar, *Life and letters of Cicero*, XII. 306
Abel, I. 30, 74
Abel, in *The Cytezen and Uplondyshman* III. 63
Abel, Niels Henrik, XIV. 258
Abelard, Peter, I. 183, 184, 191, 216; v. 38; VII. 312; IX. 71, 477, 538
Abercorn, earl of. *See* Hamilton, James
Abercrombie, H. R., XIV. Add. 9
Abercrombie, John (1780–1844), XIV. 467
Abercromby, Patrick (1656–1716?), IX. 552
Aberdare, baron. *See* Bruce, Henry Austin
Aberdeen, II. 88, 102, 127, 128, 369, 371; III. 122, 137, 155; IX. 372, 374, 542 ff.; X. 355; XII. 31, 359, 394, 513; XIV. 23, 209, 428
King's college, II. 369; VII. 254; X. 347
Marischal college, IX. 129; X. 38, 347
Aberdeen, earl of. *See* Gordon, George Hamilton
Aberdeen Breviary, IV. 412
Aberdeen Intelligencer, The, IX. 563
Aberdeen printers, IV. 547; XI. 469
Aberdeen university, X. 230; XII. 296, 333, 342
Aberdeenshire, II. 99, 100, 103, 259; IV. 253; IX. 372, 373; XIII. 431
Aberdonensis, Musa Latina, IX. 554, 555
Aberfoil, XII. 17
Abergavenny, X. 386, 387
Aberigh-Mackay, George Robert (1848–1881), XIV. 341, 574; *Twenty-one Days in India*, XIV. 340
Aberystwyth, University college, XIV. 433
Abgarus, legend of, I. 120
Abingdon, I. 113, 114; IV. 409; V. 330; VII. 454
Abingdon, Thomas. *See* Habington
Abingdon, William, VIII. 412
Abingdon Chronicle, I. 109–112
Abington, Frances (1737–1815), X. 264; XI. 257
Abishag, IV. 231
Ablancourt, Nicolas Perrot d', VII. 263; IX. 267
Ablett, J., *Literary Hours*, XII. 440
Ablewhite, Godfrey, in *The Moonstone*, XIII. 437
Abou ben Adhem, Leigh Hunt's, XIII. 308
Abra, in *Jacob and Esau*, v. 112
Abraham, I. 46; II. 424; VII. 377; XII. 321
Abraham, in Cowley's *Davideis*, VII. 66

Abraham (or Faith), in *Piers the Plowman*, II. 27
Abraham and Isaac, v. 17, 46, 390
Abraham man, the, in *The Fraternitye of vacabones*, III. 102
Abram, père, *Histoire de l'université et du Collège de Pont-à-Mousson*, IV. 256, 499
Abrey Hatch, IV. 240
Abry, Louis, II. 81
Absalom, in *Absalom and Achitophel*, VIII. 36, 38, 39
Absalom's Conspiracy, VIII. 37
'Absence, hear thou my protestation,' IV. 209
Absence, Song of, II. 283
Absolute, Sir Anthony, in Sheridan's *Rivals*, XI. 266, 267; XIII. 64; XIV. 387
Absolute, captain, in Sheridan's *Rivals*, XI. 266, 269
Abury, IX. 540
Abyndon, or Abingdon, Henry, VI. 281
Abyssinia, X. 179, 460, 461; XIV. 241, 246, 247
Abyssinians, the, X. 160
Academia Secretorum Naturae of Naples, VIII. 364
Academic, The, IX. 414
Academico, in *The Returne from Pernassus*, VI. 313
Académie des Inscriptions, X. 282
Académie Française, IX. 397; XIV. 397, 460
Academy, The, XII, 347; XIV. 200, 533
Acapulco, IV. 100
Acca, Bede's letters to, I. 80
Accent and Rhythm. See Blake, J. W.
Accoram boni, Vittoria, story of, VI. 174
Account of the sickness and death of Dr Woodward, IX. 132
Account of the state of learning in the Empire of Lilliput, IX. 132
Accursius, II. 350, 363
Aceronia, in Gray's *Agrippina*, X. 119
Achaians, IV. 33
Acheron, II. 265
Acheson, lady, in Swift's *Grand Question debated*, IX. 119
Achilles, III. 231; IV. 21; VI. 106; VIII. 25, 76
Achilles, in *The Birth of Merlin*, V. 249
Achilles, in *Confessio Amantis*, II. 148
Achilles Tatius, *Clitophon and Leucippe*, III. 351; IV. 435; VII. 489
Achitophel, in *Absalom and Achitophel*, VIII. 37, 38, 41, 75; XIV. 113
Achitophel, in *The Palice of Honour*, II. 260, 261
Acignius, in *Euphormio*, IV. 255, 258, 259
Acircius, Aldhelm's letter to, I. 76
Acis and Galatea, in *Confessio Amantis*, II. 147, 151
Ackermann, Rudolph (1764–1834), XIV. 216, 217, 221, 222
Ackermann Rudolph, the younger, XIV. 233
Acland, Sir Thos. Dyke (1809–1898), XIV. 136, 596
Acolastus. See under Gnaphaeus
Acres, Bob, in Sheridan's *Rivals*, XI. 266, 267; XIII. 64
Act for the Encouragement of Learning, XI. 314
Act of Settlement, IX. 200; XIV. 57
Act of Succession, IX. 197
Act of Supremacy, IX. 197
Act of Uniformity, IX. 573
Acta Regia, X. 280
Acta Sanctorum, X. 282
Actaeon, IV. 196
Actaeon's hounds, in Sandys's *Ovid*, VII. 51
Actium, battle of, V. 171
Activa Vita, in *Piers the Plowman*, II. 26, 27; V. 4
Acton, John Emerich Edward Dalberg-Acton, lord (1834–1902), X. 299; XII. 272, 430; XIII. 383; XIV. 100, 101, 116 ff., 484
  'Conflicts with Rome,' XIV. 118
  'Döllinger's Historical Work,' XIV. 118
  'German Schools of History,' XIV. 118
  Lectures on Modern History, XIV. 117
  Letters of Quirinus, XIV. 118
  'Mill *On Liberty*,' XIV. 118
  On the Study of History, XII. 303
  Open Letter to a German Bishop, XIV. 118
Acton common, X. 395
Actors Remonstrance, The, VI. 407, 492
Acts of the Apostles, MS. Laud. Gr. 35 at Oxford, I. 72
Adah, in Byron's *Cain*, XII. 48
Adam, I. 134, 353; V. 56; VII. 301; VIII. 341; IX. 28, 60, 327
Adam, in *As You Like It*, V. 374; VI. 248
Adam, in *Paradise Lost*, VII. 101, 119; XII. 85
Adam, in *The Cytezen and Uplondyshman*, III. 63
Adam, in *The Golden Legend*, II. 335
Adam (play), V. 11, 39, 390
Adam, Book of, I. 133
Adam, James (1860–1907), *The Religious Teachers of Greece*, XII. 333, 479; *The Vitality of Platonism*, XII. 333
Adam, Thomas (1701–1784), IX. 313; XII. 471
Adam and Eve, III. 130
Adam Bell, Clim of the Clough, and William of Cloudesley, I. 300; II. 408, 416, 501
Adam du Petit Pont, I. 185
Adam house, an, XI. 377
Adam of Domerham (d. after 1291), IX. 535
Adam of Usk (*fl.* 1400), II. 496
Adam Spencer, in *Gamelyn*, I. 298
'Adam Unparadized,' VII. 117
Adamites, the, VII. 387
Adamnan, St (625?–704), I. 82, 96, 433; II. 131; *Life of St Columba*, XII. 361, 518
Adams, Clement (1519?–1587), IV. 72
Adams, Clement (? *fl.* 1516), VI. 282

Adams, Francis, printer (*fl.* 1585), IV. 386
Adams, Francis (1796–1861), XII. 479
Adams, Francis, of Birmingham, XIV. 590
Adams, Francis William Lauderdale (1862–1893), XIII. 560; XIV. 369, 584
Adams, George (d. 1773), X. 470
Adams, Jean, IX. 374
Adams, John, XIV. 590
Adams, John Couch (1819–1892), XIV. 262, 264, 555
Adams, John Quincy, XI. 266
Adams, parson, in Fielding's *Joseph Andrews*, IX. 408; X. 24 ff., 28, 206; XI. 143; XIV. 218
Adams, Sarah Flower (1805–1848), XII. 413; XIII. 498; *Nearer, my God, to Thee*, XIII. 53, 176; *Vivia Perpetua*, XIII. 176
Adams, Thomas (*fl.* 1612–1653), VII. 423
Adams, William (d. 1620), IV. 99 ff.
Adams, William (1814–1848), XII. 447
Adams, William Davenport (1851–1904), XIII. 513
Adams, W. E., XIV. 533
Adams, William Henry Davenport (1828–1891), XIV. 515
Adamson, Henry (d. 1639), IX. 554
Adamson, John (d. 1653), IX. 542, 554
Adamson, John Ernest, XIV. Add. 4
Adamson, John William, XIV. Add. 11
Adamson, Robert (1852–1902), XIV. 467, 475
Development of Modern Philosophy, The, XIV. 49
Fichte, XIV. 48
On the Philosophy of Kant, XIV. 48
Short History of Logic, A, XIV. 48
Adderley, William, VII. 316
Addington, Henry, viscount Sidmouth (1757–1844), XIV. 506
Addison, Joseph (1672–1719), II. 163, 192, 415; III. 304, 373; IV. 30, 213, 335, 525; VII. 30, 72, 108, 109, 176, 244, 266, 388, 390; VIII. 174, 194, 220, 292, 293, 296, 303, 428, 430; IX. 5, 26, 27, 41, 43 ff. (main entry), 67, 75, 78, 86, 94, 125, 142, 151, 165, 166, 170 ff., 180 ff., 220, 237, 434 ff., 440, 442, 444, 445, 448, 483, 485, *also see* Add.; X. 1, 2, 20, 26, 27, 56, 80, 110, 119, 139, 140, 143, 172, 173, 193, 199, 205, 215, 219, 220, 226, 241, 279, 352, 353, 458, 484, *also see* Add.; XI. 2, 206, 280, 320, 330; XII. 177, 218, 221; XIII. 170, 312, 429, 445; XIV. 62, 169, 197, 209, 211, 396, 441, 442, 444, 461, 550
Campaign, The, IX. 44
Cato, IX. 63, 64, 77, 171, 184, 474; X. 69, 81, 83; XI. 273
Coverly papers, X. 178
Dialogues upon...Ancient Medals, IX. 43
Dissertatio de Romanorum poetis, IX. 43
Drummer, The, IX. 172
Essay on Travel, IX. 44
First Vision of Mirza, IX. 63
Musae Anglicanae, IX. 43
Addison, Joseph
'On the Pleasures of the Imagination,' IX. 61
Oratio de nova philosophia, IX. 43
Remarks on Italy, IX. 44
Travels in Italy, IX. 94
See, also, *Spectator, The*, and *Tatler, The*
Addison, Lancelot (1632–1703), IX. 38, 438
Adeane, Jane, *The Girlhood of Maria Josepha Holroyd*, X. 299
Adela of Louvain, II. 419
Adelaide, XIV. 365
Adelard or Aethelard of Bath (12th century), IV. 68; *De Eodem et Diverso*, etc., I. 153
Adelbright, in *Albion's England*, IV. 136
Adeline, in *La Cousine Bette*, XIII. 290
Adeline, in Mrs Radcliffe's *Romance of the Forest*, XI. 302
Adeline, Tennyson's, XIII. 29
Adis, Henry, VII. 515
Adlard, H., engraver, XII. 323
Adlington, William, *The Golden Ass*, IV. 3, 9, 435
Admetus, in *The Court of Love*, II. 220
Admirable Crichton, VII. 250, 255; VIII. 195
Admiral's company, the, V. 136, 316, 333; VI. 83, 89, 90, 93, 245, 247, 249, 250, 255, 259, 269, 274
Admonition to the Parliament, An, IV. 411
Ado of Vienne, I. 81
Adolphus, John Leycester (1795–1862), XII. 377
Adonais, in Shelley's poem, XII. 74
Adonis, XIII. 183
Adonis, in *Venus and Adonis*, V. 226
Adoptionist controversy, I. 84
Adorni, in *The Maid of Honour*, VI. 158, 164
Adraien van Berghen, printer, of Antwerp, II. 320
Adria, in the tale of *Colkelbie's sow*, II. 126
Adrian VI, pope, XIV. 100
Adrian, in *Confessio Amantis*, II. 151
Adriana, in *The Comedy of Errors*, V. 169, 178
Adrianus and Ritheus, I. 218
Adriatic sea, X. 119; XII. 33, 63
Adso, *Libellus de Antichristo*, I. 343
Adson, John, IV. 463
Adullam, in *Davideis*, VII. 67
Adurni, in *The Ladies Triall*, VI. 194
Adventurer, The, X. 171, 175, 466; XII. 363
Adventures of Dr Comicus, The, XIV. 219
Adversyte, in *Magnyfycence*, III. 77
Advertisement of a Sale of Choice Goods, VIII. 99
Advice to a Young Nobleman, XI. 371
Advices to a Painter, VIII. 91; Second and Third (1667), VII. 409; New Advice (1679), VIII. 91
Ady, Thomas, VII. 396; *A Candle in the Dark*, VII. 395, 507
Æ., XIV. 573

Aeacus, in *Locrine*, v. 240
Aecius, in *Valentinian*, vi. 122, 129, 130
Aeditio (Colet's), vii. 332
Aegeon of Syracuse, in *The Comedy of Errors*, iv. 79
Aegisthus, in *Agamemnon*, v. 79
Aeglamour, in *The Sad Shepherd*, vi. 11, 369, 370
Aelfhēah (St Alphege) (954–1012), i. 109, 127, 139, 153
Aelfhere, i. 138
Aelfnoth, i. 144
Aelfric (*fl.* 1006), i. 86, 96, 107, 113 ff., 116–129 (main entry), 131, 133, 136, 142, 143, 148, 150, 218, 221, 224, 369; ix. 536, 539; xi. 366
Advice to a Spiritual Son, trans. from St Basil, i. 124
Colloquy, i. 118, 119; xi. 367
De Veteri et de Novo Testamento, i. 126
Deuteronomy, i. 119
Grammar, i. 118, 119
Hexameron, trans. from St Basil, i. 122, 124
Homilies, i. 86, 96, 115, 116 ff., 120, 127 ff., 133; iv. 37, 397; ix. 402
Letter to the Monks of Eynsham, i. 114
Lives (*Passions*) *of the Saints, The*, i. 120, 121, 122, 128; iv. 424
Pastoral letter, i. 127
Version of Bede's *De Temporibus*, i. 122
Vita Aethelwoldi, i. 125
Vocabulary, i. 118, 119
Aelfric society, xii. 355
Aelfwine (Alboin), in *Widsith*, i. 35
Aelfwine, in *The Battle of Maldon*, i. 144
Aelian, iv. 435
Aeneas, viii. 67; ix. 45, 60, 256, 257; xiii. 123
Aeneas, in *Dido*, v. 146
Aeneas, James I described as, in *The Hue and Cry after Cupid*, vi. 347
'Aeolian lyre,' x. 128
Aeolus, vii. 370
Aeschere, in *The Battle of Maldon*, i. 145
Aeschere, in *Beowulf*, i. 23
Aeschines, vii. 147; ix. 528; xii. 493
Aeschylus, iv. 4, 248; v. 30; vii. 83; ix. 477; xii. 93, 99, 265, 324, 328, 331, 333, 480 ff., 485, 487 ff., 491, 494, 495; xiii. 191, 497; xiv. 211, 515
Agamemnon, xii. 318, 329, 334; xiii. 145
Choëphoroe, xii. 329, 334
Persae, vi. 92; xii. 329
Prometheus Bound, xii. 64, 65, 329; xiii. 70
Seven against Thebes, xii. 329
Aesculapius, in *The Faerie Queene*, iii. 234
Aeson, vi. 163
Aesop, ix. 102, 275, 391, 418, 473, 524, 525, 561; x. 196; xi. 366, 425, 479, 490, 491; *Fables*, i. 106, 355; ii. 245, 314, 334, 484; iii. 22; iv. 427, 435; v. 157; vi. 250; viii. 59
Aethelard. *See* Adelard
Aethelbriht, laws of, i. 98
Aethelflaed, the Lady of Mercia (d. 918?), i. 110, 141, 143
Aethelmaer, i. 125, 143
Aethelney, i. 89
Aethelred II, king (979?–1016), i. 112, 127, 129, 130, 145; v. 31
Aethelred, king of Mercia, i. 11
Aethelred, ealdorman of Mercia, i. 104
Aethelstan (Athelstan), king (925–940), i. 62, 108, 123, 137, 305; viii. 310
Aethelstan, abbot of Abingdon, i. 110
Aethelstan of Kent, prince, xiv. 83
Aethelweard, the ealdorman, i. 120, 122, 123
Aethelweard the chronicler (d. 998?), i. 443
Aethelwold, in *Havelok*, i. 303, 351
Aethelwold or Ethelwold, St (908?–984), bishop of Winchester, abbot of Abingdon, i. 16, 113, 114, 117, 118, 121, 125, 127, 148
Aethelwulf, i. 104
Aethilwald or Ethelbald, i. 78, 87
Aethiopians, in *The Masque of Blacknesse*, vi. 342, 343
Æþred's ring, i. 11
Aetion, v. 171
Aetna, xii. 335, 337
Affections, the, in *Pathomachia*, vi. 324
Affections, the four, in *Hymenaei*, vi. 346
Affery, in *Little Dorrit*, xiii. 331
Affirmation bill, the, xiv. 135
Affonso, Pedro, iv. 70
Afghanistan, xii. 352
Africa, ix. 19; xi. 112; xiii. 362; xiv. 192, 247, 252 ff., 434
African church, the, iii. 411
African languages, xiv. 459
Africander's War Song, The, xiv. 377
Africans, the, xi. 159
Agamemnon, in *Confessio Amantis*, ii. 148
Agape, St, i. 74
Agar, Anne (born Milton), vii. 108
Agar, Ralph (1540?–1621), vi. 462
Agatha, St, i. 74
Agathocles, xii. 316
Agathon (Plato's), iii. 216
Age, in *Nature*, v. 54
Age, in *Piers the Plowman*, ii. 25
Age, in *The Parlement of the Thre Ages*, ii. 37
Age, in *The Passetyme of Pleasure*, ii. 226
Ager, captain, in *A Faire Quarrell*, vi. 73, 74
Aggas, Edward (*fl.* 1564–1601), iv. 445, 447
Agincourt, battle of, ii. 423; iii. 314, 325; iv. 298; vii. 343; poems on, ii. 499, 501
Agincourt song, the, iv. 462
Agnellus, friar, i. 203
Agnes, in *David Copperfield*, xiii. 327
Agnes, St, i. 74
Agnes, St, Tennyson's, xiii. 29
Agnoli, G., xii. 377
Agra, iv. 90, 99

'Agra,' ship, XIII. 428
Agricola, XIV. 95
Agricola, Rodolphus, III. 50, 424
Agrigentum, IX. 332
Agrippa, Henricus Cornelius, of Nettesheim, III. 11, 112, 363, 365; VII. 370, 509 ff., 514, 517; VIII. 64; IX. 315; *De incertitudine et vanitate scientiarum*, VI. 377, 492; VII. 394; *De Occulta Philosophia*, III. 112; VIII. 67, 407
Aguecheek, Sir Andrew, in *Twelfth Night*, V. 194; XI. 266
Ahania, Blake's, XI. 194
Ahlwardt, Christian Wilhelm, X. 488
Ahmed, the cobbler, XIV. 248
Aholibamah, in Byron's *Heaven and Earth*, XII. 48
Aidan (d. 651), I. 42, 82, 121, 148
Aikin, Anna Laetitia. *See* Barbauld
Aikin, John (1747–1822), X. 385, 446, 449, 452, 455; XI. 382, 384, 477; XIV. 603
Aikin, J. and A. L., *Miscellaneous Pieces in Prose*, X. 188
Aikin, Lucy (1781–1864), XI. 477
Ailesbury, Susanna, countess of (d. 1783), XI. 282
Ailred or Ethelred of Rievaulx (1109?–1166), I. 161, 230, 337, 450
Aimonius of Fleury, II. 366
Aimwell, in Farquhar's *Beaux Stratagem*, VIII. 172
Ainderby, near Northallerton, II. 45
Ainger, Alfred (1837–1904), XI. 403, 410, 416, 419, 438; XII. 377, 418, 435, 473; XIII. 476, 542, *also see* Add. 2; XIV. 515; *Crabbe*, XI. 146, 475
Ainger, Arthur Campbell, XIV. 597
Ainsworth, Henry (1571–1623?), VII. 481, 490
Ainsworth, Robert (1660–1743), IX. 526, 568
Ainsworth, William Francis (1807–1896), XII. 429
Ainsworth, William Harrison (1805–1882), XII. 429 ff., 447, 448; XIII. 279, 307, 418
Guy Fawkes, XII. 250
Jack Sheppard, XII. 250
Lancashire Witches, The, XII. 250
Old St Paul's, XII. 250
Rookwood, XII. 250
South Sea Bubble, The, XII. 250
Tower of London, The, XII. 250
Aird, Thomas (1802–1876), XIII. 498
Airedale, XII. 421
Airy, Sir George Biddell (1801–1892), XIV. 258, 555
Airy, Osmund, IX. 203, 209
Aitken, Edward Hamilton (1851–1909), XIV. 574; *Behind the Bungalow*, XIV. 341
Aitken, George A., IX. 12, *also see* Add.; XI. 438
Aitken, J. C., XIII. 467
Aix-la-Chapelle, IX. 162; XIII. 61
Aix-la-Chapelle, treaty of, X. 40
Aix-les-Bains, II. 74
Ajax, VIII. 68
Ajax, in *Troilus and Cressida*, VI. 44
Ajax, An Anatomie of the Metamorpho-sed, IV. 533
Ajax Flagellifer, VI. 298, 317
Ajmere, IV. 90
Akenside, Mark (1721–1770), IX. 190, 220, 475; X. 39, 125, 138, 147, 152–153 (main entry), 156, 452; XI. 324; XII. 97
Epistle to Curio, X. 152, 153
Hymn to the Naiads, IX. 191; X. 152, 153
Inscriptions, X. 153
Odes, X. 153
Pleasures of Imagination, IX. 62; X. 122, 152, 153; XI. 323
Akerman, John Yonge (1806–1873), XII. 507
Akinetos, in Horne's *Orion*, XII. 118
Alabaster, William (1567–1640), *Roxana*, VI. 266, 268, 302, 463, 469, 470
Alain de Lille (1114–1203), I. 452; *Anti-Claudianus* and *De Planctu Naturae*, I. 193, 256
Alamanni, Luigi, III. 173
'Alamode Castle,' X. 250
Alane (Alesius), Alexander (1500–1565), III. 140, 141, 500
Cohortatio ad Concordiam, III. 141
Description of Edinburgh, III. 141
Epistola contra Decretum quoddam Episcoporum in Scotia, III. 141
Responsio ad Cochlaei Calumnias, III. 141
Alanius (Yong's), IV. 122
Alans, the, XIV. 302
Alarcon y Mendoza, Juan Ruiz de, VIII. 130
Alasco, Albertus, Polish prince palatine, V. 128
Alasi, prince, in Beckford's *Episodes*, XI. 291
Alba, VI. 317
Alban, Scottish settlers in, II. 89
Alban, St, Passion of, I. 81
Albanact, III. 192
Albania, X. 77; XII. 32, 42, 43; XIV. 252
Albany, duke of. *See* Stewart, John
Albemarle, earls of. *See* Keppel, Arnold; Keppel, George
Albemarle Papers, the, IX. 563
Alberic, master, I. 184
Albert, prince consort (1819–1861), XII. 311; XIV. 189, 415
Albert of Aix, II. 80
Albert of York, I. 84
Alberti, George William (1723–1758), VIII. 402
Alberti, L. B., IV. 441
Albertini di Prato, Niccolò, cardinal, V. 61
Albertino (Mussatus), *Eccerinis*, V. 62
Albertus Magnus (1193–1280), I. 200, 210, 211; II. 350; III. 494; VII. 503; *Philosophia*, II. 363
Albery, James (1838–1889), XIII. 273, 516
Albigenses, the, XIV. 79, 110
Albin, St, in Layamon, I. 234

Albina, in Racine's *Britannicus*, x. 119
Albinus of Canterbury, I. 82
Albion, in Blake's *Jerusalem*, XI. 198, 199
Albion, in *The Masque of Blacknesse*, VI. 342
Albion, The, XII. 187, 188
Albion Knight, v. 58, 124, 393
Alboin, in *Confessio Amantis*, II. 151
Alboin, in *Widsith*, I. 35
Albumazar, Galbrion, VII. 509
Alcaeus, VII. 65; XII. 329
Alcalà, IV. 69
Alcazar, battle of, VIII. 31
Alceone, in *Confessio Amantis*, II. 151
Alceste (Molière's), v. 194
Alcester, x. 112, 271
Alcester academy, x. 385
Alcestis, I. 321; VII. 105, 227; x. 108
Alcestis, in *The Court of Love*, II. 220
Alcestis, in *The Legend of Good Women*, II. 176
Alchemists, in *Mercury Vindicated*, VI. 357, 358
Alchfrith, I. 12
Alciati, Andrea, III. 423; VII. 47
Alcides, VI. 163
Alcilia, IV. 469
Alcimus Avitus, I. 76
Alcina, in *Orlando Furioso*, III. 231
Alcinous, XII. 198
Alcluyd, II. 74
Alcmaeon, v. 123
Alcmaeon, XII. Add.
Alcmena, in *Amphitruo*, v. 107
Alcmena, in *The Silver Age*, VI. 93
Alcock, John (1430–1500), bishop of Ely, II. 323, 355, 358; III. 66; IV. 494
Alcofribas, Messer, IV. 9
Alcon, in *A Looking Glasse for London and England*, v. 354
Alcon, in *The Queenes Arcadia*, VI. 318
Alcott, Louisa May, XI. 492
Alcuin or Ealhwine (735–804), I. 5, 59, 79, 84 ff., 89, 117, 121, 145, 153, 433; IV. 269; XI. 366
Alcuine's Bible, XII. 517
Aldeburgh, XI. 140, 141, 143, 144, 146, 147, 419
Alden, Raymond Macdonald, XIII. 511
Alderton, Suffolk, IV. 164, 165
Aldfrith (d. 705), king of Northumbria, I. 76, 77
Aldhelm (640?–709), bishop of Sherborne, I. 15, 17, 60, 61, 72 ff., 82, 83, 86, 87, 91, 102, 230, 433; XI. 366
Aldingar, Sir, II. 412
Aldis, Harry Gidney (d. 1919), IV. 547; XI. 469; XII. 519
Aldred, the glossator (10th century), I. 132, 460
Aldrich, Henry (1647–1710), IX. 528; XIV. 476; *Artis logicæ rudimenta*, XIV. 13
Aldus Manutius, Romanus, III. 5, 427
Aldwinkle, Northants, VII. 244; VIII. 2
Alec-Tweedie, Mrs Ethel Brilliana, XIV. 533
Aleman, M., *The Rogue, or the Life of Guzman de Alfarache*, IV. 395, 441; VI 139
Alembert, Jean B. le Rond d', XI. 354
Alembic Club Reprints, XIV. 557, 558
Aleppo, IV. 84, 90; VII. 308; x. 466
Aleppo, basha of, in *The Renegado*, VI. 156
Alesius, Aless. *See* Alane, Alexander
Alessio, IV. 441
Alethea, in Butler's *The Way of all Flesh*, XIII. 454
Alexander I, emperor of Russia, XII. 39
Alexander III, king of Scots, I. 283; II. 100, 101, 109; XIV. 95
Alexander, in Lee's *Rival Queens*, VIII. 186
Alexander, Mrs Cecil Frances, born Humphreys (1818–1895), XIII. 498; XIV. 567; *Burial of Moses, The*, XIV. 321; *Irish Mother's Lament, The*, XIV. 321; *Siege of Derry, The*, XIV. 321
Alexander, John (d. 1743), x. 385
Alexander, Patrick Proctor, XIII. 470; XIV. 525
Alexander, The Buik of, II. 104, 448
Alexander, The Wars of, I. 291, 333, 334, 466
Alexander, W. F., XIV. 584
Alexander, Sir William, earl of Stirling (1567?–1640), II. 95; III. 266; IV. 152, 311, 413, 509; v. 473; VI. 19; VII. 273; VIII. 133; IX. 554; *Anacrisis*, VII. 263; *Aurora*, III. 257, 267, 522; *Monarchick Tragedies*, v. 335
Alexander, William (1826–1894), XIII. 560
Alexander, William (1824–1911), archbishop of Armagh, XIV. 321, 567
Alexander de Villa Dei, II. 359, 366; *Doctrinale Puerorum*, II. 363
Alexander Hieronymus, IV. 259
Alexander of Blois, I. 166, 167
Alexander of Hales (d. 1245), I. 199 ff., 205, 207, 452; IV. 269, 271; VII. 504
Alexander of Lincoln, I. 156, 169, 258
Alexander the Great, x. 27; XII. 309, 313, 315, 331; XIV. 579
Alexander the Great, in romance, I. 135, 148, 169, 279, 285, 291, 307, 308, 333, 334, 342, 466; II. 112, 301; III. 24, 61; IV. 196
See, also, *Alisaunder, Secreta Secretorum*
Alexander to Aristotle, The Letter of, I. 35; II. 80
Alexandri, Historia, II. 151
Alexandria, II. 13, 131; XIII. 362; XIV. 247
Alexandrian poets, VII. 9
Alexandrines, XI. 246; XII. 88, 229; XIII. 35, 151, 238, 251
Alexis (Virgil's), III. 264
Alexis, or the young Adventurer (1746), IX. 563
Alexius, St, I. 293, 356
Alfieri, Vittorio, count, XII. 33, 40, 47, 49, 397, 438
Alford, Henry (1810–1871), XII. 340, 500; XIII. 24, 476

Alfoxden, xi. 99, 102, 405
Alfred, king of West-Saxons (849–901?), i. 19, 84, 87 ff., 109, 113, 115, 123, 128, 136, 144, 150, 198, 219, 239, 363, 380 ff., 436 ff.; ii. 341; iii. 160; iv. 74; v. 2; viii. 310; ix. 534
  Falconry attributed to, i. 106
  Handbook, i. 91
  Translations: of Augustine, i. 102, 103; of Bede, i. 96; of Boethius, i. 99 ff.; ii. 186; of Gregory, i. 91 ff.; of Orosius, i. 93 ff.
Alfred, Proverbs of, i. 218, 438, 459, 460
Alfred aetheling, i. 139, 374
Alfred of Beverley (*fl.* 1143), i. 262; ii. 76; ix. 534
Algarotti, Francesco, *Newtonianismo per le Dame*, xi. 356
Algeria, xii. 480
Algiers, vii. 364
Ali, i. 26, 27
Ali pasha, xii. 32
Alicante, xiv. 73
Alice, in Lamb's *Essays of Elia*, xii. 182, 186
Alice, in Mrs Gaskell's *Mary Barton*, xiii. 375
Alinda, in *Rosalynde*, iii. 358
Alinda, in *The Pilgrim*, vi. 123
Alington, Syr Giles, knight, iii. 57
Alipur, near Calcutta, xiii. 276
Alisaunder, King, i. 288, 306, 308, 309, 317, 356, 399
Alison, Archibald (1757–1839), xiv. 467; xiv. 57, 94, 485; *Autobiography*, xiv. 66; *History of Europe*, xiv. 66; *History of Scottish Criminal Law*, xiv. 66
Alison, Richard (*fl.* 1606), iv. 113, 463
Alison, in *Misogonus*, v. 111
Alithia (Philosophy), in Wyclif's *Trialogus* ii. 65
Alken, Henry (*fl.* 1816–1831), xiv. 225, 232 ff., 542; *National Sports of Great Britain*, xiv. 232; *Specimens of Riding*, xiv. 232; *Symptoms of being amazed*, xiv. 232
Alken, in *The Sad Shepherd*, vi. 370
Alkington academy, x. 387
Alkmaar, iv. 246
All Fools, game of, v. 179
All is True, vi. 256
All the Year Round, xiii. 178, 315, 323, 326, 332, 335, 376, 437
All wyckednes doth beginne to amende, etc., iii. 491
Allam, Andrew (1655–1685), ix. 351
Allan, David (1744–1796), ix. 567
Allan-a-Maut, ii. 279
Allardyce, Alexander (1846–1896), xiv. 574; *The City of Sunshine*, xiv. 339
Allbut, Robert, xiii. 542
Allde, Edward (*fl.* 1583–1634), iv. 384, 390; v. 158
Allde, John (*fl.* 1555–1592), v. 92, 312
Allen, Giles, vi. 252, 253
Allen, Grant (*pseud.* Cecil Power, 1848–1899), xiii. 560; xiv. 343, 467, 535
Allen, Henry Ellis, xii. 337, 479
Allen, John (1771–1843), xii. 144, 426; xiv. 54, 485, 492
Allen, John (1810–1886), archdeacon of Salop, xiii. 142
Allen, Joseph, *Punch* artist, xiv. 236
Allen, Joshua, viscount (1685–1758), ix. 121
Allen, Ralph (1694–1764), ix. 443; x. 29, 33, 276
Allen, Thomas (1803–1833), xii. 507
Allen, William (1532–1594), cardinal, iii. 422; *Modest Answer to the English Persecutors*, vii. 432
Allen, William (1770–1843), xiv. 603
Alley, William (1510?–1570), *The Poore Man's Librarie*, vi. 378, 492
Alleyn, Edward (1566–1626), iv. 407; v. 144; vi. 41, 51, 87, 247, 249, 250, 255, 258, 278, 292
Alleyn, Ellen, *pseud. See* Rossetti, Christina Georgina
Alleyn's college, Dulwich, vii. 339
Allibone, S. Austin, xii. 519
Allingham, Helen, xiii. 498
Allingham, William (1824–1889), xii. 409; xiii. 189, 498; xiv. 567; *Lovely Mary Donnelly*, xiii. 190; *Up the Fairy Mountain*, xiii. 190
Allington, Kent, iii. 167
Allison, Thomas (*fl.* 1697), iv. 453
Allison Gross, ii. 414
Alliterative revival, i. 291
All-Night, countess of, in Goldsmith's *Citizen of the World*, x. 206
Allot, Robert (*fl.* 1600), *England's Parnassus*, iv. 394, 467; v. 134, 162
Alloway, xi. 219, 435
Allsop, Thomas (1795–1880), xi. 415, 416; xii. 199, 200
Allworthy, in Fielding's *Tom Jones*, x. 28, 29, 31
Alma, battle of the, xiii. 173; xiv. 94
Alma, house of, in *The Faerie Queene*, iii. 233
Alma Mater (Aberdeen), xiv. 209
Alma redemptoris mater, in Chaucer's *The Prioress's Tale*, ii. 359
Almaigne, Song against the King of, i. 368
Almanacs, iii. 19
Almanzor, in Dryden's *Conquest of Granada*, viii. 25, 27
Almerine, in *Brennoralt*, vi. 238
Almira, in *A Very Woman*, vi. 156
Almon, John (1737–1805), x. 522, 524 ff.; *Anecdotes of Eminent Persons*, x. 400
Almond, Hely Hutchinson (1832–1903), xiv. 590, 601
Almond for a Parrat, An, vi. 393
Alms, in *The Exeter Book*, i. 428
Alne, Robert, fellow of Peterhouse, ii. 366
Alnwick, ix. 566; xi. 469; xiv. 227
Alonso, in *The Tempest*, v. 206

Alonzo, in *The Bashful Lover*, VI. 158
Aloÿse, in Rossetti's *Bride's Prelude*, XIII. 114
Alpers, O. T. J., XIV. 584
Alphabet, Irish and Roman, I. 13
Alphege, St. *See* Aelfhēah
Alphere, in *Waltharius*, I. 32
Alphonso, in *The Mourning Bride*, VIII. 152
Alphonso I, king of Aragon and Navarre, V. 137
Alphonso V, king of Aragon, Sicily and Naples, V. 137
Alphus (Mantuan's), III. 223
Alpine Journal, The, XIV. 255
Alps, the, II. 119; IV. 6; V. 101; VIII. 245; X. 119, 202, 510; XI. 96; XII. 44, 47, 61, 63, 64; XIII. 443; XIV. 254, 255, 292, 294
Alresford, VII. 207, 454
Alscrip, in Burgoyne's *Heiress*, XI. 275, 276
Alscrip, Miss, in Burgoyne's *Heiress*, XI. 275; XIV. 387
Alsop, Vincent (d. 1703), IX. 503
Alspice, in Morton's *Way to get Married*, XI. 281
Altamont, in Rowe's *Fair Penitent*, VIII. 196
Altamont, colonel, in *Pendennis*, XIII. 291
Altdorf, V. 285
Althaus, Friedrich, XIII. 70
Althorp, VI. 4, 339
Althorp, viscount. *See* Spencer, John Charles
Althorp library, XII. 365, 366
Alton, Miss, in Burgoyne's *Heiress*, XI. 275
Alton, Hampshire, XIII. 381
Altrive farm, in Yarrow, XI. 239
Altus prosator, I. 69
Alucius, History of, VI. 286
Alva, duke of, V. 344; VII. 306; VIII. 160
Alvan, Sigismund, in Meredith's *The Tragic Comedians*, XIII. 444
Alvanley, baron. *See* Arden, Richard Pepper
Alvar, in Coleridge's *Remorse*, XI. 414
Alvarez Espriella, Don Manuel, in Southey's *Letters from Spain*, XI. 163
Alys Esry, in *Cocke Lorell's bote*, III. 84
Amada, Philip, IV. 85
Amadas and Ydoine, I. 286
Amadas, Sir, I. 293, 294, 470
Amadeus, in *The Bugbears*, V. 115
Amadine, in *Mucedorus*, V. 253
Amadis, IV. 9; VII. 75, 235
Amadis and Palmerin cycles, III. 359
Amadis of Gaul, VII. 74; X. 220; XII. 422; XIII. 35
Amalekites, II. 10; VIII. 78
Amalteo, Geronimo, IV. 264
Amanda, in Sheridan's *Trip to Scarborough*, XI. 268
Amanda, in Thomson's *Seasons*, X. 95, 99, 102
Amanda, in Vanbrugh's *Relapse*, VIII. 161; XI. 268
Amaranta, in *The Spanish Curate*, VI. 134
Amarillis (Herrick's), VII. 12, 13
Amaryllis, in *The Shepheards Calender*, III. 222, 226
Amatus Lusitanus, in Burton's *Anatomy*, IV. 246
Amaziah, in Cowley's *Davideis*, VII. 67
Amazon, river, XIV. 250
'Amazon,' ship, XIV. 251
Amazonian maids in *Ralph Roister Doister*, V. 106
Amazons, the, IV. 57, 61; X. 464
Ambassadorial despatches and newsletters, VII. 436 ff.
Ambodexter, in *A Dialogue...against the fever Pestilence*, III. 109
Amboyna (Amboina), outrage at, IV. 99; VI. 183; VIII. Add.
Amboyna, A true relation of the unjust, cruel and barbarous proceeding against the English at, VII. 433
Ambroise, *Histoire de la Guerre Sainte*, II. 420, 507
Ambrosden, parish of, IX. 536; X. 517
Ambrose, St, I. 59, 74, 75; II. 365; VII. 483; XII. 266
Ambrose, in *The Example of Virtue*, II. 227
Ambrose's tavern, XII. 159
Ambrosius Aurelianus, Aurelius Ambrosius (G. of M.), Embreis Guletic (Nennius), Emrys Wledig in Welsh literature, I. 66, 247, 268
'Ambusheer,' the, X. 198
Amelia, X. 33, 34
Amelia, in George Eliot's *Amos Barton*, XIII. 388
Amelia, in Fielding's novel, X. 23, 28, 33, 34
Amelia, in Thomson's *Seasons*, X. 103
Amelotte, in Rossetti's *Bride's Prelude*, XIII. 114
America, IV. 73, 74, 86, 95, 96, 101, 311; VII. 176, 305, 308; VIII. 101, 243, 257, 314, 341, 342; IX. 19, 212; X. 43, 199, 200, 364, 504; XI. 3, 7, 10 ff., 15, 20, 75, 119, 189, 190, 235, 236, 275, 380, 383; XII. 89, 165, 316; XIII. 10, 58, 88, 107, 150, 152, 294, 321, 322, 334, 455; XIV. 86, 98, 166, 207, 255, 263, 267, 293, 318, 397, 457. *See, also*, United States
America, Central, XIV. 297
America, South, IX. 23; XI. 60; XIV. 249, 250, 252
America, discovery of, III. 97; IV. 68, 69, 75
America, first English books on, II. 330; IV. 69, 70
America, study of Shakespeare in, V. 308
American Celt, The, XIV. 318
American character, XIV. 346
American church, X. 356
American civil war, XIV. 91, 143, 182, 326
American colonies, X. 306; XI. 5, 22; XIV. 361
American congress, X. 182
American constitution, XI. 71

American declaration of independence, XI. 71
American languages, XIV. 459
American philosophy, IX. 281
American politics, XIV. 346
American scholars, XII. 340
American slang, XIV. 211
American war of independence, X. 251, 393; XI. 5, 6, 16, 24; XIV. 89
Americans, the, XI, 11, 15, 19, 52
Amersham, VII. 53, 54
Ames, Joseph (1689–1759), *Typographical Antiquities*, IX. 356, 530; XII. 362, 366, 520
Ames, William (1576–1633), VII. 308; *De Conscientia et ejus jure vel casibus*, VII. 280, 469
Amesbury, IX. 163
Amhurst, Nicholas (1697–1742), IX. 220. 411, 433, 491, 574; XI. 172
Amie, in *The Sad Shepherd*, VI. 370
Amiel, Henri Frédéric, XIII. 99
Amiens, X. 118; XII. 341
Amiens, in *As You Like It*, VII. 3; VIII. 225
Amiens, peace of, XIV. 120, 184
Aminta, in Meredith's *Lord Ormont and his Aminta*, XIII. 444
Amintor, in *The Maides Tragedy*, VI. 120, 126 ff.
Amis and Amiloun, I. 314, 315, 467
Amitiez de Ami et Amile, Li, IX. 39
Amlet, Mrs, in *The Confederacy*, VIII. 162
Amlethus (Hamlet) in Saxo Grammaticus, I. 9. *See, also, under* Hamlet
Ammianus Marcellinus, I. 35
Ammonius, Andreas, III. 14
Amner, John (d. 1641), IV. 463
Amoret (Spenser's), III. 236
Amoret (Vaughan's), VII. 38, 40
Amoret (Waller's), VII. 55
Amoretta, in *The Ladies Triall*, VI. 194
Amoretto, in *The Pilgrimage to Parnassus*, VI. 310
Amoretto, in *The Returne from Parnassus*, VI. 313
Amorgen, incantation of, XIV. 303
Amorous La-Foole, Sir, in *The Silent Woman*, VI. 22, 152
Amorphus, in *Cynthia's Revels*, VI. 41, 44
Amory, Blanche, in *Pendennis*, XIII. 290 ff.
Amory, J., in *Pendennis*, XIII. 291
Amory, Thomas (1691?–1788), X. 386, 423; XI. 285 ff. (main entry), 307; *Life of John Buncle*, X. 56; XI. 285 ff., 328, 329; *Memoirs of Several Ladies*, XI. 285, 287
Amos, Andrew, XIV. 594
Amos, hermit, I. 74
Amours, Francis Joseph, II. 113, 115, 121, 126, 450
Amphitryon, VII. 125
Amphitryon, in *Confessio Amantis*, II. 148
Amsarey, in Disraeli's *Tancred*, XIII. 351
Amsterdam, IV. 402, 403; V. 286; VI. 22, 324; VII. 286, 289, 308, 344; IX. 197, 199, 306, 515, 519; X. 296
Amsterdam, Letter from, to a Friend in England, VIII. 100
Amurath, VI. 481
Amwell, Hertfordshire, XII. 191
Amyas, in *Westward Ho!*, XIII. 364
Amyntas, in *The Cytezen and Uplondyshman*, III. 63
Amyntas, in *The Queenes Arcadia*, VI. 317
Amyot, Jacques, IV. 3, 10, 11
Anacreon, IV. 123 ff., 186; VII. 1, 2, 4, 9, 18, 83, 489; VIII. 444; IX. 526; X. 454; XI. 426; XII. 223, 410
Anacreon, the pseudo-, VII. 83
Anaides, in *Cynthia's Revels*, VI. 18, 41
Analysis of the Hunting Field, The, XIV. 232, 234
Analytical Review, The, XI. 402
Ananias, in *The Alchemist*, VI. 22
Anastasius, emperor, X. 314
Anatolia, XIV. 251
Anatolia, St, I. 74, 75
Anatomy of Wit, VI. 394
An Bispel, I. 227, 228, 458, 459
Ancient Buildings, society for the pro tection of, XIII. 128
Ancient Pistol, in *Henry IV*. *See* Pistol, Ancient
Ancor, river, IV. 169, 173 ff., 190
Ancren Riwle, I. 222, 230, 234, 398, 400, 458, 459; II. 300; III. 440
Anderdon, J., IX. 518
Andersen, Hans Christian, XI. 387, 491
Anderson, Alexander (1845–1909), XIII. 498
Anderson, George (1676?–1756), IX. 547
Anderson, James (1662–1728), IX. 552; X. 498
Anderson, James (1739–1808), IX. 560; XIV. 467; *Enquiry into the Nature of Corn-Laws*, XIV. 3
Anderson, John P., X. 421, 483; XI. 456; XII. 382, 397, 404, 407, 447; XIII. 464, 480, 531, 554
Anderson, Joseph (b. 1832), XII. 507
Anderson, Robert (1750–1830), IX. 187, 479; X. 138, 469, 473; XII. 413; XIII. 224; *The Works of the British Poets*, X. 452
André (Bernard Andreas) of Toulouse, VII. 203; *Les Douze Triomphes de Henry VII*, II. 223, 471
Andrea, ghost of, in *Jeronimo*, V. 160
Andrea, Joannes, II. 364
Andreae, Antonius, commentary on Aristotle's *Metaphysics*, II. 318
Andreae, Johann Valentin (?*fl.* 1619), *Menippus*, IV. 248; VII. Add.
Andreas, I. 51 ff., 58, 143, 430
Andreini, Giovanni Battista, *Adamo*, VII. 118; XI. 403
Andreos, in *The Purple Island*, IV. 166
’Ανδρέου καὶ Ματθαίου, Πράξεις, I. 54

Andrew, merchant in Lyme Regis, x. 21
Andrew, St, I. 54, 115. See, also, *Andreas*
Andrew Lammie, II. 412
Andrew of Wyntoun. *See* Wyntoun
Andrewe, Laurence (*fl.* 1510–1537), printer, II. 330; IV. 542
Andrewes, George, XIV. 539; *Dictionary of the Slang and Cant Languages*, XIV. 224
Andrewes, Lancelot (1555–1626), bishop of Winchester, IV. 228, 237 ff., 491, 494, 509; VII. 28, 139, 157 ff., 309, 310, 317, 333; VIII. 293, 294, 301; X. 359, 360; *Private Devotions*, IV. 238; VII. 43
Andrews, Alexander, XIV. 531; *The History of British Journalism*, XIV. 178, 184, 204
Andrews, Apology for the Life of Mrs Shamela, X. 6
Andrews, John (*fl.* 1615), IV. 473
Andrews, Joseph, in Fielding's novel, X. 24 ff.
Andrews, Thomas (1813–1885), XIV. 595
'Andrian, Solomon,' IX. 471
Andromache, in the *Iliad*, VIII. 50
Andromache, in Dryden's *Troilus and Cressida*, VIII. 29
Andromana, or The Merchant's Wife, VI. 451
Andromeda (a giant), II. 79
Andronicus, Livius, IX. 270
Andronicus Commenus, VI. 481
Androphilus, in *The Purple Island*, IV. 166
Androse, Richard (*fl.* 1569), IV. 441
Andrugio, in *Promos and Cassandra*, V. 120
Aneirin (Aneurin) (*fl.* 603?), *Gododin*, I. 248, 249, 461
Angantyr, X. 223, 224
Angel of Death, XI. 31
Angela, sister (St Beatrix), XIII. 178
Angelica, in Congreve's *Love for Love*, VIII. 151, 156
Angelica, in Farquhar's *Sir Harry Wildair*, VIII. 169
Angell, John (*fl.* 1758), X. 469
Angellier, Auguste, XI. 115, 438
Angelo, in *Measure for Measure*, V. 190
Angelo, in *The Virgin Martir*, VI. 54
Angelo, Michael, IV. 222, 223; VII. 176
Angels, The treatise of the Song of, II. 327
Anger, in *Confessio Amantis*, II. 147
Angevin reigns, the, XIV. 72
Angevins, the, VIII. 311
Angharad, in *The Misfortunes of Arthur*, V. 78
Angier of St Frideswide, II. 508
Angiolieri, Cecco, XIII. 118
Anglia, IX. 106
Anglican church, the, XII. 134, 275, 291, 299; XIII. 138
Anglican clergy, XI. 309
Anglicans, IX. 100
Angling, writers on, IV. 541
Anglo-Canadians, XIV. 345
Anglo-catholic movement, the, XIII. 435
Anglo-French law language, the, I. 407 ff.; VIII. 319
Anglo-French literature, XIV. 307
Anglo-Indian literature, XIV. 331 ff.
Anglo-Irish, the, XIV. 308
Anglomanie, the, X. 16
Anglo-Norman *chanson*, XIV. 67
Anglo-Norman works, II. 419 ff., 503 507 ff.; V. 38
Anglo-Normans, the, in Ireland, XIV. 306, 308
Anglo-Roman hierarchy, XII. 274
Anglo-Saxon chair, at Cambridge, XII. 344; at Oxford, IX. 413; XII. 344; XIV. 385
Anglo-Saxon Chronicle, XII. 344; XIV. 69
Anglo-Saxon language, I. 379 ff.; VII. 319
Angus, Archibald, 5th earl of (1449?–1514), 'Bell the Cat,' II. 259
Anian, strait of, IV. 78
Anicetus, in Gray's *Agrippina*, X. 119
Anima, in *Piers the Plowman* (also called Will, Reason, Love, Conscience), II. 19, 21, 22, 27, 28
Anima, in *Mind, Will and Understanding*, V. 52
Animalibus, De, II. 363
Anjou, Francis, duke of (formerly duke of Alençon), V. 341; VII. 191
Anlaf, I. 109, 144, 305
Anlaf Cuaran, I. 287
'Anna Matilda.' *See* Cowley, Hannah
Annalia Dubrensia, IV. 487
Annals and Magazines of Natural History, The, XIV. 288, 565
Annals of Agriculture, XI. 72
Annals of England, IV. 424
Annals of the Fine Arts, XIV. 539
Annals of the Four Masters, XII. 360, 518 XIV. 309
Annan, Dumfriesshire, XIII. 2, 3
Annand, James (1843–1906), XIV. 533
Annand, William (1633–1689), IX. 545
Annas, in the York plays, V. 46
Anne, in *The Misfortunes of Arthur*, V. 78
Anne, mastres, friend of John Skelton, III. 71
Anne, queen of Great Britain, IV. 251, 433; VIII. 96, 113, 220, 261, 373; IX. 30, 44, 72, 78, 96, 97, 103, 113, 124, 130, 131, 139, 150 ff., 155, 160, 161, 169, 175, 177, 180, 200, 202, 205, 208, 216, 217, 219, 222, 228, 231, 232, 309, 394, 395, 407, 408; X. 67 ff., 73, 139, 196, 352, 374, 502; XI. 370, 372; XII. 488; XIII. 300, 453; XIV. 212, 383, 463
Anne, queen, in *Richard III*, VI. 129; VIII. 123
Anne Boleyn, 2nd queen of Henry VIII III. 16, 26, 167, 168, 175, 332, 336, 337; V. 103; VI. 335; X. 27; XII. 477; XIII. 261
Anne of Bohemia, II. 62, 170
Anne of Cleves, III. 175
Anne of Denmark, queen consort of James I, IV. 134, 143; VI. 83, 337

339 ff., 348, 350, 361, 366; VII. 79, 205; XIV. 93; companies of, VI. 104, 254, 258
Annesley, Arthur, earl of Anglesea (1614–1686), VII. 229
Annesley claimant, the, XIII. 426
Annet, Peter (1693–1769), IX. 288, 504; *Resurrection of Jesus examined*, IX. 294
Annibal, in George Eliot's *The Spanish Gypsy*, XIII. 398
Annie of Lochryan, I. 300
Annual Register, X. 357, 474, 482, 483; XI. 145, 324; XII. 138; XIV. 228
Annual Review, The, XIV. 98
Annus Mirabilis primus et secundus, VIII. 10
῎Ανοδος, *pseud.* of Mary E. Coleridge, XIII. 183
Anselm, St (1033–1109), archbishop of Canterbury, I. 16, 128, 149, 151, 154, 162, 163, 186, 217, 222, 224, 228, 231, 234, 355, 446; II. 365; XII. 455; XIV. 113
Anson, George, baron Anson (1697–1762), XIV. 243, 550
Anson, Sir William Reynell (1843–1914), XIV. 485, 487
Anster, John (1793–1867), XIV. Add. 3
Anstey, Christopher (1724–1805), IX. 481; XI. 158, 160, 172, 424; XII. 7, 120; *New Bath Guide*, XI. 173
Anstey, John (d. 1819), XI. 424
Anstis, John (1669–1744), IX. 355, 531
Anstruther, Fife, XI. 243
Anstruther, lady Margaret, IX. 369
Answerall, lady, in Swift's *Complete Collection of...Conversation*, IX. 106
Antarctic exploration, XIV. 245
Ante Crucem Virgo Stabat, II. 383
Antenorius, in *Argenis*, IV. 259
Anthea (Herrick's), VII. 6, 9
Anthony, Now-Now, in *The Gentle Craft*, III. 370
Anthropological society, the, XII. 350
Anti-christ, VI. 374
Antichrist, in Dunbar's *Vision*, II. 256
Antichrist, in *Piers the Plowman*, II. 28
Antidote against Melancholy, IV. 536; VII. 512
Antigone, XII. 68
Antigone, in *Phoenissae*, V. 71, 72
Antigonus, in *The Humorous Lieutenant*, VI. 122
Antigonus, in *The Winter's Tale*, V. 206
Anti-Jacobin, The, XI. 39 ff., 157, 392; XII. 150; XIII. 260; XIV. 194, 214
Anti-Jacobin Review, The, XI. 392; XII. 526
Antioch, XII. 107
Antiochus, Asiatic king, in *Believe as you List*, VI. 147 ff.
Antiochus, in *The Tatler*, IX. 38
Antipodes, the, XIV. 255
Anti-projector, The, IV. 308, 509
Antiquaries, in Stuart times, VII. 232–258, 460 ff.
Antiquaries, in Tudor times, III. 313–338, 527 ff.
Antiquaries, Scottish society of, IX. 372; XII. 349
Antiquaries, society of (founded 1572), IV. 55; VII. 305
Antiquaries of London, society of (founded 1717–18), IX. 352, 357, 358, 531; XII. 506, 510
Anti-Romish propaganda in stage plays, VI. 150
'Anti-Sejanus,' X. 401
Anton, Robert (*fl.* 1616), IV. 516, 520, 533; *Moriomachia*, IV. 359
Antoninus, in *The Virgin Martir*, VI. 154
Antoninus Bassianus Caracalla, VI. 481
Antonio, in *Albumazar*, VI. 323
Antonio, in Otway's *Venice Preserv'd*, VIII. 94, 184
Antonio, in *The Case is Altered*, V. 321
Antonio, in *The Coxcombe*, VI. 133
Antonio, in *The Dutchesse of Malfy*, VI. 181, 182
Antonio, in *The Merchant of Venice*, V. 183, 355
Antonio, in *The Tempest*, V. 206
Antonio de Eslava, *Noches de Invierno*, VIII. 126
Antonius, in *A Dialogue...against the fever Pestilence*, III. 108
Antonius, in *Ignoramus*, VI. 322
Antony, in *Antony and Cleopatra*, V. 199
Antony, in *Julius Caesar*, V. 197
Antony, in *Romeo and Juliet*, V. 182
Antony, Life of, Athanasius's, I. 75
Antrobus, Dorothy, mother of Thomas Gray, X. 116
Antrobus, Mary, X. 116, 121, 127
Antrobus, Robert, X. 116, 117
Antrobus, William, X. 116
Antwerp, II. 319, 320, 329, 330; III. 18, 43, 208; IV. 69, 266, 274, 316, 324, 396, 402, 403; V. 90, 113, 114; VII. 460; VIII. 141; XII. 365; XIII. 433
Antwerp, Plantin Museum at, I. 72
Antwerpe, Tragical Historie of the citie of, IV. 324
Apelles, IV. 14
Apennines, the, XII. 63
Apicius Caelius, IX. 478
Apius and Virginia. *See* R. B.
Apocrypha, the. *See under* Bible
Apollinaris (Laodicean bishop), V. 5
Apollo, II. 78; IV. 196; VI. 368; VII. 370; VIII. 204; IX. 257; XIII. 59, 191, 213
Apollo, in Keats's *The Fall of Hyperion*, XII. 80, 86
Apollo, in Suckling's *Session of the Poets*, VII. 274
Apollo press, XI. 325
Apollodorus, III. 86
Apollonius, hermit, I. 74
Apollonius Rhodius, XI. 426
Apollonius of Tyre, in *Confessio Amantis*, II. 149, 152
Apollonius of Tyre, I. 135, 151
Apostolic Fathers, the, X. 353; XII. 501
Apostolical Constitutions, IX. 221
Apothecaries' company, the, XIV. 286

Apperley, Charles James (*pseud.* Nimrod, 1779–1843), xiv. 216, 232, 542, 598; *Life of a Sportsman, The*, xiv. 233; *Memoirs of...John Mytton*, xiv. 233
Appian, iv. 435
Applebee, John, ix. 16, 22, 433
Appleton, Charles Edward Cutts Birch (1841–1879), xiv. 533
Appletree, Thomas, in Farquhar's *Recruiting Officer*, viii. 171
Appolyn of Thyre, King, ii. 324, 325, 484
Aprile, in Browning's *Paracelsus*, xiii. 57, 59
Apsley, Lucy, viii. 270
Apthorpe, East (1753–1816), x. 507; *Letters on the Prevalence of Christianity*, x. 308
Apuleius, i. 135; iv. 9, 242, 414, 435; vi. 82; vii. 77, 370, 503
Apuleius, in *Loves Maistresse*, vi. 103
Apuleius, *The Golden Ass*, xiv. 311
Aquila, ix. 330
Aquilegiensis, Laurence, *Practica sive Usus Dictaminis* ('Complete Letter Writer'), ii. 363
Aquinas, St Thomas, i. 200, 210 ff.; ii. 350, 363; iii. 4, 9, 19, 416; vii. 277, 279, 312, 504, 510; xii. 201; *Summa*, ii. 365; iv. 272
Aquitania, in *The Masque of Blacknesse*, vi. 342
Ara Fortunae, vi. 319, 474
Arabella, in *The Pickwick Papers*, xiii. 314
Arabi pasha, xii. 342
Arabia, vi. 35; xii. 342; xiv. 252
Arabian learning, i. 153
Arabian Nights, The, i. 286; iii. 485; ix. 106; xi. 161, 291, 477; xii. 342, 499; xiii. 124, 305; xiv. 338
Arabian tales, xi. 290, 374
Arabians, ii. 362, 365
Arabic chair, at Cambridge, ix. 413
Arabic language, vii. 317 ff., 491
Arabic language and literature, ix. 291; xi. 290, 291, 355; xii. 341, 342, 362; xiv. 416, 457, 458
Arabin, dean, Trollope's, xiii. 422
Arabs, the, xiv. 238, 252, 253
Arachne, in Ovid's *Metamorphoses*, ix. 160
Arachne and Pallas, ix. 115
Aragon, v. 183
Aram, Eugene (1704–1759), ix. 574; xii. 418
Aram, Eugene, lord Lytton's, xiii. 418
Arator, i. 76
Arbaces, in *A King and no King*, vi. 120, 127
Arber, Edward (1836–1912), iv. 69, 70, 110, 388; viii. 182, 422; xi. 311, 339, 466, 467, 470, 471; xii. 357, 515
Arblay, Alexandre G. P. d', x. 63, 261
Arblay, Frances Burney, Madame d' (1752–1840), x. 46, 63 ff. (main entry), 135, 150, 254, 259 ff. (main entry), 267, 424, 473, 493, *also see* Add.; xi. 289, 296, 344, 349, 354, 458, 473; xii. 133, 447
  Camilla, x. 64, 66, 261; xii. 231
  Cecilia, x. 63, 64, 66
  Diary and Letters, x. 63, 65, 260, 261
  Early Diary, x. 260
  Evelina, x. 15, 64 ff., 259; xi. 365; xii. 233
  Wanderer, The, x. 63, 64, 66
Arbury, Warwickshire, x. 113
Arbuthnet, Alexander (d. 1585), printer, iv. 412
Arbuthnot, Alexander (1538–1583), iii. 137, 498
Arbuthnot, Archibald (*fl.* 1746), ix. 563
Arbuthnot, Charles, ix. 469
Arbuthnot, George, ix. 133
Arbuthnot, John (1667–1735), ix. 72, 78, 96, 98, 124, 127, 129 ff. (main entry), 152, 161, 163, 171, 220, 249, 445 ff., 452, 466 ff., 481, 498; xii. 168
  Account of the...death of Dr Woodward, ix. 132
  Art of Political Lying, ix. 131, 136
  Brief account of Mr John Ginglicutt's Treatise, ix. 133, 138, 464
  Essay concerning the effects of Air..., ix. 133, 138
  Essay concerning the nature of Ailments, ix. 133, 138
  Examination of Dr Woodward's Account of the Deluge, ix. 129
  History of John Bull, ix. 131, 133, 137
  Humble Petition of the Colliers, ix. 132
  John Bull in his Senses, ix. 131
  John Bull still in his Senses (and *Appendix*), ix. 131
  Know Yourself, ix. 133, 138
  Law is a Bottomless Pit, ix. 130; xiv. 212
  Lewis Baboon turned Honest, ix. 131
  Miscellaneous Works, ix. 133
  On the Usefulness of Mathematical Learning, ix. 130, 138
  Reasons humbly offered by the Company ...of Upholders, ix. 132
  Sermon...at the Mercat Cross, ix. 130, 138
  Tables of...Measures, Weights and Coins, ix. 130, 132
Arbuthnott, Robert, 2nd viscount (d. 1682), ix. 129
Arcadia, vi. 11, 317, 318, 341, 364, 368; x. 179; xi. 142, 287
Arcadia and Arcadianism, iii. 265, 340, 348, 352, 353, 356, 357 ff., 367, 370
Arcadian shepherds, in *Piers Plainnes seaven yeres Prentiship*, iii. 367
Arcana Aulica; or Walsingham's Manual, vii. 518
Archaeologia, ix. 358, 530, 531; xii. 506
Archaeologia Cambrensis, xii. 506
Archaeological association, xii. 349
Archaeological association, British, Journal, xii. 506
Archaeological Journal, xii. 506

Archangel, IX. 240
Archas, in *The Loyal Subject*, VI. 122, 130
Archdall, Mervyn (1723–1791), XII. 349
Archdeacon, Daniel (*fl.* 1588), IV. 453
Archer, in Farquhar's *Beaux' Stratagem*, VIII. 172
Archer or Frizer, or Ingram, murderer of Marlowe. *See* Frizer
Archer, Thomas (1554–1630?), VII. 344
Archer, Thomas (1894), XIII. 532
Archer, William (1856–1924), VI. 266, 269; XI. 447, 453; XIII. 513
Archer-Hind, Richard Dacre (1849–1910), XII. 333, 479
Archibald, Raymond Clare, XIII. 470
Archie o' Cawfield, II. 415
Archimago, in *The Faerie Queene*, III. 231
Architectural Magazine, The, XIV. 149
Architecture, Anglo-Norman, I. 155, 222, 223
Architecture, Elizabethan and Jacobean, V. 372
Architrenius, or Arch-Mourner, of Jean de Hauteville, I. 193
Archombrotus, in *Argenis*, IV. 258, 259
Archon, lord, in *Oceana*, VII. 299, 300
Archytas, I. 279
Arcite, in *Palamon and Arcyte*, VI. 299
Arcite, in *The Knightes Tale*, XIII. 123
Arcite, in *The Two Noble Kinsmen*, V. 256
Arctic regions, XIV. 241, 245, 248, 358
Arctic voyages, IV. 76
Ardagh, VII. 318; X. 197
Ardelia, in *The Dukes Mistris*, VI. 200
'Ardelia' (Winchilsea, Anne, countess of), IX. 169
Arden, forest of, III. 355; V. 192; VI. 27; XIII. 382
Arden, Mary, V. 167; XIV. 307
Arden, Mrs, VII. 55
Arden, Richard Pepper, baron Alvanley (1745–1804), XIV. 115, 127
Arden of Feversham, V. 162, 237, 240 ff., 324, 441, 443; VI. 95; X. 73, 436; XII. 186
Ardens, Radulphus, I. 221
Areopagus, the, VII. 140
Arethusa, in Keats's *Endymion*, XII. 82
Aretine, in Jonson's *Volpone*, VII. 274
Aretino, Leonardo, II. 325; IV. 441; *Poliscene*, V. 101
Aretino, Pietro, IV. 322
Aretino, in *The Unfortunate Traveller*, III. 366
Arfeville, Nicolas d', III. 156
Argalia, in Chamberlayne's *Pharonnida*, VII. 75
Argall, Anne, IV. 141
Argall, Thomas, IV. 141
Argante, in Layamon's *Brut*, I. 235, 236, 265, 266
Argemone, in Kingsley's *Yeast*, XIII. 360; XIV. 84
Argensola, Bartolomeo de, VI. 139
Argensola, Bartolomeo de (the younger), VIII. 129
Argentile, in *Albion's England*, III. 357 IV. 136
Argentine, Richarde (d. 1568), IV. 447, 448
Argogastis, XIV. 303
Argonauts, the, IV. 62
Argus, Arabella, XI. 477; *Adventures of a Donkey*, XI. 383; *Juvenile Spectator*, XI. 383
Argyll, Elizabeth, duchess of. *See* Gunning, Elizabeth
Argyll, dukes of. *See* Campbell, George Douglas; Campbell, John
Argyll, marquis of. *See* Campbell, Archibald
Argyll commission (Scottish schools), XIV. 421
Argyllshire, XIII. 431
Ariadne, X. 199
Ariadne, Titian's, XIV. 171
Ariana, mistress (Etherege's), VIII. 138
Arianism, IX. 295, 297; X. 360, 362, 371, 372, 377 ff., 384 ff.
Ariel, in *The Tempest*, V. 207, 317; VII. 3; VIII. 28, 225; XII. 196, 220; XIII. 62
Arimanes, spirits of, in Byron's *Manfred*, XII. 47
Ariodante and Genevora, V. 102, 116
Arion, XIII. 50
Ariosto, Ludovico, III. 23, 176, 204, 210 229 ff., 236, 244, 262, 305; IV. 23, 24, 196, 441, 540; V. 116, 132, 191, 220; VII. 74, 78, 271; VIII. 22; IX. 338, 481; X. 221, 234, 241, 435; XI. 157; XII. 3, 80; *Orlando Furioso*, III. 230 ff., 236; V. 102, 137; IX. 61; *Gli Suppositi*, V. 71, 114
Ariosto (trans.), XII. Add.
'Aristarch,' an, IX. 191
Aristarchus, XII. 332
Aristides, X. 154; XIII. 182
Aristippus, in *Damon and Pithias*, V. 118
Aristophanes, III. 20; IV. 526; V. 22; VI. 18, 24, 79, 315, 322, 327, 352, 362, 363; VIII. 38, 58, 164; IX. 336; X. 25, 34, 53, 415; XI. 392; XII. 309, 324, 325, 329 ff., 480, 483 ff., 488 ff., 494, *also see* Add.; XIII. 81, 82, 175, 445
  Birds, XII. 329
  Εἰρήνη or *Pax*, VI. 294
  Plutus, VI. 25, 294
  Wasps, The, VI. 25
Aristophanes, in D'Avenant's *First Day's Entertainment*, VIII. 117
Aristophanic comedy, XIV. 13
Aristotle, I. 153, 185, 187, 204, 205, 210, 212, 213; II. 21, 129, 186, 201, 207, 231, 301, 350, 354, 360 ff., 370, 371; III. 6, 20, 23, 50, 109, 233, 291, 305, 416, 420, 425, 430; IV. 3, 24, 269, 271, 273 ff., 286, 287, 291, 298, 430, 521; V. 65, 167, 172, 204, 206, 214, 295 ff.; VI. 6, 225, 232, 296; VII. 182, 228, 261, 265, 267, 277, 278, 282, 288, 302 ff., 323, 376, 377; VIII. 8, 29, 170, 203, 221, 277, 278, 287, 289, 291, 329, 350; IX. 51, 59, 60, 64, 383, 386, 562; X. 137, 514; XI. 17,

Aristotle
134; xii. 211, 230, 311, 476, 480 ff., 484 ff., 488, 489, 492, 494, *also see* Add.; xiii. 152, 167, 169, 172, 312; xiv. 9, 16, 23, 140, 398, 473, 475
Constitution of Athens, xii. 340
Ethics, i. 204, 213; iii. 430; iv. 5, 335, 414, 428, 435; vi. 233; xii. 334
History of Animals, i. 199
Metaphysics, i. 201; ii. 318
Nichomachean Ethics, xii. 520
Organon, i. 187, 207; iv. 276
Physics, i. 201, 204, 211, 212
Poetics, v. 70; vi. 8; vii. 265; viii. 375, 376; xii. 334
Politics, i. 213; iv. 5, 435; xii. 333, 334
Rhetoric, iv. 335, 347; xi. 16; xii. 328, 331
Aristotle, Aldine edition, iii. 5; iv. 422
Aristotle, in *The Palice of Honour*, ii. 260
Aristotle, The Letter of Alexander to, ii. 80
Aristotelian society, xiv. 39
Arithmetic, in *The Passetyme of Pleasure*, ii. 225
Arius, iv. 214
Arkinholm, ii. 113
'Arley,' Della Cruscan poet, xi. 177
Arley Regis, Worcester, i. 234
Arlington, 1st earl (1618–1685). *See* Bennet, Henry
Armada, the, iii. 188, 211, 244; iv. 136, 142; v. 77, 81, 136, 309, 345, 361; vi. 27, 53, 92, 174; vii. 157; xiii. 135, 136
Armado, don, in *Love's Labour's Lost*, v. 178, 239
Armageddon, xiii. 153
Armagh, vii. 139, 301, 318; xiv. 309, 321
Armenia, ii. 13, 79
Armida, in *Orlando Furioso*, iii. 230
Armin, Robert (1564?–1612?), vi. 273, 452
Foole upon Foole, vi. 218
Italian Taylor and his Boy, The, vi. 218
Nest of Ninnies, A, iv. 532; vi. 218
Two Maids of More-clacke, The, vi. 217
Arminianism, vii. 437; x. 367, 377, 381
Arminius, i. 20; viii. 291, 292
Armorican Bretons, i. 256
Armour, Jean, xi. 222
Armstrong, Cecil Ferard, xiii. 513; *Shakespeare to Shaw*, xi. 269
Armstrong, Edmund John (1841–1865), xiv. 567
Armstrong, G. F. Savage- (1845–1906), xiv. 567
Armstrong, John (1709–1779), x. 138, 147, 148, 452; *Art of Preserving Health, The*, x. 148; xiii. 200; *Economy of Love*, x. 148; *Epistle to Wilkes*, x. 148
Armstrong, Johnny, in *Pendennis*, xiii. 291
Armys, The Buke of the Law of, or Buke of Bataillis, ii. 284
Armytage, Mrs, Mrs Gore's, xii. 246
Arnall, William (1715?–1741?), ix. 433
Arne, Thomas Augustine (1710–1778), viii. 426; x. 109, 199, 425, 426, 429, 433, 447
Arngosk, The Lady of, ii. 411
Arno river, xiii. 136, 149
Arnold, A. S., xiii. 470
Arnold, Sir Edwin (1832–1904), xiii. 194, 203, 498; xiv. 191, 192, 574, 575; *He and She*, xiii. 201; *The Light of Asia*, xiii. 200; xiv. 340
Arnold, Fanny, xiii. 103
Arnold, Frances Lucy, born Wightman, xiii. 87
Arnold, Frank Bishop, xiii. 513
Arnold, Rev. Frederick, xiv. 493
Arnold, Frederick Octavius, xiv. 536
Arnold, Matthew (1822–1888), i. 249, 251, 254, 274, 275; ii. 107, 180; iv. 132, 135, 139; vi. 57; ix. 31, 169; x. 361; xi. 136, 161, 388, 406, 408, 411, 438; xii. 77, 108, 154, 177, 178, 207, 208, 297, 384, 392, 402, 406, 527; xiii. 85 ff. (main entry), 147 ff., 155, 159, 160, 174, 183, 188 ff., 221, 223, 486 ff. (main entry), 557, *also see* Add. 2; xiv. 141, 144, 147, 159, 172, 180, 191, 304, 306, 307, 350, 351, 420, 422 ff., 432, 433, 453, 601, 603
Balder Dead, xiii. 89, 94
Cromwell, xiii. 87
Culture and Anarchy, xiii. 88, 101; xiv. 425
Democracy, xiii. 88
Discourses in America, xiii. 87, 88, 99
Dover Beach, xiii. 89, 96
Empedocles on Etna, xiii. 89, 91, 95
Essays in Criticism, xiii. 98, 100, 101
Forsaken Merman, The, xiii. 91, 251
Fragment of an 'Antigone,' The, xiii. 90
French Eton, A, xiii. 88
Friendship's Garland, xiii. 101, 451
Geist's Grave, xiii. 89
God and the Bible, xiii. 101
Heine's Grave, xiii. 89
'Joubert,' xiii. 100
Last Essays on Church and Religion, xiii. 101
Last words on Translating Homer, xiii. 103
Letters, xiii. 85, 94, 99, 103
Literature and Dogma, xiii. 101
Memorial Verses, xiii. 94
Merope, a Tragedy, vii. 122; xiii. 89, 91, 95
Mixed Essays, xiii. 88, 99
Mycerinus, xiii. 90
New Poems, xiii. 89, 95
New Sirens, The, xiii. 90
'Numbers,' xiii. 99
Obermann, xiii. 98
Obermann Once More, xiii. 89, 94
On Translating Homer, xi. 90; xiii. 88, 98
Poems (1853), xiv. 139
Poems (1854), xiii. 98

Arnold, Matthew
Poems, Second Series, XIII. 89
Popular Education of France, XIII. 88; XIV. 422
Reports on Elementary Schools, XIII. 88
Requiescat, XIII. 96
Resignation, XII. 220; XIII. 90
Rugby Chapel, XIII. 89, 96
St Paul and Protestantism, XIII. 101
Scholar-Gipsy, The, XIII. 89, 92, 93, 96, 251
Schools and Universities on the Continent, XIII. 88; XIV. 422
Self-Dependence, XIII. 94, 97
Separation, XIII. 89
Sick King in Bokhara, The, XIII. 90, 91
Sohrab and Rustum, XIII. 89, 92, 94, 95, 251
Southern Night, A, XIII. 89, 96, 251
'Speech at Eton, A,' XIII. 99
Stanzas from the Grande Chartreuse, XIII. 95
Stanzas in Memory of the Author of 'Obermann,' XIII. 93, 94
Strayed Reveller, The, XIII. 89, 90, 252
Study of Celtic Literature, The, XIII. 88, 98, 100
Summer Night, A, XIII. 94, 251
Thyrsis, VII. 114; XIII. 89, 92, 96, 102
To a Gipsy Child, XIII. 90
Tristram and Iseult, XIII. 93, 251
Westminster Abbey, XIII. 89, 96
Arnold, Richard (d. 1521), *Chronicle*, II. 320, 329, 484; III. 532
Arnold, Samuel (1740–1802), X. 425, 428, 429
Arnold, Samuel James (1774–1852), XIII. 517
Arnold, Thomas (1795–1842), I. 167; VII. 152; X. 355; XII. 153, 259, 287–288, 292, 294, 302 ff. (main entry), 309, 318, 321, 338, 464, 474; XIII. 86, 103 ff., 109, 370, 433; XIV. 70, 409, 411, 413, 414, 594, 601, 603; *History of Rome*, XII. 303, 304, 339; *History of the later Roman Commonwealth*, XII. 303; *Life and Correspondence*, XII. 303, 304, 320
Arnold, Thomas (junior) (1823–1900), XII. 504
Arnold, William Delafield (1828–1859), XIV. 575; *Oakfield*, XIV. 338, 339
Arnold, William Thomas (1852–1904), XII. 405, 474; XIV. 533; *Roman System of Provincial Administration*, XII. 304
Arnold's Magazine, XIV. 539
Arqua, IV. 429
Arran, isles of, XIV. 312
Arrêts d'Amour, Les, VIII. 59
Arrivall, The History of the (1471), II. 302
Arrogance, in *Mirour de l'Omme*, II. 140
Arrowsmith, *Reformation* (1673), VIII. 26
Ars Moriendi, V. 53
Arsilius (Yong's), IV. 122
Art, in Cowley's *The Muse*, VII. 65
Art and Poetry, XIII. 111
Art de bien vivre et de bien mourir, L', II. 329
Art of good living and dying, The, II. 324, 328, 329
Artaban, in La Calprenède's *Cléopâtre*, VIII. 25
Artegall, in *The Faerie Queene*, II. 234; III. 231, 234, 236; VII. 209
Arthour and Merlin, I. 269, 317, 399, 467
Arthur, Death of, I. 190. See, also, under *Morte*
Arthur, king, X. 231; XII. 13, 354
Arthur, Kyng (Southey's), XI. 422
Arthur, prince, in *The Faerie Queene*, III. 230, 232 ff., 237
Arthur, prince, in *King John*, V. 185
Arthur, prince (1486–1502), son of Henry VII, III. 6, 8; VI. 332, 333
Arthur, Tennyson's, XIII. 37, 38
Arthur, The Dethe of, begynyng at Cassabelaun, II. 308
Arthur, The Misfortunes of, V. 78, 79
Arthur and the Arthurian legend, I. 70, 133, 148, 158, 169, 170, 177, 198, 223, 235 ff., 243–276 (main entry), 279, 284, 286, 296, 309, 311 ff., 326, 336, 342, 350, 351, 461 ff., 467, *also see Add.*; II. 112, 115, 116, 118 ff., 181, 184, 228, 230, 234, 307, 337 ff., 428; III. 359; IV 67; V. 10, 108, 250; X. 228; XIII. 36; XIV. 304, 306
See, also, under the separate title of the Arthurian romances, Wace, Layamon, etc.
Arthur and King Cornwall, King, II. 414
Arthur of Little Britain, II. 322, 339
Arthure, Gret Gest of, II. 116
Arthurian ballads, I. 464
Articles, Ten, III. 13
Articles, the XXXIX, XII. 260, 296
Articles of Grievance and Oppression, VI. 275
Articuli ad Novas Narrationes (1561), VIII. 465, 466
Artotrogos, in *Miles Gloriosus*, V. 106
Arundel, earls of. *See* Howard, Philip; Howard, Thomas
Arundel, Thomas, archbishop (1353–1414), II. 59, 62, 67, 68, 154, 348; III. 42
Arundel, William, earl of (1417–1487), Caxton's patron, II. 314
Arundel, the horse in *Sir Beves*, I. 292
Arviragus, in Layamon's *Brut*, I. 237
Arviragus, in *The Franklin's Tale*, II. 184
Arwaker, Edmund (d. 1730), VII. 405; VIII. 411
Aryan origin of ballads, II. 417
As I came in by Edinburgh town, IX. 363
Asbies mortgage, V. 219
Asbjörnsen, Peter Christen, XI. 491
Ascanius, VIII. 70
Ascapart the giant, in *Sir Beves*, I. 293, 343
Ascensio, V. 12
Ascension island, XIV. 242
Ascham, Anthony (*fl.* 1553), IV. 542

Ascham, Roger (1515–1568), III. 290 ff., 308, 310, 311, 317, 318, 327, 341, 348, 419, 421, 425, 431 ff., 438, 444, 446, 447, 454, 526, 549; IV. 6, 7, 276, 320, 345, 390; V. 350, 394; VI. 378, 480, 492; VII. 315, 329, 335; X. 177, 184, 469
De Imitatione, III. 433
Report and Discourse of the affairs of Germany, III. 432
Scholemaster, The, II. 213; III. 311, 341, 433 ff.; IV. 344, 397; VI. 295; IX. 55; XII. 488; XIII. 104
Toxophilus, III. 308, 433, 445; IV. 16
Aschillus, in *The Misfortunes of Arthur*, V. 78
Ascolot, maid of, I. 313
Ascue, Sir G., VIII. 218
Ascyltus, IX. 266
Asgill, John (1659–1738), IX. 11
Ashantee, XIV. 254
Ashburnham, John (1603–1671), VII. 449
Ashburnham, lady, IX. 125
Ashburton, Devonshire, XI. 39
Ashby, George (d. 1475), II. 209, 469; *Active Policy of a Prince*, II. 210
Ashby-de-la-Zouch, VII. 335; XI. 340
Ashe, St George (1658?–1718), IX. 166
Ashe, Simeon (d. 1662), *Intelligence*, VII. 351
Ashe, Thomas, *Carolina* (1682), IV. 453
Ashe, Thomas (1836–1889), XI. 412, 415, 416; XIII. 194, 498; *The Sorrows of Hypsipyle*, XIII. 206
Ashfield, dame, in Morton's *Speed the Plough*, XI. 281
Ashford, Kent, III. 395; VII. 341
Ashley, Sir Anthony (1551–1627), IV. 453
Ashley, A. Evelyn M., XIV. 505
Ashley, Sir John, IV. 383
Ashley, William James, XIV. 477
Ashley-Cooper, Frederick Samuel, XIV. 545
Ashmole, Elias (1617–1692), VII. 369; VIII. 247; IX. 355, 413, 531; XIV. 285, 558; *Antiquities of Berkshire*, IX. 353; *Theatrum Chemicum*, II. 211, 212
Ashton, John, XI. 475; XII. 418; XIV. 540
Ashton, Lucy, in Scott's *Bride of Lammermoor*, XII. 22
Ashton, Thomas (d. 1578), III. 428, 429; V. 103; VII. 337
Ashton, Thomas (1716–1775), X. 117, 119, 123, 243, 251
Ashton, Sir William, in Scott's *Bride of Lammermoor*, XII. 22
Ashworth, Caleb (1722–1775), X. 384
Ashworth, John (1813–1875), XIII. 560
Asia, XI. 16, 190; XII. 66; XIV. 246, 247, 252, 457, 458
Asia Minor, V. 37
Asiatic society, Greek, XII. 506
Asiatic society of Bengal, XII. 352; XIV. 334, 337
Aske, Christopher, Kingsley's, XIII. 366
Aske, Robert, Kingsley's, XIII. 366
Askesian society, XIV. 287
Aslackton, Nottinghamshire, III. 32
Asloan MS., II. 478
Asolo, XIII. 61, 62, 84
'Aspasia' (Lady Elizabeth Hastings (1682–1739), IX. 38
Aspatia, in *The Maides Tragedy*, VI. 120, 123, 126
Asper, in *Every Man out of his Humour*, VI. 17, 39
Aspland, Robert (1782–1845), XII. 428, 465
Aspley, William (*fl.* 1588–1637), IV. 393 ff.
Assaye, battle of, XII. 98
Asser (d. 909?), bishop of Sherborne, I. 89 ff., 101, 105; *Aelfredi regis res gestae*, IV. 397
Asses, feast of, V. 8
Assisi, I. 200, 210, 364
Assmann, I. 124
Association for the protection of the queen's person, V. 345
Assoucy, Charles Coypeau d', IX. 256
Assumptio Mariae, I. 232, 458, 459
Assurbanipal, Annals of, XII. 499
Assyria, II. 296; XII. 342, 477
Assyrian host, in *Ezechias*, VI. 298
Assyrians, IV. 31
Astarte, in Byron's *Manfred*, XII. 47, 393, 395, 396
Astell, Mary (1668–1731), IX. 244, 498; *Serious proposal to the Ladies*, IX. 404, 569
'Asteria' (lady Luxborough). *See* Knight, Henrietta
Asthall, I. 126
Astley, John (d. 1595), IV. 444, 540
Astley, Sir John Dugdale (1828–1894) XIV. 540
Astley, Philip (1742–1814), XIII. 264, 265
Aston, colonel, VIII. 211
Aston, Edward, IV. 442
Aston, John (*fl.* 1382), II. 61
Aston, lady Gertrude, IV. 194
Aston, R., *Placita Latine Rediviva* (1661) VIII. 467
Aston, Walter, baron Aston (1584–1639) IV. 173, 176, 179, 184, 188, 216
Astragon, in D'Avenant's *Gondibert*, VII 71
Astrology and occultism, VII. 508 ff.
Astronomia, in *Technogamia*, VI. 323
Astronomy, in *The Passetyme of Pleasure* II. 225
Astrophel (Waller's), VII. 54
Astrophell (*i.e.* Sidney), IV. 116
Astrophil, VIII. 61
Astrophill, V. 349
Atalantis Major, IX. 13
Até, in *Locrine*, V. 84
Ateukin, in *James IV*, V. 138
Athanase, in Shelley's *Prince Athanase* XII. 61
Athanasian controversy, X. 362
Athanasian creed, VIII. 42; X. 360

Athanasius, I. 74, 75; II. 79, 86; XI. 287; *Festal Letters*, XII. 341
Atheist's Tragedie, The (ballad), V. 143
Athelstan. *See* Aethelstan
Athelston, I. 287, 467
Athenaeum, The, IX. 106; XII. 349, 359, 365, 437; XIII. 54, 69; XIV. 144, 145, 171, 174, 193, 200, 364, 530, 531, 533, 534
Athenaeus, VII. 311; XII. 325; *Deipnosophia*, VI. 102
Athenais, in *The Emperour of the East*, VI. 158, 163
Athenian democracy, XII. 311, 312
Athenian Gazette (Dunton's), IX. 5
Athenian Letters, XI. 475
Athenian Mercury (Dunton's), IX. 5, 34, 41, 92
Athenians, the, IX. 223; XIV. 120
Athens, IV. 1, 270, 335; V. 64; VI. 308; XII. 32, 72, 312, 313; XIII. 129, 133, 135, 136, 256; XIV. 122, 205, 211
Parthenon, XII. 340
Temple of Theseus, XII. 39
Athens, in *The Anatomy of Wit*, III. 345
Atherstone, Edwin (1788–1872), XII. 129, 413; *The Fall of Nineveh*, XII. 128
Aðils, king of the Svear, I. 25 ff.
Athlone, X. 196, 197
Atholl, 3rd duke of. *See* Murray, John
Athos, mount, XIV. 252
Atkins, John Black, XIV. 535
Atkins, Samuel, VIII. 257
Atkinson, Henry George, XIV. 476
Atkinson, Joseph, *The Mutual Deception*, X. 429
Atkinson, Robert, XII. 361, 362, 515
Atkinson, Thomas (1600–1639), VI. 470
Atkyns, Sir Robert (1647–1711), *Glocestershire*, IX. 353, 531
Atkynson, William (d. 1509), translator of *Imitatio Christi*, II. 321
Atlámal, in the *Edda*, I. 21
Atlante, in *Orlando Furioso*, III. 231
Atlantic, the, IV. 68; XI. 190
Atlantic ocean, XIII. 88
Atlantis, XI. 190
Atlantis (of Plato), IV. 73
Atlas, in *Pleasure Reconciled*, VI. 359 ff.
Atlas, sign of, on the Globe theatre, VI. 256
Atlas, The, XII. 444
Atlay, James Beresford (1860–1913), XIV. 500, 507, 508, 511
Atli, the hall of, XIII. 126
Atossa, in Pope's *Characters of Women*, IX. 82, 89
Atreus, in *Thyestes*, VI. 301
Atropos, in *Filostrato e Panfila*, V. 62
Attendant spirit, the, in *Comus*, VII. 113
Atterbury, Francis (1662–1732), VII. 410, 444; VIII. 394; IX. 131, 147, 153, 176, 196, 234, 333, 334, 337, 340, 425, 525; X. 351 ff., 515, 517; XIV. 61; *Discourse on the death of the Lady Cutts*, X. 352
Attercliffe, IX. 393
Attercliffe academy, X. 386
Attey, John (*c.* 1622), IV. 463
Attic democracy, the, XIV. 134
Attic drama, V. 1, 5; VI. 232. *See, also*, Greek drama
Attic dramatists, IX. 330
Attic eloquence, XI. 13
Attic idiom, XII. 328
Attic law, XII. 327
Attic orators, XII. 329
Attic prose, XIII. 99
Attic tragedy, XIII. 90
Atticus, T. Pomponius, IX. 198
'Atticus,' in Dibdin's *Bibliomania*, XII. 365
Atticus, in Graves's *Columella*, X. 277
Attila, I. 20, 32, 34
Attilia, in *Fedele and Fortunio*, V. 315
Atwit, colonel, in Swift's *Complete Collection of...Conversation*, IX. 106
Atwood, William (d. 1705?), X. 498
Auban, Vie de Seint, XII. 362
Auberon, in *Huon of Bordeaux*, II. 339
Aubignac, abbé d', *Pratique du théâtre*, VIII. 375
Aubrey, Augusta, in Cumberland's *Fashionable Lover*, XI. 265
Aubrey, John (1626–1697), III. 323; IV. 509; V. 167; VII. 22, 38, 42, 56, 58, 59, 61, 70, 107, 118, 153, 282 ff., 290, 329, 362, 507, *also see* Add.; VIII. 295, 322, 361; IX. 267, 351 (main entry), 531, 536, 574; XI. 393
Brief Lives, IX. 308, 351
Miscellanies, IX. 351
Monumenta Britannica, IX. 354
Perambulation of Surrey, IX. 351, 353
Surrey, IV. 308
Wilts, IV. 308
Aubrey, Mary (K. Philips's 'Rosania'), VII. 88
Auburn, in Goldsmith's *Deserted Village*, X. 212
Aubusson regiment, the, X. 203
Aucassin et Nicolette, IX. 39
Auchinleck, X. 190, 191, 193; XI. 235, 236, 442
Auchinleck MS., I. 370, 465; XII. 376
Auchinleck press, XII. 357
Audax, grammarian, I. 76
Audax, in *The Floating Island*, VI. 325
Audelay, John (*fl.* 1426), II. 496, 504
Auditor, The, X. 390, 392, 522
Auditus, in *Lingua*, VI. 315
Audlem, Cheshire, VII. 341
Audley, in *Edward III*, V. 246
Audley, George, lord, IV. 161
Audley, James de (1316?–1369), II. 336
Audley, Thomas, baron Audley of Walden (1488–1544), II. 358
Audley, Thomas (*fl.* 1643), VII. 494; *Mercurius Britannicus*, VII. 350; *Mercurius Diutinus*, VII. 351
Audoin, in *Widsith*, I. 35
Audry, St, IX. 343

Aue. *See* Hartmann von
Aufidius, in *Coriolanus*, v. 198
Augsberg Interim, III. 34
Augusel, in Arthurian legend, I. 259
Augusta, princess of Wales, x. 108, XIV. 287
Augustalis, Threnodia. *See* Cornelys, Mrs Theresa
Augustan age, IV. 330
Augustan school of poetry, XII. 36, 40, 41, 43, 77
Augustine, St, of Hippo, I. 93, 94, 102, 103, 117, 120, 124, 126, 127, 213, 224, 231, 234, 355, 436, 438, 440; II. 20, 52, 53, 182, 199, 230, 308, 324, 355, 365; III. 9, 19, 400, 416; IV. 220, 241, 395, 441; VII. 312, 370, 372, 376, 504, 510; VIII. 348; XII. 260; *Confessions*, VII. 170; VIII. 103; *De Civitate Dei*, III. 15, 16; IV. 395; IX. 318; *Meditations*, II. 383
Augustine, St (d. 604), archbishop of Canterbury, I. 1, 5, 13, 41, 42, 71, 72, 351
Augustinian monastery in London, v. 104
Augustinianism, III. 12
Augustinians (Austin Friars), II. 287, 349, 367
Augustus, emperor of Rome, IV. 416; XII. 304, 493
Augustus Frederick, duke of Sussex (1773–1843), XII. 367; XIV. 411
Aulay, I. 287
Auld Guidman, The, IX. 360
'Auld Hornie,' XI. 212
'Auld Licht' clergy, XI. 212, 213, 216
Auld Maitland, II. 408, 493
Auld Nick, in Burns's *Tam o' Shanter*, XI. 219
Auld Reekie, IX. 379
Auld Rob Morris, IX. 360
Auld Wife ayont the Fire, IX. 360
Aulnoy, Mary Catherine, countess de, XI. 375, 485, 491
Aulus, in Owen's *Epigrammata*, IV. 265
Aulus Gellius, III. 20
Aungerville, Sir Richard (1281–1345), I. 213
Aurelia, duchess of Siena, in *The Maid of Honour*, VI. 152, 155
Aurelia, in *The Prophetesse*, VI. 152
Aurelian, emperor of Rome, XII. 304
Aurelian, in Congreve's *Incognita*, VIII. 146
Aurelio, in *The Ladies Triall*, VI. 194
Aurelius, Caninus, I. 67
Aurelius, Marcus, IX. 300; X. 275; XII. 307; XIII. 98; *Meditations*, XII. 335
Aurelius, in *The Franklin's Tale*, II. 184
Auria, a Genoese, in *The Ladies Triall*, VI. 194
Aurifaber, John (*fl.* 1566), VIII. 321
Aurora, in *The Penates*, VI. 341
Aurora, The, XIV. 177
Aurungzebe the Great, X. 110; XIV. 333
Ausonius, III. 173, 187; IV. 250, 267, 435; VII. 83, 489; *Collige, virgo, rosas*, VII. 2
Aust, prebend of, II. 49
Austen, Cassandra, XII. 232, 237
Austen, Charles, XII. 239
Austen, Jane, II. 192; IX. 338; XI. 285, 286; XII. 24, 231 ff. (main entry), 246, 247, 252, 379, 446, *also see* Add.; XIII. 307, 313, 377, 430, 431; XIV. 208
Elinor and Marianne, XII. 233, 236
Emma, XII. 151, 234, 239
First Impressions (*Pride and Prejudice*), XII. 233, 234
Kitty, or the Bower, XII. 233
Lady Susan, XII. 233
Mansfield Park, X. 66; XII. 234, 238, 241
Northanger Abbey, XI. 299; XII. 233 ff., 247
Persuasion, XII. 234, 235, 237, 238, 240, 241
Pride and Prejudice, XII. 233 ff., 237, 238, 241, 243
Sense and Sensibility, X. 15; XII. 233 ff., 241
Susan, XII. 234
Watsons, The, XII. 234
Austen, lady Anne, XI. 83, 87, 88
Austen-Leigh, J. E., *Memoir of Jane Austen*, XII. 233, 234, 446
Austen-Leigh, R. A., XIV. 597
Austen-Leigh, W. and R. A., *Jane Austen*, XII. 232, 234, 239
Austerlitz, battle of, XII. 166
Austin, Alfred (1835–1913), XIII. 194, 498, 499; XIV. 189; *Human Tragedy, The*, XIII. 203; *Prince Lucifer*, XIII. 203
Austin, John (1613–1669), VII. 406
Austin, John (1790–1859), VIII. 321; XIV. 468
Austin, lieutenant, XIII. 427
Austin, Mrs, *Shakespeare in Paris*, XII. 153
Austin, Sarah (1793–1867), XI. 491; XIII. 560
Austin, St, in Layamon, I. 234
Austin, William (1587–1634), VII. 423, 512
Austin, William (*fl.* 1662), IX. 429
Australasia, XIV. 289
Australasian, The, XIV. 367
Australasian languages, XIV. 459
Australia, IV. 100; XII. 119; XIV. 86, 137, 241, 289, 319, 331, 361 ff., 434, 457
Australian Journal, The, XIV. 370
Australian journalism, XIV. 371
Australian literature, XIV. 361 ff.
Australian tales, XIII. 432, 433
Austria, IX. 232; XII. 50; XIV. 383
Austria-Hungary, II. 310
Authority, in *Respublica*, v. 60
Autolycus, in *The Winter's Tale*, III. 356; v. 95, 206; XIII. 64
Auvergne, XIV. 293, 294
Auvergne (La Chaise Dieu), III. 100
Avalon, isle of, I. 243, 264, 266, 272, 311; II. 120
Avantance, in *Mirour de l'Omme*, II. 140
Avarice, in *Confessio Amantis*, II. 147, 149
Avarice, in *Nature*, v. 54
Avarice, in *Negromansir*, III. 77

Avarice, in *The Passetyme of Pleasure*, II. 226
Avarice, in *Piers the Plowman*, II. 23, 28
Avarice, in *Two Lamentable Tragedies*, V. 326
Avaritia, in *The Castle of Perseverance*, V. 52
Avaritia, in *Psychomachia*, V. 60
Avarus, in *A Dialogue...against the fever Pestilence*, III. 109
Ave Maria, II. 359
Ave maris Stella, IV. 129
Avebury, Sir John Lubbock, lord (1834–1913), XII. 511; XIV. 476, 562; *Prehistoric Times*, XII. 348; *The Origin of Civilization*, XII. 348
Averroes, II. 363
Averroists, the, I. 213
Avianus, XII. 337
Avicenna, I. 205
Avignon, I. 212, 213, 216; II. 53, 57; V. 61; IX. 245, 483; XIV. 22
Avila y Zuniga, Luis de, IV. 441
Avison, Charles (1710?–1770), musician, XIII. 84
Avitus of Vienne, I. 47
Avogadro, count Amadeo, XIV. 277, 557
Avon, river, IV. 190; X. 112
Avondale, lord, in Morton's *School of Reform*, XI. 281
Avowing of Arthur, I. 313
Awa Whigs Awa, IX. 377
Awdeley or Awdelay, John (*fl.* 1559–1577), IV. 317, 318, 320, 390; *The Fraternitye of vacabones*, III. 87, 102, 103, 104, 343, 360, 448, 484, 492; IV. 509, 521; V. 480
Awntyrs [Adventures] *of Arthure at the Terne Wathelyne*, I. 291, 312; II. 112, 116, 121 ff., 450; III. 278
Axon, William Edward Armytage, VII. 247, 462; XI. 467; XIII. 542, 549, 553
Axtell, col. Daniel (d. 1600), VIII. 470
Ayenbite of Inwyt, I. 353 ff., 388, 396, 397, 475
Aylesbury, VII. 440; X. 391
Aylesford, earl of. *See* Finch, Heneage
Aylett, Robert (1583–1655?), IV. 521; VII. 406
Ayliffe, John (1676–1732), IX. 570
Aylmer, Brabazon, XI. 319, 332
Aylmer, John (1521–1594), bishop of London, III. 145, 376, 385, 386, 397, 593; IV. 382, 410, 509; V. 482; VII. 316; IX. 496
Aylmer, Rose, XII. 441
Ayloffe, John (d. 1685), VIII. 408, 410; IX. 266, 499
Aylott and Jones, publishers, XIII. 415
Aylward, Alfred, XIV. Add. 5
Aymon, The Four Sons of, I. 292. *See, also, under* Caxton
Aynard, Joseph, XI. 416
Ayre, William (*fl.* 1744), IX. 447
Ayrer, Jacob, V. 284, 457; *Comedia von der schönen Sidea*, V. 220, 285; *Schöne Phoenicia*, V. 285
Ayres, Philip (1638–1712), VII. 88, 405, 412
Ayrshire, III. 45; X. 191; XI. 220, 235, 440 ff., 445; XIII. 432
Ayscough, George Edward (d. 1779), *Semiramis*, X. 86, 439
Aytoun or Ayton, Sir Robert (1570–1638), II. 95; VII. 412
Aytoun, William Edmonstoune (1813–1865), XII. 421; XIII. 147, 187, 189, 499; XIV. 504
Bon Gaultier Ballads, The (with Sir Th. Martin), XIII. 161
Firmilian, XIII. 160, 161
Island of the Scots, The, XIII. 160
Lays of the Scottish Cavaliers, XIII. 160
Azalais, in Morris's *Love is Enough*, XIII. 125
Azarias, I. 48, 428
Azo of Bologna, I. 181; II. 364; VIII. 312, 465; *Brocardica*, II. 364; *Summa*, II. 364
Azores, IV. 200; VI. 101; IX. 175
Azov, sea of, XIV. 294

B., Mr, in Richardson's *Pamela*, X. 5, 7
B. B. *See* Nairne, Caroline Oliphant
B. R. (*fl.* 1584), IV. 4, 436
B[oreman], R[obert] (d. 1675), VII. 342
Bab, lady, in Burgoyne's *Maid of the Oaks*, XI. 265
Babbage, Charles (1792–1871), XIV. 258, 288, 555
Babees' Boke, The, etc., II. 499; III. 341; XI. 368
Babel, tower of, in Alfred's *Boethius*, I. 101
Babes in the Wood, The, IV. 393; XI. 385
Babes in Wood, Italian version, V. 325; VI. 96
Babilon, Saudan of, in Fortescue's *Monarchia*, II. 298
Babington, Churchill (1821–1889), XII. 331, 480
Babington, Gervase (1550?–1610), IV. 495; *Very Fruitful Exposition of the Commandments*, VI. 396, 492
Babington, William (1756–1833), XIV. 287, 558
Bab-lock-hithe, XIII. 93
Baboon, Lewis, in Arbuthnot's *History of John Bull*, IX. 134, 135; IX. 134
Babrius, XI. 479; XII. 339
Babson, J. E., XII. 435
Baby-Cake, in *The Masque of Christmas*, VI. 358
Babylas, martyr, I. 74
Babylon, II. 13, 71; IV. 84; V. 49; VIII. 122; X. 117, 228; XIII. 214
Babylon, in Blake's poems, XI. 197, 199
Babylon, paynim porter of, in *Huon of Bordeaux*, II. 339
Babylon, sultan of, I. 302. *See, also,* Babilon

Babylon, II. 403, 410 ff.
Babylonia, XII. 342, 477
Babyngton, Anthony, V. 345, 371
Baby's Début, I. 289
Bacchus, III. 317; VII. 370; VIII. 203; XIII. 247
Bacchus, in Keats's *Endymion*, XII. 82
Bacchus, in *Lingua*, VI. 315
Bacchus, in *The Penates*, VI. 341
Bacchylides, XII. 332, 485; *Odes*, XII. 340
Bacha, in *Cupid's Revenge*, VI. 128
Back, John, XI. 335
Backbite, Sir Benjamin, in *The School for Scandal*, IV. 114
Backstead, IV. 360
Bacon, in Lamb's *Mr H—*, XII. 189
Bacon, lady Ann (1528–1610), IV. 278; VII. 193
Bacon, Anthony (1558–1601), IV. 123, 278, 279; VII. 343, 436; X. 295, 498
Bacon, Francis, 1st baron Verulam and viscount St Albans (1561–1626), III. 308, 324, 325, 337, 392, 417, 425, 438, 445, 459, *also see* Add.; IV. 31, 77, 237, 269, 273, 275, 277, 278–292 (main entry), 298, 318, 325, 343 ff., 348, 375, 434, 504 ff., 521, 524, 525, 542; V. 77, 167, 222, 357, 367, 477; VI. 2, 112, 356; VII. 95, 163, 193, 221, 238, 259, 264 ff., 269, 270, 272, 277, 283, 289, 290, 298, 303, 306, 319, 323, 339, 366, 379, 433, 438, 440 ff., 453, 465, 469; VIII. 8, 273, 275, 278, 317, 321, 332, 351, 367, 368, 377, 467; IX. 47, 351, 381, 385, 386, 388, 396, 508, 529, 573; XI. 11, 57, 432; XII. 363, 427, 455, 505; XIII. 169, 212; XIV. 29, 63, 82, 169, 460, 472, 506
- *A Reading on the Statute of Uses*, VIII. 316
- *Advancement of Learning*, IV. 268, 279, 282, 283, 285, 290, 291, 349; VII. 314; IX. 388
- *Augmentis Scientiarum, De*, IV. 279, 280, 283, 290, 291; VII. 190, 374; VIII. 316; IX. 388
- *Considerations Touching the War with Spain*, IV. 87
- 'Coulers of good and evill, The,' IV. 343
- *Essays*, IV. 279, 290, 343, 347, 524; V. 338, 357; VI. 8, 189; VIII. 376; IX. 44; X. 206
- *History of Henry VII*, IV. 279, 408; VI. 193; VII. 201 ff.; IX. 227
- *History of Henry VIII*, VII. 442
- *Instauratio Magna*, IV. 401; VII. 194
- *Letter to the King*, VII. 194
- *Maxims of the Law*, VIII. 316
- *New Atlantis*, IV. 280, 281; VII. 299, 303, 470; IX. 388
- *Novum Organum*, IV. 279, 284, 285, 287, 289; VII. 276, 314
- *Sapientia Veterum, De*, IV. 279; VII. 260
- *Sylva Sylvarum*, IV. 280, 283
- *Witty Apophthegms*, VII. 392

Bacon, friar, XI. 373
Bacon, Nathaniel (1593–1660), VII. Add.; VIII. 142, 467
Bacon, Sir Nicholas, IV. 278
Bacon, Robert, I. 202
Bacon, Roger (1214?–1294), I. 199 ff., 204 ff., 452, *also see* Add.; II. 50, 350, 366; IV. 269, 271, 273; VII. 367, 372, 504, 510; XIV. 82, 467, 469; *De Grammatica*, II. 363; *De multiplicatione specierum cum perspectiva ejusdem*, II. 362
Baconian philosophy, XIV. 418
Baconthorpe, John (d. 1346), the "Resolute Doctor," I. 213, 452
Bactria, VI. 302
Baden, treaty of, IX. 228
Badenoch, X. 230, 232
Badger, squire, in Fielding's *Don Quixote in England*, X. 22
Badham, Charles (1813–1884), XII. 330, 480
Badius, Jodocus, III. 59, 485
Badmington Library of Sports, The, XIV. 539
Badon, mount, I. 66, 246 ff.
Baffin, William (d. 1622), IV. 99, 107
Bagdad. *See* Baghdad
Bage, Robert (1728–1801), X. 423; XI. 295 ff., 459
- *Barham Downs*, XI. 295, 296
- *Fair Syrian*, XI. 295
- *Hermsprong, or Man as he is not*, X. 59; XI. 292, 295
- *James Wallace*, XI. 295
- *Man as he is*, XI. 295, 296
- *Mount Henneth*, XI. 295, 296

Bagehot, Walter (1826–1877), X. 509, 512; XI. 408; XII. 179, 377, 402, 431; XIII 104, 155, 476, 483, 489, 542; XIV. 141 ff., 164, 199, 493, 515
- *Biographical Studies*, XIV. 142
- *Economic Studies*, XIV. 36
- *English Constitution, The*, XIV. 36, 58, 142, 143
- *Literary Studies*, XII. 152; XIV. 142
- *Lombard Street*, XIV. 36, 142, 143
- *Physics and Politics*, XIV. 36, 142

Bagford, John (1650–1716), III. 97
Bagford Ballads, VIII. 411
Baggily hall, Cheshire, II. 40
Baghdad, I. 153
Baghdad, caliph of, XII. 55
Bagley wood, XIII. 93
Bagnet, Mrs, XII. 125
Bagstock, major, in *Dombey and Son*, XIII. 325
Bagwell, William (*fl.* 1655), VII. 515
Bailey, J. C., *The Poems of William Cowper*, XI. 83
Bailey, J. E., VII. 247
Bailey, Nathan (d. 1742), *Universal Etymological Dictionary*, X. 173 ff., 236
Bailey, Philip James (1816–1902), XIII 147, 148, 157, 161, 187, 223, 499
- *Angel World, The*, XIII. 154
- *Festus*, XII. 114; XIII. 152 ff., 159

Bailey, Philip James
Mystic, The, XIII. 154
Spiritual Legend, The, XIII. 154
Universal Hymn, XIII. 154
Bailey, Samuel (1791–1870), XIV. 468
Baillie, lady Grizel (1665–1746), XI. 231; *The Ewe-buchtin's bonnie*, IX. 364; *Were na my Heart licht*, IX. 364
Baillie, Joanna (1762–1851), XI. 149, 231 (main entry), 442, 456; XII. 12, 373, 413; XIII. 467
Chough and the Crow, The, XII. 125
De Montfort, XI. 274
Fugitive Pieces, XI. 231
Good night, XII. 125
It was on a morn, XI. 231
Metrical Legends, XI. 231
'My Bride he is winsome and bonnie,' XI. 231
On the passions, XII. 124
Poverty parts Good Company, XI. 231
Saw Ye Johnie Comin, XI. 231
Tam o' the Lin, XI. 231
Baillie, Robert (1599–1662), VII. 455; XII. 517
Baillie, Sir William, of Lamington (*fl.* 1648), VII. 455
Baily, in *Gammer Gurton's Nedle*, VI. 297
Baily, or Bayly, Lewes (d. 1631), *The Practice of Piety*, VII. 147, 423
Bain, Alexander (1818–1903), XII. 476; XIV. 5, 48, 97, 98, 468, 473, 477 ff., 495, 594, 601, 604
Education as a Science, XIV. 428
Emotions and the Will, The, XIV. 23
On teaching English, XIV. 429
Senses and the Intellect, The, XIV. 23
The British Settler's Song, XIV. 377
Bain, James, XIV. 358, 583
Bain, Joseph, XII. 515
Bainbridge, John (1582–1643), IX. 530
Baines, Edward (1774–1848), XII. 507; XIV. 533
Baines, Sir Edward (1800–1890), XIV. 604
Bajazet (Louis XIV), in Rowe's *Tamerlane*, VIII. 195
Baker, Arthur E., XIII. 476, 567
Baker, David (Augustin) (1575–1641), VII. 143, 144, 423
Baker, David Erskine (1730–1767), VIII. 423; X. 442; *Biographia Dramatica*, XIV. 334; *Companion to the playhouses*, XI. 453
Baker, E. A., IX. 327
Baker, Geoffrey (*fl.* 1350), II. 496
Baker, George (1540–1600), IV. 444
Baker, George (1781–1851), XII. 507: *History and Antiquities of Northamptonshire*, XII. 346
Baker, George Pierce, VI. 266; XIII. 542
Baker, Henry (1698–1774), IX. 24, 25, 433; X. 452
Baker, James, XIV. 601
Baker, Sir Richard (1568–1645), IV. 525; VII. Add.; *Theatrum Redivivum*, VI. 406, 460, 496
Baker, Samuel (d. 1788), XI. 336, 467
Baker, Sir Samuel White (1821–1893), XIV. 550
Baker, Thomas (1656–1740), IX. 354, 477, 531, 541, 568; XII. 481; *Reflections on Learning*, IX. 354, 531; *History of St John's College*, XII. 326, 488
Baker, Thomas, dramatist (*fl.* 1703), *The Yeoman of Kent*, XI. 321
Baker, W. T., XIII. 513
Baker, 'collonel,' *The Blazing-Star*, VII. 383
Baker, Jesuit father, X. 301
Bakewell, C. M., XIV. 472
Bala, Merionethshire, X. 115
Bala rocks, XIV. 292
Balaam, VII. 370; XIII. 170
Balaam, in Cowley's *Davideis*, VII. 66
Balaam, Sir, in Pope's *Epistles*, IX. 81
'Balaam,' newspaper, XIII. 308
Balaustion, Browning's, XIII. 80, 81
Balboa, Vasco Nuñez de, IV. 68
Balcanqual, or Balcanquhall, W. (1586?–1645), VII. 435; IX. 542
Balcarres, Fife, XI. 231
Balcarres, house of, XII. 377. *See, also*, Lindsays
Balclutha, I. 275
Baldassare, in *Romola*, XIII. 395
Balderstone, Caleb, in Scott's *Bride of Lammermoor*, XII. 23
Baldi, Octavio (*i.e.* Sir Henry Wotton), IV. 163
Baldock, Herts, VIII. 243
Baldwin (d. 1190), archbishop of Canterbury, I. 194, 195
Baldwin, Edwin, newspaper owner, XIV. 188
Baldwin, Edwin (*pseud.* of William Godwin), XI. 394
Baldwin, Prudence, VII. 6
Baldwin, Sir, I. 313
Baldwin, William (*fl.* 1547), editor of *A Mirror for Magistrates*, which also see, III. 192 ff., 198, 200, 494; *A Brief Memorial*, III. 194; *The Canticles*, III. 194; *A Treatise of Moral Philosophy*, III. 194; IV. 436, 507
Baldwin, William (*fl.* 1824–1826), XIV. 228
Bale, John (1495–1563), bishop of Ossory, II. 36, 39, 40, 152, 225, 441; III. 55, 123, 124, 531; V. 103, 104, 391, 392, 395, 399, 401; VI. 374, 482; XIV. 485; *Catalogus*, V. 58; *King John*, III. 123, 280; V. 65, 66, 152, 153; *The Three Laws*, V. 58
Bale, Robert (*fl.* 1461), III. 48, 57, 77, 81
Balfour, Alexander (1767–1829), XII. 448
Balfour, Sir Andrew (1630–1694), IX. 552, 558
Balfour, Arthur James, earl of, XIV. 509
Balfour, Francis Maitland (1851–1882), XIV. 558; *Text-book of Embryology*, XIV. 300

Balfour, lady F., XIV. 507
Balfour, Graham, XIV. 526, 590
Balfour, John, XI. 342
Balfour, Robert, 2nd baron Burleigh (d. 1663), IV. 265
Balguy, John (1686–1748), IX. 504; *Foundation of Moral Goodness*, IX. 299
Balibari, the chevalier de, in Thackeray's *Barry Lyndon*, XIII. 282
Balin and Balan, I. 269
Baliol, Edward, I. 357
Baliol, John de (1249–1315), II. 104
Balkan peninsula, XII. 32, 42
Ball, Edward. *See* Fitzball
Ball, John (d. 1381), I. 369, 477; II. 63
Ball, John (1818–1889), XIV. 553
Ball, John, in Morris's *Dream of John Ball*, XIII. 128
Ball, John, of Honiton, X. 387
Ball, Sir Robert Stawell (1840–1913), XIV. 263, 265, 500, 555
Ball, W. V., XIV. 536
Ballad in Imitation of Martial, XI. 174
Ballad society, II. 493; XII. 355, 504
Ballada, in *Fucus Histriomastix*, VI. 324
Ballade of Ballades, IV. 249
Balladino, in *The Case is Altered*, V. 314, 321
Ballads, II. 492 ff., 395–418
Ballads (street), III. 19, 491; IV. 535
Ballantine, A., XII. 377
Ballantyne, James (1772–1833), XI. 342, 469; XII. 5, 12, 372
Ballantyne, John (1774–1821), XII. 2, 366, 375
Ballantyne, Robert Michael (1825–1894), XI. 387
Ballantyne, Thomas (1806–1871), XIII. 464, 466
Ballantyne Humbug handled, The, XII. 377, 380
Ballantyne novels (the Novelist's Library), XI. 295; XII. 2, 366, 375
Ballantyne press, XI. 342, 469; XII. 377
Ballantyne's *Annual Register*, XI. 162
Ballard, Edward (d. 1796), XI. 332
Ballard, George (1706–1755), XI. 426, XIV. 599
Ballards, the, XI. 336, 337
Ballengeich, the Gudeman of (= James V of Scotland), II. 244, 270
Baller, Joseph, IX. 164
Ballincollig, county Cork, XIII. 107; XIV. 326
Balliol. *See* Baliol
Ballitore, Ireland, XI. 1
Ballymahon, X. 195, 196, 199
Ballymote, Book of, XII. 362, 515
'Balmquhapple,' Fife, XI. 242
'Balnaves,' *O Gallandis All I cry and call*, III. 131
Balochistan, XII. 352
Balormy, John, in *Lives of the Saints*, II. 128
Balsara, IV. 84
Balsham, Hugo de, I. 205
Baltic, the, IV. 67, 310
Baltimore, XIV. 263
Baltinglas, viscount, VII. 245
Balzac, Honoré de, IX. 20; XI. 290, 305; XII. 20; XIII. 286, 301, 339, 422, 456
Béatrix, XIII. 283
Chef d'Œuvre inconnu, IX. 39
Comédie Humaine, La, XII. 54; XIII. 292
Cousine Bette, La, XIII. 290
Curé de Tours, Le, XIII. 283
Eugénie Grandet, XIII. 283
Père Goriot, Le, XIII. 283
Balzac, Jean Louis Guez de, IV. 221, 525; VII. 263, 391; *Letters*, VIII. 371 ff.
Bamberg, IV. 429
Bamford, Rev., XIV. 604
Bamford, Samuel, *Passages in the Life of a Radical*, XII. 397; XIV. 202
Bampfield, Joseph (*fl.* 1639–1685), VII. 450
Bampfylde, Coplestone Warre (d. 1791), XI. 424; XIV. 214
Bampfylde, John Codrington (1754–1796), X. 453; XI. 178; XII. 132, 413
Country enjoyment, XII. 133
Evening, XII. 133
Morning, XII. 133
The Sea, XII. 133
To the River Teign, XII. 133
Bampton lectures, X. 309; XII. 273, 286, 294; XIV. 13
Banaster, Gilbert, VI. 281, 283
Banbury, XI. 373
Banbury, Roman amphitheatre at, VI. 252
Bancks, J., publisher of Prior's *Miscellaneous Works*, IX. 482; *also see* Add.
Bancroft, John (d. 1696), VIII. 400
Bancroft, Richard (1544–1610), archbishop of Canterbury, III. 391, 392, 394, 544; IV. 382, 422, 424, 425, 491, 519, 545; VII. 327, 332; *Sermon preached at Paules crosse*, III. 392, 543
Bancroft, Thomas (*fl.* 1633–1658), VII. 412
Bancrofts, the, XIII. 513
Band, Cuffe and Ruffe, VI. 481
Bandello, Matteo, III. 343; IV. 3, 6, 7, 377, 441, 442; V. 191, 220, 221, 244, 245, 247; VI. 49, 99, 100, 123, 180; VIII 126
Bandon, county Cork, XII. 165
Banff, II. 100; XII. 513
Bang, W., VI. 102
Bangor, IX. 309, 310, 541; X. 354, 362
Bangor, antiphonary hymns of, I. 65
Bangor college, XIV. 433
Bangorian controversy, IX. 17, 19, 309, 477, 510, 511
Banim, John (1798–1842), XIV. 312, 314, 567
Aileen, XIV. 316
Damon and Pythias, XIII. 259; XIV. 316
Nowlans, The, XIV. 316
Revelations of the Dead, XIV. 316
Soggarth Aroon, XIV. 316
Tales by the O'Hara Family, XIV. 316

Banim, Michael (1796–1874), XIV. 312, 314, 567; *Father Connell*, XIV. 316, 317; *Tales by the O'Hara Family*, XIV. 316; *Town of the Cascades, The*, XIV. 317
Banishment of Poverty, The, IX. 366
'Banjo Byron' (Alfred Austin), XIII. 203
Bank of England, XI. 39
Bankes, G. N., XIV. 597
'Bankes his Curtall,' IV. 366
Banks (a Scotsman), IV. 366, 367, 531, 540
Banks, John (*fl.* 1696), VIII. 21, 195, 401, 434; *The Unhappy Favourite, or the Earl of Essex*, V. 346; VIII. 194; X. 86; *Vertue Betray'd or Anna Bullen*, VIII. 194
Banks, Sir Joseph (1743–1820), VIII. 361; XIV. 245, 289, 290, 550, 558
Bannatyne, George (1545–1608?), II. 282, 478; III. 132; XII. 358, 377
Bannatyne, Richard, *The Memorials of the Transactions of Scotland*, III. 148, 149, 500
Bannatyne club, XI. 231; XII. 358, 359, 361, 370, 377, 378; XIV. 94
Bannatyne MS., II. 478; III. 122, 131, 132, 499; IX. 361, 365, 367, 369, 553, 567
Bannatyne Miscellany, IV. 414
Bannister, John (1760–1836), XII. 171; XIV. 217
Bannockburn, battle of, I. 357, 370; II. 101, 102, 109; X. 224; XII. 1; XIV. 95
Banquet of Daintie Conceits, A, IV. 467
Banquo, in an Interlude, VI. 318
Banquo, in *Macbeth*, II. 104; V. 255; VI. 318
Bansley, Charles (*fl.* 1548), IV. 317; V. 477; *The Pryde and Abuse of Women*, III. 97, 491; IV. 328
Banville, Théodore de, XIII. 162, 211
Baptist education society, X. 387
Baptist general assembly, X. 378
Baptist general association, X. 378, 387
Baptist historical society, X. 519
Baptist histories, X. 519
Baptist Rawdon college, X. 387
Baptists, X. 522
Barabas, in *The Jew of Malta*, V. 145, 326, 366; VI. 250
Barabas, in the Passion play, V. 18
Barabbas, in Marlowe's *Jew of Malta*, XII. 68
Baradoun, Henry (*fl.* 1483), II. 502
Barak, IV. 170
Barante, Pierre A. P. B., baron de, XII. 322; *Histoire des Ducs de Bourgogne*, XIV. 107
Barbadoes, XI. 279, 280
Barbarisme, in *The Tears of the Muses*, III. 241
Barbarus, Hermolas, III. 5
Barbary, IV. 4, 99; XIV. 246
Barbauld, Anna Laetitia, born Aikin (1743–1825), X. 11, 412, 452, 454; XI. 132, 343, 382, 477; XII. 4, 124, 133, 447; XIII. 324; XIV. 393, 603
  Easy Lessons, XI. 384
  Evenings at Home, XI. 384
Barbauld, Anna Laetitia
  Hymns in Prose, XI. 384
  'On Romances,' X. 188
'Barber, Francis,' X. 472
Barber, Margaret Fairless (*pseud.* Michael Fairless, 1869–1901), XIV. 515
Barber, Mary (1690?–1757), IX. 106, 460, 484; XI. 426
Barberini, cardinal, IV. 259
Barbès, Armand, XIII. 283
Barbeyrac, Jean, X. 308
Barbones parliament, IX. 386
Barbour, John (*c.* 1320–1395), II. 100 ff., 114, 117, 127, 129, 130, 447 ff.; IV. 413; X. 224
  The Bruce, I. 359; II. 88, 91, 101, 104–108 (main entry), 239, 280, 447; XII. 13, 344
  Other works attributed to Barbour: *The Brut*, II. 103; *Lives* or *Legends of the Saints*, II. 103, 127, 128, 239; *Siege of Troy*, II. 104; *The Stewartis Oryginalle*, II. 103
Barckley, Sir Richard, *A Discourse of the felicitie of man: or his Summum bonum*, IV. 268, 507, 531
Barclay, Alexander (1475?–1552), II. 210; III. 56 ff., 75, 85, 95, 185, 478 ff.; IV. 4, 322, 439, 476
  Bellum Jugurthinum, translation of, III. 56
  Chasteau de labour, Le, translation of Gringore's, II. 329; III. 56
  Codrus and Minalcus, III. 64
  Contra Skeltonum, III. 66
  Cytezen and Uplondyshman, III. 63, 64
  Eclogues, III. 56, 57, 62 ff.
  Introductory to write and to pronounce Frenche, III. 56, 57
  Myrrour of Good Maners, The, translation of, III. 57, 341
  St George, Life of, III. 57
  St Thomas of Canterbury, Life of, III. 57
  Sallust, III. 57
  Ship of Fools, The (trans. *Narrenschiff*), II. 321; III. 56, 57, 60 ff., 64 ff., 71, 74, 79, 485, 489; IV. 320, 400, 521, 531, 532
Barclay, David (1610–1686), VIII. 111
Barclay, James, X. 474
Barclay, John (1582–1621), IV. 242, 243, 253 ff., 499 ff.
  Apologia Euphormionis pro se, IV. 255 ff.
  Argenis, IV. 245, 254, 255, 257, 260; VII. 315
  Euphormionis Satyricon, IV. 254 ff.; VII. 315
  Icon Animorum, IV. 254, 257, 260
  Paraenesis ad sectarios, IV. 254
  Pietas, sive publicae pro regibus ac principibus et privatae, pro G. Barclaio contra Bellarminum Vindiciae, IV. 254
  Thebais, commentary on, IV. 253
Barclay, John (1734–1798), *Dialogue betwixt William Lickladle and Thomas Cleancogue*, IX. 373

Barclay, Robert (1648–1690), VIII. 415; IX. 520, 546; *An Apology for the True Christian Divinity*, VIII. 111, 112
Barclay, Robert (1779–1854), XIV. 230; *Religious Societies of the Commonwealth*, IX. 307
Barclay, William (1570?–1630?), IV. 253, 254; *De Potestate Papae*, IV. 254; *Nepenthes*, IV. 531
'Bard, The,' Della Cruscan poet, XI. 177
Bardell, Mrs, in *The Pickwick Papers*, XIII. 313
Bardolph, Shakespeare's, V. 187, 367; XI. 289; XIV. 125
Bardsey, near Leeds, VIII. 146
Bardus, in *Confessio Amantis*, II. 151
Bareacres, house of, in Thackeray's *Vanity Fair*, XIII. 287
Barebone's parliament, VII. 190; XIV. 452
Barents, IV. 460
Baret, John (*fl.* 1441–1446), II. 198
Baret, John (d. 1580?), III. 555
Baret, M., IV. 540
Baretti, Giuseppe, V. 293; X. 159, 468 ff.
Bargrave, John (1610–1680), VII. 35
Barham, Richard Harris (1788–1845), X. 154; XI. 160; XII. 111, 122–123 (main entry), 138, 413; XIV. 200; *As I lay a thynkynge*, XII. 122; *Ingoldsby Legends, The*, VIII. 96; XI. 38; XII. 122, 123; XIII. 161
Bari, V. 37
Barillon, Paul, marquis de Branges, X. 290
Baring, Evelyn, earl of Cromer, XIII. 546
Baring, Mrs H., XIV. 507
Baring-Gould, S., XII. 417
Barker, Christopher (1529?–1599), queen's printer, IV. 384, 386, 387, 389, 395, 398, 400
Barker, Edmund Henry (1788–1839), XII. 327, 490, 491
Barker, John (*fl.* 1464), III. 99
Barker, Matthew (1619–1698), VII. 316
Barker, Robert (d. 1645), IV. 398, 400, 406
Barker, T. (*fl.* 1651), *The Art of Angling*, VII. 463
Barker, William (*fl.* 1572), IV. 444
Barkham, John (1572?–1642), III. 324
Barkiarokh, in Beckford's *Episodes*, XI. 291
Barking, II. 157; IV. 141
Barkstead, John, 'goldsmith in the Strand' (d. 1662), VII. 512
Barkstead, William (*fl.* 1611), *Hiren, or the Faire Greeke*, VI. 49; *Mirrha, the Mother of Adonis*, VI. 49
Barlaam and Josaphat, I. 286, 467; II. 150, 507; V. 53
Barley, William (*fl.* 1596), IV. 113, 463
Barleycorn, John (*alias* 'Allan-a-Maut'), II. 279
Barlow, Arthur, IV. 85
Barlow, George, XIII. 542
Barlow, Jerome (*fl.* 1528–1533), III. 80; *upon the origin of the protestant fashions*, III. 80; *Proper Dyalogue betwene a Gentillman and a Husbandman*, III. 80; *Rede me and be not wrothe*, III. 80, 105
Barlow, Mr, in *Sandford and Merton*, XI. 381, 382
Barlow, William (d. 1613), IV. 382; VII. 316
Barn Elms, on the Thames, VIII. 377
Barnabas, Gospel of, IX. 291
Barnabas, St, VII. 318
Barnabees Journal, VII. 390
Barnaby, in *The New Inn*, IV. 361
Barnaby Bunch the botcher, in *The weak est goeth to the Wall*, V. 316
Barnacle, in *The Gamester*, VI. 202
Barnakill, in Kingsley's *Yeast*, XIII. 360
Barnard, lady Anne (lady Anne Lindsay, 1750–1825), XI. 442; XII. 377; XIV. Add. 5; *Auld Robin Gray*, XI. 231; *Why Tarries My Love*, XI. 232
Barnard, Edward, XI. 346
Barnard, Frederick, XIII. 540, 541
Barnard, Sir John, X. 84
Barnard Castle, XIII. 317
Barnes, Barnabe (1569?–1609), III. 256, 264, 265, 271, 522; IV. 115, 468; *The Devil's Charter*, VI. 150, 452; *Parthenophil and Parthenope*, III. 265
Barnes, Joseph, III. 427; IV. 410, 411
Barnes or Berners, Juliana. *See* Berners
Barnes, J. H., XIII. 513
Barnes, Robert (1495–1540), III. 27, 37, 43, 53, 474
Barnes, Thomas (? 1624), IV. 437
Barnes, Thomas (1747–1810), XIV. 386, 599, 604
Barnes, Thomas (1785–1841), XIV. 179 ff., 198
Barnes, William (1801–1886), I. 240; XII. 134, 413; XIV. 459
Barnet, VIII. 351; XIII. 276
Barnett, Percy Arthur, XIV. Add. 5
Barnfield, Richard (1574–1627), IV. 117, 121, 468; V. 224
Affectionate Shepherd, The, IV. 120, 126
Another of the same shepherd's, IV. 120
'As it fell upon a day,' IV. 119
Complainte of Poetrie for the Death of Liberalitie, The, IV. 120
Cynthia, with certaine Sonnets, III. 256, 264, 522; IV. 120
Encomion of Lady Pecunia, The, IV. 119, 120, 519
Hellens Rape, or a light Lanthorne for light Ladies, IV. 120
'If Musique and sweet Poetrie agree,' IV. 113, 119
Poems in divers Humors, IV. 119, 120
Barnham, Alice, IV. 280
Barnstaple, IX. 160
Barnwell, George, in Lillo's *London Merchant*, X. 75 ff., 79
Barnwell priory, Cambridge, II. 343, 347, 352, 500; XII. 348, 508

Barocci, Giacomo, IV. 431
Baron, George (*fl.* 1652), VII. 512
Baron, Robert (1593?–1639), IX. 542
Baron, Robert (*fl.* 1645), VII. 88, 137, 412; VIII. 434
Baron hill, X. 115
Baron o' Brackley, The, II. 412
Baron-Wilson, Margaret, XI. 462
Baroni, Leonora, VII. 99
Baronius, Caesar, cardinal, VII. 311; *Annales Ecclesiastici*, VII. 310
Baronius, Justus, IV. 249
Barontus, St, of Pistoja, I. 86
Barot, O., XIII. 465
Barratt, Alfred (1844–1881), XIV. 468
Barrels, near Henley-in-Arden, X. 271, 273, 278
Barret, Robert (*fl.* 1600), IV. 473
Barret, William (*fl.* 1609), IV. 395
Barretier, Johann Philipp, X. 164, 460, 464, 465
Barrett, Charlotte, X. 260
Barrett, E., XIII. 464
Barrett, Eaton Stannard (1786–1820), XI. 299, 459
Barrett, Edward Moulton, XIII. 70
Barrett, Elizabeth. *See* Browning, Elizabeth Barrett
Barrett, J. A. S., XIII. 465
Barrie, Sir J. M., XIII. 569; *Auld Licht Idylls*, XIV. 436; *When a Man's Single*, XIV. 447
Barrington, Daines, X. 269
Barrington, Emilie I., XIV. 515
Barrington, John Shute, 1st viscount Barrington (1678–1734), X. 380
Barrington, Sir Jonah (1760–1834), XIV. 567; *Personal Sketches*, XIV. 322
Barrington, Rutland, XIII. 513
Barrington, William Wildman, 2nd viscount Barrington (1717–1793), X. 405, 408, 410
Barrosa, X. 230
Barrow or Barrowe, Henry (d. 1593), III. 389, 390
Barrow, Isaac (1630–1677), VII. 487; VIII. 295 ff., 301, 308, 389, 458, 476; *Exposition of the Creed, Decalogue and Sacraments*, VIII. 297; *On the Pope's Supremacy*, VIII. 296; *Works*, VIII. 296
Barrow, Sir John (1764–1848), XII. 154, 426; XIV. 550; *Autobiographical Memoir*, XIV. 248; *Travels in China*, XIV. 248; *Voyage to Cochin-China, A*, XIV. 248
Barrow, John, XIV. 596
Barrow, William (1754–1836), XIV. 604
Barrowists, the, III. 408
Barry, Mrs Elizabeth (1658–1713), VIII. 136, 179, 182, 184, 191, 439
Barry, Henry Boothby, XIV. 596
Barry, Lodowick, *Ram-Alley or Merrie-Trickes*, V. 367; VI. 218, 219, 452
Barry, M. J., XIV. 572
Barry, Redmond, in Thackeray's *Barry Lyndon*, XIII. 281 ff.
Barry, Spranger (1719–1777), XI. 257, 260, 450, 454
Bartello, IV. 441
Bartello, in *Dan Bartholmew of Bathe*, III. 205, 206
Barter, Charles, XIV. Add. 5
Barth, Caspar, IV. 253; *Amphitheatrum Seriorum Jocorum*, IV. 266; *Scioppius excellens*, IV. 266
Barthélémon, François H., XI. 258
Barthélemy, E., XIII. 465, 466, 470
Bartholinus, Thomas, X. 225
Bartholomaeus Anglicus (*fl.* 1230–1250), I. 184, 452; IV. 521; *De Proprietatibus Rerum*, II. 71, 72, 74, 76, 80, 86, 311, 323, 443; IV. 320
Bartholomew, A. T., XIII. 572, *also see* Add. 1; XIV. 539
Bartholomew de Cotton (d. 1298?), I. 449
Bartholomew fair, VIII. 115, 193
Bartholus, II. 363
Bartlet, John (*fl.* 1662), IV. 113, 463
Bartolozzi, Francesco, XIV. 216
Barton, Amos, George Eliot's, XIII. 387, 388
Barton, Bernard (1784–1849), VIII. 113; XI. 483; XII. 135, 198 ff., 413, 438; XIII. 142, 143
Barton, John, Mrs Gaskell's, XIII. 373
Barton, Mary, Mrs Gaskell's, XIII. 372
Barton, in Jane Austen's *Sense and Sensibility*, XII. 241
Barton, Sir Andrew, II. 408, 414
Barty, lord Charles, in Henry Kingsley's *Austin Eliot*, XIII. 433
Basedow, Johann Bernhard (1724–1790), IX. 401; XIV. 382, 402
Basel, III. 41, 58, 100, 333, 532; IV. 374, 389, 403; V. 71, 101
Basil, St, I. 74, 75, 77, 122, 124; XII. 266
Basilisco, in *Solimon and Perseda*, V. 161, 162
Basilissa, martyr, I. 74
Basilius, in *The Ile of Guls*, VI. 212
Basilius, St, bishop of Caesarea, VII. 503
Basing, VII. 246, 454
Basire, Isaac (1607–1676), VIII. 459
Basire, James (1730–1802), XI. 181
Baskerville, John (1706–1775), XI. 341, 469
Basoche, Confrérie de la, V. 22, 25
Bassandyne, Thomas (d. 1577), IV. 412. 547
Bassanes, in *The Broken Heart*, VI. 191
Basse or Bas, William (d. 1653?), IV. 150, 479
Basset, Thomas, VIII. 464
Bassett, lady, in Reade's *A Terrible Temptation*, XIII. 426
Bassingbourne, V. 34
Bastard, Thomas (1566–1618), IV. 334, 335, 519
Bastiat, Frederick, IV. 299; XIV. 509
Baston, Robert (*fl.* 1300), II. 496
Bastwick, John (1593–1654), VII. 145, 423, 433, 456, 498

Basyn, The Tale of the, II. 501
Bat Burst, in *The New Inne*, VI. 25
Bateman, Christopher, XI. 331, 332, 336
Bateman, Thomas (1821–1861), XII. 507
Bateman, William (1298?–1355), bishop of Norwich, II. 354
Bates, Cadwallader John, XII. 507; *Border Holds of Northumberland*, XII. 349, 507
Bates, Charley, in *Oliver Twist*, XIII. 316
Bates, Henry Walter (1825–1892), XIV. 550
Bates, Miss, in Jane Austen's *Emma*, XII. 240
Bates, William, *Harmony of the divine attributes*, XI. 316
Bateson, Mary (1865–1906), XIV. 485
Borough Customs, XIV. 81
Charters of the Borough of Cambridge, The, XIV. 81
Laws of Breteuil, The, XIV. 81
Medieval England, I. 446
Origin and Early History of Double Monasteries, The, XIV. 81
Records of the Borough of Leicester, XIV. 81
Bateson, Thomas (1580?–1620?), IV. 113, 463; *First Set of English Madrigals*, VII. 8
Bath, I. 40; VIII. 159, 363; IX. 34, 163, 167, 172, 538; X. 22, 28, 29, 35, 39, 42, 206, 207, 261, 276, 277, 409, 427; XI. 149, 173, 175, 283, 344, 347, *also see* Add.; XII. 232, 236, 513; XIV. 220, 225, 324
Bath, colonel, in Fielding's *Amelia*, X. 34; XI. 265
Bath, earl of. *See* Pulteney, William
Bath, knights of the, XI. 282
Bath, marquis of. *See* Thynne, Thomas
Bath, marquis of, *Papers*, IX. 96, 99, 141, 443, 483. See, also, *Longleat Papers*
Bath Easton, X. 277, 456
Bath school, VII. 330
Bathurst, Allen, 1st earl Bathurst (1684–1775), IX. 79, 152, 228, 443, 445
Bathurst, Ralph, M.D. (1620–1704), X. 492
Batrachomyomachia, VIII. 64
Batt, in *Dan Bartholmew of Bathe*, III. 205
Battie, J., IV. 509
Battle of Falkirk Muir, IX. 378
Battle Royal, The, VIII. 92
Baucida, XII. 201
Baucis, XII. 201
Baucis and Philemon, VII. 252
Baucis and Philemon, in Sandys's *Ovid*, VII. 51
Baudelaire, Charles Pierre, IV. 218; XII. 525; XIII. 129, 133, 490
Baudissin, count, V. 303; VI. 165
Bauermeister, actor, V. 306
Bauhusius of Antwerp, IV. 266
Baumgarten, O., XIII. 470
Baur, Frederick Christian, IX. 291
Bavand or Bavande, William (*fl.* 1559), VI. 377, 409; *A Woorke of Joannes Ferrarius Montanus touchynge the good orderynge of a Common Weale*, VI. 377, 493
Bavaria, VII. 200
Baxter, Andrew (1686–1750), IX. 504
Baxter, Lucy W., XIII. 530
Baxter, Nathaniel (*fl.* 1606), IV. 473
Baxter, Richard (1615–1691), IV. 433; VII. 145, 146, 207, 424, 427, 433; IX. 574; X. 373, 377, 499, 519; XI. 334; XII. 523
Call to the Unconverted, XI. 369
Holy Commonwealth, VII. 433
Life and Times, VIII. 297
Quaker's Catechism, VIII. 110
Reliquiae Baxterianae, VII. 145; VIII. 462, 463; IX. 307, 383; XI. 316
Saints' Everlasting Rest, The, VII. 146; IX. 269; X. 383; XI. 316
Baxter, William (1650–1723), IX. 526
Baxter's Dead, A Winding Sheet for Mr, IX. 514
Bayard, in *Four Sons of Aymon*, I. 292
Bayes, in *The Rehearsal*, VII. 184; VIII. 26; IX. 147. *See, also*, IX. 476
Bayham, Frederick, in *The Newcomes*, XIII. 297
Bayle, Pierre, V. 286, 292; IX. 211, 477, 529; X. 177; *Dictionary*, XI. 320
Bayley, John [Whitcomb] (d. 1869), XII. 507
Bayly, Lewis, bishop of Bangor (d. 1631), IV. 495; *The Practice of Piety*, XI. 369
Bayly, Thomas Haynes (1797–1839), VII. 84; XII. 130, 414; XIII. 154; XIV. 200
Bayne, Alicia, XIV. 602
Bayne, Peter (1830–1896), XIII. 470, 483; XIV. 515, 522
Baynes, A. H., XIV. Add. 5
Baynes, Mrs, in Thackeray's *Adventures of Philip*, XIII. 299
Baynes, Thomas Spencer (1823–1887), XII. 402; XIV. 468, 474; *Essay on the New Analytic*, XIV. 9
Baynham, W., XIII. 513
Bayreuth, V. 305
Bazalgette, Mrs, in Reade's *Love me Little, Love me Long*, XIII. 426
Be Domes Daege, I. 129, 145 ff., 220, 227, 444
Be Merry and Wise, VII. 393
Beach, Joseph Warren, XIII. 570
Beach, Michael Hicks, XII. 143
Beaconsfield, Burke's residence, XI. 142
Beaconsfield, earl of. *See* Disraeli, Benjamin
Beadnell, Maria, XIII. 542
Beaduhild, in *Deor*, I. 36
Beagle, Sir Harry, in Colman's *Jealous Wife*, X. 89, 90
'Beagle,' ship, XIV. 250, 296, 298
Beagnoþ, owner of the Thames runic sword, I. 11
Beale, Catherine Hutton, XIV. 520
Beale, Dorothea (1831–1905), XIV. 429, 599
Bear, the, in *Mum, Sothsegger*, II. 36
Beard, Thomas (d. 1632), III. 552; VI. 492
Beardsley, Aubrey, XIII. 502
Beare, John Isaac (1857–1918), XII. Add. 3

Beare, Philip O'Sullivan (1590?–1660), xiv. 308
Beaton, David (1494–1546), archbishop of St Andrews, ii. 369
Beaton or Bethune, James (d. 1539), archbishop of St Andrews, ii. 369; iii. 160
Beatrice (Dante's), iii. 234; iv. 210, 217; xii. 85, 86
Beatrice, in Middleton's *Changeling*, vi. 76, 77; xii. 222
Beatrice, in *The Dutch Courtezan*, vi. 48
Beatrice, in *Much Ado about Nothing*, v. 191, 193, 214, 379; vi. 46, 100, 123; viii. 120, 154
Beatrix, in *Esmond*, xiii. 292, 293, 296, 298
Beatrix, St (sister Angela), xiii. 178
Beattie, James (1735–1803), x. 138, 154, 155, 347, 453, 480, 512, 514; xi. 206, 342, 350; xii. 100, 132; xiii. 235; xiv. 601, 604
Essay on Truth, x. 155, 348; xi. 351
Judgment of Paris, x. 155
Minstrel, The, ix. 374; x. 132, 154; xi. 247, 351; xiii. 149
Pastorals, x. 155
Retirement, x. 155
To Mr Alexander Ross, ix. 374
Beattie, William (1793–1875), xii. 410; xiv. 56, 595
Beatty-Kingston, William, xiv. 192
Beau Bunter, in *Sir Harry Wildair*, viii. 169
Beau Clincher, in Farquhar's *The Constant Couple*, viii. 175
Beauchamp, George Meredith's, xiii. 446
Beauchamp, Philip (*see* Bentham, Jeremy), xi. 398
Beauchamp, Richard de, earl of Warwick (1382–1439), ii. 76, 335
Beauchamp court, Warwickshire, iv. 159
Beauclerk, Charles, 1st duke of St Albans (1670–1726), viii. 376
Beauclerk, Topham, x. 207
Beaudesert, Warwickshire, x. 112
Beauford, in D'Urfey's *The Virtuous Wife*, viii. 175
Beaufort, cardinal, bishop of Winchester, in *Henry VI*, v. 186
Beaufort, duke of. *See* Somerset, Henry Charles
Beaufort, Henry (d. 1447), ii. 352, 355
Beaufort, Joan, ii. 244
Beaufort, Margaret (1443–1509), countess of Richmond and Derby, ii. 300, 309, 316, 321, 324, 325, 358; iii. 8, 13, 67; iv. 224, 226, 227, 426; xii. 488, 515
Beaumarchais, Pierre A. C. de, *Figaro*, xi. 262
Beaumaris, x. 115
Beaumont, Charles, viii. 284
Beaumont, Francis (1584–1616), iv. 55, 115, 194; v. 347; vi. 2, 5, 27, 107–140 (main entry), 145, 177, 195, 205, 208, 248, 272, 329, 435 ff., 488, *and see* Add.; vii. 7, 82, 272; viii. 13, 127, 132, 226, 425; ix. 140, 145; x. 91; xii. 89, 186, 444, 504; xiii. 144, 289. *See, also, under* Fletcher, John
Beaumont, Sir George Howland, of Coleorton (1753–1827), xi. 130, 416; xii. 376
Beaumont, Jeanne Marie, le prince de (*c.* 1775), xi. 491
Beaumont, lady, of Coleorton, ix. 328, xi. 408, 416; xii. 376
Beaumont and Fletcher, plays and poems attributed to, whether singly, jointly, or in collaboration with others, vi. 435 ff.; xi. 319; xiii. Add. 2
'All ye woods and trees and bowers,' vi. 125
'Arm, arm,' vi. 125
'Away, delights,' vi. 128
Barnavelt, Sir John van Olden, vi. 116, 123, 130, 138
'Beauty clear and fair,' vi. 125
Beggars Bush, The, v. 376; vi. 121, 125, 131, 139; viii. 121
Bloody Brother, The, vi. 26, 125, 129, 138
Bonduca, vi. 123, 128, 138; x. 429
Captaine, The, vi. 125, 128, 137
Cardenio, The History of, vi. 140; viii. 127
'Care-charming Sleep,' vi. 125
'Cast our caps and cares away,' vi. 125
Chances, The, vi. 135, 136, 140; viii. 128; x. 433
Coronation, The. See under Shirley
Coxcombe, The, v. 362; vi. 119, 120, 133, 137; viii. 128
Cupid's Revenge, iii. 355; vi. 114, 119, 127, 137
Custome of the Countrey, The, v. 366; vi. 122, 130, 138; viii. 128
Demetrius and Enanthe, vi. 138
Devil of Dowgate, The, vi. 140
Double Marriage, The, vi. 131, 139; viii. 128
Elder Brother, The, vi. 121, 125, 136, 140
Elegy on lady Penelope Clifton (daughter of Sidney's Stella), vi. 113
Elegy on lady Markham, vi. 113
Elegy on the countess of Rutland (Sidney's daughter), vi. 113
Faire Maide of the Inne, The, vi. 132, 140, 183; viii. 128
Faithfull Shepherdesse, The, vi. 31, 112, 114, 117, 125, 126, 137, 340, 353, 363 366, 367, 369, 490; viii. 18, 271
False One, The, vi. 111, 121, 123, 131, 139
Four Plays in One, vi. 119, 128, 137
'God Lyaeus, ever young,' vi. 125
'Hence, all you vain delights,' vi. 124, 134
Honest man's Fortune, The, vi. 128, 137
Humorous Lieutenant, The, vi. 134, 138
Island Princesse, The, vi. 123, 131, 139; viii. 120, 129, 443

Beaumont and Fletcher
Jeweller of Amsterdam, The, VI. 140
King and no King, A, VI. 114, 119, 120, 126, 127, 129, 137
Knight of Malta, The, VI. 130, 138
Knight of the Burning Pestle, The, I. 292; IV. 359; 363; V. 130; VI. 89, 114, 119, 133, 137, 234; VIII. 121, 128, 425; X. 220
Lawes of Candy, The, VI. 131, 139
'Let the bells ring,' VI. 125
Little French Lawyer, The, VI. 119, 134, 138, 152, 184
Lovers' Progress, The, VI. 131, 139
Loves Cure, VI. 119, 124, 136, 140; VIII. 128
Loves Pilgrimage, VI. 132, 140; VIII. 31, 128
Loyal Subject, The, VI. 100, 130, 138
Mad Lover, The, VI. 130, 138, 152
Mador, King of Great Britain, VI. 140
Maid in the Mill, The, VI. 69, 70, 132, 139; VIII. 128, 129
Maides Tragedy, The, VI. 111, 114, 119, 120, 124, 126, 127, 129, 137, 199; VIII. 120, 215
Masque of Grayes Inne and the Inner-Temple, The, VI. 137, 353, 356, 488
Monsieur Thomas, VI. 123, 135, 138
Nice Valour, The, IV. 251; VI. 119, 134, 140
Night-Walker, The, VI. 134, 135, 140
Noble Gentleman, The, VI. 136, 140
'O how my lungs do tickle,' VI. 125
Ovid's Salmacis and Hermaphroditus, IV. 20; VI. 112
Philaster, VI. 111, 113, 114, 119 ff., 126, 128, 129, 137, 190; VIII. 441; X. 429
Pilgrim, The, VI. 122, 131, 139; VIII. 31, 52, 54, 120, 396, 401, 431
Prophetesse, The, VI. 123, 131, 139, 152; VIII. 120, 128, 135, 401
Queene of Corinth, The, V. 350; VI. 130, 138; VIII. 128
Right Woman, A, VI. 140
Rule a Wife and have a Wife, V. 356; VI. 135, 139; VIII. 128
Scorneful Ladie, The, VI. 114, 119, 133, 137
Sea Voyage, The, V. 347; VI. 131, 139; VIII. 120
'Sit, soldiers, sit and sing,' VI. 125
Spanish Curate, The, VI. 125, 134, 139, 183; VIII. 20, 128
Tamer Tamed, VIII. 121
'Tell me, dearest, what is love,' VI. 125, 128
Thierry and Theodoret, VI. 114, 123, 129, 138
'Three merry boys,' VI. 125
''Tis late and cold,' VI. 125
Triumph of Death, The, VI. 128, 137
Triumph of Honour, The, VI. 128, 137
Triumph of Love, The, VI. 120, 128, 137
Triumph of Time, The, VI. 128, 137

Beaumont and Fletcher
Two Noble Kinsmen, The, VI. 132, 139, 299. See, also, under *Two Noble Kinsmen*
Valentinian, VI. 122, 123, 125, 129, 138
Wandering Lovers, The, VI. 139
Wife for a Month, The, VI. 122, 132, 139
Wild-Goose Chase, The, VI. 135, 139; VIII. 120
Wit At severall Weapons, VI. 119, 134, 138
Wit Without Money, VI. 134, 138
Woman Hater, The, VI. 27, 112, 114, 119, 124, 132, 137
Woman's Plot, A, VI. 140
Womans Prize, The, VI. 134, 135, 138
Women pleas'd, VI. 130, 138; VIII. 128
See, also, under Middleton and Shirley
Beaumont, Sir Francis (d. 1598), VI. 111
Beaumont, Sir John (1583–1627), IV. 194, 435, 436, 487; VII. 56, 57, 75, 90, 406; VIII. 228, 447; *Bosworth Field*, VI. 111; *To His Late Majesty, concerning the True Forme of English Poetry*, VII. 49
Beaumont, Joseph (1616–1699), VII. 34, 406, *also see* Add.; VIII. 283 ff., 453; *Psyche*, VIII. 283, 284
Beaupré, in *The Parliament of Love*, VI. 155
Beaupuy, Michel, XI. 98
Beauty, in *The Golden Targe*, II. 253
Beauty of the World, I. 294
Beaw or Beo, son of Scyld (Sceldwea), I. 28
Bec, monastic school at, I. 153; "Geoffrey Arthur's" book at, I. 170
Beccaria, Cesare Bonesana, marquis di, XI. 66, 70; *Crimes and Punishments*, XI. 64; *Dei Delitti e delle Pene*, IX. 302
Beche, Sir Henry Thomas de la (1796–1855), XIV. 294, 560; *A Geological Manual*, XIV. 292; *Report on the Geology of Cornwall, etc.*, XIV. 292
Becher, Anne. *See* Thackeray, Anne
Becher, Miss, XIII. 276
Becke, Edmund (*fl.* 1550), IV. 443
Becke, George Louis (1848–1913), XIV. 584
Becker, Wilhelm Adolph, *Charicles*, XII. 230; *Gallus*, XII. 230
Becket, St Thomas à, archbishop of Canterbury, I. 173, 185, 186, 191, 202, 339, 341, 448; II. 84, 87, 342; III. 12, 332; IV. 417, 418; V. 38, 56, 58; XI. 315; XII. 258, 321, 416
Becket, St Thomas à, in Caxton's *Golden Legend*, II. 334
Becket and Dehorde, booksellers, X. 191
Beckford, Peter (1740–1811), XIV. 542; *Essays on Hunting*, XIV. 232; *Thoughts upon Hare and Fox Hunting*, XIV. 232
Beckford, Richard, X. 388
Beckford, William (1709–1770), X. 485
Beckford, William (1759–1844), X. 423, *also see* Add.; XI. 289 ff., 306, 307, 459
Azemia, XI. 289
Dreams, Waking Thoughts and Incidents, XI. 289
Episodes, XI. 290 ff.

Beckford, William
History of Extraordinary Painters, XI. 289
Letters from Portugal, XI. 289
Modern Novel Writing, XI. 289
Vathek, XI. 161, 289 ff., 304
Beckington, Somerset, IV. 133
Becon, Thomas (1512–1567), III. **27**; **IV.** 380, 397, 491, 495
Bedam, Historia post, I. 174
Beddoe, John (1826–1911), XII. **507**; *Anthropological History of Europe*, XII. 351; *Contributions to Scottish Ethnology*, XII. 350; *The Races of Britain*, XII. 350
Beddoes, Thomas Lovell (1803–1849), XII. 107, 115 ff. (main entry), 126, 139, 414; XIII. 141, 149, 198, 230, 238, 517
Bride's Tragedy, The, XII. 115
Death's Jest Book or *The Fool's Revenge*, XII. 115, 116; XIII. 239
Dirge for Wolfram, XII. 116
Dream-Pedlary, XII. 116
Improvisatore, The, XII. 115
Letter from Oxford, XII. 116
Old Adam, the carrion crow, XII. 116
Pygmalion, XII. 116
Song of the Stygian Naiades, XII. 116
Bede, in *The Example of Virtue*, II. 227
Bede or Baeda, the Venerable (673–735), I. 5, 10, 14, 19, 20, 43 ff., 53, 55, 57, 59, 66, 68, 70, 71, 79–84 (main entry), 89, 96, 117, 119 ff., 131, 145, 148, 159 ff., 163 ff., 167 ff., 172, 198, 224, 257, 342, 347, 350, 351, 380, 433, 434, 436, 437, 439; IV. 67; VII. 510; XIV. 69, 302
Death Song, I. 61
De Natura Rerum, I. 80.
De Temporibus, I. 81
Historia Ecclesiastica, I. 81 ff., 93, 96, 101, 106, 110, 112, 234, 434, 436, 437, 439; IV. 37; VIII. 309; IX. 539; XII. 487
Martyrology, I. 80
Retractationes, I. 80
Other works, I. 80–81, 224
Bede, Adam, George Eliot's, XIII. 382, 389 ff.
Bede, Cuthbert, *pseud.* *See* Bradley, Edward
Bede, Seth, George Eliot's, XIII. 389, 391
Bedell, William (1571–1642), VII. 308, 318, 442; IX. 489; XII. 488
Bedford, II. 336; III. 202; VII. 167 ff., 172; IX. 169
Bedford, Arthur (1668–1745), VIII. 432; IX. 528
Bedford, countess of (d. 1627). *See* Russell, Lucy
Bedford, dukes of. *See* Lancaster, John of; Russell, Francis; Russell, John; Russell, Wriothesley
Bedford, Grosvenor, the elder, XI. 154
Bedford, Grosvenor, the younger, XI. 154, 169, 172
Bedford, H., XIII. 570
Bedford gaol, VII. 170, 172
Bedford level, IX. 343
Bedford missal, XII. 510
Bedford school, VII. 330
Bedfordshire, II. 206; VIII. 60; IX. 145; XII. 345; XIII. 145
Bedingfield, lady, XIV. 503
Bedingfield, Thomas (d. 1613), IV. 7, 398, 442, 443, 540
Bedivere. *See* Bedwyr
Bedlam, X. 56
Bedwell, William (d. 1632), IV. 453; VII. 470
Bedworth academy, X. 385
Bedwyr or Bedivere, Arthurian knight, I. 250, 254, 255, 260; II. 119
Bee, The (Anderson's), IX. 560; XI. 236
Bee, The (Budgell's), IX. 492
Bee and the Spider, The, in Swift's *Battle of the Books*, IX. 102
Beech, Robert (d. 1594), V. 325
Beeching, Henry Charles (1859–1919), XI. 434; XII. 257, 453, 455; XIV. 515; *Francis Atterbury*, X. 352
Beedome, Thomas (d. 1641?), VII. 88, 412
Beef-steak club, IX. 139
Beelzebub, V. 33
Beer-Hofmann, *Der Graf von Charolais*, VI. 165
Bees, writers on, IV. 542
Beesly, Edward Spencer (1831–1915), XIV 468
Beeston, Christopher, VI. 103
Beethoven, Ludwig van, XII. 64, 268
Beets, Heinrich, IX. 515
Beghard communities, II. 47
Begum, the, in *Pendennis*, XIII. 291
Beha-ed-din Zoheir, XII. 499
Behaim, Martin, of Nürnberg, IV. 82
Behmen, Jacob. *See* Boehme
Behmenists, IX. 306
Behn, Mrs Aphra or Aphara (1640–1689), VIII. 140, 168, 416, 422, 424, 425; IX. 18, 174; X. 72; XII. 246
City Heiress, The, VIII. 142
Debauchee, The, VIII. 141
Dutch Lover, The, VIII. 131, 141
False Count, The, VIII. 131, 142
Forced Marriage, The, VIII. 141, 181
Maximes, trans. of La Rochefoucauld's, VIII. 373
Moor's Revenge, The, VIII. 141, 195
Nun, The, or The Perjur'd Beauty, VIII. 191
Oronooko, or the Royal Slave, VIII. 141, 191
Roundheads, The, VIII. 122, 142
Rover, The, or the Banished Cavaliers, VIII. 131, 141
Town Fop, The, VIII. 142
Widow Ranter, The, VIII. 142, 401
Young King, The, VIII. 141
Beid, IV. 363
Bek, Thomas, of Castleford, I. 335, 338
Bekinsau, John (1496?–1559), VIII. 466
Bekynton, or Beckington, T. (1390?–1465, II. 303, 482
Bel-Anna, in *The Masque of Queens*, VI. 349
Belarius, in *Cymbeline*, V. 205

Belcarre, lord, xiv. 284
Belch, Sir Toby, in *Twelfth Night*, v. 194
Belcour, in Cumberland's *West Indian*, xi. 264, 265, 275
Belfast, xi. 283; xiv. 311, 317, 327
Belfast, books printed in, xi. 470
Belfast, Queen's college, xiv. 417, *also see* Add. 3
'Belfast man, the,' Francis Davis, xiv. 326
Belfastman's Journal, The, xiv. 327
Belfield, in Cumberland's *Brothers*, xi. 264
Belgarde, in *The Unnaturall Combat*, vi. 160 ff.
Belgian writers, ix. 314
Belgic Kymrys, xiv. 68
Belgioioso, duchess of, xii. 440
Belgium, ii. 310; xiii. 88, 112
Belgrade, ix. 244; xiv. 251
Belial, xii. 36
Belial, in *Paradise Lost*, vii. 121; x. 310
Belianis, don, in *The Tatler*, xi. 373
Belinda, in Congreve's *Old Bachelor*, viii. 148
Belinda, Miss Edgeworth's, xi. 297
Belinda, in Vanbrugh's *Provok'd Wife*, viii. 161
Belisante, in *Amis and Amiloun*, i. 314
Beljame, Alexandre, x. 444; xi. 466; xii. 400, 524
Bell, Alfred Henry Haynes, xiv. Add. 4; *Knight of Avelon*, xiv. 378; *Last Stand, The*, xiv. 378; *To a Sea Conch*, xiv. 378
Bell, Andrew (1753–1832), xi. 422; xiv. 395, 403, 404, 590, 601, 604; *Experiments in Education*, xiv. 401
Bell, Sir Charles (1774–1842), x. 513; xiv. 559
Bell, Charles Dent (d. 1898), xiii. 499
Bell, Henry (1767–1830), xiv. 258
Bell, Henry Glassford (1803–1874), xii. 414
Bell, Henry Thomas Mackenzie, xiii. 496
Bell, James (*fl.* 1551–1596), iv. 446
Bell, John (1691–1780), ix. 560; xi. 325, 342, 453, 456; *Poets of Great Britain from Chaucer to Churchill*, ix. 479; x. 451
Bell, Paul, *pseud.* *See* Chorley, Henry Fothergill
Bell, Peter, in Wordsworth's poem, xii. 70
Bell, Robert (1800–1867), xi. 422; xiv. 533
Bell, Thomas (*fl.* 1573–1610), iv. 509
Bell, Thomas (*fl.* 1672), ix. 545
Bell, Thomas (1792–1880), x. 269, 270
Bell's Life in London, xiv. 231, 232, 234, 235, 239
Bell's Life in Victoria, xiv. 366, 367
Bell's Weekly Messenger, xi. 325
Bellafront, in *The Honest Whore*, v. 251; vi. 53, 172
Bellafront, in *A Woman is a Weathercocke*, vi. 221
Bellair, in Etherege's *The Man of Mode*, viii. 138
Bellamia, in *The Example*, vi. 202
Bellamont, in *North-Ward Hoe*, vi. 172
Bellamy, Daniel, the elder (b. 1687), xi. 172, 424
Bellamy, David, the younger (d. 1788), xi. 424
Bellamy, Miss George Anne (1731?–1788), xi. 260, 453
Bellamy, Henry (*fl.* 1630), vi. 470
Bellamy, Thomas (1745–1800), xi. 448
'Bellamy's' in Dickens's 'Parliamentary Sketch,' xiii. 309
Bellario, in *Philaster*, vi. 126
Bellarmine, cardinal, iii. 414; iv. 500; vii. 301, 309; viii. 462; *Disputationes*, iv. 199
Bellasis, Edward (1800–1873), xii. 454
Bellaston, lady, in Fielding's *Tom Jones*, x. 31, 32, 89
Belleforest, F. de, iv. 3; v. 159, 221; *Histoires Tragiques*, vi. 180
Bellenden, Edith, in Scott's *Old Mortality*, xii. 22
Bellenden, John (*fl.* 1533–1587), iii. 131, 156, 319, 500; *The Banner of Pietie*, iii. 131; Scottish translation of Livy, ii. 285; iii. 156; translation of Boece's *History of Scotland*, ii. 285; iv. 412
Bellenden, Mary, ix. 250
Bellenden, William (*fl.* 1616), xii. 326
Bellers, John (1654–1725), *Proposals for Raising a Colledge of Industry*, ix. 406, 570
'Belleville,' Badenoch, x. 232
Bellimperia, in *The Spanish Tragedie*, v. 161 ff.
Bellingham, Northumberland, xiii. 129
Bellings, Richard (d. 1677), *History of the Irish Confederation*, vii. 212, 448
Bellisant, in *The Parliament of Love*, vi. 155
Bellmour, in Congreve's *Old Bachelor*, viii. 148
Belloc, L. Sw., xiii. 551
Bellot, J., iv. 541
Belloy, Pierre L. B. de, *Le Siège de Calais*, xi. 274
Bellum grammaticale, vi. 482; ix. 551
Belman's Brother, The, iv. 354
Beloe, William (1756–1817), x. 473; xii. 491, 520; *Anecdotes of Literature*, xii. 363; *The Sexagenarian*, xii. 363
Belphegor, in *The Devil and his Dame*, v. 329
Belphoebe, in *The Faerie Queene*, iii. 233, 237
Belsham, Thomas (1750–1829), xii. 465
Belshazzar, xii. 229, 477
Belshazzar, in *Cleanness*, i. 323
Belson, Mrs. *See* Elliott, Mary
Beltayne, At, ii. 244
Beltrees, Renfrewshire, ix. 364, 556
Belvedere Or The Garden Of The Muses, iv. 467
Belvidera, in Otway's *Venice Preserv'd*, viii. 183, 184
Belvoir, Leicestershire, xi. 143, 144

Belzoni, Giovanni Battista (1778–1823), xiv. 248, 550
Bembo, Pietro, cardinal, iii. 262; iv. 428
Bemerton, Wilts, vii. 29; viii. 348
Ben, in Congreve's *Love for Love*, viii. 150 ff.
Ben, sailor, in Congreve's *Love for Love*, x. 90
Benares, rajah of, xi. 14
Benatzi, in *The Ladies Triall*, vi. 194
Bendall, Cecil (1856–1906), xii. 502
Bendo, Alexander, *i.e.* Rochester, earl of, viii. 208
Bendz, E., xiii. 488
Benedetti, Anna, xiii. 570
Benedick, in *Much Ado about Nothing*, v. 191; viii. 120, 155
Benedict of Peterborough (d. 1193), i. 160, 173, 174, 449; iv. 417; ix. 349; *Gesta Regis Henrici*, xiv. 74
Benedict Biscop (628?–690), abbot of Wearmouth, i. 5, 71, 84, 89, 151
Benedict, St, i. 74, 105; vii. 391
Benedict XII, pope, ii. 349
Benedict XIII, pope, ii. 368
'Benedict,' Della Cruscan poet, xi. 177
Benedictbeuern, monastery in Bavaria, i. 190
Benedictines, the, ii. 2, 245, 349, 350, 354, 362; iii. 48, 51, 57; iv. 416 ff.; vii. 143; x. 282; xiv. 53
Benedix, Roderich, *Aschenbrödel*, xiii. 272
Benet, St, Rule of, i. 15, 230, 458, 459
Bengal, xi. 242; xiv. 338
Bengal army, the, xiv. 337
Bengali literature, xiv. 341
Benger, Elizabeth Ogilvy (1778–1827), xi. 460
Benham, Allen Rogers, i. Add.
Benion, Samuel (*fl.* 1706), x. 386
Benkhausen, chevalier George de, xiii. 55
Benlow (or Bruce), Mrs Marinda, in Amory's *Memoirs of Several Ladies*, xi. 287
Benlowes, Edward (1603?–1676), vii. 73, 88 ff., 94, 137, 412; xiii. 218; *Theophila or Love's Sacrifice*, vii. 90
Benn, Alfred William, xiv. 467
Bennet, Benjamin (1674–1726), ix. 476; x. 521
Bennet, Elizabeth, in Jane Austen's *Pride and Prejudice*, xii. 237 ff., 243
Bennet, Henry, 1st earl of Arlington (1618–1685), vii. 363; viii. 92, 198, 376, 379, 380, 384, 480, 482
Bennet, James (*fl.* 1761), x. 177, 469
Bennet, Jane, in Jane Austen's *Pride and Prejudice*, xii. 238
Bennet, John (*fl.* 1600), iv. 463
Bennet, Mr, in Jane Austen's *Pride and Prejudice*, xii. 238
Bennet, Mrs, in Jane Austen's *Pride and Prejudice*, xii. 238
Bennet, Mrs, in Fielding's *Amelia*, x. 33
Bennett, Edward Turner, x. 270
Bennett, James (1774–1862) and Bogue, D., *History of Dissenters*, x. 518
Bennett, Joseph, xiv. 192
Bennett, Samuel (1815–1878), xiv. 584; *History of Australian Discovery*, xiv. 371
Bennett, William Cox (1820–1895), xiii. 499
Benoit, historiographer, ii. 419, 507
Benoît de Ste More, i. 280, 306, 467; ii. 150; *Roman de Troie*, ii. 172
Bensley, Robert (1738?–1817?), xi. 257
Bensly, Robert Lubbock (1831–1893), xii. 341, 503
Benson, Arthur Christopher (1862–1925), xiii. 476, 486, 490, 497, 503, 555, 557; xiv. 523, 524
Benson, George (1699–1762), x. 386, 521
Benson, Thurston, in Mrs Gaskell's *Ruth*, xiii. 372
Benson, William (1682–1754), ix. 562
Bent, James Theodore (1852–1897), xii. 496
Bent, William (*fl.* 1770), xi. 339
Bentham, Edward (*fl.* 1748), xiv. 595
Bentham, George (1800–1884), xiv. 468
Bentham, James (1708–1794), xii. 507; *History of Ely Cathedral*, ix. 354, 532
Bentham, Jeremy (1748–1832), iii. 425; vii. 104; viii. 321; ix. 299, 301, 409; x. 335, 346; xi. 57 ff. (main entry), 136, 397; xii. 152, 309, 430; xiv. 2, 4, 8, 14 ff., 20, 59, 98, 127, 187, 194, 198, 290, 336, 407, 559, 604
Anarchical Fallacies, xi. 71
Book of Fallacies, xi. 71
Chrestomathia, xi. 72; xiv. 404
Codification Proposals, xi. 72
Constitutional Code, xi. 71
Defence of Usury, xi. 58
Deontology, xi. 61
Fragment on Government, xi. 58, 61 ff., 71
Influence of Time and Place in Matters of Legislation, xi. 72
Introduction to the Principles of Morals and Legislation, xi. 58, 59, 64, 65, 69
Introductory view of the Rationale of Evidence, xi. 61
Poor Laws and Pauper Management, xi. 72
Rationale of Evidence, xi. 61
Table of the Springs of Action, xi. 61, 65
Theory of Legislation, xi. 68
Works, xi. 60, 61
Bentham, Samuel (brother of Jeremy Bentham), xi. 58
Benthamism, xiii. 22
Bentinck, countess, viii. 272
Bentinck, lord George (1802–1848), xiii. 353, 546; xiv. 115, 129, 130, 336, 508
Bentinck, William, 1st earl of Portland (1649–1709), ix. 149, 150, 206
Bentinck, William, 2nd duke of Portland (1709–1762), x. 262; xi. 347, 389
Bentinck, William Henry Cavendish, 3rd duke of Portland (1738–1809), x. 403
Bentivoglio, cardinal, x. 291

Bentley, Richard (1662–1742), IV. 250; V. 273; VII. 109; VIII. 230, 385; IX. 80, 86, 88, 103, 132, 138, 139, 297, 329 ff. (main entry), 381, 382, 411, 412, 449, 478, 504, 524 ff., 561, 572, 574; X. 309; XI. 341, 380; XII. 324, 325, 332, 485, 488: XIV. 283
'Confutation of Atheism,' IX. 331
Dissertation on the Epistles of Phalaris, IX. 329, 330, 333, 338, 391
Epistola ad Millium, IX. 330, 331
Horace, IX. 336, 337
Manilius, IX. 338
Milton, IX. 338, 339
Remarks upon a late Discourse of Free-thinking, IX. 292, 293, 337
Terence, IX. 338
Bentley, Richard (1708–1782), X. 245, 248; XI. 456; *Designs for six Poems by Mr T. Gray*, X. 126, 450; *Philodamus*, XI. 274
Bentley and Newton correspondence, X. 466
Bentley's Miscellany, XII. 413, 447; XIII. 315, 316; XIV. 316
Bentworth, near Alton, Hampshire, IV. 154
Beowa, I. 27, 28
Beowanham, I. 27
Beowulf, I. 1 ff., 11, 12, 20, 21, 22–30 (main entry), 34, 35, 41, 43, 54, 58, 63, 99, 115, 124, 137, 143, 277, 306, 421, *also see* Add. to third impression; II. 1, 398; IV. 517; V. 26; XII. 344; XIII. 127; XIV. 453
Beppo, in Byron's poem, XII. 53
Berachyah Nakden, I. 478
Beranger, Gabriel (d. 1817), XII. 514
Berdoe, Edward, XIII. 483
Berdok, King, II. 276
Bere, Richard (d. 1524), III. 49
Bereblock or Bearblock, John (*fl.* 1566), V. 400; VI. 299
Bereker, W., IV. 441
Berengarius, I. 154
Berenger, Richard (d. 1782), XI. 362
Bergen, VIII. 202
Bergenroth, Gustav Adolph (1813–1869), XIV. 485
Bergerac, Cyrano de. *See* Cyrano
Bergers, Calendrier des, II. 328
Bergetto, in *Tis Pitty Shees a Whore*, VI. 192
Berghen. *See* Adraien van
Berinthia, in Sheridan's *Trip to Scarborough*, XI. 268
Berinthia, in Vanbrugh's *Relapse*, VIII. 161; XI. 268
Berkeley, Charles, 2nd earl of Berkeley (1693?–1746), IX. 93
Berkeley, Elizabeth, countess of, IX. 93
Berkeley, George, 1st earl of (1628–1698), II. 77
Berkeley, George (1685–1753), bishop of Cloyne, III. 416; VII. 278, 289, 290; VIII. 428; IX. 171, 279 ff., 502, *also see* Add.; X. 35, 328 ff., 342, 343, 348, 381; XI. 57, 100; XII. 60; XIV. 8, 19, 41, 43, 47, 468, 473
Alciphron, IX. 282, 283, 286, 301, 302
Analyst, The, IX. 282
Common-place Book, IX. 280, 283, 287
De Motu, IX. 280
Essay towards a new theory of vision, IX. 61, 280, 283, 284
Essay towards preventing the ruin of Great Britain, IX. 280
Miscellany, IX. 282
Principles of human knowledge, IX. 280, 284, 286, 287
Querist, The, IX. 282
Siris, IX. 282, 287
Theory of Vision, IX. 282, 284
Three Dialogues between Hylas and Philonous, IX. 131, 280, 286
Verses on the prospect of planting arts... in America, IX. 281
Works, XIV. 48
Berkeley, Hon. George (1712–1767), IX. 498
Berkeley, George Monck (1763–1793), VIII. 428; IX. 453, 470
Berkeley, Jane Martha, dowager lady, afterwards countess of Portland (1672–1751), VIII. 380
Berkeley, Sir John (d. 1678), VII. 449
Berkeley, Miles Joseph (1803–1889), XIV. 559; *Phytophthora infestans*, XIV. 290
Berkeley, Thomas, 5th lord (1353–1417), II. 74, 76, 77
Berkeley, Sir William (d. 1677), VIII. 434; *The Lost Lady*, VI. 452
Berkeley, Gloucestershire, II. 74, 77
Berkeley castle, IV. 181
Berkenhead or Birkenhead, Sir John (1616–1679), VI. 136; VII. 494; *Mercurius Aulicus*, VII. 348; *Mercurius Bellicus*, VII. 349
Berkshire, III. 368; IV. 431; IX. 531; X. 356; XIII. 367
Berkshire, 3rd earl of, father of Sir Robert Howard, VIII. 8
Berlin, VII. 309; VIII. 330; XIII. 385; XIV. 382
Berlioz, Hector, V. 302
Bermuda, IX. 281; XII. 103
Bermudas, the, IV. 78; V. 220, 347
Bernard, Charles de, XIII. 283
Bernard, Edward (1638–1696), IX. 356, 53[illegible]
Bernard, John (1756–1828), XI. 447
Bernard, Little, St, XII. 496, 497
Bernard, Mountague (1820–1882), XII. 45[illegible]
Bernard, Richard (1568–1641), IV. 440 VII. 374; *Guide to Grand Jury Men*, VII 375, 507
Bernard, Sir Thomas (1750–1818), XIV 601, 604
Bernard, St, I. 185, 221, 231, 355; II. 230 365; III. 189; IV. 235; XIV. 504; *Tracta[illegible]* II. 383; *Sayings of*, II. 425
Bernard, William Bayle (1807–1875), XIII 517; XIV. 569
Doge of Venice, The, XIII. 266

Bernard, William Bayle
Marie Ducange, XIII. 266
Passing Cloud, The, XIII. 266
Round of Wrong, The, XIII. 266
Bernard, in *Specula Stultorum*, I. 193
Bernard of Chartres, I. 184, 188
Bernard of Clugny or Morlaix, *De Contemptu Mundi*, XIII. 172, 173
Bernardo, in Shelley's *The Cenci*, XII. 69
Bernays, Jacob, *Life of Scaliger*, XIV. 109
Berners, Isopel, Borrow's, XIII. 442
Berners, Juliana (b. 1388?), IV. 538; *The Book of St Albans*, II. 318, 323, 420, 485, 496.
Berners, Lord (1467–1533). *See* Bourchier, John
Berni, Francesco, XII. 33, 52, 56
Bernier, François, XIV. 333; *Voyage*, X. 110
Bernlak de Hautdesert, *the Green Knight*. See *Sir Gawayne*
Bernstein, baroness, in *The Virginians*, XIII. 298
Bernysdale, II. 309
Beroaldus, Philippus (d. 1505), IV. 249, 429
Béroul (*c.* 1150), I. 273, 310
Berquin, Arnaud, XI. 491; *L'Ami des Enfans*, XI. 378, 382; *Le Petit Grandisson*, XI. 382
Berrow's Worcester Journal, XIV. 169
Berry, Arthur, XIV. 555
Berry, Mary (1763–1852), X. 249 ff., 494 ff.
Berry, Mrs George Meredith's, XIII. 447
Berryer, Pierre Antoine, XIV. 127
Berrys, the (Robert, Mary and Agnes), X. 495
Bert, Edmund, IV. 541
Bertha, in Keats's *Eve of St Mark's*, XII. 87
Bertha, mother of Charles the Great, V. 40
Berthe aux grands pieds, I. 468
Berthelet, Thomas, printer to Henry VIII, III. 315, 486; IV. 400, 405, 546
Bertholdi, in *The Imposture*, VI. 205
Bertoldo, in *The Maid of Honour*, VI. 155, 156, 162
Bertram, Charles (1723–1765), IX. 540; XII. 336
Bertram, Edmund, in Jane Austen's *Mansfield Park*, XII. 238, 239
Bertram, Godfrey, laird of Ellangowan, in Scott's *Guy Mannering*, XII. 29, 151
Bertram, in Scott's *Rokeby*, XII. 12
Bertram, lady, in Jane Austen's *Mansfield Park*, XII. 239
Bertram, Lucy, in Scott's *Guy Mannering*, XII. 22
Bertram, Sir Stephen, in Cumberland's *Jew*, XI. 282
Bertram, Sir Thomas, in Jane Austen's *Mansfield Park*, XII. 239, 241
Bertram, the misses, in Jane Austen's *Mansfield Park*, XII. 238, 243
Berwick Advertiser, The, XIV. 203
Berwick, siege of, II. 101
Berwick-upon-Tweed, XI. 469; XIII. 372
Berwickshire, X. 323
Berwyn mountains, X. 115
Beryn, The Tale of, or *The Second Merchant's Tale*, I. 298, 299, 467; II. 162, 164, 215, 216, 469
Besançon, Etienne de, III. 489
Besant, Sir Walter (1836–1901), XII. 507; XIII. 438, 560; *A Survey of London*, XII. 349; *All Sorts and Conditions of Men*, XIII. 458
Besler of Nürnberg, IV. 247
Bess the Gawkie, IX. 374
Besse, Joseph (1683?–1757), VIII. 413, 414
Besselaar, G., XIV. Add. 4
Bessus, in *A King and no King*, VI. 127
Bessy, the, in folk plays, V. 31 ff.
Bessy Bell and Marie Gray, IX. 368
Best, Charles (*fl.* 1602), IV. 124
Best, captain George (d. 1584), *A True discourse of the late voyages...to Cathaya*, IV. 74, 453
Best, Paul (1590?–1657), X. 377
Best, William Draper, 1st baron Wynford (1767–1845), VIII. 317
Bestiaries, Old English, I. 59; Middle English, I. 226, 227, 239, 292, 458 ff.
Beta (queen Elizabeth), in Drayton's *Idea*, IV. 172, 173, 184
Betham, Mary Matilda (1776–1852), XI. 423
Bethell, Richard, 1st baron Westbury (1800–1873), XIV. 124, 507
Bethlehem, II. 13; V. 37
Bethulia, I. 142, 143
Bethune, Alexander (1804–1843), XII. 414
Betokis bour, in *Gyre Carling*, II. 275, 277
Betraying of Christ, The, V. 17
Betsey, Miss, in *David Copperfield*, XIII. 327
Betteridge, Wilkie Collins's, XIII. 438
Betterton, Thomas (1635?–1710), VI. 47, 248, 271; VIII. 29, 31, 121, 146, 150, 166, 177, 179, 182, 184, 186, 191, 192, 194, 195, 422, 423, 439; IX. 144, 476; X. 442; XI. 257, 447, 454; *Henry IV*, version of, VIII. 120; *The Prophetesse*, VIII. 120, 401
Betty, in Phillips's *Don Quixote*, IX. 269
Betty, William Henry West (1791–1874), XI. 283, 452
Betuleius, Xystus, V. 101
Beuchame, Lewes, IV. 446
Beulah, daughters of, in Blake's *Four Zoas*, XI. 196
Beulah, land of, XII. 175, 253
Beulan, teacher of Nennius, I. 70
Beveridge, William (1637–1708), VII. 490; VIII. 298, 301, 302, 457; IX. 528
Beverley, V. 41, 45, 103
Beverley. *See* Alfred of; St John of
Beverley, in Sheridan's *Rivals*, XI. 266
Beverley, Mrs, in Moore's *Gamester*, X. 80
Beverley, Yorks., IX. 470
Beversham, James (*fl.* 1618), IV. 93

Beves or *Bevis of Hamtoun*, I. 218, 282, 287, 291 ff., 303, 305, 306, 470; II. 320, 323; V. 108; VII. 167
Bevil junior, in Steele's *Conscious Lovers*, IX. 64
Beville, William (*fl.* 1782), X. 475
Bevis, in *The Tatler*, XI. 373
Bew, M., III. 189
Beware the Cat, III. 112, 494
Bewcastle column, Cumberland, I. 12, 426
Bewick, Thomas (1753–1828), IX. 481; XI. 377, 436, 485, 487, 489, 490, 492; XIV. 201, 227, 235, 236, 540, 542
Bewick and Graham, II. 411
Bexley, 1st lord. *See* Vansittart, Nicholas
Bexley heath, XIII. 119
Beyle, Henri (De Stendhal), XII. 381, 392, 397; *Racine et Shakespeare*, X. 181
Beyrout, XIV. 251
Beza, Theodore, III. 45, 46, 174; IV. 429; VIII. 277, 363; *Abraham's Sacrifice*, V. 394; *Praefatio Poetica*, III. 174
Bhagalpur, XIV. 334
Bhagavadgītā, the, XII. 343, 503
Biagi, Guido, XIII. 552
Bianca, in *Loves Sacrifice*, VI. 192
Bianca, in *The Taming of the Shrew*, V. 181
Bianca, in *Women beware Women*, VI. 78, 176
Biberach, V. 298
Bible, the, I. 72, 89; II. 150, 151, 230, 289, 291, 314, 366, 367; III. 10, 11, 13, 25, 27, 28, 29, 31, 40 ff., 44, 45, 47, 53, 58, 86, 110, 130, 133, 140, 141, 145, 157, 163, 214, 339, 363, 400, 407, 410 ff., 416, 423, 445, 455, 462, 463; IV. 26 ff., 81, 230, 241, 248, 270, 303, 347, 389, 396, 412, 421, *also see* Add.; V. 17, 40, 44, 101, 111, 342; VI. 91, 375, 378, 401, 402, 405; VII. 6, 151, 157, 164, 169, 171, 177, 236, 253, 269, 296, 297, 303 ff., 315 ff., 321 ff., 371, 375, 382, 396; VIII. 42, 78, 86, 91, 92, 101, 103, 105, 110 ff., 164, 274 ff., 278, 294, 298, 302, 326, 346, 364; IX. 42, 118, 393, 402; X. 154, 229, 236; XI. 48, 89, 181, 188, 189, 237, 326, 363, 369; XII. 156, 177, 280, 282 ff., 293, 295, 318, 331, 488, 501, 502, 520, 521; XIII. 102; XIV. 148, 329, 405
  See, also, *Old and New Testament*
  New Testament, IX. 294, 330; XII. 286, 290, 293, 297, 298, 340 (revised version), 501; the first printed English, XII. 515; in Scots, XIV. 101
  Old Testament, IX. 296; XII. 501; XIV. 132
Bible, Versions of the:
  Authorised Version, the, III. 45, 423, 465; IV. 26–50, 185, 238, 398, 449; XIV. 435, 441, 446 ff.
  Bassandyne, the, II. 94, 285
  Bishops', the, III. 45, 423; IV. 400, 401
  Challoner's Roman Catholic, IV. 49
  Chinese, XII. 342, 500
  Coverdale's, III. 45; IV. 41, 402
  Cranmer's, III. 44
Bible, Versions of the:
  Douay, IV. 41, 49; X. Add.
  Early translations, IV. 37, 39; VII. 127
  English, III. 474, IV. 26 ff. (main entry)
  Genevan, II. 94; III. 45, 46; IV. 41, 403
  Great, the, III. 44, 45
  Greek Testament, IX. 336; XII. 340, 500
  Hebrew, IX. 330; XII. 341
  Matthew's, III. 45
  Polyglot, IV. 427
  Rheims translation of, III. 446; IV. 38, 41, 42, 49; X. Add.
  Sanskrit, XII. 343
  Septuagint, I. 77; VII. 316; IV. 46
  Syriac (*Gospels*), XII. 341
  Tindale's, III. 41 ff.; IV. 38 ff.
  Trevisa's, II. 77
  Vulgate, the, I. 46, 84, 85, 91, 97, 208, 400; II. 59, 60, 62, 94, 431; III. 41, 45, 463, 464; IV. 36, 46
  Wyclifite, II. 300, 430, 431, 440; IV. 38, 39, 42, 428
Bible, single vols. or MSS. of:
  Codex Amiatinus at Florence, I. 72
  Codex Argenteus at Upsala, I. 16
  King Philip's, IV. 427
  Metz, I. 89
  Rushworth Gospels, the, I. 132
  St Denis, I. 89
  Sir Walter Ralegh's, IV. 65
  Thomas Cromwell's, IV. 426
Bible, books and parts of:
  Acts of the Apostles, IV. 32; IX. 534; XIV. 449
  Apocalypse. See *Revelation*
  Apocrypha, the, II. 120, 230, 430; III. 43 ff.; VII. 316, 317; XII. 502
  Baruch, II. 61
  Canticles. See, post, *Song of Songs*
  Chronicles, III. 44; IV. 43
  Colossians, XII. 501
  Corinthians, IV. 38; VII. 140, 322; XI. 355
  Corinthians I, XII. 483, 501
  Corinthians II, XII. 501
  Daniel, XII. 501, 503
  Deuteronomy, IV. 170; VII. 140, 395; XII. 501
  Ecclesiastes, III. 271; VII. 317; XII. 341, 501; XIII. 138
  Ephesians, II. 234, 431; IX. 560
  Esther, VII. 316
  Exodus, IV. 30, 36, 37, 39; XII. 499, 501
  Exodus (Old English), I. 46 ff., 58, 63, 428
  Exodus (Wyclifite), II. 430
  Ezekiel, VII. 322; XII. 501
  Four Gospels, IX. 561
  Galatians, XII. 486, 501
  Genesis, II. 14; IV. 31; VII. 140; VIII. 352; XII. 48, 499, 501, 503; XIV. 149
  Genesis, A and B, Old English, I. 46 ff., 63, 428
  Genesis and Exodus, Middle English, I. 225, 376, 387, 399, 458, 459
  Gospels, the, IV. 39, 424

Bible, books and parts of:
Gospels, x. 365; xii. 280, 503, 505
Habakkuk, xii. 501
Hebrews, iv. 43; xii. 340, 503
Hosea, vii. 322
Isaiah, ii. 430; iii. 101; iv. 77, 170; xii. 501
Jeremiah, xii. 501
Job, iv. 30, 33, 47, 48; vii. 317, 322; x. 458; xi. 434; xii. 341, 416, 501, 502
Joel and Amos, xii. 501
John, epistles of St, xii. 340
John, First Epistle of St, x. 309
John, Gospel of St, ii. 365; iv. 37, 38; v. 37, 42; vii. 322; x. 463; xii. 340, 481, 489, 490
Jonah, iii. 44; vii. 46
Judges, iv. 43, 170
2 *Kings*, iv. 33
Leviticus, xii. 501
Luke, Gospel of St, iv. 41; xii. 503
Maccabees iv, xii. 503
Mark, Gospel of St, i. 132; iii. 42; v. 42; xii. 505
Matthew, Gospel of St, i. 132; iii. 42; vii. 140
Nahum, xii. 501
Paul, Epistles of St, iv. 27, 30; xii. 340, 506
Paul, speech of St, iv. 29
Pentateuch, iii. 44; iv. 39, 238; xii. 296
Philemon, xii. 501
Philippians, xii. 501
Proverbs, ii. 14; iv. 34; vii. 317
Psalm cxix, xiv. 74
Psalms, iii. 46, 101, 174; iv. 30, 33, 34, 44, 81, 131, 407; v. 21; vii. 31, 109, 215, 322; ix. 63, 78, 556, 559, 562; x. 456, 457; xi. 206, 237; xii. 419
Psalms, Buchanan's version, iii. 162, 164
Psalms in metre, iii. 476; iv. 384, 395, 397
Psalms, versions of Sternhold and Hopkins, iii. 46
Psalter, iv. 28, 31, 384
Psalter, Gallican, iv. 422
Psalter, the Genevan, iii. 46
Psalter, Irish, iv. 426
Psalter, Prayer Book version, iv. 41
Psalter, the Scots (1564), iii. 46
Revelation of St John (*Apocalypse*), ii. 60; iv. 28, 30, 47; vii. 170; viii. 286; xi. 197; xii. 501; xiii. 139; xiv. 149
Romans, iii. 45; iv. 38, 42; xii. 484, 486, 492
Samuel, iv. 33
Song of Songs, The (*Canticles, Song of Solomon*), ii. 48; iv. 170, 249; vii. 109, 317; x. 489, 522; xii. 341, 501
Thessalonians, xii. 486
Zephaniah, xii. 501
Bible societies in Scotland, xi. 469
Bible society, the, ix. 247; xi. 259; xiv. 146
Bibles, prices of, ii. 308
Biblical parodies, ix. 563
Biblical studies, vii. 311, 318, 321, 481
Bibliographical society, xii. 355, 369, 519
Bibliothèque universelle, viii. 331
Bickerstaff, Isaac (d. 1812?), ix. 35, 39, 40, 46 ff., 50, 51, 54; x. 71, 425; xi. 451; xiv. 461
Lionel and Clarissa, x. 89
Love in a Village, x. 89
Maid of the Mill, x. 89
Padlock, The, x. 89; xi. 262
Schools for Fathers, x. 89
Bickerstaff, Isaac, of *The Tatler*, xi. 373
Bickersteth, Edward (1786–1850), xii. 471
Bickersteth, Henry, lord Langdale (1783–1851), xii. 355, 356, 516
Bickham, George (d. 1758), xiv. 212, 214
Bickley, Francis, ix. Add.
Bickley, Francis L., xiii. 488
Bicknell, Alexander (d. 1796), xi. 453
Bidding prayer, iii. 31
Biddle, John (1615–1662), x. 359, 377, 378
Bideford, Devon, xiv. 84
Bidpai, fables of, xi. 479; xii. 499
Biffen, in Gissing's *New Grub Street*, xiii. 460
Big Endians, ix. 229
Bigg, Charles, ix. 321, 324
Bigg, John Stanyan (1828–1865), xiii. 499
Bigg, Mrs, x. 119
Biggs, Noah, vii. 511
Bigland, Ralph (1711–1784), xii. 510
Bigmore, E. C., xiv. 535
Bignell, Mrs, in D'Urfey's *The Modern Prophets*, viii. 175
Bignold, Thomas Francis (d. 1888), xiv. 575; *Leviora*, xiv. 340
Bigod, Ralph, in Lamb's *Essays of Elia*, xii. 188
Bijapur army, the, xiv. 338
Bilberg, John, iv. 453
Bilboe, in Wilson's *The Cheats*, viii. 122
Biliotti, Édouard, xii. 339
Bill, John, *Books printed in English*, iv. 403, 404
Bill, William (d. 1561), iii. 421
Billings, Robert William (1813–1874), xii. 507
Billingsgate, in Trevisa, ii. 78
Billingsley, Sir Henry (d. 1606), iii. 551; iv. 436, 453
Billy, Jacques de, iv. 24
'Billy, perfidious,' xiv. 116
Bilney, Thomas (d. 1531), iii. 27, 36; iv. 231
Bilson, Thomas (1547–1616), iv. 265, 491; vii. 318, 484; *Christian subjection*, iv. 411
Bindley, Charles (*pseud.* Harry Hieover, 1795–1859), xiv. 542
Binfield, ix. 67, 68, 161, 167
Bing, Thomas (*fl.* 1603), *Sorrowe's Joy*, iv. 351
Bingham, Joseph (1668–1723), x. 515; *Origines Ecclesiasticae*, x. 357
Bingham, Peregrine (1788–1864), xi. 398

Bingley, in Jane Austen's *Pride and Prejudice*, XII. 238
'Bingo,' Japan, IV. 99
Binney, E., XIV. 492
Binney, Edward William (1812–1881), XIV. 290, 559
Binning, Hugh (1627–1653), IX. 542
Binning, Thomas, IV. 453
Binns, Henry Bryan, XIV. 590, 592
Binyon, Laurence, XII. 406
Biographia Britannica, IX. 472, 530; X. 184
Biographia Dramatica, VIII. 188, 423; XI. 453
Biographical Dictionary (society for the Diffusion of Useful Knowledge), XII. 307; XIV. 409
Biographisches Jahrbuch, XII. 332
Bion, III. 218, 221, 222, 223; VII. 83, 489; IX. 526; X. 454; XI. 426; XII. 495
Bion, Greek pastoral translated by Oldham, VIII. 86
Birch, John (1616–1691), *Negotiations*, VII. 190
Birch, Samuel (1813–1885), XII. 500; *Book of the Dead*, XII. 342; *Hieroglyphical Grammar and Dictionary*, XII. 342; *History of Ancient Pottery*, XII. 342
Birch, Thomas (1705–1766), VIII. 453, 461, 462, 477, 479; IX. 529; X. 294, 498, *also see* Add.; XI. 356, 475
The Court and Times of James I, VII. 193, 433, 436
Court and Times of James I and Charles I, X. 295
History of the Royal Society, X. 466
Inquiry into Transactions of Glamorgan, X. 294
Life of Dr John Tillotson, X. 295
Life of Henry, Prince of Wales, X. 295
Memoirs of the Reign of Elizabeth, X. 295
Negotiations, X. 295
Thurloe papers, X. 294
Birch, Walter, XII. 440
Birch, Walter de Gray, I. 451; XIV. 491
Birchenough, Charles, XIV. 590
Birchington, near Margate, XIII. 112
Birckbek, Simon (1584–1656), VII. 484
Birckman, Arnold (*fl.* 1568), IV. 403
Birckmans, the, IV. 402
Bird, John, XIV. Add. 5
Bird, William (*fl.* 1780), XII. 181
Bird, in *The Muses Looking-Glasse*, VI. 234
Birde, W. (*fl.* 1602), V. 333
Birel, Robert, The Diary of, III. 149, 501
Biringaccio, Vannuccio, *Pyrotechnica*, IV. 70
Birkabeyn, in *Havelok*, I. 303
Birkbeck, George (1776–1841), XIV. 407 ff., 601
Birkenhead or Berkenhead, Sir John (1616–1679), VI. 136
Birks, Thomas Rawson (1810–1883), XII. 471
Birmingham, III. 427; X. 159, 160, 163, 176, 187, 476; XI. 338, 340, 341, 469, 484; XII. 174, 184, 279, 511; XIII. 119, 427
Birmingham, Mason's college, XIV. 432
Birmingham Journal, X. 159
Birmingham school, VII. 330
Birnam wood, in Wyntoun's *Cronykil*, II. 132
Birnie, Pat, IX. 366
Biron, in *Love's Labour's Lost*, V. 178, 315
Biron, in Southerne's *Fatal Marriage*, VIII. 191, 192
Birrell, Augustine, XI. 466; XII. 437, 445; XIII. 470, 479, 484, 488, 505, 557
Birrenswark, in Dumfriesshire, XII. 350
Birth of Merlin, The, V. 236, 238, 249 ff., 441, 443; VI. 69, 70
Birtha, in D'Avenant's *Gondibert*, VII. 71; VIII. 9
Bishop, George (*fl.* 1590), IV. 82, 389, 398
Bishop, Sir Henry Rowley (1786–1855), XIII. 264
Bishop, Isabella L., born Bird (1831–1904), XIV. 550
Bishop, Richard (*fl.* 1645), VII. 361
Bishops' Book, The, III. 13, 36
Bishop's court, Kirk Michael, X. 359
Bishop's wood, in Pecock, II. 291
Bishopsbourne, III. 406
Bisland, Elizabeth, XIV. 519
Bismarck, prince von, XIII. 20; XIV. 183, 192, 194
Bisset, James (1762?–1832), XI. 452, 484
Bisset, Robert (1759–1805), IX. 441; XI. 390
Bisset, William (d. 1747), IX. 478
Bithynia, queen of, in *Believe as you List*, VI. 148, 149
Björkman, E., XIII. 573
Blachford, lord. *See* Rogers, Frederic
Black, A. and C., publishers, XII. 372
Black, John (1783–1855), XIV. 187
Black, John Sutherland, XII. 470
Black, Joseph (1728–1799), XIV. 272 ff., 406, 557; *Magnesia alba, Quicklime, and other alcaline substances*, XIV. 274
Black, Stephen, XIV. Add. 5
Black, William (1841–1898), XIII. 431, 560; XIV. 199; *Daughter of Heth, A*, XIII. 432; *Macleod of Dare*, XIII. 432; *Strange Adventures of a Phaeton, The*, XIII. 432
Black Almaine, the (a tune), III. 190
Black Bateman of the North, V. 325
Black Book of Carmarthen, I. 243, 249 250, 251, 461
Black Death, the, I. 371; II. 41, 42, 45 70, 71, 354
Blacke Dogge of Newgate, The, III. 99
Black Friars. *See* Dominicans
Black hole of Calcutta, the, XIV. 334
Black Knight, the, in *A Game at Chesse*, VI. 79
Black Knight, the, in Scott's *Ivanhoe*, XII. 18
Black Magic, VII. 368
'Black Mill,' VIII. 212, 219

Black Prince, the, II. 22; IV. 182; VI. 330; XI. 131
Black Prince, the, in *Edward III*, V. 246
Blackall, Offspring, IX. 41; X. 354
Blackbird, The, XI. 234
Blackbourne, Richard (b. 1652), VII. Add.
Blackburn, Douglas, XIV. Add. 5
Blackburn, Henry, XIV. 536
Blackfriars, children of, VI. 292
'Blackfriars preachers,' VI. 257
'Black-Fryers, Sanctified Fraternity of,' the, VI. 234
Blackie, John Stuart (1809–1895), XI. 439; XII. 335, 480; XIV. 515, 516
Blacklock, Thomas (1721–1791), IX. 556; X. 477; XI. 233, 234, 442
Blackman, John, XIV. 601
Blackmantle, Bernard, *pseud. See* Westmacott, Charles Molloy
Blackmore, Sir Richard (d. 1729), VIII. 32, 54, 168, 428, 432; IX. 29, 78, 177, 178, 180–181 (main entry), 477, 484; X. 72, 148, 183; XII. 128
Alfred, IX. 180
Arthur, IX. 180
Creation, IX. 180, 181, 184
Eliza, IX. 180
King Arthur, VIII. 52
Prince Arthur, VIII. 163
Satyr on Wit, VIII. 52
Blackmore, Richard Doddridge (1825–1900), XIII. 560; *Lorna Doone*, XIII. 434, 435; *Springhaven*, XIII. 435
Blackstone, Sir William (1723–1780), VIII. 321; X. 275, 499; XIV. 80; *Commentaries*, VIII. 315; XI. 61, 62, 66; *Law Tracts*, XI. 61
Blackwater, river, XIV. 308
Blackwater river (*Battle of Maldon*), I. 144
Blackwell, B. H., XIV. 528
Blackwell, Thomas (1660?–1728), IX. 547
Blackwell, Thomas (1701–1757), IX. 552; *Memoirs of the Court of Augustus*, X. 466
Blackwood, Frederick Temple Hamilton-Temple, marquis of Dufferin (1826–1902), XIV. 98, 552, 568; *Letters from High Latitudes*, XIV. 240
Blackwood, Helen Selina, born Sheridan, countess of Dufferin (1807–1867), XIII. 177, 499; XIV. 309, 508; *Bay of Dublin, The*, XIV. 310; *I'm sitting on the stile, Mary*, XIV. 310
Blackwood, John (1818–1879), XII. 425
Blackwood, William (1776–1834), XII. 156, 157, 159, 161, 425; *Annals of a Publishing House*, XII. 159
Blackwood, Tales from, XII. 425
Blackwood's Edinburgh Magazine ('Maga'), XII. 36, 141, 153, 154, 155 ff. (main entry), 221, 409 ff., 425; XI. 148; XIII. 5, 160, 187, 372, 386, 396, 425; XIV. 66, 150, 161, 188, 232, 313, 319, 327, 373
Bladen, William (*fl.* 1640), IV. 414
Blades, William (1824–1890), XII. 520
Blagrave, John (d. 1611), *The Mathematical Jewel*, III. 549; IV. 453
Blague, in *The Merry Devill*, V. 252
Blague, mistress, in *Edward IV*, VI. 91
Blaiman, Irish tale, I. 293
Blair, Hugh (1718–1800), IX. 560; X. 227 ff., 324, 488; XII. 426; XIV. 604; *Lectures on Rhetoric*, XIV. 398, 399; *Sermons*, XI. 327
Blair, John (*fl.* 1300), II. 110
Blair, Robert (1593–1666), VII. 455
Blair, Robert (1699–1746), IX. 167; X. 138, 144, 147 (main entry), 453; *The Grave*, X. 147; XI. 244
Blake, J. W., *Accent and Rhythm explained by the law of Monopressures*, XIII. 249, 511
Blake, Robert (1599–1657), X. 164, 464
Blake, William (1757–1827), VI. 71; VIII. 230; X. 147, 236, 458; XI. 176, 181 ff. (main entry), 245, 250, 395, 431, *also see* Add.; XIII. 43, 108, 151, 195, 197, 198, 225, 406, 489, 495; XIV. 363, 525
Africa, XI. 194
America, XI. 189, 190, 193
Auguries of Innocence, XI. 200
Birds, The, XI. 200
Blossom, The, XI. 185
Book of Ahania, XI. 193, 194
Book of Los, XI. 193, 194
Book of Thel, XI. 186, 187
Book of Urizen, XI. 193 ff.
Chimney Sweeper, The, XI. 185, 186
Clod and the Pebble, XI. 191
Cradle Song, XI. 186, 193
Crystal Cabinet, The, XI. 199
Descriptive Catalogue, XI. 200
Divine Image, The, XI. 184
Dream, A, XI. 185
Earth's Answer, XI. 192
Echoing Green, The, XI. 185
Europe, XI. 193, 194, 197
Everlasting Gospel, The, XI. 200
Fair Elenor, XI. 182
Four Zoas, The, XI. 196, 197
French Revolution, XI. 189, 190
Ghost of Abel, XI. 199
Golden Net, The, XI. 199
Grey Monk, The, XI. 199
Holy Thursday, XI. 185, 191
'How sweet I roam'd from field to field, XI. 182
'I laid me down upon a bank,' XI. 192
I love the jocund dance, XI. 185
I told my love, XI. 193
Infant Joy, XI. 186
Infant Sorrow, XI. 192
Introduction, XI. 192
Island in the Moon, XI. 183
Jerusalem, XI. 197 ff.
King Edward the Third, XI. 183
Lamb, The, XI. 186
Land of Dreams, XI. 199
Laocoon, XI. 199, 201
Laughing Song, XI. 185
Little Black Boy, XI. 186
Little Boy Lost, XI. 192
Mad Song, XI. 170, 183

Blake, William
Marriage of Heaven and Hell, xi. 187 ff., 192, 200
Mary, xi. 200
Memorable Fancies, xi. 188
Mental Traveller, The, xi. 200
Milton, xi. 188, 197
Morning, xi. 199
My silks and fine array, xi. 183
My Spectre around me, xi. 200
Night, xi. 185
No Natural Religion, xi. 187
Note on *The Canterbury Tales*, xi. 200
On Homer's Poetry, xi. 201
On Virgil, xi. 201
Passions, The, xi. 182
Poetical Sketches, xi. 181, 182, 184, 185
Prophetic Books, xiii. 226
Public Address, xi. 201
Schoolboy, The, xi. 192
Smile, The, xi. 199
Song of Liberty, xi. 189
Song of Los, xi. 193, 194
Song of Phebe, xi. 184
Songs of Experience, xi. 190 ff.
Songs of Innocence, xi. 184 ff., 191, 192, 196, 197, 384
Spring, xi. 185
Sunflower, The, xi. 192
Tiger, The, xi. 191, 192
Tiriel, xi. 187
To My Myrtle, xi. 193
To the Christians, xi. 200
To the Deists, xi. 200
To the Muses, xi. 182
Vala, xi. 195, 196
Vision of the Last Judgment, xi. 197
Visions of the Daughters of Albion, xi. 190, 192
War Song to Englishmen, xi. 183
When old corruption first begun, xi. 184
Wild Flower's Song, xi. 193
William Bond, xi. 200
Lambeth books, xi. 189, 193, 195 ff. 199
Pickering ms., xi. 199, 432
Rossetti ms., xi. 191, 197, 199, 200, 431
Blakeney, colonel, x. 65
Blakesley, Joseph Williams (1808–1885), xii. 330, 480; xiv. 593
Blakesley, Northants., viii. 2
Blakesware, in Widford, xii. 182, 186, 189, 191
Blamire, Susanna (1747–1794), x. 453; *And ye shall walk in Silk Attire*, xi. 232; *Nabob*, xi. 232; *What ails this heart of Mine*, xi. 232
Blamsdon, Yorkshire, iii. 314
Blanchard, Edward Litt Laman (1820–1889), xiii. 517
Blanchard, Samuel Laman (1804–1845), xii. 131, 414, 419, 428, 450; xiv. 188, 192, 196
Blanche blab-it-out, in *The Disobedient Child*, v. 109
Blanche of Lancaster, ii. 170
Blanchefleur, i. 308
Blanco, E. González, xiii. 465
Bland, Tobias (*fl.* 1563?–1604), iii. Add.
Blandish, Mr and Mrs, in Burgoyne's *Heiress*, xi. 276
Blandford, x. 94
Blandy, William (*fl.* 1580), iv. 444
Blane, William, xiv. Add. 4
Blaneford, Henry (*fl.* 1330), ii. 496
Blaquiere, captain, xii. 38
Blasour, in *Gyre Carling*, ii. 275
Blastist, xiii. 214
Blaydes, Frederick H. M. (1818–1908), xii. 480
Bleek, Wilhelm Heinrich Immanuel, xiv. Add. 5
Bleheris of Wales, ii. 451
Bleking, in Ohthere's voyage, i. 94
Bleloch, William Edwin, xiv. Add. 5
Blencowe, John, vi. Add. 2
Blenerhasset, Thomas (1550?–1625?), iii. 197
Blenheim, ix. 44, 150, 151, 155, 182
Blenheim palace, viii. 163; xii. 173, 192
Blerblowan, in *Colkelbie's sow*, ii. 127
Blessednes of Brytaine, The, v. 340
Blessington, Charles John Gardiner, 1st earl of, xii. 37
Blessington, Marguerite, countess of (1789–1849), xiv. 567
Conversations, xii. 37, 384, 392, 441
Idler in France, The, xiv. 322
Idler in Italy, The, xiv. 322
Journal of Conversations with Lord Byron, xiv. 322
Bletchingley, Surrey, vi. 282
Blickling Homilies, i. 114, 129, 442
Blifil, in Fielding's *Tom Jones*, viii. 148; x. 26, 31, 89
Bligh, William (1754–1817), xiv. 550
Blimber, Dr, in *Dombey and Son*, xiii. 325
Blind, Mathilde (1841–1896), xiii. 181, 499, 553
Blind Devotion, in *A True Inventory*, vii. 382
Bliss, Philip (1787–1857), ix. 342, 535
Bliss, bower of, in *The Faerie Queene*, iii. 233, 237
Blith, Walter (*fl.* 1649), iv. 509
Bloet, Robert, bishop of Lincoln (d. 1123), i. 166
Blois, viii. 245; xi. 97
Blois. *See* Alexander, and Peter, of
Blome, Richard (d. 1705), *The Gentleman's Recreation*, xiv. 232
Blomefield, Francis (1705–1752), ix. 532; *History of Norfolk*, ix. 353
Blomfield, Alfred, xii. 481
Blomfield, Charles James (1786–1857), xii. 291, 325, 327, 328, 329 (main entry), 454, 481, 483, 488, 491
Blomfield, Edward Valentine (1788–1816), xii. 481
'Bloomerism,' xiv. 239
Bloomfield, Robert (1766–1823), xi. 484 xii. 131, 132, 139, 414, 508

Blou northerne wynd, II. 393
Bloudy Newes, IV. 389
Blougram, bishop, Browning's, XIII. 63, 72
Blount, Charles, earl of Devonshire (1563–1606), IV. 132, 133; V. 347; VI. 196; VII. 211
Blount, Charles (1654–1693), VIII. 403, *also see* Add.; IX. 288, 289, 475, 504
Anima Mundi, IX. 288
Great is Diana of the Ephesians, IX. 288
Miscellaneous Works, IX. 289
Oracles of Reason, IX. 289
Sale of Esau's Birthright, VIII. 97
Two first books of Philostratus, IX. 288
Blount or Blunt, Edward (*fl.* 1588–1632), IV. 341, 395, 443, 526, 546; V. 122, 125, 148
Blount, Sir Henry (1602–1682), IV. 453
Blount, Martha (1690–1762), IX. 71, 72, 82, 443, 444
Blount, Teresa, IX. 71, 443, 444
Blount, Thomas (1618–1679), VII. 517; VIII. 468; IX. 528
Blount, William, 4th lord Mountjoy (d. 1534), III. 3, 4, 7, 8, 14
Blow, John (1648–1708), VIII. 395
Blowbol. See *Colin Blowbol*
Blowitz, Henri G. S. A. O. de (1832–1903), XIV. 183, 533
Bloxam, John Rouse (1807–1891), XII. 459, 460
Bloxam MSS., Magd. Coll. Oxford, XII. 460
Bluebeard, XI. 375; XIII. 415
Bluebeard, a female, III. 88
Blue Stockings, the, X. 261, 268; XI. 343 ff., 473
Bluffe, captain, in Congreve's *Old Bachelor*, VIII. 147, 152
Bluhm, G. R., XIII. 542
'Blumine,' in Carlyle's *Sartor Resartus*, XIII. 3
Blundell, James (1780–1877), XIII. 53
Blundell, James, prosodist, XIII. 241
Blunden, Humphrey (*fl.* 1648), IX. 515, 517, 518
Blunderbore, giant, XI. 374
Blunderhead family, in Anstey's *New Bath Guide*, XI. 173
Blundeston, friend of Barnabe Googe, III. 185
Blundeville, M., His exercises...in Cosmographie..., III. 425, 549; IV. 453
Blundeville, Thomas (*fl.* 1561), IV. 443, 444, 540
Blunt, Henry (1794–1843), XII. 471
Blunt, John James (1794–1855), XII. 490
Blunt, Reginald, XIII. 470
Blurt, in *Blurt Master-Constable*, V. 362
Blyth, Edmund Kell, XIV. 601
'Blyth, John,' II. 279
Blyth (near Rotherham), XII. 512
Blythesome Bridal, The, IX. 363 ff.
Boaden, James (1762–1839), X. 263, 264; XI. 428, 452 ff., 461
Boadicea, VI. 128; VII. 443
Boadicea, in Milton's *England*, VII. 129
Boake, Barcroft Henry (1866–1892), XIV. 369, 584
Board of Works, XIV. 285
Boas, Frederick Samuel, IV. 164; V 414, 424; VI. Add. 2
Boas, Henrietta O'Brien, Mrs F. S., XIII. 490
Boase, George Clement (1829–1897), XII. 521; XIV. 512
Boaz, X. 104
Bobadil, captain, in *Solimon and Perseda*, V. 161
Bobadill, in Jonson's *Every Man in His Humour*, IV. 15; V. 33, 315, 361, 367; VI. 16, 26, 28, 127, 249, 272; VIII. 127, 147, 171; XI. 283
Bobbin, Tim. *See* Collier, John
Boccaccio, Giovanni, I. 199, 214, 360; II. 134, 145, 168, 174, 176, 182, 184, 199, 204, 262, 264, 321, 325; III. 65, 130, 181, 192, 198, 337, 339, 343, 375; IV. 6, 441, 442; VIII. 4, 51, 52, 183, 433; XII. 58, 168, 217, 365
Admeto, VI. 364
Decameron, I. 286; II. 177; III. 356; IV. 7, 361; V. 62, 72, 73, 75, 103, 116, 220, 221; VI. 48, 137, 138, 205, 304, 364, 484; XII. 53, 82; XIII. 400, 401
De Casibus Virorum Illustrium, III. 130, 192, 198
Fiammetta, IV. 7
Filocopo, I. 286; IV. 7
Filostrato, Il, II. 172
Olympia, I. 323
Teseide, II. 180
Boccalini, T., *Ragguagli di Parnaso*, VII. 274
Bocking, VIII. 269
Böddeker, K., I. 477; XIII. 564
Bodel, Jean, *Chanson de Saisnes*, I. 279, 302
Bodenham, John (*fl.* 1600), III. 522; IV. 117, 526; *Belvedere*, VI. 312
Bodenstedt, F. von, V. 303
Bodin, Jean, III. 145; IV. 296, 298, 509; VI. 377, 492; VII. 394, 405; *Démonomie des Sorciers*, III. 112
Bodley, John, father of Sir Thomas Bodley, IV. 429
Bodley, Sir Thomas (1545–1613), III. 425: IV. 56, 403, 406, 415, 429 ff., 433; VII. 153; IX. 342, 349, 534
Bodli, in Morris's *The Lovers of Gudrun*, XIII. 125
Bodmer, Johann Jakob, V. 290
Body and Soul. See *Soul and Body*
Boece or Boethius, Hector (1465?–1536), II. 114, 251, 370, 371; III. 131, 148, 154, 155, 156, 319, 501; *Historia Gentis Scotorum*, II. 104; III. 148, 155, 156; IV. 412; *Vitae Episcoporum Murthlacensium et Aberdonensium*, III. 155
Boeckh, Philipp August, *The Public Economy of Athens*, XII. 301, 339

Boehme, Jacob, vii. 303, 351; ix. 307, 308, 314 ff., 327, 328, 511 ff., 521 ff.; xiii. 431
Forty Questions, ix. 307
Mysterium Magnum, ix. 317
Signatura Rerum, ix. 307, 316
Three Principles, ix. 307
Threefold Life of Man, ix. 316
Boehme, Johann, iv. 442
Boeotia, iv. 10
Boeotia (*i.e.* Germany), in *Euphormio*, iv. 256
Boer war (1898), xiv. 193, 456
Boer zijn Zaterdag Aand, Die, xiv. 377
Boerhaave, Hermann, x. 164, 464
Boers, the, xiv. 173, 254
Boethius, i. 213, 355; ii. 241, 247, 355, 360, 363, 456; iv. 417, 442; *Arithmetica*, ii. 362; *De Consolatione Philosophiae*, iii. 290; iv. 409, (Alfred's version, i. 91, 99 ff., 107, 436, 437, 439)
Boffin, Mr, in *Our Mutual Friend*, xiii. 336
Bogue, David and Bennett, J. (1750–1825), *History of Dissenters*, x. 518
Bohemia, ii. 69, 292, 298; iii. 355, 357, 359; v. 167, 205, 206; vii. 344
Bohemian, the, in *The Fyrste Boke of the Introduction of Knowledge*, iii. 105
Bohemian scholars in England in Wyclif's day, ii. 67
Bohemianism, xiii. 162, 163, 290; xiv. 176
Bohemund, in *Orlando Furioso*, iii. 230
Bohn, Henry George (1796–1884), x. 410; xii. 520; xiv. 612; *Antiquarian Library*, xii. 368; *Guinea Catalogue*, xii. 368
Boiardo, Matteo Maria, xii. 3; *Orlando Innamorato*, iv. 442; xii. 422
Boiastuan, iii. 109
Boice, Sir, in *Morte Arthure*, ii. 119
Boileau, Abbé, x. 501
Boileau-Despréaux, Nicolas, v. 176; viii. 133, 203, 214, 219, 220, 373 ff., 385; ix. 140, 150, 155, 257, 473; x. 115; xii. 104
L'Art Poétique, viii. 373, 375; x. 169
Lutrin, viii. 197, 373, 436, 440; ix. 70, 179
Ode sur la Prise de Namur, ix. 148
Satire (second), viii. 63
Satire touching Nobility, viii. 88
Bois, John (1561–1644), vii. 316, 318, 482
Boisil, i. 148
Bokenam, Osbern (1393–1447?), ii. 469; *Lives* or *Legends of Saints*, ii. 198, 214
Bokyngham, John (d. 1398), *Super Sententias*, ii. 366
Bolas, Thomas, xiv. 535
Bold, Henry (1627–1683), vii. 88, 412
Bold, Samuel (1649–1737), viii. 347, 472
Boldon Buke, xii. 510
Boldrewood, Rolf, *pseud.* *See* Browne, Thomas Alexander
Boleyn, Anne. *See* Anne
Boleyn, Sir Thomas, earl of Wiltshire (1477–1539), iii. 32, 167
Bolingbroke, viscount. *See* St John, Henry
Bolingbroke, in *King Richard II*, v. 271
Bolmer, in Yorkshire, v. 90
Bologna, ii. 350, 364; iii. 5, 7, 49, 167, 423; viii. 5, 312
Bologna, schools of, i. 187, 192, 199, 200
Bolomyer, Henry, canon of Lausanne, ii. 315
Bolton, Edmund ('Philanactophil') (157? ?–1633?), iii. 199, 201, 306; iv. 117, 118, 436, 482, 543; vii. 205, 443; *Corpus Rerum Anglicarum*, vii. 205; *Florus's Epitome of Roman History* (trans.), vii. 205; *Hypercritica*, iii. 201, 528; vii. 262, 265, 273, 465
Bolton, M. P. W., xiv. 474
Bolton, Lancashire, xiv. 195
Bolton-le-Moors, Lancashire, vii. 342
Bolts, William (1740?–1808), xiv. 334, 575
Bombay, xiv. 59, 336
Bon Gaultier Ballads, The, xiii. 150, 161
Bona, Jaonnes, *Guide to Eternity*, ix. 274, 418
Bonarelli, *Filli di Sciro*, vi. 321
Bonar, Horatius (1808–1889), xii. 471
Bonaventura, St, i. 110, 154, 206; *Meditations*, v. 42
Bond, Sir Edward Augustus (1815–1898), xi. 396; xii. 356, 515
Bond, Henry, iv. 453
Bond, John (1550–1612), vii. 486
Bond, R. Warwick, v. 123, 125, 401, 402, 415
Bond, Thomas (1765–1837), xii. 508
Bond, William (*fl.* 1726), ix. 21
Bonducci, Andrea, x. 447
Bone Aventure, in *The Bowge of Courte*, iii. 73
Bonet, Honoré, ii. 284
Bongrace, in *Jacke Jugeler*, v. 107
Bonheur de ce Monde, ix. 170
Bonhill, x. 36
Boniface, in Farquhar's *Beaux' Stratagem*, viii. 171
Boniface VIII, pope, ii. 148; *Liber Sextus*, ii. 364
Boniface IX, pope, ii. 348
Boniface, St, i. 73, 78, 86, 435, *also see* Add. to third impression
Boniface, Sir, in *The Wise-woman Of Hogsdon*, vi. 83
Bonn, xii. 302
Bonn university, xiv. 410
Bonner or Boner, Edmund (1500?–1569), bishop of London, iii. 167, 186, 337
Bonner, Hypatia Bradlaugh (1833–1891), xiv. 501
Bonner, W. S., xiv. 513
Bonnie Annie, ii. 413
Bonnie Charlie, ix. 378
Bonnie Dundee, iii. 184
Bonnie James Campbell, ii. 413
Bonnie Scotch Lad, The, ix. 363
Bonnivard, in Byron's *Prisoner of Chillon*, xii. 46

Bonny Baby Livingstone, II. 411
Bonny Earl of Murray, The, II. 413
Bonoeil, John, IV. 453
Bononcini, IX. 326
Bonstetten, Charles-Victor de, X. 134
Bonwick, James (1817–1906), XIV. 531, 584, 585; *Daily Life and Origin of the Tasmanians*, XIV. 371; *Last of the Tasmanians, The*, XIV. 371
Bonwicke, Ambrose (1652–1722), XII. 488; *A Pattern for Young Students*, X. 356
Bonwicke, Ambrose (1692–1714), IX. 412, 574
Booby, lady, in Fielding's *Joseph Andrews*, X. 24
Booby, squire, in Fielding's *Joseph Andrews*, X. 24
'Boojum,' Lewis Carroll's, XIII. 167
Book of Anzac, The, XIV. 367
Book of Common Prayer, IV. 384, 396, 407, 414; VII. 149, 455, 488; XIV. 402, 444, 450, 451; Irish version of, IV. 414
Book of Kells, The, XIV. 309
Book of the Universal Kirk of Scotland, The, VII. 208, 448
Book production and distribution, II. 331 ff., 483 ff.; IV. 378 ff., 544 ff.; XI. 466 ff.
Bookbinding, 1557–1625, IV. 548–549
Booke of Honor and Armes, The, IV. 525, 543
Booker, John (1603–1667), VII. 501; *The bloudy Almanac*, VII. 352, 499, 509; *Several Speeches at a Conference*, VII. 352
Bookwit, in Steele's *Lying Lover*, IX. 30
Boole, George (1815–1864), XIV. 263, 469, 555; *The Laws of Thought*, XIV. 10
Boon, Martin James, XIV. Add. 5
Boor, John (*fl.* 1389), VI. 280
Boorde, Andrew (1490?–1549), III. 105 ff., 488, 493; IV. 343, 523; V. 359; *A Compendyous Regyment or a Dyetary of Helth*, III. 91, 106; *The Fyrst boke of the Introduction of Knowledge*, III. 105, 106; IV. 320
Booth, Barton (1681–1733), X. 21, 444; XI. 257
Booth, Edwin, V. 308
Booth, James (1806–1878), XIV. 556, 604
Booth, Junius Brutus (1796–1852), V. 308; XII. 171
Booth, William, *In darkest England and the way out*, VII. 292
Booth, in Fielding's *Amelia*, X. 23, 33
Boothby, Guy Newell (1867–1905), XIV. 370, 585
Boothby, Miss Hill (1708–1756), X. 463
Boothby, Richard, *Briefe Discovery...of Madagascar*, IV. 102, 454
Boots, in *Our Mutual Friend*, XIII. 337
Boquet, Monsieur, XI. 258
Borachia, in *A Very Woman*, VI. 157
Borachio, in *The Atheist's Tragedie*, VI. 168
Boraskie, in *The Loyal Subject*, VI. 130
Borbonius, Matthew, IV. 264
Borbonius, Nicholas, *Nugae*, IV. 264
Borck, C. W. von, V. 294, 300, 462; *Julius Caesar*, V. 290, 296
Bord-à-Plouffe, Canada, XIV. 355
Bordeaux, III. 161; VI. 295, 322; VII. 309
Bordeaux, Collège de Guyenne, III. 160, 161, 426
Border, Daniel, anabaptist (*fl.* 1643–1650), VII. 351
England's Moderate Messenger, VII. 351
Impartial Scout, The, VII. 351
Kingdoms Faithfull Scout, The, VII. 351
Kingdoms Weekly Post, The, VII. 351
Perfect Weekly Account, The, VII. 351
Weekly Accompt, A, VII. 351
Weekly Account, The, VII. 351
Border, the, II. 128, 251; VII. 26; IX. 361 568; XII. 255; XIV. 96
Border ballads, XII. 3
Borderers, the, II. 415
Boreman, Robert (d. 1675), IX. 570
Borgias, the, XIV. 99
Borkowsky, T., IX. 106
Borlase, William (1695–1772), IX. 532; X. 466
Borough muir, the, in Scott's *Marmion*, XII. 10
Boroughbridge, battle of, II. 81
Borowlaski, count, XII. 22
Borromeo, cardinal, IV. 429
Borron, Robert de, I. 268, 271
Borrow, George (1803–1881), I. 275; VI. 230; IX. 247; XIII. 442; XIV. 138, 180, 251, 516; *also see* Add. 2
Bible in Spain, The, XIV. 145, 240, 241, 250
Lavengro, XIV. 145
Romany Rye, The, XIV. 145
Wild Wales, XIV. 146
Borrowdale, XI. 110
Borsa, Mario, XIV. 531
Borthwick, Sir Algernon, lord Glenesk, XIV. 185, 533
Borthwick, Peter (1804–1852), XIV. 185
Bos, C., XIII. 466
Bosanquet, Bernard, XIV. 469
Boscan-Almogaver, Juan, VII. 83
Boscawen, Mrs F., wife of admiral Boscawen, XI. 348, 354, 361 ff.
Boscombe, near Salisbury, rectory of, III. 406
Bosham. *See* Herbert of Bosham
Bosman, H. S., XIV. 380
Bosman, John, XIV. 244
Bosman, Walter, XIV. Add. 5
Bosola, in *The Dutchesse of Malfy*, VI. 180 ff.
Bossewell, John (*fl.* 1572), IV. 376, 543
Bossuet, Jacques-Bénigne, bishop of Meaux, VIII. 303, 305, 456
Conférence avec M. Claude, VIII. 373
Discours sur l'Histoire Universelle, VIII. 373
Exposition de la Doctrine de l'Église Catholique, VIII. 373
Histoire des Variations, IX. 198
Boston, Thomas (1676–1732), IX. 548

Boston, U.S.A., XIV. 318, 322
Boston Pilot, The, XIV. 318, 322
Boswell, Sir Alexander (1775–1822), X. 192, 478; XI. 442; XII. 357, 515; XIV. 188
Ah! Mary, sweetest maid, Farewell, XI. 235
East Neuk of Fife, XI. 236
Jenny Dang the Weaver, XI. 236
Jenny's Bawbee, XI. 236
New Whig Song, XI. 236
Paddy O'Rafferty, XI. 236
Sir Albyn, XI. 236
Skeldon Haughs or the Sow flitted, XI. 236
Songs Chiefly in the Scottish Dialect, XI. 236
Taste Life's Glad Moments, XI. 236
Boswell, G. (*fl.* 1657), VII. 390
Boswell, James (1740–1795), III. 336; IV. 247; IX. 325, 330; X. 157, 158, 161, 164, 167, 168, 172, 174, 176, 181 ff., 187, 189 ff. (main entry), 200, 207, 213, 215, 216, 259, 263, 312, 459 ff., 477 ff., 482, *also see* Add.; XI. 38, 235, 326, 333, 344 ff., 364; XIV. 188, 503, 550
Account of Corsica, X. 192
Boswelliana, X. 193
British Essays in favour of the Brave Corsicans, X. 192
Critical Strictures on Malloch's Elvira (by Boswell, Erskine, and Dempster), X. 477
Cub at Newmarket, The, X. 191
Dorando, X. 191
Elegy on the death of an amiable young lady, X. 191
Essence of the Douglas Cause, X. 191
Hypochrondriack, The, X. 192
Journal of a Tour to the Hebrides, X. 194
Life of Johnson, VIII. 322; IX. 313, 340; X. 181, 184, 186, 189, 190, 193, 194, 260, 267, 289, 291; XI. 13, 253, 325, 344; XII. 363; XIV. 63
'Memoirs' (in *The European Magazine*), X. 193
No Abolition of Slavery, X. 193
Ode to Tragedy, X. 191, 193
On the Alarming Attempt to infringe the Articles of the Union, X. 193
On the present state of the Nation, X. 193
Songs in the Justiciary Opera, X. 192
Boswell, James, the younger (1778–1822), V. 276; X. 172
Boswell, John (1698–1756), X. 498
Bosworth, Joseph (1789–1876), I. 91; XII. 344, 504
Bosworth, or Boxworth, William (1607–1650?), VII. 412; *Chaste and Lost Lovers, The*, or *Arcadius and Sepha*, VII. 79, 80; *Hinc Lachrimae*, VII. 80; *To Aurora*, VII. 80
Bosworth, battle of, II. 41; VI. 301
Bosworth, battlefield of, V. 171
Botanical Magazine, The, XIV. 288, 565
Botany bay, XI. 58; XII. 195
Boteler, Nathaniel (*fl.* 1625–1627), IV. 107; *Six Dialogues about Sea Services*, IV. 108, 454
Botener, John (*fl.* 1376), IV. 423
Botero, Giovanni, IV. 442, 454
Botes, III. 482
Botfield, Beriah (1807–1863), XII. 355, 365, 515
Botha, Louis, XIV. Add. 5
Böðvarr Biarki, I. 27
Bothwell, 1st earl of. *See* Hepburn, Patrick
Bothwell Bridge, II. 415
Botolph, St, V. 49
Böttger, C., XIII. 546
Bottom, in *A Midsummer-Night's Dream*, V. 74, 317; VI. 207, 285; XIII. 64
Bouchain, IX. 455, 461
Boucicault, Dion (1820?–1890), XIII. 264, 266 ff., 517, 522; XIV. 567
Arrah-na-Pogue, XIII. 267
Colleen Bawn, The, XIII. 267
Corsican Brothers, The, XIII. 267
London Assurance, XIII. 269
Louis XI, XIII. 267
Shaughraun, The, XIII. 267
Boudoin, J., *L'Artisan de la Fortune* (trans. of Bacon's *Essays*), IV. 347
Boufflers, Louis-François, duc de, IX. 256
Bough, Samuel (1822–1878), XI. 437
Boughton hall, Boughton Malherbe, Kent, IV. 163
Boughton-under-Blee, II. 184
Bouhours, Dominique, VIII. 402; *Manière de penser sur les ouvrages de l'esprit*, VIII. 376
Boulainvilliers, count de, X. 283
Boulge, near Woodbridge, XIII. 142
Boulogne, III. 175; X. 193, 395
Boulter, Hugh (1672–1742), archbishop of Armagh, IX. 407; X. 468
Boulton, Matthew (1728–1809), XIV. 381
Bouncer, Mrs, in *Verdant Green*, XIV. 225
Bounderby, Josiah, in Dickens's *Hard Times*, XIII. 330
Bounteous Progress, Sir, in *A Mad World, My Masters*, VI. 64
Bourbon, the constable de, III. 167
Bourbon, house of, IX. 215; XIII. 258
Bourchier family, the, II. 208
Bourchier, John, 2nd lord Berners (1467–1533), II. 332, 337 ff., 484; IV. 435, 445; V. 123
Castle of Love, The, II. 322
Froissart's *Chronicle*, II. 322, 340; III. 348
Golden Book of Marcus Aurelius, The, II. 340
History of Arthur of Little Britain, II. 322, 339
Huon of Bordeaux, II. 322, 339, 340
Bourchier, Thomas (1404?–1486), archbishop of Canterbury, II. 289
Bourdaloue, Louis, VIII. 303
Bourgeois, Maurice, XIV. 571
Bourget, Louis, XIV. 484
Bourget, Paul, XI. 408

Bourgh, lady Catherine de, in Jane Austen's *Pride and Prejudice*, XII. 238
Bourignon, Antoinette (1616–1680), IX. 307, 314, 519, 523
Bourinot, Sir John George (1837–1902), XIV. 581, 582; *The Story of Canada*, XIV. 359
Bourn, Samuel (1689–1754), *Address to Protestant Dissenters*, X. 380
Bourne, Henry (1696–1733), IX. 532; *Antiquities of the Common People, The*, IX. 355; XII. 346, 508
Bourne, Henry Richard Fox, *Life of John Locke*, IX. 406; *English Newspapers*, XIV. 179, 190, 531
Bourne, Nicholas (*fl.* 1622). IV. 398; VII. 344, 345
Bourne, Vincent (1695–1747), IX. 173, 526; XI. 83
Bourne, William (d. 1583), IV. 82, 104, 454
Bournemouth, XII. 331
Boursault, Edme, VIII. 162
Boutell, Charles (1812–1877), XII. 508
Bouterwek, K. W., I. 147
Bovaldo, in *Loves Crueltie*, VI. 199
Bove, Jean de, *Des trois larrons*, IX. 39
Bow Bells, XII. 448
Bowden, John Edward, XII. 456; XIII. 502
Bowden, John William (1798–1844), XII. 258, 454, 455, 459; XIII. 507
Bowdler, Thomas (1754–1825), XI. 260
Bowdler, in *The Fayre Mayde of the Exchange*, VI. 86
Bowdlerising, V. 187
Bowen, Edward Ernest (1836–1901), XIV. 597, 601, 606
Bowen, Herbert Courthope, XIV. 590
Bower, Alexander (*fl.* 1804–1830), X. 453
Bower, Archibald (1686–1766), X. 115, 499; *History of the Popes*, X. 292, 293
Bower, George Spencer, XIV. 477
Bower, Richard (d. 1561?), VI. 282, 286, *and see* Bowyer, Richard
Bower or Bowmaker, Walter (d. 1449), II. 128, 129, 451
Bower of Bliss, in *The Faerie Queene*, VI. 335; VII. 2
Bowes, Sir Hierome, III. 315
Bowes, Sir Jerome, in Milton's *Moscovia*, VII. 128
Bowes, Robert, XI. 468
Bowes, Thomas (*fl.* 1586), III. 356, 437; *The French Academy*, III. 437, 552
Bowes's academy, IX. 393
Bowker, Richard Rogers, XIV. 536
Bowles, Caroline. *See* Southey, Mrs Caroline Anne
Bowles, John (*fl.* 1807), *Letter to Whitbread*, XIV. 403, 590
Bowles, William Lisle (1762–1850), IX. 69, 451; XI. 118, 148, 177, 413, 424; XII. 100, 133, 183, 384, 392; XIII. 46
  Bamborough Castle, XI. 178
  Fourteen Sonnets, XI. 178
  Hope, XI. 178
  Influence of Time on Grief, XI. 178
Bowles, William Lisle
  Sonnets, XI. 172
  Tynemouth, XI. 178
  Vindiciae Wykehamicae, XIV. 406, 598
Bowley, Sir Joseph, in Dickens's *The Chimes*, XIII. 324
Bowling, Tom, in Smollett's *Roderick Random*, X. 37, 50
Bowring, Sir John (1792–1872), XI. 61, 397, 398; XII. 38, 310, 430; XIV. 512, 550, 604
Bows, Mr, in *Pendennis*, XIII. 292
Bowyer, Richard, *alias* Styrley or Strylly or Strelley, VI. 282
Bowyer, W. (*fl.* 1710), VIII. 461
Bowyer, William, *The Valiant Scot* (1637), VI. 453
Bowyer, William, the younger (1699–1777), XI. 327, 471; *Literary Anecdotes of the Eighteenth Century*, XII. 345
Box hill, XIII. 440
Boxley, VII. 53
Boy, the, in *The Play of the wether*, V. 94
Boy and the Mantle, The, I. 464; II. 414
Boy bishop, V. 8; VI. 294
Boy of Battlesdon, VII. 375
Boy of Bilson, the, IV. 535; VII. 375
Boyce, Samuel (d. 1775), X. 453
Boyce, William B., XIV. Add. 5
Boycotting system, XIV. 320
Boyd, Andrew Kennedy Hutchinson (1825–1899), XIV. 516; *Last Years of St Andrews, The*, XIV. 161; *Recreations of a Country Parson*, XIV. 161
Boyd, Hugh (1746–1794), XIV. 335, 575
Boyd, Robert (1578–1627), IX. 542
Boyd, William, 4th earl of Kilmarnock (1704–1746), IX. 564
Boyd, Zachary (1585?–1653), IX. 542
Boydell, John (1719–1804), XIV. 215, 216, 221
Boyer, Abel (1667–1729), VIII. 261, 451; IX. 17, 236, 237, 433, 491
  Achilles, or Iphigenia in Aulis (Racine's), VIII. 181
  History of Queen Anne, IX. 236
  History of the Reign of Queen Anne..., IX. 236
  History of William III, IX. 236
Boyer, Clarence Valentine, VI. Add.
Boyle, Charles, 4th earl of Orrery and 1st baron Marston (1676–1731), VIII. 385; IX. 103, 139, 216, 332, 333, 391, 443, 492, 525, 572; XI. 316
Boyle, Dorothy, countess of Burlington XIV. 213
Boyle, Frederick, XIV. Add. 5
Boyle, George David (1828–1901), XIV 501
Boyle, John, 5th earl of Orrery (1707–1762), IX. 460, 467
Boyle, Miss, XII. 440
Boyle, Richard, 1st earl of Cork (1566–1643), VIII. 268
Boyle, Richard, 3rd earl of Burlington (1695–1753), IX. 79, 162, 445

Boyle, Robert (1627–1691), VII. 266, 288, 396, 470; VIII. 247, 363 ff., 476; IX. 199, 331, 332, 389, 412, 489; X. 498; XII. 363; XIV. 281, 283; *Origine of Formes...and Qualities*, VIII. 338; *Seraphic Love*, VIII. 268; *Tracts*, VIII. 338
Boyle, Robert, V. 257, 444
Boyle, Roger, lord Broghill and 1st earl of Orrery (1621–1679), VII. 23; VIII. 21, 121, 124, 133, 190, 218, 268, 420, 424, 444
Black Prince, The, VIII. 18, 22
English Adventures. By a Person of Honour (1676) (attributed to Roger Boyle), VIII. 182
Guzman, VIII. 124, 131
History of Henry the Fifth, The, VIII. 18, 22
Mr Anthony (attributed to Roger Boyle), VIII. 123
Mustapha, VIII. 18, 22
Parthenissa, IV. 260; VII. 391; VIII. 22, 185, 371
Boyle lectures, IX. 297, 298, 331, 412, 524, 529; XII. 306
Boyne, William, *The Yorkshire Library*, XII. 519
Boyne, battle of, X. 358
Boynton, P. Holmes, XIII. 567; XIV. 528
Boys, John (1571–1625), IV. 415
Boys' Own Book, The, VIII. 359
Boyse, Samuel (1708–1749), IX. 563; XI. 172, 331, 425
Boythorn, in Dickens's *Bleak House*, XII. 205, 208; XIII. 328
Bozon, Nicole, II. 420, 507
Brabant, XIII. 436
Brabant, in *Jacke Drums Entertainment*, VI. 41
Brabine, Thomas, V. 121
Brabourne, II. 134
Bracebridge, in Kingsley's *Yeast*, XIII. 360
Bracegirdle, Anne (1663?–1748), VIII. 146, 159, 166, 177
Brachiano, in *The White Divel*, VI. 176
Bracken, Thomas (1843–1898), XIV. 368, 585; *Not Understood*, XIV. 368
Brackley, III. 430
Brackyn, Francis, VI. 313, 314, 322
Bracton or Bratton, Henry de (d. 1268), I. 181, 449; VIII. 313, 465; *De Legibus et Consuetudinibus Angliae*, VIII. 312; XIV. 80
Bradamante, in *Orlando Furioso*, III. 231, 236
Bradbury, Thomas (1677–1759), X. 380
Braddon, Laurence (d. 1724), IX. 490
Braddon, Mary Elizabeth (Mrs John Maxwell, 1837–1915), XIII. 438, 560
Bradfield school, XIV. 414
Bradford, X. 385
Bradford school, VII. 330, 342
Bradford, John (1510?–1555), IV. 232 ff., 446, 448, 491, 495; *Meditations*, IV. 414
Bradlaugh, Charles (1833–1891), XIII. 107; XIV. 501
Bradley, Andrew Cecil, XI. 408; XII. 77, 402, 406, 447; XIII. 476; *A Commentary on Tennyson's* 'In Memoriam,' XIII. 33
Bradley, Arthur Granville, XIV. 598
Bradley, Edward (*pseud.* Cuthbert Bede, 1827–1889), XIII. 560; *Verdant Green*, XIV. 225, 238
Bradley, Francis Herbert (1846–1924), XIV. 469, 480
Appearance and Reality, XIV. 46
Essays on Truth and Reality, XIV. 47
Ethical Studies, XIV. 46
Principles of Logic, XIV. 46
Bradley, George Granville, XII. 470, 478
Bradley, Henry (1845–1924), I. 87, 419; II. 35, 36, 39
Bradley, James (1693–1762), XIV. 258, 556
Bradley, Katharine Harris. *See* Field, Michael
Bradley, Richard (d. 1732), XIV. 286, 559
Bradshaw, in *Arden of Feversham*, V. 241
Bradshaw, Henry (d. 1513), II. 210, 469; *Life of Saynt Werburghe*, III. 66
Bradshaw, Henry (1831–1886), II. 45, 62, 103, 167, 448; IV. 423, 425, 432; XII. 520; *Collected Papers*, XII. 369; 'Memoranda,' XII. 369
Bradshaw, John (1602–1659), VII. 219; VIII. 312; IX. 258
Bradshaw, Mrs, Gissing's, XIII. 460
Bradshaw, Richard (*fl.* 1650), VII. 438
Bradshaw, William (*fl.* 1700), XI. 329; *Parable of the Magpye*, VIII. 99; XI. 330
Bradshaw's *Guide*, III. 330
Bradsheet, Anne (1612–1672), VII. 412
Bradwardine, baron of, in *Waverley*, VII. 231
Bradwardine, Thomas, *Doctor profundus* (1290?–1349), I. 213, 452; II. 18, 31, 355; IV. 269
Brady, Nicholas (1659–1726), VIII. 91, 92, 411, 431; *Psalms*, version of, by Nahum Tate and Nicholas Brady, VIII. 41, 443
Brady, Thomas John Bellingham, XII. 494
Braes o' Yarrow, The, II. 412
Brahma, XI. 194
Brahmanical religion, XI. 18
Brāhmī alphabet, the, XII. 352
Brailsford, Henry Noel, *Shelley, Godwin and their Circle*, XI. 276
Braintree, V. 104
Brainworm, in D'Urfey's *Virtuous Wife* VIII. 175
Bramber, Sussex, VII. 22
Bramble, Matthew, in Smollett's *Humphrey Clinker*, X. 38, 43, 206
Bramble, Mrs Tabitha, in Smollett's *Humphrey Clinker*, X. 43; XI. 266
Bramdean, VII. 454
Bramhall, John (1594–1663), VII. 285, 288 289, 470; VIII. 369; *Castigations of M Hobbes*, VIII. 301; *A Defence of the Tru Liberty of Human Actions*, VIII. 301
Brampton, Thomas (*fl.* 1414), II. 496

Bramston, James (1694?–1744), IX. 189, 484
Bramston, Sir John (1611–1700), VII. 335
Brand, Hannah (d. 1821), XI. 456
Brand, John (1744–1806), IX. 532; XII. 346, 508
Brand, Robert Henry, XIV. Add. 6
Brandan, St, XIII. 199
Brandenburg, Frederick William, elector of, VIII. 329
Brandes, Georg, I. ix; V. 308; XI. 409, 416; XII. 524; XIII. 21, 546
Brandl, Alois, I. ix, 421; XI. 409, 416
Brandon, Charles, duke of Suffolk (d. 1545), IV. 182; VIII. 182
Brandon, colonel, in Jane Austen's *Sense and Sensibility*, XII. 327
Brandon, George, in Thackeray's *A Shabby Genteel Story*, XIII. 280, 299
Brandon, Richard (d. 1649), VII. 513
Branghtons, the, in Burney's *Evelina*, X. 64
Brankston (Branxton) hill or moor, II. 371; III. 70; *and see* Flodden
Brant, Sebastian, *Das Narrenschiff*, III. 57, 58, 59, 60, 61, 74, 82, 83, 85, 480; IV. 528; VIII. 59. *See, also, under* Barclay, Alexander
Brantham, Suffolk, III. 183
Brantôme, III. 94
Brantwood, XII. 372
Branwell, Elizabeth (d. 1822), XIII. 404, 405
Branwell, Maria. *See* Brontë, Maria
Branwen, daughter of Llŷr, I. 252
Brash and Reid's *Poetry Ancient and Select*, XI. 243
Brasidas, IV. 43
Brass, in Vanbrugh's *Confederacy*, VIII. 162
Brasses, the, in *The Old Curiosity Shop*, XIII. 319
Brassey, Anna, lady (1839–1887), XIV. 550
Brathwaite, Richard (1588?–1673), III. 114; IV. 520, 521, 522, 524, 525, 531, 533, 534; V. 477
Barnabae Itinerarium or Barnabee's Journal, IV. 361, 533
The Prodigals Teares: or His fare-well to Vanity, IV. 323
The Smoking Age, or the Man in the Mist, IV. 349, 531
Whimzies, IV. 102
Brattle, Carry, in Trollope's *The Vicar of Bullhampton*, XIII. 423
Braun, Mrs C., XIII. 515
Braune, Wilhelm, I. ix
Braunschweig, H., IV. 442
Brawne, Fanny, XII. 92, 406
Brawny Bishop's Complaint, The, VIII. 97
Braxfield, Robert Macqueen, lord (1722–1799), X. 478
Bray, Charles (1811–1884), XII. 465; XIII. 384, 553; *The Philosophy of Necessity*, XIII. 383
Bray, William (1736–1832), VIII. 242; XII. 508, 511
Bray, vicar of, in Prior's *Dialogues*, IX. 16
Braybrook, near Leicester, II. 67
Braybrooke, lord. *See* Neville, R. G.
Brayley, Edward Wedlake (1773–1854), XII. 345, 508
Brayne, father-in-law of J. Burbage, VI. 252
Brayne, John, VII. 509
Brazil, IV. 72; XIV. 250
Breach, mistress, XI. 332
Breca, in *Beowulf*, I. 22
Breca, in *Widsith*, I. 34
Brecon, VII. 37
Bredfield, Suffolk, XIII. 142, 143
Bredt, P., XIII. 466, 467
Brehons, XIV. 302
Breisach on the Rhine, II. 74
Brek, Simon, in Wyntoun's *Cronykil*, II. 130
Bremen, IX. 231
Bremner, Christina S., XIV. 599
Bremner, Robert, XIV. 550
Brémond, abbé, XII. 299
Brendan, St, I. 339, 474; II. 419, 507; XIV. 306
Brende, John, IV. 2; *Quintus Curtius*, IV. 4, 436
Brent, Charlotte (d. 1802), XI. 260
Brent, Sir Nathaniel (1573?–1652), IV. 448
Brent hall, Essex, VII. 89
Brentford, VI. 171; X. 385
Brentford, battle of, VIII. 245
Brentwood school, VII. 331
Brenz, J., IV. 442
Brer Rabbit, XIV. 314
Brereton, Austin, XIII. 513
Brerewood, Edward (1565?–1613), VII. 479
Brescia, IX. 245
Brest, III. 64
Bretherne and systars, The rule of the living of the, II. 325
Bretherton, print-seller, XIV. 216
Breton, Nicholas (1545?–1626?), III. 114, 203, 249, 359, 367, 487, 522, 536; IV. 114, 116 ff., 345, 360, 411, 468, 469, 473, 519, 522, 525, 526, 534; V. 478; VII. 7, 16, 390
Characters upon Essays, IV. 346
Chesse Play, The, IV. 116
Countesse of Pembrook's love, The, IV. 118
Excellent dreame of ladies, and their riddles, An, IV. 116
Miseries of Mavillia, III. 367
Passionate Shepherd, The, III. 249; IV. 118
Pilgrimage to Paradise, The, IV. 118
Poste with a Packet of Mad Letters, A, VII. 391
Soules immortall Crowne, The, IV. 118
Strange description of a rare garden plot, A, IV. 116
Strange Fortunes of two excellent princes, III. 359
Wit's Trenchmour, VII. 463
Breton, cape, IV. 66
Breton language, XIV. 458
Breton lays, I. 294

Breton saints, I. 68
Bretons, Geste des, I. 337
Brett, Thomas (1667–1744), X. 356, 515
Bretts (or 'Welsh'), II. 89
Breval, John Durant (1680?–1738), IX. 472; *Remarks on several parts of Europe*, XI. 322
Breviaries, III. 19; Roman, III. 31; Sarum, III. 30, 31
Brewer, George (b. 1766), XI. 485
Brewer, John Sherren (1810–1879), I. 202 ff., 207, 210; XII. 356; XIV. 485, 489; *English Studies*, XIV. 82; *Reign of Henry VIII, The*, XIV. 82
Brewer, Robert Frederick, *A Manual of English Prosody*, XIII. 247, 511
Brewer, Thomas (*fl.* 1624), *The Merry Devill of Edmonton*, V. 253
Brewster, Sir David (1781–1868), XIII. 4; XIV. 259, 288, 555, 556
Brewster, Thomas (*fl.* 1656), VII. 359
Briareus, legend of, IV. 347
Brice, Andrew (1690–1773), XI. 471
Bricot, III. 50
Bricriu's Feast, I. 296, 327; XIV. 307
Bridall, John (b. 1635?), VIII. 468
Bride, in *The Golden Legend*, II. 335
Bridegroom Greets when the Sun gae's doon, XI. 231
Bridekirk, IX. 170
Bridell-Fox, E. F., XIII. 498
Bridges, Besse, in *The Fair Maid Of The West*, VI. 101, 102
Bridges, G., VII. 518
Bridges, John (d. 1618), dean of Sarum, bishop of Oxford, III. 383, 384, 385, 386, 392; VI. 296; *A Defence of the Government established in the Church of England for ecclesiastical matters*, III. 383, 539
Bridges, John (1666–1724), IX. 532; X. 505
Bridges, John Henry (1832–1906), XIV. 469
Comte's General View of Positivism, XIV. 24
Comte's System of Positive Polity (trans.), XIV. 24
Essays and Addresses, XIV. 25
Five Discourses on Positive Religion, XIV. 25
The Unity of Comte's Life and Doctrine, XIV. 25
Bridges, Robert, poet laureate, XII. 406, 456; XIII. 197, 211, 246, 501, 511; *Prosody of Milton*, XIII. 249
Bridges, Thomas (*fl.* 1759–1775), IV. 18
Bridgewater, earl of. *See* Egerton, John
Bridgewater, Mrs. *See* Hazlitt, Mrs
Bridgewater treatises, XIV. 290
Bridgman, or Bridgeman, Sir Orlando (1606?–1674), VII. 42; VIII. 380, 468
Bridgman, Richard Whalley (1761?–1820), XII. 520
Bridgnorth, VII. 145; XIV. 117
Bridgnorth academy, X. 385, 387
Bridgwater, IX. 237
Bridlington, II. 211
Bridlington, Augustinian priory, I. 344
'Briefless, Mr,' *pseud.* of À Beckett, Gilbert Abbott, XIV. 237
'Briefless, Junior, A.,' *pseud.* of À Beckett, Arthur William, XIV. 238
Brierley, Benjamin (1825–1896), XIII. 560
Brigden, Mrs. *See* Richardson, Mary
Briggs, Arabella, in Thackeray's *Vanity Fair*, XIII. 287
Briggs, Henry (1561–1630), III. 426; IX. 530
Briggs, John (1785–1875), XIV. 337, 575
Briggs, William, XIV. 536
Briggs, Mr, in Burney's *Cecilia*, X. 64
Briggs, Mr, Leech's, XIV. 239
Brigham, Nicholas (d. 1558), I. 332; II. 36
Bright, Edward Brailsford, XIV. 613
Bright, John (1811–1889), XI. 31; XIV. 129, 131 ff., 179, 181, 190, 508, 509
Bright, William (1824–1901), XII. 454, 474, *also see* Add. 3; *Chapters of Early English Church History*, XII. 322; *History of the Church*, XII. 321
Bright, lady, in *Amends for Ladies*, VI. 223
Brightland, John, XI. 250
Brighton, XII. 291, 508; XIII. 287; XIV. 225, 414
Brigittine order, IV. 418
Brihtwold, bishop of Ramsbury (d. 1045), I. 133
Brill, III. 203
Brimblecombe, John, in Kingsley's *Westward Ho!*, XII. 102
Brimley, George (1819–1857), XIII. 148, 365, 367, 466, 476; XIV. 139, 208, 516
Brindley, John, XI. 323, 332
Brine, John (1703–1765), X. 387
Brine, *Punch* artist, XIV. 236
Brink, Melt J., *Grappige Stories*, XIV. 377
Brinkelow, Henry (d. 1546), III. 87, 477; IV. 317; *The Complaynt of Roderyck Mors*, III. 99, 105, 491
Brinsley, John, the elder (*fl.* 1663), IX. 387, 405, 568; *Aesop*, XI. 490; *Ludus Literarius*, VII. 314, 335, 478, 479, 491
Brinton, Sybil G., *Old Friends and New Fancies*, XII. 244
Brisbane, John, IX. 203
Briscoe, Samuel, IX. 264
Briseida, I. 306
Brisk, Fastidious, in *Every Man out of his Humour*, X. 50
Brisk, Mr, in Congreve's *Double-Dealer*, VIII. 149, 156, 375
Bristol, II. 212, 338, 423; III. 40; IV. 68, 87, 94, 106, 409; VI. 110, 281, 301, 319, 386; VII. 245, 350; IX. 163, 407; X. 165, 236, 237, 268, 269, 322, 353, 362; XI. 6, 15, 30, 132, 155, 156, 159, 283, 340, 341, 359, 361, 390, 413, 414, 420, 421, 474; XII. 340
Bristol, Colston's hospital, X. 237
Bristol, earldom of, IX. 251
Bristol, earls of. *See* Digby, George; Digby, John; Hervey, Augustus John; Hervey, John

Bristol, St Mary Redcliffe church, x. 236, 486; xii. 345, 508
Bristol academy, x. 387
Bristol Journal, xi. 133, 134, 461
Bristol university, xiv. 432
Bristow, W., ix. 574
Britain, ii. 342, 396; ix. 214
Britain, Benjamin, in Dickens's *Battle of Life*, xiii. 323
Britain, Book of, i. 70 ff.
Britain, early, xiv. 69
Britain, Roman, xii. 347
Britain's Buss, iv. 509
Britannia, ix. 154
Britannia, in Thomson's *Castle of Indolence*, x. 107
Britanniae, De Situ, xii. 336
Britanny, v. 16
Britanny, duchess of, in *Morte Arthure*, ii. 118
Britanny, duke of, in *Froissart*, ii. 338
British academy, viii. 220; xii. 332
British and Foreign school society, xiv. 403 ff., 419
British archaeological association, xii. 347
British association, the, xiv. 259, 288
British constitution, xi. 8, 10, 12, 20, 26
British empire, xi. 13, 18
British kings, line of, in *The Faerie Queene*, iii. 234
British parliament, xi. 20
British school of archaeology at Athens, xii. 340
British school of archaeology at Rome, xii. 340
British school of archaeology in Egypt, xii. 339
'British shell,' x. 143
British Album, xi. 177
British Censor, The, ix. 438
British Critic, The, xii. 259, 273, 453, 455, 460, 461
British Journal, ix. 571
British Magazine, The, x. 41, 205, 421; xi. 260; xii. 257, 453, 454; xiv. 79
British Poets, The, ix. 183; xi. 325, 326
Brito, William (d. 1356), *Quaestiones*, ii. 363; *Summa de expositione verborum Bibliae*, ii. 363
Britomart, in Spenser's *Faerie Queene*, iii. 231, 234, 236; xii. 61, 87
Briton, The, x. 41, 390 ff., 421, 522
Britons, the, xiv. 68
Britons, Caesar on, reproduced in Mandeville, ii. 80
Britton, John (d. 1275), viii. 313, 465
Britton, John (1771–1857), xii. 508
Architectural Antiquities of Great Britain, xii. 345
Beauties of England and Wales, xii. 345
Beauties of Wiltshire, xii. 345
Cathedral Antiquities, xii. 345
'Picturesque Antiquities of English Cities,' xii. 345
Brixen, xiv. 247
Broad church, xii. 464
Broadhurst, Frances, xiv. 599
Broadhurst, Thomas, xiv. 599
Broadley, Alexander Mayrick, xiv. 541
Broadley, A. M. and Seccombe, Thomas, *Doctor Johnson and Mrs Thrale*, x. 157
Broadsides and Street Ballads, iii. 490, 494; iv. 530, 535
Broadwindsor, vii. 245, 258
Brobdingnag, ix. 104, 128
Broceliande, fountain of, in *Ywain and Gawain*, i. 312
Brockett, Lawrence (*fl.* 1763), x. 131, 133
Broderip, Mrs Frances Freeling (1830–1878), xii. 418
Brodie, Alexander (1617–1680), ix. 551
Brodmeier, C., vi. 265, 266
Brodrick, George Charles, *Memorials of Merton*, ix. 411; xiv. 383
Broke, Arthur (d. 1563), iv. 441; v. 221
Brokesby, Francis (1637–1714), *Life of Hy. Dodwell*, viii. 307, 459; *Of Education*, ix. 405, 568
Brome, Alexander (1620–1666), vi. 453, 492; vii. 512
Brome, Charles (*fl.* 1687–1700), viii. 405, 412
Brome, Joanna (*fl.* 1681), viii. 412
Brome, Richard (d. 1652?), v. 311, 315; vi. 153, 211, 212, 224–232 (main entry), 234, 236, 431, 453, *and see* Add. 2; vii. 513; viii. 124, 142; xiii. Add. 2
Antipodes, The, vi. 226, 227, 231
City Witt, The, vi. 225, 226, 228
Court Beggar, The, vi. 226
Covent Garden Weeded, vi. 226
Damoiselle, The, vi. 226
English Moor, The, vi. 230
Fault in Friendship, A, vi. 224
Joviall Crew, A, vi. 229 ff.
Love-sick Court, The, vi. 230, 231
Madd Couple well matcht, The, vi. 226; viii. 141
New Academy, The, vi. 226
Northern Lasse, The, vi 224, 226 ff.
Novella, The, vi. 230
Queen and Concubine, The, vi. 230, 231
Queenes Exchange, The, vi. 230, 231
Sparagus Garden, The, vi. 226, 227
'What if a day, or a month, or a year,' vi. 231
See, also, under Heywood
Brome, Stephen (d. 1652?), vi. 224
Brome play, the (Abraham and Isaac), ii. 426
Bromion, in Blake's *Visions of the Daughters of Albion*, xi. 190
Bromley, Mrs Beatrice, xiv. Add. 4
Bromley, Sir George, vii. 438
Bromley, Thomas (d. 1691), ix. 307, 513, 515
Brommerton, William, vii. 509
Bromsgrove, xi. 340
Bromyarde, John de (*fl.* 1390), *Summa Praedicantium*, i. 367
Brontë, Anne (1820–1849), xiii. 403 ff., 409, 554, 555, 557; *Agnes Grey*, xiii

Brontë, Anne
408, 414; *Tenant of Wildfell Hall, The,* xiii. 408, 414
Brontë, Charlotte (1816–1855), xii. 446; xiii. 379, 403 ff. (main entry), 483, 495, 550, 554 ff., *also see* Add. 3; xiv. 515
Emma, xiii. 410
Jane Eyre, xiii. 404, 406 ff., 410 ff., 414, 415
Poems (by Currer, Ellis and Acton Bell), xiii. 406, 415
Professor, The, xiii. 406, 409, 414
Shirley, xiii. 408, 409
Villette, xiii. 409, 410
Brontë, Elizabeth, 2nd daughter of Patrick Brontë, xiii. 404
Brontë, Emily Jane (1818–1848), xiii. 175, 214, 404, 405, 410 ff. (main entry), 554 ff.; xiv. 349
Old Stoic, The, xiii. 412
Remembrance, xiii. 412
Stanzas, xiii. 412
Wuthering Heights, xiii. 408, 410 ff.
Brontë, Maria (born Branwell), xiii. 404
Brontë, Maria, daughter of Patrick Brontë, xiii. 404
Brontë, Patrick (1777–1861), xiii. 403, 557; xiv. 567
Brontë, Patrick Branwell (1817–1848), xiii. 404 ff., 508, 557
Brook, Benjamin (1776–1848), x. 520
Brooke, Charles Frederick Tucker, v. 237, 255
Brooke, Charlotte (d. 1793), xiv. 305, 567, 572; *Reliques of Irish Poetry,* xiv. 311
Brooke, Christopher (d. 1628), iv. 117, 121, 157, 158, 200, 201, 479
Brooke, Frances (1724–1789), x. 426; xi. 448; *The History of Emily Montague,* xiv. 359, 582
Brooke, Henry (1703?–1783), ix. 181, 184, 185, 513; x. 46, 55, 58 ff. (main entry), 423, 437, 460
Conrade, ix. 185
Fables, ix. 185
Farmer's Letters, x. 58
Fool of Quality, The, ix. 181, 184, 327, 328; x. 15, 49, 58 ff.
Gustavus Vasa, x. 175
History of Henry Earl of Moreland, ix. 328
Juliet Grenville, x. 60
Universal Beauty, ix. 184
Brooke, Henry, of Dublin, ix. 327
Brooke, lord. *See* Greville, Sir Fulke; 2nd lord. *See* Greville, Robert
Brooke, Mr, in *Middlemarch,* xiii. 299
Brooke, rajah, xiii. 364
Brooke, Ralph (1553–1625), iii. 328, 528
Brooke, Sir Robert, viii. 466; *Abridgement of the Year Books,* viii. 315
Brooke, Rupert Chawner (1887–1915), vi. Add.; xiii. 499, 574
Brooke, Samuel (d. 1632), iv. 201; vi. 470; *Adelphe,* vi. 321, 323; *Melanthe,* vi. 323; *Scyros,* vi. 321, 323
Brooke, Stopford Augustus (1832–1916), Pref. x; i. 2 ff., 47, 48, 51, 59; xi. 403, 406, 407, 409, 412, 416, 434, 439; xii. 399, 400, 402, 406, 469; xiii. 476, 484, 488 ff.; xiv. 516, 517, 573, *also see* Add. 2, 3; *The Need and Use of getting Irish Literature into the English Tongue,* xiv. 305
Brooke, William, 7th lord Cobham (d. 1597), vi. 385
Brooke, Sir William, iii. 321
Brooke family, the, iv. 216
Brookfield, Charles, xiii. 530
Brookfield, Frances, xiii. 530
Brookfield, Jane Octavia, xiii. 530
Brookfield, William Henry (1809–1874), xiii. 277
Brooks, Charles William Shirley (1816–1874), xiii. 264, 266, 517; xiv. 196, 238, 548; *The Exposition,* xiii. 271
Brooks, Henry, xiv. Add. 6
Brooks, Van Wyck, xiv. 527
Brooks's club, xi. 52
Broom o' Cowden knowes, The, ii. 413
Broome, William (1689–1745), ix. 75, 76, 181, 183, 184, 443, 484; xi. 246
Broome of Cowden Knowes, ix. 363
Broomfield Hill, The, ii. 414
Brosch, Moritz, *Lord Bolingbroke,* ix. 226
Brotanek, R., v. 85
Brother, The Cruel, ii. 412
'Brotherhood, the,' xiii. 119, 120
Brothers, Richard (1757–1824), xi. 163
Brothers, The Twa, ii. 412
Brothers club, ix. 96, 151
Brough, John, in Thackeray's *Great Hoggarty Diamond,* xiii. 281
Brough, Robert Barnabas (1828–1860), xiii. 499, 517
Brough, Westmorland, x. 133
Brougham, Henry Peter, 1st lord Brougham and Vaux (1778–1868), viii. 316; x. 513; xii. 32, 143 ff., 147, 393, 426, 427; xiv. 54, 60, 115, 116, 123 ff., 180, 186, 197, 403 ff., 418, 485, 508, 512, 555, 601, 604
Letter to Samuel Romilly...upon the abuse of charities, xiv. 405, 408
Life and Times, xiv. 112
Practical Observations upon the education of the people, xiv. 408
'The Crisis in the Sugar Colonies,' xii. 145
Brougham, John (1814–1880), *The Duke's Motto,* xiii. 525
Broughamiana, xiv. 123
Broughton, Hugh (1549–1612), iv. 491
Broughton, Jack (1705–1789), xiv. 229, 231
Broughton, John (*fl.* 1703), viii. 347, 472
Broughton, Richard (d. 1634), ix. 532
Broughton de Gyfford, lord. *See* Hobhouse, John Cam
Broughton Papers, the, xii. 390
Brouncker, lady, in *Pendennis,* xiv. 440
Brounker, William, 2nd viscount Brounker (1620?–1684), viii. 61, 218

Brounsmith, J., x. 443
Brown, Andrew (*fl.* 1700), ix. 558, 560
Brown, Charles Armitage (1786–1842), xii. 83 ff., 91, 93
Brown, Ford Madox (1821–1893), xii. 384; xiii. 110, 140
Brown, George Douglas (*pseud.* George Douglas, 1869–1902), xiii. 561
Brown, Horatio F., xiv. 527
Brown, John (1610?–1679), ix. 545
Brown, John (1715–1766), ix. 508; x. 426; xiv. 604; *The Estimate*, x. 133, 136; *Thoughts on Civil Liberty*, xiv. 400
Brown, John (1722–1787), ix. 548
Brown, John, xiv. 590
Brown, John (1810–1882), xi. 476; xiv. 517, 543, *also see* Add. 2; *Horae Subsecivae*, xiii. 437; *Rab and his Friends*, xiv. 160
Brown, John Croumbie, xiv. Add. 6
Brown, lady, x. 126
Brown, Lucky, xii. 3
Brown, M. J., xiv. 574
Brown, Mrs, of Falkland, ii. 409
Brown, Oliver Madox (1855–1874), xiii. 216, 499, 561
Brown, P. Hume, xiv. 491; *History of Scotland*, x. 281
Brown, Robert (1773–1858), xiv. 289, 290, 559
Brown, Robinson, xiii. 557
Brown, Thomas, *Nature's Cabinet Unlock'd*, 1657, vii. 510
Brown, Thomas (1663–1704), viii. 48, 168, 404, 405, 432, 445, 480; ix. 256, 260, 263 ff., 329, 499
  Amusements Serious and Comical, ix. 262, 263
  Colloquies of Erasmus, ix. 275
  Elegy on Mr Edward Millington, xi. 336
  Miscellanea Aulica, ix. 496
Brown, Thomas (1778–1820), xiv. 6 ff., 10, 12, 469; *Lectures on the Philosophy of the Human Mind*, xiv. 6; *Observations on the...Doctrine of Mr Hume*, xiv. 6; *Observations on the Zoonomia of Erasmus Darwin*, xiv. 6
Brown, Thomas Edward (1830–1897), xiii. 194 ff., 499; xiv. 145
  Bella Gorry, xiii. 196
  Betsy Lee, xiii. 194
  Dartmoor pieces, xiii. 196
  'Englishwoman on the Pincian,' xiii. 195
  Fo'c'sle Yarns, xiii. 194
  Mary Quayle, xiii. 196
  Opifex, xiii. 196
  Peel Life Boat, The, xiii. 195
  Prayer, The, xiii. 196
  Risus Dei, xiii. 196
  Roman Women, xiii. 195
  Schooner, The, xiii. 196
  Sermon at Church on Good Friday, A, xiii. 185
  Sinking of the Victoria, The, xiii. 196
Brown, Thomas Edward
  White Foxglove, xiii. 196
Brown, Vanbeest, in Scott's *Guy Mannering*, xii. 17, 18
Brown, William (*fl.* 1671), viii. 468
Brown, William (*fl.* 1768), xi. 335
Brown, William Harvey, xiv. Add. 6
Brown Dozen of Drunkards..., A, iv. 361, 522
Brown Robin, ii. 411
Brown Robyn's Confession, ii. 413
Browne, a serving man, vi. 243
Browne, Edgar A., xiii. 540
Browne, Edward (1644–1708), son of Sir Thomas Browne, vii. 233, 244
Browne, Edward Granville, xii. 503
Browne, Mrs. *See* Hemans, Felicia Dorothea
Browne, mistress Frances, wife of Sir J. Reresby, viii. 266
Browne, Frances (1816–1879), xiv. 567
Browne, George (d. 1556), archbishop of Dublin, iii. 426
Browne, Hablot Knight (*pseud.* Phiz, 1815–1882), xii. 447, 452; xiii. 540, 541; xiv. 234, 238, 545 ff.
Browne, Henry (1804–1875), xii. 454
Browne, Henry, *pseud. See* Erskine Francis Robert St Claire
Browne, Isaac Hawkins (1705–1760), ix. 484; *Pipe of Tobacco*, ix. 188, 191
Browne, Mary, wife of John Evelyn. *See* Evelyn, Mary
Browne, Ned, in *The Blacke Bookes Messenger*, iii. 361
Browne, Patrick (1720?–1790), x. 467
Browne, Peter (d. 1735), ix. 504; *Answer* (to Toland), ix. 282; *Divine Analogy*, ix. 283; *Procedure, extent and limits of human understanding*, ix. 282
Browne, Sir Richard (d. 1669), viii. 245, 246
Browne, Robert (1550?–1633?), iii. 389, 422, 548
Browne, Simon (1680–1732), x. 521, 522
Browne, Thomas (1604?–1673), translator of Camden, iii. 326, 528, 554
Browne, Sir Thomas (1605–1682), iii. 463; iv. 216, 221, 252; vi. 187; vii. 99, 130, 132, 163, 232–244 (main entry), 249, 250, 253, 256 ff., 366, 460 ff., 511, *also see* Add.; viii. 292, 357, 368, 378, 386; xi. 2, 28; xii. 169, 176, 197; xiii. 195; xiv. 457, 460
  Christian Morals, vii. 239, 241, 243; x. 177, 466, 468
  Dreams, vii. 241
  Garden of Cyrus, The, vii. 237, 241, 242; xii. 197
  Hydriotaphia or Urn Burial, vii. 237, 241, 242
  Hydriotaphia, xii. 197
  Letter to a Friend, A, vii. 241, 243
  Miscellanies, vii. 241
  Pseudodoxia Epidemica (Vulgar Errors), vii. 236, 238, 241; xii. 197

Browne, Sir Thomas
Religio Medici, IV. 246; VII. 44, 233, 234 ff., 239, 241, 313, 449; VIII. 42; XI. 318
Works, VII. 241
Browne, Tom, son of Sir Thomas Browne, VII. 234, 244
Browne, Thomas Alexander (*pseud.* Rolf Boldrewood, 1826–1915), XIV. 585
Colonial Reformer, A, XIV. 370
Miner's Right, The, XIV. 370
Robbery under Arms, XIV. 370
Squatter's Dream, The, XIV. 370
Browne, William (of Tavistock) (1591–1643?), III. 311; IV. 117, 124, 150, 154, 155, 157 ff. (main entry), 194, 479; VI. 10, 113, 329; VII. 75, 83, 112, 113; VIII. 227; XII. 79, 93; *Britannia's Pastorals*, IV. 157, 158; VI. 215; VII. 38; *Inner Temple Masque*, IV. 159; *Shepherd's Pipe*, IV. 121, 158
Browne, W., trans. of Gomberville's *Polexandre*, VII. 391
Browne medal, the, XIII. 45
Brownell, William Crary, XIII. 470, 488, 570, 574
Browning, Elizabeth Barrett (1806–1861), II. 233; X. 141; XII. 106, 118, 124; XIII. 46, 49 ff., 57, 61 ff., 70 ff. (main entry), 139, 147, 148, 160, 161, 175, 177, 180, 181, 480, 481 ff., *also see* Add. 2; XIV. 515
Aurora Leigh, XIII. 70, 72, 74, 75, 179
Battle of Marathon, The, XIII. 70
Casa Guidi Windows, XIII. 74
Child's Grave at Florence, A, XIII. 75
Cowper's Grave, XIII. 75
Cry of the Children, The, XIII. 75
Drama of Exile, XIII. 71
Essay on Mind and other Poems, An, XIII. 70
Greek Christian poets and the English poets, XIII. 69, 77
Lady Geraldine's Courtship, XIII. 69
Last Poems, XIII. 74
Lost Bower, The, XIII. 70
Poems (1844), XIII. 69, 71
Poems before Congress, XIII. 74
Rhyme of the Duchess May, XIII. 75
Seraphim and other Poems, The, XIII. 70, 71
Sonnets by E. B. B., XIII. 71
Sonnets from the Portuguese, XIII. 49, 50, 70, 71, 75
Trans. of Aeschylus's *Prometheus Bound*, XIII. 70
Browning, Oscar, XIII. Add. 3
Browning, Robert (1812–1889), V. 231; VII. 91; X. 236, 457; XI. 409; XII. 106, 113, 115, 118, 154, 177, 178, 219, 223, 402; XIII. 10, 43 ff., 47, 49 ff. (main entry), 85, 89, 108, 120, 121, 131, 147, 152, 153, 155, 157 ff., 165, 179, 180, 184, 186, 187, 190, 194, 195, 202, 219, 221, 230, 250 ff., 309, 401, 442, 448, 479 ff., 494, *also see* Add. 2; XIV. 132, 255, 320, 354, 365, 368, 445, 453, 456, 517

Browning, Robert
Agamemnon of Aeschylus, The, XIII. 58, 81
Any Wife to Any Husband, XIII. 76
Aristophanes' Apology, VI. 232; XIII. 81
Asolando, XIII. 52, 78, 84
At the 'Mermaid,' XIII. 82
Balaustion's Adventure, XIII. 80
Bells and Pomegranates, XII. 101; XIII. 61, 62, 228
Bishop Blougram's Apology, XIII. 55
Bishop orders his Tomb, The, XIII. 69
Blot in the 'Scutcheon, A, XIII. 62, 68
Caliban upon Setebos, XIII. 55, 78
Caponsacchi, XIII. 80
Christmas Eve and Easter Day, XII. 100; XIII. 75, 76
Cleon, XIII. 76
Clive, XIII. 84
Colombe's Birthday, XIII. 62, 69
Confessional, The, XIII. 63
'Confidence lit swift the forehead up,' XIII. 62
Cristina, XIII. 76
Death in the Desert, A, XIII. 78
Dramatic Idyls, XIII. 83
Dramatic Lyrics, XIII. 76
Dramatic Romances and Lyrics, XIII. 62, 63, 76
Dramatis Personae, XIII. 63, 77 ff., 81
Epilogue (in *Asolando*), XIII. 84
Ferishtah's Fancies, XIII. 55, 84
Fifine at the Fair, XIII. 50, 77, 81, 82, 251
Flight of the Duchess, The, XIII. 69
Fra Lippo Lippi, XIII. 72
Garden Fancies, XIII. 65
Glove, The, XIII. 63
Gold Hair: a Story of Pornic, XIII. 77
Guido, XIII. 80
Hervé Riel, XIII. 80
Home Thoughts from the Sea, XIII. 61
'Hope rose a-tiptoe,' XIII. 62
House, XIII. 82
How they brought the Good News, XIII. 83
In a Gondola, XIII. 76
Incondita, XIII. 53
Inn Album, The, XIII. 81, 82
Introduction to *Certain Letters of Percy Bysshe Shelley*, XIII. 75
Ivàn Ivanovitch, XIII. 83
Ixion, XIII. 84
James Lee's Wife, XIII. 55
Jocoseria, XIII. 84
Karshish, An Epistle...of, XIII. 76
King Victor and King Charles, XIII. 61, 62
Laboratory, The, XIII. 63
Last Ride Together, The, XIII. 76
Lost Mistress, The, XIII. 76
Luria, XIII. 62
Martin Relph, XIII. 83
Men and Women, XIII. 72, 75 ff.
Mr Sludge, 'The Medium,' XIII. 46, 72, 78
Muléykeh, XIII. 84

Browning, Robert
Ned Bratts, XIII. 83
Never the Time and the Place, XIII. 84
Numpholeptos, XIII. 83
One Way of Love, XIII. 76
One Word More, XIII. 72
Pacchiarotto, XIII. 64, 82, 203
Paracelsus, XIII. 55 ff., 60, 70, 75
Parleyings with Certain People, XIII. 52, 84
Pauline, XIII. 52 ff., 58, 75, 116
Pheidippides, XIII. 83
Pied Piper of Hamelin, The, XIII. 64
Pippa Passes, XIII. 61, 62, 75 ff., 84
Pompilia, XIII. 80
Pope, The, XIII. 80
Porphyria's Lover, XIII. 55
Prince Hohenstiel-Schwangau, XIII. 55, 74, 81
Prospice, XIII. 78
Rabbi Ben Ezra, XIII. 78
'Rapture drooped the eyes,' XIII. 62
Red Cotton Night-cap Country, XIII. 77, 81, 82
Return of the Druses, The, XIII. 61, 62
Ring and the Book, The, IV. 249; XIII. 50, 60, 65, 77 ff.
St Martin's Summer, XIII. 83
Saisiaz, La, XIII. 83
Saul, XIII. 76
Sibrandus Schafnaburgensis, XIII. 64
Sordello, XIII. 52, 55, 58 ff., 64, 76, 82
Soul's Tragedy, A, XIII. 62
'Still ailing, Wind?' XIII. 55
Strafford, VII. 17; XIII. 55, 58, 59
Two Poets of Croisic, The, XIII. 77, 83
Waring, XIV. 241
Woman's Last Word, A, XIII. 76
Youth and Art, XIII. 65
Browning, Robert Wiedemann Barrett, XIII. 71
Browning society, the, XII. 504
Brownists, the, IV. 52
Brownlow, William Robert, XII. 508, 512
Bruce, Alexander (brother of Robert Bruce), I. 344
Bruce, Alexander Balmain (1831–1899), XII. 465; XIV. 469
Bruce, Edward (d. 1318), II. 101; in Barbour's *Bruce*, II. 105, 106
Bruce, Henry Austin, 1st baron Aberdare (1815–1895), XIV. 107, 496, 590
Bruce, James (1730–1794), XIV. 246, 247, 550; *Travels in Abyssinia*, XIV. 241
Bruce, John (1745–1826), XII. 354, 515; XIV. 97, 485
Bruce, John (1802–1869), XIV. 486
Bruce, John Collingwood (1805–1892), XII. 508; *Lapidarium Septentrionale*, XII. 346
Bruce, Michael (1746–1767), IX. 557; X. 484; XI. 442; *Cuckoo, The*, XI. 244; *Elegy on Spring*, XI. 244; *Poems on Several Occasions*, XI. 244
Bruce, Robert (1274–1329), I. 344, 352; II. 100, 101 ff., 109, 114, 130, 280; X. 224; XIV. 95
Bruce, Robert (1559–1631), IX. 543
Bruce's *Anglo-Saxon Version of the Book of Psalms*, I. 106
Bruces, the, in *Robert, Earle of Huntington*, V. 323, 324
Brueys and Palaprat, *Le Grondeur*, VIII. 139
Bruges, II. 54, 311, 312, 338; III. 18
Brugis, Thomas (*fl.* 1640?), IV. 454
Bruliferius, III. 50
Brumoy, father, X. 469
Brumpton, lord, in Steele's *Funeral*, IX. 30
Brunanburh, battle of, I. 137, 141, 150, 167, 287, 443; II. 400
Brunanburh, X. 487
Brunellus, the donkey of Nigel Wireker, I. 192
Brunetière, Ferdinand, IX. 20
Brunetto Latini, *Trésor*, II. 80, 149, 150
Brunhalt, in *Thierry and Theodoret*, VI. 122, 129
Brunnëwake in Kestevene, I. 344
Brunnow, baron, XIV. 129
Brunnus, in *The Scourge of Folly*, IV. 334
Bruno, Giordano, *Il Candelaio*, VI. 22
Brunswick, V. 298
Brunswick-Lüneburg, VII. 438
Brunton, Mary (1778–1818), XI. 459; XIII. 561
Brunton, Thomas (*fl.* 1373–1389), bishop of Rochester, II. 55, 58
Brunty, Patrick. *See* Brontë
Brushfield, Thomas Nadauld, IV. 450
Brussels, I. 57; III. 431; VIII. 267; XII. 365; XIII. 282, 406, 409
Brussels, Rue d'Isabelle, XIII. 405
Brut, Brute, the *Bruts*, the Brutus legend, I. 170, 175, 234 ff., 258, 306, 336, 375; II. 301, 322, 482; III. 315; IV. 136; VII. 117; X. 231
Brute, The Chronicle of the, II. 313, 334, 482
Brut, Layamon's, I. 137, 170, 223, 234 ff., 265, 375, 397, 398
Brut, Tysilio's, I. 235
Brut, Wace's, I. 234, 235, 350
Brute, lady, in Vanbrugh's *Provok'd Wife*, VIII. 161
Brute, Sir John, in Vanbrugh's *Provok'd Wife*, VIII. 161, 162, 168
Bruton, William (*fl.* 1638), XIV. 333, 575
Brutus, IX. 28
Brutus, in *Julius Caesar*, V. 197, 379; VI. 127
Brutus, in Milton's *England*, VII. 129
Brutus legend, the. See *Brut*
Brutus of Troy, IX. 74
Bruyère, la, VIII. 373
Bryan, Sir Francis (d. 1550), II. 340; III. 173, 181; IV. 445
Bryan, John (d. 1676), X. 385
Bryant, Jacob (1715–1804), X. 485, 486
Bryant, Sophie, XIV. 599
Bryce, James Bryce, viscount, XII. 271; XIV. 71, 74, 525; *Studies in Contemporary Biography*, XIV. 118
Bryce, M. A. L., XIV. 483

Bryce commission (1896), XIV. 423, 433
Brydall, John. *See* Bridall
Bryden, H. Anderson, XIV. Add. 6
Brydges, Grey, 5th lord Chandos (1579?–1621), IV. 524
Brydges, James, 1st duke of Chandos (1673–1744), IX. 81
Brydges, Sir Samuel Egerton (1762–1837), IV. 54; VII. 84; XI. 471; XII. 384, 393, 520; XIV. 232, 512; *British Bibliographer, The*, XII. 364; *Censura Literaria*, XII. 363; *Restituta*, XII. 364
Brylinger, N., V. 412
Brynllywarch academy, X. 386, 387
Bryskett, Lodowick or Lewis (*fl.* 1571–1611), III. 229, 521; IV. 444, 525; *The Mourning Muse of Thestylis*, XI. 179
Brysson, George (*c.* 1649–*c.* 1730), XIV. 493, 507
Bubble, in *Greene's Tu Quoque*, VI. 219
Buc *See* Buck
Bucan, earl of. *See* Erskine, David Steuart
Buccleuch, dukes of. *See* Scott, Charles W. H.; Scott, Henry
Buccleugh, in Scott's *Lay of the Last Minstrel*, XII. 8
Bucephalus, I. 307
Bucer, Martin (1491–1551), III. 34, 53, 419, 428, 474; IV. 233; VII. 417; *De honestis ludis*, VI. 374, 492
Buchan, Peter (1790–1854), II. 409; IX. 371, 565; *Gleanings of...Ballads*, IX. 374
Buchan, the harrying of, by Robert Bruce, II. 100
Buchanan, George (1506–1582), II. 96; III. 1, 6, 16, 116, 123, 138, 143, 151, 152, 156, 157–165 (main entry), 301, 424, 466, 501; IV. 253, 254, 261, 304, 509; V. 394; IX. 526, 552, 562; XII. 520, 522
Ad Carolum V Imperatorem, III. 160
Admonition to the trew Lordis, The, III. 164
Adventus in Galliam, III. 162
Alcestis, translation of, III. 161
Baptistes, III. 16, 161; V. 82; VI. 295
Book of Elegies, III. 158
Chamaeleon, II. 285; III. 164
Detectis, III. 164
Epithalamium, an, III. 163
Franciscanus, III. 159; VIII. 85
Genethliacon, a, III. 164
Jephthes, III. 161; V. 82; VI. 296
Jure Regni apud Scotos, De, III. 165; IV. 303
Masque, a (for Mary's marriage with Darnley), III. 164
Medea, translation of, III. 161
Odes on the capture of Calais and of Metz, III. 163
Palinodia, III. 159
Psalmorum Davidis Paraphrasis Poetica, III. 162
Psalms, translation of the, III. 162 ff.
Buchanan, George
Ptolomaeum Luxium Tastaeum et Jacobum Taevium cum articulari morbo laboravit, Ad, III. 161
Quam misera sit conditio docentium literas humaniores Lutetiae, III. 158
Rerum Scoticarum Historia, III. 164; IV. 412
Sphaera, De, III. 163
Somnium (*How Dunbar wes desyrd to be ane freir*), III. 159
Buchanan, Robert Williams (1841–1901), XIII. 117, 207 ff., 217, 490, 500, 517, 561; *Ballad of Judas Iscariot, The*, XIII. 209; *Ratcliff Meg*, XIII. 209; *Vision of the Man Accurst, The*, XIII. 209
Buchanan-Hamilton, Francis (1762–1829), XIV. 575; *An account of the Kingdom of Nipal*, XIV. 335
Buchell, Arend von, VI. 260
Buck or Buc, Sir George (d. 1623), IV. 383; VII. 443; X. 291; *History of the Life and Reigne of Richard III*, III. 334
Buckbasket Mishap, The, VIII. 116
Buckeridge, John (1562?–1631), IV. 239
Buckhurst, lords. *See* Sackville, Charles; Sackville, Thomas
Buckhurst, Sir Charles, in Disraeli's *Coningsby*, XIII. 350
Buckingham, IX. 541
Buckingham, duke of, in *King Henry VIII*, V. 346
Buckingham, dukes of. *See* Stafford, Edward; Stafford, Henry; Villiers, George
Buckingham, James Silk (1786–1855), XIV. 533
Buckingham and Normanby, duchess of, IX. 82
Buckingham and Normanby, duke of. *See* Sheffield, John
Buckinghamshire, III. 11; VII. 98, 107; X. 351; XII. 511
Buckland, Charles Edward, XIV. 574
Buckland, Francis Trevelyan (1826–1880), XIV. 559
Buckland, William (1784–1856), XIV. 292 ff., 559; *Reliquiae Diluvianae*, XIV. 292
Buckle, George Earle, XIII. 345, 547; XIV. 504
Buckle, Henry Thomas (1821–1862), XIII 383; XIV. 486; *History of Civilisation in England*, XIV. 102 ff.
Buckley, Michael B., XIV. 570
Buckley, Samuel, *Daily Courant*, IX. 5
Buckman, Sydney S., XIV. 562
Buckstone, John Baldwin (1802–1879), XIII. 265, 270, 518; *Bear-hunters (The)*; *or, The Fatal Ravine*, XIII. 266; *Flower of the Forest, The*, XIII. 266; *Green Bushes (The); or, A Hundred Years Ago*, XIII. 266
Budaeus, VII. 307, 320
Budd, Thomas, IV. 454
Buddeus, Johan Franz, V. 286
Buddha, I. 286; XIII. 400

Buddhism, XIII. 200
Buddhist topes, XII. 353
Budé, Guillaume, III. 1, 18, 20, 325
Budgell, Eustace (1686–1737), IX. 86, 220, 436, 492, 568
Budleigh, Devon, IV. 51
Buelt, Builth or Buallt, I. 247
Buffer, in *Our Mutual Friend*, XIII. 337
Buffle, Sir Raffle, Trollope's, XIII. 422
Buffon, George Louis Leclerc, comte de, IX. 321; X. 135; XIII. 450
Buffone, Carlo, in *Every Man out of his Humour*, VI. 17, 40
Bufo, in Pope's *Epistle to Arbuthnot*, IX. 147
Bugbears, The, V. 115, 117, 413
Bugge, Sophus, II. 417
Bugnot, L. G. (attributed to), *Alitophilus castigatus*, IV. 257, 500
Buist, G., XIV. 496
Buke of Order of Knighthood, The, XII. 515
Bukton (Chaucer's), II. 161, 187
Bull, George (1634–1710), bishop of St David's, VIII. 308, 459; X. 359; *Harmonia Apostolica*, VIII. 305; *Judicia Ecclesiae Catholicae*, VIII. 305; *Sermon on the Fall*, VIII. 305
Bull, Henry (d. 1575?), IV. 446, 495
Bull, John (1563?–1628), IV. 464
'Bull, John,' X. 29, 182; XII. 230; XIV. 212, 213
Bull, John, in Arbuthnot's *History of John Bull*, IX. 134, 135
Bull, Mrs, in Arbuthnot's *History of John Bull*, IX. 134, 135
Bullein, William (d. 1576), III. 66, 87, 107 ff. (main entry), 493; IV. 317, 343, 523; VII. 366; *Bulwarke of Defence*, III. 107; IV. 326; *Dialogue...against the fever Pestilence*, III. 66, 107 ff.; IV. 330
Bullen, Arthur Henry (1857–1920), III. 182; IV. 110, 113, 117, 119, 125; V. 221; VI. 10, 58, 65, 102, 214, 459; VII. 453; X. 161; XII. 428
Buller, Charles (1806–1848), XIII. 5; XIV. 125, 508, 512
Buller, William Archer, XIV. 469
Bullinger, Heinrich ('Black Bullinger'), III. 127; IV. 380
Bullock, Henry (d. 1526), III. 27
Bullock, William, *Virginia Impartially examined*, IV. 96, 454, 510
Bulloign, earl of, in *Godfrey of Bulloigne*, VI. 89
Bullokar, William (*fl.* 1586), III. 444, 550; IV. 435
Bulstred, Mrs, Donne's elegy on, IV. 216
Bulstrode, Buckinghamshire, XI. 347
Bulstrode, Sir Richard (1610–1711), VII. 436; VIII. 266, 452; *Life of James II*, VIII. 267; *Memoirs and Reflections*, VIII. 267; *Original Letters*, VIII. 267
Bulteel, John (*fl.* 1683), VIII. 422
Bulwer, John (*fl.* 1654), *Anthropometamorphosis*, VII. 387
Bulwer-Lytton. *See* Lytton, lord
Bulwer, William Henry Lytton Earle (Sir Henry Bulwer) (1801–1872), XII. 384; XIV. 505
Bumble, in *Oliver Twist*, XIII. 316
Bunbury, Henry William (1750–1811), X. 215, 482; XIV. 215, 232, 542
Academy for Grown Horsemen...by Geoffrey Gambado, Esq., XIV. 216
Chop House, A, XIV. 216
Long Minuet, A, XIV. 216
Propagation of a lie, The, XIV. 216
Buncle, John, in Amory's *Life of John Buncle*, XI. 288, 296
Bungay. *See* Thomas de
Bunion, Miss, in Thackeray's *Mrs Perkins's Ball*, XII. 125
Bunn, Alfred, XIII. 513
Bunny, Edmund (1540–1619), IV. 495
Bunsen, Christian Carl Josias, baron, XII. 283, 302, 303, 500; *Biblical Researches*, XII. 295; *Memoir*, XIII. 363
Bunting, Edward (1773–1843), *Ancient Irish Music*, XIV. 311
Bunyan, John (1628–1688), I. 58; II. 201; IV. 45, 50; VII. 154, 155, 166–178 (main entry), 251, 428 ff., *also see* Add.; VIII. 105, 293; IX. 18, 98; X. 1, 9, 20, 26, 383; XI. 381, 477; XII. 169; XIII. 388; XIV. 61, 461
Book for Boys and Girls, XI. 372
Confession of my Faith, A, VII. 172
Divine Emblems, XI. 372
Grace Abounding to the Chief of Sinners, VII. 168, 170, 171, 177; VIII. 104
Holy City or the New Jerusalem, The, VII. 170, 177
Life and Death of Mr Badman, The, VII. 177
Pilgrim's Progress, The, II. 200, 229; III. 221, 230, 234; IV. 47; VII. 172–177 (main entry), 178; VIII. 284; X. 2; XI. 334, 422; XIII. 452; XIV. 444; translations of, VII. 176
Some Gospel Truths Opened, VII. 169; VIII. 110
Buonaparte, Louis, XII. 377
Burana, Carmina, I. 190
Buranic verse, II. 385
Burbage, Cuthbert, son of Richard Burbage, VI. 253, 255, 276, 277
Burbage, James (d. 1597), VI. 246, 249, 251 ff., 257, 276, 289
Burbage, Richard (1567?–1619), V. 169; VI. 170, 220, 247, 248, 253, 255, 256, 258, 272, 274, 276, 277, 289, 358, *and see* Add. 2
Burbage, Richard, in *The Returne from Pernassus*, VI. 44, 312
Burbon, in *The Faerie Queene*, II. 234
Burbridge, Thomas, XIII. 104
Burby, Cuthbert (*fl.* 1594–1600), IV. 394
Burch, R. M., XIV. 536
Burchard Wormaciensis, VII. 372, 504
Burchell, Mr, in *Vicar of Wakefield*, X. 209

Burchell, William John (1782–1863), xiv. 550
Burckhardt, John Lewis (1784–1817), xiv. 247, 248, 250, 550
Burden, Jane. *See* Morris, Jane
Burdet, Sir Nicholas (*fl.* 1541), iii. 197
Burdett, Sir Francis (1770–1844), xiv. 121, 408, 508
Burdy, Samuel (1760?–1820), xiv. 486, 567
Burel or Burrel, John (*fl.* 1590), *The Description of the Queenis Majesties most honourable entry in the Town of Edinburgh*, iii. 137; *The Passage of the Pilgrim*, iii. 137, 498
Burford, Oxfordshire, viii. 206
Bürger, Gottfried August, xi. 303; xii. 6, 7, 373, 422, 526; *Der wilde Jäger*, xii. 4; *Leonore*, xii. 4
Burgersdijk, Leendert, v. 307
Burgersdyck, Francis, x. 198
Burges, George (1786?–1864), xii. 327
Burges, Sir James Bland (Sir James Lamb) (1752–1824), xi. 177, 425
Burgess, Anthony (*fl.* 1652), vii. 322
Burgess, Cornelius (1589?–1665), vii. 314
Burgess, Thomas (1756–1837), xii. 481
Burgh, Benet or Benedict (d. 1483), ii. 199, 208, 469; iii. 277, 290
  A Christmas Game, ii. 209
  Aristotle's ABC, ii. 209
  Cato, ii. 209, 312, 427
  Poem to Lydgate, ii. 209
  Secrets of Philosophers, ii. 208
Burgh, Elizabeth de, duchess of Clarence, ii. 156
Burgh, James (1714–1775), xiv. 604
Burgh, John de, *Pupilla Oculi*, ii. 498
Burgh, Thomas (*fl.* 1447), ii. 214
Burgh, Thomas (*fl.* 1790), xi. 6
Burgh, William (1741–1808), *Enquiry*, x. 308, 507; *Political Disquisitions*, x. 308
Burgher, the, and wife, in *A Dialogue... against the fever Pestilence*, iii. 109
Burghley, lord. *See* Cecil, William
Burgon, John William (1813–1888), iv. 263; xii. 274, 455
Burgonians Tragedy, The, iv. 362
Burgos, v. 99
Burgoyne, John (1722–1792), xi. 31, 456; *Heiress, The*, xi. 275, 276; xiv. 387; *Maid of the Oaks*, xi. 265, 275
Burgundian court, ii. 312
Burgundy, Margaret, duchess of (1446–1503), ii. 307, 309
Burgundy, Philip III, duke of, ii. 311
Burhill or Burghill, Robert (1572–1641), iv. 59
Burke, Edmund (1729–1797), iii. 235, 236; viii. 56; iv. 233; x. 63, 64, 207, 215, 262, 264 ff., 306, 316, 317, 405 ff., 503, 522; xi. 1 ff. (main entry), 34, 42, 47, 48, 52, 58, 93, 139, 142, 143, 145, 146, 262, 324, 360, 388 ff., 395, 396, 399; xii. 168, 179, 175; xiii. 487; xiv. 58, 105, 110, 119, 120, 122, 143, 323, 462
Burke, Edmund
  Address to the British Colonists, xi. 5
  Address to the King, xi. 5, 21
  Appeal from the New to the Old Whigs, xi. 7, 21 ff.
  Letter...to a Member of the National Assembly, xi. 7
  Letter...to a Noble Lord, xi. 7, 29; xii. 166
  Letter...to...Sheriffs of...Bristol, xi. 5, 13
  Letter to William Smith, xi. 25
  Letters on a Regicide Peace, xi. 25, 31, 138
  Letters...on the proposals for peace, xi. 7
  Observations on...'The Present State of the Nation,' xi. 5, 7
  On American Taxation, xi. 5, 12, 21
  On moving his Resolutions for Conciliation, xi. 5, 11, 12, 20, 26
  On Mr Fox's East-India Bill, xi. 16, 18, 19
  On the Sublime, x. 202
  Philosophical Enquiry into...the Sublime and Beautiful, xi. 2, 3
  Reflections, x. 251, 344
  Reflections on the Revolution in France, xi. 4, 7, 20, 22, 138, 413
  Remarks on the Policy of the Allies, xi. 7
  Short Account of a Short Administration, x. 399
  Speech at the Guildhall in Bristol, xi. 6,15
  Speech on the...Nabob of Arcot's Private Debts, xi. 6, 16, 18, 31
  Thoughts on French Affairs, xi. 7
  Thoughts on the...Present Discontents, x. 503: xi. 5, 8, 9; xiv. 438, 439
  To a peer of Ireland on the Penal Laws, xi. 15
  To Sir Hercules Langrishe, xi. 15
  Tracts relative to the Laws against Popery, xi. 14, 24
  Two Letters...to Gentlemen...of Bristol, xi. 6, 15
  Vindication of Natural Society, ix. 232; xi. 2 ff.
Burke, Richard, brother of Edmund Burke, xi. 6, 361
Burke, Richard, son of Edmund Burke xi. 6
Burke, Robert O'Hara (1820–1881), xiv 364
Burke, Thomas Henry (1829–1882), xiv. 320
Burke, William (d. 1798), xi. 2, 6, 388
Burke, William (1792–1829), xiv. 453
Burke, W. T., viii. 54
Burleigh, Bennet (d. 1914), xiv. 192
Burleigh, lord. *See* Balfour, Robert
Burleigh or Burley, Walter (1275–1345?) i. 213, 452; ii. 363
Burleigh house, ix. 148
Burlesques, iv. 516, 533
Burleus, iii. 50
Burley, in Scott's *Old Mortality*, xii. 22

Burlington, countess of. *See* Boyle, Dorothy
Burlington, earl of. *See* Boyle, Richard
Burman, Francis, IX. 574; XII. 488
Burmann, Peter (1668–1741), IX. 336; X. 164, 465
Burn, Robert (1829–1904), XII. 496
Burnaby, Frederick Gustavus (1842–1885), XIV. 550
Burnaby, J., IX. 266, 499
Burnand, Sir Francis Cowley (1836–1917), XIV. 548
Burne, Nicol (*fl.* 1581), II. 285
Burne-Jones, Sir Edward Coley (1833–1898), XIII. 118, 119, 137, 139, 297, 493
Burnell, Arthur Coke (1840–1882), XII. 502
Burnet, Gilbert (1643-1715), bishop of Salisbury, VII. 185, 214, 476; VIII. 23, 46, 97, 202, 206, 207, 209, 213, 214, 216, 272, 298, 299, 300 ff., 360, 459; IX. 94, 112, 132, 192 ff. (main entry), 211, 213, 214, 217, 221, 234, 247, 335, 402, 488 ff., 541; X. 115, 117, 354, 373, 379; XIV. 604
Censure of M. de Meaux' History, IX. 198
Discourse of the Pastoral Care, IX. 201
Discourse on...Sir Robert Fletcher, IX. 192
Eighteen papers, IX. 199
Enquiry into the measures of submission, IX. 199
Essay on...the late Queen Mary, IX. 200
Exposition of the Thirty-nine Articles, VIII. 300; IX. 200
History of My Own Time, VIII. 48, 273, 278, 445, 463; IX. 199, 202 ff., 212
History of the Reformation, IV. 228, 239; VIII. 250; IX. 110, 195, 197, 198, 200, 210, 212
Letter...on the two papers writ by King Charles II, IX. 199
Life and Death of Sir Matthew Hale, VIII. 10; IX. 198
Memoires of the...Dukes of Hamilton and Castleherald, VII. 435; IX. 193, 194, 196
Memoirs or *Secret History*, IX. 199, 200, 202 ff.
Memorial...of the Constitution and Policy of England, IX. 201
Modest and Free Conference, IX. 192
Pastoral Care, The, VIII. 300
Reasons against Repealing the Test, VIII. 48
Reflections on the Declaration for Liberty of Conscience, IX. 199
Reflections on the pamphlet *Parliamentum Pacificum*, IX. 199
Review of the Reflections on the Prince's Declaration, IX. 200
Second Collection of Several Tracts, IX. 200
Some letters, IX. 199
Some passages in the Life and Death of the right honorable John Earl of Rochester, VIII. 300, 445
Thoughts on Education, IX. 192; XIV. 604
Utopia, trans. of, IX. 198
Burnet, Gilbert
Vindication from the two *Letters containing some Reflections on His Majesty's Proclamation*, IX. 199
Vindication of the...Church of Scotland, IX. 194
Burnet, Thomas (1635?–1715), VIII. 292, 472, 473, 474; IX. 434, 474, 572; *Sacra telluris theoria*, VIII. 347; *The Theory of the Earth*, IX. 390
Burnet, Thomas, of Kemnay, VIII. 347
Burnet, Sir Thomas (1694–1753), IX. 204
Burnet, Thomas (Sir Iliad Doggrel) (*fl.* 1715), IX. 258, 448
Burnett, James, lord Monboddo (1714–1799), IX. 562; X. 513; XI. 250
Burney, Charles (1726–1814), X. 63, 260, 263, 473
Burney, Charles (1757–1817), XII. 325
Burney, Frances. *See* Arblay, Madame d'
Burney, J., XIV. 550
Burney, Martin Charles, XII. 188, 192, 434
Burnham, baron. *See* Lawson, Edward Levy
Burnham, Cant's hall at, X. 117
Burnham Thorpe, II. 301
Burnouf, Jean Louis, XII. 343
Burns, Gilbert, XI. 436, 437
Burns, Robert (1759–1796), I. 290; II. 247, 267, 274, 278, 413; III. 129, 136, 188; IV. 112, 212; VII. 13; IX. 360, 363, 367 ff., 372 ff., 376 ff., 567; X. 224, 226; XI. 182, 183, 203 ff. (main entry), 233 ff., 237 ff., 242, 243, 408, 419, 435, 441, 469, 472, *also see* Add.; XII. 1, 19, 30, 125, 132, 134, 382, 429, 480, 505; XIII. 9, 13, 16, 178, 226, 233, 242, 465, 468; XIV. 357, 375
Address to Edinburgh, XI. 217
Address to the Deil, II. 255; XI. 212, 213
Address to the Unco Guid, XI. 218
Auld Farmer's New Year Salutation, XI. 212, 214
Auld Lang Syne, XI. 225, 228, 232
Author's Earnest Cry and Prayer, XI. 212
Banks o' Doon, XI. 230
Bard's Epitaph, XI. 208
Birthday Ode, XI. 208
Blue-eyed Lassie, XI. 230
Brigs of Ayr, IX. 380; XI. 218
Captain Matthew Henderson, XI. 211, 219
Centenary Burns, The, XIV. 148
Charlie he's my Darling, XI. 229
Chevalier's Lament, IX. 377
Comin Thro' the Rye, XI. 230
Corn Rigs, XI. 205
Cotter's Saturday Night, The, XI. 144, 206; XIV. 377
Death and Doctor Hornbook, XI. 212
Death and Dying Words of Poor Mailie, II. 255; IX. 366, 372; XI. 214
Despondency, XI. 206, 217
Dream, A, XI. 215
Duncan Davison, XI. 229
Duncan Gray, XIV. 377
Epistle to a Young Friend, XI. 218

Burns, Robert
Epistle to Davie, xi. 207, 217
Epistle to Lord Daer, xi. 218
Epistles, xi. 234
Epistles to Graham of Fintry, xi. 208
Farewell, The, xi. 217
Fintry My Stay, xi. 218
From Esopus to Maria, xi. 208
Gloomy Night, xi. 205
Green grow the Rashes o', xi. 205
Guildford Good, xi. 218
Halloween, xi. 215, 216, 235
Handsome Nell, xi. 206
'*Hear, land o' Cakes,*' xii. 349
Here's to the Health, xi. 206
Holy Fair, xi. 213, 215
Holy Willie's Prayer, xi. 212, 213
How Lang and Drearie is the Night, xi. 229
In Lamington Kirk, xi. 208
Inscribed on a Work of Hannah More's, xi. 217
Inscribed to the Hon. C. J. Fox, xi. 208
Is there for Honest Poverty, xi. 229
It was a' for our Richtfu' King, xi. 225, 229; xii. 14
James Smith, xi. 211
John Anderson My Jo, xi. 229
John Barleycorn, ii. 279
John Lapraik, xi. 211
Jolly Beggars, iii. 131, 136, 188; xi. 206, 215, 217 ff., 224
'*Ken ye ought o' Captain Grose,*' xii. 349
Kirk's Alarm, xi. 213
Lament, The, xi. 206, 217
Lass of Cessnock Banks, xi. 206
Lines on the Fall of Fyers, xi. 208
Logan Water, xi. 235
MacPherson's Farewell, xi. 228
Man was made to Mourn, xi. 206, 217
Mary Morison, xi. 230
Mauchline Wedding, xi. 215
My Father was a Farmer, xi. 206
No Churchman am I, xi. 205
O Leeze me on my Spinnin Wheel, xi. 230
O Merry Hae I been, xi. 229
O Tibbie I hae seen the Day, xi. 206
O Wert thou in the Cauld blast, xi. 230
Ode Sacred to the Memory of Mrs Oswald, xi. 208
Ode to General Washington's Birthday, xi. 208
Ode to the Departed Regency Bill, xi. 208
Ode to the Departed Year, xi. 208
Of a' the Airts, xi. 230
On a Wag in Mauchline, xi. 208
On Captain Grose, xi. 208
On Grizzel Grimme, xi. 208
On Holy Willie, xi. 208
On John Dove, Innkeeper, xi. 208
On Tam the Chapman, xi. 208
On the Death of Lord President Dundas, xi. 208
On the Death of Robert Ruisseaux, xi. 208
On the Death of Sir James Hunter Blair, xi. 208

Burns, Robert
On the Late Miss Burnet of Monboddo, xi. 208
On Willie Nicol's Mare, xi. 208
Ordination, The, xi. 213, 215
Poems (Kilmarnock, 1786), xi. 204 ff., 220, 221, 342
Poems (Edinburgh, 1787), xi. 205
Poet's Welcome to his Love-Begotten Daughter, xi. 212
Poor Mailie, xi. 211, 214
Prayer in the prospect of Death, xi, 206
Rantin Dog the Daddie O't, xi. 230
Red, Red Rose, xi. 225, 229
Remorse, xi. 206
Reply to a Trimming Epistle, xi. 211
Ruined Farmer, xi. 206
Scotch Drink, ii. 278; xi. 212
Scots Wha hae, xi. 229
Strathallan's Lament, ix. 377
Tam o' Shanter, xi. 215, 217 ff., 224, 238; xiv. 377
Tam Samson, xi. 211
To a Louse, xi. 214
To a Mountain Daisy, xi. 214
To a Mouse, xi. 214
To John Rankine, xi. 211
To Ruin, xi. 206, 217
To the Guidwife of Wauchope House, xi. 217
Tragic Fragment, xi. 206
Twa Dogs, xi. 214, 217
Twa Herds, xi. 213
Up in the Morning Early, xi. 229
Vision, The, xi. 207, 214
What can a Young Lassie, xi. 229
Who is that at My Bower Door, xi. 229
Willie Brew'd a Peck o' Maut, xi. 230
Willie Simpson, xi. 211
Works (1834–5), xi. 237
Written with a Pencil at Taymouth, xi. 208
Ye Banks and Braes, xi. 230
Yestreen I had a pint o' Wine, xi. 230
Burnt Njal, xiii. 125
Burrhus, in Racine's *Britannicus*, x. 119
Burrough or Borough, Christopher (*fl.* 1579–1587), iv. 69
Burrough, Edward (1634–1662), vii. 169, 428; viii. 110
Burrough, Sir John (d. 1643), iv. 454
Burrough, Stephen (1525–1584), iv. 84
Burroughs, Jeremiah (1599–1646), vii 322
Burroughs, John, xiii. 470
Burroughs, Ronald Montague (1867–1920), xii. Add. 2
Burrowes, Robert (*fl.* 1787), x. 475
Burstall, Sara A., xiv. 599
Burthogge, Richard (1638?–1694?), viii. 472; *An Essay upon Reason and the Nature of Spirits*, viii. 347; *Organum vetus et novum*, viii. 347
Burton, Alfred, *pseud. See* Mitford, John
Burton, Alfred Richard Edward, xiv. Add. 6

Burton, Henry (1578–1648), VII. 145, 424, 433, 441, 456, 498
Burton, Hezekiah (d. 1681), VIII. 292
Burton, Isabel, lady (1831–1896), XIV. 550
Burton, John (1710–1771), IX. 563
Burton, John Hill (1809–1881), XI. 397; XII. 445, 520; XIV. 486
Book-Hunter, The, XII. 359, 360, 371; XIV. 95
History of Scotland, XII. 371; XIV. 95
History of the Reign of Queen Anne, XIV. 95
Life of David Hume, X. 283, 284, 289, 293, 321, 323, 511; XIV. 95
Scot Abroad, The, XIV. 95
Burton, Richard, *pseud.* *See* Crouch, Nathaniel
Burton, Sir Richard Francis (1821–1890), XIV. 246, 252, 337, 551; *The Lake Regions of Central Africa*, XIV. 253
Burton, Robert (1577–1640), III. 532; IV. 242–253 (main entry), 257, 260, 261, 267, 496 ff., 519, *also see* Add.; VII. 163, 253, 366; X. 50; XIV. 460; *Anatomy of Melancholy*, IV. 244 ff. (main entry), 411, 432; VI. 187, 190, 191; VII. 313; VIII. 357, 378; XII. 86, 88, 187, 188, 434, 436; *Philosophaster*, IV. 244; VI. 470
Burton, Thomas (*fl.* 1656–9), VII. 440
Burton, William (d. 1461), IV. 496
Burton, William (1575–1645), III. 532; *Description of Leicester Shire*, IX. 352, 532
Burton, William (1609–1657), VII. 482, 487; *Commentary on Antoninus, his Itinerary*, IX. 355, 532
Burton, Annals of, I. 178
Burton Hall, VIII. 96
Burton-on-Trent, V. 97
Bury. *See* Richard of
Bury, Arthur (1624–1713), *The Naked Gospel*, X. 378
Bury, lady Charlotte Susan Maria (1775–1861), XI. 434; XII. 448
Bury, John Bagnell, X. 313 ff., 318, 506; XII. 475; XIV. 538
Bury, Richard de (1281–1345), bishop of Durham. *See* Richard of Bury
Bury St Edmunds, or St Edmundsbury, Benedictine abbey of, I. 162, 176, 182, 213; II. 197, 198, 307; IV. 418; V. 9; VI. 282; VII. 61, 234; VIII. 357; X. 464; XI. 140; XII. 192, 201, 331; XIII. 15
Bury St Edmunds, King Edward VI's school, VII. 330; XIII. 142
Busby, John (*fl.* 1600), IV. 393
Busby, Richard (1606–1695), VII. 317, 341, 486, 487; IX. 146, 272; Dryden's transl. of *Fifth Satire of Persius* ascribed to, VIII. 2
Busher, Leonard (*fl.* 1614), VII. 456; X. 520
Bushnell, Edmund, IV. 454
Busino (chaplain to Venetian embassy), VI. 181
Busirane, castle of, I. 295
Busiris, in Alfred's *Boethius*, I. 100
Busleiden (Buslidianus), Jerome, III. 7
Buss, Frances Mary, XIV. 429, 599
Bussey, H. Findlater, XIV. 533
Bussy-Rabutin, *Histoire Amoureuse de Gaule*, VIII. 385
Busteed, Henry Elmsley (1833–1912), XIV. 575; *Echoes from Old Calcutta*, XIV. 338
Bustus, Matthaeus, VII. 482
Busy Body, The, X. 205
But, John, II. 21, 22, 35
Butcher, Samuel Henry (1850–1910), IX. 64; XII. 332, 333, 481; XIV. 521
Bute, 3rd earl of. *See* Stuart, John
Bute, Mary, countess of (d. 1794), IX. 245, 246, 248, 403
Butler, Alban (1711–1773), X. Add.
Butler, Arthur Gray (1831–1909), XIII. 500
Butler, Arthur John (1844–1910), XII. 137; XIV. 501; *Dante, his Times and his Work*, XIV. 113
Butler, Charles (d. 1647), IV. 542
Butler, Charles (1750–1832), XI. 422; XIV. 55, 115, 492, 512; *The Book of the Roman Catholic Church*, XIV. 53
Butler, George (1819–1889), XIV. 598
Butler, James, 4th earl of Ormonde and earl of Wiltshire (1420–1461), II. 302
Butler, James, 1st duke of Ormonde (1610–1688), VII. 212, 224, 356, 436
Butler, John (*fl.* 1680), VII. 510; VIII. 455
Butler, Joseph (1692–1752), bishop of Durham, VIII. 296; IX. 289, 296, 303, 304, 326, 393, 394, 502, 504; X. 351, 358, 360 ff., 381, 386; XII. 269; *Analogy of Religion, The*, IX. 303, 304; X. 361, 362; XII. 270; *Sermons*, IX. 303; X. 361, 362
Butler, Josephine E. (1828–1906), XIV. 501, 598
Butler, Nathaniel (d. 1664), IV. 394; VII. 344
Butler, Pierce, II. 335
Butler, Samuel (1612–1680), III. 95; IV. 342, 522; VII. 72, 92, 167, 238, 345; VIII. 17, 26, 43, 58–79 (main entry), 88, 215, 232, 372, 373, 402, 406 ff.; IX. 119, 260; XI. 247; XIII. 218
Characters, VIII. 60, 62 ff., 75
Contradictions, VIII. 61
Critics who judge of modern plays by the rules of the Ancients, Upon, VIII. 375
Cynarctomachy, or Battle between Bear and Dogs, VIII. 65, 68
Elephant in the Moon, The, VIII. 61, 62, 366
Genuine Remains in Verse and Prose of Mr Samuel Butler, The, VIII. 60, 62, 63
Hudibras, IV. 359; VII. 167; VIII. 19, 37, 49, 59 ff., 64–67 (main entry), 90, 92, 93; IX. 145, 154, 158, 201, 259, 272, 308, 418, 476, 477 (*cf.* 499, 502, 567); X. 396; XI. 318; XIII. 233, 451; XIV. 206
Miscellaneous Thoughts, VIII. 63
Observations and Reflexions, VIII. 60
Occasional thoughts, VIII. 62

Butler, Samuel
On Philip Nye's Thanksgiving Beard, VIII. 63
Posthumous Works, VIII. 62
Reflections, VIII. 61
Repartees between Cat and Puss at a Caterwauling, VIII. 17
Small Poet, A, VII. 89
Thoughts on Learning and Knowledge, VIII. 61
Butler, Samuel (1774–1839), bishop of Lichfield, VII. 336; XII. 327 ff., 481; XIII. 449, 572; XIV. 413, 594, 598, 601; Atlas of Ancient Geography, XII. 328
Butler, Samuel (1835–1902), XI. 426; XIII. 449 ff., 570 ff., also see Add. 1
Alps and Sanctuaries, XIII. 450, 451, 454
Authoress of the Odyssey, The, XIII. 450
Darwin among the Machines, XIII. 449
Darwin on the Origin of Species, XIII. 449
Deadlock in Darwinism, The, XIII. 449
Erewhon, VII. 378; X. 42; XIII. 420, 449, 451 ff.
Erewhon Revisited, XIII. 450 ff.
Evidence for the Resurrection of Jesus Christ, XIII. 449
Evolution Old and New, XIII. 449
Ex Voto, XIII. 450
Fair Haven, The, XIII. 449, 453
First Year in a Canterbury Settlement, A, XIII. 449
God the Known and God the Unknown, XIII. 449, 453
Life and Habit, XIII. 449
Life and Letters of Dr Samuel Butler, XIII. 450, 453
Luck or Cunning, XIII. 449
Note-Books, XIII. 450, 451
On the Trapanese origin of the Odyssey, XIII. 450
Psalm of Montreal, A, XIII. 449, 451, 452
Quis Desiderio...? XIII. 455
Shakespeare's Sonnets reconsidered, XIII. 450
Unconscious Memory, XIII. 449
Way of all Flesh, The, XIII. 449, 451, 453
Butler, Thomas, earl of Ossory (1634–1680), VIII. 202
Butler, Thomas (1806–1886), XIII. 449
Butler, William Archer (1814?–1848), XIV. 37, 312, 469, 567
Butler, Sir William Francis (1838–1910), XIV. 551, 567
Butler, William John (1818–1894), XII. 454
Buttes, Henry (fl. 1599), Dyets Dry Dinner, IV. 349, 530, 543
Button, Ralph (d. 1680), X. 385
Button, Sir Thomas (d. 1634), IV. 99
Button's coffee-house, IX. 165, 171
Butts, captain Thomas, XI. 196
Buzzard, the, in Dryden's Fables, VIII. 48
Byblis, The Passion of, IX. 473
By-Ends, Mr, in Bunyan's Pilgrim's Progress, VII. 173
Byerley, Thomas (d. 1826), XI. 472
Byfield, Nicholas (1579–1622), IV. 495
Byng, John, admiral (1663–1733), IX. 185, 254; X. 244, 467
Bynneman, Henry (d. 1583), IV. 384, 398, 546
Byrd, William (1538?–1623), IV. 110, 112 ff., 121, 126, 384, 463, 464
Byrhtferth (fl. 1000), I. 131
Byrhtnoth, in The Battle of Malden, I. 41, 109, 137, 143, 144, 306
Byrhtwold, I. 137
Byrne, Desmond, XIV. 584
Byrne, Thomas (fl. 1730), X. 196, 197
Byrom, John (1692–1763), IX. 191, 309, 314, 325 ff. (main entry), 513, 515, 518, 520, 523; XI. 248; XIII. 239; XIV. 230
Enthusiasm, IX. 326; X. 350
Epistle to a Gentleman of the Temple, IX. 326
Journal, IX. 307, 313, 318, 325
Poems, IX. 322, 327
Redemption, IX. 327
Universal Beauty, IX. 327
Byron, Augusta, XII. 382
Byron, George Gordon, 6th lord (1788–1824), I. 275; IV. 89, 252; VI. 239; X. 152, 154, 155, 236, 242, 253, 254; XI. 83, 91, 102, 108, 109, 117, 124, 144, 150, 158, 166, 167, 171, 178, 179, 300, 302 ff., 306, 308, 410, 414, 420, 423; XII. 15, 30, 31 ff. (main entry), 57, 60 ff., 67, 74, 76, 81, 92, 96, 98, 100, 102, 106, 111, 120, 122, 126, 131, 135, 136, 162, 174, 179, 180, 199, 205, 219, 228, 247, 314, 318, 382 ff., 402 ff., 407, 412, 426, 441, 443, 450, 485, 505, also see Add.; XIII. 7, 10, 23 ff., 52, 94, 101, 109, 135, 136, 157, 161, 184, 203, 230, 239, 258, 259, 307, 346, 352, 417, 418, 421, 436, 495, 503, 512, 514; XIV. 56, 126, 187, 198, 206, 230, 322, 327, 373, 399
'Adieu, adieu, my native land,' XIV. 374
Age of Bronze, The, XII. 37
Assyrian came down, The, XIII. 235
Beppo, XII. 33, 34, 52, 53, 63; XIII. 236; XIV. 438
Blues, The, XII. 37
Bride of Abydos, The, XII. 32, 45
British Bards, XII. 382
Cain, XI. 106, 199; XII. 35, 47, 48
Childe Harold, II. 413; III. 246; X. 301; XI. 131; XII. 32, 34, 38, 42 ff., 60, 145, 158, 382; XIII. 236, 253; XIV. 249, 374, 436
Childish Recollections, XII. 41
Corsair, The, XII. 32, 44, 45
Darkness, XII. 51
Death of Calmar and Orla, The, XII. 40
Deformed Transformed, The, XII. 37, 50
Don Juan, VII. 79; XII. 32 ff., 37, 40, 46, 51, 52, 54 ff., 71, 95, 383; XIII. 236; XIV. 244
Dorset, To the Duke of, XII. 41
Dream, The, XII. 51
Elegy on Newstead Abbey, XII. 41
English Bards and Scotch Reviewers, XII. 32, 41, 49, 52, 147

Byron, George Gordon
Epistle to Augusta, XII. 52
Epitaph on a Friend, XII. 41
Francesca of Rimini, XII. 33, 35
Fugitive Pieces, XII. 31
Giaour, The, XII. 32, 45
Heaven and Earth, XII. 35, 37, 47, 48
Hints from Horace, XII. 382
Hours of Idleness, XII. 31, 33, 40, 147
I would I were a careless child, XII. 40, 41
Island, The, XII. 38, 45, 46, 52
'Isles of Greece,' XII. 54
Lachin y Gair, XII. 40
Lament of Tasso, The, XII. 33, 50
Lara, XII. 45, 408
Letter to John Murray Esq. on... Bowles's Strictures on the Life...of Pope, XII. 35
Letters, XII. 382
Letters and Journals, XIV. 107
Maid of Athens, XIV. 377
Manfred, XII. 34, 35, 41, 47, 48, 60
Marino Faliero, XII. 35, 47, 49
Mazeppa, XII. 34, 45, 46
Memoirs, XII. 34, 103
Ode to the Framers of the Frame Bill, XII. 390
Oscar of Alva, XII. 40
Parisina, XII. 45, 46
Prisoner of Chillon, The, XII. 34, 45, 46
Prophecy of Dante, The, XII. 33, 35, 50, 56
Romance, To, XII. 41
Sardanapalus, XII. 33 ff., 47 ff.
Siege of Corinth, XI. 127; XII. 32, 45
Some Observations, XII. 36
Sonnet on Chillon, XII. 46
Speech on Frame-work bill, XII. 382
Stanzas to Jessy, XII. 382
Trans. of Pulci's *Morgante Maggiore*, XII. 35, 37
Two Foscari, The, XII. 35, 47, 49
Venetian tragedies, XII. 48, 49
Vision of Judgment, The, V. 96; XII. 36, 37, 53
Werner, XII. 37, 47, 50
When I roved a young Highlander, XII. 40
When we two parted, XII. 51
Conversations of (Medwin's), XII. 37
Life and Works of (ed. Moore), XII. 53
See, also, Astarte
Byron, George Gordon (natural son of the poet), XII. 382
Byron, Harriet, in Richardson's *Sir Charles Grandison*, X. 10, 62
Byron, Henry James (1834–1884), XIII. 271, 518; *Cyril's Success*, XIII. 273; *Our Boys*, XIII. 273; *Uncle Dick's Darling*, XIII. 273
Byron, John, 1st baron (d. 1652), VII. 436
Byron, John (1723–1786), XIV. 244, 551
Byron, lady (Anne Isabella Milbanke), XII. 32
Byron, lady, XII. 392, 393, 396, 398
Byron, 'Mad Jack' (1756–1791), XII. 31
Byron, William, 5th lord (d. 1798), XII. 31
Byse, Mrs, Fanny, VII. 98
Bysset, Abacuck, II. 93, 479; *Rolment of Courtis*, II. 285
Bysshe, Sir Edward (1615?–1679), IV. 376
Bysshe, Edward (*fl.* 1712), VIII. 230, 231, 240; IX. 529; XIII. 228, 229, 240, 249; *Art of Poetry*, XI. 249, 250, 256; *Art of English Poetry, The*, XIII. 228, 512
'Bysshe Vanolis', *pseud.* *See* Thomson, James B. V.
Bythner, Victorinus (1605?–1670?), VII. 490
Bywater, Ingram (1840–1914), XII. 334, 481, 482, *also see* Add. 3
Bywater, Mrs Henry Wood's, XIII. 430
Byzantine empire, X. 314; XII. 315

C., C. S. *See* Calverley, Charles Stuart
C Mery Talys, A, IX. 39
Cabal ministry, VII. 42
Cabal the hound, in Nennius, I. 247
Cabala, sive Scrinia Sacra (1654), VII. 191, 433; VIII. 281
Cabala (1663), VIII. 99
Cabala, The Prince's, VII. 188, 191, 458
Cabbala, the Jewish, IX. 315
Cabbalistica, Conjectura, VIII. 455
Cabillavus, IV. 266
Cabot, John, IV. 66, 68, 69, 85
Cabot, Sebastian (1474–1557), IV. 69 ff., 75, 85
Cacurgus, in *Misogonus*, V. 111
Cade, Jack, in *Henry VI*, V. 186, 248
Cade's rebellion, II. 302, 424; IV. 137, 300, 529
Caddell, W. Waithman, XIV. Add. 5
Cadell, Jessie Ellen (1844–1884), XIV. 575; *Ida Craven*, XIV. 339
Cadell, Thomas (1742–1802), X. 213; XI. 326, 327, 361
Cadell, Thomas, the younger (1773–1836), XI. 327; XII. 234
Cadesia, battle of, X. 281
Cadiou, Andrew, II. 284
Cadiz, IV. 85, 103, 200, 221; V. 361; VII. 454
Cadmus, in *Dialogues of the Dead*, XI. 351
Cadoc, St (d. 570?), I. 262
Cadogan, William Bromley, XII. 473
Cador, in Layamon, I. 266
Cador, in *Emarè*, I. 311
Cador, in *The Misfortunes of Arthur*, V. 78, 79
Cadwalader, in Layamon, I. 234
Cadwalader, in Mannyng, I. 351
Cadwallader, X. 154
Cadwallader, Mrs, in *Middlemarch*, XIII. 399
Caedmon (*fl.* 670), I. 14, 30, 41 ff., 56, 57, 61, 63, 82, 89, 96, 119, 142, 382, 383, 428; XII. 344; XIII. 241; *Genesis*, VII. 118
Caelia, in Whitehead's *School for Lovers*, X. 86
Caelius Rhodiginus, Ludovicus, VIII. 407
Caelo et Olympo, VI. 93
Caen, VIII. 220
Caer Rigor, I. 251

Caer Sidi, I. 251
Caerleon, or Caerlleon, or Carleon, upon Usk, I. 197, 246, 260; II. 303; XII. 346, 511
Caesar, in *The False One*, VI. 131
Caesar, in *The Poetaster*, VI. 42
Caesar, Julius, I. 13, 71, 81, 93, 187, 197, 342; II. 80, 111, 339; III. 24, 164, 329, 429; VII. 159, 164, 443; VIII. 67, 76; IX. 63, 204; X. 27, 119, 284, 319; XIII. 221; *Commentaries*, IX. 297
Caesar, Julius, in Byron's *The Deformed Transformed*, XII. 50
Caesar, P., IV. 510
Caesar and Pompey, VI. 483
Caesar's Ghost, VIII. 93
Caesars, the, V. 4; XII. 182, 487
Caffyn, Matthew (1628–1714), X. 378
Cagliostro, Alessandro, count, XI. 293; XIII. 468
Cahergillagh court, in Le Fanu's story, XIII. 415
Caiaphas, V. 46, 47
Caigniez, Louis Charles, XIII. 264
Caim, II. 443
Cain, I. 30; II. 20; IV. 214; X. 376
Cain, Byron's, XI. 106, 199; XII. 45, 48
Cain, Grendel's ancestor, in *Beowulf*, I. 22
Cain, in the *Towneley Mysteries*, V. 47
Cain and Abel, V. 45, 388
Caine, Sir T. H. Hall, XIII. 491
Caird, Edward (1835–1908), XIV. 45 ff., 469; *Critical Account of the Philosophy of Kant*, XIV. 45; *Critical Philosophy of Immanuel Kant, The*, XIV. 45; *Evolution of Religion, The*, XIV. 45
Caird, John (1820–1898), XII. 465; XIV. 469; *An Introduction to the Philosophy of Religion*, XIV. 45
Cairnes, John Elliot (1823–1875), XIV. 470
Cairns, Hugh McCalmont, 1st earl (1819–1885), XIV. 124, 508
Cairo, II. 80, 82, 298; XIV. 192, 251
Caithness, bishop of, III. 194
Caius, Dr, in *The Merry Wives of Windsor*, V. 268
Caius, John (1510–1573), III. 419 ff., 466; IV. 442, 541
Caius, Thomas (d. 1572), IX. 535
Caius Cestius, VI. 37
Caius Martius, in *Coriolanus*, V. 198
Caladbolg, XIV. 307
Calahorra, Diego Ortuñez de, IV. 442
Calais, II. 338, 423, 424; III. 3, 163, 167, 328; IV. 200; VI. 185; VII. 232; VIII. 271; XI. 97; XIV. 233
Calais, siege of, Minot's poem on, I. 357, 358
Calais, Chronicle of, III. 532
Calamy, Edmund (1600–1666), VII. 145, 312, 416, 424
Calamy, Edmund (1671–1732), IX. 574; X. 373, 386, 387, 499, 519, 521; *Abridgement of the Life of Baxter*, X. 374; *Defence of Moderate Conformity*, X. 374; *Historical Account of my own Life*, X. 377
Calandrino, in *The Great Duke of Florence*, VI. 161
Calantha, in Ford's *The Broken Heart*, VI. 191, 195; XII. 190
Calcraft, John (1726–1772), X. 409, 410
Calcutta, XII. 138; XIII. 276; XIV. 334 ff.
  Hindu college, XIV. 336, 337
  Sanskrit college, XII. 343
  University, XIV. 341
Calcutta Review, The, XIV. 337, 339, 574
Caldecott, Randolph (1846–1886), XI. 478, 491
Calder, Robert (1658–1723), IX. 548, 549
Calderon de La Barca, Pedro, IV. 353; V. 207, 303; VI. 140; XIII. 143, 144, 497; XIV. 318
  Dama Duende, VIII. 120, 130
  El Maestro de Danzar, VIII. 131, 144
  El Magico Prodigioso, XIII. 146
  La Vida es Sueño, XIII. 145
  No Siempre lo Peor es Cierto, VIII. 130
Calderwood, David (1575–1650), III. 122, 141; VII. 448; *Historie of the Kirk of Scotland*, VII. 209; *Recantation* (so-called), VII. 209
Calderwood, Henry (1830–1897), XIV. 470
Calderwood, Margaret (1715–1774), X. 493
Calderwood, W., XIV. 470
Caldoro, in *The Guardian*, VI. 158
Caldwell, Mrs Anne, afterwards Marsh (1791–1874), XIII. 561; *Chronicles of Dartmoor*, XIII. 430
Caledonia, X. 231
Caledonian Musical Museum, XI. 436, 442
Caledonian Musical Repository, XI. 442
Caledonian verse, X. 232
Calendar of Letters and Papers of the Reign of Henry VIII, II. 393; XIV. 82
Calendars of State Papers, XIV. 111
Caletfwlch (Excalibur), XIV. 307
Calfhill or Calfield, James (1530?–1570), VI. 320; *Progne*, VI. 299
Caliban, Browning's, XIII. 63
Caliban, in *The Tempest*, V. 207; VIII. 28. 72; XII. 128
Caliburn, Arthur's sword, I. 266
Caliburnus (Excalibur), XIV. 307
California, XIV. 241, 245, 325
Caligula, in Orosius, I. 95
Calipso, in *The Guardian*, VI. 157
Calis, princess, in *The Mad Lover*, VI. 152
Calista, in Rowe's *Fair Penitent*, VIII. 196; X. 74
Calisto and Melebea, V. 99, 100, 409; VIII. 125
Call, Wathen Mark Wilks, XIII. 167, 500; *Bird and the Bower, The*, XIII. 174; *Manoli*, XIII. 174
Callaghan, Sir, in Macklin's *Love à-la-mode*, XI. 257
Callaman, Jeremiah John (1795–1829), XIV. 305, 567
Callander, John (d. 1789), IX. 560; X. 475, 490
Callaway, Henry, XIV. Add. 6
Calle, Richard, II. 305

Callet, Auguste, x. 485
Callianax, in *The Maides Tragedy*, vi. 127
Callidamus et Callanthia, vi. 483
Callières, François de, *Le Combat des Livres*, ix. 102
Callimachus, ix. 331; xii. 329
Callington, Cornwall, x. 244
Callio, in *Euphormio*, iv. 255
Calliope, in *The Palice of Honour*, ii. 260
Callis, Robert (*fl.* 1634), viii. 468
Calman, A. L., xiii. 560
Calne, Wiltshire, xii. 191
Calpurnia, in *Julius Caesar*, v. 197
Calton in Craven, x. 386
Calvary, hill of, v. 44
Calverley, Charles Stuart (1831–1884), iv. 249; viii. 9; xi. 379; xiii. 162, 165 ff., 246, 500, 543; xiv. 205, 537; *Fly Leaves*, xiii. 165; *Remains*, xiii. 166; *Wanderers*, xiii. 36
Calverley hall, in *A Yorkshire Tragedy*, v. 242, 243
Calvert, Adelaide H., xiii. 513
Calvert, *Judy*, artist, xiv. 239
Calvert, W., xiii. 513
Calvin, John (1509–1564), iii. 10, 46, 144, 145, 383, 399, 400, 402, 403, 407, 411, 431; iv. 21, 214, 220, 303, 380, 429, 433, 442, 510; v. 114, 365; vi. 374; vii. 152, 159, 160, 208, 308, 309, 321, 477; viii. 108, 111, 277, 279, 291, 295, 299, 306, 407; x. 370; xiv. 102; *Institutes of the Christian Religion*, iii. 145, 400; vii. 306
Calvinism, vii. 143, 148, 152, 153, 157, 279, 280; x. 364, 367, 368, 376, 381, 383; xi. 43, 213; xii. 279, 284; xiii. 431; xiv. 428
Calvinistic methodists, x. 364, 365
Calvinists, the, iv. 276, 296; xi. 19; attacked in *Loiola*, vi. 324
Cam, river, vi. 93, 327; vii. 327
Cambert, Robert, viii. 135; *Pomone*, viii. 134
Cambert and Perrin, P., *Ariane, ou le Mariage de Bacchus*, viii. 134
Cambray, congress of, ix. 221
Cambrensis, Giraldus. *See* Giraldus
Cambriae Annales, i. 246, 248, 461
Cambrian rocks, xiv. 292
Cambridge, i. 184, 382; ii. 67, 103, 104, 130, 199, 221, 305, 307, 341 ff., 367, 368, 487, 488; iii. 8, 13, 14, 26, 27, 28, 34, 36, 37, 39, 43, 50, 51, 53, 56, 67, 151, 175, 179, 183, 185, 213, 214, 290, 292, 293, 301, 318, 321, 337, 355, 362, 366, 418 ff., 427, 429 ff., 436; iv. 70, 131, 190, 198, 200, 224, 228, 229, 274 ff., 374, 381, 398, 403, 406, 409 ff., 416, 418, 419, 422 ff., 433; v. 104, 109, 121, 132 ff., 343, 363 ff., 368, 369; vi. 86, 105, 218, 220, 232, 293 ff., 300, 303, 311 ff., 316, 374; vii. 5, 9, 28, 32, 42, 46, 78, 85, 98, 143, 148, 155, 180, 189, 223, 228, 245, 305, 312, 316, 317 ff.,
Cambridge 327, 336, 364, 437, 441, 476 ff.; viii. 60, 108, 122, 273, 286, 317, 361, 472; ix. 130, 142, 150, 165, 184, 188, 195, 235, 294, 295, 308, 309, 313, 321, 325, 326, 330, 335, 336, 340, 341, 354, 355, 382, 383, 386, 387, 390, 395, 406, 410 ff., 485, 526, 532, 571, 573, 574; x. 47, 117, 118, 121, 122, 128, 130, 131, 133, 262, 300, 310, 357, 359, 360, 397, 450, 457; xi. 57, 118, 150, 173, 335, 338 340, 347, 355, 407; xii. 132, 198, 200, 256, 273, 294, 296, 298, 305, 306, 325 327 ff., 338 ff., 342, 354, 357, 369, 370 467, 488, 508, 515, 522; xiii. 23, 25, 40, 46, 143, 165, 172, 174, 203, 206, 209, 240, 277, 278, 346, 361, 362, 368, 369, 414, 449; xiv. 25, 26, 37, 64, 79, 90 ff., 100, 109, 110, 117, 119, 168, 205 ff. 215, 247, 257 ff., 262 ff., 268, 269, 284, 300, 362, 383 ff., 395, 403, 409, 414, 416, 417, 429 ff.
Cambridge, Dominicans and Franciscans at, i. 200; ii. 349, 350
Cambridge, Richard Owen (1717–1802), xi. 350, 365, 425
Cambridge, South Africa, xiv. 377
Cambridge, University of (Ackermann's), xiv. 222
Cambridge books and printers:
  Books, xi. 468
  Printers, iv. 546 ff.; xi. 468
Cambridge buildings and churches:
  Augustinian priory, iii. 37
  Benedictine school, ii. 349
  Botanic garden, xiv. 286
  Cavendish laboratory, xiv. 270
  Churches, xii. 489
  Fitzwilliam museum, xii. 498
  Gaol, x. 280
  St Bene't's church, vii. 244
  St Edward's Church, iii. 37
  St John, hospital of, ii. 353
  St Mary's church, iii. 389; vii. 34; viii. 290
  St Radegund, priory of, ii. 358
  Sedgwick museum, xiv. 291
  Senate house, xiv. 384, 412
  Sturbridge fair, iv. 409; xi. 340
  Trinity church, viii. 274
  University library, iv. 424, 426, 432; ix. 532; xii. 323, 341, 342, 369, 480, 502, 503, 518; xiv. 484
  University press, iv. 277, 409 ff.; viii. 278; xi. 341; xii. 324, 328, 329
  White Horse, the (Little Germany), iii. 34, 37
Cambridge college magazines, xiv. 538–539
Cambridge colleges:
  Bene't, or Corpus Christi college, ii. 346, 354. *See* Corpus Christi college
  Buckingham college. *See* Magdalene college
  Caius college. *See* Gonville and Caius college

Cambridge colleges:
Catherine hall, vi. 196, vii. 301, *and see* St Catharine's college
Christ's college, ii. 354; iii. 14, 328; v. 111; vi. 295, 296; vii. 91, 92, 97, 114, 279, 342; viii. 278 ff., 287, 290, 292, 360; xii. 344, 490, 516
Clare hall or college, ii. 354; iii. 36; v. 132; vi. 307, 308, 322; viii. 281, 292; ix. 250, 516
Corpus Christi college, ii. 354; iv. 4, 18, 423, 426; v. 142, 143; vi. 111; x. 131; xii. 344, 363, 498, 517; xiv. 283; Parker mss., iv. 424
Emmanuel college, iii. 432; iv. 159, 329, 424 ff.; vi. 317; vii. 224, 279, 317, 339, 340, 354; viii. 274, 276, 277, 281, 288, 290, 359, 461, 482; ix. 308; xii. 187, 326, 333, 493, 516
Girton college, xiv. 430
God's house, ii. 358
Gonville and Caius college, iii. 420, 422; vi. 216, 301, 306; vii. 188, 320, 321, 345; viii. 4, 363; ix. 386; xii. 187, 333, 341, 517; xiii. 241
Jesus college, ii. 358; iii. 20, 32; iv. 159, 424; vi. 307; vii. 310; viii. 282; ix. 240; x. 342; xii. 326; xiv. 298
King's college, ii. 288, 357, 358, 489; iii. 183, 265, 315, 431; iv. 165, 275, 407, 410; v. 70; vi. 285, 294, 298, 317, 321; vii. 53, 326, 328, 329; viii. 274, 275, 279, 292; x. 117, 243; xii. 333
King's college chapel, iii. 320
King's hall, ii. 352, 354, 358; iv. 426
Magdalene college, ii. 358; iii. 32; iv. 427; viii. 242, 253, 292, 355; x. 359; xii. 517; xiii. 355
Magdalene college, Pepysian library, ii. 224, 316, 423; iii. 133; iv. 427; viii. 242, 250, 260
Michael house, ii. 354, 358, 366; iii. 13; iv. 426; vi. 294
Newnham college, xiv. 430
Pembroke college, iv. 427; vi. 296; vii. 32, 33, 83; ix. 257; x. 117, 123, 124, 128, 131, 132, 281, 450; xii. 327, 516
Pembroke hall or college, ii. 355; iii. 213, 422; iv. 238
Peterhouse, i. 205; ii. 302, 308, 347, 352, 353 ff., 362 ff., 371; iii. 67; iv. 141, 142, 422, 423, 432; vi. 83, 99, 307; vii. 33 ff., 326, 406, 449; viii. 284, 295; ix. 341; x. 116, 117, 133; xii. 330, 516; xiii. 241; xiv. 109, 121, 385
Peterhouse, chained library at, ii. 362, 364 ff.
Queens' college, ii. 358; iii. 27; iv. 426; v. 103, 108; vi. 305, 324; vii. 244; viii. 288; ix. 169, 340; xii. 516, 522
St Catharine's college, ii. 358; iv. 426; viii. 290
St John's college, ii. 358; iii. 292, 293, 420, 422, 425, 430, 432; iv. 31, 91, 232, 274, 277, 426; v. 81, 132, 140; vi. 3, 294, 296, 301, 304, 306 ff., 312, 321, 397; vii. 4, 84, 89, 91, 329, 330, 337, 362; viii. 243; ix. 147, 152, 153, 165, 182, 330, 341, 354, 381, 411, 412, 483, 531, 573; x. 393, 525; xi. 96; xii. 280, 326, 328, 329, 331, 335 ff., 341, 345, 481, 488, 517; xiii. 45, 404
St John's college magazine, *The Eagle*, iv. 275; xii. 487
Sidney Sussex college, iii. 422; vii. 244; viii. 360
Trinity college, ii. 354, 358; iii. 202, 418, 420, 422, 424; iv. 12, 164, 274, 278, 427, 431; v. 103; vi. 232, 294, 295, 302, 305, 306, 314, 321, 322, 324 ff., 397; viii. 3, 4, 21, 185, 277, 278, 295, 297, 366; ix. 240, 241, 335, 340, 411, 412, 525; xi. 417; xii. 31, 288, 302, 308, 323, 328 ff., 335, 344, 347, 353, 369, 491, 499, 516, 523; xiii. 45, 142, 189, 276; xiv. 60, 251, 282, 283, 295; *and see* Michael house; King's hall
Trinity college library, xiii. 473
Trinity hall, ii. 354; iii. 183, 424, 426; vii. 4, 21, 27, 62, 117, 179, 317, 333, 342, 361; viii. 253; xii. 517
University hall. *See* Clare college
Cambridge English Classics, xi. 150
Cambridge Essays, xii. 324; xiv. 139
Cambridge Modern History, The, xiv. 81, 101, 119
Cambridge Observer, The, xiv. 208, 537
Cambridge Platonists, the, vii. 278, 279, 302, 316; viii. 110, 273 ff., 301, 330; ix. 209, 300, 306
Cambridge Review, The, xiv. 207, 208, 537
Cambridge Review, The Book of the, xiv. 207
Cambridge Shakespeare, The, v. 271, 275, 280
Cambridge societies:
Antiquarian, xii. 506
'Apostles,' the, xiii. 24
Philosophical, xiv. 288, 289
Cambridge University:
Clark lectures, xii. 331
'Local' Examinations, xiv. 429
Moral Sciences tripos, xiv. 416
Natural Sciences tripos, xiv. 416
Rede lecture, xiv. 81
Cambridge University Magazine, The, xiv. 208
Cambridge University Prize, Townshend's, xiv. 385
Cambridge University professors:
Anglo-Saxon (Elrington and Bosworth), xii. 344
Arabic (Lord Almoner's), ix. 413
Archaeology (Disney), xii. 331
Astronomy (Plumian), vii. 342; ix. 412, 413
Astronomy and Geometry (Lowndean), ix. 413
Chinese, xii. 343
Divinity (Lady Margaret's), iii. 13, 14
Experimental Physics (Cavendish), xiv. 269

Cambridge University professors:
Geology (Woodwardian), XIV. 291
Greek (Regius), XII. 323, 328 ff., 332
Latin (Kennedy), XII. 335
Mathematics (Lucasian), XIV. 266
Natural Philosophy (Jacksonian), XIV. 385
Sanskrit, XII. 343
Cambridgeshire, II. 197; X. 280; XI. 347; XIII. 216; XIV. 221, 282
Cambuscan, II. 184
Cambyses, IV. 232
Camden, earl of. *See* Pratt, Charles
Camden, William (1551–1623), I. 89, 381; III. 157, 237, 313, 315, 318, 321, 324 ff., 330, 331, 334, 428, 438, 451, 527; IV. 59, 159, 325, 327; V. 477; VI. 3, 6, 9; VII. 337, 338, 442, 487; VIII. 318; IX. 350 ff., 551; X. 293
Britannia, III. 327, 328, 331, 438; IV. 190, 401, 442; IX. 353, 534; XII. 345, 353
Greek Grammar, IV. 407
Remains, IV. 266
Rerum Anglicarum et Hibernicarum Annales, III. 325, 326, 550; IV. 262, 299, 510
Camden society, II. 500; IX. 212; XII. 353, 354, 368, 369; XIII. 15; XIV. 87, 88
Cameiros, necropolis of, XII. 339
Camel, river, I. 261
Camelford (Camlan), battle of, I. 248, 250, 266
Camelford, lord. *See* Pitt, Thomas
Camelot, I. 326
Camerarius, Joachim, IV. 249
Cameron, Archibald (1707–1753), IX. 563
Cameron, George Frederick (1854–1885), XIV. 357, 582
Cameron, Jenny, IX. 563
Cameron, Lucy Lyttleton (1781–1858), XI. 485
Cameron, Richard (d. 1680), IX. 549
Cameronians, the, XII. 18, 25
Camfield, B., VII. 507
Camilla, in Owen's *Epigrammata*, IV. 265
Camilla Lacey, Mme d'Arblay's house, X. 261
Camilla (Lyly's), III. 346
Camillo, in *The White Divel*, VI. 177
Camiola, in *The Maid of Honour*, VI. 150, 156, 163, 164
Camlan. *See* Camelford
Cammelli, Antonio, *Filostrato e Panfila*, V. 62, 69
Camoëns, Luis de, VIII. 271; X. 456; XII. 422
Campagna, the, XII. 69
Campan, Mme de, XIII. 343
Campanella, Tommaso, VII. 298, 470
Campania, VI. 299
Campbell, Alexander (1764–1824), XII. 373; *Albyn's Anthology*, XI. 236, 442
Campbell, Archibald, marquis of Argyll and 8th earl (1598–1661), XII. 21, 29
Campbell, Archibald, bishop of Aberdeen (d. 1744), X. 355
Campbell, Archibald (1691–1756), IX. 548
Campbell, Archibald (1726?–1780), X. 131, 474
Campbell, Colin Turing, XIV. Add. 6
Campbell, Duncan, IX. 21, 428; *Secret Memoirs*, IX. 22
Campbell, Frank B. F., *The Battle of Bibliography*, XII. 519
Campbell, George (1719–1796), IX. 561; X. 347, 512; *Dissertation on Miracles*, X. 348; *Philosophy of Rhetoric, The*, X. 348; XIV. 399, 605
Campbell, George Douglas, 8th duke of Argyll (1823–1900), XIV. 468
Campbell, James Dykes, XI. 412, 416
Campbell, John, 2nd duke of Argyll (1678–1743), XII. 19
Campbell, John, 1st lord (1779–1861), XIV. 124, 186, 501, 508; *Lives of Lord Lyndhurst and Lord Brougham*, XIV. 112; *Lives of the Lord Chancellors*, XIV. 112; *Lives of the Lord Chief Justices*, XIV 112
Campbell, John Francis (1822–1885), *Popular Tales of the West Highlands*, I. 294; XIII. 561
Campbell, John McLeod (1800–1872), XII. 283, 289, 465; *The Nature of the Atonement*, XII. 284
Campbell, Lawrence Dundas, XIV. 575
Campbell, Lewis (1830–1908), XII. 220, 409, 468, 479, 480, 482, 486; XIII. 310; XIV. 503, 594
Campbell, major, in Kingsley's *Two Years Ago*, XIII. 365
Campbell, Thomas (1733–1795), X. 473
Campbell, Thomas (1777–1844), VII. 73; IX. 451, *also see* Add.; XI. 148, 150, 178; XII. 95, 96, 98 ff. (main entry), 102, 126, 138, 139, 148, 384, 385, 409, 429; XIII. 186, 230; XIV. 186, 410 ff., 595
Argyllshire, Lines on Revisiting a Scene in, XII. 99
Battle of the Baltic, The, VIII. 11; XII. 99
Gertrude of Wyoming, XII. 100
Hohenlinden, XII. 99, 101; XIV. 437
How delicious is the winning, XII. 99
Last Man, The, XII. 99, 161
Lectures on Poetry, XII. 161
Life and Letters, XIV. 56
Lochiel's Warning, XII. 98, 99
Lord Ullin's Daughter, XII. 98, 99
Pilgrim of Glencoe, The, XII. 100
Pleasures of Hope, The, XII. 41, 100
Soldier's Dream, The, XII. 99
Song of Hybrias the Cretan, The, XII. 99
Specimens, XII. 99, 100
Theodoric, XII. 100
Withdraw not yet those lips and fingers, XII. 99
Ye Mariners of England, XII. 99
Campbell, William Wilfred, XIV. 582
Campion, Edmund (1540–1581), IV. 127, 237, 411, 536; XIV. 118, 308; *Description of Ireland*, III. 319
Campion, John (d. 1576), IV. 141
Campion, Lucy, afterwards Steward (d. 1580), IV. 141

Campion, M., A true reporte of the death... of, vi. 387, 498
Campion, Rose, iv. 141
Campion, Thomas (d. 1619), iii. 178, 295, 306, 307, 526; iv. 112, 113, 124 ff., 141 ff. (main entry), 266, 463, 478; vi. 231, 329, 354; viii. 229, 231, 237, 239; xi. 160, 161, 179; xiii. 245
Ayres that were sung and played at Brougham Castle, iv. 143
Book of Ayres, iv. 142, 143, 146
'Follow your Saint,' iv. 148
'Harke, al you ladies,' iv. 145, 148
Lords' Maske, iii. 353; iv. 143, 145, 146
Man of Life upright, The, iv. 126
Masques, vi. 488
'My sweetest Lesbia,' vii. 2
New Way of Making Fowre Parts in Counter-point, A, iv. 143, 144
'Now hath Flora,' iv. 145
Observations in the Art of English Poesie, iii. 306; iv. 133, 142, 144
Poemata, iv. 142
'So be it ever,' iv. 145
Songs of Divers Noblemen and Gentlemen, iv. 145
Songs of Mourning, iv. 143
'There is a garden in her face,' iv. 145; vii. 8
'Young and simple though I am,' iv. 145
Campion, in *Westward Ho!* xiii. 364
Canaanites, in *The Silver Age*, vi. 93
Canace, in *Confessio Amantis*, ii. 151, 152
Canada, xiii. 449; xiv. 125, 293, 318, 323, 331, 343 ff., 434
Canada balsam, xiv. 445
Canadian Fiction, Bibliography of, xiv. 359
Canadian house of commons, xiv. 359
Canadian literature, xiv. 343 ff.
Canaries, the, iii. 358; v. 139; xiv. 293
Canby, Henry Seidel, xiii. 567
Cancer: Comoedia, vi. 483
Cancioneros, Spanish, ii. 268
Cancrone, in *Sicelides*, vi. 323
Candido, in *The Honest Whore*, vi. 172
Candidus (Mantuan's), iii. 223 ff.
Candish, Richard. *See* Cavendish
Candlemas, ii. 378
Candlish, Robert Smith (1806–1873), xii. 471
'Candor,' x. 399, 400, 405, 523
Candy, Pennyloaf, in Gissing's *The Nether World*, xiii. 458
Canmore, Malcolm, ii. 130
Cannae, viii. 11
Cannan, Gilbert, xiii. 572
Canne, John (d. 1667), vii. 360, 361
Cannes, x. 42
Canning, Hon. Albert S. G., xiii. 542
Canning, Elizabeth (1734–1773), x. 34
Canning, George (1770–1827), viii. 38; xi. 39, 40, 42, 52, 174, 175, 392; xii. 120, 136, 150, 155; xiii. 24, 161, 166, 238; xiv. 123, 126, 128, 134, 188, 214,
Canning, George
506, 508, 597; 'On unlawful Societies in Ireland,' xiv. 122; *Speeches*, xiv. 122; *The New Morality*, xi. 42
Canning, Stratford, 1st viscount Stratford de Redcliffe (1786–1880), xiv. 179, 182
Canon or Canonicus, John (*fl.* 1329), i. 211, 452
Canonbury tower, x. 212
Canons, iv. 424
Canons, ix. 81
Canons-Ashby, Northants, viii. 2
Cantalupo, in *The Bugbears*, v. 115
Canterbury, i. 50, 71, 127, 139, 202; iii. 30, 49, 375, 407; iv. 381, 382, 409; v. 21, 56, 103, 371; vii. 157, 301, 309; viii. 3, 302, 303, 305; ix. 151, 210, 532, 539; x. 362; xi. 354; xii. 320, 340, 364, 478; xiv. 390
Christ church priory, iii. 5; iv. 417, 424
King's school, v. 102, 142
Lee Priory, xii. 520
St Augustine's abbey, iv. 417, 424
Shrine of Thomas à Beckett, iii. 12
Canterbury, convocation of, x. 360
Canterbury, early school and culture of, i. 13, 79, 87
Canterbury, Franciscans at, i. 202; iii. 57
Canterbury, in *Euphues and his England*, iii. 345
Canterbury, in Shakespeare's *King Henry V*, ii. 77
Canterbury, monk-chronicler of, ii. 301
Canterbury Chronicle at Christ church, i. 109
Canters' college, the, in *The Staple of Newes*, vi. 25
Cantilenae, v. 26, 29 ff., 34
Cant's hall, Burnham, x. 117
Canute, king of the English (994?–1035), i. 111, 127, 150, 337; viii. 310
Canute Song, The, i. 219, 458; ii. 397 ff.
Canutus, Benedict, *Regimen contra pestilentiam*, ii. 319
Canynge's coffer, x. 236
Canynges, the, x. 485, 486
Canzonets to foure voyces, vii. 2
Cape Argus, The, xiv. 588
Cape Colony, xiv. 372, 374, 377
Cape Monthly Magazine, The, xiv. 588
Cape of Good Hope, xiv. 192, 241
Cape Town, xiv. 373
Cape-Dutch language and literature, xiv. 373, 374, 377, 458
Capel, of Hoxton square academy, x. 385
Capel family, xiv. 286
Capell, Edward (1713–1781), v. 267, 274, 275; x. 433; xii. 369; *Prolusiones*, v. 243; *Shakespeare*, xi. 320
Caper Sauce, xiv. 377
Caperwit, in *Changes*, vi. 202
Capgrave, John (1393–1464), ii. 287, 295, 479; iii. 440
Annals, ii. 287
Chronicle, ii. 287
Famous Henries, ii. 287
Guide to Rome, ii. 287

Capgrave, John
Life of Humphrey, duke of Gloucester, II. 287
Life of St Augustine, II. 480
Life of St Gilbert of Sempringham, II. 287
Life of St Katherine, II. 287
Life of St Norbert, II. 480
Capheaton, Northumberland, XIII. 129
Capodistrias, Joannes Antonios, count, XII. 314
Capon's Tale, in *The Miscellany*, IX. 85
Caponsacchi, in *The Ring and the Book*, XIII. 64, 66, 80
Caporali, VII. 274
Capriccio, in *The Masque of the Middle Temple*, VI. 355
Capro, in Marston's *Scourge of Villanie*, IV. 332
Captain Car, II. 406, 408, 412
Captain Stukeley, VIII. 125
Captain Wedderburn's Courtship, II. 409
Capuchin friars, X. 499
Capulet, in *Romeo and Juliet*, V. 172, 182
Capystranus, metrical romance, II. 326
Carabas, in Disraeli's *Vivian Grey*, XIII. 349
Caracalla, baths of, XII. 67
Caracona, in Casti's *Il Poema Tartaro*, XII. 55
Caractacus, VI. 128
Caradoc or Caradog of Llancarvan (d. 1147?), I. 65, 262
Carados, in *Conte del Graal*, I. 328
Carannog, St (*fl.* 450), I. 262
Carathis, in Beckford's *Vathek*, XI. 290, 291
Carbery, lady, VIII. 456
Carbery, earl of. *See* Vaughan, Richard
Carbonari movement, XII. 33, 36, 38, 51
Carcani, Giulio, V. 306
Card or rutter of the Sea lyenge betwene Holland and Ffryseland, IV. 399
Cardan, Jerome, III. 113, 420; IV. 249
Cardano, Girolamo, IV. 442
Cardenio, in *Don Quixote*, IX. 269
Carder, Peter (*fl.* 1577–1586), IV. 93
Cardiff, IV. 192
Cardiff castle, IV. 421
Cardiff, University college, XIV. 433
Cardross, X. 36
'Cards, Monopolies of,' VII. 440
Care, Henry (1646–1688), VIII. 403, 412; *Pacquet of Advice from Rome*, IX. 4; *Weekly Pacquet*, IX. 4
Carew, Sir George (d. 1612), VIII. 468
Carew, Sir George, afterwards lord Carew of Clopton and earl of Totnes (1555–1629), VII. 211, 437, 438, 448; *Relation of the State of France*, VII. 190
Carew, John (d. 1660), VIII. 470
Carew, lady, IV. 211
Carew, Sir Matthew (d. 1618), VII. 16
Carew, Peter (*fl.* 1566), VI. 287
Carew, Richard (1555–1620), IV. 18, 23, 445, 448, 510; VI. 89; IX. 352; *The Excellency of the English Tongue*, III. 305, 330, 446, 526; *A Survey of Cornwall*, III. 330, 528; V. 15
Carew, Thomas (1598?–1639?), IV. 139, 168, 197, 213, 214; VI. 11, 363; VII. 4, 7, 13, 15 ff. (main entry), 22, 23, 25, 57, 81, 87, 398; VIII. 141
'Ask me no more where Jove bestows, VII. 19
Boldness in Love, VII. 18
Coelum Britannicum, VI. 363; VII. 16, 19
Elegy upon the Death of Dr Donne, VII. 17, 18
'Fair copy of my Celia's face,' VII. 19
'He that loves a rosy lip,' VII. 19
'I'll gaze no more on her bewitching face,' VII. 17
'Mark how the bashful morn, in vain,' VII. 18
Murdering Beauty, VII. 18
Rapture, The, IV. 210; VII. 19
Spring, The, VII. 20
'Sweetly breathing vernal air,' VII. 19
Upon the Death of the King of Sweden, VII. 20
Carew papers, VII. 436
Carey, David, XIV. 225, 542
Carey, George, 2nd lord Hunsdon (1547–1603), VI. 247, 385
Carey, George Saville (1743–1807), XI. 451
Carey, Henry (d. 1743), II. 272; IX. 484; X. 71, 426; *Chrononhotonthologos*, IX. 190; X. 83; *Dragon of Wantley*, X. 83; *Sally in our Alley*, IX. 165, 190
Carey, Henry, 1st lord Hunsdon (1524?–1596), VI. 247
Carey, James, XIV. 320
Carey, John, 3rd lord Hunsdon (d. 1617), IV. 19, 161; VI. 161
Carey, Patrick (*fl.* 1651), VII. 412; XII. 376; XIII. 211; *Trivial Poems and Triolets*, VII. 88
Carey, Robert, earl of Monmouth (1560?–1639), VII. 449; *Memoirs*, VII. 221, 449
Carey, William (1761–1834), XII. 343, 502
Cargill, Daniel or Donald (1619?–1681), IX. 549
Carinthia, George Meredith's, XIII. 444 ff.
Carinus, in *The Prophetesse*, VI. 152
Carisbrooke, VII. 39
Carisophus, in *Damon and Pithias*, V. 118
Carker, James, in *Dombey and Son*, XIII. 317, 325, 331
Carle an' the King come, IX. 377
Carlell, Lodowick (*fl.* 1629–1664), VI. 239, 240; VIII. 119, 400; Corneille's *Héraclius* translated by, VIII. 133, 180
Carleton, Sir Dudley, viscount Dorchester (1573–1632), VI. 3, 291; VII. 16, 152, 193, 343, 394, 437; X. 502
Carleton, George (1559–1628), ΑΣΤΡΟΛΟΓΟΜΑΝΙΑ: *the madness of astrologers*, VII. 377, 508
Carleton, captain George (*fl.* 1728), IX. 23; XII. 376; *Military Memoirs*, XII. 16
Carleton, William (1794–1869), XIV. 312, 314 ff., 567

Carleton, William
Anne Cosgrave, xiv. 315
Black Prophet, The, xiv. 315
Fardorougha the Miser, xiv. 315
Tales of Ireland, xiv. 315
Traits and Stories of the Irish Peasantry, xiv. 315
Valentine McClutchy, xiv. 315
Carlia, in Whitehead's *School for Lovers*, x. 86
Carlile, Richard (1790–1843), xi. 395; xiv. 187, 470
Carlisle, ii. 116, 122, 411; x. 193, 352; xi. 240; xii. 511; xiii. 196; xiv. 100
Carlisle, in Arthurian romance, i. 312, 313
Carlisle, bishop of, in *Richard II*, v. 249
Carlisle, lady, in Browning's *Strafford*, xiii. 59
Carlisle, Lucy Hay, countess of (1599–1660), vii. 17, 55
Carlisle, Nicholas (1771–1847), vii. 333; ix. 408; xii. 419; *Endowed Grammar Schools*, vii. 333; xiv. 389
Carlo Alberto, king, xii. 440
Carlton or Carleton, Richard (1560?–1638?), iv. 113, 463
Carlton house, xii. 232
Carlyle, Alexander ('Jupiter' Carlyle) (1722–1805), ix. 561; xi. 220; xii. 472; xiii. 467, 470
Carlyle, John Aitken (1801–1879), xii. 137, 522
Carlyle, J. E., xiv. Add. 6
Carlyle, Jane Welsh (1801–1866), xiii. 5, 6, 467, 470
Carlyle, Thomas (1795–1881), iii. 147; iv. 45; vi. 239; vii. 91, 189, 191, 194, 225, 356, 440, 501; x. 42, 66, 288, 315, 316, 476, 480; xi. 28, 137, 209, 218, 228 ff., 409, 417, 439, 491; xii. 23 ff., 97, 159, 162, 177, 178, 219, 253, 273, 283, 378, 430, 431, 445, 505; xiii. 1 ff. (main entry), 57, 58, 71, 77, 81, 86, 128, 143, 158, 185, 320, 343, 355, 361, 362, 364 ff., 420, 422, 425, 436, 442, 447, 451, 458, 464 ff. (main entry), 483, 552; xiv. 1, 14, 42, 63, 83, 84, 86, 112, 113, 138, 144, 153, 180, 318*a*, 462, 470, 486, 515, 518
Characteristics, xiii. 8
Chartism, xiii. 14
Critical and Miscellaneous Essays, xiii. 5
Early Kings of Norway, The, xiii. 20
Essay on Goethe's *Faust*, xiii. 4
Frederick the Great, xiii. 17 ff.
German Romance, xiii. 4, 5
History of the French Revolution, xiii. 11 ff., 17, 19, 278, 332, 333, 384; xiv. 15
Latter Day Pamphlets, xiii. 15
Lectures on Heroes, xiii. 3
Letters and Speeches of Oliver Cromwell, xiii. 17, 19
Life of John Sterling, xi. 136; xiii. 18
Life of Schiller, xiii. 1, 4
On Heroes, Hero-Worship and the Heroic in History, xiii. 12 ff.
Carlyle, Thomas
On the Choice of Books, xiii. 19
Past and Present, i. 176; xiii. 14
Reminiscences, xiii. 2
Sartor Resartus, ix. 100; xii. 163, 431; xiii. 2, 3, 5 ff., 9 ff., 60; xiv. 416
Trans. of Goethe's *Wilhelm Meister's Apprenticeship*, xiii. 4, 5
Trans. of Goethe's *Wilhelm Meister's Travels*, xiii. 5
Trans. of Legendre's *Elements of Geometry and Trigonometry*, xiii. 4
Wotton Reinfred, xiii. 9
Carmarthen, x. 386
Carmarthen, Presbyterian college, x. 387
Carmarthen, Roman walls at, i. 197
Carmarthen. See *Black Book of*
Carmelites, the, i. 213; ii. 349, 350; iv. 419
Carmen Heroicum, iii. 293
Carmichael, Grace Jennings (1867?–1904), xiv. 369, 585
Carmichael-Smyth, major, xiii. 276
Carnan, Thomas, xi. 377
Carnarvon castle, xi. 131
Carnarvon, earls of. *See* Dormer, Robert; Herbert, H. H. M.
Carnarvonshire, iv. 262; x. 115
Carnatic, the, xi. 19
Caro (Flesh), in *Piers the Plowman*, ii. 19
Carol, in *The Masque of Christmas*, vi. 358
Carolina, South, ix. 12
Caroline, in Thackeray's *A Shabby Genteel Story*, xiii. 280, 299
Caroline (1683–1737), queen of George II, ix. 132, 175, 187, 222, 249 ff., 281, 338; x. 274, 353; xii. 19
Caroline (1768–1821), queen of George IV, xiv. 121, 201
Caroline divines, xii. 253, 255, 261, 262, 265, 277
Caroline dramatists, x. 108
Caroline essayists, ix. 36
Caroline literature, viii. 222, 227, 389
Caroline poetry, xiii. 192, 218, 237
Caroline poets, vii. 1, 2, 10, 17; x. 151; xii. 127, 221
Carolingian empire, viii. 310
Carolingian romances, i. 302, 309. *See, also, under* Charlemagne
Carolings, the, v. 4
Carolles, Christmasse (Wynkyn de Worde's), ii. 393
Carolostadius, iii. 363
Carols, ii. 373 ff.
Carols, Christmas, iii. 19
Carols sung at Queen's College, Oxford, ii. 326
Carové, Friedrich Wilhelm, xi. 491
Carow, black nuns at, v. 8
Carow, in *Phyllyp Sparowe*, iii. 71
Carpenter, Agricola, *Pseuchographia Anthropomagica* (1652), vii. 509
Carpenter, J. Estlin, xii. 468; xiv. 470, 477
Carpenter, Nathaniel (1589–1628?), *Philosophia libera*, iv. 278, 507
Carpenter, Richard (d. 1670?), vii. 509

Carpenter, William Benjamin (1813–1885), xiv. 296, 470, 559
Carpenter's Tools, Debate of the, ii. 501
Carr, Henry, iv. 390
Carr, James Anderson, xiv. 572
Carr, J. Comyns, xiii. 522
Carr, Robert, earl of Somerset (d. 1645), iv. 202; vi. 31, 37, 344; vii. 441
Carré, H., *Histoire de France*, x. 283
'Carré, Jérôme,' v. 292
Carre, Thomas, *pseud. See* Pinkney, Miles
Carric, i. 236
Carroll. *See under* Centlivre, Susannah
Carroll, Lewis, *pseud. See* Dodgson, Charles Lutwidge
Carroll, William, viii. 473
Carrow. *See* Carow
Carruthers, R. (1799–1878), xi. 439; xiv. 517, 574
Carsons, the, in Mrs Gaskell's *Mary Barton*, xiii. 374
Carstares, William (1649–1715), ix. 492; x. 295; xiv. 507
Cartagena, x. 36, 37, 41
Carte, Thomas (1686–1754), x. 291, 293, 355, 498 ff.; *History of England*, x. 280; *Life of James, Duke of Ormond*, x. 280, 294, 295
Carte mss., the, xiv. 96
Carter, Elizabeth (1717–1806), x. 171, 464, 473; xi. 343, 350 ff., 354 ff. (main entry), 361, 363, 365, 473
Epictetus, xi. 356 ff.
Examination of Mr Pope's Essay on Man, xi. 356
Memoirs, xi. 356
Ode to Wisdom, xi. 356
Sir Isaac Newton's Philosophy Explained, xi. 356
Carter, Huntley, xiii. 513
Carter, Matthew (*fl.* 1660), ix. 532
Carter, Nicholas (*fl.* 1717), xi. 354
Carter, Thos. Fortescue, xiv. Add. 6
Carter, William (d. 1584), iv. 381
Carteret, John, 1st earl Granville (1690–1763), ix. 88, 172, 458, 459, 465
Carteret, lady, ix. 457, 459, 463
Carteret, Philip (d. 1796), xiv. 244
Cartesian philosophy, xi. 57
Cartesianism, vii. 303. *See, also*, Descartes
Carthage, ii. 74; viii. 65; ix. 258; xii. 301, 316, 475, 478, 480
Carthage, in Alfred's *Orosius*, i. 95
Carthusian order, i. 189; ii. 61; vii. 338; xiii. 95
Cartier, J., iv. 442
Cartmell, Lancashire, xii. 514
Carton, Sydney, in *A Tale of Two Cities*, xiii. 333
Cartwright, Christopher (1602–1658), vii. 424
Cartwright, Mrs, xiv. 599
Cartwright, Thomas (1535–1603), iii. 213, 214, 389, 405, 413, 422, 426, 548; iv. 411, 433; ix. 235; xi. 32
Cartwright, Thomas (1634–1689), xii. 516
Cartwright, William (1611–1643), v. 371; vi. 11, 28, 109, 240; vii. 4, 39, 272
Lady Errant, The, vi. 237
Ordinary, The, vi. 237
Royall Slave, The, vi. 237, 326; viii. 118
Siedge or Love's Convert, The, vi. 237
Cartwright, William (d. 1687), vi. 83, 480
Cartwright, William Cornwallis, xiv. 485
Carve, Thomas (1590–1672?), vii 453
Carver, Jonathan (1732–1780), xiv. 551
Carving, book on, iii. 19
Cary, Elizabeth L., xiii. 476, 491, 493, 496, 574
Cary, Sir George, vi. 257
Cary, Sir Henry, 1st viscount Falkland (d. 1633), *The Marriage Night*, viii. 130, 418
Cary, Henry Francis (1772–1844), xi. 402; xii. 137, 415; *Dante*, xii. 85, 202; xiii. 174
Cary, Lettice, wife of 2nd viscount Falkland, vii. 151, 155
Cary, Sir Lucius, 2nd viscount Falkland (1610?–1643), vi. 6; vii. 21, 52, 88, 143, 150 ff., 218, 305, 424, 441, 484; viii. 63, 298; *Discourse of Infallibility*, vii. 150, 151
Cary, Sir Robert, *Memoirs*, xii. 16
Caryl, Joseph (1602–1673), vii. 316, 322
Caryll, John (1666?–1736), ix. 70, 73, 82, 84, 85, 443
Casa, G. della, *Il Galateo*, iii. 341
Casa Guidi, Florence, xiii. 70, 73, 79
Casa Magni, xii. 76
Casas, Bartolomé de las, ix. 500
Casaubon, Isaac (1559–1614), iii. 424; iv. 161, 238, 353, 500, 521; vii. 109, 250, 307 ff., 311, 312, 314, 319, 320, 324, 477, 485 ff.; viii. 63; ix. 331; xiv. 109; *De rebus sacris et ecclesiasticis exercitationes XVI ad Baronii annales*, vii. 310, 484
Casaubon, Meric (1599–1671), vii. 109, 322, 477, 486, 487, 488, 510, 517
Commentary on the Hebrew and (Anglo-Saxon language, vii. 319
Epictetus, vii. 319
Marcus Antoninus, vii. 319
Of Credulity and Incredulity, vii. 395, 484, 507
Treatise concerning Enthusiasm, A, vii. 393
Casaubon, Mr, in *Middlemarch*, xiii. 399
Casby, Flora, in *Little Dorrit*, xiii. 331
Casby, Mr, in *Little Dorrit*, xiii. 331
Casca, in *Julius Caesar*, v. 197
Case, John (d. 1600), iv. 507; vi. 398; *Speculum moralium questionum in universam ethicen Aristotelis*, iv. 274; vi. 398
Casere, in *Widsith*, i. 35
Casey, Elizabeth Owens Blackburne (1845?–1894), xiv. 567; *A bunch of Shamrocks*, xiv. 327

Casey, John (1820–1891), xiv. 555
Casimir, vii. 87
Casimir, in Coleridge's *Zapolya*, xi. 414
Casket, The, a Miscellany (1829), xi. 419
Casket letters, vii. 161
Caspian sea, iv. 84
Cassandra, iv. 120
Cassandra, in *Promos and Cassandra*, v. 119
Cassano library, xii. 366
Cassell, John (1817–1865), xiv. 533, 612
Cassels, Walter Richard (1826–1907), xii. 465
Cassilis, Catherine, in Black's *A Daughter of Heth*, xiii. 432
Cassillis, earls of. *See* Kennedy, Gilbert
Cassio, in *Othello*, v. 202
Cassiodorien, in *Richard Coeur de Lion*, i. 307
Cassiodorus, i. 20, 213; ii. 363, 366; xii. 272, 322, 476; xiii. 461
Cassius, in *Julius Caesar*, v. 197; vi. 127; xiii. 221
Cassius Longinus, Gaius, ix. 28
Cassius Severus, iv. 349; vii. 272
Castabala, xiv. 53
Castalio, in Otway's *Orphan*, viii. 183
Castalio, Sebastian, iii. 145
Castamela, in *The Fancies*, vi. 193, 194
Castanheda, Hernan Lopes de, iv. 442
Castelain, Maurice, vi. 5, 9, 10, 362, 370
Castell, Edmund (1606–1685), vii. 490, 491
Castelvetro, Lodovico, vii. 265
Casti, Giambattista, xii. 33, 51, 52, 56; *Il Poema Tartaro*, xii. 55
Castiglione, Balthazar or Baldasarre, iii. 174, 344; iv. 135, 159, 342, v. 132; *Il Cortegiano*, iii. 171, 235, 341, 434, 437, 438, 505, 550; iv. 7, 397, 443; v. 124, 349; ix. 396
Castillo, John (1792–1845), xii. 415
Castle, Egerton, xiv. 503
Castle Howard, viii. 162
Castle inn, in *The Fair Maid Of The West*, vi. 101
Castle of Perseverance, The, v. 52, 391, 392
Castle of Pleasure, The, ii. 327
Castlemaine, countess of. *See* Villiers, Barbara
Castlemaine, earl of. *See* Palmer, Roger
Castlereagh, viscount. *See* Stewart, Robert
Castlewood, lady, in *Esmond*, xiii. 293, 296, 407
Castlewood family, in *The Virginians*, xiii. 298
Castro, Guillen de, vi. 124, 136, 140; viii. 128
Caswall, Edward (1814–1878), xii. 455
'Cataline, Colonel,' x. 393
Catalogi Librorum Manuscriptorum, ix. 356
Catalogue, complete, of modern books, xi. 339
Catalogue of all the Books...since the Dreadful Fire, xi. 339
Catalogue of Books (term catalogue), xi. 339
Catalogue of the most vendible Books, xi. 338
Catalogues, xi. 470
Catalogus Bibliothecae Harleianae, x. 166
Cataneo, Girolamo, iv. 443, 454
Catch, Nehemiah, viii. 122
Catchpole, in Rabelais, viii. 67
Catesby, Monsignore, in Disraeli's *Lothair*, xiii. 350
Catharine II, empress of Russia, v. 308; x. 246, 266, 288; xi. 358, 430; xii. 52, 55
Catharine, St, in *Tyrannick Love*, viii. 22
Catharine of Alexandria, St, v. 7, 37, 38
Catharine of Braganza, queen, ix. 278
Cathay, iv. 66, 71 ff., 76, 86
Cathcart, lord, in Glover's *Boadicea*, xi. 258
Catherine, in Emily Brontë's *Wuthering Heights*, xiii. 411
Catherine, in Thackeray's novel, xiii. 280
Catherine de' Medici, iv. 429
Catherine of Aragon (1485–1536), 1st queen of Henry VIII, iii. 15, 16; v. 201; vi. 332, 333; ix. 197
Catherine of Aragon, queen, in *Henry VIII*, v. 195; vi. 231
Catherine of Aragon, queen, song in praise of, ii. 394
Catherine of Valois, queen of Henry V, iv. 182
Catherine Parr (1512–1548), 6th queen of Henry VIII, iv. 231, 495
Catherlough, Robert Knight, earl of (lord Luxborough), x. 272, 273
Catholic emancipation, xiii. 24
Catholic reaction, the, v. 337
Catholic Standard, The, xii. 463
Catholicon Anglicum, ii. 483; iii. 555
Catiline, in *The Palice of Honour*, ii. 261
Catley, Ann (1745–1789), xi. 450, 453
Catling, Thomas, xiv. 533
Catnach, James (1792–1841), xi. 373, 469; xiv. 226 ff., 540, 542
Cato, ix. 28, 63, 64
Cato, in *Caesar and Pompey*, vi. 35
Cato, Distichs of, i. 119
Cato street conspiracy, xiv. 201, 228
Cats, Vader, *Maechden-Pflicht*, vi. 87
Cattaro, Dalmatia, iii. 262
Cattraeth, i. 249
Cattuna, empress, in Casti's *Il Poema Tartaro*, xii. 55
Catullus, i. 362; iv. 197, 334, 516; vi. 346; vii. 1, 12, 13, 36; xii. 337, 483, 488, 490; xiii. 42, 45, 175; *Attis*, xiii. 449; *Vivamus, mea Lesbia, et amemus*, vii. 2; *Luctus in morte passeris*, vii. 9
Caucasus, the, xii. 65, 70
Caulah, in Ockley's *History of the Saracens*, x. 281
Causidicade, The, x. 28
Caussin, N., vi. 140
Caustic, in Morton's *Way to get Married*, xi. 281
Cavalcanti, Guido, iv. 197; xiii. 118

Cavalier songs and jests, VII. 512
Cavaliers Catechisme and confession of his faith, The, VII. 383
Cavaliers' Catechisme, or the Reformed Protestant catechising the anti-christian Papist, VII. 382
Cavaliers' Diurnall, The, VII. 388
Cavaliers Letanie, The, VII. 383
Cavall, the hound. *See* Cabal
Cavallilly Man, The, VIII. 96
Cave, Edward (1691–1754), X. 162 ff., 175, 465, 466; XI. 323, 355, 467; XII. 428; XIV. 169
Cave, Henry, *Narration of the Fall of Paris Garden*, VI. 393
Cave, R., XII. 428
'Cave of Adullam,' the, XIV. 133
Cave of Envy, in Sandys's *Ovid*, VII. 51
Cave of Harmony, the, in *The Newcomes*, XIII. 296
Cave of Mammon, in *The Faerie Queene*, VI. 335
Cavenagh, F. A., XIV. 525
Cavendish family, VII. 282, 289. *See, also, under* Devonshire and Newcastle
Cavendish, lord Frederick Charles (1836–1882), XIV. 320
Cavendish, George (1500–1561?), III. 198, 325, 334 ff., 528; IV. 428; VII. 514; *Life and Death of Thomas Woolsey*, III. 325, 335; *Metrical Visions*, III. 198
Cavendish, Georgiana, duchess of Devonshire (1757–1806), XI. 456
Cavendish, Gilbert, IV. 524
Cavendish, Henry (1731–1810), XIV. 258, 272, 274, 275, 556, 557
Cavendish, Margaret, duchess of Newcastle (1624?–1674), IV. 193; VII. 229, 452; VIII. 124, 149, 419, 424; *The ccxi Sociable Letters*, VII. 228; *The Life of William Cavendish, duke of Newcastle*, VII. 227; *True Relation of the Birth, Breeding and Life of Margaret, duchess of Newcastle*, VII. 228
Cavendish, Richard (d. 1601), IV. 436
Cavendish, Spencer Compton, 8th duke of Devonshire, marquis of Hartington (1833–1908), XIV. 131, 509
Cavendish, Thomas (1560–1592), III. 358, 359; IV. 78, 92; V. 139
Cavendish, William, 1st duke of Devonshire (1640–1707), VIII. 411
Cavendish, William George Spencer, 6th duke of Devonshire (1790–1858), XII. 368
Cavendish, Sir William, 7th duke of Devonshire (1808–1891), XIV. 270
Cavendish, William, marquis and 1st duke of Newcastle (1592–1676), VI. 6, 197; VII. 226, 227, 229, 285; VIII. 17, 149, 398, 420, 424; *The Humorous Lovers*, VIII. 124; *The Triumphant Widow*, VIII. 124
Cavendish, Sir William (d. 1557), III. 335
Cavendish, William, 1st earl of Devonshire (d. 1626), VII. 282
Cavendish, William, 2nd earl of Devonshire (1591?–1628), VII. 287
Cavendish, William, 3rd earl of Devonshire (1617–1684), VII. 284
Cavour, Camillo, count di, XIII. 73
Caw, G., *Poetical Museum*, IX. 565
Cawarden, Sir Thomas (d. 1559), VI. 257
Cawline, Sir, II. 414
Cawood, John (1514–1572), III. 59; IV. 397, 400
Caxton, William (1421-8–1491), I. 245, 285; II. 73, 77, 97, 160, 161, 198, 209, 228, 245, 264, 310 ff., 316, 332 ff., 421, 429, 483 ff.; III. 19, 67, 289, 290, 308, 339, 439 ff., 443 ff., 459, 460, 526; IV. 343, 353, 427, 428, 523; V. 53; IX. 536; XII. 520; XIV. 491
  Aesop's *Fables*, II. 314, 334
  Art of good living and good dying, II. 324
  Aymon, The History of the Four Sons of, II. 316, 332, 484; IV. 397
  Blanchardyn and Eglantine, The History of, 316
  Bonne meurs, Le livre des, II. 315
  Cato, II. 209, 314
  Charles the Great, The Life of, II. 314, 315
  Chesse, Game and playe of the, II. 309, 312, 313; IV. 300, 510
  Chivalry, The Order of, II. 228, 314
  Chronicle of Brute, II. 313, 334
  Curtesye, Book of, II. 313, 427
  Dictes and Sayings of the Philosophers, II. 313, 427, 485
  Eneydos, II. 316; III. 19, 67; IV. 39
  Fayttes of Arms, The, II. 316
  Godfrey of Bologne, The History of, II. 313
  Golden Legend, The, II. 314; IV. 39
  Good Manners, The Book of, II. 314, 333, 420
  Knight of the Tower, The Book of, II. 314, 333, 420
  Mirror of the World, The, II. 313
  Paris and Vienne, The History of, II. 314, 315, 319, 332
  Recuyell of the Histories of Troy, II. 230, 311 ff.; III. 289; IV. 397
  Reynard the Fox, II. 245, 313, 314, 332
  Royal Book, The, II. 315
  Trevisa's Higden's *Polychronicon*, Caxton's revision of, II. 313
  Vitae Sanctorum Patrum, II. 323
Caxton society, XII. 355
Cayet, Pierre Victor Palma, VI. 148, 149
Cayley, Arthur (1821–1895), XIV. 262, 264, 556
Cayley, Charles Bagot, XIII. 246, 247
Cayley, George John (1826–1878), XIV. 551
Cazamian, L., XIII. 470, 545, 546, 548, 551; *Le Roman Social en Angleterre*, XIII. 344, 348
Ceadda (Chad), IV. 421. *See, also*, Chad
Cearbhall (d. 888), Irish king, I. 287
Cebes, X. 468
Cebes his Table, VII. 489
Cecil, Edward, *Aemilia*, VI. 321
Cecil, in Kelly's *False Delicacy*, X. 91; XI. 263

Cecil, Richard (1748–1810), XII. 471
Cecil, Sir Robert, 1st earl of Salisbury (1563?–1612), IV. 82, 83, 94, 225; V. 345; VII. 331. 435, 438, 440; X. 501
Cecil, William, lord Burghley (1520–1598), III. 185, 241, 242, 319, 326, 380, 419, 421; IV. 1, 8, 10, 225, 275, 277 ff., 281, 300 ff., 307, 308, 312, 382, 386, 401, 405, 410, 510; V. 64, 89, 90, 341, 343, 345, 362; VI. 47, 305, 381, 382, 384; VII. 191, 325, 328, 331; VIII. 8; X. 500; XIV. 86; *Precepts*, IV. 343, 344, 523
Cecilia, St, I. 74
Cecilia, St, The Life of, II. 503
Cecilia de Chaumpaigne, II. 159
Cecils, the, IV. 278, 279; VI. 6
Cedd, St (d. 664), I. 82
Ceix, in *Confessio Amantis*, II. 151
Celadon, in Dryden's *Secret Love*, VIII. 20
Celadon, in Thomson's *Seasons*, X. 103
Celand, in *Britannia's Pastorals*, IV. 157
Celesia, Dorothea (Mallet, 1738–1790), XI. 263; *Almida*, X. 86, 439; XI. 456
Celestial Hierarchy, The, III. 6, 214
Celestina, in *Calisto and Melebea*, V. 99, 100
Celestina, in *The Lady of Pleasure*, VI. 202
Celestine, pope, II. 148
Celia, in *As You Like It*, I. 298
Celia, in *The Humorous Lieutenant*, VI. 123
Celia (Carew's), VII. 17, 20
Celia (Waller's), VII. 55
Celimène, in *The Spectator*, IX. 57
Cellier, François A., XIII. 519
Celling. *See* Tilly, William
Cellini, Benvenuto, *Memoirs*, XIV. 108
Celsus, XII. 521
Celtic ancestry, XIII. 122, 440
Celtic influence on English literature, I 274 ff.
Celtic language and literature, XII. 327, 343, 344, 361, 362; XIII. 100, 101, 196; XIV. 303, 307. 434, 457
Celtic legend, XIII. 36, 42
Celtic minstrels, V. 27
Celtic mysticism, VII. 15, 42
Celtic scholars, XIV. 307
Celtic society, XII. 361
Celtic tales, II. 407
Celticism, X. 230, 296
Celts, XIV. 68, 69
Cenci, Beatrice, in Shelley's *The Cenci*, XII. 67 ff., 113
Cenci, count, in Shelley's *The Cenci*, XII. 68
Cenci, Francesco, VI. 159
Cenci family, the, VI. 153
Cenci palace, XII. 70
Cenis, Mont, XII. 496
'Censor of Great Britain,' IX. 41
Censure of the Rota on Mr Dryden's Conquest of Granada, The, VIII. 4
Centlivre, Susannah (1667?–1723), VIII. 132, 168, 176, 426; X. 71 ff., 427; XI. 322
Artifice, The, X. 72
Bold Stroke for a Wife, X. 72
Centlivre, Susannah
Busy-Body, The, X. 72
Marplot in Lisbon, X. 72
Perjur'd Husband, The, X. 72
Perplexed Lover, The, VIII. 131
Wonder, The, X. 72
Ceolfrid, saint (642–716), I. 55, 82
Ceolwulf, saint (d. 764), king of Northumbria, I. 82
Cephalonia, island of, XII. 38
Cephalus, in *Confessio Amantis*, II. 152
'Cerbera' (Mrs Schwellenberg), X. 260
Cerberon, in Drayton's *Eglogs*, IV. 173 176
Cerberus, in *Hudibras*, VIII. 73
Cerdic, I. 236
Cerdogni, Camillo, VII. 100
Cerdon, the cobbler, in *Hudibras*, VIII. 68, 69
Ceres, VII. 370
Ceres, in *Lingua*, VI. 315
Ceriol, Federico Furió, IV. 443
Cerne, abbey of, in Dorsetshire, and *Book of*, I. 86, 116, 120, 125, 150, 434
Cervantes-Saavedra, Miguel de, VI. 132, 135, 136, 138, 140, 154; VIII. 67, 425; X. 26, 44, 50 ff., 414; XII. 168
Curioso Impertinente, VI. 133, 137, 223, 236
Don Quixote, IV. 360, 395, 443; VI. 133, 137, 223, 236; VIII. 65, 68, 70, 126 ff., 189, 191; IX. 268, 269, 272, 275, 278, 500 ff., 529; X. 25, 40, 51, 52, 417; XI. 280, *also see* Add.; XIII. 305; XIV. 249, 251
El Viejo celoso, VIII. 129
La Fuerza de la Sangre, VIII. 129
La Gitanilla, VIII. 129
Los Baños de Argel, VIII. 129
Novelas Exemplares, IV. 9; VI. 123, 139, 140; VIII. 128, 129
Persiles y Sigismunda, VI. 123, 130, 138; VIII. 128
Voyage to Parnassus, VII. 274
Cesario, in *The Faire Maide of the Innc*, VI. 140
'Cesario,' Della Cruscan poet, XI. 177
Cesarotti, X. 488
Cespedes, Gonzalo de, VIII. 128, 129; *Gerardo*, VI. 123, 139, 183
Cestre, C., XI. 417
Ceylon, II. 80
Chabot, Madame, X. 248
Chad, St (d. 672), I. 82; IV. 421
Chad, St, in *The Golden Legend*, II. 335
Chadderton, William (1540?–1608), XII. 493
Chaderton, Laurence (1536?–1640), VII. 317, 340
Chadwick, Esther E., XIII. 557
Chadwick, Hector Munro, I. 419, 425
Chaeronea, IV. 10
Chaffanbrass, Trollope's, XIII. 422
Chagford, VII. 86
Chalcedon, XII. 262
Chalcondylas, Demetrius, III. 5, 6
Chaldea, XII. 477
Chaldee language, IX. 393

Chaldee learning, vii. 318, 319; viii. 364
'Chaldee ms., the,' xii. 156, 157, 160, 163
Chaldee Targums, vii. 319
Chalfont St Giles, Bucks., vii. 107, 120
Chaliz, vii. 173
Chalk farm, xii. 161
Chalkhill, John (*fl.* 1600), vii. 77 ff., 81, 113, 252; viii. 227; xiii. 237; *Thealma and Clearchus*, ii. 218; vii. 76, 78, 250, 412
'Challenger,' H.M.S., xiv. 297
Challoner, Luke (*fl.* 1603), iv. 433
Challoner, Richard (1691–1781), iv. 49; x. Add.
Chalmers, Alexander (1759–1834), vi. 1; ix. 187, 190, 480; x. 138, 153, 154, 172, 452, 462, 476, 478; xi. 467; xiii. 224
Chalmers, George (1742–1825), ix. 562; x. 459, 463; xi. 395, 470; xii. 508
Caledonia, xii. 350
'Political Annals of the Colonies,' xii. 350
'Treaties,' xii. 350
Chalmers, James (1841–1901), xiv. 551
Chalmers, J. A., xiv. Add. 7
Chalmers, Thomas (1780–1847), xii. 472; xiv. 119, 470
Chalmers, William, xiv. 517
Chalmers's *Poets*, ii. 199
Chalon-sur-Saône, i. 34
Chaloner, Sir Thomas (1521–1565), iv. 443; *De Re Publica Anglorum instaurranda*, iv. 261
Chaloner, Sir Thomas (1561–1615), iv. 84
Cham, the Great, ii. 79, 86
Chamber, John (1546–1604), iv. 535; vii. 394; *A Confutation of Astrological Demonology*, vii. 377; *A Treatise against Judicial Astrologie*, vii. 376, 508
Chambéri, ix. 245
Chamberlain or Chamberlayne, Edward (1616–1703), vii. 514
Chamberlain, John (1553–1627), vi. 291, 324; vii. 193, 343, 345, 437
Chamberlain, Joseph, xiv. 134, 186
Chamberlain, Robert, xiii. 244
Chamberlaine, Frances. *See* Sheridan, Frances
Chamberlain's company, the lord, v. 309; vi. 3, 4, 40, 182, 245, 247, 250, 253, 255, 256, 258, 274, 275, 312
Chamberlayne, Dr, ix. 464
Chamberlayne, Edward (1616–1703), *Angliae Notitia*, ix. 352, 532
Chamberlayne, John (1666–1723), *Magnae Britanniae Notitia*, ix. 353, 532
Chamberlayne, William (1619–1689), vii. 73, 81, 94, 113, 412; viii. 227, 435; xiii. 237
England's Jubile, vii. 74; viii. 229
Love's Victory, vii. 74
Pharonnidia, vii. 49, 74, 76 ff., 80; viii. 229; xiii. 238, 244
Wits led by the Nose, vii. 74
Chamberlen, P., *The Poore Man's Advocate*, iv. 510
Chambers, Edmund Kerchever, vi. 267; *Mediaeval Stage, The*, ii. 380
Chambers, Raymond Wilson, i. Add.
Chambers, Robert (1802–1871), ix. 566; xi. 437, 440, 442; xii. 378, 425, 465; xiii. 500; xiv. 159, 517, 533, 559, 612; *Vestiges of Creation*, xiv. 298
Chambers, Sir William, x. 199
Chambers, William (1800–1883), xii. 425; xiv. 159, 533, 612
Chambers's Cyclopaedia of English Literature, i. ix; xiv. 145, 527, 528, 574
Chambers's Journal, xii. 425; xiv 159, 326
Chambray, Roland Fréart, Sieur de, viii. 449
Chamfort, Nicolas, xi. 175
Chamier, Anthony (1725–1780), x. 405
Chamier, Frederick (1796–1870), xii. 251, 448; xiv. 490
Chamisso de Boncourt, L. C. A. von, xiii. 192
Chamont, in Otway's *Orphan*, viii. 184
Champfleury (*pseud.*), xiv. 540
Champion, The, x. 23, 24, 27, 417; xii. 171, 434
Champneys, Arthur Charles, xiv. 598
Champneys, Basil, xiii. 507, 508
Chance, J. F., x. 295
Chancellor, Richard (d. 1556), iv. 68, 71, 72, 84, 88
Chancery, court of, xi. 315
Chandler, Edward (1668?–1750), viii. 282, 453
Chandler, Frank Wadleigh, iv. 530; xiii. 513; xiv. 540; *The Literature of Roguery*, xiii. 437
Chandler, Henry William (1828–1889), xii. 520
Chandler, Richard (1738–1810), xii. 496; *Antiquities of Ionia*, xii. 338
Chandler, Samuel (1693–1766), ix. 476, 570; x. 386, 499, 521; *Case of Subscription*, x. 374; *History of Persecution*, x. 374
Chandler, or Chaundler, T. (1418?–1490), vii. 326
Chandos, duke of. *See* Brydges, James
Chandos, lord. *See* Brydges, Grey
Chandra Sen, Keshab, xiv. 341
Channel islands, iv. 190; xiv. 434
Channing, William Ellery, xii. 378
Chansons de geste, i. 279, 291, 447; v. 3, *and see* 34
Chanteloup, ix. 226
Chantrey, Sir Francis Legatt (1781–1842), xi. 242; xii. 323
Chantries act (1547), iii. 418; vii. 326
Chapbook editions of children's books, xi. 477
Chapbooks, xi. 475, 476
Chapel Royal, the, vi. 279. *See, also, under* Children of the Chapel Royal
Chapel Royal, The Old Cheque Book of the, vi. 280, 282
Chapelain, Jean, vii. 268; viii. 374; x. 220; *La Pucelle*, vii. 268

Chapman, George (1559?–1634), III. 191, 199, 271, 292, 305, 449, 452, 526, 550; IV. 22, 266, 393 ff.; V. 148, 224, 311, 312, 344, 371, 422; VI. 2, 16, 19, 28–57 (main entry), 147, 202, 225, 250, 329, 353 ff., 420 ff., 451, 488, *also see* Add.; VII. 51, 465; IX. 75; XII. 191; XIII. 448, 495, *also see* Add. 2
Achilles Shield, VI. 37
Al Fooles, VI. 15, 32, 290
Alphonsus Emperour of Germany, VI. 35
Amorous Zodiac, The, VI. 30, 31
Andromache Literata, VI. 31
Batrachomyomachia, VI. 37
Blinde begger of Alexandria, The, VI. 15, 31
Byron, The Conspiracie, And Tragedie of Charles Duke of, VI. 30, 33 ff., 175, 258
Caesar, trans. of, IV. 435
Caesar and Pompey, VI. 35, 172
Chabot, Admirall of France, VI. 35, 207
Comodey of Umers, The, VI. 32
Coronet for his Mistress Philosophy, A, VI. 31
De Guiana Carmen, IV. 88
Eastward Hoe, III. 191; V. 255; VI. 4, 20, 30, 32, 43, 47, 48, 171, 173, 258, 355; VII. 433
Euthymiae Raptus, VI. 29
Fatal Love, a French tragedy, VI. 36
Gentleman Usher, The, VI. 32, 290
Gyles Goosecappe, Sir, VI. 35, 290, 459
Hesiod's *Works and Days*, Chapman's trans. of, IV. 436; VI. 37
Homer, III. 305; IV. 2, 19, 21, 394, 437, 516, 526; VI. 29, 30, 32, 37; XI. 90; XII. 79, 190
Homeric *Epigrams*, VI. 37
Homeric *Hymns*, VI. 37
Humerous Dayes Myrth, An, V. 331; VI. 15, 31
Marlowe's *Hero and Leander*, Chapman's continuation of, VI. 31
Masque...of the Middle Temple and Lyncolnes Inn, VI. 36, 353
May-Day, III. 199; V. 34; VI. 32, 290
Monsieur D'Olive, VI. 32
Musaeus, translation of, VI. 30
Ovid's Banquet of Sence, IV. 19, 439; VI. 31
Revenge for Honour, VI. 35
Revenge of Bussy D'Ambois, The, VI. 33 ff., 178, 223
Shadow of Night, The, VI. 31
Tears of Peace, The, VI. 31
Widdowes Teares, The, VI 32
World runs on Wheels, The (*Al Fooles*), VI. 32
Yorkshire Gentlewoman and her Son, The, VI. 36
See, also, under Marston and Shirley
Chapman, George (1723–1806), XIV. 605
Chapman, John (1822–1894), XII. 430; XIII. 383, 385
Chapman, Maria Weston, XIII. 343, 554
Chapman and Hall, publishers, XIII. 440
Chapone, Mrs Hester, born Mulso (1727–1801), X. 171, 270; XI. 356, 473; XIV. 599; *Letters*, XI. 365, 379
Chappell, Jennie, XIV. 517
Chappell, William (1582–1649), VII. 97, 98
Chappell, William, X. 233
Chappell, W., *Popular Music of the Olden Time*, IX. 361 ff., 568
Chapter books, XI. 325
Character of a Coffee-house, The, VII. 389
Character of Italy, The, VII. 392
Character of Spain, The, VII. 392
Character of Warre, The, VII. 386
Character sketches, VII. 517
Character writers, IV. 521, 522
Charissa, in *The Faerie Queene*, VI. 335
Chariton, *Chereas and Callirrhoe*, III. 351
Charity, in *Confessio Amantis*, II. 148
Charity, in *The Example of Virtue*, II. 227, 228
Charity, in *The Passetyme of Pleasure*, II. 228
Charity, the tree of, in *Piers the Plowman*, II. 24, 27
Charity commission, XIV. 422, 433
Charity schools, IX. 570, 571
Charivari, XIV. 235, 326
Charlemagne in romance, I. 169, 281, 283, 284, 302, 342, 467
Charlemont, in *The Atheist's Tragedie*, VI. 168
Charles I, IV. 92, 107, 195, 238 ff., 265, 301, 302, 312, 366, 381, 411, 426; V. 222, 348, 360; VI. 6, 7, 83, 147 ff., 201, 203, 208, 232, 237, 238, 240, 243, 245, 246, 271, 278, 321, 324 ff., 336, 359, 360, 363, 403; VII. 1, 6, 16, 17, 24, 29, 35, 39, 50, 52 ff., 59, 61, 63, 79, 80, 106, 140, 142, 144, 146 ff., 154, 159, 161 ff., 165, 179, 188, 191, 192, 194, 195, 198, 205, 212, 214, 215, 218, 219, 221 ff., 229, 254, 280, 300, 306, 335, 340, 352, 353, 361, 382, 383, 392, 433, 435, 436, 438 ff., 447, 449, 450, 455; VIII. 2, 67, 101, 119, 130, 134, 245, 246, 267, 277, 294, 295, 297, 312, 318, 319, 323, 358, 361, 371, 383, *also see* Add.; IX. 27, 201, 222, 233, 235, 240, 250, 307, 309, 403; X. 279, 283, 286, 287, 290, 295, 318, 355, 498 ff.; XI. 280, 311; XII. 253, 260, 521; XIV. 93, 396
Charles I, in Shelley's drama, XII. 75
Charles I, Just Defence of the Royal Martyr King, VII. 225
Charles I, pamphlets on, VII. 513
Charles II, I. 282; IV. 204; V. 237, 375; VI. 250, 271; VII. 61, 62, 150, 161, 179, 180, 183, 188, 196, 197, 206, 213 ff., 219, 234, 250, 254, 285, 314, 360, 365, 434, 436, 441, 455; VIII. 6, 7, 9, 18, 20, 21, 30, 34, 35, 37, 39, 43 ff., 61, 62, 64, 77, 80, 82, 88, 92 ff., 97 ff., 118, 122, 123, 131, 132, 155, 158, 174, 185, 198, 199, 206, 207, 213, 247, 248, 254, 256, 261, 262, 264 ff., 269, 272, 291, 293, 295, 297, 302, 304, 358, 370, 372, 382,

Charles II
387, 481, 482; IX. 2, 194, 199, 201, 203, 205, 206, 208, 213, 225, 233, 234, 239, 307, 362, 363; X. 287, 290, 351, 373; XIII. 434
Charles II, king of Spain, IX. 8, 133; XIV. 212
Charles V, emperor, X. 504
Charles V, king of Spain, II. 83, 338, 340; III. 32, 160
Charles VIII, king, in *Romola*, XIII. 394
Charles VIII, king of France, X. 303
Charles IX, king of France, VIII. 87
Charles XII, king of Sweden, IX. 19; X. 169
Charles, archduke of Austria, IX. 134
Charles Edward, prince (the Young Pretender), IX. 371, 373, 563 ff.; XII. 26; XIV. 360
Charles, Edwin, XIII. 537
Charles, Émile, I. 208 ff.
Charles Frederick, king of Prussia, X. 463
Charles Lewis (Karl Ludwig), elector Palatine, V. 284; VII. 231
Charles the Bald, I. 88, 89; IV. 270
Charles the Bold, II. 307
Charles the Great (Charlemagne), I. 5, 84, 88 ff.; II. 112, 181, 339, 416; III. 211, 245, 437; IV. 24, 269; V. 40; X. 314; XII. 322, 476
For Romances, *see under* Charlemagne *and* Carolingian
Charles the Great, in *Rauf Coilȝear*, II. 125, 126
Charles the Great, Life of, II. 314, 315, 485
Charles's men, prince, VI. 232
Charleton, Walter (1619–1707), VIII. 362, 395, 476; *Chorea Gigantum*, IX. 354, 532
Charlett, Arthur (1655–1722), IX. 57, 470
Charley, in Mrs Gaskell's *Mary Barton*, XIII. 376
Charlie is my Darling, IX. 376
Charlotte, in Cumberland's *West Indian*, XI. 264
Charlotte, in Goethe's *Werther*, X. 227
Charlotte, in *Oliver Twist*, XIII. 317
Charlotte, in Thackeray's *Adventures of Philip*, XIII. 299
Charlotte, Augusta, princess (1796–1817), XI. 166; XII. 401; XIII. 276; XIV. 227
Charlotte, Sophia (1744–1818), queen of George III, X. 63, 65, 260
'Charlotte Elizabeth.' *See* Tonna, Charlotte Elizabeth
Charlton, Sir Job (1614–1697), IX. 392
Charlton, Stephen, VII. 438
Charlton, Wilts., VIII. 9
Charlwood, John (d. 1592), IV. 394
Charm for Barren Land, I. 64
Charmer, The, IX. 371, 566
Charms, Old English, I. 40, 422, 423
Charnock, Richard, prior, III. 3, 4, 11, 49
Charolais, in *The Fatall Dowry*, VI. 158
Charon, VII. 381
Charon, in *Dialogues of the Dead*, XI. 351
Charon, in *Friar Rush*, VI. 53
Chart, near Leeds in Kent, I. 353
Charter, Elizabeth (*fl.* 1815–1825), XI. 419
Charter Rolls, the, XII. 516
Charterhouse, XII 288, 329, 332; XIII. 276; XIV. 404, 422
Charteris, Francis (1675–1732), IX. 469, 470
Charteris, Henry (d. 1599), III. 123; IV. 413
Chartier, Alain, II. 164, 216, 485; III. 489, 502; IV. 443; VIII 59; *Le Quadrilogue Invectif*, III. 152, 153
Chartley, in *The Wise woman of Hogsdon*, VI. 99
Chartres, school of, I. 183 ff., 216
Chase, John Centlivres, XIV. Add. 6, 11
Chase side, Enfield, XII. 201
Chasles, Ph., XII. 524
Chastitie, in *Ane Pleasant Satyre*, III. 125, 126
Chastity, tower of, in *The Passetyme of Pleasure*, II. 231
Chateaubriand, François René, vicomte de, IV. 43; V. 301; XII. 396, 524; XIV. 107; *Génie du Christianisme*, XI. 108; XII. 254
Chatham, VIII. 249, 381
Chatham, earl of. *See* Pitt, William
Chatteris, Cambridgeshire, XIII. 216
Chatteris, in Thackeray's *Pendennis*, XIII. 276
Chatterji, Bankim Chandra, XIV. 341
Chatterton, Thomas (1752–1770), X. 234 ff. (main entry), 239, 485, 486, 525, *also see* Add.; XI. 181, 245, 250, 390, 422; XII. 81, 86; XIII. 225, 226; XIV. 504
Bristowe Tragedie, X. 234
Consuliad, X. 399
Elinoure and Juga, X. 235, 238
Excelente Balade of Charitie, X. 235
Revenge, The, X. 237
Ryse of Peyncteyning in Englande, X. 237
Saxon Atchievements, X. 237
Songe to Ælla, X. 235
Unknown Knight, The, X. 236
Works, XII. 146
See, also, Rowley, Thomas, and the Rowley Poems
Chattuarii, the, I. 26
Chaucer, Agnes, wife of John Chaucer, II. 156
Chaucer, Elizabeth, II. 157
Chaucer, Geoffrey (1340?–1400), I. 16, 99, 155, 170, 177, 193, 213, 270, 275 ff., 280, 282, 283, 288, 289, 292, 298, 299, 309, 316, 319, 332, 335, 348 ff., 355, 366, 367, 380, 382, 386 ff., 394 ff.; II. 18, 39, 41, 72, 92 ff., 103, 110, 134, 135, 142, 143, 145, 146, 150 ff., 156–196 (main entry), 197, 198, 200, 204, 205, 207, 208, 210, 211, 213 ff., 222, 225, 227 ff., 236, 239, 240, 243 ff., 247, 248, 250, 252 ff., 257, 258, 261, 263 ff., 272, 295, 308, 314, 317, 323, 332, 334, 337, 340, 351, 352, 355, 364, 391, 403, 412, 416, 422, 429, 455 ff., 488; III. 24, 68, 70, 73, 79, 98, 108, 116, 117, 119, 120, 130, 138, 149, 168, 169, 173, 174, 177, 178, 188, 192, 200, 212, 227, 239, 244,

Chauncer, Geoffrey
246, 273 ff., 280 ff., 286, 287, 289, 290 ff., 296 ff., 301, 303, 308, 324, 325, 327, 435, 439, 441 ff., 448, 449, 555; IV. 22, 194, 207, 246, 248, 421, 432; V. 22, 96, 98, 103, 196, 220, 221, 226, 227, 234, 327; VI. 52, 113, 137, 299, 311; VII. 75, 132, 135, 156, 173, 235; VIII. 20, 48, 51, 52, 55, 222, 227, 228, 230, 232, 233, 433; IX. 68, 151, 158, 362, 369, 446; X. 183, 218, 219, 221, 223, 227, 236, 239, 241, 491; XI. 161, 251, 255, 368, 394, 431; XII. 54, 98, 120, 168, 177, 344, 354, 443; XIII. 104, 119, 128, 211, 238, 242, 423

Chaucer, Geoffrey, works by, or attributed to:
A.B.C., II. 161, 162, 164, 167, 170
Anelida and Arcite, II. 161, 162, 164, 167, 171, 217, 312; III. 116
Assembly of Fowls, The. See *Parliament*
Assembly of Ladies, The, II. 162, 164, 215, 217, 223
Astrolabe, II. 157, 161, 162, 185
Ballade in Commendation of our Lady, A, II. 162
Boethius, II. 160 ff., 185, 186, 317; IV. 422
Bukton, The Envoy to, II. 162, 187
Canon's Yeoman's Tale, The, II. 211
Canterbury Tales, I. 16, 193, 213, 286, 298, 352; II. 135, 143, 145, 160 ff., 167, 168, 174, 177, 180, 185, 187, 194, 215, 216, 218, 313, 314, 320, 323; III 235, 241, 285, 290, 298; IV. 330; XI. 200
Circumstance, II. 162
Clerk's Tale, The, II. 183, 188, 192, 350, 413; V. 117
Complaint of Mars, The, II. 161, 162, 164, 167, 170
Complaint of Venus, The, II. 161, 162, 164, 187
Complaint to his Lady, The, II. 167, 170
Complaint unto Pity, The, II. 161, 164, 167, 170
Cook's Tale, The, II. 181
Death of Pity, The, II. 162
Dream, The. See *Duchess, The book of*
Duchess, The book of the [Death of Blanche], II. 160 ff., 164, 167, 168, 170; XIII. 124
Empty Purse, Complaint of Chaucer to his, II. 161, 162, 187
Flower of Courtesy, The, II. 162
Former Age, The, II. 161, 186
Fortune, II. 161, 162, 186
Franklin's Tale, The, II. 184
Gentilesse, II. 161, 186
Good Counsel, Ballad of. See *Truth*
Goodly Ballade of Chaucer, A, II. 162
House of Fame, I. 170; II. 160 ff., 167, 174, 175, 187, 188, 261, 314, 412; III. 70, 117; XIII. 124
Knight's Tale, The, II. 168, 171, 174, 176, 178, 180, 188, 191, 193, 243; V. 256; VI. 139, 299, 300; X. 230; XIII. 122, 123

Chaucer, Geoffrey, works by, or attributed to:
Lack of Steadfastness, II. 161, 162, 186
Legend of Good Women, The, II. 145, 150, 160 ff., 164, 167 ff., 174, 175, 217, 219; (prologue), III. 71
Lion, The book of the, II. 160, 161
Man of Law's Prologue and *Tale, The*, I. 181, 292; II. 161, 181
Man of Law's Tale, IX. 185
Manciple's Tale, The, II. 184
Melibeus, The tale of, II. 180, 182, 185; III. 178
Merchant's Prologue and *Tale, The*, II. 184, 215
Merciles Beaute, II. 187
Miller's Tale, The, II. 216; V. 19
Monk's Tale, The, II. 216; III. 192
Nun's Priest's Tale, The, I. 193, 290; II. 183, 187; III. 241
Palamon and Arcite, II. 161
Pardoner's Tale, The, II. 183, 215
Parliament of Fowls, The, II. 160 ff., 164, 167, 170, 172, 312; III. 98; IV. 184
Parson's Prologue and *Tale, The*, I. 355; II. 160, 185, 194, 216
Phyllis and Demophoon (*Legend of Good Women*), II. 217
Physician's Tale of Virginia, II. 182, 183
Praise of Women, A, II. 162
Prioress's Tale, The, II. 169, 180 ff., 190 ff., 359
Prologue, The, II. 168, 178 ff., 182, 185, 191, 193; III. 441
Reeve's Tale, The, II. 216
Romaunt of the Rose, II. 161, 162, 164 167 ff., 170, 240, 244
Rosemounde ballade, The, II. 161, 186
St Cecily. See *Second Nun's Tale, The*
Sapience, II. 162
Scogan, The Envoy to, II. 187
Second Nun's Tale, The, II. 174, 178 184; IV. 38
Shipman's Tale, The, II. 181
Sir Thopas, I. 277, 281, 282, 289, 291, 292, 295, 299, 319, 365 ff.; II. 167, 180, 181, 188, 189, 195, 196; III. 289; IV. 173; V. 3; X. 154; XI. 218
Squire's Tale, The, I. 3, 9; II. 174; III. 130
Temple of Brass, II. 312
Troilus and Criseyde, I. 332; II. 135, 145, 160 ff., 167, 168, 170 ff., 176, 185, 188, 193, 230, 308, 314, 391, 474; VII. 78, 314, 487; XIII. 124
Truth, II. 161, 162, 186
Wife of Bath's Prologue and *Tale, The*, I. 177, 295; II. 169, 179, 180, 183, 192, 218, 254, 413; III. 88, 486; IV. 340; VI. 138
Yeoman's Tale, The, I. 298

Chaucer, John (d. 1366), II. 156, 159
Chaucer, Philippa, wife of Geoffrey Chaucer, II. 157
Chaucer, Robert le, II. 156
Chaucer, Thomas (1367?–1434), II. 157
Chaucer society, II. 166, 216; XII. 355, 504

Chaucer's 'little Lewis,' II. 157, 185
Chaucerian school, I. 321, 334
Chauceriana, II. 215 ff., 469, 470
Chaucerians, the English, II. 197 ff., 467 ff.
Chaucerians, the Scottish, II. 239 ff., 471 ff.
Chauncy, Sir Henry (1632–1719), *Antiquities of Hertfordshire*, IX. 353, 532
Chauncy, Isaac (1632–1712), X. 384; *Neo-Nomianism Unmasked*, X. 377
Chaundler, Thomas (1418?–1490), dean of Hereford, III. 5
Chaunteclere, in *Phyllyp Sparowe*, III. 71
Chaworth, Mary Ann, XII. 31, 51
Chawton, Hampshire, XII. 236
Cheadle, Walter Butler, XIV. 553
Cheats of London, The, IX. 264
Cheddar Hole, III. 322
Chedreux, VIII. 375
Cheem, Aliph, *pseud.* *See* Yeldham, Walter
Cheerybles, the, in *Nicholas Nickleby*, XIII. 318
Cheke, Sir Hatton, VII. 232
Cheke, Henry (1548?–1586?), IV. 441
Cheke, Sir John (1514–1557), III. 290, 291, 293, 348, 418, 419, 424, 425, 430 ff., 446 ff., 550, 555; IX. 496
Cheldrich, in *The Misfortunes of Arthur*, V. 78
Chelmsford school, VII. 330
Chelsea, VIII. 269; XIII. 107
Chelsum, James (1740?–1801), *Remarks on... Mr Gibbon's History*, X. 307, 507
Cheltenham, X. 277; XIII. 46, 287; XIV. 225, 414
Chelwood, Knightly (1650–1720), VIII. 446
Chenery, Thomas (1826–1884), XIV. 182, 183
Chenevix, Richard (1698–1779), bishop of Waterford, X. 256, 257
Cheney, Sir Thomas, III. 167
Chénier, Marie-Joseph, V. 294
Chepman, Walter (1473?–1538?). *See* Chepman and Myllar
Chepman and Myllar, II. 92, 123, 284, 478, 479; IV. 412; IX. 359
Cherbuliez, Victor, XIII. 470
Cherokee, X. 57
Cherry, in Farquhar's *Beaux' Stratagem*, VIII. 172
Cherry, Andrew (1762–1812), XIV. 567
Cherry, Francis (1665?–1713), X. 356
Cherry, J. L., *Life of John Clare*, XII. 132, 415
Chertsey, Andrew (*fl.* 1508–1532), II. 324, 329
Craft to live well and to die well, II. 324
The Flower of commandments of God, II. 324
The Lucydarye, II. 324
The Ordinary of Christian Men, II. 324
The Treatise of the Passion of Christ, II. 324
Chertsey, Cowley at, VII. 63; VIII. 378
Chertsey abbey, Denham on, VII. 59
Cherwell, vale of the, X. 112
Cheshire, III. 319; VII. 214, 232, 341; IX. 166, 536; XI. 469; XII. 355, 509, 511, 512, 514; XIII. 372, 377
Cheshire (and Lancashire) Record society, XII. 506
Chesney, Sir George Tomkyns (1830–1895), XIV. 575; *Battle of Dorking, The*, XIV. 339; *Dilemma, The*, XIV. 339
Chess, in *Reason and Sensuality*, II. 202
Chess, The Book of the, XII. 515
Chesse, A Game at (1624), VII. 433
Chesse, The Game of (1643), VII. 385
Chessington hall, X. 260
Chester, II. 71, 210; III. 429; IV. 190, 408; VII. 319; VIII. 297, 313, 369; IX. 167; X. 309; XI. 12, 469; XII. 329, 509; XIII. 103, 369; XIV. 74
Chester, Charles, VI. 40
Chester, St Werburgh's, II. 71, 210
Chester, Sir John, in *Barnaby Rudge*, X. 255; XIII. 321, 333
Chester, Philippa, in Reade's *The Wandering Heir*, XIII. 426
Chester, Robert (1566?–1640?), *Loves Martyr*, IV. 473; V. 224; VI. 423
Chester Plays (or Mysteries), II. 426; III. 91; V. 12 ff., 17, 19, 20, 46 ff., 124, 389
Chester Rolls, XII. 355
Chesterfield, earl of. *See* Stanhope, Philip Dormer, and Stanhope, Philip
Chesterfield free school, IX. 393
Chesterton, near Harbury, X. 112
Chesterton, Gilbert Keith, XII. 476, 484, 532, 539, 543
Chesterton, George Luval, XIV. 551
Chestre, Thomas (*fl.* 1430), *Launfal Miles*, I. 295
Chetham, Humphrey (1580–1653), IV. 432, 433
Chetham society, IX. 322; XII. 355
Chettam, Sir James, in *Middlemarch*, XIII. 399
Chettle, Henry (d. 1607?), III. 114, 367, 536; IV. 514; V. 117, 138, 166, 171, 219, 221, 310 ff., 319, 321 ff., 330 ff., 361, 473, 475; VI. 12, 13, 51, 54, 97, 218, 424, 459; VII. 395
Black Bateman of the North, VI. 96
Englandes Mourning Garment, IV. 184, 351; V. 328
Hoffman, The Tragedy of, V. 310, 323, 324, 326, 327; VI. 178, 217
Italian Tragedy, The, VI. 96
Kind Hart's Dream, III. 545; IV. 363, 530; V. 323; VI. 397, 492
Matilda's Tragedy, V. 327
Patient Grissill, V. 117, 323
Piers Plainnes seaven yeres Prentiship, III. 367
Shore, VI. 90
See, also, under Day
Chettle and Dekker, *Kinge Sebastiane of Portingalle*, VIII. 126
Chetwood, William Rufus (d. 1766) VIII. 190; X. 442; XI. 317, 448
Chevalerie, L'Ordre de, II. 284

Chevalier de Coucy, I. 300
Chevallier (of Geneva), IV. 429
Chevelere Assigne (Swan-Knight), I. 291, 467
Cheveril, in Holcroft's *Deserted Daughter*, XI. 277
Cheviot, II. 398, 408, 415
Chevrillon, André, XII. 427
Chevy Chase, II. 395, 415; III. 280, 300; VIII. 96; IX. 59, 370; X. 219, 220, 226, 484
Chew, Samuel C., XIII. 514
Cheyne, Elspeth, in Scott's *Antiquary*, XIII. 234
Cheyne, George (1671–1743), IX. 307, 325, 513, 519
Cheyne, Thomas Kelly (1841–1915), XII. 465, *also see* Add. 4
Cheynell, Francis (1608–1665), VII. 495; X. 175, 466
Chicheley, or Chichele, Henry (1362?–1443), II. 358; VII. 326
Chichester, II. 288; IV. 422; VII. 377, 459; VIII. 301; IX. 530; XI. 403, 427; XII. 86, 274, 327; XIV. 112
Chicksands, VIII. 15
Chiffinch, William (1602?–1688), IX. 240
Child, Francis James, X. 233; *Ballads*, I. 295; II. 395, 399 ff., 408, 409, 413 ff.
Child, Sir Josiah (1630–1699), VIII. 342, 473
Child Christ, the, II. 380 ff., 392, 427
Child Maurice, II. 410, 412
Child of Ell, II. 410
Child Waters, II. 413
Childe, L., IV. 454
Childe Harold, in Byron's poem, XII. 43, 45
Childe of Bristowe, The, II. 500
Childers, Robert Caesar (1838–1876), XII. 502
Childhood of Jesus, I. 368
Children in the Wood, The, II. 408; IX. 59, 166; X. 226
Children of the Chapel Royal and other children's companies, V. 64, 118, 122 ff., 161; VI. 4, 41, 212, 220, 221, 246, 258, 262, 279–292 (main entry), 402, 467
Children of the Chapel Stript and Whipt, The, VI. 280
Children's books, XI. 475 ff.
Children's books, magazine articles on, XI. 476
Childrey, Joshua (1623–1670), VII. 509
Childric, in Layamon, I. 237
Chile, XIV. 243
Chillingworth, William (1602–1644), IV. 433; VII. 150, 153, 157, 163, 218, 424, 427; IX. 401; *The Religion of Protestants*, VII. 151, 304, 484; XIV. 102
Chillip, Mr, in *David Copperfield*, XIII. 327
Chilmead, Edmund (1610–1654), VII. 488
Chimenti, F. è G., XIII. Add. 2
China, II. 79; IV. 92, 98; IX. 391; X. 465; XII. 188; XIV. 169
China goods, IX. 263, 271
Chinaman, Goldsmith's, XIII. 445
Chinese imperial yellow dye, XIV. 286
Chinese language and literature, XI. 381; XII. 342, 343, 362; XIV. 421
Chinese Letters, X. 205, 206
Chinese poetry, X. 489
Chinese room, Mrs Montagu's, XI. 348
Chionia, St, I. 74
Chippenham, III. 430
Chipping Campden, X. 113
Chipping Wycombe, VII. 54
Chisholm, John, XII. Add. 1
Chiswell, Richard (1639–1711), XI. 323
Chiswick, VII. 333; IX. 566
Chit-Chat, IX. 442
'Chits,' VIII. 94
Chivalry, tower of, in *The Passetyme of Pleasure*, II. 225
Chloe, XII. 133
Chloe, in Pope's *Characters of Women*, IX. 82
Chloris (Waller's), VII. 55
Chohilaicus (Chlochilaicus) or Huiglaucus, I. 26
Choice Drollery (1656), VII. 512
Choice Song-Books, XI. 218
Chorley, Henry Fothergill (*pseud.* Paul Bell, 1808–1872), XII. 417; XIII. 483; XIV. 517
Chorlton, John (1666–1705), X. 385, 386
Chrestomathic day school, XIV. 404
Chretien de Troyes, I. 263, 268, 269, 271, 273, 279 ff., 285, 299, 462
  Chevalier de la Charrette, I. 270
  Cligès, I. 286
  Conte del Graal, I. 253, 269, 271, 284, 294, 328
  Erec, I. 250, 253, 274
  Le Chevalier au Lion (*Yvain*), I. 253, 274, 279, 280, 284
  Perceval le Gallois, II. 124, 450
  Tristan (ascribed to C. de T.), I. 273
Chrisoganus, 'Master Pedant,' in *Histriomastix*, VI. 40
Christ, in religious plays, V. 15, 37, 41, 42, 44 ff., 49
Christ, Bull on, VIII. 305
Christ, Bunyan on, VII. 169
Christ, hymns of, II. 426. *See, also, under* Child Christ *and* Jesus
Christ, life of (Cornish play), V. 15
Christ (Milton's), VII. 119, 121, 136
Christ, On Serving I. 227, 458
Christ, on the lowering of, from the cross (play), V. 43
Christ, R. Barclay on, VIII. 112
Christ, The Passion of (various works), II. 266, 284, 324, 328, 329
Christ, The Suffering (Χριστὸς πάσχων), V. 5
Christabel, I. 148, 376
Christchurch, Hampshire, VI. 38
Christchurch, New Zealand, XIII. 449
Christendome, The present estate of, VII. 385
Christian, in Bunyan's *Pilgrim's Progress*, I. 58; VII. 173, 177
Christian IV, of Denmark, IV. 151; VI 189; VII. 231

Christian Brethren, association of, III. 40
Christian commonwealth of Hobbes, VII. 296 ff.
Christian doctrine, XII. 259, 264, 275, 278 ff., 292, 295 ff.
Christian drama, V. 36, 37
Christian mysticism, VIII. 108, 110
Christian scholarship, XII. 280, 298
Christian science, VIII. 359
Christian socialism, XIII. 359
Christian socialist, XII. 290
Christian Examiner, The, XIV. 315
Christian Instructor, XII. 472
Christian Observer, The, XI. 404; XII. 281
Christian Paradoxes, VIII. 276
Christian Remembrancer, The, XII. 454 ff., 459
Christian Socialist The, XIII. 358
Christiana, in Bunyan's *Pilgrim's Progress*, VII. 177
Christianity, V. 21, 29; VI. 373; VII. 305, 367; VIII. 42, 100, 102, 276, 346, 389; IX. 28, 83, 100, 101, 108, 112, 290 ff., 300, 305, 331; X. 7, 114, 308, 309, 313, 317, 363; XI. 18, 48, 194, 196, 198, 199, 286, 287, 380; XII. 254, 269, 270, 276 ff., 282, 283, 290 ff., 297 ff., 322; XIII. 24, 40, 75, 76, 113, 138, 174, 366, 436; XIV. 13, 46, 110, 253, 302, 303, 401, 402, 409, 411, 414
Christianorum Tractatus de decem nationibus, II. 330
Christians, in *Tyrannick Love*, VIII. 22
Christians, Duty of, I. 228
'Christianus Presbyteromastix' = Sir Thomas Urquhart, VII. 253
Christie, Albany, XII. 460
Christie, Jonathan, XII. 161, 163
Christie, Richard Copley (1830–1901), XII. 333, 369, 515, 520; XIV. 501; *Étienne Dolet*, XII. 334; XIV. 109
Christie, Robert (1788–1856), XIV. 358, 582
Christie, William Dougal (1816–1874), VIII. 3, 4; IX. 212; XIV. 501; *Life of the First Earl of Shaftesbury*, XIV. 113
Christie's sale room, X. 471
Christina, queen, in Milton's *Defensio*, VII. 130
Christina, queen of Sweden, VII. 230; VIII. 20
Christina, St, I. 74, 75; V. 49
Christine de Pisan, II. 208, 316; III. 90; *City of Ladies*, II. 327; *Moral Proverbs of*, II. 313, 485
Christis Kirk on the Grene, II. 244, 250, 270, 271, 273, 274, 471, 473; III. 130, 135; IX. 366, 367, 379, 560; X. 223, 226; XI. 215, 218
Christmas, in *The Masque of Christmas*, VI. 355, 358
Christmas, tracts against, VII. 514
'Christmas Abbess,' V. 8
Christmas carols, XIII. 125, 140
Christmas eve, XIII. 111
'Christmas lord,' V. 8
Christmas numbers, XIII. 376
Christmas plays, V. 15, 32, 37 ff., 44, 47, 48, 68
Christmas stories, XIII. 323, 326, 334, 335
Christmas Prince, The, VI. 319, 474
Christopher, in Dickens's *Somebody's Luggage*, XIII. 335
Christopher, The, English warship, I. 357
Christopherson, John (d. 1558), *Jephtha*, VI. 295
Christ's college, Attercliffe, X. 386
Christ's Descent into Hell, I. 428
Christus Patiens, V. 6
Chronica Monasterii de Melsa, XII. 356
Chronicle, the Old English, I. 5, 62, 89, 90, 104, 107 ff., 137 ff., 145, 150, 161, 167, 219, 236, 245, 317, 352, 369, 374, 443; II. 400, 420; III. 458; VIII. 313 *See, also, under* Peterborough, Winchester, etc.
Chronicle, English (1377–1461), II. 301, 482
Chronicle, The, XIV. 118
Chronicle of the Brute, The, II. 313, 334, 482
Chronicle plays, IX. 136; V. 35, 142, 151 ff., 199, 425
Chronicle to Edwarde the iii, II. 308
Chroniclers, transition, I. 335 ff.
Chroniclers, 14th and 15th century, II. 496 ff.
Chroniclers in Tudor times, III. 313 ff., 527 ff.
Chronicles and Memorials of Great Britain and Ireland, XII. 356
Chronicles of England, The, II. 301, 318, 319
Chronicon Boguphali Episcopi, I. 32
Chrysanthus, martyr, I. 74
Chrysoloras, Manuel, grammar of, III. 14
Chrysostom, St John, I. 154; II. 365; III. 4, 431; IV. 235, 265, 325, 411; VII. 304; VIII. 449; XII. 266, 501; Eton edition of his works, VII. 312
Chrystal, George, XII. 470
Chubb, Thomas (1679–1747), IX. 288, 294, 504; X. 521
Chudleigh, Devon, IV. 418
Chudleigh, James (d. 1643), VII. 348
Chudleigh, John (*fl.* 1650), VII. 31
Church, Frederick John (1854–1888), XII. 455
Church, Mary C., XII. 455
Church, Nathanael, *Cheap Riches*, 1654, VII. 517
Church, Richard William (1815–1890), XII. 255, 261, 271 ff. (main entry), 319, 453 ff., 459, 460; XIV. 113, 486, 501; on Anselm, I. 164; VII. 210; *The Oxford Movement*, XII. 256, 265, 272
Church, Holy, in *Piers the Plowman*, II. 2, 6 ff., 11, 17, 32
Church, The Last Age of the, II. 49
Church Missionary society, the, XII. 471
Church of England Quarterly Review, The, XII. 491
Church of Evil Men and Women, The, II. 324

Churchill, Awnsham, xi. 323
Churchill, Charles (1731–1764), x. 40, 207, 393 ff., 522, 524; xi. 34, 42, 78, 82, 246, 450
Apology, The, x. 395
Author, The, x. 397
Bard, The, x. 394
Candidate, The, x. 397
Conclave, The, x. 394
Conference, The, x. 397
Duellist, The, x. 396, 397
Epistle to William Hogarth, x. 396, 398
Farewell, The, x. 397
Ghost, The, v. 273; x. 179, 397
Gotham, x. 397
Independence, x. 397, 398
Journey, The, x. 397
Night, x. 395
Prophecy of Famine, The, x. 394, 396, 398
Rosciad, The, x. 394, 395, 398
Times, The, x. 397
Churchill, G. B., v. 82
Churchill, Henrietta, duchess of Marlborough, wife of Francis Godolphin, viii. 159; ix. 82
Churchill, J., collection of voyages, iv. 103
Churchill, John (publisher), xi. 323
Churchill, John, 1st duke of Marlborough (1650–1722), viii. 220; ix. 44, 94, 96, 124, 130, 134, 139, 174, 200, 206, 217, 218, 261, 336, 435, 494; x. 502; xiv. 65
Churchill, lord Randolph (1849–1894), xiv. 509
Churchill, Sarah (born Jennings), duchess of Marlborough (1660–1744), viii. 208; ix. 82, 98, 130, 185, 217, 218, 220; x. 465
Churchill, Winston Spencer, xiv. 509
Churchyard, Thomas (1520?–1604), iii. 114, 182, 183, 189, 197, 198, 201, 506; iv. 114, 322, 411, 434, 456
Churchyardes Chippes, iii. 182
Myrrour of man, The, iii. 182; xii. 357, 515
Ovid's De Tristibus, iv. 20, 439
Praise of Poetrie, The, iii. 183
Shore's Wife, in *A Mirror for Magistrates*, iii. 182, 198; iv. 134; vi. 90
Sieges of Leith and Edinburgh, descriptions of, iii. 182
Warres, A Generall Rehearsall of (*Churchyard's Choise*), iii. 182
Wofull Warres in Flaunders, The, iii. 182
Worthines of Wales, The, iii. 183
Churne, William, xi. 374
Churton, Edward, *Life of Joshua Watson*, xii. 256
Chusi, in *Absalom*, vi. 296
Chuzzlewit, Jonas, Dickens's, xiii. 317, 322
Chuzzlewit, Martin, Dickens's, xiii. 322
Cibber, Colley (1671–1757), viii. 146, 151, 152, 159, 166, 189, 426, 431; ix. 86, 88, 89, 449; x. 21, 39, 67, 68, 81, 92, 216, 425, 428, 442
Cibber, Colley
An Apology for his Life, viii 177, 179; ix. 143
Apology, x. 24, 70, 71
Careless Husband, viii. 168; x. 72
Hamlet, xi. 258
Love's Last Shift, viii. 160, 176; xi. 321
Non-Juror, x. 89
Richard III, v. 298
She Would and She Would Not, viii. 132
Cibber, Susannah Maria, viii. 191; x. 264; xi. 260
Cibber, Theophilus (1703–1758), viii. 422; ix. 480; x. 24, 85, 444, 445; *Lives of the Poets*, x. 77, 184
Ciccotti-D'Errico, Ernestina, xiii. Add. 2
Cicero, M. Tullius (Tully), i. 76, 100, 185, 187; ii. 359, 360, 363; iii. 20, 23, 24, 90, 92, 157, 180, 187, 345, 416, 424, 429; iv. 255, 260, 322, 342, 435, 436, 470, 525; v. 123; vi. 406; vii. 131, 261, 313, 390, 392; viii. 273, 278, 282; ix. 28, 54, 55, 204, 218, 229, 334, 337, 340, 418, 527, 528; x. 159, 197, 319, 509, 510; xi. 2, 30, 31; xii. 230, 326, 338, 476, 479, 483, 485, 487, 492 ff., *also see* Add.; xiv. 303
De Amicitia, ii. 308; iii. 345; iv. 5, 264
De Natura Deorum, iii. 345
De Officiis, iii. 180; iv. 5, 6, 24; ix. 274, 525, 526; xii. 332
De Oratore, xi. 13; xii. 335, 337
De Senectute, iv. 5; vii. 61
In Verrem, xi. 16, 17, 274
Letters, iii. 67, 429; vii. 315
Life and Letters, xii. 306
Pro Milone, ii. 331
Second Philippic, xii. 336
Speeches against Catiline, xii. 337
Tusculan Questions, iv. 5
Cicero, Don, in *The Pilgrimage to Parnassus*, vi. 310
Cicero, in *Catiline*, vi. 19, 20
Cicero, translators of, iv. 5
Ciceronian manner, the, xiv. 121
Cid, The, ii. 412; xi. 422
Cieza, Peter de, ix. 501
Cigarette, in *Under Two Flags*, xiii. 436
Cincinnati, xiv. 165
Cinderella, xi. 380
Cino da Pistoia, xiii. 118
Cinqbars, lord, Thackeray's, xiii. 280
Cinque ports, iv. 84; ix. 536
Cinque ports, barons of the, xi. 282
Cinric, i. 236
Cinthio, Giambattista Giraldi, iv. 443; v. 63, 65, 220, 221, 409; vi. 139, 199; *Hecatommithi*, v. 119, 137, 138; *Orecche*, v. 62
Cintra convention, the, xiv. 187
Cinus of Pistoja (d. 1336), ii. 363
Cipriano, in Calderon's *El Magico Prodigioso*, xiii. 144
Circe, vii. 370
Circle of the Sciences, xi. 367, 376
Circumcision, feast of, v. 8

Circumlocution office, the, in *Little Dorrit*, XIII. 331
Cirencester, VI. 237; VIII. 106
Cirencester, Richard of (d. 1401?), XII. 366
Cis, the shoemaker's wife, in *Piers the Plowman*, II. 16
Cistercian nuns, II. 45
Cistercians, I. 189; II. 351; III. 51
Citherea, palace of, in *The Court of Love*, II. 220
Citizen of the World, Letters from a, X. 53, 171, 199, 206, 207, 209, 229
City Dames Petition, The, VII. 382
City of Prague, The. *See* Prowse, W. J.
Civil (Civil Law), in *Piers the Plowman*, II. 7
Civil war, the, III. 87, 114; IV. 55, 156, 342, 363; XIV. 57, 59, 87
Civil war pamphlets and broadsides, VII. 512, 514, 515; XI. 470
Civis, in *A Dialogue...against the fever Pestilence*, III. 109
Civyle and uncivyle life, On, V. 349
Clack, Miss, Wilkie Collins's, XIII. 438
Clack the miller, in *The Devil and his Dame*, V. 329
Claire, in Rousseau's *La Nouvelle Héloïse*, X. 17
Clairmont, Allegra, XII. 37
Clairmont, Clara Mary Jane (1798–1879), XII. 37, 401
Clairmont, Mary Jane. *See* Godwin, Mrs
Clairon, Mlle, X. 264
Clanvowe, Sir Thomas, *The Cuckoo and the Nightingale*, II. 162, 164, 166, 215 ff.
Clapham, VIII. 258
Clapham, John Harold, XIII. 545
'Clapham sect,' the, XII. 281; XIV. 110
Clapp, H. A., XIII. 514
Clapperton, *In Bowdin on Blak Monanday*, III. 132
Clara, in Bailey's *Festus*, XIII. 153
Clara, in *The Scowrers*, IX. 362
Clara, in Scott's *Marmion*, XII. 11
Clara, Sta., XII. 260
Clarange, in *The Lovers Progress*, VI. 131
Clare. *See* Osbert de
Clare, Allan, in Lamb's *Rosamund Gray*, XII. 185, 186
Clare, Elinor, in Lamb's *Rosamund Gray*, XII. 186
Clare, Elizabeth de (1291?–1360), II. 354
Clare, in Mrs Gaskell's *Wives and Daughters*, XIII. 381
Clare, John (1793–1864), XII. 131, 134, 415; *The Last of March*, XII. 132
Clare, Robert Nugent. *See* Nugent, Robert, earl Nugent
Clarence, George, duke of (1444–1478), III. 334
Clarence, George, duke of, in *Richard III*, V. 186
Clarence, Reginald, XIII. 516
Clarendon, Constitutions of, I. 337
Clarendon, earls of. *See* Hyde, Edward; Villiers, George W. F.
Clarendon commission (Public Schools), XIV. 413, 421, 422
Clarges, Sir Thomas (d. 1695), VII. 362, 363
Clarice, in *Piers the Plowman*, II. 16
Clarinda. *See* Maclehose, Mrs Agnes (1759–1841)
Clariodus, I. 291, 467
Clarissa, in *Loves Crueltie*, VI. 199
Clarissa, in Richardson's novel, X. 2, 7 ff., 17; XIII. 288
Clarissa, in *The Tatler*, IX. 50
Clark, Andrew, IX. 346; *Life of Anthony Wood*, IX. 341, 382, 383, 413, 541
Clark, George Thomas (1809–1898), XII. 508; *Mediaeval Military Architecture in England*, XII. 349
Clark, Mrs Godfrey, XI. 348
Clark, James (d. 1724), IX. 546
Clark, John (*fl.* 1759), VIII. 62
Clark, John (d. 1807), X. 471
Clark, John, XIV. Add. 4
Clark, J. S., *Life of James the Second*, IX. 213
Clark, John Willis (1833–1910), XII. 508; XIV. 539, 563; *The Care of Books*, XII. 348
Clark, William (*fl.* 1685), IX. 556
Clark, William George (1821–1878), V. 280; XIV. 516; *Peloponnesus*, XII. 331
Clarke, Abraham, VII. 107
Clarke, Adam (1762?–1832), XII. 491, 520; XIV. 567
Clarke, Charles (1787–1877) and Mary Cowden (1809–1898), XI. 437; XII. 79, 406, 437, 444; *and see* Clarke, Mary Cowden
Clarke, Sir Edward, XIII. 543
Clarke, Edward Daniel (1769–1822), XII. 484, 491; XIV. 241, 551; *Travels*, XIV. 247
Clarke, Sir Ernest, VIII. 28; X. Add.
Clarke, Sir G. S., XIV. 491
Clarke, Helen A., XIII. 479
Clarke, Henry Butler (1863–1904), XIV. 486
Clarke, Herbert Edwin, XIII. 500
By the Washes, XIII. 216
Chant d'Amour, XIII. 216
Failure, XIII. 216
Nocturn at Twilight, A, XIII. 216
Poems and Sonnets, XIII. 215
Poems in Exile, XIII. 215
Storm-Drift, XIII. 215
Tannhäuser and other Poems, XIII. 215
Voluntary, A, XIII. 216
Clarke, Hyde (b. 1815), XII. 508
Clarke, John, *Paroemiologia* (1639), VII. 479
Clarke, John (1682–1757), IX. 505
Clarke, John (1687–1734), IX. 568
Clarke, John (d. 1730), IX. 505
Clarke, John, XIV. 604
Clarke, Joseph (d. 1749), IX. 505
Clarke, J. S., X. 295, 454; XII. 232

Clarke, Marcus Andrew Hislop (1846–1881), xiv. 367, 585; *His Natural Life*, xiv. 370; *Long Odds* (*Heavy Odds*), xiv. 370
Clarke, Mary Cowden (1809–1898), xi. 485
Clarke, Matthew (1664–1726), x. 386
Clarke, Samuel (1599–1683), vii. 479, 484
Clarke, Samuel (1625–1669), vii. 319
Clarke, Samuel (1675–1729), viii. 473; ix. 279, 281, 289, 293, 294, 296, 297 ff. (main entry), 394, 505, 507; x. 345; xi. 481; xiv. 37
Being and Attributes of God, ix. 292, 297
Boyle Lectures, ix. 297, 298
Discourse concerning...Natural Religion, ix. 297
Lives, viii. 278
Scripture Doctrine of the Trinity, ix. 297; x. 359, 379
Clarke, T. E. S., *Life of Gilbert Burnet*, ix. 202
Clarke papers at Worcester college, Oxford, vii. 347, 435, 438
Clarkson, Laurence (1615–1667), vii. 509
Clarkson, Mrs, xi. 121
Clarkson, Thomas (1760–1846), xiv. 373, 486
Classus, in *The Scourge of Folly*, iv. 334
Claude, in Kingsley's *Two Years Ago*, xiii. 365
Claude de Pontoux, iii. 258, 263; *L'Idée*, iii. 263
Claude Lorraine, xii. 172, 173
Claudia, in *Gismond of Salerne*, v. 75
Claudian, i. 68; iv. 250, 417, 436
Claudio, in *Measure for Measure*, i. 1
Claudio, in *Much Ado about Nothing*, xiii. 262
Claudius, in *Hamlet*, v. 200 ff., 211
Claus, P., xiv. 524
Clavell, John (1603–1642), iv. 530
Clavell, Robert (d. 1711), xi. 339, 471
Claverhouse, John Graham of. *See* Graham, John, viscount Dundee
Clavering, in *Pendennis*, xiii. 276, 291
Clavering, Mary. *See* Cowper, countess
Claverton, x. 276
Clavis Apocalyptica, viii. 286
Clavius, C., vii. 320
Clay, James (1805–1873), v. 173
Clay, Mrs, in Jane Austen's *Persuasion*, xii. 240
Clay, William F., xiv. 557
Claypole, Noah, in *Oliver Twist*, xiii. 317
Clayton, J., viii. 468
'Clean contrary way, The,' viii. 96
Cleanness, i. 320 ff., 343, 472
Cleanness, lady, in *The Example of Virtue*, ii. 227, 234
Cleges, Sir, i. 315, 470
Cleland, J., *The Institution of a Nobleman*, iii. 437
Cleland, William (1661?–1689), viii. 408; ix. 556
Clem, in *The Fair Maid Of The West*, vi. 102
Clemens, S. L. *See* Twain, Mark
Clement IV, pope, i. 206
Clement VI, pope, v. 13
Clement VII, pope, ii. 56
Clement VIII, pope, iii. 415
Clement, Gregory (d. 1660), viii. 470
Clement, Justice, in *Every Man in His Humour*, v. 350
Clément, Nicolas, v. 285
Clement, saint, xii. 266, 340
Clement, William Innell (d. 1852), xiv. 228, 235
Clement of Alexandria, iii. 409, 416
Clement of Llanthony (d. 1190?), *Harmony of the Gospels*, ii. 60
Clement of Rome, i. 74, 118; xii. 501; *Recognitions of*, i. 75
Clementina, in Richardson's *Sir Charles Grandison*, x. 10
Clementines, ii. 364
Clenard, Nicholas, iii. 429
Clene Maidenhod, ii. 503
Clennan family, in *Little Dorrit*, xiii. 331
Clennell, Luke (1781–1840), xiv. 227
Cleobulus, in *Argenis*, iv. 259
Cleobury Mortimer, ii. 2
Cléomadès, French romance, ii. 184
Cleopatra, i. 95; ii. 177; viii. 216
Cleopatra, in *Antony and Cleopatra*, v. 180, 183, 199, 213, 214; vi. 72, 273
Cleora, in *The Bond-man*, vi. 154, 155, 157, 158
Clephane, Dr John (d. 1758), x. 284
Clergy (Learning), in *Piers the Plowman*, ii. 20, 21, 27
Clerical subscription act, xii. 296
Clericus and Puella, dialogue between, i. 365; v. 25, 55, 91
Clerimont, in Steele's *Tender Husband*, ix. 30
Clerk, John, ii. 274
Clerk, Sir John, of Penicuik (1684–1755), ix. 553; xii. 350; *Merry may the Maid*, ix. 371
Clerk Colvill, ii. 413
Clerk Saunders, ii. 413
Clerk of Tranent, ii. 122
Clerke, Agnes Mary, xiv. 265, 555
Clerke, Gilbert (1626–1697?), x. 359, 377
Clerke, Henry (d. 1687), viii. 358
Clerkenwell News, The, xiv. 193
Clerk-Maxwell, James (1831–1879), xiv. 261, 265, 266, 268 ff., 556
Clerselius, viii. 455
Cléry, Jean Baptiste, xiv. 66
Cleveland, Yorkshire, xi. 174
Cleveland, or Cleiveland, John (1613–1658), iv. 342, 522; vii. 73, 85, 88, 91 ff., 111, 356, 412, 495, 496, 502, 513, 516 ff.; viii. 80, 88, 91
Character of a London Diurnall, vii. 348, 384
Mark Antony, vii. 93; viii. 231
Mercurius Politicus, Character of, vii. 358

Cleveland, or Cleiveland, John
Mercurius Politicus, The Second Character of, VII. 353
Mixed Assembly, The, VII. 92
Rebel Scot, The, VII. 92
Square-Cap, VIII. 231
Cleveland, duchess of. *See* Villiers, Barbara
Clèves, la princesse de, XII. 381
Cliefdon. *See* Cliveden
Clifford, lady Anne (1590–1676), IV. 132, 133, 138
Clifford, Arthur (1778–1830), XII. 376
Clifford, Christopher, IV. 368; *The Schoole of Horsemanship*, IV 369, 540
Clifford, George, 3rd earl of Cumberland (1558–1605), IV. 455
Clifford, Margaret, countess of Cumberland, IV. 132, 133
Clifford, Martin (d. 1677), VIII. 23, 25, 26, 48, 402, 404
Clifford, Paul, lord Lytton's, XIII. 418
Clifford, Thos. (1630–1673), VIII. 380
Clifford, William Kingdon (1845–1879), XIV. 34, 470, 556
Clifford, in Burgoyne's *Heiress*, XI. 275, 276
Clifford, in *Henry VI*, V. 186
Clifford Chambers, near Evesham, IV. 174
Clifton, Henry (*fl.* 1587–1600), VI. 290, 291
Clifton, Thomas (b. 1587), VI. 290, 291
Climenson, Emily J., *Elizabeth Montagu*, XI. 328
Clincher, in Farquhar's *The Constant Couple*, VIII. 169, 170
Clinker, Humphrey, in Smollett's novel, X. 43
Clinton, Henry Fiennes, 9th earl of Lincoln (1720–1794), X. 244
Clinton, Henry Fynes (1781–1852), XII. 496; *Fasti Hellenici*, XII. 310, 339; *Fasti Romani*, XII. 310, 339
Clinton, H. P. F. Pelham, 5th duke of Newcastle (1811–1864), XIV. 510
Clinton, Mr, in Brooke's *Fool of Quality*, IX. 327, 328
Clinton (pirate), in *Fortune by Land and Sea*, VI. 104
Clio, XII. 136
Clisthenes, XII. 313
Clithero, Yorks., XII. 514
Clive, Caroline Archer, 'V' (1801–1873), XII. 448; XIII. 180, 500, 561
Death, XIII. 176
Heart's Ease, XIII. 176
I watched the Heavens, XIII. 176
Paul Ferroll, XIII. 175, 437
Valley of the Morlas, The, XIII. 176
Venice, XIII. 176
Why Paul Ferroll killed his Wife, XIII. 176
IX Poems by V, XIII. 176
Clive, Catherine (1711–1785), X. 22, 254, 264, 439; XI. 257
Clive, Robert Clive, lord (1725–1774), XIV. 63, 578
Cliveden, X. 108, 109
Clodd, Edward, XIII. 569
Cloe, in *The Faithfull Shepherdesse*, VI. 368
Cloete, Henry, XIV. Add. 6
Clogher, IX. 166
Clogy, or Clogie, Alexander (1614–1698), VII. 442
Clokyd Colusyon, in *Magnyfycence*, III. 77
Cloncurry, lord, XIV. 324
Clongowes college, XIV. 316
Clonmacnoise, XIV. 312
'Clootie,' II. 409; XI. 212
Clorin, in *The Faithfull Shepheardesse*, VI. 368
Clorinda, in *Orlando Furioso*, III. 230
Cloris, in *The Queenes Arcadia*, VI. 317, 318
Close, Francis (1797–1882), XII. 472; XIV. 590, 598
Close, John (1816–1891), XIII. 500
Close Rolls, XII. 355, 516
Closet, A, for ladies and gentlewomen, IV. 543
Cloten, in Layamon, I. 237
Cloth-Breeches, in *A Quip for an Upstart Courtier*, III. 361
Clough, Arthur Hugh (1819–1861), XI. 409; XII. 255, 293; XIII. 87, 91, 102 ff. (main entry), 174, 245 ff., 488, 489 (main entry)
Ambarvalia, XIII. 104
Amours de Voyage, XIII. 104
Bothie of Tober-na-Vuolich, The, XIII 103 ff.
Dipsychus, XIII. 104, 105
Duty, XIII. 104
Higher Courage, The, XIII. 104
Mari Magno, XIII. 104, 105
New Sinai, The, XIII. 104
Prose Remains, XIII. 91
Qua Cursum Ventus, XIII. 104
Questioning Spirit, The, XIII. 104
Qui Laborat Orat, XIII. 104
Say not the struggle nought availeth, XIII. 106
Sic Itur, XIII. 104
Songs in Absence, XIII. 104, 106
Clough, Blanche Athena, XIII. 103; XIV. 599
Clouston, W. A., II. 216
Clove, in *Every Man out of His Humour*, VI. 225
Clovesho, synod of, I. 50
Clovis, I. 20, 21; XIV. 68
Clowes, Alice A., XIV. 613
Clowes, John, VII. 352
Clowes, Sir William Laird (1856–1905), XIV. 486
Clown, the, in a broadside, III. 87
Cloyne, IX. 166
'Club, The,' X. 181, 187, 192, 207, 212, 214, 260, 261, 264
Club-Law, VI. 307, 308, 313, 315, 327, 483
Clubs, Varlet of, in *Terminus et non Terminus*, VI. 307

Clumsey, Sir Tunbelly, in Vanbrugh's *The Relapse*, VIII. 161, 162
Cluniac order, the, IV. 419
Clust, son of Clustveinad, I. 255
Clustveinad, I. 255
Clutterbuck, Robert (1772–1831), XII. 509
Clutton-Brock, Arthur, XIII. 493, 572
Cluverius, Philippus, VII. 307; X. 305
Clwyd, vale of, 115
Clyde, the, II. 89
Clytemnestra, in *Agamemnon*, V. 79
Clytemnestra, in Thomson's *Agamemnon*, X. 108
Clytemnestra, in *Horestes*, V. 64, 65
Clytophon, VI. 483
Cnidos, XII. 339
Cnitthon. *See* Knighton
Cnossos, palace of, XII. 339
Cobalt, Canada, XIV. 356
Cobb, James (1756–1818), XI. 281, 456
Cobbe, Frances Power (1822–1904), XIV. 470, 517, 599
Cobbes Prophecies, IV. 534
Cobbett, William (1762–1835), I. 370; XI. 49 ff., 393; XII. 170, 179; XIV. 125, 137, 197, 202, 461; *Political Register*, XI. 49; XIV. 197; *Rural Rides*, XI. 51; *State Trials*, XI. 49
Cobbold, Thomas Spencer (1828–1886), XIV. 301
Cobden, Richard (1804–1865), XIV. 78, 131–132 (main entry), 137, 173, 179, 181, 190, 509, 512
Cobet, Carel Gabriel, XII. 330
Cobham, Eleanor, duchess of Gloucester (d. 1446?), IV. 182
Cobham, lady, X. 126
Cobham, lord. *See* Brooke, William
Cobham, lord. *See* Oldcastle, Sir John
Cobham, Thomas de (d. 1327), IV. 430
Cobham, viscount. *See* Temple, Sir Richard
Cobler of Canterburie, The, IV. 362, 521, 523, 531
Coburg, house of, IX. 338; XII. 232
Cocai, Merlin (Teofilo Folengo), *Baldus*, VIII. 59
Cochrane, John George (1781–1852), XII. 378
Cochrane, Thomas, 10th earl of Dundonald (1775–1860), XIV. 502, 552
Cock and the Jewel, in Henryson's *Fables*, II. 246
Cock lane ghost, X. 179, 206, 465, 481
Cock Lawrel (tune), VIII. 96
Cock up your Bonnet, IX. 377
Cockayne, Oswald, I. 105, 135, 136
Cockayne, or Cokayne, Thomas (1587–1638), VII. 316
Cockburn, Sir Alexander J. E. Cockburn, lord (1802–1880), XIV. 124, 509, 513
Cockburn, Alison (1712?–1794), XI. 231, 232; '*I have seen the Smiling*,' IX. 373
Cockburn, Mrs Catherine (born Trotter) (1679–1749), VIII. 347, 435, 473
Cockburn, Henry Thomas Cockburn, lord (1779–1854), XII. 426; XIV. 501
Journal, X. 324
Life of Jeffrey, X. 188
Memorials of His Time, XIV. 112
'Scottish Criminal Jurisprudence,' XII. 153, 378
Cockburn, John (1652–1729), IX. 520, 551
Cocke, J., IV. 339, 518
Cocke Lorell's bote, III. 61, 83 ff., 482; IV. 362, 521, 529
Cocker, Edmund (*fl.* 1664), VIII. 256
Cockeram, Henry (*fl.* 1650), IX. 529
Cockeram, Richard (*fl.* 1468–1482), IV. 432
Cockerell, Sydney Carlyle, XIII. 491, 493
Cockerell, Thomas, XI. 332
Cockermouth, XI. 94
Cockledemoy, in *The Dutch Courtezan*, VI. 46
Cocklorrel's song, in *The Masque of the Metamorphos'd Gypsies*, VI. 362
Cockney school of poetry, XII. 157, 160
Cockshutt of the Inner Temple, friend of Henry More, VIII. 456
Cockton, Henry (1807–1853), XII. 448
Cockwood, lady (Etherege's), VIII. 138
Codex Alexandrinus, XII. 501
Codex Augiensis, the, XII. 501
Codex Bezae, the, XII. 501
Codex Galeanus, XII. 325, 491
Codlin and Short, in *The Old Curiosity Shop*, XIII. 319
Codlo, Antonio, *Los Empeños de Seis Horas*, VIII. 130
Codronchus, IV. 247
Codrus, in Juvenal's *Third Satire*, VIII. 89
Codrus, in *Misogonus*, V. 111
Coelia, in *The Faerie Queene*, VI. 335
Coelum, in *Lingua*, VI. 315
Coffee (1727), IX. 434
Coffee, A Brief Description of the Excellent Virtues o that sober and wholesome drink called, VII. 389, 390
Coffee, A Cup of, VII. 389
Coffee pamphlets, VII. 516
Coffee-House Dialogue, A, VII. 390; IX. 32
Coffee-house, News from the, VII. 389
Coffee-house, Rules and Orders of the, VII. 390
Coffee-houses, VII. 389
Coffee-houses Vindicated, The, VII. 389
Coffee-Scuffle, The, VII. 390; IX. 32
Coffey, Charles (d. 1745), X. 439; XIV. 567; *The Beggar's Wedding*, XI. 218
Coffin, Robert Aston (1819–1885), XII. 460
Coffin for King Charles, A, VII. 381
Cogan, Thomas (1545?–1607), VII. 486, 488
Coggeshall. *See* Ralph of
Coghill, Mrs Harry, XIII. 565
Coghlan, C. H., *A Quiet Rubber*, XIII. 525
Cohen, Francis. *See* Palgrave, Sir Francis
Cohen, H. T., XIV. 509
Coignet, Matthieu. IV. 443
Coillard, François, XIV. Add. 6
Coimbra, III. 162
Cokaygne. See *Land of*

Cokayne or Cokain, Sir Aston (1608–1684), vi. 114, 142, 144, 145; viii. 417
Cokayne, Sir Thomas (1519?–1592), iv. 541
Coke, Sir Edward, lord Coke or Cooke (1552–1634), iii. 424; iv. 265; v. 367; viii. 309, 312 ff., 321, 465, 466, 468; *Institutes*, viii. 317, 320; *Law Reports*, viii. 316, 317; *The Lord Coke his Speech & charge*, vi. 400, 492
Coke, Thomas (1747–1814), x. 518
Cokes, a booby, in *Bartholomew Fayre*, vi. 23
Coketown, in Dickens's *Hard Times*, xiii. 330
Cokwold's Daunce, The, i. 464; ii. 501
Colax, in *The Queenes Arcadia*, vi. 317
Colbrand, in *Guy of Warwick*, i. 304 ff., 343
Colburn, Henry (d. 1855), xii. 161, 200
Colburne, v. 108
Colby and Mrs Colby, in *Club Law*, vi. 308
Colchester, ii. 208; iii. 428: vii. 82; viii. 101, 363; ix. 537
Colchester, lord. *See* Abbot, Charles
Coldicott, H. R. S., 'How Cowper got his pension,' xi. 90
Cole, Alfred Whaley, xiv. Add. 6
Cole, Charles Nelson (1723–1804), ix. 533
Cole, Sir Henry ('Felix Summerly,' 1808–1882), xi. 462, 478; *The Home Treasury*, xi. 386
Cole, John (1792–1848), xi. 474
Cole, John William, xiii. 514
Cole, Thomas (d. 1571), iv. 491
Cole, Thomas (1627?–1697), x. 385
Cole, William, *A Rod for the Lawyers* (1659), vii. 515
Cole, William (1714–1782), ix. 354, 532; x. 249, 255, 495
Colebrooke, E., xiv. 576
Colebrooke, Henry Thomas (1765–1837), xii. 502; xiv. 335; *Essays on Sanskrit literature*, xii. 343
Coleman, Edward (d. 1669), viii. 117
Coleman, John, xiii. 514, 566
Coleman, Mrs (*fl.* 1656), viii. 118
Coleman, Thomas (1598–1647), ix. 544
Colenso, Durnford E., xiv. Add. 6
Colenso, Frances, Ellen (1849–1887), xiv. Add. 6
Colenso, John William (1814–1883), bishop of Natal, xii. 296, 297, 314, 465, 474; xiv. Add. 6
Coleorton, xi. 410, 416, 423; xii. 376
Colepeper, John, 1st baron (d. 1660), vii. 218
Coleridge, Derwent (1800–1883), xi. 412, 415, 417; xii. 415, 421; xiii. 355
Coleridge, Ernest Hartley, xi. 412, 416; xii. 385, 388; *also see* Add. 1
Coleridge, Hartley (1796–1849), xi. 127, 162, 417; *also see* Add.; xii. 104, 107–108 (main entry), 124, 127, 415; xiii. 183
Homer, xii. 108
Medley, A, xii. 108

Coleridge, Hartley
Poietes Apoietes, xii. 108
Prayer, xii. 108
Prometheus, xii. 107
Shakespeare, xii. 108
Youth, xii. 108
Coleridge, Henry Nelson (1798–1843), xi. 405, 415, 417
Coleridge, Sir John Duke, 1st lord (1820–1894), xiv. 596
Coleridge, Sir John Taylor (1790–1876), xii. 153, 429, 457; xiii. 504
Coleridge, Mary Elizabeth (1861–1907), xiii. 182 ff., 197, 198, 500, 501
Day-dream, A, xiii. 184
Difference, A, xiii. 184
He came unto His Own, xiii. 184
On the Arrival of a Visitor, xiii. 184
Other Side of a Mirror, The, xiii. 184
Unwelcome, xiii. 183
Witch, The, xiii. 184
Coleridge, Samuel Taylor (1772–1834), i. 148, 376; ii. 186, 190, 205; iii. 465; iv. 43, 46, 50, 236, 241, 259, 260; v. 209, 222, 270, 304; vi. 23, 129, 131; vii. 163, 236, 247; viii. 298; ix. 106, 277, 328; x. 137, 186, 316, 526; xi. 28, 71, 99 ff., 104, 112, 113, 117 ff. (main entry), 150, 154 ff., 162, 163, 168, 171, 172, 178, 201, 202, 250, 294, 305, 308, 309, 341, 405, 407, 409, 411, 412, 421, 423, 468; xii. 39, 48, 57 ff., 77, 78, 93, 95, 101, 107, 120, 147, 158, 159, 166, 169, 170, 175, 176, 178, 180 ff., 187, 188, 191, 196, 197, 201, 203, 205, 211, 218, 219, 223, 255, 280, 282–283, 289, 399, 402, 405, 434, 436, 445, 465, 471, 527, *and see* Add. 1; xiii. 7 ff., 18, 23 ff., 40, 46, 52, 57, 86, 148, 183, 196, 198, 225, 230 ff., 241, 243 ff., 258 ff., 276, 312, 318, 420, 442; xiv. 1, 8, 15, 16, 40, 138, 144, 146, 170, 177, 180, 275, 373, 374, 471, 518, 560
Aids to Reflexion, ix. 328; xi. 138; xii. 283
Ancient Mariner, x. 217, 234; xi. 101, 120, 123 ff., 130, 132, 160, 169, 170, 201; xii. 71, 108, 110, 113, 124, 133; xiii. 231, 233, 244, 324; xiv. 255
Anima Poetæ, xi. 129, 130
Biographia Literaria, ix. 328; xi. 122, 123, 126, 133, 135 ff., 176, 304; xii. 157; xiv. 184, 403
Christabel, iii. 286; x. 236; xi. 120, 126 ff., 131, 132, 169, 170, 200, 201; xii. 7, 8, 46, 62, 71, 87, 108; xiii. 184, 228, 231, 233, 244
Collection of Political Tracts, ix. 223
Conciones ad populum, xi. 138
Confessions of an Enquiring Spirit, xii. 282, 283, 288
Constitution of Church and State, xi. 138
Dejection, xi. 104, 120, 123, 129, 130
Devil's Thoughts, The, xiv. 184
Eolian Harp, xi. 119
Essays on his own Times, xi. 139; xiv. 184

Coleridge, Samuel Taylor
Fall of Robespierre, XI. 161
Fears in Solitude, XI. 115
Friend, The, XI. 122, 138, 139
Kubla Khan, X. 153; XI. 120, 124, 125, 169; XII. 59, 108
Lay Sermons, XI. 139
Letters, XI. 122, 131, 139
Lyrical Ballads, X. 217; XI. 86, 101, 123, 150, 151; XII. 40, 42
Nightingale, The, XI. 129
Ode to France, XI. 115
Ode to the Departing Year, XI. 124
Poems (Oct. 1797), XII. 184
Poems on Various Subjects, XII. 183
Preliminary Treatise on Method, XI. 133
Religious Musings, XI. 124; XII. 183
Sibylline Leaves, XI. 119
Spiritual Philosophy, XI. 121
Statesman's Manual, XI. 139
Table Talk, IV. 139; XI. 131
This lime-tree bower, my prison, XI. 129
Three Graves, The, XI. 132
Wallenstein (trans.), XIII. 260
Watchman, The, XI. 138
Coleridge, Mrs Sara (1802–1852), born Fricker, XI. 119, 412, 415, 417; *also see* Add.; XII. 124, 128, 415; XIII. 183
Envoy, XII. 127
False Love, too long thou hast delayed, XII. 127
One face alone, XII. 127
Phantasmion, XII. 127
Coles, Francis (*fl.* 1626–1681), VII. 347
Coleshill, VII. 53
Colet, John (1467?–1519), II. 48, 61, 341, 367, 489; III. 1, 3, 4, 6, 8–13 (main entry), 15, 17, 18, 26, 66, 428, 466; IV. 224, 225, 227, 228, 491; VII. 332 ff.; IX. 529; *An Exposition of St Paul's First Epistle to the Corinthians*, III. 11; *An Exposition of St Paul's Epistle to the Romans*, III. 11; lectures on the *Epistle to the Romans*, III. 10
Colet, John (d. 1637), XIV. 79
Colgan, John (d. 1657?), XIV. 308, *also see* Add. 3
Colgrim, in Layamon, I. 237
Colin, in *The Shepheards Calender*, III. 222, 224, 226, 228. *See, also, under* Spenser
Colin (or *Colyn*) *Blowbol's Testament*, II. 501; III. 84, 86, 483
Colkelbeis Feist, II. 277
Colkelbie, Stewarton, Ayrshire, in *Colkelbie's sow*, II. 126, 127
Colkelbie's sow, II. 126, 127
Collatinus, in *The Rape of Lucrece*, VI. 101
Collbrande (Excalibur), in *Morte Arthure*, II. 119
Collection of Fundamental Liberties and Laws, VIII. 319
Collection of Original Poems, by the Rev. Mr Blacklock and other Scottish Gentlemen, X. 191
College, Stephen (1635?–1681), VIII. 36, 97, 188
College of Arms, IX. 344, 355
Colles, H. Cresswell, IV. 111
Collet, Collet Dobson, XIV. 590
Collet, Mary, IV. 406; VII. 154
Collett, John (1725?–1780), XIV. 214
Collier, Arthur (1680–1732), IX. 287, 288, 505; *Clavis Universalis*, IX. 287
Collier, James, XIV. 481
Collier, Jeremy (1650–1726), VI. 408, 492; VIII. 33, 52, 54, 145, 146, 157, 164 ff., 194, 427, 432 ff.; IX. 29, 141, 142, 210 ff. (main entry), 492; X. 70, 72; XI. 282
Dissuasive from the Playhouse, VIII. 167
Duelling, IX. 211
Ecclesiastical History, VIII. 32; IX. 211, 212
Essays, IX. 211
Historical Dictionary, IX. 211, 212
Of Lying, IX. 211
Office of a Chaplain, IX. 211
Short view of the...English Stage, VIII. 32, 163, 197; IX. 211; X. 67
Collier, John ['Tim Bobbin'] (1708–1786), X. 453
Collier, John Payne (1789–1883), V. 10, 13, 54, 143, 146, 277 ff., 286, 314, 315; VI. 33, 50, 89, 249, 281, 398; XI. 133; XII. 353, 520
Extracts from the Registers of the Stationers' Company, XII. 368
Notes on Rare English Books, XII. 368
Roxburghe Ballads, The, XII. 368
Shakespeare's Library, XII. 368
Collier, Thomas (*fl.* 1691), X. 377
Collier, The Historie of the, V. 329
Collin (i.e. Spenser), IV. 180
Collings, Samuel (*fl.* 1780–1790?), X. 479
Collingtree, X. 365
Collingwood, Ralph, dean of Lichfield, IV 225
Collingwood, Stuart Dodgson, XIII. 501
Collingwood, William Gershom, XIV. Add. 3
Collins, Anthony (1676–1729), VIII. 332, 471; IX. 111, 288, 292, 293, 505, 512
Discourse of Free-thinking, IX. 292, 293, 337, 456
Discourse of the...Christian Religion, IX. 293
Essay concerning the use of Reason, IX. 293
Philosophical Inquiry concerning Human Liberty, IX. 293
Priestcraft in perfection, IX. 293
Collins, Arthur (1690?–1760), VIII. 267; IX. 496; X. 500; *Peerage*, XI. 327
Collins, Benjamin (*fl.* 1762), X. 207, 209, 210, 482
Collins, Charles Allston (1828–1873), XIII. 326, 332, 561
Collins, Charles MacCarthy, XIV. 573
Collins, F. H., XIV. 481
Collins, John Churton (1848–1908), IV. 43; V. 133 ff.; VI. 166; IX. 230; X. Add.; XII. 504; XIII. 476, 486, 488; XIV. 517, 518, 594; *Bolingbroke*, IX. 218, 224

Collins, Mortimer (1827–1876), XIII. 500; *British Birds, The,* XIII. 163; *To F. C.,* XIII. 163
Collins, Mr, in Jane Austen's *Pride and Prejudice,* XII. 234, 238, 240, 243, 245
Collins, Thomas (*fl.* 1615), VII. 406
Collins, William (1721–1759), V. 205; IX. 167, 169, 179, 191, 481; X. 60, 87, 93, 132, 138, 142 ff. (main entry), 147, 149, 153, 156, 164, 183, 186, 230, 447, 453, 454, 469, *also see* Add.; XI. 77, 86, 124, 158, 160, 161, 248, 250, 255; XII. 101, 177
Dirge in Cymbeline, X. 126, 144
Eclogues, X. 143
Evening, XII. 124
'How sleep the brave,' X. 143, 144
Ode...death of Mr Thomson, X. 109
Ode to Evening, X. 125, 143, 144, 218; XI. 85, 179
Ode to Liberty, X. 144
Ode to Simplicity, X. 128
Odes, X. 142 ff.
Superstitions of the Highlands, X. 144
Collins, William Edward (1867–1911), XIV. 101, 486
Collins, William Lucas, XIV. 597
Collins, William Wilkie (1824–1889), XIII. 326, 335, 336, 420, 423, 425, 437–438 (main entry), 538, 541, 542, 561
Antonina, XIII. 434
Moonstone, The, XIII. 437
No Name, XIII. 437
Woman in White, The, XIII. 437
Collinson, James (1825?–1881), XIII. 110
Collinson, John (1757?–1793), XII. 509
Collis, Ramsay, XIV. 533
Collison-Morley, L., *Giuseppe Baretti,* X. 159
Collop, John (*fl.* 1660), VII. 88, 412, 465
Collyer, N., XIV. 591
Colman, Francis (d. 1733), X. 430
Colman, George, the elder (1732–1794), X. 77, 89 ff., 211, 214, 428 ff., 432, 436, 441, 474; XI. 78, 270; XIII. 269; XIV. 590, 594
Clandestine Marriage, X. 91 ff.
Connoisseur, The, XI. 448, 451; XIV. 590, 594
Deuce is in Him, X. 90
English Merchant, X. 86
Jealous Wife, X. 89 ff.
Man of Business, XI. 265
Musical Lady, X. 90
New Brooms, XI. 282
Philaster, X. 90
Polly Honeycombe, X. 89
Ut Pictura Poesis, XI. 282
Colman, George, the younger (1762–1836), XI. 276, 278 ff., 453, 455, 457
Battle of Hexham, XI. 280
Heir at Law, XI. 280
Inkle and Yarico, XI. 279
Iron Chest, The, XI. 280, 393
John Bull, XI. 280
Mountaineers, The, XI. 280
Siege of Paris, XI. 257
Coleman, George, the younger
Surrender of Calais, XI. 280
Turk and no Turk, XI. 279
Two to One, XI. 279
Colne river, VII. 98
Cologne, II. 311, 312, 321; III. 42; IV. 402, 403; VI. 295; VII. 212; VIII. 261, 262
Cologne, Three Kings of, II. 323, 335, 486, 503
Colombe, Browning's, XIII. 64
Colomies or Colomesius, Paul (1638–1692), VII. 484
Colon, the ostler, in *Hudibras,* VIII. 68
Colonial and Indian Exhibition, XIV. 369
Colonial Monthly, The, XIV. 367
Colonna palace, XII. 67
Colour, in *Lingua,* VI. 315
Colquhoun, Archibald Ross, XIV. Add. 6
Colquhoun, John (1805–1885), XIV. 542
Colquhoun, John Campbell (1803–1870), XIV. 605
Colquhoun, Patrick (1745–1820), XIV. 605
Colson, Nathaniel, IV. 454
'Colson, Tom,' in *The Tatler,* IX. 34
Colt, the, in *Mum, Sothsegger,* II. 36
Colton, John (d. 1404), XII. 518
Columba, St (521–597), I. 42, 69, 435; XII. 518
Columban, St (543–615), I. 65, 435
Columbus, Christopher, I. 209; IV. 68, 70–82, 86, 92, 101; VII. 305; X. 289
Columbus, in *Perfidus Hetruscus,* VI. 302
Columella, II. 363; IV. 371
Columne, Jacob, IV. 454
Coluthus, VII. 87
Coluthus, in *The Rape of Helen,* V. 143
Colvile, George (*fl.* 1556), IV. 442
Colvill, Robert (d. 1788), IX. 557
Colvill, Samuel (*fl.* 1681), IX. 499, 556
Colvin, Ian D., XIV. Add. 6
Colvin, Sir Sidney, XII. 219, 405 ff., 439, 441, 499, *also see* Add. 2; XIII. 484; XIV. 526
Colwell, Thomas, IV. 390; V. 116; VI. 296
Colyton academy, X. 385
Combe, George (1788–1858), XIV. 414, 471, 542, 543, 605
Combe, William (1741–1823), XIV. 217 ff., 542, 543
Anti-Diabo-lady, The, XIV. 217
Dance of Life, The, XIV. 219
Diabo-lady, The, XIV. 217
Diaboliad, The, XIV. 217
English Dance of Death, The, XIV. 219
Johnny Quae Genus, XIV. 220
Letters of the late Lord Lyttelton, XIV. 217
Letters of Sterne to Eliza, XIV. 217
Life of Napoleon, XIV. 223
Second Tour of Dr Syntax, The, XIV. 220
Third Tour of Dr Syntax, The, XIV. 220
Tour of Dr Syntax, The, XIV. 218, 219, 221
Combe abbey, IV. 175
Comber, Thomas (1645–1699), VII. 342
Comedies of Italian or Romantic origin, Anonymous, V. 413

Comedus, in *Lingua*, VI. 315
Comedy, early English, V. 401 ff.
Comedy, in *Mucedorus*, V. 254
Comedy, in *The Muses Looking-Glasse*, VI. 233
Comedy, in *A Warning for Faire Women*, V. 326
Comenius, John Amos, IX. 381, 403, 569; *Didactica Magna*, IX. 388; *Opera Didactica Omnia*, IX. 388, 568, 573
Comestor, Peter, *Magister Historiarum, Historia Scholastica* of, II. 365; IV. 39, 60
Comet, The, XIV. 318a
Comic dialogues, VII. 516
Comic Magazine, The, XIV. 235
Comines, Philippe de, *Mémoires*, XII. 26
Coming of Antichrist, The, V. 15
Comment, Cuthbert. *See* Tucker, Abraham
Commines or Comines, Philippe de, III. 315; IV. 3, 443
Commodus, I. 95
Common Conditions, V. 117, 130, 138, 413; VI. 284
Common Thift, in *Ane Pleasant Satyre*, III. 128
Commons, house of, III. 402; IV. 162, 279, 305, 306; IX. 64, 194, 195, 216, 219, 225, 232, 240, 281; X. 3, 84, 94, 163, 244, 283, 284, 296, 306, 320, 399, 401, 404; XI. 2, 5, 8, 9, 12, 13, 21, 29, 34, 50, 52; XII. 307; XIII. 305
Commons Journals, The, VIII. 255
Commonwealth, the, IV. 396, 433; XI. 394
Commonwealth acts, VIII. 468
Commonwealth pamphlets, etc., XI. 470
Communis Sensus, in *Lingua*, VI. 314, 315
Comnenus, Andronicus, VII. 248
Comoedia, in *Fucus Histriomastix*, VI. 324
Compassio Mariae and *Assumptio Mariae*, I. 232, 458
Compendious Booke of Godly and Spirituall Songs, IX. 361, 362
Complaint, in Davison's *Rapsody*, IV. 124
Complaint of a lover's life, The, II. 485
Complaynt of Scotlande, The, II. 93, 94, 97, 98, 251, 268, 279, 280, 285; III. 131, 152, 153, 502
Complaynte of the Heart, The, II. 326
Compleat Devotions, X. 356
Compleat History of England, IX. 233, 234
Complete Courtier, IV. 344
Compters Common Wealth, III. 99
Compton, Charles, 7th earl of Northampton (d. 1763), X. 113
Compton, Henry (1632–1713), bishop of London, IX. 170; *Episcopalia*, VIII. 305, 459
Compton, Spencer, earl of Wilmington (1673?–1743), IX. 252; X. 94
Compton Wynyates, X. 113
Comput. See Thaun, P. de
Comte, Auguste, XIII. 22, 385, 457; XIV. 22, 24, 32, 33, 102 ff., 468, 469, 471, 475 ff.; *Cours de philosophie positive*, XIV. 17; *Système de Politique Positive*, XIII. 397
Comus, in Milton's *Comus*, VII. 113
Comus, in *Pleasure Reconciled*, VI. 359 ff.
Comyns, the, II. 100
Conan, in *The Misfortunes of Arthur*, V. 78, 79
Conant, John (1608–1694), VII. 317
Concanen, Matthew (1701–1749), IX. 434; XIV. 568
Conceits, in Cowley's *The Muse*, VII. 65
Concini, marshal d'Ancre, IV. 259, VI. 181
Concordia Regularis, V. 36, 37
Concupiscencia-carnis, in *Piers the Plowman*, II. 25
Condé, Louis II de Bourbon, prince de, VIII. 246
Conde Lucanor, VIII. 126
Condell, Henry (d. 1627), V. 169; VI. 248, 249, 276 ff.
Conder, Claude Reignier (1848–1910), XIV. 551
Conder, Eustace R., XIV. 533
Conder, Josiah (1789–1855), XII. 415
Condillac, Etienne Bonnot de Marly de, VIII. 335, 336
Condorcet, marquis de, XI. 399, 414; *Esquisse d'un tableau historique*, XI. 73, 276
Conestaggio, G., IV. 443
Coney-Catching pamphlets, IV. 515
Confessio, in *The Castle of Perseverance*, V. 52
Confession, in *Every-man*, V. 54
Confucian canon, the, XII. 343
Confucius, XII. 500
Conger, the, XI. 325
Congleton, IX. 166
Congleton, lord. *See* Parnell, Henry Brooke
Congo, the, XIV. 192
Congregational Historical society, X. 519
Congregational histories, X. 519
Congreve, Richard (1818–1899), XII. 334; XIV. 471; *The Catechism of Positive Religion translated*, XIV. 24
Congreve, William (1670–1729), IV. 185; V. 127, 189; VI. 492; VIII. 57, 137, 139, 146 ff. (main entry), 161, 163, 165 ff., 171, 172, 176, 189, 191, 423, 427, 428, 430, 432, 433, 442; IX. 38, 69, 75, 91, 124, 131, 163, 228, 270, 436, 439, 440, 473, 475; X. 21, 22, 67, 185, 446; XI. 248; XII. 168, 443; XIII. 269
Amendments, VIII. 168
Double Dealer, The, VIII. 55, 148, 149, 375, 396
Incognita, or Love and Duty Reconciled, VIII. 146
Love for Love, VIII. 150, 152, 157, 158, 168; X. 90
Mourning Bride, The, VIII. 152, 166, 168; X. 218
Ode to the Queen, X. 127
Old Bachelor, The, VIII. 146, 147
Way of the World, The, VIII. 150, 153 155 ff., 168

Congreve, Vanbrugh and Walsh, *Squire Treloobу*, VIII. 157
Coningham, James (1670–1716), X. 385
Coningsby, Disraeli's, XIII. 350
Coningsby, Sir Thomas (d. 1625), VII. 449
Conington, John (1825–1869), IX. 74; X. 124; XII. 334, 337, 482; XIII. 175, 500
Conjecture, Essays of, IV. 524
Connoisseur, The, X. 171, 202, 429; XI. 402
Connolly, Daniel, XIV. 573
Connor, Ireland, XII. 361
Connycatching, The Groundworke of, V. 480
Conquest, the Norman, III. 193, 196, 197, 440; IV. 60, 137
Conrad, in Byron's *Corsair*, XII. 46
Conscience, in an *estrif* by Barnfield, IV. 120
Conscience, in *Mirour de l'Omme*, II. 140 ff.
Conscience, in *Piers the Plowman*, II. 8 ff., 16, 19, 20, 26 ff.
Conscience, in *Robin Conscience*, III. 97
Conscience, in *The Palice of Honour*, II. 261
Consolation, The Rote or mirror of, II. 323
Constable, Archibald (1774–1827), XI. 342, 459, 469; XII. 142, 144, 155, 156, 378, 427, 450; XIV. 612
Constable, George, XII. 350
Constable, Henry (1562–1613), III. 522; IV. 117, 124; *Diana*, III. 247, 256, 260, 261, 271
Constable, Thomas (1812–1881), XI. 477; XII. 378, 427, 450; XIV. 612
Constable country, XII. 305
Constance, Browning's, XIII. 64
Constance, council of, II. 69
Constance, in *Confessio Amantis*, II. 147
Constance, in *King John*, V. 185
Constance, in Scott's *Marmion*, XII. 10
Constance, in *The Man of Law's Tale*, I. 311; II. 181, 182
Constance, in *The Northern Lasse*, VI. 226
Constancy, legend of, in *The Faerie Queene*, III. 238
Constantina, St, I. 74
Constantine, *Breviary* (*Viaticus*) of, II. 365
Constantine, in *Confessio Amantis*, II. 148, 151, 152
Constantine, in Layamon, I. 266
Constantine, in *Morte Arthure*, II. 120
Constantine, *Lexicon graeco-latinum*, IV. 429
Constantine, the donation of, III. 179
Constantine of Devon and Cornwall, I. 67
Constantine the Great, I. 55; II. 58, 293; V. 16; X. 317; XII. 305, 321
Constantinople, II. 131; IV. 90; VII. 437; VIII. 291, 295; IX. 240, 244, 246, 391; X. 391; XII. 273; XIV. 251
'Constantinus Afer,' X. 204
Constantius, *Life of St Germanus of Auxerre*, I. 81
Constantius Chlorus, I. 34
Constanza, in *The Spanish Gipsie*, VI. 77
Constitutional, The, XIII. 278; XIV. 196
Consultation, The, of Hermann of Wied, III. 31
Contarine, Jane (Mrs Lawder) (*fl.* 1750), X. 199, 481
Contarine, Thomas (uncle of Goldsmith, Oliver), X. 198, 200, 209
Contarini, Gaspar, IV. 443
Contemplacio, in Coventry plays, V. 12, 49
Contemporary Review, The, XIV. 523, 534
Contention, The First Part of the, IV. 393
Contention, The, betwixt the two famous Houses of Yorke and Lancaster, V. 135, 147, 153, 184, 220, 237, 238, 260, 397, 433
Contention between Liberalitie and Prodigalitie, V. 394
Contes de ma mère l'Oie, XI. 374, 375
Con-Test, The, X. 389, 390, 522
Conti, Antonio, *Il Cesare*, V. 288, 289
Contrition, in *Piers the Plowman*, II. 28
Contrition, in *The Passetyme of Pleasure* and *The Example of Virtue*, II. 228
Conventicle Act of 1593, VII. 170, 172
Conversion of St Paul, The, V. 19
Conway, Anne, viscountess (d. 1679), VIII. 110, 280
Conway, Edward, 1st viscount (d. 1631), VII. 434; VIII. 280
Conway, George, X. 199
Conway, Gilbert, *Treatise of Versification*, XIII. 248, 512
Conway, Henry Seymour (1721–1795), X. 245, 249, 251, 399, 495, 523; XI. 12
Conway, Hugh, *pseud.* *See* Fargus, Frederick John
Conway, lord. *See* Seymour-Conway
Conway, Moncure Daniel, XI. 395; XIII. 470
Conybeare, William John (1815–1857), XII. 293, 464, 472
Conyngton. *See* Richard de
Cook, Albert Stanburrough, I. 50, 57, 59, 419, Add.; X. Add.; XIII. 507
Cook, Dutton, XIII. 514
Cook, Eliza (1818–1889), XIII. 177, 189, 500
Cook, Ernest Thomas, XIV. 153, 524, 533, 534
Cook, George (1772–1845), XIV. 487
Cook, captain James (1728–1779), IV. 102
Cook, James, XIII. 531; XIV. 244, 289, 459, 551; *Narrative*, XIV. 241; *To the Pacific Ocean*, XIV. 245; *Towards the South Pole*, XIV. 245
Cook, John (d. 1660), VIII. 470
Cook, John Douglas (1808?–1868), XIV. 533
Cook, William (*fl.* 1632–1641), VII. 347
Cook, William (d. 1824), XI. 448
Cooke, Sir Anthony (1504–1576), IV. 175, 177, 278
Cooke, George Frederick (1756–1811), XI. 453
Cooke, George Wingrove (1814–1865), XII. 426; XIII. 553
Cooke, J. (*fl.* 1614), *Greene's Tu Quoque or The Cittie Gallant*, VI. 219, 454
Cooke, Sir J., *Unum necessarium* (1648), IV. 510
Cooke, John (1731–1810), XI. 326; XIV. 573

Cooke, Thomas (1703–1756), VII. 430; IX. 78, 220, 526
Cooke, Thomas Potter (1786–1864), XIII. 264, 265
Cooke, W. (d. 1814), X. 195, 445, 470, 471, 483
Cookery books, II. 483, 500; III. 19
Cookery, Boke of, IV. 543
Cookesley, William, XI. 40
Cookson, Anne. *See* Wordsworth, Anne
Coolidge, William Augustus Brevoort, XIV. 552
Coolin district, Skye, XIII. 209
Cooling Carde for all Fond Lovers, A, in *The Anatomy of Wit*, III. 345, 346
Coolney, XIV. 304
Cooper, Anthony Ashley, 1st earl of Shaftesbury (1621–1683), VII. 451; VIII. 17, 30, 36 ff., 40, 75, 90, 92 ff., 97, 100, 184, 188, 190, 329, 330, 440; IX. 3, 234
Cooper, Anthony Ashley, 3rd earl of Shaftesbury (1671–1713), VIII. 457, 471; IX. 204, 288, 295, 299 ff. (main entry), 302, 303, 506, 508, *also see* Add.; X. 122, 337, 426, 469
  Characteristics, VIII. 329; IX. 300
  Inquiry concerning Virtue, IX. 300
  Letter concerning Enthusiasm, IX. 204, 300
  Miscellaneous Reflections, IX. 300
  Moralists, The, IX. 300
  Notion of the Historical Draught...of the Judgment of Hercules, IX. 300
  Sensus Communis, IX. 300
  Soliloquy: or Advice to an Author, IX. 300
Cooper, Charles A. (1829–1916), XIV. 533; *Fifty Years of Newspaper Work*, XIV. 176
Cooper, Charles Henry (1808–1866), XII. 488, 515
  Annals of Cambridge, XII. 357
  Athenae Cantabrigienses, XII. 357
  Memoir of Margaret Countess of Richmond and Derby, XII. 357
  Memorials of Cambridge, XII. 357
Cooper, Charles Purton (1793–1873), XII. 515; *An Account of the Public Records*, XII. 354
Cooper, Edith Emma. *See* Field, Michael
Cooper, Edward Herbert (1867–1910), XIII. 561
Cooper, Elizabeth (*fl.* 1737), *The Muses' Library*, VII. 193, 199
Cooper, John Gilbert (1723–1769), X. 452
Cooper, Lane, XI. 409
Cooper or Couper, Thomas (1517?–1594), III. 385 ff., 391, 392, 537; *An Admonition to the People of England*, III. 386, 387, 391, 392, 537; *Advertisement touching the Controversies of the Church of England*, III. 392
Cooper, Thomas (*fl.* 1626), IV. 535; VII. 506
Cooper, Thomas (*fl.* 1744), XI. 323, 375
Cooper, Thomas (1805–1892), XIII. 500; XIV. 471, 601
Cooper, Thompson, XIII. 564
Cooper, William (d. 1689), XI. 335, 336
Cooper, William Durrant (1812–1875), XI. 429, 485; XII. 511
'Cooper,' earl, *A Letter to Isaac Bickerstaffe, Esq.*, IX. 217
Cooper's hill, VII. 59
Coorson, Margery, in *The foure P. P.*, V. 96
Coote, Edmund (*fl.* 1597), *The English Schoolmaster...*, III. 556
Coote, Henry Charles (1815–1885), XII. 515
Cope, Sir Antony (d. 1551), IV. 4, 438
Cope, Edward Meredith (1818–1873), XII. 331, 475, 482
Cope's Tobacco Plant, XIII. 108, 489
Copeland, C. T., XIII. 470
Copeland, William John (1804–1885), XII 454, 459
Copenhagen, V. 283, 307; IX. 165; XII. 336, 344
Coperario or Coprario, Giovanni, or John Cooper (d. 1626), IV. 463
Copernicus, Nicholas, III. 163, 425; IV. 66, 278, 290; VII. 238, 314; VIII. 283, 350, 352; IX. 391; XIV. 27
Copinger, Walter Arthur (1847–1910), XII. 427, 520; XIV. 536; *Incunabula Biblica*, XII. 369
Copland, Robert (*fl.* 1508–1547), II. 312, 324, 325, 329; III. 62, 82, 94, 101, 102, 105, 360; IV. 317, 397, 521, 546
  Art of good living and dying, II. 329
  Helias Knight of the Swan, II. 325
  Hye Way to the Spyttell House, The, II. 324, 485, 501; III. 62, 101, 360, 492
  Jyl of Braintford's Testament, II. 324, 485
  Kalendar of Shepherds, II. 324
  Kynge Appolyn of Thyre, II. 324
  Mirror of the Church, The, II. 324
Copland, William (*fl.* 1556–1569), IV. 397, 448, 518, 542; V. 92
Cople Hoo, near Bedford, VIII. 60
Cople Woodend, VII. 167
Copleston, Edward (1776–1849), XII. 284, 427; XIV. 596, 601; *Replies* (to the *Edinburgh Review*), XIV. 410
Copleston, Reginald Stephen, XIV. 209
Copley, Anthony (1567–1607?), IV. 119, 469
Copley, John Singleton, lord Lyndhurst (1772–1863), XIII. 347; XIV. 112, 124 510
Copperfield, David, Dickens's, XIII. 305, 307, 326, 339
Coppin, Richard (*fl.* 1646–1659), X. 377
Coptic language, XII. 362
Copyright act, the, XI. 313 ff., 317, 342; XIV. 89
Coquerel, J. G., XI. 430
Corah (Titus Oates), in Dryden's *Absalom*, VIII. 39
Coran. *See* Koran
Corantos, IV. 389; VII. 345, 346, 385 IX. 1, 5
Corbet, John (1603–1641), IX. 543

Corbet, Richard (1582–1635), IV. 362; VII. 412; XI. 374; *The Fairies Farewell*, X. 233
Corbie. *See* John of
Corbould, E. H., XII. 448
Corbulo, in *Appius and Virginia*, VI. 182
Cordelia, in *King Lear*, V. 203, 204
Cordella, in *King Leir*, V. 83, 84
Corder, William (1804–1828), XIV. 228
Cordier, Mathurin, III. 429; *Pueriles Confabulatiunculae*, XI. 367
Cordifiamma, in Kingsley's *Two Years Ago*, XIII. 365
Cordova, in Alfred's *Orosius*, I. 95
Cordus, Euricius, IV. 264
Cordyale, II. 313
Corfe castle, XII. 508
Corfesgeat, I. 138
Coridon, in Barclay's *Epilogues*, III. 65
Corineus, in Layamon, I. 237
Corineus, in *Locrine*, V. 240
Corineus of Cornwall, IV. 190
Corinna (Herrick's), II. 393; VII. 6
Corinth, VI. 163, 317
Corinthian pillars, X. 110
Coriolanus, III. 24; IV. 11
Coriolanus (Shakespeare's), IV. 11
Corippus, I. 76
Cork, III. 244; IX. 282; XII. 159; XIII. 107; XIV. 263, 311, 316
Cork, countess of. *See* Monckton, Mary
Cork, county, XII. 165; XIV. 326
Cork, earl of. *See* Boyle, Richard
Cork, Queen's college, XIV. 417
Corkine, William, IV. 113, 463
Cormac, Irish scholar (831–903), I. 246
Corn law, the, XIV. 132
Corn law agitation, XIII. 14
'Corn Law Rhymer,' XII. 136, 416
Cornaro, Luigi (1475–1566), VII. 402
Cornbury, viscount. *See* Hyde, Henry
Corneille, Pierre, V. 292, 293, 295; VI. 49; VII. 275; VIII. 14, 18, 24, 30, 31, 33, 56, 131, 134, 165, 376, 422, 424, 483; IX. 256; X. 83, 444; XI. 353
  Cid, Le, VIII. 13, 180, 371; X. 69
  Cinna, X. 69
  Discours, VIII. 23, 374
  Examens, VIII. 23, 374
  Héraclius, VIII. 133, 180
  Horace, VII. 88; VIII. 180; IX. 276, 499; X. 86
  Lyer, The, VIII. 373
  Médée, VIII. 13
  Menteur, Le, VIII. 13, 373; IX. 30; see also, *The Lyer* and *The Mistaken Beauty*
  Mistaken Beauty, The, VIII. 373
  Nicomède, VIII. 180
  Polyeucte, VIII. 180
  Pompée, VII. 88; VIII. 133, 180
Corneille, Thomas, X. 86
Cornelia, in *The White Divel*, VI. 177, 187
Cornelius, in *Memoirs of Martinus Scriblerus*, IX. 136
Cornelius Agrippa, IV. 249
Cornelius Nepos, I. 195
Cornelius Tacitus, in *The City Witt*, VI. 225
Cornelys, Mrs Theresa (Threnodia Augustalis) (1723–1797), X. 482
Cornford, L. C., XIII. 503; XIV. 526
Cornhill Magazine, The, X. 204, XI. 90; XII. 426, 431; XIII. 299, 300, 380, 425; XIV. 143, 152, 194, 316
Corniche road, X. 42
Cornish, bishop, III. 56
Cornish, Francis Warre, XII. 447, 464; XIII. 503
Cornish, Joseph (1750–1823), XIV. 605
Cornish dialect, XIV. 434
Cornish drama, XII. 512
Cornish giant, a, XIII. 278
Cornish miracle plays, V. 15, 16, 391
Cornish 'rounds,' VI. 252
Cornishman, the, in *The Fyrste Boke of the Introduction of Knowledge*, III. 105
Cornix, in Barclay's *Eclogues*, III. 65
Cornix, in Barnabe Googe's *Eclogues*, III. 186
Cornwall, IV. 190, 200; VI. 242; VII. 16, 86; VIII. 119; IX. 532; X. 77, 193, 244, 365, 490; XI. 37; XII. 346, 417, 521; XIV. 434
Cornwall. *See* John of
Cornwall, Barry, *pseud.* *See* Procter, Bryan Waller
Cornwallis, Caroline Frances (1786–1858), XIV. 471
Cornwallis, Frederick (1713–1783), archbishop of Canterbury, X. 308
Cornwallis, Sir William (d. 1631), IV. 343 ff., 362, 517, 524, 525; VI. 341; VII. 389
Cornyshe, or Cornish, William (d. 1524?), VI. 281 ff., 287; *Triumphe of Love and Bewte, The*, VI. 284, 287
Coromandel, X. 204
Coronation stone, the, II. 130
Corporation act, X. 374
Corpus Christi, feast of, III. 81; and plays, V. 9, 12, 13, 44, 45, 48, 52, 56, 389
Corpus Historicum, XII. 355
Corpus juris, II. 350, 363; VIII. 312
Corpus Poetarum Infantilium, XI. 375
Correggio, Antonio, VII. 176
Correspondence between Frances Countess of Hertford and Henrietta Louisa Countess of Pomfret, X. 274
Correspondent, The, IX. 460
Corrupt Doctrine, in *A True Inventory*, VII. 382
Corry, Isaac (1755–1813), XI. 156
Corsica, X. 190, 192, 477, 479
Corsica, the Syracusan, in *The Bond-man*, VI. 157
Corstopitum, Corbridge, Northumberland, XII. 509
Corstorphine, George Stewart, XIV. Add. 7
Corte, Claudio, IV. 443
Cortes, Martin, *Breve compendio de la Sphera y de la arte de navigar*, IV. 71, 104, 443, 455
Coruisk district, Skye, XIII. 209

Coruns, raisins of, II. 305
Cory, G. E., XIV. Add. 6
Cory, William Johnson (1823–1892), XIII. 189, 503; XIV. 597, 606; *Invocation, An*, XIII. 193; *Ionica*, XIII. 193; *Mimnermus in Church*, XIII. 193
Coryate, George (father of Thomas), IV. 89
Coryate, Thomas (1577?–1617), IV. 89 ff., 392, 454; V. 350; VI. 138, 219; XIV. 333
Coryats Cramb, IV. 90
Coryats Crudities, IV. 89, 203; VII. 201; X. 200
Odcombian Banquet, The, IV. 90
Thomas Coriate Traveller for the English Wits: Greeting, IV. 90
Coryate, T., in *Love Restored*, VI. 351
Corydon (Vergil's), III. 264
Cosimo II, grand duke of Tuscany, VIII. 358
Cosin, John (1594–1672), IV. 421; VII. 34, 424, 482; VIII. 294 ff., 459; IX. 530; X. 360; *A Collection of Private Devotions*, VII. 147; VIII. 294; *Correspondence*, VIII. 296; *Historia Transubstantionis Papalis*, VIII. 296
Cosin Cutpurse, VI. 285
Cosma, in *Sicelides*, VI. 323
Cosmas, martyr, I. 74
Cosmo, in *The Traytor*, VI. 199
'Cosmopolis,' IX. 292
Cosroe, in *Tamburlaine*, V. 151
Cossacks, XII. 46
Cossé, Charles du, comte de Brissac, III. 163
Cossé, Timoleon du, III. 163
Costar Pearmain, in Farquhar's *Recruiting Officer*, VIII. 171
Costard, in *Love's Labour's Lost*, V. 178
Coste, Pierre (1668–1747), VIII. 472; IX. 400
Costeker, John Littleton, *The Fine Gentleman*, IX. 397, 569
Costigan, captain, Thackeray's, XIII. 283, 292, 296
Costlie Whore, The, III. 81
Costume, poems on, II. 502
Cotentin, the, II. 118
Cotes, Roger (1682–1716), IX. 335, 412
Cotgrave, John (*fl.* 1655), VII. 512; *Le Mercure Anglois*, VII. 360
Cotgrave, Randle (d. 1634?), *Dictionary*, IX. 255, 271, 529
Cotswolds, the, IV. 190; VIII. 83; X. 113; XII. 256, 257, 265
Cotta, in Owen's *Epigrammata*, IV. 265
Cotta, John (1575?–1650?), IV. 535; VII. 375, 394, 506, 511; *Discovery of... Ignorant Practicers of Physice*, VII. 374; *The Triall of Witchcraft*, VII. 374
Cottenham, manor of, II. 343
Cottin, Sophie, *Elisabeth*, XIII. 522
Cottington, Francis, lord (1578?–1652), VII. 215
Cottle, Amos Simon (1768?–1800), X. 487
Cottle, Joseph (1770–1853), X. 485, 486; XI. 341, 409, 417, 422, 423, 468; *Early Recollections*, XI. 133
Cotton. *See* Bartholomew de
Cotton, Charles (1630–1687), IV. 16, 18; VI. 115; VII. 251, 463; IX. 257, 272, 276, 277, 499
Burlesque upon Burlesque, IX. 257
Compleat Gamester, IX. 277
Horace, Corneille's, translation of, VIII. 180
Montaigne, VIII. 387
Planter's Manual, IX. 277
Scarronides, or Virgil Travestie, VIII. 372; IX. 257
Transactions, IX. 276
Cotton, Geo. Edw. Lynch (1813–1866), XIV. 598
Cotton, Sir Henry, VII. 442
Cotton, Henry (1789–1879), XI. 468; XII. 520
Cotton, John (1584–1652), III. 422
Cotton, Sir John (1621–1701), IX. 196, 197
Cotton, Nathaniel (1705–1788), XI. 186
Cotton, Sir Robert Bruce (1571–1631), III. 55, 324, 326; IV. 55, 59, 60, 429; VII. 203; VIII. 318, 323; IX. 357; XIV. 285, 566; *Henry III*, VII. 433, 514
Cotton, Sophia Anne, XIV. 598
Cottoni Posthuma (1651), VIII. 470
Cottonian library, IX. 349, 357; XIV. 52, 560
Cottrell, Sir Charles (1615–1687), translation of La Calprenède's *Cléopâtre*, VIII. 371
Coucy, Raoul de, XI. 274
Coues, Elliott, XIV. 583
Coulson, Walter (1794?–1860), XIV. 533
Council, the King's, II. 286
Counsel, in *The Passetyme of Pleasure*, II. 225
Countenance, in *The Assembly of Ladies*, II. 217
Counterfesaunce, in *The Tears of the Muses*, III. 241
Counterfet Countenaunce, in *Magnyfycence*, III. 77
Country Gentleman, The, IX. 220
Country pursuits and pastimes, writers on, IV. 364 ff., 537 ff.
Couper, A. S., XIV. 557
Courage, in *The Example of Virtue*, II. 227
Courier, The, XIII. 259; XIV. 172, 184, 187, 188, 194
'Court of Good Company,' II. 208
Court of High Commission, V. 371, 372
Court of Love, The, II. 162, 164, 166, 167, 215, 217, 218, 220, 221, 223, 240, 243, 261
Court Poems, IX. 78, 247; XI. 328
Courtall, in *She Would if She Could*, VIII. 138
Courtenay, Edward, earl of Devonshire (1526?–1556), IV. 447
Courtenay, John (1741–1816), X. 472, 480

Courtenay, Thomas Peregrine (1782–1841), xiv. 513
Courtenay, William (1342?–1396), ii. 55, 56
Courtes, The Booke of the Diversities of (1561), viii. 465, 466
Courtesy, in *The Pastyme of Pleasure*, ii. 229, 234
Courtesy, in *The Faerie Queene*, ii. 234
Courtesy books, ix. 569
Courthope, William John (1842–1917), i. 419; ix. 76; xii. 524; *History of English Poetry*, i. 240; ii. 139; iii. 180, 181; iv. 146; viii. 423; ix. 153
Courtier's Calling, The, ix. 396, 570
Courtly Abusyon, in *Magnyfycence*, iii. 77
Courtly Nice, Sir (Crowne's), viii. 188 ff.
Courtney, William Leonard, xiii. 514; xiv. 478
Courtney, William Prideaux (1845–1913), ix. 191; xii. 521; xiv. 508, 512, 531; *A Register of National Bibliography*, xii. 369
Courts of Justice Corrected and Amended, The, vii. 388
Cousin, Victor, xiv. 11; *History of Modern Philosophy*, xii. 371
Coutances, André de, *Roman des Franceis*, i. 236
Coutts, Jas., xiv. 595
Covenant, the, vii. 455
Covent Garden Drolery (1672), viii. 395
Covent-Garden Journal, x. 33, 34, 39, 417
Coventry, ii. 61; iii. 381, 382, 386; iv. 190, 409; vi. 37; ix. 196; xiii. 276, 383, 384
Coventry, Francis (d. 1759?), xi. 459; *Pompey the Little*, ix. 245, 391, 409, 574
Coventry, Mick Parke, iv. 174
Coventry, Thomas, 1st baron (1578–1640), vii. 219
Coventry, Sir William (1628?–1686), viii. 255, 256, 259, 387, 481
Coventry academy, x. 385
Coventry family, vii. 87
Coventry grammar school, iv. 12
Coventry Plays, ii. 425; v. 10, 12, 13, 16, 17, 19 ff., 30, 31, 44, 46, 48, 49, 56, 69, 389, *and see* Add. 1
Coveras, don Francisco de las (imaginary author), viii. 141
Coverdale, Miles (1488–1568), iii. 27, 43, 44, 79, 96, 473, 486; iv. 41, 380, 402, 421, 442; *Goostly Psalmes and Spiritual Songes*, iii. 79
Coverdale's Bible, xii. 521
Coverley, Sir Roger de, iv. 342; ix. 50 ff.; x. 56; xi. 146
Coverly hall, xiv. 231
Coverly papers, x. 56
Coverte, Robert, iv. 455
Covetousness, in an *estrif* by Barnfield, iv. 120
Covetousness, in *Ane Pleasant Satyre*, iii. 127, 128
Covetousness, in *Piers the Plowman*, ii. 12
Covetousness, Ballet agaynst, iii. 491
Covetyse-of-eyes, in *Piers the Plowman*, ii. 25
Covilla, in Landor's *Count Julian*, xii. 211
Coward, William (1657?–1725), viii. 394
Coward, William (*fl.* 1729–1751), x. 384
Coward trustees, x. 384
Cowden Knowes, x. 233
Cowell, Edward Byles (1826–1903), xii. 343, 489, 502; xiii. 143, 145; xiv. 487
Cowell, John (1554–1611), iii. 424; iv. 510; viii. 468; *Institutiones Juris Anglicani*, viii. 317; *Interpreter, The*, law dictionary, vi. 322, 477; vii. 433; viii. 317
Cowen, Joseph (1831–1900), xiv. 533
Cowes, xiv. 225
Cowes castle, vii. 70
Cowley, Abraham (1618–1667), iv. 163, 187, 223, 261; vi. 471; vii. 61–70 (main entry), 89, 91, 109, 268, 275, 315, 407, 411, 465, 467; viii. 4, 5, 43, 51, 56, 84, 228, 233, 234, 239, 292, 366, 369, 371, 376 ff., 381, 386, 389, 390, 417, 480, *also see* Add.; ix. 47, 119, 158, 168, 264, 406, 570; x. 96, 127, 183, 219, 225; xii. 182; xiii. 429; xiv. 281, 448
Anacreontiques, vii. 63
Battle of Newbury, vii. 63
Change, The, vii. 64
Chronicle, The, vii. 63
Complaint, The, vii. 69
Constantia and Philetus, vii. 62
Cutter of Coleman-Street, vi. 326; vii. 62, 63; viii. 122, 377
Danger of Procrastination, The, viii. 378
Dangers of an Honest Man in Such Company, The, viii. 378
Davideis, vii. 63, 66, 67, 269; viii. 229
Discourse by way of Vision concerning the Government of Oliver Cromwell, vii. 63, 68; viii. 377
Extasie, The, vii. 66
Garden, The, viii. 378
Guardian, The, vi. 326; vii. 62; viii. 122
Hymn to Light, ix. 176
Inconstant, The, vii. 64
Love and Life, vii. 64
'Love in her Sunny Eyes does basking play,' vii. 64
Love's Riddle, vii. 62
Miscellanies, vii. 63
Mistress, The, vii. 25, 63, 64
Muse, The, vii. 65, 66
Naufragium Joculare, vi. 102, 326; vii. 62
Ode Sitting and Drinking in the Chair, made out of the Reliques of Sir Francis Drake's Ship, vii. 68
Ode upon His Majesties Restoration and Return, vii. 68
Odes, vii. 70
Of Agriculture, viii. 378
Of Greatness, viii. 378
Of My Self, vii. 61; viii. 378
Of Obscurity, viii. 378
Of Solitude, viii. 378

Cowley, Abraham
On the Death of Mr Crashaw, VII. 35, 63
On the Death of Mr William Hervey, VII. 63; VIII. 362
Parting, The, VII. 64
Passions, The, VII. 64
Pindarique Odes, VII. 63, 64, 264
Poeticall Blossomes, VII. 35, 62
Poeticall Revenge, A, VII. 62
Prophet, The, VII. 64
Proposition for the Advancement of Experimental Philosophy, VII. 68; VIII. 365; IX. 389, 390
Puritan and the Papist, The, VII. 68
Pyramus and Thisbe, VII. 62
Resurrection, The, VII. 65
Several Discourses by way of Essays in Verse and Prose, VII. 68, 69; VIII. 379
Shortness of Life and uncertainty of Riches, The, VIII. 378
Spring, The, VII. 64
Sylva, VII. 62
To Dr Scarborough, VII. 65
To Mr Hobs, VII. 65
To the Royal Society, VII. 68
Verses on Several Occasions, VII. 68
Vote, The, VII. 62
Written in Juice of Lemmon, VII. 64
Cowley, Hannah, 'Anna Matilda' (1743–1809), XI. 273, 425; *Belle's Stratagem*, XI. 177, 275; *Bold Stroke for a Husband*, XI. 275; *Runaway, The*, XI. 274
Cowper, Ashley, XI. 78
Cowper, Harriet. *See* Hesketh, lady
Cowper, John, XI. 79
Cowper, John, Ramsay's elegy on, IX. 367, 370
Cowper, Mary, countess (1685–1724), IX. 249, 497
Cowper, Spencer, IX. 249, 497
Cowper, Theodora, XI. 78
Cowper, major William, XI. 79
Cowper, William, 1st earl Cowper (d. 1723), IX. 249
Cowper, William (1731–1800), III. 184; IV. 260, 267; VII. 176; VIII. 230; IX. 154, 162, 169, 410; X. 60, 242, 300, 397, 521; XI. 77 ff. (main entry), 145, 150, 152, 167, 175, 176, 179, 246, 247, 251, 252, 254, 259, 327, 362, 401, 427; XII. 132, 177, 231, 473; XIII. 239, 244; XIV. 435, 498, 590
Absence and Bereavement, XI. 78
Anti-Thelyphthora, XI. 81
Boadicea, XI. 83
Castaway, The, XI. 90
Charity, XI. 81
Colubriad, The, XI. 88
Conversation, XI. 81
Dog and the Water-lily, XI. 87
Expostulation, XI. 81
Garden, The, XI. 86
God moves in a mysterious way, XI. 80
Hark, my soul! it is the Lord, XI. 80
Homer, XI. 88 ff.
Hope, XI. 81
Cowper, William
Invitation into the Country, XI. 83
Jesus! where'er thy people meet, XI. 80
John Gilpin, XI. 79, 87; XIV. 438
Letters, XI. 85
Oh for a closer walk with God, XI. 80
'Old Tiney, surliest of his kind,' XI. 88
Olney Hymns, XI. 80
On her endeavouring to conceal her Grief at Parting, XI. 78
On receipt of my Mother's Picture, XI. 78, 87
On the Loss of the Royal George, XI. 88
Poems (1782), XI. 83
Poplar Field, The, XI. 88
Progress of Error, XI. 81, 82
Retirement, XI. 81 ff.
Rose, The, XI. 87
Shrubbery, The, XI. 79, 83
Sofa, The, XI. 84 ff.
Table Talk, XI. 81
Task, The, XI. 81, 83 ff.
There is a fountain filled with blood, XI. 80
Time-piece, The, XI. 86, 87
Tirocinium, XI. 78, 87; XIV. 386
To Mary, XI. 80, 88
To Mrs Unwin, XI. 80, 88
Truth, XI. 81
Verses supposed to be written by Alexander Selkirk, XI. 83
Winter Evening, XI. 86
Winter Morning Walk, XI. 86
Winter Walk at Noon, XI. 86
Yardley Oak, XI. 248
Cowper manuscripts, IX. 249
Cowslip green, XI. 363
Cox, captain (*fl.* 1575), III. 489, 496
Cox, E. G., II. 407
Cox, Geo. Valentine (1786–1875), XIV. 596
Cox, Sir George William (1827–1902), XII. 465, 474; XIV. 70, 488; *History of Greece*, XII. 313, 314; *Poems Legendary and Historical*, XII. 314
Cox, Harold, XII. 426
Cox, Richard (1500–1581), VII. 327, 328, 516
Cox, Sir Richard (1650–1733), IX. 476; X. 293
Cox, Robert, VIII. 417; *Humours of Simpleton the Smith*, VIII. 116; *John Swabber*, VIII. 116
Cox, Samuel (1826–1893), XII. 465
Cox, Thomas (d. 1734), *Magna Britannia et Hibernia*, IX. 353, 537
Cox of Collumpton, V. 325
Coxe, Leonard, of Reading, III. 290, 550
Coxe, William (1747–1828), IX. 481; XI. 430; XIV. 501; *House of Austria, The*, XIV. 89; *Memoirs of the Duke of Marlborough*, XIV. 89; *Memoirs of Sir Robert Walpole*, XIV. 88
Coxeter, Thomas (1689–1747), X. 429
Coxhoe hall, Durham, XIII. 70

Coy, dame, in *Jacke Jugeler*, v. 107
Coyne, Joseph Stirling (1803–1868), XIII. 266, 270, 518; XIV. 236
Coysevox, Antoine, IX. 153
Crabbe, George (1754–1832), IX. 154, 161; X. 277; XI. 86, 111, 140 ff. (main entry), 418, *also see* Add.; XII. 36, 42, 95, 136, 231, 232, 268; XIII. 40, 186, 191, 230, 373, 497; XIV. 200, 515
  Amusements, XI. 151
  Ancient Mansion, The, XI. 150
  Birth of Flattery, The, XI. 147
  Borough, The, XI. 140, 146 ff., 151
  Confidant, The, XI. 148
  Delay has Danger, XI. 149, 151
  Ellen Orford, XI. 140
  Epistle from the Devil, XI. 141
  Epistle to Mira, XI. 142
  Equal Marriage, The, XI. 150
  Farewell and Return, The, XI. 150
  Foes of Mankind, XI. 141
  Frank Courtship, The, XI. 148
  Gentleman Farmer, The, XI. 148
  Hall of Justice, The, XI. 147
  His Mother's Wedding-Ring, XI. 150
  Inebriety, XI. 140, 141
  Library, The, XI. 143, 145
  Lover's Journey, XI. 141
  Midnight, XI. 141
  Natural Death of Love, XI. 149
  Newspaper, The, XI. 145
  Parham Revisited, XI. 150
  Parish Register, The, XI. 140, 145 ff.
  Parting Hour, The, XI. 148; XIII. 38
  Patron, The, XI. 143, 148, 151
  Readings from Crabbe, XIII. 143
  Silford Hall, XI. 150
  Sir Eustace Grey, XI. 147
  Smugglers and Poachers, XI. 149
  Tales, XI. 141, 148, 149, 151
  Tales of the Hall, XI. 149, 151; XIII. 377, 380
  'To the Authors of the *Monthly Review*,' XI. 142
  Village, The, X. 186; XI. 143 ff., 150
  Widow, The, XI. 149
  Wish, The, XI. 140
  Works, XI. 143
  World of Dreams, The, XI. 147
Crabbe, George (1785–1857), XI. 150
Crabbe, George, grandson of the poet, XIII. 143
Crabbe, Maria, XI. 383
Crabbe, Mrs Sarah, born Elmy (d. 1813), XI. 140 ff., 145, 148
Crabs, earl of, Thackeray's, XIII. 279
Crabshaw, Timothy, in Smollett's *Sir Launcelot Greaves*, X. 41
Crackanthorpe, Hubert (d. 1897), XIII. 500; XIV. 518, *also see* Add. 2
Crackstone, captain, in *Fedele and Fortunio*, V. 314, 315; VI. 304
Cradle of Security, The, V. 57, 394
Cradock, Catherine, X. 23
Cradock, Charlotte. *See* Fielding, Charlotte
Cradock, Mrs Harriet, *Hulse House*, XII. 247
Cradock, Joseph (1742–1826), X. 473; *Zobeide*, X. 86, 439; XI. 265
Cradock, Samuel (1621–1706), X. 387
Cradok, Sir, in *Morte Arthure*, II. 120
Craft of Deyng, II. 284, 479
Craftsman, The, IX. 98, 132, 219 ff., 252, 433, 491, 492, 497; X. 389. *See, also*, Amhurst, Nicholas
Crafty Conveyaunce, in *Magnyfycence*, III. 77
Craig, Alexander, of Rosecraig (1567?–1627), IX. 555
Craig, Isa. *See* Knox, Isa
Craig, John (1512?–1600), III. 502
Craig, R. S., XIII. 470
Craig, Sir Thomas (1538–1608), IX. 549
Craig-Ereri, in *Pleasure Reconciled*, VI. 361
Craigenputtock, XIII. 5, 10
Craigie, Pearl Mary Teresa (*pseud.* John Oliver Hobbes, 1867–1906), XIII. 561
Craigie, William Alexander, XI. 438, 439; XIV. 611
Craik, Dinah Maria. *See* Mulock, Dinah Maria
Craik, George Lillie (1798–1866), I. viii; XII. 504; XIV. 487, 612
Craik, Sir Henry, VII. 241; XIV. 502, 590
Crakanthorp, Richard (1567–1624), VII. 470, 484 *bis*; *Logicae libri quinque de Praedicabilibus*, VII. 276
Crake, Augustine David (1836–1890), XI. 485
Crambe, in *Memoirs of Martinus Scriblerus*, IX. 137
Cramer, John Anthony (1793–1848), XII. 496
Cramond, cocks of, II. 276
Cranborne Chase, XII. 512
Crane, mistress, III. 379, 380
Crane, Ralph (*fl.* 1625), VII. 406
Crane, Walter (1845–1915), XI. 476, 491
Crane, William (*fl.* 1530), VI. 282, 284
Cranfield, Lionel, earl of Middlesex (1575–1645), VII. 440
Cranford, VII. 246
Cranford, Mrs Gaskell's, XIII. 372
Cranley, Thomas (*fl.* 1635), VII. 412
Cranmer, George (1563–1600), III. 406
Cranmer, Thomas (1489–1556), II. 62; III. 13, 26, 30 ff., 38, 44, 471; IV. 41, 298, 301, 380; V. 58; VII. 250; IX. 235, 496
  Answer, III. 33
  Appeal to a Council, III. 35
  Defence of the true and Catholic Doctrine of the Sacrement of the Body and Blood of Christ, III. 33
  Homilies, III. 35
  Institution of a Christian Man, The, III. 35
  Reply to the Three Articles, III. 33
Cranmer's Bible, XII. 521
Crape, Sir, in Oldham, *Satyr address'd to a Friend*, VIII. 88

Crashaw, Richard (1613?–1649), I. 232; IV. 218, 260; VII. 15, 26, 32 ff. (main entry), 42, 47, 63, 91, 142, 317, 400, 467, 489, *also see* Add.; X. 369; XI. 81, 318; XIII. 431; XIV. 460
An Apologie, VII. 34
Carmen Deo Nostro, VII. 34, 35
Come and let us live my dear, VII. 36
Death, what dost? o hold thy Blow, VII. 33
Delights of the Muses, The, VII. 36
Dies Irae, VII. 36
Epigrammatum Sacrorum Liber, VII. 33
Flaming Heart, The, VII. 37; XIII. 113
Hymne to St Teresa, VII. 33, 36; XIII. 113, 218
'Know you faire on what you look,' VII. 32
Loves Horoscope, VII. 36
Musicks Duell, VII. 36
Odes to John Tournay, VII. 33
On a Treatise of Charity, VII. 33, 153
Sospetto d'Herode, VII. 36
Steps to the Temple, VII. 29, 32, 34, 35
To the Countess of Denbigh, VII. 37
To thy Lover, Deere, discover, VII. 36
Translations of Latin hymns, VII. 36
Vexilla Regis, VII. 36
Weeper, The, VII. 31, 33, 37
Wishes. To his (supposed) Mistresse, VII. 36
Crashawe or Crashaw, William (1572–1626), VI. 375, 492; VII. 32, 33; VIII. 324; *The Honour of Vertue*, VII. 32; *The Jesuittes Gospel*, VII. 33; *A Manuall for true Catholickes*, VII. 33
Crassus,' in *The Examiner*, IX. 218
Crasy, Mr, in *The City Witt*, VI. 228, 229
Cratander, Ephesian captive, in *The Royall Slave*, VI. 326
Cratchits, the, in *A Christmas Carol*, XIII. 324
Crathie, IX. 373
Crauford, in Lytton's *The Disowned*, XIII. 418
Craven, Henry Thornton (1818–1905), XIII. 518
Craven, James Brown, X. 357
Craven, Pauline M. A. A., XIII. 562
Craven scholar, XII. 323
Craven, Yorks., XII. 514
Crawfoot, J. R., VIII. 461
Crawford, Charles, V. 85, 87, 238; VI. 180, *see also* Add.
Crawford, David (1665–1726), IX. 559
Crawford, earl of. *See* Lindsay, J. L.
Crawford, Mrs Emily, XIV. 190
Crawford, Francis Marion (1854–1909), XIII. 562
Crawford, Henry, in Jane Austen's *Mansfield Park*, XII. 239
Crawford, Isabella Valancy (1850–1886), XIV. 348 ff., 582
Helot, The, XIV. 349
Love's Forget Me Not, XIV. 349
Malcolm's Katie, XIV. 349
Old Spookses' Pass, XIV. 349
Crawford, Miss, in Jane Austen's *Mansfield Park*, XII. 238
Crawford, Robert (d. 1733), IX. 370, 566
Allan Water, IX. 371
Bush aboon Traquair, IX. 371
Down the Burn Davie, IX. 371
Tweedside, IX. 371
Crawfurd, George (d. 1748), X. 500
Crawfurd, Thomas (d. 1662), IX. 550
Crawley, Josiah, Trollope's, XIII. 424
Crawley, lady Jane, in *Vanity Fair*, XIII. 289
Crawley, Sir Pitt, in *Vanity Fair*, VIII. 162; XIII. 287, 289
Crawley, Rawdon, in *Vanity Fair*, XIII. 287 ff.
Crawleys, the, in *Vanity Fair*, XIII. 286 ff.
Crawleys, the, Trollope's, XIII. 422
Crayke, near York, monastery at, I. 86
Crayon, Geoffrey. *See* Irving, Washington
'Crazy Castle,' XI. 174
Creakle, Mr, in *David Copperfield*, XIII. 325
Creation, the, IV. 59 ff.
Crecy, battle of, I. 357, 359; II. 120
Credenhill, Herefordshire, VII. 42
Crediton, X. 375
Crediton school, VII. 330
Credo à l'userier, La, III. 90, 487
Creech, Thomas (1659–1701), VIII. 408; IX. 526
Creech, William (1745–1815), XI. 220, 221, 342, 469
Creed, a play on the, V. 52
Creede, Thomas (d. 1616?), IV. 377
Creevey, Thomas, XIV. 116, 501; *The Creevey Papers*, XIV. 115
Creichton, captain John, IX. 459
Creighton, Charles, VI. 284
Creighton, Louise, XII. Add.; XIV. 487; *Life and Letters of Mandell Creighton*, XIV. 101, 487
Creighton, Mandell (1843–1901), bishop of London, VII. 208; XII. 271; XIV. 81, 99 ff., 487, 500, 605; *History of the Papacy*, XIV. 99, 100
Creizenach, Wilhelm, V. 284, 341, 344, 345, 365, 367
Creole, in Miss Edgeworth's *Belinda*, XI. 297
Creon, V. 72
Creon, in *The Bond-man*, VI. 157
Cresseid, in Henryson's *Testament of Cresseid*, II. 247, 248
Cressy, father Hugh Paulinus (1605–1674), VII. 143, 424; *Sancta Sophia, or Holy Wisdom*, VII. 142, 143
Crete, V. 64; XII. 339
Crèvecœur, J. Hector St John (1731–1813), XI. 399
Crewe hall, XI. 390
Crewe, marquess of, X. 193
Creweltie of a Stepmother, The, V. 117, 325
Crib, Tom (1781–1848), XII. 411; XIV. 231

Crichton, Admirable, VII. 254, 255; VIII. 195
Crichton, Andrew, XIV. 493
Crichton castle, in Scott's *Marmion*, XII. 10
Crichton-Browne, Sir J., XIII. 467, 471
Cricket, in *Club Law*, VI. 308
Crimean war, the, XII. 154, 227; XIII. 103, 156, 363 ff., 433; XIV. 165, 173, 176, 181, 182, 187, 190, 196, 239, 251
Crimsworth, in Charlotte Brontë's *The Professor*, XIII. 414
Cripple, the, in *The Fayre Mayd of the Exchange*, VI. 86, 100
Cripps, Arthur Shearley, XIV. Add. 4
Crisp, Samuel (miscalled Henry, d. 1783), X. 260, 430
Crisp, Tobias (1600–1643), X. 376, 377
Crispinella, in *The Dutch Courtezan*, VI. 48
Crispinus, in *The Poetaster*, VI. 18, 42, 43
Crist. See Cynewulf
Crist and Satan, I. 48, 49, 428
Crites, in *Cynthia's Revels*, VI. 39, 41
Crites (Sir Robert Howard), in Dryden's *An Essay of Dramatick Poesie*, VIII. 21, 24
Critical Remarks on Capt. Gulliver's Travels, by Doctor Bantley, IX. 132
Critical Review, The, X. 40, 201, 395, 421, 467, 474; XI. 339, 353
Critici Sacri, VII. 322, 481
Criticisms of the Rolliad, XI. 34
Crito Cantabrigienses, *A Vindication of the Literary Character of Prof. Porson*, XII. 325
Croaker, in *The Good-Natur'd Man*, X. 211, 212
Crochallan club, XI. 221
Crocker, Thomas, VII. 513
Crockett, Samuel Rutherford (1860–1914), XIII. 467
Croese, G., *The General History of Quakers* (1696), VIII. 413
Croft, Sir Herbert (1751–1816), X. 183, 476, 486; *Love and Madness*, XI. 231
Crofts, H. H. S., III. 302
Crofts, John (*fl.* 1629), VII. 17
Croisic, XIII. 77
Croisnel, Renée de, in Meredith's *Beauchamp's Career*, XIII. 446
Croke, Richard (1489?–1558), III. 27, 467
Croker, John Wilson (1780–1857), IX. 250, 252; X. 158, 473, 476, 478; XI. 346; XII. 150, 154, 155, 162, 163, 363, 380, 412, 429; XIII. 240, 350; XIV. 63, 129, 322, 323, 501; *The Croker Papers*, XIV. 115
Croker, Thomas Crofton (1798–1854), XII. 353, 412, 516; XIV. 312, 315, 568, 572
Fairy Legends and Traditions, XII. 360
Fairy Legends and Traditions of Ireland, XIV. 314
Legends of the Lakes, XII. 360
Popular Songs, XII. 360
Researches in the South of Ireland, XII. 360
Crole, Robert. See Crowley
Croly, George (1780–1860), XII. 416, 448; *also see* Add.; *Marston*, XII. 249: *Salathiel*, XII. 249
Cromarty, VII. 253, 254, 258
Cromarty, earl of. *See* Mackenzie, George
Crome, the shrine of Our Lady at, V. 97
Cromek, Robert Hartley (1770–1812), IX. 566; X. 456; XI. 436, 437, 441, 443; *Remains of Nithsdale and Galloway Songs*, IX. 374, 377; XI. 234, 242
Cromer, earl of. *See* Baring, Evelyn
Crompton, Richard (*fl.* 1573–1599), VIII. 466
Crompton, proprietor of *The Morning Post*, XIV. 185
Cromwell, Henry (1628–1674), VII. 436; VIII. 343; IX. 34, 68, 73, 83 ff., 447
Cromwell, Oliver (1599–1658), IV. 64, 141, 156, 310, 421, 426, 432, 434; VI. 316; VII. 54, 56, 68, 85, 91, 105, 148, 178, 187, 189, 190, 191, 194, 197, 218, 225, 227, 231, 254, 299, 306, 344, 349, 350 ff., 365, 383, 434, 449, 450, 451, 455, 458, 460, 513, *also see* Add.; VIII. 2, 3, 5, 7, 21, 60, 68, 73, 74, 116, 119, 198, 265, 267, 360; IX. 2, 160, 203, 212, 234, 258, 267, 269, 387, 392, 443; X. 279, 372, 373, 464; XI. 312; XIII. 13, 17, 19, 268, 469; XIV. 88, 91, 96, 113, 114, 242, 507; *Proclamation*, VIII. 274
Cromwell, Richard (1626–1712), IV. 64; VII. 190; VIII. 3, 118, 119
Cromwell, Thomas (1485?–1540), earl of Essex, I. 211; III. 42, 43, 160, 167, 244, 332, 336, 337, 490; IV. 8, 297; V. 58, 59, 102, 104; X. 233
Cromwell, Milton's, in *Defensio*, VII. 130
Cromwell, Vindication of Oliver, VII. 225
Cromwell's Nose, A Case for Nol, VII. 383
Cromwell's widow, VIII. 121
Cronica duo Anglica, I. 110
Cronke, Dickory (the 'Dumb Philosopher'), IX. 21
Crooke, Andrew, VII. 235; XI. 318
Crooke, William (*fl.* 1682), IX. 385
Crooke, W., XIV. 576
Crosfeild, Robert (*fl.* 1693), IV. 102, 455
Cross, John Walter, XIII. 402, 553; *George Eliot's Life*, XIII 373, 381 ff., 388, 389, 391 ff.
Cross, Lancelot, *pseud.* Carr, F., XII. 442
Cross, Mary Ann, born Evans. *See* Eliot, George
Cross, Thomas, *The Autobiography of a Stage Coachman*, XIV. 233, 540
Cross, Wilbur L., X. Add.; XIII. 567
Cross, festivals and legends of the, I. 55, 56, 134; Aelfric's homily, I. 118. See, also, *Dream of the Rood*
Crosse, Mrs Andrew, XII. 441
Crossen, siege of, VII. 22
Crossley, James (1800–1883), IV. 252; VI. 105; IX. 15
Crossman, Samuel (1624?–1684), VII. 406; XI. 370, 478
Crosthwaite, X. 386
Crotch, W. Walter, XIII. 543

Crouch, Edward Heath, xiv. 377, 588, *also see* Add. 4
Crouch, John (*fl.* 1660–1681)
Fumigosus, vii. 357
Man in the Moon, vii. 357
Mercurius Democritus, vii. 357
Mercurius Melancholicus, counterfeit of, vii. 357
Pragmaticus, counterfeit of, vii. 357
Crouch, Nathaniel ('Richard Burton') (1632?–1725?), ix. 18; xi. 330, 478; *Winter Evening Entertainments*, xi. 370
Croucher, John (*fl.* 1408–1453?), iv. 432; vi. 280
Crousaz, Jean-Pierre de, ix. 83, 449; x. 465; xi. 356
Crow, William (*fl.* 1663), vii. 479
Crow and Pie, ii. 414
Crowdero, in *Hudibras*, viii. 68, 70
Crowdy, Wallace Lowe, xiii. 540
Crowe, captain, in Smollett's *Sir Launcelot Greaves*, x. 41
Crowe, Catherine (1800?–1876), xii. 448; xiii. 430; *Adventures of Susan Hopley*, xii. 249; *Night Side of Nature, The*, xii. 248; *Story of Lilly Dawson, The*, xii. 249
Crowe, Sir Joseph Archer (1825–1896), xiv. 533
Crowe, William (1745–1829), x. 454; xii. 416; xiii. Add. 2; *Treatise on English Versification*, xiii. 240, 512
Crowland, xiii. 366
Crowley (Crole or Croleus), Robert (1518?–1588), iii. 87, 100, 101, 492; iv. 324, 328, 334, 382; ix. 51
Epigrams, The one and thirty, iii. 100; iv. 328, 334
Information and Peticion agaynst the oppressours of the pore commons of the realme, iii. 101
Pleasure and pain, heaven and hell, iii. 101
Voice of the Last Trumpet, The, iii. 100
Way to Wealth, The, iii. 100
Crowne, Dryden and Shadwell, *Notes and Observations*, viii. 193, 441
Crowne, John (d. 1703?), viii. 21, 133, 213, 214, 400, 401, 435, 441
Ambitious Statesman, The, viii. 188
Andromache, viii. 181, 187
Caligula, viii. 189
Calisto, or the Chast Nymph, viii. 187
City Politiques, viii. 122, 188
Country Wit, The, viii. 134, 188
Darius, viii. 189
Destruction of Jerusalem, The, viii. 188, 190
English Frier, The, viii. 134, 188, 189
Henry the Sixth, the First Part With the Murder of Humphrey, Duke of Glocester, viii. 188
History of Charles the Eighth of France, The, viii. 187
Juliana, or the Princess of Poland, viii. 187
Crowne, John
Justice Busy, viii. 189
Married Beau, The, viii. 189
Misery of Civil-War, The, viii. 188
Pandion and Amphigenia, vii. 391; viii. 187
Regulus, viii. 189
Sir Courtly Nice, or It cannot be, viii. 131, 179, 188, 189
Thyestes, viii. 188
Crowne, William, father of Crowne, John, viii. 187
Crowned King, The, ii. 40, 432, 435
Crowquill, Alfred, *pseud. See* Forrester, Alfred Henry
Crowther, Joseph, vi. Add. 2
Croxall, Samuel (d. 1752), xi. 172, 425, 490; *Fables*, xiii. 52
Croxton play, the, v. 391
Croydon, iii. 57; v. 119, 141; vi. 287; xiv. 406
Croydon, Whitgift's school, viii. 83
Croyland, abbey of, i. 89; ii. 343; iv. 417; forged chronicle of, ii. 399, 497
Croyland. *See* Felix of
Crozier, John Beattie, xiii. 470
Cruden, Alexander (1701–1770), *Concordance*, xi. 327, 467
Cruelty, in Chronicle plays, v. 151
Cruikshank, George (1792–1878), x. 416, 418, 421; xi. 386, 402, 478, 491; xii. 447; xiii. 526, 540, 542; xiv. 188, 221 ff., 232, 234, 237, 520, 539, 541, 543 ff.; *Comic Almanac*, xiv. 235; *George Cruikshank's Magazine*, xiv. 234; *Table Book*, xiii. 284
Cruikshank, George and Robert, ix. 567
Cruikshank, Isaac Robert or Robert (1789–1856), xiv. 222, 223, 225, 226, 235, 236, 543
Crummleses, the, in *Nicholas Nickleby*, xiii. 317, 318
Crump, Charles G., xii. 439, 440
Crump, James, xi. 334
Crump, Mrs Lucy, xiv. 503
Crump, Mrs and Miss, in Thackeray's *The Ravenswing*, xiii. 281
Cruncher, Jerry, in *A Tale of Two Cities*, xiii. 332
Crusade, first, in Wm. of Malmesbury, i. 165
Crusades, the, ii. 337
Cruso, Aquila, vi. 471
Crusoe, Robinson, x. 66; xiii. 438
Crux de te Volo Conqueri, ii. 383
Cuchulinn, in *Fled Bricrend* (*Bricriu's Feast*), i. 296, 327
Cuchullain, x. 231; xiii. 188; xiv. 307
Cuculo, in *A Very Woman*, vi. 161
Cuddie, in *The Shepheards Calender*, iii. 225
Cuddy, in Davison's *Rapsody*, iv. 125
Cudworth, Ralph (1617–1688), vii. 279, 302; viii. 273, 274, 279 ff., 286, 290 ff. 330, 453 ff.; ix. 299, 401; x. 345; xi. 57

Cudworth, Ralph
Moral Good or Evil, or Natural Ethics, VIII. 281; *Treatise concerning Eternal and Immutable Morality,* VIII. 282; *The true Intellectual System of the Universe,* VIII. 287
Cuffe or Cuff, Henry (1563–1601), IV. 114; VII. 329, 343
Cuirass. See *Lorica*
Cujas, Jacques de, III. 423
Cujus contrarium verum est, VII. 381
Cul de Jatte, in *The Cloister and the Hearth,* XIII. 429
Culdees at St Andrews, II. 367
Cullercoats, XIV. 297
Cullinan, Maxwell Cormac, XII. 494
Culloden, IX. 563 ff.
Culpeper, Nicholas (1616–1654), VII. 509
Culpeper, Sir Thomas, the elder (1578–1662), IV. 510
Culpeper, Sir Thomas (1626–1697), *Morall Discourses and Essayes,* VII. 517
Culross, II. 131
Culross, lady (Elizabeth Melville) (*fl.* 1603), IX. 555
Culverwel, Nathaniel (d. 1651), VII. 280; VIII. 287, 292, 454; *Commonplaces,* VIII. 290; *Light of Nature,* VII. 279, 470; VIII. 288, 289
Cumberland, IX. 170; XI. 232, 410; XII. 17, 511; XIII. 426; XIV. 221
Cumberland, ship, X. 36
Cumberland, countess of. *See* Clifford, Margaret
Cumberland, duke of. *See* William Augustus (1721–1765)
Cumberland, earl of. *See* Clifford, George
Cumberland, Richard (1631–1718), bishop of Peterborough, VI. 9; IX. 506, 525; X. 351; *De Legibus Naturae,* VII. 303, 470; VIII. 292, 468
Cumberland, Richard (1732–1811), IX. 574; X. 90, 473, 483; XI. 263 ff., 270, 272, 448, 457, *also see* Add.; XIV. 592
Brothers, The, XI. 263, 264, 277, 279, 414
Choleric Man, The, XI. 265
Fashionable Lover, The, XI. 265
Jew, The, XI. 282
Timon of Athens, XI. 265
West Indian, The, X. 92, 214; XI. 257, 264
Cumbrian dialect, XII. 413
Cumming, fiddler, X. 196
Cumming, Joseph George (1812–1868), XII. 509
Cumner hills, XIII. 93
Cundall, Joseph, XI. 386
Cuneburga, abbess, I. 79
Cuneglasus, king, I. 67
Cuningham or Cunningham, William (*fl.* 1586), *The Cosmographical Glasse,* III. 550; IV. 400
Cunliffe, John William, V. Add. 2; XIII. 572, *also see* Add. 1
Cunningham, Alexander, 5th earl of Glencairn (d. 1574), *Epistle direct from the Holy hermit of Allarit,* III. 132
Cunningham, Alexander (1655?–1730), IX. 561
Cunningham, Sir Alexander (1814–1893), XII. 352, 509
Ancient Geography of India, XII. 353
Architecture of the Temples of Kashmir, XII. 353
Bhilsa Topes, The, XII. 353
Corpus Inscriptionum Indicarum, XII. 353
Cunningham, Allan (1784–1842), IX. 566; XI. 234, 434, 437, 439, 443; XIII. 54
Biographical and Critical History of British Literature, XII. 365, 378, 437
Bonnie Lady Anne, XI. 243
Hame Hame, Hame, XI. 243
John Grumlie, XI. 243
Maid of Elvar, XI. 242
My Nannie O, XI. 243
She's Gane to dwell in Heaven, XI. 243
Sir Marmaduke, XI. 242
Songs of Scotland, XI. 242
Wee, Wee German Lairdie, IX. 377; XI. 243
Wet Sheet and a Flowing Sea, XI. 243
Young Maxwell, XI. 242
Cunningham, lady Elizabeth, XI. 223
Cunningham, Francis (1820–1875), V. 143
Cunningham, James, 14th earl of Glencairn (1749–1791), XI. 220, 223
Cunningham, John William (1780–1861), XI. 401
Cunningham, Mary (d. 1615), IV. 152
Cunningham, Peter (1816–1869), X. 247, 249; XII. 409
Cunningham, Thomas Mounsey (1776–1834), *Hairst Kirn,* XI. 243; *Hills o' Gallowa,* XI. 243
Cunningham, William, 9th earl of Glencairn (1610?–1664), XII. 377
Cupar-Fife, III. 123; XII. 513
Cupid, III. 17; IV. 196, 330; XII. 90; XIV. 311
Cupid (lap-dog), IX. 46
Cupid, god of love, in *Confessio Amantis,* II. 146
Cupid, in *Gismond of Salerne,* V. 73 ff.
Cupid, in *The Hue and Cry after Cupid,* VI. 346, 347
Cupid, in *Love Restored,* VI. 351, 352
Cupid, in *Loves Maistresse,* VI. 103
Cupid, in *The Masque of Christmas,* VI. 358, 359
Cupid, in *The Palice of Honour,* II. 260
Cupid, in *The Testament of Cresseid,* II. 248
Cupid God of Love, The book of, II. 216
Cupid's Court of Salutations, XI. 334
Cupids, in *The Masque of Beauty,* VI. 347
Cur, Sir John, in Barnabe Googe's *Eclogues,* III. 186
Curan, in *Albion's England,* III. 357; IV. 136
Curchod, Suzanne. *See* Necker
Cures for the Itch, III. 487
Cureton, William (1808–1864), XII. 341, 503

'Curious Impertinent, The,' in *Don Quixote*, vi. 133, 137, 223, 236; viii. 189, 191
Curle, James, xii. 509
Curle, Richard H. P., xiii. 570
Curlicism, xi. 328
Curll, Edmund (1675–1747), ix. 78, 83, 84, 86, 123, 165, 247, 446, 447, 452, 462, 469, 475, 535; xi. 288, 327 ff., 467
Curran, John Philpot (1750–1817), xiv. 311; *Cushla ma Chree*, xiv. 319; *Deserter's Meditation*, xiv. 319
Curran, William Henry, *Sketches of the Irish Bar*, xiv. 319
Currawn, county Leitrim, xiv. 355
Currie, A. E., xiv. 584
Currie, James (1756–1805), xi. 408, 436, 437
Currie, Mary Montgomerie, lady, born Lamb (*pseud.* Violet Fane, 1843–1905), xiii. 180, 504
Curson of Kedleston, cardinal (d. 1218), i. 199, 453
Cursor Mundi, i. 134, 341 ff., 348, 399, 474; ii. 189; iii. 289; v. 15, 389
Curtasy, The Boke of, ii. 502
Curteis, T., ix. 463
Curtin, *Hero Tales of Ireland*, i. 293
Curtis, William (1746–1799), xiv. 288, 559
Curtius, Ernst, xii. 322, 476
Curtius, George, *Principles of Greek Etymology*, xii. 337; *The Greek Verb*, xii. 337
Curtius, Quintus, iv. 2, 4, 436
Curwen, Henry (1845–1892), xi. 466; xiv. 339, 575
Curzon, lord, of Kedleston, xiv. 597
Curzon, Robert, lord Zouche (1810–1873), xiv. 551; *The Monasteries of the Levant*, xiv. 252
Cusack, Mary Frances, xiv. 510
Cusanus, C., vii. 517
Cussans, John Edwin (1837–1899), xii. 509
Cust, Lionel, xii. 499
Custance, dame, in *Ralph Roister Doister*, v. 105, 106
Cut pursses, A ballett..., iii. 492
Cutchery court, xi. 12
Cute, alderman, in Dickens's *The Chimes*, xiii. 324
Cuthbert, abbot of Wearmouth and Jarrow, i. 61, 79
Cuthbert Cutpurse, ii. 232
Cuthbert, St, of Lindisfarne (d. 687), i. 64, 80, 82, 83, 85, 117, 118 148, 435; iv. 421; xii. 10
Cuthbertson, James Lister (1851–1910), xiv. 369, 585
Cuthwin, i. 61, 71, 79
Cutter, in Cowley's *Cutter of Coleman Street*, viii. 122
Cutting Capers, xiv. 377
Cuttle, captain, in *Dombey and Son*, xiii. 325
Cutts, John, lord (1661–1707), viii. 410
Cutwode, Thomas, *Caltha Poetarum*, iv. 469
Cuvelier de Trye, Jean G. A., xiii. 264
Cuvier, Georges L. C. F. D., xiv. 295
Cybele, in Keats's *Endymion*, xii. 82
Cyclope, in *Mercury Vindicated*, vi. 357
Cyclopes, in *The Hue and Cry after Cupid*, vi. 347, 348
Cymbeline, in Geoffrey of Monmouth, i. 171
Cymmodorion, Honourable society of, xii. 506
Cymric language and literature, i. 464
Cynara, Dowson's, xiii. 220
Cynewulf (*fl.* 1750), i. 38, 41, 49 ff., 133, 134, 143, 325, 428, 430; xi. 366; *also see* xiii. Add. 2
Crist, i. 49, 52, 53, 56, 58, 59, 63, 64; runes in, i. 12; Cook's edn., i. 59; iv. 37
Elene, i. 50 ff., 55, 57, 62, 63, 134, 143; runes in, i. 12
Fata Apostolorum, i. 52 ff.; runes in, i. 12
Juliana, i. 52, 53; runes in, i. 12
Cynewulf, bishop of Lindisfarne, i. 49, 430
Cynewulf, king, in O.E. *Chronicle*, i. 107 443
Cynthia, iv. 196
Cynthia, in Congreve's *Double-Dealer*, viii. 148, 150
Cynthia, in *Endimion*, v. 341
Cynthia, in *The Faerie Queene*, iii. 233, 238
Cynthia, in Mrs Gaskell's *Wives and Daughters*, xiii. 381
Cynthio, ix. 50, 57
Cynulf of Clovesho, i. 50
Cynus super Codicem, ii. 364
Cyprian, bishop of Toulon, xii. 487
Cyprian, St, ii. 365; iii. 411; vi. 375; ix. 527; xii. 266
'Cyprians,' xiv. 227
Cyprianus (Juvencus), i. 76
Cyprus, xiv. 251, 253
Cyrano de Bergerac, S., *Histoire comique*, ix. 106
Cyrene, xii. 339
Cyril, xii. 503
Cyril, in Tennyson's *The Princess*, xiii. 31
Cyrus, iii. 437
Cyrus, Le Grand, i. 280
Cytherea: or poems upon Love and Intrigue, ix. 78
Cythna, in Shelley's *Revolt of Islam*, xii. 61

Daantjie Gouws, xiv. 377
Daborne, Robert (d. 1628), vi. 116, 146, 454; *A Christian turned Turke*, v. 366
Dacia, in Geoffrey of Monmouth, i. 259
Dacier, André, ix. 75; Aristotle's *Poetics*, trans. of, viii. 375; *Essai sur la Satire*, viii. 374
Dacier, Madame, x. 27
Dacier, in Meredith's *Diana of the Crossways*, xiii. 445
Dacre, lord, friend of Gavin Douglas, ii. 260

Dacre, Mary, in Disraeli's *The Young Duke*, XIII. 348
Dacres, Edward, IV. 8, 446
Daedalus, III. 86
Daeghrefn, in *Beowulf*, I. 24, 27
Daffy's Elixir Salutis, XI. 335
Dagon's Fall, VIII. 97
Dahlia, in Meredith's *Rhoda Fleming*, XIII. 447
Dahra, XIV. 238
Daillé, John, *Traité de l'employ des saincts pères*, VII. 313, 484
Daily Advertiser, The, XI. 391
Daily Chronicle, The, XIV. 192, 193
Daily Courant, The, IX. 5; XI. 333
Daily Express, The, XIV. 193
Daily Gazetteer, The, X. 467
Daily Graphic, The, XIV. 201
Daily Mail, The, XIV. 193
Daily News, The, XIII. 324; XIV. 90, 173, 188 ff., 316, 530, 535
Daily Post, The, IX. 21, 433; XIV. 201
Daily Telegraph, The, XIV. 180, 183, 188, 190 ff., 196, 328, 530, 534
Daily Universal Register, The, XIV. 177
Dakins, William (d. 1607), VII. 316
Dalbeattie, XI. 444, 445
Dale, Alfred William Winterslow, XII. 465
Dale, David (1739–1806), XIV. 404
Dale, Edmund, I. Add.
Dale, Robert William (1829–1895), XII. 465, 471
D'Alembert, J. le Rond, V. 293
Dales, the, in Trollope's novels, XIII. 422
Daley, Victor James (1858–1905), XIV. 369, 585
Dalgairns, John Dobree (1818–1876), XII. 275, 456, 460
Dalgetty, Dugald, in Scott's *Legend of Montrose*, X. 43; XII. 21, 25, 29
Dalhousie, marquis J. *See* Ramsay, J. A. B.
Dalila, in *Samson Agonistes*, VII. 122, 137; VIII. 154
Dalkeith, XI. 469
Dalkeith, countess of, XII. 7
Dallas, Rev. Alexander Robert Charles (1791–1869), XII. 386
Dallas, Eneas Sweetland (1828–1879), XII. 398; XIII. 245, 512; XIV. 142, 147, 518; *Gay Science, The*, XIV. 140; *Kettner's Book of the Table*, XIV. 140; *Poetics, an Essay on Poetry*, XIV. 139
Dallas, Robert Charles (1754–1824), XII. 384, 386
Dallas, William Sweetland, XIV. 559
Dallaway, James (1763–1834), IX. 246
Dalquhurn, Cardross, X. 36
Dalrymple, Sir David, lord Hailes (1726–1792), VIII. 262; IX. 553; X. 192, 245, 294, 501, 507; XI. 273, 341
Ancient Scottish Poems, XI. 204
Annals of Scotland, X. 290
Inquiry, X. 310
Memorials and Letters, X. 290
Dalrymple, James (*fl.* 1596), II. 398; III. 155
Dalrymple, James, viscount Stair (1619–1695), VIII. 468; IX. 560
Dalrymple, Sir James (*fl.* 1714), IX. 551
Dalrymple, Sir John, 1st earl of Stair (1648–1707), IX. 495
Dalrymple, John, 2nd earl of Stair (1693–1747), IX. 152, 495
Dalrymple, Sir John, 4th baronet of Cranstoun (1726–1810), IX. 553; X. 294, 500; *Memoirs of Great Britain and Ireland*, X. 290, 291
Dalrymple of Orangefield, XI. 220
Dalton, in Norton's *Ordinall*, II. 213
Dalton, tutor to lady Hertford's son, X. 272
Dalton family, the, patrons of Rolle, II. 44
Dalton, Sir Cornelius Neale, IX. Add.
Dalton, John (1766–1844), XIV. 259, 261, 271, 272, 275 ff. (main entry), 556, 557, 605; *A new system of Chemical Philosophy*, XIV. 275
D'Alton, John (1792–1867), XIV. 312, 568; *Annals of Boyle, The*, XIV. 325; *Dermid*, XIV. 325; *History of County Dublin, The*, XIV. 325
Dalton, Michael (d. 1648?), VIII. 468
Dalyell, Sir John Graham (1775–1851), XII. 516; *The Darker Superstitions of Scotland*, XII. 350
Dalyell, in *Perkin Warbeck*, VI. 193
Dalziel, Edward George, XIV. 239
Damascus, XIV. 251
Damasus, pseudo-, II. 293
D'Ambois, Clermont, in *The Revenge of Bussy D'Ambois*, VI. 34
D'Ambra, *Cofanaria*, V. 69
Dame and her Donkey's Five, XI. 386
Dame Siriz, I. 365, 366, 479
Dame Wiggins of Lee, XI. 386
Damerval, IV. 527
Dametas, in Sidney's *Arcadia*, III. 353
Dametas, in *The Ile of Guls*, VI. 213
Damian, martyr, I. 74
Dammee Cavaliers Warning piece (1643), VII. 382
Damocles, in *The Usurper*, VIII. 21
Damoetas, in Barnabe Googe's *Eclogues*, III. 186
Damon, in Thomson's *Summer*, X. 104
Dampier, H., X. 485
Dampier, William (1652–1715), IX. 106, 492, *also see* Add.; XIV. 242, 551; *Journals*, XIV. 241
Dampit, in *A Trick to catch the Old-one*, VI. 65
D'Amville, in *The Atheist's Tragedie*, VI. 167
Dan Michel of Northgate, Kent, I. 353 ff., 400, 475
Dan Robert of Malton, I. 350
Danaë, in *The Bird in a Cage*, VI. 204
Danaides, in *Phoenissae*, V. 71
Dance of Death, The, III. 87, 100, 484; XIV. 219

Dancer, John (*fl.* 1675), VI. 490; *Nicomède* (Corneille's), translated by, VIII. 180
D'Ancourt, Florent Carton, *Les Bourgeoises à la Mode*, VIII. 162, 431
D'Ancre, marshal, VI. 138
Dane Hew Monk of Leicestre, A Mery Jest of, II. 501
Danelaw, the, VIII. 311
Danes, the, IV. 417, 418; V. 31; IX. 354; laws and customs of, VIII. 311, 318
Danes, the, in *Morte Arthure*, II. 120
Danett, Thomas (*fl.* 1566–1601), IV. 3, 443, 445; *Commines*, IV. 8
'Dangerus Fortrees,' VI. 283
Dangle, in Sheridan's *Critic*, XI. 272
Daniel, I. 74; V. 48; X. 222
Daniel, bishop of Winchester (d. 745), I. 82
Daniel, Charles Henry Olive (b. 1836–1919), XII. Add. 5
Daniel, George, of Berwick (1616–1657), VII. Add.
Daniel, George (1789–1864), XIII. 516; XIV. 518
Daniel, John (*fl.* 1625), *Songs for the Lute, Viol and Voice*, IV. 113, 133, 134, 463
Daniel, Mary, X. 28
Daniel (Donellan), Nehemias (d. 1609?), archbishop of Tuam, IV. 414
Daniel, Old English poem, I. 46, 48, 428; runes in, I. 11
Daniel, Peter Augustin, V. 85
Daniel, Samuel (1562–1619), III. 198, 247, 256, 260, 261, 264 ff., 270, 295, 304, 306, 307, 312; IV. 24, 25, 88, 115, 118, 127, 132–140 (main entry), 158, 159, 179 ff., 191, 248, 265, 266, 398, 434, 444, 474; V. 63, 226, 338, 371, 473; VI. 4, 23, 37, 39, 40, 44, 317, 337, 339, 343, 345, 350, 366, 471, 489, 490; VII. 444; VIII. 237, 239
  Certaine Small Poems, IV. 134
  Civil Wars, The, III. 198; IV. 132 ff., 136 ff., 140
  Cleopatra, IV. 133, 139; V. 334
  Complaynt of Rosamund, The, III. 198; IV. 133, 134, 140, 176
  Defence of Ryme, III. 304, 306, 307, 526; IV. 132, 133, 135
  Delia, III. 256, 260, 522; IV. 133, 177
  England, history of, IV. 134
  Epistle to the Lady Margaret, IV. 126, 137, 138
  Epistles, IV. 138
  Hymen's Triumph, IV. 134, 138, 140; VI. 190, 366
  Musophilus, or a General Defence of Learning, III. 446; IV. 88, 133, 135, 140
  Octavia to Marcus Antoninus, Epistle of, IV. 133, 138, 140
  Panegyrike Congratulatorie, IV. 132, 134, 135, 140
  Philotas, IV. 132, 134, 135; V. 334, 346, 371; VI. 339; VII. 122
  Poeticall Essayes, IV. 133
Daniel, Samuel
  Queenes Arcadia, The, IV. 134; VI. 317, 318, 327, 366
  Senecan tragedies, IV. 134
  Sonnets to Delia, IV. 139
  Tethys Festival, IV. 134; VI. 350
  Ulisses and the Syren, IV. 134, 138, 140; XIII. 141
  Vision of Twelve Goddesses, The, IV. 134; VI. 337, 345, 350
Daniel, Story of, by Hilarius, I. 191
Daniel of Morley, I. 153
Daniell, John Frederick, XIV. 557
Daniell, John Jeremiah, VII. 28, 403
Daniello, III. 290
Danish fleet, the, XIV. 120, 122
Danish Tragedy, The, V. 327
Danse Macabre, II. 199, 256; III. 87
Dante, Alighieri, I. 43, 99, 199, 200, 227, 232, 270, 363; II. 80, 133, 134, 161, 175, 179, 180, 188, 231, 258, 435; III. 200, 234, 245, 300, 305, *also see* Add.; IV. 23, 45, 196, 197, 210, 217, 527; V. 213, 214, 324; VII. 95, 101, 122, 136 ff., 240; VIII. 67, 78, 351; X. 9, 220, *also see* Add.; XII. 50, 58, 137, 221, 222, 229, 272, 394, 396, 398, 403, 415, 525; XIII. 13, 42, 195, 312; XIV. 113, 306
  Commedia, XII. 51, 85
  De Monarchia, XII. 455
  De vulgari eloquentia, XIII. 186
  Inferno, X. 240; XII. 202
  La Divina Commedia, XIII. 30
  La Vita Nuova, XII. 73; XIII. 112, 118
  Paradiso, I. 99, 154; V. 233, 339; XII. 76
  Purgatorio, XIII. 32
Danter, John, IV. 393; V. 322, 323
Danton, Georges Jacques, XIII. 12
'D'Anvers, Caleb' (N. Amhurst), IX. 220, 225, 491
Danvers, Jane (wife of George Herbert), VII. 29
Danvers, lady (mother of George Herbert), IV. 240; VII. 28
Danzig, V. 283
Dapper, in *The Alchemist*, VI. 22
Dapper, Tim, in *The Tatler*, IX. 41
Darbishire, Arthur Duckinfield, XIII. 572
D'Arblay, Frances Burney, Mme. *See* Arblay, Madame d'
Darbyshire, Thomas (1518–1604), IV. 127
Darch, Robert, X. 386
Darcie, Abraham (*fl.* 1625), III. 326, 528
Darcy, in Jane Austen's *Pride and Prejudice*, XII. 237, 238, 243, 247
D'Arcy, Robert, 4th earl of Holdernesse (1718–1778), X. 118
Dares Phrygius, I. 170, 467, 469; II. 172
Daria, martyr, I. 74
Darien expedition, IX. 214, 215, 542
Darius, I. 307
Dark Blue, The, XIV. 206
Darley, George (1795–1846), XII. 107, 114–115 (main entry), 139, 201, 416; XIII. 230, 238; XIV. 214
  Beckett, XII. 114

Darley, George
Enchanted Lyre, The, xii. 115
Errors of Ecstacie, xii. 114
Ethelstan, xii. 114
It is not Beauty I demand, xii. 115
I've been roaming, xii. 115
Labours of Idleness, xii. 114
Maiden's Grave, The, xii. 115
Nepenthe, xii. 114, 119; xiii. 204
Sylvia, xii. 114, 115; xiii. 239
Darling, James (1797–1862), xii. 521
Darlington, xiv. 193
Darlow, Thomas Hult, xiv. 516
Darmesteter, James, xi. 409
Darnal, Sheffield, vii. 353
Darnaway (Moray), ii. 112, 115
Darnley, earl of. *See* Stewart, Henry
Darrell, John (*fl.* 1562–1602), iv. 535
Dart, John (d. 1730), ix. 532
Darter, Adrian, xiv. Add. 6
Dartle, Rosa, in *David Copperfield*, xiii. 327
Dartmoor, vii. 5; x. 115
Dartmouth, x. 387
Dartmouth, earl of. *See* Legge, William
Darton, F. J. Harvey, xi. 482; xiv. 590
Darton, William, xi. 377, 485
Darton and Clarke, publishers, xi. 481
Darwin, Charles Robert (1809–1882), iv. 290; xi. 75, 426; xiii. 470, 571, 572, *also see* Add. 1; xiv. 28, 29, 34, 35, 296, 298 ff. (main entry), 479, 501, 551, 559
Descent of Man, The, xiv. 32
Expression of the Emotions, The, xiv. 32
Life and Letters, xiv. 293
Origin of Species, The, xiv. 27, 293, 298 ff., 381
Voyage of the Beagle, The, xiv. 241, 250
Darwin, Erasmus (1731–1802), xi. 41, 172, 175 ff., 180, 246, 425; xii. 247; xiii. 450; xiv. 298, 469, 560; *Botanic Garden*, xi. 175; *Loves of the Plants*, xi. 41, 175, 176
Darwin, Sir Francis, xiv. 284, 501, 559
Darwin, Sir George Howard (1845–1912), xiv. 265, 556
Darwinism, xii. 154, 269; xiii. 451
Dasent, Sir George Webbe (1817–1896), xi. 491
Dashall, Dick, in Morton's *Way to get Married*, xi. 281
Dashall, Tom, in *Real Life in London*, xiv. 227
Dashwood, Elinor, in Jane Austen's *Sense and Sensibility*, xii. 237, 241, 243
Dashwood, John, in Jane Austen's *Sense and Sensibility*, xii. 237
Dashwood, Marianne, in Jane Austen's *Sense and Sensibility*, xii. 235, 237, 241
Dashwood, Mrs, in Jane Austen's *Sense and Sensibility*, xii. 237
Dassent, Arthur Irwin, xiv. 533
Dastin or Daustin, John (*fl.* 1320), i. 453
Daubeny, Mr, Trollope's, xiii. 423
D'Aubigny, lord, v. 370; vi. 4, 6
Daudet, Alphonse, xiii. 544
D'Audiguier, vi. 123, 139
Daughters of God, the Four, in *Piers the Plowman*, ii. 27
D'Aulnoy, countess, *Travels into Spain*, viii. 191
Daunce and Song of Death, The, iii. 87
Daunger, in *The Bowge of Courte*, iii. 73
Daunses, A Treatise of, vi. 391, 498
Dauphine, Sir, in *The Silent Woman*, vi. 22
Daus, John (*fl.* 1561), iv. 448
D'Auvergne, Martial, vi. 154
Davenant, Charles (1656–1714), viii. 400, 473; ix. 11; *An Essay on the East India Trade*, viii. 342
Davenant, Judith (mother of Thomas Fuller), vii. 244
D'Avenant, Sir William (1606–1668), iv. 115, 159; vi. 212, 262, 271, 454, 489; vii. 16, 39, 105, 106, 267, 269, 270, 274, 275, 333, 408, 411, 465, 467; viii. 26, 34, 116 ff., 132 ff., 179, 398, 417, 418, 422, 423, 424; ix. 157; x. 78; xi. 318
Albovine, viii. 226
Britannia Triumphans, vii. 433
Cruelty of the Spaniards in Peru, The, viii. 118
Fair Favourite, The, vi. 240
First Day's Entertainment at Rutland House, The, viii. 117, 118
Gondibert, vii. 70, 71, 73, 263, 266 ff.; viii. 9, 371, 374
History of Sir Francis Drake, The, viii. 118
Law Against Lovers, The, viii. 120
Love and Honour, vi. 240; viii. 120, 121, 132
Macbeth, D'Avenant's alteration, viii. 20
Platonick Lovers, The, vi. 240; viii. 120, 132
Playhouse to be Let, The, viii. 118, 134
Preface to Gondibert, viii. 9
Rivals, The, viii. 120
Romeo and Juliet, viii. 120
Salmacida Spolia, vi. 363
Siege, The, x. 73; xi. 282
Siege of Rhodes, viii. 18, 117, 118, 121, 137, 194, 261
Sir Martin Mar-all, viii. 134
Tempest, The, or The Enchanted Island (with Dryden), viii. 28, 120
Temple of Love, The, viii. 132
Unfortunate Lovers, The, vi. 240
Wits, The, viii. 120
Davenport, Elizabeth, viii. 261
Davenport, J., *The Witches of Huntingdon* (1646), vii. 507
Davenport, Mrs, in Mrs Gaskell's *Mary Barton*, xiii. 375
Davenport, Robert (*fl.* 1623), vi. 235, 236, 454; *The City-Night-Cap*, vi. 236, *also see* xiii. Add. 2; *A New Tricke to Cheat the Divell*, vi. 236
Davenport, William Bromley (1821–1884), xiv. 543
Daventry, x. 384
Davers, lady, in Richardson's *Pamela*, x. 5

Davey, Samuel, XIII. 470
David, I. 74, 93, 134, 147; II. 15, 106; III. 174; IV. 33, 195, 231; X. 229; XIII. 369
David, in Cowley's *Davideis*, VII. 66, 67
David, in Watson's *Absalom*, VI. 296
David I, king of Scotland, II. 100, 101, 129
David II, king of Scotland, II. 102, 117, 129
David, king, in *Absalom and Achitophel*, VIII. 37, 39
David, St (d. 601), I. 67
Davids, C. A. F. Rhys, XIV. 479
Davidson, Andrew Bruce (1831–1902), XII. 341, 501
Davidson, James (d. 1866), XII. 519
Davidson, John (printer, 1541), IV. 412
Davidson, John (1549?–1603), III. 122, 150, 502; *Ane Schort Discurs of the Estaitis quha hes caus to deploir the Deith of this excellent Servand of God*, III. 150
Davidson, John (1857–1909), XII. 113; XIII. 216 ff., 223, 501
Ballad of Heaven, A, XIII. 217
Bruce, XIII. 216
Fleet Street Eclogues, XIII. 217
For Lovers, XIII. 217
Kinnoull Hill, XIII. 217
London, XIII. 217
Lutanist, The, XIII. 217
Scaramouch in Naxos, XIII. 216
Smith, XIII. 216
Davidson, Samuel (1806–1898), XII. 466
Davidson, Thomas (1838–1870), XIII. 501
Davidson, Thomas (1840–1900), XIV. 472
Davidson, W. L., XIV. 468
Davies, Emily, XIV. 429, 430, 599
Davies, Evan, X. 386
Davies, George, XIV. 591
Davies, Sir John (1569–1626), III. 201, 268; IV. 123, 150, 161 ff., 166, 311, 334, 479, 480, 519; V. 422, 477; VII. 110, 211, 432, 448, 470
Contention betwixt a Wife, a Widdow and a Maide, A, IV. 161, 357
Dialogue between a Gentleman Usher and a Poet, A, IV. 161
Discoverie of the true causes why Ireland has never been intirely subdued, IV. 161, 162; VII. 212
Epigrammes, III. 201; VII. 432
Hymns to Astræa, IV. 161, 163
Lark, To the, IV. 163
Lottery, A, IV. 161
Nosce Teipsum, IV. 131, 161, 162; VII. 277, 278; VIII. 9
Orchestra, IV. 161, 162
Davies, John (1627?–1693), IV. 455; VII. 390, 505
Davies, John (1679–1732), IX. 340, 526, 528
Davies, John, of Hereford (1565?–1618?), IV. 132, 146, 158, 159, 161, 335, 475, 487, 520, 521, 533; VI. 248; VII. 501
Microcosmos, IV. 131, 411
Davies, John, of Hereford
Mirum in Modum, IV. 131
Scourge of Folly, The, IV. 334, 517; VI. 137
Summa Totalis, IV. 131
Davies, John, of Kidwelly, *Clélie*, trans. of, VIII. 372; *Cléopâtre*, trans. of, 372
Davies, John Llewelyn, XIV. 591
Davies, Myles (1662–1715?), *The Critical History of Pamphlets*, X. 166
Davies, Richard (1635–1708), VIII. 106, 415
Davies, Richard (d. 1762), XIV. 592
Davies, Robert (1793–1875), XI. 468; XIV. 531
Davies, Sneyd (1709–1769), X. 454
Davies, Thomas, chaplain at Aleppo (*fl.* 1624–1627), VII. 308
Davies, Thomas (1712?–1785), VIII. 423; X. 191, 212, 433, 436, 445, 471, 483; XI. 327, 448, 453; *Dramatic Miscellanies*, VIII. 159; *Life of Garrick*, XI. 326, 333; *Miscellaneous and Fugitive Pieces*, X. 459, 463
Davies, William, XIV. 525
Davila, Enrico Caterino, VIII. 30
Davis, Alexander, XIV. Add. 6
Davis, Francis, XIV. 326, 327, 568
Davis, Henry Edwards (1756–1784), *Examination of...Mr Gibbon's History*, X. 308, 507
Davis, James, XIV. 51
Davis, John (d. 1622), III. 327
Davis, Sir John Francis (1795–1890), XII. 500
Davis, Lockyer (1719–1791), XI. 336
Davis, Miss, VII. 103
Davis, Nathan (1812–1882), XII. 316, 475
Davis, Richard, X. 371
Davis, Thomas Osborne (1814–1845), XIV. 317 ff., 568
Boatman of Kinsale, XIV. 317
Lament for Owen Roe O'Neill, XIV. 317
My Grave, XIV. 317
O the Marriage, XIV. 317
Sack of Baltimore, The, XIV. 317
Davis strait, IV. 76
Davison, Francis (*fl.* 1602), III. 523
Davison, Francis and Walter (*fl.* 1602), *In praise of a beggar's life*, IV. 124; *A Poetical Rapsody*, IV. 109, 117, 118, 123 ff., 138, 196, 357, 467; *Relation of Saxony*, IV. 123
Davison, John (1777–1834), XII. 466; XIV. 596
Davison, William (1541?–1608), IV. 123, 124
Davisson, John (d. 1721), X. 387
D'Avolos, in *Loves Sacrifice*, VI. 192
Davy, Adam (*fl.* 1308?), I. 335, 353, 355, 474
Davy, Sir Humphry (1778–1829), XIV. 260, 272, 278 ff., 287, 294, 557
Davy Diceplayer, II. 232
Davy Drunken-nole, II. 232
Davyd ap Gwilym, I. 275

Davys, John (1550?–1605), IV. 78, 455; *The Seaman's Secrets*, IV. 76, 82, 104; *The Worlde's Hydrographical Description*, IV. 76
Daw, in *The Silent Woman*, VI. 22
Dawes, Richard (1708–1766), IV. 265; XII. 325; *Miscellanea Critica*, IX. 341, 526
Dawes, Richard (1793–1867), XIV. 414, 601, 605
Dawes, Sir William (1671–1724), archbishop of York, X. 360
Dawks, Ichabod (1661–1730), IX. 5
Dawkyn, in *Turnament of Totenham*, I. 366
Dawley, IX. 81, 226
Dawney, Edmund, XIV. 533
Dawson, Coningsby William, XIV. 501
Dawson, George (1821–1876), XII. 472
Dawson, Phoebe, in Crabbe's *Parish Register*, XI. 146
Dawson, S., XIII. 471
Dawson, T., *The good huswifes jewell*, IV. 543
Dawson, William Harbutt, XIII. 488
Dawson, William James, XIV. 501
Dawsonfield, Westmorland, X. 386
Daxara, in Thomson's *Edward and Eleonora*, X. 109
Day, Angell (*fl.* 1586), IV. 438, 525; *English Secretary*, VII. 391
Day, Isaac, XI. 383, 485
Day, John, printer (1522–1584), III. 80, 333, 494; IV. 384, 386, 389, 397, 399, 400, 546
Day, John (*fl.* 1606), V. 147, 311, 312, 323, 326, 328, 332 ff., 361, 332, 474; VI. 211–217 (main entry), 231, 309, 371, 455
Blind Beggar of Bednal Green, The, V. 332, 474
'Characters,' VI. 216
'Colloquies,' VI. 216
Cox of Collumpton, VI. 96
Humour out of Breath, VI. 215
Ile of Guls, The, III. 355; VI. 212 ff.
Italian Tragedy, The, V 325
Law Trickes, VI. 215
Maiden's Holiday, The, V. 146
Orphan's Tragedy, The, VI. 96
Parliament of Bees, The, V. 332, 334; VI. 212, 215 ff., 233
Peregrinatio Scholastica, VI. 216
Thomas Merry, VI. 96
Travailes of The three English Brothers, The, VI. 69
See, also, under Chettle, Dekker *and* Marlowe
Day, John, Hathway, R. and Haughton, W., *The Conqueste of Spayne by John a Gaunt*, VIII. 126
Day, Lal Behari, XIV. 575, 576; *Folk Tales of Bengal*, XIV. 342; *Govinda Sámanta*, XIV. 342
Day, Thomas (1748–1789), X. 424; XI. 478; XIV. 601; *Sandford and Merton*, XI. 381, 382; XIV. 392, 393; *History of Little Jack*, XI. 382
Day (a lady's name), in *The Lover asketh pardon of his dere*, III. 180
Day and Chettle, *Orphan's Tragedy*, V. 325
Day and Haughton, *Thomas Merry, or Beech's Tragedy*, V. 325, 326
Day and William Rowley, *Travailes of The three English Brothers*, V. 366
Daye or Day, Richard (1552–1607?), IV. 495; V. 394
Dayot, Armand, XIV. 540
Dayrolles, Solomon, X. 257
Deacon, Thomas (1697–1753), X. 355, 356, 516
Dead Man's Song, The, IV. 353
De adventu Normannorum in Angliam et de jure quod habuit Willelmus bastardus ad regnum Angliae, II. 366
Deakin, Mary H., XIII. 553
Deal, XI. 354, 358
Dean Prior, Dartmoor, VII. 5 ff., 11, 13, 17
Deane, Sir Anthony (1638?–1721), VIII. 257
Deans, David, in Scott's *Heart of Midlothian*, XII. 25
Deans, Jeanie, in Scott's *Heart of Midlothian*, XII. 18, 25
Death, I. 227, 458
Death, in a broadside, III. 87
Death, in *Death and Liffe*, II. 40
Death, in *Every-man*, V. 53
Death, in folk plays, V. 31
Death, in *Mirour de l'Omme*, II. 140
Death, in *Piers the Plowman*, II. 22, 27, 28, 38
Death, in *The Example of Virtue*, II. 227
Death, in *The Parlement of the Three Ages*, II. 38
Death, in *The Passetyme of Pleasure*, II. 226
Death, in *The Wonderfull Yeare*, IV. 351
Death, king of, in *The Pride of Life*, V. 3
Death, The Doctrinal of, II. 323
Death and Liffe, II. 40, 41, 432, 435
Death-Song of Ragnar Lodbrok, X. 221, 222, 224; XIV. 51
Debarrys, the, in *Felix Holt*, XIII. 397
Debates, II. 500, 501. See, also, *The Controversy between a lover and a Jay*, II. 224, 326
Debates and speeches in Jacobean times, XII. 439 ff.
Débats, I. 239; V. 2, 31, 92, 94
Debauched Cavalier, The, VII. 382
Deben, river, XIII. 142
Debet, Sir Daniel, in *The Serving Man's Comfort*, V. 374
De Bonnefons, F., VIII. 449
Deborah, IV. 170
Deborah, in *Jacob and Esau*, V. 112
Deceit, in *The World tost at Tennis*, VI. 75
'Declaration of the Rights of Man and the Citizen,' XI. 71
Declaratory act, XI. 10
Decle, Lionel, XIV. 192
Decretals of Gregory IX, VIII. 312

Dedekind, Friedrich, III. 82; *Grobiana's Nuptials*, III. 82; *Grobianus* (trans. as *The School of Slovenrie*), III. 82; IV. 355, 443, 528; *Grobianus et Grobiana*, III. 82
Dedlock, lady, in *Bleak House*, XIII. 329
Dee, John (1527–1608), IV. 73, 436, 453, 455, 534; V. 377, 477; VI. 294; VII. 222, 369, 510, 511; VIII. 350; IX. 530; *British Monarchy*, IV. 95
Dee valley, X. 115
Deer, The Book of, XII. 513
Deeside, XII. 31
Defence for Mylke Maydes, A, III. 486
De Flores, in Middleton's *The Changeling*, VI. 76, 77, 80; XII. 222
Defoe, Daniel (1661?–1731), I. 257; II. 82; III. 363; IV. 93, 108; VI. 51, 56; VII. 167; VIII. 141; IX. 1 ff. (main entry), 80, 110, 394, 415 ff., 465, 476, 546, 569, 570; X. 1, 2, 5, 14, 18, 20, 26, 46, 386, 412; XII. 175, 201, 231, 250, 522; XIII. 314, 427; XIV. 197, 213, 461
Appeal to Honour and Justice, IX. 14 ff.
Atalantis Major (attr. to Defoe), IX. 13
Augusta Triumphans, IX. 23
Captain Singleton, IX. 22
Colonel Jacque, IX. 22
Complete English Gentleman, IX. 24, 398, 404
Complete English Tradesman, IX. 24
Consolidator, The, IX. 12, 19
Dissenters in England Vindicated, IX. 547
Due Preparations, IX. 22
Dyet of Poland, The, IX. 12
Enquiry into the occasional Conformity, X. 374
Essay on...Apparitions, IX. 24
Essay upon Projects, IX. 7, 397, 404
Experiment, The, IX. 12
Family Instructor, The, IX. 16, 19
Farther Adventures of Robinson Crusoe, IX. 19
Fortunate Mistress. See *Roxana*
Four Years Voyages of Capt. George Roberts, IX. 23
Friendly Demon, IX. 21
General History of Trade, IX. 15
Giving Alms no Charity, IX. 11
Great Law of Subordination Considered, IX. 23
History of...Mr Duncan Campbell, IX. 21
History of Peter the Great, IX. 22
History of the Union, IX. 13
History of the Wars of Charles XII, IX. 16
Hymn to the Pillory, IX. 9
Impartial History of Peter Alexowitz, IX. 22
Journal of the Plague Year, IX. 22
Jure Divino, IX. 12
Legion's Address, IX. 8
Letter to Mr Howe, X. 374
Manufacturer, The, IX. 14
Defoe, Daniel
Memoirs of a Cavalier, IX. 22
Memoirs of Captain George Carleton, IX. 23
Memoirs of the Church of Scotland, IX. 17
Mercator, IX. 14, 15
Minutes of Mesnager, IX. 17
Moll Flanders, IX. 22; X. 48
Mrs Veal, IX. 19
New Test, IX. 9
New Voyage round the World, IX. 23
Of Royall Educacion, IX. 406
Original Power of the Collective Body, IX. 8
Periodicals with which he was connected, IX. 432
Plan of the English Commerce, IX. 24
Political History of the Devil, IX. 24
Reasons against the Succession of the House of Hanover, IX. 14
Religious Courtship, IX. 22
Review, The, IX. 1, 4, 5, 10, 11, 13, 14, 34, 432
Robinson Crusoe, IX. 1, 11, 17, 19, 20, 21, 25, 106, 141, 142; X. 84; XI. 323, 366, 373, 477; XII. 251; XIII. 201, 265; XIV. 255, 438
Roxana, IX. 22 ff.
Secret History of the October Club, IX. 19
Secret History of the White Staff, IX. 15, 16
Serious Reflections during the Life... of Robinson Crusoe, IX. 19
Shortest Way with the Dissenters. IX. 7 ff., 19; X. 374
System of Magic, IX. 24
Tour thro' the Whole Island of Great Britain, IX. 21, 23
True-Born Englishman, IX. 8
True Relation of the Apparition, IX. 12
Defoe, Daniel, the younger, IX. 24
Defoe, Hannah, IX. 21
Defoe, Sophia, IX. 24
Degare, Sir, I. 311, 471
Degge, Sir Simon (1612–1704), VIII. 468
Degrevant, Sir, I. 289, 471
Deguileville, Guillaume, II. 170, 200, 201, 503; *Pilgrimage of the Soul*, IV. 353
De Heretico Comburendo, II. 67, 422
Deianeira, in *Confessio Amantis*, II. 148
d'Eichthal, G., XIV. 477
Deimling, Hermann, ed. of *Chester Plays*, II. 426
Deirdre's Lament, XIV. 304
Deism, XI. 286, 287
Dekker, Thomas (1570?–1641?), III. 114, 371, 485; IV. 115, 323, 351 ff., 363, 393, 434, 526 ff., 532, 534; V. 117, 184, 251, 254, 311, 312, 319, 323, 327, 332, 334, 345, 371; VI. 4, 13, 18, 29–57 (main entry), 64, 66, 68, 69, 95 ff., 142, 145, 146, 165, 168 ff., 184, 190, 195, 218, 226 ff., 231, 250, 345, 424 ff., 427, 443, *and see* Add.; VII. 389, 395; VIII. 162; IX. 32, 51, 262
Belman of London, The, IV. 354, 517
Canaan's Calamitie, IV. 324

Dekker, Thomas
Civil Wars in France, The, VI. 55
Dead Tearme, The, VI. 57
Dekker his Dreame, VI. 51, 57
Fowre Birds of Noahs Arke, VI. 57
Friar Rush, VI. 53
Gul's Hornbooke, III. 82; IV. 356; VII. 379; IX. 263
Honest Whore, The, VI. 53, 54, 62, 95, 173
If It Be Not Good, the Divel is in it, VI. 53; VIII. 123
Knight's Conjuring, A, IV. 354
Lady Jane, VI. 168
Lanthorne and Candle-light, IV. 354
Match mee in London, VI. 53, 98
Newes from Hell, IV. 352, 353; VII. 381
North-Ward Hoe, VI. 54, 170 ff.
Old Fortunatus, VI. 52
Page of Plymouth, VI. 12, 54, 96
Patient Grissill, VI. 54, 97, 100, 231
Phaeton, VI. 51, 54
Robert the Second, VI. 13, 54
Rod for Runawayes, A, VI. 56
Satiro-Mastix, VI. 4, 42, 53, 171, 173
Seven Deadly Sinnes of London, The, IV. 352, 510, 516; VIII. 10
Shoemaker's Holiday, The, III. 371; V. 255, 357, 373; VI. 52
Spanish Moor's Tragedy, The, VI. 55
Strange Horse Race, A, IV. 356
Sun's Darling, The, V. 125
Troilus and Cressida, VI. 51
West-Ward Hoe, VI. 54, 170 ff., 212
Whore of Babylon, The, VI. 53, 91, 150
Wonder of A Kingdom, The, VI. 54, 215
Wonderfull Yeare, The, IV. 351; VI. 56
Worke for Armourours, VI. 56
Wyat, The Famous History of Sir Thomas, VI. 54, 169, 173
Delacour, lady, in Miss Edgeworth's *Belinda*, XI. 297
Delacroix, Eugène, V. 302
Delamere, Lord, II. 414
Delane, John Thaddeus (1817 1879), XIV. 172, 180 ff., 533
Delany, Mrs Mary Granville (1700–1788), XI. 343, 347, 354, 365, 473
Delany, Patrick (1685?–1768), IX. 97, 459, 464, 466, 467
Delap, John (1725–1812), XI. 457; *Royal Suppliants*, XI. 274
De La Quintinye, VIII. 449
De La Ramée, Louise. *See* Ouida
de la Rochejaquelin, XII. 377
Delectable Demaundes, III. 489
Delft, II. 327
Delgan, in Layamon, I. 236
Delight, in *The Playe of Playes and Pastimes*, VI. 392
Delight, in *The Tears of the Muses*, III. 241
De l'Isle, Alain, *Anti-Claudianus*, VIII. 59
De Lisle, Ambrose Lisle March Phillipps (1809–1878), XII. 276, 454
Delitiae Poetarum Scotorum, IX. 550, 554 ff.
Delius, Nicolaus, V. 257, 278, 279, 305
Dell, William (d. 1664), VII. 316; IX. 386, 570, 571
Della Cruscan poets, XI. 40, 158, 172, 176 (main entry), 178, 180; XII. 124
Della Porretta family, in Richardson's *Sir Charles Grandison*, X. 11
Della Porta, G. B., *L'Astrologo*, VI. 322, 479; *La Cintia*, VI. 305; *La Fantesca*, VI. 305; *Trappolaria*, VI. 322, 477
Delolme, Jean-Louis, X. 500; *The Constitution of England*, X. 296
Deloney, Thomas (1543?–1607?), II. 415; III. 340, 343, 359 ff., 367 ff., 533; IV. 390, 536
The Gentle Craft, III. 368, containing the following tales: *Crispine and Crispinus*, III. 368; *Jack of Newbury*, III. 368; *Master Peachey and his men*, III. 369; *Richard Casteler*, III. 369; *Simon Eyre*, III. 368, 369, 371; *Sir Hugh*, III. 368; *Thomas of Reading*, III. 368, 370, *also see* Add.; V. 373
Deloraine, in Scott's *Lay of the Last Minstrel*, XII. 46
Delphic Oracle, in *Saturnalia*, VI. 319
Delphium (*i.e.* Pont-à-Mousson), in *Euphormio*, IX. 256
Deluge, the, XIV. 192
Delves, in Norton's *Ordinall*, II. 213
Demands, Budget of, III. 489
Demaundes joyous, III. 95, 489
Dembley, John Malham, XIII. 557
De Méré, chevalier (afterwards marquis), VIII. 376
Demetrias, St, I. 74
Demetrius, in *Confessio Amantis*, II. 147
Demetrius, in *The Poetaster*, VI. 18, 42, 44
De Mille, James (1836–1880), XIV. 360, 581
Democritus, VIII. 338
Democritus, riddles of, III. 489
Demogorgon, in Shelley's *Prometheus Unbound*, XII. 67
Demonio, in Calderon's *El Magico Prodigioso*, XIII. 144
Demonology, VII. 367 ff., 503 ff.
De Morgan, Augustus (1806–1871), IV. 263; XII. 370, 521; XIV. 10, 262, 263, 472, 474, 556
Demosthenes, III. 420, 429; IV. 1, 436; VII. 130, 131, 313, 316; IX. 229, 528; XI. 13; XII. 329, 332, 481, 485, 486, 489, 493, 495; *De Falsa Legatione*, XII. 330
Dempster, George (1732–1818), X. 191, 477
Dempster, Thomas (1579?–1625), IV. 253; VII. 315, 486; XII. 522
Dempster, in George Eliot's *Janet's Repentance*, XIII. 387
Denania, X. 237
Denbigh, earl of. *See* Feilding, William
Dence, Jael, in Reade's *Put Yourself in his Place*, XIII. 425
Denham, Henry (*fl.* 1591), IV. 400, 546
Denham, Sir John, father of the poet (1559–1639), VII. 59

Denham, Sir John (1615–1669), IV. 156; VII. 58 ff., 63, 67, 69, 70, 409, 431, 465; VIII. 3, 91, 247, 371, 410; IX. 67
Aeneid, trans. of second book, VII. 59
Cooper's Hill, VII. 38, 59, 60; IX. 69, 179; X. 111
Destruction of Troy, The, VII. 59, 61
Elegy on the Death of Henry, Lord Hastings, VII. 61
Essay on Translation, VII. 264
Horace (Corneille's), begun by Mrs Philips, finished by Sir John Denham, VIII. 180
Instructions to a Painter, VIII. 81, 408
Of Justice, VII. 61
Of Old Age, VII. 61
Of Prudence, VII. 61
On Mr Abraham Cowley's Death, VII. 61
Passion of Dido for Aeneas, The, VII. 61
Poems, VII. 61
Second Western Wonder, VII. 350
Sophy, The, VII. 59, 61
Version of the Psalms of David, A, VII. 61
Western Wonder, VII. 348
Deniehy, Henry (1828–1865), XIV. 362, 585
Denino, Fife, XI. 243
Denis, St, II. 102
Denison, Gedge Anthony (1805–1896), XIV. 591
Denison, John Evelyn, 1st viscount Ossington (1800–1873), XII. 307
Denman, admiral Joseph, XIV. 512
Denman, Thomas Denman, lord, 'Parliament and the Courts,' XII. 153
Denmark, V. 171, 200, 222, 307; VII. 197; VIII. 267; XII. 351; XIV. 293
Denmark, king of, in *Faire Em*, V. 252
Dennis, John (1657–1734), V. 189; VI. 28; VII. 265; VIII. 4, 143, 428, 433, 436, 438; IX. 73, 78, 122, 140, 142 (main entry), 143, 168, 435, 442, 448, 456, 473 ff., 512; XI. 250
Advancement and Reformation of Modern Poetry, IX. 142, 143
A Plot and No Plot, VIII. 194
Essay on...Shakespeare, IX. 142
Essay on the Operas, IX. 142
Grounds of Criticism in Poetry, IX. 143
Impartial Critic, The, VIII. 375
Reflections on Pope's Essay on Criticism, VIII. 61
Reflections upon...An Essay upon Criticism, IX. 77
Rinaldo and Armida, VIII. 194
Three Letters on the Genius and Writings of Shakespeare, VIII. 193
Usefulness of the Stage, VIII. 167
Dennis, John (1873), IX. Add.; XI. 423
Dennis, Ned, in *Barnaby Rudge*, XIII. 321
Denny, Sir Anthony (1501–1549), VII. 329, 330
Dennys, John (d. 1609), *Secrets of Angling*, IV. 374, 541; VII. 464
Dent, John Charles (1841–1888), XIV. 583; *Last Forty Years, The*, XIV. 358; *Story of the Upper Canadian Rebellion, The*, XIV. 358
Denward, Mrs E., XIV. 390
Denys, in *The Cloister and the Hearth*, XIII. 420
De Oculo Morali, II. 365
Deor, Complaint of, I. 4, 19 ff., 36, 373, 423, 428; II. 397; V. 26
De Palacio Garcia, IV. 455
Depazzi, in *The Traytor*, VI. 199
Depden, Suffolk, X. 294
De Phillide et Flora, I. 460
Deptford, V. 142; VIII. 260
De Quincey, Thomas (1785–1859), X. 476, 483; XI. 246, 344, 409, 417, 423; XII. 159, 160, 164, 174, 178, 203 ff., 219, 223, 224 ff. (main entry), 249, 430, 433, 437, 441, 444 (main entry), 490, *also see* Add.; XIII. 148, 158; XIV. 184, 203, 313, 462, 532
Autobiography, XII. 204
Confessions of an Opium-Eater, XI. 147
Confessions of an English Opium Eater, XII. 160, 194, 215, 224
Miscellanea, XII. 206
On Murder as one of the Fine Arts, XII. 175, 225
Our Ladies of Sorrow, XII. 226
Suspiria de Profundis, XIII. 109
De Raaf, V. 53
Derar, in Ockley's *History of the Saracens*, X. 281
Derby, X. 28; XI. 426, 431; XIV. 28, 437
Derby Ale-house, IX. 261
Derby, countess of. *See* Stanley, Alice
Derby, earl of, in *Edward III*, V. 246
Derby, earls of. *See* Stanley
Derbyshire, VII. 289; VIII. 106; IX. 277; X. 2, 131, 386; XII. 230, 507, 511; XIII. 390
De Refuge, E., IV. 526
Derham, William (1657–1735), IX. 506, 529; X. 512; *Physico-Theology*, X. 346
Derham, William (1846), XIV. 563
Dering, Edward (1540?–1576), IV. 236, 492; VII. 316
Dering or Deering, Sir Edward (1598–1644), VII. 440
Dermody, Thomas (1775–1802), XIV. 568
Dermot and the Earl, II. 502
Deronda, Daniel, George Eliot's, XIII. 400
De Ros, William L. L. Fitz-G., lord, XII. 509
Derosne, C. B., XIII. 546
Derozio, Henry Louis Vivian, XIV. 575; *The Fakeer of Jungheera*, XIV. 336
Derrick, Samuel (1724–1769), X. 442; XI. 448
Derry, IV. 311; VII. 285, 301
Derry, deanery of, IX. 281
Derwent river, XI. 95
'De Sawdust, Thomas' (De Quincey), XII. 225
Descartes, René, VII. 266, 284, 292, 302, 303, 394; VIII. 279, 285, 286, 290, 329, 334, 338, 340, 347, 348, 455, 472; IX. 61, 229, 282, 285, 287, 298, 314; X. 322, 348; XIV. 8, 268

Descartes, René
Dioptrique, VII. 285
Discours de la Méthode, VII. 285
Meditationes de prima philosophia, VII. 285, 286
Objectiones, VII. 285
Traité des passions de l'âme, VIII. 372
Deschamps, Eustache, II. 159, 467
Deschamps, J., IX. 435, 436
Deschapelles, V. 173
Desdemona, in *Othello*, IV. 78; V. 202, 203; VI. 95; VIII. 164
Desire, in prince Arthur's marriage pageant, VI. 332
Desire, in *The Bowge of Courte*, III. 73
Desire, in *Tom Tyler*, V. 117
Des Maizeaux, Pierre (1673?–1745), VIII. 471, 481; IX. 509
Desmarets de Saint Sorlin, J., VII. 270
Desmond, earl of. *See* Fitzthomas, Maurice
Despair, in *Piers the Plowman*, II. 28
Despair, cave of, in *The Faerie Queene*, III. 237
Despair, giant, in Bunyan's *Pilgrim's Progress*, VII. 173
Despauterius, Johannes, III. 429
Despenser or Spencer, Henry le (d. 1406), bishop of Norwich, II. 56
Desportes, Philippe, III. 251, 257, 258, 260, 261, 262, 263, 264, 523, *also see* Add.; IV. 24, 196, 223, 377, 443; IX. 167; *Diane*, III. 258, 261
Despréaux, Boileau, IX. 482. *See, also,* Boileau
De Stefani, A., XIII. Add. 2
Destiny, in *Tom Tyler*, V. 117
Destouches, Philippe-Néricault, X. 68, 78; *Philosophe marié*, X. 79
D'Estrades, count, VIII. 263
De Tabley, lord. *See* Warren, John Byrne Leicester
Detection of Damnable Drifts, VII. 373
Detraction, in *Confessio Amantis*, II. 147
Detraction, in *The Faerie Queene*, II. 234
Deuceace, Thackeray's, XIII. 277, 279 ff.
Deusdedit (d. 663/4), I. 82
Deuteromelia, III. 84; IV. 536
Deutschbein, M., *Englische Sagengeschichte*, I. 293
Deventer, III. 13
De Vere, Sir Aubrey (1788–1846), XI. 409; XII. 416
De Vere, Aubrey Thomas (1814–1902), XII. 441, 456; XIII. 188, 501
Devereux, lady Jane, of Merivale, IV. 170
Devereux, Penelope (lady Rich), VI. 189
Devereux, Robert, 2nd earl of Essex (1566–1601), III. 212, 254, 508; IV. 103, 114, 132, 133, 135, 142, 163, 164, 170, 200, 214, 215, 239, 276, 282, 376, 466; V. 346, 361, 371; VI. 30, 37, 101, 166, 248, 339, 344, 385; VII. 194, 343, 447, 454; XII. 440; XIV. 308
Devereux, Robert, 3rd earl of Essex (1591–1646), VII. 383, 447; VIII. 71
Devereux, Walter, 1st earl of Essex (d. 1576), III. 254, 508, *also see* Add.; IV. 466; V. 346
Devereux, Walter (brother of Robert, earl of Essex), IV. 376
de Vigny, Alfred, XII. 412
Devil, the, II. 366, 409
Devil, The, seen at St Albans, VII. 507
Devil, in *Mirour de l'Omme*, II. 140
Devil o'er Stirling, The, IX. 376
Devils, The Parliament of, II. 325, 501
Devine, Molly, Charlotte Eccles's, XIV. 325
Devizes. *See* Richard of
Devon booksellers and printers, XI. 468
Devonian system, the, XIV. 294
Devonshire, IV. 157, 190, 235, 314; V. 255; VI. 188, 237; VII. 1, 6, 9, 17, 386; IX. 162, 538; X. 21, 385, 490; XI. 34, 39; XII. 132. 345, 346, 514, 519; XIII. 276, 355, 360, 363, 364, 368; XIV. 84, 292
Devonshire, duchesses of. *See* Cavendish, Georgiana; Cavendish, Margaret
Devonshire, dukes of. *See* Cavendish, Spencer Compton; Cavendish, William
Devonshire, earls of. *See* Blount, Charles; Cavendish, William
Devotion, in *Ane Pleasant Satyre*, III. 125
Devotion, in *Mirour de l'Omme*, II. 142
De Waal, Daphne, XIV. Add. 4
Dewart, E. H., XIV. 582
Dewes, Giles (d. 1535), III. 550
D'Ewes, Sir Simonds (1602–1650), VI. 486; VII. 440, 441, 449; *Autobiography*, VII. 223, 224
De Wet, Christiaan Rudolf, XIV. Add 6
De Witt, Dutch traveller, VI. 252, 260, 261
Dewsbury, William (1621–1688), VIII. 110, 415
Dey, Lal Behari, XIV. 575, 576
Deyverdun, George (*fl.* 1768–1783), X. 311, 507, 508
Dialogue between James II and his Italian queen, VIII. 93
Dialogue between the devil and George II, IX. 371
Dialogus duarum sororum, III. 81
Dialogus linguae et ventris, II. 321
Diana, III. 179; IV. 122, 196; VI. 163
Diana, in *Colin Blowbol's Testament*, III. 86
Diana, in *Frier Bacon*, V. 340
Diana, in *The Flower and the Leaf*, II. 219
Diana, in *Reason and Sensuality*, II. 202
Diana, George Meredith's, XIII. 444
Diaper, William, *Eclogues*, IX. 126
Diaries and personal memoirs in Jacobean times, VII. 449
Dibben, Thomas (d. 1741), IX. 482
Dibdin, Charles (1745–1814), VIII. 423; X. 89, 425, 426, 443; XI. 281, 448, 453, 457; XIV. 224
Dibdin, James C., *Annals of the Edinburgh Stage*, X. 192, 444; XIII. 514
Dibdin, Thomas Frognall (1776–1847), XII. 350, 362, 520, 521
Aedes Althorpianae, XII. 366
Bibliographical Decameron, The, XII. 367

Dibdin, Thomas Frognall
Bibliographical Tour, A, xii. 367
Bibliomania, xii. 365, 366
Bibliophobia, xii. 367
Bibliotheca Spenceriana, xii. 366
Introduction to the Greek and Latin Classics, xii. 366, 367
Library Companion, The, xii. 367
Reminiscences of a Literary Life, i. 216; xii. 367
Dibdin, Thomas John (1771–1841), xi. 447; xiii. 514, 516
Dibelius, W., xiii. 543; *Englische Romankunst*, xiii. 341
Diccon, in *Gammer Gurtons Nedle*, vi. 297
Dice Play, ix. 51
Diceto. *See* Ralph of
Dicey, Albert Venn, xiv. 536
Dicey, Edward, xiv. 192
Dick, Ernst, xiii. 570
Dick, in Mrs Trimmer's *Robins*, xi. 379
Dick, Mr, in *David Copperfield*, xiii. 327
Dick Amlet, in Vanbrugh's *Confederacy*, viii. 162
Dick o' the Cow, ii. 415
Dicke Droom, in *The Glasse of Governement*, v. 113, 114
Dicke of Devonshire, vi. 432; vii. 453
Dickens, Charles (1812–1870), ii. 177; vi. 24, 28, 359; vii. 137; viii. 20; x. 37, 64; xi. 287, 385, 478; xii. 25, 219 ff., 250 ff., 431; xiii. 57, 178, 263, 265, 267, 275, 294, 301, 303 ff. (main entry), 344, 351, 376, 377, 386, 388, 420, 422, 423, 427, 442, 447, 458, 459, 461, 470, 495, 514, 516, 518, 523, 530 ff., 573, *also see* Add. 3; xiv. 148, 163, 170, 187, 189, 190, 236, 326, 444, 445
All the Year Round, xii. 441
American Notes, xiii. 322, 323; xiv. 348
Barnaby Rudge, x. 255; xiii. 318, 320, 325, 332, 457
Battle of Life, The, xiii. 323
Bleak House, xiii. 328, 332
'Boots at the Holly Tree Inn,' xiii. 335
Child's History of England, A, xiii. 320, 329
Chimes, The, xiii. 323, 324
Christmas Books, xiii. 323, 326
Christmas Carol, A, xiii. 323, 324
Christmas stories, xiii. 305
Cricket on the Hearth, The, xiii. 323, 324
David Copperfield, xiii. 305, 322, 326 ff., 331, 333, 337, 391
Doctor Marigold's Prescriptions, xiii. 335
Dombey and Son, xiii. 317, 324, 325
Edwin Drood, The mystery of, xiii. 310, 334, 335
George Silverman's Explanation, xiii. 323, 334
'Ghost in Master B's room, The,' xiii. 335
Great Expectations, xiii. 314, 328, 330, 333, 421
Hard Times, xiii. 310, 313, 328 ff., 332, 336, 337, 375, 378
Haunted House, The, xiii. 335
Dickens, Charles
Haunted Man, The, xiii. 323, 324, 326
Holiday Romance, A, xiii. 334
Hunted Down, xiii. 334
'Island of Silver-store, The,' xiii. 335
Letters of Charles Dickens to Wilkie Collins, xiii. 438
Little Dorrit, xiii. 317, 330, 331
Martin Chuzzlewit, xiii. 322, 324, 325
Master Humphrey's Clock, xiii. 308, 318, 321
Message from the Sea, A (with Wilkie Collins), xiii. 335
Mrs Lirriper, xiii. 335
Mudfog Papers, The, xiii. 308
Mugby Junction, xiii. 335
Nicholas Nickleby, xiii. 314, 315, 317, 325
No Thoroughfare (with Wilkie Collins), xiii. 335
Old Curiosity Shop, The, xiii. 318, 319, 325
Oliver Twist, x. 49; xiii. 315 ff., 325, 334
Our Mutual Friend, xiii. 314, 319, 334 ff.
'Our Parish,' xiii. 309, 313
'Parliamentary Sketch,' xiii. 309
Perils of Certain English Prisoners, The, xiii. 335
Pickwick Papers, The, x. 45; xii. 119; xiii. 305, 307, 308, 310 ff., 318, 319, 322, 323, 325, 333, 377, 418; xiv. 218, 234, 255
Pictures from Italy, xiii. 314, 324
Seven Poor Travellers, The, xiii. 335
Sketches by Boz, xii. 221; xiii. 305, 307 ff., 319
Sketches of Young Couples, xiii. 308
Sketches of Young Gentlemen, xiii. 308, 313
Somebody's Luggage, xiii. 335
Tale of Two Cities, A, xiii. 268, 313, 320, 332, 333, 337
Tom Tiddler's Ground, xiii. 335
Uncommercial Traveller, The, xii. 119; xiii. 307, 332, 335
Works (Rochester ed.), xiii. 456
Wreck of the Golden Mary, The, xiii. 335
Dickens, Charles, Forster's *Life* of, xiii. 305
Dickens, Mary, xiii. 532
Dickenson, John (*fl.* 1594), iii. 350, 367, 536; iv. 117, 469; *Shepheardes Complaint*, iv. 119
Dickins, Bruce, i. Add.
Dickinson, Francis Henry, xiv. 488
Dickinson, Henry, viii. 42
Dickinson, William (1746–1823), xiv. 216
Dickson, David (1583–1663), ix. 543
Dickson, Robert, xii. 521
Dickson, William Purdie (1823–1901), xii. 371, 521
Dictionaries, English-Latin, iii. 444
Dictionary, The New English, iv. 46
Dictionary of National Biography, ix. 236, 346, 347; x. 269; xii. 307, 309; xiv. 111, 143
Dictys Cretensis, i. 170, 467; ii. 172
Dicuil (*fl.* 825), i. 434

Didactic Literature, Old French, II. 507
Diderot, Denis, I. 209; V. 292; VI. 82; IX. 301; X. 68, 78, 79, 81, 264; XI. 292, 295, 296; XIII. 9, 468
De la Poésie Dramatique, X. 79
Éloge de Richardson, X. 17, 413
Fils Naturel, Le, X. 79
Paradoxe sur le Comédien, XI. 448
Père de Famille, Le, X. 79; XI. 275
Dido, IX. 45, 60, 257, 258; XIII. 123
Dido, in *The Legend of Good Women*, II. 264
Dido, in *The Shepheards Calendar*, III. 224
Dido, queen of Carthage, IV. 18; V. 74, 102; VIII. 65
Dido, tragedy on, in Vergilian hexameters, VI. 300
Dido, V. 70
Didot, printing press of, IV. 267
Didot Percival, in the Graal legend, I. 271
'Didymus Mountain' (*i.e.* Thomas Hill), IV. 375
Diego, in Arbuthnot's *History of John Bull*, IX. 135
Diego di Miranda, Don, in *Don Quixote*, IX. 269
Dieppe, IV. 142; XIII. 381
Dies Irae, IX. 178; XII. 9; XIII. 170
Dietary of ghostly health, The, II. 327
Dietrich, Franz, I. 49, 123
Dietrich von Bern, I. 36
Dieu save Dame Emme, in *Piers the Plowman*, II. 5
Diffidence, in Bunyan's *Pilgrim's Progress*, VII. 173
Digby, Everard (*fl.* 1590), IV. 274 ff., 507; VII. 278
Arte natandi, De, IV. 275
Dissuasive from taking away the lyvings and goods of the Church, IV. 275
Duplici methodo, De, IV. 275
Theoria analytica, viam ad monarchiam scientiarum demonstrans, IV. 275
Digby, George, 2nd earl of Bristol (1612–1677), VII. 440; *Elvira*, VIII. 130, 417
Digby, John, 1st earl of Bristol (1580–1653), VII. 440
Digby, Sir Kenelm (1603–1665), IV. 432; VII. 223, 238, 281, 302, 449, 470; VIII. 64, 76, 323, 354, 359, 407; XIV. 281; *Journal of a Voyage into the Mediterranean*, VII. 222; *Observations on Religio Medici*, VII. 235; *Private Memoirs of*, VII. 222
Digby, Kenelm Henry (1800–1880), XII. 448
Digby, Venetia, lady (born Stanley) (1600–1633), VII. 222
Digby plays, V. 19, 44, 390
Digby's Farewell, VIII. 96
Digges, Sir Dudley (1583–1639), IV. 310, 510; VII. 441, 456; *The Compleat Ambassador*, V. 477; VII. 191, 437
Digges, Dudley, the younger (1613–1643), VII. 456, 457
Digges, Leonard (1588–1635), IV. 436; VIII. 129
Diggon Davie, in *The Shepheards Calender*, III. 224
Dighton, Robert (1752?–1814), XIV. 225
Diligence, in *Ane Pleasant Satyre*, III. 125, 126, 127, 128
Diligence, in *The Assembly of Ladies*, II. 217
Dilke, Charles Wentworth (1789–1864), IX. 84; XI. 390; XII. 407
Dilke, Sir Charles Wentworth (1843–1911), XIV. 184, 200, 551; *Greater Britain*, XIV. 98, 255; *Problems of Greater Britain*, XIV. 255
Dillenius, John James (1687–1747), XIV. 286, 560
Dillingham, John (*fl.* 1649), VII. 360; *The Moderate Intelligencer*, VII. 349; *The Parliament Scout*, VII. 349
Dillon, John Blake (1816–1866), XIV. 317
Dillon, Peter (1785?–1847), XIV. 551
Dillon, Wentworth, 4th earl of Roscommon (1633?–1685), VII. 109; VIII. 219 ff., 409, 444, 446; IX. 70, 181, 473, 476; X. 183, 465; *Ars Poetica*, VIII. 221; *Essay on Translated Verse*, VIII. 220, 221, 395
Dilly, Charles (1739–1807), X. 479; XI. 326, 327
Dilly, Edward (1732–1779), X. 203, 481; XI. 325 ff.
Dilnot, Frank, XIV. 533
Dilworth, W. H., IX. 447, 466
Dimnet, Ernest, XIII. 557
Dingelstedt, Franz, V. 306
Dingley, Francis, of Munston, III. 197
Dingley, Rebecca, IX. 93, 95, 99, 126; XIV. 197
Dinmont, Dandie, in Scott's *Guy Mannering*, XII. 17, 25
Dinsdale, Frederick T., IX. Add.
Dio Cassius, VI. 154
Dio Chrysostomus, XII. 495
Diocletian, I. 309
Diocletian, in *The Prophetesse*, VI. 139
Diodati, Charles (1608?–1638), VII. 100. 131; X. 122
Diodati, Giovanni, VII. 481, 482
Diodati, villa, XII. 60
Diodorus Siculus, III. 67; VII. 488; XIV. 579; *Bibliothecae Historicae*, XII. 49
Diogenes, in D'Avenant's *First Day's Entertainment*, VIII. 117
Diogenes, in *The Palice of Honour*, II. 260
Diogenes Laertius, V. 125
Diogenes Laertius, in *The City Witt*, VI. 225
Diomed, VIII. 76
Diomed, in *Confessio Amantis*, II. 148
Diomede, in *The Testament of Cresseid*, II. 248
'Dion, Halicarnasseus,' VII. 65
Dionysia, in *Alls Lost by Lust*, VI. 72
Dionysius, IV. 436
Dionysius Longinus, XII. 494

Dionysius the Areopagite, I. 204; III. 6, 214; IV. 270; IX. 314
Dionysius of Halicarnassus, VI. 182
Dionysius, in *Damon and Pithias*, V. 118
Dionysius, Pseudo-, III. 6, 9, 216
Dionysius the Tyrant, The History of, III. 122, 141
Dionysius's Geography, IX. 393
Diotima (Plato's), III. 216
Directioun, in Douglas's *Aeneid*, II. 264
Director, The, IX. 433
Directorium Sacerdotum, II. 315
Disciplina Clericalis, I. 365; II. 150
Discipline, The First Book of, III. 146. *See, also, under* Knox, John
Discobolus, XIII. 452
Discordia, in Arbuthnot's *History of John Bull*, IX. 134
Discourse of Poesy, A, VIII. 240
Discovery of 29 Sects, A, VII. 386
Discretion, in *Ane Pleasant Satyre*, III. 125
Discretion, in *Piers the Plowman*, II. 19
Discretion, in *The Example of Virtue*, II. 227, 230
Discretion, in *The Palice of Honour*, II. 261
Disdain, in *The Faerie Queene*, III. 230
Disdain, in *The Passetyme of Pleasure*, II. 234
Disney, John, XIV. 593
Disobedience, in *Mirour de l'Omme*, II. 140
Dispatch, in Thomson's *Castle of Indolence*, X. 106
Disputational learning, 1600–1660, VII. 484
Disraeli, Benjamin, earl of Beaconsfield (1804–1881), IX. 243; XIII. 20, 258, 340, 345 ff. (main entry), 400, 423, 545 ff.; XIV. 115, 124, 127, 129, 130, 164, 183, 195, 196, 198, 488, 508
Alroy, XIII. 347, 349
Coalition, XIII. 353
Coningsby, XII. 155; XIII. 288, 346 ff., 352, 360, 373
Contarini Fleming, XIII. 346, 352
Count Alarcos, XIII. 353
Endymion, XIII. 348 ff.
Henrietta Temple, XIII. 346 ff., 350, 352
Infernal Marriage, The, XIII. 351
Ixion in Heaven, XIII. 351
Letters of Runnymede, XIII. 347, 348
Lothair, XIII. 348 ff.
Popanilla, XIII. 351
Revolutionary Epick, The, XIII. 352
Rise of Iskander, The, XIII. 347
Runnymede Letters, The, XIV. 181
Spirit of Whiggism, The, XIII. 347
Sybil, XIII. 347, 348, 350, 352, 373
Tancred, XIII. 345, 346, 348 ff., 352
Venetia, XIII. 346, 347, 352
Vindication of the English Constitution, XIII. 347
Vivian Grey, XIII. 346, 349, 351, 352, 436
Whigs and Whiggism, XIII. 348
Young Duke, The, XIII. 347, 350
Disraeli, Isaac (1766–1848), III. 78; XI. 466; XII. 366, 367, 521
Amenities of Literature, XII. 364
Calamities of Authors, XII. 364
Curiosities of Literature, XII. 353, 364
Literary Miscellanies, XII. 370
Quarrels of Authors, XII. 364
Diss, Norfolk, II. 258; III. 67, 70, 72, 93
Dissait, in *Ane Pleasant Satyre*, III. 124
Dissertation sur la poésie anglaise, V. 287
'Dissidence of Dissent,' the, XIII. 101
Dissimulation, in *Kynge Johan*, V. 66
Distaff, Jenny, in *The Tatler*, IX. 39, 40, 53
Distaff-lane, in *The Masque of Christmas*, VI. 359
Distracted Emperor, The, VI. 459
Ditchley, near Woodstock, VIII. 206
Diu Krône, by Heinrich von dem Türlin. I. 269
Diurnall of Remarkable Occurents, The, III. 149, 502
Diurnalls, VII. 346, 385
Dives and Pauper, II. 321, 323
Dives Pragmaticus, V. 355
Divine Correctioun, in *Ane Pleasant Satyre*, III. 126, 128
Divine Poems, XI. 370
Divinity, lady (in an anti-Martinist play), III. 393
Divyāvadāna, XII. 489
Dixie, Sir Woolstone (1525–1594), V. 131
Dixon, Henry Hall, 'The Druid' (1822–1870), XIV. 543
Dixon, Richard Watson (1833–1900), XIII. 119, 184, 194, 203, 501; XIV. 487
Fallen Rain, XIII. 197
Feathers of the Willow, The, XIII. 197
Last Poems, XIII. 196
Love's Consolation, XIII. 197
Mano, XIII. 196, 197
Ode on Advancing Age, XIII. 198
Poems, XIII. 197
To Shadow, XIII. 198
Dixon, Robert (d. 1688), VII. 507; IX. 499
Dixon, William Hepworth (1821–1879), XII. 451; XIV. 193, 253, 501, 551, 570
Dixon, William Macneil, XIII. 476, 488, 497, 570; *Edinburgh Book of Scottish Verse*, XI. 443
Dixon, W. W., XIV. 533
Dobbin, major William, in Thackeray's *Vanity Fair*, XIII. 287, 289, 293
Dobell, Bertram (1837–1914), VI. 5; VII. 42; XII. 400 ff.; XIII. 108, 489, 501
Dobell, Sydney Thompson (1824–1874), XIII. 156 ff., 411, 501, 557, 558
Balder, XII. 114; XIII. 158 ff.
England in Time of War, XIII. 159
Keith of Ravelston, XIII. 159
Nuptial Song, A, XIII. 159
Roman, The, XIII. 159
Tommy's Dead, XIII. 159
Do-best, in *Piers the Plowman*, II. 2 ff., 18 ff., 24, 26, 28

Do-better, in *Piers the Plowman*, II. 2 ff., 18 ff., 24, 26, 28
Dobree, Peter Paul (1782–1825), XII. 325, 327, 328, 482, 491; *Adversaria*, XII. 328; *Lexicon rhetoricum Cantabrigiense*, XII. 328; *Notes on Inscriptions*, XII. 328
Dobson, Austin (1840–1923), IX. 73; X. 3, 12, 261, 413, 418, 483, *also see* Add.; XI. 374, 458, 468, 469, 475; XII. 444, 446; XIII. 211, 504; XIV. 540; *Horace Walpole*, X. 245
Dobson, William (*fl.* 1734), IX. 482
Doctor, in *Ane Pleasant Satyre*, III. 128
Doctor Syntax in Paris, XIV. 219
Doctrinal of Death, The, II. 323
Doctrine, tower of, in *The Passetyme of Pleasure*, II. 225, 231
Dodd, A., IX. 79
Dodd, William (1729–1777), X. 470
Dodd, in Reade's *Hard Cash*, XIII. 428
Doddridge, Philip (1702–1751), IX. 563; X. 371, 381 ff., 521; *Rise and Progress of Religion in the Soul*, X. 383
Doderidge, Sir John (1555–1628), VIII. 468, 470
Dodger, the, in *Oliver Twist*, XIII. 316
Dodgson, Charles Lutwidge (*pseud.* 'Lewis Carroll,' 1832–1898), XI. 477, 478; XIII. 501; XIV. 163, 206, 472
Alice in Wonderland, VII. 30; XI. 387; XIII. 166
Hunting of the Snark, The, XIII. 167
Jabberwocky, XIII. 167
Rhyme? and Reason? XIII. 167
Sylvie and Bruno, XI. 387; XIII. 167
Walrus and the Carpenter, The, XIII. 167
Dodington, George Bubb, lord Melcombe (1691–1762), IX. 86, 188, 253, 254, 497; X. 94, 103; *Diary*, IX. 254
Dodoens, Rembert, IV. 542; *A Niewe Herball*, III. 551; IV. 374, 408; *Pemptades*, IV. 374
Dodona, site of, XII. 329
Dodsley, James (1724–1797), XI. 142, 324
Dodsley, Robert (1703–1764), V. 41, 54; IX. 177, 188, 189, 190–191 (main entry), 475, 484; X. 123, 124, 132, 135, 138, 144, 167, 170, 177, 245, 271, 273, 439, 445, 456; XI. 318, 323, 324, 327, 332, 334, 468, 490
Collection of Poems, VIII. 44; IX. 190, 191; X. 274, 454, 496; XI. 324
Compendium of Voyages, X. 41
Muse in Livery, IX. 190
Select Collection of Old Plays, VIII. 129; IX. 190; XI. 324
The Toyshop, XI. 323
Dodsworth, Roger (1585–1654), IX. 342, 343, 348, 350, 532, 533, 539; XII. 349
Dodwell, Edward (1767–1832), XII. 496; *Classical and Topographical Tour through Greece*, XII. 338
Dodwell, Henry, the elder (1641–1711), VIII. 306, 307, 459; IX. 329, 330, 505, 506, 515, 527, 534; X. 308, 356, 516, 521; *De Cyclis*, IX. 330
Dodwell, Henry, the younger (d. 1784), IX. 288; *Christianity not founded on argument*, IX. 295, 506, 507
Dodwell, Miss, IX. 511
Doe, Charles, VII. 430
Doeg, in *The Second Part of Absalom and Achitophel*, VIII. 41, 42, 192
Doesborch or Desborowe, John of, II. 329, 330; III. 82; IV. 69; (printed by), *Of the newelandes and of ye people founde by the messengers of the Kynge of Portyngale named Emanuel*, II. 330; IV. 70, 71
Dogberry, in *Much Ado about Nothing*, IV. 360; V. 191, 362; VI. 46, 217; XI. 266; XIII. 64
Doggrel, Sir Iliad [Burnet, Thomas], IX. 258, 448
Dol Common, in *The Alchemist*, V. 377; VI. 22
Dolben, Digby Mackworth (1848–1867), XII. 271, 276, 456; XIII. 502
Dolben, John (1625–1686), VIII. 302
Dolby, George, XIII. 532
Dolce, Lodovico, III. 359; V. 63, 72, 76
Didone, V. 74 ff.
Giocasta, V. 71
Phoenissae, IV. 4
Troiane, V. 69
Dole, Nathan Haskell, XIII. 497
Dolet, Etienne, IV. 322, 517
Do-little Lane, in *The Masque of Christmas*, VI. 358
Doll, in *Henry IV*, V. 187
Dolléans, Edouard, XIV. 478
Dolling, Robert William Radclyffe (1851–1902), XIV. 502
Döllinger, Johann J. I., XIV. 117
Dolman, John (*fl.* 1551), IV. 5, 435
Dolman, Miss, X. 273, 496
Dombey, Paul, Dickens's, XIII. 325
Domesday, Fifteen Signs before, I. 356, 458
Domesday Book, I. 390; VIII. 313; XII. 509, 511
Domestic drama, English, VI. 97, 133
Domestic tragedies, English, V. 376
Domett, Alfred (1811–1887), XIII. 502; XIV. 585
'Centuries ago,' XIII. 187
Christmas Hymn, A, XIII. 187
Flotsam and Jetsam, XIV. 368
Ranolf and Amohia, XIII. 186; XIV. 368
Dominic, St, I. 200, 339
Dominica, XIV. 214
Dominicans, I. 200, 355; II. 370; III. 68, 70; VI. 257; VIII. 59; X. 282
Dominicans, in Cambridge and Oxford, II. 349
Dominicans, in Paris, II. 349, 350
Dominichi, Lodovico, III. 93
Dominis, Antonio de, VII. 308
Dominus, in *Saturnalia*, VI. 319
Domitia, in *The Roman Actor*, VI. 155, 159
Domitian, I. 226; III. 433
Domitian, in *The Roman Actor*, VI. 153, 155, 159

Domitilla, in *The Royall Master,* VI. 205
Don Armado, in *Love's Labour's Lost,* VIII. 127
Don Diego, in Jonson's *The Alchemist,* VIII. 127
Don Gayferos, I. 293
Don Juan, in Shadwell's *Libertine,* VIII. 174
Don Quixote, I. 293; VIII. 67, 68, 70
Dôn, the children of, I. 252
Donald, in Holcroft's *Deserted Daughter,* XI. 277
Donaldson, Alexander, XI. 315, 342
Donaldson, Augustus Blair, XIII. 504
Donaldson, David, II. 118
Donaldson, James (*fl.* 1713), IX. 559
Donaldson, Sir James, XIV. 538, 597
Donaldson, John William (1811–1861), XII. 482
Classical Scholarship and Classical Learning, XII. 331
New Cratylus, The, XII. 330
Theatre of the Greeks, The, XII. 330
Varronianus, XII. 330
Donati, Eduardo, III. 296
Donatists, the, XII. 260
Donatus, grammars of, I. 114, 118; II. 359
Doncaster, II. 45, 88, 321; XI. 168; XII. 516; XIII. 351; XIV. 225
Doncaster, viscount. *See* Hay, James
'Done oracio,' V. 160
Doni, IV. 443
Donne, John (1573–1631), III. 173, 426; IV. 55, 145, 163, 169, 187, 196–223 (main entry), 224, 226, 239 ff., 329, 390, 434, 488 ff., 492, 495; V. 338; VI. 2, 9 ff., 15, 72, 177, 185, 187; VII. 3, 10, 17, 19, 26, 38, 46, 49, 62, 64, 69, 81, 82, 85, 86, 130, 148, 157, 163, 166, 180, 250, 252, 258, 463, 488; VIII. 228, 229, 238, 292, 293, 365, 366; IX. 157, 446; X. 226; XII. 259; XIII. 191, 219, 448; XIV. 460, 491
Aire and Angels, IV. 210
Anatomy of the World, The, IV. 204
Anniversaries, IV. 212 ff., 216, 217
Annunciation and Passion, IV 217
Apparition, The, IV. 210
'At Court,' IV. 200
Autumnal, IV. 209
Bait, The, VII. 8
ΒΙΑΘΑΝΑΤΟΣ, IV. 202, 208, 219
Blossom, The, IV. 211
Break of Day, The, IV. 212
'By our first strange and fatal interview,' IV. 212
Calme, The, IV. 200, 215
Canonization, The, IV. 212
Chain, The, IV. 210, 215
(?) 'Come Fates,' IV. 209
'Dear Love, continue nice,' IV. 209
Death be not proud, IV. 216
Death I recant, IV. 216
Death's Duel, IV. 204
Devotions, IV. 204, 219
Donne, John
Dialogue, IV. 209
Divine Poems, IV. 204, 205; VII. 27, 31
Dream, The, IV. 210, 212
Ecstacy, The, IV. 212
Eighty Sermons, IV. 241
Elegie on Prince Henry, IV. 204
Elegies, IV. 203, 205, 208 ff., 213
Epigrams, IV. 205
Epistles to Wotton, IV. 215
Epithalamiums, IV. 203, 205
Essays in Divinity, IV. 219
Expiration, The, IV. 212
'For Godsake hold your tongue,' IV. 212
Funerall, The, IV. 211
Funerall Elegies, IV. 202, 205, 213, 215
'Go catch a falling star,' IV. 210; VII. 23
Holy Sonnets, IV. 217
Ignatius his Conclave, IV. 203, 218
'I love to talk with some old lover's ghost,' VII. 23
Indifferent, The, IV. 210
'Kind pity checks my spleen,' IV. 197
La Corona, IV. 217
Lamentations of Jeremy, The, IV. 205, 217
Letters to countess of Bedford, IV. 216
Letters to Severall Personages, IV. 205, 215
Litany, The, IV. 217; VII. 15
Love's War, IV. 209
'Now thou hast loved me one whole day,' VII. 23
Paradoxes, IV. 203, 208, 218
Perfume, The, IV. 210
Picture, The, IV. 210
Primrose, The, IV. 211
Problems, IV. 203, 218
Progresse of the Soule, The, IV. 203, 205, 214
Pseudo-Martyr, IV. 203, 208, 217 ff.
Satyres, IV. 203, 205, 213
'Send home my long stray'd eyes to me,' IV. 210
Sermons, IV. 204
Songs and Sonets, IV. 205, 208, 209; VII. 2
'Soul's joy,' IV. 209
Storm, The, IV. 200, 215
Sun-rising, The, IV. 212
To Christ, IV. 217
To God, my God, IV. 217
To God the Father, IV. 217
'To make the doubt clear,' IV. 209
To Sir Nicholas Smith, IV. 206
Twickenham Garden, IV. 211
Upon Mr Thomas Coryat's Crudities, IV. 204
Valediction: forbidding Mourning, IV. 212
Valediction: of Weeping, IV. 211
Woman's Constancy, IV. 210
Donne, John (1604–1662), IV. 240
Donne, William Bodham (1807–1882), XII. 475; XIII. 142; *Essays on the Drama,* XII. 305

Donusa, in *The Renegado*, vi. 155 ff.
Doolittle, Thomas (1632?–1707), x. 386; *Sufferings of Christ*, iv. 388
Doomsday, i. 227, 458
Doomsday (a broadside), iv. 414
Doomsday poems, i. 444
Doon, river, xi. 235
Doones, the, in Blackmore's *Lorna Doone*, xiii. 434
Dora, in *David Copperfield*, xiii. 327, 331
Doran, Cecily, Gissing's, xiii. 461
Doran, John (1807–1878), xi. 447, 474; xiv. 518
  A Lady of the last Century, x. 261, 262
  Knights and their Days, xiv. 139
  Mann and Manners at the Court of Florence, x. 249
  Their Majesties' Servants, xiv. 139
Dorastus, in *Pandosto*, iii. 356
Dorax, in Dryden's *Don Sebastian*, viii. 31
Dorchester, xii. 326; Roman amphitheatre at, vi. 252
Dorchester, viscount. *See* Carleton, Sir Dudley
Dorigen, in *The Franklin's Tale*, ii. 184
Dorilant, Sir John, in Whitehead's *School for Lovers*, x. 86
Dorimant, in Etherege's *Man of Mode*, viii. 138, 214
Dorislaus of Holland, iv. 159
Dorlandus, Petrus, *Elckerlijk*, ii. 329
Dormer, Robert, 1st earl of Carnarvon (d. 1643), iv. 157; vi. 143
Dormer's News Letter, ix. 432
Dornton, in Holcroft's *Road to Ruin*, xi. 277
Dorothea, i. 74, 75
Dorothea, in *James IV*, v. 137, 138
Dorothea, in Massinger's *The Virgin Martir*, vi. 54, 150, 154, 165; xii. 68
Dorothea, in *Middlemarch*, xiii. 392, 398
Dorrington, Edward (? pseudonym), xi. 489
Dorrits, the, Dickens's, xiii. 320, 331
D'Orsay, Alfred Guillaume Gabriel, count (1801–1852), xiv. 115
Dorset, ii. 414; vii. 74; ix. 146; x. 20, 25; xi. 99; xii. 346, 511, 513, 520; xiii. 320; xiv. 292
Dorset dialect, xii. 413
Dorset, Catherine Ann (1750?–1817?), xi. 476, 478; *Lion's Masquerade*, xi. 386; *Peacock at Home*, xi. 386
Dorset, countess of, ix. 148
Dorset, earls of. *See* Sackville, Charles, Richard, Thomas
Dort, iv. 402, 403
Dort, synod of, vii. 152, 322, 437
D'Orville, xii. 484
Dory, John, ii. 414
Dostöevsky, F. M., *The Brothers Karamazov*, xiii. 462
Dotheboys hall, in *Nicholas Nickleby*, xiii. 317
Douady, Jules, xii. 343
Douay, iii. 426; iv. 127, 274, 402; vii. 302, 303; xiv. 53
Douay commentary, vii. 481
Double Falsehood, v. 444
Doubledick, Richard, in Dickens's *Seven Poor Travellers*, xiii. 335
Douce, Francis (1757–1834), ii. 122, 329
Douglas, in Mrs Oliphant's *Kirsteen*, xiii. 431
Douglas, captain (1667), viii. 381
Douglas, Catherine, duchess of Queensberry (d. 1777), ix. 162 ff.
Douglas, Charles, 3rd duke of Queensberry (1698–1778), ix. 163, 164; x. 102; xi. 317
Douglas, Charles Mackinnon, xiv. 478
Douglas, Francis (1710?–1790?), ix. 557, 563; x. 477, 478, 479
Douglas, Gawin or Gavin (1475?–1522), ii. 91, 92, 94, 96 ff., 126, 239, 244, 249 ff., 258–265 (main entry), 275, 476 ff.; iii. 115, 116, 117, 119, 120, 138, 185, 200, 278; x. 223, 239; xi. 203, 204, 431
  Aeneid, trans. of, ii. 240, 259, 261 ff.; iv. 397
  Aurae Orationes, ii. 259
  Conscience, ii. 259, 262
  King Hart, ii. 228, 259, 262
  Palice of Honour, The, ii. 126, 259, 260, 262, 266, 268; iii. 117, 119; iv. 397, 412; vii. 174; ix. 359
  Vergil, ix. 359, 562
Douglas, George, *pseud.* *See* Brown, George Douglas
Douglas, Sir George Brisbane Scott, ii. 396; xii. 453; *Book of Scottish Poetry, The*, xi. 443
Douglas, Sir James (1286?–1330), ii. 114
Douglas, James, xiii. 510
Douglas, James, 4th duke of Hamilton (1658–1712), ix. 424
Douglas, Dr James (1675–1742), xii. 363
Douglas, James of, in *Bruce*, ii. 101, 105
Douglas, John (1721–1807), x. 292, 293, 499; *Criterion of Miracles*, x. 346, 512
Douglas, lady Juliana, in Susan Ferrier's *Marriage*, xii. 245, 246
Douglas, M. A., xiv. 599
Douglas, William, 8th earl of Douglas (1425?–1452), ii. 113
Douglas, William (*fl.* 1660), ix. 543
Douglas, William Scott (1815–1883), xi. 438, 440
Douglas ballad, the, ii. 398
Douglas cause, x. 191
Douglas family, ii. 113, 114, 115; iii. 118
Douglas Tragedy, i. 300; ii. 410
Douglas-Albany quarrels, the, ii. 259
Douglasdale, ii. 105
Douglass, Arthur, xiv. Add. 6
Douse, Francis, xii. 376
Dove, Sir Benjamin and lady, in Cumberland's *Brothers*, xi. 264, 279
Dove, Dr Daniel, in Southey's *Doctor*, xi. 168

Dove, Jane Frances, xiv. 599
Dove cottage, xi. 102, 103, 409
Dover, iii. 3; iv. 418; vii. 183; viii. 202, 263; ix. 240, 268; x. 118, 201, 244, 395
Dow, Alexander (d. 1779), xiv. 576; *Sethona*, xiv. 334; *Zingis*, xiv. 334
'Doway,' university of, v. 113
Dowden, Edward (1843–1913), xi. 404, 406, 409, 412, 413, 417, 420, 422, 423; xii. 399, 401 ff., 415, 423; xiii. 65, 464, 465, 476, 480, 487, 495, 553; xiv. 211, 487, 518, 527; *Life of Shelley*, xiv. 147; *Shakespeare...his Mind and Art*, xiv. 147
Dowel, John, vii. 470
Do-well, in *Piers the Plowman*, ii. 2 ff., 15, 18 ff., 24, 26, 28
Dowland, John (1563?–1626?), iv. 114, 463, 464; xiv. 307; *A Pilgrim's Solace*, iv. 113
Dowland, Robert (17th cent.), iv. 113, 464
Dowler, Mr, in *The Pickwick Papers*, xiii. 314
Dowling, Richard, xiv. 568; *Mystery of Killard, The*, xiv. 327; *On Babies and Ladders*, xiv. 327
Down, county, xii. 361; xiii. 404
Down, Kent, xiv. 298
Down hall, Essex, ix. 152, 153
'Down Survey,' the, of forfeited lands, viii. 343
Downefall of Dagon, The, vii. 382
Downefall of temporizing poets, The, vii, 386
Downes, Andrew (1549?–1628), iii. 425; vii. 312, 488; *De Caede Eratosthenis*, vii. 316; *De Pace*, vii. 316
Downes, John (*fl.* 1662–1710), *Roscius Anglicanus*, viii. 189, 192, 423
Downey, Edmund, xiv. 569
Downing, Emanuel (*fl.* 1650), vii. 353
Downing, Sir George (1684?–1749), viii. 253
Downman, Hugh (1740–1809), xi. 451
Dowsabell, in Drayton's *Eglogs*, iv. 173
Dowsing, William (1596?–1679?), vii. 34
Dowson, Ernest (1867–1900), xiii. 212, 220, 502; *I have been faithful to thee, Cynara*, xiii. 219
Dowson, John (1820–1881), xii. 516; xiv. 337
Dowson, M. E. *See* Palmer, William Scott
Doyle, Sir Francis Hastings Charles (1810–1888), xiii. 45, 502; xiv. 597; *Private of the Buffs, A*, xiii. 186; *Red Thread of Honour, The*, xiii. 186
Doyle, James E. (1822–1892), xiv. 502
Doyle, John Andrew (1844–1907), xiv. 98, 487
Doyle, Martin, xiv. 312
Doyle, Richard (1824–1883), xi. 480, 487; xiii. 294, 499; xiv. 238, 548, 549
D'Oyly, Christopher, x. 405, 410
Dracontius, i. 76
Drage, William (1637?–1669), vii. 507
Draghi, John Baptist (17th cent.), viii. 394
Drake, Sir Francis (1540?–1596), iii. 52, 327; iv. 1, 68, 72, 73, 78, 85 ff., 92, 93, 96, 102, 103, 261, 299, 454, 510; v. 345, 361; vii. 248; x. 164, 464; xiii. 364
Drake, Sir Francis (the younger), *Sir Francis Drake Reviv'd*, iv. 96, 455
Drake, Francis (1696–1771), *York*, ix. 353, 532
Drake, James (1667–1707), viii. 91, 410, 433
Drake, Nathan (1766–1836), *Essays illustrative of the Rambler*, x. 172, 461, 476, 483
Drake, The, vi. 53
Drakenberg, the, xiv. 372
Drama and the stage in the age of Johnson, the, x. 67 ff., 425 ff.
Drames v. 192
Drane, Augusta Theodosia (1823–1894), xiv. 601
Drant, Thomas (d. 1578?), iii. 201; iv. 23, 437, 492, 518; v. 156
Draper, Mrs Eliza (1744–1778), x. 47
Draper, Sir William (1721–1787), x. 403, 407, 526
Drapier, M. B. (Swift's pseudonym), ix. 115
Drawcansir, in *The Rehearsal*, viii. 27
Drawcansir, Sir Alexander (Fielding's pseudonym), x. 34
Drayton, Michael (1563–1631), i. 170; iii. 183, 220, 247, 256, 258, 260, 263 ff., 268, 270, 286, 305, 523, 526; iv. 87, 95, 117, 118, 121, 136, 138, 153, 158, 168–195 (main entry), 211, 248, 266, 351, 357, 401, 434, 455, 485 ff., 530; v. 148, 226, 228, 236, 311, 312, 319, 323, 332, 338, 371, 474; vi. 2, 61, 113, 250, 312; vii. 50, 52, 56, 58, 250, 264, 387, 465; viii. 226, 228, 237, 239
  Agincourt, Ballad of, iv. 170, 188, 192
  Agincourt, The Battaile of, iv. 192
  Amours, iv. 178
  'An evill spirit,' iv. 179
  Baron's Wars, The, iii. 198, 305; iv. 174, 181, 182, 191, 192
  Cromwell, The Legend of Great, iii. 198; iv. 176, 177, 188
  David and Goliah, iv. 194
  Eclogues, iii. 220; iv. 118, 172, 173
  Elegies upon sundry occasions, iv. 192, 194
  Endimion and Phoebe, iv. 173, 175, 176, 180, 181, 183, 195
  England's Heroicall Epistles, iii. 198; iv. 169, 175, 182 ff., 206; vii. 49
  Epistle to George Sandys, iv. 184
  Harmonie of the Church, The, iv. 170, 171, 173, 357
  Heavenly Harmonie of Spirituall Songs, A, iv. 171
  'How many paltry,' iv. 179
  Hymn to his Ladies Birth-Place, iv. 174
  Idea, the Shepheard's Garland, iii. 256, 258, 260; iv. 118, 170 ff., 184, 193

Drayton, Michael
Ideas Mirrour, III. 263; IV. 177, 178, 180
'Into these loves,' IV. 179
Man in the Moone, The, IV. 181, 185
'Many there be excelling,' IV. 179
Matilda, III. 198; IV. 176, 177, 182
Miseries of Queene Margarite, The, IV. 193
Moone-Calfe, The, IV. 185, 194
Mortimeriados, III. 305; IV. 175, 176, 181, 182
Moses, his Birth and Miracles, IV. 185, 194
Moyses in a Map of his Miracles, IV. 185, 194
Muses Elizium, The, IV. 193, 194
Noah's Floud, IV. 194, 195
Nymphidia, I. 289; IV. 193
Odes, IV. 174, 185 ff., 193
Of his Ladies not Coming to London, IV. 194
Of Poets and Poesy, Epistle to Henry Reynolds, III. 201; IV. 138, 194; VII. 273
Owle, The, IV. 184, 185
Paen Triumphall, IV. 184
Piers Gaveston, III. 198; IV. 176, 177, 182
Poems, Lyric and Pastoral, IV. 118, 168, 172
Polyolbion, II. 209; III. 183; IV. 136, 174, 177, 183, 188 ff., 401
Quest of Cynthia, The, IV. 193
Remedy for Love, His, III. 264
Robert, Duke of Normandy, III. 198; IV. 175 ff., 182
Shepheards Sirena, The, IV. 193
'Since there's no help,' IV. 179
To his Coy Love, IV. 187
To His Rivall, IV. 186
To the Majestie of King James, IV. 184
To the New Yeere, IV. 186
To the Virginian Voyage, IV. 187
'Whilst thus my pen,' IV. 179
See, also, under Middleton, Rowland
Drayton Beauchamp, III. 406
Dread, in *Piers the Plowman*, II. 8
'Dread Maria's Universal Fall,' IX. 148
Dream of the Cabal, VIII. 81
Dream of the Rood (? Cynewulf), I. 42, 51 ff., 56, 57, 63, 133, 430
Dream of the Rood, Ruthwell Cross, I. 12; II. 88
Drede, in *The Bowge of Courte*, III. 73
Drelincourt, Charles (1644–1722), IX. 12
Drennan, William (1754–1820), XIV. 311, 568; *Erin*, XIV. 310; *Letters of Orellana*, XIV. 310; *Wake of William Orr, The*, XIV. 310
Dresden, VI. 165; IX. 515; XIII. 388
Drift, Adrian, IX. 149, 151, 153, 217, 482, *also see* Add.
Dring, Thomas, VII. 123
Drinkwater, John, XIII. 493, 495
Driver, Samuel Rolles (1846–1914), XII. 466, 501; *Introduction to the Literature of the Old Testament*, XII. 341
Droeshout, E. P., V. 89
Drogheda, VII. 196, 351, 353, *also see* Add.
Drogheda, lady (d. *c.* 1681), wife of Wycherley, W., VIII. 143
Drogheda, St Peter's church, VII. 354
Dromios, in *The Comedy of Errors*, V. 178
Dromodotus, in *Pedantius*, VI. 306
Dromore, deanery of, IX. 280
Dromore, Ireland, VIII. 290; XII. 354, 361
'Drone Hall,' Oxford, IX. 414
Drosomell (Herrick's), VII. 12
Droyn, Jehan, III. 59
Druce, George Claridge, XIV. 560, 562
Drugger, Abel, in *The Alchemist*, VI. 22; X. 265; XI. 257
Druidism, IX. 352, 354
Druids, I. 13
Drummond, Henry (1851–1897), XII. 466
Drummond, J., XIII. 467
Drummond, John, 1st earl Melfort (1649–1714), VIII. 263
Drummond, Sir John (d. 1610), IV. 150
Drummond, Margaret (1472?–1501), II. 253, 281
Drummond, Peter Robert (1802–1879), XIII. 507
Drummond, William, of Hawthornden (1585–1649), III. 267, 269, 523, *also see* Add.; IV. 130, 138, 139, 150 ff. (main entry), 157, 159, 166, 189, 196, 197, 201, 205, 209, 214, 413, 434, 480; V. 343; VI. 1, 2, 5, 11, 36, 38, 39, 44, 47, 58, 112, 221, 353; VII. 30, 273, 274, 466; VIII. 227, 322; IX. 69; X. 484
Cypress Grove, The, IV. 153
Flowers of Sion, IV. 153, 154
Forth Feasting, IV. 152
Hymn of the Fairest Fair, IV. 153
Madrigals and Epigrams, VII. 14
Tears on the Death of Moeliades, IV. 151, 152
Drummond, William Hamilton (1778–1865), XIV. 568, 573
Drummond, William Henry (1854–1907), XIV. 343, 354 ff., 360, 582
Canadian Country Doctor, XIV. 355
Great Fight, The, XIV. 355, 356
Habitant, The, XIV. 354, 356
Johnnie Courteau, XIV. 356
Ole Doctor Fiset, XIV. 355
Philorum's Canoe, XIV. 356
Vieux Temps, Le, XIV. 355
Voyageur, The, XIV. 356
Wreck of the Julie Plante, The, XIV. 355
Drumsoy, IX. 370
Drunkard's Character, The, VII. 384
Drury, Elizabeth (d. 1610), IV. 202, 214, 216
Drury, Joseph (1750–1834), XIV. 386
Drury, Sir Robert (*fl.* 1574?–1613), IV. 202
Drury, Robert (b. 1687), XIV. 551; *Journal*, IX. 23
Dryburgh abbey, I. 333
Dryden, Elizabeth, IX. 91
Dryden, Erasmus, VIII. 2
Dryden, Sir Erasmus Henry (1669–1710), IX. 91

Dryden, Honor, daughter of Sir John Dryden, VIII. 4
Dryden, John (1631–1700), I. 283; II. 165, 168, 186, 195, 219, 220; III. 157, 165, 312; IV. 2, 4, 25, 131, 140, 168, 177, 183, 208, 214; V. 174, 206, 209, 222, 347; VI. 7, 9, 11, 25, 28, 34, 57, 109, 111, 112, 122, 125, 126, 133, 240, 323, 479; VII. 7, 12, 61, 68, 72, 73, 76, 87 ff., 92, 93, 105, 107, 109, 126, 138, 176, 183, 184, 244, 259, 262, 264, 268, 270; VIII. 1–57 (main entry), 62, 75, 79, 89, 90, 92, 94, 121, 130, 136, 139, 143, 146, 150, 158, 166, 168, 174, 178, 179, 181, 185, 193, 201, 202, 204, 205, 209, 212, 214, 215, 217, 219 220, 222, 227, 229, 231 ff., 292, 293, 302, 369, 372 ff., 389, 391 ff., 410, 411, 418, 427, 428, 434, 437, 441, 442, 447, *also see* Add.; IX. 67 ff., 73, 77, 119, 122, 141, 146, 147, 157, 173 ff., 177, 180, 184, 185, 187 ff., 199, 237, 263, 264, 266, 267, 270, 271, 348, 362, 444, 473, 482; X. 27, 67, 120, 126, 145, 153, 156, 158, 167, 169, 185, 202, 218, 219, 221, 226, 232, 398, 432, 433, 484; XI. 27, 40, 170, 171, 174, 201, 206, 316, 318, 320, 466; XII. 41, 88, 108, 136, 177, 207, 221, 224, 253, 376, 494; XIII. 86, 96, 122, 233, 237 ff., 253, 312, 552; XIV. 113, 396, 436, 448, 501
Absalom and Achitophel, VIII. 31, 35 ff. (main entry), 40, 41, 77, 142, 192, 235; XI. 36
Account of the Ensuing Poem, in a letter to Sir Robert Howard, An, VIII. 9
Aeneis, VIII. 50, 239
Albion and Albanius, VIII. 30, 135, 375
Alexander's Feast, VIII. 44, 53, 234
All for Love, VIII. 28, 33, 235, 375, 386; IX. 140; XI. 171
Amboyna, VIII. 7, 27
Amphitryon, VIII. 17, 134
Annus Mirabilis, VII. 71; VIII. 8 ff., 34, 38, 238; IX. 169; X. 124
Apology for Heroick Poetry, VIII. 374
Assignation, or Love in a Nunnery, The, VIII. 17, 140
Astraea Redux, VIII. 6; XIV. 444
Aureng-Zebe, VIII. 16, 21, 22, 27, 235
Author's Apology for Heroick Poetry and Poetic Licence, The, VIII. 27
Boccaccio, reproductions of, VIII. 51
Britannia Rediviva, VIII. 44, 49
Character of a Good Parson, VIII. 52
Charleton, To my Honoured Friend Dr, VIII. 8, 362
Chaucer, reproductions of, VIII. 51
Cleomenes, the Spartan hero, VIII. 31, 53, 190
Congreve, on his Comedy Called The Double Dealer, To my dear Friend, Mr, VIII. 55
Conquest of Granada, The, VIII. 22, 25 ff., 53, 235
Dedication of Examen Poeticum, VIII. 375
Dedication of the Aeneis, VIII. 239
Dryden, John
Defence of an Essay of Dramatick Poesie, A, VIII. 16, 24
Defence of the Epilogue, A, VIII. 17, 25, 370
Discourse Concerning the Original and Progress of Satire, A, VIII. 19, 26, 36, 39, 40, 44, 49, 373, 374
Don Sebastian, VIII. 31, 32, 164; XIII. 523
Duke of Guise, The (with Lee), VIII. 16, 30, 186
Epigrams, lines by 'J. Dryden of Trin. C.' in, VIII. 4
Epilogue to the Second Part of the Conquest of Granada, VIII. 25
Essay of Dramatick Poesie, An, II. 163; VI. 136; VII. 275; XI. 171; XIV. 460
Essay of Heroick Plays, VIII. 18, 22 ff., 26
Evening's Love, An, VIII. 16, 17, 53, 127, 131, 134, 367
Examen Poeticum, VIII. 50, 57
Fables, Ancient and Modern, VII. 48, 53, 57; VIII. 32, 51, 433; X. 241; XI. 171; XII. 46; XIII. 238
Granville, on his excellent Tragedy, called 'Heroick Love,' To Mr, VIII. 55
Heroick Stanzas, VIII. 5 ff.
Hind and the Panther, The, VIII. 43, 45 ff., 235
His Sacred Majesty, To, VIII. 7
History of the League, Maimbourg's, translation of, VIII. 34
Iliad, VIII. 51
Indian Emperor, The, VIII. 21, 22, 24, 53
Indian Queen, The, VIII. 21, 123, 235
Killigrew, To the Pious Memory of the Accomplisht Young Lady, Mrs Anne, VIII. 32, 45, 53, 57, 234
Lachrymae Musarum, contribution to, VIII. 2
Letter to Sir George Etherege, VIII. 49
Limberham, or the Kind Keeper, VIII. 17
Love Triumphant, VIII. 20
Lucian, life of, VIII. 402
Mac Flecknoe, VIII. 36, 40, 41, 235; IX. 79, 179
Mall, The, or the Modish Lovers, VIII. 399
Marriage-à-la-Mode, VIII. 17, 20, 140
Medal, The, VIII. 35, 39, 40, 188
Miscellanies, VII. 86; VIII. 44, 49, 50, 231, 375; IX. 148, 455; X. 223
Mistaken Husband, The, VIII. 399, 401, 422
My Lord Chancellor, To, VIII. 7
Œdipus, King of Thebes (with Lee), VIII. 30, 186
Palamon and Arcite, X. 120
Parallel of Poetry and Painting, A, VIII. 20, 29, 49
Plutarch, preface to a translation of, VIII. 44
Poem upon the Death of His Late Highness, Oliver, Lord Protector of England, Scotland and Ireland, A, VIII. 5
Preface concerning the Grounds of Criticism in Tragedy, VIII. 29

Dryden, John
Preface to the Fables, VIII. 52, 56, 57, 235, 390
Prologue, addressed to Oxford, VIII. 3, 4
Prologue to Secret Love, VIII. 24
Prologue to the Duchess [of York], VIII. 34
Prosodia, VIII. 50
Religio Laici, IV. 197; VIII. 15, 41 ff., 46, 235
Rival Ladies, The, VII. 48; VIII. 4, 17, 19, 123, 131, 137, 370; XIV. 460
St John's Eve, VIII. 54
Satire on the Dutch, VIII. 7
Secret Love, or the Maiden Queen, VIII. 20, 426
Secular Masque, VIII. 31
Sir Geoffrey Kneller, To, VIII. 50
Sir Martin Mar-all, VIII. 17, 134, 420
Song for St Cecilia's Day, VIII. 53
Southern, on his Comedy Called 'The Wives' Excuse,' To Mr, VIII. 55
Spanish Fryar, The, VIII. 20, 33, 49
State of Innocence and Fall of Man, The, VIII. 27, 422; IX. 58
Sylvae, VIII. 44
Te Deum, translation of, VIII. 54
Tempest, The (with D'Avenant), VIII. 28, 120, 398, 418
Threnodia Augustalis, VIII. 44
Translations of: *Juvenal*, VIII. 49, 77; *Latin Hymns*, VIII. 397; *Lucretius*, VIII. 396; *Ovid*, VIII. 50, 51, 396, 397; *Persius*, VIII. 2, 49, 77; *Tacitus*, VIII. 402; *Theocritus*, VIII. 397; *Vergil*, VIII. 50, 397
Troilus and Cressida, VIII. 29; XI. 319
Tyrannick Love, VIII. 21, 22, 235
Veni Creator Spiritus, paraphrase of, VIII. 54
Verses to Her Royal Highness the Duchess (of York), VIII. 8
Vindication of the Duke of Guise, VIII. 30
Wild Gallant, The, VIII. 16, 17, 131
Works, XII. 16
Dryden, John, junior (1668–1701), VIII. 400, 402
Dryden, Sir John, VIII. 4
Drydeniana, VIII. 404 ff.
Drystan, son of Tallwch (Tristram), I. 273
Drythelm, vision of, I. 82, 86
Drywood, Mr, of Trinity, VI. 397
Du Bartas, William de Salluste, IX. 269; *Semaines* (trans. as *Divine Weekes and Workes*), IV. 23, 131, 331, 443
Du Baudrier, Sieur, IX. 455
Du Bellay, Joachim, III. 250, 251, 258, 263; IV. 24, 264, 443; *Les Antiquités de Rome*, III. 250
Dublin, IV. 142, 161, 414, 434; VI. 197, 200, 203, 205, 206; VII. 58, 148, 197, 355; VIII. 122, 220; IX. 79, 84, 91, 93, 96 ff., 118, 126, 166, 327, 330, 406, 413, 452 ff.; X. 58, 257, 258, 379, 408; XI. 1, 283, 288, 340, 342, 373; XII. 285, 351, 361; XIII. 240, 258; XIV. 96, 104, 173, 261, 269, 311, 315, 318*a*, 319, 321, 323, 348, 397, 417
Dublin society. *See* Royal Dublin society
Historical society, XIV. 317
Mountrath court, X. 199
Parliament square, X. 198
Phoenix park, XIV. 317
Record office, XII. 360, 361
Reindeer tavern, X. 199
St Patrick's cathedral, IX. 93, 96, 99, 100, 119, 132
Smock (or Smoke) Alley theatre, VIII. 170; X. 426 ff.; XI. 455
Theatre royal, VIII. 180; X. 425 ff.
Trinity college, III. 426; IV. 276, 433; VII. 148; VIII. 146, 170, 332; IX. 91, 92, 166, 280, 282, 362; X. 58, 197, 198, 293, 356, 358; XI. 1, 2; XII. 159, 338, 342, 360, 362, 494; XIV. 211, 263, 309, 313, 318, 571, *also see* Add. 3
Dublin, archbishopric of, XII. 272
Dublin, books printed and published in, XI. 470
Dublin Penny Journal, The, XIV. 312, 315, 318*a*
Dublin printers, IV. 547, 548
Dublin Review, The, XII. 260, 426, 460, 461, 463
Dublin Translations into Greek and Latin Verse, XIV. 211
Dublin University Magazine, The, XIII. 407, 414, 415; XIV. 313, 319, 326
Dublin University Review, The, XIV. 211, 538
Dubricius, archbishop of the "City of Legions," I. 259
Ducarel, Andrew Coltee (1713–1785), IV. 422; IX. 532
Ducci, L., IV. 526
Du Chaillu, Paul B. (1835–1903), XIV. 551
Duchal, James (1697–1761), X. 521
Ducis, Jean François, V. 294, 298, 299, 301, 306 ff.
Duck, Sir Arthur (1580–1648), VIII. 317, 468
Duck, Stephen (1705–1756), IX. 187, 448, 485
Du Deffand, madame, X. 248, 250, 495
Dudley, earl of. *See* Ward, John William
Dudley, Edmund (1462?–1510), IV. 297, 510
Dudley, lord Guilford (d. 1554), IV. 169, 182
Dudley, Sir Henry Bate (1745–1824), XIV. 188
Dudley, John, 1st duke of Northumberland (1502?–1553), VII. 325, 326
Dudley, Louisa, in Cumberland's *West Indian*, XI. 264, 265
Dudley, Robert, earl of Leicester (1532?–1588), III. 207, 241, 421, 422, 424; IV. 1, 8, 10, 20, 116, 172, 274, 384, 390, 401, 406, 410; V. 341, 345, 346, 365; VI. 246, 247, 302, 336, 381, 393; VII. 191, 306

Dudleys, the, in Cumberland's *West Indian*, xi. 264, 265
Duelling, vii. 204
Duessa, in *The Faerie Queene*, iii. 231, 234
Duff, James Grant (1789–1858), xiv. 490, 576; *A History of the Mahrattas*, xiv. 337
Duff, Sir Mountstuart Elphinstone Grant, xii. 147; xiii. 497
Dufferin, lady. *See* Blackwood, Helen Selina
Dufferin, marquis of. *See* Blackwood, Frederick Temple
Duffet, Thomas (*fl.* 1678), viii. 422
Duffy, Sir Charles Gavan (1816–1903), xiii. 471; xiv. 317 ff., 370, 568, 572
Innishowen, xiv. 318
Irish Chief, The, xiv. 318
Irish Library, xiv. 325
Lay Sermon, xiv. 318
Patriot's Bride, The, xiv. 318
Dufresnoy, Charles-Alphonse, viii. 49, 402; ix. 256, 444, 538
Dugdale, Sir William (1605–1686), vii. 438; viii. 318, 469; ix. 342 ff., 348, 355, 356, 533, 539, 540
Antiquities of Warwickshire, ix. 341, 342, 345, 352
Baronage of England, ix. 344
History of Imbanking, iv. 308, 510; ix. 343
History of St Paul's Cathedral, ix. 343, 354
Life, Diary and Correspondence, ix. 343
Monasticon Anglicanum, ix. 342, 343, 350; xii. 346, 349
Origines Juridicales, viii. 320, 464; ix. 344
Short view of the late troubles, ix. 344
Duglas river, battle of, i. 259
Du Guérins, the, xiii. 98, 99
Du Halde, Jean Baptiste, x. 206, 465
Dukas, Jules, iv. 257
Duke, Richard (1658–1711), viii. 408, 409, 446; ix. 174, 176, 485
Duke and the Emperor, The Meeting of the, ii. 308
Duke of York's company, the, vi. 262
Duke Rowland and Sir Ohiel of Spayne, i. 470
Dukes, Ashley, xiii. 514
Dulcimer, in *The Faune*, vi. 48
Dulcinea, in *Don Quixote*, x. 51
Dulcinea del Toboso, in *Don Quixote*, viii. 70
'Dulness's Laureate Son,' in Pope's *Dunciad*, ix. 88
Dulwich, vi. 249, 278
Dumas, Alexandre, *père*, v. 302; xi. 307, 458; xii. 212, 381, 525; xiii. 257, 263
Du Maurier, George Louis Palmella Busson (1834–1896), xiii. 562; xiv. 235, 239, 548
History of the Jack Sprats, The, xiii. 433
Martian, The, xiii. 433
Peter Ibbetson, xiii. 433
Trilby, xiii. 433
'Dumb Philosopher,' the, ix. 21
Dumb Wyf, The, ii. 280
Dumbarton, x. 36
Dumbartonshire, x. 36
Dumbiedykes, laird of, in *The Heart of Midlothian*, viii. 355
Dumbleton, John (*fl.* 1340), *Summa*, ii. 363
Dumfries, ix. 565; xi. 225, 235, 237, 470
Dumfries Journal, The, xi. 235
Dumfriesshire, xi. 222, 242, 444, 445; xii. 350; xiii. 2 ff., 10
Dumfriesshire, The Poets of, ix. 568
Dumont, Étienne, xi. 59, 60, 70, 397, 398
Du Moulin, Peter, vii. 309, 418, 420; *Regii Sanguinis Clamor*, vii. 105
Dun Monidh, xiv. 304
Dunalbius, in *Argenis*, iv. 295
Dunbar, Elizabeth, countess of Moray (d. 1591), ii. 113
Dunbar, William (1460?–1520?), i. 292; ii. 91, 93, 121, 122, 126, 154, 192, 221, 239, 244, 249, 250 ff., 259, 261, 265, 266, 269, 275, 276, 278, 280, 331, 401, 475, 507; iii. 115 ff., 119, 121, 122, 131, 133 ff., 159, 179, 486; iv. 322, 517, 527; vii. 351; ix. 359; xi. 203, 204; xii. 95, 517
Beauty and the Prisoner (Sen that I am a presoneir), ii. 253
Black Lady, ii. 255
Blitheness, ii. 256
Complaint to the King, ii. 257
Dance of the Sevin Deidlie Synnis, ii. 228, 255, 256
Dreme, The, iii. 116
Epitaph on Donald Owre, The, ii. 255; iii. 133
Flyting of Dunbar and Kennedie, The, ii. 90, 99, 250, 256, 266; iii. 72, 490
Freiris of Berwick, The, ii. 253, 279; viii. 226
General Satire, ii. 255
Golden Targe, The, ii. 228, 231, 252, 253, 260; iii. 116; vii. 174
Good Counsel, ii. 256
How Dunbar wes desyrd to be ane freir, ii. 251
Interlude of the Droichis Part of the Play, The, ii. 253, 255, 275; iii. 122
Joustis of the Tailȝeour and the Sowtar, ii. 255; iii. 121, 135
Kynd Kittok, Ballad of, ii. 255, 275
Lament for the Makaris, ii. 109, 116, 245, 256, 257, 266, 268
London thou art the flower of cities all, ii. 252, 331
Petition of the Grey Horse, iii. 120
Satire on Edinburgh, ii. 255
Testament of Mr Andro Kennedy, ii. 256, 278, 501; iii. 85, 483, 484
Thrissil and the Rois, The, ii. 253; iii. 116, 120
Tidings from the Session, ii. 255
Tretis of the Tua Mariit Wemen and the Wedo, ii. 192, 254
Vision, ii. 256

Dunbar, William, friend of Burns, xi. 222, 223
Dunblane, ii. 275; viii. 298
Duncan, in Boece, iii. 156
Duncan I, ii. 89
Duncan, Andrew (1744–1828), xi. 442
Duncan, David, xiv. 481
Duncan, Geilis, vii. 372
Duncan (Holinshed's), v. 241
Duncan, William, xiv. 533
Duncan Gray, ii. 274
Dunckley, Henry (1823–1896), *Crown and Cabinet*, xiv. 189, 504
Duncombe, John (1729–1786), ix. 477
Duncombe, William (1690–1769), ix. 477; *Brutus*, x. 82, 439
Duncombe, in Mrs Gaskell's *Mr Harrison's Confessions*, xiii. 372
Duncon, John (*fl.* 1648), vii. 155 ff.; *Life of Lettice Falkland*, vii. 151
Duncumb, John (1765–1839), xii. 509
Dundas, iii. 69
Dundas, Henry, 1st viscount Melville, xi. 16, 31, 35; xiv. 179
Dundee, iii. 122, 142; xi. 399; xii. 350; xiii. 51
Dundee, University college, xiv. 432
Dundee, viscount. *See* Graham, John, of Claverhouse
Dundee Advertiser, The, xiv. 531, 534
Dundee Book, The, iii, 141
Dundonald, earl of. *See* Cochrane, Thomas
Dundreary, lord, in *Our American Cousin*, viii. 176
Dunfermline, ii. 245, 250
Dunk, George Montague, 2nd earl of Halifax (1716–1771), x. 243, 245, 249, 251, 495
Dunkeld, ii. 259; iv. 277
Dunkin, William (1709?–1765), ix. 466
Dunkirk, ix. 135, 440, 455, 461; xiv. 387
Dunkirk, battle of, vii. 24, 452
Dunlop, Andrew, xiv. 533
Dunlop, Mrs Frances Anne Wallace (1730–1815), xi. 222, 223, 438
Dunlop, John Colin (d. 1842), xiv. 487
Dunlop, Robert, xiv. 510
Dunmow flitch, the, ii. 20
Dunn, Henry, xiv. 605
Dunn, William, xiv. 512
Dunnere, in *The Battle of Maldon*, i. 145
Dunois of Orleans, v. 83
Dunraven, earl of. *See* Quin, Edwin Wyndham
Duns Furens, vi. 307
Duns Scotus, John, *Doctor subtilis* (1265?–1308?), i. 200, 210 ff., 453; ii. 350, 355; iii. 4, 19, 48, 50, 416; iv. 269, 272; vii. 505
Dunsinane, in *Orygynale Cronykil*, ii. 132
Dunstable, v. 7, 38
Dunstable, annals of, i. 178
Dunstan, St (924–988), i. 113, 114, 118, 127, 131, 150, 151, 153, 243, 446; ii. 76; xiv. 76; *Memorials of*, xiv. 74
Dunstan, St, in *The Devil and his Dame*, v. 329
Dunstaple, ix. 535
Dunster, Somerset, iii. 188
Dunton, John (1659–1733), iv. 388; viii. 99; ix. 4, 41, 267; xi. 320, 329, 334, 340, 468; *Athenian Gazette*, ix. 5; *Athenian Mercury*, ix. 5, 34, 41, 92; *Life and Errors*, ix. 5; xi. 327, 330
Dupatys Lettres sur l'Italie, xii. 395
Dupely, in Burgoyne's *Maid of the Oaks*, xi. 265
Du Plessis, J., xiv. Add. 6
Dupont de Nemours, Pierre Samuel, x. 336
Du Pontavice de Heussey, R., xiii. 543
Duport, James (1606–1679), iv. 427; vii. 317, 488
Duport, John (d. 1617), vii. 316
Duport, Paul, v. 302
Duppa, Bryan (1588–1662), bishop of Winchester, vi. 7
Duppa, Richard (1770–1831), x. 455, 463
Durand, David (1680–1763), ix. 235, 495
Durand, Sir H. Mortimer, xiii. 505; xiv. 493
Durand, W. Y., v. 64
Durand, Durandus, William (d. 1296), *Speculum Juris* or *Speculum Judiciale*, ii. 364
Durandus, bishop of Meaux, commentary of, ii. 363
Durant, Gilles, iv. 24
Durastanti, Signora Margarita, ix. 468
Durazzo, in *The Guardian*, vi. 161
Dürer, Albert, vi. 333
D'Urfé, Honoré, *Astrée*, vi. 123, 138, 239
D'Urfey, Thomas (1653–1723), ii. 414; vi. 33; viii. 96, 166 ff., 174 ff., 408, 411, 428; ix. 264, 475, 499
Campaigners, The, viii. 167
Famous History of the Rise and Fall of Massaniello, The, viii. 175
Modern Prophets, The, viii. 175
New Reformation, The, viii. 167
Pills to Purge Melancholy, viii. 232
Scotch Wedding, ix. 363
Sea Voyage, The, viii. 120
Siege of Memphis, The, viii. 175
Trimmer, The, viii. 97
Durham, iii. 49; iv. 416, 418, 421; vii. 84; viii. 282, 295; ix. 249, 303, 387, 392, 393; x. 127; xi. 244; xii. 10, 327, 340, 348, 354, 508, 510 ff., 515; xiii. 70, 427
Durham, Benedictine priory at, ii. 349
Durham, earl of. *See* Lambton, John George
Durham, James (1622–1658), ix. 543
Durham. *See* Simeon of
Durham cathedral, xii. 507
Durham university, vii. Add.; xiv. 411, 431
Durham, Book of (or *Lindisfarne Gospels*), i. 14
Durham Field, ii. 415
Durham, Poem on the city of, i. 147

Durham Ritual, runes in, I. 12
Durie. *See* Dury, John
Durlavon, prebend of, IX. 93
Dursley, lord, IX. 148
Dury, Giles (*fl.* 1649), VII. 363
Dury, John (1596–1680), IV. 549; IX. 194; *The Reformed School* (1650), VII. 479; IX. 389, 568
Duse, Eleanora, V. 307
'Dusky Night rides down the sky,' X. 22
Düsseldorf, V. 305
Duszeperez, II. 116
Dutch, the, IX. 134; in the East Indies, VI. 183
Dutch, Howell's satire against the, VII. 200
Dutch, Low, XIII. 112
Dutch Annotations on the Bible, VII. 322
Dutch artists, XIV. 212
Dutch church, the, XIV. 380
Dutch drama, V. 109, 284, 285, 307
Dutch India company, the, IV. 99
Dutch language and literature, IX. 331, 385; X. 19, 291; XIV. 457 ff.
Dutch paper, XI. 377
Dutch people, VIII. 7, 27, 140, 202, 247, 272, 342, 381, 382, 384
Dutch printing presses, VII. 308, 344
Dutch scholars, VII. 263, 307
Dutch towns, English actors in, V. 283
Dutch trade in the far east, V. 345
Dutch wars, VII. 183, 184, 234, 306, 434; VIII. 10, 81, 218, 249, 252, 254, 329
'Dutch sublime, the,' XI. 126
Dutchman, the, in *A Woman will have her Will*, V. 329
Dutchman, the, in *The Weakest Goeth to the Wall*, V. 316
Du Toit, S. J., XIV. Add. 6
Dutt, Gorrind Chandra, XIV. 342, 576
Dutt, Michael Madhu Sadan, XIV. 576; *The Captive Ladie*, XIV. 342
Dutt, Romesh Chunder, XIV. 576; *Lays of Ancient India*, XIV. 341
Dutt, Sasi Chandra, XIV. 342, 576
Dutt, Torulata, XIV. 576; *Ancient Ballads and Legends of Hindustan*, XIV. 342; *Sheaf Gleaned in French Fields, A*, XIV. 342
Dutton, John, VI. 249
Dutton, Sir Thomas (step-father of Sir Thomas Browne), VII. 232, 233
Duty, in *Horestes*, V. 64, 65
Du Vair, Guillaume, *Moral Philosophy of the Stoics*, IX. 276, 499
Duval, Dennis, Thackeray's, XIII. 300
Dux Morand, V. 390
Dwerga, in Darley's *Becket*, XII. 114
Dyaloge betwene ij Beggers, A, III. 492
Dyalogue du fol et du sage, V. 93
Dyboski, R., *Tennyson's Sprache und Stil*, XIII. 29
Dyccon of Bedlam, VI. 296
Dyce, Alexander (1798–1869), V. 129, 247, 278 ff.; VI. 58, 138, 169; IX. 145; X. 452, 454; XII. 353, 408, 491; XIII. 175, 497
Dyer, Sir Edward (d. 1607), III. 217, 303, 507; IV. 113, 114, 116, 117, 163, 164, 466; VII. 271; XI. 247; 'My mind to me a kingdom is,' IV. 126; *The Prayse of Nothing*, VIII. 213
Dyer, George (1755–1841), XII. 183, 186, 187, 196, 198, *also see* Add. 2
Dyer, Sir James (1512–1582), *Law Reports*, VIII. 316, 466
Dyer, John (1700?–1758), VIII. 230; IX. 5, 169; X. 138, 144 ff. (main entry), 156, 452, 454
Country Walk, The, X. 145
Fleece, The, X. 145
Grongar Hill, IX. 191; X. 97, 136, 137, 145, 146
Ruins of Rome, The, X. 145
Dymock, Cressy, IV. 511
Dymock, Edward, IV. 445; VI. 490
Dymok, Roger (*fl.* 1390), II. 441
Dysdayne, in *The Bowge of Courte*, III. 74
Dysert castle, IX. 280
Dyson, Jeremiah (1722–1776), X. 452
Dyspare, in *Magnyfycence*, III. 77

'E. B.' (probably Edmund Bolton), IV. 118
E. C., III. 256
E. I. O., III. 283
E. K. *See* Kirke, Edward
E. S. (? Edward Sharpham), *Discoverie of the Knights of the Poste*, IV. 350, 354
Eachard, John (1636?–1697), VII. 156, 301, 471; IX. 418
Eadberg, I. 148
Eadfrith, I. 148
Eadgils, *Beowulf* and *Widsith*, I. 24, 25, 35
Eadmer (d. 1124?), I. 162 ff., 168, 172, 449
Eadric, I. 126
Eadwine, in *Widsith*, I. 35
Eagle, the, Henry of Lancaster in *Mum, Sothsegger*, II. 36
Eagle, The, St John's college magazine, IV. 275; VI. 3; VIII. 243; XII. 487
Eagles, John (1783–1855), XII. 425
Eagles, Thomas (1746–1812), X. 485
Eaha, in *Finnsburh*, I. 31
Eahfrid, I. 73
Ealhhild, in *Widsith*, I. 34, 35
Ealing, X. 35
Eames, John (d. 1744), X. 384
Eames, W., XI. 470
Eanmund, in *Beowulf*, I. 24, 26
Eanred's ring, I. 11
Earl Brand, II. 410, 411
Earle, John (1601–1665), bishop of Salisbury, III. 114; IV. 521; VI. 113; VII. 156, 218, 329, 366, 379; VIII. 245, 407; *Microcosmographie*, IV. 260, 341, 342, 395, 522; V. 368, 477; VII. 151; VIII. 63, 64
Earle, John (1824–1903), I. 104, 141, 418; XII. 504; XIV. 611; *Philology of the English Tongue*, XIII. 248, 512
Early English dialect, IX. 361
Early English Text society, II. 41, 166 199, 500; XI. 368; XII. 344, 355, 504

Earth upon Earth, II. 502
Earthquake council, the, II. 64, 443
Earwaker, John Parsons (1847–1895), XII. 509
Easden, John, IV. 464
East, Thomas (1540?–1608?), IV. 400, 546
East Anglia, XIV. 78
East Grinstead, IX. 150
East India bill, XI. 6
East India company, the, IV. 98; VIII. 342; XI. 6, 16, 17; XIII. 275; XIV. 97, 248, 332
East Indies, VI. 183; VIII. 23; XIV. 241, 250, 434, 457
East Molesey, III. 379, 380
East Ruston, Norfolk, XII. 323
East Stour, X. 20, 23
Eastbrook, IX. 146
Eastbury Park, X. 94, 103
Easter controversy, I. 73, 81, 82
Easter liturgical drama and plays, V. 11, 36 ff.
Eastern church, XII. 478
Easthealon, I. 126
Eastlake, Sir Charles Lock (1793–1865), XIV. 238
Eastlake, Elizabeth, lady, born Rigby (1809–1893), XIII. 414, 558; XIV. 523
Eastland company, the, IV. 310
Eastwell, IX. 168, 169
Eastwood, IV. 91
Easy, Sir Charles, in *The Careless Husband*, VIII. 176
Easy, Mr, in Marryat's *Mr Midshipman Easy*, XII. 250
Easy club, IX. 369
Eatanswill, in *The Pickwick Papers*, XIII. 304
Eatanswill journalism, XIV. 170
Eaton, John Richard Turner, XII. 334
Ebbaac, G.,' XI. 140
Ebionite heresy, I. 224
Eblis, in Beckford's *Vathek*, XI. 290, 291; XIII. 357
Ebrington, X. 113
Ebsworth, Joseph Woodfall, IX. 361, 364; *Roxburghe Ballads*, IX. 378
Eccho, in *The Glasse of Governement*, V. 113, 114
Ecclefechan, XIII. 2, 9, 20
Eccles, Charlotte O'Conor (1860?–1911), XIV. Add. 3
Aliens of the West, XIV. 325
Matrimonial Lottery, A, XIV. 325
Rejuvenation of Miss Semaphore, The, XIV. 325
Tom Connolly's Daughter, XIV. 325
Eccles division of Lancashire, XII. 337
Ecclesdown castle, in Arbuthnot's *History of John Bull*, IX. 135
Ecclesiastes, II. 242
Ecclesiastical learning (1600–1660), VII. 484, 485
Ecclesiastick, The, XIV. 70
Ecclesiologist, The, XIV. 70
Eccleston, Thomas de. *See* Thomas de
Ecgfrith, I. 10
Ecglaf, I. 145
Ecgtheow, Beowulf's father, I. 22
Echard, Laurence (1670?–1730), IX. 237, 238, 492; *History of England*, IX. 235, 494
Échecs amoureux, II. 202
Echo, in *Narcissus*, VI. 316
Echo, The, XIV. 195
Eckel, John C., XIII. 531
Eckermann, Johann Peter, XII. 379
Eckhart, *Meister* (1260?–1329?), IX. 315
Eclectic Review, The, XIII. 61
École de Chartes, XIV. 53
Economist, The, XIV. 28, 141, 199
Edda, The, I. 8, 21, 62; X. 202, 228, 490
Eddius Stephanus (*fl.* 669), I. 85, 434
Eden, garden of, III. 231, 244; IV. 60, 61; VII. 370
Eden, Richard (1521?–1576), IV. 79, 80, 101, 107, 455
Arte of Navigation, The, IV. 71, 443
Compendium, IV. 104
History of Travayle, etc., The, IV. 75
Trans. of Peter Martyr's *The Decades of the Newe World*, IV. 70, 71, 75, 441
Treatyse of the Newe India, A, IV. 70, 71
Edern, son of Nuð, I. 255
Edgar, Sir James (1841–1899), XIV. 357, 582
Edgar, Sir John (*fl.* 1720), IX. 439, 442, 473, 475
Edgar, king of the English (944–975), I. 110, 113, 114, 121, 123, 137 ff., 305; II. 76; IV. 68; V. 36; VIII. 310; X. 111
Edgar, Matilda, lady (1844–1910), XIV. 583; *Colonial Governor in Maryland, A*, XIV. 359; *Life of Brock*, XIV. 359; *Ten Years of Peace and War*, XIV. 359
Edgar, in *King Lear*, III. 448
Edgcumbe, mount, X. 115
Edgcumbe, R. P., XIV. 537
Edge-hill, X. 112, 113, 271, 272
Edgehill, battle of, VII. 195; VIII. 361
Edgeman, Clarendon's secretary, VII. 188
Edgeworth, F. A., XI. 460
Edgeworth, Honora, born Sneyd (d. 1780), XIV. 393
Edgeworth, Jane, born Lovell, XIV. 392
Edgeworth, Maria (1767–1849), XI. 286, 296 ff. (main entry), 304, 381, 459, 475; XII. 2, 241, 245, 447; XIII. 376, 377, 425; XIV. 392, 598, 599, 605
Absentee, The, X. 66; XI. 297
Amie Inconnue, La, XI. 299
Belinda, XI. 285, 297, 299
Castle Rackrent, XI. 297
Frank, XI. 382
Harry and Lucy, XI. 382
Helen, XI. 148, 297
Letters for Literary Ladies, XIV. 395
Moral Tales, XI. 296, 382
Ormond, XI. 297
Parent's Assistant, The, XI. 382; XIV. 393, 394
Practical Education (with R. L. Edgeworth), XIV. 393
Simple Susan, XI. 299, 382

Edgeworth, Richard Lovell (1744–1817), xi. 296, 460; xiv. 601, 605
  Harry and Lucy, xiv. 393
  Memoirs, xiv. 392
  Practical Education (with M. Edgeworth), xiv. 393
  Professional Education, xiv. 394
  Rational Primer, A, xiv. 394
Edgeworths, the, xiv. 391, 601
Edgeworthstown, x. 197; xiv. 391
Edgware, x. 212, 214
Edgworth, Roger (d. 1560), iii. 51
Edial, near Lichfield, x. 160, 161
Edinburgh, ii. 92, 109, 126, 128, 284, 370; iii. 120, 182, 426; iv. 150, 151, 215, 267, 409, 412 ff., 547; vi. 5, 47, 369; vii. 197, 452, 455; ix. 130, 214, 290, 359, 366, 367, 369, 371, 379, 380, 537; x. 40, 42, 55, 87, 94, 182, 190 ff., 200, 201, 230, 281, 283, 290, 296, 322, 324, 336; xi. 75, 149, 220 ff., 233 ff., 238, 315, 327, 338, 341, 342; xii. 2, 5, 11, 18, 19, 23, 143, 155, 156, 158, 159, 321, 349, 370; xiii. 3, 4, 5, 9, 10, 362, 372; xiv. 139, 159, 176, 199, 204, 257, 263, 267, 274, 294, 373, 374, 406
  Advocates' library, iii. 137; xii. 26, 358, 370 ff., 372
  Apollo press, xi. 325
  Bibliographical society, xi. 469, 470
  Botanic garden, xiv. 286
  Bruntsfield-links, ix. 366
  Calton hill, iii. 123
  Canongate, ix. 366; xii. 2
  Castle, iii. 122, 148
  College of Justice, iii. 150
  Corporation buildings, xi. 435
  Cowgate, xii. 2
  George street, xii. 149
  High school, xii. 3, 4; xiv. 404
  Holyrood house, viii. 394, 395
  Holyrood palace, xii. 29
  Infirmary, xiii. 213
  Leith Walk, xiii. 6
  New college, xii. 371; xiv. 47
  Periodical Press, the, vii. 502; xi. 469
  Portrait Gallery, xi. 435
  Printers and booksellers, xi. 469
  Register house, xii. 359
  Royal society, xiv. 288; *Transactions*, xi. 76
  St Andrew's church, xi. 233
  St Giles, ii. 259
  Signet library, xii. 358, 371, 521; xiv. 101
  Theatre Royal, x. 479
  Tolbooth, xii. 17, 18
  University, iv. 150, 434; viii. 298; ix. 550; x. 93, 287; xi. 222, 244; xii. 332, 335, 350, 359, 372, 484; xiii. 2, 3, 19; xiv. 6, 7, 209, 210
  University library, xi. 435
Edinburgh Annual Register, The, xii. 13, 373
Edinburgh Courant, The, ix. 432; x. 479; xiv. 203
Edinburgh Encyclopaedia, xiii. 4
Edinburgh Magazine, The, xi. 243, 439
Edinburgh Magazine and Review, x. 258
Edinburgh Monthly Magazine, The, xii. 425; xiv. 373
Edinburgh Review, The (1755–1756), ix. 561; x. 173, 474; xii. 426
Edinburgh Review, The (1802–), x. 232, 239; xi. 442; xii. 32, 33, 92, 141 ff. (main entry), 151 ff., 155, 156, 158, 162, 163, 288, 293, 310, 325, 426; xiii. 5, 8, 29, 35, 38, 78, 241, 245, 359, 374, 467; xiv. 5, 7, 8, 54, 59 ff., 71, 97, 138, 194, 395, 403, 405, 407, 409 ff., 416, 596, 605, 609
Edinburgh University Magazine, The, xiv. 210, 538
Edith, in *Dombey and Son*, xiii. 325
Edith, in *The Bloody Brother*, vi. 129, 138
Edith, in *Widow Edith*, iii. 88, 89
Edkins, Joshua, xiv. 572
Edmond, John Philip (1850–1906), xii. 521
Edmondes, Sir Clement (1564?–1622), iv. 435
Edmondes, Sir Thomas (1563?–1639), vii. 436; x. 498
Edmonds, Charles, xi. 392
Edmonton, v. 252; xii. 118, 201 ff.
Edmund, in *King Lear*, v. 204, 213, 262
Edmund Ironside (981?–1016), i. 127, 140, 337
Edmund Ironside, v. 399
Edmund, king of the East Angles (841–870), viii. 310
Edmund of Abingdon (d. 1240), i. 200
Edmund, St (1170?–1240), i. 121; v. 10
Edmund, St, in *The Example of Virtue*, ii. 227
Edmund, St, in *The Golden Legend*, ii. 33
Edmund (922?–946), son of Edward th Elder, i. 137
Edmundson, Henry (d. 1659), vii. 486
Ednam, Roxburghshire, x. 93
Edom o' Gordon, x. 233
Edomites, in Cowley's *Davideis*, vii. 67
Edstone, near Henley-in-Arden, x. 10 112, 271
Education, books on, ix. 568 ff.
Education, early books of, ii. 499
Education, English and Scottish, i 341 ff., 487 ff.
Education act (1870), xiv. 415, 42 (1902–3), xiv. 433
Education department, xiv. 420, 421, 4
Education society of the northern cou ties, x. 385
Edward I, king of England, i. 350, 35 370; ii. 103, 130, 132; iii. 104, 13 ix. 535; x. 129; xiv. 75, 81, 101
Edward I, Elegy on, i. 370
Edward II, i. 342, 355, 356, 370; ii. 8 352, 421, 502; iii. 421; iv. 181; i 222, 535; x. 287
Edward II, Evil Times of, i. 370

Edward III, I. 213, 284, 292, 338, 344, 353, 357 ff.; II. 22, 37, 102, 117, 156, 157, 296, 311, 356, 358, 421; III. 440; IV. 181; V. 244; VI. 330; VII. 206; VIII. 313; IX. 535
Edward III, V. 146, 237, 238, 243, 245, 398, 441, 443
Edward III, in Barbour's *Bruce*, II. 106
Edward the Third, The Raigne of King, IV. 394
Edward IV, II. 211, 287, 298, 317, 338, 482; III. 196; IV. 137, 182; V. 28; VI. 279, 280, 301; VII. 327; VIII. 314; IX. 535
Edward V, VIII. 314
Edward VI, II. 503; III. 30, 31, 33, 34, 36, 50, 51, 80, 81, 94, 107, 110, 143, 162, 181, 195, 198, 287, 338, 400, 403, 419, 427, 428, 430, 477; IV. 229, 230, 232, 234, 300, 314, 379, 380, 396; V. 56, 59, 90, 104, 108, 109; VI. 297; VII. 208, 325 ff., 330, 331, 336, 337; IX. 197, 210; XII. 355; XIV. 111
Edward VII, king of Great Britain, XII. 321
Edward (ballad), II. 412
Edward, prince, in *Henry VI*, V. 186
Edward, prince of Wales (1453–1471), II. 210, 297
Edward, son of Edgar, I. 138, 139
Edward aetheling, I. 140
Edward the Confessor (St Edward), I. 111, 140, 149, 180, 337, 355, 390, 449; V. 31; VIII. 310; XIV. 72
Edward the Confessor, in *The Example of Virtue*, II. 227
Edward the Elder, I. 137; VIII. 310
Edwardes, Sir Herbert Benjamin, XIV. 495
Edwardian commissioners, IV. 427
Edwards, Amelia Blandford (1831–1892), XIII. 562; XIV. 552
Edwards, Edward (1812–1886), XII. 521; *Lives of the Founders of the British Museum*, XII. 368; *Memoirs of Libraries*, XII. 368
Edwards, Eliseus James, XIV. Add. 7
Edwards, Henry Sutherland, XIV. 238
Edwards, John (1637–1716), VIII. 471, 473
Edwards, Jonathan (1629–1712), IX. 281
Edwards, Richard (1523?–1566), V. 120, 126, 396, 402; VI. 283 ff.
  Damon and Pithias, V. 63, 64, 70, 77, 118 ff., 123; VI. 284, 286, 299, 300
  In going to my naked bed, III. 189
  Palamon and Arcyte, V. 70, 118, 256; VI. 284, 286, 299, 300, 471
  Paradyse of Daynty Devises, The, III. 98, 189, 523
Edwards, Thomas (*fl.* 1595), *Cephalus and Procris*, IV. 469
Edwards, Thomas (1599–1647), *Gangraena*, VII. 386, 514
Edwards, Thomas (1699–1757), V. 273; IX. 475; *Canons of Criticism*, IX. 144; *Gangraena*, IX. 307
Edwards, Thomas (*fl.* 1810), X. 310, 507
Edwin, John (1749–1790), XI. 257, 453
Edwin, monk, I. 390
Edwin and Paulinus story, in Milton's *History of England*, VII. 128
Edwin of Northumbria (585?–633), I. 81; IV. 67
Edwy, Dunstan and, II. 76
Egan, Pierce (1772–1849), XIII. 418; XIV. 222 ff., 230, 233, 543
  Anecdotes, XIV. 226
  Book of Sports, XIV. 231
  Boxiana, XIV. 231
  Finish to the Adventures of Tom, Jerry, and Logic, The, XIV. 226
  Life in London, XIII. 265; XIV. 222 ff., 229, 238
  Life of an Actor, The, XIV. 226
  Pierce Egan's Life in London and Sporting Guide, XIV. 231
Egbert, bishop of Lindisfarne, I. 86
Egbert or Ecgberht of York (d. 766), I. 5, 80, 83, 84, 87
Eger, Sir, I. 291, 467
Egerton, lady Alice, VII. 113
Egerton, Hugh Edward, XIV. 563
Egerton, John, 1st earl of Bridgewater (1579–1649), VII. 113
Egerton, John, bookseller, XI. 336
Egerton, Sir Thomas, baron Ellesmere and viscount Brackley (1540?–1617), IV. 138, 161, 199, 200, 214, 215, 221, 265; VII. 112
Egerton, Thomas, IV. 200
Egerton, T. and J., *Theatrical Remembrancer, The* (1787), XI. 448
Egerton Papers, V. 477
Egeus, in *A Midsummer-Night's Dream*, V. 172
Egham, VII. 59
Egidia, step-sister of Robert II, II. 117
Egidius Romanus (d. 1316), II. 363
Egil Skallagrimsson, I. 9, 62; X. 224
Egilssaga, XII. 484
Egisthus, in Thomson's *Agamemnon*, X 108
Egistus, in *Horestes*, V. 65
Eglamor, XIII. 59
Eglamour of Artois, Sir, I. 316, 471; II. 182
Eglantine, Archibald, in Thackeray's *The Ravenswing*, XIII. 281
Egypt, II. 79, 87; IV. 89; VI. 301; X. 503; XII. 198, 317, 320, 339, 340, 351, 478; XIV. 246, 247, 252
Egypt, Frederick Tennyson's ode on, XIII. 45
Egypt, khedive of, XIV. 195
Egypt exploration fund, XII. 339, 340
Egyptologists, XII. 342
Egyptology, VII. 318
Ehangwen, Arthur's hall, I. 254
Eichler, A., XIII. 502
Eight Letters, VIII. 277
Eighty-eight, VIII. 96
Eikon Basilike. *See* Gauden, John
Eilhart von Oberge, I. 273
Einaudi, L., XIII. Add. 2
Einenkel, Eugen, I. 118

Einhart's *Life of Charles the Great*, I. 90
Ekkehard of St Gall, I. 32, 33; V. 37
Elaine, Tennyson's, XIII. 37
Elbing, in Alfred's *Orosius*, I. 94
Elbodugus. *See* Elfoð
Elckerlijk, the Dutch, V. 53
Eld, in *Confessio Amantis*, II. 148
Eld, George, IV. 394
Elder, John (*fl.* 1555), III. 194
Elderton, William (d. 1592), III. 201; IV. 169, 390, 535; V. 102; VI. 218; *Doctor Stories stumblinge into Englonde*, IV. 380
Eldon, earl of. *See* Scott, John
Eleanor, in Thomson's *Edward and Eleonora*, X. 108
Eleanor, duchess of Augustine, queen of Henry II, I. 264
Eleanor, lady, in Mrs Inchbald's *Every one has his Fault*, XI. 279
Eleanor of Castile, queen of Edward I, VIII. 125
Eleanor of Provence, queen of Henry III, I. 194, 361
Electra (Herrick's), VII. 6
Elegant Extracts, XI. 472
Elena, in Taylor's *Philip van Artevelde*, XII. 113
Elford, Staffordshire, XII. 277
Elflēdes Boc, I. 110. *See, also*, Aethelflaed
Elfoð, or Elbodugus, bishop of Bangor (d. 809), I. 70, 246
Elgin, II. 100
Elginbrod, David and Margaret, in George Macdonald's novel, XIII. 432
Elia. *See* Lamb, Charles
Elias of Jerusalem, I. 106
Elicea, in *Celestina*, V. 99
Elidure, king, in *No-Body, and Some-Body*, VI. 92
Elidure the Just, IV. 190
Elie de Beaumont, J.-B.-J., X. 61
Eliensis, Historia, II. 397
Elijah, I. 67, 74
Elijah, in Cowley's *The Muse*, VII. 66
Elinor, queen, in *Robert, Earle of Huntington*, V. 324
Eliot, Francis Perceval (1756?–1818), XIV. 513
Eliot, George (Mary Ann Cross, born Evans, 1819–1880), XI. 146; XII. 154, 292, 446; XIII. 108, 175, 292, 341, 345, 373, 379, 381 ff. (main entry), 422, 431, 442, 445, 446, 551 ff., 570, *also see* Add. 3; XIV. 199
Adam Bede, XIII. 382, 383, 386, 388 ff.
Address to Working-Men, XIII. 396
Agatha, XIII. 401
Amos Barton, XIII. 386 ff.
Armgart, XIII. 401
'Brother and Sister,' XIII. 382
Brother Jacob, XIII. 401
Daniel Deronda, XIII. 384, 394 ff.
Evangelical Teaching of Dr Cumming, The, XIII. 385
Felix Holt, the Radical, XIII. 396, 397
How Lisa loved the King, XIII. 400
Eliot, George
Impressions of Theophrastus Such, The, XIII. 382, 386, 401
Janet's Repentance, XIII. 386 ff.
Legend of Jubal, The, XIII. 401
Lifted Veil, The, XIII. 401
'Looking Backward,' XIII. 382
Middlemarch, XIII. 382, 398 ff.
Mill on the Floss, The, XIII. 391, 392, 394
Minor Prophet, The, XIII. 401
Mr Gilfil's Love Story, XIII. 386 ff.
Poems, XIII. 382, 401
Romola, XIII. 393 ff., 398
Scenes of Clerical Life, XIII. 386 ff.
Silas Marner, XIII. 393, 401
Spanish Gypsy, The, XIII. 396, 397, 400
Tales from Clerical Life, XIII. 386
Translations by, XIII. 383, 385
Wise, Witty, and Tender Sayings of George Eliot, XIII. 388
Works, XIII. 382
Life of. See Cross, J. W.
Eliot, Sir John (1592–1632), VII. 440; X. 287
Elipandus of Toledo, I. 85
Elisabeth of Schönau, St, I. 229
Elisha, I. 74
Eliza, in Barnfield's *Cynthia*, IV. 120
Eliza, in Wycherley's *Country Wife*, VIII. 145
Elizabeth, countess of Kent. *See* Grey, Elizabeth
Elizabeth, Epitaph on the lady, VII. 40
Elizabeth, princess (1635–1650), daughter of Charles I, IX. 403
Elizabeth, princess (1596–1662), daughter of James I, afterwards queen of Bohemia, IV. 143, 145, 154, 203; VI. 112, 250, 318, 353; VII. 46, 437, 439; the company of, VI. 261, 262
Elizabeth, queen of England, I. 99, 319, 381; II. 359; III. 1, 34, 35, 45, 54, 81, 96, 97, 114, 145, 148, 172, 181, 198, 201, 207, 212, 215, 219, 224, 226, 243, 245 ff., 252, 254, 264, 267, 290, 311, 314, 322, 326, 327, 331, 332, 337, 351, 374, 375, 377, 399 ff., 405, 406, 412, 418, 420 ff., 426, 432, 433, 437, 449, 454; IV. 1, 3, 6, 9, 16, 23, 51 ff., 57, 60, 64, 84, 87, 94, 95, 98, 104, 110, 111, 113, 120, 124, 126, 127, 132, 135, 142, 144, 150, 160, 163, 165, 172, 173, 176, 184, 193, 195, 208, 214, 232, 234, 298, 299, 301, 302, 305 ff., 312, 320, 329, 333, 351, 360, 380, 384, 391, 401, 405, 442; V. 29 ff., 35, 56, 60, 65, 66, 68, 77, 78, 102, 104, 109, 117, 118, 124, 152, 170, 247, 253, 256, 262, 309, 311, 328, 336 ff., 345, 347, 348, 354, 360, 361, 363, 366, 371, 376, 377, 480 ff.; VI. 33, 53, 91, 110, 141, 175, 212, 217, 241 ff., 246, 251, 264, 270, 272, 278, 285, 286, 291, 292, 297 ff., 301, 305, 309, 316, 320, 321, 326, 327, 335, 336, 365, 374, 380, 396, 400, 401; VII. 4, 28, 77, 157, 166, 190, 191, 196,

Elizabeth, queen of England
203, 221, 304 ff., 309, 314, 325, 326, 331, 333, 337, 338, 343, 366, 369, 386, 432; VIII. 44, 115, 350, 351, 356, 371; IX. 222, 271, 306, 534; X. 174, 287, 498, 499, 504; XI. 106, 350, 368; XII. 354, 355, 512, 514; XIII. 366; XIV. 52, 55, 84, 86, 93, 100, 101, 396; trans. of Boethius, II. 186
Elizabeth (1465–1503), queen of Henry VII, II. 391; III. 17
Elizabeth Brownrigge, XIII. 278
Elizabeth de Burgh. *See* Burgh, Elizabeth de; Clare, Elizabeth de
Elizabethan age, VII. 26, 150, 440, 449; X. 142; XI. 248, 369; XII. 80, 93, 168, 169, 358; XIII. 255, 364, 423; XIV. 443 ff.
Elizabethan church settlement, VII. 208
Elizabethan criticism, III. 289 ff., 526 ff.
Elizabethan divines, VII. 306
Elizabethan drama, IX. 56; X. 1, 5, 68, 69, 73, 78, 86, 92; XI. 258; XII. 68, 69, 112, 186; XIII. 257, 259
Elizabethan English, X. 180, 236
Elizabethan grammar schools, VII. 317
Elizabethan literature, II. 200, 209, 267, 387, 429; VII. 1, 7 ff., 17, 20, 23 ff., 48, 73, 93, 135, 148, 149, 155, 188, 256, 261, 263, 264, 270, 275, 323, 387; VIII. 25, 28, 125 ff., 130, 152, 179, 180, 184, 187, 195, 222, 308, 321, 387; IX. 265, 266; X. 184, 218, 221, 238; XII. 107, 113, 116, 253, 262, 364; XIII. 233, 238, 241, 269; XIV. 171, 460
Elizabethan lyrists, I. 362
Elizabethan moralities, V. 393
Elizabethan poets, X. 130; XI. 182, 183; XII. 47, 58, 79, 81; XIII. 130, 244, 245
Elizabethan prose fiction, III. 339 ff., 533 ff., *also see* Add.
Elizabethan public, XI. 262
Elizabethan sonnet, the, III. 247 ff., 522 ff.; XIII. 117
Elizabethan wars, VII. 447
Ellangowan, XIII. 234
Ellangowan, laird of. *See* Bertram, Godfrey
Ellen, in *Child Waters*, II. 413
Ellen, in Scott's *Lady of the Lake*, XII. 12
Ellena, in Mrs Radcliffe's *Italian*, XI. 302
Ellenberger, D. Frederic, XIV. Add. 7
Ellenborough, earl of. *See* Law, Edward
Elleray, lake Windermere, XII. 158
Ellesmere, lord. *See* Egerton, Sir Thomas
Ellicott, Charles John (1819–1905), IV. 46; XII. 340, 500
Elliot, Anne, in Jane Austen's *Persuasion*, XII. 240, 242
Elliot, the Hon. Arthur Ralph Douglas, XII. 426
Elliot, Charles, XI. 327, 342
Elliot, Edward Elliot, lord, X. 306
Elliot, Sir Gilbert (1722–1777), *My Apron Dearie*, IX. 373
Elliot, Sir Henry Miers (1808–1853), *History of India*, XIV. 337, 576
Elliot, Hugh S. R., XIV. 477
Elliot, Jane (1727–1805), XI. 231, *Ewe 'I've heard them Lilting at the* 232; *Milking*,' IX. 373
Elliot, Miss, in Jane Austen's *Persuasion*, XII. 240, 243
Elliot, Sir Walter, in Jane Austen's *Persuasion*, XII. 240
Elliot, Sir Walter (1803–1887), XII. 509
Elliott, Charlotte (1789–1871), XII. 416
Elliott, Ebenezer (1781–1849), XII. 135, 416; XIII. 156, 418; XIV. 327; *Battle Song*, XII. 136
Elliott, Mary (Mrs Belson, *fl.* 1810–1820), XI. 382, 478; *Aunt Mary's Tales*, XI. 383; *Rambles of a Butterfly*, XI. 383; *Tales for Boys*, XI. 383
Ellis, Alexander John (1814–1890), XII. 504; XIII. 248; XIV. 611; *Early English Pronunciation*, XIV. 441
Ellis, Annie Raine, X. 260
Ellis, Clement (1630–1700), IX. 395, 569; *The Gentile Sinner*, IX. 397
Ellis, Edmund, *Dia Poemata* (1655), VII. 412
Ellis, Edwin J., XI. 431, 433, 434
Ellis, F. S., XII. 403, 405
Ellis, George (1753–1815), VII. 73, 86; X. 234, 487, 491; XI. 35, 36, 39, 53, 391, 392; XII. 144, 149 ff., 357; *Early English Poets*, XII. 146; *Specimens of Early English Romances in Metre*, XI. 172; XII. 368
Ellis, Sir Henry (1777–1869), XII. 508, 509; *Introduction to Domesday Book*, XII. 346; *Original Letters, illustrative of English History*, XII. 346
Ellis, Hercules, XIV. 572, 573
Ellis, James (1763?–1830), XII. 376
Ellis, John (1643?–1738), IX. 495
Ellis, Robert (1820–1885), XII. 496
Ellis, Robert Leslie (1817–1859), IV. 280
Ellis, Robinson (1834–1913), XII. 483; XIII. 175, 502; *Appendix Vergiliana*, XII. 337; *Catullus* (trans.), XII. 337
Ellis, Thomas, in *The merry jests of the widow Edith*, II. 327
Ellis, Thomas, "sailer," IV. 456
Ellis, Thomas Flower (1796–1861), XIV. 493
Ellis, William (1800–1881), XIV. 414, 415, 601
Ellisland, Dumfriesshire, XI. 222
Ellison, Henry, XIII. 502
Ellison, O., XIII. 532
Elliston, Robert William (1774–1831), XII. 189
Ellistone, John (*fl.* 1651), IX. 515, 517
Ellwood, Thomas (1639–1713), VII. 107, 118, 120, 121; VIII. 104 ff., 110, 414, 415; IX. 406; *A Collection of Poems on Various Subjects*, VIII. 113; *The History of the Life of Thomas Ellwood, written by his own hand*, VIII. 105
Elmham, Thomas (d. 1440?), II. 496; IX. 535
Elmsley, Peter (1736–1802), XI. 327
Elmsley, Peter (1773–1825), XII. 327 ff., 333, 483

Elmy, Sarah. *See* Crabbe, Mrs
Eloisa, IX. 71
Elphin (*i.e.* Sir P. Sidney), in Drayton's *Idea*, IV. 172
Elphin, Roscommon, X. 196, 197, 199
Elphinstone, Mountstuart (1779–1859), XIV. 487, 552, 576; *The History of India*, XIV. 337
Elphinstone, William (1431–1514), II. 251, 369
Elrington, Charles Richard (1787–1850), XIV. 572
Elrington, Thomas (1688–1732), IX. 457
Elsinore, V. 159
Elstob, Elizabeth (1683–1756), IX. 402, 533; *Grammar*, IX. 355; *Homily on the Birthday of St Gregory*, IX. 355
Elstob, William (1673–1715), IX. 355
Elstow, Beds., VII. 167
Elsynge, Henry (1598–1654), X. 491
Eltham, VI. 283
Elton, Charles Isaac (1839–1900), XII. 401, 403, 521; XIV. 199
Elton, Mary Augusta, XII. 521
Elton, Mr, in Jane Austen's *Emma*, XII. 234, 243
Elton, Mrs, in Jane Austen's *Emma*, XII. 239, 240, 243
Elton, Oliver, I. 425; IV. 168, 178, 179, 180, 183, 186, 188, 195; XII. 230, 433, 524; XIII. 477, 495, 570, 572, *also see* Add. 1, 3; XIV. 497; *Survey of English Literature*, XI. 20, 434, 439
Elton, Richard (*fl.* 1650), IV. 456
Eltraine, IV. 363
Elwin, Whitwell (1816–1900), IX. 84; X. 422, *also see* Add.; XI. 404; XII. 153, 429
Elwina, in Hannah More's *Percy*, XI. 274
Elwood, Anne K., XI. 473, 463 ff.
Ely, II. 342, 347, 350, 352, 353, 358; IV. 190, 224, 238, 409, 422; VIII. 288, 301; IX. 330, 335, 339, 343, 356, 532; XII. 305, 325, 507; XIII. 366; monastery of, I. 16, 114, 140; II. 397
Ely, Mr, in George Eliot's *Amos Barton*, XIII. 387
Ely. *See* Thomas of
Elyot, Sir Thomas (1490?–1546), III. 21 ff. (main entry), 107, 302, 341, 423, 433, 445, 467, 486; IV. 437, 439, 495; VI. 492; VII. 304
Bankette of Science, The, III. 23
Castel of Helth, The, III. 23, 107, 445
Dictionary of Syr T. Eliot, Knyght (*Bibliothecae Eliotae*), III. 23; VII. 315
Doctrine of Princes, made by the noble oratour Isocrates, The, III. 23
Education or Bringinge up of Children, translated out of Plutarche, The, III. 23
Governour, The Boke named the, III. 21 ff., 105, 302, 341, 433
Holy Saynt Ciprian, A swete and devout sermon of, III. 23
Image of Governance, compiled of the actes and sentences notable of the moste

Elyot, Sir Thomas
noble Emperour Alexander Severus, The, III. 23
Of the Knowledge which maketh a wise man, IV. 5
Rules of a Christian lyfe made by Picus, The, III. 23
Elysian fields, XI. 107, 352
Elysium, Dekker's, IV. 354
Elze, Karl, V. 305
Elzevir press, Amsterdam, VII. 286
Elzevir texts, VII. 315
Elzevirianum, the, X. 245
Emancipation act, XIV. 54
Emarè, I. 310, 311, 316, 467
Emaricdulfe (E. C.'s), III. 256, 523
Emblem books, VII. 405, 479
Emdale, county Down, XIII. 404
Emelye, in *The Knightes Tale*, XIII. 123
Emerson, Oliver Farrar, XIV. 611
Emerson, Ralph Waldo, XI. 153, 171, 409, 439; XII. 440, 441; XIII. 10, 15, 465, 466, 469, 471
Emery, Thomas, XIV. 591
Emilia, in *Othello*, V. 202
Emilia, in *The Two Noble Kinsmen*, V. 256
Emilie, in *The Knight's Tale*, II. 243; V. 256
Emily, in *Palamon and Arcyte*, VI. 299
Emily, in Mrs Cowley's *Runaway*, XI. 274
Emily, in Mrs Radcliffe's *Mysteries of Udolpho*, XI. 302, 303
Emily, in Richardson's *Sir Charles Grandison*, X. 10
Emily, in Wordsworth's *White Doe of Rylstone*, XI. 106, 107
Emily, lady, in Burgoyne's *Heiress*, XI. 275
Emily, little, in *David Copperfield*, XIII. 327
Emin pasha, XIV. 192
Emlyn, in *The boke of Mayd Emlyn*, III. 88
Emlyn, Thomas (1663–1741), X. 386; *Humble Enquiry*, X. 379
Emma, in Jane Austen's novel, XII. 239, 243
Emmanuel, in *The Weakest goeth to the Wall*, V. 316
Emmaus, V. 39
Emmeline, in Dryden's *King Arthur*, VIII. 31
Empire, The, XIV. 364
Empiric, The, VI. 28
Emulo, in *Patient Grissill*, VI. 40
Encyclopaedia Biblica, XII. Add.
Encyclopaedia Britannica, XI. 76, 23[illegible]; XII. 296, 370, 375; XIV. 5, 13, 59, 6[illegible], 63, 98, 144
Encyclopaedia Metropolitana, XI. 133, 41[illegible]; XII. 474; XIV. 26, 428
Encyclopédie, L', I. 207; V. 292
'Endeavour,' ship, XIV. 289
Endimion (Lyly's), V. 341
Endor, witch of, VII. 370
Endowed Schools acts, XIV. 422

Endowed Schools commission, xii. 336; xiv. 421, 422, 429, 430
Endymion, in *The Faithfull Shepheardesse*, vi. 368
Endymion, in Keats's poem, xii. 57, 81, 82
Énéas, Roman d', i. 285
Eneydes, Le livre des, ii. 316
Enfans sans souci, v. 22, 25
Enfield, xii. 79, 182, 186, 200, 201
Enfield chase, v. 253
Enfield, William (1741–1797), x. 385; xiv. 606; *The Speaker*, xiv. 399
Engagement, The, viii. 275
Engel, Carl (1818–1882), xii. 521
Engelbrecht, Johann, ix. 519
England, church of, iv. 204, 305; v. 365; vi. 3, 150; vii. 142 ff., 208, 214, 217, 223, 310, 321, 340; viii. 43, 46, 273, 286, 292, 293 ff.; ix. 210; x. 287, 351, 352, 359, 362, 364, 366, 370, 375, 377 ff., 381; xi. 1, 167; xii. 254, 259 ff., 266, 267, 274 ff., 295; xiii. 103, 348, 453; xiv. 76, 383, 402, 411
England, The Political History of, xii. 322
England's Helicon, iii. 178; iv. 52, 109, 113, 116 ff., 121, 122, 125, 159, 222, 467, 487; v. 148; vii. 2
England's Joy, vi. 263
England's Miserie, vii. 385
England's Parnassus, v. 129, 134, 148, 162; xii. 113
Englefield, Sir Henry C. (1752–1822), xii. 509
English association, the, xiii. 377
English canon law, xiv. 80
English dialect society, xii. 344
English, earliest documents in, iii. 440
English grammar, xiv. 396 ff., 440 ff.
English, history and literature, Old, xii. 344
English language, i. 379 ff., 480; xiv. 434 ff.
English language, Middle, i. 481
English language, Old, i. 480
'English Men of Letters' series, xiv. 144
English Annotations of the Bible, vii. 322
English Courtier and the Countrey Gentleman, The, iii. 489; v. 349, 351, 478
English Historical Review, The, x. 295, 409; xiv. 100, 118
English Miscellany, An, iv. 119
English Poets, xi. 325
English Post, The, xi. 333
English Review, x. 310
English Rogue, The (1665), vii. 516
English Spy, The, xiv. 238
Englishman, The, ix. 220, 441
Englishman, the, in *The Fyrste Boke of the Introduction of Knowledge*, iii. 105
Englishman's Magazine, The, xii. 437
Enid, i. 280
Enitharmon, Blake's, xi. 194 ff.
Ennius, iv. 17, 264; viii. 58
Ennui, in Reynolds's *Dramatist*, xi. 281
Enoch, in Byron's *Cain*, xii. 48
Enoch, Book of, i. 133
Enquirer, The (1797), xi. 394
Ensor, George (1769–1843), xiv. 605
Ent, Sir George (1604–1689), viii. 356, 363, 476; xiv. 281
Entepfuhl, in Carlyle's *Sartor Resartus*, xiii. 9
Entick, John (1703?–1773), x. 522; *Latin and English Dictionary*, x. 388; *Spelling Dictionary*, x. 388
Entries (legal) (1546), viii. 466
Envy, in *Confessio Amantis*, ii. 147, 148
Envy, in *Mucedorus*, v. 254
Envy, in *Piers the Plowman*, ii. 12
Envy, in *The Passetyme of Pleasure*, ii. 229, 234
Eoganesius, Janus Julius, ix. 292
Eormenric, in *Beowulf* and *Widsith*, i. 26, 34 ff.
Epaminondas, xii. 313
Epeircte, in *Argenis*, iv. 259
Ephraim, xiii. 149
Epicharmus, iii. 433
Epicoene. *See* Jonson, *Silent Woman, The*
Epictetus, i. 286; ii. 308; iv. 436, 523; vi. 34, 50; vii. 489; ix. 54, 300; xi. 356 ff., 473; xii. 335, 487; xiii. 90; *Enchiridion*, ix. 246; xi. 357
Epicurus, viii. 288, 289; xii. 340
Epigrams and satires, iv. 518
Epinasse, Francis, xiv. 519
Epiphany, festival of, ii. 378
Epistolae Cantuarienses, xiv. 74
Epistolae Obscurorum Virorum, iii. 91, 106, 107, 398, 496; vii. 370
Eppie Morrie, ii. 411
Epsom, viii. 136, 199; ix. 130, 268; x. 260
Epternach, i. 83
Epworth, x. 364
Equatoria, xiv. 192
Erasmus, Desiderius (1466?–1536), i. 363; ii. 67, 325, 330, 367, 369, 370; iii. 1 ff., 7, 8, 11 ff., 18, 26 ff., 32, 40 ff., 49, 52, 59, 67, 80, 93, 96, 104, 113, 155, 346, 347, 363, 365, 429, 433, 466 ff., 487, 496, *also see* Add.; iv. 225, 227, 228, 322, 358, 414, 420, 422, 428, 430, 443, 444, 491, 492, 530; vi. 9; vii. 261, 304, 310, 315, 331, 366; viii. 23; ix. 418, 529; xi. 367; xii. 324, 332, 468, 477, 485; xiv. 79, 86
Adagia, iii. 4, 20, 347; viii. 59, 407
Apophthegmata, iii. 93, 347
Colloquia, iii. 1, 4, 20, 81, 104, 346, 347, 429; iv. 347; vi. 87; vii. 370; ix. 273 ff.; xiii. 428
Compendium vitae, xiii. 428
Constructione, De, iii. 20, 21
Convivium Fabulorum, iii. 93
Copia, iii. 4, 12, 20, 21
Ecclesiastes, sive concionator Evangelicus, iv. 224
Enchiridion Militis Christiani, iii. 4, 20, 27
Encomium Moriae, iii. 4, 18, 19, 96; v. 9, 13; vii. 376; viii. 36, 59, 407
Institutio Principis Christiani, iii. 4

Erasmus, Desiderius
Jerome and Chrysostom, editions of and commentaries on, III. 4
Laudibus Britanniae, De, III. 67
Novum Instrumentum, III. 4, 12
Paraphrase of the New Testament, V. 104
Paraphrases, III. 4
Erastianism, VII. 296; IX. 193; X. 355, 370, 372; XII. 256
Erce, "the mother of the Earth," I. 40
Erceldoune, Thomas of. *See* Thomas de
Erckmann-Chatrian, XIV. 322
Erdeswicke, Sampson (d. 1603), III. 532; IX. 533
'Erebus,' ship, XIV. 296
Erec (Geraint), Sir, I. 284
Eremyt and the Outlawe, The, II. 503
Erewhon, Butler's, XIII. 453
Erichto, in *The Wonder of Women*, VI. 49
Erick, Abigail, IX. 91
Erigena, John. *See* Scotus
Erin, port, Isle of Man, XIV. 297
Erkenwald, I. 333, 334
Erl of Tolous and the Emperes of Almayn, I. 471
Erlinton, II. 411
Ermyn, in *Beves*, I. 305
Ernley or Arley Regis, Worcester, I. 234
Ernulf (1040–1124), I. 449; *Textus Roffensis*, IX. 535
Ernulphus, in Sterne's *Tristram Shandy*, X. 53, 55
Eromena, VII. 74
Erondelle, Peter, IV. 456
Errand, Tom, in Farquhar's *Constant Couple*, VIII. 169
Error, in *Time's Complaint*, VI. 320
'Ersch,' or 'Yrisch' speech, II. 90, 99
Erse poetry, X. 487
Erskine, Andrew, X. 191, 477
Erskine, David Steuart, 11th earl of Buchan (1742–1829), XI. 220; XII. 149
Erskine, Ebenezer (1680–1754), IX. 548
Erskine, Francis Robert St Claire, earl of Rosslyn (1853–1890), XIII. 502
Erskine, Henry (1746–1817), XI. 220; XII. 149
Erskine, J., XIV. Add. 3
Erskine, Ralph (1685–1752), IX. 548
Erskine, Thomas, 1st lord Erskine (1750–1823), XI. 139; XII. 149; XIV. 509, 513; *Defence of the Whigs*, XIV. 121
Erskine, Thomas, of Linlathen (1788–1870), IX. 328, 521; XII. 283, 466; *Brazen Serpent, The*, XII. 289; *Letters*, XII. 284; *Unconditional Freeness of the Gospel, The*, XII. 284
Erskine, William, lord Kinneder (1769–1822), XII. 13, 375
Erythraeus, *Eudemia*, IV. 260
Esau, VI. 93; XIII. 208
Esau, in *Jacob and Esau*, V. 111, 112
Eschenbach. *See* Wolfram von
Eschenburg, Johann Joachim, V. 298, 304
Escott, Thomas Hay Sweet, XIII. 564, 567; XIV. 185, 531, 533; *Masters of English Journalism*, XIV. 180, 187
Esdaile, Arundell, *A chronological list of George Meredith's publications*, XIII. 440, 568
Esher, III. 337
Esmond, colonel, in *The Virginians*, XIII. 298
Esmond, Henry, Thackeray's, XIII. 292, 293, 297, 300, 407
Esmond, lady Maria, in *The Virginians*, XIII. 298
Español Gerardo, El, VI. 123
Espinasse, Francis, IX. 236; XIV. Add. 2
Espriella, Don Manuel Alvarez (*i.e.* Southey), XI. 421
Espronceda, XII. 393
Esquemeling, John, IV. 456
Essay, the, IV. 523 ff.
Essay concerning the Origin of Sciences, IX. 137
Essay on Tragedy (1749), X. 161
Essay to revive the antient education of Gentlewomen, IX. 403
Essays and Reviews, XII. 285, 294 ff., 466; XIII. 452
Essays on a liberal education, XIV. 425
Essex, II. 208; IV. 127; VII. 37, 46, 58, 89, 454; IX. 152, 153, 537, 539; X. 386, 393; XII. 305, 513, 514; XIV. 74, 221
Essex, countess of. *See* Howard, Frances
Essex, earls of. *See* Cromwell, Thomas; Devereux, Robert; Devereux, Walter
Essex-Head club, X. 187, 471
Estcourt, Richard (1668–1712), VIII. 158, 177
Este, house of, III. 305
Este, Isabella de, V. 69
Este, Italy, XII. 63
Este, Leonora de, XII. 50
Este, Michael, IV. 113, 464
Estella, in *Great Expectations*, XIII. 330, 334
Estesian 'proofs,' XI. 163
Esther, V. 106
Estienne, Charles, VI. 484
Estienne, Henri, III. 157, 162, 424; IV. 8, 403, 408, 444; VII. 479
Estienne, Robert, III. 162
Estlin, John Prior (1747–1817), XI. 416
Estmere, King, II. 410, 411, 414
Esto Perpetua club, XI. 34, 35
Estrifs, V. 2, 27, 31
Estrild, in *Locrine*, V. 239, 240
État des hommes, II. 139
Eternity, in *The Passetyme of Pleasure*, II. 226
Etesia (Vaughan's), VII. 40
Ethelbald. *See* Aethilwald
Ethelbert, king of Kent, VIII. 309, 310
Ethelburga, St (d. 676?), I. 82
Etheldreda, St (630?–679), I. 82; II. 210
Ethelred. *See* Aethelred
Ethelwold. *See* Aethelwold
Ethelwulf's poem on ? Crayke, I. 86, 434

Etherege, Sir George (1635?–1691), VIII. 136 ff., 142 ff., 155, 214, 401, 418, 423, 424, 445; IX. 474; X. 67
Comical Revenge or Love in a Tub, The, VIII. 18, 136, 137, 139, 143
Letter books, VIII. 137, 138
Man of Mode, The, or Sir Fopling Flutter, VIII. 136
She Would if She Could, VIII. 136, 138
Ethiopians, IX. 138
Ethiopic learning, VII. 319
Etiquette, book on table, III. 19
Eton college, II. 305, 321, 355, 357, 359, 489; III. 183, 315, 418, 420, 426 ff., 433, 434; IV. 164, 165, 275, 406, 431; V. 102, 104, 105; VI. 246; VII. 53, 152, 192, 312, 326 ff., 331, 334, 341, 492; VIII. 279, 281; IX. 392, 405, 408 ff., 573; X. 20, 113, 114, 116, 117, 242, 247, 272; XI. 173, 341, 346; XII. 58, 323, 324; XIII. 24, 45, 129; XIV. 56, 121, 207, 225, 251, 386, 387, 390, 413, 422
Eton Greek grammar, III. 429
Eton, printing press, IV. 400, 411
Etonian, The, XIV. 539
Ettrick, XI. 239
Ettrick Banks, IX. 374
Ettrick shepherd, the. *See* Hogg, James
Etty, William (1787–1849), XIV. 203
Etymologicum Magnum, XII. 328
Eubulus, in *Damon and Pithias,* V. 118
Eubulus, in F. Davison's eclogue, IV. 124
Eubulus, in *The Anatomy of Wit,* III. 345
Eubulus, in *The Picture,* VI. 161
Eucharist, Aelfric on the, I. 117, 127, 128
Eucharist, Cranmer on the, III. 33, 34, 404
Eucharist, Lanfranc on the, I. 154
Eucharist, the, X. 354, 360; XII. 299
Eucherius, bishop of Lyons, VII. 405
Euclid, I. 153; II. 362; III. 420; VII. 266, 284, 287, 320; VIII. 360; IX. 305, 410
Euclid, first English translation, III. 425, 551; IV. 436
Euclio, in Pope's *Epistles,* IX. 82
Euganean hills, XII. 63; XIV. 293
Eugenia, in *The Duke of Millaine,* VI. 155
Eugenia, St, I. 74
Eugenius, in Sterne's *Tristram Shandy,* X. 47, 50; XI. 174
Eugonus, in *Misogonus,* V. 110, 111
Eulalia, queen, in *The Queen and Concubine,* VI. 231
Eulalia, St, I. 74
Eulenspiegel, III. 79, 81, 82, 94, 490; IV. 356, 360, 448, 533
Eulogium, Latin compendium, II. 301
Eumolpus, IX. 266
Eunapius Sardianus, IV. 436
Eunomia, in *The Masque of the Middle Temple,* VI. 355
Eupelas, in *Misogonus,* V. 110
Euphorion, in Goethe's *Faust,* XII. 34
Euphormio (John Barclay's), IV. 255
Euphrasia, in *Philaster,* VI. 120, 126
Euphrates, the, IV. 90
Euphuism, IV. 145, 146, 194, 328; V. 214, 378; VI. 142, 163, 189, 387, 392. *See, also, under* Lyly
Euripides, III. 161, 420, 429, 430; IV. 348, 436; V. 5; VI. 296; VII. 334; VIII. 164, 194; IX. 477, 524, 527; XII. 68, 325, 330 ff., 475, 480, 483, 488, 489, 491, 493 ff.
Alcestis, XII. 329; XIII. 81
Bacchae, XII. 318, 327, 338
Hecuba, XII. 324, 326
Heraclidae, XI. 274; XII. 327
Hippolytus, XII. 329
Iphigenia, XII. 329
Medea, X. 124; XII. 101, 324, 327
Orestes, XII. 324
Phoenissae, IV. 4; V. 71; XII. 324
European literature, X. 14, 16, 17
European studies, X. 176
European Magazine, X. 192, 193, 471, 473, 479, 483
Euryalus and Lucrece, II. 329
Eurydice, I. 295, 311; X. 114
Eurydice, in *King Orfeo,* II. 414
Eurydice, in a Shetland ballad, II. 417
Eurymachus, in *Ulysses Redux,* VI. 303
Eusden, Laurence (1688–1730), IX. 181, 188, 448, 485
Eusebius, I. 66, 75; II. 293; XII. 484, 503
Eusebius (Hwaetberct), I. 60, 78, 79
Eusebius of Emesa, III. 416
Eustace, count, I. 111
Eustace, legend of St, I. 292, 315
Eustace, lord, in Mrs Griffith's *School for Rakes,* XI. 263
Eustace the Monk, II. 507, 508
Eustathius, IX. 75
Eustochium, St, I. 74
Eutheo, in *The Third Blast of Retreat from Plays and Theatres,* V. 313
Eutropius, I. 81; IV. 436
Evadne, in *The Jealous Lovers,* VI. 325
Evadne, in *The Maides Tragedy,* VI. 120, 126, 127
Evadne, in Sheil's play, XIII. 259
Evander, II. 231
Evans, Anne (1820–1870), XIII. 180, 198, 210, 502; *Pevensey and Hurstmonceaux,* XIII. 177; *Roses and Rosemary,* XIII. 177
Evans, Arise (b. 1607), VII. 509
Evans, Sir Arthur (b. 1851), XII. 316, 339, *also see* Add. 4
Evans, Arthur William, XIII. 471
Evans, Caleb, X. 387
Evans, Elizabeth, XIII. 389
Evans, Evan (1731–1789), X. 487
Evans, George Essex (1863–1909), XIV. 585; *Australian Symphony,* XIV. 369; *Repentance of Magdalene Despar, The,* XIV. 369
Evans, Gwenogvryn, I. 252
Evans, Henry, VI. 258, 289 ff.
Evans, Hugh, X. 387
Evans, Sir Hugh, in *The Merry Wives of Windsor,* V. 189; XIV. 307
Evans, Isaac, XIII. 382
Evans, John (1680?–1730), IX. 212

Evans, John (1767–1827), XI. 486
Evans, Sir John (1823–1908), XII. 509; XIII. 198; *Ancient Bronze Implements*, XII. 347; *Ancient Stone Implements*, XII. 347; *Coins of the Ancient Britons*, XII. 347
Evans, Lewys, *How to Wyve well*, III. 486
Evans, Margaret, XIV. 595
Evans, Marian or Mary Ann. *See* Eliot, George
Evans, Mary, XI. 118
Evans, Maurice S., XIV. Add. 7
Evans, Robert Wilson (1789–1866), *Treatise of Versification*, XIII. 244, 512
Evans, Sebastian (1830–1909), I. 258, 260, 271; XIII. 194, 198, 502; *Brother Fabian's Manuscripts*, XIII. 199; *High History of the Holy Graal, The*, XIII. 199; *Shadows*, XIII. 199
Evans, Thomas, VI. 276
Evans, Thomas (1742–1784), IX. 482; XI. 327
Evans, Thomas Saunders (1816–1889), XII. 483
Evans, William (d. 1718), X. 387
Evanthe, in *A Wife for a Month*, VI. 122, 132
Eve, I. 134; IV. 214; IX. 28, 60
Eve, in Dryden's *The State of Innocence*, VIII. 28
Eve, in *Paradise Lost*, VII. 101; XII. 85
Eve, in the *Coventry play*, II. 425
Eve, in *The Cytezen and Uplondyshman*, III. 63, 64
Eve, in *The Golden Legend*, II. 335
Eve, in the mystery plays, V. 56, 390, 391
Eveleigh, John (1748–1814), XII. 284
Eveleigh, William, XIV. Add. 7
Evelina, in Mason's *Caractacus*, XI. 273
Evelyn, George, brother of John, VIII. 244
Evelyn, John (1620–1706), IV. 426, 456; VII. 54, 99, 234, 270, 394, 482, 486, 496, 518; VIII. 10, 163, 209, 241 ff. (main entry), 258, 259, 264, 308, 354, 355, 359, 365, 369, 371, 378, 448 ff., 477; IX. 32, 276, 331, 387, 396; XIV. 281
Diary, VIII. 134, 265, 301; IX. 389, 574
Fumifugium, or The inconvenience of the Air and Smoke of London dissipated, VIII. 247
Gardening, VIII. 378
Golden Book of St John Chrysostom, The, translation of, VIII. 247
Kalendarium Hortense, VIII. 378
Liberty and Servitude, translated from an essay by François de la Mothe Le Vayer, VIII. 246
Life of Margaret Godolphin, VIII. 250, 251
Sylva, VIII. 248, 355
Tyrannus, or the Mode, VIII. 248
Evelyn, lady, VIII. 242
Evelyn, Mrs John, born Browne, VIII. 245, 246
Evelyn, Richard, eldest child of John Evelyn, VIII. 246
Evelyn, Richard, father of John, VIII. 244
Evelyns, the, IX. 243
Evening News, The, XIV. 195
Evening Standard, The, XIV. 188, 189
Evening Star, The, XIV. 190
Everard, John (1575?–1650?), VII. 488
Everett, George, IV. 456
Everett, James (1784–1872), XII. 420
Everie Woman in her Humor, VI. 27, 459
Eversfield, Sir Thomas, IV. 157
Eversfield, Tymothy, IV. 157
Eversley, Hampshire, XIII. 355, 365, 369
Every-man, II. 328; V. 17, 53, 54, 392
Evesham, II. 67; IV. 174, 190; IX. 535; XIV. 185
Evesham, battle of, I. 336, 338
Evesham, monastery of, I. 89
Evesham, vale of, X. 111
Evesham, Vision of the Monk of, II. 318, 486, 503
Evesham or Worcester *Chronicle*, I. 109, 111
Evesham. *See* Walter of
'Ewaipanoma race,' the, IV. 78
Ewald, Georg Heinrich August von, XII. 321
Ewart, Nanty, in Scott's *Redgauntlet*, XII. 21
Ewen, John (1741–1821), *O weel may the Boatie Row*, IX. 374
Ewing, Alexander (1814–1873), XII. 466
Ewing, Juliana Horatia (1841–1885), XI. 387, 478; XIV. 163
Examen Miscellaneum (1702), VIII. 444
Examen Poeticum Duplex, IX. 434
Examiner, The, IX. 95, 131, 151, 217, 218, 220, 440, 455, 446, 461, 465, 470, 491; XI. 128; XII. 157, 171, 172, 193, 194, 432, 434, 436; XIII. 258, *also see* Add. 1; XIV. 177, 197, 198, 324
Excalibur, XIV. 307
Excalibur, in *Morte Arthure*, II. 120
Excellencie of a Free State, The, VII. 359
Exceptiones ad Caesandum Brevia, VIII. 465
Exchange, The, VII. 449
Exchange Ware, VI. 481
Exchequer, Dialogue of the, IV. 511
Excise bill, IX. 224
Exclusion bill, the, VIII. 36, 90; IX. 225
Exempla, collections of, III. 92, 93, 489; IV. 343
Exeter, IV. 235, 350, 408, 422; V. 55; VI. 241; VII. 245, 246, 309; VIII. 360; IX. 164, 538; X. 379, 380, 384; XIII. 276
Exeter, duke of. *See* Holland, John
Exeter, earl of, IX. 147
Exeter academy, X. 384
Exeter Book, The, I. 12, 34, 39, 48, 52, 53, 60 ff., 151, 374, 428
Exeter meetings, X. 373
'Exodus, Desert of the,' the, XII. 342
Exoniensis, Liber, IV. 422
Expedients for Publique Peace, VII. 386
'Extravagants,' the, II. 364
Eynsham, abbey of, I. 125, 127, 133
Eynsham, Aelfric's letters, I. 114, 125, 126

Eynsham, synod of, I. 129, 130
Eyrbiggia Saga, The, XII. 375
Eyre, Sir James, X. 406
Eyre, Jane, Charlotte Brontë's, XIII. 408
Eyre, Simon, in *The Shomakers Holiday*, VI. 52, 172
Eyton, Robert William (1815–1881), XII. 509
Eyton, Shropshire, IV. 292
Eyzat, Edward, IX. 560
Ezechias, V. 104
Ezekiel, I. 92; IV. 238; V. 48; X. 130
Ezra, fourth book of, XII. 341

Fabell, Peter, in *The Merry Devill*, V. 252, 253
Faber, Frederick William (1814–1863), XII. 259, 275, 456, 460; XIII. 167, 502; *Cherwell Water Lily, The*, XIII. 171; *Pilgrims of the Night, The*, XIII. 172; *Sorrowful World, The*, XIII. 172
Fables, XI. 479
Fables bestiaires, VIII. 59
Fabliaux, I. 158, 365; II. 279, 280; III. 91, 93, 487, 489; VII. 380
Fabricius, II. 106
Fabula Atellana, Old Italian (Campanian), V. 24
Fabyan, Robert (d. 1513), *Chronicles*, I. 477; II. 101, 302, 322, 485, 496; VII. 203
Fabyl, The Merry Pranks of, V. 253
Fabyl's Ghoste, V. 253
Face, in *The Alchemist*, VI. 22
Facetiae, III. 92, 93, 95, 489
Facetie et motti arguti di alcuni eccellentissimi ingegni et nobilissimi signori, III. 93
Faery, king of, in *Gyre Carling*, II. 275, 276
Fag, in Sheridan's *Rivals*, XI. 266, 267
Fagan, Louis Alexander, XIV. 540
Faggus, Tom, in *Lorna Doone*, XIII. 434
Fagin, in *Oliver Twist*, XIII. 316, 317, 319
Fagius, Paul (1504–1549), III. 34, 53
Faiel, Eudes de, XI. 274
Fainall, in Congreve's *Way of the World*, VIII. 153, 154
Fainall, Mrs (Congreve's), VIII. 155
Fair Annie, II. 410
Fair Flower of Northumberland, The, II. 411
Fair Janet, II. 412
Fair Margaret and Sweet William, II. 412
Fair Quiet (Marvell's), VII. 181
Fairbairn, John, XIV. 378
Fairbridge, Charles Aiken, XIV. Add. 4
Fairbridge, Kingsley, XIV. Add. 4
Fairbrother, William Henry, XIV. 473
Faire Em, V. 136, 161, 237, 238, 251, 252, 419, 441, 443
Faire Maide of Bristow, The, VI. 96
Fairfax, Edward (d. 1635), IV. 23, 448; VII. 83; VIII. 234
Discourse of Witch-craft, A, VII. 374, 506
Fairfax Correspondence, The, VII. 194
Godfrey of Bulloigne, VII. 57, 374; IX. 418
Memorials of the Civil War, VII. 194
Tasso, translation of, VII. 374; VIII. 227
Fairfax, Jane, in Jane Austen's *Emma*, XII. 240
Fairfax, Mary (b. 1638), VII. 180
Fairfax, Thomas, lord (1612–1671), VII. 178, 190, 225, 449, 512, 513
Fairfax, William, VII. 83
Fairfax Correspondence, the, VII. 439
Fairhaven, IV. 93
Fairholt, Frederick William (1814–1866), XII. 509
Fairless, Michael, *pseud.* *See* Barber, Margaret Fairless
Fairy Queen, II. 182
Fairy Queen, in Spenser, II. 234
Fairy tales, XI. 479
Faith, in *Piers the Plowman*, II. 27
Faith, in *Portuus of Noblines*, etc., II. 284
Faith of one God Who is only the Father, X. 378
Faithful Friends, The, VI. 132, 140
Faithorne, William (1616–1691), VII. 487
Falconbridge the bastard, in *Edward IV*. VI. 90
Falconbridge, in *The Merchant of Venice*, V. 359
Falconer, C. M., XIV. 522
Falconer, Edmund. *See* O'Rourke, Edmund
Falconer, Lanoe, *pseud.* *See* Hawker, Mary
Falconer, Thomas (1738–1792), *Strabo*, XIV. 409
Falconer, William (1732–1769), X. 154 (main entry), 155, 398, 453, 454, 525; *The Shipwreck*, X. 154
Falkiner, Caesar Litton (1863–1908), VII. 209, 436; XII. 410; XIV. 97, 487
Falkirk, battle of, II. 108
Falkland, in Godwin's *Caleb Williams*, XI. 46, 293
Falkland, lady. *See* Cary, Lettice
Falkland, viscount. *See* Cary, Sir Henry; Cary, Sir Lucius
Falkland islands, X. 404, 462, 474
Fall, The, V. 391
Fallaw, Lance, XIV. Add. 4
False, in *Piers the Plowman*, II. 7, 8, 32
False Bachelor, the tale of, in *Confessio Amantis*, II. 148
False Semblant, in *Confessio Amantis*, II. 148
Falsehood of Man (Bi manne lease), I. 62
Falset, in *Ane Pleasant Satyre*, III. 124
Falstaff, Sir John (Shakespeare's), III. 371; IV. 78; V. 187, 189, 194, 239, 269, 315, 316, 321, 358, 367; VI. 15, 23, 249; VII. 204; XII. 196, 280, 349; XIII. 39, 64, 72
Falstaff, Sir John, Original Letters, etc., of, XII. 438
Falstaff, The Bouncing Knight, VIII. 116
Fame, in Drayton's *Robert of Normandy*, IV. 177
Fame, in *Hudibras*, VIII. 70
Fame, in *The Masque of Queens*, VI. 349

Fame, in *The Passetyme of Pleasure*, II. 225, 226
Family Library, The, XII. 318; XIV. 67
'Family of Love' books, IV. 402
Famous Battel of the Catts, The, VII. 409
Famous Flower of Serving Men, The, II. 411
Fancy, in *Magnyfycence*, III. 77
Fancy, in *The Floating Island*, VI. 325
Fancy, The, XIV. 231
Fane, Charles Fane, 2nd viscount, X. 249
Fane, Sir Francis (d. 1689?), VIII. 204, 422
Fane, Mildmay, 2nd earl of Westmorland (d. 1665), VII. 5, 407
Fane, Violet, *pseud. See* Currie, Mary Montgomerie, lady
'Fannikin' (Fanny Burney), X. 260
Fanny, in Fielding's *Joseph Andrews*, X. 26
Fanny, in Parnell's *Elegy*, IX. 167
Fanshawe, lady Anne (born Harrison), (1625–1680), VIII. 270, 359; *Memoirs*, VIII. 270, 452
Fanshawe, Catherine Maria (1765–1834), XII. 416
Fanshawe, Sir Henry (1569?–1616), IV. 265
Fanshawe, Sir Richard (1608–1666), VIII. 130, 452; *La Fida Pastora*, Latin translation of Fletcher's *Faithfull Shepheardesse*, VIII. 271; version of Luis de Camoëns' *Lusiads*, VIII. 271; translation of Guarini's *Pastor Fido*, VI. 490; VII. 61, 264; VIII. 271, 441
Fantosme, Jordan, *Chronicle of the Scottish Wars*, I. 446; II. 420, 508
Faques, Richard, ballads of Flodden printed by, II. 327; *The booke of the pylgrymage of man* (*Le Pelerinage de l'homme*), II. 327
Faraday, Michael (1791–1867), XIV. 259 ff., 267 ff., 270, 280, 556, 557
Farces, V. 22, 91, 92, 97, 98, 115
Farces, A Collection of (1809), XI. 456
Fareham, XIII. 276
Farel, William, III. 411
Faret, N., *L'Art de plaire à la Cour*, IV. 345, 526
Fargus, Frederick John (*pseud.* Hugh Conway, 1847–1885), XIII. 562
Faria y Sousa, M. de, IX. 501; *The Portuguese Asia*, IX. 278
Faricius, I. 72
Farindon, Antony (1598–1658), VII. 152
Farish, William (1759–1837), XIV. 385
Farjeon, Benjamin Leopold (1838–1903), XIV. 370, 585
Farley, F. E., XII. Add. 1
Farley's *Bristol Journal*, XI. 133, 134
Farman, priest of Harewood, Leeds, I. 132
Farmer, John (*fl.* 1591–1601), IV. 113, 464
Farmer, Priscilla, XII. 436
Farmer, Richard (1735–1797), XII. 365, 493
Farnaby, Giles (*fl.* 1598), IV. 113, 464; VII. 2
Farnaby, Thomas (1575?–1647), VII. 307, 335, 486, 488
Farnham, IX. 91
Farnham castle, Surrey, IV. 156
Farnworth, Richard (d. 1666), VII. 507
Faro, Portugal, IV. 56
Faroe version of *The Maid Freed from the Gallows*, II. 405
Faron, Jean, II. 312
Farquhar, George (1678–1707), VIII. 146, 168 ff., 178, 423, 427, 429, 430; X. 67, 72, 202, 211, 216; XII. 443
Adventures of Covent Garden, The, VIII. 166, 170
Beaux' Stratagem, The, VIII. 171, 172, 173; XI. 322
Constant Couple, The, VIII. 169, 170, 175
Inconstant, The, VI. 135; VIII. 120
Love and a Bottle, VIII. 169, 170
Recruiting Officer, The, VIII. 171
Sir Harry Wildair, VIII. 169
Stage-Coach, The (with P. A. Motteux), VIII. 171
Twin Rivals, The, XI. 322
Farr, Dr Samuel (1741–1795), X. 209
Farra, Alessandro, VII. 264
Farrar, Frederic William (1831–1903), XII. 466; XIV. 425, 426, 606
Farrell, John (1851–1904), XIV. 369, 585
Farren, Robert, XII. 357
Farrer, John, *Virgo Triumphans* (1650), IV. 462
Fastidious, British bishop, I. 65
Fastidious Brisk, in Jonson's *Every Man Out of his Humour*, IV. 207; VI. 40, 44
Fastnachtsspiele, III. 58, 81
Fastolf, Sir John (1378?–1459), II. 68, 308, 309; V. 187
Fates of Men (Bi manna wyrdum), I. 61, 428
'Father of Candor, The,' X. 399
Father's Blessing Penn'd for the Instruction of his Children, XI. 370
Father's Instruction, A, I. 62, 219, 363, 428
Fathers, Lives of the, II. 127, 317, 323
Fathers, the, II. 129; III. 11, 92, 145, 212, 409, 410, 416; VII. 305, 312, 313, 316, 318, 321, 482, 483; VIII. 112, 294, 296, 302; IX. 211; XII. 269, 277, 298, 355, 454
Fathers of the Holy Catholic Church, XII. 259
Fathom, count, in Smollett's novel, X. 39
Fatum Vortigerni, VI. 483
Faucit, Helena, afterwards lady Martin (1817–1898), XIII. 59, 69, 261; XIV. 112
Fauconbridge, Sir Richard, in *Looke About You*, V. 321
Faulkland, in Sheridan's *Rivals*, XI. 267
Faulkner, George (1699?–1775), IX. 123, X. 257; XI. 342
Fauntelte (childishness), in *Piers the Plowman*, II. 25
Fauntleroy, Henry (1785–1824), XIII. 41[illegible]
Faust, XIII. 153, 274
Faust, E. K. R., *Richard Brome*, VI, 225
Faust, in Goethe's drama, XII. 34, 47
Faust legend, the, VII. 369
Faustulus (Mantuan's), III. 224

Faustus, in (?) Ralegh's *Dialogue*, IV. 109
Faustus, in *The Cytezen and Uplondyshman*, III. 63
Fauvel, Henri, XIII. 465
Favel, in *Piers the Plowman*, II. 7, 8
Faversham, Kent, V. 240; IX. 536; XII. 347
Favine, André, IV. 543
'Favonius' (Richard West), X. 118, 121
Favour, in *The Bowge of Courte*, III. 73
Favourite, The, VI. 28
Fawcett, Henry (1833–1884), XIV. 472, 509, 513, 606
Fawcett, Millicent Garrett, XIV. 606
Fawconbridge, in *The Troublesome Raigne of King John*, V. 83
Fawkes, Francis (1720–1777), X. 183, 454, 469; XI. 172, 426, 431
Fawnia, in *Pandosto*, III. 356, 357
Fawsley, III. 380, 386
Fay, Eliza, XIV. 576; *Original Letters from Calcutta*, XIV. 335
Fear, in *Mirour de l'Omme*, II. 140
Featherston, of Ardagh, X. 197, 214
Featley, Daniel (1582–1645), IV. 382, 495; VII. 484, 502; *Britanicus Vapulans*, VII. 351; *Dipper Dipt, or the Anabaptist Duck't and Plung'd over Head and Ears in a Disputation, The*, VII. 145; *Mercurius Urbanus*, VII. 351
Featley, John (1605?–1666), VII. 308
Fécamp, monks of, I. 202
Fedalma, in George Eliot's *The Spanish Gypsy*, XIII. 398
Fedele, in *Fedele and Fortunio*, V. 315
Feenix, cousin, in *Dombey and Son*, XIII. 325
Fehr, Bernhard, XIII. 570
'Feilding, Beau,' in *The Tatler*, IX. 34
Feilding, Mary, IX. 243
Feilding, Susan, countess of Denbigh, VII. 35
Feilding, William, 3rd earl of Denbigh, IX. 243
Felice, in *Guy of Warwick*, I. 304 ff.
Felismena, in Montemayor's *Diana*, VIII. 126
Felix, anti-pope, IV. 322
Felix, Don, in Mrs Centlivre's *The Wonder*, X. 72
Felix, in Montemayor's *Diana*, VIII. 126
Felix, St (d. 647?), I. 74, 75
Felix and Philiomena, The History of, VIII. 126
Felix of Croyland, *Life of St Guthlac*, I. 58, 85, 131, 434
Felix of Urgel, I. 85
Fell, John (1625–1686?), VII. 457, 488; IX. 265, 329, 345, 348, 527; XI. 341
Fell Smith, Miss C., VIII. 270
Fellmar, lord, in Fielding's *Tom Jones*, X. 89
Fellowes, Robert (1771–1847), XI. 312; XII. 466
Fellows, Sir Charles (1799–1860), XII. 339, 496
Fellowship, in *Every-man*, V. 53
Felltham, Owen (1602–1668), *Resolves*, IV. 248, 348, 524, 525
Felpham, Sussex, XI. 195, 197
Felsted, VII. 454; VIII. 269, 359
'Female dream,' the, in Blake's poems, XI. 194
Fencer, the, in *Pan's Anniversarie*, VI. 355, 361
Fénelon, François de Salignac de la Mothe, IV. 260; VII. 176; VIII. 303; IX. 307, 520, 521; X. 114, 134, 420, XI. 424, 491; *Aventures de Télémaque*, XII. 190
Fenian Sagas, XIV. 304
Fenians, XIV. 313, 318, 321, 322
Fenn, Eleanor, lady (1743–1813), XI. 479, 480; *Cobwebs to Catch Flies*, XI. 379
Fennell, Charles Augustus Maude, XIII. 537
Fennor, William, IV. 518; *The Compter's Commonwealth*, IV. 350, 530
Fens, the, IV. 190, 308, 509; XII. 417
Fenton, Elijah (1683–1730), VII. 410, 414; VIII. 446; IX. 76, 181, 183, 184, 484, 485; XI. 246; *Mariamne*, X. 83, 430
Fenton, Sir Geoffrey (1539?–1608), IV. 441, 445; VI. 390, 492; *Forme of Christian pollicie gathered out of French*, VI. 377, 386; *Tragicall Discourses*, III. 343, 536; IV. 2, 6, 7; VI. 377
Fenton, Mr, in Brooke's *Fool of Quality*, IX. 327
Fenton, Richard (1746–1821), XII. 509
Fenton, Roger (1565–1615), IV. 313, 510; VII. 316
Fenwick, John, XII. 188
Fenwick, Mrs, XI. 486
Ferars, in *A Challenge for Beauty*, VI. 103
Ferdia, XIII. 188
Ferdinand, in *The Doubtfull Heir*, VI. 205
Ferdinand, in *The Dutchesse of Malfy*, VI. 182
Ferdinand, in *The Tempest*, V. 201, 206 VIII. 9; XII. 54
Ferdinand, Don, in *Don Quixote*, IX. 269
Ferdinand I, grand duke of Tuscany, IV 163; VI. 175
Ferdinand II, emperor, IV. 259; VII. 453
Ferentes, in *Loves Sacrifice*, VI. 192
Fergus, in *Gorboduc*, V. 67
Fergus's Gaist, Laying of Lord, II. 277
Ferguson, Adam (1723–1816), IX. 561; X. 285, 501, 512; XI. 450; *Essay on the History of Civil Society*, X. 296, 319; *History of the Roman Republic*, X. 296, 319, 320
Ferguson, John, *Bibliotheca Chemica*, XII. 371, 519; *Some Aspects of Bibliography*, XII. 371, 519; *Witchcraft Literature of Scotland*, XII. 371, 519
Ferguson, J. W., XIV. 238
Ferguson, Mary Catherine, lady, born Guinness (1823–1905), XII. 360; *Sir Samuel Ferguson*, XIV. 319; *Story of Ireland*, XIV. 319
Ferguson, Robert, 'the Plotter' (d. 1714), VIII. 41

Ferguson, Sir Samuel (1810–1886), xii. 516; xiv. 305, 319 ff., 568
At the Polo Ground, xiv. 320
Conary, xiv. 320
Congal, xiv. 320
Curse of the Joyces, The, xiv. 320
Deirdre, xiv. 320
Forging of the Anchor, The, xiv. 319
In Carey's Footsteps, xiv. 320
Lays of the Western Gael, xiv. 320
Ogham Inscriptions, xii. 360
Return of Claneboy, The, xiv. 319
Tain Quest, The, xiv. 320
Thomas Davis, xiv. 319
Welshmen of Tirawley, The, xiv. 320
Fergusson, James (1621–1667), ix. 543
Fergusson, James (1808–1886), xii. 510
Cave Temples of India, xii. 353
Illustrated Hand-book of Architecture, xii. 353
Rock-cut Temples of India, xii. 353
Tree and Serpent Worship, xii. 353
Fergusson, Robert (1750–1774), i. 290; ii. 267; ix. 378 ff., 562, 566; x. 226; xi. 204 ff., 209, 211, 217, 221, 228
Auld Reekie, ix. 380
Bill of Fare, ix. 380
Death of Scots Music, ix. 378
Elegy on John Hogg, ix. 378
Farmer's Ingle, The, ix. 379, 380; xi. 206
Gowdspink, The, ix. 379
Hallow Fair, ix. 379; xi. 215
Leith Races, ix. 379; xi. 215, 216
Planestanes and Causeway, ix. 380
To the Bee, ix. 379
Ferishta, Mohamed Kasim, *Muhammedan Power in India*, xiv. 337
Ferishtah, Browning's, xiii. 84
Fermor, Arabella, ix. 70
Fermor, Henrietta Louisa, countess of Pomfret (d. 1761), ix. 248; x. 274, 496
Fernandez, Jerónimo, iv. 444
Fernando, in *Loves Sacrifice*, vi. 192, 194
Ferndean, Charlotte Brontë's, xiii. 408
Ferne, Sir John (d. 1610), iv. 376, 543
Ferrabosco, Alphonso (*fl.* 1544–1587), iv. 113, 464; v. 125; vi. 348
Ferrar, Nicholas (1592–1637), iv. 406; vii. 27 ff., 32, 46, 153 ff., 162, 402, 424, 427, 482; xii. 488
Ferrara, iii. 5, 7, 167; v. 62, 69, 114; vi. 365; vii. 100; xii. 50
Ferrara, duke of, in *The Imposture*, vi. 205
Ferrarius. *See under* Montanus
Ferrars, Edward, in Jane Austen's *Sense and Sensibility*, xii. 237, 239, 241
Ferrers, George (1500?–1579), iii. 193, 195, 494
Ferret, in Smollett's *Sir Launcelot Greaves*, x. 41
Ferrex, in *Gorboduc*, v. 66, 67
Ferrex and Porrex, v. 396
Ferriar, John (1761–1815), iv. 252; viii. 442; x. 422; *Bibliomania*, xii. 366; *Illustrations of Sterne*, xii. 366
Ferrier, James Frederick (1808–1864), xii. 160, 425, 487; xiv. 40 ff., 472
Institutes of Metaphysic, The, xiv. 40, 41
Lectures on Greek Philosophy, xiv. 41
'Philosophy of Consciousness, The,' xiv. 40
Scottish Philosophy, xiv. 7
Ferrier, James Walter, xiv. 210
Ferrier, Susan Edmonstone (1782–1854), xii. 246, 449; xiii. 431, 432
Destiny, xii. 245
Inheritance, The, xii. 245
Marriage, xii. 245
Ferris, Richard (*fl.* 1600), *The Most dangerous and memorable Adventure*, iv. 361
Ferumbras, Sir, i. 288, 291, 293, 302, 303, 465, 471
Feste, in *Twelfth Night*, v. 190, 193; vii. 3
Festing, Gabrielle, xiii. 503
Festiniog, vale of, x. 115
Festive songs of the 16th and 17th centuries, v. 477
Festus, Bailey's, xiii. 153
Festus, in Browning's *Paracelsus*, xiii. 57
Fet Asaver, viii. 465
Fethe, Fethy or Futhy, Sir John, Scots poet, ii. 282; iii. 131
Fetherstone, Henry, iv. 398, 403
Feuerbach, Ludwig, *Essence of Christianity*, xiii. 385, 553
Feuillerat, Albert, v. 341, 478, *and see* Add. 2; vi. 270; vii. 454
Fever, in *Piers the Plowman*, ii. 22
Feverel, Sir Austin, Meredith's, xiii. 445
Feverel, Richard, Meredith's, xiii. 443, 444
Few may fend for falsett, ii. 280
Feylde, Thomas, *The Controversy between a Lover and a Jay*, ii. 224, 326
'Fiall,' in *The Fair Maid Of the West*, vi. 101
Fichte, Johann Gottlieb, xi. 136; xiii. 7, 13; xiv. 9, 41, 467, 478
Ficino, Marsilio, iii. 8, 214 ff., 221
Fickle, madame (D'Urfey's), viii. 175
Fiddes, Richard (1671–1725), *Body of Divinity*, xi. 322
Fidelia, in *The Faerie Queene*, vi. 335
Fidelia, in Wycherley's *Country Wife*, viii. 145
Fidelity, in *The Passetyme of Pleasure*, ii. 229
Fidge, George, *The English Gusman* (1652), vii. 516
'Fidget' (Elizabeth Montagu), x. 262
Fidus, in *Euphues and his England*, iii. 345
Field, Barron (1786–1846), vi. 104; xii. 182, 199; xiv. 586; *First Fruits of Australian Poetry*, xii. 194; xiv. 362; *Kangaroo, The*, xii. 195
Field, Elizabeth. *See* Lamb, Mrs Elizabeth
Field, Frederick (1801–1885), xii. 341, 501
Field or Feilde, John (d. 1588), iii. 377, 378, 385, 390, 403, 548; vi. 220, 224; *Admonition to Parliament*, vi. 393
Godly Exhortation, vi. 393, 493

Field, Kate, XII. 441; XIII. 514, 543
Field, Michael, *pseud.* (Katharine Harris Bradley and Edith Emma Cooper), XIII. 502; *Callirrhoe*, XIII. 181
Field, Mrs, Charles Lamb's grandmother, XII. 182
Field, Nathaniel (1587–1633), IV. 360; V. 370; VI. 28, 33, 116, 128, 137, 138, 140, 145, 146, 165, 211, 212, 220–225 (main entry), 232, 274, 402, 403, 443, 455, 491; VIII. 195; *Amends for Ladies*, VI. 223; *Woman is a Weathercocke, A*, VI. 221
Field, Richard (1561–1616), *Of the Church*, VII. 323, 484; VIII. 276, 277
Field, Richard (*fl.* 1579–1624), IV. 394, 400, 401
Field, The, XIV. 201
Field, Theophilus (1574–1636), bishop of Hereford, VI. 220, 402
Field, William (1768–1851), XII. 490
Field of the Cloth of Gold, II. 228, 338; III. 57, 175, 317; VI. 284, 334
Fielde, J., IV. 447
Fielding, Charlotte (d. 1744), X. 22, 23, 27, 28
Fielding, Edmund, X. 20
Fielding, Henry (1707–1754), IV. 246, 255; VI. 24, 28; VIII. 162, 168; IX. 243, 248, 254, 471; X. 16, 20 ff. (main entry), 36, 37, 39, 41 ff., 50, 56, 71, 77, 78, 88, 211, 216, 317, 413 ff., 438, 440, *also see* Add.; XI. 264, 288, 296, 331; XII. 2, 168, 177, 231, 242, 251; XIII. 285, 305, 307, 310, 352, 386, 388, 398; XIV. 223, 552
Amelia, X. 21, 23, 33, 34; XI. 262, 265, 279, 324
'Apology for the Clergy,' X. 24
Author's Farce, The, X. 21, 22; XI. 329
Charity, essay on, X. 24
Coffee-House Politician, The, X. 21
Covent Garden Tragedy, X. 22, 83
Don Quixote in England, X. 22
Enquiry into the causes of the late Increase of Robbers, X. 33
'Essay on Conversation,' X. 23
Examples of the Interposition of Providence, in the Detection...of Murder, X. 34
Good-Natured Man, The, X. 23
Historical Register, The, X. 23, 84
Intriguing Chambermaid, The, X. 22
Jonathan Wild, X. 27, 30, 39; XIII. 279, 280
Joseph Andrews, IX. 405, 407; X. 6, 20, 24 ff., 30, 44; XII. 235; XIII. 295; XIV. 213
Journey from this World to the Next, X. 27
Love in Several Masques, X. 21
Miscellanies, X. 21, 23, 26 ff.
Miser, The, X. 22
Mock Doctor, The, X. 22
Pasquin, X. 23, 24, 84
Pleasures of the Town, X. 21
Proposals for erecting a country workhouse, X. 29, 34
Fielding, Henry
Proposals for making an effectual provision for the poor, X. 34
Provoked Husband, The, X. 92
Temple Beau, The, X. 21
Tom Jones, IX. 405; X. 9, 15, 20, 22, 26, 28 ff., 39, 48, 89, 92, 272, 508; XI. 260, 448; XIII. 295; XIV. 255
Tom Thumb, X. 22, 26, 73, 83
Tragedy of Tragedies, X. 22, 83
Voyage to Lisbon, X. 35, 252
Wedding Day, The, X. 23
Fielding, Sarah (1710–1768), XI. 479, *also see* Add.; *David Simple*, X. 20, 28, 415; *Governess or Little Female Academy, The*, XI. 376, 380; XIV. 600
Fielding, William, X. 28
Fields, James T., XIII. 543, 565
Fiennes, Madame de, VIII. 248
Fiennes, Nathaniel (1608–1669), VII. 450
Fient a crum of thee she faws, IX. 360
Fierabras, I. 284
Fiesole, XIII. 73
Fife, II. 89, 131, 371; IX. 364, 367, 552; XI. 242, 243; XII. 513
Fifeshire, XIII. 3
Fifteen Tokens, The (*L'Art de bien mourir*), II. 329
Figaro, XIV. 235
Figaro in London, XIV. 235, 236
Figg, James (d. 1734), IX. 191; XIV. 229, 231
Figgis, John Neville, XIV. 484
Figures, in Cowley's *The Muse*, VII. 65
Fikenhild, in *Horn*, I. 304
Filidh (Filé), XIV. 302
Fillingham, T., X. 492
Filmer, Edward (*fl.* 1707), VIII. 433
Filmer, Sir Robert (d. 1653), VII. 301, 420, 471, 507; VIII. 341; *An Advertisement to the Jury-men of England*, VII. 395; *Originall of Government*, VII. 300; *Patriarcha*, VII. 300
Filon, Augustin, XIII. 514
Finch, Anne, countess of Winchester (d. 1720), IX. 483, 484; X. 145; XII. 124
Fanscombe Barn, IX. 169
Lines to Prior, IX. 169
Nocturnal Reverie, IX. 168
Sigh, The, IX. 169
Spleen, The, IX. 169
To Mr F now Earl of W, IX. 169
To Mr Jervas, IX. 169
To Mr Pope, IX. 169
To the Nightingale, IX. 169
Finch, Daniel, 2nd earl of Nottingham (1647–1730), IX. 9, 95, 135
Finch, Heneage, 1st earl of Aylesford (1647?–1719), VIII. 410
Finch, Heneage, 4th earl of Winchilsea, IX. 168
Finch, Sir Henry (1558–1625), VIII. 468
Finch, Sir John (1584–1660), VIII. 110
Finch-Hatton Correspondence, VII. 196
Finchley, XIII. 52
Findern, Derbyshire, X. 386

Findlay, John Ritchie (1824–1898), XII. 445
Findlay, Joseph John, XIV. 601
Fine Arts Quarterly, XIV. 539
Fingal, X. 227, 229, 231, 232, 487
Finglass, IX. 166
Finical, Father, in Crowne's *English Frier*, VIII. 189
Finland, II. 405
Finlason, Thomas, IV. 547
Finlay, George (1799–1875), XII. 475
Greece under the Romans, XII. 314
History of Greece, XII. 314, 315
History of the Byzantine and Greek Empires, XII. 314
History of the Greek Revolution, XII. 314
Finlayson, James (1840–1906), XII. 521
Finn, in *Beowulf*, *Finnsburh* and *Widsith*, I. 23, 31, 34
Finn, Irish tales of, X. 231
Finn, Phineas, Trollope's, XIII. 423
Finnsburh, I. 30, 47, 423, *also see* Add.; X. 223, 224
Fiordespina, in *Orlando Furioso*, III. 231
Fiorinda of Urbino, in *The Great Duke of Florence*, VI. 156
Fiormonda, in *Loves Sacrifice*, VI. 192
Firdusi, I. 293
Fire of London, the great, VII. 289
Firebrace, lady, X. 464
Firenzuola, Agnolo, III. 252
Firmin, Giles (1614–1697), VII. 424; X. 359; *A Brief Vindication of Mr Stephen Marshal*, VII. 145
Firmin, Philip, in Thackeray's *Adventures of Philip*, XIII. 299, 300
Firmin, Thomas (1632–1697), X. 377
Firouzkah, princess, in Beckford's *Episodes*, XI. 291
Firth, Charles Harding, VII. 214, 218, 219, 432, 451; VIII. 352; IX. 202, 204, 208; XIV. 88, 493, 594
Fischer, Lisbeth, Balzac's, XIII. 287
Fischer, Thomas A., XIII. 465, 466, 471
Fish, Simon (d. 1531), III. 473; *Sum of Scripture, The*, III. 39; *Supplication for the beggars*, III. 26, 101, 105; IV. 314, 510; VII. 432
Fisher, George William, *Annals of Shrewsbury School*, XIV. 413, 598
Fisher, Herbert Albert Laurens, XIV. 494
Fisher, Jasper (*fl.* 1639), VI. 472
Fisher, John (1459–1535), bishop of Rochester, III. 7, 12 ff., 19, 27, 36, 53, 332, 468, 473; IV. 224 ff., 231, 232, 492, 495, *also see* Add.; IX. 197, 531; XII. 488
Assertio septem Sacramentorum, a defence of Henry VIII's, III. 15
Confutatio Assertionis Lutheranae, III. 15
De Eucharistia contra Johannem Oecolampadium libri quinque, III. 15
Funeral sermon on Henry VII, II. 325
Mourning Remembrance, II. 325
Penitential Psalms, Sermons on the, II. 325; IV. 226
Fisher, John
Sacri Sacerdotii Defensio contra Lutherum, III. 15
Fisher, John (1569–1641), VIII. 300
Fisher, John, of Warwick (*fl.* 1500), IV. 309, 510
Fisher, Joseph Robert, XIV. 536
Fisher, Payne (1616–1693), VII. Add.; XI. 317
Fisher, Robert, III. 3, 7
Fisher, Samuel (1605–1665), VIII. 111, 416
Fishing with an angle, II. 323
Fishwick, Henry (1835–1914), XII. 519
Fitch, Sir Joshua Girling (1824–1903), XIII. 48; XIV. 601, 606
Fitch, Ralph (*fl.* 1583–1606), XIV. 332, 576
Fitch, Walter Hood, XIV. 561
Fitela, in *Beowulf*, I. 23, 26
Fitton, Anne, VII. 196
Fitton, Mary (*fl.* 1600), V. 229, 231; VII. 196
Fitz-Alan, house of, II. 103
Fitzball, Edward (1792–1873), XIII. 257, 264, 518
Fitz-Boodle, George Savage, *pseud.* of W. M. Thackeray, XIII. 281
Fitzdottrel, 'duke of Brownlands' and Mrs Fitzdottrel, in *The Divell is an Asse*, VI. 24
Fitzgeffry, Charles (1575?–1637), IV. 168, 360, 475; VII. 406
Fitzgerald, Edward (1809–1883), XI. 147, 418, 439; XII. 135, 199, 305, 413, 438; XIII. 31, 35, 47, 142 ff. (main entry), 172, 253, 277, 497 (main entry), 530; XIV. 146, 519
Agamemnon, XIII. 145
Bird's-eye View of Faríd-Uddín Attar's Bird-Parliament, XIII. 145
Euphranor, XIII. 143, 146
Meadows in Spring, The, XIII. 143
Mighty Magician, The, XIII. 144
Oedipus at Athens, XIII. 144
Oedipus at Thebes, XIII. 144
Painter of his own Dishonour, The, XIII. 144
Polonius, XIII. 143
Readings in Crabbe, XIII. 143
Rubáiyát of Omar Khayyám, XIII. 145, 146, 174
Salámán and Absál of Jámí, XIII. 145
Six Dramas of Calderon, XIII. 143
Such Stuff as Dreams are Made of, XIII. 144
Fitzgerald, lord Edward (1763–1798), XII 412
Fitz-Gerald, lady Elizabeth (1528?–1589) III. 176
Fitzgerald, George Francis (1851–1901) XIV. 269, 556
Fitzgerald, Gerald, 9th earl of Kildare (1487–1534), III. 176
Fitzgerald, Percy H., XIII. 514, 519, 532 543
FitzGerald, Shafto Justin Adair, XIII. 54[illegible]
Fitz-hamon, Robert (d. 1107), I. 256

Fitzherbert, Sir Anthony (1470–1538), IV. 309, 369, 510; VIII. 466; *Abridgment of the Year Books*, VIII. 315
Fitzherbert, John of Norbury, IV. 307, 364, 371, 510, 541; *Book of Husbandry*, IV. 300, 369, 370, 510; *Book of Surveying* IV. 369, 370
Fitz-James, Richard (d. 1522), bishop of London, III. 9
Fitzmaurice, Edmund George Petty, 1st lord, XIV. 510
Fitzmaurice Kelly, James, VIII. 126, 129
Fitz-Neale or -Nigel, Richard, bishop of London (d. 1198), I. 173, 449; IV. 510; *Dialogus de Scaccario*, I. 174
Fitzpatrick, Sir Percy, XIV. Add. 7
Fitzpatrick, Richard (1747–1813), XI. 35; *Lyars*, XI. 36
Fitzpatrick, T., XI. 450
Fitz-Patrick, William John (1830–1895), XII. 379, 451; XIV. 568, 569
FitzRalph, Richard (d. 1360), archbishop of Armagh, II. 42, 44, 52, 53, 74, 308, 355; *Defensio Curatorum, De Pauperie Salvatoris*, II. 53
Fitzroy, Augustus Henry, 3rd duke of Grafton (1735–1811), X. 133, 402, 404 ff., 523, 526, 527
Fitzsimons, Frederick William, XIV. Add. 7
Fitz-Stephen, William (d. 1190?), I. 449; II. 505; V. 7, 38
Fitzthomas, Maurice, 1st earl of Desmond (d. 1356), X. 20
Fitztraver, in Scott's *Lay of the Last Minstrel*, XII. 9
Fitzwarine, Fulk, II. 399, 428, 503, 507
Fitzwater, in *Robert, Earle of Huntington*, V. 318, 324
Fitzwater, lady, III. 357
Fitzwater, Matilda, IV. 182, 183
Fitzwilliam, John (d. 1699), VIII. 272
Fitzwilliam, William, viscount Milton (1839–1877), XIV. 553
Fitzwilliam, William Wentworth, 2nd earl Fitzwilliam (1748–1833), XI. 4, 388
Five Joys of the Virgin, I. 231, 458
Five Plays in One, VI. 87, 128
Five Starches, the, in *The World tost at Tennis*, VI. 75
Flacius Illyricus, XIII. 172
Flagellant, The, XI. 155; XIV. 387
Flamboroughs, the Miss, in *The Vicar of Wakefield*, X. 210
Flamineo, in *The White Divel*, VI. 175
Flaminius, in *Believe as you List*, VI. 148
Flaminius, in *Laelia*, VI. 305
Flamsteed, John (1646–1719), VIII. 477; IX. 470
Flanders, II. 56; VI. 3; X. 51, 200; XII. 43
Flandria (Flanders), in *Colkelbie's sow*, II. 127
Flannislie, in *Colkelbie's sow*, II. 126
Flapsy, in Mrs Trimmer's *Robins*, XI. 379
Flatman, Thomas (1637–1688), VII. 88, 241, 251, 412; VIII. 412, 444
Flatterie, in *Ane Pleasant Satyre*, III. 124, 125, 126, 128, 129
Flattery, A Discourse against, IX. 524
Flattery, in *Piers the Plowman*, II. 28
Flaubert, Gustave, XI. 293; XIII. 456; *Salammbô*, XIII. 461; *Trois contes*, IX. 39
Flavel, John (1630?–1691), X. 387
Flavia, in Law's *Serious Call*, IX. 323
Flavia, in *The Fancies*, VI. 194
Flavia, in *The Spectator*, IX. 57
Flavia (Waller's), VII. 55
Flaxman, John (1755–1826), XI. 181; XII. 172
Fleance, son of Banquo, II. 104
Fleay, Frederick Gard (1831–1909), III. 206; V. 146, 316, 318, 332; VI. 4, 5, 9, 17, 23, 83 ff., 89, 90, 92, 93, 98, 100, 102, 103, 204, 216, 224, 228, 232, 233, 235, 240, 274, 287, 288, 345, 348, 358, 459
Flecker, James Elroy (d. 1915), XIII. 502
Flecknoe, Richard (d. 1678?), VII. 183, 412; VIII. 40, 422; *Short Discourse of the English Stage*, VII. 238, 251, 272, 441
Fled Bricrend (the feast of Bricriu), I. 327
Fleet, publisher, XI. 375
Fleet prison, the, IV. 78
Fleetwood, in Meredith's *The Amazing Marriage*, XIII. 445
Fleetwood, Charles (d. 1692), VIII. 121; XI. 449
Fleetwood, E., VII. 514
Fleetwood, George (1605–1667), VII. 450
Fleetwood, William (1535?–1594), VI. 382, 393
Fleming or Flemming, Abraham (1552?–1607), IV. 435, 437, 439, 442
Fleming, Caleb (1698–1779), X. 521
Fleming, Contarini, Disraeli's, XIII. 346, 348, 361
Fleming, Francis, XIV. Add. 7
Fleming, John (*fl.* 1726), X. 385
Fleming, Marjorie (1803–1811), XI. 476 XIV. 228, 229, 543
Fleming, Mary, Scott's, XII. 27
Fleming, Rhoda, George Meredith's, XIII. 447
Fleming, Richard (d. 1431), II. 358
'Fleming,' *Be Merry Brethren*, III. 131
Fleming, the, in *The Fyrste Boke of the Introduction of Knowledge*, III. 105
Flemings, VII. 306
Flemish clothmakers, II. 311
Flemish towns, trade in, V. 355
Flemming or Fleming, Robert (d. 1483), dean of Lincoln, III. 5; IV. 428
Flesh of Man, in *Mirour de l'Omme*, II. 140
Fleta (*c.* 1290), VIII. 313, 465
Fletcher, Andrew, of Saltoun (1655–1716), IX. 492; X. 449
Account of a Conversation, IX. 215
Discorso delle cose di Spagna, IX. 215
Discourse of... Militias, IX. 214
Political Works, IX. 214
Speech upon the State of the Nation, IX. 215
Two Discourses, IX. 215

Fletcher, Charles Robert Leslie, XIII. 465
Fletcher, Francis, IV. 87, 456
Fletcher, Giles, the elder (1549?–1611), III. 198, 256, 264, 265; *Licia*, III. 265, 523; *Richard III*, III. 198
Fletcher, Giles, the younger (1588?–1623), IV. 150, 164 ff. (main entry), 456, 481; VI. 111
Christs Victorie, IV. 164
Death of Eliza, Canto upon the, IV. 164, 165
Description of Encolpius, A, IV. 164
Prince Henry's Death, IV. 164
Fletcher, John (1579–1625), IV. 115; V. 148, 181, 195, 217, 218, 256 ff., 347, 356, 362, 364, 371; VI. 2, 26, 27, 36, 65, 69, 89, 107–136 (main entry), 142, 144, 145, 151, 152, 157, 177, 182, 184, 185, 195, 199, 205, 206, 208, 211, 223, 231, 234, 235, 239, 240, 248, 272, 340, 353, 363, 366 ff., 371, 372, 427, 435 ff., 490; VII. 3, 39, 272, 275; VIII. 12, 13, 29, 31, 116, 119, 127, 128, 132, 133, 141, 150, 162, 184, 192, 202, 219, 226, 425; IX. 140, 145; X. 91, 145; XII. 89, 186, 444; XIII. 144, 218, 260, 289; *Thierry and Theodoret*, XII. 190. *See, also*, Beaumont and Fletcher
Fletcher, John William (1729–1785), X. 365 ff., 516; *Scriptures Scales*, X. 367; *Zelotus and Honestus*, X. 367
Fletcher, Phineas (1582–1650), IV. 150, 164 ff. (main entry), 481; VI. 111, 321; VII. 46; XII. 79; XIII. 218
Brittain's Ida, IV. 165
Elisa, IV. 166
Locusts or Apollyonists, The, IV. 166, 167
Piscatorie Eclogues, IV. 165
Purple Island, The, IV. 164, 166
Sicelides, IV. 165
Fletcher, Richard (father of John), VI. 110
Fletcher, Sir Robert, IX. 192, 488
Fletcher, R. H., *The Arthurian Material in the Chronicles*, I. 257
Fletcher, William Younger, XII. 519
Fletching church, X. 312
Fleury, religious revival of, I. 113. *See, also*, Abbo of
Fleury's Ecclesiastical history, XII. 460
Fleury-sur-Loire, V. 37
Flexney, bookseller, X. 191
Flinders, Matthew (1774–1814), XIV. 289
Flint, Robert (1838–1910), XIV. 472
Flint cottage, Box hill, XIII. 440
Flintwinch, in *Little Dorrit*, XIII. 331
Flodden, battle of, II. 40, 41, 109, 251, 327, 369; III. 70, 197; XII. 10, 11; XIV. 185
Flodden Field, II. 415
Flood, Henry (1732–1791), XIV. 311
Flood, the, III. 130, 318
Flora, in Beaumont's masque, VI. 356
Flora, in Owen's *Epigrammata*, IV. 265
Flora, in *The Flower and the Leaf*, II. 219
Flora, in *The Penates*, VI. 341
Flora, in *The Vision of the Twelve Goddesses*, VI. 338
Florabell (Herrick's), VII. 12
Florac, in *The Newcomes*, XIII. 295, 297
Floras dames, The glyttering showes of, III. 190
Florence, II. 350; III. 5, 6, 8, 167; IV. 69, 163; V. 61, 69, 115, 247, 350; VI. 144; VII. 99, 100, 284; X. 41, 119, 122, 249, 303; XII. 204, 324, 327, 401; XIII. 46, 54, 70, 72, 73, 77, 79, 103, 393 ff.
Laurentian library, IV. 429
San Marco, XIII. 394
Florence of Rome, I. 467
Florence of Worcester (d. 1118), I. 90, 91, 160 ff., 451; IV. 68
Florence wine, IX. 412
Florent, tale of, in Gower, II. 183
Florentine, in *The Seven Sages*, I. 309
Florentine academy, XI. 176
Florentine nobleman, in Congreve's *Incognita*, VIII. 146
Florentine renascence, IX. 306
Flores, Juan de, *Historia de Aurelio y de Ysabela*, VI. 123, 138; VIII. 128
Flores and Blancheflour, I. 286, 303, 308, 309, 465, 468
Flores Historiarum, I. 449
Florestan, king, in Disraeli's *Endymion*, XIII. 350
Florida, IV. 70, 81
Floridan peat, X. 392
Florimel, in Dryden's *Secret Love*, VIII. 20
'Florimel,' in *The Tatler*, IX. 34
Florinda, in *Count Julian*, XII. 211
Florio, John (1553?–1625), IV. 442; VI. 221; VIII. 387; *A Worlde of Wordes*, IV. 15, 395; XIV. 448; *Montaigne*, IV. 8, 15, 248, 395, 447, 523; IX. 265, 276, 277
Floripas, in *Sir Ferumbras*, I. 302, 303
Florizel, in *The Winter's Tale*, V. 217
Florus, Lucius Annaeus, IV. 436
Florus of Lyons, I. 81
Floud, Rachel (d. 1640), VII. 250
Flower, Benjamin (1755–1829), XIV. 533
Flower, Eliza (1803–1846), XIII. 53
Flower, 'Maister,' V. 77
Flower, Sir William Henry (1831–1899), XIV. 295, 560
Flower and the Leaf, The, II. 162, 164, 166, 167, 215, 217 ff., 221, 223, 429
Flowerdales, the, in *The London Prodigall*, V. 254
Flowerdew, mistress, in *The Muses Looking-Glasse*, VI. 234
Flowers of the Forest, The, IX. 373; XI. 232
Fludd, Robert (1574–1637), IV. 278, 508; VII. 378; IX. 386
Fluellen, in *Henry V*, V. 189, 195; XIV. 307
Flügel, Ewald, XIII. 470, 471
Flute, in *A Midsummer-Night's Dream*, VI. 285
Flutter, Sir Fopling, in Etherege's *Man of Mode*, VIII. 138
Fly, in *The New Inne*, VI. 25

Flying Island, in *Gulliver's Travels*, IX. 104
Flying Post, IX. 5, 15, 432; XI. 333; XIV. 230
Flyting between Thomas Smith and William Gray, the, III. 490
Flytings, IV. 517
Foe, James, father of Defoe, Daniel, IX. 6
Foersom, P., V. 307
Fogg, Peter Walkden, XI. 250; XIII. 240
Foggo, A., XIII. 546
Fog's Weekly Journal, IX. 433
Foigny, Gabriel de, *Journey of Jacques Sadeur*, IX. 106
Foix, count of, in Froissart, II. 338
Foker, Henry, in *Pendennis*, XIII. 291, 292
Folio, Tom, in *The Tatler*, IX. 46
Foliot, Gilbert (d. 1187), I. 173, 449
Folk-drama and early pageantry, V. 24, 385
Folk-Lore Journal, The, XII. 518
Folk-lore Society, XII. 506
Follett, Sir William Webb (1798–1845), XIV. 509
Folly, in *Ane Pleasant Satyre*, III. 124, 129
Folly, in *Magnyfycence*, III. 77
Folly, in *The World and the Child*, II. 233; V. 54
Fonblanque, Albany, XIII. 558; XIV. 186, 198, 533
Fonblanque, E. B. de, XIV. 533
Fondlewife, in Congreve's *Old Bachelor*, VIII. 147, 149
Fonseca, Jeronymo Osorio da, IV. 444
Fontainebleau, V. 284
Fontainebleau, library at, IV. 429
Fontenelle, Bernard le Bovyer de, VIII. 261; IX. 477, 572; X. 464; *Dialogues of the Dead*, IX. 143; *Les Anciens et les Modernes*, IX. 390
Fonthill abbey, XI. 289; XII. 345, 508
Foolish Virgins, The, V. 11
Fools, feast of, V. 8
Foot, Jessé (1744–1826), X. 438
Foote, G. W., XIII. 489
Foote, Samuel (1720–1777), X. 82, 83, 87, 317, 430, 441; XI. 257, 260, 262, 448, 451, 453, 454; XIII. 514
  The Cozeners, XI. 278
  Maid of Bath, X. 88
  Minor, The, X. 88; XI. 451
  Piety in Pattens, X. 214
Fopling Flutters, X. 90
Foppington, lord, in Sheridan's *A Trip to Scarborough*, XI. 269
Foppington, lord, in Vanbrugh's *The Relapse*, VIII. 76, 160, 161, 164, 165, 170; X. 90; XI. 257, 269, 283
Forbes, Alexander Penrose (1817–1875), XII. 456
Forbes, Archibald (1838–1900), XIV. 173, 190
Forbes, Edward (1815–1854), XII. 339, 498; XIV. 210, 296, 560
Forbes, James (1749–1819), *Oriental Memoirs*, XIV. 334
Forbes, James David (1809–1868) XIV. 552
Forbes, John (1593–1648), IX. 544
Forbes, Patrick (1564–1635), IX. 544
Forbes, Robert (1708–1775), IX. 563, 564; *Journals*, X. 356
Forbes, Robert, in Pennecuick's *Presbyterian Pope*, IX. 370
Forbes, Sir William (1739–1806), X. 453, 480, 512; XIV. 601
Forbes, William Henry (1851–1914), XII. 483
Forçade, Eugène, XIII. 558
Forcellini, Egidio, XII. 335
Forcet, or Forsett, Edward, VI. 306, 481
Ford, in *The Merry Wives of Windsor*, V. 206
Ford, Charles (*fl.* 1726), IX. 103
Ford, E., *Fair Play in the Lottery* (1660), VII. 516
Ford, Emanuel (*fl.* 1607), *Parismus*, III. 359, 536; VI. 305; *Parismenos*, III. 359, 536
Ford, John (*fl.* 1639), IV. 353, 527; VI. 69, 96, 144, 182, 188–209 (main entry), 226, 424, 425, 447 ff.; VII. 3; XII. 415; XIII. 426
  Beauty in a Trance, VI. 195
  Bristowe Merchant, The, VI. 195
  Broken Heart, The, V. 347; VI. 186, 191; XII. 190
  Elegy on death of Charles Blount, earl of Devonshire, VI. 189
  Elegy on Mountjoy's death, V. 347
  Fairy Knight, The, VI. 54, 195
  Fame's Memorial, VI. 189, 191
  Fancies, Chart and Noble, The, VI. 193
  Honor Triumphant, VI. 189
  Ill Beginning has a Good End, An, VI. 195
  Ladies Triall, The, VI. 194
  Line of Life, A, VI. 189
  London Merchant, The, VI. 195
  Lover's Melancholy, The, VI. 190; VII. 36
  Loves Sacrifice, VI. 192
  Masque of Melancholy, VI. 190
  Monarches Meeting, The, VI. 189
  Perkin Warbeck, VI. 193
  Royal Combat, The, VI. 195
  Sun's Darling, The: A Moral Masque, V. 125; VI. 54, 190
  Tis Pitty Shees a Whore, VI. 192
  See, also, under Rowley, W. and Webster
Ford, joint lessee of Drury Lane theatre, X. 265
Ford, mistress, in *The Merry Wives of Windsor*, V. 169, 189
Ford, Richard (1796–1858), XIV. 251, 552; *Handbook for travellers in Spain*, XIV. 250
Ford, Thomas (d. 1648), IV. 113, 115, 464
Ford Lectures, XIV. 81
Forde, Thomas (*fl.* 1660), VII. 439, 457, 514, 517; VIII. 481; *Lusus Fortunae*, VIII. 377; *Times Anatomised*, VII. 384; *Virtus Rediviva*, VII. 444

Fordhook, Fielding's house, x. 35
Fordoun, Kincardineshire, II. 128
Fordun, John (d. 1384?), II. 128, 129, 132, 280, 451; *Scotichronicon*, IX. 535
Fordyce, William, XII. 510
Foreign Quarterly Review, The, XIII. 5
Foreign Review, The, XIII. 5
Foresight, in Congreve's *Love for Love*, VIII. 151
Foresight, in *King Hart*, II. 262
Foresight, Mrs, in Congreve's *Love for Love*, VIII. 152
Forest, in *Fortune by Land and Sea*, V. 361
Forest of Reason, in *Reason and Sensuality*, II. 202
Forfarshire, IX. 372; XIV. 436
Forgues, F. D., XIII. 549, 551
'Forland' (Caxton's egg-story), II. 316
Form of Living, The, or *Mending of Life* (school of Rolle), II. 46, 47
Forman, Harry Buxton, XII. 399 ff., 403 ff.; XIII. 480, 481, 491, 570; XIV. 527
Forman, Simon (1552–1611), V. 204; VI. 23, 460; VII. 369; VIII. 357
Forme of Cury, II. 71, 500
Formey, J. H. S., X. 482
Formosus, in *The Bugbears*, V. 115
Forneron, H., *Histoire de Philippe II*, X. 291
Forres, II. 100
Forrest, David William, XIV. 517
Forrest, Edwin, V. 308
Forrest, Old, in *Fortune by Land and Sea*, VI. 104
Forrest, Thomas (*fl.* 1580), IV. 437
Forrest, William (*fl.* 1581), IV. 476
Forrester, Alfred Henry ('Alfred Crowquill'), XIV. 201, 238
Forrester, Thomas (1635?–1706), IX. 546
Forsett, Edward (d. 1630?). *See* Forcet
Forshall, Frederick Hale, XIV. 598
Forshall, Josiah (1795–1863), II. 45, 73, 431; XII. 517
Forster, John (1812–1876), X. 195, 201, 202, 483; XII. 206, 211, 230, 303, 439, 441; XIII. 57, 58, 69, 471, 484, 485, 513, 530 ff.; XIV. 190, 198, 502, 598
Life of Charles Dickens, XIII. 305; XIV. 114
Life of Oliver Goldsmith, XIV. 113
Life of Swift, XIV. 114
Life of Walter Savage Landor, XIV. 114
Lives of the statesmen of the Commonwealth, XIV. 114
On English Freedom under Plantagenets and Tudors, XIV. 114
Förster, Max, I. 117; III. 277
Forster, William Edward (1818–1886), XIV. 427, 505, 509
Forster collection, X. 263
Forsyth, Joseph (1763–1815), XIV. 552
Forsyth, J. M., XIV. 467
Forsyth, William (1812–1899), XIV. 518
Forsyth, William (1818–1879), XIV. 533
Fortescue, George Knottesford (1847–1912), XII. 521
Fortescue, Sir John (1394?–1476?), II. 286, 296 ff., 307, 336, 481, 482; VIII. 315, 318, 465, 466, 469
De Laudibus Legum Angliae, II. 297; IV. 297, 511; VIII. 314
De Natura Legis Naturae, II. 296
Declaration, etc., II. 298
Monarchia (*The Difference between an Absolute and a Limited Monarchy*), II. 297
Understanding and Faith, II. 299
Fortescue, Sir John (1531?–1607), VI. 290
Fortescue, Lucy. *See* Lyttelton, Lucy
Fortescue, Thomas, *Foreste or Collection of Histories*, trans. from French, III. 536; IV. 446; VIII. 126
Fortescue, William (1687–1749), IX. 251
Forth, firth of, II. 88, 89, 100, 131; IX. 552; XII. 11; XIII. 6
Fortias-Santarelli, XIV. 490
Fortitude, in *The Passetyme of Pleasure*, II. 229
Fortnightly Review, The, XII. 296; XIII. 425, 440, 467
'Fortoun buik, Ane lytill,' IV. 414
Fortrey, Samuel (1622–1681), VIII. 367, 477
Fortune, in *Ara Fortunae*, VI. 319
Fortune, in *Ira seu Tumulus Fortunae*, VI 320
Fortune, in Drayton's *Robert of Normandy*, IV. 177
Fortune, in *Locrine*, V. 240
Fortune, in *Reason and Sensuality*, II. 203
Fortune, in *The Bowge of Courte*, III. 73
Fortune, in *The Example of Virtue*, II. 227, 228, 234
Fortune, in *The Kingis Quair*, II. 241, 242
Fortune, in *The Passetyme of Pleasure*, II. 228, 231, 234, 235
Fortune, in *Piers the Plowman*, II. 25, 26 28
Fortune, lady, in *Old Fortunatus*, VI. 52
Fortune, Sir Edward, in *Jacke Drums Entertainment*, VI. 41
Fortunia (play), VI. 486
Forty-one, VIII. 96
Forum, the (debating society), XI. 239
Fosbroke, Thomas Dudley (1770–1842), XII. 510
Foscari, in Byron's *The Two Foscari*, XII. 49
Foscari, in *The Gratefull Servant*, VI. 203
Fosco, count, in Wilkie Collins's *Woman in White*, XIII. 438
Foscolo, Ugo, XII. 384, 525; *Lettere di Jacopo Ortis*, XI. 288
Foskett, Bernard, X. 387
Foster, Elizabeth, Milton's grand-daughter (d. 1754), VII. 107; X. 461
Foster, Ernest, XIV. 531
Foster, George, VII. 509
Foster, Gregory, I. 143
Foster, James (1697–1753), X. 381, 521
Foster, John (1731–1774), XI. 250

Foster, John (1770–1843), XII. 286, 466, 472; XIV. 518; *On the Aversion of Men of Taste to Evangelical Religion*, XII. 281
Foster, Sir Michael (1836–1907), XIV. 295, 560
Foster, Myles Birket (1825–1899), XIV. 201
Foster, Samuel (d. 1652), VII. 488
Foster, W., XIV. 580
Fotherby, Martin (1549?–1619), *Atheomastix*, VII. 277, 471
Fotherby, Robert (*fl.* 1615), IV. 93
Fotheringay, Miss, in *Pendennis*, XIII. 276, 291
Fotheringham, Alma, Gissing's, XIII. 460
Fotheringham, James, XIII. 484
Fouché, Leo, XIV. Add. 7
Foulis, Andrew (1712–1775), XI. 342, 470
Foulis, Robert (1707–1776), XI. 342, 470
Foulis, R. and A., XII. 324, 530
Foulis press, IX. 262, 562, 567; X. 132
Fountain, Lucy, in Reade's *Love me Little, Love me Long*, XIII. 426
Fountainhall, lord. *See* Lauder, Sir John
Fouqué, Friedrich Karl Heinrich de la Motte, XIII. 4, 192, 465
Four Elements, A New Interlude and a Merry of the nature of the, IV. 70
Four Sirens, the, in *Filostrato e Panfila*, V. 62
Four Sons of Aymon, I. 292. *See under* Caxton
Foure Ages of England, The, VII. 408
Fourier, baron de, XIV. 267
Fowell, Frank, XIV. 536
Fowler, Sir Henry Hartley, viscount Wolverhampton (1830–1911), XIV. 511
Fowler, Thomas (1832–1904), XIV. 472
Fowler, William (*fl.* 1603), *The Triumphs of Petrarch*, III. 137
Fowler, William (1761–1832), XII. 510
Fowler, William Warde (1847–1921), XII. Add. 3; XIV. 521
Fowles, William, IV. 437
Fox, Caroline (1819–1871), XIV. 502
Fox, Charles James (1749–1806), X. 306; XI. 1, 2, 19, 34, 35, 51, 52 ff. (main entry), 143, 146, 389, 396, 405; XII. 151, 326, 439, 495; XIII. 24; XIV. 98, 119 ff., 132, 184, 214, 502
Fox, Edward Long, XI. 414
Fox, Elizabeth, countess of Ilchester, XI. 174
Fox, George (1624–1691), VII. 169, 509; VIII. 101, 110, 413, 414; XI. 167; XII. 198, 476; *Journal*, VII. 352; VIII. 103 ff.; IX. 307, 523; *The Great Mystery*, VIII. 111
Fox, Henry, 1st lord Holland (1705–1774), X. 388, 389
Fox, Henry Richard Vassall, 3rd lord Holland (1773–1840), XI. 174; XIV. 503
Fox, Joseph, XIV. 606
Fox, capt. Luke (1586–1635), IV. 107, 456; *North West Fox; or Fox from the North-West Passage*, IV. 106
Fox, Stephen, 1st earl of Ilchester, XI. 174
Fox, William Johnson (1786–1864), XII. 428, 466; XIII. 53, 54, 57; XIV. 132, 137, 509, 591, 601
Foxcroft, A. B., XIV. 584
Foxcroft, H. C., *Life of Gilbert Burnet*, IX. 195, 198, 202 ff., 208; *Supplement to Burnet's History*, IX. 201, 204, 205
Foxe, John (1516–1587), I. 124; II. 60, 294; V. 247; VI. 374; *Actes and Monuments* (*Book of Martyrs*), III. 26, 331 ff., 447, 528; IV. 389, 397, 400, 403, 433; VII. 322; *Book of Martyrs, The*, XI. 326, 369; XIV. 79; *Christus Triumphans*, V. 394
Foxe or Fox, John, of Woodbridge (*fl.* 1577), IV. 84
Foxe or Fox, Richard (1448?–1528), III. 468
Foxwell, Herbert Somerton, XIV. 4
Foy, VI. 101
Fracastor, Girolamo, IX. 60
Fracastorius, IV. 261
Fragmenta Aulica, VIII. 470
Fragmenta Regalia, XII. 376
Frail, Mrs, in Congreve's *Love for Love*, VIII. 152
Framlingham, II. 305
Frampton, in Mrs Griffith's *School for Rakes*, XI. 263
Frampton, John (*fl.* 1577–1596), IV. 446, 530
Frampul, lord and lady, in *The New Inne* VI. 25
France, II. 340; V. 25 ff., 34, 38, 43, 44, 49, 55, 58, 91, 121, 123, 137, 140, 222, 262, 284 ff., 288, 291, 299, 303, 306, 308, 334, 341, 344, 355, 359; VI. 5, 90, 175, 270, 271, 365; VII. 21, 22, 54, 61 ff., 180, 191, 197, 200, 205, 214, 221, 234, 282, 283, 285, 286, 301, 306 ff., 338, 381, 437; VIII. 11, 142, 206, 245, 256, 263, 265, 267, 296, 314, 330, 342, 364, 380, 384, 385; IX. 6 ff., 11, 13, 37, 81, 89, 95, 118, 130, 132, 142, 216, 218, 224 ff., 228, 229, 231, 232, 237, 256, 257, 265, 280, 332, 365, 390, 395, 396, 401, 406; X. 16, 17, 41, 47, 49, 63, 78, 79, 115, 119, 159, 182, 200, 219 ff., 261, 264, 274, 282, 283, 302, 306, 322, 323, 335, 336, 353, 388; XI. 1, 7, 22 ff., 25, 26, 30, 39, 42, 44, 47, 50, 71, 73, 97, 98, 118, 136, 189, 344, 374, 380, 382; XII. 26, 27, 30, 31, 43, 59, 174, 254, 276, 282, 343, 367; XIII. 20, 88, 119, 132, 211, 238, 357, 372, 428, 437, 444, 445; XIV. 42, 53, 57, 60, 110, 122, 151, 178, 179, 182, 183, 188, 192, 215, 292 ff., 322, 324, 382, 383, 388, 392, 399, 404, 419, 437
France, Hazlitt in, XII. 432
France, Martin de, *Le Champion des Dames*, VIII. 59
France, trials for sorcery in, VI. 183
France and Byron, XII. 392, 394 ff.
France and Shelley, XII. 403
Frances, Madame, in *The Tatler*, IX. 50
Francesca, I. 363

Francesco, in *Never too late*, III. 360
Francesco, grand duke of Florence, VI. 174, 175
Francillon, Robert E., XIII. 567; XIV. 528
Francis I, king of France, III. 46, 158, 160, 163, 224, 437; X. 105
Francis, John (1811–1882), XIV. 200, 534; *History of the Athenaeum*, XIV. 174
Francis, Philip (1708?–1773), X. 389, 408, 455, 523; *Letter from the Cocoa-Tree*, X. 390
Francis, Sir Philip (1740–1818), X. 400, 401, 405, 408 ff., 522, 526, 527; XI. 17; XIV. 513
Francis, St, I. 200, 201, 339; III. 159; X. 367
Franciscans, the (Minorites, Grey Friars), I. 200 ff., 209; II. 66, 71, 251, 255, 349, 350; III. 57, 92, 123, 159, 162; IV. 419; V. 13; VII. 303, 337; VIII. 59; IX. 538
Franciscans in Cambridge, I. 200; II. 349, 350
Franciscans in Oxford, I. 200 ff., 452 ff.; II. 349, 350
Franciscans in St Andrews, II. 370
Francisco, in *The Duke of Millaine*, VI. 155, 159
Francisco, in *The Renegado*, VI. 157
Francisco, in *The White Divel*, VI. 176
Francison, A., XIII. 471
Franck, Richard (1624?–1708), XII. 376
Franck, Sebastien, IX. 315
Francklin, Richard (1624?–1708), IX. 220, 221
Francklin, Thomas (1721–1784), X. 41, 128, 420, 431; *Orestes*, X. 86, 439
Franckton, John, IV. 414
Franco-Prussian war, XIV. 173, 182, 190, 192, 328
Francorum, Gesta Regum, I. 26. *See, also*, Gregory of Tours
Franeker university, in Friesland, VII. 308
Frank, in *The Witch of Edmonton*, VI. 190
Frank, Elizabeth, XII. 505
Frank, Mark (1613–1664), VII. 147, 424
Frankenstein, in Mary Shelley's novel, XII. 248
Frankford, Mrs, in *A Woman Kilde with Kindnesse*, VI. 84, 98
Frankfort-on-the-Main, III. 144, 434; IV. 366, 403, 545, 548; *also see* Add.; VII. 304, 308; XI. 331
Frankish law, VIII. 311
Frankland, Sir Edward (1825–1899), XIV. 272, 277, 557
Frankland, Richard (1630–1698), IX. 392; X. 386
Franklin, in *Arden of Feversham*, V. 240
Franklin, Benjamin, XII. 165; XIV. 394
Franklin, Sir John (1786–1847), XIV. 245, 552, 583
Franks, in *Beowulf*, etc., I. 25, 26, 32, 34
Franks, Sir Augustus Wollaston (1826–1897), XII. 347, 510
Franks casket, I. 12, 426
'Frantics,' in *The Lords' Masque*, VI. 353
Fraser, Alexander Campbell (1819–1914), IX. 280; XIV. 473
Berkeley, XIV. 47
Berkeley and Spiritual Realism, XIV. 47
Biographia Philosophica, XIV. 48
Essays in Philosophy, XIV. 47
Locke, XIV. 47
Philosophy of Theism, The, XIV. 48
Fraser, James (1818–1885), XIV. 606
Fraser, Peter, XIV. 180
Fraser, Simon, 12th lord Lovat (1667?–1747), IX. 563, 564
Fraser's Magazine, XII. 159, 163, 427, 431, 441; XIII. 10, 95, 278 ff., 347, 356, 360, 362, 465; XIV. 20, 86, 152, 161, 316
Fraunce, Abraham (*fl.* 1587–1633), III. 425, 432, 551; IV. 436, 476; VIII. 238
Aminta, VI. 365, 490
Arcadian Rhetorike, The, III. 432
Countess of Pembrokes Emanuell, The, IV. 131
Countess of Pembrokes Yvychurch, The, IV. 131
Nativity, The, IV. 131
Victoria, VI. 304, 472
Fraunhofer, Joseph von, XIV. 266
Fraus Pia, VI. 483
Frazer, Hugh, XIV. 536
Frazer, James (1818–1885), bishop of Manchester, XIII. 553
Frazer, Sir James George, XI. 85
Frazer, Robert Watson, XIV. 574
Frazer, William (1817–1879), XIV. 602
Fréchette, Louis, XIV. 356
Frederica, in Jane Austen's *Lady Susan*, XII. 233
Frederick, in *A Wife for a Month*, VI. 122, 132
Frederick, in Mrs Gaskell's *North and South*, XIII. 378
Frederick, in *The Weakest goeth to the Wall*, V. 316
Frederick II, emperor, I. 199; VII. 102, 159
Frederick V, elector Palatine and king of Bohemia, IV. 259; VI. 148, 149, 250, 321, 353
Frederick, Don, in *The Chances*, VI. 135
Frederick, duke, in *As You Like It*, V. 192
Frederick, lord, in *Nicholas Nickleby*, XIII. 317
Frederick, Louis, prince of Wales (1707–1751), IX. 230, 251; X. 94, 95, 108, 110; XIV. 287
Frederick, Sir, in *The Returne from Pernassus*, VI. 313
Frederick, William III, king of Prussia, XIV. 416
Frederick the Great, XII. 410; XIII. 18, 19; XIV. 63, 382, 416
Frederick of Jennen, II. 329

Freedom, in *She Would if She Could*, VIII. 138
Freedom's Farewell, IX. 376
Freeholder, The, IX. 437
Freelove, lady, in Colman's *Jealous Wife*, X. 89, 90
Freeman, in *Discoverie of the Knights of the Poste*, IV. 350
Freeman, in Wycherley's *Country Wife*, VIII. 145
Freeman, Anthony, in *The Spectator*, IX. 57
Freeman, Edward Augustus (1823–1892), I. 163, 171, 197, 199; II. 399; VII. 330; X. 313; XII. 261, 271, 321, 379, 475; XIV. 62, 67, 69 ff. (main entry), 76, 85, 86, 99, 101, 198, 487
Greek People and the Greek Kingdom, The, XIV. 71
Historical Essays, XII. 308, 316
Historical Geography, XIV. 72
History and Conquests of the Saracens, XIV. 71
History of Architecture, XIV. 71
History of Federal Government, XII. 315; XIV. 71
History of the Norman Conquest, XII. 316; XIV. 71 ff.
History of Sicily, XII. 316
History of Wells Cathedral, XII. 348
Old English History for Children, XIV. 72
Poems, legendary and historical (with G. W. Cox), XII. 314; XIV. 70
Reign of William Rufus, The, XIV. 73
Freeman, Thomas (*fl.* 1614), IV. 520
Freeman's Journal, The, XIV. 318
Freemantle, H. E. S., XIV. Add. 7
Freeport, Sir Andrew, in *The Spectator*, IX. 51, 52
Freher, Dionysius (1649–1728), IX. 308, 520
Freiligrath, Ferdinand, V. 303
Freind, Robert (1667–1751), IX. 151, 153, 217, 250
Freiris of Berwick, IX. 367
Freke, Harriot, in Miss Edgeworth's *Belinda*, XI. 297
Freke, William (1662–1744), X. 377
French, Samuel, XIII. 516
French, the, X. 40, 255, 264, 282, 294; XI. 28; XII. 326; XIII. 282, 283, 339, 446; XIV. 173, 195, 213, 223, 225, 230, 247, 328
French academy, V. 293, 294; VIII. 369, 371; X. 173; XI. 354; XIV. 264
French actresses, VI. 404; VIII. 118
French artists, XIV. 214
French characters in English plays, VIII. 144
French constituent assembly, XI. 71
French dancers, XI. 282
French directory, XI. 26
French drama, X. 78, 81, 86, 211; XI. 281, 354; XIII. 265, 267, 270, 272
French economists, XIV. 381
French education, IX. 399; X. 283: XIV 391, 423, 428
French *émigrés*, X. 66, 261
French empire, XI. 103
French fleet, X. 291
French historians, IX. 227; XII. 271; XIV. 102
French institutions, X. 42
French interest in Shakespeare, V. 209, 287–296
French invasion panic, the, XIV. 137
French July revolution, XIII. 357
French king, the, in *The Duke of Millaine*, VI. 158, 163
French lady, in *Godfrey of Bulloigne*, VI. 89
French language and literature: IX. 4, 26, 30, 214, 233, 267, 276, 331, 385, 390, 393, 395, 402 ff., 410, 412, 413; X. 17, 60, 69, 71, 90, 114, 120, 123, 135, 173, 174, 202 ff., 241, 250, 257, 259, 281, 283 ff., 288 ff., 296, 302, 303, 305, 313, 316, 317, 319, 323; XI. 58, 59, 181, 224, 289, 291, 292, 295 ff., 327, 330, 332, 334, 347, 353 ff., 359, 382; XII. 3, 154, 208, 247, 254, 308, 328; XIII. 99, 124, 129, 162, 199, 208, 213, 219, 259, 263, 346; XIV. 62, 107, 185, 224, 306, 327, 333, 342, 358, 360, 385, 387, 388, 391, 406, 408, 434, 438, 442, 455, 457, 458; (French, Old): no more spoken in England, II. 70; influence on our medieval poetry, (carols), II. 376, (songs), 377, 384 ff., 388 ff.; in legal works, VIII. 313 ff., 319; writers of, II. 507 ff.; (Renascence): influence of, on Chapman, VI. 33, 172; on Hobbes, VII. 266, 268, 269; and translation, VII. 263; (17th century): influence of, VIII. 124, 186 ff., 194, 214, 270, 321, 322, 332, 371 ff.; on Dryden, VIII. 23, 56; on satire, VIII. 59; on Temple, VIII. 381, 383, 385; *see, also*, Hamilton, Anthony. *See, also*, French poets and poetry; French stage, etc.
French encyclopedists, XIII. 19; XIV. 402
French *fabliaux*, XI. 175
French fiction, XIII. 283, 442, 456
French novelists, X. 18
French octave, the, or ballad royal, XI. 217
French law, XII. 354
French mathematicians, XIV. 258
French *mélodrame*, XIII. 263, 264
French music, in *Albion and Albanius*, VIII. 30
French mysticism, VII. 155
French national assembly, XI. 12, 21 ff., 26; XII. 144
French national convention, IX. 386; XI. 47
French opera, IX. 163; XIII. 256
French oratory, XII. 268
French periodicals, VII. 360
French *philosophes*, X. 296
French pietism, XII. 262

French poets and poetry, IX. 67; X. 79, 217, 219; XI. 209; XII. 4, 354; XIII. 129, 140, 210 ff., 252
French prosody, VIII. 239
French romances, V. 314; VI. 239, 240; VII. 74, 391
French romantic school, X. 181; XIII. 9
French sonnet writers, V. 173, 230
French translations, VI. 124; VII. 263; VIII. 123, 126 ff.
French troubadours, IX. 365
French press, V. 286, 295
French prints, XIV. 215
French publicists, XI. 42
French queen, in *The Conspiracie and Tragedie of Charles Duke of Byron*, VI. 30
French 'Reign of Terror,' XIV. 459
French revolution, II. 81; V. 197, 294; IX. 213, 233; X. 43, 59, 251, 318; XI. 4, 6, 14, 16, 19, 21, 22, 25 ff., 39, 44, 47, 79, 97, 106, 117, 118, 138, 155, 190, 194, 225, 236, 430, 433, *also see* Add.; XII. 39, 107, 149, 164, 249, 279, 310, 429; XIII. 2, 10, 11, 19, 257, 258, 300, 345, 420; XIV. 50, 66, 187, 214, 215, 382
French society, IX. 243
French stage, the:
Classical, V. 1, 61, 63, 76, 91
Medieval, V. 36, 39 ff., 46, 52
Influence on English drama, VIII. 13 ff., 28, 29, 31, 131 ff., 157, 162, 179 ff., 187; X. 108
French theatres, XI. 265
French theology, XII. 254
French wines, V. 358
French-Canadians, XIV. 348, 354
Frenchman, in *A Woman will have her Will*, V. 329
Frend, William (1757–1841), XII. 279, 466, 467; XIV. 591, 593
Frere, Sir Bartle (1815–1884), XI. 392
Frere, John Hookham (1769–1846), XI. 39, 40, 392; XII. 52, 394; XIII. 175, 236, 238, 241, 246, 502; XIV. 206, 387; *Brunanburh*, X. 487
Frere and the Boye, The, II. 501, 502
Fréron, Élie Catherine, X. 264
Frescobaldi, in *Cromwell*, V. 247
Freund, Wilhelm, XII. 335
Freyr (Old Norse alphabet), I. 10
Friar, The, and the Boy, XI. 334
Friar Rush, II. 507; III. 94, 488
Friars, poems against, II. 443
Friars Minor. *See* Franciscans
Fribourg, XIV. 404
Fricker, Edith. *See* Southey, Mrs
Fricker, Sara. *See* Coleridge, Mrs
Frideswide, in *The Golden Legend*, II. 335
Friedrich, J., X. 454
Friend, Sir John (d. 1696), VIII. 163
Friends, society of, VIII. 112, and *ante*; XIV. 271
Friendship's Offering, XIV. 149
Frigidianus, bishop, I. 105
Frische Haff, the, I. 94
Frisco, in *A Woman will have her Will*, V. 330
Friscobaldo, Orlando, in *The Honest Whore*, VI. 53
Friscus, in Marston's *Scourge of Villanie*, IV. 332
Frisians, XIV. 68
Frisians, the, in *Beowulf*, I. 24 ff., 31
Frisius, Gemma, IV. 73, 74
'Frissis, Duk of,' in Wyntoun's *Chronicle*, II. 131
Frith, John (1503–1533), III. 26, 31, 40, 41, 140, 473; IV. 40; *Disputation of Purgatory*, III. 40; *The Revelation of Anti-Christ*, III. 39; *The Supper of the Lord*, III. 40
Friuli, IX. 150
Frizer, Ingram, V. 142
Frobel, John, of Basel, III. 41
Froben, J., II. 322; IV. 403
Frobisher, Martin (1535?–1594), IV. 73, 74, 76, 85, 88, 456; VII. 305
Froda, in *Beowulf*, I. 24, 25
Froebel, Friedrich, IX. 389; XIV. 394, 600, 608
Frog, Nicholas, in Arbuthnot's *History of John Bull*, IX. 134, 135
Frogges of Egypt, IV. 530
Frohman, Daniel, XIII. 514
Froissart, Jean, I. 213, 358; II. 159; V. 244; IX. 236; X. 133, 135; XIII. 428; *Chronicles*, II. 228, 322, 336, 338, 340: V. 246; XII. 146
Frollicke, Sir Frederick, in Etherege's *She Would if She Could*, VIII. 138
Frollo, I. 236
Fronia, in *The Misfortunes of Arthur*, V. 78
Frontinus, II. 366
Froschover, C., II. 322; III. 44
Frost, Thomas, XIII. 543; XIV. 534
Frost, Walter, *A Briefe Relation*, VII. 354
Frost, The Great, IV. 532
Frost's Lives of Eminent Christians, XIII. 455
Froth, Abraham, in *The Spectator*, IX. 57
Froth, lady, in Congreve's *Double-Dealer*, VIII. 149, 375; XI. 266
Froth, lord, in Congreve's *Double-Dealer*, VIII. 149, 156
Fróði (Frotho IV), I. 25
Frotho I, I. 28
Froude, James Anthony (1818–1894), IV. 45, 96; VII. 178; XII. 179, 255, 292, 319, 430, 445, 456, 460, *also see* Add. 1, 2; XIII. 17, 18, 358, 424, 467, 469, 471, 547; XIV. 83 ff., 96, 152, 488, 552
Council of Trent, The, XIV. 86
England's Forgotten Worthies, XIV. 84
English in Ireland, The, XIV. 86, 105
English Seamen in the Sixteenth Century, XIV. 86
History of England, XIII. 369; XIV. 84 ff.
Life and Letters of Erasmus, XIV. 86
Life of Carlyle, XIV. 86
Nemesis of Faith, The, XIV. 84
'Scientific Method Applied to History, The,' XIV. 85

Froude, James Anthony
Short Studies, XIV. 85, 86
Froude, Richard Hurrell (1803–1836), XII. 257 ff., 454 ff., 461; *Remains*, XII. 258, 259
Froumond, I. 101
Frugal, Luke, in *The City Madam*, VI. 160
Fry, Elizabeth (1780–1845), VIII. 114
Fry, Francis (1803–1886), XII. 521
Fry, John (1609–1657), X. 377
Fryer, John (d. 1733), XIV. 576; *New Account of East India and Persia*, XIV. 333
Fryer Bacon, The Famous Historie of, I. 210
Fuess, Claude Moore, *Lord Byron as a Satirist in Verse*, XII. 55
Fueter, E., XIV. 484; *Geschichte der neueren Historiographie*, XIV. 107
Fugitive tracts in verse, 1403–1600, V. 478
Fulbecke, William (1560–1603?), III. 551; VIII. 468
Fulke, William (1538–1589), III. 446, 473; IV. 508; *Confutation of the Rhemish Testament*, IV. 389
Fuller, XII. 434
Fuller, Nicholas (1557?–1626), VII. 317, 482
Fuller, Robert H., XIV. Add. 7
Fuller, Thomas (1608–1661), II. 190, 353; III. 50, 324, 328, 332, 426, 463, 473; IV. 12, 14, 245, 370, 420; VII. 158, 232, 244–249 (main entry), 253, 256 ff., 462; XIV. 460
Abel Redivivus, VII. 248
Andronicus, VII. 248
Appeal of Injured Innocence, VII. 246
Church History, VII. 207, 246 ff.; VIII. 15
Davids Heinous Sin, VII. 244
Good Thoughts in Bad Times, VII. 245, 247
History of the University of Cambridge, The, VI. 307; VII. 248
Holy and Profane State, The, VII. 245, 247, 248
Holy War, The, VII. 245, 247, 248
'Pisgah Sights,' VII. 248
Worthies of England, The, IV. 308, 511; VII. 246 ff.
Fuller, Thomas, father of Thomas Fuller, VII. 244
Fuller, Sir Thos. E., XIV. Add. 7
Fullerton, lady Georgiana Charlotte (1812–1885), XIII. 562
Fulman, William (1632–1688), IX. 533
Fulmers, the, in Cumberland's *West Indian*, XI. 264
Fulston St Peter's, Wilts., VII. 29
Fulwell, Ulpian (*fl.* 1586), *Like will to Like*, V. 57, 393; VI. 284
Fun, XIV. 196, 239
Fungoso, in *Every Man out of His Humour*, VI. 40
Furetière, Antoine, IX. 256; *Le roman Bourgeois*, X. 26
Furlong, Thomas (1794–1827), XIV. 312, 568
Furly, Benjamin (1636–1714), VIII. 414
Furneaux, Henry (1829–1900), XII. 483
Furness, Horace Howard, V. 308; VI. 305
Furnivall, Frederick James (1825–1910), I. ix, 344; II. 166, 216, 424 ff.; VI. 375; IX. 361; X. 233; XII. 504; XIII. 484; XIV. 408, 506; *An English Miscellany* presented to, II. 504
Fursey, the Irish hermit, vision of, in Bede, I. 82, 86
'Fusbos,' *pseud.* *See* Plunkett, Henry Grattan
Fuscara (Cleiveland's), VII. 93
Fuscus, in *The Scourge of Folly*, IV. 334
Fuseli, Henry (1741–1825), XIV. 214
Futhy. *See* Fethe
Fy, let us all to the Bridal, X. 233
Fyfe, Thomas Alexander, XIII. 543
Fyffe, Charles Alan (1845–1892), XIV. 488
Fyfield elm, the, XIII. 93
Fyn, in Dunbar's *Interlude*, II. 255
Fyshe, Simon. *See* Fish
Fyve Bestis, Talis of the, II. 279, 280

G. Al., V. 72
G. S. B., *A Study of the Prologue and Epilogue in English Literature*, VIII. 34
Gaberlunzie Man, The, III. 130; IX. 560; XI. 218
Gaboriau, Émile, XIII. 437
Gabriel, in Cowley's *Davideis*, VII. 66, 67
Gabriel, in *The Example of Virtue*, II. 227
Gabriel, the angel, I. 115; II. 382
Gabrielson, Arvid, XIII. 512
Gace, William (*fl.* 1580), IV. 446
Gadbury, John (1627–1704), VII. 509
Gaddesden. *See* John of
Gadshill place, XIII. 332
Gaelic language and literature, I. 464; IX. 377, 559; X. 225, 229 ff., 487; XII. 24; XIV. 302 ff., 357, 457, 458
Gaelic league, the, XIV. 305
Gage, Sir Henry (1597–1645), VII. 454
Gage, Thomas (d. 1656), *A New Survey of the West Indies*, IV. 97, 456
Gager, William (*fl.* 1580–1619), V. 82; VI. 318, 324, 378, 399, 409, 472, 491
Dido, VI. 303
Meleager, VI. 302
Oedipus, VI. 303
Rivales, V. 128; VI. 302, 303, 398
Ulysses Redux, VI. 303, 327, 398
Gaguin, Robert, III. 71
Gahagan, major Goliah O'Grady, *pseud.* of W. M. Thackeray, XIII. 279
Gailhard, Jean, *The Compleat Gentleman*, IX. 397, 569
Gaillard, Michel, IV. 527
Gaimar, Geoffrey (d. 1140), *Estorie des Engles*, etc., I. 104, 170, 236, 264, 446; II. 420, 508
Gainsborough, Thomas (1727–1788), X. 267
Gainsford, captain Francis, VII. 345
Gainsford, Thomas, VI. 493; *Perkin Warbeck*, VI. 193

Gair, J., IX. 371
Gairdner, James (1828–1912), II. 67; XII. 356; XIV. 485, 489
Divine Right of Kings, The, XIV. 83
Historical Element in Shakespeare's Falstaff, The, XIV. 83
History of the English Church, vol. iv, XIV. 83
Life of Richard III, XIV. 82
Lollardy and the Reformation, XIV. 83
Studies in English History (with J. Spedding), XIV. 82, 83
Gaisford, Thomas (1779–1855), XII. 327, 328, 333, 483, 484, 491
Gaius, XII. 492
Galafridus de Vino Salvo. *See* Geoffrey de Vinsauf
Galahad, in Arthurian legend, I. 271
Galahad, Sir, Tennyson's, XIII. 29
Galán escarmentado, El, VIII. 16
Galaor, VII. 75
Galatea, III. 224
Galathea, in Lyly's *Galathea*, V. 126
Gale, Roger (1672–1744), IX. 355, 358, 533, 534; XII. 350
Gale, Samuel (1682–1754), IX. 358, 533
Gale, Theophilus (1628–1678), VII. 471, *also see* Add.; X. 385; *Court of the Gentiles*, VII. 303
Gale, Thomas (1507–1587), IV. 444
Gale, Thomas (1635?–1702), IX. 355, 534
Galen, Claudius, I. 192, 193; II. 365; III. 5, 6, 20, 21, 23, 427, 433; IV. 444; VIII. 350; XII. 521
Galeron of Galloway, in *Awntyrs of Arthure*, I. 312; II. 122, 123
Gali, Francisco de, *Discourse of the East and West Indies*, IV. 78
Galicia, XIV. 294
Galignani's Messenger, XII. 383
Galileo Galilei, IV. 278, 290; VII. 100, 283, 292; VIII. 276, 282, 338, 350, 352, 358; XIV. 27; *Dialogue*, VII. 284
Galiot, in *Golagros and Gawane*, II. 124
Gall, Richard (1776–1801), *Farewell to Ayrshire*, XI. 234; *Now Bank and Brae*, XI. 234; *Poems and Songs*, XI. 234, 443
Gallant, A Treatise of a, III. 98, 491
Gallant Grahams, The, IX. 373
Galley late come into England from Terra Nova, III. 87, 482
Gallia Christiana, X. 282
Gallican liberties, VIII. 308
Gallienus Redivivus, XIV. 65
Gallio, in Hall's *Virgidemiarum*, IV. 331
Gallipoli, XIV. 367
Galloway, II. 99, 101, 104; VII. 79; XI. 446
Galloway, lady, X. 64
'Galloway poet,' the. *See* Nicholson, William
Gallus, III. 224
Gallus, Evaldus, *Pueriles Confabulatiunculae*, XI. 367
Gally, Henry (1696–1769), XI. 250
Galt, John (1779–1839), X. 445; XII. 30, 384, 385, 394, 449; XIII. 377; XIV. 188
Annals of the Parish, The, XI. 64; XII. 251
The Ayrshire Legatees, XII. 251
The Entail, XII. 251
The Last of the Lairds, XII. 251
Galton, Arthur Howard, XIII. 488
Galton, Sir Francis (1822–1911), XIV. 473, 560
Galvano, Antony, *Discoveries of the World*, IV. 83, 444, 457
Galway, Queen's college, XIV. 417
Gama, Vasco da, IV. 68, 82, 86
Gamba, count Pietro, XII. 35, 36, 38, 384
Gamba family, the, XII. 36, 37
Gambado, Geoffrey. *See* Bunbury, Henry William
Gamble, John (d. 1687), VII. 83
Gamble, William, XIV. 532
Gambol, in *The Masque of Christmas*, VI. 358, 359
Game, The Master of, II. 286
Game of Cardes, Comedie or Morrall devised on, VI. 286
Gamelyn, Tale of, I. 289, 298, 299, 367, 468; II. 162, 164, 178, 194 ff., 211, 215, 216, 467; III. 279, 358; V. 193, 220; XIII. 252
Gammer Gurton's Garland, XI. 375
Gammer Gurton's Needle, II. 233; V. 111; VI. 296, 297, 478
Gamp, Sarah, in *Martin Chuzzlewit*, XIII. 304, 323
Gandersheim, V. 6, 7
Gandy, Henry (1649–1734), X. 355
Ganymede, II. 175
Ganymede (Barnfield's), III. 264; IV. 120, 126
Gaping Wide-mouthed Waddling Frog, XI. 386
Garbett, James (1802–1879), XIII. 171
Garçon et l'Aveugle, Le, V. 25
Garden, Francis (1810–1884), XII. 454
Garden, George (1649–1733), IX. 519, 520
Garden, James (1647–1726), IX. 520
Garden of Delight, in *Reason and Sensuality*, II. 202
Gardening, writers on, IV. 542
Gardiner, Edmund, *The Triall of Tabacco*, IV. 349, 531
Gardiner, col. James (1688–1745), IX. 563
Gardiner, R., *England's Grievance Discovered*, VII. 507
Gardiner, Samuel Rawson (1829–1902), IV. 42; VI. 148, 149; VII. 190; IX. 193; XIII. 480; XIV. 99, 489, 500
Cromwell's Place in History, XIV. 88
History of England, XIV. 87
Letters and Documents illustrating the relations between England and Germany, XIV. 88
Parliamentary Debates in 1610, XIV. 87
Thirty Years' War, The, XIV. 88

Gardiner, Stephen (1483?–1555), bishop of Winchester, III. 33, 81, 194, 418 ff., 444, 474; V. 365; VI. 91, 296, 397, 475; *Contra Turneri vulpem*, III. 81; *Explication and Assertion of the true Catholic Faith*, III. 33
Gardiner and Mullinger, *Introduction to the Study of English History*, XII. 356
Gardner, Alan Gardner, 1st lord (1742–1809), XIV. 245
Gardyne, Alexander (1585?–1634?), IX. 555
Gareth, in Malory, I. 295
Garfit, Arthur, XIV. 591
Gargantua (Rabelais), II. 256, 258; IV. 8
Gargantua his Prophecie, IV. 9
Gargantua's mare, VIII. 67
Gargery, Joe, in *Great Expectations*, XIII. 334
Garibaldi, Giuseppe, XIII. 132
Garland, John, *Organum*, XIV. 308
Garlandia, Joannes de (*fl.* 1230), I. 193, 194, 453; III. 84
Garnesche, Christopher. *See under* Skelton
Garnett, Edward, XIV. 527, 601
Garnett, Henry (1555–1606), IV. 127; VIII. 85, 86
Garnett, Richard (1835–1906), IV. 111; XI. 412, 434, 462, 463; XII. 159, 248, 399 ff., 412, 435, 444, 521; XIII. 194, 464, 467, 471, 476, 481, 499, 503; XIV. 509, 518, 601; *Twilight of the Gods, The*, XIV. 144
Garnett, Robert S., XIII. 530
Garnier, Robert, V. 63, 163; VI. 366; VIII. 13, 133; *Marc-Antoine*, V. 334; *Cornélie*, V. 157, 334; *Porcie*, V. 157
Garnier de Pont-Sainte-Maxence, *Vie de St Thomas Becket*, II. 420, 508
Garonne, river, XIV. 302
Garraway, Anne, VII. 232
Garret (a London character), IV. 360
Garrett, Edmund, XIV. 534
Garrett, F. E., XIV. Add. 7
Garrick, David (1717–1779), V. 291, 298; VI. 28, 262, 323; VIII. 184, 191, 196; X. 36, 39, 40, 71, 72, 82, 83, 85 ff., 90, 91, 128, 161, 172, 204, 211, 212, 214, 215, 260, 261, 263 ff. (main entry), 268, 395, 405, 426, 428, 429, 432 ff., 437 ff., 441, 445, 460, 461, 471, 483, 493; XI. 257 ff., 264, 265, 271, 282, 284, 360 ff., 448 ff., 453, 454; XII. 180, 200
  Bon Ton, X. 88
  Cymon, XI. 282
  Gamesters, X. 86
  Irish Widow, X. 88
  Lethe, X. 85
  Lying Valet, X. 88
  Miss in her Teens, X. 88
Garrick, Eva Marie Violetti, X. 268
Garrick and Colman, *The Clandestine Marriage*, X. 211
Garrick collection (British Museum), V. 35
Garrick plays, XII. 436
'Garrison, The,' in Smollett's *Peregrine Pickle*, X. 38
Garter, Order of the, I. 328; II. 38; IX. 355
Garth, Caleb, in *Middlemarch*, XIII. 382
Garth, Sir Samuel (1661–1719), VIII. 410, 411; IX. 75, 151, 175, 177 ff. (main entry), 485; X. 156; XI. 246; *Claremont*, IX. 179; *Dispensary, The*, IX. 179, 333
Gartha, in D'Avenant's *Gondibert*, VII. 71
Garulf, in *Finnsburh*, I. 31
Gascoigne, George (1525?–1577), III. 201–210 (main entry), 248, 249, 281, 282, 284, 285, 296 ff., 302, 303, 312, 447, 448, 517 ff., 526, *also see* Add.; IV. 52, 73, 329, 441; V. 70 ff., 120, 181, 344, 386, 394, 402 ff.; VII. 271; XI. 248; XIII. 253
  Adventures of Master F. J., The, III. 205, 206
  Certayne notes of Instruction in English, III. 206, 207, 281, 296
  Complaint of Phylomene, The, III. 207
  Councell given to Master Bartholmew Withipoll, III. 203, 205, 206
  Dan Bartholmew of Bathe, III. 203, 205, 210, 484
  Delicate Diet, for daintie mouthd Droonkardes, A, III. 207
  Droome of Doomes daie, The, III. 207, 208
  Dulce Bellum inexpertis, III. 202, 206
  Ferdinando Jeronimi, VI. 192
  Fetters, The fruite of, III. 206
  Glasse of Government, The, III. 207; V. 113, 114
  Gloze upon this text, Dominus iis opus habet, A, III. 207, 208
  Grief of Joye, The, III. 207
  Hemetes the heremyte, The Tale of, III. 202, 205, 207, 208
  Hollande, Voyage into, III. 203, 206
  Hundreth sundrie Flowers, A, III. 205; IV. 399
  Jocasta, III. 203, 206; IV. 4; V. 70 ff., 76, 77, 396, 399
  Posies, IV. 399
  Princelye Pleasures, The, III. 210
  Spoyle of Antwerp, The, III. 208; IV. 324
  Steele Glas, The, III. 202, 205, 207, 209; VIII. 223
  Supposes, III. 203, 204, 206; V. 114, 115, 220; VIII. 126
  Weedes, III. 202
Gascoigne, Sir John (father of George Gascoigne), III. 202
Gascoigne, Thomas (1403–1458), chancellor of Oxford university, II. 66, 157, 294, 496; IV. 419, 428
Gascony, II. 293
Gascoyne-Cecil, Robert A. T., 3rd marquis of Salisbury (1830–1903), XII. 155, 430; XIV. 134, 196, 198, 511
Gashford, in *Barnaby Rudge*, XIII. 320
Gaskell, Elizabeth Cleghorn (1810–1865), XIII. 326, 345, 371 ff. (main entry), 386, 408, 431, 458, 549 ff., 555, 558
  Cousin Phillis, XIII. 371, 380, 403, 406
  Cranford, XIII. 371, 376 ff., 381, 403, 430

Gaskell, Elizabeth Cleghorn
Life of Charlotte Brontë, XIII. 379, 403, 414
Lizzie Leigh, XIII. 371, 373
Manchester Marriage, The, XIII. 379
Mary Barton, XIII. 362, 371 ff., 381, 403
Moorland Cottage, The, XIII. 377
Mr Harrison's Confessions, XIII. 371, 376, 377
My Lady Ludlow, XIII. 379
North and South, XIII. 375, 378, 381
Round the Sofa, XIII. 372, 379
Ruth, XIII. 371, 372, 377 ff., 381, 403
Sketches among the Poor, XIII. 372
Sylvia's Lovers, XIII. 378 ff., 403
Wives and Daughters, XIII. 372, 377, 378, 380, 381
Gaskell, William, XIII. 372
Gasquet, cardinal Francis Aidan, XIV. 484
Gassendi, Pierre, VII. 284, 286
Gataker, Thomas (1574–1654), VII. 308, 315 ff., 320, 321, 488, 490; *Annotations on the Bible*, VII. 322; *Cinnus*, VII. 318; *Marcus Antoninus*, VII. 316
Gate House, the, in *The Martin Marprelate Controversy*, III. 387
Gath, VII. 67
Gatherer, J., IX. 550
Gatty, Margaret (1807–1873), XI. 248, 479
Gatty, mistress (Etherege's), VIII. 138
Gatty laboratory, XIV. 297
Gau, John (1493?–1553?), *Richt Vay*, II. 285, 479
Gaubius, Hieronymus David, X. 200
Gauchos, the, XIV. 250
Gauden, John (1605–1662), bishop of Worcester, III. 407; VII. 160 ff., 425; VIII. 269; *Anti-Baal-Berith*, VII. 161; *Eikon Basilike*, VII. 140, 161, 162; VIII. 67; X. 355, 517
Gaudifer, in *Golagros and Gawane*, II. 124
Gaufridus, Arturus, I. 257
Gaul, XIV. 110
Gaul, *joculatores* in, II. 386
Gaul, women of, I. 151
Gaule, John (*fl.* 1646–1660), VII. 507, 509; *Πῦς-μαντια, The Mag-astromancer*, VII. 394
Gaulish scholars, XIV. 302, 303
Gaulmin, Gilbert, IV. 249, 259
Gauls, the, IV. 13
Gaultier, abbé, IX. 151, 152
Gaunt, Griffith, Charles Reade's, XIII. 426
Gaunt, John of, duke of Lancaster (1340–1399). *See* John
Gaunt house, in Thackeray's *Vanity Fair*, XIII. 287
Gauss, Karl Friedrich, XIV. 258, 268
Gaussen, Alice, *Percy: Prelate and Poet*, X. 206
Gaussen, François S. R. L., XII. 283
Gaussin, Mlle, X. 118
Gautar, the, in Old Norse literature, I. 26
Gautier, archbishop of Sens, I. 190
Gautier, Théophile, XIII. 129, 307; XIV. 349; *La Chimère*, XIII. 208
Gautier de Doulens, I. 328; II. 450
Gaveston, in *Edward II*, V. 154
Gaw, A., VIII. 131
Gawain, Gawayne (Walgainus), I. 243, 260, 261, 269, 270, 295, 297, 309, 311 ff., 336, 468; II. 100; III. 68; VII. 75. See, also, *Gawayne and the Grene Knight*
Gawain, Sir, in *Awntyrs of Arthure*, II. 116, 121, 122
Gawain, Sir, in *Golagros and Gawane*, II. 123, 124, 450
Gawain, Sir, in *Morte Arthure*, II. 119, 120
Gawain, Wedding of, I. 295, 312, 471
Gawaine, The Marriage of Sir, II. 414
Gawane, Anteris of, II. 116, 121
Gawayn, Syr, XIV. 307
Gawayne, Sir, and the Grene Knight, I. 281, 284, 285, 287, 296, 297, 312, 320, 325 ff., 330 ff., 333, 334, 378, 462, 468, 471, 472; II. 133, 272, 308, 379; VII. 75; XIV. 307
Gawdy, Philip (*fl.* 1601), VI. 291
Gawdyfer at Gaddris, Alexander story of, II. 112
Gawin, in *The Misfortunes of Arthur*, V. 78
Gay, Florence, XIV. 584
Gay, John (1685–1732), IX. 78, 98, 103, 106, 137, 139, 152, 160 ff. (main entry), 169, 220, 247, 249, 442, 446, 447, 452, 468, 472, 480, 483; X. 80, 84, 102, 202, 429, *also see* Add.; XI. 88, 173, 248, 479; XII. 122; XIII. 239, 265
Beggar's Opera, IX. 163; X. 71, 83, 428; XI. 218, 260
Birth of the Squire, IX. 164
Black-eyed Susan, IX. 161
Eclogues, XI. 36
Fables, IX. 162
Fan, The, IX. 161
Funeral, The, IX. 164
Ladies' Petition, IX. 164
Mr Pope's Welcome from Greece, IX. 75, 164
Polly, IX. 163
Rural Sports, IX. 160
Shepherd's Week, IX. 131, 161, 162, 164, 165; XI. 144
Tea-Table, The, IX. 164
Three Hours after Marriage, VIII. 168; IX. 72, 132; XI. 322
Toilette, The, IX. 164
Tragical Comical Farce, IX. 160
Trivia, or The Art of Walking the Streets of London, IX. 161, 164; XI. 322
'Twas when the Seas were roaring, IX. 161
What D'ye-Call-it, IX. 161; X. 83
Wife of Bath, IX. 161; XI. 322
Wine, IX. 160
Gay, John (1699–1745), *Dissertation*, X 342; *Gazetteer, The*, X. 400, 525
Gay, Joseph, XI. 330
Gay, Thomas, IX. 160
Gay, William (d. 1695), IX. 160
Gay, William (1865–1897), XIV. 369, 586
Gay Lussac, XIV. 557
Gay Goshawk, The, II. 411
Gayley, Charles Mills, V. 134 ff., 418; VI. Add

Gaynour, queen (Guinevere), in *Awntyrs of Arthure*, II. 122
Gay's Chair, IX. 164
Gayton, Edmund (1608–1666), VII. 516
Gayville, lord, in Burgoyne's *Heiress*, XI. 275
Gaza, Theodorus, grammar of, III. 14
Gazeau, J., XIII. 471
Gazet, in *The Renegado*, VI. 161
Gazette, The, IX. 2, 4
Gazette, The (Manchester), XIV. 169
Gazetteer, The, XIV. 186
Gazettes, VII. 345
Geat, in *Deor*, I. 36
Geatas, the, in *Beowulf*, I. 24 ff.
Geddes, Alexander (1737–1802), XII. 467
Charming Highlandman, IX. 372
Iliad, IX. 372
Lewie Gordon, IX. 372
Linton, IX. 372
Wee Wifukie, IX. 372
Geddes, John (1735–1799), XI. 223
Geddes, William (1600?–1694), IX. 546
Geddes, Sir William Duguid (1828–1900), XII. 335, 484
Gedell-Glaiss, son of Sir Newill, in *Orygynale Cronykil*, II. 130
Gedike, Friedrich, XIV. 382
Gee, J., VIII. 453
Geesh (Abyssinia), XIV. 246
Geffe, or Goffe, N., *The Perfect Use of Silk-wormes*, IV. 487, 542
Geikie, Sir Archibald, XIV. 291, 559, 561
Geikie, Walter (1795–1837), II. 270
Geiler von Kaisersberg, John, III. 14, 59, 482, 490
'Geist,' Matthew Arnold's dachshund, XIII. 96
Gelasimus, Herod's fool in *Archipropheta*, VI. 295
Gell, Sir William (1777–1836), XII. 497; *Pompeiana*, XII. 338
Gellert, Christian Fürchtegott, *Das Leben der schwedischen Gräfen von G.*, X. 18
Gelli, Giovanni Battista, IV. 444
Gellia, in Owen's *Epigrammata*, IV. 265
Gellibrand, Henry (1597–1636), IV. 456
Gellius, Aulus, IV. 6, 249, 348
Gelon, Sicilian ruler, XII. 316
General Advertiser, The, X. 466
General assembly, the (1650), VII. 254
General assembly of the Church of Scotland, IX. 129
Generous, in *The Late Lancashire Witches*, VI. 105
Generydes, I. 291, 468
Genest, John (1764–1839), VIII. 123, 124, 168, 188; XI. 447, 456; *Some Account of the English Stage*, X. 85, 161, 443
Geneva, III. 45, 53, 144, 145, 399, 400, 402, 403; IV. 163, 276, 303, 402, 403, 429; V. 113; VI. 374; VII. 100, 304, 306, 308; VIII. 245, 291; X. 296; XI. 59; XIII. 383
Geneva, lake of, XII. 44
Geneviève, St, IX. 68
Gengiscan the Great, X. 110
Genius, priest of Nature, in *Roman de la Rose*, II. 150
Genius, priest of Venus, in *Confessio Amantis*, II. 146, 150
Genius of the Wood, the, in *Arcades*, VII. 113
Genlis, comtesse de, XI. 491; XIII. 273; XIV. 606; *Adèle et Théodore*, XI. 382; XIV. 388; *Tales of the Castle*, XI. 382
Genoa, II. 79, 118, 157, 305; IV. 68; VII. 99; IX. 245; X. 41, 469
Genoa, villa Saluzzo, XII. 37
Genovino, in D'Urfey's *Famous History of Massaniello*, VIII. 175
Gent, Thomas (1693–1778), XI. 341, 469
Gentile Christians, IX. 291
Gentiles, the, XII. 209
Gentili, Alberico (1552–1608), VI. 399; VII. 309; VIII. 466; *De Jure Belli*, III. 423, 424; VIII. 316; *De Legationibus*, III. 423
Gentillet, Innocent, *Discours sur les moyens de bien gouverner et maintenir de bonne paix un royaume*, IV. 8, 444
'Gentle river,' X. 233
Gentleman, Francis (1728–1784), X. 443
Gentleman, Tobias (*fl.* 1614), IV. 511
Gentleman's Calling, The, IX. 397, 570
Gentleman's Journal, IX. 270; X. 163
Gentleman's Magazine, The, IX. 191; X. 144, 159, 161 ff., 168, 171, 173, 175, 181, 183, 193, 460, 461, 463, 464, 467, 471 ff., 479, 480; XI. 323, 324, 339, 355; XII. 140, 181, 193, 345, 347, 365, 428; XIV. 230, 594
Gentleman's Magazine Library, XII. 506, 519
Gentûs, the, XI. 17
Gentylnes and Nobylyte, V. 409
Gentz, Friedrich von, IX. 233; X. 306
Geoffrey de Vinsauf (*fl.* 1200), *Art of Poetry*, I. 193, 453
Geoffrey of Monmouth (1100?–1154), I. 68, 71, 158, 159, 168 ff., 175, 235, 237, 245 ff., 250, 252, 257 ff., 264, 266 ff., 284, 336, 338, 350, 351, 450, 451, 461; II. 118; III. 234, 237, 314; IV. 67, 422; V. 67, 68, 78, 239; VI. 92; X. 231; XIV. 307
Geoffrey of Waterford, II. 508
Geoffrey the cripple, in *Tale of Beryn*, I. 298
Geoffrey the grammarian or Starkey (*fl.* 1440), *Promptorium Parvulorum*, II. 483, 496; III. 555
Geoffrey the Norman, bishop of St Albans, V. 7
Geological Magazine, The, XIV. 289, 566
Geological society of London, XII. 347; XIV. 287
Geometry, in *The Passetyme of Pleasure*, II. 225
George I, king of Great Britain (elector of Hanover), IV. 251; VIII. 299; IX. 132, 231, 235, 237, 238, 243, 249, 308, 309, 330, 407, 408; X. 283; XIV. 229

George II, king of Great Britain, IX. 87, 104, 230, 243, 249, 250, 252 ff., 381, 407, 408, 410, 413; X. 44, 295, 388; XIV. 57, 381
George III, king of Great Britain, V. 208; IX. 230, 252, 253; X. 66, 136, 184, 206, 363, 389 ff., 400, 404, 406, 463, 469, 477; XI. 5, 11, 13, 37, 52, 166, 261; XII. 36, 53, 475; XIV. 60, 90, 213, 215, 244, 328, 386, 389
George IV, king of Great Britain, IX. 213; XI. 49, 54; XII. 36, 70; XIII. 295, 342; XIV. 114, 201, 222, 229, 432
George, duke of Saxe-Meiningen, V. 306
George, prince, in the mummers' play, V. 33
George, prince, of Denmark (1653–1708), IX. 33, 130
George, St, VII. 167; XI. 373
George, St, in early drama, II. 309, 406; V. 32 ff., 49
George, St, in *Richard Coeur de Lion*, I. 308
George inn, the, in the *Paston Letters*, II. 309
George of Gorbals, in *The Bon Gaultier Ballads*, XIII. 161
George tavern at Edmonton, V. 252
Georgia, IX. 324, 325
Georgian drama, XI. 257 ff., 272, 447, *also see* Add.
Georgian era, IX. 192: X. 1, 142; XI. 284, 372, 373, 377
Georgian poets, XII. 106
Georgian public, XI. 259, 267, 268, 270
Georgian theatre, XI. 269, 273
Geraint (Sir Erec), I. 274, 284
Gerald of Wales. *See* Giraldus Cambrensis
Geraldine. *See* Fitz-Gerald, lady Elizabeth
Geraldine, in Coleridge's *Christabel*, XII. 88
Geraldine, in Heywood's *History of Women*, VI. 102
Geraldine, in *The English Traveller*, VI. 102
Geraldine, in *The Unfortunate Traveller*, III. 363
Geraldine (Surrey's), IV. 182
Geraldines of Wales, the, I. 94
Gerard, in *The Cloister and the Hearth*, XIII. 428, 429
Gerard, John (1545–1612), *Herball or generall historie of Plantes*, III. 551; IV. 374, 542
Gerard, John (1564–1637), VII. 444
Gerard of Cremona, II. 365
Gerbel, V. 308
Gerbelius, Nicholas, IV. 250
Gerbert of Aurillac, I. 209
Gerbier, Sir Balthazar (1591?–1667), VII. 353
Gerbier, Charles, VII. 514
Geree, John (1601?–1649), VII. 509, 517
Gereint or Geraint, son of Erbin, in *The Black Book*, I. 250, 253, 255
Gerhoh of Reichersberg, VI. 374
Germ, The, XIII. 111, 112, 114, 120, 138; XIV. 139
Germain, George Sackville, 1st viscount Sackville (1716–1785), X. 526
German ballads, XII. 5
German criticism, XIV. 140
German doctor in *Hymenaeus*, VI. 304
German drama, XI. 41, 281; XII. 372; XIII. 265, 272
German education, XIV. 382, 391, 423
German flute, X. 198
German historians, IX. 227; XII. 271; XIII. 18; XIV. 102
German history, XIV. 92, 99
German interest in Shakespeare, V. 167, 283, 284, 285, 289, 298
German language and literature, IX. 314, 331, 400; X. 18, 60, 79, 80, 217, 291, 296; XI. 177, 300, 355, 356, 414; XII. 4, 113, 154, 157, 221, 247, 254, 288, 302, 308, 340; XIII. 3 ff., 10, 12, 53, 227, 244, 247, 259, 263, 323, 383; XIV. 306, 318 *a*, *b*, 391, 406, 434, 457 ff.
German philosophy, XII. 270; XIV. 9, 13, 40, 41
German politics, X. 388
German reformation, XIV. 108
German reforming princes, the, VII. 103
German romanticism, XIII. 7 ff., 192, 259, 261
German stage, Massinger and, VI. 165
German stage (medieval), V. 36, 39, 41, 44, 48
German stage (modern), V. 346; VI. 49, 374
German theology, XII. 254, 318
German universities, XIII. 2, 9; XIV. 382, 410 ff.
Germanic kingdoms, the, XIV. 68
Germanic origins in Britain, XIV. 69, 70, 79
Germanist historical school, XIV. 51, 68, 69, 75
Germanus, St, of Auxerre, I. 70, 81
Germany, V. 25, 33, 43, 55, 101, 171, 222, 284, 286, 294 ff., 298, 299, 303, 306, 359; VI. 35; VII. 201, 283, 306, 309, 314, 345, 378; VIII. 182, 265, 330; IX. 6, 22, 70, 89, 106, 222, 315, 401, 406; X. 18, 19, 41, 63, 78, 79, 148, 200, 234, 353; XI. 102, 121, 136, 284, 303; XII. 34, 174, 263, 280, 282, 315, 343, 365, 367; XIII. 3, 20, 22, 156, 277, 281, 441, 455, 457; XIV. 8, 42, 53, 184, 293, 294, 382, 383
Germany and Byron, XII. 392 ff.
Germany and De Quincey, XII. 445
Germany and Shelley, XII. 402
Gernutus, X. 234
Gerrard, in *The Triumph of Love*, VI. 120
Gerrold, W., XIV. 536
Gerson, Jean, VIII. 59
Gerstenberg, H. W. von, V. 297, 298
Gert Beyers, XIV. 377
Gertrude, in *Hamlet*, V. 169
Gervase of Canterbury (*fl.* 1188), I. 173, 175, 449; II. 34
Gervase (Gervasius) of Tilbury (*fl.* 1211), *Otia Imperialia*, I. 173, 176, 192, 449, 453; VII. 504

Gervasius, I. 75
Gervinus, Georg Gottfried, V. 305
Gesner, Conrad, IV. 444
Gessner, Salomon, XI. 181; *Death of Abel*, XI. 182; XII. 48
Gesta Grayorum, V. 78
Gesta Romanorum, I. 135, 365, 367, 477; II. 85, 151, 207, 299, 300, 301, 314, 338, 482; III. 92, 489, 490, 494; V. 49; VI. 138, 139; XI. 366, 372
Geta, in *Confessio Amantis*, II. 148
Get Up and Bar the Door, II. 414
Geulincx, Arnold, VIII. 347
Geystes of Skoggan, The, IV. 327
Ghent, II. 338; V. 37; VIII. 160; XII. 365; XIII. 61
Ghent, church of Saint-Baron, XIII. 112
Ghibellines, XIII. 59, 60
Ghismonda (Boccaccio's), V. 72, 73
Ghose, J. C., XIV. 580
Ghost, the, in *Hamlet*, VI. 248
Ghost of King Charles II, The, VIII. 93
Ghulam Hussein Khan, *Siyar-ul-Muta'akhkhirin*, XIV. 335
'Giant Walker, The,' XIV. 320
Gibb, Elias John Wilkinson (1857–1901), XII. 503; *History of Ottoman Poetry*, XII. 342
Gibbet, in Farquhar's *Beaux' Stratagem*, VIII. 171
Gibbon, Edward (1666–1736), IX. 308
Gibbon, Edward, father of the historian, X. 299, 301, 305
Gibbon, Edward (1737–1794), I. 165, 244; VII. 220, 248; IX. 323, 381, 436, 574; X. 216, 240, 248, 280, 288 ff., 294, 297 ff. (main entry), 319, 320, 335, 390, 489, 506 ff., 527, *also see* Add.; XI. 260, 327, 400; XII. 300, 305, 318, 319, 322, 324, 477; XIII. 461; XIV. 461, 504
  Address (on *Scriptores Rerum Angl.*), X. 312
  Antiquities of the House of Brunswick, X. 311
  Critical Enquiries concerning the Title of Charles VIII, X. 305
  Decline and Fall of the Roman Empire, III. 332; X. 281, 298, 300, 304, 306 ff., 312 ff., 317, 318; XI. 71, 326
  Essai sur l'Étude de la Littérature, X. 302
  Introduction à l'Histoire...des Suisses, X. 304, 305
  Letters (1814), X. 299
  Mémoire Justificatif, X. 306
  Memoirs, IX. 308, 313, 326, 414; X. 279, 289, 292, 297 ff., 302 ff., 306, 307, 310 ff., 316, 317
  Miscellaneous Works, X. 304 ff., 308, 310, 312
  Nomina Gentesque Antiquae Italiae, X. 305
  Observations on the...VIth Book of the Aeneid, X. 305
  Outlines of the History of the World—Ninth Century to Fifteenth, X. 305
Gibbon, Edward
  Private Letters, X. 299, 301, 306, 311
  Remarks on Blackstone's Commentaries, X. 305
  Vindication of some Passages, X. 308, 315
Gibbon, Hester, IX. 308, 514
Gibbon, Perceval, XIV. Add. 4
Gibbon Commemoration, Proceedings, X. 299
Gibbons, Grinling (1648–1720), VIII. 250
Gibbons, Orlando (1583–1625), IV. 113, 464
Gibbs, J. W. M., XIV. 477, 506
Gibicho, in *Waltharius*, I. 32
Gibraltar, XIV. 101
Gibson, Charles Dana, XIII. 540
Gibson, Edmund (1669–1748), bishop of London, IV. 422; VIII. 469; IX. 351, 353, 355, 512, 534, 539; X. 223, 226, 484
Gibson, John (d. 1852), XIII. 74
Gibson, J. Y., XIV. Add. 7
Gibson, Leon, *Tantara*, III. 191
Gibson, Mr, in Mrs Gaskell's *Wives and Daughters*, XIII. 381
Gichtel, Johann Georg, IX. 515, 523
Gide, André, XIV. 528
Gideon, IV. 43
Gideon, in *Confessio Amantis*, II. 151
Gife Langour makis men licht, III. 131
Giffard, lady Martha, VIII. 382; IX. 92, 98, 467; *Letters*, VIII. 380; *Life of Sir William Temple*, VIII. 379, 482, 483
Giffard, Stanley Lees (1788–1858), XIV. 534
Gifford, Edwin Hamilton (1820–1905), XII. 484
Gifford, George (d. 1620), VII. 371, 372, 390, 394, 395, 506; *A Dialogue of Witches and Witchcraft*, V. 478; VII. 371; *Discourse of the subtile Practises of Devilles*, IV. 325, 534, 535; VII. 371
Gifford, Humfrey (*fl.* 1580), III. 114, 188; VIII. 231; *For Souldiers*, III. 188; *Posie of Gilloflowers*, III. 188
Gifford, John (1758–1818), XI. 392
Gifford, William (1756–1826), VI. 1, 339, 341, 346, 359, 361; XI. 37, 39, 166, 177, 392, 393; XII. 142, 150 ff., 170, 175, 193, 429, 430, 432, 443, 526; XIV. 138; *The Baviad*, XI. 40; XII. 41; *The Maeviad*, XI. 40; XII. 41
Gifford lectures, XII. 333; XIV. 45, 48
Gifica (Gibicho), in *Widsith*, I. 34
Gifts of Men (Bi monna craeftum), I. 61, 428
Gil Brenton, II. 411
Gilbert, in *The Sparagus Garden*, VI. 227
Gilbert, Henry March, XII. 519
Gilbert, Sir Humphrey (1539?–1583), III. 114, 341, 438; IV. 67, 74, 76, 85, 86, 88; *Discourse of a Discoverie for a new passage to Cataia*, IV. 73, 456; *Queene Elizabethes Achademy*, III. 341, 438, 551; IV. 355
Gilbert, Sir John (1817–1897), XI. 483; XII. 448; XIV. 201, 238

Gilbert, Sir John Thomas (1829–1898), XII. 515; XIV. 489, 568
Celtic Records and Historic Literature of Ireland, XII. 361
Facsimiles of the National Manuscripts of Ireland, XII. 361
Historic and Municipal Documents of Ireland, XII. 361
History of Dublin, The, XIV. 328
History of the Irish Confederation, The, VII. 212; XIV. 96
History of the Viceroys of Ireland, The, XIV. 96
Gilbert, Mrs. *See* Taylor, Ann
Gilbert, William (1540–1603), IV. 278, 286, 508; VIII. 350; *De Magnete, magneticisque corporibus*, III. 425; IV. 277
Gilbert, William (1760?–1825?), XII. 416
Gilbert, William (1804–1890), XIII. 562
Gilbert, Sir William Schwenck (1836–1911), XIII. 162, 513, 518; XIV. 206, 544
Bab Ballads, The, XIII. 274
Broken Hearts, XIII. 273
Engaged, XIII. 274
Grand Duke, The, XIII. 274
Gretchen, XIII. 274
Palace of Truth, The, XIII. 273
Pygmalion and Galatea, XIII. 273, 274
Sweethearts, XIII. 274
Trial by Jury, XIII. 274
Wicked World, The, XIII. 273
Gilbert de la Porrée, I. 184, 185
Gilbert of Sempringham (1083?–1189), I. 229, 364
Gilbert the Englishman (*fl.* 1250), I. 453
Gilbertine order, I. 344
Gilby, Anthony (d. 1585), III. 45
Gilby, Goddard (*fl.* 1561), IV. 436
Gilchrist, Alexander (1828–1861), XI. 434; XIV. 525
Gilchrist, Mrs Anne (1828–1885), XII. 433, 437
Gilchrist, John, *Collection of Scottish Ballads*, IX. 373
Gilchrist, J. D. F., XIV. Add. 7
Gilchrist, Octavius Graham (1779–1823), IX. 451
Gildas (516?–570?), I. 5, 65 ff., 70, 71, 81, 247, 262, 350, 435, 461; III. 314
Gildemeister, Otto, V. 303
Gildon, Charles (1665–1724), VIII. 423, 428, 444, 445; IX. 86, 141, 142, 289, 475, 479, 504; X. 146; XI. 250; *A Comparison between the Two Stages*, IX. 141; *Life... of Mr D— De F—*, IX. 141; *Lives of the English Dramatic Poets*, IX. 141, 479
Gilds, English, V. 389
Giles, Jacob, VIII. 373, 428
Giles, Miss, X. 409
Giles, Nathaniel (d. 1634), V. 125; VI. 221, 257, 258, 283, 287 ff.
Giles, Peter (Aegidius), III. 18
Giles, Thomas (*fl.* 1608), VI. 344, 346
Gilfillan, George (1813–1878), XI. 390, 393, 402, 409, 417, 419, 423, 424, 437 ff., 442, 443; XII. 372, 379, 403, 407, 410, 412, 418, 431, 433, 437, 441, 445, 452, 472; XIII. 471, 477, 484, 499, 501, 509, 530; XIV. 481, 525, 555
Gilfillan, Robert (1798–1850), XI. 443; *O Why Left I my Hame*, XI. 243
Gilkes, Arthur H., XIV. 606
Gill, Abraham, IX. 12
Gill, Alexander, the elder (1565–1635), VII. 97, 98; *Logonomia Anglica*, VII. 332
Gill, Alexander, the younger (1597–1642), VII. 98
Gill, Sir David, XIV. Add. 7
Gill, Dr John (1697–1771), X. 387
Gill, John (1818–1910), XIV. 606
Gill, William Archer, XIII. 504
Gilla Coemgin, I. 70
Gillamor, in *The Misfortunes of Arthur*, V. 78
Gillespie, George (1613–1648), IX. 544
Gillian, in *Richard Casteler*, III. 369
Gillies, John (1712–1796), X. 518
Gillies, Robert Pearse (1788–1858), XII. 379, 445; XIV. 502
Gilliland, Thomas (*fl.* 1804–1816), X. 443
Gillingham, Kent, IV. 99; X. 25
Gilliver, Lawton, IX. 79; XI. 323
Gillman, James, XI. 121, 129, 417
Gillmans, the, of Highgate, XI. 417
Gillmore, Parker, XIV. Add. 7
Gillray, James (1757–1815), VIII. 160; XI. 392; XIV. 214, 216, 223, 225, 235, 540
Gillus. *See* Gildas
Gillyflower, Matthew, XI. 332
Gil Morrice (Percy's *Reliques*), X. 137
Gilpin, Bernard (1517–1583), IV. 225, 234, 492
Gilpin, William (1724–1804), XIV. 217, 543, 544; *Observations on the River Wye*, XIV. 221; *Picturesque Remarks*, XIV. 221; *Remarks on Forest Scenery*, XIV. 221
Gilpin, William Sawrey (1762–1843), XIV. 221
Gilpin Horner, border legend, XII. 7, 8
Gilpin's Rig (1783?), XI. 402
Gilston, XII. 182
Ginevra, in Rogers's *Italy*, XII. 98
'Gingerbread, Giles,' XI. 377
Ginsburg, Christian David (1831–1914), XII. 501; *Facsimiles of MSS. of the Hebrew Bible*, XII. 341
Gioliti's publishing house, V. 71
Giordano, Paolo, duke of Bracciano, VI. 173
Giovanna of Naples, XII. 212
Giovanni, in *The White Divel*, VI. 175, 177
Giovanni, in *Tis Pitty Shees a Whore*, VI. 195
Giovanni, prince, in *The Great Duke of Florence*, VI. 156, 158
Giovio, Paolo, IV. 132, 444
Giraffi, Alessandro, VII. 446
Giraldo, Baptista, IV. 444
Giraldus, X. 293

Giraldus Cambrensis (1146?–1220?), I. 160, 171, 173, 176, 177, 188 ff., 194 ff., 202, 243, 292, 449, 451, 453; II. 76; III. 314, 319; IV. 67; XII. 5, 10; *Topographia Hibernica*, II. 342, 483, 488
Girard, father, XIV. 404
Girard, Guillaume, *Life of the Duke of Espernon*, IX. 276, 499
Girardin, Émile de, XIII. 273
Girls' Public Day School company, XIV. 430
Girondists, the, XI. 157
Gisborne, Thomas (1758–1846), XII. 472
Gisippus, V. 103
Gismond of Salerne, V. 72, 73, 75 ff., 399
Gissing, George Robert (1857–1903), XIII. 455 ff., 533, 543, 573
Born in Exile, XIII. 455, 458, 459
By the Ionian Sea, XIII. 456, 461
Charles Dickens: A Critical Study, XIII. 456
Crown of Life, The, XIII. 456, 460
Demos, XIII. 455, 458
Denzil Quarrier, XIII. 455
Dickens in Memory, XIII. 456
Emancipated, The, XIII. 455, 460
Eve's Ransom, XIII. 456, 458, 460
Forster's Life of Dickens (abridgment), XIII. 456
House of Cobwebs, XIII. 456, 458
Human Odds and Ends, XIII. 456, 458
In the Year of Jubilee, XIII. 455, 458
Isabel Clarendon, XIII. 455, 457, 460
Letters from George Gissing to Edward Clodd, XIII. 457
Life's Morning, A, XIII. 455, 460
'Mount of Refuge, The,' XIII. 461
Nether World, The, XIII. 455, 458
New Grubb Street, XIII. 455, 458 ff.
Odd Women, The, XIII. 455, 458 ff.
Our Friend the Charlatan, XIII. 456, 460
Paying Guest, The, XIII. 456
Private Papers of Henry Ryecroft, The, XIII. 456, 462
Sleeping Fires, XIII. 455
Thyrza, XIII. 455, 458, 459
Town Traveller, The, XIII. 456, 459
Unclassed, The, XIII. 455
Veranilda, XIII. 456, 461
Whirlpool, The, XIII. 456, 460
Will Warburton, XIII. 456, 459
Workers in the Dawn, XIII. 455
Given, John L., XIV. 531
Gladstone, John Hall, XIV. 557
Gladstone, Mary, XIV. 484
Gladstone, William Ewart (1809–1898), X. 358, 361; XI. 4; XII. 152, 155, 255, 312, 426, 484; XIII. 23, 24, 31, 38, 477; XIV. 119, 128, 131, 132, 134 ff. (main entry), 195, 198, 199, 509, 513
Bulgarian Horrors, XIV. 136
Homeric Synchronism, XII. 334
Juventus Mundi, XII. 334
Lessons in Massacre, XIV. 136
Letters to the Earl of Aberdeen, XIV. 136
Gladstone, William Ewart
State in its Relations with the Church, The, XIV. 135
Studies on Homer, XII. 334
Vatican Decrees, The, XIV. 136
Vaticanism, XIV. 136
Glamorganshire, XII. 512
Glanvill, Joseph (1636–1680), VII. 471, 507, 517, *also see* Add.; VIII. 292, 454, 456; IX. 436
Antifanatick Theologie, and Free Philosophy, VII. 303
Lux Orientalis, VIII. 291
Philosophical Considerations touching Witches and Witchcraft, VII. 395
Plus Ultra, VIII. 291
Sadducismus Triumphatus, VIII. 291
Scepsis Scientifica, VII. 302
Vanity of Dogmatizing, The, VII. 302, 393
Glanville, Ernest, XIV. Add. 7
Glanville, Ranulf de (d. 1190), I. 173, 181, 195, 449; VIII. 311, 312, 465
Glanville, Sir Reginald, in Lytton's *Pelham*, XIII. 417
Glapthorne, Henry (*fl.* 1639), VI. 240, 456; VII. 88
Albertus Wallenstein, VI. 240
Argalus and Parthenia, III. 355; VI. 240
Ladies Privilege, The, VI. 240
The Paraside, a Revenge for Honour, VI. 35
Glas, John (1695–1773), IX. 548
Glas Keraint, the Welsh, II. 412
Glascock, William Nugent (1787?–1847), XII. 251, 449
'Glascurion,' in Chaucer's *House of Fame*, II. 412
Glasgerion, II. 412
Glasgow, VIII. 298; IX. 133, 193; X. 132, 188, 191, 335, 348; XI. 237, 244, 341, 373; XII. 17, 29, 350, 358, 370, 419, 513, 515; XIII. 161, 194; XIV. 279, 286, 410
Glasgow, Andersonian institution, XIV. 407
Glasgow, Mechanics' institution, XIV. 407, 408
Glasgow, university of, II. 245, 369, 371; III. 151, 426; IV. 276; IX. 290, 301; X. 36; XII. 143, 157, 158, 165, 330, 332, 371, 409, 521; XIV. 7, 43, 45, 267
Glasgow Courier, The, XI. 237
Glasgow Herald, The, XIV. 531
Glasgow press, XI. 470; XII. 520
Glasgow Sentinel, The, XI. 236
Glasgow Theatrical Register, The, XI. 452
Glasgow University Magazine, The, XIV 209, 538
Glasscock, Thomas, X. 386
Glastonbury, I. 150, 164, 198, 243, 262, 272, 313; IV. 417; IX. 535; X. 20
Glastonia, abbey of, in *Life of Gildas*, I. 262
Glaucilla, in *Sicelides*, VI. 323
Glaucus, in Keats's *Endymion*, XII. 82
Gleanings from an Old Portfolio, XI. 348

Gleig, George Robert (1796–1888), XII. 303, 449, *also see* Add.
Glen, William (1789–1826), XI. 443; XII. 416; *Wae's me for Prince Charlie*, XI. 243
Glencairn, earls of. *See* Cunningham, Alexander; Cunningham, James
Glencoe, massacre of, IX. 564; XIV. 65
Glendower, Owen, in *Henry IV*, V. 187; XIV. 307
Glenesk, lord. *See* Borthwick, Sir Algernon
Glenfallen, lord and lady, in Le Fanu's story, XIII. 415, 416
'Glenkroden,' river, XI. 287
Glenriddell MSS. (Burns), XI. 435, 438
Glewlwyd Gavaelvawr or Glewlwyd of the Mighty Grasp, one of Arthur's porters, I. 251
Gliddon, George Robins (1809–1857), XII. 500
Glisson, Francis (1597–1677), VIII. 359, 363, 473, 477; XIV. 281
Globe, Le, V. 302
Globe, The, XIV. 185, 194, 316, 530, 533
Globe and Blackfriars company, XIII. 256
Glogau, siege of, VII. 22
'Glomery, Master of' (*Magister Glomerial*), II. 346, 347, 356
Gloriana, in *The Faerie Queene*, III. 234, 236, 246; V. 183
Glories of Ireland, The, XIV. 307
Glorious Tipto, Sir, in *The New Inne*, VI. 25
Glossaries, IV. 424
Glossin, in Scott's *Guy Mannering*, XII. 21
Gloster, earl of, in *Looke about You*, V. 320, 323
Gloster, earl of, in Thomson's *Edward and Eleonora*, X. 109
Gloucester, II. 349; VIII. 245; IX. 296, 341, 393, 531; XI. 484; XII. 329, 340, 510; XIV. 389
Gloucester, duke of, in *Henry VI*, V. 186
Gloucester, dukes of. *See* Henry (1639–1660); Humphrey (1391–1447); Thomas (1355–1397); William (1689–1700)
Gloucester, earl of, in *King Lear*, III. 355; V. 204, 262
Gloucester, earl of. *See* Robert (d. 1147)
Gloucester, or *South English Legendary*. *See* Legendary
Gloucester academy, X. 386
Gloucester Chronicle. *See* Robert of Gloucester
Gloucester Journal, The, XIV. 169
Gloucestershire, III. 39; V. 187; VII. 312; X. 111; XII. 346
Glover, Arnold, X. 44; XI. 150; XII. 167, 431
Glover, James Mackey, XIII. 514
Glover, Jean (1758–1801), IX. 374
Glover, Julia (1779–1850), VIII. 186
Glover, Richard (1712–1785), IX. 183; X. 148, 434, 455; XI. 402
  Admiral Hosier's Ghost, X. 148, 233
  Atheniad, The, X. 148
Glover, Richard
  Boadicea, XI. 258
  Leonidas, X. 148; XI. 323
  Medea, XI. 179
Glover, Robert (1544–1588), III. 528
Glover, Stephen (d. 1869), XII. 501, 507
Glover, William, X. 195, 482, 483
Gloys, James, chaplain to Margaret Paston, II. 306
Glutton, in *Piers the Plowman*, II. 12, 16, 23
Gluttony, in *Confessio Amantis*, II. 147, 149
Gluttony, in *The Passetyme of Pleasure*, II. 236
Gnaphaeus, William, *Acolastus*, III. 363; V. 101, 109, 110, 112, 113, 410, 412
Gnomaticus, in *The Glasse of Governe-ment*, V. 113
Gnomic Verses, O.E., I. 218, 428, 432
'Go from my Window,' IX. 362
Goad, Caroline, X. Add.
Gobble, Mrs, in Smollett's *Sir Launcelot Greaves*, X. 41
Gobbo, in *The Merchant of Venice*, V. 183
Gobelive, Godfrey, in *The Passetyme of Pleasure*, II. 225, 232, 233, 235
Gobrias, in *Argenis*, IV. 259
God Ureism of ure Lefdi, On (A Good Orison of Our Lady), I. 232, 450
Godard, in *Havelok*, I. 303
Godard, J. G., XIV. 601
Goddard, William (*fl.* 1615), IV. 520
Godden, Gertrude M., X. 29, 418
Godefroy of Le Mans, V. 38
Godfrey, in *Orlando Furioso*, III. 230
Godfrey, captain, XIV. 229, 544; *The Useful Art of Self-defence*, XIV. 230
Godfrey, Sir Edmund Berry (1621–1678), VIII. 86, 189, 257; IX. 6
Godfrey, G. W., XIII. 519
Godfrey, Walter H., VI. 269
Godfrey of Bologne, II. 313, 485
Godfrey of Bouillon, cycle of, I. 291
Godfrey of Cambrai and Winchester, I. 191, 454
Godfrey of Viterbo, II. 144, 150
Godiva, lady, I. 364; IV. 174
Godkin, Edwin Lawrence, XIV. 534
Godley, Alfred Denis, XII. 410, 421, 422
Godley, A. D., XIV. 537
Godly Queene Hester, V. 393
Godman, Frederick Du Cane, XIV. 297
Godolphin, Cornwall, VII. 86
Godolphin, Francis, 2nd earl of (1678–1766), VIII. 159
Godolphin, John (1617–1678), IV. 456; VIII. 468
Godolphin, Mrs (Margaret Blagge) (1652–1678), VIII. 250, 251, 264
Godolphin, Sidney (1610–1643), VII. 87, 218; VIII. 133, 215
  Aeneid, trans., VII. 86
  Chorus, VII. 86
  Meditation, VII. 86
  'No more unto my thoughts appear,' VII. 86

Godolphin, Sidney
'Or love me less or love me more,' vii. 86
Poem to Sandys, vii. 86
Psalms, paraphrase of the, vii. 86
''Tis Affection but dissembled,' vii. 86
Godolphin, Sidney, 1st earl of (1645–1712), viii. 251; ix. 12, 13, 44, 94, 95, 150, 151
Godolphin, Sir William (d. 1613), vii. 86
Godolphin, Sir William (1634?–1696), viii. 380
Godric, in *Battle of Maldon*, i. 145
Godric, St (1065?–1170), i. 375; *Cantus Beati Godrici*, i. 220, 458
Godrich, household of, in *Havelok*, i. 303, 304
Godstow bridge, xiii. 93
Godwin, i. 111, 139
Godwin, F., *Voyage of Domingo Gonsalez*, ix. 106
Godwin, Francis (1562–1633), vii. 444
Godwin, Mrs Mary Jane (Mrs Clairmont), xi. 294; xii. 189, 191
Godwin, Mrs Mary Wollstonecraft (1759–1797), xi. 43 ff., 189, 293, 394, 395; *also see* Add.; xii. 61, 191; xiv. 388, 600; *Vindication of the Rights of Women*, xi. 43, 44; xiv. 400
Godwin, Mary Wollstonecraft (1797–1851). *See* Shelley, Mrs
Godwin, William (1756–1836), vii. 452; xi. 24, 43 ff., 48, 98, 119, 189, 277, 292 ff. (main entry), 393, 395. 399, *also see* Add.; xii. 39, 59, 60, 64, 65, 67, 73, 93, 188, 190, 248, 401 ff.; xiii. 258, 427; xiv. 137, 237, 606
Caleb Williams, x. 59; xi. 43, 46, 280. 292 ff.; xiii. 418, 437
Cloudesley, xi. 292
Enquiry concerning political justice. xiv. 400
Fleetwood, xi. 292
Juvenile Library, xi. 385
Life of Chaucer, xii. 146
Mandeville, xi. 292
Political Justice, xi. 43, 46, 73, 276, 292, 294
St Leon, xi. 43, 46, 285, 292, 293; xiii. 419
See, also, Baldwin, Edwin
Godwine, earl, xiv. 72
Goertz, baron de, ix. 20
Goethe, Johann Wolfgang von, v. 209, 298 ff., 305, 465; viii. 49; x. 52, 227, 228, 232, 422, 488; xi. 42, 135, 416; xii. 7, 38, 42, 64, 157, 168, 254, 375, 377, 379, 380, 392, 394, 397, 402, 403, 480, 526, 527; xiii. 1, 6, 7, 9, 10, 18, 21, 90, 93, 94, 105, 153, 277, 417, 442, 464, 465; xiv. 109, 113
Faust, v. 20; xi. 131; xii. 34, 47, 48, 86; xiii. 360, 467; xiv. 138, 367
Goetz von Berlichingen, v. 301; xii. 4
Hermann und Dorothea, xiii. 105, 380
Shakespeare als Dichter überhaupt, xi. 284
Goethe, Johann Wolfgang von
Shakespeare als Theaterdichter, xi. 283
Sprüche in Prosa, x. 52
Werther, x. 19, 60
Wilhelm Meister, v. 299, 300, 304; x. 49, 52; xiii. 4, 5, 346
Goffe, Thomas (1591–1629), vi. 144, 369, 473, 491; viii. 436; *The Careless Shepherdess*, vi. 366
Gog and Magog, in Dickens's *Master Humphrey's Clock*, xiii. 319
Gog Magog, ii. 275, 278
Golagros and Gawane, i. 312, 333, 334, 468; ii. 112, 121, 123, 124, 126, 450
Goldberg, Isaac, xiii. 519
Goldburgh, in *Havelok*, i. 303, 304, 351
Golden Cross, the, in *The Pickwick Papers*, xiii. 310
'Golden Hind' (ship), iv. 74
Golden Legend, The, i. 55, 134, 343; ii. 80, 127, 300, 314. 316, 333 ff., 482, 485; v. 15
Golden Rump, The, x. 84
Golden Treasury, The, xiii. 192
Golden Treasury series, xiii. 95, 196
Goldey (*i.e.* Lodge), iv. 180
Goldfinch, in Holcroft's *Road to Ruin*, xi. 277
Goldfinch, The, ix. 566
Goldhan, A. B., xiii. 564
Golding, Arthur (1536?–1605?), iii. 302, 303, 446, 448; iv. 4 ff., 8, 19 ff., 24, 397, 435, 437 ff., 441, 442, 445, 447, 448; v. 394
Translations:
Caesar's *Gallic War*, iv. 4, 21, 397, 435
Histories of Trogus Pompeius, The abridgment of the, iv. 21
Ovid's *Metamorphoses*, iv. 19, 20, 397, 438
Politicke, Moral and Martial Discourses, iv. 21
Worke concerning Benefyting, The, iv. 6
Goldingham, William, vi. 473
Goldoni, Carlo, x. 19, 411
Goldring, Maude, xiii. 558
Goldsborough, Miles, vi. 307
Goldsmith, Catharine, x. 198
Goldsmith, Charles, x. 196
Goldsmith, Henry, x. 197, 199, 201, 205, 207, 209, 212
Goldsmith, Oliver (1728–1774), ii. 413; iv. 40; vi. 51; viii. 137; ix. 166, 167, 173, 220, 223, 325, 481; x. 39, 47, 68, 195 ff. (main entry), 263, 317, 318, 344, 422, 475, 480 ff., 489, 501, *also see* Add.; xi. 32, 163, 206, 207, 246, 252, 260, 262, 265, 266, 271, 376, 377, 385, 448, 466, 479, 489; xii. 43, 97, 132; xiii. 226, 244, 269, 445; xiv. 61, 169, 223, 313, 320, 439, 446, 448, 451, 552
Adventures of a Strolling Player, x. 205
Beauties of English Poesy, x. 210
Bee, The, x. 205, 206, 208
Captivity, The, x. 207, 480
City Night-Piece, A, x. 205

Goldsmith, Oliver
Description of an Author's Bedchamber, x. 205
Deserted Village, The, x. 134, 212, 213, 470; xi. 2, 144, 145, 361
Double Transformation, x. 198, 208
'Edinburgh, 1753,' x. 205
Elegy on Mrs Mary Blaize, x. 201, 205
English Grammar, x. 210
Enquiry into the Present State of Polite Learning, x. 92, 203 ff., 207, 211
Essay on the Theatre, x. 92
Essays, x. 208, 210
Fame Machine, The, x. 205
Gift, The, x. 205
Good-Natur'd Man, The, x. 91, 92, 211, 212, 214, 465, 470; xi. 261, 263
Haunch of Venison, The, x. 214, 215
Hermit (The) or Edwin and Angelina, x. 209
History of Animated Nature, x. 212
History of England, x. 212, 293, 501
History of England in Letters from a Nobleman to his Son, x. 207
History of Mecklenburgh, x. 206
History of Philosophy, x. 210
Life of Bolingbroke, x. 213
Life of Richard Nash, x. 206
Memoirs of a Protestant, x. 203
Memoirs of Voltaire, x. 204, 206
New Simile, The, x. 208
Old House, a New Inn (*She Stoops to Conquer*), x. 214
On the Death of Wolfe, x. 205
'On the Stage,' x. 204
Plutarch's Lives, x. 206
Poems for Young Ladies, x. 210
Present State of Polite Learning, The, xi. 323, 331
Retaliation, x. 215
Reverie in the Boar's Head Tavern, x. 205
Roman History, x. 212, 213
She Stoops to Conquer, x. 91, 197, 214, 479; xi. 265
Traveller, The, x. 128, 170, 201, 205, 207, 208, 210, 213, 467, 470; xii. 42
Vicar of Wakefield, The, x. 15, 25, 44, 195, 200, 203, 206 ff.; xi. 2; xiii. 524
Vida's Game of Chess, x. 480
Golgotha, v. 45
Goliardi, v. 27
Goliardic literature, ii. 256, 499
Golias, bishop, and *Goliardic Poems*, i. 177, 189, 190, 364
Goliath, in Cowley's *Davideis*, vii. 67
Goliath, in *Cursor Mundi*, i. 343
Gollancz, Sir Israel, i. 58, 61, 428; ii. 37
'Golldyn Arber in the Arche yerd of Plesyer, the,' vi. 283
Gómara, Francisco Lopez de, iv. 444
Gomberville, M. Le Roy de, viii. 15; *Polexandre*, vii. 391; viii. 371
Gomersal, Robert (1602–1646?), vii. 88, 412
Gomme, Sir Laurence, xii. 506
Goncourt, Edmond de, xiii. 457
Goncourt, Jules de, xiii. 457
Gondibert, in D'Avenant's *Gondibert*, vii. 71
Gondomar, don S. de Acuña, marquis de, ambassador, v. 365, 478; vi. 58, 79, 248; vii. 205
Goneril, in *King Lear*, v. 169
Gongora y Argote, Luis de, iv. 213; vii. 83
Gongorism, iii. 348; iv. 213
Gonville, Edmund (d. 1351), ii. 354
Gonzalo, in *The Tempest*, v. 207
Gooch, George Peabody, xiii. 545; xiv. 484; *English History and Historians*, xii. 313; xiv. 117
Good, John Mason (1764–1827), x. 526
Good Counsel, ii. 472, 473
Good Hope, cape of, iv. 85, 86, 99
Good Hope, in *The Kingis Quair*, ii. 242
Good Old Cause Revived, viii. 91
Good Words, xii. 472; xiii. 366
Goodall, Walter (1706?–1766), x. 501; *Examination of the* [Casket] *Letters*, x. 288
Goodcole, Henry (1586–1641), iv. 535
Goodcoll, in *Discoverie of the Knights of the Poste*, iv. 350
Good-deeds, in *Every-man*, v. 54
Goode, William (*fl.* 1644), *Intelligence*, vii. 351
Goode, William (1801–1868), xii. 472
Goodere, Anne (*fl.* 1595), iv. 174 ff., 190, 194, 211
Goodere, Frances, iv. 174
Goodere, Sir Henry, of Powlsworth, iv. 169, 174, 204, 205, 216, 221, 265
Goodere, Sir Henry, the younger, iv. 170
Goodhope, in *Magnyfycence*, iii. 77
Goodluck, in *Ralph Roister Doister*, v. 106
Goodman, Christopher (1520?–1603), iv. 303, 511
Goodman, Gabriel (1529?–1601), vii. 333, 450
Goodman, Godfrey (1583–1656), iv. 431; vii. 450
Goodman, W., xiii. 514
Goodrich, ix. 91
Goodrich, Samuel Griswold, xi. 387, 481. *See, also*, Parley, Peter
Goodwill, in Bunyan's *Pilgrim's Progress*, vii. 173
Goodwin, Charles Wycliffe (1817–1878), xii. 294, 466
Goodwin, Philip (d. 1699), vii. 510
Goodwin, Thomas, junior (1650?–1716), x. 385
Goody Two Shoes, xi. 376
Googe, Barnabe (1540–1594), iii. 177, 185, 186, 187, 219, 302, 508; iv. 110, 121, 171, 370, 447, 538
Cupido Conquered, ii. 228; iii. 185
Eclogs, Epytaphes and Sonettes, iii. 185, 186, 523
Four bookes of Husbandry, iv. 371, 511
Zodiacus Vitae, translation of, iii. 185
Goose, mother, xi. 375

Goranson, x. 490
Gorboduc, III. 284, 301; IV. 397; V. 66 ff., 85, 152, 155, 239, 337, 395; VII. 271; VIII. 223, 224; X. 70; XII. 190
Gordale scar, x. 101
Gordon, Ada, XII. 32
Gordon, Adam Lindsay (1833–1870), XIV. 365 ff., 371, 586
Ashtaroth, XIV. 367
Bush Ballads, XIV. 366, 367
Doubtful Dreams, XIV. 367
How we beat the Favourite, XIV. 367
Ride from the Wreck, The, XIV. 367
Sea Spray and Smoke Drift, XIV. 367
Sick Stockrider, The, XIV. 366, 367
Whisperings in Wattle-Boughs, XIV. 367
Wolf and Hound, XIV. 366, 367
Gordon, Alexander (d. 1752), IX. 553
Gordon, Alexander (1692?–1754?), IX. 355; *Itinerarium Septentrionale*, IX. 352, 534
Gordon, Catherine, of Gight, XII. 31
Gordon, Sir Cosmo, XII. 394
Gordon, lord George (1751–1793), XIII. 320; XIV. 121
Gordon, George Hamilton, 4th earl of Aberdeen (1784–1860), XIV. 134, 181, 182, 184, 420, 508
Gordon, James (1615?–1686), IX. 550
Gordon, Jane, duchess of (1749?–1812), XI. 220
Gordon, Margaret, XIII. 3
Gordon, Mrs Mary, XII. 445
Gordon, Patrick (*fl.* 1614–1650), IX. 555
Gordon, surgeon in Glasgow, X. 36
Gordon, Thomas (d. 1750), IX. 462, 471
Gordon, William (*fl.* 1726), IX. 553
Gordon riots, XI. 27. *See, also*, Gordon, lord George
Gore, Catherine Grace Frances (1799–1861), XII. 449; *Mothers and Daughters*, XII. 246; *Mrs Armytage, or Female Domination*, XII. 246
Gorges, lord, IX. 343
Gorges, Sir Arthur (d. 1625), IV. 438
Gorges, Sir Tristram, IV. 94
Gorges, William, IV. 456
Gorgious Gallery of Gallant Inventions, A, III. 190, 191, 248, 511, 523; IV. 471. *See, also*, Proctor, Thomas
Gorgo, in *The Adoniazusae*, III. 226
Gorgonius, in *The Scourge of Folly*, IV. 334
Gorhambury, IV. 279; VII. 203, 283
Goring, Charles, *Irene, or the Fair Greek*, X. 161
Goring, George, lord (1608–1657), VII. 22
Gorion, Joseph Ben, IV. 323
Görlitz, IX. 314
Gorlois, in Arthurian legend, I. 259
Gorlois, in *The Misfortunes of Arthur*, V. 77, 78
Goscelin (*fl.* 1099), II. 479
Gosnold, Bartholomew (d. 1609), IV. 94
Gospels, Early English, I. 444
Gosse, Edmund, IV. 203, 217, 241; VIII. 18; IX. 169; XI. 491; XII. 115, 173, 414, 432; XIII. 53, 211, 482, 484, 486, 494, 495, 508, 558, *also see* Add. 2; XIV. 526, 576; *Questions at Issue*, XIII. 457
Gosson, Stephen (1554–1624), III. 491; IV. 317, 323, 492, 518; V. 139, 359, 478; VI. 397, 461, 493
Apologie for the Schoole of Abuse, An, VI. 389, 392
Captain Mario, The Comedie of, V. 116; VI. 387
Catalines Conspiracy, VI. 387
Ephemerides of Phialo, The, VI. 388, 389
Playes Confuted in five Actions, V. 116; VI. 391, 392, 406
Pleasant Quippes for Upstart Gentlewomen, IV. 329; VI. 392
Pleasaunt invective against Poets, Pipers, Plaiers, Jesters and such like Caterpillers of a Commonwealth, VI. 387
Praise at Parting, VI. 387
School of Abuse, The, III. 299, 300, 526; V. 360; VI. 387 ff., 391
'Gossouin, Maistre,' II. 313
Goswell street, in *The Pickwick Papers*, XIII. 310
Gosynhyll, Edward (*fl.* 1560), III. 486; *The Prayse of all women, called Mulierum paean*, III. 90; *The Schole-house of women*, III. 84, 89, 90, 97
Götaland, I. 26, 27
Götar (Gautoi), I. 27
Gothic architecture, X. 217, 218, 238; XIV. 151, 246
Gothic art, X. 219; XI. 181
'Gothic Castle, The,' X. 245
Gothic gospels, X. 223, 225
Gothic language, XII. 326, 327, 343
Gothic nations, X. 222
'Gothic' romances, X. 233
Gothic rule in Italy, XII. 322
Gothic taste, X. 239
'Gothick' manner, the, X. 219
Goths, the, I. 21, 35; XIII. 363; XIV. 302
Gott, Samuel, VII. 421, 517
Gottfried von Strassburg, I. 268, 273, 316
Göttingen, II. 327
Gottlieb, T., IV. 419
Gottsched, J. C., V. 286, 290, 295
Gouda, II. 314
Gouge, William (1578–1653), VII. 322
Gough, Richard (1735–1809), IX. 530; X. 255; XII. 510; *Anecdotes of British Topography*, XI. 335; XII. 344, 345; 'History of the Society of Antiquaries,' XII. 345; *Sepulchral Monuments of Great Britain*, XII. 345
Goujon, French cadet, X. 203
Goulart, *Histoires Admirables*, VI. 183
Gould, G. M., XIII. 471; XIV. 166, 519
Gould, Robert (d. 1709?), VIII. 91, 404, 410
Gouldman, Francis (d. 1688?), VII. 486
Gouldsbury, Cullen, XIV. Add. 4, 7
Goupy, Joseph (d. 1763), XIV. 213
Gourgand, General, XII. 379

Gourlaw, Robert (d. 1585), IV. 414
Governance, a greyhound, in *The Passetyme of Pleasure*, II. 229
Governesses' Benevolent institution, XIV. 429
Government of Princes, the pseudo-Aristotelian, II. 284
Gow, Niel, XI. 233
Gowans, the, in *Little Dorrit*, XIII. 331
Go-well, in *Piers the Plowman*, II. 19
Gower, John (1325?–1408), I. 191, 204, 277, 280, 282, 332, 389; II. 133–155 (main entry), 159, 162, 164, 174, 183, 197, 210, 214, 225, 227, 228, 243, 252, 261, 262, 419, 422, 452 ff.; III. 57, 68, 70, 192, 273 ff., 281, 301, 440; V. 221; VI. 144, 311; VIII. 232; X. 239; XII. 504; XIII. 211, 238
 Carmen de pacis commendacione, In Praise of Peace, II. 153
 Cinkante Balades, II. 138, 154
 Confessio Amantis, I. 135, 286, 291, 347, 352; II. 134, 142, 143, 145 ff. (main entry), 155, 214, 219, 230, 314; III. 57
 Cronica Tripertita, II. 137, 154
 Henry IV, English poem to, II. 153
 Mirour de l'Omme (*Speculum Hominis, Speculum Meditantis*), II. 134, 137 ff., 147, 174; III. 192
 Vox Clamantis, II. 136 ff., 143 ff., 154
Gower, Sir Robert, of Brabourne, II. 134
Gownsman, The, XIII. 277; XIV. 207
Gowrie conspiracy, the, VI. 347; VII. 454
Gowther, Sir, I. 311, 314, 471
Grabbe, Christian, V. 303
Grabut, monsieur, VIII. 135
'Gracchus,' XIV. 513
Grace, a greyhound, in *The Passetyme of Pleasure*, II. 229
Grace, in *The Example of Virtue*, II. 227, 228
Grace-dieu (Leicestershire), VI. 111
Grâce Dieu, house of, in de Guileville's *Pilgrimage of the Sowle*, VII. 173
Gradgrinds, the, in Dickens's *Hard Times*, XIII. 330
Gradus ad Parnassum, VIII. 216
Graeci, Poetae Minores, XII. 328
Graelent, I. 295
Graevius, John George, IX. 331, 332, 524
Graf, Urs, II. 329
Grafton, III. 337
Grafton, duke of. *See* Fitzroy, Augustus Henry
Grafton, Richard (d. 1572), I. 170; III. 44, 316, 323, 332, 334, 337, 529; IV. 400;
 Abridgemen of the Chronicles of England, IV. 396; *A Chronicle at Large*, IV. 396; *Grammar of Oxford and Cambridge*, IV. 407
Graham, colonel, of Gartmore, XI. 232
Graham, Dougal (1724–1779), IX. 564, 566
 Comical Transactions of Lothian Tam, IX. 373
 Full...Account of the Rebellion, IX. 373
 History of Buchhaven, IX. 373
Graham, Dougal
 Jocky and Maggie's Courtship, IX. 373
 Turnimspike, The, IX. 373
Graham, George (d. 1767), *Telemachus*, X. 467
Graham, H. G., XIV. 535
Graham, James (1612–1650), 1st marquis of Montrose, IX. 193, 550, 556; XII. 21
Graham, James (d. 1742), 4th marquis and 1st duke of Montrose, IX. 215; X. 94
Graham, Sir James, VI. 47
Graham, Sir James Robert George (1792–1861), XIV. 130, 181, 326, 510
Graham, John, of Claverhouse, viscount Dundee (1649?–1689), IX. 264, 363, 564; XII. 21; XIV. 65
Graham, Patrick (d. 1478), II. 369
Graham, Richard (*fl.* 1680–1720), IX. 444
Graham, R. B. Cunningham, XIII. 493
Graham, Thomas, lord Lynedoch (1748–1843), X. 230
Graham, Thomas (1805–1869), XIV. 272, 279, 557
Graham, William (1839–1911), XIV. 473
Graham of Balgowan, X. 230
Graham's Town, XIV. 377
Grahame, James (1765–1811), XI. 443;
 Birds of Scotland, XI. 244; *Mary Queen of Scots*, XI. 244; *The Sabbath*, XI. 244
Grahame, Simion (1570?–1614), VII. 406; IX. 555
Grail, Gilbert, in Gissing's *Thyrza*, XIII. 459
Grail, the Holy (St Graal), in Arthurian romance, I. 261, 270 ff., 462, 469
Grail, the Holy, Malory on, II. 336, 337
Grail, the Holy, Map and the prose *Quest of*, I. 190, 270 ff.
Grainger, James (1721?–1766), X. 40, 455, *also see* Add.; *The Sugar Cane*, X. 204, 467
Grammar, lady, in *The Passetyme of Pleasure*, II. 225
Grammar schools, English, II. 70, 356 ff., VII. 491 ff.
Gramont, marshal de, brother of P. de Gramont, VIII. 263
Gramont, Philibert, comte de, VIII. 207, 209, 262, 266, 359; key to the *Memoirs of the Comte de Gramont*, VIII. 261; *Mémoires de Gramont*, VIII. 199, 268; IX. 236
Grampian club, X. 193
Grampians, the, XII. 31
Gramsbergen, Matthus, V. 285
Granada, IV. 9
Granada, Luis de, IV. 444
Granard, XIV. 311
Granby, marquis of. *See* Manners, John
Grand Combatant, mounsier, French braggadocio, in *Club Law*, VI. 309
'Grand Council,' The, X. 403
Grandcourt, in *Daniel Deronda*, XIII. 399, 400
Grande Chartreuse, VII. 338; X. 119, 127

Grandison, Sir Charles, in Richardson's novel, VIII. 308; X. 2. 10, 11, 14, 18, 31, 62; XI. 356; XII. 128; XIII. 390
Grandison, Charlotte, in Richardson's novel, X. 11
Grandison, John (1292?–1369), bishop of Exeter, V. 25, 55
Granger, James (1723–1776), XIV. 502
Grant, Sir Alexander (1826–1884), XII. 334, 484, 487; XIV. 595
Grant, Mrs Anne, of Laggan (1755–1838), XI. 443; XIV. 502
Eighteen Hundred and Thirteen, XI. 232
Letters from the Mountains, XI. 232
O Where tell me Where, XI. 232
Poems, XI. 232
Grant, Charles, baron Glenelg (1778–1866), XII. 417
Grant, or Graunt, Edward (1540?–1601), *Spicilegium*, III. 429
Grant, Mrs Elizabeth, of Carron (Mrs Murray: 1745?–1814), *Roy's wife of Aldivalloch*, XI. 232
Grant, George Monro (1835–1902), XIV. 359, 583
Grant, James (1802–1879), XIV. 531; *The Newspaper Press*, XIV. 177
Grant, James (1822–1887), XIII. 471, 562
Grant, James (1840–1885), XIV. 591
Grant, James Augustus (1827–1892), XIV. 552
Grant, Sir Robert (1779–1838), XII. 417
Grant, Robert Edmond (1793–1874), XIV. 298, 560
Grant, Roger, IX. 41
Grant Duff, James. *See* Duff, James Grant
Grant Duff, Sir Mountstuart Elphinstone (1829–1906), XIV. 494, 502, 594
Granta, The, XIV. 207, 208, 537
Grantham, IV. 23; VIII. 279
Grantham, Henry, IV. 441, 443
Grantham school, VII. 330
Grantly, archdeacon, Trollope's, XIII. 422
Granville, Augustus Bozzi, *Travels in Russia*, XII. 302
Granville, Sir Bevil (d. 1706), IX. 175
Granville, earls of. *See* Carteret, John; Leveson-Gower, Granville George
Granville, George, baron Lansdowne (1667–1735), VIII. 221, 436, 444, 445; IX. 69, 174 ff., 476, 486; X. 432, 458
British Enchanters, The, VIII. 53, 194
Heroick Love, VIII. 55, 194, 396
'Love is by Fancy led about,' IX. 175
Merchant of Venice, The, VIII. 194
'Myra,' IX. 174, 175
She-Gallants, The, VIII. 194
'Thoughtful nights and restless waking,' IX. 175
Graphic, The, XIV. 196, 201, 530, 535
Grasby, Lincolnshire, XIII. 46
Grasmere, XI. 102, 103, 109; XII. 337
Grasse, admiral de, XIV. 214
Grassi, Giacomo, IV. 457
Gratian, III. 50, 416
Gratian's *Decretum*, II. 350; VIII. 312
Grattan, Henry (1746–1820), XI. 55, 56, 396; XIV. 126, 311, 510
Grattan, Henry ('Fusbos'). *See* Plunkett, Henry Grattan
Grattan, Thomas Colley (1792–1864), XIV. 552
Gratton, John (1641–1712), VIII. 106, 416
Graund Amour, in *The Passetyme of Pleasure*, II. 225, 226, 228, 229, 232, 234, 235, 238
Graunt, John (1620–1674), VIII. 473, 477; *Natural and Political Observations*, VIII. 367
Grave, The, I. 147
Grave Diggers' Colloquy, The, VIII. 116
Gravelot, H., XIV. 212
Graves, Alfred Perceval, XII. 361; XIII. 556; XIV. 573, 574
Graves, Charles (1812–1899), XII. 516; XIV. 328
Graves, Charles Edward (1839–1920), XII. Add. 3
Graves, James (1815–1886), XII. 510
Graves, Richard (1715–1804), IX. 412; X. 273, 275 ff., 497
Columella, or the Distressed Anchoret, X. 276, 277
Eugenius or Anecdotes of the Golden Vale, X. 277
Euphrosyne, X. 275
Festoon, The, X. 275
Plexippus, X. 277
Recollection of...Shenstone, X. 275
Spiritual Quixote, X. 276, 277
Graves, Stanzas of the, I. 243, 249, 250
Gravesend, III. 203; IV. 362
Gray, Andrew (1633–1656), IX. 544
Gray, D., IV. 457
Gray, David (1838–1861), XIII. 194, 503
Gray, Dorothy, mother of Thomas Gray, X. 116
Gray, G. J., X. 457
Gray, James (d. 1830), XI. 408
Gray, John Hamilton, XIV. 593
Gray, Philip, father of Thomas Gray, X. 116
Gray, Rosamund, in Lamb's *Rosamund Gray*, XII. 186
Gray, Sir Thomas (d. 1369?), *Scalacronica*, II. 128, 451
Gray, Thomas, parson of Liberton, II. 110
Gray, Thomas (1716–1771), I. 275; II. 204, 410; VIII. 234; IX. 169, 173, 189 ff., 412, 481; X. 87, 93, 109, 116 ff. (main entry), 147, 149, 155, 198, 205, 220, 239, 241 ff., 251, 450, 475, 489, *also see* Add.; XI. 77, 91, 124, 140, 207, 248, 250 ff., 255; XII. 133, 177, 208; XIII. 27, 29; XIV. 109, 117, 385, 453, 507, 517
Agrippina, X. 119, 120
Alliance of Education and Government, X. 123
Bard, The, X. 127 ff., 132, 136, 137, 186, 225
De Principiis Cogitandi, X. 122

Gray, Thomas
Descent of Odin, x. 120, 132, 221, 225, 227
Elegy, vi. 189; ix. 167; x. 118, 123 ff., 128, 132, 185, 186, 208, 273; xi. 85, 144, 206, 248, 323; xii. 41; xiii. 44, 149, 170
Fatal Sisters, The, x. 129, 132, 221, 225
Hymn to Adversity, x. 121
Hymn to Ignorance, x. 121
Journal in the Lakes, x. 101
Letters, x. 134
Long Story, A, x. 126, 127, 132
Metrum, x. 131; xi. 252
Observations on the poems of Lydgate, x. 131
Ode on the Death of a Favourite Cat, x. 123
Ode on a Distant Prospect of Eton College, ix. 409; x. 121, 122; xi. 323
Ode on the Spring, x. 121
Odes, x. 202
On the pleasure arising from Vicissitude, x. 128, 129
Poems (1898 ed.), x. 123
Progress of Poesy, x. 119, 127 ff.
Sonnet on the Death of Richard West, x. 121
Stanzas to Richard Bentley, x. 126
Gray, Thomas and Erasmus, iii. 7
Gray ms., ii. 478
Gray and his Friends, x. 121
Grayes-Inne, Certaine devises and Shewes presented to her Majestie by the Gentlemen of, v. 77
Gray's Inn Journal, x. 466
Grazzini, A. F., v. 413; *La Spiritata*, v. 115; *La Strega*, v. 69
Great Baddow, iii. 57
Great Berkhampstead, xi. 78
Great Braxted, viii. 321
Great Malvern, x. 276
Great North road, the, xii. 19
Great Parham, xi. 144
Great Rissington, ix. 145
Great Tew, vii. 150 ff., 155, 305; viii. 63, 298
Great Assizes holden in Parnassus, The, vii. 387
Great Silkie of Sule Skerry, The, ii. 413
Greaves, John (1602–1652), vii. 488; viii. 360; ix. 530
Greaves, J. P., ix. 328
Greaves, Sir Launcelot, in Smollett's novel, x. 41
Greaves, Thomas (*fl.* 1604), iv. 113, 154, 464
Grech, W. L., xiii. 543
Greece, ii. 238; iv. 3, 64; v. 24, 29, 30; vi. 8; vii. 99, 303; ix. 112, 138, 256; x. 104, 107, 128, 154, 202, 318; xi. 57, 72; xii. 32, 38 ff., 44, 46, 56, 62, 82, 89, 90, 93, 209, 272, 302, 304, 314 ff., 329 ff., 338, 339, 411, 417; xiii. 130. 461; xiv. 8, 23, 70, 71
Greece, history of, xii. 300, 302, 307 ff.
Greece and Byron, xii. 392, 394 ff.
Greedy, in *A New Way to pay Old Debts*, vi. 161
Greek anthologists, the, xiii. 193
Greek anthology, xii. 420, *also see* Add.
Greek architecture, xii. 339
Greek atomic theory, xiv. 272
Greek chair at Cambridge, ix. 341
Greek chorus, xi. 265; xiii. 445
Greek church, viii. 297
Greek coins, xii. 338
Greek drama, v. 1, 5, 61, 62, 65, 71, 182, 296, 297, 334; vi. 14, 215, 232, 294 ff.; x. 78, 108; xii. 68, 113, 327; xiii. 130, 133
Greek epigram, xiii. 387
Greek heroes, xiii. 354
Greek history, xiv. 175
Greek hymns, xii. 273
Greek inscriptions, xii. 339
Greek kings, in *The Four Ages*, vi. 92
Greek language and literature, v. 362; vii. 3, 7, 9, 13, 14, 74, 80, 130, 164, 165, 237, 282, 283, 312, 313, 315 ff., 319, 320, 323, 329, 333, 340 ff., 348; viii. 58, 86, 112, 229, 287, 353, 364; ix. 75, 144, 266, 267, 270, 273, 331, 334, 336, 337, 341, 382, 383, 385, 388, 390, 391, 393, 396, 403, 404, 409, 410, 562; x. 202, 335; xi. 2, 58, 90, 181, 343, 354 ff.; xii. 40, 60, 83, 89, 94, 208 ff., 212, 215, 230, 278, 308, 317, 323 ff., 329, 330, 334, 338, 340, 343; xiii. 53, 71, 81, 90, 92, 126, 129, 165, 175, 187, 245, 249, 353; xiv. 209, 302, 307, 327, 382, 385, 388, 391, 405, 406, 413, 416, 426, 440, 454, 455, 457, 458
Greek learning (1600–1660), vii. 487 ff.
Greek manuscripts, xii. 323
Greek mythology, xii. 65, 111; xiii. 271; xiv. 154
Greek poetry, ix. 67, 331; xii. 58, 329, 330, 332, 333; xiii. 36, 45, 95
Greek press, Early Parisian, xii. 522
Greek printing, 15th century, xii. 523
Greek pronunciation, ix. 210
Greek revolution, xii. 314
Greek, study of, ii. 359, 367, 370, 371
Greek Testament, vii. 317, 339; ix. 336
Greek war of liberation, xii. 38, 75
Greek and Latin Measures in English Poetry, xiii. 244
Greeks, the, xi. 30, 273, 352, 363; xii. 38, 45, 69, 80; xiii. 90, 205
Greeks, the, in Milton's *England*, vii. 129
Green, Alice S. A., xiv. 77, 490
Green, Mrs Everett, vii. 189
Green, George (1793–1841), xiv. 265 ff., 556
Green, Henry, xiii. 549
Green, John (1706?–1779), ix. 571
Green, J. A., xiii. 549
Green, John Richard (1837–1883), i. 196, 201; vii. 168, 305; xii. 321; xiii. 465; xiv. 64, 74, 76 ff. (main entry), 100, 198, 490
Conquest of England, The, xiv. 77
Making of England, The, xiv. 77

Green, John Richard
Short History of the English People, A, XIV. 76, 77
Studies from England and Italy, XIV. 76
Green, Joseph Henry (1791–1863), XI, 417; XIV. 471
Green, Mary Anne Everett, born Wood (1818–1895), XIV. 502; *Letters of Queen Henrietta Maria,* XIV. 111; *Letters of Royal Ladies of Great Britain,* XIV. 111; *Lives of the Princesses of England,* XIV. 111
Green, Matthew (1696–1737), X. 137, 138, 144, 146 (main entry), 156, 455, 480; *The Spleen,* IX. 191; X. 146
Green, rector of Kilkenny West, X. 196
Green, Robert, Ἐγκυκλοπαιδεία, IX. 411
Green, Thomas Hill (1836–1882), X. 511; XII. 298, 467; XIV. 38, 43 ff., 473
Lectures on the Principles of Political Obligation, XIV. 44
Prolegomena to Ethics, XIV. 43
Works, XIV. 43
Green, William Charles (1832–1914), XII. 484
Green willow, Sing all of, III. 190
Greenaway, Kate, XI. 475, 483, 485
Greene, Edward Burnaby (d. 1788), X. 485
Greene, John, *A Refutation of the Apology for Actors,* VI. 401
Greene, Robert (1560?–1592), III. 114, 208, 241, 243, 305, 340, 342, 343, 350, 351, 355 ff., 359 ff., 366, 367, 370, 371, 395, 396, 534, 545, 546; IV. 116 ff., 317 ff., 323, 324, 358, 363, 469, 470, 472, 473, 514 ff., 517, 521, 527, 528, 530, 535; V. 63, 85, 87, 121–141 (main entry), 147, 166, 169, 170, 175, 185, 206, 219, 239, 246, 251, 309, 327, 353, 364, 370, 418 ff., 439, *and see* Add. 2; VI. 13, 14, 249, 287, 300, 301, 365, 494; VII. 395; VIII. 223; IX. 26, 51, 161; XI. 262; XIV. 234
? A most rare and excellent dreame, IV. 116
Alcida, III. 357
Alphonsus King of Arragon, V. 134 ff.; VIII. 125
Arbasto, III. 357
Battell of Alcazar, VIII. 125
Black Booke's Messenger, The, III. 361
'Cupid abroad was lated in the night,' VII. 2
Defence of Conny-Catching, A, III. 361; IV. 319
Disputation between a He Conny-Catcher and a She Conny-Catcher, A, III. 361; IV. 319
Edward I, VIII. 125
Euphues his Censure to Philautus, III. 350, 356
Farewell to Folly, V. 133, 252
Francesco's Fortunes, IV. 118; VI. 396
Frier Bacon and Frier Bongay, I. 210; V. 135 ff., 252, 316, 340
Greene, Robert
George a Greene, the Pinner of Wakefield, V. 35, 135, 373, 418
Greenes Mourning Garment, V. 133, 137
Groatsworth of Wit, III. 357, 360, 545; IV. 320; V. 322
Gwydonius, III. 357
James IV, V. 135, 137, 138, 245
Job, V. 134
Looking Glasse for London and England, A, V. 135, 354
Mamillia, III. 350; IV. 398; V. 133, 161
Menaphon, III. 208, 256, 357, 545; IV. 118; V. 80, 121, 133, 134, 140, 157
Morando, V. 133
Mourning Garment, III. 360
Myrrour of Modestie, The, III. 350, 356
Never too late, III. 356, 360
Notable Discovery of Coosnage, A, III. 360, 361; IV. 319; V. 132
Orlando Furioso, V. 134 ff.; VI. 250
Orpharion, III. 357; VII. 2
Pandosto, III. 356; V. 133, 220
Penelope's Web, III. 350
Perimedes the Blacksmith, III. 356; V. 133, 134, 136
Philomela, III. 357; V. 133; VI. 137
Planetomachia, III. 356, 357; V. 133
Quip for an Upstart Courtier, A, III. 361, 396, 545; IV. 319
Repentance of Robert Greene, The, III. 360; V. 133, 136
Spanish Masquerado, III. 357; V. 133
Vision, V. 133, 137
Trans. of Anacreon, from *Orpharion,* IV. 124
See, also, *Faire Em* and *Selimus*
Greene, Thomas, actor, VI. 219
Greene, Thomas (1658–1738), bishop of Ely, IX. 335, 339
Greenham or Grenham, Richard (1535?–1594?), III. 389
Greenhill, William (1591–1671), VII. 322
Greenhill, William Alexander (1814–1894), VII. 235
Greenland, VII. 64; XII. 420
Greenock, IX. 374; XI. 410
Greenough, George Bellas (1778–1855), XIV. 287, 560, 611
'Greensleeves,' III. 190
Greenwell, Dorothy (Dora) (1821–1882), XIII. 177, 503
Greenwell, William (b. 1820), XII. 354, 510; *British Barrows,* XII. 348; *The electrum coinage of Cyzicus,* XII. 348
Greenwey, Richard, IV. 5, 440
Greenwich, II. 158; III. 80; V. 90, 170, 219; VIII. 260; IX. 281
Greenwich hospital, VIII. 249
Greenwood, Frederick (1830–1909), XIV. 189, 194, 195, 534
Greenwood, G., XIV. 561
Greenwood, James (d. 1737), IX. 474
Greenwood, John (d. 1593), III. 390
Greenwood, T., XIV. 543
Greenwood, William, *Philalethes,* IV. 251

Greevous Grones for the Poore, IV. 513
Greg, Walter Wilson, V. 253, 331; VI. 96, 274, 365
Greg, William Rathbone (1809–1881), XII. 291, 467; XIII. 359, 373, 377, 471, 548; XIV. 519
Creed of Christendom, The, XIV. 164
Enigmas of Life, XIV. 164
Essays, XIII. 374
Mistaken Aims, XIII. 374; XIV. 164
Rocks Ahead, XIV. 164
Grego, J., XIII. 530; XIV. 540
Gregorian Gospels at Corpus Christi college, Cambridge, I. 72
Gregory VII, pope, XII. 418
Gregory IX, pope, I. 203; VII. 367; VIII. 312
Gregory XI, pope, II. 49
Gregory, David (1661–1708), IX. 378
Gregory, George (1754–1808), X. 485; 486; XIII. 241
Gregory, lady Isabella Augusta, XIII. 514
Gregory, John, M.D. (1724–1773), XI. 486; XIV. 600
Gregory, Olinthus Gilbert (1774–1841), XI. 399
Gregory, Padraic, XIV. 574
Gregory, Robert, XIV. 591
Gregory, T., VIII. 459
Gregory, Saint, XII. 266
Gregory, St, Trentals of, I. 312
Gregory, William (d. 1467), II. 302, 482
Gregory the Great, I. 53, 61, 81, 85, 91, 92, 96, 117, 224, 231, 347, 355; II. 76, 264, 365; III. 9; IV. 424; *Cura Pastoralis*, I. 91, 92; *Dialogues*, I. 75, 86, 103, 105, 436, 437, 439; VII. 391
Gregory the Great and the English boy slaves, I. 234, 351, 379, 380
Gregory Nazianzen, St, I. 74; II. 75; V. 5
Gregory of Tours, I. 26, 67, 117
Grein, C. W. M., I. ix, 48, 91, 420
Grelot, Guillaume Joseph, *Voyage to Constantinople*, IX. 268, 500
Grendel, in *Beowulf*, I. 2, 11, 22, 23, 28, 115; II. 398
Grendles mere, Wiltshire, I. 27
Grenville, George (1712–1770), X. 399, 402 ff., 408, 409, 523, 527; XI. 5, 7, 10 ff.
Grenville, George (master of Magdalene college, Cambridge), VIII. 242
Grenville, lord George (Nugent Temple) (1753–1813), VIII. 242
Grenville, Sir Richard (1541?–1591), IV. 10, 56; VII. 75
Grenville, Richard Temple, earl Temple (1711–1779), X. 402, 409, 410, 523
Grenville, William Wyndham, lord Grenville (1759–1834), XIV. 513
Grenville Correspondence, X. 400, 402
Grenville library, XII. 368
Grenville party, the, XIV. 120
Gresham, Sir Thomas (1519?–1579), III. 426; V. 354; VI. 84, 91, 300; VII. 333; IX. 530; XIV. 186
Gresham's law, XIV. 186
Greshams, the, in Trollope's novels, XIII. 422
Gresset, Jean-Baptiste-Louis, X. 137; *Sur ma convalescence*, X. 129
Greswell, William, XIV. Add. 7
Greswell, William Parr (1765–1854), XII. 522
Greta hall, XII. 188
Greta hall, Keswick, XI. 156, 168
Gretchen, XIII. 153
Grete herball, The, IV. 542
Grettir, I. 27; XIII. 125
Grettis Saga, I. 27, 28; XIII. 125
Greville, Charles Cavendish Fulke (1794–1865), XIV. 123, 124, 171, 184, 187, 503; *The Greville Memoirs*, XIV. 114, 115, 181, 182, 189; *The Policy of England to Ireland*, XIV. 115
Greville, Sir Fulke, lord Brooke (1554–1628), III. 189, 257, 267; IV. 114, 117, 132, 133, 150, 159–161 (main entry), 465, 482; V. 204, 335, 474; VI. 19; VII. 278, 337, 471, *also see* Add.; VIII. 133
Alaham, IV. 159; V. 334
Caelica, III. 257, 267; IV. 160, 523, 551
Certaine learned and elegant workes, IV. 159
Inquisition upon Fame and Honour, An, IV. 159
Monarchy and Religion, IV. 160
Mustapha, IV. 159; V. 334
Of Fame and Honour, IV. 160
Of Humane Learning, IV. 160
Of Warres, IV. 160
Remains, IV. 160
Treatie of Warres, A, IV. 159
Treatise of Humane Learning, A, IV. 159
Greville, Robert, 2nd lord Brooke (1608–1643), VII. 277 ff.; *The Nature of Truth*, VII. 278, 471; *A Discourse...of...Episcopacy*, VII. 278
Greville, Mrs, *Prayer for Indifference*, XII. 124
'Grewellers,' VIII. 98
Grew, Nehemiah (1641–1712), VIII. 477; XIV. 282, 560
Grew, Obadiah (1607–1689), X. 385
Grey, Arthur (1536–1593), baron Grey de Wilton, III. 202, 206, 207, 212, 229; IV. 51, 53; VII. 211
Grey, Charles, 2nd earl Grey (1764–1845), XI. 52; XIV. 116, 120, 124, 125, 172, 510
Grey, Douglas, XIV. 536
Grey, Elizabeth, countess of Kent (1581–1651), VIII. 60
Grey, Elizabeth, queen of Edward IV, IV. 137
Grey, Sir George (1812–1898), XIV. 487
Grey, lady Jane (1537–1554), III. 431; IV. 169, 182; VI. 54
Grey, Vivian, Disraeli's, XIII. 346, 417
Grey, William (d. 1478), bishop of Ely, II. 303, 496, 499; III. 5; IV. 427
Grey, Mrs William [Maria Georgina Grey, born Shirreff], XIV. 600, 606

Grey, Zachary (1688–1766), v. 273; viii. 59; ix. 145, 212, 476, 494, 531
Grey collection, the (South Africa), xiv. Add. 4
Grey Friars, church of, ii. 335
Gride, Arthur, in *Nicholas Nickleby*, xiii. 322
Grierson, Constantia (1706?–1733), xi. 172, 426
Grierson, Sir George Abraham (b. 1851), xii. Add. 4
Grieve, Mrs, in Foote's drama, x. 88
Griff house, xiii. 382
Griffin, Bartholomew (*fl.* 1596), iii. 256, 264, 266; v. 224; *Fidessa*, iii. 256, 266, 523; *Venus and Adonis*, iii. 266
Griffin, Gerald (1803–1840), xiv. 568; *Collegians, The*, xiv. 320; *Gisippus*, xiv. 320
Griffin, maker of Arthur's spear, in *Layamon*, i. 265
Griffin, Mrs, vii. 360, 361
Griffin, Sir, in *John a Kent*, v. 317
Griffin, W., publisher, x. 212
Griffin, W. H. and H. C. Minchin, *The Life of Robert Browning*, xiii. 71
Griffith, Mrs Elizabeth (1720?–1793), xi. 457; *School for Rakes*, xi. 263
Griffith, Matthew (1599?–1665), vii. 106, 141, 416
Griffith, Ralph Thomas Hotchkin (1826–1906), xii. 502
Griffith, Roger, x. 387
Griffith and Farran, xi. 377
Griffiths, Ralph (1720–1803), ix. 563; x. 40, 201 ff., 206, 483
Griffiths, Vavasor, x. 386
Grignan, château de, x. 248
Grillparzer, Franz, v. 303
Grim, in *Damon and Pithias*, v. 119
Grim, in *Havelok*, i. 303, 304
Grim, the collier, in *The Devil and his Dame*, v. 329
Grimald or Grimoald, Nicholas (1519–1562), iii. 179 ff., 185, 508; iv. 5, 24, 435; v. 394; vi. 473
Archipropheta, v. 82; vi. 295, 327
Christus Redivivus, vi. 295
Funerall song upon the deceas of Annes his mother, iii. 180
The Garden, iii. 180
The Lover asketh pardon of his dere, iii. 180
Grimaldi, Joseph, xiii. 514
Grimalfi, in *Perfidus Hetruscus*, vi. 302
Grimbald of St Bertin (820?–903), abbot of Winchester, i. 89, 92
Grime, in Holcroft's *Deserted Daughter*, xi. 277
Grimefield, J., *The Sage Senator Delineated*, vii. 518
Grimeston, Edward, *Admirable and Memorable Histories*, iii. 536; translation of de Serres's *Inventaire Général de l'Histoire de France*, iv. 448; vi. 33; translation of *History* of Polybius, vii. 488
Grimm, H., xiii. 470
Grimm, Jacob, i. 55, 383, 420; xii. 344
Grimm, Jacob Ludwig Carl and Wilhelm Carl, xi. 381, 491; *German Popular Stories*, xi. 386
Grimm, Samuel Hieronymus (1734–1794), xiv. 214
Grimmelshausen, H. J. C. von, *Simplicissimus*, iv. 256
Grimoard, comte, ix. 217
Grimsby, in *Havelok*, i. 303, 351, 364
Grimshawe, Thomas Shuttleworth (1778–1850), xi. 401, 402; xii. 472
Grimston, Sir Harbottle (1603–1685), ix. 194
Grindal, Edmund (1519?–1583), archbishop of Canterbury, iii. 213, 214, 374, 375, 468; iv. 493; v. 56, 482; vi. 297, 381; ix. 496
Gringoire, Pierre, xiii. 428; *Chasteau de labour*, ii. 329; iii. 56
Grinsell, Thomas, vii. 250
Grischow, J. H., x. 515
Griselda (Chaucer's), v. 243
Griselda (Petrarch's), ii. 184
Griseldis, in school plays, v. 103
Griseldis-Motiv, in English drama, vi. 97
Grisone, iv. 444
Gritsch, Johan, iii. 489
Grizzle, Dr Syntax's mare, xiv. 218, 219
Grobian, St, ix. 32, 46
Grobiana's Nuptialls, vi. 483
Grobianism, iv. 517, 528
Grobianus, in *Das Narrenschiff*, iii. 82
Grobianus, in *Grobiana's Nuptials*, iii. 82
Grocer's Play, The, v. 390
Grocyn, William (1446?–1519), ii. 367; iii. 3, 6, 10, 12, 13, 15, 17, 430; vii. 326
Grolier, Jean, iv. 406
Grolier club, xiii. 476
Gronovius, J. F., vii. 307; ix. 527
Groome, Francis Hindes (1851–1902), xiv. 519; *In Gypsy Tents*, xiv. 146; *Kriegspiel*, xiv. 145, 146; *Suffolk Parson, A*, xiv. 146
Grosart, Alexander Balloch (1827–1899), iv. 165; v. 85; vii. 11, 29, 34, 35; xi. 407, 442, 445; xiii. 508
Grose, captain, ii. 275
Grose, Francis (1731?–1791), xii. 510
Ancient Armour and Weapons, xii. 349
Antiquities of England and Wales, xii. 349
Antiquities of Ireland, xii. 349
Antiquities of Scotland, xii. 349
Dictionary of the Vulgar Tongue, xiv. 224, 540
Grose, T. H., x. 511; xiv. 473
Grosseteste, Robert (d. 1253), bishop of Lincoln, i. 203, 204 ff., 209, 210, 342, 353; ii. 42, 44, 48, 52, 345, 348, 350, 365; iv. 269, 307, 369, 370; v. 8, 39; vi. 374; *Château d'Amour*, i. 204, 343, 454; ii. 26
Grosvenor, Richard Grosvenor, 1st earl (1731–1802), xi. 40

Grote, George (1794–1871), XI. 72, 398; XII. 307 ff., 318, 322, 475, 476; XIV. 14, 187, 407, 473
Essentials of Parliamentary Reform, XII. 310
Fragments on Ethical Subjects, XIV. 23
History of Greece, XII. 311, 312
Plato and the Companions of Sokrates, XII. 311
Seven Letters on the Recent Politics of Switzerland, XII. 311
Statement of the Question of Parliamentary Reform, XII. 310
Grote, Harriet, *Personal Life of George Grote*, XII. 309, 476
Grote, John (1813–1866), XII. 493; XIV. 26, 473; *Examination of the Utilitarian Philosophy*, XIV. 25; *Exploratio Philosophica*, XIV. 25; *Treatise on the Moral Ideals*, XIV. 25
Grotius, Hugo, III. 157, 423; IV. 259, 293; VII. 52, 99, 281, 300, 518; VIII. 316; IX. 331, 525; X. 291; *Adamus Exul*, VII. 118; *Mare Liberum*, VII. 307; VIII. 318
Groto, Luigi, V. 62; *Pentimento Amoroso*, VI. 317; *La Dalida*, VI. 302
Groundolf, Agnes (Gower's wife), II. 135
Grove, Sir George (1820–1900), XII. 493
Grove, Henry (1684–1738), X. 386
Grove, Matthew (*fl.* 1587), III. 508; *Epigrams, songes and sonnettes*, III. 188; *The History of Pelops and Hippodamia*, III. 188
Grove, Sir William Robert (1811–1896), XIV. 556
Grove, The, IV. 209
Grover, Henry Montague (1791–1866), XIII. 261, 519
Groves, a Jesuit, VIII. 266
Growoll, A., *Three centuries of English booktrade bibliography*, XI. 339, 470, 471
Grub, George (1812–1892), XII. 513; XIV. 490
Grub, J., XIV. 497
Grub street, VIII. 91, 174; IX. 118, 122, 256, 258, 261, 262, 264, 265, 268, 271, 272; X. 139, 201, 389; XI. 317, 329, 330; XII. 204; XIII. 163; XIV. 168
Grub-street Journal, The, IX. 80, 449; X. 162; XI. 466; XIV. 200
Gruffydd ap Cynan, XIV. 307
Grumio, in Lacy's *Sawny the Scot*, VIII. 140
Grumio, Shakespeare's, XIV. 443
Grundtvig, S. H., II. 398, 413, 417
Grundy, Frances H., XIII. 558
Grundy, Mrs, in Morton's *Speed the Plough*, XI. 281
Grundy, Sydney (1848–1914), XIII. 519
Grunnius Corocotta, Testament of, III. 482
Gruter, J., IV. 261
Gryphius, Andreas, V. 285, 290, 458
Gryphius, Sebastian, III. 427
Guala, cardinal, I. 238
Gualter, Katherine, in Burton's *Anatomy*, IV. 246
Guardeloop, in *The Tatler*, IX. 41
Guardian, The, IX. 64, 69, 77, 161, 165, 437 ff., 441, 446, 456, 462; XII. 454, 459; XIV. 67, 71, 199, 202
Guardian of Education, The, XI. 380; XIV. 402
Guarini, in Jonson's *Volpone*, VII. 274
Guarini, Gian Battista, *Pastor Fido*, IV. 134, 445; VI. 21, 137, 317, 365, 366, 371, 485, 490; VIII. 271, 441
Guarino, Battista, III. 5; IV. 323
Guarna, A., *Grammaticale Bellum*, VI. 482
Guarsi, Andrew, VI. 38
Guary miracles, V. 15
Guayaquil, XIV. 242
Guazzo Stefano, *Civile Conversation*, III. 432, 551; IV. 445
Guben, siege of, VII. 22
Gude and Godlie Ballatis, The, III. 138, 141, 502; IX. 359, 360, 365
Gude Counsell, in *Ane Pleasant Satyre*, III. 124, 125, 126
Gude Wallace, II. 399
Gudgeon Credulous, Sir, in Wilson's *The Projectors*, VIII. 123
Gudius, X. 457
Gudrun, in Morris's *Sigurd the Volsung*, XIII. 126
Gudrun, in Morris's *The Lovers of Gudrun*, XIII. 125
Guelphs, XIII. 59
Guenevora, in *The Misfortunes of Arthur*, V. 78, 79
Guericke, Otto von, VIII. 364
Guernsey, XII. 328; XIII. 135
Guernsey, A. H., XIII. 471
Guest, Edwin (1800–1880), I. 333; XII. 510; XIII. 241 ff., 247, 248, 512; *A History of English Rhythms*, XI. 170; XIII. 228, 232, 240, 512
Guest, lady Charlotte, *Mabinogion*, I. 247, 252, 253, 276, 461
Guest, Stephen, in *The Mill on the Floss*, XIII. 392
Guevara, Antonio de, II. 340; III. 341, 344 ff., 348, 551; IV. 9, 445, 525; *El Relox de Principes*, III. 341; V. 123; VI. 377; VII. 390
Guiana, IV. 56, 57, 59, 61, 88; XIV. 249
Guiboux, Carolingian heroine, I. 303
Guicciardini, F., IV. 445
Guiccioli, count, XII. 34
Guiccioli, Theresa, countess, XII. 33 ff., 37, 49, 50, 383, 395
Guido, in Browning's *The Ring and the Book*, XIII. 66
Guido de Baysio's *Rosarium*, II. 364
Guido delle Colonne, I. 170; *Hystoria Troiana*, II. 104, 118, 150, 172, 201, 363
Guido Reni, XII. 67
Guiffardière, M. de, X. 65, 254
Guild, William (1586–1657), IX. 544
Guildenstern, in *Hamlet*, V. 201, 262
Guildford, III. 428
Guildford. *See* Nicholas of
Guildford, Sir Richard (1455?–1506), IV 457; *Pilgrimage of*, II. 321

Guileville, G. de, *Pilgrimage of the Sowle*, VII. 173, 430
Guilford, earls of. *See* North, Francis; North, Frederick
Guillaume de Lorris, II. 169, 219
Guillaume de Machault, II. 467
Guillaume de Palerme. See *William of Palerne*
Guillaume de Tignoville, *Les ditz moraulx des philosophes*, II. 313
Guillaume de Twicé, II. 509
Guillaume le Roy, II. 316
Guillaume le Maréchal, L'Histoire de, I. 477; II. 420
Guillemard, G., IX. 435
Guillemins, church of the, Mandeville's burial place, II. 81
Guillim, John (1565–1621), *Display of Heraldrie*, IV. 376, 543
Guilpin, Edward, IV. 332, 362, 363; *Skialetheia, or A Shadowe of Truth*, IV. 138, 331, 519, 533; VI. 461
Guilsborough, XII. 256
Guinea, IV. 72, 75, 88
Guinevere or Guenever, I. 261, 262, 266, 270, 312, 313, 327; II. 122, 176; VII. 75
Guinevere, Tennyson's, XIII. 37, 38
Guiney, Louise Imogen, XIII. 503
Guingelot, Wade's boat, I. 218
Guinicelli, IV. 196
Guinnion, castle of, I. 246
Guiomar, in *The Custome of the Countrey*, VI. 131
Guirimir, or miracle-plays, VI. 252
Guisburn, priory of, I. 181
Guiscard, in *Gismond of Salerne*, V. 75 ff.
Guiscard, marquis de, IX. 461
Guise, duke of, in *The Massacre at Paris*, V. 145
Guise, Henry, duke of, IV. 259; VI. 34
Guise, John (d. 1765), XII. 377
Guisnes, I. 356; III. 175
Guizot, François Pierre Guillaume, V. 301, 302; X. 314, 317, 507; XII. 304; *Histoire de la Civilisation*, XIV. 56, 102
Gules, Thomas, in *The Tatler*, IX. 53
Gull, Arctic, in *King Berdok*, II. 276
Gulley, John (1783–1863), XIV. 231
Gullio, in *The Returne from Parnassus*, VI. 311, 312
Gulnare, in Byron's *Corsair*, XII. 46
Gummere, Francis Barton, V. 130
Gundicarius (Gundaharius), king of the Burgundians, I. 33
Gunnar, in Morris's *Sigurd the Volsung*, XIII. 126
Gunnell, Doris, *Stendhal et l'Angleterre*, X. 181
Gunning, Elizabeth, duchess of Argyll (1734–1790), XI. 451
Gunning, Henry (1780–1854), XIV. 601
Gunnings, the, XI. 260
Gunpowder, plot, the, IV. 166, 254; VII. 45, 162; VIII. 85, 86
Gunter, Edmund (1581–1626), IV. 457; VIII. 356, 477
Guntharius, in *Waltharius* (*Waldhere*), I. 32
Gunthorpe, John (d. 1498), III. 5
Gunton, Simon (1609–1676), *History of the Church of Peterborough*, IX. 354, 534
Gurney, Edmund (1847–1888), XIII. 248, 512; XIV. 473
Gurney, Mary, XIV. 600
Gurney, William Brodie (1777–1855), VIII. 243
Gurton, Gammer, XI. 375
Gurwood, John (1790–1845), XIV. 107
Gustavus Adolphus, king of Sweden, VII. 20, 21, 231; VIII. 111; IX. 194
Gustus, in *Lingua*, VI. 315
Gutch, John (1746–1831), IX. 346, 541
Gutch, John Mathew (1776–1861), XII. 187; XIV. 534
Guthere, in *Waldhere* and *Widsith*, I. 33, 35
Guthkelch, Adolph Charles Louis, IX. Add.
Guthlac, St, in Old English, I. 51, 52, 58, 428, 430
Guthlac, St, Life of, I. 85, 86, 131. *See, also*, Felix of Croyland
Guthlaf, in *Beowulf* and *Finnsburh*, I. 31
Guthrie, Henry (1600?–1676), bishop of Dunkeld, X. 500
Guthrie, Thomas (1803–1873), XII. 472
Guthrie, William (1620–1665), IX. 546
Guthrie, William (1708–1770), IX. 553; X. 163, 501, 523; *History of England*, X. 291
Guthry, Henry (1600?–1676), VII. 455
Guy Faux, in *Friar Rush*, VI. 53
Guy of Warwick, the traditional, I. 218; III. 68; IV. 190, 191; V. 108; VIII. 68; XI. 373
Guy of Warwick, I. 282, 293, 294, 303 ff., 468; II. 199, 308, 320, 321, 323, 500; VII. 96
Guy, The Goste of, II. 320, 485
Guy and Colbronde, II. 308
Guy's Porridge Pot, XII. 439
Guye, P. A., XIV. 557
Guyon, abbé de, X. 464
Guyon, madame (1648–1717), VIII. 103; IX. 307, 314, 520, 523; XI. 90, 401, 403
Guyse, John (1680–1761), XI. 479
Guystarde and Sygysmonde, The History of, II. 325, 486
Gwalchmei = Gawain, in the Welsh Triads and in the *Mabinogion*, I. 269
Gwendolen, in *Daniel Deronda*, XIII. 392, 399, 400
Gwestad, I. 255
Gwevyl, son of Gwestad, I. 255
Gwinne or Gwynne, Matthew (1558?–1627), VI. 318, 473; *Vertumnus sive Annus Recurrens*, VI. 317
Gwyneth, Owen, in Southey's *Madoc*, XI. 162
Gwynn, John (d. 1786), X. 469, 470
Gwynn, Nell (1650–1687), VIII. 20, 93, 99, 199, 213
Gwynn, Stephen, XII. 410, 412; XIII. 477

Gwynn, son of Nuð, I. 254
Gwynne, John (*fl.* 1660), XII. 377
Gybbys, J., VII. 511
Gyles Goosecappe, Sir. See under Chapman
Gyliane, in *Rauf Coilȝear*, II. 125
Gyngalyn, in *Libeanus Desconus*, I. 312
Gyraldus, Lilius, IV. 249
Gyre Carling, II. 275

H. B., *The Craftsmans Craft*, VII. 386
H. G., IV. 7
Haak, Theodore (1605–1690), VII. 322, 481
Habbie Simson, piper of Kilbarchan, I. 290
Habbie Simson, IX. 365, 366, 374, 378, 379
Habeas Corpus act, VII. 441
Haben's (or Hyberdine's) *A Sermon in praise of thieves*, V. 480
Habert, P., *Le Temple de la Mort*, VIII. 443
Habington or Abingdon, Thomas (1560–1647), VII. 445, 479; IX. 530
Habington, William (1605–1654), IV. 522; VII. 25, 26, 38, 401
Castara, V. 277; VI. 30; VII. 4, 45, 46, 445
Cupio dissolvi, VII. 46
Et exultavit Humiles, VII. 46
History of Edward IV, begun by Thomas, and completed by William, Habington, VII. 45
Nox nocti indicat Scientiam, VII. 46
Queene of Arragon, The, VI. 456; VII. 46
Hack, Maria (1777–1844), XI. 479; *Fireside Stories*, XI. 384; *Harry Beaufoy*, XI. 384
Hacker, col. Francis (d. 1660), VIII. 470
Hacket, John (1592–1670), IV. 422; VII. 329, 333, 342, 477, 491; *Life of Archbishop Williams*, VII. 334; IX. 165; *Loiola*, VI. 324, 473
Hacket, Thomas (*fl.* 1550), V. 105
Hackluyt, John (*fl.* 1644), VII. 356, 494
Hackman, James (1752–1779), X. 479
'Hackney, Iscariot' (Richard Savage), XI. 330
Hackney academy, X. 385; XII. 166
Hackwood, Frederick William, XIV. 520
Haddan, Arthur West (1816–1873), XIV. 75, 499
Haddeby, in the Baltic, I. 94
Hadden, R. H., XIV. 609
Haddington, XIII. 5
Haddington, hens of, II. 276
Haddingtonshire, III. 151; IX. 214
Haddon, Walter (1516–1572), III. 423; VII. 328
Hades, in Byron's *Cain*, XII. 48
Hades, king of, in *Preiðeu Annwvn*, I. 251
Hadington, viscount. *See* Ramsay, Sir John
Hadleigh, Suffolk, VIII. 284; XII. 256, 257
Hadley, near Barnet, XIII. 276
Hadow, James (1670?–1764), IX. 548, 549
Hadow, William Henry, XIII. 514
Hadrian, abbot, I. 5, 71 ff., 77, 82
Hadrian, emperor, X. 314
Hadrian IV, pope (Nicholas Breakspear), I. 185
Haethcyn, in *Beowulf*, I. 24
Hafiz, X. 144; XIV. 318 *b*
Hagall (Old Norse alphabet), I. 10
Hagano, in *Waldhere* and *Waltharius*, I. 32, 33
Hagberg, Carl August, V. 307
Hagena, in *Waldhere* and *Widsith*, I. 33
Haggard, A. M., XIV. 515
Haggard, Sir Henry Rider, XIV. 208
Hagley park, X. 101, 102, 113, 115, 150
Hagthorpe, John (*fl.* 1625), IV. 457; VII. 406
Hague, the, IV. 430; V. 286; VII. 16, 152, 188, 434, 437; VIII. 267, 380; IX. 148, 149, 158, 199, 208, 235, 236
Hahn, Theophilus, XIV. Add. 4
Hahn-Hahn, countess, XIV. 138
Haidée, in Byron's *Don Juan*, XII. 46, 54
Haig Brown, William (1823–1907), XIV. 597, 601
Haigh, Arthur Elam (1855–1905), XII. 484
'Hail to the Knight of the post,' ballad, VIII. 95
'Hail to the Myrtle Shades,' ballad, VIII. 95
Haile, Martin, XIV. 492
Hailes, lord. *See* Dalrymple, Sir David
Haileybury, XIV. 59
Hain, Ludwig, *Repertorium Bibliographicum*, XII. 369, 520
Hake, Edward (*fl.* 1579), III. 199; *Newes out of Poules Churcheyarde*, IV. 329, 518
Hake, Thomas Gordon (1809–1895), XIII. 156, 187, 503; *Maiden Ecstasy*, XIII. 185; *Old Souls*, XIII. 185; *Palmist, The*, XIII. 185
Hakewill, George (1578–1649), VII. 323, 425, 465, 471; *An Apologie or Declaration of the Power and Providence of God*, VII. 277
Hakluyt, Richard (1552?–1616), I. 95; II. 424; III. 187, 438; IV. 9, 66, 69, 71 ff., 78 ff., 87, 91 ff., 101, 103, 191, 457, *also see* Add.; V. 338; XIV. 332
Divers Voyages touching the Discoverie of America, IV. 81
Miraculous Victory achieved by the English flete, IV. 84
Notable Historie...voyages made by... French Captains unto Florida, A, IV. 81
Principal Navigations, III. 438, 551; IV. 67, 76, 78, 79, 80, 82, 88, 94, 398
Virginia Richly Valued, IV. 94
Hakluyt, Richard (uncle of above), IV. 85
Hakluyt society, the, IV. 81, 107; XII. 355
'Hal wes thu, folde, fira modor,' I. 3
Haldane, Elizabeth S., XIV. 472
Haldenstone, or Haldenstoun, or Haddenston, James (d. 1443), II. 368
Hale, Lancashire, II. 122
Hale, Sir Matthew (1609–1676), VII. 234, 323, 392, 476; VIII. 319 ff., 357, 466, 468; IX. 198, 240, 489; *London Liberties*, VIII. 319
Hale, Thomas, IV. 457
Hales. *See* Alexander of; Thomas de

Hales, John (d. 1571), *Discourse of the Commonweal*, IV. 300, 307, 511; V. 478
Hales, John (*fl.* 1589), III. 381, 383
Hales, John (1584–1656), IV. 431; V. 222; VII. 21, 151 ff., 157, 163, 218, 316, 425, 465; *Golden Remains*, VII. 152, 479
Hales, John Wesley (1836–1914), V. 346; X. 233; XI. 409; XII. 504; XIV. 426, 606
Hales, Stephen (1677–1761), X. 466; XIV. 283, 284, 560
Halévy, Elie, *Formation du radicalisme philosophique*, XI. 69, 397
Halfdan, I. 25
Halga, in *Beowulf*, I. 25
Halgoland, I. 94
Hali Meidenhad, I. 229, 234, 362, 458
Haliburton, Thomas Chandler (*pseud.* Sam Slick, 1796–1865), XII. 449; XIV. 343, 345 ff., 581, 583
Attaché, The, XIV. 348
Bubbles of Canada, The, XIV. 359
Clockmaker, The, XIV. 348
Historical and Statistical Account of Nova Scotia, XIV. 359
Nature and Human Nature, XIV. 348
Rule and Misrule of the English in America, XIV. 359
Wise Saws, XIV. 348
Halicarnassus, mausoleum of, XII. 339
Halidon hill, battle of, I. 357
Halifax, earl of. *See* Montague, Charles
Halifax, marquis of. *See* Savile, Sir George
Halifax, Nova Scotia, XIV. 346, 347
Halifax, Yorkshire, VII. 233, 235
Halkett, George (d. 1756), IX. 371, 372; *Logie O'Buchan*, IX. 371, 372; *Occasional Poems*, IX. 371; *Wherry Whigs Awa*, IX. 371
Halkett, Sir James, VII. 450
Halkett, lady (Ann Murray) (1622–1699), VII. 450
Halkett, Samuel (1814–1871), XII. 522; *Dictionary of Anonymous... Literature*, XII. 371
Halkirk, Caithness, II. 115
Hall, Anna Maria (Mrs S. C. Hall) (1800–1881), XI. 486; XIV. 312, 568
Hall, Anthony (1679–1725), XII. 7
Hall, Arthur (*fl.* 1563–1604), IV. 23, 437; VI. 37
Hall, Arthur Vine, XIV. 374, *also see* Add. 4
Hall, Basil (1788–1844), XIII. 562; XIV. 249, 552; *Schloss Hainfeld*, XIII. 432
Hall, Edward (d. 1547), II. 339; III. 315 ff.; VI. 333 ff.; *Union of the two Noble and Illustre famelies of Lancastre and Yorke* (*Chronicle*), III. 315 ff., 320, 325, 334, 529; IV. 396; V. 58, 83, 247; VII. 432
Hall, Hubert, V. 354
Hall, John (1575–1635), V. 219
Hall, John (1627–1656), VII. 86, 87, 94, 111, 359, 412, 501, 517; VIII. 229
Call, The, VII. 85
Crystal, The, VII. 85
Dithyramb, A, VII. 85
Epicurean Ode, An, VII. 85
Hall, John
Epilogue, The, VII. 85
Height of Eloquence, The, VII. 85
Horae Vacivae, VII. 84, 392, 517
Julia Weeping, VII. 85
Lure, The, VII. 85
Mercurius Brittanicus, VII. 357
Mercurius Censorius, VII. 357
Morning Star, The, VII. 85
Ode, 'Descend, O Lord,' VII. 85
Ode from an undergraduate to his tutor, Pawson, VII. 85
Ode, 'Lord, send thine hand,' VII. 85
Of Beauty, VII. 85
Poems, VII. 84
Sedition Scourg'd (probably by John Hall), VII. 344
Self, VII. 85
Hall, John, of Gray's Inn, VII. 488, 489
Hall, John Richard Clark, I. 421, Add.
Hall, Joseph (1574–1656), bishop of Exeter and Norwich, III. 173, 199, 207; IV. 129, 206, 207, 239, 329 ff., 336 ff., 341, 342, 357, 363, 376, 519, 525; V. 338; VI. 15, 38, 59; VII. 105, 124, 139, 250, 265, 383, 425, 450, 471, 481; VIII. 63
Characters of Virtues and Vices, IV. 336, 521; VII. 280
Decisions of Diverse Practicall Cases of Conscience, VII. 280
Episcopacy by Divine Right Asserted, VII. 158
King's Prophecie, The, IV. 351
Meditations and Vowes, IV. 265, 336
Mundus alter et idem, IV. 336
Occasional Meditations, VIII. 270
Quo Vadis? A Just Censure of Travell, IV. 345
Six Decads of Epistles, VII. 391
Hall, Joseph, *Satires*, IX. 87; *Virgidemiarum*, III. 173; IV. 329, 330, 337, 511, 519; VII. 432
Hall, Robert (1764–1831), XI. 399; XII. 472
Hall, R. N., XIV. Add. 7
Hall, Samuel Carter (1800–1889), XII. 410; XIV. 519
Hall, sergeant, in *The Tatler*, IX. 41
Hall, Theophilus D., XII. 335
Hall, Thomas (1610–1665), IX. 571
Hall, William (1748–1825), XII. 417
Hall-Stevenson, John (1718–1785), X. 47
Hallam, Arthur Henry (1811–1833), XIII. 23, 24, 32, 40, 477
Hallam, Henry (1777–1859), III. 417; IV. 45, 241, 264; V. 173, 234, 276; VI. 115; VII. 175; VIII. 262, 295; X. 284, 288; XII. 144, 311, 433; XIV. 56 ff., 75, 102, 143, 490; *Constitutional History of England*, XIV. 57 ff.; *Introduction to the Literature of Europe*, XIV. 58; *View of the state of Europe during the Middle Ages*, XIV. 56, 57
Hallam, Henry Fitzmaurice (1824–1850), XIV. 494
Hallamshire, XII. 516
Halle, Adam de la (*c.* 1235–1287), V. 34

Halle, John (d. 1479), III. 107, 108, 482, 493
Halle, Joseph, *The Chyrurgens Book*, V. 369, 478
Hallett, Joseph (1628?–1689), X. 384
Hallett, Joseph (1656–1722), X. 379, 384
Hallett, Joseph (1691?–1744), X. 381, 521
Halley, Edmund (1656–1742), VIII. 361, 477
Halliburtons, Memorials of the, XII. 376
Halliwell, Edward, VI. 303; *Dido*, VI. 298
Halliwell, J. O. *See* Halliwell-Phillipps
Halliwell-Phillipps (Halliwell), James Orchard (1820–1889), II. 199, 204, 422, 425; V. 165, 278, 314, 315; VI. 276; XI. 475; XII. 353, 369, 522; *Dictionary of Archaic and Provincial Words*, XII. 369; *Dictionary of Old English Plays*, XII. 369
Halloran, Henry, XIV. 362, 586
Hallward, N. L., XII. 437
Hallywell, Henry, VIII. 456
Halyblude, The, III. 122
Hama, in *Beowulf* and *Widsith*, I. 26, 35
Haman, in Biblical plays, V. 101
Hamauorum, pagus, I. 34
Hambden, Mr (John Hampden the younger?), VIII. 411
Hamber, captain, XIV. 180, 196
Hamburg, III. 42, 43; IV. 310; V. 298, 299, 307; XI. 259; XII. 4; XIV. 201
Hame, Hame, Hame, IX. 377
Hamerton, Philip Gilbert (1834–1894), XII. 524
Hamilton, IX. 193, 194
Hamilton, Alexander (d. 1732?), XIV. 576; *A New Account of the East Indies*, XIV. 333
Hamilton, Alexander (1762–1824), XII. 144, 343
Hamilton, Anne, duchess of (1636–1716), IX. 193
Hamilton, Anthony (1646?–1720), VIII. 208, 210, 262; XI. 290, 291, 307, 309; *Mémoires de la Vie du Comte de Gramont*, VIII. 261, 445, 446, 451; IX. 270; X. 245
Hamilton, Archibald, printer, X. 40, 201
Hamilton, Charles, marquis of, VII. 21
Hamilton, Charles (1753?–1792), XIV. 334, 576
Hamilton, Elizabeth, sister of Anthony, married comte de Gramont, VIII. 262, 263, 266
Hamilton, Elizabeth (1758–1816), XI. 460; XIII. 431; XIV. 600; *Cottagers of Glenburnie*, XI. 232; *My Ain Fireside*, XI. 232
Hamilton, Emma, lady (1761?–1815), XIV. 213
Hamilton, Gavin, XI 213
Hamilton, Sir George (d. 1679), VIII. 261, 263
Hamilton, James, 1st earl of Abercorn (d. 1617), VIII. 261
Hamilton, James, 1st duke of Hamilton (1606–1649), IX. 193, 194, 488
Hamilton, Janet (1795–1873), XII. 417
Hamilton, John (1511?–1571), archbishop of St Andrews, II. 369; *Catechism*, III. 153, 503
Hamilton, John (*fl.* 1568–1609), *Ane Catholik and Facile Traictise*, II. 94
Hamilton, John (1761–1814), XI. 234, 440
Hamilton, J. A., XIV. 509 ff.
Hamilton, Mary, II. 414
Hamilton, Nicholas, V. 278
Hamilton, Patrick (1504?–1528), III. 138, 140, 503; *Patrikes Places*, III. 140
Hamilton, Richard (*fl.* 1688), VIII. 263
Hamilton, Richard Winter (1794–1848), XIV. 606
Hamilton, Thomas (1789–1842), XII. 449
Hamilton, Thomas, 6th earl of Haddington (1680–1735), IX. 422
Hamilton, Walter, XIII. 491
Hamilton, Sir William (1788–1856), X. 274, 514; XI. 400; XII. 158; XIV. 1, 2, 7 ff. (main entry), 16, 29, 40, 41, 47, 139, 140, 411, 412, 473, 474, 476, 477, 481, 483, 596
Discussions on Philosophy and Literature, XII. 370; XIV. 7, 9
Lectures on Logic and Metaphysics, XII. 370; XIV. 8, 9
'Logic,' XIV. 7
'Philosophy of Perception, the,' XIV. 7, 10, 12
'Philosophy of the Unconditioned, the,' XIV. 7, 11
Hamilton, William, of Bangour (1704–1754), IX. 566; *Braes of Yarrow*, IX. 371; *Ode to the battle of Gladsmuir*, IX. 371
Hamilton, William, of Gilbertfield (1665?–1751), II. 108; IX. 372, 566, 567; XI. 204, 211; *Bonnie Heck*, IX. 364, 366; *Willie was a Wanton Wag*, IX. 364
Hamilton, W. D., XIV. 486
Hamilton, William, 2nd duke of Hamilton (1616–1651), IX. 194, 488
Hamilton, William Gerard (1729–1796), XI. 5, 173; *Parliamentary Logic*, X. 181, 463
Hamilton, Sir William Rowan (1805–1865), XIV. 262, 263, 556
Hamilton papers, VII. 435; IX. 194; XI. 290
Hamilton-King, Harriet Eleanor, XIII. 503; *The Disciples*, XIII. 179
Hamlet, Shakespeare's, I. 292; IV. 336; XII. 196; XIII. 34, 39, 60, 146
Hamlet, W. H. W. Betty as, XI. 283
'Hamlet's Aunt,' XIII. 327
Hamley, Sir Edward Bruce (1824–1893) XIII. 471
Hammer, Sir Thomas, XIV. 558
Hammersmith, IX. 254; X. 3, 95
Hammerton, J. A., XIII. 533, 544, 570
Hammond, Anthony (1668–1738), IX. 188, 485
Hammond, Henry (1605–1660), IV. 228; VII. 148, 151, 157, 425; VIII. 276, 293; *Paraphrase and Annotations on the New*

Hammond, Henry
Testament, VII. 147; *Poor Man's Tithing, The*, VII. 147; *Practical Catechism, A*, VII. 147; VIII. 277
Hammond, James (1710–1742), IX. 188, 485
Hammond, Mary, VII. 83
Hammond, Col. Robert (1621–1654), X. 499
Hammond, William (*fl.* 1655), VII. 88, 412; IX. 188
Hamond, Walter (*fl.* 1643), IV. 457
Hampden, John (1594–1643), IV. 54, 55; VII. 219, 439; VIII. 312
Hampden, Renn Dickson (1793–1868), XII. 259, 286 ff., 467
Hampden's, Mr, Speeches occasioned upon the Londoner's Petition for Peace (1642), VII. 385
Hamper, William (1776–1831), IX. 343, 344
Hampole. *See* Rolle, Richard
Hampole, near Doncaster, II. 45, 47, 88
Hampole's *Pricke of Conscience*, XII. 504
Hampshire, III. 46; V. 103; XI. 49; XII. 231, 236, 346; XIII. 355, 381; XIV. 221, 294
Hampshire militia, X. 303, 320
Hampstead, XI. 149; XII. 79, 89, 91
Hampsthwaite, XIII. 275
Hampton, Benjamin, VIII. 474
Hampton, James (1721–1778), X. 466
Hampton, Middlesex, VII. 4; XI. 362
Hampton court, III. 208; V. 102; VI. 237, 274, 326, 337; VII. 4, 6, 42; VIII. 245
Hampton court conference, III. 34, 45
Hanan, in *Jacob and Esau*, V. 111
Hanbury, David T., XIV. 583
Handel, George Frederick (1685–1759), VIII. 428; IX. 326; XIII. 250; XIV. 213; *Ariadne*, X. 199; *Scipio*, XI. 88
Handefull of pleasant delites, A, III. 190, 191, 249, 511, 512, 524; IV. 111
Handley, Clement, XIV. Add. 7
Hangman's Tree, The, II. 396
Hanky and Panky, in Butler's *Erewhon Revisited*, XIII. 453
Hanmer, Sir Thomas (1677–1746), V. 271, 272, 274; IX. 145, 476; X. 167, 454, 460, 465
Hanna, William (1808–1882), XII. 472
Hannah, in Swift's *Grand Question debated*, IX. 119
Hannah, John (1818–1888), IV. 52, 53; VII. 82
Hannay, D., X. 421; XII. Add.
Hannay, James (1827–1873), XI. 392, 439, 463; XIII. 162, 466; XIV. 140, 203, 238, 519, 583; *Satire and Satirists*, XIV. 141; *Singleton Fontenoy*, XIV. 141
Hannay, James (1842–1910), XIV. 583; *History of Acadia*, XIV. 359; *The War of* 1812, XIV. 359
Hannay, Patrick (d. 1629?), VII. 412
Anne of Denmark, elegies on, VII. 79
Happy Husband, The, IV. 521; VII. 79
Hannay, Patrick
Philomela, VII. 79
Sheretine and Mariana, VII. 79
Hannes, Edward (d. 1710), IX. 478
Hannibal, IV. 62; X. 510
Hannibal's passage of the Alps, XII. 496, 497
Hanover, V. 33; VIII. 50; IX. 45, 161, 200, 201, 251, 309; X. 311
Hanover, elector of. *See* George I
Hanover, Sophia (princess), electress of, V. 284; VIII. 220, 452
Hanover archives, VIII. 272; X. 295
Hanover club, IX. 165
Hanoverian period, X. 355; XIV. 88
Hanoverian protestantism, X. 352
Hanoverian queens of England, XIV. 111
Hanoverian succession, IX. 14, 192, 440; X. 354, 374
Hansard, Thomas Curson (1776–1833), XI. 49
Hansard's Analytical Parliamentary Digest, XIV. 508
Hansard's Parliamentary Debates, XIV. 508
Hanseatic league, II. 100; IV. 310; V. 355; VII. 198; XIV. 72
Hanserd Knollys society, X. 520
Hanway, Jonas (1712–1786), X. 467
Hanway, Mary Ann, X. 475
Haphazard, in *Apius and Virginia*, V. 64
Harapha, in *Samson Agonistes*, VII. 122, 137
Harbord, William (1635?–1692), VIII. 257
Harbury, X. 112, 271
Harcourt, Lewis Vernon, XIV. 506
Harcourt, Robert (1574?–1631), IV. 97, 457
Harcourt, Simon, 1st viscount Harcourt (1661?–1727), IX. 162
Harcourt, Simon (1684–1720), VIII. 410
Harcourt, Sir William Vernon, XIV. 198
Hardcastle, Ephraim, *pseud.* *See* Pyne, William Henry
Hardcastle, Mr, in *She Stoops to Conquer*, X. 214
Hardcastle, Miss, in *She Stoops to Conquer*, X. 482
Harden, W. T., XIII. 481
Hardenberg, Friedrich Ludwig von. *See* Novalis
Harder, H., IV. 267
Hardicanute, V. 31
Hardie, in Reade's *Hard Cash*, XIII. 428
Hardie, M., XIV. 540
Hardie, William Ross (1862–1919), XII. Add. 3
Hardiman, James (1790?–1855), XIV. 568; *Irish Minstrelsy*, XIV. 305, 325
Harding, Septimus, Trollope's, XIII. 422
Hardinge, George (1743–1816), X. 244, 248, 250; XI. 390
Hardinge, Henry Charles, viscount Hardinge (1857–1924), XIV. 505
Hardres court, Canterbury, XIV. 390

Hardwick, vii. 283, 289
Hardwicke, earls of. *See* Yorke, Philip
Hardy, Alexandre (c. 1570–1631), *Marianne*, viii. 13
Hardy, Laetitia, in Mrs Cowley's *Belle's Stratagem*, xi. 275
Hardy, Thomas, i. 240; ii. 414; iv. 48; xiii. Add. 2; xiv. 121
Hardy, Sir Thomas Duffus (1804–1878), xii. 516; *Descriptive catalogue of materials relating to the history of Great Britain and Ireland*, xii. 355
Hardyng, John (1378–1465?), x. 498; *Chronicle*, ii. 496; iii. 334; iv. 396
Hare, Augustus J. C. (1834–1903), xi. 460; xiv. 503, 519
Hare, Augustus William (1792–1834), iv. 40; xii. 467; *Guesses at Truth*, x. 218; xii. 301
Hare, Christopher, xiii. 18
Hare, David, xiv. 336
Hare, Francis (1671–1740), ix. 336, 455, 525
Hare, Julius Charles (1795–1855), xi. 491; xii. 282, 289, 308, 425, 467, 478;
Guesses at Truth, x. 218; xii. 301;
Mission of the Comforter, The, xii. 288;
Vindication of Niebuhr's History, xii. 302
Hare, Thomas, ix. 216
Haredales, the, in *Barnaby Rudge*, xiii. 320
Harefield, Middlesex, vii. 113
Harewood, Leeds, *Rushworth Gospels*, written by a priest of, i. 132
Harflete, Henry (*fl.* 1653), iv. 503; vii. 509, 517
Hargraves, the, in Mrs Cowley's *Runaway*, xi. 274
Hargrove, William (1788–1862), xii. 510
Harington. Sir John (1561–1612), iii. 199, 231, 252, 268, 270, 304, 305, 425, 509; iv. 24, 263, 265, 267, 328, 334, 520, 533; v. 82, 345, 478; vi. 314, 480; vii. 271
An Apologie of Poetrie, ix. 61
Ariosto, iii. 199, 526; iv. 23, 248, 401, 441
Epigrams, iii. 270, 523
Nugae Antiquae, iv. 55
Treatise of Playe, vi. 397
Hark, the thund'ring Cannons roar, viii. 96
Harland, Henry (1851–1905), xiii. 563
Harlaw, ii. 415; xiii. 234
Harleian *Collection of Voyages and Travels*, x. 166
Harleian library, ix. 357; x. 465, 468; xi. 336, 467; xii. 363
Harleian manuscripts, ix. 356; xii. 491, 522
Harleian Miscellany, iv. 65; vii. 455; viii. 411; ix. 357, 534; x. 166, 468
Harleian society, xii. 355
Harley, Edward, 2nd earl of Oxford (1689–1741), ix. 79, 84, 87, 152, 153, 357, 482; x. 166, 262; xi. 347
Harley, George Davies (d. 1811?), xi. 452
Harley, Henrietta, countess of Oxford, ix. 248
Harley, lady Henrietta-Cavendish Holles, ix. 483
Harley, Margaret, duchess of Portland, x. 262
Harley, Margaret Cavendish Holles, ix. 153, 155
Harley, Mrs, in Kelly's *False Delicacy*, x. 91; xi. 263
Harley, Robert, 1st earl of Oxford (1661–1724), iii. 97; ix. 5, 8, 10 ff., 20, 77, 78, 94 ff., 99, 113, 117 ff., 124, 130, 131, 151 ff., 161, 166, 167, 217, 219, 336, 357, 443, 444, 455, 461, 465; x. 280, 386; xi. 317; xiv. 168, 462, 463
Harlot, the, in a broadside, iii. 87
Harlow, ix. 153
Harlowe family, in Richardson's *Clarissa*, x. 9
Harman, Thomas (*fl.* 1567), iii. 85, 87, 103, 104, 320; iv. 317, 318, 320, 354; vii. 395; *A Caveat or Warening for Commen Corsetors*, iii. 103, 104, 320, 343, 448, 482, 492; iv. 521; v. 480
Harmar, John (1555?–1613), vii. 316, 482
Harmer, Anthony. *See* Wharton, Henry (1664–1695)
Harmer, Florence Elizabeth, i. Add.
Harnack, Adolf, xii. 467
Haro, Don Lewis de, vii. 391
Harold I, king of the English, i. 149, 150, 278; xiii. 366; xiv. 72
Harold the Fair-haired, i. 26
Haroun, in Beckford's *Vathek*, xi. 290
Haroun, Abraschid, xii. 499
Harp of Caledonia, xi. 443
Harpagon, Molière's, xiii. 446
Harpalus, in Owen's *Epigrammata*, iv. 265
Harper, Charles George, xiv. 540
Harper, Thomas Norton (1821–1893), xiv. 474
Harpsfield, John (1516–1578), iv. 493
Harpur, Charles (1817–1868), xiv. 586
Bushrangers, The, xiv. 363
Creek of the Four Graves, The, xiv. 363
Thoughts, xiv. 363
Tower of the Dream, The, xiv. 363
Words, xiv. 363
Harrington, James (1611–1677), vii. 300, 362, 389, 421, 471, 472, 518, *also see* Add.; ix. 201, 384, 570; *Oceana*, vii. 298, 299; ix. 385; *Political Aphorisms*, vii. 299
Harrington, John, 1st baron of Exton (d. 1613), iv. 175
Harrington, John, 2nd baron of Exton (1592–1614), iv. 216
Harrington, or Harington, John (*fl.* 1550), trans. of Cicero *On Friendship*, iv. 5, 436
Harriot, in Colman's *Jealous Wife*, x. 89, 90
Harriot, Thomas (1560–1621), iv. 55, 59, 452, 508
Harris, Benjamin, viii. 98
Harris, Edwin, xiii. 543

Harris, F., XIII. 465
Harris, Furlong Elizabeth Skipton, XII. 456
Harris, James (1709–1780), X. 512
Harris, James (*Hermes* Harris), XI. 250
Harris, James, 1st earl of Malmesbury (1746–1820), XIV. 504
Harris, James Howard, 3rd earl of Malmesbury (1807–1889), XIV. 504
Harris, John, alias Sirrahniho or Oxford Jack, VII. 494, 495; *Anti Mercurius*, VII. 357; *Mercurius Militaris*, VII. 357
Harris, John (1667?–1719), VII. 266; IX. 534
Harris, John (1756–1846), XI. 377
Harris, John, XIV. 552
Harris, Joseph (1661–1702), VIII. 401, 436; IX. 264
Harris, J. F., XIII. 572
Harris, Thomas (d. 1820), XI. 451, 452; XII. 69
Harris, Thomas Lake, XIV. 165
Harris, William (1675?–1740), X. 381, 521
Harrison, Elizabeth, X. 467
Harrison, Frederic (1831–1923), X. 299, 302, 312, 316; XIII. 471, 477, 509, 543. 548, 558, 573; XIV. 24, 469
Harrison, George, XIV. 606
Harrison, Ralph (1748–1810), XIV. 599
Harrison, Robert (d. 1585), III. 106
Harrison, Thomas (1606–1660), VII. 219; VIII. 470
Harrison, William (1534–1593), *Chronologie*, VI. 381; *Description of England and Scotland*, III. 319, 320, 321, 323, 328, 331; IV. 308, 511; V. 342, 348, 350, 352 ff., 357, 358, 360 ff., 367, 373 ff., 478; VI. 394, 462
Harrison, William (1685–1713), VIII. 158; IX. 125, 485; X. 140
Harrison, William (1802–1884), XII. 519
Harrison, Rev. William, XIII. 548
Harrovian, The, XIV. 539
Harrow school, VII. 326, 336, 492; IX. 142, 408; XII. 31, 41, 326, 329, 333; XIII. 241; XIV. 386, 390, 413, 422
Harrow-upon-the-Hill, VII. 336
Harrowby, earl of. *See* Ryder, Dudley
Harrowby, lady, XIV. 115
Harrowing of hell, in *Piers the Plowman*, II. 27
Harrowing of Hell, The, I. 48, 99, 251, 465; V. 2, 14, 15, 20, 27, 41, 390
Harruney, Luke, *i.e.* Henry Walker, VII. 351, 352, 499
Harry, Blind, or Henry the Minstrel (*fl.* 1460–1492), II. 108 ff.; IV. 412, 413; *Wallace*, II. 108 ff., 124, 239, 251, 280, 399, 447, 449; IV. 412; XI. 204, 237
Harsnett, Samuel (1561–1631), IV. 535
Hart, Andro (d. 1621), IV. 151, 413, 547
Hart, Charles (d. 1683), VIII. 186
Hart, John (d. 1574), III. 556; *An orthographie*, IV. 397
Hart, S. Hopgood, XIII. 564
Hart, W. H., *Index Expurgatorius Anglicanus*, V. 482
Harte, Bret, XIII. 543; XIV. 349, 368, 369; *Heathen Chinee, The*, XIV. 206
Harte, Walter (1709–1774), IV. 368; XI. 472; *Essay on Husbandry*, IV. 371
Hartington, marquis of. *See* Cavendish, Spencer Compton
Hartis Tale, in *Talis of the Fyve Bestis*, II. 280
Hartleborough, X. 386
Hartley, David (1705–1757), X. 345, 513; XI. 100, 137; XII. 168, 431; XIV. 5, 23, 393, 477; *Observations on Man*, X. 342, 343
Hartley, Elizabeth (1751–1824), XI. 273
Hartley, Thomas (1709?–1784), IX. 512
Hartlib, Samuel (d. 1670?), VII. 305, 310, 472; IX. 388; *Considerations...of England's reformation*, IX. 389; *Macaria*, IX. 389, 570
Hartly House, XIV. 335, 574
Hartmann, M., I. 102
Hartmann von Aue, I. 268, 280
Hartog, Philippe Joseph, XIV. 597
Hartop, Job, IV. 73
Hartshill, Warwickshire, IV. 168
Hartshorne, Charles Henry (1802–1865), XII. 369, 522
Hartson, Hall (d. 1773), X. 534
Hartwell, A. (the elder?), VI. 298
Hartwell, Abraham (the younger) (*fl.* 1600), IV. 382, 445, 446
Harun-ar-Rashid, I. 153
Harvard, VII. 29; X. 386
Harvard, Elizabethan stage at, VI. 266
Harvard, John (1607–1638), VII. 339
Harvard college library, XII. 401, 405
Harveian oration, IX. 132
Harvey, Baldwin, *Bustorum Aliquot Reliquiae*, VIII. 362
Harvey, Charles, VII. 356, 501
Harvey, Christopher (1597–1663), VII. 405; *Synagogue*, VII. 44, 406
Harvey, Clarence, in Miss Edgeworth's *Belinda*, XI. 297
Harvey, Gabriel (1545?–1630), III. 179, 190, 201, 202, 213, 214, 217, 219, 220, 229, 252, 271, 293, 294, 302, 305, 392, 393, 395, 396, 520, 526, 545, 546; IV. 8, 17, 18, 23, 54, 125, 131, 134, 322, 327, 360, 399, 514, 517, 523; V. 122, 140, 372, 394, 478; VI. 218, 288, 480, 494; VII. 316; IX. 32
  A New Letter, III. 546
  Advertisement to Papp-Hatchet, IV. 395, 537
  Gratulationes Valdinenses, III. 201
  Have with you to Saffron-Walden, IV. 326
  Musarum Lachrymae, VI. 306
  Pierces Supererogation, III. 252, 546; IV. 323
  Trimming of Thomas Nashe, III. 546; VI. 307
Harvey, Gilbert, VI. 307
Harvey, John (d. 1592), III. 545
Harvey, John (*fl.* 1729), IX. 557

Harvey, Joseph, xi. 377
Harvey, Richard (d. 1623?), iii. 393, 394, 396; iv. 322; vi. 307; *Plaine Percevall the Peace-maker of England*, iii. 393, 396, 543; *A Theologicall Discourse of the Lamb of God and his enemies*, iii. 396, 540
Harvey, Thomas, translator of Owen's *Latin Epigrams*, iv. 503
Harvey, William (1578–1657), iv. 278, 290, 292; vii. 314, 396, 478, 479; viii. 276, 350, 351, 359, 361 ff., 477; ix. 391; xiv. 281, 283, 284; *Exercitatio*, viii. 361; *Exercitationes de Generatione Animalium*, viii. 362
Harvey, William Henry, xiv. Add. 7
Harvey-Nashe controversy, iii. 395, 545; iv. 322, 332
Harward, Simon (*fl.* 1572–1614), iv. 542
Harwich, viii. 257
Harwood, Edward (1729–1794), xii. 522
Harwood, Sir Edward (1586?–1632), iv. 457
Harwood, Isabella (*pseud.* Ross Neil, 1840?–1888), xiii. 180, 503, 519
Harwood, Philip (1809–1887), xiv. 534
Haselrigge, Sir Arthur, ix. 258
Hasely, village of, iii. 380, 382
Haslewood, Joseph (1769–1833), xii. 516
Hassall, Arthur, xiv. 508
Hasted, Edward (1732–1812), xi. 426; xii. 510
Hastings, vii. 54
Hastings, battle of, i. 111, 149 ff., 157; xi. 34
Hastings, Charles, xiii. 514
Hastings, lady Elizabeth (1682–1739), ix. 38
Hastings, Francis Rawdon, 2nd earl Moira (1754–1826), xii. 103
Hastings, Henry, lord, vii. 7; viii. 2
Hastings, Lucy, countess of Huntingdon, iv. 161, 216
Hastings, Selina, countess of Huntingdon (1707–1791), x. 365, 366
Hastings, Warren (1732–1818), x. 260, 408; xi. 6, 14, 16 ff., 20, 25, 54, 78, 167, 389, 390, 396; xii. 343, 515; xiv. 63, 98, 333, 334, 493
Hastings, William, lord (1430?–1483), iii. 335; x. 291
Haswell, in Mrs Inchbald's *Such Things Are*, xi. 278
Hatch, Edwin (1835–1889), xii. 467
Hatch, F. H., xiv. Add. 7
Hatcham, xiii. 61
Hatcher, Henry (1777–1846), xii. 510
Hatcher, Orie Latham, vi. 122
Hatchett, William, *Rival Father*, x. 86
Hatchway, lieutenant, in Smollett's *Peregrine Pickle*, x. 38
Haterius, iv. 349
Hatfield, vii. 435; x. 126
Hatfield, Thomas of (d. 1381), xii. 510
Hatfield Broadoak, ii. 198
Hathaway, Agnes, v. 168
Hatherton, lord. *See* Littleton, Edward John
Hathwaye, or Hathway, Richard (*fl.* 1602), v. 311, 312, 319, 328; viii. 126; *King Arthur*, vii. 331
Hathwey or Hathaway, Anne, v. 168, 219
Hatred, in *Pathomachia*, vi. 324
Hatter, Richard (*fl.* 1649), vii. 354
Hatteraick, Dirk, in Scott's *Guy Mannering*, xii. 21
Hatto, bishop (ballad), iii. 81
Hatton, Sir Christopher (1540–1591), iv. 1; v. 72; vii. 196
Hatton, Christopher, 1st viscount (1632–1706), vii. 196; ix. 344
Hatton, Correspondence of the Family of, vii. 196, 439
Hatton, Joseph (1841–1907), xii. 428; xiii. 563; xiv. 532, 549
Hatton, Warwickshire, xii. 326
Hatton house, viii. 115
Hattuariorum, pagus, i. 34
Haughton, William (*fl.* 1598), v. 117, 311, 312, 326, 328, 474; vi. 54, 96, 97, 219, 424
Conquest of Spayne, The, viii. 126
English Men For My Money, v. 328
Grim the Collier of Croyden; or, The Devil and his Dame, v. 328; viii. 123
Roben Hood's penerthes, v. 35
Woman will have her Will, A, v. 328 ff.
See, also, under Day, Dekker *and* Marlowe
Haukin, John, in *The merry jests of the widow Edith*, ii. 327
Haultain, Arnold, xiv. 498
Hausted, Peter (d. 1645), vi. 473, 474; *The Rival Friends*, vi. 324
Hávamál, i. 62
Havard, William (1710?–1778), xi. 257; *Regulus*, xi. 273
Havell, Ernest Binfield (b. 1861), xii. Add. 5
Havelok the Dane, Lay of, i. 218, 277, 286, 287, 288, 303, 305, 306, 309, 315, 351, 360, 364, 367, 399, 468; ii. 420; iii. 372; xii. 517
Haverfield, Francis John (1860–1919), xii. 507, *also see* Add. 5
Haverfordwest, x. 386
Havergal, Frances Ridley (1836–1879), xi. 479
Haversham, lord. *See* Thompson, Sir John
Haviland, John, vii. 361
Havisham, Miss, in *Great Expectations*, xiii. 334
Havre, Le, xiii. 119
Haward, Nicolas (*fl.* 1569), iv. 436
Haweis, Rev. Hugh Reginald, xiii. 483
Hawes, Stephen (d. 1523?), ii. 223, 225, 231, 265, 325, 330, 428, 470, 471; iii. 168, 282, 291
Comfort of Lovers, The, ii. 224
Conversion of Swearers, The, ii. 224, 226, 230, 325
Example of Virtue, The, ii. 224, 22[illegible], 228, 233

Hawes, Stephen
Joyful Meditation to all England of the Coronation of Henry the Eighth, A, II. 224, 226, 325
Passetyme of Pleasure, The, II. 223 ff., 228 ff., 325; VII. 174
Hawes, William (1736–1808), X. 483
Hawick, IX. 565
Hawk, Sir Mulberry, in *Nicholas Nickleby*, XIII. 317
Hawke, Sir John, *The Englishman's Right* (1680), VIII. 469
Hawke, Michael, *The Groundes of the Laws of England* (1657), VIII. 469
Hawker, Mary (*pseud.* Lanoe Falconer, 1848–1908), XIII. 563
Hawker, Robert Stephen (1803–1875), XII. 417
'And shall Trelawney die?' XII. 134
Morwenna poems, XII. 134
Pater Vester Pascit illa, XII. 134
Queen Gwennyvar's Round ('Naiad for Grecian Waters'), XII. 134
Quest of the Sangraal, The, XII. 134
Sea-Bird's Cry, The, XII. 134
Silent Tower of Bottreau, The (*Bells of Bottreau*), XII. 134
Song of the Western Men, XII. 134
Hawkesworth, John (1715?–1775), VIII. 191, 442; IX. 124, 453; X. 175, 188, 465, 466; XI. 457; XIV. 244, 552; *Account of Voyages*, XI. 327
Hawkesworth, Walter (d. 1606), VI. 474; *Labyrinthus*, VI. 305; *Leander*, VI. 305
Hawking, writers on, IV. 541
Hawkins, Alexander (*fl.* 1601), VI. 290
Hawkins, Henry (1571?–1646), *Parthenia Sacra*, VII. 88, 412
Hawkins, Sir John (1532–1595), III. 327; IV. 1, 68, 77, 85, 88; VII. 305; *A True Declaration of the Troublesome voyage of Mr John Hawkins...in the years... 1567 and 1568*, IV. 72, 458
Hawkins, Sir John (1719–1789), X. 157, 158, 161, 163, 215, 459, 466, 471, 472; XI. 333; XII. 490; *Life of Johnson*, X. 189, 190, 483
Hawkins, Laetitia M., X. 473; XI. 473
Hawkins, Sir Richard (1562?–1622), IV. 77 ff.; *Observations of Sir R... H..., in his voiage into the South Sea*, IV. 77, 78, 458
Hawkins, William (d. 1554?), IV. 72
Hawkins, capt. William, IV. 99
Hawkins, W., VIII. 460
Hawkins, son-in-law of Izaak Walton, VII. 256
Hawkshead grammar school, XI. 95
Hawkyn and Dawkyn and Tomkyn, in *The Turnament of Totenham*, I. 366
Hawley, Henry (1679?–1759), IX. 378
Haworth, Yorkshire, XIII. 404 ff.
Haworth, Miss Euphrasia Fanny, XIII. 61
Hawthorn, Jerry, in Egan's *Life in London*, XIV. 223, 227, 230
Hawthornden, IV. 151, 153; VIII. 322
Hawthorne, Nathaniel, XI. 439, 492
Hawthorne, The Testament of the, III. 483
Hawtrey, Edward Craven (1789–1862), XIV. 413
Haxey-hood contest, Lincolnshire, V. 30
Hay, Sir Gilbert (*fl.* 1456), II. 284, 479; *Buik of King Alexander*, I. 291; II. 448; *Buke of the Law of Armys, The*, or *Buke of Bataillis*, II. 284; *Buke of the Order of Knichthood, The*, II. 284
Hay, James, 1st viscount Doncaster (d. 1636), IV. 202, 203; VII. 437
Hay, John Barras, XIV. 595
Hay, Thomas, 8th earl of Kinnoul (1710–1787), X. 408; XI. 351
Hay, William, XIV. Add. 5
Hay Now the Day daws, IX. 362
Haydn, Joseph, XI. 232
Haydocke, Richard (*fl.* 1605), IV. 445
Haydon, Benjamin Robert (1786–1846), XII. 79, 81, 172, 173, 407, 433; XIV. 519; *Autobiography*, XIV. 156, 157; *Lectures on Painting and Design*, XIV. 156
Hayes, Edward, XIV. 573
Hayes, lord (*fl.* 1607), IV. 143, 144
Hayes Barton, Budleigh, IV. 51
Hayley, William (1745–1820), XI. 90, 172, 176 ff., 180, 195, 401 ff., 426, 457; *Triumph of Temper*, XI. 176
Hayman, Henry (1823–1904), XII. 484
Hayman, Robert (d. 1631?), IV. 502, 520
Haymo, I. 117
Haynie, Henry, XIV. 534
Hayward, Abraham (1801–1884), X. 473, 484; XI. 344, 392; XII. 408; XIV. 198, 491, 519; *Art of Dining, The*, XIV. 138; *Faust* (trans.), XIV. 138; *More about Junius*, X. 409; XIV. 139
Hayward, Frank Herbert, XIV. 480
Hayward, Sir John (1564?–1627), III. 318, 334, 337, 338, 529, 530; IV. 302, 511
Henry IV, III. 338
Lives of the Three Normans, Kings of England, III. 338
The Beginning of the Reigne of Queene Elizabeth, III. 338
The Life and Reigne of King Edward the Sixt, III. 338
Hayward, W., translator, VI. 482
Haywood, Mrs Eliza (1693?–1756), IX. 18, 21, *also see* Add.
Haywood, Ralph, IV. 160
Hazard-Wilding plot, in *The Gamester*, VI. 202
Hazlitt, John, brother of W. Hazlitt, XII. 166
Hazlitt, Margaret, sister of W. Hazlitt, XII. 165
Hazlitt, Mrs (formerly Mrs Bridgewater), XII. 167
Hazlitt, Sarah (born Stoddart), XII. 167, 188
Hazlitt, William (1778–1830), III. 255; IV. 132; V. 222, 234, 252; VI. 53, 278; VII. 104; IX. 70, 87, 451; X. 43, 118; XI. 99, 112, 120, 128, 151, 159, 168, 171, 284,

Hazlitt, William
288, 391, 393, 394, 409, 417, 423, 439, 447, 461; XII. 77, 79, 104, 108, 118, 160, 164 ff. (main entry), 188, 192, 199, 203, 219, 223, 379, 410, 412, 430 ff., 438, 442, 444; XIII. 148, 275 ff., 311, 429, 513, 515; XIV. 138, 170, 171, 198, 230
Cant and Hypocrisy, XII. 177
Conversations of James Northcote, XII. 173
Disagreeable People, On, XII. 174
Essay on the Principles of Human Action, XII. 168
Familiar Style, On, XII. 174
Fear of Death, On the, XII. 174
Feeling of Immortality in Youth, The, XII. 174, 176
Fight, The, XII. 174, 175
Genius and Common Sense, XII. 177
Going a Journey, On, XII. 174, 176
Lectures on the Dramatic Literature of the Age of Elizabeth, VIII. 185
Lectures on the [English] Comic Writers, VIII. 162; X. 44
Letter to William Gifford, XII. 175
Liber Amoris, XII. 167
My First Acquaintance with Poets, XII. 166, 174, 176
Past and Future, XII. 177
Patronage and Puffing, XII. 177
Persons One Would Wish to have Seen, Of, XII. 174
Reading New Books, On, XII. 174
Reading Old Books, On, XII. 174
Review of the English Stage, A, XII. 171
Sick Chamber, The, XII. 174
Spirit of the Age, The, XI. 150; XII. 170
Taste, On, XII. 174
Thought and Action, XII. 177
Wit and Humour, XII. 177
Writing and Speaking, XII. 177
Hazlitt, William, unitarian minister, father of above, XII. 165
Hazlitt, William Carew (1834–1913), XII. 433, 438, 522; *Remains of the Early Popular Poetry of England*, II. 500
Hazlitts, the, XII. 192
Head, Barclay Vincent (1844–1914), XII. 497
Head, Sir Francis Bond (1793–1875), XIV. 249, 552
Head, G. O. A., Disraeli's, XIII. 351
Head, Richard (1637?–1686?), VII. 516; IX. 500
Headda, or Hedda, I. 77
Headlam, Walter George (1866–1908), XII. 485, *also see* Add.; *A Book of Greek Verse*, XII. 333
Headley, Henry (1765–1788), X. 455
Headpiece, Sir Francis, in Vanbrugh's *Journey to London*, VIII. 162
Headrigg, Cuddie, in Scott's *Old Mortality*, XII. 25
Headrigg, Mause, in Scott's *Old Mortality*, XII. 25
Headstrong, Jonathan, VIII. 122
Healey, John (d. 1610), III. 487; IV. 395, 436, 441, 521; VII. 482, 489
Healfdene, in *Beowulf*, I. 22, 25, 31, 32
Health, in *The Pride of Life*, V. 52
Heardred, in *Beowulf*, I. 24
Hearn, Lafcadio (1850–1904), XIV. 138, 519, *also see* Add. 3
Glimpses of Unfamiliar Japan, XIV. 166
Japan: an Attempt at Interpretation, XIV. 166
Karma, XIV. 166
Two Years in the French West Indies, XIV. 165
Hearne, Thomas (1678–1735), I. 143; VIII. 241, 463; IX. 57, 167, 170, 171, 342, 349 (main entry), 391, 413, 467, 534, 536, 541; X. 220, 355, 356; *Ductor Historicus*, IX. 349; *Reliquiae Bodleianae*, IX. 349, 574
Hearniana, Bibliotheca, XII. 515
Heart, king, in *King Hart*, II. 262
Heartfree, in Congreve's *Old Bachelor*, VIII. 147
Heartfree, in Fielding's *Jonathan Wild*, X. 27
Hear-well, in *Piers the Plowman*, II. 19
Heath, Benjamin (1704–1766), V. 273; IX. 477; XII. 365; XIV. 386; *A Revisal of Shakespeare's Text*, IX. 144, 145
Heath, Charles (1785–1848), XIV. 225
Heath, Douglas Denon, IV. 282
Heath, John (*fl.* 1615), IV. 520; VII. 486
Heath, Robert (*fl.* 1650), *Clarastella*, VII. 88, 412
Heathcliff, in Emily Brontë's *Wuthering Heights*, XIII. 411, 412
Heathobeardan, the, in *Beowulf*, I. 24, 25
Heaviness, in *The Goldyn Targe*, II. 253
Heavitree, Exeter, III. 405
Heavysege, Charles (1816–1876), XIV. 350, 582; *Saul*, XIV. 357
Hebbel, Christian Friedrich, V. 304
Heber, Reginald (1783–1826), XII. 365, 417, 467; XIV. 576; *If thou wert by my side, my love*, XII. 139; *Morte d'Arthur*, XII. 138; *Narrative of a Journey*, XIV. 336
Heber, Richard (1773–1833), XII. 5, 365, 366, 377, 522
Heberden, William (1710–1801), XI. 333
'Hebraism and Hellenism,' XIII. 101
Hebraists, XII. 262, 341
Hebrew, knowledge of, in Elizabethan days, V. 362
Hebrew, study of, II. 370
Hebrew language and literature, VII. 53, 316 ff., 333, 341, 348, 353, 490; VIII. 75, 112, 281, 288, 307, 323, 364; IX. 337, 382, 385, 393, 403, 558; X. 229, 237; XI. 181, 354; XII. 341, 362; XIV. 406, 459
Hebrew poetry, II. 406
Hebrew professor at Cambridge, IX. 335
Hebrew prophets, XI. 32; XIII. 36
Hebrews, the, IV. 27 ff.
Hebrides, the, IX. 560; XI. 287; XIII. 432

Hebron, in *Absalom and Achitophel,* VIII. 37
Hecate, in *Macbeth,* VI. 76
Hecate, in *The Witch of Edmonton,* VI. 76
Hecht, G., XIII. 470
Hecht, Hans, IX. 360; *Songs from David Herd's Manuscript,* IX. 374
Heckmondwike academy, X. 385
Hector, in Dryden's *Troilus and Cressida,* VIII. 29
Hector, in *Iliad,* VIII. 50
Hector, in *The Birth of Merlin,* V. 249
Hector, Edmund (*fl.* 1732), X. 159
'Hector of Sarum' (Burnet), IX. 217
Hedderwick, J., XIII. 503
Hedelin, François, abbé d'Aubignac, VII. 368, 504
Hedon, in *Cynthia's Revels,* VI. 41, 42, 44
Hedwig, I. 229
Hedworth, Henry, X. 377
Heenan, John C., pugilist, XIV. 183
Heep, Uriah, in *David Copperfield,* XIII. 327; XIV. 437
Hegel, Georg Wilhelm Friedrich, V. 304, 305; IX. 328, 522; XI. 121, 139; XIV. 1, 9, 11, 16, 40 ff., 47, 48, 479, 481, 483; *Encyclopaedia,* XIV. 45
Hegelian philosophy, XI. 57
Héger, Constantin, XIII. 405, 406
Heichen, Paul, XIII. 532
Heidegger, Gotthard, XIV. 213
Heidegger, John James (1659?–1749), IX. 477
Heidelberg, IV. 159
Heidelberg, Mrs, in Colman's *Clandestine Marriage,* X. 90
Heimskringla, the, XIII. 127
Heine, Heinrich, XI. 307; XII. 169, 396, 397; XIII. 9, 98, 99, 108, 552
Heinse, Johann J. W., XI. 303
Heinsius, Daniel, VI. 9; VII. 261, 307
Heinsius, N., VII. 307
Helen, in *Dr Faustus,* V. 155
Helen, in Goethe's *Faust,* XII. 34
Helen, in Shelley's *Rosalind and Helen,* XII. 62
Helen, in Tennyson's *Helen's Tower,* XIII. 177
Helen of Kirkconnel, IX. 364
Helen of Troy, VII. 101
Helena, in *A Midsummer-Night's Dream,* V. 180, 272
Helena, St, finder of the Cross, I. 55, 56, 133, 134
Helfta, in Saxony, convent, I. 229
Helgakviđa Hiörvarđssonar, Old Norse poem, I. 21
Helgakviđa Hundingsbana II, Old Norse poem, I. 21
Helgi, son of Halfdan, I. 25
Heliand, I. 46, 47
Helias of Jerusalem, I. 136
Helias, Knight of the Swan, The History of, II. 325, 485
Helicon, VI. 310; VIII. 201
Hélie de Barron, I. 273
Helinand de Froidmont, *Vers de la Mort,* II. 140, 142
Heliodorus, III. 351; IX. 536; *Aethiopian Historie,* IV. 3, 19, 436
Hell, XI. 188
Hell, Eleven Pains of, I. 227, 458
Hellena, in *A Challenge for Beauty,* VI. 103
Hellenic studies, society for the promotion of, XII. 340
Hellenism, XII. 34, 40; XIII. 26, 36, 101, 123
Hellfire club, X. 391
Hello, Ernest, V. 208, 209, 222
Hellowes, Edward (*fl.* 1574–1600), IV. 445, 458
Helm, William Henry, XIII. 543
Helmgisl, I. 87
Helmholtz, Hermann von, XIV. 269
Heloise, IX. 477, 538
Helps, Sir Arthur (1813–1875), XIV. 98, 503, 519, 520, *also see* Add. 3
  Brevia, XIV. 164
  Friends in Council, XIV. 163, 164
  Realmah, XIV. 164
  The Spanish Conquest of the New World, XIV. 99
Helston, VII. 86
Helston school, Cornwall, XIII. 355
Helstone, Caroline, in Charlotte Brontë's *Shirley,* XIII. 408, 409
Helstonleigh, Mrs Henry Wood's, XIII. 430
Helvétius, Claude Adrien, IX. 401; XI. 70; XII. 168, 431; XIV. 8; *De l'Esprit,* XI. 63
Hemans, Felicia Dorothea (1793–1835), XI. 442; XII. 124 ff., 129, 417; XIII. 149, 175, 177; XIV. 311
  Better Land, The, XII. 127
  Casabianca, XII. 125, 127
  England's Dead, XII. 127
  They grew in beauty side by side, XII. 127
Heming, or Hemminge, or Heminge, John (d. 1630), V. 169; VI. 248, 249, 276, 358
Hemingburgh. *See* Walter of
Hemingford, Walter de (*fl.* 1300), IX. 535
Hemming (*fl.* 1096), IX. 535
Hempstead, IV. 411
Henbury, Gloucestershire, X. 111
Henchman, Humfrey (1592–1675), bishop of London, VIII. 302
Henderson, Alexander (1583?–1646), IX. 544
Henderson, Andrew (*fl.* 1734–1775), IX. 564, 565; X. 475, *also see* Add.
Henderson, Archibald, XIII. 515, 570
Henderson, John (1747–1785), XI. 402, 454
Henderson, May J. S., XIII. 570
Henderson, Thomas Finlayson, II. 413; XI. 438, 439, 445; XII. 373, 451
Hendley, William (1691?–1724), IX. 571
Hendon, IX. 155; X. 214
Hendred, Dane William, prior of Leominster, II. 327
Hendyng, Proverbs of, I. 219, 363, 477

Hengest, in *Finnsburh*, I. 31, 32. *See, also*, I. 104, 246
Hengham, Ralph de (d. 1311), VIII. 465, 469
Hengo, in Fletcher's *Bonduca*, VI. 128; VIII. 31
Henley, John (1692–1756), X. 21
Henley, Samuel (1740–1815), X. 423; XI. 289, 291, 460
Henley, W. E. (1849–1903), X. 418; XI. 161, 438, 440; XII. 167, 179, 225, 384; XIII. 194, 197, 207, 211, 214 ff. (main entry), 477, 499, 503, 523, 570; XIV. 199, 520, 535
Beau Austin (with R. L. Stevenson), XIV. 163
Bric-à-Brac, XIII. 213
Echoes, XIII. 214
Essay in *The Century Burns*, XIV. 148
Hawthorn and Lavender, XIII. 214
Hospital Verses, XIII. 213
I loved you once in Old Japan, XIII. 213
In Hospital, XIII. 214
In the year that's come and gone, XIII. 214
London Voluntaries, XIII. 214
Love, his flying feather, XIII. 214
Lyra Heroica, XIII. 195
Out of the Night that covers me, XIII. 214
Pro rege nostro, XIII. 214
Rhymes and Rhythms, XIII. 214
Song of the Sword, The, XIII. 214
Views and Reviews, XIV. 147
What is to come? XIII. 213
Henley, Walter of, IV. 541
Henley-in-Arden, X. 109, 112, 271
Henman, Charles, XII. 512
Hennell, Charles Christian (1809–1850), XII. 467; *Origin of Christianity, The*, XIII. 383
Hennell, Mrs Charles, XIII. 383
Hennell, Sara, *Thoughts in Aid of Faith*, XIII. 383
Henneman, IV. 119
Henning, Archibald S., XIV. 236
Henning, F. W. J., XIV. 540
Henri II, king of France, III. 156
Henri III, king of France, III. 437; IV. 259, 376
Henri IV (Henry of Navarre), king of France, III. 244; IV. 142, 256, 259, 312; V. 341; VIII. 370
Henrietta, duchess of Orleans (1644–1670), daughter of Charles I, VII. 245; VIII. 180, 248, 266
Henrietta, queen, in Shelley's *Charles I*, XII. 75
Henrietta Maria (1609–1669), queen of Charles I, V. 348; VI. 83, 148, 149, 197, 237, 240, 262, 324 ff., 404; VII. 13, 35, 53 61, 189, 195, 218, 439, 449; VIII. 262, 294, 358, 371; X. 499; XIV. 93
Henriot, in Lytton's *Zanoni*, XIII. 420
Henrique, Don, in *The Spanish Curate*, VI. 139
Henry I, king of England, I. 151, 154, 157, 162, 222, 256, 278, 336; II. 343, 419; III. 368; V. 320; VIII. 310; XIV. 73
Henry II, king of England, I. 156, 157, 167, 171 ff., 176, 181, 185, 188, 189, 191, 197, 198, 202, 238, 243, 258, 264, 272, 307, 337, 397, 398, 449; II. 342, 504; IV. 182; VII. 206; VIII. 311; IX. 535; X. 115, 292, 502; XIV. 72; *Gesta Regis Henrici Secundi*, I. 449
Henry II, in *Looke about you*, V. 320, 321
Henry III, king of England, I. 180, 184, 194, 233, 238, 337, 368; II. 343; VI. 33; VII. 386; X. 287; XI. 301
Henry IV, king of England, I. 322; II. 36, 70, 137, 138, 153, 154, 206, 217, 284, 287, 303, 422; III. 316, 317; V. 44, 340; VII. 189, 190
Henry V, king of England, II. 40, 206, 286, 287, 303; IV. 137, 298; V. 373; VI. 280; IX. 534, 535; X. 303
Henry VI, king of England, II. 210, 296, 297, 355, 357 ff.; III. 334; IV. 193, 243, 428; V. 9, 340; VII. 247, 248, 327; X. 291
Henry VII, king of England, II. 223, 224, 226, 228, 316, 325, 329, 338, 358, 375; III. 5, 7, 8, 13, 17, 65, 67, 70, 97, 152, 175, 316, 325; V. 29, 50; VI. 246, 280, 332; VII. 203; IX. 211; X. 283, 284; XIV. 53, 83
Henry VIII, king of England, II. 161, 224, 325, 338, 354, 358, 375, 388, 389; III. 6, 14 ff., 23, 26, 30, 31, 32, 36, 39, 41 ff., 46, 50, 57, 61, 65, 67, 69, 70, 78, 95 ff., 110, 111, 160, 166, 167, 172, 181, 182, 188, 316, 320, 328, 332, 368, 403, 418, 478; IV. 63, 66, 72, 109, 113, 196, 225 ff., 293, 299, 400, 405, 409; V. 10, 50, 54, 56 ff., 90, 91, 102, 109, 124, 247, 375; VI. 91, 241, 256, 268, 280, 333 ff.; VII. 59, 103, 124, 192, 203, 333, 337, 442; VIII. 125; IX. 197, 210, 355; X. 184, 290; XIV. 52, 59, 82, 84, 85, 329
Henry VIII, in *When you see me, etc.*, V. 333
Henry VIII, *Book of Payments*, V. 89
Henry VIII, Household Book of, VI. 283
Henry VIII, Letters and Papers of, II. 393; XIV. 232
Henry, Alexander (1739–1824), XIV. 583; *Travels and Adventures*, XIV. 358
Henry, Aurelia, VI. 22
Henry, D., XII. 428
Henry, duke of Gloucester (1639–1660), VII. 58; VII. 383; VIII. 254
Henry, Frederick, prince of Wales (1594–1612), IV. 58, 59, 68, 90, 135, 143, 151, 154, 157, 188, 216, 263, 265, 366, 429, 431; VI. 30, 31, 37, 185, 250, 316, 318, 339, 345, 348, 350, 353; VIII. 363; X. 499
Henry, James (1798–1876), *Aeneidea*, XII. 338
Henry, Robert (1718–1790), *History of England*, X. 290, 502, 505; XI. 326
Henry, William Charles, XIV. 557, 601
Henry (Benedictine monk), IV. 417
Henry de Bracton. *See* Bracton
Henry of Ghent (d. 1293), *Questiones*, II. 365

Henry of Huntingdon (1084?–1155), I. 159, 160, 162, 166 ff., 170, 172, 174, 191, 218, 257, 262, 336, 337, 450, 454, 461; II. 399
Henry of Saltrey (*fl.* 1150), I. 191, 454, 474
Henry of Susa (d. 1271), cardinal of Ostia, commentary of, II. 364
Henry the Fifth, The Famous Victories of, V. 82, 152, 187, 220, 398
Henry's (King) Mirth or Freemen's Songs, III. 84
Henryson, Robert (1425?–1500?), II. 91, 93, 115, 204, 239, 244, 245, 248, 249, 252 ff., 263 ff., 473 ff.; III. 85, 173, 484; IV. 413; XI. 203
Age, II. 249
Bludy Serk, The, II. 249
Death, II. 249
Hasty Credence, II. 249
Morall Fabillis of Esope, II. 245 ff., 263; IX. 359
Orpheus and Eurydice, II. 247, 260
Prayer for the Pest, A, II. 249
Robene and Makyne, II. 245, 249; XI. 215
Sum Practysis of Medecyne, II. 249, 269
Testament of Cresseid, II. 162, 164, 240, 245, 247, 253, 264, 266
Uponlandis Mous and the Burges Mous, The, II. 246
Want of Wise Men, II. 249
Hensel, P., XIII. 471
Henshaw, Thomas (1618–1700), VII. 360; VIII. 247
Henslow, John Stevens (1796–1861), XIV. 289, 290, 560
Henslowe, Francis (*fl.* 1593–1595), VI. 277
Henslowe, Philip (d. 1616), V. 35, 135, 136, 143, 145, 157, 158, 160, 161, 236, 251, 256, 309 ff., 316, 319, 321 ff., 327, 328, 330 ff., 382, 473; VI. 3, 4, 7, 12, 17, 32, 33, 40, 45, 51, 53, 54, 83, 97, 141, 146, 168, 178, 210, 212, 216, 247, 250, 254, 255, 258, 261, 267, 269, 271, 275, 278, 290, 395, 411, 454; VIII. 123, 125
Hentzner, Paul, V. 356, 365, 369, 379, 478; *A Journey into England*, X. 245
Heoden (Heðinn), in *Deor*, I. 37
Heodeningas, the, in *Deor*, I. 37
Heorogar, in *Beowulf*, I. 25
Heorot, Hrothgaishall, in *Beowulf*, I. 22
Heoroweard, in *Beowulf*, I. 25
Heorrenda, minstrel, in *Deor*, I. 37
Hepburn, George (*fl.* 1695), IX. 560
Hepburn, John (d. 1522), II. 369, 370
Hepburn, Patrick (d. 1508), 1st earl of Bothwell, II. 251
Hephaestion, *Manual of Greek Metre*, XII. 328
Hepple, Norman, XI. 409
Her Trippa, in Rabelais's *Pantagruel*, VIII. 67
Heraclitus, IV. 31; VIII. 386; XIII. 193
Heraclitus' Dream, VII. 381
Heraclitus, riddles of, III. 489
Herald, the, in *Horestes*, V. 64
Heraldes, Debate Betwene the, IV. 296
Heraldry, writers on, IV. 543
Heraud, John Abraham (1799–1887), XII. 128, 129, 417, 428; XIII. 520
'Heraudee, Jawbrahim,' XII. 129
Herball, Grete, IV. 374
Herbals, IV. 542
Herbarium, Old English, I. 135
Herbarum, De virtutibus, II. 364
Herbert, prosodist, XIII. 241
Herbert, Arthur, earl of Torrington (1647–1716), IX. 490
Herbert, Auberon E. W. M. (1838–1906), XIV. 474
Herbert, Charles, lord, VI. 144
Herbert, Edward, 1st baron Herbert of Cherbury (1583–1648), IV. 292 ff., 508; VII. 16, 26, 29, 222, 277, 278, 283, 412, 413, 445; VIII. 352, 353, 355; IX. 288; XIII. 32
Appendix ad Sacerdotes, IV. 293
Autobiography, VII. 204, 205
De Causis Errorum, IV. 293
De Religione Gentilium, IV. 293
De Religione Laici, IV. 293; VIII. 42
De Veritate, IV. 293
Dialogue between a Tutor and his Pupil, IV. 293
Life of, X. 245
Life and Reign of King Henry the Eighth, VII. 201, 204, 205
Herbert, Sir Edward (1591?–1657), IV. 265
Herbert, Edward, earl of Powis (1785–1848), XIV. 578
Herbert, George (1593–1633), I. 232; IV. 123, 203, 240, 292; VII. 15, 26 ff. (main entry), 42, 45, 47, 153, 162, 163, 252, 401 ff., 425, 463, *also see* Add.; VIII. 229, 299; X. 360, 369; XI. 79; XIII. 169
Aaron, VII. 30
Antiphon, VII. 31
Avarice, VII. 30
Church, The, VII. 32
Church Porch, The, VII. 32
Collar, The, VII. 30, 32
Dawning, The, VII. 31
Decay, VII. 30
Eastern Song, XIII. 139
Heaven, VII. 30
Home, VII. 30
Hygiasticon, VII. 32
Jordan, VII. 30
Justice, VII. 30
Man, VII. 32
Odour, The, VII. 3
Outlandish Proverbs, 32
Parentalia, VII. 27
Prayer, VII. 30
Priest to the Temple, A, VII. 26, 155, 156
Providence, VII. 31
Pulley, The, VII. 30
Quip, The, VII. 30
Temple, The, II. 226; IV. 218; VII. 26, 27, 29, 30, 32, 40, 44
Throw away thy rod, VII. 32
'Shaped' verses, VII. 30

Herbert, George Robert Charles, 13th earl of Pembroke (1850–1895), xiv. 554
Herbert, Henry, 2nd earl of Pembroke (1534?–1601), iii. 188; iv. 265
Herbert, Sir Henry (1595–1673), iv. 383; vi. 102, 147, 202, 246; viii. 118, 119
Herbert, Henry Howard Molyneux, 4th earl of Carnarvon (1831–1890), x. 259
Herbert, Lucy, vii. 45
Herbert, Mrs Magdalen, afterwards lady Danvers (b. 1565), iv. 197, 203, 210, 211, 240; vii. 27
Herbert, Mary, countess of Pembroke (1561–1621), iii. 241, 254; iv. 116, 124, 132, 135, 172, 390, 434, 447; v. 63, 157, 334, 476; vi. 9; *Antonie*, iv. 133; *Dialogue between two shepheards*, iv. 124
Herbert, Matthew, vii. 37
Herbert, Sir Percy, vii. 515
Herbert, Philip, earl of Montgomery and 4th earl of Pembroke (1584–1650), v. 347; vi. 143, 144, 149; vii. 5, 29, 450, 513
Herbert, Philip, 5th earl of Pembroke (1619–1669), vii. 61
Herbert, Sidney, lord Herbert of Lea (1810–1861), xiv. 131, 510
Herbert, Thomas (*fl.* 1642), iv. 389
Herbert, Sir Thomas (1606–1682), vii. 450
Herbert, Thomas Martin (1835–1877), xiv. 474
Herbert, William, 3rd earl of Pembroke (1580–1630), iv. 123, 132, 209, 390, 431; v. 174, 225, 347; vi. 143, 149, 150; vii. 219; viii. 377
Herbert, William (1718–1795), ix. 531; xii. 520, 522
Herbert, William (1778–1847), xiv. 298, 561
Herbert family, the, iv. 157; v. 370; vi. 141
Herbert of Bosham (*fl.* 1162–1186), i. 448
Herbert's *Typographical Antiquities*, ii. 319
Herbes, A Boke of the properties of, iv. 397
Herbier, Grand, iv. 374
Herculaneum, xii. 340, 413
Hercules, viii. 68; ix. 136, xiii. 81
Hercules, in *Confessio Amantis*, ii. 148
Hercules, in *Dialogues of the Dead*, xi. 351
Hercules, in *Pleasure Reconciled*, vi. 360, 361
Hercules, in *Saturnalia*, vi. 319
Hercules, in *The Masque of Christmas*, vi. 359
Hercules, captain, in *The Champion*, x. 23
Hercules, duke, in *Parasitaster*, vi. 48
'Hercules,' ship, xii. 38
Herd, David (1732–1810), ii. 409; ix. 360, 362 ff., 373, 374, 566; x. 487, 490; *Ancient and Modern Scottish Songs*, xi. 204, 218
Herd ms., xi. 229, 235
Herder, Johann Gottfried von, v. 290, 297, 298, 304; x. 232
Here awa there awa, ix. 374
Here Prophecy, i. 218, 459
Herebeald, in *Beowulf*, i. 24
Hereford, ii. 61; iii. 28; iv. 131, 190, 421; vi. 220; vii. 42, 444; ix. 538; xii. 286; xiv. 414
Hereford, Henry of. *See* Henry V
Hereford, Nicholas (*fl.* 1390), ii. 60, 61, 63, 73
Herefordshire, ii. 216; xi. 430; xii. 509; xiii. 70
Heremod, in *Beowulf*, i. 23, 26
Heresye's Testament, iii. 483
Hereward the Wake (*fl.* 1070–1071), i. 111, 287, 364, 478; ii. 399, 428, 507; v. 27; ix. 343
Hereward the Wake, Kingsley's, xiii. 366
Herford, Charles Harold, vi. 17; xi. 409; xii. 433, 524; xiii. 52, 56, 62, 79, 480, 484
Herford, John (*fl.* 1534), iv. 409
Hergest. See *Red Book of*
Heriot, George (1766–1844), xiv. 583; *History of Canada*, xiv. 358; *Travels through the Canadas*, xiv. 358
Heriricus, in *Waltharius*, i. 32
Herkomer, Sir Hubert von, xii. 330
Herman, Guillaume, v. 21
Herman, Henry (1832–1894), xiii. 524
Herman, Hugo, *Pia Desideria*, vii. 47
Herman of Wied, archbishop of Cologne, iii. 31
Hermann, Johann Gottfried Jakob, xii. 324, 325
Hermegild, in D'Avenant's *Gondibert*, vii. 71
Hermenegild, St, i. 105
Hermes, iv. 45
Hermes, Johann Timotheus, *Geschichte der Miss Fanny Wilkes*, x. 18
Hermes, Trismegistus, vii. 488
Herminia, in *Orlando Furioso*, iii. 230
Hermione, in *Horestes*, v. 65
Hermione, in *The Winter's Tale*, v. 169, 189, 206
Hermogenes, iii. 420
Hermsprong, Bage's, xi. 295
Herne, Hierome, vi. 348, 349
Hernishowe, in Trevisa, ii. 78
Hero, in *Much Ado about Nothing*, v. 191
Hero and Leander (Nashe's burlesque), iv. 327
Herod, iii. 78; v. 17, 46, 50, 87, 151; vi. 154, 295; x. 83
Herodas, *Mimes*, xii. 340
Herodian, iv. 436
Herodias, vi. 295
Herodotus, iii. 430, 433; iv. 4, 6, 436 ix. 39, 43; x. 135; xii. 328, 330, 334, 477, 479, 480, 484; xiv. 85
Heroic Virtue, in *The Masque of Queens*, vi. 349
Heroical adventures of the Knight of the Sea, iv. 359
Herolt's *Promptuarium*, iii. 489
Heron, Robert (1764–1807), x. 446, 526; xi. 440, 472

Heron, The Vows of the (*leus veus du hairon*), II. 421
Herondas, XII. 492
Herrenhausen, IX. 249
Herrera, Antonio de, IX. 501
Herrick, Nicholas (d. 1592), VII. 4
Herrick, Robert (1591–1674), II. 393; IV. 193; VI. 1, 11, 27, 215; VII. 1, 4–16 (main entry), 22, 23, 81, 180, 398, *also see* Add.; VIII. 3, 229, 231; XI. 318, 383; XII. 223; XIII. 495
'Alas! for me, that I have lost,' VII. 11
'Among the myrtles as I walked,' VII. 7
Apparition of his Mistress calling him to Elysium, The, VII. 7
Canticles to Bacchus, VII. 9
Cherry Ripe, IV. 145; VII. 8
Christian Militant, The, VII. 10
Corinna's Going a-Maying, VII. 8, 13
Country Life: to his Brother, Mr Tho. Herrick, A, VII. 4, 9, 11, 12
Cruel Maid, The, VII. 9
Description of a Woman, The, VII. 7
Dirge of Jephthah's Daughter, VII. 15
Farewell to Sack, A, VII. 6, 7
Hesperides, VII. 1, 6 ff., 11, 13, 15, 19
His Age, VII. 9, 11
His Content in the Country, VII. 6
His Creed, VII. 15
His Departure Hence, VII. 11
His Farewell unto Poetry, VII. 5
His Ode for Ben Jonson, VII. 11
His Litany to the Holy Spirit, VII. 15
His Request to Julia, VII. 10
Hock-Cart, The, VII. 12
Mad Maid's Song, VII. 8
May-pole is up, The, VII. 8
Night-Piece to Julia, VII. 10, 13
Noble Numbers, VII. 7, 10, 14
Nuptial Song on Sir Clipseby Crew, A, VII. 11
Oberon's Diet, VII. 7
Ode to Endymion Porter upon his Brother's Death, An, VII. 11
Panegyric to Sir Lewis Pemberton, VII. 10
Primrose, The, VII. 7
Thanksgiving to God for his House, A, VII. 6, 15
Tinker's Song, The, VII. 8
To Anthea, VII. 13
To Daffodils, VII. 13, 14
To his Book, VII. 14
To Keep a true Lent, VII. 15
To Phyllis to love and live with him, VII. 8, 13
To Primroses filled with Morning Dew, VII. 11 ff.
To the reverend Shade of his religious Father, VII. 10
Upon Himself, VII. 14
Upon the Death of his Sparrow, VII. 9
'When a daffodil I see,' VII. 14
Herrick, Sir William (1562–1653), VII. 4, 5
Herries, John, XI. 250; XIII. 250
Herring, Thomas (1693–1757), IV. 251; X. 362, 516
Herringman, Henry, VIII. 6, 392; XI. 318, 319
Herrington, Sir Jasper, in Fanny Burney's *Wanderer*, X. 65
Herriott, Frank I., *Sir William Temple on the Origin and Nature of Government*, VIII. 384
Herrys, William, VII. 33
Herschel, Sir John Frederick William (1792–1871), XIV. 258, 288, 474, 555; *Discourse on the Study of Natural Philosophy*, XIV. 17
Herschel, Sir William (1738–1822), XIV. 258, 556
Hertford, III. 330
Hertford, earl of. *See* Seymour, Edward
Hertford, lady. *See* Somerset, Frances
Hertford, marquis of. *See* Seymour-Conway, Francis Charles
Hertfordshire, VI. 29, 196; VII. 252; IX. 532, 538; X. 120; XI. 78; XII. 180, 182, 183, 201, 509; XIV. 79
Hertogenbosch, III. 2
Hertz, Heinrich Rudolf, XIV. 269
Hervarar Saga, I. 35
Hervet, Gentian, IV. 440, 543
Hervey, Augustus John, 3rd earl of Bristol (1724–1779), IX. 252
Hervey, Carr (1691–1723), IX. 250
Hervey, James (1714–1758), IX. 506; X. 365 ff., 369
Contemplations, X. 365, 366
Meditations, X. 124, 365; XI. 325
Reflections, X. 365
Theron and Aspasia, X. 365
Hervey, John, 1st earl of Bristol (1665–1751), IX. 250, 496
Hervey, John, lord (1696–1743), IX. 85, 250 ff., 449, 497
Letters from a nobleman, IX. 86, 251
Memoirs, IX. 250 ff.
Miscellaneous Thoughts, IX. 252
Three Speeches, IX. 252
Hervey, Mary, lady (1700–1768), IX. 85, 250, 251; X. 248
Hervey, Sir Thomas (1698–1775), IX. 250. 496; XI. 394
Herveys, the, IX. 248, 251
Hervier, Paul Louis, XIII. 532
Hervor, X. 223, 224
Hesiod, I. 77; III. 429; IV. 436; IX. 220, 526, 527; XII. 331, 484, 489
Hesketh, Harriet, lady (born Cowper) (1733–1807), XI. 78, 88, 89, 91, 402, 404
Hesperus, X. 137
Hesse-Cassel, X. 466
Hester, in Mrs Inchbald's *To Marry or not to Marry*, XI. 279
Hesternit, in Mandeville, II. 84
Hesychius, IX. 330
Hetel (Heðinn), in *Kudrun*, I. 37
Hetherington, Henry (1792–1849), XIV. 534

Heðinn, I. 37
Heton, Northumberland, II. 128
Hettner, H., I. viii
Hetware (Chattuarii), in *Beowulf*, I. 25, 26
Heurodys, in *Sir Orfeo*, I. 311
Hew, Sir, of Eglintoun (*c.* 1376), II. 103, 116, 117, 123, 451
Hewer, William, VIII. 258
Hewes, John, IV. 170, 186, 188
Hewett, Mrs, IX. 248
Hewitt, Bob, in Gissing's *The Nether World*, XIII. 458
Hewlett, Esther, XI. 383, 486
Hewlett, Henry Gray, XIV. 517
Hewlett, Maurice (1861–1923), XIII. 572, *also see* Add. 1
Hewson, the shoemaker, in the *Mercuries*, VII. 356
Hewson, John (d. 1662), VIII. 121
Hexham, Henry (1585?–1650?), VII. 454
Hey, boys, Up we go! VIII. 96
Heydon, Sir Christopher (d. 1623), IV. 535; VII. 508, 510; *A Defense of Judiciall Astrologie*, VII. 377
Heydon, John (*fl.* 1667), VII. 378, 510
Heylyn, Peter (1600–1662), III. 478; IV. 458; VII. 246 ff., 427, 445, 447, 479, 518
Aerius Redivivus, VII. 208
Cosmography, VII. 207
Cyprianus Anglicus, VII. 208
Ecclesia Restaurata, VII. 207
Examen Criticum, VII. 207
Geography, VII. 207
Mercurius Aulicus, VII. 207
Microcosmus: a little Description of the Great World (later edition *Cosmographie*), IV. 89
Heyne, Christian Gottlob, XII. 490; XIII. 468
Heyse, Paul, V. 303
Heywood, Elizabeth (daughter of John Heywood), IV. 198
Heywood, Elizaeus (1530–1578), V. 90
Heywood, Jasper (1535–1598), III. 189, 198; IV. 440; V. 89, 395
Heywood, John (1497?–1580?), II. 269, 328; III. 124, 179, 279; IV. 198, 334, 518; V. 25, 89 ff., 97, 110, 404 ff., 409 ff., *and see* Add. 2
Foure P. P., The, V. 92, 95, 97
Johan the husbande Johan Tyb his wyfe and Syr Jhãn the priest, V. 92, 96 ff., 105, 111
Pardoner and the frere, The, V. 92, 96, 97, 108
Play of Love, A, V. 92 ff.
Proverbs, V. 105
Wether, The, V. 92 ff., 97
Witty and Witless, V. 92 ff., 99
Heywood, Oliver (1630–1702), XI. 486
Heywood, Samuel (1753–1828), XIV. 490
Heywood, Thomas (d. 1650?), II. 202; IV. 4, 115, 434, 438, 439, 458; V. 145, 158, 222, 224, 243, 254, 259, 263, 311, 312, 361, 370, 371, 373; VI. 80–106 (main entry), 168, 204, 219, 378, 389,
Heywood, Thomas
409, 430 ff., 445, 487, *and see* Add. 2; VIII. 169; XI. 286; XII. 191
Actor's Vindication, The, VI. 83, 408
Ambrosius Merlin, Life of, VI. 88
Apology for Actors, An, VI. 83 ff., 241, 401, 408, 461, 494
Blind eats many a fly, The, VI. 97
Bold Beachams, The, VI. 89
Brazen Age, The, VI. 93
Captives, or The Lost Recovered, The, VI. 102
Challenge for Beautie, A, VI. 82, 103
Christmas comes but once a year, VI. 97
Edward IV, VI. 84, 88, 90
England's Elizabeth, V. 342; VI. 86, 91
English Traveller, The, V. 351; VI. 81, 84, 94, 97, 102; VIII. 172
Fair Maid of The West, The, VI. 85, 97, 101
Fayre Mayde of the Exchange, The, VI. 84, 86, 99
Fortune by Land and Sea, VI. 69, 104
Four Ages, The, VI. 92
Foure Prentises of London, The, With the Conquest of Jerusalem, VI. 84, 88, 89
General History of Women, The, VI. 86, 102, 103, 138
Godfrey of Bulloigne, VI. 89
Golden Age, The, VI. 93, 97
Hercules, VI. 92
Hierarchy of the Blessed Angels, VI. 86, 87
If you know not me, You know no bodie: Or, The troubles of Queene Elizabeth, V. 342, 344, 345, 354, 365; VI. 84, 85, 91, 97, 300; VIII. 125
Iron Age, The, VI. 84, 92, 93
Jew of Malta, The, Heywood work in, VI. 103
Joan and my Lady, VI. 97
Late Lancashire Witches, The, VI. 104
Lives of all the Poets, VI. 86
Loves Maistresse, VI. 84, 103
Marshal Osric, VI. 100
Mayden-Head well lost, A, VI. 84, 103
Nine Most Worthy Women of the World, VI. 91
Pleasant Dialogues and Drammas, VI. 87, 88
Porta Pietatis, VI. 88
Rape of Lucrece, The, V. 367; VI. 19, 101
Royall King, The, and the Loyall Subject, VI. 81, 83, 97, 100, 102, 138
Silver Age, The, VI. 93
Sovereign of the Seas, The, pamphlet on, VI. 84
Troicus Britannicus, or Great Britain's Troy, VI. 86
Wise-woman of Hogsdon, The, VI. 83, 93, 97, 99
Woman Kilde with Kindnesse, A, V. 252; VI. 84, 92 ff., 97, 99, 101; VII. 3; X. 73
Hezekiah, English verse play on, VI. 300
Hezekiah, in *Ezechias*, VI. 298

Hiarrandi, father of Heðinn, I. 27
Hiaðningar, I. 37
Hiatt, Charles, XIII. 515
Hibernian society, XIV. 397, 398
Hibernica, VII. 211
Hichyns (Tindale, William), III. 39
Hick, in *Piers the Plowman*, II. 16
Hick Scorner, V. 54, 392
Hickathrift, XI. 373
Hickeringill, Edmund (1631–1708), IV. 458; VIII. 403
Hickes, Francis (1566–1631), IV. 438; VII. 316
Hickes, George (1642–1715), I. 31, 147, 382; VII. 43; VIII. 258, 306, 460; IX. 212, 355, 535; X. 220, 224 ff., 229, 355, 356; *Constitution of the Catholic Church*, IX. 310, 511; Icelandic grammar, X. 223; *Linguarum veterum septentrionalium thesaurus grammatico-criticus et archaeologicus*, VIII. 307; X. 223, 225, 484
Hickes, William, *Coffee-house Jests*, VII. 390, 516
Hickes, Sir William, VIII. 83
Hickford, R., X. 485
Hickman, Francis (*fl.* 1690), VIII. 394
Hickman [? Henry], X. 387
Hickman, Thomas, XIV. 230
Hickes, G. Dawes, XIV. 467, 474
Hicks, Thomas, *Dialogue between a Christian and a Quaker*, VIII. 110
Hickson, William Edward (1803–1870), XII. 430
Hicky, James Augustus (*fl.* 1780), XIV. 334
Hicky's Bengal Gazette, XIV. 334
Hidaspes, in *Cupid's Revenge*, VI. 128
Hiero (Mantuan's), III. 224
Hierocles, X. 464
Hieroleander, in *Argenis*, IV. 259
Hieron Osorius, bishop, library of, IV. 56
Hieronimo, in *The Spanish Tragedie*, V. 158, 162, 164, 240; VI. 13; VIII. 87
Hierophilus, *pseud.* *See* McHale, John
Higden, Betty, in *Our Mutual Friend*, XIII. 336
Higden, Henry (*fl.* 1693), VIII. 395
Higden, Ranulf (d. 1364), *Polychronicon*, II. 71, 72, 74 ff., 313, 333, 334, 444; IV. 320, 521; XII. 480
Higford, William (1581?–1657), *Institutions of a Gentleman*, IX. 396, 570
Higgins, John (*fl.* 1570–1602), III. 196, 197; V. 407
Higgins, Matthew James ('Jacob Omnium,' 1810–1868), XIV. 238, 534
'Higgins, Mr, of St Mary Axe,' XI. 43
Higgs, in Butler's *Erewhon Revisited*, XIII. 453
Higgs, Griffin or Griffith (1589–1659), *Thomas Tucker*, VI. 318, 320, 474
High Dutch, VII. 314
High Ercall, Shropshire, VII. 27
High Wycombe, VII. 53
Highland Scots, IX. 373
Highlanders, the, X. 28, 182, 230, 231
Highlands, the, IX. 215; XII. 19, 24, 26, 83, 84, 255; XIII. 106; XIV. 65, 434
'Hightest thou Urse,' I. 460
Highwaymen, Lives of the, XI. 352
Hilarion, I. 74
Hilarius or Hilary (*fl.* 1125), I. 191, 454; V. 7, 8, 11, 38; *Image of St Nicholas*, I. 191; *The Raising of Lazarus*, I. 191; V. 11
Hilda or Hild, St (614–680), abbess of Streoneshalh, Whitby, I. 42, 43, 45, 82
Hildebrandslied, the, I. 36
Hildeburh, in *Beowulf*, I. 31
Hildegard, St, of Bingen, I. 229
Hildesham, Hildersam, or Hildersham, Arthur (1563–1632), VII. 322, 482
Hildilid, or Hildelitha, St, abbess of Barking (*fl.* 700), I. 74
Hildr, daughter of Högni, I. 37
Hildreth, Richard, XI. 68, 398
Hilgay, Norfolk, IV. 165
Hill, Aaron (1685–1750), IX. 160, 187, 447, 485; X. 94, 434, 439; *Alzira*, X. 82; *Merope*, X. 82, 86; *Zara*, X. 81, 82
Hill, Abigail (d. 1734), IX. 130
Hill, Abraham (1635–1721), VIII. 296, 458
Hill, Constance, XI. 365, 460; XII. 447
Hill, David Octavius (1802–1870), XI. 437
Hill, Eleanor M., XIV. 599
Hill, Frederic (1803–1896), XIV. 591, 601
Hill, George (1810–1900), XIV. 568
Hill, George Birkbeck (1835–1903), IX. 308, 313, 326; X. 181, 184, 186, 267, 279, 289, 297, 317; XI. 13, 344; XIV. 503, 606
Hill, John (d. 1765), IX. 455
Hill, John (1716?–1775), XI. 472
Hill, Joseph, XI. 87, 402
Hill, Richard (*c.* 1500), II. 500
Hill, Richard, III. 189
Hill, Rowland (1744–1833), XII. 472
Hill, Sir Rowland (1795–1879), XIV. 606
Hill, Samuel Charles, XII. 437
Hill, Thomas ('Didymus Mountain') (*fl.* 1590), III. 484; IV. 542; *A most briefe and pleasaunt treatyse, etc.*, IV. 375; *The proffitable arte of gardening*, IV. 375
Hill, Thomas, uncle of Southey, XI. 155
Hill, Wills, 1st earl of Hillsborough (1718–1793), X. 403
Hillard, George Stillman, XIII. 73
Hillier, Alfred P., XIV. Add. 8
Hills, Henry, XI. 330
Hillsborough, earl of. *See* Hill, Wills
Hiltgund, in *Waldhere* and *Waltharius*, I. 32 ff.
Hilton, Arthur Clement (1851–1877), XIV. 537; *Heathen Pass-ee, The*, XIV. 206; *Octopus, The*, XIV. 206; *Vulture and the Husbandman, The*, XIV. 206
Hilton, John (d. 1657), IV. 464
'Hinchinbroke, lord,' in *The Tatler*, IX. 34
Hinchingbrooke, X. 133
Hincks, Edward (1792–1866), XII. 342, 499
Hind, Arthur Mayger, XIV. 539

Hind, Henry Youle, xiv. 583
Hind, James (d. 1652), ix. 258
Hind Horn, ii. 410, 411, 414
Hindley, Charles, xiv. 540, 544
Hindlip hall, near Worcester, vii. 45
Hindoos, the, xi. 17
Hindshaw, W., xiv. 592
Hindu religion, xiv. 98
Hindu romance, xi. 164
Hindustan, xi. 12
Hindustani language, xi. 242; xiii. 279
Hine, Henry George (1811–1895), xiv. 238
Hingston, Edward Perron, xiii. 515
Hinkson, Henry Albert, xiv. 573
Hinkson, Katharine Tynan, xiv. 316, 573
Hinnom, xii. 82
Hinton, James (1822–1875), xii. 467; xiv. 475
Hinton, John Howard (1791–1873), xiv. 591
Hinxman, John (*fl.* 1760), xi. 341
Hiordis, in Morris's *Sigurd the Volsung*, xiii. 126
Hiörvarðr, brother-in-law of Hrólfr, i. 25
Hippel, x. 422
Hippocrates, ii. 365; iii. 427; iv. 436; vii. 488; viii. 350, 363; xii. 521
Hippolito, in *Loves Crueltie*, vi. 199
Hippolyta, in *A Midsummer-Night's Dream*, v. 183; vi. 213, 214
Hippolyta, in *The Custome of the Countrey*, vi. 122, 131
Hippolytus, vi. 163
Hippomedon. See *Ipomedon*
Hiram's hospital, in Trollope's *The Warden*, xiii. 422
Hislop, Andrew, xi. 237
Hispanus, play, vi. 484
Hisperica Famina, i. 69, 70, 435
Histoire Littéraire de la France, xi. 172
Historia, in *Technogamia*, vi. 323
Historia Brittonum. See Nennius
Historical mss. commission, ix. 119, 141; xiv. 89, 97
Histories and tragedies, early printed, and in mss., v. 395 ff.
History of Henry Earl of Moreland, ix. 328
History of Savarambes, ix. 106
History of the Sixteen Wonderful Old Women, xi. 386
History of the Union (1698), x. 377
History of the Works of the Learned, x. 176
Hitchcock, Richard, translator of Sansovino, iv. 448
Hitchcock, Robert (*fl.* 1580–1591), iv. 309, 511
Hitchcock, Robert (d. 1809), x. 443
Hitchener, Elizabeth, xii. 401, 402
Hitchin, v. 103; vi. 29; xiv. 430
Hitchman, Francis, xiii. 545, 547
Hitopadesa, the, xii. 343, 502, 503
Hnaef, in *Beowulf* and *Widsith*, i. 23, 31, 32, 34
Hoadley or Hoadly, Samuel (1643–1705), vi. 482
Hoadly, Benjamin (1676–1761), ix. 20, 41, 221, 309 ff., 428, 505, 506, 511; x. 354, 355, 357, 516, 517
Nature of the Kingdom of Christ, ix. 310, 311; x. 354
Plain Account of the...Sacrament, x. 354
Preservative against the...Non-Jurors, ix. 310; x. 354
Reasonableness of Conformity, x. 374
Hoadly, Benjamin (1706–1757), x. 87, 435
Hoadly, John (1711–1776), x. 87, 433, 439
Hoare, Prince (1755–1834), x. 276; xi. 281, 457; xii. 473
Hoare, Sir Richard Colt (1758–1838), xii. 510; *Wiltshire*, xii. 346
Hoares, the, xi. 149
Hobbes, John Oliver, *pseud. See* Craigie, Pearl Mary Teresa
Hobbes, Thomas (1588–1679), iv. 292, 297; vii. 54, 70, 71, 84, 85, 217, 259, 260, 265 ff., 275, 276–298 (main entry), 409, 465, 469 ff., *also see* Add.; viii. 462, 469, 475; ix. 75, 269, 301 ff., 351, 384, 386, 397, 571; x. 325, 332, 335; xi. 7, 32, 57, 318; xiv. 16, 24, 29, 479
Behemoth, vii. 289, 445; ix. 385
De Cive, vii. 286, 291
De Corpore, vii. 287, 288, 291
De Corpore Politico, vii. 285
De Homine, vii. 287
Decameron Physiologicum, vii. 289
Dialogue between a Philosopher and a Student of the Common Laws of England, vii. 289
Elements of Law natural and politic, vii. 284, 285, 291, 294
Heresy, vii. 289
Historia Ecclesiastica, vii. 289
Homer, vii. 267, 289
Human Nature, vii. 285
Latin works, vii. 289, 291
Leviathan, The, vii. 286 ff., 296, 297, 301, 371; ix. 385; x. 372
Of Liberty and Necessity, vii. 288
Philosophical Rudiments concerning Government and Society, vii. 286, 291
Short Tract on First Principles, vii. 284
Thucydides, vii. 284
Tractatus Opticus, vii. 286
Hobbinol, in *The Shepheards Calender*, iii. 224
Hobby-horse, v. 33
Hobhouse, John Cam, lord Broughton de Gyfford (1786–1869), xii. 32, 34, 382 ff., 387, 393, 395; xiv. 407, 550
Hobhouse, Leonard T., xiv. 469
Hobhouse, Thomas, x. 472
Hobie Noble, ii. 415
Hoblyn, Robert (1710–1756), xii. 522
Hobs, the tanner of Tamworth, in *Edward IV*, v. 373; vi. 90, 91

Hobson (a London character), IV. 360
Hobson, Mrs Carey, XIV. Add. 8
Hobson, Paul, X. 377
Hobson, Thomas (1544?–1631), VII. 244
Hoby, Sir Edward (1560–1617), IV. 443, 446
Hoby, Sir Thomas (1530–1566), III. 290, 433, 437, 444; IV. 3; *The Courtier*, III. 437, 505, 550; IV. 3, 7, 397, 443
Hoccleve. *See* Occleve
Hocken, Thomas Morland, XIV. 587
Hockenhull, prosodist, XIII. 244
Hockley, William Browne (1792–1860), XIV. 338, 557; *Pandurang Hari*, XIV. 337; *Tales of the Zenana*, XIV. 337
Hockliffe, or Hocelyve, in Bedfordshire, II. 206
Hocktide plays, V. 30, 31
Hocus, in Arbuthnot's *History of John Bull*, IX. 134
Hoddesdon, John (*fl.* 1650), VIII. 395
Hodell, Charles W., XIII. 484
Hodge, in *Cromwell*, V. 247
Hodge, in *Horestes*, V. 64
Hodge, in *Piers the Plowman*, II. 16
Hodge, D., XIII. 471
Hodges, Anthony, VII. 489
Hodges, Richard, XIV. 441
Hodges, Sir William (1645?–1714), IV. 102, 458
Hodgetts, John, *Terra Australis incognita*, IV. 101, 458
Hodgkin, Thomas (1831–1913), XII. 476, *also see* Add.; *Italy and her Invaders*, XII. 322
Hodgkins, John, III. 382
Hodgson, Francis (1781–1852), XII. 395
Hodgson, George B., XIV. 533
Hodgson, Geraldine Emma, XIV. 591
Hodgson, John (d. 1684), XII. 16, 376
Hodgson, Shadworth Hollway (1832–1912), XIII. 248; XIV. 40, 474
Metaphysic of Experience, The, XIV. 39
Philosophy of Reflection, The, XIV. 39
Theory of Practice, The, XIV. 39
Time and Space, XIV. 39
Hodgson, William Ballantyne (1815–1880), XIV. 414, 600, 601, 606, 607
Hodnet, XII. 365
Hody, Humphrey (1659–1707), X. 354, 516
Hoefuðlausn of Egill Skallagrimsson, I. 62
Hoel, in *The Misfortunes of Arthur*, V. 78
Hoel, king of Brittany, I. 259, 260
Hoey, J. C., XIV. 510
Höffding, H., XIV. 467
Hoffmann, Ernst Theodor Wilhelm, XIII. 4, 465
Hoffmann, F., IX. 442
Hoffmanswaldau, Christian Hofman von, III. 348
Hofland, Mrs Barbara (1770–1844), XI. 480; *Clergyman's Widow*, XI. 384; *Son of a Genius*, XI. 384; *Theodore*, XI. 384
Hofmeyr, J. H., XIV. Add. 8
Hog, James (1658?–1734), IX. 520, 548, 549
Hog (Hogaeus), Latin translations of Milton, VII. 118, 414
Hogarth, David George, XIV. 551
Hogarth, George, XIII. 542
Hogarth, William (1697–1764), IX. 122, 145; X. 22, 263, 354, 396, 429, 524; XII. 177, 182, 192, 434; XIII. 458; XIV. 212 ff., 540, 541
Beer Street, XIV. 213
Calais Gate, XIV. 213
England, XIV. 213
Enraged Musician, The, XI. 282; XIV. 213
France, XIV. 213
Gin Lane, X. 33; XIV. 213
Harlot's Progress, X. 24, 75; XIV. 213
Marriage-à-la-Mode, X. 90; XII. 432
Rake's Progress, X. 24; XIV. 213, 214
Hogben, John, XIV. 534
Hogg, Alexander, XI. 326
Hogg, Ethel M., XIV. 602
Hogg, James (1770–1835), XI. 237 ff., 437, 443, *also see* Add.; XII. 5, 95, 96, 156, 159, 160, 373, 379, 425, 444, 445, 449; XIII. 108
Bonny Kilmeny, XI. 241
Cam Ye by Athol, XI. 242
Fate of Macgregor, XI. 241
Forest Minstrel, XI. 241, 243
Gathering of the Clans, XI. 242
Haunted Glen, XI. 242
Jacobite Relics, IX. 371 ff., 375 ff., 566
Lock the Door Lauriston, XI. 242
M'Kinnon, XI. 242
Mador of the Moor, XI. 241
Mountain Bard, XI. 239
O Weel Befa', XI. 242
Pilgrims of the Sun, XI. 241
Queen Hynde, XI. 241
Queen's Wake, XI. 239 ff.
Rise Rise Lowland and Highland Man, XI. 242
Skylark, The, XI. 242
Spy, The, XI. 239
When the Kye comes Hame, XI. 242
Witch of Fife, XI. 240
Hogg, Quintin (1845–1903), XIV. 602
Hogg, Thomas Jefferson (1792–1862), XII. 60, 79, 401, 403
Hoggarty, Mrs, in Thackeray's *Great Hoggarty Diamond*, XIII. 281
Hoggins, Mary Ann, in Thackeray's Contributions to *Punch*, XIII. 279
Hogglestock, Trollope's, XIII. 424
Högni, I. 37
Hogsden. *See* Hoxton
Hogsflesh, in Lamb's *Mr H—*, XII. 189
Hohenstiel-Schwangau, prince, Browning's, XIII. 72
Hoker, John, *Piscator, or The Fisher Caught*, VI. 294
Holberg, Ludwig, X. 200
Holborn, II. 233
Holbroke, John (d. 1437), II. 347, 362

Holcot, Robert (d. 1349), III. 489
Holcroft, Thomas (1745–1809), X. 443, 480; XI. 119, 189, 270, 276 ff., 281, 295, 454, 457, 461, *also see* Add.; XII. 432
Alwyn, XI. 294
Anna St Ives, XI. 292, 294
Autobiography, XI. 294
Crisis, The, XI. 277
Deserted Daughter, The, XI. 277, 278
Duplicity, XI. 277
Hugh Trevor, XI. 294
Road to Ruin, The, XI. 277
Holden, Hubert Ashton (1822–1896), XII. 331, 485
Holdernesse, earl of. *See* D'Arcy, Robert
Holdsworth, Dr, VIII. 473
Holdsworth, Philip Joseph (1849–1902), XIV. 369, 586
Holdsworth, Richard (1590–1649), IV. 425, 426, 434
Hole, Richard (1746–1803), X. 487
Hole, Samuel Reynolds, XIV. 238, 503
Hole, William (*fl.* 1600–1630), IV. 168
Holiday, Barten, *Technogamia, or The Marriage of the Arts*, VI. 323, 474
Holiness, house of, in *The Faerie Queene*, II. 234; VI. 336
Holiness, in *Piers the Plowman*, II. 25
Holinshed, Raphael (d. 1580?), I. 170; II. 104, 339; *Chronicles of England, Scotland and Ireland*, III. 111, 156, 237, 316, 318 ff., 438, 530; IV. 7, 192, 398 ff.; V. 100, 220, 221, 239 ff., 244, 271, 371; VI. 138, 301; XIV. 308
Holkot, Robert, *Moralitates*, I. 214, 454
Holland, V. 101, 286, 288, 308; VII. 64, 180, 261, 285, 307, 360, 453, 456, 460; IX. 3, 199, 203, 213, 214, 231, 255, 300, 306, 350, 515; X. 203; XI. 19, 25, 321; XII. 165; XIII. 88, 429; XIV. 212, 423, 459
Holland, Abraham (d. 1626), VII. 502
Holland, Bernard, XIV. 509
Holland, earl of. *See* Rich, Sir Henry
Holland, Henry (d. 1604), *A Treatise against Witchcraft*, IV. 325, 534; VII. 371, 506, 511
Holland, Henry (1583–1650?), III. 324; *Basiliologia*, IV. 543
Holland, Henry Scott, XII. 453, 455, 458
Holland, Henry Wilkinson, XIV. 591
Holland, John, duke of Exeter (1352?–1400), II. 170
Holland, John (1794–1872), XII. 420
Holland, lords. *See* Fox, Henry; Fox, Henry Richard Vassall
olland, Mary Sibylla, XIII. 549
Holland, Philemon (1552–1637), III. 324, 328, 528; IV. 1, 3 ff., 15, 21, 266, 438 ff., 442, 446, 523, 527; VII. 487; IX. 267; *Plutarch*, IX. 265; Plutarch's *Moralia*, VII. 316; Xenophon's *Cyropaedia*, VII. 316
Holland, Sir Richard (*fl.* 1450–1482), *Buke Hof the Howlat*, II. 100, 112, 114, 115, 120, 272, 449
Holland, lady Saba (d. 1866), XII. 427
Holland, Thomas (d. 1612), VII. 312, 317
Holland family, XIII. 372
Hollar, Wenceslaus (1607–1677), VI. 262; VII. 487
Holles, Denzil, lord (1599–1680), VII. 225, 451, 457; IX. 194
Hollingford, in Mrs Gaskell's *Wives and Daughters*, XIII. 372
Hollingshead, John, XIII. 515
Hollway, H. C. Schunke, XIV. Add. 4
Hollyband, Claudius, IV. 446
Hollybush, J., IV. 442
Holm, in Norway, I. 179
Holman, in Mrs Gaskell's *Cousin Phillis*, XIII. 372, 380
Holme, Randle (1627–1699), *Academy of Armory*, IX. 355, 535
Holmes, Arthur (1837–1875), XII. 485
Holmes, George (1662–1749), IX. 495
Holmes or Homes, Nathaniel (1599–1678), VII. 507, 515
Holmes, Oliver Wendell, XIV. 378; *The Last Leaf*, XIII. 164
Holmes, Thomas Rice Edward, XIV. 496
Holmes, William (*fl.* 1582), IV. 386
Holofernes, I. 142
Holofernes, in *Love's Labour's Lost*, V. 178; VI. 30, 336
Holroyd, A., XIII. 558
Holroyd, John Baker, 1st earl of Sheffield (1735–1821), X. 299, 301, 302, 310, 312, 508, 509
Holroyd, Maria Josepha (lady Stanley of Alderley), X. 509
Holt, Felix, George Eliot's, XIII. 342, 397
Holt, Joseph (1756–1826), XII. 516
Holt, L. H., VI. 5
Holwell, John Zephaniah (1711–1798), XIV. 577; *India Tracts*, XIV. 334; *Narrative of the...Black Hole*, XIV. 334
Holy alliance, the, XI. 108; XII. 39, 40
'Holy Club,' the, X. 364
Holy Ghost, The Emission of the, V. 17
Holy Grail, the, XII. 518
Holy island, XII. 10
Holy land, the, IV. 89
Holy Roman empire, I. 318; III. 244
Holy Rood, The, I. 445
Holy Sepulchre, the, IV. 201; XIV. 252
Holy week carols, II. 378
Holybourne, Hampshire, XIII. 381
Holyhead, IX. 99
Holyoake, George Jacob, XIV. 478, 534
Holyoke, Francis (1567–1653), *Dictionary*, VII. 315, 486
Holyoke, Thomas (1616?–1675), VII. 486
Holyrood, IV. 239; VII. 435
Holyrood press, the, XI. 470
Holywood. *See* Johannes de Sacro Bosco
Home, Daniel D., XIII. 72
Home, Henry, lord Kames (1696–1782), IX. 561, 547; X. 190, 513, 514; XI. 250; XIV. 606; *Elements of Rhetoric*, XIV. 398; *Loose Hints upon Education*, XIV. 391

Home, John (1722–1808), v. 297; ix. 557, 561, 564; x. 435; xi. 450, 457; *Douglas*, ii. 410; ix. 549; x. 87, 202, 230, 369; xi. 273; xiii. 258; *Siege of Aquileia*, xi. 273
Home and Foreign Review, The, xiv. 118
Home office, the, xiv. 328
Home Rule, xiv. 136, 198
Homer, i. 77, 170; ii. 109, 110; iii. 22, 229, 230, 271, 272, 305, 420, 429, 452; iv. 21 ff., 33, 42, 43, 47, 414, 418, 429, 437, 516, 526; v. 51, 71, 138, 214; vi. 18, 31, 36, 82, 86, 93, 101, 197, 303, 347; vii. 70, 117, 138, 267, 268, 274, 289, 317, 334, 381; viii. 205, 219, 221, 372, 375, 433; ix. 44, 59, 68, 72, 74 ff., 88, 183, 256, 258, 338 ff., 366, 443, 446, 448, 474, 481, 483, 484, 527; x. 27, 128, 167, 180, 186, 220, 227, 232, 415; xi. 79, 88 ff., 355, 403, 433; xii. 99, 256, 310, 311, 422, 480, 482, 484, 485, 487 ff., 491, 492, 496, *also see* Add.; xiii. 35, 90, 92, 104, 312; xiv. 135, 164, 252, 365, 375
Iliad, i. 293; viii. 9, 25, 50, 64; ix. 297, 372, 410; x. 231, 232, 240; xi. 88, 320, 322, 401; xii. 54, 280, 331, 334, 477; xiii. 450; xiv. 329
Odyssey, ix. 410; xi. 321, 322; xii. 190, 333, 334, 500; xiii. 125 ff., 175, 450
Homeric hexameter, the, xiii. 127
Homerides, by 'Sir Iliad Doggrel,' ix. 258, 448
Homerton, x. 384
Homes and Haunts of Famous Authors, xiii. 456
Homicide, in *Two Lamentable Tragedies*, v. 326
Homilies (1547 and later), iii. 35; iv. 304, 511
Homilies, Middle English, i. 221, 474
Homilies, Old English (*see, also*, Aelfric, Wulfstan, etc.), i. 218, 458, 459; iv. 424
Hone, Percy F., xiv. Add. 8
Hone, William (1780–1842), xiv. 520; *Every-Day Book*, xii. 181; *Table Book*, xii. 200, 436, 437
Hone's Year-Book, xiii. 143
Honeycomb, Will, in *The Spectator*, ix. 51
Honeycombe, Polly, in Colman's drama, x. 89
Honeyman, Charles, in *The Newcomes*, xiii. 295
Honeyman, Martha, in *The Newcomes*, xiii. 297
Honiton, x. 387
Honor, in *The Masque of the Middle Temple*, vi. 355
Honoria, in Dryden's *The Rival Ladies*, viii. 4
Honoria, in *The Picture*, vi. 156, 158
Honorius I, ii. 347
Honorius of Autun, *Elucidarium* of, i. 343
Honour, in *Portuus of Noblines*, etc., ii. 284
Honour, in *The Faerie Queene*, iii. 236
Honour, lady, in *Amends for Ladies*, vi. 223
Honour, prince of, in *The Palice of Honour*, ii. 261, 262
Honourable society for the Advancement of Experimental Philosophy, ix. 389
Honyman, Andrew (d. 1676), ix. 546
Hood, Edwin Paxton, xiii. 471
Hood, Thomas (*fl.* 1582–1598), iv. 458
Hood, Thomas (1799–1845), x. 135; xi. 160; xii. 107, 108 ff. (main entry), 119 ff., 129, 131, 139, 418, 429, 449; xiii. 161, 230, 238
Bridge of Sighs, The, xii. 109, 110; xiii. 239
Clapham Academy, xii. 109
Comic Annual, xiv. 235
Death Bed, A, xii. 110
Desert Born, The, xii. 111
Elm Tree, The, xii. 110
Eugene Aram, xii. 110
Fair Ines, xii. 111
Farewell, Life, xii. 110
Giver of glowing light, xii. 111
Haunted House, The, xii. 110, 111; xiii 239
Hero and Leander, xii. 110
It was not in the Winter, xii. 110
Lake and a Fairy Boat, A, xii. 111
Lycus the Centaur, xii. 110
Miss Kilmansegg, xii. 109, 111
Plea of the Midsummer Fairies, The, xii. 110, 111
Serious Poems, xii. 109
Song of the Shirt, The, xii. 109; xiv. 238
Spring it is cheery, xii. 111
Stars are with the Voyager, xii. 111
United Family, The, xii. 121
Up the Rhine, xii. 121
Works, xii. 109
Hood, Thomas, the younger (1835–1874), xiii. 512; xiv. 339; *The Rules of Rhyme*, xiii. 248
Hood's Magazine, xiii. 69
Hooghe, Pieter de, xiv. 212
Hook, Theodore Edward (1788–1841), xii. 103, 123, 429, 449; xiii. 307 ff.; xiv. 200; *Gervase Skinner*, xii. 251; xiii. 309; *Sayings and Doings*, xii. 251
Hook, Walter Farquhar (1798–1875), xii. 274, 457; xiv. 101, 503, 507, 591; *Lives of the Archbishops of Canterbury*, xiv. 112
Hooke, Nathaniel (d. 1763), x. 509; *Account of the...Duchess of Marlborough*, x. 319; *Observations on the Roman Senate*, x. 319; *Roman History*, x. 319
Hooke, Robert (1635–1703), viii. 250, 364; xiv. 561; *Micrographia*, viii. 356, 477; xiv. 283
Hooker, Joan, iii. 406
Hooker, John (1526?–1601), iii. 406
Hooker, Sir Joseph Dalton (1817–1911), xiv. 296, 299, 300, 550, 561

Hooker, Richard (1554–1600), II. 290; III. 319, 399–417, 459; IV. 221, 226, 235 ff., 239, 268, 303, 411, 493, 511; V. 338; VII. 125, 146, 158, 163, 236, 252, 280, 295, 463; VIII. 72, 308; X. 174, 360; XI. 28, 32; XII. 253; *Christian Letter, The*, III. 415; *Of the Laws of Ecclesiastical Polity*, III. 399–417 (main entry), 547; VII. 323; VIII. 336
Hooker, Sir William Jackson (1785–1865), XIV. 290, 561
Hookham, Edward, XI. 463
Hoole, Charles (1610–1667), V. 80; VII. 480; *New Discovery of the Old Art of teaching Schoole*, IX. 387, 569
Hoole, John (1727–1803), X. 435, 469, 473; XI. 246; *Cyrus*, X. 87, 435, 439; XI. 263; *Timanthes*, XI. 263
Hooly and Fairly, IX. 374
Hooper, John (d. 1555), bishop of Gloucester and Worcester, sermons upon *Jonah*, III. 36, 474; IV. 232, 493
Hooper, Richard, VII. 51
Hoosier writers, XIV. 349
Hope (Spes), in *Piers the Plowman*, II. 27
Hope, in prince Arthur's marriage pageant, VI. 332
Hope, Thomas (1770?–1831), XI. 461; *Anastasius*, XI. 306, 307
Hope, Sir William, IV. 369
Hope, Sir William Henry St John (1854–1919), XII. Add. 5
Hope End, Herefordshire, XIII. 70
Hopeful, in Bunyan's *Pilgrim's Progress*, VII. 173
Hope-Scott, James Robert (1812–1873), XII. 454; XIV. 505
Hopewell, the Rev. Mr, Haliburton's, XIV. 346
Hopkins, Charles (1664–1700), VIII. 437
Hopkins, Ellice, XII. 467
Hopkins, Gerard, XIII. 207, 210
Hopkins, J. Castell, XIV. 581
Hopkins, John (d. 1570), III. 46; *Psalms*, VIII. 41
Hopkins, Matthew (d. 1647), *The Discovery of Witches*, VII. 375
Hopkins, Richard (d. 1594?), IV. 444
Hopkins, Robert Thurston, XIV. 528
Hopkins, William (1793–1866), XIV. 265, 561
Hoppner, John (1758–1810), XII. 323
Hoppus, John, XIV. 591
Hopton, Ralph, lord (1598–1652), VII. 86, 245, 246, 348, 454
Horace, I. 76, 193, 221; II. 264; III. 20, 113, 173, 232, 259; IV. 2, 17, 23, 30, 124, 186, 197, 206 ff., 235, 248, 250, 329, 332, 418, 437; V. 65; VI. 221, 313, 348, 362, 406; VII. 1, 4, 12, 62, 69, 180, 181, 265, 267, 334, 370; VIII. 44, 58, 61, 85, 89, 203, 214, 215, 220, 271, 278, 408, 446; IX. 39, 46, 58, 59, 72, 85 ff., 119, 146, 158, 264, 269, 277, 336 ff., 445, 449, 455, 456, 458 ff., 462, 473, 478, 482, 484, 497, 499, 525, 526, 528, 561; X. 117, 124, 128, 197, 201, 430, 457, 464, *also see* Add.; XI. 2, 81, 82, 90, 134, 136, 403, 426; XII. 73, 318, 326, 335, 363, 419, 482, 484, 486 ff., 490, 491, 493 ff., 497, *also see* Add.; XIII. 294; XIV. 205
  Ars Poetica, VI. 6, 8; VIII. 221; IX. 70
  Beatus ille, VII. 9
  Coelum non animum, VII. 100
  Carmina, X. 130
  Epistles, XII. 337
  Integer vitae, VII. 2
  Odes, XI. 359
  Translations from, by Sir Richard Fanshawe, VIII. 271
Horace, in *The Poetaster*, VI. 18, 39, 42
Horae Subsecivae, IV. 524
Horant, in *Kudrun*, I. 37
Horatio, in Rowe's *Fair Penitent*, VIII. 196
Horatio, in *The Dukes Mistris*, VI. 200
Horatio, don, in *The Spanish Tragedie*, V. 158, 163, 240
Horatius Cocles, in *The Rape of Lucrece*, VI. 101
Horm, Danish viking, I. 287
Horman, William (d. 1535), II. 321; III. 555
Horn, cape, XIII. 16
Horn, John, II. 66
Horn, The Gest of King, I. 218, 281, 286, 287, 291 ff., 299, 303 ff., 309, 468
Horn Childe, I. 282, 291, 468
Hornby, near Lancaster, XIV. 54
Horne, Andrew (d. 1328), VIII. 465
Horne, George (1730–1792), IX. 512; X. 472; XII. 467
Horne, John. *See* Tooke, John Horne
Horne, Richard Henry or Hengist (1803–1884), XI. 410; XII. 107, 117, 418, 428, 441; XIII. 471, 483, 484, 520, 543; XIV. 365, 520, 586
  Australian Autobiography, XIV. 371
  Australian Facts and Fancies, XIV. 371
  Cosmo de' Medici, XII. 118; XIII. 262
  Death of Marlowe, The, XII. 118; XIII. 262
  Gregory VII, XIII. 262
  Judas Iscariot, XIII. 262
  Laura Dibalzo, XII. 118
  New Spirit of the Age, A, XII. 118
  Orion, XII. 118; XIV. 363
Horne, Thomas (1610–1654), VII. 480
Horne, Thomas Hartwell (1780–1862), IV. 426; XII. 472, 522
Horneck, Anthony (1641–1697), VIII. 301, 302, 460
Hornecks, Mrs and the Miss, X. 213
Horner, Francis (1778–1817), XII. 144, 426; 'The Paper credit of Great Britain, XII. 145
Horning, L. E., XIV. 581
Horologium, Old English, I. 136
Horrocks, Jeremiah (d. 1641), VIII. 477
Horsa, I. 104
Horse, book on care of, III. 19

Horse, the, in *Mum, Sothsegger*, II. 36
Horses, writers on, IV. 540
Horsfield, Thomas Walker (d. 1837), XII. 511
Horsham, Sussex, X. 378; XII. 58
Horsham school, VII. 342
Horsley, John (1685–1732), *Britannia Romana*, IX. 355, 536
Horsley, Samuel (1733–1806), XI. 399; XII. 279, 280
Horsleydown, X. 382
Horsman, Edward (1807–1876), XIV. 133, 172, 510
Horstmann, Carl, I. 338, 340
Hort, Fenton John Anthony (1828–1892), XII. 340, 465, 467, *also see* Add.; *The Way the Truth the Life*, XII. 298
Hort, Josiah (1674?–1751), IX. 465; X. 385
Hortense, in Charlotte Brontë's *Shirley*, XIII. 409
Hortensio, in *The Bashful Lover*, VI. 155, 158
Hortensius, in Grave's *Columella*, X. 277
Horton, Bucks., VII. 98, 99, 107, 113
Hosack, John (d. 1887), XIV. 503; *Mary Queen of Scots and her Accusers*, XIV. 94
Hosein, in Ockley's *History of the Saracens*, X. 281
Hoskins, John (1566–1638), IV. 59, 209, 265
Hoskins, Sir John (1634–1705), VIII. 247
Hoskins, William (*fl.* 1591), V. 322
Hospitall of incurable fooles, The, III. 482
Hospitallers. *See* St John, knights of
Host, the, in the *Canterbury Tales*, III. 192
Hôtel de Rambouillet, VII. 391
Hotham, Charles (1615–1672?), IX. 515, 517, 518
Hotham, Durant (1617?–1691), IX. 515, 518; *The Spie*, VII. 351
Hotham, Sir John (d. 1645), VII. 351
Hothbroddus, I. 25
Hothead, in Crowne's *Sir Courtly Nice*, VIII. 189
Hotspur, II. 415; V. 256
Hotspur, in *Macbeth*, XI. 284
Hotten, John Camden (1832–1873), XII. 506; XIII. 467, 532
Hottentots, X. 160; XIV. 375
Houbraken, X. 498
Houdancourt, Mlle La Motte, VIII. 262
Houghton, X. 246
Houghton, lord. *See* Milnes, Richard Monckton
Houghton Conquest, Beds., IX. 145
Hounslow heath, VIII. 93
Hour, The, XIV. 196
Hour before Marriage, An, XI. 265
Hours, Books of, II. 315; IV. 426
House of Commons, II. 286, 303
Household books, II. 503
Household Words, XII. 221; XIII. 178, 315, 323, 326, 328, 329, 332, 335, 373, 375 ff., 379
Housewifery, writers on, IV. 543
Housman, Laurence, XI. 433
Houyhnhnms, in *Gulliver's Travels*, IX. 105
Hoveden, John (d. 1275), I. 194, 454
Hoveden, Roger of (d. 1201?), I. 160, 161, 172 ff., 178, 450; III. 314; IV. 68
How, Frederick Douglas, XIV. 599
How a man may chuse a good Wife from a bad, VI. 93, 96, 432
How a Merchande dyd hys Wyfe Betray, II. 501
How the Good Wife taught her Daughter, II. 501, 502
How the Plowman lerned his Pater Noster, II. 501
How the Wise man taught his Son, II. 501, 502
How unhappy is Phyllis in love, VIII. 96
Howard, Charles, of Effingham, admiral, 1st earl of Nottingham (1536–1624), IV. 82; VI. 249, 250
Howard, Charles, 11th duke of Norfolk (1746–1815), XIV. 186
Howard, Edward (*fl.* 1669), VIII. 217, 422; *The Usurper*, VIII. 21; *The Women's Conquest*, V. 277; version of Rochester's *British Princes*, VII. 267
Howard, Sir Edward, lord high admiral (d. 1513), III. 64
Howard, Edward Granville George (d. 1841), XII. 449
Howard, lady Elizabeth, Dryden's wife, VIII. 8
Howard, Frances, countess of Essex (and Somerset), IV. 143, 145, 202, 259; VI. 31, 344
Howard, Frederick, 5th earl of Carlisle (1748–1825), XI. 392
Howard, Henrietta, countess of Suffolk (1681–1767), IX. 82, 249, 470, 498; X. 257; *Letters*, IX. 250
Howard, Henry, earl of Surrey (1517?–1547), II. 213, 331; III. 23, 24, 168, 169, 171, 174 ff. (main entry), 201, 210, 212, 227, 247 ff., 281 ff., 285, 287, 293, 294, 298, 300, 302, 303, 363, 365, 442, 447, 509; IV. 108, 110, 116 ff., 130, 138, 182, 183, 196, 197; VII. 1; VIII. 222, 223
  Aeneid, V. 155; VII. 133
  Beautie, Frailtie and hurtfulnesse of, III. 176
  Complaint of a dying lover, III. 176
  Complaint of the absence of her lover, III. 177
  Complaint that his ladie after she knew of his love kept her face alway hidden from him, III. 176
  Liricks, VII. 271
  Phylida was a fayer mayde, III. 178
  Richmond, Elegy on the Duke of, III. 178
  Spring, wherein eche thing renewes, III. 176
  Vow to love faithfully howsoever he be rewarded, III. 176
Howard, Henry, 1st earl of Northampton (1540–1614), VI. 4; VII. 435

Howard, James (*fl.* 1674), VIII. 422; *All Mistaken*, VIII. 21; version of *Romeo and Juliet*, VIII. 21, 120
H[oward], J., *Panegyric on King William*, VIII. 92
Howard, John (1726?–1790), XI. 16, 278, 424, 427
Howard, lady Margaret, VII. 23
Howard, Philip, 1st earl of Arundel (1557–1595), *Fourefould Meditation, of the foure last things*, IV. 130
Howard, Sir Robert (1626–1698), VIII. 6, 8, 26, 395, 398, 419, 444
Committee, The, VIII. 20, 121
Foure New Plays, VIII. 23
Great Favourite, The, VIII. 21, 24
Indian Queen (with Dryden), VIII. 123
Howard, Thomas, 2nd duke of Norfolk (1443–1524), II. 503; III. 56, 174
Howard, Thomas, 3rd duke of Norfolk (1473–1554), III. 174
Howard, Thomas, 1st earl of Suffolk (1561–1626), IV. 427; VI. 344; VII. 338
Howard, Thomas, 2nd earl of Arundel and Surrey (1586–1646), VII. 219, 307
Howe, Frederick A., V. 250
Howe, John (1630–1705), X. 379; *Calm and Sober Enquiry*, X. 378; *Some Considerations*, X. 374
Howe, Joseph (1804–1873), XIV. 346, 357, 359, 582
Howe, Miss, in Richardson's *Clarissa*, X. 8, 17
Howe, Percival Presland, XIII. 515
Howe Johan Splynter made his testament, A mery gest, II. 327
Howell, James (1594?–1666), VII. 84, 99, 197, 359, 439, 446, 457, 458, 466, 480, 513; IX. 416
Brief Character of the Low Countries, A, VII. 200
Dendrologia, Dodona's Grove, or the Vocall Forest, VII. 200
England's Teares for the present Warres, VII. 200
Familiar letters, VII. 197 ff.; XIV. 168
Instructions for Forreine Travell, VII. 200, 201
Londinopolis, VII. 201
Perfect Description of the Country of Scotland, A, VII. 200
Howell, Thomas, translator of Ovid, IV. 438
Howell, Thomas (*fl.* 1568), III. 509
A Dreame, III. 188; XI. 217
Arbor of Amitie, The, III. 187
Devises, III. 188; XI. 217
Newe Sonets and pretie Pamphlets, III. 188
Howes, Edmund (*fl.* 1607–1631), VI. 254
Howgill, Francis (1618–1669), VIII. 416
Howie, John (1735–1793), IX. 549
Howitt, Mary (1799–1888), XI. 387, 480, 491; XIII. 373; XIV. 520
Howitt, Samuel (1765?–1822), *The British Sportsman*, XIV. 232, 544
Howitt, William (1792–1879), XI. 387, 410, 440, 480; XII. 379; XIII. 549; XIV. 371, 520, 586; *A Boy's Adventures in the Wilds of Australia*, XIV. 369
Howleglass, Tyll Howleglas, II. 329; III. 82, 94, 488
Howson, Edmond W., XIV. 597
Howson, John Saul (1816–1885), XII. 472
Hoxton (Hogsden), III. 316; IV. 361, 362; X. 384; XII. 183
Hoy, Thomas (1659–1718?), VIII. 404
Hoyden, Miss, in Vanbrugh's *Relapse*, VIII. 161
Hoyden, Miss, in Vanbrugh's *Relapse* and Sheridan's *Trip to Scarborough*, XI. 269
Hoyden, Timothy, in *The Sparagus Garden*, VI. 227
Hoyle, Joshua (d. 1654), VII. 322
Hrethel, in *Beowulf*, I. 24
Hrethric, in *Beowulf*, I. 25
Hróarr (Roe), son of Halfdan, I. 25
Hroerekr (Roricus), I. 25
Hrólfr, I. 25
Hrólfr Kraki, I. 25, 27
Hrólfs Saga Kraka, I. 25, 27
Hrothgar, in *Beowulf* and *Widsith*, I. 20, 22, 23, 24, 25, 29, 32, 34; V. 26
Hrothwulf, in *Beowulf* and *Widsith*, I. 23, 25, 34
Hrotsvitha, Roswitha, Benedictine abbess of Gandersheim, V. 6, 101; VII. 503
Huarte Navarro, J. de D., *Examen de Ingenios*, IV. 445; VII. 260
Hubba, X. 237
Hubbard, Frank Gaylord, V. 85, 87
Hubbard, John, X. 384
Huber, Victor Aimé, XIV. 593
Hubert, in *King John*, V. 185
Hübner, XII. 523
Huchon, R., XI. 419, 420, 474; *Un Poète Réaliste Anglais*, XI. 142
Huchoun of the Awle Ryale (*fl.* 14th cent.) I. 284, 333; II. 100, 115 ff., 121, 123, 450, 451
Hucknall Torkard, XII. 39, 393
Huddesford, George (1749–1809), XII. 418
Huddesford, William (1732–1772), IX. 535, 541
Hudibrastic couplet, the, XI. 247
'Hudibrastics,' X. 151; XIII. 233
Hudson, Henry (d. 1611), IV. 99, 107
Hudson, Henry Norman, V. 277
Hudson, John (1622–1719), *Dionysius*, XI. 341
Hudson, Thomas (*fl.* 1610), IV. 443
Hudson, William Henry, XIII. 488, 489
Hue, François, XIV. 66
Hue de Rotelande (*c.* 1185), I. 190, 270, 285, 470; *Ipomedon*, I. 190, 270, 281, 285, 286, 291, 313, 314, 465, 468
Hue and Cry after those rambling protonotaries of the times, Mercurius Elencticus, Britanicus, Melancholicus and Aulicus, The, VII. 359, 502, 514
Hueffer, Ford H. Madox, XIII. 499, 561, 574

Hueil or Huel, king of Scotland, I. 262
Huff, Ruff and Snuff, in *Cambises*, v. 64
Hügel, baron von, XII. 275
Hugessen, Edward Hugessen Knatchbull, 1st lord Brabourne. *See* Knatchbull-Hugessen
Huggins, William (1696–1761), x. 492
Huggins, Sir William (1824–1910), XIV. 556
Hugh, in *Barnaby Rudge*, XIII. 320, 321
Hugh, Sir, II. 414
Hugh de Campden's *Boctus and Sidrac*, II. 214
Hugh of Kirkstall (*fl.* 1200), I. 450
Hugh Spencer's Feats in France, II. 414
Hughes, A. M. D., XIII. Add. 2
Hughes, Charles, VII. 201
Hughes, H. R., of Kinmel, IV. 262
Hughes, Jabez (1685?–1731), VIII. 405
Hughes, John (1677–1720), VIII. 395, 410, 411, 437; IX. 57, 71, 143 ff., 181, 183, 437, 438, 477; *Apollo and Daphne*, VIII. 194; *Calypso and Telemachus*, VIII. 194; *The Siege of Damascus*, VIII. 194; IX. 144, 184; x. 73
Hughes, J. L., XIII. 543
Hughes, Michael (*fl.* 1746), IX. 564
Hughes, Patrick, x. 197
Hughes, Thomas (*fl.* 1587), *The Misfortunes of Arthur*, v. 77 ff., 152, 239, 397
Hughes, Thomas (1822–1896), XI. 480; XIII. 355, 358, 547, 553; XIV. 408; *Tom Brown's School Days*, XIII. 370, 435; XIV. 413
Hughes, Thomas McKenny, XII. 508
Hughes, W., *Abridgment* (1660–1662), VIII. 469
Hughes, William Richard, XIII. 543
Hugo, Herman, *Pia Desideria*, VII. 405
Hugo, Thomas, XIV. 540
Hugo, Victor, I. 279; v. 222, 234, 303; x. 221; XII. 208, 395; XIII. 129, 134, 137, 283, 425, 427, 428, 495
Art d'être Grandpère, L', XIII. 135
Châtiments, Les, XIII. 132
Cromwell, v. 302; XIII. 133
Égout de Rome, L', XIII. 133
Les Misérables, x. 49
Notre Dame de Paris, x. 218; XIII. 419
Roi s'amuse, Le, XIII. 267
Scott's *Quentin Durward*, XII. Add. 1
Hugo de Balsham (d. 1286), II. 346, 347, 350, 351, 353, 355
Hugo de Petra, in *The Usurper*, VIII. 21
Hugo de St Victor, I. 228, 232, 234, 355; II. 365
Huguccio, bishop of Ferrara (d. 1213), *Dictionary*, II. 363, 366
Huguenots, the, v. 286; VII. 306, 308, 322; VIII. 174, 261; IX. 236, 240; XI. 354
Hugues of Saxe-Gotha, Master, Browning's, XIII. 67
Huish, Robert (1777–1850), XI. 393
Hull, IV. 106, 310; VII. 184, 224
Hull, Eleanor, XIV. 574
Hull, Thomas (1728–1808), x. 273, 274 447; XI. 457
Hull Packet, The, XIV. 203
Hull grammar school, VII. 179
Huloet, Richard (*fl.* 1552), III. 555
Hulsean lectures, XII. 298
Hulton, Samuel Fletcher, XIV. 541
Humanities, the study of the, II. 366, 370
Humanity, in *The Palice of Honour*, II. 261
Humanum Genus, in *The Castle of Perseverance*, v. 52
Humber, the, II. 88, 100
Humble Address of the Atheists, The, VIII. 100
Humboldt, Alexander von, XIV. 249
Hume, Abraham (1814–1884), XII. 511
Hume, or Home, Alexander (1560?–1609), *Hymns and Sacred Songs*, III. 137, 498
Hume, Alexander (*fl.* 1612), IX. 558
Hume, Alexander (1811–1859), XIII. 503
Hume, Anna (*fl.* 1644), IX. 555
Hume, David, of Godscroft (1560?–1630?), IX. 550; *History of Douglas and Angus*, IX. 555
Hume, David (1711–1776), IV. 57, 292; VII. 278, 289, 290; VIII. 328, 335, 336, 340, 472; IX. 287, 547, 561, 565; x. 41, 87, 190, 263, 280, 281, 282 ff., 288, 291 ff., 296, 297, 301, 303, 305, 307, 313, 316 ff., 321 ff. (main entry), 337, 341 ff., 347 ff., 502, 505, 507, 510; XI. 57, 70, 71, 73, 74, 137, 139, 351; XII. 300; XIV. 5, 8, 17 ff., 41, 48, 469, 470, 473, 606
Dialogues concerning Natural Religion, x. 324, 332, 333
Enquiry concerning Human Understanding, x. 323, 327, 328, 331, 332
Enquiry concerning the Principles of Morals, x. 323, 332
Essay on Miracles, x. 332; XII. 285
Essays, x. 322 ff., 362; XIV. 398
Four Dissertations, x. 324
History, XI. 324, 326
History of England, x. 40, 283 ff., 289, 290, 293, 323, 362; XIV. 50, 54
History of Great Britain, x. 283 ff.
Letters to Strahan, x. 290, 303
Natural History of Religion, IX. 296; x. 332, 333
'Of Morals,' x. 322
'Of the Origin of Government,' x. 334
Own Life, x. 321, 324
Philosophical Essays, x. 323
Political Discourses, x. 323
Treatise of Human Nature, IX. 285; x. 282, 322 ff., 330 ff., 335, 342; XI. 63, 64; XIV. 43
Hume, David (1757–1838), x. 324
Hume, Joseph (1777–1855), XIV. 198, 407, 510
Hume, Martin Andrew Sharp, XIV. 490
Hume, Hugh, 3rd earl of Marchmont (1708–1794), x. 185
Hume, Patrick (*fl.* 1695), VII. 109

Hume, Patrick, 1st earl of Marchmont (1641–1724), III. 136, 137; IX. 364
Hume, capt. Tobias (d. 1645), IV. 113, 464
Humfrey or Humphrey, Laurence (1527?–1590), III. 421, 422, 445; IV. 429; *Optimates*, III. 445
Humil, in *The two Maids of More-clacke*, VI. 217
Humilitas, in *Psychomachia*, V. 51
Humility, in *Piers the Plowman*, II. 10
Humility, in *The Example of Virtue*, II. 227, 234
Humiltá, in *The Faerie Queene*, II. 234; VI. 335
Hummun's Turkish bath, IX. 263
Humourist, The, XIV. 223
Humours, the four, in *Hymenaei*, VI. 345
Humours, The Comedy of, V. 331
Humphrey, R., VII. 483
Humphrey, duke of Gloucester (1391–1447), II. 198, 286 ff., 318, 362, 497; IV. 182, 430; V. 367
Humphrey, Master, in Dickens's *Master Humphrey's Clock*, XIII. 318
Humphrey, squire, in Vanbrugh's *Journey to London*, VIII. 162
Humphris, E., and Sladen, D., *Adam Lindsay Gordon*, XIV. 365, 586
Huna, V. 31
Hundred Merry Tales, A, II. 327; III. 90, 93, 104, 109, 486, 487, 489; IV. 327, 340, 360
Hundred Years' war, XI. 280
Hunferth (Unferth), king's "orator," in *Beowulf*, I. 22
Hungarian language, XIV. 458
Hungary, II. 80; V. 308; VII. 79, 453
Hunger, in *Piers the Plowman*, II. 14, 22
Hungerford, XIV. 230
Hungerford, Margaret Wolfe (1855?–1897), XIV. 568
Hungerford academy, X. 386
Hunnis, John, VI. 283
Hunnis, Thomas, VI. 283
Hunnis, William (d. 1597), III. 189; IV. 121, 473, 495; V. 411; VI. 283, 286, 288, 291, *and see* Add. 2
Huns, the, I. 33, 35; XIV. 302
Hunsdon, lords. *See* Carey, George; Carey, Henry; Carey, John
Hunt, F. Knight, XIV. 532
Hunt, Henry (1773–1835), XIV. 125, 510
Hunt, James Henry Leigh (1784–1859), VI. 58, 76; VIII. 166, 167, 170; IX. 446; X. 483; XI. 326, 391, 449, 454; XII. 70, 74, 79 ff., 157, 160, 162, 171, 172, 178, 192, 194, 199, 204 ff., 219, 220 ff. (main entry), 227, 384, 395, 396, 399 ff., 403, 407, 428, 433, 437, 441 ff., *also see* Add.; XIII. 148, 258, 259, 337 ff., 328, 401, 469, 484, 513; XIV. 171, 180, 191, 198, 202
Abou ben Adhem, XII. 222
Autobiography, XIV. 197
Captain Sword and Captain Pen, XII. 223
Hunt, James Henry Leigh
Chat of the Week, The, XII. 443
Companion, The, XII. 443
Examiner, The, XII. 442, 444
Feast of the Poets, The, XII. 223
Feast of the Violets, The, XII. 223
Glove, The, XII. 223
Hero and Leander, XII. 222
Indicator, The, XII. 442, 443
Jenny kissed me, XII. 222
Journal, XII. 443
Liberal, The, XII. 36, 37, 443
Literary Examiner, The, XII. 443
Literary Pocket-Book, The, XII. 442
London Journal, XII. 443
Man, Fish and Spirit, XII. 222
Monthly Repository, The, XII. 440, 443
Old Court Suburb, The, XII. 223
Palfrey, The, XII. 223
Poetical Works, XII. 222
Reflector, The, XII. 223, 442
Story of Rimini, The, XII. 222; XIII. 237
Tatler, The, XII. 223, 443
Hunt, John (*fl.* 1805), XIV. 197
Hunt, John, D.D., *Religious Thought in England*, IX. 294
Hunt, Joseph, XIV. 201
Hunt, Mary, XIV. 490
Hunt, Thornton Leigh (1810–1873), XII. 443; XIV. 191, 196, 202
Hunt, Tufton, in Thackeray's *Adventures of Philip*, XIII. 299
Hunt, William, XIV. 83, 101, 532
Hunt, William Holman, XIII. 110 ff., 491
Hunter, Mrs Anne (1742–1821), XI. 444; *Adieu Ye Streams*, XI. 232; *My Mother bids me bind my hair*, XI. 232; *Poems*, XI. 232
Hunter, John (1728–1793), XIV. 286, 561
Hunter, Joseph (1783–1861), XII. 516; *Hallamshire*, XII. 346; *South Yorkshire*, XII. 346
Hunter, Mrs Leo, X. 277
Hunter, Sir William Wilson (1840–1900), XIII. Add. 2; XIV. 338, 490, 577
Annals of Rural Bengal, The, XIV. 339
History of British India, A, XIV. 339
Imperial Gazetteer, The, XIV. 339
Old Missionary, The, XIV. 339
Thackerays in India, The, XIV. 339
Hunterian club, XII. 358
Hunterian collection, XIV. 286
Hunterian professor, XIV. 295
Hunting, writers on, IV. 541
Hunting of the Cheviots, XI. 215
Hunting of the Hare, II. 502; III. 483
Huntingdon, XI. 80
Huntingdon. *See* Henry of
Huntingdon, countesses of. *See* Hastings, Lucy; Hastings, Selina
Huntingdon grammar school, VIII. 253
Huntingdonshire, VII. 342
Huntingford, George Isaac (1748–1832), XII. 490
Huntly, in *Perkin Warbeck*, VI. 193
Huntly, earl of (Holland's *Howlat*), II. 11

Hunton, Philip (1604?–1682), VII. Add.
Hunt's Up, The, IX. 362
Huon of Bordeaux, I. 292; II. 322, 339; V. 220
Hupe, I. 343
Hurault, Jacques, *Politicke, Moral and Martiall Discourses*, IV. 8, 21, 445
Hurd, Richard (1720–1808), IX. 509; X. 241, 363, 516; XI. 133, 449; *Letters on Chivalry and Romance*, X. 240, 484
Hurdis, James (1763–1801), XI. 427
Hursley, XII. 277
Hurstmonceaux rectory, XII. 288
Hurtado, Luis, IV. 445
Hurwitz, Hyman (1770–1844), XI. 413
Hus, John (1369–1415), II. 59, 69; III. 39, 69
Husbandman, Song of the, I. 370
Husbandry, writers on, IV. 541
Husbands, J., *A Miscellany of Poems by Several Hands*, X. 159, 467
Husband's Message, The, I. 4, 39, 424, 428; runes in, I. 12
Huskisson, William (1770–1830), XIV. 131
Hussey, Edward, XI. 174
Hussey, Thomas (1741–1803), bishop of Waterford, XI. 6
Hutcheon, William, XIII. 348, 547
Hutcheson, Francis (1694–1746), IX. 301, 302, 506, 508, 548; X. 122, 332, 335, 337; XI. 63, 67; *Essay on the... Passions and Affections*, IX. 301; *Inquiry into... Ideas of Beauty and Virtue*, IX. 301; *System of Moral Philosophy*, IX. 301
Hutcheson, Mrs, IX. 308
Hutcheson, W. G., XIV. 488
Hutchins, John (1698–1773), XII. 511
Hutchinson, John (1615–1664), IV. 523; VII. 225, 226, 227
Hutchinson, Julius, VII. 226
Hutchinson, Lucy (b. 1620), VI. 402, 403; VII. 225, 226, 451; VIII. 270
Hutchinson, Mary, XI. 103
Hutchinson or Hutchenson, Ralph (1553?–1606), VII. 316
Hutchinson, Roger (d. 1555), IV. 493
Hutchinson, Thomas (1698–1769), XII. 490
Hutchinson, Thomas (d. 1919), editor of Wordsworth and Lamb, XI. 405 ff., 410, 413; XII. 399, 434 ff.
Hutchinson, William (1732–1814), XII. 511
Hutten, Leonard (1557?–1632), III. 80; VI. 482
Hutton, Arthur Wollaston, XIV. 509
Hutton, Catherine (1756–1846), XI. 469; XIV. 520
Hutton, Charles (1737–1823), XIV. 556
Hutton, Hon. C. W., XIV. Add. 10
Hutton, Henry (*fl.* 1619), IV. 520; V. 478
Hutton, James (1726–1797), XIV. 290 ff., 561
Hutton, Luke (d. 1598), IV. 529, 530; *The Blacke Dogge of Newgate*, IV. 350
Hutton, Richard Holt (1826–1897), XI. 410; XII. 461, 467; XIII. 91, 189, 394, 471, 477, 484, 488, 489, 553; XIV. 197, 198, 515, 520, 521, 534; *Aspects of Religious and Scientific Thought*, XIV. 141; *Essays, Theological and Literary*, XIV. 141
Hutton, William (1723–1815), XI. 338, 340, 469; XII. 511; XIV. 521
Hutton, William Holden, XI. 420; XIV. 486, 488, 499
Huxley, Leonard, XIV. 603
Huxley, Thomas Henry (1825–1895), IV. 42, 50; VIII. 352; X. 511; XII. 297; XIV. 296, 300, 474, 606
Collected Essays, XIV. 299
Ethics and Evolution, XIV. 34
Life of Hume, XIV. 34
'On the Hypothesis that Animals are Automata,' XIV. 34
'Physical Basis of Life, The,' XIV. 34
'Science and Morals,' XIV. 34
Huyche, William, translator of Calvin's *Common Praiers*, IV. 442
Huygens, Christian, IX. 129
Hwaetberct. *See* Eusebius
Hwon holy chirche is under uote, I. 226, 458
Hyatt, Stanley Portal, XIV. Add. 8
Hyberdine, parson, IV. 319
Hyde, near Winchester, Benedictine abbey at, IV. 417
Hyde, Anne, duchess of York (1637–1671), VII. 220
Hyde, Douglas, XIV. 314, 573
Hyde, Edward, 1st earl of Clarendon (1609–1674), V. 364; VI. 6, 235; VII. 16, 85, 150, 183, 184, 212 ff. (main entry), 226, 229, 296, 434, 436, 438, 439, 441, 443, 449, 453, 454; VII. Add.; VIII. 7, 8, 23, 38, 81, 206, 271, 295, 308, 323, 368, 384, 480; IX. 209, 214, 221, 226, 237, 238, 347; X. 113, 315; XI. 12, 28
A Collection of Some of the Massacres and Murthers committed on the Irish, VII. 212
Against Multiplying Controversies, VII. 217
An Active and Contemplative Life, VII. 217
Brief Survey of the dangerous and pernicious Errors to Church and State in Mr Hobbes's book, VII. 301
Concerning Education, IX. 396
Contemplations and Reflections upon the Psalms of David, VII. 215, 217
Essays Divine and Moral, VII. 217, 221
History of the Rebellion, VII. 188, 202, 212, 214 ff.; VIII. 63, 389; IX. 204, 206, 208, 227, 394; X 280; XI. 341
Life (autobiography), VII. 213, 216 ff., 221; VIII. 322; IX. 208
Miscellaneous Works, VII. 215, 217
Of Contempt of Death, VIII. 389
Of Friendship, VIII. 389
Of Human Nature, VII. 217
Of Liberty, VII. 217
Of Repentance, VII. 217; VIII. 389
Of the Want of Respect due to Age, IX. 396

Hyde, Edward
On Education, VII. 217, 220
On the Reverence due to Old Age, VII. 217
Reflections upon several Christian Duties, VIII. 389
Short View of the State and Condition of the Kingdom of Ireland, A, VII. 212
State Papers, VII. 188
Vindication, VII. 217
Hyde, Edward, 3rd earl of Clarendon (1661–1724), IX. 161
Hyde, Henry, 2nd earl of Clarendon (1638–1700), VIII. 249, 250; IX. 534
Hyde, Henry, viscount Cornbury and lord Hyde (1710–1753), IX. 226, 227
Hyde, Jane, lady, IX. 162
Hyde, Lawrence, 1st earl of Rochester (1641–1711), VII. 218; VIII. 43, 97, 268
Hyde, Thomas (1636–1703), IX. 529
Hyder Ali, XI. 17, 18
Hye Way to the Spyttel Hous, The, II. 324, 485, 501; III. 492
Hygd, in *Beowulf,* I. 23, 24
Hygeia, in Garth's *Dispensary,* IX. 180
Hygelac, in *Beowulf,* I. 23, 24, 25, 26, 29, 41
Hyland, Inez K. (1863–1892), XIV. 586
Hylton, or Hilton, Walter (d. 1396), II. 482; *Ladder of Perfection* or *The Devout book to a temporal man,* II. 299, 300; *The Treatise of the Song of the Angels,* II. 327
Hymen, in *Hymenaei,* VI. 345, 346
Hymen, in *The Hue and Cry after Cupid,* VI. 347
Hymen, in *The Jealous Lovers,* VI. 325
Hymenaeus, VI. 304, 327, 484
Hynd, James, VII. 513
Hynde, S., *Iter Lusitanicum,* IV. 458
Hyndluliöð, Old Norse poem, I. 23
Hypatia, Kingsley's, XIII. 363
Hyperides, XII. 331, 340
Hyperion, in Keats's poem, XII. 86
Hypermnestra, II. 177
Hypochondriack, The, X. 479
Hypocrisy, in *Ane Pleasant Satyre,* III. 127
Hypocrisy, in Medwall's interlude, V. 54
Hypocrisy, in *Mirour de l'Omme,* II. 140
'Hypolito, cardinall, of Est,' in *The Famous Whore,* IV. 376
Hyslop, James (1798–1827), XII. 418; *Cameronian's Dream,* XI. 243
Hyspanus (Petrus), IV. 445

'I canna come every day to Woo,' XI. 235
I had a horse, IX. 374
I mak it kend, he that will spend, II. 279
'I saw a Peacock with a fiery Tail,' XI. 370
I sing of a maiden, III. 280
Iachimo, in *Cymbeline,* V. 205
Iago, in *Othello,* III. 188; V. 202, 203, 213; VI. 274; XII. 171
Ianthe, in *The Siege* (D'Avenant's), VIII. 118
Ibbitson, Robert (*fl.* 1650), VII. 352, 355, 356
Ibbotson, J., VIII. 463
Ibburranes, in *Argenis,* IV. 259
Ibrahim Mollac, in Lyttelton's *Persian Letters,* X. 114
Ibrahim pasha, XIV. 252
Ibsen, Henrik, X. 77; XII. 116; XIII. 273
Iceland, IV. 325; XIII. 125; XIV. 289
Icelanders, the, X. 222
Icelandic language and literature, X. 220, 223 ff., 489 ff.; XIII. 124 ff.; XIV. 458. *See, also,* Norse and Scandinavian
Icelus, XIII. 330
Icilius, in *Appius and Virginia,* VI. 182
Ickworth, IX. 251, 252
Ida, in *James IV,* V. 138, 245
Iden, Henry, IV. 444
Ider, I. 297
Idler, The, XIV. 594
Idolatry, in *A True Inventory,* VII. 382
Idumeans, the, VII. 382
Iffley, river, XIV. 209
Igerna, in Arthurian legend, I. 259
Igerna, in *The Misfortunes of Arthur,* V. 78
Ignatius, St, VII. 318; XII. 340; *Epistles,* VII. 149; VIII. 297; XII. 341, 503
Ignatius, *Epistles,* rendering by Grosseteste, I. 204
Ignatius of Antioch, IX. 329
Ignorance, in Medwall's interlude, X. 54
Ignorance, in *The Nature of the Four Elements,* V. 57
Ignorance, in *The Tears of the Muses,* III. 241
'Ignoto,' IV. 52, 116, 117; V. 224; *The Nymph's Reply,* VII. 8
Ilchester, I. 205; VII. 54
Ilissus, river, XIV. 132
Ilium (*i.e.* Paris), in *Euphormio,* IV. 256
'I'll tell thee, Dick,' VIII. 96
Illtyd, St, St Iltut or Iltutus (*fl.* 520) of Lantwit Major, Wales, I. 66, 67, 69
Illustrated London News, The, XIV. 192, 196, 201
Illustrated Sporting and Dramatic News, The, XIV. 201
Illustrated Times, The, XIV. 196
Illustrations of Northern Antiquities, XII. 358
Illyrians, the, IV. 43
Ilmington, I. 126
Ilsington (Devonshire), VI. 188
Imaginative, in *Piers the Plowman,* II. 27
Imlay, Gilbert (*fl.* 1793), XI. 44, 395
Imma, in Bede, I. 10
Immalee, in Maturin's *Melmoth,* XI. 305
Immerito, in *The Returne from Pernassus,* VI. 314
Immerito and G. H., *Three proper and wittie familiar Letters,* VI. 388
Immermann, Karl, V. 305
Imogen, in *Cymbeline,* V. 169, 189, 205, 206; XII. 87
Impartial Trimmer, The, VIII. 92
Impatient Poverty, V. 60, 393
Imperial Dictionary of Universal Biography, XIV. 326

Imperial Tragedy, The (1669), VIII. 434
Impey, Sir Elijah (1732–1809), XI. 78
In and In Medley, in *A Tale of a Tub*, VI. 26
In Diebus Dominicis, I. 227, 458
In January last, IX. 360
In May in a morning, II. 282
Inamorato and Misogamos, VII. 512
Incest, in *Confessio Amantis*, II. 149
Inchbald, Mrs Elizabeth (1753–1821), IX. 435; XI. 224, 270, 276, 281, 294–295 (main entry), 454, 456, 457, 461
Every one has his Fault, XI. 279
I'll tell you What, XI. 278
Mogul Tale, The, XI. 278
Nature and Art, X. 49, 59; XI. 294
Simple Story, A, XI. 279, 292, 294
Such Things Are, XI. 278
To Marry or not to Marry, XI. 278
Wives as they Were, XI. 279
Inchbald, Joseph (d. 1779), XI. 278
Inchcolm, Firth of Forth, II. 128, 129
'Inche of Lowchlewyn,' II. 131
Inderwick, Frederick Andrew (1836–1904), XIV. 503
Index Expurgatorius Anglicanus, VII. 432
Index librorum prohibitorum, XIV. 108
India, II. 79; IV. 92, 98, 99, 102; IX. 138; X. 294, 408, 491 (poems), 503, 504; XI. 3, 5, 6, 11, 12, 14 ff., 27, 242, 381; XII. 343, 352, 353, 361; XIII. 199; XIV. 59, 61, 64, 78, 97, 98, 130, 133, 221, 331 ff.
India office, XII. 502
Indian alphabets, XII. 352
Indian antiquities, XII. 512
Indian architecture, XII. 509, 510
Indian army, the, XIV. 253
Indian civil service, XIII. 202
Indian geography, XIV. 334
Indian languages, XIV. 457, 458
Indian law, XII. 327
Indian mutiny, the, XII. 227; XIV. 176, 339
Indian mythology, XIV. 339
Indian poetry, XIV. 340
Indian princes, in *The Masque of the Middle Temple*, VI. 355
Indian rebels, XIII. 40
Indian sage, IX. 317
Indians, in *The Moonstone*, XIII. 437
Indians, the, in Cowley's *The Passions*, VII. 64
Indicator, The, XII. 194, 436
Indolence, in Thomson's *Castle of Indolence*, X. 107
Ine, king of Wessex (d. 726), VIII. 310
Ine, laws of, I. 97, 98
Infant School society, XIV. 405
Infida, in *Never too late*, III. 357
Infidelity, in *The Faerie Queene*, III. 234
Ingannati, Gl', V. 115; VI. 305; VIII. 126
Ingeld, in *Beowulf* and *Widsith*, I. 24, 25, 34
Ingelend, Thomas (*fl.* 1560), *The Disobedient Child*, V. 109, 404; VI. 94
Ingelow, Jean (1820–1897), XI. 387, 487; XIII. 503; *Divided*, XIII. 179
Ingenioso, in *The Pilgrimage to Parnassus*, VI. 310
Ingenioso, in *The Returne from Parnassus*, VI. 311
Ingialdr, I. 25
Ingleborough, X. 101
Ingler, William (*fl.* 1643), *Certaine Informations*, VII. 350
Inglis, Sir James, abbot of Cambus Kenneth, III. 153
Inglis, Sir James, abbot of Culross (d. 1531), III. 131, 153
Inglis, Sir Robert Harry, XIV. 596
Ingoldsby, Lincolnshire, VIII. 456
Ingram and Marlowe. *See* Frizer
Ingram, David, IV. 73
Ingram, Herbert, XIV. 201
Ingram, J. Forsyth, XIV. Add. 5, 8
Ingram, John H., XIII. 484, 499, 561
Ingram, John Kells (1823–1907), XIV. 568; *Who fears to speak of Ninety-Eight?* XIV. 318
Ingram, Robert Acklon (1763–1809), XIV. 606; *Necessity of introducing divinity, The*, XIV. 385; *Remarks upon the enormous expense*, XIV. 385
Ingram, Thomas Dunbar (1826–1904), XIV. 490
Ingram, William (*fl.* 1601), IV. 517
Ingulph of Croyland, Chronicle of the pseudo, II. 497; IV. 417
Iniquity, in *Nice Wanton*, V. 110
Inis Eogain, IX. 292
Inishowen, IX. 292
Injunctions given by the Queenes Majestie, IV. 380, 381
Inkle, in Colman's *Inkle and Yarico*, XI. 279
Innes, Alexander (*fl.* 1728), IX. 548
Innes, Cosmo (1798–1874), XII. 516; *Lectures on Scotch Legal Antiquities*, XII. 359
Innes, captain Robert, VII. 361
Innes, Thomas (1662–1744), IX. 553
Innholders' play, V. 46
Innocence, in Marvell's *The Garden*, VII. 181
Innocent III, I. 193; VIII. 296; *De Contemptu Mundi*, III. 208
Innocent IV, I. 201
Innocent VIII, III. 5
Innocents, Boy bishop at the feast of the, V. 8
Innocents, murder of, in early plays, V. 50
Inns of Court, II. 305
Inns of Court Masque (1623), VII. 230
Innsbruck, V. 283
Inny river, X. 199
Inquisition, the, III. 16, 162; XI. 414
Insolence, in *Respublica*, V. 60
Institoris, H., VII. 368, 504
Institucion of a Gentleman, The, III. 552
Intellectus Agens, in *The Floating Island*, VI. 325
Intelligencer, The, IX. 458

Interludes, anonymous, of Heywood's period, v. 409
Intermedii, v. 69
Inverness, II. 100; VII. 254
Inverquharity, IX. 376
'Invisible College,' the, IX. 389
Inwit, Sir (Discretion), in *Piers the Plowman*, II. 19
Iolante, in *The Guardian*, VI. 157
Iona, I. 30, 42
Iona society, XII. 361
Ionian sea, XIII. 38
Iphigenia, VII. 371
Iphigenia, in *The Bugbears*, v. 115
Iphigenia, schoolboy play, v. 123
Iphis, in *Confessio Amantis*, II. 152
Ipreswel, or Hipswell, near Richmond, Yorkshire, II. 49
Ipsden, lord, in Reade's *Christie Johnstone*, XIII. 425
Ipsen, A., XIII. 532
Ipswich, II. 156; IV. 409; X. 355; XI. 140, 418; XIV. 190
Ipswich, queen Elizabeth's school, XII. 331
Ipswich, Wolsey's school at, II. 358; III. 428, 429
Ipswich Journal, The, XIII. 440
Ira, in *Psychomachia*, v. 51
Ira seu Tumulus Fortunae, VI. 320, 474
Irato, in *The Floating Island*, VI. 325
Irby, Adeline P., XIV. 553
Irby, Sir Antony, IV. 166
Ireland. *See* John of
Ireland, I. 71; II. 423; IV. 67; V. 137, 344, 347; VI. 197; VII. 46, 58, 78, 79, 114, 148, 149, 190, 207, 209 ff., 223, 225, 233, 253, 355, 358, 436, 442, 451, 458; VIII. 122, 169, 170, 190, 267, 342, 343; IX. 91 ff., 110, 114 ff., 121, 123, 126, 130, 132, 139, 166, 167, 171, 280, 282, 290; X. 58, 195, 200, 202, 203, 231, 256, 293; XI. 1, 3 ff., 12, 14 ff., 19, 39, 342, 343; XII. 165, 337, 344, 351, 360, 361, 433; XIII. 207, 348, 357, 364; XIV. 86, 115, 128, 133, 201, 302 ff., 343, 391, 392, 417, 434, 437
Ireland, Alexander (1810–1894), XII. 444
Ireland, Annie E. (d. 1893), XIII. 52, 467
Ireland, John (d. 1808), XI. 454; *Letter to Henry Brougham*, XIV. 406, 604
Ireland, Richard (*fl.* 1600), VII. 27
Ireland, Samuel (d. 1800), XII. 490
Ireland, William Henry (1777–1835), XI. 414, 457; XII. 364; XIV. 203
Ireland, Anglo-Irish political relations, VIII. 21
Ireland, books printed in, XI. 470
Ireland, church of, X. 358; XII. 272
Ireland, National University, XIV. Add.
Ireland, poems on, II. 502, 508
Ireland, printers in, IV. 547
Ireland, Ancient Laws of, XII. 360, 361
Ireland, English Conquest of, II. 483
Ireland, Good Newes from, IV. 389
Ireland, The Glories of, XIV. 307
Ireland's Eye, XIV. 327
Irena, a Tragedy, X. 161
Irenaeus, Aelfric's homily on, I. 118
Irenaeus (*i.e.* Edmund Spenser), VII. 210
Irene, Middleton's, XIII. 220
Irene, St, I. 74
Ireton, Henry (1611–1651), VII. 383, 513
Iris, in Beaumont's masque, VI. 356
Iris, in *The Vision of the Twelve Goddesses*, VI. 337, 338
Irish airs, XIV. 314
Irish archaeological society, XII. 361
Irish archaeology, XII. 351, 352, 360
Irish bar, the, XIV. 126
Irish booksellers, X. 11; XI. 342
Irish catholics, X. 58; XI. 7, 108
Irish channel, IX. 126
Irish church, the, XIV. 126
Irish clergy, IX. 394
Irish cronan, IX. 362
Irish dances, XIV. 328
Irish dialect, XIV. 447
Irish drama, XIII. 264; XIV. 330
Irish education, XIV. 328, 393
Irish expedition, Essex's, v. 346
Irish folk-songs, XIV. 328
Irish harpers, XIV. 311
Irish history, X. 280; XI. 15; XII. 360; XIV. 96, 105, 328
Irish land acts, XIV. 97
Irish language and literature, VII. 318; X. 196; XII. 360 ff.; XIV. 302 ff., 458
Irish literary societies, XIV. 319
Irish literary theatre, XIV. 329
Irish manners, XIII. 426
Irish music, X. 232
Irish national anthem, XIV. 321
Irish orators, XIV. 127, 128
Irish Ossianic poems, X. 232
Irish parliament, IX. 290, 291; XI. 6, 55, 344; XIV. 393
Irish people, the, XIV. 127
Irish place names, XIV. 328
Irish poets and poetry, XII. 114; XIII. 188, 190, 234; XIV. 211, 302 ff.
Irish policy, X. 403
Irish politics, XIV. 211, 311, 317
Irish potato famine, XIV. 318, 320
Irish rebellion of 1848, the, XIV. 242, 318
Irish 'revolution,' XI. 24
Irish saints, XIV. 303
Irish scenery, XIII. 283
Irish scholars, X. 231
Irish sea, XIII. 414
Irish sees, the, XII. 257
Irish State papers, VII. 436
Irish stories, XI. 297; XIII. 42, 415, 421
Irish Text society, XII. 516, 518; XIV. 305, 309
Irish trade, XI. 5, 6
Irish university system, XIV. 432
Irish Citizen, The, XIV. 326
Irish Hudibras, The, IX. 258, 502
Irish Liber Hymnorum, XII. 515
Irish Monthly, The, XIV. 329
Irish Penny Journal, The, XIV. 312, 315
Irish People, The, XIV. 321

Irish-Canadians, xiv. 345
Irishman, the stage, xi. 257
Irishmen, xiii. 283, 284, 404
'Irishmen, the Society of United,' xiv. 310, 325
Irnerius, of Bologna, ii. 349; viii. 312
Irnham, Simon, lord, xiv. 217
Ironmongers' company, vii. 250
Ironsides, Cromwell's, vii. 460
Irus, in *Ulysses Redux*, vi. 303
Irvine, Christopher (*fl.* 1638–1685), vi. 482; ix. 551
Irving, David (1778–1860), xi. 440, 445; xii. 522; *History of Scottish Poetry*, xii. 370; *Lives of Scottish Poets*, xii. 370; *Memoirs of...George Buchanan*, xii. 370
Irving, Edward (1792–1834), xii. 472; xiii. 3 ff., 467, 468
Irving, Sir Henry (1838–1905), v. 306; xi. 448; xiii. 474, 513, 514
Irving, Washington, x. 483; xii. 379, 409; *Bracebridge Hall*, xiii. 323; *The Sketch Book*, xiii. 429
Irwin, in Mrs Inchbald's *Every one has his Fault*, xi. 279
Irwin, Sidney, x. 202
Irwin, Sidney Thomas, xiii. 499; xiv. 145, 521
Irwin, Thomas C. (1823–1892), xiv. 569
Irwine, Mr, in *Adam Bede*, xiii. 390
Isaac, i. 46, 123
Isaac, Arabian physician, ii. 364, 365
Isaac, in the religious plays, ii. 424, 426, 427
Isaac, in *Jacob and Esau*, v. 111, 112
Isabel, in *The Decameron*, xii. 82
Isabel, in *Misogonus*, v. 111
Isabel of Castille, duchess of York, ii. 170
Isabel, Lady, and the Elf-Knight, ii. 410, 411
Isabella, in Emily Brontë's *Wuthering Heights*, xiii. 411
Isabella, in Keats's poem, xii. 86, 88
Isabella, in *Laelia*, vi. 305
Isabella, in *Measure for Measure*, i. 1; v. 190, 191, 245
Isabella, in Southerne's *Fatal Marriage*, viii. 191, 192
Isabella, in *The White Divel*, vi. 176, 177
Isabella, countess of Swevia, in *The Insatiate Countesse*, vi. 45, 49
Isabella, queen, in *A Challenge for Beautie*, vi. 103
Isabella, queen, in *Edward II*, v. 153
Isabella of France (1292–1358), queen of Edward II, ii. 338
Isabella of France (1389–1409), queen of Richard II, iv. 169, 181, 182
Isaiah, ii. 106; ix. 69; x. 229
Isenbarth, M., xiii. 553
Iseo, Lago di, ix. 245
Iseult, i. 272 ff., 298, 310. *See, also*, Tristram
Isidora, in Maturin's *Melmoth*, xi. 305
Isidore of Seville, i. 71, 75, 80, 224, 343, 436; ii. 86, 319, 365; iii. 109; *Etymologies* of, i. 119; ii. 86, 363
'Isis Idols,' xiv. 208
Isis river, vii. 327
Isis, The, xiv. 208, 537
Islam, ix. 184; xiii. 13; xiv. 252, 338
Island of Sorcerers, in *Gulliver's Travels*, ix. 105
Islands expedition (Azores, 1597), iv. 103, 200, 201
Isle of Birds, i. 339
Isle of Man, in *Horn*, i. 304
Isle of Wight, xii. 509
Isleworth, iv. 418
Isley, Henry, vi. 112
Isley, Ursula (wife of Beaumont), vi. 112
Islington, iii. 316, 371
Islip, John (d. 1532), iii. 69
Ismael, in *The Loyal Brother*, viii. 190
Ismail, siege of, in Byron's *Don Juan*, xii. 55
Isocrates, iii. 429; iv. 437; x. 202
Isola, Agostino, ix 412; xiv. 385
Isola, Charles, xii. 200
Isola, Emma. *See* Moxon, Mrs Emma
Ispahan, x. 114
Israel, in Cowley's *Davideis*, vii. 67
Israel, people of, iv. 311; viii. 78; xii. 299
Israel, royal house of, in *Absalom*, vi. 296
Istakar, in Beckford's *Vathek*, xi. 289, 290
Isumbras, Sir, i. 289, 292, 315, 465, 471
Isyphena, in Amory's *Memoirs of Several Ladies*, xi. 287
It cannot rain but it pours, ix. 132
It was a' for our Rightfu' King, ix. 376
It was a lover and his lass, ii. 393
Italian art, xii. 33
Italian characters, xiii. 447
Italian epic, xi. 39
Italian historians, ix. 227
Italian history, xiv. 99
Italian humanists, xiv. 100
Italian interest in Shakespeare, v. 289, 290
Italian language and literature, v. 61, 69 ff., 75, 76, 88, 114 ff., 314, 361; vi. 64, 96, 125, 302, 310, 317, 334, 335, 366, 387; vii. 2, 3, 7, 10, 34, 155, 265, 266, 268, 269, 271, 273, 308, 318, 439; viii. 58, 126, 127, 135, 239, 352; ix. 54, 214, 384, 385, 402 ff., 412, 413; x. 159, 254, 303; xi. 181, 347, 355, 359; xii. 3, 52, 83, 137, 202, 308; xiii. 110, 118, 231; xiv. 128, 135, 385, 391, 434, 457 ff.
Italian medley-poets, xii. 51, 52
Italian *novella*, xii. 53
Italian novels attacked, vi. 378
Italian opera, viii. 134; ix. 58, 88, 163; x. 70, 71, 83, 84; xiii. 256; xiv. 213
Italian oratory, xii. 268
Italian peasantry, xiii. 453
Italian poets and poetry, ix. 67; xi. 134; xii. 4, 33, 55, 71; xiii. 116, 118, 236
Italian renascence, xiii. 259; xiv. 108

Italian romances, v. 127, 254, 319, 350, 413
Italian sonnet writers, v. 173, 230
Italian sonnets, xiii. 46, 117, 252
Italian sources and influence, v. 124, 127, 157, 181, 191, 220, 225, 314; vi. 45, 46, 94, 102, 174, 218, 304, 305, 322, 323, 345, 364, 365, 377; viii. 14. *See, also, under* Boccaccio, Bandello, etc.
Italian theatre, xi. 266
Italian theology, xii. 254
Italian, the, in *A Woman will have her Will*, v. 329
Italianate Englishman, vi. 219
Italians, the, xiii. 306
'Italomania,' xiii. 159, 179
Italy, ii. 238, 310; v. 61, 63, 101, 110, 121, 123, 132, 140, 286, 288, 301, 304, 306, 313, 350, 359; vi. 154, 158, 159, 175, 199, 203, 271; vii. 21, 100, 116, 154, 180, 201, 261, 283, 318; viii. 206, 245, 296, 364, 365; ix. 6, 138, 142, 245, 256, 280, 300, 396; x. 19, 41 ff., 47, 104, 115, 128, 200, 221, 249, 274, 292, 304; xi. 302, 344; xii. 33 ff., 42 ff., 49, 50, 52, 54, 57, 62, 64, 67, 82, 92, 248, 338, 422; xiii. 44, 46, 59, 61, 69 ff., 73 ff., 83, 84 132, 133, 260, 324, 372, 393, 436, 441, 449, 461; xiv. 77, 102, 108, 118, 151, 184, 217, 292 ff., 322 ff.
Italy and Byron, xii. 392, 395 ff.
Italy, Hazlitt in, xii. 432
Italy and Landor, xii. 440, 441
Italy and Shelley, xii. 402
Item, in Holcroft's *Deserted Daughter*, xi. 277
Ithaca, ix. 76; xii. 338
Ithamore, in *The Jew of Malta*, v. 326
Ithocles, in *The Broken Heart*, vi. 191
Itinerarium...Regis Ricardi, xiv. 74
Itis, vi. 320
Ivan the Terrible, in Milton's *Moscovia*, vii. 128
Ive, Paul (*fl.* 1602), iv. 443
Ivernian society, *Journal*, xii. 351, 360
Ivry, duchesse d', in *The Newcomes*, xiii. 295
Iwain and Gawain, i. 468
Izarde, John, vi. 287
Izoulet-Loubatières, J., xiii. 466

J. B., *Heroick Education*, vii. 393, 517
J. C. R., The, xiv. 537
J. D. (1597), iv. 5, 435
J. D. (1656), viii. 47, 238, 447
J. H. (John Hoskins), 'Absence, hear thou my protestation,' iv. 209
J. K. S. *See* Stephen, James Kenneth
Jacinta, in *Alls Lost by Lust*, vi. 72
Jacinta, in *The Brothers*, vi. 203
Jack, in Arbuthnot's *History of John Bull*, ix. 135
Jack, in *Damon and Pithias*, v. 119
Jack, in Swift's *Tale of a Tub*, ix. 100
Jack, A. E., ii. 34, 435
Jack, Chaffing, Disraeli's, xiii. 351
Jack, Sir T. Gresham's nephew, in *If you know not me*, vi. 91
Jack and Jill, xi. 303, 385
'Jack in the Box,' iii. 80
Jack of Dover, iv. 532
'Jack of Lent,' iii. 80
Jack of Newbery, xi. 334
Jack Napes, The Dirge of, ii. 288, 424
Jack Presbyter, vii. 383
Jack Straw, v. 152, 397, 426
Jack the Giant Killer, xi. 374
Jacke Drums Entertainment, vi. 41
Jacke Jugeler, v. 107, 411
Jacke Upland, ii. 39, 40, 162, 432, 434
Jacke Upland, The Rejoinder of, ii. 40
Jackman (traveller), iv. 88
Jacks, Lawrence Pearsall, xiv. Add. 2
Jackson, Andrew, xi. 327
Jackson, B. D., xiv. 566
Jackson, chaplain, in Foote's drama, x. 88
Jackson, Henry (1586–1662), vii. 312, 486
Jackson, Henry, xiii. 537
Jackson, John (1686–1763), ix. 507
Jackson, John (*fl.* 1761–1792), x. 443; xi. 452
Jackson, John, pugilist, xiv. 223, 230, 231
Jackson, Mason, *The Pictorial Press*, xiv. 201, 532, 541
Jackson, Thomas (1579–1640), vii. 425
Jackson, Thomas (d. 1646), viii. 276, 277
Jackson, Thomas (1783–1873), *Life of Charles Wesley*, ix. 325
Jackson, William Hatchett, xiv. 300, 563
Jacob, xiii. 208
Jacob, Edward (1710?–1788), v. 240
Jacob, Giles (1686–1744), viii. 159; ix. 260; *The Poetical Register*, 1719–1720, xi. 425
Jacob, Hildebrand (1693–1739), ix. 188, 486
Jacob and Esau, v. 39, 111 ff., 411
Jacobean dramatists, x. 108
Jacobean essayists, ix. 28, 36
Jacobean poets, xii. 221; xiii. 237
Jacobi, Karl Gustav Jacob, xiv. 258, 264
Jacobinism, xi. 1, 7, 25 ff., 30, 32, 119, 138, 155, 156, 165, 380
Jacobins, x. 119; xi. 40, 98, 118, 139, 157
Jacobite literature, ix. 563 ff.
Jacobite rising, x. 251; xii. 1, 26; xiv. 95
Jacobite songs, ix. 371, 372, 375 ff.; xi. 233, 242, 243, 443; xiii. 190
Jacobites, viii. 92, 99, 122, 194; ix. 11, 13 ff., 110, 113, 117, 201, 211, 218, 219, 223, 226, 249, 325, 407, 413; x. 28, 58, 251, 281, 300, 335, 338, 352, 360
Jacobites' Journal, The, x. 29, 417
Jacobitism, xi. 233
Jacobs, Joseph, xi. 480, 491
Jacobs, J. and Wolf, L., *Bibliotheca Anglo-Judaica*, xi. 428
Jacobus a Voragine. *See* Voragine
Jacobus de Cessolis, *Liber de ludo scacchorum*, ii. 312
Jacomo, in *The Gratefull Servant*, vi. 204
Jacques de Vitry (d. 1240), ii. 80, 504

Jacquier, Nicholas (*fl. c.* 1458), VII. 368, 504
Jacuppus, in *Machiavellus*, VI. 315
Jaffa, II. 79
Jaffier, in Otway's *Venice Preserv'd*, VIII. 183, 184
Jaffray, Alexander (1614–1673), IX. 551
Jaggard, Isaac, IV. 395
Jaggard, William (1567?–1623), III. 266; IV. 394, 395, 548; V. 221, 223, 224. 234
Jaggers, Mr, in *Great Expectations*, XIII. 334
Jago, Richard (1715–1781), X. 110, 271 ff., 275, 448
Adam, X. 112
Edge-Hill, X. 112, 113
Goldfinches, The, X. 112
To William Shenstone, esq., X. 112
Jahangir, court of, XIV. 333
Jahaziel, IV. 43
Jamaica, VIII. 158; X. 36, 467; XI. 37, 222; XIV. 241, 242
James I of England and VI of Scotland, II. 93; III. 34, 136, 137, 150, 160, 164, 198, 271, 378, 498, 503; IV. 53, 57, 59, 63, 64, 95, 132, 134, 135, 137, 149 ff., 154, 155, 161, 163, 165, 184, 187 ff., 203, 237, 239, 253, 254, 256, 259, 266, 276, 279, 293, 302, 304 ff., 310 ff., 334, 351, 374, 392, 403, 405, 406, 427, 428, 531; V. 56, 219, 253, 262, 333, 340, 341, 348, 349, 352, 354, 358 ff., 365, 375, 376, 478, 480 ff.; VI. 4, 5, 7, 38, 47, 86, 101, 107, 108, 147, 149, 172, 217, 220, 234, 243, 245, 250, 254, 255, 258, 262, 271, 272, 278, 283, 290, 298, 314, 316 ff., 321 ff., 327, 333, 336, 337, 342 ff., 358, 360 ff., 401, 403; VII. 4, 21, 49, 54, 158, 166, 188, 190, 191, 196, 199, 203, 205, 206, 208, 209, 219, 223, 309, 310, 312, 314, 327, 331, 337, 340, 343, 366, 390, 394, 433, 435, 436, 438, 439, 441, 450, 451, 454, 455, 458, 506, *also see* Add.; VIII. 127, 128, 130, 132, 143, 277, 316, 319, 323, 356, 363, 470; IX. 202, 222, 235, 357, 359, 360, 558, *also see* Add.; X. 84, 283, 286, 290, 295, 499 ff.; XI. 217, 235; XII. 18, 21, 376; XIII. 256; XIV. 55, 83, 84, 93, 95, 333, 396
Ane Schort Treatise, II. 285
Basilicon Doron, IV. 384
Counterblast to Tobacco, A, IV. 349, 531; VI. 318
Demonology, IV. 535; VII. 372, 373
Essays of a Prentice in the Divine Art of Poetry, I. 291; III. 137, 271
King's Majesties Declaration to his Subjects concerning Lawful Sports to be used, The, IV. 339
Poetical Exercises, III. 137
True Lawe of Free Monarchies, The, IV. 301, 304, 511
Secret History of, XII. 16
James II, king of England, II. 77; IV. 426, 458; VII. 96, 183, 365; VIII. 10, 30, 31, 39, 46, 49, 82, 90, 92 ff., 99, 100, 113, 189, 202, 216, 221, 228, 249, 254, 256, 266, 267, 302, 304, 305, 452; IX. 4, 7, 148, 175, 199, 200, 202, 203, 207, 233, 235, 236, 253; X. 287, 295, 351, 373, 503; XI. 313, 396; XIV. 55, 64, 65, 98
Memoirs, IX. 213, 214, 493
James I (1394–1437), king of Scotland, II. 129, 171, 239 ff., 283, 284, 368; III. 138, 154, 197; *The Kingis Quair*, II. 91, 94, 154, 171, 219, 240, 241, 243, 244, 250, 253, 267, 270, 281, 471 ff.
James II (1430–1460), king of Scotland, II. 113, 285; III. 148
James III (1451–1488), king of Scotland, II. 284
James IV (1473–1513), king of Scotland, II. 94, 251, 253, 260, 369; III. 61, 70, 135, 152, 197; X. 193
James IV and Flodden Field, The Lamentation of, III. 197
James V (1512–1542), king of Scotland, II. 270; III. 116, 123, 130, 132, 138, 149, 156, 159, 160; IV. 322; V. 59
James VI, king of Scotland. *See* James I, king of England
James (1688–1766), prince of Wales (the Old Pretender), IX. 150, 201, 211, 213, 218, 219, 222, 223, 231; X. 353
James, in *Witty and Witless*, V. 92, 93
James, C. C., XIV. 581
James, George Payne Rainsford (1799–1860), I. 287; XII. 250, 449; XIII. 307; *Richelieu*, XII. 249
James, Henry (1843–1916), XIII. 499, 553, 558, 567, 574, *also see* Add. 3; XIV. 526, 548, *also see* Add. 2
James, John (d. 1680), VIII. 257
James, John, XIV. 595
James, John, seaman, IV. 76
James, Montague Rhodes, IX. 424; XII. 516
James, Richard (1592–1638), VII. 316, 489
James, Robert (1705–1776), X. 467
James, R. A. Scott, XIV. 532
James, St, I. 118, 231; II. 12; IV. 237
James, St, shrine of, at Compostella, II. 313
James, Stephen (d. 1725), X. 386
James, Thomas (1573?–1629), IV. 431, 550; *Catalogus...T. Bodleius*, III. 552
James, Thomas (1593?–1635?), *The Strange and Dangerous Voyage of Captain Thomas James in his Intended Discovery of the North West Passage*, IV. 105 ff., 458
James, Thomas (1748–1804), IX. 408; XIV. 386
James, William (1635?–1663), VII. 486
James, William (d. 1827), XIV. 490
James the Sext, The History and Life of, III. 149
James's powder, X. 215

Jameson, Mrs Anna Brownell, born Murphy (1794–1860), xi. 487; xiv. 503, 521, 569, 583
Characteristics of Women, xiv. 157
Diary of an Ennuyée, The, xiv. 323
Loves of the Poets, The, xiv. 157
Winter Studies and Summer Rambles, xiv. 323, 358
Jameson, Robert, xiv. 323
Jameson, William (*fl.* 1689–1720), ix. 546
Jámi, *Salámán and Absál*, xiii. 145
Jamie, Don, in *The Spanish Curate*, vi. 139
Jamieson, John (1759–1838), xiv. 611; *Barbour's Bruce*, xii. 517
Jamieson, Robert (1780?–1844), xii. 358, 517; *Popular Ballads and Songs*, xii. 357
Jamnes, legend of, i. 135
Jane, in *A Chast Mayd*, vi. 75
Jane, dame, v. 33
Jane (Seymour) (1509?–1537), queen of Henry VIII, iii. 175
Jane, servant of S. Pepys, viii. 254
Janet, in George Eliot's *Janet's Repentance*, xiii. 387, 388
Janeway, James (1636?–1674), xi. 480; *Token for Children*, xi. 371
Janeway, Richard, viii. 98
Janin, Jules, v. 302
Janina, in Albania, xii. 43
Januarius, saint, xiv. 247
Janus, xii. 139; xiii. 460
Janus, temple of, i. 95
Janusa, in Chamberlayne's *Pharonnida*, vii. 75
Japan, iv. 75, 92, 99, 100; x. 42; xiv. 138, 165, 166
Japan wares, ix. 271
Japanese language, xiv. 421, 459
Japp, Alexander Hay, xii. 444, 445; xiii. 471
Jaques, in *Alls Lost by Lust*, vi. 70
Jaques, in *As You Like It*, iii. 349; v. 192, 193
Jardine, David (*fl.* 1750), x 386
Jardine, Sir William (1800–1874), x. Add.
Jarley, Mrs, in *The Old Curiosity Shop*, xiii. 319
Jarrow, i. 5, 72, 78, 79, 83, 85, 89; iv. 418
Jarvie, Baillie Nicol, in Scott's *Rob Roy*, xii. 25
Jasher, the lost book of, xii. 331
Jason, William Morris's, xiii. 123, 134
Jason, in *Confessio Amantis*, ii. 151
Jason, or Joshua, in *Parlement of the Thre Ages*, i. 333
Jason, The History of, ii. 313, 319
Jatāka, xii. 489
Javanese language, xiv. 459
Jawleyford, Mr, Surtees's, xiv. 234
Jay, Harriet, xiii. 500, 517
Jeaffreson, John Cordy (1831–1891), xiii. 567; xiv. 503
Jeake, Samuel (1623–1690), ix. 536; *Charters of the Cinque Ports*, xi. 322
'Jeames,' Thackeray's, xiii. 279, 284
Jean à la Barbe. *See* Jehan de Bourgoigne
Jean de Hauteville (*fl.* 1184), i. 193, 454
Jean de Meun, i. 99; ii. 169; iii. 90; vii. 367
Jean d'Outremeuse, *Myreur des Histors*, ii. 81, 82
Jean de Vignay, ii. 312
Jean de Waurin, ii. 508
Jeanroy, Alfred, ii. 392
Jeany where has thou been, ix. 360
Jebb, John (1736–1786), xiv. 385, 593
Jebb, John (1775–1833), bishop of Limerick, xii. 256, 457
Jebb, Sir Richard Claverhouse (1841–1905), xii. 324, 485, 486, 492; xiii. 477; xiv. 493
Attic Orators, The, xii. 332
Bentley, xii. 332
Introduction to Homer, xii. 332
Pindaric Odes, xii. 332
Jebb, Samuel (1694?–1772), i. 207
Jed valley, x. 93
Jedburgh, x. 93; xi. 444
Jefferies, Richard (1848–1887), xi. 480, xiv. 521
Field and Hedgerow, xiv. 166
Gamekeeper at Home, The, xiv. 166
Hodge and his Master, xiv. 166
Story of my Heart, The, xiv. 166
Wood Magic, xiv. 166
Jefferson, Samuel (1809–1846), xii. 511
Jeffery, John (1647–1720), viii. 457
Jeffes, Abel (*fl.* 1595), iv. 383; v. 158
Jeffrey, Alexander (1806–1874), xii. 511
Jeffrey, Francis, lord Jeffrey (1773–1850), ix. 127; x. 188, 413; xi. 149, 440; xii. 8 ff., 42, 92, 103, 142 ff., 152, 153, 156, 158, 161, 163, 378, 379, 384, 411, 426, 427; xiii. 8, 467; xiv. 112, 138; *Contributions to the Edinburgh Review*, xii. 146; 'Don Cevallos, and the French Usurpation in Spain,' xii. 149
Jeffrey, in *Edward IV*, vi. 91
Jeffrey or Jeffreys, Sarah, vii. 96
Jeffreys, George, 1st baron Jeffreys (1648–1689), vii. 365; viii. 410, 411; ix. 5, 6, 240; x. 274; xiii. 434
Jeffreys, John Gwyn (1809–1885), xiv. 296, 561, 562
Jehan de Bourgoigne (John ad barbam), in the Mandeville myth, ii. 80 ff.
Jehan de Bel, i. 478
Jehovah, xi. 194, 199
Jekyll, Sir Joseph (1663–1738), x. 385
Jena, xiv. 416
Jeninges, Edward (*fl.* 1593), iv. 309, 511
Jenkin Careaway, in *Jacke Jugeler*, v. 107
Jenkin, Henry Charles Fleeming (1833–1885), xiii. 248
Jenkins, Elijah. *See* Mottley, John
Jenkins, Herbert, xiv. 516
Jenkins, J., x. 386
Jenkins, Sir Leoline (1623–1685), ix. 213
Jenkins, Mrs Winifred, in Smollett's *Humphrey Clinker*, x. 43; xiii. 279
Jenkinson, Anthony (d. 1611), iv. 84, 88
Jenkinson, Ephraim, x. 202

Jenkinson, Robert Banks (1770–1828), 2nd earl of Liverpool, xi. 154; xii. 439; xiv. 407
'Jenks,' *pseud. See* Beckford, William
Jenkyns, Patheryke, or Patrick, vii. 88, 413
Jenner, Thomas, *Sea Coasts of England, The*, iv. 458
Jenner, Sir T., Speech to his Wife and Children, viii. 97
Jennings, David (1691–1762), x. 384
Jennings, John (d. 1723), x. 384
Jennings, Mrs, in Jane Austen's *Sense and Sensibility*, xii. 236
Jennings, Theodore (*fl.* 1647), vii. 515
Jenny, Jenny, ix. 363
Jenyns, Soame (1704–1787), x. 461, 523, 525; xi. 350; *Free Enquiry into the Nature and Origin of Evil*, x. 177
Jephson, Henry, xiv. 536
Jephson, Robert (1736–1803), xi. 457; *Count of Narbonne*, xi. 274
Jephthah, ii. 151
Jeppe, Carl, xiv. Add. 8
Jerdan, William (1782–1869), xi. 463; xii. 418; xiv. 177, 200, 534
Jeremiah, i. 74
Jeremy, in Congreve's *Love for Love*, viii. 151
Jermyn, Henry, 1st earl of St Albans (d. 1684), vii. 22, 63, 70, 219
Jerningham, Edward (1727–1812), vii. 84; x. 487
Jerome, in *Witty and Witless*, v. 93
Jerome, Don, in Sheridan's *Duenna*, xi. 257
Jerome, Jerome K., xiii. 543
Jerome, St, and writings of, i. 66, 70, 75, 103, 117, 120, 189, 355; ii. 293, 365; iii. 4; iv. 36, 37; vii. 304; xii. 496; *Vitae Sanctorum Patrum*, ii. 317, 323
Jerome, St, in *The Example of Virtue*, ii. 227
Jeronimo, in *The Spanish Tragedie*, v. 160 ff.
Jeronimo, The First Part of, v. 158 ff.; vi. 23; viii. 125
Jerrold, Wm Blanchard, xiv. 541
Jerrold, Douglas William (1803–1857), xiii. 268, 520; xiv. 193, 196, 236 ff., 544, 548
Blackey'd Susan; or, 'All in the Downs,' xiii. 265; xiv. 237
Catspaw, The, xiii. 269
Men of Character, xiv. 237
Mrs Caudle's Curtain Lectures, xiv. 237
Punch's Complete Letter-writer, xiv. 237
Punch's letters to his son, xiv. 237
Prisoner of War, The, xiii. 269
Time Works Wonders, xiii. 269
Jerrold, Walter, xiii. 530, 533, 570; xiv. 548
Jerrold, William Blanchard (1826–1884), xiii. 563; xiv. 193
Jersey, vii. 196, 214, 215, 217, 218, 316; xiii. 46
Jersey, earl of. *See* Villiers, Edward, 1st earl
Jerusalem, i. 134; ii. 79, 80, 85, 114, 299, 321; iii. 230; iv. 90, 323, 324; v. 49; vi. 84, 89; viii. 23; xii. 107, 249, 260, 321, 514; xiv. 251
Jerusalem, in *The Faerie Queene*, iii. 231
Jerusalem, Battle of, i. 356
Jervas, Charles (1675?–1739), ix. 169, 171, 444, 529; x. 40
Jervois, Miss, in Richardson's *Sir Charles Grandison*, x. 11, 18
Jespersen, Otto, xiv. 611
'Jessamy Bride,' the, x. 213
Jesse, Edward (1780–1867), x. Add.; xiv. 544
Jesse, John Heneage (1815–1874), xiv. 503
Jessica, in *The Merchant of Venice*, v. 183
Jessopp, Augustus (1824–1914), ix. 198, 238, 494; xiv. 490; *Arcady for better for worse*, xiv. 78
Jest-books, iii. 487 ff.; iv. 531; vii. 516
Jesu Christ, The Seven Sheddings of the blood of, ii. 325
Jesuit printing press, iv. 411
Jesuits, the, iii. 162; iv. 100, 127, 167, 202, 218, 220, 244, 255, 256, 296, 429; v. 89, 90, 344, 345, 365, 371; vi. 150, 157, 302, 324, 377; vii. 33, 36, 47, 88, 151, 236, 305, 309, 311, 320, 335, 336, 353, 392; viii. 85, 86, 88, 173, 175, 266, 300, 305, 449; ix. 197; x. 282, 283, 292, 300, 319, 322; xiii. 210, 366, 435; xiv. 101, 127, 253, 308, 316, 329, 382
Jesus, Orm's treatment of the name of, i. 225. See, also, *Childhood of*, and under Christ
Jesus (a Samaritan), in *Piers the Plowman*, ii. 27
Jesus, in Cowley's *Davideis*, vii. 66
Jesus, in Douglas's *Aeneid*, ii. 264
Jesus, in *Mirour de l'Omme*, ii. 141
Jesus, in transition songs, ii. 383
Jesus, in Wyclif's *Dialogus*, ii. 65
See, also, under Christ *and* Child Christ
Jesus Christ, ix. 28, 29, 312, 325, 327; x. 371, 378; xi. 185, 194, 196 ff., 326, 369; xii. 40, 65, 67, 256, 259, 273, 284, 287, 290, 295 ff.; xiii. 102; xiv. 444
Jesu's Psalter, v. 323
Jeux, v. 4, 27
Jevons, Harriet A., xiv. 475
Jevons, William Stanley (1835–1882), xiv. 475
Principles of Science, The, xiv. 23
Pure Logic, xiv. 23
Substitution of Similars, The, xiv. 23
Theory of Political Economy, The, xiv. 23
Jew, in *Machiavellus*, vi. 305
Jew, the, in Sheridan's *Duenna*, xi. 267
Jewel, John (1522–1571), bishop of Salisbury, iii. 406, 548; iv. 236, 433, 493; Challenge sermon, iv. 235

Jewell for Gentrie, A, 1614, IV. 541
Jewish antiquities, IX. 393
Jewish Christians, IX. 291
Jewish church, XII. 321, 478
Jewish doctor, in *The Duke of Millaine*, VI. 159
Jewish faith, XII. 14
Jewish history, IX. 227
Jewish religion, XI. 48
Jewish writers, I. 478
Jewitt, Llewellyn Frederick William (1816–1888), X. 473; XII. 511
Jewkes, Mrs, in Richardson's *Pamela*, X. 5
Jews, the, I. 63, 133, 176; II. 24, 343, 345, 350, 362, 365; V. 44, 49, 366; VI. 86, 154; VII. 102, 147, 198, 200, 281, 300, 319; VIII. 274; IX. 297; X. 362; XII. 318, 477, 478; XIII. 349, 353, 384, 400; XIV. 2, 67, 136, 309
Jews, the Council of the (*Coventry Mysteries*), V. 19
Jews, queen of the, in *Gyre Carling*, II. 276
Jewsbury, Geraldine Endsor (1812–1880), XIII. 563
Jhan, Sir, the priest, in *Johan Johan*, V. 98, 99
Jingle, Alfred, in Dickens's *Pickwick Papers*, X. 41; XIII. 310, 351
Jo, in *Bleak House*, XIII. 328, 329
Joab, IV. 231
Joab, in Cowley's *Davideis*, VII. 67
Joan, in *The Devil and his Dame*, V. 329
Joan, pope, II. 131; VII. 240
Joan Go-to-'t, in *The Birth of Merlin*, V. 249, 251
Joan of Naples, VII. 248
Joan of Navarre (1370?–1437), queen of Henry IV, II. 217
Joanna, in Holcroft's *Deserted Daughter*, XI. 277
Joanna, in Middleton's *Changeling*, XII. 222
Joannes de Garlandia. *See* Garlandia
Joannides, A., XIII. 515
Job, VII. 370; XII. 64
Job, in school plays, V. 103
Jobson, Richard (*fl.* 1620–1623), IV. 458
Jocelin of Brakelond (*fl.* 1200), I. 176, 450, 451, 458; XIII. 15
Jocelyn, Rose, Meredith's, XIII. 426
Jock o' the Side, II. 415
Jockey club, X. 191
Jockie, in *Edward IV*, VI. 91
Jocky Fou and Jenny Fain, IX. 360
Jocky met with Jenny fair, IX. 360
Jocky said to Jeany, IX. 360
Joculatores. See *Jongleurs*
Jodelle, Étienne, IV. 124; *Cléopatre Captive*, V. 63
Joel, II. 106
Joffred, abbot of Crowland, II. 343
Johan Baptistes, Enterlude of, V. 391
Johan the Evangelist, V. 60, 391
Johannes de Hese's *Itinerarius*, II. 330
Johannes de Sacro Bosco (d. 1252), or John of Holywood, I. 200, 456; II. 185
Johannes Secundus, IV. 264; XII. 223
Johannesburg, XIV. 380
Johannicius, *Isagoge*, II. 364, 365
John, in *Witty and Witless*, V. 92, 93
John, in *The Wowing of Jok and Jynny*, II. 275
John, Don, in *The Chances*, VI. 123, 135
John, Don, in *The two Maids of Moreclacke*, VI. 217
John, Dr, in Charlotte Brontë's *Villette*, XIII. 409
John, king of England, I. 175, 194, 198; II. 342; IV. 182, 183; V. 318; VII. 194
John, king (Shakespeare's), V. 153, 213, 318
John, king, in *Robert, Earle of Huntington*, V. 323, 324
John, king of England, The Troublesome Raigne of, V. 82, 135, 147, 153, 236 ff., 344, 397, 434
John, king of France, II. 307
John II, king of Portugal, IV. 69
John III, king of Portugal, III. 162
John XXII, pope, I. 212
John XXIII, pope, II. 348
John, Passion of, by Pseudo-Melito, I. 75
John, prince, in *Looke about you*, V. 321, 323
John, prior of Hexham (*fl.* 1180), I. 161, 450
John, St, the Baptist, I. 74, 126; VI. 295
John, St, the Baptist, tragedy on, III. 141
John, St, the Baptist, in *Baptistes*, III. 161
John, St, of Beverley, I. 82
John, St, evangelist, I. 74, 198, 354; II. 79, 383; V. 37, 48
John, Sir, the priest, in *Misogonus*, V. 110
John, Sir, the priest, in *The Merry Devill*, V. 252
John Bull, XIV. 200
John Chrysostom, St. *See* Chrysostom
John come kisse me, IX. 362
John de Cella, I. 178
John de Janua, *Catholicon*, II. 363
John de Oxenedes, or Oxnead (d. 1293?), I. 450
John de Tayster or Taxster (d. 1265), I. 182, 450
John George, elector of Saxony, VII. 453
John Lemouicensis, *Pharaoh's Dream*, II. 363
John Ochiltree, IX. 360
John Uponlandis Complaint, II. 280
John of Basingstoke (d. 1252), I. 204, 207
John of Bridlington, II. 443
John of Bury (*fl.* 1460), II. 497
John of Corbie, abbot of Aethelney, I. 89, 92
John of Cornwall, II. 70, 504
John of Doesborch. *See* Doesborch
John of Doncaster, I. 357
John of Dunstable, IV. 462, 463

John of Gaddesden (d. 1361), I. 453
John of Gaunt, duke of Lancaster (1340–1399), II. 55, 60, 73, 135, 157, 158; XI. 394
John of Gaunt, in *Richard II*, IV. 78
John of Glastonbury (*fl.* 1400), IX. 535
John of Guildford, I. 238
John of Hainault, Sir, II. 338
John of Hildesheim, *Historia Trium Regum*, II. 323, 503
John of Ireland, II. 94, 97; *Opera Theologica*, II. 284; On the Passioun, II. 284
John of Leyden, IV. 528
John of Lindebergh, I. 343
John of Salisbury (d. 1180), I. 173, 176, 183 ff., 202, 214, 216, 450, 454; IV. 269; VII. 376, 505
John of Trokelowe (*fl.* 1330), I. 181, 450; IX. 535
John of Usk (*fl. c.* 1360), abbot of Chertsey, II. 54
John of Worcester, I. 162
John the Common Weill, in *Ane Pleasant Satyre*, III. 128, 129
John the Common Weill, in *The Dreme*, III. 117
John the Reeve, I. 468; II. 126, 280
Johnie Cock, II. 416
Johnnie Cope, IX. 373
Johnny Armstrong, II. 413; IX. 166
Johns, Claude Hermann Walter (1857–1920), XII. Add. 4
Johnson, in Buckingham's *Rehearsal*, IX. 147
Johnson, Memoirs of the Life and Writings of, X. 177
Johnson, Abraham, VII. 340
Johnson, Charles (1679–1748), VI. 471; X. 89, 435; *Caelia*, X. 80, 414
Johnson, Charles (*fl.* 1724–1736), IX. 500
Johnson, Charles Plumptre, XIII. 531, 534
Johnson, Esther (1681–1728) (Swift's 'Stella'), IX. 93 ff., 97 ff., 120, 124, 126, 166; X. 168; XI. 332; XIV. 197
Johnson, E. Pauline (1862–1913), XIV. 582; *A Prodigal*, XIV. 357
Johnson, James (1787–1803), *Scots Musical Museum*, IX. 360, 361, 368, 373, 376, 377, 566; XI. 225, 226, 231 ff., 435, 444; XII. 14
Johnson, James (1850), XIV. 188
Johnson, John, father of Aphra Behn, VIII. 140
Johnson, John (1662–1725), X. 516; *The Unbloody Sacrifice*, X. 360
Johnson, John, LL.D. (d. 1833), XI. 403, 404, 427
Johnson, Joseph (1738–1809), XI. 189, 327
Johnson, Joseph (1905), XIII. 564
Johnson, J. P., XIV. Add. 8
Johnson, Laurence or Laurentius Baricona of Ketteringe (*fl.* 1603), *Cometographia*, V. 110
Johnson, Lionel Pigot (1867–1902), XIII. 503, *also see* Add. 2; *Postliminium*, XI. 30
Johnson, Michael, father of Samuel Johnson, XI. 340
Johnson, Nathaniel, brother of Samuel Johnson, X. 159
Johnson, Richard (1573–1659?), IV. 532, 536; *Anglorum Lachrymae*, IV. 351; *Looke on me, London*, IV. 530; *Seven Champions*, V. 34
Johnson, Reginald Brimley, XIII. 477
Johnson, Robert (1540–1625), IV. 442, 525; VII. 340; *Essaies or Rather Imperfect Offers*, IV. 345, 524; *The Traveller's Breviat*, IV. 89, 458
Johnson, Samuel (1649–1703), rector of Corringham, IX. 507; X. 355, 464, 517; *Julian the Apostate*, X. 351; *Reflections on the History of Passive Obedience*, X. 351
Johnson, Samuel (1691–1773), X. 439; *Hurlothrumbo*, X. 463
Johnson, Samuel (1709–1784), III. 157; IV. 247, 252; V. 209, 222, 235, 267, 270, 273 ff.; VI. 7; VII. 31, 72, 89, 115, 119, 135, 176, 235; VIII. 40, 42, 47, 48, 52, 146, 151, 152, 159, 196, 197, 210, 213, 217, 218, 220, 230, 237, 322, 323, 366, 386; IX. 133, 137, 140, 143, 144, 146, 164 ff., 171 ff., 178 ff., 185, 186, 188 ff., 243, 254, 313, 325, 330, 340, 357, 380, 538, *also see* Add.; X. 36, 39, 48, 63, 64, 66, 95, 96, 120, 124, 138, 140, 145 ff., 149, 157 ff. (main entry), 198, 201, 206 ff., 210, 212 ff., 231, 252, 255, 260, 262, 263, 266 ff., 274, 285, 289, 290, 312, 315, 355, 363, 392, 397 ff., 406, 407, 438, 452, 454, 459 ff., 482, 484, 523, *also see* Add.; XI. 2, 27, 31, 32, 38, 143, 145, 146, 246, 247, 251 ff., 260, 331, 333, 334, 345, 346, 350 ff., 355, 360 ff., 364, 365, 448 ff., 472, 473, 475, 476; XII. 218, 357, 363, 490; XIII. 13, 96, 224, 226, 232, 250, 465, 468; XIV. 61, 120, 122, 144, 160, 168, 169, 209, 216, 437 ff., 448, 452, 454, 461 ff., 503, 552, 554, 607
Account of the Harleian Library, X. 166
Charles of Sweden, X. 162
Choice of Life, The, X. 178
Compleat Vindication of the Licensers of the Stage, X. 165
Considerations on the Corn Laws, X. 181
Dictionary of the English Language, VII. 307; X. 167, 169, 173 ff., 177, 184, 187, 205, 350; XI. 324; XII. 504; XIV. 396, 439, 447, 463
Dictionary (abridgement), X. 177
'Dissertation on Pope's Epitaphs,' X. 183
'Easy Writing,' X. 178
'Engaging in Politicks with H—n,' X. 181
Essay on Epitaphs, X. 164
Essay on...Small Tracts, X. 166
Falkland's Islands, X. 181
False Alarm, The, X. 181, 182
Friendship, An Ode, X. 168

Johnson, Samuel
Γνῶθι σεαυτὸν *post Lexicon Anglicanum auctum et emendatum*, x. 177
'Grammar of the English Tongue,' x. 176
'Hard Words,' x. 178
'History of the English Language,' x. 176
Idler, The, x. 171, 178, 179, 184
Irene, x. 86, 161, 162, 170, 181
Journey to the Western Islands of Scotland, x. 181, 194
Life of Collins, x. 125
Life of Cowley, VII. 69; VIII. 379
Life of Denham, VII. 61; x. 167
Life of Dryden, VIII. 38
Life of Gray, x. 188
Life of Hammond, x. 475
Life of Milton, VI. 302; x. 161; XI. 84
Life of Pope, x. 168, 186
Life of Prior, x. 162
Life of Savage, x. 162, 165, 166, 169, 170, 183
Life of Thomson, x. 96
Lives of the Poets, IX. 170, 438, 448, 453, 466, 477, 479, 480; x. 165, 172, 182 ff., 292; XI. 325; XII. 137; XIII. 487; XIV. 447
London, x. 136, 168, 172; XI. 323
Marmor Norfolciense, x. 165
Miscellaneous Observations on the Tragedy of Macbeth, x. 167
Patriot, The, x. 181
Plan of a Dictionary of the English Language, x. 167, 173, 174, 176
Prayers, x. 170
Prince of Abissinia. See Rasselas
Proposals (for an edition of Shakespeare), x. 167, 177, 460
Proposals (for printing the Harleian Catalogue), x. 166
Proposals (for printing the *Harleian Miscellany*), x. 166
Rambler, The, x. 11, 157, 160, 170 ff., 175, 178, 181, 187, 188, 192, 205; XI. 253, 356, 365
Rasselas, x. 49, 159, 172, 178, 179
Shakespeare, x. 172, 179, 180, 186; XI. 320, 352
'Sufficiency of the English Language,' x. 178
Taxation no Tyranny, x. 181, 182
To Miss Hickman, playing on the Spinnet, x. 168
Trans. of Pope's *Messiah*, x. 168
Urbane, nullis fesse laboribus, x. 163
Vanity of Human Wishes, The, IV. 329; IX. 191; x. 160, 167 ff., 178
Verses (on the opening of Garrick's theatre), x. 136
Vision of Theodore, the Hermit of Teneriffe, x. 170
Voyage to Abyssinia, x. 159, 176, 179, 187
Written at the request of a gentleman, x. 168

Johnson, Samuel
'Young Authour, The,' x. 167
See, also, the bibliography by Courtney, W. P., revised by Smith, D. Nichol
Johnson, Samuel (of New York), x. 463
Johnson, Samuel (of Shrewsbury), x. 463
Johnson, Thomas (d. 1644), IV. 375
Johnson, T. (*fl.* 1649), VII. 368
'Johnson, Will.' (viscount Bolingbroke), IX. 220
Johnson, William, *Valetudinarium*, VI. 474
Johnson, William (*fl.* 1574), actor, VI. 246
Johnson, William (*fl.* 1774), bookseller, XI. 325
Johnson, William (1784–1864), XI. 406
Johnson, William. *See* Cory, William Johnson
Johnson, William Savage, XIII. 471
Johnson's literary club, XI. 345
Johnston, Alexander Keith, XIV. 485
Johnston, Arthur (1587–1641), IX. 550, 554, 555
Johnston, Sir Harry Hamilton, XIV. 192
Johnston, James (1643?–1737), IX. 203
Johnston, Robert (1567–1639), IX. 550
Johnston's Edinburgh Magazine, XII. 430
Johnstone, Charles (1719?–1800?), XI. 461; *Chrysal*, x. 524
Johnstone, Christian Isobel (1781–1857), XIII. 563
Johnstone, Christie, Charles Reade's, XIII. 425
Johnstone, John (1768–1836), XII. 490; XIV. 602
Johnstone, Maggie, IX. 366
Johny's Escape from Bonny Dundee, IX. 363
Joici et Sales...ab Ottomaro Luscinio, III. 93
Joinville, John, Sieur de, IV. 30
Jolles, Sir John (*fl.* 1617), VII. 339
Jollie, Timothy (1659?–1714), x. 386
Jolly, colonel, in *Cutter of Coleman Street*, VIII. 122
Jolly, William, XIV. 609
Jolly Beggar, The, II. 414; IX. 364; XI. 218
Jolly Beggars, tune of, VIII. 96
Jolly's academy, IX. 393
Jolter, in *Peregrine Pickle*, IX. 410
Joly, Charles Jasper (1864–1906), XIV. 263, 556
Jonah, XIV. 282
Jonah, in *Pearl* and *Patience*, I. 323, 325
Jonathan, in Cowley's *Davideis*, VII. 66
Jones, D., VIII. 380
Jones, Ebenezer (1820–1860), XIII. 503
Face, The, XIII. 157
Hand, The, XIII. 157
Rain, XIII. 157
Studies of Sensation and Event, XIII. 156
Jones, Ernest Charles (1819–1869), XIII. 157, 504; *Poet's Parallel, The*, XIII. 156; *Song of the Lower Classes, The*, XIII. 156; *Songs of Democracy*, XIII. 156
Jones, Evan Rowland, XIV. 533

Jones, Henry (1721–1770), *The Earl of Essex*, x. 86, 435
Jones, Henry, Sir, xiii. 477, 484
Jones, Henry Arthur, xiii. 515
Jones, H. Bence, xiv. 557
Jones, Henry Festing, xiii. 450, 570 ff., *also see* Add. 1
Jones, Inigo (1573–1652), v. 125, 372, 481; vi. 6, 26, 30, 271, 326, 333, 335, 342, 348, 350, 353, 354, 361; ix. 354, 536; *Britannia Triumphans*, vii. 433
Jones, Jeremiah (1693–1724), x. 521
Jones, John, of Neyath, Brecon, vii. 515
Jones, John, servant (*fl.* 1827), xi. 423
Jones, col. John (d. 1660), viii. 470
Jones, Oliver (*fl.* 1740), x. 196
Jones, Richard (*fl.* 1564–1602), iv. 390; v. 144
Jones, Richard (1790–1855), xiv. 475
Jones, Robert (*fl.* 1616), iv. 113, 464; *Second Book of Songs and Airs*, iv. 109
Jones, Rufus Matthew, *Studies in Mystical Religion*, ix. 306, 307
Jones, Samuel (1680?–1719), ix. 393, 394; x. 386, 387
Jones, Stephen (1763–1827), *Biographia dramatica*, xi. 453, 457
Jones, Sir Thomas (d. 1692), viii. 90
Jones, Tom, in Fielding's novel, x. 30 ff., 89
Jones, William (1559), iv. 383
Jones, William (1593), v. 145
Jones, William (1690), x. 378
Jones, William (1726–1800), ix. 512; xii. 453
Jones, Sir William (1631–1682), viii. 312; ix. 196
Jones, Sir William (1746–1794), xi. 427; xii. 343, 353, 502; xiv. 334, 577, 602; *Asiatic Researches*, xii. 327; *From the Persian*, xi. 180; *Ode in imitation of Alcaeus*, xi. 180
Jones, William Basil (1822–1897), xiv. 488
Jongleurs, v. 3, 26, 41
Jonson, Benjamin (1573?–1637), iii. 68, 81, 114, 228, 269, 271, 288, 308, 312, 444, 458, 482; iv. 46, 55, 59, 63, 115, 130, 138, 145, 153, 158, 185, 198, 199, 206, 207, 209, 214 ff., 248, 266, 349, 390, 392, 395, 406, 434, 437, 481, 501, 517, 520, 521, 524, 529, 533; v. 125, 142 ff., 148, 158, 161, 164, 166, 167, 171, 206, 222, 224, 254, 311, 312, 314, 315, 323, 328, 330, 334, 338, 343, 344, 347, 355, 361, 368, 370 ff.; vi. 1–30 (main entry), 32, 36, 38, 44, 47, 51, 53 ff., 58, 69, 85, 95, 96, 107, 111, 116, 118, 120, 121, 129, 133, 134, 138, 144, 151, 177, 188, 196, 198, 202, 206, 210, 211, 213, 214, 219 ff., 232 ff., 237, 239, 249, 250, 267, 271, 274, 291, 313, 329 ff., 339–355 (masques), 372, 376, 413 ff., 422, 423, 427, 458, 487, 488, 489, 491, *also see* Add.; vii. 2 ff., 7, 9, 14, 16 ff., 23, 25, 26, 33, 38, 49, 77, 81, 82, 85, 176, 184, 250, 259, 261 ff., 272 ff., 283, 335, 387, 413, 466, 467, 477, 502, *also see* Add.; viii.
Jonson, Benjamin
13, 16 ff., 25, 32, 116, 122 ff., 127, 132, 133, 137, 138, 141, 142, 145, 147, 150, 155, 157, 173, 174, 214, 227, 229, 233, 368, 443, 447; ix. 351; x. 50, 219, 220, 505; xi. 170, 248, 266; xii. 105, 125, 177, 224; xiii. 32, 108, 233, 495; xiv 444, 527
Alchemist, The, v. 365, 369; vi. 5, 22 ff., 26, 28, 222; viii. 357, 366
Apologetical Dialogue, vi. 4
Ars Poetica (trans. of), with commentary from Aristotle, vi. 6
Bartholomew Fayre, v. 158, 365, 376; vi. 2, 4, 5, 19, 22 ff., 26, 28, 220, 224, 261, 337; viii. 121
Case is Altered, The, v. 321; vi. 4, 5, 13, 17, 290
Catiline, vi. 5, 19, 20, 112, 221, 235; viii. 85; xiv. 448
Celebration of Charis, A, vi. 10
Celia, To ('Drink to me only with thine eyes'), vi. 10
Challenge at Tilt, A, vi. 357
'Come, leave the loathed Stage,' vi. 25
'Come, my Celia, let us prove,' vii. 17
Conversations with William Drummond, iii. 269; v. 343; vi. 7; viii. 238, 322
Cooke Laurell, iii. 482
Court Worm, vi. 9
Cynthia's Revels, iv. 337; v. 158, 359; vi. 4, 18, 25, 41, 42, 170, 171, 220, 290, 336, 337; vii. 19; viii. 118
Discourse of Poesy, viii. 238, 239
Divell is an Asse, The, v. 252, 358; vi. 5, 24; viii. 123
Dreame, vi. 10
English Grammar, An, ii. 152; vi. 6 ff.; viii. 238
Epicoene, x. 429
Epigrams, vi. 5, 9
Epistle to a Friend, An, to perswade him to the Warres (*Master Colby*), vi. 10
Eupheme; or, the faire fame...of...Lady Venetia Digby, vi. 10
Every Man in His Humour, iv. 137; v. 219, 331, 350; vi. 2, 3, 13, 15, 16, 20, 26, 28, 39, 248; x. 432
Every Man out of His Humour, iv. 333, 358; v. 358; vi. 4, 16 ff., 40, 170, 225; viii. 16
Execration upon Vulcan, An, vi. 6, 10
Expostulation with Inigo Jones, v. 372
Fall of Mortimer, The, vi. 7, 19
Fit of Rhyme against Rhyme, vii. 3
For the Honour of Wales, vi. 361, 371
Forest, The, vi. 5, 9; vii. 18
Fortunate Isles, The, vi. 362
Golden Age Restored, The, vi. 358
Gipsies, The, iv. 361
Henry V, A history of, vi. 6
Hesperus's song in *Cynthia's Revels*, vi. 10
Hot Anger Soon Cold, vi. 12
Hue and Cry after Cupid, The, marriage masque for lord Haddington, vi. 346, 347

Jonson, Benjamin
'Humbler gleanings in divinity,' VI. 6
Hymenaei, VI. 344, 345, 347
Induction, The, IV. 333
Irish Masque, The, VI. 357, 361, 371
Jeronimo, Jonson's additions to, V. 311
Love freed from Ignorance and Folly, VI. 350, 351
Love Restored, VI. 351, 357, 358, 371
Lovers Made Men, VI. 359
Magnetic Lady, The: Or Humors Reconcil'd, IV. 333; VI. 6, 25
Magnificent Entertainment, The: Given to King James, VI. 55
Masque of Augures, The, VI. 345, 350; VII. 3
Masque of Beauty, The, VI. 344
Masque of Blacknesse, The, VI. 5, 341, 344, 347
Masque of Christmas, The, VI. 355, 357 ff.
Masque of Lethe, The, i.e. *Lovers made Men*, VI. 359
Masque of Owls, The, VI. 361
Masque of Queens, The, VI. 344, 345, 347, 348, 370
Masque of the Metamorphos'd Gypsies, A, VI. 361; VII. 10
May Lord, The, VI. 11, 369 ff.
Mercury Vindicated from the Alchemists, VI. 357; VII. 3
Miscellanies, XI. 181
Neptune's Triumph, VI. 361
New Inn, The, IV. 361; VI. 6, 15, 25, 132, 140, 370
Newes from the New World discovered in the Moone, VI. 361
Nymphs Passion, A, VI. 10
Oberon the Faery Prince, VI. 340, 350, 351; X. 429
Ode to Himself, VI. 2
Pan's Anniversarie, VI. 355, 361, 362
Penates, The, VI. 341
Penshurst, To, VI. 9; VII. 10, 20
Philological collections, VI. 6
Pindaric ode on the death of Sir H. Morison, VI. 10
Pleasure Reconciled to Virtue, VI. 359, 361, 363
Poetaster, V. 187, 239; VI. 4, 18, 39 ff., 53, 166, 171, 172, 220, 290
Proserpine, a poem on the rape of, VI. 6
Prosodia, VIII. 239, 240
'Queen and huntress' in *Cynthia's Revels*, VI. 10, 11
Richard Crookback, VI. 13, 18
Sad Shepherd, The, V. 34; VI. 7, 11, 366, 369 ff., 491
Satyr, The, VI. 339
Scotland, poetical narrative of his journey to, VI. 6
Sejanus, V. 371; VI. 4, 19, 20, 28, 43, 152, 235, 248
Shakespeare, poem to, VI. 10
Shift, Lieutenant, epigram on, VI. 9
Silent Woman, The (*Epicoene*), VI. 5, 22, 24, 28, 112, 153; VII. 275; VIII. 120, 357, 401
'Slow, slow, fresh fount, keep time with my salt tears,' VII. 19
Spanish Tragedie, The, additions to, VI. 13, 17, 18, 369, 370
Staple of News, The, III. 81; IV. 137; VI. 6, 25; VII. 345
Tale of a Tub, A, VI. 4, 6, 26, 290
Timber: or, Discoveries made upon men and matter, IV. 25, 336, 348, 524; VI. 2, 6 ff.; VII. 262, 272, 273, 307, 466
Time Vindicated, VI. 362
'To my Bookseller,' XI. 335
Twelfth Night Masque, VI. 357
Underwoods, VI. 6, 9, 10; VII. 18; XI. 181
Vision of Delight, The, VI. 359
Volpone, III. 269; VI. 5, 21, 22, 28, 112, 194, 221, 222, 348; VII. 261, 274
Voluptuous Beast, Sir, epigram on, VI. 9
Wroth, sonnet to Lady Mary, VI. 10
See, also, under Beaumont and Fletcher, Chapman, Dekker and Middleton
Jonson and Porter's *Hot Anger soon Cold*, V. 331
Jonson's son, VI. 224
Jonsonus Virbius, VI. 7, 235, 237; VII. 3, 261, 272, 401, 466
Jónsson, Arngrim, I. 31
Jonston, Arthur (1587–1641), *Delitiae Poetarum Scotorum*, IV. 261
Joppa, IV. 68
Jordan, in *Absalom and Achitophel*, VIII. 37
Jordan, Denham ('A Son of the Marshes'), XIV. 166, 521
Jordan, Dorothea or Dorothy, born Bland (1762–1816), XI. 452, 454
Jordan, Thomas (1612?–1685), VII. 413, 514; VIII. 422; *The Plotting Papists' Litany*, VIII. 97
Jordanes, I. 35
Jorrocks, Mr, Surtees's, X. 111; XIII. 311; XIV. 234, 239
Jortin, John (1698–1770), IX. 75; XII. 468
Joseph, I. 74; IX. 42
Joseph, in Emily Brontë's *Wuthering Heights*, XIII. 411
Joseph, in the mysteries, V. 42, 47
Joseph I, emperor, IX. 228
Joseph of Arimathaea, I. 133, 271, 272, 462, 468
Joseph of Arimathea, V. 15
Joseph of Exeter (*fl.* 1190), *Flos Regum Arthurus* (*Antiocheis*), I. 195, 454, 467, 468
Josephine, empress of the French, XIII. 366
Josephus, I. 224; II. 334; III. 173, 416; IV. 427, 437; VI. 206; IX. 273, 275, 295, 418; XI. 326
Joshua, II. 231
Joshua, in *The Silver Age*, VI. 93
Josian, in *Beves*, I. 305, 306
Josselin, in *Edward IV*, VI. 90

Josselin, or Joscelyn, John (1529–1603) secretary to Matthew Parker, III. 55
Josselyn, John (*fl.* 1675), IV. 458
Joubert, André, XIII. 532
Joubert, Joseph, IX. 175; XII. 527; XIII. 98, 99
Joule, James Prescott (1818–1889), XIV. 261, 556
Jourdan, Philip, XIV. Add. 8
Journal Britannique, X. 173
Journal Encyclopédique, Le, V. 292
Journal littéraire, Le, V. 287
Journal of Anatomy and Physiology, The, XIV. 289, 566
Journal of Association, The, XIII. 358
Journal of Horticulture, The, XIV. 289
Journalism, the beginnings of English, VII. 494 ff.. *also see* Add.
Journalism, English, VIII. 412
Jove, in *Gismond of Salerne*, V. 75
Joviall Crew, A, V. 376
'Jovian Ferreri Piedmontese,' III. 319
Jovis et Iunonis nuptiae, VI. 484
Jovius, Paulus, III. 478; VI. 137; VII. 406
Jowett, Benjamin (1817–1893), XII. 292 ff., 333, 334, 442, 466, 468, 479, 482, 486; XIV. 503, 607; *The Epistles of St Paul*, XII. 293
Joy for another's grief, in *Confessio Amantis*, II. 147
Joyce, in Greene's *Tu Quoque*, VI. 219
Joyce, in the *Mercuries*, VII. 356
Joyce, Patrick Weston (1827–1914), XII. 517; XIV. 569
Ancient Irish Music, XII. 361
Irish Music and Song, XII. 361
Irish Names of Places, XII. 361
Irish Peasant Songs, XII. 361
Old Celtic Romances, XII. 361; XIV. 306, 328
Social History of Ancient Ireland, XII. 361; XIV. 328
Joyce, Robert Dwyer (1836–1883), XIV. 569; *Blacksmith of Limerick, The*, XIV. 321; *Blanaid*, XIV. 321; *Deirdre*, XIV. 321
Joye, George (d. 1553), III. 39, 40, 43, 473
Joyner, William (1622–1706), VIII. 437
Juan, Browning's, XIII. 72
Juan, Don, in Byron's poem, XII. 46, 54, 55
Juan, G., XIV. 552
Juan Fernandez, XIV. 242, 243
Juba, in Addison's *Cato*, IX. 63, 64
Juby, Ed., V. 135
Judaea, IX. 274
Judaic law, VIII. 75
Judaism, XII. 521
Judas, XIII. 199
Judas, in *The Second Part of Absalom and Achitophel*, VIII. 41
Judas, in *The York Plays*, V. 46
Judas (ballad), II. 194, 408
Judas Iscariot, I. 340; VIII. 86; IX. 234; XIV. 306
Judd, John W., *The Coming of Evolution*, XIV. 298, 299, 301
Jude, St, I. 354
Judge, the, in *The Daunce and Song of Death*, III. 87
Judicio, in *The Returne from Parnassus*, IV. 139; VI. 311
Judicium Essoniorum, VIII. 465
Judith, IV. 170
Judith, I. 48, 49, 77, 110, 123, 137, 141 ff., 150, 230, 445
Judith, in Amory's *Memoirs of Several Ladies*, XI. 287
Judith, in Biblical plays, V. 101, 103
Judith, daughter of Charles the Bald, I. 88
Judy, XIV. 239
Jugge, Richard (*fl.* 1531–1577?), IV. 384, 400, 401
Juigné, Antoine É. L. Leclerc de, archbishop of Paris, XI. 189
Julia, in Morton's *Way to get Married*, XI. 281
Julia, in *The Dutchesse Of Malfy*, VI. 182
Julia, in *The Poetaster*, VI. 18
Julia, in *Two Gentlemen of Verona*, V. 180; VI. 157; VIII. 126
Julia (Herrick's), VII. 6, 9, 17
Julian, in Aldhelm's treatise on virginity, I. 74
Julian, in Landor's *Count Julian*, XII. 211
Julian, coffee-house haunter, VIII. 89
Julian, emperor, IX. 507; X. 27, 318; XII. 416, 497
Julian, Epistle to Mr, VIII. 394
Julian, J., XIII. 498
Julian house, the (*Aeneid*), III. 305
Julian of Toledo, I. 76
Juliana, lady, in Susan Ferrier's *Marriage*, XII. 245
Juliana, St, I. 53, 229, 459
Juliana of Norwich (1342–1442), *Revelations of Divine Love*, II. 300, 482
Julianus, in *Alls Lost by Lust*, VI. 77
Julie, XII. 60
Juliet, in *Romeo and Juliet*, V. 169, 193, 331; VI. 265, 335; XII. 54
Julio, Don, in Mrs Cowley's *Bold Stroke for a Husband*, XI. 275
Julius Agricola, IX. 552
Julius Caesar, XII. Add.
Julius Caesar (Shakespeare's), II. 337
Julius Caesar, translation of, IV. 4, 21, 435
Julius Valerius, I. 135
Julleville, L. Petit de, I. ix
Jullien, A., *L'Histoire du Costume au Théâtre*, XI. 258
'Jumping Jenny,' the, in Scott's *Redgauntlet*, XII. 21
Junge, H., XIII. 558
Jungfrau, the, XII. 47
Jung-Stilling. *See* Stilling
Junia, in Racine's *Britannicus*, X. 119
Junilius, I. 76
Juniper hall, X. 63, 261
Junius, X. 133, 182, 509; XI 34; XII. 54; XIV. 335, 496
Junius, *Letters* of, X. 305, 399 ff., 455, 525 ff.; XI. 55; XIII. 52, 347; XIV. 186

Junius, Franciscus (1589–1677), VII. 118, 480; IX. 355, 536; X. 223, 225; XII. 504; Caedmon, edition of, VII. 307; *De Pictura Veterum*, VII. 307; Moeso-Gothic text of Ulfilas, VII. 307
Juno, VII. 370
Juno, in *Hymenaei*, VI. 345, 346
Juno, in *Troiane*, V. 69
Juno (Herrick's), VII. 13
Jupiter, II. 276; III. 71, 433; VI. 313; XII. 64, 80
Jupiter, in Alfred's *Boethius*, I. 101
Jupiter, in *Amphitruo*, V. 107
Jupiter, in Shelley's *Prometheus Unbound*, XII. 65, 66
Jupiter, in *The Four Ages*, VI. 92, 93
Jupiter, in *The Play of the Wether*, V. 93, 94, 95
Jupiter's satellites, VIII. 350
Jupps, Mrs, in Butler's *The Way of all Flesh*, XIII. 454
Jusserand, J. J., I. ix, 2; II. 2, 3, 24, 28 ff., 32, 34; IV. 246; V. 4, 17, 285, 289, 293; VI. 2; XIV. 518
Justamond, John Obadiah, X. 494
Justice, in Fortescue's *De Natura Legis Naturae*, II. 296
Justice, in *Pathomachia*, VI. 324
Justice, in *The Example of Virtue*, II. 227, 228
Justice, in *The Faerie Queene*, II. 234; III. 233; VII. 209
Justice, in *The Passetyme of Pleasure*, II. 229, 234
Justin, IV. 437, 438; XIV. 579; *The abridgemente of the Histories of Trogus Pompeius*, IV. 21
Justina, St, I. 74
Justinian, VIII. 312; XII. 488, 492
Codex, II. 364; III. 113
Digestum, II. 364
Pandects, II. 350
Parvum Volumen, II. 364
Institutes, IV. 151
Justiniano, in *West-Ward Hoe*, VI. 171 ff.
Justitia, in the *Coventry Plays*, V. 21
Juvenal, I. 68, 76; III. 68, 429; IV. 17, 206, 207, 250, 321, 329, 331 ff., 349; VII. 335, 487, 503; VIII. 58, 61, 85, 87, 88, 165; IX. 63, 87, 257, 269, 473; X. 21; XI. 40, 81, 393; XII. 487, 493; *Third Satire*, X. 169, 460
Juvencus. *See* Cyprianus
Juxon, William (1582–1663), IV. 306, 425; VI. 319; VII. 159
Jyl of Breyntford's Testament, II. 324, 485; III. 84, 85, 88, 483, 484

Kabbalah, the, XII. 501
Kaermerðin, I. 266
Kaffirs, the, XIV. 376
Kai or Kay, Sir, a knight of Arthur, I. 250, 254, 255, 260, 312, 313
Kaisersberg. *See* Geiler von
Kaled, in Byron's *Lara*, XII. 46
Kalenborowe, The Parson of, II. 329, 486
Kalendar of Shepherds, II. 233, 324, 328, 329, 485
Kalendar of the new legend of England, II. 322
Kalendrier des Bergers, III. 221, 226; IV. 353
Kalidasa, *Sakuntala*, XIV. 334; *Vikramorvasi*, XII. 502
Kalilah, in Beckford's *Episodes*, XI. 292
Kalote, in *Piers the Plowman*, II. 34
Kaltoff, mechanician, VIII. 359
Kaluza, Max, XIII. 512; XIV. 611
Kames, lord. *See* Home, Henry
Kant, Immanuel, IV. 292; VIII. 333; X. 333, 348, 511, 512; XI. 121, 136 ff. XIV. 8, 9, 11, 12, 37, 40, 42, 43, 45, 404, 467, 469, 478, 483
Kantian philosophy, XI. 57
Kapur-di-Giri rock-inscription, XII. 352
Karlamagnus Saga, I. 283
Karlemeyne and the Duzeper, I. 226
Karolin, in *The Sad Shepherd*, VI. 370
Karroo, the, XIV. 372
Kashinath Trimback Telang, XIV. 341
Kastrill, in *The Alchemist*, VI. 22
Kate, in *Cocke Lorell's bote*, III. 84
Kate, Corinthian, in Egan's *Life in London*, XIV. 226
Katharine, in *A Woman is a Weathercocke*, VI. 222
Katharine, in *The Taming of the Shrew*, V. 181
Katharine, in *The Womans Prize*, VI. 135
Katharine, St, Life of, I. 229, 459, 460
Katharine, the, a ship, VIII. 202
Katharine Jaffray, II. 411
Katherine, in *Perkin Warbeck*, VI. 193
Katherine of Senis, The life of St, II. 327
Katrine, loch, XII. 11, 12
Kaufmann, Moritz, *Charles Kingsley*, XIII. 356, 358, 548
Kavanagh, Julia (1824–1877), XIII. 563; XIV. 569; *French Women of Letters*, XIV. 324; *Natalie*, XIV. 324; *Summer and Winter in the Two Sicilies, A*, XIV. 324
Kavanagh, Morgan Peter (d. 1874), XIV. 324
Kavanagh, Rose, XIV. 329
Kay, in *Golagros and Gawane*, II. 123
Kay, Joseph (1821–1878), XIV. 607
Kay-Shuttleworth, Sir James Phillip (1804–1877), XIV. 419, 420, 607
Kaye, Sir John William (1814–1876), XII. 450; XIV. 491, 495, 577, 579; *A History of the Sepoy War*, XIV. 337
Keach, Benjamin (1640–1704), X. 522; *Travels of True Godliness*, XI. 334; *War with the Devil*, XI. 334
Keach in the Creel, The, II. 414
Kean, Charles John (1811?–1868), XIII. 69, 255, 514
Kean, Edmund (1787–1833), V. 302; VIII. 186, 423; IX. 190; XI. Add.; XII. 171, 421; XIII. 255, 259
Kearney, John (d. 1600?), *ABC and Catechism*, IV. 384, 386, 397, 409, 412, 414

Kearsley, George (*fl.* 1785), x. 459
Keary, Annie (1825–1879), xi. 480; xiv. 569
Castle Daly, xiv. 324
Doubting Heart, A, xiv. 324
Heroes of Asgard, The, xiv. 324
York and Lancaster Rose, A, xiv. 324
Keate, George (1729–1797), xi. 427
Keate, John (1773–1852), xiv. 387
Keating, Geoffrey (1570?–1644?), xiv. 308, 569; *Geoffrey Keating to his Letter*, xiv. 309; *The History of Ireland*, xiv. 304, 309
Keatly, Joseph (*fl.* 1704), viii. 157
Keats, George (1797–1842), xii. 84, 90
Keats, Georgiana (born Wylie), wife of Keats, George, xii. 81
Keats, John (1795–1821), i. 275; iii. 246; vii. 73, 75, 77, 109; viii. 227; x. 122; xi. 102, 117, 129, 150, 171, 182, 192, 202, 410, 440; xii. 40, 57, 58, 79 ff. (main entry), 106, 107, 113, 117, 126, 139, 157, 160, 162, 205, 221, 222, 395, 399, 400, 403, 404, 405 ff. (main entry), 433, 438, 445, *also see* Add. 2; xiii. 25 ff., 44, 101, 122, 185, 197, 198, 208, 219, 229, 230, 236, 250, 420; xiv. 311, 350, 373, 453
Adonais, xiii. 53
Autumn, To, xii. 72, 81, 89, 91
Bards of Passion and of Mirth, xii. 89
Belle Dame sans Merci, La, xi. 183; xii. 87, 88, 94; xiii. 238
Bright star! xii. 92
Cap and Bells, The, xii. 88
Endymion, vi. 367; vii. 76; xii. 58, 81 ff., 88, 89; xiii. 237, 238, 240, 251
Eve of Saint Agnes, The, xi. 131; xii. 81, 86 ff.; xiii. 114, 237, 238
Eve of St Mark's, The, xii. 87; xiii. 237, 238, 252
Fall of Hyperion, The, xii. 85, 86
Fancy, xii. 89
Fanny, Ode to, xii. 92
Grecian Urn, Ode on a, xii. 58, 72, 90
Homer, To, xii. 92
Hymn to Pan, xii. 82
Hyperion, xii. 74, 84 ff., 92, 94, 305, 477; xiii. 237, 238
I stood tiptoe, xii. 80
Isabella, xii. 58, 83, 88; xiii. 238
June's sea, xii. 92
King Lear, On sitting down to read, once again, xii. 58, 83, 91
Lamia, iv. 252; viii. 237; xi. 132; xii. 88, 194; xiii. 135, 237, 238; xiv. 436
Maia, Ode to, xii. 89
Melancholy, Ode on, xii. 90
Mermaid Tavern, Lines on the, xii. 89
Nightingale, Ode to a, xii. 91, 92; xiv. 352
O Sorrow, xii. 82
Otho the Great, xii. 88
Oxford, On, xii. 202
Psyche, Ode to, xii. 89, 90
Robin Hood, xii. 89
Keats, John
Sleep, To, xii. 92
Sleep and Poetry, xii. 80, 81, 85
Spenser, Imitation of, xii. 79
Stephen, xii. 88
Teignmouth, xii. 202
The Day is gone, I cry you mercy, xii. 92
To..., xii. 92
To some ladies, xii. 80
When I have fears, xii. 91
Kebbel, Thomas Edward, xiii. 471, 509, 547; xiv. 508, 509
Keble, John (1792–1866), vii. 147; viii. 308; x. 369, 518; xii. 153, 253 ff., 264 ff. (main entry), 271, 274, 277, 380, 454 ff.; xiii. 147, 167 ff. (main entry), 504
Christian Year, The, xii. 257, 261, 264; xiii. 167, 169 ff.
Evening Hymn, xiii. 170
O for a sculptor's hand, xiii. 170
Praelections, xiii. 168
Red o'er the forest peers the setting sun, xiii. 170
See Lucifer like lightning fall, xiii. 170
What went ye out to see, xiii. 170
Keble, Thomas (1793–1875), xii. 454, 457
Keeling, William (d. 1620), iv. 99
Keene, Charles Samuel (1823–1891), xiv. 239, 548
Keene, Henry George (1825–1915), xiv. 338, 339, 577, 578
Keepsake, The, xiv. 149
Keightley, Thomas (1789–1872), xii. 306, 476; xiv. 569
Fairy Mythology, xi. 475; xii. 368
History of Greece, xii. 302
History of the War of Greek Independence, xii. 302
Mythology of Ancient Greece and Italy, xii. 302
Outlines of General History, xii. 302
Keill, John (1671–1721), viii. 474
Keith, George (1639?–1716), ix. 546
Keith, Sir George, of Cowburn, iv. 151
Keith, Robert (1681–1757), x. 467
Keith of Ewern, in Rossetti's *Sister Helen*, xiii. 115
Keith-Falconer, Ion Grant Neville (1856–1887), xii. 499
Kelke, Roger (1524–1576), vi. 297
Keller, W., v. 82
Kellett, Ernest Edward, xiv. 537
Kellner, Leon, xiv. 528, 611
Kelly, Charles Arthur, xiv. 339, 340, 578
Kelly, Cornelius (*fl.* 1740), x. 197
Kelly, Edward (1555–1595), v. 377; vii. 369; viii. 350
Kelly, Frances Maria (Fanny) (1790–1882), xii. 194
Kelly, Hugh (1739–1777), x. 90 ff., 436; xi. 451
Clementina, x. 91
False Delicacy, x. 91, 92, 212; xi. 263
Man of Reason, x. 92
School for Wives, x. 92; xi. 263

Kelly, Hugh
Word to the Wise, x. 91
Kelly, Michael (1764?–1826), xi. 454
Kelmscott manor-house, xiii. 120
Kelmscott press, the, xii. 405; xiii. 127, 491 ff.
Kelsall, Thomas Forbes, xii. 115, 414
Kelso, xi. 342, 444; xii. 5; xiv. 373
Kelso, A. P., xiii. 488
Kelvin, lord. *See* Thomson, Sir William
Kemble, Charles (1775–1854), v. 302; viii. 186, 196
Kemble, Frances Anne (Fanny) (1809–1893), xiii. 142, 177, 497, 504; xiv. 504
Kemble, John Mitchell (1807–1857), xiii. 142, 177; xiv. 52, 68, 491; *Codex Diplomaticus Aevi Saxonici*, xii. 344; xiv. 69; *Horae Ferales*, xii. 347; *Saxons in England, The*, i. 420; xii. 344; xiv. 69
Kemble, John Philip (1757–1823), viii. 184, 196, 437, 439, 440, 442; ix. 435; x. 458; xi. 260, 262, 283, 428, 454, 456, 457; xiii. 255; xiv. 319, 440; *Coriolanus*, xi. 274; *The Tempest*, xi. 274
Kembles, the, xii. 119, 171
Kemerton, near Evesham, ii. 67
Kemnay, Aberdeenshire, viii. 347
Kemp, in *The Returne from Pernassus*, vi. 44, 312
Kemp, Flora van, in Le Fanu's story, xiii. 416
Kemp, William (*fl.* 1600), v. 313, 316, 329; vi. 217, 247, 248, 273, 276, 467; *Kemp's nine days wonder*, iv. 361, 533
Kemp Owyne, ii. 414
Kemp's Jigge, iv. 362
Kempe, Alfred John, *Losely Manuscripts*, iv. 221
Kempe, ancresse of Lynn, The book of Margery, ii. 327
Kempis, Thomas à, i. 99; ii. 300; iii. 291; viii. 458; ix. 519; *Imitatione Christi, De*, ii. 482
Ken, Anne, wife of Isaac Walton, vii. 250
Ken, Thomas (1637–1711), bishop of Bath and Wells, vii. 241, 250; viii. 460; *Ichabod*, viii. 306; Sermon for the Funeral of the Right Hon. the Lady Margaret Mainard, viii. 307
Kendal, v. 56; xi. 408; xiv. 203
Kendal, duchess of. *See* Schulenburg, countess Ehrengard
Kendal academy, x. 385, 386
Kendall, Edward Augustus (1776?–1842), xi. 480
Kendall, Henry Clarence (1841–1882), xiv. 368, 369, 586
Leaves from an Australian Forest, xiv. 364
Poems and Songs, xiv. 364
Songs from the Mountains, xiv. 364
To a Mountain, xiv. 365
Kendall, Thomas (*fl.* 1601), vi. 290
Kendall, Timothy (*fl.* 1577), *Floweres of Epigrammes*, iv. 23, 434, 438, 519
Kendals, the, xiii. 515
Kenealy, Edward Vaughan Hyde (1819–1880), xiv. 197, 238
Kenelm, St, i. 336, 339
Kenilworth, iii. 207, 210; iv. 181; v. 30
Kennedy, Benjamin Hall (1804–1889), xii. 331, 332, 336, 419, 486; *Between Whiles*, xii. 329; *Latin Primer*, xii. 329; *Public School Latin Grammar*, xii. 329
Kennedy, Charles Rann (1808–1867), xii. 329, 419, 486; xiii. 175, 504
Kennedy, Edward Shirley, xiv. 553
Kennedy, Gilbert, 2nd earl of Cassillis (d. 1527), iii. 154
Kennedy, Gilbert, 3rd earl of Cassillis (1517?–1558), iii. 158, 159
Kennedy, H. A., xiv. 236
Kennedy, James (1406?–1465), bishop of St Andrews, ii. 368, 369, 370
Kennedy, John (1789–1833), xii. 419
Kennedy, Patrick (1801–1873), xiv. 569
Banks of the Boro', xiv. 315
Bardic Stories, xiv. 315
Evenings in the Duffrey, xiv. 315
Fireside Stories, xiv. 315
Legendary Fictions of the Irish Celt, xiv. 315
Kennedy, Quintin (1520–1564), iii. 119, 153, 154, 503; iv. 322, 412; *The Compendius Tractive*, iii. 154; *Ressoning*, iii. 154
Kennedy, Rann (1772–1851), xii. 419; xiii. 175
Kennedy, Walter (1460?–1508?), ii. 250, 261, 266, 268; xi. 203
Ane agis Manis invective against Mouth-thankless, ii. 266
Ane Ballat in praise of Our Lady, ii. 266
Pious Counsale, ii. 266
The Passioun of Christ, ii. 266
The Praise of Aige, ii. 266
Kennett, Basil (1674–1715), x. 319
Kennett, White (1660–1728), bishop of Peterborough, vii. 442; ix. 212, 234, 235, 493, 536, 539, 541; x. 356, 517; *Compleat History of England*, viii. 384; ix. 143; *Parochial Antiquities of Ambrosden, The*, x. 354; *Register and Chronicle*, ix. 234
Kenney, James (1780–1849), xiii. 520; xiv. 569
Kenrick, John (1788–1877), xii. 511; *Ancient Egypt*, xii. 348; *Phoenicia*, xii. 348; *Primeval History*, xii. 348
Kenrick, William (1725?–1779), v. 274; x. 455, 474, 479; xi. 451, 458, 472; *Duellist*, xi. 265
Kensington, vii. 360
Kent, ii. 134, 158, 311, 424; iii. 321, 344; iv. 190; v. 343; vi. 112; vii. 23, 24, 28, 53, 83, 176, 341, 361; viii. 309, 310; ix. 24, 534, 536, 539; x. 249; xi. 426; xii. 347, 510, 513; xiii. 447; xiv. 128, 221, 298
Kent, laws of, i. 98

Kent, Maid of, II. 330
Kent, William (1684–1748), IX. 162
Kent, William Charles Mark, XIII. 543
Kentish Chronicle, I. 111, 112. See, also, under *Chronicle*
Kentish petitioners, IX. 8
Kentish Sermons, Old, I. 221, 459
Kenulph, bishop of Winchester, I. 125
Kenwigses, the, in *Nicholas Nickleby*, XIII. 318
Kenyon, Sir Frederick G., XIII. 479, 480, 481, 484, 485, 502
Kenyon, John (1784–1856), XII. 419; XIII. 69, 72, 74
Keper, John (*fl.* 1580), III. 438; IV. 448
Kepler or Keppler, Johann, IV. 278, 290; VIII. 361
Keppel, Arnold Joost van, 1st earl of Albemarle (1669–1718), VIII. 202
Keppel, George Thomas, 6th earl of Albemarle (1799–1891), XIV. 500, 598
Ker, John, of Kersland (1673–1726), IX. 493; *Memoirs*, XI. 328
Ker, John, 3rd duke of Roxburgh (1740–1804), XII. 365
Ker, Robert, 1st earl of Roxburgh (1570?–1650), VI. 366
Ker, William Pater (1855–1923), I. 420, VIII. 49; XI. Add.; XIII. 239, 477, 484; XIV. 487
Kerouaile, Louise Renée de, duchess of Portsmouth (1649–1734), VIII. 93, 99, 268
Kerr, John, X. 385
Kerr, J. (1887), XIII. 472
Kerr, Robert (1755–1813), XI. 440, 470
Kerr, Robert (*fl.* 1811–1824), XIV. 552
Kersal moor, Manchester, XIII. 373
Kersey, John, *Dictionarium Anglo-Britannicum*, X. 236
Kester, in Mrs Gaskell's *Sylvia's Lovers*, XIII. 380
Kestevene, I. 344
Keswick, X. 133; XI. 156, 161; XII. 84
Kethe, William (d. 1608?), III. 46
Kett, Francis (d. 1589), V. 143
Kett, Rev. George, XIV. Add. 5
Kettering, V. 110
Kettlewell, John (1653–1695), VIII. 306, 307, 460, 461; IX. 574
Kettner, Gustav, VII. 176
Kew, IV. 374
Kew, earl of, in *The Newcomes*, XIII. 295
Kew, lady, in *The Newcomes*, XIII. 296
Kew gardens, XIV. 286, 287, 289
Key, Thomas Hewitt (1799–1875), XII. 486; *Latin Dictionary*, XII. 335; *Latin Grammar*, XII. 335
Keyber, Conny, X. 411
Keymor or Keymer, John (*fl.* 1610–1620), IV. 309, 511
Keynes, Geoffrey, XI. 431
Kharosthi alphabet, the, XII. 352
Khatmanda, XIV. 165
Kiartan, in Morris's *The Lovers of Gudrun*, XIII. 125
Kibworth academy, X. 384
Kickham, Charles Joseph (1826–1882), XIV. 321, 569; *Irish Peasant Girl, The*, XIV. 322; *Knocknagow*, XIV. 322
Kidd, Dudley, XIV. Add. 8
Kidd, Thomas (1770–1850), X. 508; XII. 327, 486, 491
Kidder, Richard (1633–1703), VIII. 460
Kidderminster, VII. 145, 146
Kidderminster school, VII. 342
Kidwelly, VIII. 372
Kiel, V. 286
Kiffin, William (1616–1701), XII. 523
Kiftsgate, Gloucestershire, X. 111
Kilbarchan, I. 290; IX. 364
Kilburne, Richard (1605–1678), IX. 536
Kilburne, William, VII. 496
Kilby or Kilbye, Richard (1561?–1620), VII. 317
Kilcolman castle, III. 229, 244
Kildare, earl of. *See* Fitzgerald, Gerald
Kildare. *See* Michael of
Kildare, Satire on the people of, II. 502
Kilima-njaro, XIV. 192
Kilkenny, VII. 436; VIII. 146; XII. 510; XIV. 316
Kilkenny, Roman Catholic council of 1650, VII. 190
Kilkenny archaeological society, XII. 351
Kilkenny school, IX. 91, 280
Kilkenny West, X. 196, 207
Killaloe, bishopric of, X. 257
Killearn, Stirlingshire, III. 157
Killiecrankie, IX. 373, 376
Killigrew, Anne (1660–1685), VIII. 395, 444; IX. 168
Killigrew, Henry (1613–1700), VI. 456; VIII. 419; *Conspiracy, The*, VIII. 120; *Pallantus and Eudora*, first published as *The Conspiracy*, VIII. 120, 139
Killigrew, Thomas, the elder (1612–1683), VI. 240, 456; VIII. 118, 119, 207, 419
Cecilia and Clorinda, VIII. 119
Claracilla, VIII. 119
Parson's Wedding, The, VIII. 120, 130
Princess, The, VIII. 119
Prisoners, The, VIII. 119
Thomaso the Wanderer, VIII. 141
Killigrew, Thomas, the younger (1657–1719), VIII. 120; *Chit-Chat*, XI. 322
Killigrew, Sir William (1606–1695), VIII. 419, 434
Ormasdes, or Love and Friendship, VIII. 120
Pandora, VIII. 120
Selindra, VIII. 120
Siege of Urbin, The, VIII. 120
Killing no Murder, VII. 358
Killychrankie, XI. 218
Kilmarnock, XI. 342, 435, 438 ff.
Kilmarnock, earl of. *See* Boyd, William
Kilmore, VII. 318, 442
Kilner, Dorothy, XI. 480; *Adventures of a Pincushion*, XI. 378; *Jemima Placid*, XI. 379; *Memoirs of a Peg-top*, XI. 378
Kilner, Mary Jane, XI. 480
Kilpin, Ralph, XIV. Add. 8

Kilroot, IX. 92
Kilwardby, Robert (d. 1279), I. 210, 454; II. 363
Kilyð, I. 254
Kimber, Isaac (1692–1755), VIII. 459
Kimcote, near Lutterworth, X. 112
Kinbelin, in Layamon, I. 237
Kincardineshire, IX. 129
Kinch, Horace, in Dickens's *Uncommercial Traveller*, XII. 119
Kind (God), in *Piers the Plowman*, II. 19
Kind-Wit (Natural Intelligence), in *Piers the Plowman*, II. 10, 21
'Kinde-Kit of Kingstone,' IV. 361
Kindred, in *Every-man*, V. 53
King, Charles William (1818–1888), XII. 335, 497
King, Daniel (d. 1664?), IX. 536
King, Edward (1612–1637), VII. 114, 131, 415; XII. 74
King, Henry (1592–1669), VII. 81 ff., 413, 425, *also see* Add.
Dirge, The, VII. 82
Exequy, The, VII. 82
Legacy, The, VII. 82
Poems, VII. 82
Sic Vita, VII. 82
Silence, VII. 82
'Tell me no more how fair she is,' VII. 82
King, John (1559?–1621), IV. 91, 92, 203, 383; VII. 250
King, John (1696–1728), IX. 527
King, J. E., XIV. 597
King, Leonard William (1869–1919), XII. Add. 4
King, Richard John (1818–1879), XII. 517; XIV. 613
King, Thomas, actor (1730–1805), XI. 257
King, Tom, prizefighter (1835–1888), XIV. 231
King, William (1650–1729), archbishop of Dublin, VIII. 347, 474; IX. 97, 127, 139, 166, 461, 507; *Origin of Evil*, X. 342
King, William (1663–1712), IX. 174, 478
Art of Cookery, IX. 139, 176
Dialogue showing the way to Modern Preferment, IX. 139
Dialogues of the Dead, IX. 139
Journey to London, IX. 139
Miscellanies in Prose and Verse, IX. 139
Molly of Mountown, IX. 139
Orpheus and Eurydice, IX. 176
Rufinus, IX. 139
Transactioner, The, IX. 139
Useful Miscellanies, IX. 140
Useful Transactions in Philosophy, IX. 139
King, William (1685–1763), IX. 174; *The Toast*, IX. 139
King, W., bishop of Rochester, XI. 388
King, Zoe, XII. 116
King and the Barber, The, II. 451, 500
King and the Cobbler, The, XI. 334
King and the Miller, The, II. 451, 500
King Arthur, or the British Worthy, VIII. 30
King Darius, V. 393
King Estmere, X. 233
King James and Brown, II. 414
Kingcote, Bernard, in Gissing's *Isabel Clarendon*, XIII. 457
Kinghorn, IX. 367
Kinglake, Alexander William (1809–1891), XI. 307; XII. 199, 491, 552; *Eothen*, XIII. 346; XIV. 94, 240, 251, 252; *Invasion of the Crimea*, XIV. 94
King's Book, The, III. 36
King's Cliffe, IX. 308, 309, 326
King's College Miscellany, The (Aberdeen), XIV. 209
King's companies, the, VI. 221, 247, 256 ff., 274, 275
'King's Friends,' the, IX. 230, 231
King's Head society academy, X. 384
King's pamphlets, the British Museum, VII. 455
Kingsborough, lady, XI. 43
Kingsford, William (1819–1898), XIV. 491, 583; *History of Canada*, XIV. 358, 359
Kingsland, W. G., XIII. 483, 484
Kingsley, Charles (1819–1875), XI. 387, 481; XII. 102, 267, 290, 291, 430, 431, 460, 468; XIII. 147, 158, 160, 340, 345, 353 ff. (main entry), 378, 384, 397, 547, 548; XIV. 86, 323, 408, 552, 607
Alexandria and her Schools, XIII. 362
Alton Locke, XIII. 189, 358 ff.
Ancien Régime, The, XIII. 369
Andromeda, XIII. 245, 368
At Last, XIII. 369
Cheap Clothes, and Nasty, XIII. 358, 359
Friends of Order, The, XIII. 359
Glaucus, XIII. 363
Hereward the Wake, XIII. 366
Hypatia, XIII. 362 ff., 394
Hypotheses Hypochondriacae, XIII. 356
Lectures delivered in America, XIII. 369
Letters and Memories, XIII. 354, 356, 358, 365, 366
Life and Works, XIII. 368
Limits of Exact Science as applied to History, XIII. 368
Nun's Pool, The, XIII. 358
Phaethon, XIII. 363
Plays and Puritans, XIII. 356, 369
Prose Idylls, XIII. 366, 369
Psyche, a Rhapsody, XIII. 356
Roman and the Teuton, The, XIII. 368
St Maura, XIII. 368
Saint's Tragedy, The, XIII. 356, 426
Sands of Dee, The, XIII. 368
Three Fishers, The, XIII. 368
Two Years Ago, XIII. 364 ff., 399
Village Sermons, XIII. 369
Water-Babies, The, XIII. 369
Westward Ho! XIII. 363, 364, 366; XIV. 84, 255
Who causes Pestilence? XIII. 365
Why should we fear the Romish Priests, XIII. 356
Yeast, XIII. 359 ff., 363, 420; XIV. 84
Kingsley, George Henry (1827–1892), XIV. 552, 554

Kingsley, Henry (1830–1876), XIII. 563; *Austin Elliot*, XIII. 433; *Geoffrey Hamlyn*, XIII. 432; XIV. 369; *Ravenshoe*, XIII. 433
Kingsley, Mary Henrietta (1862–1900), XIV. 240, 552; *Travels in West Africa*, XIV. 254
Kingsmill, Sir William (*fl.* 1661), IX. 168
Kingston, dukes of. *See* Pierrepont, Evelyn; Pierrepont, William
Kingston, Felix, IV. 400
Kingston-on-Thames, III. 379, 370, 383, 385, *also see* Add.; X. 300
Kingswood school, IX. 313
Kingussie, X. 230
Kinneder, lord. *See* Erskine, William
Kinnoul, 8th earl of. *See* Hay, Thomas
Kinross, IX. 552
Kinsale prison, XII. 165
'Kinsayder' (Marston), VI. 39, 43
Kintyre, Scotland, XII. 514
Kinwelmersh or Kindlemarsh, Francis (d. 1580?), III. 203; IV. 4, 113, 436; V. 70; *A Vertuous Gentlewoman in the praise of her love*, III. 189; *From Virgin's wombe*, III. 189; Ode to Concord, V. 71
Kiomi, Meredith's, XIII. 442, 446
Kipling, Rudyard, XIV. 208, 211, 372, 373, 380
Kippis, Andrew (1725–1795), X. 384; XI. 472; XIV. 593. See, also, *Biographia Britannica*
Kirby, Margaret (Margaret of Ainderby), II. 45, 47
Kirby, Thomas Frederick, XIV. 598
Kirby, William (1817–1906), XIV. 581; *Le Chien d'Or*, XIV. 360
Kirbye, George (d. 1634), IV. 113, 464
Kirchhoff, Gustav Robert, XIV. 267
Kirchmayer, Thomas (Naogeorgos), *Pammachius*, II. 28; V. 101, 392; VI. 296, 397, 474
Kirchner, E., XIV. 490
Kirk, John Foster, XII. 519
Kirk, Robert (1641?–1692), IX. 559
Kirk of Field, XIII. 133
Kirk Michael, X. 359
Kirkbride, XI. 470
Kirkby, T., artist, XII. 323
Kirkcaldy, X. 335, 336; XIII. 3
Kirkcaldy, Sir William, of Grange (d. 1573), III. 503; *Ane Ballat of the Captane of the Castell*, III. 150
Kirkcudbrightshire, XI. 234
Kirke, Edward (1553–1613), III. 220, 227, 240, 304, 526
Kirkham, Edward (*fl.* 1601), VI. 290, 292
Kirkham, monastery of, I. 342
Kirkham's children of the queen's revels, IV. 132
Kirkley, J. (1705–1754), VIII. 476
Kirkman, Francis (*fl.* 1674), V. 249, 251; VI. 69, 86, 185, 464; VIII. 116, 417; *The Wits*, VI. 266
Kirkman, James Thomas, *Memoirs of Charles Macklin*, XI. 258
Kirkpatrick, John, X. 385
Kirkpatrick, Mr, in Mrs Gaskell's *Wives and Daughters*, XIII. 381
Kirkstall. *See* Hugh of
Kirkstall abbey, X. 131
Kirkton, James (1620?–1699), IX. 551; XII. 518
Kirkwood, Sidney, in Gissing's *The Nether World*, XIII. 458
Kirsteen, Mrs Oliphant's, XIII. 431
Kit, in *The Old Curiosity Shop*, XIII. 319
Kitcat club, the, VIII. 160; IX. 151, 456; XI. 320
Kitchener, Francis Elliot, XIV. 602
Kitchin, George William (1827–1912), XII. 354, 517; *History of France*, XII. 348
Kitchin, John, *Jurisdictions*, 1605, VIII. 469
Kitely, in *Every Man in His Humour*, VI. 16
Kitte, in *Piers the Plowman*, II. 34
Kitto, John (1804–1854), XII. 472
Kitton, Frederick George (1856–1903), XIII. 531, 532, 533, 539, 540, 543, 573; XIV. 549
Kittredge, George Lyman, I. ix; II. 400, 405, 408; XIV. 611
Kiuprili, in Coleridge's *Zapolya*, XI. 414
Klaas Gezwint en Zijn Paert, XIV. 377
Kleist, H. von, V. 303
Klesmer, in *Daniel Deronda*, XIII. 401
Klinger, Friedrich Maximilian von, V. 303
Klopstock, Friedrich Gottlieb, X. 18, 232
Knack to Know a Knave, A, V. 313; VI. 217
Knapdale, Scotland, XII. 514
Knapp, Andrew, and Baldwin, William, *The Newgate Calendar*, XIV. 228, 229; *The New Newgate Calendar*, XIV. 228, 229
Knapp, William Ireland, XIV. 516
Knapton, James, XI. 323
Knapton, J. and P., IX. 76
Knaresborough, VII. 224; XII. 421; XIII. 275
Knatchbull, Sir Norton (1602–1685), VII. 341
Knatchbull-Hugessen, Edward Hugessen, 1st lord Brabourne (1829–1893), XI. 486
Knebworth, XIII. 417
Kneller, Sir Godfrey (1646–1723), VIII. 50; IX. 483; XI. 319
Knichthood, the Buke of the Order of, II. 284
Knight, Charles (1791–1873), V. 279; XII. 445; XIV. 93, 409, 491, 495, 534, 597, 612; *English Cyclopaedia*, XII. 345; *Penny Cyclopaedia*, XII. 307; *Shadows of the Old Booksellers*, XI. 337, 466
Knight, Ellis Cornelia (1757–1837), X. 461; XII. 450
Knight, Henrietta, lady Luxborough (d. 1756), X. 271 ff., 277, 278, 496
Knight, Joseph, XII. 428; XIII. 490, 491, 515; *David Garrick*, XI. 258, 453
Knight, Richard Payne (1750–1824), XII. 490; XIII. 241; *Progress of Civil Society*, XI. 41

Knight, Robert. *See* Catherlough, earl of
Knight, Robert, lord Luxborough, IX. 217
Knight, Samuel (1675–1746), IX. 529
Knight, the, in the *Canterbury Tales*, III. 192
Knight, The Baffled, II. 414
Knight, William, editor of Wordsworth, XI. 406 ff., 407, 408, 410, 411, 416, 423; XIII. 487; XIV. 472; *Memorials of Coleorton*, IX. 328
Knight, William A., XIII. 507
Knight and Shepherd's Daughter, II. 413
Knight of Arts and Industry, in Thomson's *Castle of Indolence*, X. 107
Knight of Curtesy, I. 300, 468
Knight of the Red Shield, I. 294
Knight of the Sea, The, IV. 533
Knightley, in Jane Austen's *Emma*, XII. 239
Knightley, Sir Richard (1533–1615), III. 380, 381, 383
Knighton, or Cnitthon, Henry (*fl.* 1363), II. 30, 38, 59, 497
Knighton, Sir William (1776–1836), XIV. 504
Knight's Quarterly Magazine, X. 320; XIV. 60
Knock, Duncan, in Scott's *Heart of Midlothian*, XII. 19
Knolles, Richard (1550?–1610), IX. 247; *Generall Historie of the Turkes*, IV. 58, 88, 89, 458; X. 161
Knott, Edward (1582–1656), VII. 151
Knowell, in *Every Man in His Humour*, VI. 16
Knowle, X. 150
Knowledge, in *Every-man*, V. 54
Knowles, Sir Charles (d. 1777), X. 40
Knowles, Herbert (1798–1817), XII. 419
Knowles, James Sheridan (1784–1862), XIII. 267, 268, 520; XIV. 309, 310, *also see* Add. 3
  Beggar's Daughter of Bethnal Green, The, XIII. 269
  Caius Gracchus, XIII. 261
  Hunchback, The, XIII. 269
  Virginius, XIII. 261
  Wife, The, XIII. 261
  William Tell, XIII. 261
Knowles, Sir James Thomas (1831–1908), XIV. 534
Knowles, John (*fl.* 1646–1668), X. 377
Knowles, Mrs Mary (1733–1807), X. 472
Knox, Alexander (1757–1831), XI. 422; XII. 256, 457
Knox, Isa, born Craig, XIII. 178, 501; *The Woodruff*, XIII. 179
Knox, John (1505–1572), III. 45, 116, 122, 132, 138 ff. (main entry), 154, 155, 157, 385, 503; IV. 232; VII. 209; IX. 359; XII. 517; XIII. 13, 133, 268, 467, 469; XIV. 491, 493
  Answer to a great Nomber of blasphemous cavillations, An, III. 145
  Declaration of the True Nature and Object of Prayer, A, III. 143
Knox, John
  Epistle on Justification, The, III. 143
  Epistle to the Congregation of the Castle of St Andrews, An, III. 143
  Exposition upon the Sixth Psalm of David, The, III. 143
  Faithful Admonition to the Professors of God's Truth in England, A, III. 144
  First Blast of the Trumpet against the Monstruous Regiment of Women, The, III. 144, 385; IV. 303, 512
  First Book of Discipline, The, III. 146
  Harborowe for Faithfull and Trewe Subjects agaynst the late blowne Blaste concerning the Government of Women, III. 145
  History of the Reformation in Scotland, The, II. 285; III. 132, 141, 146, 148, 149
  Narrative of the Proceedings and Troubles of the English Congregation at Frankfurt, III. 144
  Ressoning, III. 154
  Summary according to the Holy Scriptures of the Sacrament of the Lord's Supper, A, III. 143
  Two comfortable Epistles to his afflicted Brethren in England, III. 144
  Vindication of the Doctrine that the Sacrifice of the Mass is Idolatry, A, III. 143
Knox, Robert (1640?–1720), IX. 493
Knox, Vicesimus (1752–1821), VIII. 230; XI. 472; XIV. 385, 593, 600, 607; *Essays, Moral and Literary*, XIV. 383; *Letter to Lord North, A*, XIV. 334; *Liberal Education*, XIV. 384, 388, 399
Knutsford, XIII. 372
Knyveth, Sir Henry, IV. 512
Koeppel, Emil, V. 85, 238, 366; VI. 140, XIII. 480
Kögel, R., I. 21
Kok, Abraham, V. 307
Kolax, in *The Muses Looking-Glasse*, VI. 233
Kolbe, F. C., XIV. Add. 5
Kölbing, E., I. ix
Königsberg, V. 283
Koran, the, I. 153; IV. 42; VIII. 291; XII. 499
Korea, IX. 248
Körting, G. E., I. 420; IV. 257
Kosciusko, in Campbell's *Pleasures of Hope*, XII. 100
Koszue, A., XI. Add.
Koszul, A. H., XII. 401, 403
Kottabos, XIV. 211
Kottabos, Echoes from, XIV. 211
Kotzebue, August F. F. von, XI. 42, 281, 414, 455; XII. 526; XIII. 260
Kraszewski, J. I., V. 308
Krebs, H., I. 105
Kretschmar, A. von, XIII. 464
Kreyssig, Friedrich, V. 305
Kritchev, Russia, XI. 58
Kruger, S. J. P., XIV. Add. 8, 10
Ktesias, the Knidian, XIV. 579
Küchler, F., XIII. 465

Kudrun, Austrian poem, I. 37
Kuffler, Dr, VIII. 355
Kulhwch and Olwen, I. 247, 250 ff
Künzelsau, V. 48
Küster, Ludolf, IX. 335
Kyd, Benjamin, VI. 312
Kyd, Francis, V. 156
Kyd, John, V. 158
Kyd, Thomas (1558?–1594), V. 63, 81, 85, 127, 134, 138, 142–164 (main entry), 239, 240, 242, 324, 327, 334, 370, 371, 424; VI. 13, 167, 178, 316, *also see* Add.; VIII. 133
Cornelia, VII. 122
Hamlet, V. 157 ff., 164; VI. 178
Householders Philosophie, The, V. 157
Murthering of John Brewer, The, V. 157
Pompey the Great, V. 157
Richt Fontane of hailfull Sapience, The, III. 131
Solimon and Perseda, V. 158, 159, 161, 162
Spanish Tragedie, The, V. 134, 138, 142, 146, 156 ff., 239, 240; VI. 4, 45, 46, 178, 300, 316, 370; VIII. 125
See, also, under *Jeronimo* and Jonson
Kyffin, Maurice (d. 1599), IV. 440
Kylie, Edward, I. Add.
Kyllour, friar, his play against the Papists, III. 122; *The History of Christ's Passion*, III. 141, 504
Kymry, early poetry of, I. 249
Kynaston, Sir Francis (1587–1642), II. 163, 474; VII. 34, 73, 80, 85, 87, 278, 413, 487
'April is past, then do not shed,' VII. 81
Cynthiades or Amorous Sonnets, VII. 81
'Dear Cynthia, though thou bear'st the name,' VII. 81
'Do not conceal those radiant eyes,' VII. 81
Leoline and Sydanis, VII. 78
'Look not upon me with those lovely eyes,' VII. 81
Troilus, Kynaston's version of, II. 165; VII. 78, 79, 314
'When I behold the heaven of thy face,' VII. 81
Kynaston, Herbert (1835–1910), XII. 486
Kynðylan, hall of, I. 275
Kynge, John (d. 1561?), III. 90
Kyngeston, Richard (*fl.* 1403), VI. 280
Kyrle, John (1637–1724), X. 277
Kyteler or Kettle, Alice (*fl.* 1324), II. 500

'L. E. L.' *See* Landon, Laetitia Elizabeth
Laban, II. 293
Labbé's *Concilia*, I. 190
Labeo (Hall's), IV. 332
Labouchere, Henry, XIV. 173, 190, 200, 534
Labourers, statutes of, II. 61
Labrador, IV. 66, 73
La Broue, Solomon de, *Le cavalerice François*, IV. 368
La Bruyère, Jean de, IV. 523; XIII. 447; *Caractères*, VIII. 373, 389; *Des Ouvrages de l'Esprit*, VIII. 376
La Butte, René, IX. 412
La Calprenède, G. de C. de, VII. 391; *Cassandre*, VIII. 185, 371, 434; *La Cléopâtre*, VII. 439; VIII. 15, 25, 185, 272, 371; *Pharamond*, VIII. 371; IX. 55, 268, 500
La Chaises, Father, Project for the Extirpation of Heretics, VIII. 100
La Chalotais, Louis René de, IX. 401, XIV. 382
La Chapelle, Jean de, *Les Carrosses d'Orléans*, VIII. 171
La Chaussée, Pierre Claude Nivelle de, X. 68, 79
Lachrymae Musarum, VII. 180; VIII. 395
Lackington, James (1746–1815), XI. 337, 338, 340, 468; *Confessions*, XI. 327, 472; *Memoirs*, XI. 327, 337, 338
Lacordaire, Jean Baptiste Henri, XII. 254
Lacroix, P., XII. 380
Lactantius, I. 58, 76; III. 416; VII. 505; IX. 489
Lacy, in *Frier Bacon*, V. 137
Lacy, in *The Shomaker's Holiday*, V. 255
Lacy, Alexander, IV. 390
Lacy, earl of Kent, in *The Devil and his Dame*, V. 329
Lacy, J., *The Steeleids* (1714), IX. 442
Lacy, John (d. 1681), VIII. 419
Dumb Lady, The, VIII. 140
Old Troop, The, VIII. 122, 140
Sawny the Scot, VIII. 140
Sir Hercules Buffoon, VIII. 140
Lacy, Margaret de, countess of Lincoln (*c.* 1240), IV. 370
Lacy, T. H., XIII. 516
Ladder of Perfection, The, II. 299, 300
Ladies Collegiate, the, in *The Silent Woman*, VI. 22
Ladislaus, in *The Picture*, VI. 158
Ladislaw, Will, in *Middlemarch*, XIII. 399
Lads of Wamphray, The, II. 415
Lady, the, in *Comus*, VII. 113, 137
Lady, the, in *Hudibras*, VIII. 77
Lady Jane, VI. 168
Lady of the Fountain, I. 253, 274
Lady's Magazine, The, X. 205, 206; XIII. 430
Ladysmith, South Africa, XIV. 193
Laelia, VI. 305, 327, 484
Laertes, in *Hamlet*, V. 201, 262
Laertius, Diogenes, IV. 5, 436
La Fayette, countess de, *La Princesse de Clèves*, VIII. 15, 186, 373; X. 58
Lafeu, in *All's Well that Ends Well*, V. 180
La Flèche, X. 282, 322
La Flechère, J. W. *See* Fletcher, John William
La Fontaine, Jean de, VIII. 373, 376, 427; IX. 162, 168; X. 202; XI. 38, 175, 491
Laga Eadwardi. See *Leges*
Lagado, in *Gulliver's Travels*, IX. 106
Lagden, Sir Godfrey, XIV. Add. 8
Lagrange, Joseph Louis, comte, XIV. 258
La Harpe, V. 293, 302

Lahore, IV. 90
Lai du Corn, La, I. 464
Laidlaw, William (1780–1845), XI. 238; XII. 5; XIII. 504; XIV. 278; *Lucy's Flittin*, XI. 241
Laily Worm, The, II. 414
Laing. David (1793–1878), II. 115, 126, 276; IV. 412; XI. 444, 446; XII. 358, 372, 517, 520
Laing, John (1809–1880), XII. 371, 522
Laing, Malcolm (1762–1818), X. 229, 232, 487, 502; XIV. 491
Laing, Samuel, the elder (1780–1868), XIV. 552
Lairesse, Gerard de, XIII. 84
Lake, Sir Francis (*fl.* 1556), VI. 242
Lake, J. W., XII. 383, 395, 410
Lake, Osmund, *A Probe Theologicall*, VI. 375, 494
Lake, William Charles (1817–1897), XII. 454
Lake poets, XI. 308
Lake school, X. 363
Lakes, the, X. 133; XI. 302; XIV. 220, 221, 291, 292
Laleham, XII. 302; XIII. 86
Lamarck, Chevalier de, XIII. 450
Lamartine, A. M. L. de, V. 302
Lamb, lady Caroline (1785–1828), XII. 383, 397, 450
Lamb, Charles (1775–1834), III. 255; IV. 154, 155, 160, 252, 327, 328; V. 145, 222, 239, 252; VI. 45, 55, 58, 61, 73, 76, 100, 129; VII. 72, 185, 228, 236; VIII. 386; IX. 22, 24, 86, 277, 300; X. 78, 216, 242, 358; XI. 40, 91, 118, 126, 200, 201, 284, 286, 407, 410, 413, 417, 453; XII. 110, 114, 130, 131, 135, 164, 166, 167, 172 ff., 176, 178, 179, 180 ff. (main entry), 219, 221 ff., 282, 421, 433 ff., *also see* Add.; XIII. 9, 135, 143, 148, 158, 188, 198, 299, 307, 429; XIV. 109, 138, 160, 161, 169 ff., 186, 198, 313, 361, 515, 591, 597
Adventures of Ulysses, The, XII. 189, 190
Album Verses, XII. 202
Blakesmoor in H—shire, XII. 182
Blank Verse, by Charles Lloyd and Charles Lamb, XII. 184
Confessions of a Drunkard, XII. 193
Convalescent, The, XII. 200
Curious Fragments, XII. 187, 188
Dissertation on Roast Pig, XII. 160
Dream Children, XII. 182, 202
Essays of Elia, IV. 250; XII. 160, 183, 193, 196, 197, 201, 202
Extracts from the Garrick plays, VIII. 188
First Going to Church, XII. 191
Genius and Character of Hogarth, The, XII. 193
Gipsy's Malison, The, XII. 202
Going or Gone, XII. 202
Hester, XII. 194
Hypochondriacus, XII. 187
Imperfect Sympathies, XII. 198
In His Own Album, XII. 202
Lamb, Charles
In the Album of Lucy Barton, XII. 202
John Woodvil (*Pride's cure*), XII. 186 ff., 191, 194; XIII. 276
King and Queen of Hearts, The, XI. 385
'Lady Blanch,' XII. 187
Last Essays of Elia, XII. 200, 201
Macbeth, in *Tales from Shakespear*, XII. 189
Mr H—, XII. 188, 189, 194
New Year's Eve, XII. 197
Newspapers Thirty-five years ago, XII. 188; XIV. 184
Old China, XII. 186
Old Familiar Faces, The, XII. 184, 202
On the Artificial Comedy of the Last Century, VIII. 156
On the Inconveniences Resulting from being Hanged, XII. 193
Othello, in *Tales from Shakespear*, XII. 189
Oxford in the Vacation, XII. 187
Poems, XI. 385
Popular Fallacies, XII. 197, 200
Pride's Cure, XII. 186
Prince Dorus, XI. 385; XII. 191
Quaker's Meeting, A, XII. 198
Recollections of Christ's Hospital, XII. 193, 197
Recollections of the South-Sea House, XII. 195
Shakespeare, Tragedies of, XII. 193
Specimens from the Writings of Fuller, XII. 193
Specimens of English Dramatic Poets, XII. 190, 191
Starkey, Captain, XII. 181
Superannuated Man, The, XII. 200
Table-Talk, XII. 193
Tale of Rosamund Gray and Old Blind Margaret, XII. 185, 186, 194
Theses quaedam theologicae, XII. 185
Two Races of Men, The, XII. 198
Wife's Trial, The, XI. 148
Witch Aunt, The, XII. 191
Witches and other Night Fears, XII. 191
Works (1818), XII. 194
See, also, Tremebundus
Lamb, Charles and Mary, XII. 433 ff.; *Mrs Leicester's School*, XI. 385; XII. 182 191; *Poetry for Children*, XI. 384; XII. 191; *Tales from Shakespeare*, XI. 385 481; XII. 188 ff.
Lamb, Mrs Elizabeth (born Field), XII. 18[illegible]
Lamb, Sir James. *See* Burges, Sir James Bland
Lamb, John, father of Charles Lamb *Poetical Pieces on Several Occasions*, XII 180
Lamb, John, brother of Charles Lamb, XII 181 ff., 195
Lamb, Mary Ann (1764–1847), XII. 167 173, 181 ff. (main entry), 434 ff.; XIV 198; 'Highborn Helen,' XII. 182, 18[illegible] 188; *Visit to the Cousins*, XII. 191 *Young Mahometan, The*, XII. 182, 191

Lamb, Mary Montgomerie. *See* Currie, lady
Lamb, Sarah (d. 1797), XII. 184
Lamb, William, 2nd viscount Melbourne (1779–1848), XIV. 61, 115, 124, 125, 181, 194, 419, 510
Lambarde, William (1536–1601), III. 530; VIII. 467; IX. 352
Archaionomia, VIII. 315
Archeion, VIII. 315
Eirenarcha, VIII. 315
Perambulation of Kent, IV. 84
Lambe, John (d. 1628), VII. 369, 509
Lambert, Hetty, in *The Virginians*, XIII. 298, 299
Lambert, John (1619–1683), VII. 230, 353; VIII. 121
Lambert, lady, VIII. 121
Lambert, Martin, in *The Virginians*, IV. 253
Lambert, Theo, in *The Virginians*, XIII. 298, 299
Lambeth palace, II. 55; VII. 356
Lambinus, VII. 307; XII. 326
Lambton, lady Betty, in Kelly's *False Delicacy*, XI. 263
Lambton, John George, 1st earl of Durham (1792–1840), XIV. 125, 509
Lambwell, Sir, I. 295
Lamennais, Hugues Félicité Robert de, XII. 254
Lament of Gudrun, The, X. 228
Lamentable Lory, VIII. 97
Lamentation of Souls, I. 356
Lami, E., XII. 525
Lamia, in Keats's poem, XII. 88
Lamia, in *Promos and Cassandra*, V. 120
Lamia, in *The Glasse of Government*, V. 113
Lamilia, in *A Groatsworth of Wit*, III. 357; IV. 320
Lamkin, II. 412
Lamont, John (*fl.* 1671), IX. 551
Lamont, L. M., XIII. 562
Lamont, T. R., XIII. 433
La Motte Fouqué, F. H. C. de, baron. XI. 491; XII. 411
Lamp, The, XIV. 326
Lampatho, in *What You Will*, VI. 43
Lampe, John Frederick (1703?–1751), X. 426, 427, 440
Lampman, Archibald (1861–1899), XIV. 343, 350 ff., 582
Alcyone, XIV. 353
Among the Millet, XIV. 351
April, April in the Hills, XIV. 352
Athenian Reverie, An, XIV. 351
Between the Rapids, XIV. 353
By an Autumn Stream, XIV. 353
City of the End of Things, The, XIV. 354
Comfort of the Fields, The, XIV. 352
Frogs, The, XIV. 353
Heat, XIV. 353
June, XIV. 353
Land of Pallas, The, XIV. 353
Lyrics of Earth, XIV. 353
Meadow, The, XIV. 352
Lampman, Archibald
Monk, The, XIV. 351
Morning on the Lièvre, XIV. 352
September, XIV. 353
Snow, XIV. 353
Solitude, XIV. 353
Lampranus, in *Perfidus Hetruscus*, VI. 302
Lanarkshire, IX. 366; XIV. 66
Lancashire, III. 215, 448; IV. 190, 232; VI. 104; VII. 342, 373; X. 358; XI. 469; XII. 337, 346, 355, 507, 514, 519; XIII. 372, 373, 376; XIV. 185, 195
Lancashire and Cheshire Record society, XII. 506
Lancashire witches, VII. 374
Lancaster, II. 325; XI. 383; XIV. 54
Lancaster, duke of, in *Richard II*, V. 185
Lancaster, house of, II. 296; V. 340; X. 254
Lancaster, Henry Hill (1829–1875), XIII. 467; XIV. 607
Lancaster, Sir James (d. 1618), IV. 85, 92, 98, 99
Lancaster, John of, duke of Bedford (1389–1435), II 336
Lancaster, John, V. 77
Lancaster, Joseph (1778–1838), XIV. 404, 405, 591, 602, 607, 610; *Improvements in Education*, XIV. 390, 393, 401 ff.
'Lancaster,' *pseud.* of lord *de Tabley*, XIII. 204
Lancastrian court, the, VIII. 314
Lancastrian kings, IX. 222
Lancastrian system of education, XI. 133
Lancastrian writers, X. 291
Lancelot, I. 236, 261, 267, 270, 313; II. 337; III. 68; VII. 75
Lancelot, Tennyson's, XIII. 37
Lancelot, prose romance of (*Lancelot de Lake, du Lac*), I. 190, 264, 270, 271, 363. 462
Lancelot and Guinevere, II. 174
Lancelot of the Laik, I. 469; II. 91, 94
Land of Cockaygne, I. 365, 477; X. 225
Landells, Ebenezer (1808–1860), XIV. 236
Lander, Richard Lemon (1804–1834), XIV. 552
Landon, Laetitia Elizabeth, 'L. E. L.' (1802–1838), XII. 124 ff., 129, 380, 419, 450; XIII. 175, 177; *Ethel Churchill*, XII. 247
Landor, Robert Eyres (1781–1869), XII. 228 ff. (main entry), 442
Count Arezzi, XII. 228
Earl of Brecon, The, XII. 228
Faith's Fraud, XII. 228
Fawn of Sertorius, The, XII. 228 ff.
Ferryman, The, XII. 228
Fountain of Arethusa, The, XII. 229, 230
Impious Feast, The, XII. 229
Landor, Walter Savage (1775–1864), VII. 137; IX. 159; XI. 153, 164, 396, 410, 423; XII. 204 ff. (main entry), 223, 266 ff., 404, 407, 439 ff. (main entry); XIII. 57, 73, 129, 132, 148, 181, 187, 188, 193, 228, 230, 328, 463; XIV. 462, 598
Acts and Scenes, XII. 211 ff., 215

Landor, Walter Savage
Andrea of Hungary, XII. 212
Browning sonnet, XII. 214
'Cenci' scenes, XII. 213
Citation and Examination of Shakespeare, The, XII. 215, 216, 220
Coresus and Callirrhoe, XII. 212
Count Julian, VI. 71; XII. 209, 211, 212, 214
Dirce, XII. 214
Dream of Boccaccio, XII. 226
Dry Sticks, XII. 214
Duke de Richelieu, Sir Firebrace Cotes, etc., XII. 216
Essex and Spenser, XII. 220
Euthymedes, XII. 217
Gebir, XI. 300; XII. 209 ff., 229
Guidone and Lucia, XII. 214
Gunlaug, XII. 214
Hamadryad, XII. 213
Hellenics, XII. 212, 213
Ianthe poems, XII. 214
Imaginary Conversations, XII. 205, 209, 211, 215, 217, 230
Menelaus and Helen, XII. 212
Miscellanies, XII. 205
Neapolitan trilogy, XII. 211, 212
Pentameron, The, XII. 215
Pericles and Aspasia, XII. 215, 217
Poems, XII. 205, 211, 217
Rose Aylmer, XII. 214, 220
Rose the Third, XII. 215
Sensible Girl's Reply, A, XII. 215
Works, XII. 212
Landors, the, XII. Add.
Landrecy, siege of, III. 175
Landseer, Sir Edwin (1802–1873), XIV. 545
Land's End, XIII. 204
Lane, Edward William (1801–1876), XII. 342, 499
Lane, John (*fl.* 1620), V. 478
Lane, John, XIII. 568
Lane, Theodore (1800–1828), XIV. 225, 226
Laneham, John (*fl.* 1574), VI. 246, 249
Laneham, Robert (*fl.* 1575), III. 496. 518 IV. 472; V. 30, 31, 386; VI. 466, 494
Lanercost Chronicle, II. 497
Lanferth, letter of, I. 120
Lanfranc (1005?–1089), archbishop of Canterbury, I. 128, 149, 153, 154, 222, 446
Lanfranc's *Chirurgia Parva*, II. 483; V. 478
Lang, Andrew (1844–1912), II. 398, 408, 414; XI. 374, 438 ff., 481, 491, 492; XII. 154, 362, 373, 374, 380, 430, 433. 436, 493, 522; XIII. 207, 210 ff., 467, 477, 504, 509, 530, 533, 537, 543, 566; XIV. 191, 206, 210, 491, 521, 522, 526, 538
Ballade of his Choice of a Sepulchre, XIII. 210
'Bibliomania in France,' XII. 371
Books and Bookmen, XII. 371
Colonel Burnaby, XIII. 210
'Elzevirs,' XII. 371
Helen of Troy, XIII. 210
Lang, Andrew
History of Scotland, XIV. 96
Library, The, XII. 371
Life and Death of Jeanne D'Arc, XIV. 96
Lockhart, Life of J. G., XII. 162
Odyssey, The, XIII. 210
Orange Fairy Book, XIV. 164
Lang, John, XIV. 339, 578
Lang, John Dunmore (1799–1878), XIV. 586; *Aurora Australis*, XIV. 362; *Historical Account of New South Wales*, XIV. 371
Langar, Nottingham, XIII. 449
Langbaine, Gerard, the elder (1609–1658) VII. 316, 485, 489; IX. 536
Langbaine, Gerard, the younger (1656–1692), IV. 376; VI. 69, 122, 200, 202; VIII. 131, 141, 183, 423; *Account of the English Dramatic Poets*, IX. 141, 357, 475, 479
Langcake, Thomas (*fl.* 1764–1781), IX. 318, 511, 512, 515, 516
Langdale, lord. *See* Bickersteth, Henry
Langelye, Robertus, alias Robertus Parterick, II. 35
Langer, Ernst Theodor, X. 311
Langford Magna, IX. 287
Langham, W., *The garden of health*, IV. 542
Langhorne, John (1735–1779), X. 455
Langhorne, William (1721–1772), X. 455
Langland or Langley, William (1330?–1400?), I. 292; II. 2, 34, 35, 38, 433, 435, 436; XI. 368; XIII. Add. 2. See, also, *Piers Plowman*
Langley, Francis (*fl.* 1589), VI. 259
Langley, Henry (1611–1679), X. 387
Langres, I. 34
Langrishe, Sir Hercules (1731–1811), XI. 6, 389
Langtoft. *See* Peter of
Langton, Bennet (1737–1801), X. 207, 215; XI. 333, 346, 365; XIV. 590, 594
Langton, Robert, XIII. 532
Langton, Stephen (d. 1228), archbishop of Canterbury, I. 200, 455; II. 365; V. 21, 65, 151
Language, the English, from Chaucer to Shakespeare, III. 439 ff., 555 ff.; since Shakespeare, XIV. 434 ff., 611
Languet, Hubert, III. 351; *Vindiciae contra Tyrannos*, VII. 353, 499
Languish, Lydia, in Sheridan's *Rivals*, X. 89; XI. 266
Langwith, Benjamin (1684?–1743), IX. 469, 472
Laniere, Nicholas (1588–1666), VII. 5
Lanier, Sidney, XIII. 553
La Noue, François de, IV. 8, 445
Lanquet, Thomas, III. 530
Lansdowne, baron. *See* Granville, George
Lansdowne, marquises of. *See* Petty-Fitzmaurice, Henry; Petty, William
Lanson, G., XII. 525
Lantwit, major (Wales), I. 66
Lanum, IV. 360

Lanval, I. 295
Laocoon, XI. 432
Laodamia, Wordsworth's, XI. 107
Laon, in Shelley's *Revolt of Islam*, XII. 61
Laon, monks of, I. 250
La Pérouse, J. F. G. de, XIV. 553
Lapidaries, I. 460
La Place, P. A. de, V. 290 ff., 296
Laplace, Pierre Simon, marquis de, XIV. 258, 261; *Mécanique Céleste*, XIV. 409
Lapraik, John (1727–1807), *Jenny was Frail and Unkind*, XI. 234; *Poems*, XI. 234; *When I upon thy Bosom Lean*, XI. 234
La Primaudaye, Pierre de, IV. 8, 445
Laputans, the, in *Gulliver's Travels*, XIII. 452
Lār, I. 146
Lara, in Byron's poem, XII. 46
Laracor, IX. 93
La Ramée, Louise de. *See* Ouida
Lardner, Dionysius (1793–1859), XIV. 556, 613
Cabinet Cyclopaedia, XII. 303, 376, 412; XIV. 59
Critical Library, XII. 303
Cyclopaedia, XII. 308
Edinburgh Cabinet Library, XII. 303
Lardner, Nathaniel (1684–1768), IX. 507; X. 380, 381, 513; *Credibility of the Gospel History*, X. 346, 521
Large, Robert (*fl.* 1438), II. 311
Lariche, Benjamin, V. 302
Lark, The, IX. 373, 566; XI. 206, 232
Larkbeare, Devon, XIII. 276
Larkins, Miss, in *David Copperfield*, XIII. 327
Larminie, W., I. 294, 465
Larmor, Sir Joseph, XIV. 269
La Roche, Sophie, *Geschichte des Fräuleins von Sternheim*, X. 18
La Rochefoucauld, François, duc de, IV. 523; V. 169; VIII. 385, 386; XII. 97; *Maximes*, VIII. 373
La Rochelle, VII. 306
Larum for London or the siedge of Antwerpe, A, IV. 324; V. 146, 344
Lascelles, Anne, wife of Smollett, X. 36
Lasco, Albertus, VI. 303
Las Coveras, *Don Fenise*, VIII. 141
Lashmar, Dyce, Gissing's, XIII. 460
Laska, in Coleridge's *Zapolya*, XI. 414
Lassalle, Ferdinand, XIII. 444
Lasseran-Massencone, B. de, IX. 499
Last, Joseph, XIV. 236
Last Judgment, The, I. 428; XI. 198
'Last Sorrowful Lamentations,' XIV. 228
Last Will and Testaments, III. 483
Latey, John (1842–1902), XIV. 534
Lathacan, Laidcenn or Loding, Irish prince, I. 68
Latham, Robert Gordon (1812–1888), XII. 504; XIII. 245
Latham, Simon (*fl.* 1618), *Falconry*, IV. 374, 541
Lathbury, near Newport Pagnell, II. 61
Lathbury, Daniel Conner, XII. 455
Lathom almshouse, X. 358
Latimer, Hugh (1485?–1555), bishop of Worcester, II. 334; III. 27, 31, 36 ff., 42, 51, 81, 432, 471, 496, 532; IV. 227 ff., 238, 300, 324, 380, 493; VII. 236; X. 365; XIII. 184; *Conferences*, III. 38; *Sermon on the Plough*, IV. 234; *Sermons on the Card*, III. 36; IV. 229
Latimer, William (1460?–1545), III. 6, 12
Latin, early study of, II. 70, 283, 359, 367, 370, 371
Latin, on the medieval stage, V. 37, 39, 43, 46
Latin, written in Britain (to the time of Alfred), I. 65 ff., 433 ff.
Latin chroniclers, I. 156 ff., 448 ff.
Latin drama, V. 2, 24, 26, 37, 38, 61, 62, 69, 70, 72, 75, 80, 82, 100 ff., 103, 108 ff., 117 ff., 394; VI. 14, 21, 26, 64, 293 ff., 300, 398; XI. 266
Latin grammar, IX. 382, 390, 562
Latin Heptateuch, XII. 487
Latin hymns, XI. 217; XII. 273; XIII. 135, 172, 173
Latin hymns and carols, II. 375, 377, 383
Latin language and literature, VII. 3, 4, 7, 9, 18, 78, 90, 125, 165, 201, 204, 206, 220, 221, 230, 235, 237, 241, 261, 263, 267, 272, 280, 282, 283, 302, 307, 308, 313 ff., 320, 322 ff., 326, 332, 335, 339 ff., 453; VIII. 49 ff., 58, 61, 87, 88, 112, 271, 277, 279, 281, 282, 310, 313, 314, 319, 332, 353, 378, 381; IX. 43, 67, 68, 76, 253, 264, 266, 270, 292, 329 ff., 337, 341, 382, 385, 388, 390, 393, 396, 402 ff., 409; X. 14, 97, 133, 137, 158, 159, 163, 178, 187, 188, 205, 225, 257, 276, 289, 308, 335; XI. 2, 54, 58, 83, 90, 181, 334, 343, 347, 354, 355, 359; XII. 40, 106, 134, 208, 223, 230, 265, 278, 308, 317, 326, 327, 330, 335 ff., 343, 354; XIII. 23, 29, 45, 53, 124, 164, 165, 168, 169, 175, 249; XIV. 91, 120, 209, 249, 302, 303, 306, 308, 309, 316, 327, 374, 382, 385, 383, 391, 394, 405, 406, 410, 413, 424, 426, 454, 455, 457, 460, 461
Latin poets, X. 119
Latin Prayer Book, VII. 327
Latin terms, on the stage, V. 255; VI. 93, 162, 163, 225, 229, 354, 372
Latin verse, X. 159, 177; XII. 58, 265, 305, 329
Latmus, in *The Faithfull Shepheardesse*, VI. 368
La Tour Landry, G., II. 483, 485, 508. *See, also*, Caxton, *Knight of the Tower*
Latria, shrine of (Day's), VI. 216
Latta, Robert, XIV. 479
Laube, Heinrich, V. 306, 346
Laud, William (1573–1645), archbishop of Canterbury, III. 388, 420; IV. 204, 239, 306, 411, 424, 426, 432; V. 365; VI. 196, 319, 326, 405; VII. 35, 98, 115, 147, 148, 150, 152, 154, 157 ff., 162, 163, 182,

Laud, William
187, 207, 208, 216, 218, 223, 225, 334, 349, 350, 425, 427, 441, 445, 459, 498, *also see* Add.; VIII. 274, 293, 301, 462; IX. 306; *Diary*, VII. 160, 451; *Relation ...Pretended Answer to T. C.*, VIII. 300
Lauder, George (*fl.* 1677), IX. 555
Lauder, Sir John, lord Fountainhall (1646–1722), IX. 553; XII. 376
Lauder, Sir Thomas Dick (1784–1848), XII. 450
Lauder, William (1520?–1573), II. 497; III. 498; *Tractate concernyng the office and dewtie of Kyngis, etc.*, III. 132
Lauder, William (d. 1771), VII. 109, 118; IX. 557; X. 175, 468
Lauderdale, duke of. *See* Maitland, John
Lauderdale, earls of. *See* Maitland, James; Maitland, John
Laudian movement, the, XII. 253
Laudian statutes, at Oxford, IX. 383
Laudine, in *Ywain and Gawain*, I. 312
Laughter, in *The Tears of the Muses*, III. 241
Laughton, Sir John Knox (1830–1915), XII. 427; XIV. 491
Launce, in *The Two Gentlemen of Verona*, V. 180, 190; XIII. 64
Launcelot, in Kingsley's *Yeast*, XIII. 360, 361
Launcelot, in *The Merchant of Venice*, V. 190
Launceston, VII. 348
Launfal (Landavall), I. 295
Launfal, Sir, I. 281, 291, 294, 295, 299, 310, 462, 471
'Launsknights,' V. 31
Laura, in *Pendennis*, XIII. 290, 291, 293, 295, 296
'Laura,' Della Cruscan poet, XI. 177
Laura (Petrarch's), III. 225, 251, 252, 254, 265, 268, 272; IV. 210
Laura, the, in Kingsley's *Hypatia*, XIII. 363
Laurence (actor), VI. 249
Laurence, friar, in *Romeo and Juliet*, V. 357
Laurence, French (1757–1809), XI. 35, 388, 391
Laurence, R. V., XIV. 484
Laurence, St, V. 49
Laurentian manuscripts, XII. 324, 327, 328
Laurie, Simon Somerville (1829–1909), XIV. 475, 607
Laurie, William Ferguson Beatson, XIV. 574
Lausanne, II. 315; X. 298, 301, 302, 304, 311, 312
Lavater, J.-G., XI. 432
Laveleye, Emile de, XIV. 477
Lavenham, Richard (*fl.* 1380), I. 455; II. 61
Lavensforth, in Mrs Inchbald's *To Marry or not to Marry*, XI. 279
Lavington, John (1690?–1759), X. 384
Lavinia, in Thomson's *Autumn*, X. 104
Lavoisier, Antoine Laurent, XIV. 271, 273, 278
Law, in *Piers the Plowman*, II. 10
Law, Edmund (1703–1787), VIII. 474; IX. 507; X. 131, 342
Law, Edward, 1st earl of Ellenborough (1790–1871), XII. 401; XIV. 124, 130, 502
Law, John, of Lauriston (1671–1729), IX. 492, 559
Law, Robert (d. 1690?), IX. 551; XIII. 518
Law, Thomas Graves (1836–1904), XII. 522; XIV. 101, 491 *Collected Essays*, XII. 371
Law, William (1686–1761), IV. 342, 522; VI. 494; VII. 155; VIII. 433; IX. 305 ff. (main entry), 404, 507, 510 ff., 515, 519, 520, 569; X. 354, 355; XII. 284
Absolute Unlawfulness of the Stage, The, X. 70
Appeal to all that Doubt, IX. 318 ff., 328
Case of Reason, IX. 302, 311, 312
Malebranche, and the Vision of All Things in God, IX. 313
Practical Treatise upon Christian Perfection, IX. 312, 318, 323, 325
Remarks on the Fable of the Bees, IX. 302, 311, 322 ff.
Serious Call, VI. 408; IX. 308, 309, 312, 313, 318, 321 ff., 402; X. 350, 362; XII. 282
Some Animadversions upon Dr Trapp's late Reply, IX. 313, 326
Spirit of Love, IX. 314
Spirit of Prayer, IX. 319, 320, 322 ff., 326
Three Letters to the Bishop of Bangor, IX. 310
Way to Divine Knowledge, IX. 307, 318 ff., 321
Law, William John (1787–1869), XII. 497
Lawder, Mrs (Jane Contarine), X. 481
Lawes, Henry (1596–1662), VI. 325, 326; VII. 5, 22, 52, 113, 116, 123, 409, 413; VIII. 117
Lawes, William (d. 1645), VII. 5
Lawford, Essex, XII. 305
Lawkerry, Neh., VII. 499
Lawless, Emily (d. 1913), XIV. 569
Grania, XIV. 324
Hurrish, XIV. 324
With Essex in Ireland, XIV. 324
With the Wild Geese, XIV. 324
Lawley, Francis, XIV. 543
Lawrence, bishop of Durham (d. 1154), I. 191, 455
Lawrence, George Alfred (1827–1876), XIII. 563; *Guy Livingstone*, XIII. 436
Lawrence, Sir Henry (1806–1857), XIV. 495
Lawrence, John (1753–1839), XIV. 544
Lawrence, John Laird Mair, 1st baron Lawrence (1811–1879), XII. 316, 478
Lawrence, Leonard, *Arnalte and Lucenda* VII. 80, 413
Lawrence, Polly, of Bath, XI. 175
Lawrie, Sir Archibald Campbell (1837–1914), XII. 517; *Annals of Malcolm and William*, XII. 360; *Early Scottis*

Lawrie, Sir Archibald Campbell
Charters, XII. 360; *Index to the Scots Acts*, XII. 360
La Writ, in *The Little French Lawyer*, VI. 134
Laws, Old English, I. 130. *See, also*, the chapter on Alfred, I. 97 ff., 436, 437, 439
Laws, Bute MS. of, II. 284
Lawson, Edward Levy, lord Burnham, XIV. 191
Lawson, George (d. 1678), VII. 473
Lawson, Sir John (d. 1665), VIII. 11, 218
Lawson, William (*fl.* 1618), *A New Orchard and Garden*, IV. 373, 375, 542
Laxdaela saga, XIII. 125
Lay by your pleading, VIII. 96
Lay Folk's Mass Book, I. 353; II. 48
Layamon (*fl.* 1200), I. 137, 139, 170, 218, 222, 234 ff., 264, 265, 278, 287, 288, 292, 337, 375, 378, 393, 398, 458, 459, 462; II. 103, 189, 420; V. 6; *Brut*, XII. 356, 517
Layard, Sir Austen Henry (1817–1894), XII. 339, 497; XIV. 552; *Early Adventures in Persia, Susiana and Babylonia*, XIV. 253; *Popular account of Discoveries at Nineveh, A*, XIV. 253
Layard, George Somes, XII. 441; XIII. 536; XIV. 548
Lays of Helgi, X. 228
Layton, in Strype's *Ecclesiastical Memorials*, I. 212
Lazarillo, in *Blurt Master-Constable* (Middleton), VIII. 127
Lazarillo de Tormes, III. 94, 342, 364; VIII. 127
Lazarus, in school plays, V. 103
Lea, James, IV. 458
Leabhar Breac, the, XII. 362, 515
Leabhar na g-Ceart, the Book of Rights, XII. 518
Leach, Arthur Francis, VII. 336; XIV. 591; *History of Warwick School*, IV. 261
Leach, Edmund, VII. 515
Leach, Francis (*fl.* 1643), VII. 347
Lead, Jane (1623–1704), IX. 307, 513 ff., 523
Leadbeater, Mary, born Shackleton (1758–1826), XIV. 569
Annals of Ballitore, XIV. 323
Cottage Dialogues, XIV. 323
Extracts and Original Anecdotes, XIV. 323
Leadbeater Papers, The, XIV. 323
Leader, The, XIII. 385; XIV. 199
Leader-Haughs and Yarrow, IX. 364
Leadhills, Lanarkshire, IX. 366
Leaf, Walter, XIV. 522
League, the (French), III. 398; IV. 142; VI. 174; VIII. 16
Leake, William Martin (1777–1860), XII. 497; XIV. 552
Numismata Hellenica, XII. 338
Researches in Greece, XII. 338
Topography of Athens, XII. 338
Travels, XII. 338
Leakey, Caroline Woolmer (1827–1881), XIV. 587
Lean, Florence (born Marryat). *See* Marryat, Florence
Leanchops, in Wilson's *Projectors*, VIII. 123
Leander, Hero and, in Nashe's *Prayse of the Red Herring*, IV. 327
Leandro, in *The Spanish Curate*, VI. 134, 139
Leanthe, in Farquhar's *Love and a Bottle*, VIII. 169
Leapor, Mary (1722–1746), XI. 172, 427
Lear, in Shakespeare's play, XII. 47
Lear, Edward (1812–1888), XI. 386, 481; XIII. 167, 504; *Book of Nonsense*, XI. 377; XIII. 163; *Jumblies*, XIII. 163; *Owl and the Pussy-Cat, The*, XIII. 163
Lear, Garrick as, X. 265; XI. 360
Lear or Leir, in the *Bruts* and *Chronicles*, I. 171, 235, 237, 336. *See, also*, Leir, Llŷr
Learning (Clergy), in *Piers the Plowman*, II. 20
Learning-with-Money, in *All for Money*, V. 57
Learning-without-Money, in *All for Money*, V. 57
Leask, W. Keith, XIV. 538, 594
Leasowes, X. 149, 271, 275, 276, 456
Leathley, Mrs, XI. 487
Lebanon, IV. 33
Le Blanc, abbé, V. 289, 290
Le Bossu, René, VIII. 375; *Du poème Épique*, VIII. 374; IX. 59
Le Brun, N., IV. 266
Lecher, in *Piers the Plowman*, II. 12
Lechery, in *Confessio Amantis*, II. 147
Lechery, in *Piers the Plowman*, II. 20
Lechery, in *The Example of Virtue*, II. 234
Lecky, William Edward Hartpole (1838–1903), VIII. 167, 291, 292; X. 503; XI. 396; XII. 464; XIII. 552; XIV. 86, 89, 96, 103 ff. (main entry), 492, 509, 510
Declining Sense of the Miraculous, The, XIV. 104
Democracy and Liberty, XIV. 106
History of England in the Eighteenth Century, XIV. 86, 105
History of European Morals, XIV. 104
History of the Spirit of Rationalism in Europe, XIV. 104
Leaders of Public Opinion in Ireland, XIV. 104
Map of Life, The, XIV. 106
Religious Tendencies of the Age, The, XIV. 104
Memoir of, by his Wife, XIV. 104
Leclerk, George Louis. *See* Buffon, comte de
Le Clerc, Jean, or Johannes Clericus, VIII. 472; IX. 336, 435, 495, 525; X. 177; *Bibliothèque universelle*, VIII. 330
L'Ecluse (Clusius), IV. 374
Leconte de Lisle, Charles-Marie, *L'Épée d'Angantyr*, X. 223; *Poëmes barbares*, X. 223
Lecount, Mrs, in Wilkie Collins's *No Name*, XIII. 437

Lediard, Thomas (1685–1743), x. 502; *History of the Reigns of William III and Mary, and Anne*, IX. 235; *Life of John Duke of Marlborough*, IX. 235; *Naval History of England*, IX. 235
Lee, Edward (1482?–1544), archbishop of York, III. 20, 42
Lee, Elizabeth, XIII. 565
Lee, Francis (1661–1719), IX. 307, 514, 515
Lee, Harriet (1757–1851), XI. 306, 461
Lee, Sir Henry (1530–1610), IV. 113
Lee, Henry (*fl.* 1712), VIII. 347, 474
Lee, Miss Jane, v. 129, 135
Lee, John (1779–1859), XI. 469
Lee, John Edward (1808–1887), XII. 511; *Imperial Profiles*, XII. 346
Lee, Nathaniel (1653?–1692), VI. 49; VIII. 16, 21, 30, 185 ff., 189, 190, 194, 235, 395, 398, 400, 401, 437, 438; x. 67, 73
Alexander the Great, VIII. 179
Brutus, x. 82
Caesar Borgia, VIII. 186
Constantine the Great, VIII. 186
Gloriana, VIII. 185
Guise, Duke of (with Dryden), VIII. 16, 30, 186
Lucius Junius Brutus, VIII. 186, 187
Massacre of Paris, The, VIII. 186
Mithridates, King of Pontus, VIII. 185
Nero, Emperour of Rome, VIII. 185
Oedipus, King of Thebes (with Dryden), VIII. 30, 186
Princesse of Cleve, The, VIII. 186
Rival Queens, The, VIII. 185, 186, 261, 426
Theodosius, or the Force of Love, VIII. 186
Lee, Samuel (18th century bookseller), XI. 330
Lee, Samuel (1783–1852), XII. 341, 501; XIV. 593, 602
Lee, Sir Sidney, v. 165, 173, 225, 230, 368; XI. 385, 447; *Elizabethan Sonnets*, IV. 24; *Memoir of George Smith*, XIV. 111
Lee, Sophia (1750–1824), XI. 306, 461
Lee, Sophia and Harriet, *Canterbury Tales*, XII. 37, 50
Lee, William (d. 1645), VII. 407
Lee, William (1869), IX. 13, 15 ff., 24, 418; XII. 522; XIV. 498
Lee Priory press, XII. 364, 520
Lee-Hamilton, Eugene (1845–1907), XIII. 504
Leech, H. J., XIV. 508
Leech, John (*fl.* 1623), VII. 487
Leech, John (1817–1864), XIV. 201, 232, 234, 236 ff., 541, 546 ff.
Leech-book, The, I. 106, 135, 136
Leeds, IX. 540; XI. 340, 341; XII. 274, 507, 514; XIV. 112
Leeds, Yorkshire college, XIV. 432
Leeds Mercury, The, XIV. 169, 199, 529, 533, 534
Leeds school, VII. 330
Lees, Abraham, x. 384
Leesehing, L F., XIV. 522
Leeu, Gerard, of Antwerp, II. 314, 319
Chronicles of England, The, II. 319
Dialogue or communing between the wise king Solomon and Marcolphus, II. 319
History of Jason, The, II. 319
History of Paris and Vienne, The, II. 319
Leeward islands, x. 95
Lee-Warner, Sir William, XIV. 578
Le Fanu, Joseph Sheridan (1814–1873), XIII. 407; XIV. 309, 569
A Chapter in the History of a Tyrone Family, XIII. 414
Beatrice, XIV. 310
House by the Churchyard, The, XIV. 310
Legend of the Glaive, The, XIV. 310
Phaudrig Crohoore, XIV. 310
Purcell Papers, The, XIII. 414, 555, 556
Room in the Dragon Volant, The, XIV. 310
Shamus O'Brien, XIV. 310
Song of the Bottle, The, XIV. 310
Uncle Silas, XIV. 310
Watcher, The, and other Weird Stories, XIII. 414; XIV. 310
Le Fanu, W., XIV. 569
Lefebvre, Denys (Syned), XIV. Add. 5
Le Felure, VIII. 354
Le Fevre, in Sterne's *Tristram Shandy*, x. 54
Le Fèvre, Jean, III. 90
Lefèvre d'Étaples, Jacques, III. 20
Leffmann, H., XIII. 543
Lefroy, Edward Cracroft (1855–1891), XIII. 216, 504
Le Gallienne, Richard, XIII. 570
Legate, John (d. 1620), IV. 410
Legeay, U., XIV. 485
Legenda Aurea. See *Golden Legend* and Voragine
Legendaries, I. 317, 335 ff., 474. *See, also*, under various saints
Legendary, South English, I. 134, 335 ff., 340, 341
Légende de St Julien l'Hospitalier, IX. 39
Legendre, Adrien Marie, *Elements of Geometry and Trigonometry*, XIII. 4, 464
Leger, Augustin, *John Wesley's Last Love*, x. 368
Leges Edwardi Confessoris, VIII. 310, 465
Leges Henrici, VIII. 310, 311, 465
Leges Willelmi I, VIII. 310, 465
Legge, Cantrell, IV. 164, 410
Legge, George, 1st baron Dartmouth (1648–1691), VIII. 257
Legge, James (1815–1897), XII. 343, 500
Legge, Thomas (1535–1607), *Richardus Tertius*, v. 81, 82; VI. 301, 304, 327, 475
Legge, William, 1st earl of Dartmouth (1672–1750), IX. 209, 216, 483
Legh, Gerard (d. 1563), *Accedens of Armory*, IV. 376, 543
Leghorn, x. 43; XII. 37, 38
Legion, *Smec*, in Butler's *Hudibras*, VIII. 72

Legouis, Emile, xi. 410; xiii. 570; *The Early Life of Wordsworth*, xiii. 418
Legrand, Antoine, vii. 303, 474
Legrand, Jacques, *Le livre de bonnes meurs*, ii. 315
Legrand, Joachim, ix. 197, 488; x. 160, 460
Le Grice, Charles Valentine (1773–1858), xii. 419
Le Grys, Sir Robert (d. 1635), iv. 501
Lehmann, Max, xiv. 92
Lehmann, Rudolph Chambers, xiii. 542; xiv. 537
Leibbrandt, Hendrick Carel Vos, xiv. Add. 8
Leibniz, Gottfried Wilhelm von, iv. 260, 292; viii. 50, 300, 361; ix. 200, 290, 291, 297, 301, 400, 505; x. 220, 312; xiv. 8; *Annales imperii occidentis Brunsvicenses*, x. 311; *Nouveaux Essais*, viii. 347; *Reflexions*, viii. 347
Leicester, ii. 67; iii. 337; vii. 4, 340; ix. 91, 532; xi. 431; xii. 512
Leicester, earl of, in *Robert, Earle of Huntington*, v. 318, 324
Leicester, earls of. *See* Dudley, Robert; Sidney, Philip; Sidney, Robert
Leicester play, v. 391
Leicester's company, vi. 246, 249, 251, 383
Leicestershire, vi. 111; x. 159
Leicht, A., i. 102
Leigh, Sir Amyas, in *Westward Ho!* xiii. 364
Leigh, Augusta, xii. 34
Leigh, Edward (1602–1671), vii. 480, 484; *Advice on Travel*, vii. 314; *Critica Sacra*, vii. 319, 482, 490
Leigh, Elizabeth Medora, xii. 396
Leigh, George (*fl.* 1788), xi. 336
Leigh, Henry Sambrooke (1837–1883), xiii. 162, 505; xiv. 549
Leigh, John (1689–1726), viii. 177
Leigh, Percival (*pseud.* Paul Prendergast, 1813–1889), xiii. 162, 505; xiv. 239, 549; *The Comic Latin Grammar*, xiv. 236
Leigh, Richard (b. 1649), viii. 403
Leigh on Thames, iv. 91
Leighton, Alexander (1568–1649), vi. 403
Leighton, Robert (1611–1684), viii. 298, 299, 460; ix. 193; xi. 415; xii. 283, 284
Leighton, Sir William (*fl.* 1603–1614), vii. 406
Leighton Ecclesia, prebend of, vii. 28
Leinster, viii. 384
Leinster, Book of, xii. 362, 515
Leipzig, iv. 267; v. 284, 290; vii. 20, 21, 308; xii. 280
Leir, King, The True Chronicle History of, v. 83, 310, 399, 434; vi. 92
Leire, Danish royal residence, i. 27
Leith, siege of, iii. 182
Leith, South, xi. 244
Leitrim, county, xiv. 355
Le Kain, Henri Louis, x. 264
Le Keux, John Henry, xii. 357
Lekpreuik, Robert (*fl.* 1561–1588), Scots printer, ii. 126; iii. 149; iv. 412; ix. 359
Leland or Leyland, John (1506?–1552), i. 131; ii. 49, 399; iii. 48, 54, 55, 313, 321, 328, 330, 468, 530; iv. 461; v. 103; ix. 345, 352, 534, 535, 541; *Collectanea*, iii. 328; ix. 349; *Itinerary*, iii. 328, 330; iv. 66, 308, 512; ix. 349; xii. 518; *Journey and Serche*, iii. 329
Leland, John (1691–1766), ix. 502, 507; x. 520, 521
Leland, Thomas (1722–1785), *History of Ireland*, x. 293, 502
Lelia, in *The Captain*, vi. 122, 128
Le Long, Gautier, *La Veuve*, iii. 88
Lely, Sir Peter (1618–1680), ix. 241
Lembcke, E., v. 307
Lemercier, N., v. 301
Le Moine, *Peintures Morales*, iv. 523
Lemoine, Henry (1756–1812), xi. 472
Lemon, Mark (1809–1870), xi. 387, 487; xiii. 516; xiv. 236, 238, 548, 549
Lemoyne, P., *Saint Louis*, vii. 268
'Lend me Half-a-Crown,' x. 206
Le Neve, John (1679–1741), ix. 536; *Fasti Ecclesiae Anglicanae*, xii. 355, 516
Le Neve, Peter (1661–1729), ix. 353, 358
Leng, Sir John (1828–1906), xiv. 534
Leng, Sir William Christopher (1825–1902), xiv. 534
Lennox, in Barbour's *Bruce*, ii. 107
Lennox, Charles, 3rd duke of Richmond, xi. 36
Lennox, Charlotte (1720–1804), x. 467, 469; xi. 462; xiii. 561; *The Female Quixote*, x. 175, 468; *Shakespear Illustrated*, x. 175; *The Sister*, xi. 275
Lennox, earls of. *See* Stewart, Esmé; Stewart, Matthew
Lennox, lord William Pitt (1799–1881), xiii. 563; xiv. 238
Le Noir, Elizabeth Anne (1755?–1841), xii. 450
Lent, in Christmas carol, ii. 379
Lenthall, William (1591–1662), vii. 190, 439, 443
Lenz, v. 298, 303
Leo IV, pope, i. 88
Leo X, pope, iv. 334; xiv. 99
Leo XII, pope, xiv. 54
Leo, emperor, ii. 115
Leo Africanus (Leo, John), iv. 445
Leofric (d. 1072), 1st bishop of Exeter, i. 151; iv. 422
Leon, count Reginald de St, xi. 394
Leonard, St, v. 97
Leonardo da Vinci, xii. 187
Leoni, Michele, v. 306
Leonid shooting stars, xiv. 264
Leonides, Nicolaus, iii. 6
Leonora, in Fielding's *Joseph Andrews*, x. 30
Leonora, in *The Devils Law-case*, vi. 183, 187
Leonora, in *The Gratefull Servant*, vi. 204
Leonora, in *The Parliament of Love*, vi. 154
Leonore, in *The Gamester*, vi. 202

Leontes, in *The Winter's Tale*, v. 206
Leontius, in *The Humorous Lieutenant*, vi. 122
Leopardi, count Giacomo, xii. 72, 393, 395, 396, 402, 405, 525; xiii. 489
Leopold, prince, of Coburg, xii. 232
Leosthenes, in *The Bond-Man*, vi. 155, 158
Leoven, my Lady of, vi. 291
Lepanto, xii. 38
Lepell, Mary. *See* Hervey, lady Mary
Lepidus, i. 95
Lepointe, E. L., xiii. 469
Leprohon, Rosanna Elenora (1832–1879), xiv. 581, 582; *Antoinette de Mirecourt*, xiv. 360
Lerici, xii. 37
Leroy, Loys (*dit* Regius), iv. 3, 5
Le Sage, Alain-René, viii. 162; ix. 35 x. 17, 216; xii. 168; *Gil Blas*, x. 37, 420
Le Sage, J. M., xiv. 191
Lesbia, in *The Returne from Pernassus*, vi. 311
Lesbia (Catullus's), vii. 2, 9
Lescarbot, M., iv. 456
Lescurel, Jehannot de, xiii. 211
Leslie, Alexander, 1st earl of Leven (1580?–1661), vii. 22
Leslie, Charles (1650–1722), ix. 11, 475, 507, 564; x. 355, 356; *Rehearsal*, ix. 5; *Short and Easy Method*, ix. 289; *Snake in the Grass*, ix. 201, 520
Leslie, Charles Robert (1794–1859), xii. 380
Leslie, Forbes, xii. 511
Leslie or Lesley, John (1527–1596), bishop of Ross, ii. 285, 398, 415; *De Origine, Moribus et Rebus Scotorum*, iii. 154, 155, 504
Leslie, Mary E., xiv. 339, 578
Leslie, Thomas Edward Cliffe (1827?–1882), xiv. 475; *Essays in Political Economy*, xiv. 36
Lesse, Nicholas (*fl.* 1550), iv. 441
Lessing, Gotthold Ephraim, iv. 265, 267; v. 287, 288, 290, 293 ff., 300, 463; vi. 82; viii. 172, 430; ix. 61, 450, 466; xi. 121, 449; xii. 526, 527; *Laocoon*, xi. 3; *Minna von Barnhelm*, xi. 262; *Miss Sara Sampson*, x. 76, 79
Lessingham, Mrs, xi. 451
Lessius (1564–1623), vii. 402
Lester, John Ashby, v. 63
L'Estrange, Alfred Guy, xiii. 565
L'Estrange, Hamon (1605–1660), vii. 445, 446, 447
L'Estrange, Sir Roger (1616–1704), vii. 197, 363 ff., 390, 416, 496, *also see* Add.; viii. 68, 387, 388, 412, 445, 481; ix. 2 ff., 265, 273 ff., 415 ff., xi. 312, 313, 331, 466; xiv. 461
  Bona's *Guide to Eternity*, ix. 274
  Colloquies of Erasmus, ix. 273 ff.
  Considerations...Regulation of the Press ix. 2
  Discourse of the Fishery, ix. 3
  Fables and Storyes Moralized, ix. 4
L'Estrange, Sir Roger
  Fables of Æsop, ix. 4, 275
  Intelligencer, The, vii. 365
  Josephus, ix. 273, 275
  L'Estrange his Apology, ix. 2
  News, The, vii. 365
  No Blinde Guides, ix. 2
  Observator, The, vii. 365; ix. 3, 4
  Seneca's *Morals*, ix. 273, 275
  Spanish Decameron, ix. 274
  Tully's *Offices*, ix. 274
  Visions of Quevedo, ix. 3, 274
Le Sueur, Gordon, xiv. Add. 8
Le Tourneur, Pierre Félicien, v. 292, 293, 296, 301
Let us a' to the Bridal, ix. 379
Leti, Gregorio, x. 291
Letter concerning Libels, Warrants, etc., x. 399
Letter from a Blacksmith, xi. 216
Letter from a friend of the universities, ix. 411
Letter from Avignon, ix. 218
Letter to a schoolmaster in the country, A, xiv. 398
Letter to Henry Brougham...from an M.A. of Queen's College, Oxford, xiv. 407
Letter to...Lord John Russell, A, xiv. 416
Letter to The Public Advertiser, x. 399
Letters between the Hon. Andrew Erskine and James Boswell, Esq., x. 191
Letters from a Tutor to his Pupils, xi. 371
Letters from Corsica, xiv. 180
Letters of the Insurgent Leaders, ii. 432, 434
Letters, private and domestic, in Jacobean times, vii. 438, 439
Letters...to Sir Joseph Williamson, ix. 212
Letton, John (*fl.* 1480), ii. 318; viii. 314
Leucippus, in *Cupid's Revenge*, vi. 128
Leusden, Jan, iv. 47
Levant, the, iv. 67, 80, 84, 98; vii. 201
Levant company, vii. 308
Levantine traveller, in *The Fair Maid Of The West*, vi. 102
Le Vayer, François de la Mothe, *Liberty and Servitude*, viii. 246
Leve, Antoine De, Testament of, iii. 483
Levellers, the, vii. 190
Leven, loch, xi. 244
Leven, vale of, x. 36
Lever, Charles James (1806–1872), xiii 307; xiv. 255, 314, 569; *Cornelius O'Dowd*, xiv. 313; *Lord Kilgobbin*, xiv 313
Lever, Christopher (*fl.* 1627), vii. 406
Lever or Leaver, Ralph (d. 1585), *Arte of Reason rightly termed Witcraft*, vii. 276 474
Lever, Robert (*fl.* 1641), vii. 342
Lever or Leaver, Thomas (1521–1577) iii. 419, 473; iv. 232, 233, 493
Leverrier, Urbain J. J., xiv. 264
Leveson-Gower, Granville George, 2nd earl Granville (1815–1891), xiv. 131, 51
Levett, Robert (1701?–1782), x. 187, 465 467, 479

Levey, R. M., xiii. 515
Levi, Leone (1821–1888), xiv. 475
Levi-Lawson family, xiv. 191
Levidolche, in *The Ladies Triall*, vi. 194
Levins, Peter, iii. 555
Levis, Howard L., xiv. 541
Levison, Sir Richard, vii. 438
Levitt, William, vii. 515
Levy, Amy (1861–1889), xiii. 181, 505
Levy, Joseph Moses (1812–1888), xiv. 534
Lévy-Bruhl, L., xiv. 477
Lewes, battle of, i. 368
Lewes, George Henry (1817–1878), v. 276; xiii. 391, 393, 396, 401, 513, 515, 516, 558; xiv. 171, 199, 475, 504
Aristotle, xiv. 32
Biographical History of Philosophy, The, xiv. 32, 113
Comte's Philosophy of the Sciences, xiv. 32
Foundations of a Creed, The, xiv. 33
Life of Goethe, xiii. 385; xiv. 113
On Actors and Acting, xiii. 257
Problems of Life and Mind, xiv. 33
Lewine, J., xiv. 541
Lewinsky (German actor), v. 306
Lewis, Charles Lee, xiii. 552
Lewis, David (1683?–1760), ix. 188, 436, 445; *Miscellany*, x. 145; *My Winifreda*, xii. 139
Lewis, Erasmus (1670–1754), ix. 103, 456
Lewis, Sir George Cornewall (1806–1863), xii. 301, 310, 311, 426, 498
Astronomy of the Ancients, xii. 339
Credibility of Early Roman History, xii. 305, 339
Essays on the administration of Great Britain, 1864, xi. 396
'Legislation for the Working Class,' xii. 153
Lewis, John (1675–1747), ii. 54; ix. 536
Lewis, Leopold David (1828–1890), xiii. 520
Lewis, Matthew Gregory ('Monk' Lewis) (1775–1818), i. 287; x. 223; xi. 160, 283, 286, 300, 303 ff., 414, 458, 462; xiii. 260, 264; *Alonzo the Brave*, xi. 304;
Monk, The, xi. 303, 304; xiii. 418
Tales of Wonder, xii. 5, 373, 405
Lewis, William Thomas (1748?–1811), xi. 260
'Lewis Baboon' (Louis XIV), xiv. 212
Lewis of Bavaria, i. 212
Lewis de Bretaylles, ii. 313
Lewis the Pious, i. 47
Lewkenor, Lewis, iv. 443
Lewte, in *Piers the Plowman*, ii. 10, 25, 32
Lex Ecclesiae, in *The Passetyme of Pleasure*, ii. 226
Lexicon rhetoricum Cantabrigiense, xii. 328
Leybourn, William (1626–1700?), iv. 459; vii. 509
Leycester, Sir Peter (1614–1678), ix. 536
Leyden, iv. 402; vii. 233, 307, 308, 310, 322; ix. 290; xiv. 282, 290
Leyden, John (1775–1811), xi. 444; xii. 5, 419; xiv. 334, 578
Cout of Keeldar, The, xi. 242
Lord Soulis, xi. 242
Mermaid, The, xi. 242; xii. 133
Ode to an Indian Gold Coin, xiv. 335, 340
Ode to Scottish Music, xi. 242
Scenes of Infancy, xi. 242; xii. 133
Leyden riddle, i. 61
Leyden, university, viii. 347; x. 21, 22, 200, 390
Leyds, Willem Johannes, xiv. Add. 8
Leyland, Francis A., xiii. 557, 558
Leyser, Polycarp, xiii. 172
Lhwyd, Edward (1660–1709), ix. 412, 536
Liancourt, duc de, x. 66
Liar, in *Piers the Plowman*, ii. 8
Libanius, vi. 22
Libeanus Desconus, or *Sir Libeanus*, or *Libius Disconius*, i. 282, 284, 289, 295, 312, 469
Libel of English Policy, The, ii. 423, 424; iv. 67, 84
'Libell' (Otway's), viii. 94, 95
Liber Hymnorum (Irish), xii. 362
Liber Monstrorum, i. 26
Liber Niger Domus Regis, vi. 279, 280
Liber Vagatorum, xiii. 428
Liberal, Letitia, xiv. 591
Liberal, The, xii. 36, 37, 389, 391, 392
Liberal Theology, The Growth of, xii. 464 ff.
Liberate Rolls, xii. 355, 516
Liberton, ii. 110
Liberty, in *Cooper's Hill*, vii. 60
Liberty, in Thomson's poem, x. 104, 107
Liberty vindicated against slavery, vii. 388
Libido, in *Psychomachia*, v. 51
Libius Disconius, x. 233
Libraries, the foundation of, iv. 415 ff., 549 ff.
Library of Entertaining Knowledge, The, xiv. 409
Library of the Fine Arts, The, xiv. 539
Library of the Fathers, The, xii. 274, 454
Library of Useful Knowledge, The, xiv. 409
Licensing act (1662), viii. 89, 90; xi. 312
Licensing act (1737), x. 23, 24; xi. 335
Licensing act, ix. 5
Licentiousness of the Times, The, viii. 90
Lichfield, iv. 225, 421, 472; v. 38; vii. 278; ix. 196, 530; x. 158 ff.; xi. 340; xii. 124, 328; xiii. 449
Lichfield, Henry, iv. 464
Lichfield, John, iv. 411
Lichfield, Nicholas, iv. 442, 448
Lichfield school, vii. 330
Lichtenberg, G. C., ix. 467
Lichtounis Dreme, ii. 277, 278
Liddell, Henry George (1811–1898), xii. 333, 487
Liddesdale, xii. 4, 19
Liddon, Henry Parry (1829–1890), xii. 254, 273, 454, 457, 458, 462
Lidia, in *The Great Duke of Florence*, vi. 156, 158, 163, 164

Lidius, in *The Lovers Progress*, VI. 131
Liebermann, Felix, XIV. 494
Liège, II. 80 ff.
Lien Chi Altangi, X. 206, 207
Lieven, princess, XIV. 115, 172
Life, in *Death and Life*, II. 40
Life, king of, in *The Pride of Life*, V. 2
Life (lady Anima), in *Piers the Plowman*, II. 19, 21, 22, 28
Life, in *The Playe of Playes and Pastimes*, VI. 391
Life in London (Catnach's), XIV. 227
Life in Paris, XIV. 225
Life of James the Second, IX. 213; X. 295
Liggan Waters, The, IX. 363
Light Green, The, XIV. 206
'Light Within,' the, VIII. 105, 110, 112
Lightfoot, John (1602–1675), VII. 319, 482, 490
Lightfoot, Joseph Barber (1828–1889), XII. 298, 340, 468, 501
Lighthall, William Douw, XIV. 582
Lightwood, James T., XIII. 544
Ligon, Richard, *History of Barbadoes*, XI. 280
Lilburne, John (1614?–1657), VII. 456, 458, 459, 509; VIII. 75
Lilius Giraldus, II. 160
Lilley, Alfred Leslie, XIV. 601
Lilliburlero, X. 233
Lillie, Charles (*fl.* 1725), IX. 56
Lilliput, IX. 104, 128
Lilliput, Account of the state of learning in the Empire of, IX. 132
Lilliputian Magazine, The, XI. 376
Lillo, George (1693–1739), VII. 176; X. 68, 73 ff., 92, 436
  Arden of Feversham, X. 78, 84
  Britannia and Batavia, X. 78
  Christian Hero, The, X. 77
  Elmerick, or Justice Triumphant, X. 78
  Fatal Curiosity, X. 77, 79, 80, 83, 84, 414, 429
  London Merchant, or The History of George Barnwell, IX. 163; X. 73 ff., 78 ff., 84
  Marina, X. 78
  Silvia, X. 73
Lilly, William (1602–1681), VII. 357, 369, 394, 446, 447, 501, 509; *Observations*, VII. 207, 510
Lilly, W. S., XII. 459; XIII. 492
Lily, William (1468?–1522), III. 11, 13, 14, 67, 72, 429, 468, 552; IV. 322; VII. 335; *Eton Latin Grammar*, II. 367; III. 12; *Latin Syntax*, VII. 332; IX. 384
Limber Magna, Lincolnshire, I. 343
Limborch, Philip van, VIII. 330
Limerick, X. 293; XIII. 364; XIV. 127, 311
'Limerick,' the, XIII. 163
Linacre, Thomas (1460?–1524), II. 367; III. 2, 3, 5, 6, 7, 11, 12, 13, 15, 20, 158, 468, 469, 532; IV. 428; *Grammar*, III. 158
Linche or Lynche, Richard (*fl.* 1596–1601), *Diella*, III. 256, 266, 523
Lincke, O., XIII. 465
Lincoln, II. 49, 57, 116, 307, 341, 344, 348, 358; IV. 190, 224, 228, 369, 382, 422, 428; V. 39, 48, 50, 56; VII. 280, 338; X. 387; XII. 180, 329, 330, 340, 507
Lincoln, Abraham, IV. 50
Lincoln, countess of. *See* Lacy, Margaret de
Lincoln, earl of. *See* Clinton, Henry Fiennes
Lincoln, earl of, the mad lord, VIII. 380
Lincoln castle, in *Havelok*, I. 351
Lincoln cathedral, VII. 28
Lincoln grammar school, IV. 275
Lincolnshire, V. 30, 32, 33; VI. 82; VII. 330; XIII. 23, 46; XIV. 101
Lincolnshire, Rebellion in (1470), II. 302, 482
Lincus, in *The Queenes Arcadia*, VI. 318
Lindelöf, I. 132
Lindesay or Lindsay, Robert, of Pitscottie (1500?–1565?), *The Historie and Cronicles of Scotland*, II. 285; III. 147, 148, 504
Lindisfarne, I. 5, 83, 86, 89; XII. 10
Lindisfarne Gospels, The, I. 14, 72, 132
Lindley, John (1799–1865), XIV. 290, 562
Lindsay, lady Anne. *See* Barnard, lady Anne
Lindsay, James Ludovic, earl of Crawford (1847–1914), XII. 521; XIV. 541
Lindsay, lord, in Scott's *Abbot*, XII. 27
Lindsay family, XI. 231
Lindsays of Balcarres, the, XII. 377
Lindsey, Theophilus (1723–1808), X. 380, 519
Lingard, John (1771–1851), VII. 356; XIV. 52 ff., 71, 492; *Antiquities of the Anglo-Saxon Church*, XIV. 53; *History of England*, XIV. 53 ff.; *Vindication, A*, XIV. 54
Linger, Sir John, in Swift's *Complete Collection of... Conversation*, IX. 107
Linlathen, IX. 328
Linley, Elizabeth Anne, afterwards Mrs Sheridan (1754–1792), X. 88
Linley, Thomas (1732–1795), X. 265
Linlithgow, III. 123; IX. 552
Linnaean society, XIV. 287, 566
Linnaean system, XIV. 287, 290
Linnaeus (Carl Linné), X. 135; XIV. 287
Linnell, John (1792–1882), XI. 432
Linschoten, John Huighhen van, IV. 78, 460
Linskill, Mary (1840–1891), XIII. 563
Linton, in Emily Brontë's *Wuthering Heights*, XIII. 411
Linton, A., IV. 459
Linton, Elizabeth Lynn (born Lynn) (1822–1898), XIII. 563; XIV. 198
Linton, Kent, X. 249
Linton, William James (1812–1898), XII. 424; XIII. 186, 505; *A Dream*, XIII. 187; *Epicurean*, XIII. 187
Lintot, Barnaby Bernard (1675–1736), IX. 162, 445, 446; XI. 318, 320 ff., 327, 335, 471; *Miscellaneous Poems and Translations*, IX. 70, 160; XI. 320; *Monthly Catalogue*, XI. 339

Lintot, Henry (1703–1758), xi. 323
Linwood, William (1817–1878), xii. 487
Linz, iv. 163
Lion and the Mouse, in Henryson's *Fables*, ii. 246
'Lion of the fold of Judah, The,' xiv. 329
Lion, The book of the, ii. 160, 161
Lionardi, Alessandro, *Dialogi della Inventione Poetica*, ix. 60
Lionel, duke of Clarence, son of Edward III (1338–1368), ii. 156, 170
Lionel, Sir, ii. 414
Lipscomb, George (1773–1846), xii. 511
Lipsius, Justus, iv. 248, 250, 260; vi. 9; vii. 261, 315
Lisbon, x. 35, 91, 466; xi. 155, 156
Lisbon inquisition, iii. 16
Liskeard, x. 306
Lisle, William (1569?–1637), i. 123, 442; ix. 536
Lismahago, captain, in Smollett's *Humphrey Clinker*, x. 38, 43
Lismore's Book, the Dean of, x. 488
Lisobeta, in *The Decameron*, xii. 82
Lissoy, in Westmeath, x. 196, 209, 212
List of goods for Sale, viii. 99
Lister, Joseph Lister, lord, xiii. 213
Lister, Martin (1638?–1712), ix. 139, 478
Lister, Thomas Henry (1800–1842), *Granby*, xii. 247, 450
Litany, the, iii. 30 ff.; vi. 407
Litchfield, William (d. 1447), ii. 497
Literary club, x. 91, 181, 207
Literary Garland, The, xiv. 360
Literary Gazette, The, xii. 348, 523; xiv. 177, 199
Literary Journal, The, xii. 301
Literary Magazine, x. 177, 181, 203, 463, 466
Literary Miscellany (Ollier's), xii. 74
Literature of dissent, the (1660–1760), x. Add.
Lithgow, William (1582–1645?), ix. 366, 555
Lithuanians, rebel, in *Brennoralt*, vi. 238
Little, A. G., *Grey Friars at Oxford*, i. 209, 210. *See, also*, Add. to third impression
Little, Richard, *Mercurius Academicus*, vii. 351
Little Easton, Essex, viii. 307
Little Endians, ix. 229
Little Gidding, iv. 406, 548; vii. 32, 34, 153 ff.; xiii. 435
Little Gidding story books, vii. 154, 427
Little Horkesley, Essex, vii. 58
Little John, in legend of Robin Hood, ii. 110, 402; v. 35, 108; xii. 3
Little Leighs park, Essex, viii. 268, 269
Little Musgrave and Lady Barnard, ii. 412
Little Pretty Pocket Book, xi. 376
Little Sister, in Thackeray's *Adventures of Philip*, xiii. 288, 299
Little Sodbury, iii. 39
Littlebury, Isaac, vii. 451
Littledale, H., xiii. 477
Littlemore, Oxfordshire, xii. 260, 261
Littleton, Adam (1627–1694), ix. 527
Littleton, Edward John, 1st baron Hatherton (1791–1863), xiv. 323
Littleton, Sir Thomas (1402–1481), ii. 497; viii. 315; *Tenures*, viii. 314, 317, 466
Littlewit, in *Bartholomew Fayre*, vi. 23
Litton, Edward Arthur, xii. 472
Lively, Edward (1545?–1605), vii. 317
Liverpool, xi. 338; xiii. 89, 103, 348, 372 xiv. 115, 122, 134, 414
Liverpool, earl of. *See* Jenkinson, Robert Banks
Liverpool, University college, xiv. 432
Liverpool Athenaeum, xi. 435
Liverpool Courant, The, xiv. 169
Lives of the English Saints, xiv. 83
Livia, in *Women beware Women*, vi. 78
Livia (Lyly's), iii. 346
Livingston, Luther S., xii. 434
Livingstone, Christian, vii. 253
Livingstone, David (1813–1873), xiii. 553; xiv. 253, 375, 552, *also see* Add. 8
Livingstone, Guy, in Lawrence's novel, xiii. 436
Livingstone, James, 1st earl of Callander (d. 1674), ix. 556
Livingstone, John (1603–1672), ix. 546
Livingstone, Michael (*fl.* 1680), ix. 556
Livio, in *The Fancies*, vi. 193, 194
Livy, iii. 131, 156, 164, 314, 337, 429, 432; iv. 1, 4, 6, 13, 15, 438; vi. 49, 182, 225; x. 119, 197; xii. 493; xiv. 91, 98, 106
Lizie Wan, ii. 412
Llanbedr, xii. 440
Llandaff, iv. 421; ix. 540
Llangattock, vii. 37
Llangynwyd, x. 386, 387
Llansantffread, vii. 37, 42
Llongborth (viz. Portsmouth), i. 250
Lloyd, Charles (1735–1773), x. 399, 523, 526
Lloyd, Charles (1775–1839), xi. 413, 417; xii. 187, 419, 434, 436, 438; xiv. 184; *Blank Verse, by Charles Lloyd and Charles Lamb*, xii. 184; *Edmund Oliver*, xii. 185; *Nugae Canorae*, xii. 194
Lloyd, David (1635–1692), ix. 493; *Statesmen and Favourites of England*, iv. 54
Lloyd, Edward (1745), xi. 78
Lloyd, Edward (1815–1890), xiv. 192, 193, 534
Lloyd, Lodowick (*fl.* 1573–1610), iii. 189
Lloyd, Lucy C., xiv. Add. 8
Lloyd, Pierson, x. 394
Lloyd, Robert (1733–1764), x. 394, 395, 455, 524
Lloyd, Robert, xii. 181, 185, 193
Lloyd, William (1627–1717), viii. 297; ix. 196, 329, 335, 527
Lloyd's Illustrated London Newspaper, xiv. 192
Lloyd's Weekly London Newspaper, xiv. 192, 530, 533, 534
Lloyd's Weekly Newspaper, xiv. 192, 193

Lluð and Llevelys, I. 252
Lluelyn, Martin (1616–1682), IV. 497
Llwyd, Humphrey (1527–1568), III. 531; IV. 436, 445
Llwyd, Morgan (1619–1659), IX. 514
Llwynllwyd, X. 386
Llŷr, I. 252, 255. *See, also*, Lear
Llywarch Hen (496?–646?), I. 248, 249, 275, 461
Llywelyn, in Mannyng, I. 351
Llywelyn, prince of Wales, I. 180
Llywelyn ap Gruffuð (d. 1282), I. 263
Lobb, Stephen (d. 1699), X. 377, 386
Lobb, Theophilus (1678–1763), X. 385
Lobban, John Hay, XI. 473; XIII. 476
Lobeira, Vasco de, IV. 445; *Amadis of Gaul*, XI. 422
L'Obel, Matthias de, IV. 374
Löber, Valentine, IV. 266
Lobo, Jerome, X. 160, 179, 460
Locabara, X. 237
Local Education authorities, XIV. 433
Locher, Jacob, III. 59, 60
Lochlee, IX. 372
Lochleven castle, XII. 27
Lochlin, king of, X. 231
Lochmaben Gate, IX. 377
Lochnagar, XII. 31
Locke, Alton, Kingsley's, XIII. 156, 160
Locke, John (1632–1704), VII. 266, 300, 301, 396; VIII. 295, 328–348 (main entry), 367, 372, 384, 472 ff., *also see* Add.; IX. 61, 146, 150, 159, 180, 181, 233, 279, 282, 283, 286, 287, 292, 293, 297 ff., 301, 314, 331, 388, 390, 406, 412, 569, 574; X. 122, 296, 324 ff., 332, 342 ff., 347 ff., 350, 378, 379, 385; XI. 22, 57, 65, 136; XIV. 8, 17, 41, 43, 383, 384, 391 ff., 397, 399, 405, 421, 428, 461, 472, 473
  Commentary on the Pauline epistles, VIII. 332
  Common-Place Book, VIII. 344
  Conduct of the Understanding, The, VIII. 332, 346; IX. 400
  Discourse on Miracles, VIII. 332
  Epistola de Tolerantia, VIII. 330, 331
  Essay concerning Human Understanding, VIII. 328, 330 ff., 336, 346, 347; IX. 58, 282, 285, 290, 393, 400, 401, 411; XIV. 16, 48
  Examination of Father Malebranche's Opinion of Seeing all things in God, An, VIII. 332
  Further Considerations on Value of Money, VIII. 332, 344
  Letter on Toleration, First, VIII. 344
  Letter on Toleration, Second, VIII. 331
  Letter on Toleration, Third, VIII. 331
  Letter on Toleration, fragment of a fourth, VIII. 332
  Letter to the Bishop of Worcester, VIII. 331
  Letters on Toleration, X. 372
  Reasonableness of Christianity, The, VIII. 332; IX. 289, 290
Locke, John
  Some Considerations of the Consequences of the Lowering of Interest, VIII. 332, 344
  Some Thoughts concerning Education, VII. 341; VIII. 332, 346; IX. 396 ff.; XIV. 396
  Two Treatises of Government, VIII. 331, 341
  Vindication, A, VIII. 332
Locke, Matthew (1630?–1677), *Psyche*, VIII. 135
Locke, owner of Norbury Park, X. 261
Locker, John (1693–1760), IX. 529
Locker-Lampson, Frederick (1821–1895), XII. 121; XIII. 505, 558
  London Lyrics, XIII. 163
  My Guardian Angel, XIII. 165
  My Neighbour Rose, XIII. 165
  Our Photographs, XIII. 165
  Patchwork, XIII. 163, 164
  To My Grandmother, XIII. 164
Lockhart, Charles Stewart Montgomery XII. 380
Lockhart, George (1673–1731), IX. 493
Lockhart, John Gibson (1794–1854), IV. 45; XI. 166, 305, 410, 419, 437, 439, 440, 459, *also see* Add.; XII. 2, 7, 10, 19, 20, 26, 28, 153, 154, 156 ff., 161 ff., 372, 373, 376, 377, 380, 384, 425, 429, 430, 433, 449, *also see* Add. 2; XIII. 25, 207, 353, 434, 477, 563; XIV. 233, 313, 327, 491, 504
  History of Napoleon, XIV. 106
  History of the late War, XIV. 106
  Life of Scott, XIV. 106, 278
  Peter's Letters to his Kinsfolk, XII. 158
  Valerius, XIII. 419
Lockhart, John Hugh, XII. 375, 376
Lockhart, Laurence William Maxwel (1831–1882), XIII. 563
Lockhart, Milton, XII. 430
Lockier, Lionel, VII. 518
Lockit, in Gay's *Beggar's Opera*, IX. 163
Lockwood, in Emily Brontë's *Wuthering Heights*, XIII. 411
Lockwood, Edward, XIV. 598
Lockwood, Sir Frank (1846–1897), XIII. 544
Lockyer, Sir Norman, XIII. 477
Lockyer, Winifred L., XIII. 477
Locrine, V. 84 ff., 129, 146, 152, 236, 238 ff., 398, 417, 442, 443
Loda, spirit of, X. 228, 229
Lodge, Thomas (1558?–1625), I. 298; III. 114, 198, 249, 251, 256, 261, 262, 265, 299, 340, 342, 350, 351, 355, 358, 363, 367, 370, 526, 534; IV 2, 6, 24, 25, 86, 116 ff., 121, 122, 139, 318, 437, 440, 444, 470, 471, 473, 516, 517, 519, 521, 523, 528; V. 71, 85, 121–141 (main entry), 322, 353, 371, 420, 431; VI. 40, 249, 250, 378, 409, 494; IX. 275
  Alarum against Usurers, An, III. 363; IV. 317, 512; VI. 392
  Barginet of Antimachus, VII. 2
  Defence of Poetry, Music and Stage-Playes, A, VI. 389, 391, 401

Lodge, Thomas
Euphues Shadow, III. 350; V. 139
'Fatall starre that at my birthday shined, The,' IV. 116
Fig for Momus, A, IV. 180, 328, 329; V. 139; XII. 515
Forbonius and Prisceria, III. 358; V. 139
Honest Excuses, VI. 379
'Like desart woods,' IV. 116
Looking Glasse for London and England, A, V. 134, 139
Margarite of America, III. 358; IV. 77, 118; V. 139
'My bonnie Lasse thine eie,' IV. 117
Phyllis, III. 262, 523; IV. 116, 118; V. 139
Prosopopeia, IV. 357
Robert, Second Duke of Normandy, Surnamed Robin the Divell, V. 139
Rosalynde, III. 355, 358; IV. 77, 118; V. 139, 193, 220; VI. 365, 389
Scillaes Metamorphosis, V. 139, 140
Seneca, IX. 265
Tragical Complaynt of Elstred, The, III. 198; V. 239
William Longbeard, III. 367; V. 139
Wounds of Civill War, The, V. 139; VI. 19
Lodovico, in *The White Divel*, VI. 176, 177
Lodowick, in *Edward III*, V. 244
Lodowick, in *The Gratefull Servant*, VI. 204
Loe, William (d. 1645), VII. 407
Lofft, Capel, the younger (1806–1873), XIII. 505
Lofsong of ure Lefdi, On, I. 232, 458
Lofsong of ure Louerde, On, I. 233, 459
Loftus, Adam (1533?–1605), archbishop of Armagh and Dublin, III. 426
Loftus, Smyth, *Reply to the Reasonings of Mr Gibbon*, X. 308, 507
Lofty, in *The Good-Natur'd Man*, X. 211, 212
Logan, George (1678–1755), IX. 561, 562
Logan, James (1794?–1872), XII. 511; *Clans of the Scottish Highlands*, XII. 350; *The Scottish Gael*, XII. 350
Logan, John (1748–1788), IX. 557; XI. 442, 444; *Braes of Yarrow, The*, XI. 244; *Cuckoo, The*, XI. 244; *Runnamede*, XI. 244
Logan, Sir Robert, of Restalrig (d. 1606), IX. 551
Logan Water, IX. 363
Logan Water, XI. 235
Logic, in *The Passetyme of Pleasure*, II. 225
Logic, Bob, in Egan's *Life in London*, XIV. 223, 224, 226, 230
Logic land, in *The Pilgrimage to Parnassus*, VI. 310
Logie, Margaret, II. 129
Logres, in Arthurian legend, I. 279
Lohenstein, Daniel Caspar von, III. 348
Loir, river, X. 282; XIV. 302
Lok or Lock, Henry (1553?–1608?), III. 523; IV. 159; *Sundrie Sonets of Christian Passions*, III. 271
Lok, Michael (*fl.* 1615), IV. 82, 84, 459
Loliée, Frédéric, XIII. 567
Lollards, I. 364, 371; II. 40, 43, 47, 49, 53, 57, 62, 63, 66 ff., 162, 288, 289, 290, 292 ff., 348, 422, 441 ff.; III. 25, 26, 45; XIV. 83
Lollards, An Apology for the, II. 49
Lollards, poems against, II. 443, 502
Lollio, in Hall's *Virgidemiarum*, IV. 331
Lollius, in Chaucer's *Troilus and Criseyde*, II. 172
Lomas, Mrs S. C., VII. 189, 190, 434
Lomazzo, G. P., IV. 445
Lombard, Peter (c. 1100–1164), Master of the Sentences, I. 201, 211, 212; II. 46, 350, 365, 366, 371; *Sentences*, I. 208; II. 350, 365; III. 50, 400; VII. 405
Lombards, the, V. 24, 248
Lombards, the, in *Confessio Amantis*, II. 148
Lombardy, VIII. 245; XII. 63
Lombart, Pierre (1620?–1681), VII. 487
Londesborough, XII. 509
London, II. 302, 318, 320, 322, 496, 505, 508; III. 3, 15, 18, 40, 63, 71, 183, 213, 244, 267, 316, 317, 321, 330, 359 ff., 367 ff., 371, 379, 381 ff., 386, 393, 395, 396, 399, 406, 427, 436, 440; IV. 3, 76, 80 ff., 98, 106, 151, 154 ff., 161, 168, 190, 191, 198, 202 ff., 207, 224, 233, 243, 253, 255, 292, 293, 300, 310, 311, 316 ff., 321, 323 ff., 327, 328, 334, 338, 341 ff., 349, 360 ff., 378 ff., 402, 407 ff., 424 ff., 514 ff., 531 ff., 544 ff.; V. 30, 35, 38, 44, 57, 68 ff., 80, 104, 110, 128, 134, 139, 143, 166, 169 ff., 248, 253 ff., 290, 293, 306, 310, 312, 316, 320 ff., 325, 330, 342, 353, 358, 361, 366 ff., 371, 376, 378; VI. 4, 13, 15, 16, 23, 27, 28, 50, 52 ff., 60, 72, 92, 104, 107, 110, 134, 135, 141, 149, 151, 196, 201, 211, 220, 233, 242, 243, 249 ff., 259 ff., 281, 323, 330 ff., 345, 362, 365, 376, 378, 381 ff., 386 ff., 397 ff., 400; VII. 6, 7, 9, 54, 78, 88, 91, 98, 120, 151, 157, 183, 188, 190, 200, 201, 227, 230, 283, 284, 286, 287, 289, 305, 314, 322, 343, 346, 348, 379, 380, 383, 437, 453; VIII. 3 ff., 12, 37, 53, 60, 81, 83, 89, 94, 108, 113, 117, 118, 122, 127, 134, 160, 170, 180, 182, 187, 190, 210, 247, 249, 250, 263, 265, 286, 297, 301, 302, 305, 329, 330, 333, 363, 373, 377; IX. 3, 6, 11, 24, 26, 27, 31 ff., 36, 43, 44, 46, 51, 52, 57, 58, 62, 64, 65, 67, 94 ff., 112, 120, 126, 129 ff., 146, 149, 153, 160, 170, 194, 202, 212, 213, 215, 220, 234, 240, 246, 249, 256, 261 ff., 277, 280 ff., 290, 331, 336, 345, 353, 354, 357, 359, 363, 369, 394, 406, 537, 539; X. 2, 21, 23, 28, 35, 36, 39, 42, 77, 87, 94, 120, 149, 157, 160, 161, 169, 182, 192, 193, 200, 237, 261, 262, 276 ff., 296, 303, 305, 307, 311, 312, 323, 324, 344, 356, 358, 375 ff., 382, 385 ff., 391, 394, 404, 408, 409, 460; XI. 37, 44, 58, 59, 80, 81, 96, 104, 130, 133, 148, 156, 181, 195, 263 ff., 270 ff.,

London
278, 283, 286, 315, 325, 338, 340 ff., 346, 360, 363; xii. 18, 31, 32, 37, 38, 57, 81, 142, 150, 164, 166, 167, 169, 172, 181, 203, 232, 234, 290, 291, 310, 323, 325, 329, 341, 347, 349, 511; xiii. 5, 12, 14, 18, 20, 55, 72, 77, 84, 107, 142, 202, 216, 259, 260, 266, 295, 325, 357, 358, 373, 383, 384, 409, 423, 455, 458; xiv. 13, 23, 34, 77, 91, 100, 101, 119, 167 ff., 173, 177, 179, 186, 189, 193, 195, 199, 202 ff., 206, 213 ff., 217, 220, 225, 252, 257, 263, 279, 293, 295, 298, 311, 312, 323, 327, 332, 344, 346, 362, 369, 373, 406, 407, 410
Adelphi, the, xi. 362
Aldermanbury, vi. 278
Aldermary churchyard, xi. 373
Aldersgate, iv. 399; vii. 100
Aldgate, Chaucer's house in, ii. 157, 158
All Hallows, Lombard street, iii. 57
Angel sign, xi. 335
Antelope, sign of the, iv. 389
Antiquities, xii. 507, 513
Arcade (the New Exchange), viii. 138
Arches, court of, iv. 426
Arlington street, x. 243, 246
Artillery garden, vi. 89
Artillery row, vii. 107
Axe yard, Westminster, viii. 254
Baldwin's gardens, xiv. 404
Bankside, Southwark, vi. 111, 255, 258, 259, 261; x. 201
Barbican, vii. 103, 116
Barbican chapel, x. 381
Bartholomew fair, ix. 263
Bedford college, xiv. 429
Bedlam, vi. 172; viii. 186
Bell, the, Gracechurch street, vi. 251
Bell Savage, the, Ludgate hill, vi. 251
Berkeley square, x. 246, 248
Bible, sign, xi. 332
Billingsgate, iii. 371; iv. 361; vii. 130; viii. 95, 372; ix. 257, 263, 272
Birkbeck college, xiv. 408
Birkbeck schools, xiv. 414, 415
Bishopsgate, vi. 251; ix. 263
Bishopsgate street, ix. 393, 471
Black Boy, sign, xi. 335
Blackfriars, vi. 251, 257, 352; viii. 118; xi. 330
Blackfriars bridge, x. 179, 467
Black Swan, Tower street, viii. 208
Blue Coat school. *See* Christ's hospital
Bolt court, x. 187
Bolton row, xi. 345
Bond street, xiv. 223
Bow, vii. 339
Bow street, viii. 34, 199; xii. 128; xiv. 188
Brainford, iv. 361
Bread street, vii. 96, 107
Bread street, the Mermaid, iv. 90, 91
Brick court, x. 212
British museum, iii. 190; iv. 117, 429; ix. 11, 124, 234; x. 95, 131, 253, 295;

London
xi. 295; xii. 200, 339, 340, 342, 345 ff., 356, 368, 372, 382, 521, 523; xiii. 54, 140, 455, 483, 486, 507, 531, 555, 571, 572; xiv. 51, 80, 87, 153, 226, 281, 284, 285, 295, 524, 539, 558, 560, 566, 580, 610
Broad street, Golden square, xi. 433
Bromley-St-Leonard, vii. 339
Bryanstone square, xiii. 295
Buckingham palace, viii. 358; xiv. 415
Bunhill fields, vii. 107; ix. 25
Burlington gardens, ix. 163
Burlington house, xiv. 281, 287
Calf's Head club, vii. 124
Camberwell, xiii. 51
Camden town, xiii. 305
Cannon street, vii. 334
Caversham house, iv. 143
Chancery lane, vi. 354; vii. 250; xii. 187
Channel row, ix. 146
Chapel Royal, the, v. 122
Chapel street, xii. 184
Chapter coffeehouse, xi. 325
Charing Cross, vii. 513; viii. 409; ix. 146, 260
Charles street, xi. 142
Charterhouse, the, v. 17; viii. 26, 38, 193, 292, 403; ix. 45; x. 364; xiv 222, 422
Charterhouse school, vii. 24, 33, 338, 492
Cheapside, iii. 371; v. 9, 366; vi. 330; vii. 96, 382; xi. 332, 402
Chelsea, vii. 310; ix. 126, 132; x. 39; xiii. 10, 440
Chelsea, college at, iii. 391; iv. 424
Chelsea physic garden, xiv. 286
Chester's inn, Strand, ii. 206
Cheyne row, xiii. 10, 21
Cheyne walk, xiii. 372
Chiswick mall, xiii. 276
Christ church, vii. 361
Christ's hospital (Blue Coat school), iii. 327; vii. 143, 326, 337, 492; viii. 450; xi. 118; xii. 181, 183, 434
Clapham, x. 385
Clarges street, xi. 345, 359
Clerkenwell, vi. 262; x. 385, 390; xiii. 457
Cleveland row, ix. 168
Clifford's inn, iv. 157; xiii. 449
Clink liberty, Southwark, the, vi. 254
Colebrook row, xii. 198
College street, x. 300
Colonial office, xiv. 109
Conduit close, vii. 336
Cork street, ix. 133
Cornhill, ix. 6; x. 116; xi. 141, 332, 335
Counter in the Poultrey, the, vi. 51
Coutts old bank, Strand, vii. 363
Covent garden, vii. 246; viii. 34, 172, 218; ix. 160, 348; xi. 333, 336; xii. 187, 194
Cripplegate, vi. 251, 253, 258
Crosbie house, vi. 84

London
Cross Keys inn, Gracechurch street, VI. 247, 251
Cross Keys, sign, XI. 320
Crown inn, Islington, X. 212
Crown Office row, XII. 181
Curtain close, VI. 253
Curtain road, Shoreditch, VI. 251, 253
Denmark house, VI. 103
Devereux court, XI. 376
Devil tavern, XI. 326
Devil tavern, Temple Bar, Apollo room in, VI. 6; VII. 3
Doctors' Commons, IX. 139; XIII. 305, 327
Dog tavern, VII. 5
Dover street, IX. 132; XI. 348
Downing street, VIII. 253; X. 36
Drury lane, VI. 262; IX. 63; XI. 327
Duck lane, XI. 325, 331
Dulwich college, XII. 336
Dulwich gallery, XIII. 52
Earl street, XIV. 226
East India house, XII. 183, 192, 198, 200
Essex street, XII. 279
Eyebright, IV. 361
Fetter lane, XII. 181
Finsbury, XIV. 326
Finsbury fields, VI. 251 ff., 255, 257
Finsbury pavement, XII. 79
Finsbury square, XI. 337
Fire, the Great, IV. 433; VIII. 9, 10, 11, 249, 253, 320
Fish lane, IX. 263
Fish-market, the Old, II. 35
Fish street hill, X. 201
Fishmongers' company, IV. 386
Fleet, the, X. 393, 395
Fleet prison, the, II. 209; III. 175, 389; V. 140, 320; VII. 197, 199; IX. 139; XIII. 322
Fleet street, II. 159; III. 371; IV. 390, 398; VI. 218; VII. 61, 120, 250; X. 206, 207, 397; XI. 323, 339; XII. 188, 205; XIV. 185
Fleet street, sign of the Sun in, III. 194
Fleet tavern, the, V. 321
Flesh-shambles, the, II. 35
Free-masons hall, XI. 402
Freemasons' tavern, XIV. 287
Fulham, X. 12; XII. 201
Fulwood rents, IX. 260
Furnival's inn, III. 15
Gatehouse prison, Westminster, VII. 24, 357; VIII. 258
Gerrard street, X. 212
Globe tavern, VII. 38
'Globe,' Paternoster row, XI. 323
Gloucester place, XIII. 70
Goldsmiths' alley, VII. 335
Goldsmiths' company, IV. 184
Goldsmiths' row, Cheapside, V. 366; VII. 4
Gore house, XIV. 322
Gough square, X. Add.
Gower street, XIV. 290, 411

London
Gracechurch street, VI. 247, 251
Gray's inn, III. 202, 315; V. 58, 70, 71, 77, 78, 114, 219, 357, 367; VI. 112, 197, 356; VII. 21; VIII. 369; IX. 211, 220
Gray's-inn-gate, IX. 274
Gray's inn gateway, XI. 332
Great Coram street, XIII. 278
Great Eastern street, VI. 251
Great George street, IX. 246
Great Portland street, XIV. 226
Great St Andrew street, XIV. 227
Green Arbour court, X. 204
Greenstreet house, East Ham, IV. 412
Gresham college, III. 426; VII. 309, 320; VIII. 61, 249, 355, 365; IX. 385, 386, 390, 530, 573; XIV. 284
Grosvenor chapel, IX. 246
Guildhall, III. 324
Gunpowder alley, VII. 24
Guy's hospital, XIII. 53
Hackney, IX. 393; XII. 184
Hammersmith, XIII. 120, 128
Hampstead, IX. 133; X. 212
Hanson street, IX. 166
Haymarket, X. 87
Heralds' college, VII. 207
Hickford's dancing-room, IX. 483
Highgate, VI. 341; XI. 121; XII. 201; XIII. 112
Highgate academy, X. 385
Hill street, X. 262; XI. 348, 350
Holborn, VI. 168; VII. 104; X. 191; XI. 329, 332; XII. 183
Holywell lane, VI. 251
Holywell, priory of, VI. 251, 253
Homer's Head, Fleet street, XI. 323
Howard house, VII. 338
Hoxton, XIII. 457
Hoxton academy, XI. 43
Hoxton square academy, X. 385
Hyde park, XIII. 20
India office, Westminster VIII. 254; XII. 305; XIV. 14
India office library, XIV. 574
Inner Temple, IV. 157; V. 68, 70, 72, 73, 77; VI. 112, 356; VII. 221; VIII. 116, 142; IX. 51; XII. 180, 181, 183
Inner Temple lane, X. 207; XII. 191, 192
Inns of Court, III. 424; IV. 208; V. 368; VI. 218; VII. 62
Islington, IX. 261, 393; X. 207, 212; XII. 184, 196, 198, 200, 201
Islington academy, X. 385, 386
Jermyn street, XIII. 294
Jermyn street museum, XIV. 292, 294
Jewin street, X. 385
Kelmscott house, XIII. 128
Kennington, manor of, VI. 330
Kensington, XII. 331, 440, 444; XIII. 294, 300
Kensington gardens, IX. 483
Kent street, IX. 269
King's Bench prison, XIV. 217
King's college, XII. 290; XIII. 355; XIV. 82, 411, 429

London
Kingsland, VIII. 253
Knightrider street, IV. 398
Knightsbridge, VIII. 211
Lambeth, IV. 422, 424; XI. 189, 432; XII. 507, 508; XIII. 457
Lambeth palace, X. 223, 498
Lambeth palace library, VIII. 463; XII. 367; XIV. 74, 79
Lant street, XIII. 305
Latine coffee-house, VII. 389
Leadenhall, III. 369; XII. 198, 200
Leadenhall street, XII. 183
Leathersellers' company, IV. 391
Leicester fields, XI. 333, 364
Limehouse, IV. 73, 99
Lincoln's inn, III. 15; IV. 199, 203, 219, 240; V. 273; VI. 404; VII. 46, 59, 226; VIII. 320, 369; X. 362; XII. 354; XIV. 251
Lincoln's inn fields, VI. 262; VII. 104; VIII. 150, 153, 195
Lindsay row, Chelsea, XIII. 372
Little Bartholomew's Well-yard, XI. 334
Little Britain, IV. 390; IX. 274; X. 385; XI. 331, 332, 335
Little Old Bailey, X. 204, 206
Little Queen street, XII. 183
Lombard street, XI. 330
London academy, X. 386
London bridge, IV. 390, 399, 546; VI. 330; VII. 339; VIII. 11; XI. 332, 335, 467
London institution, XII. 323
London library, XII. 519
London wall, IV. 418
Lower mews, XI. 333
Ludgate hill, VI. 251
Maiden lane, VI. 255
Mall, the, IX. 256, 263
Marshalsea, the, IV. 155, 156; XIII. 305, 331; XIV. 194
Marylebone gardens, IX. 369
Mechanics' institution, XIV. 408, 415
Mercers' company, III. 11, 12
Mercers' school, the, VII. 332
Merchant Taylors' school, III. 213, 428, 435; IV. 238; V. 102, 116, 122, 156; VI. 196, 221, 246, 288; VII. 326, 334, 335, 493; XIV. 422
Mermaid tavern, VI. 1, 5, 112; VIII. 322; XII. 89
Middle Temple, the, IV. 80, 141; V. 220; VI. 37, 188; VII. 16; VIII. 146, 464; X. 23; XI. 2; XIII. 277
Miles's coffee-house in Palace-yard, VII. 389
Milk street, II. 307
Mitre court buildings, XII. 187
Monmouth court, XIV. 227
Monmouth house, X. 39
Moorfields, IX. 25, 260; X. 385, 386
Moorfields academy, X. 384
Moorgate, VI. 251
Mulberry gardens, VIII. 9, 138
Munimenta Gildhallae Londoniensis (*Liber custumarum*), II 428
National gallery, XIV. 154, 238

London
National Portrait gallery, XIV. 89
New Bond street, XI. 323, 332
New Exchange, Strand, VII. 363; VIII. 6, 138
Newgate (prison), II. 336; IV. 156, 381; V. 54; VI. 330
Newgate, IX. 2, 9, 10, 30, 163, 263, 272; X. 27, 351; XIV. 178, 228
Newington butts, VI. 58
Newington green, IX. 393
Old Bailey, XII. 279
Old Kensington palace, X. Add.
Onslow square, XIII. 294
Palace green, XIII. 300
Palace yard, VII. 389
Pall Mall, X. 266; XI. 323, 332, 333
Paper office, IX. 197
Paris garden, VI. 220, 255, 259, 383, 393, 402
Park lane, XIII. 295
Park street, VI. 256
Parliament, houses of, XII. 508
Parson's dock, IX. 257
Parson's green, X. 12
Paternoster row, II. 307; IV. 398; X. 201, 202; XI. 323, 325, 327, 332, 339; XII. 205
Paul's Cross, II. 288, 289, 302; III. 406; IV. 234, 235; VI. 375, 379, 386; VII. 146, 147
Peacock, sign, XI. 339
Pelican, sign, XI. 335
Pentonville, XII. 184, 186, 187, 194; XIV. 51
Petre house, Aldersgate, VII. 24
'Petty France,' or York street, VII. 104
Pewter Platter inn, XI. 329
Physicians, royal college of, III. 6, 107
Pimlico, IV. 362; XII. 365
Pinners' hall, X. 377
Pipe office, the, VI. 257
Poor Jewry lane, X. 381
Pope's Head alley, Cornhill, VI. 358; VII. 344
Portman square, X. 262
Poultry, VI. 51; XI. 326, 332
Primrose hill, XIII. 269
Prince's Arms, sign, XI. 318
Priory, the, Regent's park, XIII. 396
Pudding lane, VI. 358
Quaker's tavern, IX. 263
Queen-hive, IV. 361
Queen's college, XIII. 355; XIV. 429
Ram-alley, VI. 217, 219; IX. 268
Ranelagh, XI. 259, 352
Ranelagh house, X. 425
Record office, XIV. 87, 111
Red Lion square, XIII. 119
Red Pale, Westminster, sign of the, II. 312
Regent's park, XIV. 289
Rhenish tavern, IX. 146
Rolls chapel, IX. 195, 198
Ropemakers' alley, IX. 25; X. 385
Rota club and coffee-house, VII. 362, 389

London
Royal Caledonian asylum, XIII. 107
Royal Cockpit, the, XIV. 222
Royal college of surgeons, XIV. 286, 295
Royal Exchange, III. 395; VI. 83, 100, 300; IX. 49, 260; XI. 141, 327, 332
Royal institution, XII. 343; XIII. 369; XIV. 259 ff.
Rummer tavern, IX. 146
Russell street, VIII. 34; XI. 333; XII. 194, 198
St Andrew's, Holborn, IV. 141; VI. 168
St Augustine's, X. 377
St Bartholomew's hospital, VII. 361
St Clement Danes, IV. 237; IX. 195
St Dunstan's church, XII. 191
St Dunstan's churchyard, XI. 318
St Dunstan's in the West, IV. 143, 219; VII. 250
St Giles's in the Fields, VI. 30
St Giles without Cripplegate, VI. 258; VII. 107
St Giles, Cripplegate, IX. 6
St Helen's, II. 306
St James's, XIII. 269
St James's, court of, XIV. 348
St James's coffeehouse, IX. 247, 463, 471
St James's palace, VIII. 266; IX. 78, 249, 250, 331
St James's park, VIII. 7; XIV. 284
St James's street, XIII. 294
St John street, Clerkenwell, VI. 262
St John's, Westminster, X. 393
St Lawrence, Jewry, III. 15; VIII. 369
St Leonard's, Eastcheap, VII. 223
St Magnus, church of, XI. 467
St Margaret Pattens, X. 294
St Margaret's church, XII. 319
St Martin's, Ludgate, IV. 91
St Martin in the Fields, VIII. 250
St Martin's lane, VIII. 173
St Martin's vintry, VII. 355
St Mary's, Aldermanbury, VI. 278
St Mary's, Westminster, Chaucer's house at, II. 158
St Mary Overy, VI. 224
St Matthew's, Friday street, VII. 456
St Michael-le-Quern, Cheapside, VII. 232
St Mildred, Poultry, parish of, III. 183
St Olave's school, VII. 339
St Pancras, IX. 257
St Paul's cathedral, II. 208, 365, 367; III. 9, 11, 183; IV. 203, 204, 219, 225, 232, 240, 265, 320, 330, 332, 356, 366, 388, 398, 433, 546; V. 90, 122, 255, 367, 374; VI. 57, 84, 251; VII. 59, 82, 345, 458; VIII. 299, 304, 369; IX. 330, 343, 533; X. 358; XI. 332; XII. 271 ff., 319, 320, 477; XIII. 34, 260; XIV. 13, 403
St Paul's churchyard, III. 11; IV. 393, 398, 403; VII. 146; X. 205; XI. 318, 325, 331, 339, 376
St Paul's school, II. 489; III. 13, 428, 435; V. 58, 102, 125; VI. 40, 41, 246, 287, 288; VII. 96, 97, 326, 329, 332, 334; VIII. 253; IX. 573; X. 408; XIV. 422

London
St Paul's, Covent garden, VIII. 301
St Peter's, Cornhill, VIII. 301
St Saviour's church, Southwark, VI. 111, 144
St Saviour's school, Southwark, III. 428; VII. 339
St Stephen's, Westminster, II. 208
Salisbury court, X. 201
Salisbury court in Whitefriars, theatrical company at, VIII. 118
Salisbury square, X. 12
Salter's hall, X. 377, 379, 380
Savoy, the, VII. 63; VIII. 319
Savoy chapel, VII. 245, 246; VIII. 301
Savoy hospital, VIII. 249, 377
Savoy hospital, church of the, IV 156
'Saynt Magnus Corner,' IV. 399
Seething lane, VIII. 255
Seven Dials, XI. 469; XIV. 226, 227
Seven Stars, Strand, VII. 363
Shakespear's Head, sign, XI. 319, 320
Shoreditch, III. 316; VI. 251, 253
Sion college, IV. 418, 433
Skinner street, XII. 191
Smithfield, II. 422; VII. 304; IX. 263
Smyrna coffee-house, IX. 471
Snow hill, VII. 361
Soho square, X. 482
Somerset house, VI. 366; VII. 353; XIV 284
Somerset place, X. 266
South Audley street, IX. 246
South Kensington museum, XIV. 284, 285
South Molton street, XI. 432
Southampton buildings, XII. 187, 191
Southampton street, Camberwell, XIII. 51
South-Sea house, XII. 183, 195
Southwark, IV. 361, 374; VI. 111, 144, 247, 250, 254, 255; VII. 339; IX. 269
Spencer house, XII. 356
Spital, the, IV. 225; VII. 146
Spread Eagle, the, Bread street, Cheapside, VII. 96
Staining-lane, II. 35
Stationers' hall, III. 393, 397; IV. 170, 171, 180, 184
Stationers' register and court, III. Add.
Stepney, IV. 547
Stock exchange, XIV. 2
Stocks market, XI. 332
Stoke Newington, IX. 393
Strand, II. 206; IV. 202; V. 9, 366; VII. 38, 362; XI. 319, 323, 325, 332; XII. 181, 188
Stratford, VII. 339
Stratford-le-Bow school, VII. 339
Sun tavern, VII. 5
Surgeon's hall, X. 204
Swan tavern, XI. 328
Synagogue, the Great, St James's place, Aldgate, XI. 413
Taverns, VI. 101

London
Temple, the, III. 406; IV. 236, 237; VI. 218; VII. 83; X. 212, 358; XI. 79; XII. 183, 187, 194
Temple bar, XI. 326, 332
Temple church, VI. 38; VII. 197; VIII. 251, 304, 370; X. 215; XII. 191
Tenter alley, X. 384
Thames, the, II. 145, 233; III. 238, 380; IV. 72, 77, 177, 392, 532; VI. 252, 258; VII. 38, 59, 60, 334; VIII. 24
Thames embankment, IV. 418
Thames street, II. 156; V. 98
Thavies's inn, IV. 199
Threadneedle street, XI. 280
Three-legs, sign, XI. 332
Three Pigeons, sign, XI. 332
Tottenham Court road, XIII. 450; XIV. 229
Tottenham cross, IX. 403
Tower, the, III. 16, 17, 167, 176, 431; IV. 53, 57 ff., 103, 143, 181, 230, 425; VI. 90; VII. 203, 226, 254, 453; VIII. 36, 107, 111, 207, 253, 257, 259; IX. 175, 348, 356; X. 352; XII. 507, 509
Tower hill, VII. 224
Tower street, VIII. 208
Triple Tun tavern, VII. 5
Tully's Head, sign, XI. 323
Turk's Head coffee-house in Palace yard, VII. 362
Turk's Head inn, X. 215
Tuttle fields, III. 369
Tyburn, IV. 128, 381; VII. 2; VIII. 163; IX. 268; X. 351
University, XII. 350; XIV. 411, 412, 414, 417, 429, 430, 432
University college, XII. 297, 309, 335, 336; XIII. 53; XIV. 24, 290, 412, 426, 429
University College hospital, XIII. 107
Vauxhall gardens, XI. 352
Victoria and Albert museum, X. 263; XIII. 482, 483, 516, 530, 531; XIV. 539
Walpole house, XIII. 276
Walworth, XIII. 51
Wapping, XII. 362
Wapping academy, X. 385
Warwick lane, XI. 323
Watling street, V. 255
Well Close square, X. 384; XI. 452
Westminster, IX. 139, 146, 147, 397, 539; X. 29, 33, 351, 352, 393, 394, 397, 470; XII. 272, 275, 294, 411, 507, 513; XIV. 181
Westminster abbey, IX. 55, 153, 164, 532; X. 187, 232, 265; XI. 181; XII. 312, 319, 365, 383, 478, 508; XIII. 20, 84, 369; XIV. 222, 295
Westminster hall, IX. 160, 247; XI. 332, 467; XIV. 124
Westminster school, IX. 158, 188, 250, 333, 390, 405, 408 ff., 414, 483, 573; X. 300, 393; XI. 78, 83, 155, 157, 328, 421, 423; XII. 334; XIV. 225, 283, 386, 387, 422

London
White Horse tavern, Strand, VIII. 266
Whitefriars, VII. 349; VIII. 174; IX. 268
Whitefriars monastery, VI. 262
Whitehall, IV. 219; V. 64, 70, 253; VI. 36, 112, 237, 342, 348, 350, 351, 354, 356, 361, 404; VII. 1, 4, 5, 13, 16, 17, 20, 104, 215, 254, 264; VIII. 11, 115, 199, 206, 249, 268, 269, 358; IX. 215; X. 307
Williams library, VII. 29
Willis's rooms, XIII. 294
Will's coffee-house, VIII. 34, 159, 172, 212, 370, 376
Wimpole street, XIII. 70
Winchester house, VI. 356
Wine Office court, X. 206, 207
Wits' coffeehouse, IX. 263
Wood street, Cheapside, VII. 4
York buildings, Buckingham street, VIII. 258
York house, IV. 278
York street, XI. 336
York street, or 'Petty France,' VII. 104
Young street, XIII. 294
See, also, under Islington, Lambeth, Southwark, Westminster, etc.

London, XIV. 162
London, William (*fl.* 1658), VII. 480; VIII. 464; *Catalogue of the most vendible Books*, XI. 338, 470
London and the development of popular literature, IV. 316 ff., 514 ff.
London Chanticleer (1659), VII. 512
London Chronicle, III. 532; X. 177, 467
London Corresponding society, XIV. 121
London Cries, XI. 487
London Daily Chronicle, The, XIV. 193
London Evening Courier, The, XIV. 176
London Gazette, The, VII. 363, 364; IX. 1; XI. 333; XIV. 167
London Journal, IX. 221
London life, VI. 225, 226, 228
London Magazine, The, X. 192, 467, 474, 479; XI. 339; XII. 141, 160–161 (main entry), 171, 193, 195, 199, 200, 428; XIII. 4, 257, 465
London Magazine, The, or *Gentleman's Monthly Intelligencer*, XII. 428
London Magazine, The, and Monthly Chronologer, XII. 428
London merchant, a, in *A Woman will have her Will*, V. 329
London Missionary society, XIII. 51
London Monthly Miscellany, The, XIV. 149
London Packet, X. 474
London Post, IX. 432
London Prodigall, The, V. 236, 238, 254, 332; VI. 97
London Review, The, XII. 430, 440; XIV. 199
London Star, The, XI. 235
London theatres, XII. 508
Adelphi, XII. 171; XIII. 265, 270; XIV 224
Aquatic, XII. 171

London theatres
Astley's, xiv. 222, 224
Blackfriars, v. 256; vii. 59
Coburg, xii. 171
Cockpit, Drury lane, viii. 115, 116, 118, 180
Covent garden, x. 89, 91, 211, 212, 214, 425 ff., 444; xi. 244, 259 ff., 264, 273, 277, 278, 283, 448, 450 ff.; xii. 69, 171; xiii. 256, 258; xiv. 227, 319
Dorset garden, viii. 119, 182, 193; x. 70
Drury lane, viii. 134, 148, 150, 189, 400; x. 21, 40, 70, 73, 85, 87 ff., 91, 161, 167, 209, 212, 265, 425 ff.; xi. 258 ff., 263, 264, 271, 273, 277, 283, 304, 393, 402, 449 ff., 454 ff.; xii. 35, 171, 189, 194, 386, 390, 434; xiii. 256, 265, 514, 515; xiv. 334
Drury lane Theatre Royal, Covent garden (1663), viii. 119
Duke's, viii. 400
East London, xii. 171
Globe, v. 218, 242
Goodman's fields, x. 21, 427, 432, 440
Haymarket, viii. 162, 163; ix. 471; x. 21, 23, 426 ff., 444; xi. 259, 278, 279, 451, 452, 454; xii. 171; xiii. 256
King's, xii. 171
Lincoln's Inn fields, x. 426, 428, 430, 434, 436, 439, 440; xi. 258
Little theatre in the Haymarket, x. 23, 87; xi. 452
Lyceum, xii. 171; xiii. 513 ff.
Newington, v. 256
Olympic, xiv. 224
Portugal row, Lincoln's Inn fields, vi. 262; viii. 119, 152, 399
Prince of Wales's, xiii. 271
Red Bull playhouse, viii. 115; theatrical company at, viii. 118
Rose, v. 316
Royalty, xi. 452
Sadler's wells, viii. 184; xiii. 264
Salisbury court, Fleet street, viii. 119
Surrey, xii. 171; xiii. 264, 265
Whitefriars, v. 346; vi. 220, 251
Winter, xi. 452
London Topographical society, xii. 506
London and Westminster Review, xi. 398; xii. 430
Londonderry, viii. 122, 170; ix. 290
Long, Mrs Anne (1681?–1711), ix. 126, 456
Long, George (1800–1879), xii. 487, *also see* Add.; *Decline of the Roman Republic, The*, xii. 307, 335
Long, Kingsmill, translator of *Barclay His Argenis*, iv. 501
Long, loch, xi. 236
Long, Roger (1680–1770), *Life of Mohammed*, x. 281
Long Life, i. 228, 458
Long Meg of Westminster, in *Richard Casteler*, iii. 369, 487
Long Megg of Lincoln, ix. 268
Long parliament, the, iii. 397; iv. 299; vi. 235; vii. 6, 22, 24, 54, 206, 223, 224, 230, 285, 346, 440, 441, 456, 458; viii. 79, 80, 323; ix. 387; xi. 311
Longcastell (Lancaster), in *Wallace*, ii. 110
Longe, Julia G., ix. 92
Longfellow, Henry Wadsworth, i. 147; xiii. 245, 246; xiv. 365, 378; *Children of the Lord's Supper*, xiii. 244; *Evangeline*, xiii. 241, 244
Longford county, x. 195
Longing, the land of, in *Piers the Plowman*, ii. 25
Longinus, vii. 85, 316, 489; ix. 51, 59, 188, 527; x. 144; xii. 324; *On the Sublime*, v. 234
Longland, John (1473–1547), bishop of Lincoln, iii. 36, 38; iv. 228, 493, 494; *Tres Conciones*, iv. 226
Longleat, ix. 153, 443
Longleat Papers, ix. 147, 156, 443, 483. *See, also*, Bath, marquis of, *Papers*
Longman, Thomas (1699–1755), xi. 323
Longman, Thomas Norton (1771–1842), xi. 327
Longman and Rees, publishers, xii. 142
Longman's Magazine, xii. 427
Longmore, George, xiv. Add. 5
Longmuir, John (1803–1883), xii. 517
Longside, ix. 372
Long-tongue, in *The Disobedient Child*, v. 109
Longueville, Charles, viii. 62
Longueville, William (1639–1721), viii. 60, 62
Longus, iv. 438; vii. 489
Longwood, St Helena, xiii. 276
Looke about you, v. 35, 320, 328, 329, 476
Looking Glass for George Fox, ix. 307
Looking Glass for the Mind, xi. 382
Looking glasse for all proud, ambitious, covetous and corrupt Lawyers, A, vii. 388
Lope de Vega, *Don Lope de Cardona*, vi. 204; *El Mayordomo de la Duquesa de Amalfi*, vi. 180; *El Peregrino en su patria*, vi. 139
Lopes, Duarte, iv. 445
Lopez, in *The Merchant of Venice*, v. 181
Lopez, in *The Spanish Curate*, vi. 139
Lopez, Trollope's, xiii. 422
Lopez de Gomara, Francisco, *Istoria de las Indias y conquista de Mejico*, iv. 69
Lorain, P., xiii. 545
Loram, Charles Templeman, xiv. Add. 8
'Lord Fanny,' in Pope's *Imitations of Horace*, ix. 85, 251
Lord Governaunce, v. 58
Lord Love went maying, xiii. 133
Lord Lovel, ii. 412
Lord Maxwell's Last Good Night, ii. 413
Lord Randal, ii. 407, 412
Lord Thomas and Fair Annet, ii. 412
Lord's Prayer, xi. 368
Lord's Prayer, exposition on the, in *Speculum Christiani*, ii. 319
Lord's Prayer, Rolle, ii. 48

Lords, house of, III. 11; IV. 279; IX. 195, 251; X. 192, 246, 397; XI. 17, 29, 34, 79, 315, 328; XII. 32, 285
Loreau, Mme H., XIII. 550
Lorens, frère, I. 354
Lorenz, Theodor, XIV. 532
Lorenzo, in Keats's *Isabella*, XII. 86
Lorenzo, in *May Day*, III. 199
Lorenzo, in *The Bashful Lover*, VI. 152
Lorenzo, in *The Decameron*, XII. 82
Lorenzo, in *The Merchant of Venice*, V. 183
Lorenzo, in *The Spanish Tragedie*, V. 240
Lorenzo, in *The Traytor*, VI. 199
Loreto, litany of, IV. 129
Loretto, VII. 35, 63
Lorica, or *Cuirass*, I. 68, 69
Lorimer, of Hoxton square academy, X. 385
Lorraine, Claude, VIII. 217
Lorraine, duke of, IX. 149
Lorrington, Mrs, in Marston's *Favourite of Fortune*, XIII. 269
Lorrique, in *The Tragedy of Hoffman*, V. 327
Lorris, Guillaume de, II. 169, 219
Lort, Michael (1725–1790), X. Add.
Los, Blake's, XI. 194 ff., 199
Loseley MSS., the, V. 408
Losely, IV. 200
Loserth, J., II. 54, 69, 440
Losinga, Herbert de (1054?–1119), II. 497
Lot, F., I. 262
Lot, Parson (Charles Kingsley), XIII. 358
Loth, or Lot, in Arthurian legend, I. 259, 326
Lothair, Disraeli's, XIII. 352
Lothario, XIII. 378
Lothario, in Rowe's *Fair Penitent*, VIII. 196
Lothian, XI. 244
Lothians, the, II. 89, 90, 95, 259, 368, 371
Loti, Pierre, IX. 248
Lotos Eaters, I. 373
Lot's wife, in Bunyan's *Pilgrim's Progress*, VII. 173
Loudon, John Claudius (1783–1843), XIV. 562; *Magazine of Natural History*, XIV. 149
Loughborough, VII. 91
Loughborough, Alexander Wedderburn, lord. *See* Wedderburn, Alexander
Louis IX (St Louis), king of France, I. 336, 354; II. 284; III. 160; IV. 30
Louis XI, VI. 90; XII. 21, 26
Louis XII, V. 93
Louis XIII, IV. 254, 257, 259; VII. 205
Louis XIV, VII. 24; VIII. 14, 132, 195, 246, 248, 262, 263, 272, 276; IX. 148, 150, 151, 153, 391; X. 105; XI. 355; XIV. 110, 212
Louis XVI, X. 306, 507; XI. 28, 189, 430; XIV. 66
Louis XVII, XIII. 343
Louis XVIII, X. 261
Louis-Philippe, king of the French, XIII. 283; XIV. 60
Louisa, in Dickens's *Hard Times*, XIII. 329, 330
Louisa, princess, IX. 162
Louise de Gonzague, queen of Poland, V. 201
Lounger, The, X. 55; XI. 440, 449; XIV. 591, 600
Lounsbury, Thomas R., XIII. 477, 484; XIV. 611; *Shakespeare and Voltaire*, X. 81, 82; *The first editors of Shakespeare*, IX. 77, 78
Louth, Robert, XIV. 607
Louth grammar school, XIII. 23, 45
Louth school, Lincolnshire, VII. 330
Louvain, II. 245, 311; III. 67; IV. 402; V. 90; X. 200; XIV. 313
Louverture, Toussaint, XI. 114
Louverture, Toussaint, in Martineau's *The Hour and the Man*, XIII. 343
Lovat, lord. *See* Fraser, Simon
Lovato de' Lovati, V. 61
Love, in *Complaint upon Love to Reason*, III. 187
Love, in *Filostrato e Panfila*, V. 62
Love, in *Love Restored*, VI. 352
Love, in *Pathomachia*, VI. 324
Love, in *Piers the Plowman*, II. 10, 27, 28
Love, in *The Shepheards Calender*, III. 222
Love, in prince Arthur's marriage pageant, VI. 332
Love, Prety parables and proverbs of, III. 190
Love, Sir Anthony, in Southerne's *Sir Anthony Love*, VIII. 191
Love, the king of, in *The Example of Virtue*, II. 227
Love Prevented, V. 330
'Lovechild, Mrs,' XI. 377, 379
Loveday, Robert (*fl.* 1655), VII. 439 IX. 57
Lovel, in Lamb's *Elia*, XII. 180
Lovel, lord, in *The New Inne*, VI. 25
Lovelace, in Richardson's *Clarissa Harlowe*, VIII. 196; X. 8, 17
Lovelace, Dudley, VII. 24
Lovelace, earl of. *See* Milbanke, Ralph
Lovelace, Richard (1618–1658), VII. 4, 23 ff. (main entry), 178, 399
  Althea from Prison, To, VII. 24, 25
  Ellinda's Glove, VII. 25
  Going to the Wars, VII. 25
  Grasshopper, The, VII. 25
  Loose Saraband, A, VII. 25
  Lucasta: Epodes, Odes, Sonnets, Songs, etc., VII. 24, 25
  Lucasta going beyond the Seas, To, 25
  Lucasta Posthume Poems, VII. 24
  Lucasta Weeping, VII. 25
  Lucasta's Muff, VII. 25
  Pastoral: to Amarantha, VII. 25
  Poems, VII. 180
  Scholar, The, VII. 24
  Snail, The, VII. 25
  Soldier, The, VII. 24
  To Lucasta, XIV. 436
Lovelace, Sir William, VII. 23

Loveless, in Vanbrugh's *Relapse*, VIII. 161; XI. 268
Loveless, in Sheridan's *Trip to Scarborough*, XI. 268
Loveless, in *The Scornful Ladie*, VI. 133
Lovelich, Henry, I. 469
Lovell, Robert (1770?–1796), XI. 161, 420
Lovely Lass of Inverness, IX. 377
Lover, Samuel (1797–1868), XI. 440; XIV. 313 ff., 321, 569, 573; *Gridiron, The*, XIV. 314; *Handy Andy*, XIV. 314; *Paddy's Pastoral Rhapsody*, XIV. 314
Lover, the, in *Confessio Amantis*, II. 146 ff., 152
Lover Loved, the, in Heywood's *Love*, V. 93
Lover not Loved, the, in Heywood's *Love*, V. 93
Lovere, IX. 245
Loves of the Triangles, The, XI. 41, 175
Love's Garland IV. 467
Lovett, William (1800–1877), XIV. 414, 602
Lovibond, Edward (1724–1775), X. 455
Low, Frances, XIII. 551
Low Countries, II. 311, 320, 329; V. 113, 143, 344, 361; VII. 306, 345; VIII. 267
Lowde, James (*fl.* 1694–1696), VIII. 474
Lowe, John (1750–1798), X. 456; *Mary's Dream*, XI. 234
Lowe, Peter (1550?–1612?), XII. 521
Lowe, Robert, viscount Sherbrooke (1811–1892), XIV. 133, 137, 420, 511, 512, 607
Lowe, Robert W., X. 67; XI. 447, 449, 452; XII. 522; XIV. 518
Lowe, W. E., XIII. 513
Lowell, James Russell, II. 250; X. Add.; XI. 407, 410; XII. 179, 399; XIII. 143, 371, 472; XIV. 349
Lower, Richard (1631–1691), VIII. 363, 477
Lower, Sir William (1600?–1662), VIII. 119, 438; *Horatius* (Corneille's), translated by, VIII. 133, 180; *Polyeucte* (Corneille's), translated by, VIII. 133, 180
Lowin, John (1576–1659), VI. 139, 248, 249, 276, 277
Lowman, Moses (1680–1752), X. 521
Lowndes, William (1652–1724), *An Essay for the amendment of the Silver Coins*, VIII. 344, 474, 476
Lowndes, William Thomas (d. 1843), XII. 445, 522; *The Bibliographer's Manual*, X. 410; XII. 368; *The British Librarian*, XII. 368
Lowood, in *Jane Eyre*, XIII. 404
Lowry, J. M., XIV. 573
Lowth, Robert (1710–1787), II. 406; X. 136; XII. 468; *A Short Introduction to English Grammar*, XIV. 396
Lowther, Sir James, X. 131; XI. 95
Loyal Garland, The (1686), VII. 512
Loyal Observer, The, IV. 65
Loyal Songs, IX. 566
Loyal Subject's Litany, VIII. 96
Loyalist, The, IX. 566
Loyaltie and Bewtie, History of, VI. 286, 287
Loyalty, in *Assembly of Ladies*, II. 217
Loyalty, in *Piers the Plowman*, II. 10, 25, 32
Loyalty, in *Portuus of Noblines*, II. 284
Loyola, Ignatius de, VIII. 86
Loyola, Ignatius, in *A Game at Chesse*, VI. 150
Luard, Henry Richards (1825–1891), I. 182, 204; XII. 324, 356, 491, 492
Lubbock, John, baron Avebury (1834–1913), XII. 348, 511; XIV. 476, 562
Lubbock, Percy, XIII. 484
Luby, T. Clarke (1821–1901), XIV. 321, *also see* Add. 3
Lucan, I. 76; II. 366; III. 20, 113; IV. 23, 395, 438; VII. 206, 263, 267, 268, 270, 503; VIII. 61; IX. 44, 182, 256, 337, 338, 525; XII. 67, 306, 402; *Pharsalia*, IV. 138; VI. 37, 235; VIII. 197, 440
Lucar, Cyprian (*fl.* 1590), IV. 448
Lucas, Charles (1713–1771), X. 466; XIV. 569
Lucas, Sir Charles Prestwood, XIV. 509
Lucas, Edward Verrall, X. Add.; XI. 395, 417, 459, 475, 483, 484, 488, 492; XII. 414, 422, 433 ff., 437, 438; XIV. 521, *also see* Add. 3
Lucas, S., *Life of Peter Borthwick*, XIV. 185
Lucas, Samuel (1811–1865), editor of *The Morning Star*, XIV. 196
Lucas, Samuel, editor of *The Press*, XIV. 196
Lucas, Theophilus (*fl.* 1714), IX. 500
Lucas, Thomas (d. 1740), X. 387
'Lucasia,' K. Philips's, VII. 88
Lucasta, *alias* Lucy Sacheverell, VII. 24, 25
Lucca, XII. 62
Luce, Morton, XIII. 477
Luce, in *The London Prodigall*, V. 254, 255; VI. 97
Lucentio, in *The Taming of the Shrew*, V. 181
Luces, the two, in *The Wise-woman of Hogsdon*, VI. 99
Luces de Gast, I. 273
Lucia, in Addison's *Cato*, IX. 63
Lucian, III. 15, 20, 22; IV. 438, 516, 527; V. 221; VI. 18, 21, 87; VII. 131, 263, 274, 316, 318, 489; IX. 106, 159, 257, 266, 267, 500, 528; X. 474; XI. 332; XIII. 351; *Dialogues*, VIII. 36; *Menippus*, IV. 354; *Timon*, VI. 137
Lucianic reverie, X. 205
Lucifer, II. 30; III. 17, 76; IV. 166, 167; IX. 327
Lucifer, in Bailey's *Festus*, XIII. 153
Lucifer, in Byron's *Cain*, XII. 48
Lucifer, in Byron's *Vision of Judgment*, XII. 53
Lucifer, in FitzGerald's *The Mighty Magician*, XIII. 144
Lucifer, in religious plays, V. 15, 57
Lucifer, in *The Black Book*, VI. 60
Lucifer, in *The foure P.P.*, V. 96
Lucilius, VIII. 58

Lucilla, in *The Anatomy of Wit*, III. 345, 346
Lucina, in *The Birth of Merlin*, v. 249
Lucina, in *Valentinian*, VI. 122
Lucinda, in *Don Quixote*, IX. 269
Lucio, in *Measure for Measure*, v. 190
Lucius, in *The Rival Friends*, VI. 325
Lucius, king, III. 332
Lucius Iberius, in *Morte Arthure*, I. 313; II. 115, 118
'Lucius' (Junius), x. 403, 410
Luckin, M. W., XIV. Add. 8
Luckless, in Fielding's *Pleasures of the Town*, x. 21
Lucky Spence's Last Advice, IX. 366
Lucrece, in *Confessio Amantis*, II. 152
Lucrece, in *Gismond of Salerne*, v. 73, 75
Lucrece, The Play of, v. 100, 410
Lucretia, XII. 68
Lucretius, IV. 347; VII. 268, 451, 486; VIII. 61, 277, 288, 449; IX. 55, 526; XII. 67, 326, 335, 488, 492, 495; XIII. 25, 40, 45, 145; XIV. 276, 374
Lucullus, IX. 270
Lucy, in Charlotte Brontë's *Villette*, XIII. 410
Lucy, in Congreve's *Old Bachelor*, VIII. 147, 152
Lucy, in Meredith's *Richard Feverel*, XIII. 444, 446
Lucy, in Sheridan's *Rivals*, x. 89; XI. 266
Lucy, in Wordsworth's poems, XI. 113
Lucy, Sir Henry W., XIV. 534
Lucy, St, I. 74, 356
Lucy, William (1594–1677), VII. 474
Ludi or 'disgysynges,' VI. 294
Ludlow, Edmund (1617?–1692), VII. 451; *Diary*, VII. 225
Ludlow, John Malcolm, XIII. 355; XIV. 408
Ludlow castle, VI. 363; VII. 113; VIII. 60
Ludlow school, VII. 330
Ludolphus, J., *History of Aethiopia*, IX. 268
Ludovicus Vives, VI. 225
Ludus Accidiae, v. 52
Ludus Coventriae. See *Coventry Plays*
Ludwig, Lavaterus, *Of Ghostes and Spirits*, III. 495
Ludwig, Otto, v. 304
Ludwig the Pious, Life of, by Thegan, I. 90
Luft, Hans, III. 472
Lufton, lord, Trollope's, XIII. 422
Lugwardine, Antony, in Robert Landor's *Fountain of Arethusa*, XII. 230
Luick, K., II. 32, 436
'Luitprandus,' x. 204
Luke, St, I. 74; II. 15
Luke, Sir Samuel (d. 1670), VII. 167; VIII. 60, 63, 64, 66
Luke is losse, My (poems signed), III. 189
Lukin, Henry, *Practice of Godliness*, XI. 334
Lul, letter from, I. 79
Lulli, J.-B. de, musician to Charles I, and Quinault, P., *Cadmus and Hermione*, VIII. 134; *Les Fêtes de l'Amour et de Bacchus*, VIII. 134
Lully, or Lulle, Raymond, VII. 277
Lumby, Joseph Rawson (1831–1895), I. 146; II. 284; XII. 487
Lumen, in *Lingua*, VI. 315
Lumfanane, in Wyntoun's *Cronykil*, II. 132
Lumley, Eliza, afterwards Sterne, x. 47
Lumley, Richard, 2nd earl of Scarborough (d. 1721), x. 256
Lumond, sea of, in Layamon, I. 236
Lumpkin, Tony, in Goldsmith's *She Stoops to Conquer*, x. 206, 214
Luna, in Hawes's *A Joyful Meditation*, etc., II. 226
'Lunatics,' in *The Lords' Masque*, VI. 353
Lund, Thomas William Moy, XIII. 488
Lunenburg, duke of, in *The Tragedy of Hoffman*, v. 327
Luntowski, A., XIII. 465, 476
Lupset, Thomas (1498?–1530), III. 20, 105, 474
Lupton, Donald (d. 1676), VI. 494; *London and Country Carbonadoed*, IV. 351, 522
Lupton, Roger (d. 1540), VII. 329, 330
Lupton, Thomas (*fl.* 1583), *All for Money*, v. 57, 393
Lurewell, lady, in Farquhar's *The Constant Couple*, VIII. 176, 178
Luria, Browning's, XIII. 67
Lushington, Edmund Law (1811–1893), XII. 487; XIII. 24; *On the Study of Greek*, XII. 330
Lushington, Sir Franklin, XIV. 494
Lusitania, in *The Masque of Blacknesse*, VI. 342
Lutel Soth Sermun, I. 226, 458
Luther, Martin, II. 69; III. 7, 53, 69, 127, 139, 151, 363, 365, 472, 492; IV. 215, 224, 301, 380, 445, 446, *also see* Add.; v. 58, 103; VII. 103; VIII. 291, 321 ff.; XII. 273, 281; XIII. 13, 20, 388, 428; XIV. 99; *Table Talk, or Colloquies (Colloquia Mensalia)*, VII. 391; VIII. 321 322
Lutheran drama, VI. 374
Lutheranism, III. 31, 37, 140, 142
Lutherans, VII. 124, 378
Luton, IX. 169
Lutonsky, Paula, XIII. 489
Lutterworth, II. 65, 66; x. 112
Luttrell, Henry (1765?–1851), XII. 419 XIV. 115
Luttrell, Narcissus (1657–1732), *Brief Historical Relation of State Affairs*, VII 241, 451
Lutwidge, in Miss Edgeworth's *Belinda* XI. 297
Luvah, in Blake's *Vala*, XI. 195
Luvaris Lament, The, II. 282
Lux Mundi, XII. 299
Luxborough, earl of. *See* Catherlough, R. I
Luxborough, lady. *See* Knight, Henriet
Luxborough, lord. *See* Knight, Robert
Luxuria, in *The Castle of Perseverance*, v.
Luxury, in *The Cradle of Security*, v. 57
Luynes, C., duc de, VII. 205

Lyall, Sir Alfred Comyn (1835–1911), XIII. 194, 477, 505; XIV. 93, 493, 500, 578
Asiatic Studies, XIV. 98, 340
Badminton, XIII. 203
British Dominion in India, The, XIV. 340
Land of Regrets, The, XIII. 203; XIV. 340
Old Pindaree, The, XIII. 202
Retrospection, XIII. 203
Rise and Expansion of the British Dominion in India, XIV. 98
Siva, XIV. 340
Theology in Extremis, XIII. 202
Verses written in India, XIII. 202; XIV. 340
Lyall, Sir Charles James (1845–1920), XII. Add. 4
Lyberte, in *Magnyfycence*, III. 77
Lycanthropy, belief in, I. 316
Lyce, an elderly Lady, To, X. 168
Lycia, XII. 339
Lycidas (Herrick's), VII. 12
Lycogenes, in *Argenis*, IV. 258, 259
Lycophron, IX. 527
Lycosthenes, Conrad, *Prodigiorum ac Ostentorum Chronicon*, III. 111
Lycurgus, X. 59
Lydd, V. 34
Lydgate, John (1370?–1450?), I. 285; II. 104, 159, 161, 163, 164, 166, 175, 197–205 (main entry), 206 ff., 214, 218 ff., 224 ff., 231, 237, 239, 245, 246, 252, 253, 258, 261, 266, 332, 467, 468, 470; III. 68, 70, 168, 192 ff., 198, 199, 227, 277, 282, 292, 301, 411 ff., 441 ff.; IV. 441; X. 239; XIII. 211
Aesop, II. 199, 204
Albon and Amphabel, II. 199
Assembly of Gods, The, II. 199, 203
Balade of the Goos, A, II. 308
Ballade of the Midsummer Rose, II. 204
Bochas, John, Tragedies of, II. 202
Churl and the Bird, The, II. 199, 204, 312; IV. 409
Complaint of the Black Knight, The, II. 162, 164, 166, 204
Court of Sapience, The, II. 199, 231
Danse Macabre, II. 199; V. 12
De Duobus Mercatoribus, II. 199
December and July, II. 199
Edmund and Fremund, II. 199, 203
Falls of Princes, The, II. 199, 200, 202, 204, 321; III. 192, 194, 195
Flower of Courtesy, The, II. 199
Horse, the Sheep and the Goose, The, II. 199, 204, 312
Jak Hare, II. 505
Life of our Lady, II. 199, 203, 314
London Lickpenny, II. 200, 201, 204, 206, 470, 505
Lyfe and Passion of Saint Alban, IV. 409
Minor Poems, II. 199
Miracles of St Edmund, II. 199
Nightingale Poems, II. 199, 204
Pilgrimage of the Life of Man, The, II. 199, 200
Lydgate, John
Prioress and her Three Sisters, The, II. 204
Reason and Sensuality, II. 199, 202
St Austin, II. 199
St Giles, II. 199
St Margaret, II. 199, 203
Saints' Loves, II. 203
Secrets of the Philosophers, The, II. 199, 208
Serpent of Dissension, The, V. 66
Stans Puer ad mensam, II. 313
Temple of Glass, The, II. 199, 202, 225, 230, 231, 235, 308, 312
Testament, II. 199, 204
Thank God of all, II. 204
Thebes, Story of, II. 164, 199 ff.
Troy Book, II. 199, 202; V. 221
Lydgate, in *Middlemarch*, XIII. 399
Lydia, in Gissing's *Thyrza*, XIII. 459
Lydia, in Jago's *Edge-Hill*, X. 113
Lydia, in *Pedantius*, VI. 306
Lye, Edward (1694–1767), IX. 536; X. 225; XII. 344, 504
Lyell, Sir Charles (1797–1875), XIV. 292, 562
Antiquity of Man, The, XIV. 293
Elements of Geology, The, XIV. 293
Principles of Geology, The, XIV. 293, 299
Second Visit to the United States, A, XIV. 293
Travels in North America, XIV. 293
Lyle, Eustace, in Disraeli's *Coningsby*, XIII. 350
Lykewakes, I. 124
Lyly, John (1554?–1606), III. 241, 300, 340, 341, 344 ff., 349, 350, 354 ff., 358, 364, 365, 370, 392, 395, 397, 534, 544; V. 120, 121–141 (main entry), 142, 149, 177, 414 ff.; VI. 13, 18, 215, 288, 336, 387; VII. 154; VIII. 127; XI. 262; XIV. 460
Alexander and Campaspe, IV. 115; V. 125, 126; VI. 287
'Cupid and my Campaspe played at cards for kisses,' IV. 115; V. 125
Endimion, V. 122, 124, 341
Euphues, II. 340; III. 344 ff., 365, 366; IV. 344, 523; V. 114, 122, 127, 193, 338; VI. 388, 389
Euphues and his Ephoebus, III. 346
Galathea, IV. 77; VI. 365
Love's Metamorphosis, V. 122; VI. 287, 365
Midas, IV. 115; V. 122, 124, 345, 369
Mother Bombie, IV. 394; V. 122; VI. 14, 99
Pappe with a Hatchet, III. 394, 395, 397, 543
Sapho and Phao, V. 122, 124, 341; VI. 287
'Sing to Apollo,' IV. 115
Lyme Regis, VIII. 30; X. 20, 387; XII. 241
Lymington, X. 306
Lymne, XII. 347
Lynam, Robert (1796–1845), X. 459

Lynch, Hannah, XIII. 570
Lynch, Thomas Toke (1818–1871), XIII. 167, 174, 505
Lyndhurst, lord. *See* Copley, John Singleton
Lyndon, lady, in Thackeray's *Barry Lyndon*, XIII. 282
Lyndsay, Sir David (1490–1555), II. 91, 94, 249, 250, 265, 279; III. 115–130 (main entry), 135, 138, 142, 153, 156, 159, 498; IV. 322, 412 ff., 527; V. 392, 394; IX. 359; XI. 203, 204, 215; XII. 10, 350, 508, 517
Answer, An, III. 121
Deploratioun of the Death of Queen Magdalene, The, III. 130
Description of Pedder Coffeis, Ane, III. 121
Dialog betwix Experience and Ane Courteour, III. 130, 133
Dreme, The, III. 116, 138
Epistle to the Kingis Grace, III. 116
Exhortation to the King, An (epilogue to *The Dreme*), III. 118
Exclamatioun to the Redar, II. 283
Historie of the Squyer Meldrum, The, I. 291; II. 245; III. 130
John the Commonweill, II. 280
Justing betwix James Watson and Johne Barbour, The, III. 121, 135
Kitteis Confessioun, III. 121
Pleasant Satyre of the Thrie Estaitis, Ane, III. 122 ff.; V. 59; IX. 365
Publict Confessioun of the Kingis auld Hound callit Baysche, Ane, III. 121
Supplicatioun againis Syde Taillis, Ane, III. 121
Testament and Complaynt of our Soverane Lordis Papyngo, The, II. 266; III. 118, 119, 131, 484
Tragedie of the Cardinal, The, III. 130
Lyndwood, William (1375?–1446), II. 62, 498; VIII. 466
Lyne, Charles E., XIV. 587
Lynedoch, lord. *See* Graham, Thomas
Lynn, Norfolk, II. 287; IX. 2; X. 244, 460
Lynn, Elizabeth. *See* Linton, Elizabeth Lynn
Lynne, Walter (*fl.* 1550), III. 81
Lynton, in *Lorna Doone*, XIII. 434
Lynton, Thomas de, VI. 280
Lyon, John (1514?–1592), VII. 336
Lyon, John, 9th earl of Strathmore (1737–1776), X. 131
Lyonesse, I. 279
Lyons, II. 316, 323
Lyra, II. 365
Lyra Apostolica, XII. 257, 454, 456, 457; XIII. 171
Lyra Heroica, XIII. 195
Lyrical Ballads, X. 234
Lyrick, the poet, in Farquhar's *Love and a Bottle*, VIII. 170
Lyrics, Harleian (B.M. 2253), I. 360 ff., 370, 378
Lysias, VII. 316; IX. 528
Lysons, Daniel (1762–1834), XII. 511; *Magna Britannia*, XII. 345; *Environs of London*, XII. 345
Lysons, Samuel (1763–1819), XII. 511; *Reliquiae Britannico-Romanae*, XII. 345
'Lyster, Lynn,' XIV. Add. 5
Lyte, Henry (1529?–1607), III. 551; *A Niewe herball*, IV. 374, 542
Lyte, Henry Francis (1793–1847), XII. 419
Lyttelton, Charles (1714–1768), X. 247, 251
Lyttelton, George, 1st baron Lyttelton (1709–1773), IX. 220, 229, 230, 313; X. 29, 34, 36, 39, 94, 95, 100, 102 ff., 110, 113 ff. (main entry), 262, 263, 292, 448, 450, 456, 502; XI. 347, 349, 474
Dialogues of the Dead, IX. 159, 160; X. 20, 114, 115; XI. 351
History of Henry II, IX. 160; X. 114, 292, 311; XI. 345
Monody, X. 113, 114
Observations on the Conversion of St Paul, X. 114
Persian Letters, X. 114
Progress of Love, X. 114
Lyttelton, George William, 4th baron (1817–1876), XII. 484
Lyttelton, Lucy, born Fortescue, wife of Lyttelton, George, 1st baron, X. 113
Lyttelton, Sir Thomas (1647?–1710), X. 113
Lytteltons, the, X. 273
Lytton, Edward George Earle Lytton Bulwer-Lytton, 1st baron (1803–1873), XI. 304, 387; XII. 131, 414, 428, 429, 432; XIII. 307, 340, 386, 391, 392, 417 ff. (main entry), 427, 431, 432, 434, 516, 520, 563, 564; XIV. 174, 196, 238, 510
Asmodeus at Large, XIII. 420
Caxtons, The, XIII. 420
Coming Race, The, XIII. 417, 420
Devereux, XIII. 419
Disowned, The, XIII. 418
Eugene Aram, XIII. 418, 419
Falkland, XIII. 417
Glenallan, XIII. 419
Godolphin, XIII. 419
Harold, XIII. 419
Haunted and the Haunters, The, XIII 420
Ishmael and other Poems, XIII. 417
Kenelm Chillingly, XIII. 417, 420
Lady of Lyons, The, XIII. 419
Last Days of Pompeii, The, XIII. 419
Last of the Barons, The, XIII. 419
Lucretia, XIII. 418, 420
Money, XI. 82; XIII. 419
Mortimer, XIII. 417
My Novel, XIII. 420
New Timon, The, XIV. 129
Parisians, The, XIII. 417, 421
Paul Clifford, XIII. 418, 419
Pausanias the Spartan, XIII. 419
Pelham, X. 39; XIII. 417 ff., 421, 436
Pilgrims of the Rhine, The, XIII. 417

Lytton, Edward George Earle Lytton Bulwer-Lytton
Richelieu, XIII. 419
Rienzi, XIII. 419
Sea-Captain, The, XIII. 279
Strange Story, A, XIII. 420
What will he do with it? XIII. 420
Zanoni, XIII. 419
Zicci, XIII. 419
Lytton, Edward Robert Bulwer, 1st earl of Lytton (Owen Meredith) (1831–1891), XIII. 194, 199, 204, 505
After Paradise, XIII. 200
Astarte, XIII. 200
Chronicles and Characters, XIII. 200
Fables in Song, XIII. 200
Fata Morgana, XIII. 200
Glenaveril, XIII. 200
King Poppy, XIII. 200
Love Letter, A, XIII. 200
Lucile, XIII. 200
Marah, XIII. 200
Selenites, XIII. 200
Wanderer, The, XIII. 200
Lytton, Bulwer, lady, XII. 441
Lytton, Victor Alexander George Robert, 2nd earl of Lytton, XIII. 564

M.P., *pseud.*, XI. 379, 480
Maasdorp, A. F. S., XIV. Add. 8
Mab, in *The Satyr*, VI. 340
Mab, queen, in *Romeo and Juliet*, VII. 8; XIV. 307
Mabbe, James (1572–1642?), IV. 395, 441, 443, 447
Mabbott, Gilbert, VII. 351; *Mercurius Britannicus*, VII. 357; *The Moderate*, VII. 357
Mabel, daughter of Robert Fitz-hamon, I. 256
Mabillon, Jean, IV. 419; XIV. 53
Mabinogion, I. 249, 252, 253, 255, 269, 271, 276, 461. *See, also*, Lady C. Guest
Macalister, R. A. S., XII. 351, 352, 360
Macartney, George, 1st earl Macartney (1737–1806), XI. 350
Macaulay, Mrs Catharine, born Sawbridge (1731–1791), X. 502; XI. 390; XIV. 600
Macaulay, George Campbell (1852–1915), X. 449; XII. 504
Macaulay, Thomas Babington, 1st baron Macaulay (1800–1859), IV. 45, 480; VII. 129, 177, 218, 220; VIII. 107, 159, 167, 242, 273; IX. 31, 127, 182, 240, 263; X. 66, 153, 242, 243, 298, 315, 320, 476, 480, 483; XI. 167, 286, 410, 423; XII. 129, 141, 152, 153, 155, 163, 178, 221, 262, 319, 396, 420, 426, 444, 447, 477, 480; XIII. 8, 43, 147 ff. (main entry), 189, 230, 238, 320, 328, 487, 505; XIV. 55, 58, 59 ff. (main entry), 71, 77, 88, 89, 115, 125, 159, 170, 180, 336, 337, 365, 462, 493, 504, 506, 509, 510
Battle of the Lake Regillus, The, XIII. 149
Epitaph on a Jacobite, XIII. 148, 239
Essays, XII. 326; XIV. 5, 61 ff.
Macaulay, Thomas Babington
Essays: Gladstone on Church and State, XIII. 24
History (essay), XIV. 59
History of England, XIII. 11; XIV. 60 ff., 84
Last Buccaneer, The, XIII. 178, 239
Lays of Ancient Rome, XII. 30; XIII. 148, 149, 152, 153, 239; XIV. 61
Miscellaneous Writings, XIV. 59
Prophecy of Capys, The, XIII. 149
Virginia, XII. 261
Westminster Reviewer's Defence of Mill, The, XIV. 59
Macaulay, Zachary (1768–1838), XI. 259, 475; XIV. 60
Macbean, Alexander (d. 1784), X. 470
Macbean, Lachlan, XIV. 541, *also see* Add. 2
Macbeth, in Boece, III. 156
Macbeth, in Wyntoun, II. 132
Macbeth, Garrick as, XI. 284
Macbeth, lady, in Shakespeare's play, XII. 68, 171; XIV. 157
Macbeth, Shakespeare's, II. 89; VIII. 120; XIII. 67
Macbeth, W. H. W. Betty as, XI. 283
MacCabe, W. Gordon, XIII. 477
Maccallum, Mungo William, XIII. 477
McCalmont, Hugh. *See* Cairns, 1st earl
MacCarthy, Denis Florence (1817–1882), XIV. 569; *Pillar Towers of Ireland, The*, XIV. 318; *Shelley's Early Life*, XIV. 318; *Waiting for the May*, XIV. 318
MacCarthy, Desmond, XIII. 572
McCarthy, Justin Huntley (1830–1912), XIV. 493, 511, 528, 532, 569
McCaul, John, XII. 511
MacCaura clan, XIV. 318
Macclesfield, earl of. *See* Parker, Thomas
McClintock, Sir Francis Leopold (1819–1907), XIV. 245, 553
MacColl, Evan (1808–1898), XIV. 582; *Poems and Songs*, XIV. 357
MacColl, Malcolm (1831–1907), XIV. 513
Maccoll, Norman (1843–1904), XIV. 534
McCombie, Thomas, XIV. 587
McCormick, Charles (1755?–1807), XI. 390
McCormick, Joseph (1733–1799), IX. 492; X. 503; *State Papers and Letters*, X. 295
McCosh, James (1811–1894), XIV. 467, 476
MacCowl, Finn, X. 231
McCoy, Sir Frederick (1823–1899), XIV. 563
McCracken, Henry Noble, II. 468, 470
McCrie, Thomas (1772–1835), XIV. 493, 507; *Life of Andrew Melville, The*, XIV. 101; *Life of John Knox, The*, XIV. 101
McCrindle, John Watson, XIV. 338, 339, 579
MacCullagh, James (1809–1847), XIV. 261, 556
MacCullagh Torrens. *See* Torrens
MacCulloch, John Ramsay (1789–1864), XII. 522; XIV. 3, 476, 513

MacCunn, John, XIII. 21, 472
M'Cutcheon, the name, II. 117
MacDermott, Martin, XIV. 573
MacDonagh, M., XIV. 541
Macdonald, Flora (1722–1790), IX. 563
Macdonald, George (1824–1905), XI. 387, 481; XII. Add. 5; XIII. 189 ff., 431, 505, 564
Lilith, XIII. 183, 432
Phantastes, XIII. 183, 192, 432
Portent, The, XIII. 183, 192
Robert Falconer, XIII. 432
MacDonald, Ronald, XIII. 564
Macdonald, William, XII. 435
Macdonell, James (1842–1879), XIV. 534
McDow, in Susan Ferrier's *Destiny*, XII. 245
Macduff, in Wyntoun, II. 132
Macedon, XII. 309
Macedonia, IV. 59
Macer (herbalist), II. 364; IV. 542
Macfarlan, James (1832–1862), XIII. 505
Macfarlane, Alexander, XIV. 263
Macfarlane, Charles (d. 1858), XIII. 564; XIV. 487, 494, 612
Macfie, Ronald F., XIV. 538
M'Gibbon, Edinburgh musician, IX. 371, 379
McGie, Thomas D'Arcy (1825–1868), XIV. 318, 322, 357, 569, 582
Celts, The, XIV. 318
Home Thoughts, XIV. 318
I left two loves, XIV. 318
My Irish Wife, XIV. 318
Sea-divided Gaels, The, XIV. 318
McGill university, Montreal, XIV. 355
Macgillivray, Evan James, XIV. 536
MacGregor, James Comyn, XIV. Add. 7
Macgregor, John (1825–1892), XIV. 552, 553
Macgregor, Malcolm (William Mason), X. 398, 525
McHale, John (1791–1881), XIV. 328, 329, 569
Machar (Mauricius), St, II. 127
Machiavelli, in *Romola*, XIII. 394
Machiavelli, Niccolò, III. 245, 315, 432; IV. 342, 347, 446; VI. 167; VIII. 123; IX. 225; XI. 32
Arte of Warre, IV. 4, 7, 8
Florentine Historie, IV. 7, 8, 398
Prince, The, IV. 7, 8, 297
Relazioni, III. 432
Machin, Lewis (*fl.* 1608), VI. 100; *Dumbe Knight, The*, IV. 377, 539
Machlinia, William de (*fl.* 1482–1490), VIII. 314
Books printed by, II. 318 ff.: *Monk of Evesham*, II. 318; IV. 353; *Speculum Christiani*, II. 319; *Treatise of the Pestilence*, II. 319
Machyn or Machin, Henry (1498?–1563?), III. 478; V. 70; VI. 461; X. 492
Macilente, in *Every Man out of His Humour*, VI. 17
MacIlwaine, William, XIV. 573
MacIntyre, Hector, in *The Antiquary*, X. 231
MacIvor, Fergus, in *Waverley*, XII. 26
MacIvor, Flora, in *Waverley*, XII. 22
Mackail, John William, XI. 416; XII. 407; XIII. 493, 495
Mackaile, Matthew (*fl.* 1657–1696), IX. 559
Mackarness, Matilda Anne, born Planché (1826–1881), XI. 489
Mackay, Angus M., XIII. 558
Mackay, Charles (1814–1889), XII. 380; XIII. 505; XIV. 199; *Cholera Chant*, XIII. 189; *O Ye Tears!* XIII. 188
Mackay, Sir Donald, 1st baron Reay (1591–1649), VII. 231
Mackay, Robert William (1803–1882), XII. 468
Mackay, Thomas, XIV. 506
Mackaye, Saunders, in Kingsley's *Alton Locke*, XIII. 361, 362
Mackechnie, James, XIII. 569
Mackelvie, William (1800–1863), XI. 442
Mackenzie, Sir Alexander (1755–1820), XIV. 583; *Voyages from Montreal*, XIV. 358
Mackenzie, George, 1st earl of Cromarty (1630–1714), IX. 215, 492, 551, 561
Mackenzie, Sir George (1636–1691), IX. 493, 551, 561; XIV. 491; *Aretina, or the Serious Romance*, VII. 391; VIII. 372
Mackenzie, George (1669–1725), IX. 553
Mackenzie, Henry (1745–1831), X. 46, 55 ff., 424, 436, 451, *also see* Add.; XI. 440, 442, 449, 457; XII. 245; XIII. 326; XIV. 600
Julia de Roubigné, X. 57, 58
Man of Feeling, X. 15, 55 ff.; XI. 206
Man of the World, X. 57
Prince of Tunis, X. 55
Mackenzie, Sir James Dixon, XII. 511; *The Castles of England*, XII. 349
Mackenzie, John, XIV. Add. 8
Mackenzie, Mrs, in *The Newcomes*, XIII. 296, 297, 299
Mackenzie, Robert James, XIV. 601
Mackenzie, Rosey, in *The Newcomes*, XIII 296, 299
Mackenzie, William Mackay, XIV. 522
McKerrow, Ronald Brunlees, IV. 171; XI. 466
Mackery End, XII. 183, 194
Mackinder, Halford John, XIV. 596
Mackintosh, Sir James (1765–1832), VII 203; XI. 75, 76, 396, 399; XII. 187, 303 310; XIII. 418; XIV. 58, 110, 184, 186 494
Dissertation on the Progress of Ethical Philosophy, XIV. 5, 59
History of England, XIV. 59
History of the Revolution in England in 1688, XIV. 59
Memoirs, XI. 53
Mackintosh, Robert James, XI. 53
Macklin, Charles (1697?–1797), X. 85, 445 XI. 258, 260, 262, 447, 449, 450, 454 XIV. 569; *Love à-la-mode*, XI. 257

Macknight, Thomas, XIII. 547; XIV. 508; *Life of Bolingbroke*, IX. 217, 226, 227, 230
Mackshane, in Smollett's *Roderick Random*, X. 37
Mackworth, Sir Humphry (1657–1727), IX. 11, 420
Macky, John (d. 1726), VIII. 219; IX. 494; *Journey through England*, XI. 332
McLachlan, Alexander (1818–1896), XIV. 357, 582
Maclaren, Charles (1782–1866), XIV. 535
Maclaren, Elizabeth T., XIV. 517
Maclaurin, Colin (1698–1746), XIV. 257, 556
Maclean, Neil N., XIV. 594
M'Lean, T., XIV. 540
Macleane, Arthur John (1812–1858), XII. 487
Maclehose, Mrs Agnes ('Clarinda,' 1759–1841), XI. 222, 436, 437; *Talk not of Love*, XI. 232; *To a Blackbird*, XI. 232
McLennan, John Ferguson (1827–1881), XIV. 476; *Primitive Marriage*, XII. 348
M'Lennan, Murdoch, *Race of Sheriffmuir*, IX. 373
McLennan, William (1856–1904), XIV. 581
In Old France and New, XIV. 360
Songs of Old Canada, XIV. 360
Span o' Life, The, XIV. 360
Spanish John, XIV. 360
Macleod, Fiona. *See* Sharp, William
Macleod, Henry Dunning (1821–1902), XIV. 476
Macleod, Mary, *The Shakespeare Story Book*, XI. 385
Macleod, Norman (1812–1872), XI. 481; XII. 472
Maclis (a beast), III. 315
Maclise, Daniel (1806–1870), XII. 410, 428; XIII. 474
MacMechan, Archibald, XIII. 465, 466
Macmillan, Daniel (1813–1857), XIII. 553
Macmillan, Hugh (1833–1903), XII. 472
Macmillan's Magazine, XIII. 98; XIV. 324
MacMorough, II. 301
MacMurchy, Archibald, XIV. 581
Macnab, Henry Grey (1761–1823), XIV. 607, 608
Macnally, Leonard (1752–1820), XI. 281, 458
MacNeil, Hector (1746–1818), XI. 444
Come Under my Plaidie, XI. 234
Dinna think Bonnie Lassie, XI. 234
Donald and Flora, XI. 234
Harp, The, XI. 234
Mary of Castle Cary, XI. 234
My Boy Tammy, XI. 234
Scotland's Scaith, XI. 234
Waes of War, XI. 234
Macnicol, Donald (1735–1802), X. 475
Macnish, Robert (1802–1837), XII. 450
Macpherson, David (1746–1816), XII. 517
Macpherson, Geraldine, XIV. 521, 569
Macpherson, James (1736–1796), I. 275; IX. 185, 564; X. 55, 130, 222, 227 ff., 230 ff. (main entry), 234, 237, 320, 487 ff., 503, 510; XI. 229
Berrathon, X. 227
Carric-thura, X. 228
Cath-Loda, X. 130
Death of Oscar, The, X. 230
Fingal, X. 137, 225, 231
Fragments of Ancient Poetry, X. 230
Highlander, The, X. 230, 238
History of Great Britain, X. 232, 295
Hunter, The, X. 237
Iliad (translation), X. 232
Introduction to the History of Great Britain and Ireland, X. 295
Original Papers, X. 295
Ossian, XII. 40; XIII. 52, 101, 226
Temora, X. 231
See, also, under Ossian
Macray, William Dunn, VI. 309
Macready, William Charles (1793–1873), V. 302; XI. 447; XII. 171; XIII. 58, 59, 61, 68, 69, 255, 261; XIV. 319
Macro-plays, the, V. 391, 392
Macrobius, II. 366; X. 205, 481
Mac Roig, Fergus, XIV. 307
Macropedius, George, V. 412; *Asotus*, V. 101; *Rebelles*, V. 101, 110, 113
MacSpadden, Joseph Walker, XIII. 544
McWard, Robert (1633?–1687), IX. 546
Madagascar, IV. 101, 102; IX. 23
Madan, Falconer, XI. 469; XII. 462
Madan, Martin (1726–1790), XI. 81
Madden, D. D., XIV. 510
Madden, Sir Frederic (1801–1873), I. 269, 322, 326, 328; II. 45, 73, 431; XII. 356, 517
Madden, Richard Robert (1798–1886), XIII. 544; XIV. 532, 567, 569, 573
Madden, Samuel (1686–1765), X. 468
Madden, Virginia (Gissing's), XIII. 460
Maddison, Sir Ralph (1571?–1655?), VII. 515
Maddox, Isaac (1697–1759), IX. 212, 494
Maddox, Thomas (1666–1727), IX. 537; *Formulare Anglicanum*, IX. 355; *History of the Exchequer*, IX. 355
Madeira, XIV. 244, 293
Madeley, X. 365
Madeley, Eve (Gissing's), XIII. 459
Madeline, in Keats's *Eve of Saint Agnes*, XI. 131; XII. 86 ff.
Madeline, in *Nicholas Nickleby*, XIII. 318
Mademoiselle, in Vanbrugh's *Provok'd Wife*, VIII. 162
Madge, in *Misogonus*, V. 111
Madido, in *The Pilgrimage to Parnassus*, VI. 310
'Madonella' (Mary Astell), IX. 404
Madras, XIV. 336
'Madras' system of education, XIV. 403, 404
Madrid, VI. 203; VII. 215; VIII. 130, 141, 271
Maecenas, VII. 164
'Maecenas of Hill street,' XI. 350

Maeldun, the voyage of, XIV. 306
Maeldune. See *Maldon, The Battle of*
Maeterlinck, Maurice, XI. 384
Maevius, IV. 331
Maffei, Scipione, V. 289
'Maga.' See *Blackwood's Edinburgh Magazine*
Magazine of Zoology and Botany, XIV. 565
Magdeburg, siege of, VII. 22
Magellan, Ferdinand, IV. 69, 75, 78, 86, 92
Magellan, straits of, III. 358; IV. 77, 99
Maggie, in Burns's *Auld Farmer's Salutation*, XI. 214
Maggie, in Mrs Gaskell's *The Moorland Cottage*, XIII. 377
Maggie Lauder, IX. 364, 365
Maggie's Tocher, IX. 360
Magi, the, XII. 275
Magic, illustrations of, III. 495
Magicians, The Twa, II. 409
Maginn, William (1793–1842), XII. 123, 157 ff., 425, 428; XIII. 162, 163, 189, 292; XIV. 177, 236, 313 ff., 570; *Daniel O'Rourke*, XIV. 314; *Irishman and the Lady, The*, XIV. 313; *St Patrick*, XIV. 313
Magister Fabre, *praelector linguae Gallicanae*, IX. 412
Magistrates, A Mirror for. See *Mirror*
Maglocunus, king of Anglesey, I. 67
Magna Britannia et Hibernia, IX. 353, 537
Magna Carta, I. 151, 154, 174; VIII. 317, 465; X. 464; XIV. 75
Magna Charta, On the King's Breaking his Confirmation of, I. 376
'Magna Lilliputia,' X. 163, 464, 465
Magnano, in Butler's *Hudibras*, VIII. 68
Magnin, Charles, V. 302
Magnus, L., XIII. 486
Magnus de la Gardie, VIII. 20
Magnússon, Eiríkr, XIII. 125, 127, 492
Magomastix, H., VII. 507
Maguire, Trollope's, XIII. 422
Magyar versions of ballads, II. 405
Mahābhārata, XII. 503
Mahaffy, Sir John Pentland (1839–1919), V. 71; XII. 440, 485, 489, *also see* Add. 3
Mahan, Alfred Thayer, XIV. 486
Mahomet, IV. 214, 215; VIII. 291; IX. 54; X. 281, 503: XI. 18; XIII. 13
Mahon, viscount. *See* Stanhope, 5th earl
Mahony, Francis Sylvester (*pseud.* Father Prout, 1804–1866), XII. 123, 138, 428; XIII. 162; XIV. 185, 194, 549, 570; *Bells of Shandon, The*, XIV. 316; *Reliques of Father Prout*, XIV. 316; *Sabine Farmer's Serenade, The*, XIV. 316
Mahoun, in *Gyre Carling*, II. 276
'Mahownde,' V. 49
Mahrattas, the, XI. 17
Maia, in Keats's *Ode to Maia*, XII. 90
Maia, in *The Penates*, VI. 341
Maid Freed from the Gallows, The, II. 396, 405, 410
Maiden, Joseph Henry, XIV. 558
Maidens' tower, in *The Elegy on the Duke of Richmond*, III. 178
Maidment, James (1795?–1879), XII. 358, 517
Maidment's *Court of Session Garland*, X. 478
Maidstone, XII. 165
Maidwell, Laurence, *The Loving Enemies* (1680), VIII. 422
Maidwell, Lewis (*fl.* 1700), IX. 386, 387 397, 398, 411, 413, 570
Maigron, L., XII. 380
Maimbourg, L., VIII. 402, 456; *History of the League*, VIII. 34, 44
Main, Alexander, *Wise, Witty, and Tender Sayings of George Eliot*, XIII. 388, 551
Mainard, lady Margaret, VIII. 307
Maine, Sir Henry James Sumner (1822–1888), VIII. 312; XIV. 194, 198, 494, 502; *Ancient Law*, XII. 348; XIV. 36, 78; *Early History of Institutions, The*, XIV. 78; *Village Communities*, XII. 348; XIV. 78
Maintenon, Madame de, X. 135
Mainwaring, Edward, XI. 250
Mainwaring, Roger (1590–1653), VII. 160, 425, 433
Mainz, II. 310
Mais, Stuart Petre Brodie, XIII. 573
Maisey, Lady, II. 412
Maison Tellier, VI. 63
Maistre, Joseph de, XII. 254
Maitland, Edward (1824–1897), XIII. 564
Maitland, Frederic William (1850–1906), I. 363; VIII. 313; XIV. 79, 481, 485, 494
'Anglican Settlement and the Scottish Reformation,' XIV. 81
'Anglo-French Law Language, The,' XIV. 80
Bracton and Azo, XIV. 80
Bracton's Notebook, XIV. 80
Constitutional History of England, The, XIV. 81
Domesday Book and Beyond, I. 446; XIV. 80
English Law and the Renaissance, XIV. 81
Ford Lectures, XIV. 81
History of the English Law (with Sir F. Pollock), XIV. 80
Materials for English Legal History, The, XIV. 80
Roman Canon Law in the Church of England, XIV. 80
Year Books of Edward II, XIV. 81
Maitland, James, 8th earl of Lauderdale (1759–1839), XI. 29, 389; XII. 426, 427
Maitland, Sir John, 1st baron Maitland of Thirlstane (1545?–1595), III. 149, 150, 504
Works attributed to: *Aganis Sklanderous Tungis*, III. 150; *Ane Admonition to my Lord Regent's Grace*, III. 150; *Ane Schort Invectyve*, III. 150
Maitland, John, 2nd earl and 1st duke of Lauderdale (1616–1682), VII. 219, 435; VIII. 17, 250, 307; IX. 193, 194, 202
Maitland, Sir Richard, lord Lethington (1496–1586), III. 132 ff., 164, 499; IX. 365

Maitland, Sir Richard
Advyce to lesum Merynes, III. 134
Againis Discord among the Lordis, III. 133
Againis the Division of the Lordis, III. 133
Againis the Theives of Liddis-daill, III. 133
Assemblie of the Congregation, Of the, III. 133
Ballat of the Greatness of the World, III. 133
Chronicle and History of the House and Surname of Seaton, A, III. 133
Folye of Ane auld man maryand ane Young Woman, III. 133
Gude Counseillis, III. 134
Lament for the Disorders of the Cuntrie, III. 133
Miseries of the Tyme, III. 133
Na Kyndes without Siller, III. 134
On the New Year, III. 133
Quhair in the Blytheness that has been, III. 133
Satire of the Aige, The, III. 133
Satire of the Toun Ladies, The, III. 133
Solace of Aige, III. 134
Union among the Lordis, On, III. 133
Maitland, Samuel Roffey (1792–1866), XII. 367, 453, 522; XIV. 79, 495; *The Dark Ages*, X. 288
Maitland, Thomas, III. 165
Maitland, William (1528?–1573), III. 133; XII. 27
Maitland, William (1693?–1757), IX. 537
Maitland club, XII. 358, 359
Maitland MSS., II. 478; III. 132
Maittaire, Michael (1668–1747), IX. 529, 538
Major or Mair, John (1469–1550), II. 109, 244, 251, 260, 369, 371, 488; III. 151, 152, 155, 157, 319, 504; *Art of Making Puddings, The* (in *Pantagruel*), III. 151; *Commentary on the Four Books of the Sentences*, III. 151; *Historia Majoris Britanniae*, III. 151, 155
Mak, in *Secunda Pastorum*, V. 19, 47
Makculloch MS., II. 478
Makers of Canada series, XIV. 359
Makin, Mrs Bathsua (*fl.* 1673), IX. 403, 569
Makluire, John (*fl.* 1630), IX. 558
Maknab, in *Bruce*, II. 105
Makower, S. V., XIV. 208, 528
Makyne (Malkin), in *Robene and Makyne*, II. 249
Malabari, Bahramji, XIV. 341, 578; *The Indian Muse*, XIV. 342
Malacca, IV. 85
Malaprop, Mrs, in Sheridan's *Rivals*, X. 90, 91; XI. 266, 267, 277; XIV. 122, 387
Malay archipelage, XIV. 250
Malay language, XIV. 457, 459
Malbecco, in *The Devil and his Dame*, V. 329
Malbecco, in *The Faerie Queene*, V. 329
Malbie, N., IV. 540
Malchus, St, I. 74, 75, 191
Malcolm, in *Macbeth*, V. 213
Malcolm, in Wyntoun, II. 132
Malcolm, James Peller (1767–1815), XII. 507, 511
Malcolm, Sir John (1769–1833), XIV. 248, 491, 495, 553, 573, 578; *Central India*, XIV. 335; *History of Persia*, XIV. 335; *Political History of India*, XIV. 335
Malcolm of Scotland (Malcolm III), I. 140
Malden, John, X. 387
Malden, Surrey, II. 353; VII. 373
Maldon, The Battle of, I. 48, 109, 125, 137, 143, 144, 150, 278, 443
Malebranche, Nicolas, VIII. 347, 474, 476; IX. 282, 287, 521; *Recherche de la Vérité*, VIII. 348, 373; IX. 314
Malecasta, in *The Faerie Queene*, III. 231
Maleforts, the, in *The Unnaturall Combat*, VI. 153, 159
Malelas, Joannes, IX. 330, 524
Malespini, *Ducento Novelle*, VI. 202
Malet, Sir Alexander (1800–1886), XIV. 598
Malet, Harold Esdaile, XIV. 544
'Malet, Lucas,' XIII. 547
Malfato, in *The Ladies Triall*, VI. 194
Malfi, duchess of, in Webster's drama, XII. 68
Malgo, IV. 67
Malherbe, François de, VII. 2; VIII. 376
Malim, William (1553–1594), *Consuetudinary*, V. 102
Malines, V. 89, 90
Malkin, Benjamin Heath (1769–1842), *A Father's Memoir of his Child*, XI. 181, 182, 434
Malkin and Jankin, in *Lutel Soth Sermun*, I. 226
Mall, in *The Two Angry Women*, V. 330
Mallard, in Gissing's *The Emancipated*, XIII. 460
Malleson, George Bruce (1825–1898), XIV. 338, 495, 511, 578, 579; *History of the French in India*, XIV. 339
Mallet or Malloch, David (1705?–1765), IX. 181, 185–6 (main entry), 227, 295, 443, 449, 486, 504, *also see* Add.; X. 94, 107, 109, 301, 433, 437, 447, 449
Amyntor and Theodora, IX. 186
Birks of Endermay, IX. 186
Edwin and Emma, IX. 186
Elvira, X. 191, 477
Excursion, The, IX. 186
William and Margaret, IX. 182, 185, 186
Mallet, Sir Louis (1823–1890), XIV. 509, 512
Mallet, Paul Henri (1730–1807), X. 489; *Introduction à l'histoire du Dannemarc*, X. 225, 490; *Mythology of the Celtes*, X. 202; *Northern Antiquities*, XII. 368
Mallett, Mrs, VIII. 207
Malleus Maleficarum, III. 112
Malloch, David. *See* Mallet
Malmesbury, VII. 268, 282; VIII. 246
Malmesbury, earls of. *See* Harris, James; Harris, James Howard
Malmesbury, monk of (chronicler), II. 301

Malmesbury, William of. *See* William
Malmesbury abbey, I. 78, 159
Malone, Edmund (1741–1812), V. 143, 146, 275 ff.; VI. 1, 249; VIII. 4, 56, 424; IX. 477; X. 181, 194, 201, 462, 463, 465, 473, 478, 480, 485, 494; XI. 390; XII. 365; *Life of Dryden*, VIII. 3
Malory, Sir Thomas (*fl.* 1470), I. 243, 245, 268, 269, 273, 294, 295, 299; II. 315, 334 ff., 340; III. 339; IV. 227; VII. 75, 127; XIII. 119, 128, 199; *Morte d'Arthur*, II. 230, 314, 315, 332, 334 ff., 340, 486; IV. 397; V. 78; XIII. 35
Malpighi, Marcello, VIII. 362; XIV. 282
Malta, XI. 121, 393
Maltby, Edward (1770–1859), XII. 327, 487, 491
Maltby, William (1763–1854), XII. 408
Malthus, Daniel (father of T. R. Malthus), XI. 73
Malthus, Thomas Robert (1766–1834), X. 276; XI. 73 ff., 394, 399; XII. 431; *Essay on the Principle of Population*, XI. 74, 75; XIV. 298; *Inquiry into the Nature and Progress of Rent*, XI. 75; XIV. 3; *Principles of Political Economy*, XI. 75
Malvern, IV. 190; X. 134
'Malvern, John,' III. 325
Malvern, school of Benedictine monastery at, II. 2
Malvern hills, II. 2, 4, 5, 15; XIII. 49
Malvina, X. 227, 229
Malvolio, in *Twelfth Night*, IV. 78; V. 193, 194; VII. 101
Maly Stewart, IX. 376
Malynes or Malines, Gerard (*fl.* 1586–1641), IV. 297, 309, 313, 512; VIII. 469
Mambres, legend of, I. 135
Mambrun, Pierre, *De Poemate Epico*, VII. 270
Mammon, Sir Epicure, in *The Alchemist*, V. 356, 377; VI. 22, 23
Mammon, house of, in *The Faerie Queene*, III. 233, 237
Man, in *Mirour de l'Omme*, II. 140, 141, 144
Man, isle of, IV. 190; X. 193; XII. 509, 512, 519; XIV. 297
Man in Black, in Goldsmith's *Citizen of the World*, X. 198, 206
Man in the Moon, The (1609), III. 487
Man in the Moon, The (1660), VII. 360
Man of Law (Chaucer's), IV. 207
Man of no Honour, The, VIII. 92
'Man of Ross' (John Kyrle), X. 277
Man of the Hill, in Fielding's *Tom Jones*, X. 30
Mananan's mantle, XIV. 320
Manawyδan, Son of Llŷr, I. 252, 255
Manchester, III. 428; V. 251; VIII. 62; IX. 325, 386; X. 510, 516; XII. 337, 366; XIII. 351, 373, 374; XIV. 23, 152, 169, 179, 195, 204, 259, 275
  Academy, X. 385, 386; XIV. 386
  Baron's hall, IV. 433
Manchester
  Chetham library, IV. 432; XII. 369, 514, 522
  College of Arts and Science, XIV. 386
  Cross street unitarian chapel, XIII. 372
  John Rylands library, XII. 365, 523
  Literary and Philosophical society, XIV. 386
  Moss Side library, XII. 445
  Newton's lane, III. 392
  Owens college, XII. 333; XIII. 455; XIV. 290, 432
  Plymouth grove, XIII. 372
  Victoria university, XII. 369; XIV. 432
Manchester, duke of. *See* Montagu, Charles
Manchester, earl of. *See* Montagu, Edward
Manchester, Isabella, duchess of, XI. 174
Manchester Examiner and Times, The, XIV. 189
Manchester Guardian, The, XIII. 373; XIV. 91, 203, 531, 535
Mancini, VII. 61
Mancinus, Dominicus, III. 57, 187
Mandeville, Bernard (1670?–1733), IV. 299; IX. 309, 507, 512, 571; *Essay on Charity*, IX. 407; *Fable of the Bees*, IX. 302, 311, 323, 474, 507, 510, 512, 548; *Grumbling Hive, The*, IX. 302, 311
Mandeville, Sir John, XIII. 124
Mandeville, Travels of Sir John, I. 307; II. 70 ff., 78 ff., 231, 286, 298, 321, 323, 338, 429, 445, 446; IV. 68, 414
Manette, Lucie, in *A Tale of Two Cities*, XIII. 333
Manfred, in Byron's drama, XII. 45, 47
Mangan, James Clarence (1803–1849), XIV. 305, 318*a*, 318*b*, 570
Mangin, Edward (1772–1852), *Essay on Light Reading*, X. 195, 411, 483
Maniere de langage que t'enseignera bien a droit parler et escrire doulz françois, II. 421
Manifest detection of the most vyle and detestable use of dice play, A, III. 98
Manila, IV. 100; XIV. 242, 243
Manilius, III. 113; IX. 338, 525, 526
Manilla, X. 403
Maning, Frederick Edward (1812–1883), XIV. 587
Manipulus curatorum, II. 325
Manitius, I. 83
Mankynd, V. 52, 392
Manley, Mrs Mary de la Rivière (1663–1724), VIII. 438; IX. 462, *also see* Add.; XIV. 197; *New Atalantis*, IX. 18; *Royal Mischief, The*, VIII. 195
Manley, Thomas (1628–1690), *Temporis Angustiae*, VII. 392, 517
Manlius, M., IV. 13
Manly, John M., V. Add. 2
Manly, in Wycherley's *Country Wife*, VIII. 143, 145, 165
Mann, Sir Horace (1701–1786), IX. 246; X. 245, 247, 249 ff., 253, 256, 495; XI. 259, 260; XIV. 607

Mann, Dr R. J., XIII. 478; XIV. Add. 6, 8
Mannering, Julia, in Scott's *Guy Mannering*, XII. 22
Manners, Catherine (d. 1711), wife of 2nd duke of Rutland, VIII. 272
Manners, Charles, 4th duke of Rutland (1754–1787), XI. 143
Manners, John, marquis of Granby (1721–1770), X. 197, 403, 407
Manners, lord Robert (1758–1782), XI. 145
Manners, Roger, 5th earl of Rutland (1576–1612), V. 222
Manning, Anne (1807–1879), XII. 450; *Mary Powell*, XIII. 434
Manning, Henry Edward (1808–1892), cardinal, XII. 275, 276, 458, *also see* Add.; XIV. 513
Manning, Mr, VIII. 411
Manning, Owen (1721–1801), XII. 344, 504, 511
Manning, Thomas (1772–1840), XII. 181, 187 ff.
Manning, William (1630?–1711), X. 378
Manning, William Oke (1809–1878), XIV. 594
Manningham, John (d. 1622), *Diary*, IV. 262; VI. 461; VII. 221, 451
Mannington, G., *Sorrowful Sonet made at Cambridge Castle*, III. 191
Manningtree, Essex, XII. 305
Mannyng, Robert, of Brunne (*fl.* 1288–1338), I. 204, 335, 340, 341, 344–352 (main entry), 358, 399, 475; II. 133, 139, 150, 378, 420; III. 275; IX. 535; *Chronicle of England*, I. 350 ff.; III. 289; *Handlyng Synne*, I. 341, 344 ff., 350, 352; II. 139, 143, 378; *Medytacyuns of þe soper of oure lorde Jhesu*, etc., I. 352
Manorbier castle, Wales, I. 194
Mansbridge, Albert, *University Tutorial Classes*, XIV. 409, 591
Mansel, Henry Longueville (1820–1871), XII. 289, 469; XIV. 29, 197, 474, 476
Letters, Lectures and Reviews, XIV. 13
Limits of Religious Thought, The, XIV. 13
Metaphysics, XIV. 13
Philosophy of the Conditioned, XIV. 13
Phrontisterion, XIV. 13
Prolegomena Logica, XIV. 13
Mansell of Ottery, in *The Ship of Fools*, III. 60
Mansfeld, count E. von, VII. 453
Mansfield, Charles Blackford (1819–1855), XIV. 558
Mansfield, earl of. *See* Murray, William
Mansfield, Sir James (1733–1821), XI. 58
Mansfield park, in Jane Austen's novel, XII. 241
Mansfield Woodhouse, X. 257
Mansion, Colard, II. 311
Manso, Giovanni Baptista, marquis of Villa, VII. 99
Mansoul, in *The Holy War*, VII. 177
Mant, Alicia Catherine, XI. 488
Mant, Richard (1776–1848), X. 238, 240, 473, 492, 493; XII. 420
Mantalinis, the, in *Nicholas Nickleby*, XIII. 318
Mantoux, Paul, XIV. 591
Mantua, V. 369
Mantua, duchess of, in *The Humorous Courtier*, VI. 205
Mantua, duke of, in *The Imposture*, VI. 205
Mantuan or Mantuanus (Johannes Baptista Spagnuoli), III. 62 ff., 185, 187, 219, 221, 223 ff., *also see* Add.; IV. 121, 169, 171, 446; VI. 364; *De Consuetudine Divitum erga Poetas*, III. 224; *Religio*, III. 223, 224
Mantzius, Karl, XI. 447
Manuale ad usum Sarum, IV. 427
Manuel, king of Granada, in Congreve's *Mourning Bride*, VIII. 152
Manuel, Niclas, *Krankheit der Messe*, III. 80
Manufacturer, The, IX. 14, 433
Manutius, VII. 315
Manutius, in *The Bugbears*, V. 115
Manwayring, Sir Henry, *The Sea-man's Dictionary*, IV. 107, 459
Manwood, Elegy on, V. 148
Manwood, John (d. 1610), IV. 541; VIII. 467
Manzoni, Alessandro, *I promessi Sposi*, XII. 254
Maoris, the, XIV. 368
Map or Mapes, Walter (*fl.* 1200), I. 157, 160, 173, 176, 177, 188 ff., 264, 270, 271, 272, 367, 450, 455; III. 485; VII. 380; *De Nugis Curialium*, I. 177, 189, 264, 450, 455; VII. 370, 505; *Lancelot du Lac*, I. 190, 264, 270; *Quest of the Holy Grail*, I. 190, 270, 271, 272
Mapheus Vegius, 13th book of *Aeneid*, II. 262, 263
Mapledurham, IX. 443, 448
Maplet, John (d. 1592), IV. 543
Mappa Mundi, IV. 421
'Maps' (John Nicholson), XI. 338
Mar, countess of, IX. 248
Maraffi, B., IV. 446
Marathas, the, XIV. 337, 338, 341
Marathon, I. 95
Marbeck, Roger (1536–1605), VI. 286
Marble hill, IX. 250
Marbod of Rheims, I. 232
Marburg, III. 43
Marcelia, in *The Duke of Millaine*, VI. 154, 158, 159
Marcella, in *Gorboduc*, V. 67
Marcelline, G., IV. 540
Marcellinus, Ammianus, IV. 4, 438
Marcellinus Comes, I. 81
Marcello, in *The White Divel*, VI. 175, 176
'Marcellus allowance,' XIII. 219
March, earl of, letter to Henry IV of England, II. 284, 503
March, John (1612–1657), VII. 515

Marchant, John, *History of the Present Rebellion*, 1746, IX. 564; *Puerilia*, 1751, XI. 372
Marchioness, the, in *The Old Curiosity Shop*, XIII. 320
Marchmont, earls of. *See* Hume, Hugh; Hume, Patrick
Marchmont, Miss, in Kelly's *False Delicacy*, XI. 263
Marcia, in Addison's *Cato*, IX. 64
Marcia (*i.e.* Venice), in *Euphormio*, IV. 256
Marcius, in Addison's *Cato*, IX. 63
Marcks, Erich, V. 339
Marco Polo, II. 184; IV. 68, 446
Marcolf, I. 63
Marcolphus, II. 319
Marconi, G., XIV. 453
Marcus, in Owen's *Epigrammata*, IV. 265
Marcus, *The Vision of Tundale*, XIV. 306
Marcus Aurelius, III. 199, 346; IV. 435; VII. 487; VIII. 277; XII. 487
Marcus Aurelius, The Golden Book of, II. 340
Marcus Germinus, V. 70; VI. 299
Mardonius, in *A King and no King*, VI. 127
Mardontius, in Digby's *Memoirs*, VII. 222
Mare of Collington, The, IX. 366
Marfisa, in *Orlando Furioso*, III. 231, 236
Margam, chronicle of the abbey of, I. 256
Margaret, in *Faust*, V. 20
Margaret, in *Henry VI*, V. 186
Margaret, in *James IV*, V. 138
Margaret, in Mrs Gaskell's *North and South*, XIII. 378
Margaret, in Mrs Oliphant's *Kirsteen*, XIII. 431
Margaret, in *Much Ado about Nothing*, V. 191
Margaret, in *Richard III*, V. 186
Margaret, in *The Cloister and the Hearth*, XIII. 429
Margaret (d. 1093), daughter of Edward Aetheling, I. 140
Margaret, duchess of Burgundy (1446–1503), II. 307, 309, 311, 312
Margaret (Tudor), princess, queen of Scots (1489–1541), II. 252, 253, 281; III. 98; VI. 333
Margaret, queen, the 'riding against,' at Coventry, V. 10
Margaret, St, Life of, I. 229, 459; II. 321
Margaret Beaufort (lady Margaret). *See* Beaufort
Margaret of Anjou, queen of England (1430–1482), II. 199, 209, 210, 303, 358, 500
Margaret of Fressingfield, in *Frier Bacon*, V. 137
Margaret of Valois, queen of Navarre, IV. 6, 169, 182, 259; *Heptameron*, VI. 99, 199, 202
Margate, XIII. 112
Marguerite, in Godwin's *St Leon*, XI. 293
Marguerite, in *Pearl*, I. 321
Marguerite d'Angoulême, III. 1
Maria, in Lillo's *George Barnwell*, X. 75, 79
Maria, in Sheridan's *School for Scandal*, XI. 270, 271
Maria, in *Twelfth Night*, IV. 78; V. 194
Maria Grey Training college, XIV. 430
Mariamne, VI. 154
Marian, in *John a Kent and John a Cumber*, V. 317
Marian, in *The Sad Shepherd*, VI. 370
Marian, maid, V. 32, 35, 318
Marian persecution, IV. 429
Marian system of dating, VI. 255
Mariana (Tennyson's), V. 190; XIII. 29
Mariana, in *Perimedes the Blacksmith*, III. 356, 357
Mariana, Juan de, VI. 494; *Contra los Juegos Publicos*, VII. 377; *De Rege et Regis Institutione*, VII. 377; *History of Spain*, IX. 278, 501
Marianus, Scotus (1028–1082?), I. 161
Marie, in Kingsley's *Two Years Ago*, XIII. 365
Marie de France, I. 238, 239, 270, 274, 281, 294, 295, 300, 462, 469; II. 183, 420; XIII. 140; *Lai le Freine*, I. 281, 300, 465; II. 410; *Lanval*, I. 274; *Le Chèvrefeuille*, I. 274
Marie-Antoinette, queen of France, X. 251; XI. 24, 157
Maries, the three, at the tomb, V. 39
Marillier, Harry Currie, XIV. 539
Marina, in *Britannia's Pastorals*, IV. 157
Marine Biological association, XIV. 297
Marinell, in *The Faerie Queene*, III. 240
Marino, Giambattista, IV. 213; VII. 34, 83; *Adone*, VII. 268; VIII. 374; *Strage degli Innocenti*, IV. 36
Marino Faliero, in Byron's drama, XII. 49
Marion (type name of French shepherdess), V. 34, 35
Marionnettes, V. 27
Marivaux, Pierre C. de C. de, X. 68, 89, *also see* Add.; *Jeu de l'Amour*, X. 79; *Marianne*, X. 3, 26; *Paysan Parvenu*, X. 26
Mark (March) ab Meirchion, king of Cornwall, I. 273, 274, 310; II. 337
Market Bosworth, X. 159
Markham, Sir Clements Robert, XIV. 486, 553, 554
Markham, Gervase (1568?–1637), IV. 308, 364 ff., 537 ff.; V. 351, 478; VI. 456; XIV. 232
Cavelarice, or the English Horseman, IV. 365 ff.
Cheap and Good Husbandry, IV. 372
Complete Farriar, The, IV. 368
Country Contentments, IV. 372, 373
Country Housewifes Garden, IV. 375
Country-mans Recreation, IV. 375
Devoreux, or vertues tears, IV. 376, 377
Discource of Horsemanshippe, A, IV. 365
Dumbe Knight, The, IV. 377
English Arcadia, The, IV. 377
English Husbandman, IV. 375
English Huswife, IV. 373
Famous Whore, The, IV. 376

Markham, Gervase
Gentlemans Academie, IV. 375
Grinvile, Knight, The Most Honourable Tragedie of Sir Richard, IV. 376
Herod and Antipater, IV. 377
How to chuse, ride...both hunting horses and running horses, IV. 365
How to trayne and teach horses to amble, IV. 365
Inrichment of the Weald of Kent, The, IV. 373
Maister-peece, IV. 367
Marie Magdalens lamentations, IV. 376
Markhams Faithfull Farrier, IV. 368
Markhams Farewell to Husbandry, IV. 373
Markhams Method: or Epitome, IV. 367
Poem of poems, IV. 376
Rodomonths Infernall, IV. 377, 443
Teares of the Beloved, IV. 376
Thyrsis and Daphne, IV. 365
Way to get Wealth, A, IV. 369, 372, 373
Whole Art of Angling, The, IV. 373
Markland, Jeremiah (1693–1776), IX. 341, 527; XII. 483
Markolf legend, III. 81, 94
Marlay, Richard, XI. 365
Marlborough, duchesses of. *See* Churchill, Henrietta; Churchill, Sarah
Marlborough, dukes of. *See* Churchill, John; Spencer, George
Marlborough college, XII. 332; XIII. 118; XIV. 414
Marlowe, Christopher (1564–1593), III. 241, 300, 517; IV. 23, 55, 88, 117, 248, 330, 395, 438, 517, 519; V. 81, 85, 87, 103, 134, 140, 142–164 (main entry), 177, 179, 182, 183, 188, 215, 224, 239, 240, 242, 244, 309, 324, 327, 333, 347, 366, 370, 371, 373, 377, 420 ff., *and see* Add. 2; VI. 13, 14, 45, 167, 234, 272, 295, 300, 301, 335; VII. 7 ff., 16, 49, 110, 133, 273; VIII. 223, 226; XII. 418; XIII. 153, *also see* Add. 2
Dido Queene of Carthage, V. 140, 145, 146; VI. 287, 288
Dr Faustus, IV. 321; V. 134, 143 ff., 147, 154, 163, 252, 253, 333, 353, 377; VI. 250; VIII. 88
Edward II, V. 145, 152 ff., 163, 185, 186, 246; XIV. 443
Hero and Leander, IV. 180, 222, 395; V. 147, 148; VI. 112; VIII. 227
'I walked along a stream,' V. 148
Jew of Malta, The, V. 145, 155, 156, 326; VI. 249
Lucan, V. 147
Lusts Dominion, V. 146; VI. 55, 183; VIII. 125, 195
Massacre at Paris, The, V. 145, 344; VI. 33
Ovid's Elegies, IV. 19, 328; V. 143, 147; VII. 432
Passionate Shepherd to his Love, The, V. 148; VII. 8, 17, 251
Tamburlaine the Great, III. 178; V. 82, 84, 134 ff., 142 ff., 147, 150, 154, 162, 163, 316; VI. 29, 250; VIII. 126
Marlow-on-Thames, XII. 61, 62
Marly, IX. 153
Marmaduke, in Wordsworth's *Borderers*, XI. 99
Marmion, lord, in Scott's poem, XII. 10 ff.
Marmion, Shakerley (1603–1639), VI. 456; VII. 113, 413; VIII. 227, 419; *Antiquary, The*, VI. 239; *Cupid and Psyche*, VI. 239; VII. 77, 78
Marmontel, Jean-François, X. 264; XI. 296, 492; *Contes Moraux*, X. 57; *Les Incas*, XI. 280; *Moral Tales*, XI. 385
Marneffe, Valérie, Balzac's, XIII. 286, 287
Marney, Sir Henry, II. 325
Marnock, Robert (1800–1889), XIV. 289
'Marocco' (horse), IV. 366, 531, 540
Marot, Clément, III. 46, 65, 219, 221, 222, 224, 226, 249, 250; IV. 24; X. 105
Complaincte d'un Pastoureau Chrestien, III. 219
Eglogue au Roi, III. 219, 222, 224
Elegie sur Mme Louise de Savoye, III. 219, 224
Epigrammes, III. 249
Visions de Petrarque, Les, III. 251
Marphoreus, III. 394, 395
Marplot, in Centlivre's *Busy-Body*, X. 72
Marprelate, Martin, III. 213, 374 ff., 412, 537 ff., *also see* Add.; V. 140, 322; VI. 296, 384, 391, 393, 396, 478; VII. 144, 161, 517; X. 367
Admonition to Parliament, An, III. 378, 403, 404
Admonition to the People of England, An. See under Cooper, Thomas
Advertisement touching the Controversies of the Church of England. See under Cooper, Thomas
Almond for a Parrat, An, III. 397, 544
Answere to a certaine libel supplicatorie, An. See under Sutcliffe, Matthew
Answere unto a certaine calumnious letter, An. See under Sutcliffe, Matthew
Anti-Martinus, III. 393
Appelation of John Penri, Th'. See under Penry, John
Character of a Puritan, III. 389
Commission sente to the Pope, III. 376, 388
Countercuffe given to Martin Junior, A, III. 394
Defence of the Government established in the Church of England, A. See under Bridges, John
Demonstration of Discipline, A. See under Udall, John
Dialogue concerning the strife of our Church, A. See under Udall, John
Dialogue wherein is plainly laide open the tyrannicall dealing of L. Bishopps against Gods children, A, III. 381, 382, 397
Diotrephes, or, The State of the Church of Englande. See under Udall John

Marprelate, Martin
Epistle, The, III. 379, 384, 385, 389, 391, 392
Epitome, The, III. 381, 385 ff.
Exhortation, An. See under Penry, John
Friendly Admonition to Martin Marprelate, A. See under Wright, Leonard
Hay any worke for Cooper, III. 381, 387, 390, 397
Lives of the Saints, The, III. 394
M. Some laid open in his coulers, III. 381, 383
Mar-Martine, III. 388, 393
Marre Mar-Martin, III. 393
Martin Junior, The just censure and reproofe of, III. 382, 387, 388, 393, 394
Martin Senior, or The just censure and reproofe, III. 388
Martins Months Minde, III. 394, 396, 397, 544
Minerall Conclusions, The, III. 381, 386
More worke for the Cooper, III. 382
Myrrour for Martinists, A. See under T. T.
Owles Almanack, The, III. 394
Papp-Hatchet, Advertisement to. See under Harvey, Gabriel
Pappe with a Hatchet. See under Lyly, John
Petition directed to her most excellent Majestie, A, III. 391, 392
Plaine Percevall the Peace-maker of England. See under Harvey, Richard
Protestation, The, III. 382, 383, 387 ff., 393, 394, 397
Returne of Pasquill, The, III. 394, 395
Sermon preached at Paules crosse, A. See under Bancroft, Richard
Supplication to the Parliament, A. See under Penry, John
Theologicall Discourse of the Lamb of God, A. See under Harvey, Richard
Theses Martinianae, or Martin Junior, III. 382, 387 ff., 394, 396
Treatise, containing the Aequity of an humble supplication, A. See under Penry, John
Whip for an Ape, III. 393
Marprelate controversy, IV. 230, 321, 322, 332, 379, 382, 412, 547
Marprelate tracts, VII. 432
Marquis, Thomas G., XIV. 581
Marriage, The Fifteen Joys of, II. 325, 326
Marriage, The pain and sorrow of evil, II. 326, 502; III. 486
Marriage Feast, parable of, in *Cleanness*, I. 323
Marriage of Witte, The, V. 393
Married, The complaint of the too late, II. 326; III. 486
Married, The complaint of the too soon, II. 326; III. 486
Marriot, Richard (*fl.* 1653), XI. 318
Marriott, Charles (1811–1858), XII. 261, 274, 454, 458
Marriott, John Arthur Ransome, XIII. 548
'Marrow men,' IX. 549
Marryat, Florence (1838–1899), XII. 451; XIII. 564
Marryat, Frederick (1792–1848), XI. 387, 480, 481; XII. 451, *also see* Add.; XIII. 307, 322, 329; XIV. 141
Jacob Faithful, XII. 250
Japhet in search of a Father, XII. 250
Masterman Ready, XII. 251
Mr Midshipman Easy, XII. 251
Peter Simple, XII. 250
Settlers in Canada, XII. 251
Marryat, Zephaniah, X. 384
Mars, VIII. 76
Mars, temple of (Chaucer's), II. 179
Mars' hill, IV. 29, 270
Marsden, John Howard (1803–1891), XII. 497
Marseilles, V. 49; VI. 378, 383; VIII. 245
Marsh, Adam (Adam de Marisco) (*fl.* 1257?), I. 205, 206, 455; II. 350
Marsh, Anne. *See* Caldwell, Mrs Anne
Marsh, George Perkins, IV. 37, 450
Marsh, Herbert (1757–1839), XII. 280, 468; XIV. 403, 592
Marsh, Narcissus (1638–1713), IX. 330
Marsh or Marshe, Thomas, III. 194 ff.; IV. 384, 398
Marshall, the, in *The Royall King and the Loyall Subject*, VI. 100
Marshall, Anne, VIII. 261
Marshall, Arthur Milnes (1852–1893), XIV. 562; *Practical Zoology*, XIV. 300
Marshall, Emma (1830–1899), XIII. 564
Marshall, Sir John Hubert (b. 1876), XII. Add. 5
Marshall, Roger, IV. 423
Marshall, Stephen (1594?–1655), VII. 145, 147, 416, 425
Marshall, William (d. 1219), 1st earl of Pembroke and Striguil, regent of England, II. 420
Marsham, Sir John (1602–1685), IX. 196, 529
Marshman, John Clark (1794–1877), XIV. 338, 339, 495, 579
Marsiglio of Padua, I. 212
Marston, John (1575?–1634), III. 173, 191, 199, 207; IV. 6, 115, 185, 207, 266, 331 ff., 363, 434, 533; V. 81, 311, 322, 327, 371; VI. 2, 4, 17, 18, 28, 29–57 (main entry), 59, 154, 166, 170 ff., 182, 186, 239, 290 422, 423, 459, *and see* Add.; VII. 383; VIII. 87
Antonio and Mellida, VI. 15, 41, 45, 170
Antonio's Revenge, VI. 45, 167, 178
Certaine Satyres, IV. 331
Dutch Courtezan, The, VI. 46, 184
Eastward Hoe. See under Chapman
Entertainment for a visit of the countess of Derby to her son-in-law, lord Huntingdon, An, VI. 49
Histrio-Mastix (revision of), V. 321
Insatiate Countesse, The, V. 362; VI. 49
Latin pageant for the visit of king Christian of Denmark to England, a, VI. 49
Love's Martyr, VI. 43

Marston, John
Malcontent, The, v. 259; vi. 15, 39, 43, 46, 48, 169, 178
Metamorphosis of Pygmalion's Image, The, iv. 331, 332; vi. 38
Mountebank's Masque, vi. 50
Parasitaster, or The Fawne, vi. 48, 171
Reactio, iii. 199
Revenge, or the Match in Newgate, The, vi. 47
Scourge of Villanie, The, iv. 332, 333, 517, 519; vi. 38 ff.
What You Will, vi. 43
Wonder of Women, Or the Tragedie of Sophonisba, The, vi. 49
Marston, John Westland (1819–1890), xiii. 152, 267 ff., 515, 516, 521, 541
Favourite of Fortune, The, xiii. 269
Life for Life, xiii. 263
Life's Ransom, A, xiii. 263
Marie de Méranie, xiii. 263
Patrician's Daughter, The, xiii. 262
Strathmore, xiii. 263
Marston, Philip Bourke (1850–1887), xiii. 109, 140, 215, 489, 506
Marston moor, xii. 13
Marston moor, battle of, vi. 197; vii. 198, 227, 229; viii. 130
Marsyas, xiii. 90
Marteilhe, Jean, *Memoirs*, x. 203
Marten, Anthony (d. 1597), iv. 459
Marten, Henry (1602–1680), and his mistresses, in the *Mercuries*, vii. 356, 359, 513
Martha, in Le Fanu's story, xiii. 416
Martial, i. 191; iii. 429; iv. 23, 124, 206, 242, 250, 262, 266, 334, 438; vi. 221; vii. 13, 131; ix. 55, 264, 499; xi. 174; xii. 489; *Epigrammata*, vii. 20; *To Bassus, on the Country-House of Faustinus*, vii. 20
Martianus Capella's *de Nuptiis Philologiae et Mercurii*, ii. 231, 359, 363
Martin, in Kingsley's *Hereward the Wake*, xiii. 366
Martin, in Swift's *Tale of a Tub*, ix. 100
Martin, the (father Petre), in *The Hind and the Panther*, viii. 48, 189
Martin, Arthur Patchett (1851–1902), xiv. 368, 511, 584, 587
Martin, Benjamin (1704–1782), *Biographica Philosophica*, viii. 458, 463
Martin, Frederick (1830–1883), xii. 415
Martin, George, xiv. 582
Martin, Humfrey (*fl.* 1575), v. 30
Martin, James, of Dunkeld (*fl.* 1577), iv. 277
Martin, lady. *See* Faucit, Helena
Martin, Richard (1570–1618), iv. 161, 162
Martin, Robert, in Jane Austen's *Emma*, xii. 240
Martin, St, i. 74, 118
Martin, Samuel, x. 396
Martin, T., translator of Prior's *Alma* into Latin, ix. 482
Martin, Sir Theodore (1816–1909), xiii. 161, 499, 515; xiv. 504
Helena Faucit (Lady Martin), xiv. 112
Life of Lord Lyndhurst, xiv. 111
Life of the Prince Consort, xiv. 111
Memoir of W. E. Aytoun, xiv. 111
Martin, William (1801–1867), xi. 481
Martin de Franc, iii. 90
Martin's office, ix. 132
Martineau, Harriet (1802–1876), xi. 387, 481; xii. 380, 433, 445; xiii. 397, 553, 554, 558; xiv. 190, 429, 476, 495, 607
A History of England during the Thirty Years' Peace, xiv. 93
Autobiographical Memoir, xiii. 343
Crofton Boys, xiii. 343
Deerbrook, xiii. 343, 399
Feats on the Fiord, xiii. 343
Hour and the Man, The, xiii. 343
Illustrations of Political Economy, xiii. 343
Illustrations of Taxation, xiii. 343
Peasant and the Prince, The, xiii. 343
Playfellow, The, xiii. 343
Settlers at Home, The, xiii. 343
Trans. of Comte's *Positive Philosophy*, xiv. 24
Martineau, James (1805–1900), viii. 287; xii. 465, 468; xiv. 26, 477, 607; *Seat of Authority in Religion, The*, xiv. 27; *Study of Religion, A*, xii. 298; xiv. 27; *Types of Ethical Theory*, xii. 298; xiv. 27
Martineau, John, xiv. 510
Martinique, xiv. 165
Martinius, monk, i. 105
Martinius, P., iii. 552
Martinus, in *Loiola*, vi. 324
'Martinus Scriblerus' (George Crabbe), xi. 142
Martyn, Henry (1781–1812), xi. 381
Martyn, Joseph (*fl.* 1619), iv. 520
Martyn, J., one of the chief contributors to *The Grub Street Journal* (1730–1737), xi. 466
Martyr, Peter (Anglerius), iv. 69, 70–1, 74, 75, 80–2, 441, 455, 459
Martyr, Peter (Vermigli), iii. 33–4, 35, 419
Martyria, v. 38
Martyrology, Bede's, i. 80
Martyrology, The, West Saxon, i. 105, 106, 436, 438
Marullo, in *The Bond-Man*, vi. 154, 155
Marullus, in *Julius Caesar*, v. 197
Marvell, Andrew, the elder (1586?–1641), vii. 178
Marvell, Andrew, the younger (1621–1678), iv. 214, 222; vi. 235; vii. 7, 102, 105 ff., 166, 178–185 (main entry), 430 ff.; viii. 3, 40, 82, 89, 90, 91, 94, 213, 214, 408, 409, 410, 411, 412; ix. 416; xii. 202
Advice to a Painter, viii. 81
Black List of Government Pensioners, x. 213

Marvell, Andrew, the younger
Britannia and Raleigh, viii. 81
Controversial Essays, vii. 179
Coronet, The, vii. 181
Dialogue between the Resolved Soul and Created Pleasure, vii. 182
Dialogue between the Soul and the Body, vii. 181
Dialogue between two Horses, viii. 93
Farther Instructions to a Painter, viii. 81
Fleckno, an English Priest at Rome, viii. 40
Garden, The, vii. 181; viii. 99
Greek poems, vii. 179
His Majesty's Most Gracious Speech to Both Houses of Parliament, viii. 98
Historical Poem, An, vii. 183; viii. 81
Horatian Ode upon Cromwell's Return from Ireland, vii. 180
Last Instructions to a Painter, vii. 183; viii. 81
Latin poems, vii. 179, 181, 183
News-letters, vii. 179, 184
Poem on the Statue in Stocks-market, viii. 93
Poems, vii. 179, 183, 184
Rehearsal Transpros'd, The, vii. 178, 184, 185
Satires, vii. 179, 182, 183
'Where the remote Bermudas ride,' iv. 187; vii. 182
Marvin, F. S., xiii. 487
Marwood, in Lessing's *Miss Sara Sampson*, x. 76
Marwood, Mrs, in Congreve's *Way of the World*, viii. 154, 155
Mary, in *Monsieur Thomas*, vi. 123
Mary, the Blessed Virgin, i. 64, 74, 115, 146, 147, 220, 248, 297, 321, 342, 343, 353, 356; ii. 114, 264, 375, 376, 380 ff., 426, 507; iii. 12, 59; iv. 217; v. 2, 17, 18, 40 ff., 49, 50, 53, 56, 59; vii. 33, 37, 63; xii. 291; xiv. 304
Mary, princess of Orange (1631–1660), viii. 206
Mary I (1516–1558), queen of England, iii. 1, 6, 50, 51, 53, 81, 96, 107, 145, 179, 181, 183, 194 ff., 213, 316, 332, 335, 386, 403, 420, 421, 424, 427, 432; iv. 71, 127, 198, 225, 234, 379, 380, 382, 384; v. 56, 59, 60, 90, 104, 107, 356, 365; vii. 304, 306, 325, 326, 331, 337; viii. 267; ix. 210, 235; xiv. 55
Mary II (1662–1694), queen of England, viii. 49, 306, 307, 380; ix. 169, 200, 208, 233; x. 502
Mary II, Memoirs of Queen, viii. 272, 452
Mary (1542–1587), queen of Scots, ii. 414; iii. 1, 122, 144, 146 ff., 153 ff., 163, 164, 234, 326, 327; iv. 136, 253, 303, 396; v. 77, 341, 344, 345; x. 288, 289, 465, 498, 500, 501, 504, 505, 510; xi. 443; xii. 21, 27, 350, 416, 508, 513; xiii. 130, 133; xiv. 55, 85, 94, 161
Mary de' Medici, vii. 222
Mary de St Paul, ii. 355
Mary de Valentia, ii. 355
Mary of Egypt, St, Life of, i. 131
Mary of France, queen of Louis XII (1496–1533), iv. 182
Mary of Lorraine, iii. 121, 123, 144
Mary of Modena (1658–1718), queen of James II, ix. 168
Mary of Nemmegen, ii. 329
Mary Ambree, viii. 231, 232; xiii. 234
Mary Magdalen, The Lamentation of, ii. 162, 164
Mary Magdalene, in *Christus Redivivus*, vi. 295
Mary Magdalene, St, i. 341
Mary Magdalene plays, v. 19, 42, 44, 49
Maryland, xii. 350; xiv. 359
Marys, 'the four,' xii. 27
Marzials, Sir Frank T., x. Add.; xi. 291, 459; xiii. 485, 530, 532, 544
Mascall, Leonard (d. 1589), iv. 368 ff., 540 ff.
Book of Fishing, A, iv. 370
Government of Cattell, The, iv. 370
Husbandlye ordering...Poultrie, The, iv. 370
Of the arte and manner how to plant... trees, iv. 370
Masefield, John, ix. Add.; xii. 406; xiv. 551
Maseres, Francis (1731–1824), vii. 456
Masham, Abigail, lady Masham (d. 1734), ix. 124
Masham, Damaris, lady Masham (1658–1708), viii. 330
Masham, Sir Francis, 3rd baronet, viii. 330
Masham, Samuel, 2nd baron Masham (1712–1776), ix. 130
Maskell, William, iii. 48
Maskwell, in Congreve's *Double-Dealer*, viii. 148, 149
Mason, Arthur James, xiv. 486
Mason, Edward Tuckerman, xiv. 528
Mason, Francis (1566?–1621), vii. 309; *Vindex Ecclesiae Anglicanae*, vii. 329, 485
Mason, George, iv. 464
Mason, James, *Anatomy of Sorcery*, vii. 506
Mason, John (1645?–1694), vii. 407
Mason, John (1706–1763), xi. 251 ff., 255
Mason, John Monck (1726–1809), v. 277
Mason, Peter Hamnett (1827–1912), xii. 341, 501
Mason, Stuart, xiv. 528
Mason, William, *A handfull of Essaies* (1621), iv. 524
Mason, William (1724–1797), vii. 164; ix. 574; x. 120, 122, 123, 126 ff. (main entry), 137, 244, 248 ff., 398, 450, 495, 525; xi. 145, 458; xiv. 507
Caractacus, x. 136; xi. 273
Elfrida, x. 136; xi. 265
Isis, x. 136, 492
Life of Gray, x. 190
Musaeus, a Monody on...Pope, x. 136

Mason, William Shaw (1774–1853), x. 483
Masque of Cupid, in *The Faerie Queene*, vi. 335
Masquerado, in *Love Restored*, vi. 351, 352
Masques, vi. 487 ff.
Massachusetts, xii. 165
Massachusetts' Bay company, iv. 311
Massaniello, in D'Urfey's *Fall of Massaniello*, viii. 175
Masseck, C. J., xiv. 521
Massey, Sir Edward (1619?–1674?), vii. 356
Massey, Gerald (1828–1907), xiii. 189, 506
Massey, William Nathaniel (1809–1881), xiv. 495; *A History of England during the reign of George III*, xiv. 90
Massie, Joseph (d. 1784), x. 523
Massillon, Jean Baptiste, viii. 303
Massinger, Arthur, father of P. Massinger, vi. 141
Massinger, Miss (d. 1762), vi. 144
Massinger, Philip (1583–1640), iv. 6, 115; v. 195, 258, 344, 347, 366, 368, 370; vi. 61, 111, 114 ff., 118, 121, 124, 128 ff., 134, 136, 137–140, 141–165 (main entry), 196, 211, 427, 442 ff., 458; vii. 387; viii. 132; x. 429; xii. 68, 415; xiii. 144, 260, 289, *also see* Add. 2; xiv. 88
- *Bashful Lover, The*, vi. 152, 155
- *Believe as you List*, vi. 146, 147
- *Bond-Man, The*, vi. 143, 149, 155, 157, 161, 164; viii. 121
- *City Madam, The*, v. 357; vi. 152, 160
- *Duke of Millaine, The*, vi. 142, 153 ff., 159, 161, 162
- *Emperour of the East, The*, vi. 165
- *Fatall Dowry, The*, vi. 146, 158, 165, 223; viii. 129, 195, 441; xiii. 259
- *Great Duke of Florence, The*, vi. 154, 156, 165
- *Guardian, The*, vi. 157, 165; viii. 142
- *King and the Subject, The*, vi. 147
- *Lover's Progress, The*, v. 257
- *Maid of Honour, The*, iv. 299; vi. 149, 152, 155, 156, 162
- *New Way to Pay Old Debts, A*, vi. 143, 151, 152, 160, 165
- *Parliament of Love, The*, vi. 152, 154, 155, 184
- *Picture, The*, vi. 156, 164
- *Renegado, The*, vi. 150, 154, 155; viii. 129
- *Roman Actor, The*, vi. 152 ff., 161, 164
- *Unnaturall Combat, The*, vi. 142, 153, 160
- *Very Woman, A*, vi. 116, 132, 140, 146, 156, 157; viii. 129
- *Virgin Martir, The*, vi. 54, 142, 146, 150, 154
- *See, also, under* Beaumont and Fletcher and Middleton

Masson, Arthur, *Collection of English Prose and Verse*, xi. 206
Masson, Charles, 'Memoir on the Topes,' xii. 352
Masson, David (1822–1907), vii. 95, 117; x. 122, 481; xi. 410, 466; xii. 206, 380, 403, 407, 444, 445; xiii. 245, 472; xiv. 95, 467, 504; *Life of Milton*, xi. 312; xiv. 112, 113; *Recent British Philosophy*, xiv. 1
Masson, Emile, xiii. 464, 470
Masson, Flora, xiii. 558
Massorah, the, xii. 341, 501
Master, John, of Sinclair, xii. 377
Master of Game, The, ii. 286, 479
Masterman, Charles Frederick Gurney, xiii. 478
Masters, Mrs Mary (d. 1759?), x. 468
Masters, Robert (1713–1798), ix. 477, 531; x. 255, 505
Masterson, George, vii. 495
Matamoros, Alfonso Garcia, v. 214
Matelant, Richard de, ancestor of Sir Richard Maitland, iii. 132
Matey, in Meredith's *Lord Ormont and his Aminta*, xiii. 444
Math, son of Mathonwy, i. 252
Matheo, in *The Honest Whore*, vi. 53
Matheolus, iii. 90
Mather, Cotton (1663–1728), vii. 507
Mather, Increase (1639–1723), vii. 507
Mathers, Edward P., xiv. Add. 8
Mathesis, xii. 114
Mathew, Mrs, xi. 181, 184
Mathews, Charles James (1803–1878), xiii. 521
Mathias, in *The Picture*, vi. 156, 158
Mathias, Thomas James (1754?–1835), x. 450 ff., 486, 489; xi. 177, 427; *The Pursuits of Literature*, xii. 364
Matilda, in Law's *Serious Call*, ix. 402
Matilda, in *Robert, Earle of Huntington*, v. 318, 319, 322 ff., 326
Matilda, in *The Bashful Lover*, vi. 152, 155
Matilda, in Walpole's *Castle of Otranto*, x. 61
Matilda (1080–1118), queen of Henry I. i. 151, 157
Matthew, in *Every Man in His Humour*, vi. 4
Matthew, Gospel of pseudo-, v. 49
Matthew, Patrick, xiv. 298, 562
Matthew, St, i. 54
Matthew, St, Gospel of, ii. 14, 76, 431
Matthew, Thomas. *See* Rogers, John
Matthew, Tobias (1546–1628), iv. 421; vii. 334
Matthew, Sir Toby or Tobie (1577–1655), iv. 441, 489; vi. 3; vii. 194
Matthew of Westminster, i. 179
Matthews, Charles James, xiii. Add. 2
Matthews, J. Brander, xiii. 515
Matthews, John William, xi. 410
Matthews, Josiah Wright, xiv. Add. 8
Matthews, Miss, in Fielding's *Amelia*, x. 33, 34
Matthieu, *Histoire de France*, vi. 33

Matty, Miss, in Mrs Gaskell's *Cranford*, XIII. 377
Maturin, Charles Robert (1782–1824), XI. 300, 304, 462; XIII. 257, 259 ff., 521
Albigenses, The, XI. 305
Bertram: or, The Castle of St Aldobrond, XI. 176, 304; XIII. 259, 260
Fatal Vengeance or The Family of Montorio, XI. 304
Fredolfo, XIII. 259, 260
Manuel, XIII. 259, 260
Melmoth the Wanderer, XI. 304, 305; XIII. 418 ff.
Milesian Chief, XI. 304
Wild Irish Boy, XI. 304
Women, or Pour et Contre, XI. 304; XII. 146
Maty, Matthew (1718–1776), *Journal Britannique*, X. 173; *Memoirs of Lord Chesterfield*, X. 259, 494
Maty, Paul Henry (1745–1787), X. 302
Matz, Bertram Waldrom, XIII. 514, 532, 533
Mätzner, Eduard, I. ix; XIV. 611
Mauchline, XI. 213, 216, 219, 220
Maucroix, F. de, IX. 196
Maud, empress, I. 166
Maude, Cyril, XIII. 515
Maudlin, in *The Compleat Angler*, VII. 251, 252
Maudlin, the witch of Paplewick, in *The Sad Shepherd*, VI. 11
Maugham, Reginald Charles Fulke, XIV. Add. 8
Maulette, Genevefve Petau, IV. 376
Maundeville, J., rector of Burnham Thorpe, II. 301
Maunsell, Andrew (d. 1595), *Catalogue of English Printed Bookes*, IV. 404, 548
Maupassant, Guy de, XII. 244; XIII. 454, 457
Maurer, Georg Ludwig von, XIV. 78
Mauretania, IV. 259
Maurice, Charles Edmund, II. 38
Maurice, Sir Frederick, XIV. 602
Maurice, Frederick Denison (1805–1872), IX. 328; XI. 136; XII. 283, 288, 289 ff. (main entry), 295, 296, 465 ff., 471; XIII. 344, 345, 355, 357, 358, 368, 370, 378, 547; XIV. 82, 136, 408, 429, 477, 592, 596, 600, 602, 607
Moral and Metaphysical Philosophy, XIV. 26
Prophets and Kings, XII. 284
Religions of the World, XII. 289
Theological Essays, XII. 284, 290
Maurice, Thomas (1754–1824), XI. 428
Maurice of Nassau. *See* Orange
Mauritania, in *The Masque of Blacknesse*, VI. 342
Mavor, Wm Fordyce (1758–1837), XI. 488; XIV. 553
Mavrocordatos, prince Alexander, XII. 38
Maw, game of, VI. 98
Max Müller, F. *See* Müller, F. Max
Maxen Wledig, Dream of, I. 252
Maxentius, VII. 371, 395
Maxima, abbess, I. 75
Maximilian I, duke of Bavaria, VII. 200
Maximilian I, emperor, I. 53; III. 61, 112; VI. 333
Maximilla, martyr, V. 15
Maximin, in *Tyrannick Love*, VIII. 22
Maximus, in *Valentinian*, VI. 129
Maximus Tyrius, VII. 404
Maxse, Frederick Augustus (1833–1900), XIV. 608
Maxton, 'the new poete,' V. 311
Maxwell, Sir H., XIV. 501
Maxwell, James (1720–1800), XI. 440
Maxwell, James Clerk. *See* Clerk-Maxwell
Maxwell, John (1590?–1647), IX. 544
Maxwell, William Hamilton (1792–1850), XIII. 564; XIV. 570; *Stories of Waterloo*, XIV. 313; *Wild Sports of the West of Ireland*, XIV. 313
May, Sir Humphrey (1573–1630), IX. 250
May, John (*fl.* 1613), IV. 309, 512
'May, Phil,' XIV. 549
May, Thomas (1595–1650), IV. 438, 501; VI. 28, 144, 457; VII. 315, 446, 517
Antigone, the Theban Princess, VI. 235
Cleopatra, VI. 235
Heir, The, VI. 235
Historical Discourses, VII. 207
History of the Parliament of England, VII. 206, 226
Julia Agrippina, VI. 235
Julius Caesar, VII. 206
Lucan, VII. 359
Mirrour of Minds, The (Barclay), IV. 254
Old Couple, The, VI. 235
Pharsalia (trans.), VI. 235
May, Sir Thomas Erskine (1815–1886), XIV. 495; *Constitutional History of England*, XIV. 58; *Rules, Orders and Proceedings of the House of Commons*, XIV. 58
May-game, V. 34, 35
May poems, II. 374, 392, 393
Mayberrys, the, in *North-Ward Hoe*, VI. 172
Mayd Emlyn, The Boke of, III. 88, 486; IV. 340; VII. 382
Maydes Metamorphosis, The, VI. 365, 490
Maydman, Henry, IV. 102, 459
Mayer, John (1583–1664), VII. 481
Mayer, Samuel Ralph Townshend, XIII. 483
Mayerne, Sir Théodore Turquet de (1573–1655), VIII. 477; XIV. 283; *Notes*, VIII. 363
Mayfield, XII. 103
Mayhew, Anthony Lawson, XIV. 611
Mayhew, Henry (1812–1887), XIV. 236, 544, 548
Mayhew, Horace (1816–1872), XIV. 236
Mayiola, or Mayok, in *King Berdok*, II. 276
Maynard, Constance L., XIV. 600
Maynard, Edward (1654–1740), IX. 533

Maynard, Sir John (1602–1690), VIII. 466; X. 373
Mayne, Jasper (1604–1672), VI. 240, 457; *Amorous Warre, The,* VI. 237; *City Match, The,* V. 367; VI. 237; *Lucian* (trans.), VI. 237
Mayne, John (1759–1836), XI. 444; XII. 420; *Halloween,* XI. 216, 235; *Logan Water,* XI. 235; *Siller Gun, The,* XI. 235
Maynial, Guillaume, II. 315
Maynooth, XIV. 315, 329
Maynwaring, Arthur (1668–1712), IX. 437
Mayo, Charles (1792–1846), XIV. 608
Mayo, Charles Herbert, XII. 520
Mayor, John Eyton Bickersteth (1825–1910), IX. 354; X. 356; XII. 326, 357, 481, 487, 488, 515, 523; *First Greek Reader,* XII. 336; *Juvenal,* XII. 336
Mayor, Joseph Bickersteth (1828–1910), XII. 403, 523; XIII. 512; *Chapters on English Metre,* XIII. 248, 512; *Handbook of Modern English Metre,* XIII. 248, 512
Mayow, John (1640–1679), VIII. 354, 363, 478; XIV. 283
Mazarin, cardinal, IV. 434; VII. 189
Mazarin blue, XI. 364
Maze Pond school, X. 382
Mazzini, in George Meredith's *Vittoria,* XIII. 445, 447
Mazzini, Giuseppe, XIII. 15, 132, 349, 465, 472, 492
Mazzoni, Giacomo, VII. 265
Mead, Matthew (1630?–1699), VII. 316
Mead, Robert (1616–1653), VI. 475
Mead, W. E., *Outlines of the History of the Legend of Merlin,* I. 268
Meade, Jacob (*fl.* 1613), VI. 261, 275
Meadows, Joseph Kenny (1790–1874), XIV. 201, 236
Meagher, Thomas Francis (1823–1867), XIV. 570
Meagles family, in *Little Dorrit,* XIII. 331
Meander, in *Tamburlaine,* V. 151
Mease, Peter, VI. 475
Meath, county, XII. 351; XIV. 246
Mecca, XIV. 252
Mechanics' institutions, XIV. 407 ff.
Mechanics' Magazine, The, XIV. 408, 409
Medalle, Mme (Lydia Smollett), X. 47, 422
Medb, queen, XIV. 307
Mede or Mead, Joseph (1586–1638), IV. 433; VII. 318, 345, 482, 490; VIII. 458; *Works,* VIII. 286
Medea, VI. 163
Medea, in *Confessio Amantis,* II. 151
Medea, in Euripides's drama, XII. 68
Medea, in Morris's *Jason,* XIII. 123, 134
Medea, in Sandys's translation of Ovid's *Metamorphoses,* VII. 51
Medhurst, Walter Henry (1796–1857), XII. 342, 500
Media, XII. 477
Medici, Cosmo de', XII. 418
Medici, Lorenzino de', III. 5; VI. 199; VIII. 358; XIV. 108
Medici, Marie de', VI. 175
Medici, Piero and Giovanni de', III. 5
Medici, the, VI. 175; VIII. 358; X. 303; XIV. 99
Medicine, books on, II. 365
Medicus, in *A Dialogue...against the fever Pestilence,* III. 108
Medina (Arabia), XIV. 252
Medina, Pedro de, IV. 446
Mediocrity, in *The Muses Looking-Glasse,* VI. 233
Mediolano, Johannes de, IV. 446
Mediterranean sea, II. 75; IV. 68, 69, 92; VI. 203; XII. 32, 257
Medley, in Etherege's *Man of Mode,* VIII. 138
Medley, The, IX. 437, 461
Medmenham abbey, X. 391, 394, 524
Medows, Sir Philip, the elder (1676–1718), IV. 459
Medraut, or Modred, or Mordred, I. 248
Medusa, in *Fedele and Fortunio,* V. 315
Medwall, Henry (*fl.* 1486), II. 328; V. 410; *Nature,* V. 54, 392
Medway, in *The Faerie Queene,* III. 238
Medway, river, IV. 190; VII. 183; VIII. 11, 252
Medwin, Thomas (1788–1869), XII. 50, 54, 384, 385, 396, 403, 407; *Journal of the Conversations of Lord Byron,* XII. 36
Meed, lady, in *Piers the Plowman,* II. 2 ff., 7 ff., 32
Meehan, Charles Patrick (1812–1890), XIV. 570, 573
Meeke, Mrs Mary (? 1816), XI. 488
Meekly, Mr, in Brooke's *Fool of Quality,* IX. 327
Meeting of Gallants at an Ordinarie, The, V. 367, 479
Megaera, in *Gismond of Salerne,* V. 75, 76
Megaera, in *Thyestes,* V. 75, 76
Mégha Dūta, trans. of the, XII. 503
Mehemet Ali, pasha of Egypt, XIV. 252
Meighen, John, VII. 337
Meiklejohn, John Maller Dow, XIV. 601
Meilan, Mark Anthony (*fl.* 1812), XI. 491
Meilyr, story of, in *Giraldus Cambrensis,* I. 171
Meinecke, XIV. 484
Meiningen, V. 306
Meissner, V. 347
Meistersingers, the, V. 25
Mela, Pomponius, III. 420
Melancholico, in *The Floating Island,* VI. 326
Melanchthon, Philip, III. 36, 50, 113, 127, 143, 151, 290, 419, 421, 430; IV. 380, 446; VI. 374; *Inita Doctrinae physicae,* III. 113
Melanchthoniana, VII. 391
Melantha, in *Marriage-à-la-Mode,* VIII. 17
Melantho, in *Ulysses Redux,* VI. 303
Melantius, in *The Maides Tragedy,* VI. 126 ff.
Melayne, Sege of, I. 469
Melbancke, Brian (*fl.* 1583), *Philotimus,* III. 349, 536

Melbourne, International exhibition, XIV. 369
Melbourne, viscount. *See* Lamb, William
Melchior, in *William of Palerne*, I. 316
Melchisedech, in *The Palice of Honour*, II. 260
Melchizedek, I. 74; V. 48
Melcombe, lord. *See* Dodington, George Bubb
'Meldrum, Squire,' VII. 254
Meleager, XII. 485
Meleander, in *Argenis*, IV. 258, 259
Melebea, in *Calisto and Melebea*, V. 100
Mélesville (A. H. J. Duveyrier), *Sullivan*, XIII. 271
Melford, Jerry, in Smollett's *Humphrey Clinker*, X. 43
Melford, Lydia, in Smollett's *Humphrey Clinker*, X. 43
Melfort, earl. *See* Drummond, John
Melibaeus, in school plays, V. 103
Meliboeus (Vergil's), III. 224
Meliboeus, in Barnabe Googe's *Eclogues*, III. 186
Meliboeus, in ? Ralegh's *Dialogue*, IV. 109
Melicertus, in *Menaphon*, III. 357
Melior et Idoine, I. 460
Meliora Speramus, Day's 'Islands,' VI. 216
Melisea (Yong's), IV. 122
Melissa, in *Misogonus*, V. 110
Melizius, in *The Passetyme of Pleasure*, II. 225, 228, 231, 233, 234
Mellidus, in *Jacke Drums Entertainment*, VI. 41
Mellisant, in *Frier Bacon*, V. 137
Mellyagraunce, of Malory, I. 262
Melmoth, Maturin's, XI. 305
Melmotte, Trollope's, XIII. 422
Melnotte, Claud, in Lytton's *The Lady of Lyons*, XIII. 419
Melros state papers, VII. 435
Melrose, chronicle of, I. 174, 449
Melrose abbey, XII. 9, 46
Melusine, I. 470; II. 483
Melvill, Henry (1798–1871), XII. 472
Melvill, James, *Diary*, IV. 276
Melville, Andrew (1545–1622), III. 426; IV. 276, 304; IX. 556; *Anti-Tami-Cami-Categoria*, VII. 27
Melville, Elizabeth. *See* Culross, lady
Melville, George John Whyte. *See* Whyte-Melville
Melville, Helen, XIII. Add. 2
Melville, Sir James (1535–1617), of Halhill, *Memoirs*, III. 148, 505
Melville or Melvill, James (1556–1614), II. 370, 488; *Diary*, III. 148, 505
Melville, Lewis, X. 422, *also see* Add.; XI. 290, 291, 393, 459; XIII. 525, 530, 564, *also see* Add. 2
Melville, Sir Robert (1527–1621), XII. 27
Melville, viscount. *See* Dundas, Henry
Melwas, king of Somerset, I. 262
Melyonek, John, VI. 282
Memling, Hans, XIII. 112
Memnon, in *The Mad Lover*, VI. 122, 130, 152
Mémoires Littéraires de la Grande Bretagne, X. 291, 292, 311
Memoirs, Personal, in Jacobean times, VII. 449
Memoirs of a Parish Clerk, IX. 137
Memoirs of Martinus Scriblerus, IX. 103, 131, 136, 137, 139, 308, 447, 463, 469, 470
Memoirs of the Society of Grub-street, X. 162
Memorial of suche Princes as since the tyme of King Richard the Seconde have been unfortunate in the Realme of England, A, III. 194
Memorials of Coleorton, IX. 328
Memorie of the Somervilles, XII. 16
Ménage, Gilles, VIII. 321
Menai straits, X. 115
Menander, V. 5; VIII. 155; IX. 336, 525; XII. Add.
Mencke, Johann Burchard, V. 286
Mendacium (=Satan), in Wyclif's *Dialogus*, II. 65
Mendax, in *A Dialogue...against the fever Pestilence*, III. 109
Mendelssohn, Sidney, XIV. 588, *also see* Add. 4, 7, 9
Mendez, Moses (d. 1758), XI. 172, 428
Mendoza, in *The Court Secret*, VI. 206
Mendoza, Antonio de, *Fiestas de Aranjuez*, VIII. 130; *Querer por solo querer*, VIII. 130
Mendoza, Bernardino de, IV. 446
Mendoza, Daniel (1764–1836), XIV. 229, 231
Mendoza, Diego Hurtado de, III. 341; IV. 446
Mendozo, in *The Malcontent*, VI. 46
Menenius, in *Coriolanus*, V. 198
Menger, A., *The Right to the Whole Produce of Labour*, XIV. 4
Mennes or Mennis or Minnes, Sir John (1599–1671), VIII. 260; *Musarum Deliciae*, VII. 512; VIII. 231, 408
Menologium, I. 145, 445
Mensa philosophica, III. 95, 489
Mentone, XIV. 78
Mentz (Mainz), VII. 231
Meopham, Simon, archbishop of Canterbury (d. 1333), I. 353
Mephistopheles, XII. 50, 54
Mephistopheles, in *Faust*, V. 20, 187; XIII. 105
Mercator (Defoe's), IX. 14, 15, 432
Merchant, in *Ane Pleasant Satyre*, III. 128
Merchant Adventurers, IV. 71, 310; VII. 305, 308
Merchant Taylors' company, VI. 168
Mercia, I. 50, 125; II. 210
Mercia, laws of, I. 98; VIII. 310, 311
Mercian annals (or *Chronicle of Aethelflaed*), I. 109, 110. *See, also, under* Aethelflaed the lady of Mercia
Mercier, Sébastien, V. 292, 298
Merck, X. 488
Mercure Galant, Le, IX. 270; X. 163
Mercuriale, Girolamo, III. 436

Mercuries, VII. 385
Mercurius Academicus, VII. 348
Mercurius Aulicus, VII. 351, 361
Mercurius Bifrons (1681), VIII. 412
Mercurius Britannicus, VII. 344; IX. 433
Mercurius Civicus to Mercurius Rusticus, A Letter from, VII. 502
Mercurius Democritus, VII. 356
Mercurius Diabolicus or Hell's Intelligencer, VII. 381
Mercurius Elencticus, VII. 355
'Mercurius Gallobelgicus,' VII. 344
Mercurius Latinus, IX. 434
Mercurius Librarius, XI. 339
Mercurius Melancholicus or Newes from Westminster, VII. 352, 381
Mercurius Politicus, IX. 21, 432
Mercurius Rusticans, VI. 484
'Mercurius Spur,' X. 471
Mercurius Teutonicus, IX. 518
Mercurius Trismegistus, III. 416
Mercury, II. 276
Mercury, in *Amphitruo*, V. 107
Mercury, in Carew's *Coelum Britannicum*, VII. 19
Mercury, in *Dialogues of the Dead*, XI. 351, 352
Mercury, in *Mercury Vindicated*, VI. 357, 358
Mercury, in *Pleasure Reconciled*, VI. 360
Mercury, in Shelley's *Prometheus Unbound*, XII. 65
Mercury, in *The Penates*, VI. 341, 351
Mercutio, in *Romeo and Juliet*, III. 268; V.182, 268; VII. 8
Mercy, in Anglo-Norman plays, V. 21
Mercy, in *Piers the Plowman*, II. 13
Mercy, in *The Example of Virtue*, II. 227, 228
Mercy, in *The Passetyme of Pleasure*, II. 228
Mercy, house of, in *The Faerie Queene*, VII. 173
Mercy, oil of, legend of, V. 15
Merdle household, the, in *Little Dorrit*, XIII. 331
Meredith, George (1828–1909), V. 127; VIII. 154; XI. 447; XII. 24; XIII. 413, 426, 440 ff. (main entry), 451, 458, 489, 568 ff.
Adventures of Harry Richmond, The, XIII. 441
Amazing Marriage, The, XIII. 441
Attila, XIV. 249
Ballad of Fair Ladies in Revolt, A, XIII. 444, 448
Ballads and Poems of Tragic Life, XIII. 442
Beauchamp's Career, XIII. 441, 446
Case of General Ople and Lady Camper, The, XIII. 441, 445
Celt and Saxon, XIII. 441
Day of the Daughter of Hades, The, XIII. 448
Diana of the Crossways, XIII. 441, 443, 446; XIV. 309
Meredith, George
Dirge in Woods, XIII. 444
Earth and a Wedded Woman, XIII. 443
Earth and Man, XIII. 443, 448
Egoist, The, XIII. 441, 445
Emilia in England, XIII. 441
Empty Purse, The, XIII. 442
Essay on Comedy, An, XIII. 445, 515
Evan Harrington, XIII. 441
Faith on Trial, A, XIII. 440, 448
Farina, XIII. 441
Gentleman of Fifty and the Damsel of Nineteen, The, XIII. 441
House on the Beach, The, XIII. 441
Hymn to Colour, XIII. 448
Lark Ascending, The, XIII. 448
Last Poems, XIII. 442
Lord Ormont and his Aminta, XIII. 441
Love in a Valley, XIII. 440, 448
Lucifer in Starlight, XIII. 448
'Maxims for Men,' XIII. 447
Meditations under Stars, XIII. 444
Modern Love, XIII. 440, 441, 444, 448
Nuptials of Attila, The, XIII. 448
Ode to the Spirit of Earth in Autumn, XIII. 444
Odes in Contribution to the Song of French History, XIII. 442, 445, 447
On the Idea of Comedy, XIII. 441
One of Our Conquerors, XIII. 441, 446, 448
Ordeal of Richard Feverel, The, XIII. 441, 446, 454, 460
Phaéthón, XIII. 448
Phoebus with Admetus, XIII. 449
'Pilgrim's Scrip, The,' XIII. 447
Poems (1851), XIII. 440
Poems and Lyrics of the Joy of Earth XIII. 442
Reading of Earth, A, XIII. 442
Reading of Life, A, XIII. 442
Rhoda Fleming, XIII. 441, 447
Sage Enamoured and the Honest Lady, XIII. 444
Sandra Belloni, XIII. 441
Shaving of Shagpat, The, XIII. 441
Tale of Chloe, The, XIII. 441
Test of Manhood, The, XIII. 443
Thrush in February, The, XIII. 443, 448
Tragic Comedians, The, XIII. 441
Vittoria, XIII. 441, 447
Woods of Westermain, The, XI. 85; XIII. 443, 448
Meredith, Mary, born Vulliamy, XIII. 440
Meredith, Mary Ellen, born Peacock, XIII. 440
Meredith, Owen. *See* Lytton, earl of
Meredith, R., *Mr Steele Detected*, IX. 440
Meredith, Sir Rowland, in Richardson's *Sir Charles Grandison*, X. 11
Meredith, W. M., XIII. 569
Meres, Francis (1565–1647), III. 305, 359, 526; IV. 444, 526; *Palladis Tamia*, IV. 18, 139, 168, 183, 376, 394; V. 82, 166, 170, 172 ff., 181, 184, 187 ff., 194, 195 215, 219 ff., 223, 312, 323, 331; VI. 3, 30, 39, 302, 387

Meres, Sir J., IX. 440
Meriasek, Saint, Bishop and Confessor, The Life of, V. 16, 391
Merie Tales of the Mad Men of Gotam, The, III. 95, 488
Merione, in *The Queen of Corinth*, VI. 131
Merionethshire, X. 115
Meritt, Paul (d. 1895), XIII. 521
Merivale, Charles (1808–1893), XII. 313, 406, 476, 477
Autobiography, XII. 307
Conversion of the Northern Nations, The, XII. 306
Conversion of the Roman Empire, The, XII. 306
Fall of the Roman Republic, The, XII. 305
General History of Rome, XII. 306
History of the Romans under the Empire, The, XII. 305
Merivale, Herman (1806–1874), XII. 305; XIV. 495; 'Lyall's Travels in North America,' XII. 153
Merivale, Herman Charles (1839–1906), XIII. 506, 521, 530, 544; *Thaisa's Dirge*, XIII. 194
Merivale, John Herman (1779–1844), XII. 420
Merlette, Germaine-Marie, XIII. 485
Merlin (the prose), I. 269
Merlin, in legend and romance, I. 235, 259, 263, 266, 268, 269, 271, 461, 462, 469; III. 106, 234
Merlin, in *The Rolliad*, XI. 34
Merlin, Ambrose, VII. 207
Merlin, prophecies of, I. 169, 170, 193, 258, 356; IV. 363
Merlin, The Birth of, II. 325
Merlin, The Birth of (16th century version), V. 249 ff.
Merlin de St Gelais, V. 62
Mermedonians, I. 53
Merrick, James (1720–1769), X. 456; *Cameleon*, IX. 191
Merrilies, Meg, in Scott's *Guy Mannering*, XII. 18, 25, 29
Merriman, Henry Seton, *pseud.* See Scott, Hugh Stowell
Merry, J., of Pembroke College, X. 472
Merry, Robert (1755–1798), XI. 172, 176, 177, 428
Merry, Thomas (*fl.* 1594), V. 325
Merry, William Walter (1835–1918), XII. Add. 3
Merry Beggars, The, XI. 218
Merry Conceits of Bottom the Weaver, VIII. 116
Merry Devill of Edmonton, The, V. 237, 238, 251 ff., 332, 442, 443
Merry Drollery, VII. 512
Merry Jeste of a Shrewde and Curste Wyfe lapped in Morelles skin, The, III. 84, 91, 487
Merry Muses, The, IX. 360, 363, 567; XI. 229
Merry Riddles, The Booke of, III. 95, 488
Merryweather, John (*fl.* 1644), VII. 235
Mersenne, Marin, VII. 284 ff.
Merton. *See* Walter de
Mery demandes, III. 489
Mery Jests of the Widow Edith. *See* Smith, Walter
Mery Tales and Quicke Answers, III. 93, 94, 487; IV. 334, 343, 523
Merygreeke, Matthewe, in *R. Roister Doister*, V. 106
Meryon, Charles Lewis (1783–1877), XIV. 506
Merz, John Theodore, XIV. 467
Mesmer, Friedrich Anton, XI. 293
Mesnager, Nicolas, IX. 151
Mesneví of Mevlána, The, XII. 504
Meso-Gothic language, VIII. 307
Mesolonghi, XII. 38, 314
Mesopotamia, IV. 90
Messahala, II. 185
Messena, in *Sicelides*, VI. 323
Messiah, the, in Cowley's *Davideis*, VII. 67
Messina, V. 191; VII. 199
Mess-Katalog (of Frankfurt-a.-M.), IV. 403
Meston, William (1688?–1745), IX. 471, 500, 567
Metamorphosis Anglorum, VII. 391
Metamorphosis of Tobacco, The, IV. 349, 530
Metastasio, Pietro, X. 161; XI. 263, 359
Metcalfe, Charles Theophilus, 1st lord Metcalfe (1785–1846), XIV. 491
Meteor, The, XIV. 223
Meteren, E. van, X. 291
Meteyard, Eliza (1816–1879), XIV. 504
Metham, John, II. 498; *Amoryus and Cleopes*, II. 502
Methold, William (d. 1653), XIV. 579; *Relations of the Kingdome of Golconda*, XIV. 333
Metre, Bede's *tracts on*, I. 80
Metrical romances, I. 277 ff., 464 ff.
Metz, III. 163; V. 101
Metz, siege of, in *Morte Arthure*, II. 119
Meung, Jean de, I. 99; II. 169; III. 90; VII. 367
Mewe, William, VI. 475
Mexia, Pedro, IV. 446; *Silva de varia lección*, VIII. 126
Mexican language, XIV. 457
Mexico, VIII. 23; XI. 72, 162
Meyer, Paul, II. 420
Meyer-Franck, Helene, XIII. 485
Meynell, Alice, XIII. 475, 476, 503, 507; XIV. 524
Meynell, Hugo, XIV. 233
Meynell, Wilfrid, XII. 461; XIII. 510
Meyrick, Sir Samuel Rush (1783–1848), XII. 511
Mezeray, François Eudes de, *History of France*, IX. 150, 153
Mézières, Alfred, V. 302
Miall, L. C., *The Early Naturalists*, XIV. 283
Micah, II. 293
Micawber, Mr, in *David Copperfield*, VI. 22; XIII. 327

Michael, in Byron's *Vision of Judgment*, XII. 53
Michael, in *The Example of Virtue*, II. 227
Michael, in Wordsworth's poem, XI. 113
Michael, James Lionel (1824–1865), XIV. 364, 365, 587; *John Cumberland*, XIV. 363
Michael, St, I. 134, 227, 339
Michael of Kildare, II. 425
Michaelis, Johann David, *Introduction to the New Testament*, XII. 280
Michaelis, Sebastian (*fl.* 1613), VI. 183
Michal, in Browning's *Paracelsus*, XIII. 57
Michal, in Cowley's *Davideis*, VII. 66, 67
Michel, Francisque, V. 302; *Critical Inquiry into the Scottish Language, with the view of illustrating the Rise and Progress of Civilisation in Scotland* (1882), II. 95, 96
Michel, Guillaume, *Lasne Dore*, IV. 3
Michel Angelo, X. 266
Michell, John (1724–1793), XIV. 257
Michell, Sir Lewis, XIV. Add. 9
Mickle, William Julius (1735–1788), X. 456, 470; XIII. 226; *Cumnor Hall*, IX. 374
Mickleham, X. 261
Mickleton, X. 271
Microcosm, The, XI. 392; XIV. 387
Microcosm of London, The (Ackermann's), XIV. 222
Micro-cynicon, Sixe Snarling Satyres, IV. 519; VI. 59
Micrologia, III. 95
Midas, III. 64; IV. 10, 327
Midas, in *Loves Maistresse*, VI. 103
Middelburg, VI. 398
Middle-Age, in *The Parlement of the Thre Ages*, II. 37
Middle Ages, the, I. 99, 153, 161, 187, 278, 294, 299, 300, 306, 363, 366, 371; II. 43, 51, 52, 61, 76, 120, 169, 172, 181, 183, 197, 210, 231, 239, 240, 245, 301, 334, 335, 339, 350, 359, 366, 423, 506; III. 31, 83, 89, 94, 100, 106, 108, 114, 138, 155, 200, 218, 418; IV. 70, 110, 269, 319, 353; V. 5, 9, 16, 21, 38, 41 ff., 50, 51, 53, 55, 56, 152, 369; VI. 328, 372, 373; VII. 102, 367, 376 ff., 384, 391; VIII. 319, 351; X. 217 ff., 287, 288, 355, 484 ff.; XI. 273, 372
Middle Ages, the literary influence of the, X. 217 ff., 484 ff.
Middle English, X. 225; XIV. 435 ff., 442, 444 ff.
Middle English verse, XIII. 241, 242, 249
Middle Temple revels, VIII. 244
Middleburg, IV. 64, 402
Middlesex, III. 330; VI. 259, 292, 385; VII. 4, 77, 113; VIII. 37, 39, 166; X. 29, 360, 385, 391, 399, 404; XI. 8, 183
Middlesex, earl of. *See* Cranfield, Lionel
Middleton, Christopher (1560?–1628), IV. 487
Middleton, Clara (George Meredith's), XIII. 446
Middleton, Conyers (1683–1750), IX. 295, 497, 505, 525, 527; X. 123, 262, 308, 509; XI. 347; *Free Inquiry into the Miraculous Powers*, IX. 296, 340; *Life of Cicero*, IX. 253, 340; X. 319; *Miscellaneous Works*, X. 319
Middleton, David (d. 1615), IV. 92, 99
Middleton, John Henry (1846–1896), XII. 498
Middleton, Richard, XIII. 219, 220, 506, 564, *also see* Add. 3
Middleton, Thomas (1570?–1627), IV. 515, 519; V. 184, 252, 254, 255, 311, 319, 362, 371; VI. 6, 26, 28, 55, 57, 58–60 (main entry), 95, 115, 138, 145, 151, 154, 168, 196, 211, 218, 219, 250, 329, 426 ff.; VIII. 124, 127, 162; XIII. 495
Any Thing for a Quiet Life, VI. 78
Black Book, The, V. 252; VI. 60
Blurt Master-Constable, VI. 15, 61
Caesar's Fall, VI. 61, 168
Changeling, The, VI. 67, 68, 76, 79, 80; VIII. 121; XII. 222
Chast Mayd in Cheapeside, A, VI. 65, 74
Chester Tragedy, The, VI. 61
Defiance to Envy, VI. 59
Devereux, lord, dedication to, VI. 59
Faire Quarrell, A, VI. 61, 67, 68, 73, 75
Famelie of Love, The, V. 365; VI. 62, 67
Father Hubberd's Tales, VI. 59
Game at Chesse, A, V. 344, 365; VI. 58, 68, 79, 80, 147, 150, 248; VII. 433
Inner-Temple Masque, The, VI. 70, 75
Mad World, My Masters, A, V. 125; VIII. 142
Mayor of Quinborough, The, V. 187, 250, 251; VI. 60, 61, 70
Micro-cynicon, Sixe Snarling Satyres, IV. 519; VI. 59
More Dissemblers besides Women, VI. 78
Old Law, The, VI. 15, 61, 67, 68, 145
Phoenix, The, VI. 63
Roaring Girle, The, VI. 54, 62, 65
Spanish Gipsie, The (with W. Rowley), VI. 68, 77; VIII. 129
Two Harpies, The, VI. 61, 168
Widdow, The, VI. 26, 65, 140
Wisdom of Solomon Paraphrased, The, VI. 59
Witch, The, VI. 75, 76; XII. 190
Women beware Women, VI. 68, 78, 176, 180, 192
World tost at Tennis, The, VI. 62, 68, 75
Your five Gallants, VI. 63, 68
See, also, under Beaumont and Fletcher, Dekker, Jonson *and* W. Rowley
Middleton and William Rowley's *A Faire Quarrell*, V. 349
Midgley, Robert (1653–1733), IX. 500
Midianites, IV. 43
Mido, Isaac's 'boy,' in *Jacob and Esau*, V. 112
Miège, Guy (1644–1718?), *The New State of England*, IX. 353, 537; *Present State of Great Britain*, XI. 333

Mielot, Jean, secretary of Philippe le Bon, II. 313
Miggs, in *Barnaby Rudge*, XIII. 321
Mignault, Claude, VII. 406
Migne, *Patrologia*, I. 186, 202, 250
Mignet, François A. M., XIV. 56, 57, 61
Milan, V. 207, 306; VI. 17; VII. 47; XII. 220
Milan, Ambrosian library, IV. 429
Milbanke, Anne Isabella. *See* Byron, lady
Milbanke, Ralph (earl of Lovelace), *Astarte*, XII. 396
Milbourne, Luke (1649–1720), VIII. 54, 404; *Aeneid*, VIII. 51
Mildmay, friend of John Byrom, IX. 325
Mildmay, Sir Walter (1520?–1589), VII. 340
Mildred, in *Eastward Hoe*, VI. 48
Mildred, Browning's, XIII. 65, 67
Mileham, Dorothy, VII. 233
Miles, keeper of Turk's head coffee-house, VII. 362
Miles, Alfred Henry, XIII. 497
Miles, Henry Downes, *Pugilistica*, XIV. 231, 541
Miles, William Augustus (1753?–1817), XIV. 513
Milford, Humphrey Sumner, XIII. 489
Milford Haven, VII. 353
Militia Bill, X. 466
Mill, James (1773–1836), X. 342, 513; XI. 60, 61, 398; XII. 152, 301, 309, 430; XIV. 2, 4 ff., 13, 14, 23, 119, 187, 336, 403, 407, 477, 495, 580, 608
  Analysis of the Phenomena of the Human Mind, XIV. 5
  Fragment on Mackintosh, A, XIV. 5, 59
  Government (essay), XIV. 59
  History of India, XIV. 97, 98, 337
  Political Economy, XIV. 4
Mill, John (1645–1707), IX. 330, 508, 524
Mill, John Stuart (1806–1873), XI. 61, 70, 136, 398, 410, 417; XII. 275, 285, 289, 430, 438; XIII. 11, 15, 54, 385, 465, 478; XIV. 2, 5, 8, 13 ff. (main entry), 35 ff., 43, 59, 103, 133, 187, 432, 469, 474, 477, 486, 608
  Auguste Comte and Positivism, XIV. 22
  Autobiography, XI. 64; XIV. 14, 22, 425
  Considerations on Representative Government, XIV. 20
  Dissertations and Discussions, XIV. 1
  Essays on some Unsettled Questions of Political Economy, XIV. 20
  Examination of Sir William Hamilton's Philosophy, XIV. 19
  Inaugural Address (St Andrews), XIV. 424, 425
  On Liberty, XIV. 20, 21
  On the Subjection of Women, XIV. 20
  Political Economy, XIII. 397
  Principles of Political Economy, XIV. 21, 153
  System of Logic, XIV. 16, 17, 21, 23
  Thoughts on Parliamentary Reform, XIV. 20
  Three Essays on Religion, XIV. 22
  Utilitarianism, XI. 64; XIV. 20
Mill, William Hodge (1792–1853), XII. 341
Millais, Sir John Everett (1829–1896), XI. 489; XIII. 110, 474; XIV. 363
Millamant, in Congreve's *The Way of the World*, VII. 20; VIII. 155, 156
Millamant, Mrs, in Congreve's *The Way of the World*, VIII. 148, 154
Millar, Andrew (1707–1768), X. Add.; XI. 315, 317, 323, 324, 326
Millar, John (1735–1801), IX. 553
Millar, John Hepburn, IX. Add.; XIII. 497, 561; XIV. 532; *Scottish Prose of the 17th and 18th centuries*, XI. 445
Millayn, The Duke of, and the Marques of Mantua, V. 116
Millefont, in Congreve's *Double-Dealer*, VIII. 148 ff., 156
Millenary petition, III. 34
Miller, lady Anna (1741–1781), X. 277, 456
Miller, Hugh (1802–1856), XII. 380; XIV. 160, 203, 515, 522; *My Schools and Schoolmasters*, XIV. 159; *Old Red Sandstone, The*, XIV. 159
Miller, James (1706–1744), X. 440; *Mahomet*, X. 81, 433, 439
Miller, Philip (1691–1771), IX. 182
Miller, Sanderson, X. 271, 272
Miller, T., *The O.E. Version of Bede's Ecclesiastical History*, I. 44, 96, 437
Miller, Thomas (1807–1874), XIII. 506
Miller, William (1810–1872), XIII. 506
Miller of Abingdon, The Jest of the, II. 326, 499
Miller's Daughter of Manchester, The, V. 252
Milles, bookbinder, IV. 406
Milles, Jeremiah (1714–1784), X. 255, 485, 486, 505
Milles, Thomas (d. 1627), IV. 309, 512, 543; *Catalogue of Honor* (1610), III. 528
Millicent, in *The Merry Devill*, V. 252
Milligan, William (1821–1893), XII. 469
Milliken, Richard Alfred (1767–1815), XIV. 570
Millington, Edward (*fl.* 1690), XI. 336, 340
Millington, Thomas (*fl.* 1594), IV. 393
Millington, William (d. 1466?), II. 288, 303
Millwood, in Lillo's *George Barnwell*, X. 75, 76
Milly, in Dickens's *The Haunted Man*, XIII. 324
Milly, in George Eliot's *Amos Barton*, XIII. 388
Milman, Henry Hart (1791–1868), X. 314, 317, 506, 508; XII. 211, 317 ff., 322, 384, 477; XIII. 257, 261, 521; XIV. 103, 493
  Annals of St Paul's, XII. 319
  Anne Boleyn, XIII. 260
  Belshazzar, XIII. 260
  Fall of Jerusalem, The, XIII. 260
  Fazio, XIII. 260
  History of Christianity, The, XII. 318
  History of Latin Christianity, The, XII. 317
  History of the Jews, The, XII. 318
  Martyr of Antioch, The, XIII. 260

Milne, William (1785–1822), XII. 342, 500
Milner, Dr, of Peckham, X. 201
Milner, Isaac (1750–1820), XII. 281, 472
Milner, John (1628–1702), VIII. 474
Milner, John (1752–1826), XIV. 53 ff., 514
Milner, Joseph (1744–1797), *Gibbon's Account of Christianity considered*, X. 309, 507; *History of the Church of Christ*, XII. 281, 472; XIV. 79
Milnes, Richard Monckton, 1st lord Houghton (1809–1885), X. 478; XI. 462; XIII. 184, 467, 506; XIV. 505, 606; *Brookside, The*, XIII. 185; 'Political State of Prussia, The,' XII. 153, 405, 406, 441; *Strangers Yet*, XIII. 185
Milo, island of, VII. 222
Milsand, Joseph, XIII. 71, 72, 75
Miltiades, XII. 363
Milton, Anne, Milton's eldest daughter, VII. 107
Milton, Anne, Milton's sister, VII. 96, 108
Milton, Christopher (1615–1693), VII. 96, 99, 108
Milton, Deborah (d. 1727), youngest stepdaughter of Milton, VII. 107, 108
Milton, John (1608–1674), I. 43, 164, 370; II. 184, 195, 217, 220; III. 165, 168, 178, 212, 224, 295, 438; IV. 23, 45 ff., 64, 128, 136, 165, 167, 168, 186, 195, 201 ff., 238, 355, 359; V. 5, 92, 150, 151, 154, 156, 213, 214, 217, 350, 394; VI. 36, 348, 356, 489, 491; VII. 36, 75, 76, 88, 91, 95–141 (main entry), 162 ff., 166, 171, 178, 185, 240, 244, 259, 269, 276, 300, 307, 309, 314 ff., 332, 393, 413–423, 434, 466, 474, *also see* Add.; VIII. 51, 98, 106, 219, 221, 222, 229 ff., 237 ff., 279, 351, 368, 384, 394, 410, 447; IX. 1, 2, 28, 42, 64, 69, 73, 148, 167, 182, 201, 233, 265, 267, 382, 390, 410, 435, 437, 449, 473, 486, 505, 508, 525, 557, 569; X. 1, 96 ff., 101, 102, 105 ff., 109, 110, 113, 120, 127, 134, 143, 145, 148, 149, 155, 224, 232, 235, 239, 240, 304, 378, 383, 432, 462, 475, 476, 492; XI. 13, 28, 77, 84, 90, 124, 133, 140, 157, 159, 171, 179, 181, 182, 188, 193, 201, 206, 207, 224, 247, 250, 252, 254, 255, 290, 380, 394, 401 ff., 409, 415, 427, 432 ff., 466, *also see* Add.; XII. 85, 86, 94, 106, 133, 136, 137, 145, 168, 169, 177, 208, 210, 303, 407, 441; XIII. 26, 27, 29, 35, 36, 50, 66, 92, 130, 170, 173, 191, 230, 232, 237, 238, 242, 250, 253, 448; XIV. 62, 88, 112, 133, 306, 397, 440, 446, 448, 453, 460
  Ad Joannem Rousium, VII. 122, 132, 135
  Ad Patrem, VII. 131
  Animadversions upon the Remonstrant's defence, VII. 127, 139, 141
  Apology...Smectymnuus, An, VIII. 127, 139
  Arcades, VII. 111 ff., 141; VIII. 230

Milton, John
  Areopagitica, VII. 124, 127, 129, 130, 139, 359; IX. 307; X. 372, 446; XI. 311, 312; XII. 504; XIII. 49; XIV. 439
  At a Vacation Exercise, VII. 110, 123
  Brief Notes upon a late Sermon...by Matthew Griffith, VII. 141
  Cambridge list of poems, VII. 117, 121, 141
  Colasterion, VII. 140
  Comus, V. 92, 239; VI. 126, 329, 337, 349, 359 ff., 363, 366 ff.; VII. 98, 100, 111 ff., 116, 123, 127, 128, 133, 137, 138, 141; VIII. 117, 226, 230; X. 238, 429, 461, 465, 466; XII. 68; XIII. 38, 177
  Cromwell sonnet, VII. 115, 123, 141
  Dagonalia, VII. 121
  De Doctrina Christiana, VII. 129, 141
  Defensio Pro Populo Anglicano, III. 165; VII. 105, 131, 140; VIII. 312
  Defensio Secunda, VII. 105, 131, 140
  Doctrine and Discipline of Divorce, The. VII. 139, 140
  Eikonoklastes, VII. 105, 127, 140, 141
  Epitaph on the Marchioness of Winchester, An, VII. 111
  Epitaphium Damonis, VII. 100, 131; X. 122
  Fairfax sonnet, VII. 115, 123, 141
  First poems, VII. 109
  Greek works, VII. 132
  History of Britain, IX. 233
  History of England, VII. 124, 128, 141, 206
  History of Moscovia, VII. 124, 128, 141, 206
  Hobson poems, VII. 111
  Il Penseroso, IV. 251; VII. 98, 114, 133, 137; VIII. 230; X. 97, 238; XIII. 44
  In quintum Novembris, Anno aetatis 17, VII. 131
  Italian poems, VII. 115
  Judgement of Martin Bucer Concerning Divorce, The, VII. 140
  L'Allegro, IV. 251; VI. 215; VII. 12, 98, 111, 114, 133; VIII. 230; X. 97; XII. 89; XIII. 44
  Latin poems, VII. 117
  Latin works, VII. 127, 129, 130, 131, 132, 135, 140, 141, 221
  Lawes, sonnet to, VII. 115
  Lawrence, sonnet to, VII. 108, 115, 121, 141
  Letter to a Friend, A, VII. 106, 140
  Likeliest Means to Remove Hirelings, VII. 140, 321
  Lycidas, IV. 121, 171; VII. 97, 98, 112 ff., 123, 131, 135, 137, 141; X. 114, 185, 186; XII. 74
  Mansus, VII. 131
  Methought I saw, XII. 91
  Monck, a letter to, VII. 106
  Nativity Ode, XII. 90
  Nightingale sonnet, VII. 141
  Observations upon the Articles of Peace with the Irish Rebels, VII. 140

Milton, John
Of Education, VII. 100, 123, 124, 127, 139, 265; IX. 384, 389
Of Prelatical Episcopacy, VII. 139
Of Reformation touching Church-Discipline in England, VII. 100, 125, 127, 139, 246; VIII. 78
Of True Religion etc. against the growth of Popery, VII. 141
On the Death of a fair Infant, VII. 109, 123
On the late Massacher in Piemont, VII. 115, 141
On the Morning of Christ's Nativity, VII. 110, 111, 132, 133
On the new forcers of Conscience, VII. 115
On the Religious Memory of Mrs Catherine Thomson, VII. 115
Paradise Lost, III. 178, 246, 295; VII. 103, 107, 108, 112, 116 ff. (main entry), 125, 127, 133, 136, 141, 180; VIII. 27, 28, 79, 105, 226, 230, 238, 352, 422; IX. 59 ff., 140, 182, 269, 338 ff.; X. 112, 185, 266, 468; XI. 197, 212, 251, 315, 319, 327, 332; XII. 48, 84, 102, 476, 518; XIII. 30, 33, 238; XIV. 113
Paradise Regained, VII. 107, 120, 121, 123, 136; VIII. 105; XII. 98
Passion, The, VII. 110
Poems, VII. 104, 116
Poems (1645), XI. 318
Poems etc., upon Several Occasions, 2nd ed., VII. 123; X. 238
Psalm-paraphrases, VII. 109
Ready and Easy Way to Establish a Free Commonwealth, The, VII. 106, 140
Reason of Church-Government urg'd against Prelaty, The, VII. 139
Reflections on the Civil War in England, VII. 206
Samson Agonistes, V. 335; VII. 107, 111, 120 ff., 132, 133, 135, 136, 265; VIII. 154, 231, 238; XII. 68; XIII. 95
Second Defence, XI. 312
Skinner, Cyriak, sonnet to, VII. 115, 121, 123, 141
Smectymnuus, VII. 92, 96, 127, 139, 141
Sonnet IX, VII. 103
Sonnet on his blindness, VII. 115, 141
Sonnets, VII. 112, 115
Tenure of Kings and Magistrates, The, VII. 140
Tetrachordon, VII. 140
Tetrachordon Sonnets, VII. 115
Treatise of Civil Power in Ecclesiastical Causes, VIII. 344
Vane, sonnet to, VII. 123, 141
Wife, poem to his dead, VII. 116
Milton, John, the elder (1563?–1647), VII. 96, 98
Milton, Keynes, X. 351
Milton, Mary (d. 1652), VII. 102, 104, 107
Milton, viscount. *See* Fitzwilliam, William
Miltoun, Francis, XIII. 544
Milus, St, I. 106
Milward, Richard (1609–1680), VII. 392; VIII. 321, 322, 324
Mime, in *The Muses Looking-Glasse*, VI. 233
Mimus, V. 24 ff.
Minadoi, G. T., IV. 446
Minalcas, in *Codrus and Minalcas*, III. 64
Minced-Pie, in *The Masque of Christmas*, VI. 358
Minchin, Anne (d. 1711), IX. 166
Minchin, Thomas, IX. 166
Mind, XIV. 23, 24
Mind of Man (Bi manna mode), I. 62
Mind, Will and Understanding, V. 52
Mindelheim, IX. 174
Minerva, II. 231; IX. 60; XIII. 151
Minerva, in *Ira seu Tumulus Fortunae* VI. 321
Minerva, in *The Kingis Quair*, II. 242
Minerva, in *The Passetyme of Pleasure*, II. 225, 235
Minim, Dick, in Johnson's *Idler*, X. 178
Minns, Ellis Hovell, XII. Add. 5
Minorite convent, XIII. 282
Minos, III. 343, 433; X. 27
Minos, in *Locrine*, V. 240
Minot, Laurence (1300?–1352?), I. 290, 335, 352, 356, 476; II. 398, 422; III. 274; X. 490
Minsheu, John (*fl.* 1617), VII. 480; *Ductor in linguas*, IV. 392
Minshull, captain, XIV. 214
Minshull, Elizabeth (3rd wife of John Milton, d. 1727), VII. 107
'Minstrel Burn,' IX. 364
Minstrels, II. 506; V. 3, 24, 26, 91, 385
Minto, IX. 373
Minto, William (1845–1893), VI. 30; XI. 410, 440; XII. 373, 380, 445; XIII. 508, 551; XIV. 146, 209, 522, 528
Minturno, Antonio Sebastiano, III. 301; IX. 59
'Mira' (Sarah Elmy), XI. 140, 141
Mirabeau, Honoré Gabriel de Riquetti, count, X. 503, 505; XI. 59; XIII. 12, 469
Mirabel, in Disraeli's *Henrietta Temple*, XIII. 350
Mirabel, in *The Wild-Goose Chase*, VI. 123, 135
Mirabell, in Congreve's *The Way of the World*, VIII. 154 ff., 158
Mirabilis Annus, or the Year of Prodigies and Wonders, VIII. 10
Miracle of Saint Thomas, VI. 283
Miracle-plays, V. 36, 388 ff., *and see* Add.
Miracle-plays, sermons against, II. 502
Miracles of Our Lady, The, II. 323
Miraclis pleyinge, Tretise of, V. 25; VI. 374
Mirah, in *Daniel Deronda*, XIII. 400
Miranda, in Law's *Serious Call*, IX. 323
Miranda, in *The Knight of Malta*, VI. 130
Miranda, in *The Tempest*, V. 169, 172, 194, 207; VII. 71; VIII. 9, 28; XII. 54
Mirandola, Giovanni Pico della, III. 8, 214; VII. 264, 376

Mirk, John (*fl.* 1403?), II. 317; *Liber Festivalis*, II. 317, 498; *Instructions for Parish Priests*, II. 427
Mirobolant, Alcide, in *Pendennis*, XIII. 292
Mirror, The, X. 55; XIV. 592
Mirror for Magistrates, A, II. 202; III. 182, 183, 192 ff., 207, 228, 282, 296, 298, 300, 495, 514 ff.; IV. 134, 176; V. 83, 152; VII. 271; XII. 516
Contributors to, and editors of (under whose names also refer): Baldwin, William; Blenerhasset, Thomas; Ferrers, George; Higgins, John; Niccols, Richard; and Sackville, Thomas
Lives and Tragedies contained therein: Albanact; Alfred; Alurede; Arthur; Blacksmith, the; Bladud; Buckingham; Burdet, Sir Nicholas; Cade; Cadwallader; Caligula; Cambridge; Caracalla; Carassus; Chirinnus; Clarence; Claudius; Clifford; Collingbourne; Cordila; Curthose, Robert; Ebbe, Lady; Edric; Edward II; Edward IV; Edward V; Egelrede; Eleanor, duchess; Elstride; Emerianus; England's Eliza (queen Elizabeth); Forrex; Fulgentius; Galba; Geta; Glendower, Owen; Gloucester; Godwin; Guiderius; Hamo; Harold; Hastings; Helena; Henry, duke of Buckingham; Henry VI; Humber; Humphrey, duke of Gloucester; Iago; Irenglas; Ironside, Edmund; James I, of Scotland; James IV; John; Julius Caesar; Kimarus; Locrinus; Londricus; Madan; Malin; Mempricius; Morgan; Morindus; Mortimer; Mowbray; Nennius; Nero; Northumberland; Otho; Pendragon, Uther; Pinnar; Porrex; Richard I; Richard II; Richard III; Rudacke; Sabrine; Salisbury; Severus; Shore's Wife; Sigebert; Somerset; Stater; Suffolk; Tiberius; Tresilian; Varianus; Vitellius; Vortiger; Werwick; Wolsey, cardinal; Woodville; Worcester and York, III. 192–197
Mirror of Justices, The, VIII. 313, 317; XIV. 80
Mirror of St Edmund, The (Rolle), II. 47
Mirror of the Church, The, II. 324
Mirror of the periods of man's life, The, II. 502
Mirror of the World, The, II. 313
Mirrors, III. 198, 341
Mirrour of Worldly Fame, The, IV. 524
Mirza, in Lyttelton's *Persian Letters*, X. 114
Mirza Abdullah, XIV. 252
Misaubin, John, X. 22
Miscellanea Aulica, VIII. 379, 480; IX. 496
Miscellanies (Pope and Swift), IX. 78, 85, 131
Miscellany of Popular Scottish Poems (1841), XI. 444
Miser, the, in *The Daunce and Song of Death*, III. 87
Misericordia, in the *Coventry Plays*, V. 21
Misogonus, V. 110, 112, 113, 117, 119, 411
Misrule, in *The Masque of Christmas*, VI. 358, 359
Misrule, lord of, V. 8
Misselden, Edward (*fl.* 1608–1654), IV. 297, 512
Missolonghi, IV. 89
Mist, Nathaniel, IX. 16, 17; *Weekly Journal*, IX. 19, 21, 448
Mister, Mary, XI. 488; *The Adventures of a Doll*, XI. 383
Misyn, Richard (d. 1462?), II. 438
Mitcham, IV. 202
Mitchel, John (1815–1875), XIV. 570; *History of Ireland*, XIV. 326; *Jail Journal*, XIV. 325, 326; *Life of Hugh O'Neill*, XIV. 325
Mitchell, Sir Arthur (1826–1909), XII. 511
Mitchell, C., XIV. 532
Mitchell, Joseph (1684–1738), X. 434
Mitchell, Thomas (1783–1845), XII. 488; XIII. 175, 506
Mitford, Algernon Bertram Freeman, baron Redesdale (1837–1916), XIII. 495
Mitford, Bertram, XIV. Add. 9
Mitford, John (1781–1859), III. 298; X. 119, 451, 454, 458, 481; XI. 401; XII. 396, 420
Mitford, John (*pseud.* Alfred Burton, 1782–1831), XIV. 221, 544; *The Adventures of Johnny Newcome*, XIV. 220; *The Poems of a British Sailor*, XIV. 220
Mitford, John Freeman, 1st baron Redesdale (1748–1830), X. 510
Mitford, John Thomas Freeman, earl of Redesdale (1805–1886), XIII. 241, 245, 512
Mitford, Mary Russell (1787–1855), XI. 410, 458, 459, 461, 465; XII. 239, 242, 433, 453; XIII. 258, 377, 564; XIV. 200
Atherton, XIII. 429
Belford Regis, XIII. 430
Our Village, XIII. 429, 430
Recollections of a Literary Life, XIII. 429
Rienzi, XIII. 430
Mitford, William (1744–1827), XI. 251 ff., 255; XII. 302, 313; *History of Greece*, X. 320, 510; XII. 310
Mithridates, VII. 317
Mivart, St George (1827–1900), XII. 469
Moab, king of, in Cowley's *Davideis*, VII. 67
Moabite stone, the, XII. 501
Moallakat, laws of, XII. 502
Moberly, George (1803–1885), XII. 454, 457; XIII. 504
Moccum moccabitur, game of, V. 93
Mock Testaments, VII. 513
Mocket, Richard, (?) *God and the King*, IV. 382
Modder, river, XIV. 372
Model [army], the New, VII. 434
Moderate Intelligencer, The, VII. 355
Moderation, in *Piers the Plowman*, II. 20
Modern Theatre, The (1809), XI. 456

Modish, lady Betty, in Cibber's *Careless Husband*, VIII. 176
Modish, Mrs, in *Dialogues of the Dead*, XI. 352
Modus Componendi Brevia, VIII. 465
Modus Tenendi Parliamentum, XII. 355
Moe, J., XI. 491
Moetjen's *Recueil de pièces curieuses et nouvelles*, XI. 374
Moffat (Bannatyne MS.), II. 274
Moffat (Scotland), X. 230
Moffat, James, XIII. 570
Moffat, Sir John (attributed to), *Beware, I red you now*, III. 131; *The Wyf of Auchtirmuchty*, III. 132
Moffat, Robert, XIV. Add. 9
Moffett or Moffat, Thomas (1553–1604), IV. 519, 543; *Insectorum sive minimorum animalium theatrum*, IV. 374; *Silkewormes*, IV. 374
Mogridge, George (1787–1854), XI. 482
Mogul, the great, IV. 90, 91, 99; VII. 437; X. 110
Mogul empire, the, XIV. 332
Mogul government, XI. 16
Mohacz, battle of, VII. 79
Mohammadans (*Hudibras*), VIII. 65
Mohammed. *See* Mahomet
Mohammedan law, a, II. 292
Mohammedan learning, I. 153
Mohammedan religion, X. 313, 314
Mohammedanism, XI. 18, 194; XII. 191; XIII. 202, 362
Mohammedans, X. 377; XI. 17
Mohawks, the, XI. 261
Mohl, Mme, XIII. 381
'Mohock Magazine, the,' XII. 160, 161
Mohocks, the, IX. 126, 160
Mohun, Charles, 5th lord Mohun (1675?–1712), IX. 424
Mohun, Michael (1620?–1684), VIII. 186
Moir, David Macbeth (1798–1851), XII. 380, 450, 451; XIII. 431; *The Curate of Suverdiso*, XII. 252; *The Life of Mansie Wauch*, XII. 251
Moira, earl. *See* Hastings, Francis Rawdon
Molesey, III. 381
Molesworth, Robert, 1st viscount Molesworth (1656–1723), IX. 457, 463, 494
Molesworth, Sir William (1810–1855), XIV. 196
Molesworth, William Nassau (1816–1890), XIV. 495; *The History of England from 1830*, XIV. 93
Moleynes, lord (*Paston Letters*), II. 304
Molière, J. B. Poquelin de, I. 371; V. 189, 293; VI. 160, 214; VII. 366; VIII. 14, 134, 137 ff., 157, 159, 162, 165, 373, 374, 376, 428; IX. 29, 30; X. 88, 202, 417; XI. 322; XIII. 442, 445
Don Garcie de Navarre, XII. 211
Fourberies de Scapin, VIII. 181, 182
L'Avare, VIII. 174; X. 22; XI. 277
Le Bourgeois Gentilhomme, VIII. 140, 169
L'École des Femmes, VIII. 144
Molière, J. B. P. de
L'École des Maris, VIII. 139, 144, 183
L'Étourdi, VIII. 17, 133, 398; X. 72
Le mariage forcé, IX. 41; XI. 265
Le Médecin Malgré Lui, X. 22, 427
Le Misanthrope, VIII. 145; X. 226; XI. 269; XIII. 446
Les Fâcheux, VIII. 174
Les Précieuses Ridicules, VIII. 131, 174
Le Sicilien, ou l'Amour Peintre, VIII. 188
Monsieur de Pourceaugnac, VIII. 140, 431
Tartuffe, VIII. 189; X. 425
Molina, Tirso de, VIII. 130; *El Castigo del Pensèque*, VI. 204; VIII. 129
Molineaux, pugilist, XIV. 231
Molineux, Sir Richard, III. 265
Molinists, the, XIII. 435
Molitoris, U., *Dialogus de Pythonicis Mulieribus*, VII. 370, 505
Moll Cutpurse, in *The Roaring Girle*, VI. 54, 66, 223
Molle, H., VI. 480
Mollineux, Mary (born Southworth) (d. 1695), *Fruits of Retirement*, VIII. 114, 416; *Meditations in Trouble*, VIII. 114
Molloy, Charles (1646–1690), IV. 459
Molloy, Charles (d. 1767), XIV. 570
Molloy, Gerald, *The Irish Difficulty*, XIV. 447
Molloy, Joseph Fitzgerald, XIII. 515
Molly, in Mrs Gaskell's *Wives and Daughters*, XIII. 377, 378, 381
Moloch, XII. 36
Molteno, Sir Charles, XIV. Add. 9
Molteno, Percy Alport, XIV. Add. 9
Moluccas, the, IV. 99
Molyneux, William (1656–1698), VIII. 332, 339, 474; IX. 180, 181, 283; XIV. 570
Molza, III. 178
Momerie, Alfred Williams (1848–1900), XII. 469
Momford, lord, in *The Blind Beggar of Bednal Green*, V. 361
Mommsen, Theodor, I. 65, 66, 68, 70; XII. 306, 322; XIII. 469
Momure, in *Huon of Bordeaux*, II. 339
Momus, in *Wisdom of Solomon Paraphrased*, VI. 59
'Monarcho, fantastical,' VIII. 127
Monarchy or no Monarchy in England, VII. 207
Monardes, Nicolas, IV. 446
Monboddo, lord. *See* Burnett, James
Monçada, in Maturin's *Melmoth*, XIII. 420
Monck, George, 1st duke of Albemarle (1608–1670), VII. 140, 219, 229, 230, 360, 361, 364; VIII. 118, 121, 254
Monck, James Bury (1784–1856), XIV. 514
Monck, Mrs, VII. 362
Monck, William Henry Stanley, XIV. 474
Monckton, Mary, countess of Cork and Orrery (1746–1840), XI. 364
Moncrieff, William Thomas (1794–1857), XIII. 270, 418, 516, 521; XIV. 224;

Moncrieff, William Thomas
Cataract of the Ganges; or, The Rajah's Daughter, XIII. 265; *Dandy Family, The*, XIII. 265; *Tom and Jerry*, XIII. 265
Moneta, in Keats's *The Fall of Hyperion*, XII. 86
Money, in *Worke for Armorours*, VI. 56
Money-without-Learning, in *All for Money*, V. 57
Monica, St, VII. 247, 248
Monier-Williams, Sir Monier (1819–1899), XII. 343, 503
Monimia, in Otway's *Orphan*, VIII. 183, 184
Monitor, The, IX. 432; X. 388 ff., 522
Monk, James Henry (1784–1856), XII. 327 ff., 488, 491; XIV. 595; *Life of Bentley*, XII. 329
Monkhouse, Mrs, in Amory's *Memoirs of Several Ladies*, XI. 287
Monkhouse, William Cosmo (1840–1901), XII. 444; XIII. 207, 506
Monks, in *Oliver Twist*, XIII. 317, 325
Monkshaven, in Mrs Gaskell's *Sylvia's Lovers*, XIII. 380
Monmouth. *See* Geoffrey of
Monmouth, duchess of, IX. 161
Monmouth, duke of. *See* Scott, James
Monmouth, earl of. *See* Carey, Robert
Monmouth, lord, in Disraeli's *Coningsby*, XIII. 288, 349
Monmouth, Humphrey (*fl.* 1523), III. 40
Monmouth, Robert Carey, 1st earl of (1560?–1639), V. 479; XII. 376
Monmouthshire, XI. 430
Monnet, Jean, XI. 258
Monod, Adolphe, XII. 283; XIV. 490
Monod, Gabriel, XIV. 490
Monro, Alexander (d. 1715?), IX. 547
Monro, Charles Henry (1835–1908), XII. 488
Monro, David Binning (1836–1905), XII. 488, 492; *Grammar of the Homeric dialect*, XII. 334
Monro, Edward (1815–1866), XII. 472
Monro, H. A. J., XII. 482
Monro, Robert (d. 1633), *Expedition with the worthy Scots Regiment called M'Keyes Regiment*, VII. 231, 451
Monro, Robert (d. 1680?), VII. 452
Monro, Thomas (1764–1815), X. 472
Monsey, R., *Scarronides*, IX. 257, 500
Monson, Sir Thomas (1564–1641), IV. 143
Monson, Sir William (1569–1643), VII. 446; *Naval Tracts*, IV. 103, 104
Mont Blanc, XIV. 236
Mont Cenis, IX. 245; X. 115
Mont St Michel, II. 112
Montagu, Andrew, XIV. 185
Montagu, Anne Wortley, IX. 244
Montagu, Basil (1770–1851), XIV. 514
Montagu, Charles, earl of Halifax, IX. 44, 45, 86, 150, 244; *The Hind and the Panther Transvers'd*, IX. 147
Montagu, Charles, 1st duke of Manchester (1660?–1722), VIII. 274; IX. 149, 150
Montagu, Edward, 2nd earl of Manchester (1602–1671), IV. 425; VII. 351, 434
Montagu, Edward, 1st earl of Sandwich (1625–1672), VIII. 202, 249, 253, 254; IX. 244; X. 262; XI. 348
Montagu, Edward (d. 1775), X. 262; XI. 347, 348, 350
Montagu, Edward Wortley (d. 1761), IX. 244, 246, 248
Montagu, Edward Wortley (1713–1776), IX. 248; XIV. 553
Montagu, Mrs Elizabeth (1720–1800), V. 293; VII. 176; IX. 246; X. 261, 264, 268, 494; XI. 272, 328, 343, 346 ff. (main entry), 358, 360, 361, 364, 365, 474; *Dialogues of the Dead*, XI. 351, 352; *Essay on Shakespeare*, X. 262; XI. 352 ff.
Montagu, George. *See* Dunk
Montagu or Mountague, James (1568?–1618), VII. 316; VIII. 293
Montagu, John (1655?–1728), IV. 239
Montagu, John, 4th earl of Sandwich (1718–1792), X. 397, 401
Montagu, lady Mary Wortley (1689–1762), IX. 71, 191, 243 ff. (main entry), 250, 251, 402 ff., 449, 497, 574; X. 273, 274; XI. 348; XIII. 467
'Basset-table, The,' IX. 247
Constantinople Letters, IX. 246 ff.
Court Poems by a Lady of Quality, IX. 247
'Drawing Room, The,' IX. 247
Letters and Works, IX. 248
'On a maxim of La Rochefoucauld,' IX. 249
'Toilet, The,' IX. 247
Town Eclogues, IX. 247, 248
Translation of the *Enchiridion* of Epictetus, IX. 246, 248
Turkish Letters, IX. 244
Montagu, Matthew, X. 261
Montagu, Ralph, 1st duke of Montagu (1638?–1709), VIII. 156
Montagu or Mountague, Richard (1577–1641), VII. 312, 426, 459, 483, 484, 485
A New Gag for an old Goose, VII. 158
Analecta Exercitationum Ecclesiasticarum, VII. 311
Appello Caesarem, VII. 158, 433
Immediate Address unto God alone, VII. 158
Montagu, Walter (1603?–1677), VII. 517
Montague, in *Romeo and Juliet*, V. 182
Montague, Mrs Basil, XIII. 469
Montague, Charles Edward, XIV. 533
Montague, Francis Charles, XIV. 493, 536
Montague, Sir James (1666–1723), IX. 147
Montaigne, Michel Eyquem seigneur de, III. 160, 438, 453; IV. 10, 15, 16, 246, 248, 254, 343, 344, 347, 395, 447, 523; V. 207; VI. 21, 377; VII. 199, 366, 379, 389; VIII. 28, 52, 56, 58, 374, 376 ff., 385 ff., 389, 390, *also see* Add.; IX. 47, 159, 233, 237, 265, 399; X. 50; XII. 168, 174, 175; XIII. 467; XIV. 160, 421, 428; *Essays*, IX. 276, 277, 499
Montalembert, Charles Forbes de, XII. 276

Montalto, in the *Dunciad*, v. 271
Montalvan, J. P. de, VII. 83
Montalvo, García Ordoñez de, IV. 447; XI. 422
Montano, Reginaldo Gonzalez, IV. 447
Montanus (Lodge's), IV. 122
Montanus, Joannes Ferrarius, Latin treatise on Commonweal, VI. 377, 493
Montausier, duchess of (Julia de Rambouillet), VIII. 142
Monte. *See* Robert de
Monte Cassino, I. 214
Monteagle, lord. *See* Parker, William
Montégut, Émile, v. 302; IX. 71, 72; XIII. 551, 558
Monteith, Robert (*fl.* 1621–1660), IX. 550
Montemayor, George, III. 341; IV. 447; *Diana*, III. 186, 219, 351, 352; IV. 9, 117; V. 220; VI. 365
Montesquieu, Charles Louis de Secondat, baron de la Brède et de, IV. 295; v. 288; VIII. 292; X. 114, 135, 206, 334; XI. 163; XIII. 467; *Considérations*, X. 304; *Esprit des Lois*, X. 123, 296
Montfort, in Disraeli's *Endymion*, XIII. 349
Montfort, Simon de, I. 180, 204, 205, 338, 339, 368; XIV. 100
Montgomerie, Alexander (1556?–1610?), III. 134, 135, 188, 499, *also see* Add.; IV. 322, 517; IX. 359, 365; XI. 203
  Ane Answer to ane Helandmains Invective, III. 136
  Bankis of Helicon, The, III. 136; XI. 217
  Cherrie and the Slae, The, III. 133, 136; IX. 366, 367; XI. 217
  Flyting betwixt Polwart and Montgomerie, The, III. 136, 137, 491
  Night is near Gone, The, III. 137
Montgomery, VII. 27
Montgomery, countess of, *Urania*, VI. 200
Montgomery, H. R., XII. 412; XIV. 572
Montgomery, James (1771–1854), XII. 420; XIV. 203; *Go to dark Gethsemane*, XII. 135; *Songs of praise the angels sang*, XII. 135
Montgomery, Jemima (1807–1893), afterwards baroness Tautphoeus, XIII. 565
Montgomery, Robert (1807–1855), XII. 420; *Satan*, XII. 129; *The Omnipresence of the Deity*, XII. 129
Monthly Catalogue, The, XI. 339
Monthly Chronicle, The, XI. 374
Monthly Magazine, The, XII. 428
Monthly Magazine of Politics, Literature, The, and the Belles-Lettres, XII. 428
Monthly Magazine: or, British Register of Literature, Sciences, The, and the Belles-Lettres, XII. 428
Monthly Repository, The, XII. 428; XIII. 53 ff.
Monthly Repository of Theology and General Literature, The, XII. 428
Monthly Review, The, IX. 472; X. 40, 171, 176, 201 ff., 474, 483; XI. 142, 339, 353, 418 ff.; XII. 428
Monthly Review, The (*or Literary Journal*), XII. 428
Monticelso, in *The White Divel*, VI. 176
Montluc, Blaise de, *Commentaries*, IX. 276
Montoni, in Mrs Radcliffe's *Mysteries of Udolpho*, XI. 303
Montpellier, II. 364; III. 419; VII. 217, 233; VIII. 330, 389
Montpensier, Mlle de, IV. 523
Montreal, XIV. 357, 358
  Bishop's college, XIV. 355
  Shakespeare club, XIV. 355
Montreville, in *The Unnatural Combat*, VI. 159
Montrose, duke of. *See* Graham, James, 1st duke
Montrose, marquis of. *See* Graham, James, 1st marquis
Monumenta Germaniae Historica, XIV. 53
Monypenny, William Flavelle (1886–1912), XIV. 504; *The Life of Benjamin Disraeli, Earl of Beaconsfield*, XIII. 345, 346, 547
Moodie, Donald, XIV. Add. 9
Moodie, Duncan C. F., XIV. Add. 5, 9
Moodie, Susanna (1803–1885), XIV. 360, 581, 583; *Life in the Clearing*, XIV. 358; *Roughing it in the Bush*, XIV. 358
Moody, John (1727?–1812), XI. 257, 261
Moody, John, in Vanbrugh's *A Journey to London*, VIII. 162
Moor, James (1712–1779), IX. 562
Moor, John (*fl.* 1688), X. 387
Moor park, IX. 91 ff., 126
Moore, Arthur (1666?–1730), IX. 14
Moore, Arthur William (1853–1909), XII. 512
Moore, Dugald (1805–1841), XII. 420
Moore, Edward (1712–1757), X. 81, 92, 423, 437; XI. 324; *Foundling, The*, X. 80; *Gamester, The*, X. 80, 81; *Gil Blas*, X 80
Moore, Edward, XIV. 596
Moore, Henry (1751–1844), X. 518
Moore, H. Kingsmill, XIV. 592
Moore, James (1702–1734), IX. 86
Moore, John (1646–1714), IX. 330, 335, 356
Moore, John (*fl.* 1721), X. 387
Moore, John (1729–1802), XI. 207, 462; XIII. 467; *Zeluco*, X. 38
Moore, Sir John (1761–1809), XIII. 467; XIV. 107, 294
Moore, John Howard, XIV. 553
Moore, J. Sheridan, XIV. 363, 587
Moore, Louis, in Charlotte Brontë's *Shirley*, XIII. 408
Moore, Peter (1753–1828), XIII. 276
Moore, Robert, in Charlotte Brontë's *Shirley*, XIII. 408, 409
Moore, Thomas (1779–1852), XI. 396, 456; XII. 34, 42, 44, 74, 95, 102 ff. (main entry), 110, 115, 120, 122, 126, 129, 130, 136, 138, 150, 163, 223, 303, 383 ff., 410, 444; XIII. 25, 154, 161, 166, 230, 234, 306; XIV. 180, 186, 198, 310, 314, 318*a*, 322, 365, 504

Moore, Thomas
At the mid hour of night, XII. 105; XIII. 235
Corruption, XII. 104
Epicurean, The, XII. 104
Eveleen's Bower, XIII. 235
Fables for the Holy Alliance, XII. 40
Fudge Family, The, XII. 104, 105
I saw from the beach, XII. 105
Intolerance, XII. 104
Irish Melodies, XII. 41, 102, 105; XIV. 311, 316, 329
Lalla Rookh, XII. 102, 105
Last Rose of Summer, The, XII. 105
Life of Lord Byron, XII. 53, 103
Life of Lord Edward Fitzgerald, XIV. 107
Life of Sheridan, XIV. 107
Loves of the Angels, The, XII. 48, 102
Minstrel Boy, The, XII. 105
National Airs, XII. 105
Oft in the stilly night, XII. 105
'Paradise and the Peri,' XII. 105
'Phelim Connor' letters, XII. 104
Poems, XII. 103, 104
Poetical works of the late Thomas Little, XII. 103
Tell me the witching tale again, XIV. 311
Two-penny Post Bag, The, XII. 105
Moore, Zachary, XI. 174
Moore Smith, G. C. *See* Smith, G. C. Moore
Moorish wars in Spain, XI. 280
Moors, the, XIII. 258
Mopsa, in Sidney's *Arcadia*, III. 353
Mopus, in Wilson's *The Cheats*, VIII. 122
Moral Ode. See *Poema Morale*
Moralities, V. 36, 391 ff.
Moralities, Latin, V. 58
Moran, Patrick Francis (1830–1911), XIV. 570
Morand, duke, in a religious play, V. 40, 43
Morant, Philip (1700–1770), IX. 537
Moravian school, Neuwied, XIII. 440
Moravians, the, IX. 324; X. 60, 350, 364
Moray, II. 115
Moray, earl of. *See* Stewart, James
Moray, Sir Robert (d. 1673), IX. 193
Morayshire, XIII. 431
Morcelli, Stefano Antonio, XII. 326
Mordaunt, Charles, 3rd earl of Peterborough (1685–1735), VIII. 411; IX. 23, 249, 250
Mordent, in Holcroft's *Deserted Daughter*, XI. 277
Mordred or Modred, in Arthurian legend, I. 235, 248, 260 ff., 266
Mordred, in *Morte Arthure*, I. 313; II. 118, 120
Mordred, in Malory's *Morte d'Arthur*, V. 78
Mordred, in *The Misfortunes of Arthur*, V. 78, 79
More, Anne (afterwards Anne Donne), IV. 200
More, Cresacre (1572–1649), V. 247; XII. 516
More, Edward (1537?–1620), *The Defence of Women*, III. 90, 486
More, Elizabeth (afterwards Rastell), IV. 198
More, George, IV. 535
More, Sir George (of Losely), IV. 200, 201, 221
More, Hannah (1745–1833), X. 250, 251, 267 ff. (main entry), 494; XI. 260, 300, 350, 359 ff. (main entry), 365, 458, 474; XII. 124, 445; XIV. 60, 390, 600, 608
Bas Bleu, or Conversation, XI. 346, 348, 362
Bishop Bonner's Ghost, XI. 363
Bleeding Rock, The, XI. 361
Cheap Repository Tracts, XII. 281
Fatal Falsehood, The, XI. 274, 362
Inflexible Captive, The, XI. 273
Memoirs, X. 184
Percy, XI. 272, 273, 362
Preface to Tragedies, XI. 259
Repository Tracts, XI. 362
Sacred Dramas, XI. 379
Search after Happiness, The, XI. 360
Sensibility, X. 268; XI. 362
Sir Eldred of the Bower, X. 213; XI. 361
Thoughts on the importance of the Manners of the Great, XI. 362
Village Politics, XI. 362
More, Henry (1614–1687), VII. 84, 90, 279, 302, 407, 507, 510; VIII. 110, 273, 278 ff., 283, 290, 291, 347, 453 ff., 474; IX. 184, 518; XI. 57
Antidote against Atheism, VIII. 285, 287
Conjectura Cabbalistica, VIII. 285
Divine Dialogues, VIII. 286
Enchiridion Ethicum, VIII. 282
Enchiridion Metaphysicum, VIII. 286
Enthusiasmus Triumphatus, VIII. 285; IX. 326
Grand Mystery of Godliness, VIII. 285
Immortality of the Soul, The, VIII. 280, 285
Mystery of Iniquity, VIII. 286
Philosophicall Poems, VIII. 282, 283
Song of the Soul, VIII. 282, 283, 285
More, John (d. 1592), V. 133
More, P. Elmer, XI. 420; *The Shelburne Essays*, XII. 433
More, Richard (d. 1643), VII. 482
More, Sarah, X. 268
More, Sir Thomas (1478–1535), II. 62, 327; III. 2, 6, 7, 12, 13, 15–21 (main entry), 26, 40, 43, 47, 49, 52, 80, 187, 314, 332, 334, 363, 365, 469, 532; IV. 198, 228, 261, 320, 512; V. 57; VII. 158, 278, 304, 366, 392, 474; VIII. 125; IX. 160, 197, 489, 534; X. 184; XI. 422, 427; XIV. 494
Apology, The, III. 17
Dialogue, The, II. 60; III. 17, 26
Mery geste of a Sergeaunt and Frere, The, II. 326
Frith, A Letter against, III. 17
Luciani...compluria opuscula...ab Erasmo Roterodamo et Thoma Moro...traducta, III. 16

More, Sir Thomas
Picus, Life of John, III. 17
Progymnasmata, III. 13, 16
Rueful Lamentation, A, III. 17
Salem and Bizance, The Debellacyon of, III. 17
Supper of the Lord, An Answere to the, III. 17
Supplication of Souls, The, III. 17, 26
Tindale's Answere, A Confutation of, III. 17
Utopia, III. 16 ff., 109, 332, 334; IV. 67, 300; V. 90; VII. 298, 299; XIII. 452
Works, IV. 397
More, Sir Thomas, V. 237, 238, 246 ff., 332, 399, 442, 444
More, Sir William, VI. 289
Morea, the, VII. 75
Morecroft, in *The Scornful Ladie*, VI. 133
Morell, John Daniel (1816–1891), XIV. 478
Morell, Thomas (1703–1784), *Thesaurus*, XII. 327
Moréri, Louis, *Grand Dictionnaire historique*, V. 286; IX. 211, 492
Moreto, A., *No puede ser guardar una mujer* (No holding a Woman), VIII. 131, 189
Moreton Pinckney, X. 271
Morfill, William Richard (1834–1909), XIV. 495
Morgam, chronicle of the abbey of, I. 256
Morgan, in Smollett's *Roderick Random*, X. 37
Morgan, earl of London, in *The Devil and his Dame*, V. 329
Morgan, Henry, IV. 76
Morgan, Henry James, XIV. 581
Morgan, J., *Phoenix Britannicus*, X. 166
Morgan, James, in *Pendennis*, XIII. 291
Morgan, McNamara, III. 355
Morgan, N., *The Perfection of Horsemanship*, IV. 540
Morgan, lady Sydney (born Owenson) (1783–1859), XII. 451; XIV. 570
Book without a Name, The, XIV. 322
France, XIV. 322
Italy, XIV. 322
Kate Kearney, XIV. 323
St Clair, XIV. 322
Wild Irish Girl, The, XIV. 322
Morgan, Sylvanus (1620–1693), IX. 537
Morgan, Thomas (d. 1743), IX. 288, 508; X. 521; *Moral Philosopher, The*, IX. 294
Morgan, Thomas, F.S.A., XII. 512; *Romano-British Mosaic Pavements*, XII. 347
Morgan, Sir Thomas (d. 1679?), VII. 452
Morgan, Sir Thomas Charles (1783–1843), XIV. 322
Morgan le Fay, I. 265, 327
Morgans, the, XI. 121
Morhof, Daniel Georg, V. 286
Morice, Sir William (1602–1676), VII. 364
Morier, James Justinian (1780?–1849), XII. 451
Morier, Sir Robert Burnett David (1826–1893), XIV. 504
Morin, Lewis, X. 164, 464
Moriomachia, VII. 390
Morison, James Augustus Cotter (1832–1888), XIII. 467; XIV. 62, 493, 504; *Gibbon*, X. 300, 304, 305, 314, 509; XIV. 504
Morison, Jeanie, XIII. 485
Morison, Robert (1620–1683), VIII. 478; XIV. 282, 562
Morisot, Claude, *Alitophili Veritatis Lachrymae*, IV. 257
Morland, Catherine, in Jane Austen's *Northanger Abbey*, XI. 299, 300; XII. 235, 236
Morland, George (1763–1804), VIII. 66
Morland, Sir Samuel (1625–1695), VIII. 478
Morley. *See* Daniel of
Morley, George (1597–1684), bishop of Winchester, IV. 422; VII. 151, 250, 426, 518; VIII. 294, 295, 460
Morley, Henry (1822–1894), I. viii, 47, 218; II. 28, 35; XI. 392, 407, 418; XII. 427, 504; XIII. 472, 515; XIV. 198, 504
Morley, John, viscount Morley of Blackburn, IX. 153; XI. 390, 406; XII. 396; XIII. 495; XIV. 123, 195, 493, 509, 592; *Life of Gladstone*, XIV. 135; *Life of Richard Cobden*, XIV. 179
Morley, Thomas (1557–1604?), IV. 113, 121, 464, 465, 487
Mormon, Book of, IV. 47
Mornay, Philippe de, IV. 447; *Work concerning the trewnesse of the Christian Religion*, Sidney's trans., IV. 21
Morning Advertiser, The, XIV. 177, 189
Morning Chronicle, The, X. 467; XII. 171, 183, 187, 323, 432, 490; XIV. 170, 171, 177, 178, 184 ff., 189, 190
Morning Herald, The, XI. 34, 391; XIV. 188, 189
Morning Post, The, XII. 187, 188, 434; XIII. 347, 440; XIV. 177, 179, 183 ff., 529, 533
Morning Star, The, XIV. 173, 188, 190
Morocco, V. 183
Morocco, Notes and Observations on the Empress of, VIII. 3
Morose, in Jonson's *The Silent Woman*, VI. 22, 227; X. 50
Morpeth, XIII. 129
Morpeth, Ontario, XIV. 350
Morpeth school, VII. 330
Morrice, D., XIV. 598
Morris, Charles (1745–1838), XII. 420
Morris, Dinah, in *Adam Bede*, XIII. 383, 390, 391
Morris, Jane (born Burden), XIII. 119
Morris, John Brande (1812–1880), XII. 454
Morris, Sir Lewis (1833–1907), XIII. 194, 201 ff., 221, 506
Epic of Hades, An, XIII. 201
Gwen, XIII. 202
Gycia, XIII. 202
Ode of Life, The, XIII. 202

Morris, Sir Lewis
Songs of Two Worlds, XIII. 201
Songs Unsung, XIII. 202
Morris, Marshall, Faulkner and Co., XIII. 119
Morris, Miss May, XIII. 493
Morris, Richard (1833–1894), I. 115, 218; II. 166; XII. 504; XIV. 611; *Specimens of Early English*, XII. 344
Morris, William (1834–1896), I. 420; VIII. 227; XII. 275; XIII. 112, 118 ff. (main entry), 134, 137, 139, 147, 178, 193, 205, 251, 442, 448, 451, 458, 491 ff. (main entry); XIV. 537
Aeneids of Virgil, The (translation), XIII. 125, 126
Bellerophon at Argos, XIII. 125
Bellerophon in Lycia, XIII. 125
Beowulf (translation), XIII. 127
Cupid and Psyche, The Story of, XIII. 124
Defence of Guenevere, The, X. 217, 220; XIII. 121, 122, 124, 125, 129
Doom of King Acrisius, The, XIII. 124
Dream of John Ball, A, XIII. 127
Earthly Paradise, The, XIII. 120, 123, 125, 128, 252
Hollow Land, The, XIII. 121
House of the Wolfings, The, XIII. 127
'I know a little garden close,' XIII. 125
King Arthur's Tomb, XIII. 121
Land East of the Sun and West of the Moon, The, XIII. 124, 125
Life and Death of Jason, The, XIII. 122, 124, 125, 252
Lindenborg Pool, XIII. 121
Love is Enough, XIII. 125, 126, 135, 252
Lovers of Gudrun, The, XIII. 125
News from Nowhere, XIII. 127
Odyssey (translation), XIII. 125 ff.
'Outlanders, whence come ye last?' XIII. 140
Poems by the Way, XIII. 127
Rapunzel, XIII. 121
Roots of the Mountains, The, XIII. 127
Sailing of the Sword, The, XIII. 121
Sigurd the Volsung and the Fall of the Niblungs, The Story of, XIII. 126, 127, 252
Sir Peter Harpdon's End, X. 217; XIII. 121
Song of the Gillyflower, The, XIII. 121
Story of the Glittering Plain, The, XIII. 127
Story of the Unknown Church, The, XIII. 120
Sundering Flood, The, XIII. 128
Two Red Roses across the Moon, XIII. 121
Water of the Wondrous Isles, The, XIII. 128
Well at the World's End, The, XIII. 128
Welland River, XIII. 121
Wood beyond the World, The, XIII. 128
Morris dancers, V. 32
Morrison, Robert (1782–1834), XII. 342, 500
Mors, in *A Dialogue...against the fever Pestilence*, III. 109
Mors, Roderyck, The Complaint of, VII. 514
Morsbach, L., II. 152
Morse or Mosse, M., IV. 512, 518
Morte Arthure (English rime and alliterative versions), I. 235, 270, 281, 284, 290, 313, 333, 470; II. 116, 118, 119, 122, 123, 230, 314, 315, 332, 334 ff., 340, 486; III. 233, 237; IV. 6, 397; V. 78; X. 218, 228; XIII. 35; *also see* Malory
Mortgage, in *The Staple of Newes*, VI. 25
Mortimer, Mrs Favell Lee (1802–1878), XI. 481
Mortimer, Roger de, 8th baron Wigmore and 1st earl of March (1287?–1330), IV. 181, 182
Mortlake, IV. 73
Morton, Charles (1627–1698), IX. 6, 393, 394; X. 386
Morton, earl, in *John a Kent*, etc., V. 317
Morton, Henry, in Scott's *Old Mortality*, XII. 27
Morton, John (1420?–1500), archbishop of Canterbury (bishop of Ely), III. 15, 66, 334, 335; V. 54
Morton, John Maddison (1811–1891), XIII. 521; *Box and Cox*, XIII. 270
Morton, Thomas (1564–1659), bishop of Durham, IV. 202, 203, 206; VII. 323, 426, 515
Morton, Thomas (1764?–1838), XI. 270, 276, 458; XIII. 270
Columbus, XI. 280
Cure for the Heartache, XI. 281
School of Reform, XI. 281
Speed the Plough, XI. 281
Way to get Married, XI. 280, 281
Morus or Moir, Alexander, VII. 105, 125, 130, 131
Morven, X. 222
Morwenstow, XII. 134
Morwent, Charles (d. 1675), VIII. 84
Moryson, Fynes (1566–1617?), IV. 459; VI. 466; VII. 446; *History of Ireland*, VII. 211; *Itinerary*, VII. 201, 211
Mosaic code, the, XI. 194
Mosbie, in *Arden of Feversham*, V. 242
Moscheles, Felix, XIII. 562
Moschus, III. 218, 222, 265; VII. 83, 489; IX. 526; X. 454; XI. 426; XII. 495
Moseley, Henry Nottidge (1844–1891), XIV. 297, 562
Moseley, Humphrey (d. 1661), VI. 114; VII. 116, 458; XI. 318, 319
Mosellanus, *Figurae*, III. 429
Moses, I. 134, 226; IV. 61, 170; VII. 296; IX. 296; X. 130; XII. 299
Moses, in *The Three Laws*, V. 58
Moses, Belle, XIII. 501
Mosheim, J. L. von, VIII. 453
Moslems, XII. 45; XIV. 182, 252
Moss, Joseph William (1803–1862), XII. 523
Mossgiel, XI. 220, 224, 440

Mossop, Henry (1729?–1774?), xi. 450, 454
Most wonderful wonder that ever appeared, ix. 132
Mothe Le Vayer, Sieur F. de la, viii. 449
Mother Goose's Melody, xi. 375, 376, 488
Mother Goose's Tales, xi. 376
Mother Redcap, v. 319
Mother Shipton, xi. 334
Motherwell, William (1797–1835), ii. 409; xi. 437, 443, 444; xii. 6
Harp of Renfrewshire, xi. 237
Jeanie Morrison, xi. 237
Minstrelsy Ancient and Modern, xi. 237
Poems Narrative and Lyrical, xi. 237
Mottershead, Edward (*fl.* 1660), vii. 361
Motteux, Peter Anthony (1660–1718), vii. 256; viii. 171, 385, 438; ix. 256, 260, 263, 270 ff. (main entry); x. 163; *Gentleman's Journal*, ix. 270; *Rabelais*, ix. 270
Mottley, John (1692–1750), ix. 500
Motto, in Drayton's *Idea*, iv. 172
Mottram, William, xiii. 552
Mouldy, in *Henry IV*, v. 360
Moulton, James Hope (1863–1917), xii. Add. 4
Moulton, Louise C., xiii. 496
Moulton, Richard Green, xiv. 528
Moulton, William Fiddian (1835–1898), xii. 501
Moultrie, John (1799–1874), xii. 420
Mounier, Jean Joseph, xii. 144
Mountcastle, Clara H., xiv. 582
Mountferrat, in *The Knight of Malta*, vi. 130
Mountfort, Harriet, in Mrs Griffith's *School for Rakes*, xi. 263
Mountfort, Mrs (Susanna Verbruggen) (1667?–1703), viii. 191
Mountfort, William (*c.* 1664–1692), vi. 7; viii. 189
Mounth, the, in Wyntoun, ii. 132
Mountjoy, lord. *See* Blount, William
Mouse, the clown, in *Mucedorus*, v. 253
Mowbray, John, 3rd duke of Norfolk (1415–1461), ii. 304, 305, 503
Mowbray, John de, viii. 313
Mowcher, Miss, in *David Copperfield*, xiii. 336
Moxon, Edward (1801–1858), xii. 200, 201, 222, 421, 435; xiii. 61
Moxon, Mrs Emma (born Isola), xii. 200 ff., 435
Moxon, Joseph (1627–1700), iv. 459
Moyle, John (d. 1714), v. 459
Moyle, Walter (1672–1721), ix. 267
Moyra, xiv. 320
Moysie, David (*fl.* 1582–1603), vii. 455; *Memoirs of the Affairs of Scotland*, iii. 149, 505
Mozart, iv. 162
Mozley, Anne (1809–1891), xii. 459, 461
Mozley, James Bowling (1813–1878), xii. 256, 261, 273, 454, 456, 459, 464; xiii. 466
Mozley, Thomas (1806–1893), xii. 453, 459, 460; xiv. 596, 599; *Reminiscences*, xii. 273
Mr Bailey, Grocer, in Gissing's *New Grub Street*, xiii. 460
'Mr F.'s aunt,' in *Little Dorrit*, xiii. 331
'Mtesa, king of Uganda, xiv. 254
Mucedorus, v. 135, 237, 238, 251, 253, 442, 443
Mucius, consul, i. 95
Muddiman, Henry, vii. 349, 362 ff., 495; ix. 2
Current Intelligence, The, vii. 364
Gazette, London, vii. 365
Mercurius Publicus, vii. 362
Parliamentary Intelligencer, The, afterwards *The Kingdom's Intelligencer*, vii. 362
Muddiman, H. and Thomas Henshaw, *Nouvelles Ordinaires de Londres*, vii. 360
Mudford, William (1782–1848), x. 476; xi. 457; xiv. 188
Mudge, Zachariah (1694–1769), x. 467
Muggins, Dick, x. 199
Muggleton, Ludowicke, x. 377
Muir, William (1799–1860), xii. 498
Muir, Sir William (1819–1905), xiv. 339, 505, 579; *The Life of Mahomet*, xiv. 338
Muir, W. M., xi. 432, 433
Muir Mackenzie, Georgina Mary, xiv. 553
Muirland Willie, ix. 360
Mulberie trees and...silkeworms, iv. 543
Mulcaster, Richard (1530?–1611), iii. 311, 435, 436, 444, 446, 552, 556; iv. 238; v. 102, 123; vi. 221; vii. 332, 492; xiv. 608; *Elementarie*, iii. 311, 435; *Positions*, iii. 311, 435
Mulciber, in *Thersites*, v. 108
Mule sans Frein, La, i. 296
Mulgrave, John Sheffield, earl of. *See* Buckingham and Normanby, duke of
Mulholland, Rosa, xiv. 329
Müller, Friedrich Max (1823–1900), xii. 314, 502, 503; xiii. 354, 368, 469, 470, 548; xiv. 478; *Lectures on the Science of Language*, xii. 343
Müller, Johann, of Königsberg, *Ephemerides*, iv. 74, 82
Müller, Karl Ottfried, xii. 300, 483, 498; *History of Greek Literature*, xii. 331; *The Doric Race*, xii. 301, 312
Mulligan, the (Thackeray's), xiii. 283
Mullinger, James Bass (1834–1918), ii. 347, 367; vi. 3; vii. 316, 320; xiv. 489, 594
Mullisheg of Fesse, king, in *The Fair Maid of the West*, vi. 101
Mulock, Dinah Maria (Mrs Craik) (1826–1887), xi. 488; xiii. 178, 506, 565; *John Halifax, Gentleman*, xiii. 435
Mulso, Hester. *See* Chapone, Mrs Hester
Mum, Sothsegger (*i.e.* Hush, Truthteller) (*Richard the Redeless*), ii. 3, 36, 432, 434
Mumby, Frank Arthur, xi. 466
Mumford, in *King Leir*, v. 84

Mumming, in *The Masque of Christmas,* VI. 358, 359
Mun, Thomas (1571–1641), IV. 512; *Discourse of Trade to the East Indies,* IV. 310; *England's Treasure by Foreign Trade,* IV. 310
Munby, Arthur Joseph, XIII. 189, 506
Munchausen, Baron, XI. 492; XIII. 279
Munchausen romance, V. 95
Münchner Brut, I. 236
Munday, Anthony (1553–1633), III. 68, 302, 341, 349, 359, *also see* Add.; IV. 117 ff., 390, 439, 445, 447, 448, 471, 487, 525, 532, 533, 536; V. 236, 310–322 (main entry), 328, 329, 331 ff., 344, 370, 371, 474; VI. 4, 17, 41, 61, 329, 365, 391. 395, 459
'A Caveat to the Reader,' V. 313
Amadis de Gaule (trans. of), V. 314
Ballad against Plays, A, IV. 323
Banquet of Dainty Conceits, A, IV. 119
'Beauty sat bathing by a spring,' IV. 119
English Romayne Life, The, V. 313
'Fair nymphes sit ye here by me,' IV. 119
Fedele and Fortunio, V. 314 ff., 474; VI. 304
Funeral of Richard Cœur de Lion, The, V. 319
John a Kent and John a Cumber, V. 311, 315 ff., 320; VI. 347
Metropolis Coronata, V. 35
Palladino of England, V. 314, 323
Palmerin of England (trans. of), V. 314
Primaleon (trans. of), IV. 119
Robert, Earle of Huntington, V. 35, 310, 318 ff., 325, 326; VI. 236
Set at Tennis, The, V. 319
Third Blast of Retreat from Plays and Theatres, The (? by Munday), V. 313
View of Sundry Examples, A, V. 315
Woodman's Walk, The, IV. 119
Zelauto, III. 349, 536
See, also, under Chettle and Middleton and *Third Blast*
Munden, Joseph Shepherd (1758–1832), XI. 454; XII. 436
Mundus, in *Confessio Amantis,* II. 151
Mundy, John (d. 1630), IV. 113, 465
Munich, V. 306
Munich, Fugger collection at, IV. 429
Munro, Hugh Andrew Johnstone (1819–1885), X. 125; XII. 327, 337, 488; *Criticisms and Elucidations of Catullus,* XII. 335; *Translations into Latin and Greek Verse,* XII. 335
Munro, W. A., XIII. 544
Munro. *See also* Monro
Munster, Ireland, III. 229, 244; IV. 433; VII. 209, 211, 438; IX. 136; XIV. 314
Münster, in *The Unfortunate Traveller,* III. 363
Münster, bishop of (C. Bernhard von Galen), VIII. 381
Münster, Sebastian, III. 109; *Cosmographia,* III. 141; IV. 70
Muralt, Béat de, V. 287
Muratori, Ludovico Antonio, X. 220, 311, 312
Murchison, Sir Roderick Impey (1792–1871), XIV. 291, 293, 294, 562
Murcia, in *The Doubtfull Heir,* VI. 205
Murderous Mychaell, V. 117, 325
Murdoch, Patrick (d. 1774), X. 105, 446, 447
Murdoch, W. M., XIII. 495
Murdstone and Grinby, in *David Copperfield,* XIII. 327
Mure, William (1799–1860), *Critical History of the Literature of Ancient Greece,* XII. 339
Mure, Sir William, of Rowallan (1594–1657), IX. 542, 556
Murger, Henri, *Scènes de la Vie de Bohème,* XIII. 433
Murillo, Bartolomeo Esteban, XIII. 52
Murimuth, Adam (1275?–1347), II. 498
Murner, III. 59
Murning Maiden, The, II. 281
Murphy, Anna. *See* Jameson, Mrs Anna
Murphy, Arthur (1727–1805), IX. 435; X. 20, 89, 163, 189, 264, 389, 390, 393, 413, 437, 439, 441, 459, 466, 472, 474, 522; XI. 453; XIV. 570
All in the Wrong, X. 88
Grecian Daughter, X. 88
Know your own Mind, XI. 269
No One's Enemy but his Own, X. 86
Orphan of China, X. 86
School for Guardians, X. 88
Upholsterer, The, X. 88
Way to keep him, X. 88
Zenobia, X. 88
Murphy, Denis Brownell (d. 1842), XIV. 323
'Murphy,' *pseud. See* Maturin, Charles Robert
Murray, Alexander Stuart (1841–1904), XII. 498
Murray, Sir David, of Gorthy (1567–1629), IV. 487; IX. 556; *Bibliography: its Scope and Methods,* XII. 363, 370, 520; *David Laing,* XII. 350, 358, 517, 520; *R. and A. Foulis,* XII. 324, 520
Murray, David Christie (1847–1907), XIII. 544, 565
Murray, Mrs Elizabeth. *See* Grant, Mrs Elizabeth
Murray, E. C. Grenville, XIV. 194
Murray, George, XIV. 582
Murray, lord George (1700?–1760), IX. 565
Murray, Grace, X. 368
Murray, Henry, XIV. 534
Murray, Sir James Augustus Henry (1837–1915), XII. 505; XIV. 454, 611; *Dialect of the Southern counties of Scotland,* II. 96, 99
Murray, John, 3rd duke of Atholl (1729–1774), X. 274
Murray, Sir John, of Broughton (1718–1777), IX. 564
Murray, John (1745–1793), XI. 327

Murray, John (1778–1843), XI. 327, 423, 468; XIV. 613
Murray, John (1808–1892), XII. 34, 47, 52, 149 ff., 154, 155, 161, 387, 396, 430; XIII. 346, 353; XIV. 613; *Memoir of*, XII. 150
Murray, Sir John (1841–1914), XIV. 297, 562
Murray, Sir John Archibald, lord Murray (1779–1859), XII. 144
Murray, Lindley (1745–1826), XII. 505; XIII. 240; XIV. 608; *English Grammar*, XIV. 397
Murray, Patrick James, XIV. 567
Murray, Sir Robert (d. 1673), VII. 435
Murray, R. F., XIV. 209, 538; *The Scarlet Gown*, XIV. 210
Murray, Thomas (1792–1872), XI. 446
Murray, William, 1st earl of Mansfield (1705–1793), X. 285, 375, 399, 404, 405, 470, 527
Murrell, John (*fl.* 1630), IV. 543
Murry, John Middleton, XIII. 573
Musa, in Ouida's *In Maremma*, XIII. 436
Musa Cantabrigiensis, VII. 180
Musae Etonenses, XIV. 56
Musaeus, IV. 438; VII. 489; X. 454; XI. 426; XIII. 465
Musaeus (*i.e.* John Daniel), IV. 180
Musarum Anglicanarum Analecta, IX. 434
Musarum Deliciae, VII. 413
Musäus, Johann Karl August, XIII. 4, 465; *Grandison der Zweite*, X. 19
Muscovy voyages, IV. 67, 71, 75, 80, 84, 92, 93
Muses Farwel to Popery and Slavery, The (1689), VIII. 410
Muses Merriment, The (1656), VII. 512
Museum, The, XI. 324
Museum Criticum, XII. 329
Museum Minervae, VII. 78
Musgrave, Samuel (1732–1780), X. 270; XII. 483
Musgrave, Tom, in Jane Austen's *The Watsons*, XII. 234
Musgrave, Sir William, VIII. 263
Musgrove, Louisa, in Jane Austen's *Persuasion*, XII. 241
Musgrove, Mr and Mrs Charles, in Jane Austen's *Persuasion*, XII. 240
Music, in *The Passetyme of Pleasure*, II. 225, 229, 230
Music, Elizabethan, V. 372
Music of the 17th century, the, VIII. 424
Music, Old English popular, VIII. 411
Musical Miscellany, the, IX. 567
Musical Repository, IX. 567; XI. 444
Musicians of London, corporation of the, V. 28
Musidora, in Thomson's *Summer*, X. 104
Musidorus, in Sidney's *Arcadia*, III. 352
Musidorus (a poem in memory of James Thomson), X. 450
Musonius, in *Club Law*, VI. 308, 309
Musophilus (Daniel's), IV. 135
Mussatus (*see* Albertino), V. 62
Musselburgh, IX. 370
Musset, Alfred de, V. 302; XII. 392; XIII. 272; *Carmosine*, XIII. 401
Mustapha, in *Solymannidae*, VI. 301
Mustapha, Haji. *See* Raymond
Mutability, in *The Faerie Queene*, II. 234; III. 238
Mutimers, the, in Gissing's *Demos*, XIII. 459
Muto, in Marston's *Scourge of Villanie*, IV. 332
Muzzle for Cerberus, A, VII. 502
My Hart is quhyt, III. 132
My Jocky blyth, IX. 360
My Laddie, IX. 375
'My Uncle Toby,' X. 206
My Winifreda, IX. 188
Mycene, in *Horestes*, V. 64, 65
Mychell, John (*fl.* 1556), IV. 409
Myddleton, William (1556?–1621), V. 92
Mydlerd, a mirror called (*i.e.* the World), in *Piers the Plowman*, II. 25
Myers, E., XIV. 522
Myers, Frederic (1811–1851), XII. 466, 469
Myers, Frederic William Henry (1843–1901), XI. 110, 410; XII. 404; XIII. 43, 207, 478, 491, 506, 553; XIV. 473; *St Paul*, XIII. 209
Myll, G. (1492), II. 285
Myllar, Androw (*fl.* 1503–1508), VI. 412; IX. 359; *and see* Chepman and Myllar
Mylne, Robert (1643–1747), IX. 559
Mynshul, Geffray (1594?–1668), VII. 387; *Essayes and Characters of a Prison and Prisoners*, III. 99; IV. 345, 350, 522, 530; VII. 388
Myra (Fulke Greville's), III. 267
Myrania (Greene's), III. 357
Myrgingas, the, in *Widsith*, I. 34, 35
Myrrha, in Byron's *Sardanapalus*, XII. 49
Myrrour for Martinists, A, III. 397
Myschefe, in *Magnyfycence*, III. 77
Mysore war, the, XIV. 338
Mysteries, V. 388 ff., *and see* Chester plays, Coventry plays, etc.
Mystery plays, Non-cycle, V. 391
Mysticism in English literature, VII. Add.
Mytton, John (1796–1834), XIV. 233

'N—, Miss,' X. 274
N. G. *See* Grimald, Nicholas
Nabbes, Thomas (*fl.* 1638), VI. 28, 240, 457; XIII., *also see* Add. 2
Bride, The, VI. 236
Covent Garden, VI. 236
Hannibal and Scipio, VI. 236
Microcosmus, VI. 236
Totenham-Court, VI. 236
Naboth, II. 297
Naboth's vineyard, X. 150
Naden, Constance Caroline Woodhill (1858–1889), XIII. 181, 506
Nairn, II. 100
Nairne, Caroline Oliphant, baroness (1766–1845), XI. 232, 233, 444
Auld Hoose, The, XI. 233
Caller Herrin, XI. 233

Nairne, Caroline Oliphant
Charlie is My Darling, xi. 233
Here's to them that are Gane, xi. 233
He's O'er the Hills, xi. 233
Hundred Pipers, xi. 233
Hunting Tower, xi. 233
John Tod, xi. 233
Laird of Cockpen, The, xi. 233; xiv. 377
Land of the Leal, xi. 233
Lass of Gowrie, xi. 233
Rowan Tree, The, xi. 233
Wha'll be King but Charlie, xi. 233
Will he no come back again? ix. 377; xi. 233
Nala, the tale of, xii. 490, 503
Nalson, John (1638?–1686), vii. 434
'Namby-Pamby' Philips. *See* Philips, Ambrose
Nancarrow, Totty, in Gissing's *Thyrza*, xiii. 459
Nancy, ix. 149
Nancy, in *Oliver Twist*, xiii. 316
Nannini, Remigio, iv. 447
Nanny O, ix. 363
Nano, in *James IV*, v. 138
Nantes, edict of, v. 286; viii. 385; ix. 270; x. 203; xiv. 117
Nantwich, vii. 107
Naomi, iv. 43
Naphtali, ix. 547
Napier, Arthur Sampson, i. 53, 55, 125, 129, 133
Napier, Sir Charles (1786–1860), xiv. 107, 496
Napier or Neper, John, laird of Merchiston (1550–1617), iii. 426; iv. 290, 508; viii. 350, 478
Napier, Macvey (1776–1847), xii. 147, 153, 162, 426, 427; xiv. 5
Napier, Mark (1798–1879), xiv. 495
Napier, Sir William Francis Patrick (1785–1860), xi. 167; xiv. 495, 496
Conquest of Scinde, The, xiv. 107
History of Sir Charles Napier's Administration of Scinde, xiv. 107
History of the War in the Peninsula, xiv. 107
Life of Sir Charles Napier, xiv. 107
Naples, ii. 276; iv. 163, 249; v. 207; vi. 305; vii. 99, 131; viii. 141, 188, 364; x. 254; xii. 36, 63; xiii. 435; xiv. 247, 293
Naples, in *The Anatomy of Wit*, iii. 345
Napleton, John, xiv. 596
Napoleon I, emperor of the French, iv. 310; x. 27, 227; xi. 27, 54, 103, 108, 115, 117; xii. 38, 39, 61, 164, 166, 178, 192, 237, 300, 343, 378, 379, 395, 429, 431, 432, 438, 470; xiii. 13, 255, 276, 366, 435, 445, 447; xiv. 106, 148, 179, 188, 213, 223, 327; *Code Napoléon*, xi. 26
Napoleon III, emperor of the French, xiii. 73, 74, 81, 132, 133; xiv. 171, 182, 185
Napoleonic war, xiv. 89, 176
Napoleonisms, xiii. 405
Narborough, Sir John (1640–1688), iv. 459; vii. 364
Narcissa, in Colman's *Inkle and Yarico*, xi. 279, 280
'Narcissa' (Mrs Oldfield), in Pope's *Epistles*, ix. 81
Narcissus, ii. 151
Narcissus, in Racine's *Britannicus*, x. 119
Narcissus, Confessor, i. 74
Narcissus, school play, v. 123; vi. 286, 287
Narcissus, university play, vi. 316, 484
Nares, Robert (1753–1829), x. Add.; xi. 250; xii. 505
Naseby, battle of, vii. 35; xiii. 143
Naseby, the ship, viii. 7, 254
Nash, Richard (1674–1762), x. 481
Nash, Thomas Arthur, xiv. 507
Nashe, Thomas (1567–1601), ii. 415; iii. 114, 176, 183, 208, 256, 259, 293, 305, 359, 362 ff., 367, 370, 371, 392, 395 ff., 526, 535, 543 ff.; iv. 8, 17, 18, 21, 115, 133, 134, 142, 317, 321 ff., 332, 333, 343, 345, 363, 514, 515, 516, 517, 523, 534; v. 80 ff., 129, 130, 134, 137, 138, 144 ff., 148, 157 ff., 315, 322, 371, 420, 421; vi. 218, 250, 288, 300, 310 ff., 384, 385, 409; ix. 32, 51, 262; xiv. 234
Anatomie of Absurditie, The, iii. 362; iv. 318, 325; v. 140; vi. 394, 396, 494
Apologie of Pierce Pennylesse, iv. 322
Christs Teares over Jerusalem, iii. 362, 546; iv. 323, 324, 357
Haue with you to Saffron Walden, iii. 546; v. 314; vi. 306, 480
Isle of Dogs, iii. 362; v. 140; vi. 212
Lenten Stuff, iii. 363; iv. 319, 327, 328
Pierce Penilesse, his Supplication to the Divell, iii. 259, 362, 545; iv. 321, 322, 328, 352; vi. 60, 310, 311, 396, 461, 495
Strange Newes, iii. 546; vi. 306, 480
Summer's Last Will and Testament, v. 140; vi. 287
Terminus et non terminus, vi. 307, 310
Terrors of the Night, iii. 363; iv. 325; vii. 371, 395, 506
'To the Gentlemen Students,' v. 121
Unfortunate Traveller, or the life of Jack Wilton, The, iii. 176, 363 ff.; v. 141
See, also, under Marlowe
Nasmith, James (1740–1808), ix. 540
'Naso Scarronomimus,' ix. 259, 502
Nassau, count of, and the parrot, in Temple's *Memoirs*, viii. 383
Nasse, Erwin, xiv. 78
Nassyngton, William (*fl.* 1375?), ii. 46, 47, 439
Nathan, Isaac (1791?–1864), xii. 384
Nathan, Manfred, xiv. Add. 9
Nathaniel, Sir, in *Love's Labour's Lost*, v. 178
Nation (Dublin), xiv. 317 ff., 321, 325, 327
Nation (New York), xiv. 318
Nation, The (London), xiv. 199
National Observer, The, xiv. 199
National Reformer, The, xiii. 107, 108

National Review, The, XIV. 141
National society for promoting the Education of the Poor, XIV. 403, 404, 419
National Standard, The, XIII. 277
National Union for improving the education of women, XIV. 430
Nativity, carols of the, II. 373, 376, 378
Nativity plays, V. 389
Natland, near Kendal, X. 386
Natura naturata, in *The Nature of the Four Elements*, V. 57
Natural history, writers on, IV. 542, 543
Natural Intelligence (Kind-Wit), in *Piers the Plowman*, II. 21
Nature, in Cowley's *The Muse*, VII. 65
Nature, in *The Example of Virtue*, II. 227
Nature, in *Horestes*, V. 65
Nature, in *Mercury Vindicated*, VI. 358
Nature, in *Piers the Plowman*, II. 26
Nature, in *Reason and Sensuality*, II. 202
Nature of the Four Elements, The, III. 96, 105, 445
Naudens, Gabriel, VIII. 449
Naumachia or Hollands Sea-fight, IV. 487
Naunton, Sir Robert (1563–1635), IV. 51; VII. 27, 452; XII. 376; *Fragmenta Regalia*, V. 345, 479; VII. 221
Nausicaa, V. 172
Navarre, V. 101
Navarrenus, Francis Mildapettus, *pseud.* *See* Temple, Sir William (1555–1627)
Navern (Strathnaver), II. 276
Navestock, Essex, XIV. 74
Navigation, The Art of, IV. 399
Navy List (1689), IV. 459
Navy Records society, IV. 103; XII. 355
Nayler, James (1617?–1660), VIII. 109, 416
Nazareth, VIII. 78
Neal, Daniel (1678–1743), IX. 476, 494; X. 518; *History of New England*, IX. 212; *History of the Puritans*, VII. 356; IX. 212
Neal, Samuel (1826–1901), XIV. Add. 3
Neal, W. G., XIV. Add. 7
Neale, John Mason (1818–1866), XI. 488; XII. 277, 353, 459; XIII. 167, 171, 506
  Art thou weary, art thou languid, XIII. 173
  Jerusalem the Golden, XIII. 172, 173
  The day is past and over, XIII. 173
  Theodora Phranza, XII. 273
Neale, Sir Paul, VIII. 61, 62
Neale, Thomas (*fl.* 1643), VI. 475
Neander, in Dryden's *Essay of Heroick Plays*, VIII. 24, 370
Neander, in *The Rival Friends*, VI. 325
Neander, J. A. W., XII. 464
Neapolitan government, the, XIV. 136
Nearchus, prince of Argos, in *The Broken Heart*, VI. 191
Neate, Bill, prizefighter, XIV. 230
Neave, Richard, VII. 513
Neaves, Charles Neaves, lord (1800–1876), XII. 425; XIII. 507; XIV. 210
Nebo, VII. 67
Nebuchadnezzar, VII. 370
Necessary Doctrine and Erudition of a Christian man, III. 36
Nechtan, king of the Picts, I. 82
Neckam, Alexander (1157–1217), I. 193, 227, 238, 239, 367, 455; II. 144; *De Naturis Rerum*, I. 193, 227, 239
Neckar river, XIII. 372
Necker, Jacques, XI. 28; XIII. 467
Necker, Suzanne, X. 264, 302, 307
Nectabanus, II. 75
Nectabanus, in *Confessio Amantis*, II. 149
Necton, Humphrey (d. 1303), II. 350
Nedham, Marchamont (1620–1678), VII. 353, 355, 362, 363, 495, 496, 513; IX. 1
  Interest will not lie, VII. 360
  Mercurius Britanicus, VII. 351, 358, 360
  Mercurius Poeticus, VII. 360
  Mercurius Politicus, VII. 140, 358, 359, 361
  Mercurius Pragmaticus, VII. 358, 360
  The Observator, VII. 360
  The Publick Adviser, VII. 360, 361
  The Publick Intelligencer, VII. 360, 361
Need, in *Piers the Plowman*, II. 28
Needy Knife-Grinder, The, XI. 40, 41
Neele, Henry (1798–1828), *The Romance of History*, XIV. 59
Neil, Robert Alexander (1852–1901), XII. 489
Neil, Ross, *pseud.* *See* Harwood, Isabella
Neilson, George (b. 1858), II. 104, 117, 118, 120, 122; XII. 512
Neither Loved nor Loving, in Heywood's *Love*, V. 93
Neither Lover nor Loved, in Heywood's *Love*, V. 93
Neither-Money-nor-Learning, in *All for Money*, V. 57
Nell, in *Henry IV*, V. 187
Nell, Little (Dickens's), XIII. 319, 325
Nelson, Abraham, VII. 513
Nelson, Horatio, viscount Nelson (1758–1805), XIII. 435, 467; XIV. 201, 213
Nelson, James (1710–1794), XIV. 608
Nelson, Robert (1665–1715), VIII. 301, 305, 459, 460, 463; IX. 514; X. 356; *Companion for the Festivals and Fasts*, VIII. 308
Nelson, Thomas (*fl.* 1580), IV. 390
Nemnivus, I. 70
Nennius or Nynniaw (*fl.* 796), *Historia Brittonum*, I. 31, 65, 66, 68, 70, 71, 81, 169, 245 ff., 250, 257, 258, 268, 336, 435, 461
Neoplatonism, VII. 264, 273, 278, 367 370; IX. 287, 306
Neot, St, XIV. 83
Neot, St, Lives of, I. 90, 131
Nepos Cornelius, IX. 198
Neptune, VII. 370
Neptune, in *Troiane*, V. 69
Neptune, planet, XIV. 264
Neptune to England, IV. 96
Nereus, in Horace's *Carmina*, X. 130
Nero, I. 226; IV. 30; VII. 371, 443; IX. 274; X. 119, 317
Nero, in *Octavia*, VI. 301
Nero, The Tragedy of, VI. 235, 459

Nessus, in *Confessio Amantis*, II. 148
Nest, daughter of Rhys ap Tewdwr, I. 194, 256
Nestor, X. 51
Nether Stowey, Somersetshire, XI. 99, 120, 126, 416; XII. 166, 203
Netherbury, VII. 244
Netherlands, the, II. 310; III. 244, 441; V. 89, 139, 344; VI. 29, 42, 123; VII. 198, 453; VIII. 265; X. 291; XIV. 72. *See, also*, Low Countries
Netherlands, United Provinces of the, XII. 316
Nethersole, Sir Francis (1587–1659), VII. 27, 28
Netley abbey, X. 132
Nettlebed academy, X. 385
Nettleship, Archibald Lewis (1846–1892), XII. 467; XIV. 473
Nettleship, Henry (1839–1893), XII. 469, 489; XIV. 505, 594; *Contributions to Latin Lexicography*, XII. 337; *Essays*, XII. 337
Nettleship, John T., XIII. 485
Neuberg, A., XIII. 466
Neuberg, J., XIII. 466
Neue Erweiterungen der Erkenntnis und des Vergnügens, V. 295
Neugise, in *Robin Conscience*, III. 97
Neuha, in Byron's *The Island*, XII. 46
Neuhof, Switzerland, XIV. 383, 390
Neuwied, Germany, XIII. 440
Neverout Tom, in Swift's *Complete Collection of...Conversation*, IX. 106, 107
Nevile, Henry (1620–1694), VII. 514
Nevill, in *A Woman is a Weathercocke*, VI. 221
Nevill or Neville, George (1433?–1476), II. 211
Neville, lady Mary, daughter of the 4th earl of Dorset, IV. 265
Neville, Richard Griffin, 3rd lord Braybrooke (1783–1858), VIII. 243, 263
Neville, Thomas (d. 1615), IV. 264, 427
Neville, William (*fl.* 1518), *The Castle of Pleasure*, II. 327
Neville's Cross, battle of, I. 357
Nevinson, Henry W., XIII. 472, 570
Nevizanus, Johannes, *Silva nuptialis*, VIII. 59
Nevyle, Alexander (1544–1614), IV. 440; V. 80, 395
Nevynson, Stephen (d. 1581?), III. 202
New Conger, the, XI. 325
New Custom, V. 60, 393
New Edinburgh Review, The, XIII. 4
New England, IX. 281; X. 386
New England colonies, IV. 95; VII. 339
New Englanders, XIV. 345, 346
New English Art club, the, XIV. 208
New English Dictionary, XII. 293
New Fair, the, a game in *Piers the Plowman*, II. 16
New Forest, IV. 190
New Hebrides, the, IV. 101
New Holland, XIV. 241
New Institution for the Formation of Character, XIV. 404, 405
New Irish Library, The, XIV. 319
New Lanark, XIV. 404, 405
New lands found by the messengers of the King of Portugal named Emanuel, Of the, II. 330, 486
New Monthly Magazine, The, XII. 161, 200, 429, 431; XIII. 279; XIV. 230, 319
New Monthly Magazine and Humorist, The, XII. 429
New Monthly Magazine and Literary Journal, The, XII. 429
New Monthly Magazine and Universal Register, The, XII. 429
New Notbroune Mayd, II. 328; III. 491
New Presbyterian Ballad, A (1681), VIII. 97
New Quarterly Magazine, XI. 463
New Review, X. 302
New river, the, XII. 182, 198
New Scots Spy, IX. 562
New South Wales, XII. 194; XIV. 362
New Spalding club, XII. 359
New Sporting Magazine, The, XIV. 233
New Sydenham society, XII. 355
New Times, The, XII. 198
New Tunbridge Wells, IX. 261
New World, the, IV. 311
New Year's letter, II. 389
New York, XIII. 10; XIV. 318, 325, 326, 358
New York, the Bowery, XIV. 285
New York Herald, The, XIV. 192
New Zealand, XIII. 186, 364, 449; XIV. 368, 434
New Zealander, IX. 263
Newark, VII. 91
Newark, William, VI. 281, 282
Newark castle, XII. 7
Newbery, Elizabeth, XI. 377
Newbery, Francis (d. 1780), X. 207, 209, 210, 215, 482; XI. 377, 468
Newbery, Francis (1743–1818), XI. 377
Newbery, John (1713–1767), X. 41, 205, 207 ff., 476, 484; XI. 367, 374 ff., 468, 476, 490
Newbery, Ralph (*fl.* 1590), IV. 82, 398
Newbold Revell, II. 315, 335
Newburgh. *See* William of
Newbury, III. 368; VII. 55, 74
Newcastle, duchess of. *See* Cavendish, Margaret
Newcastle, dukes of. *See* Cavendish, William; Clinton, H. P. F. Pelham-Holles
Newcastle under Lyme, IV. 162
Newcastle-upon-Tyne, III. 383; IV. 310; V. 46, 391; VII. 435, 450; IX. 532, 563; X. 470; XI. 338, 341, 445, 469, 470; XII. 346, 508; XIII. 372
Newcastle Chronicle, The, XIV. 529, 533
Newcastle commission, XIV. 420 ff.
Newcastle Courant, The, XIV. 169
Newcastle Express, The, XIV. 193
Newce, Thomas, IV. 440

Newcome, Barnes (Thackeray's), v. 213; xiii. 296, 297
Newcome, Sir Brian (Thackeray's), xiii. 295, 297
Newcome, Clive (Thackeray's), xiii. 295, 296, 299, 300
Newcome, colonel (Thackeray's), xiii. 292, 296, 297
Newcome, Ethel (Thackeray's), xii. 130; xiii. 296, 297, 299
Newcome, Henry (1627–1695), x. 385
Newcome, Hobson (Thackeray's), xiii. 295, 297
Newcome family (Thackeray's), xiii. 295
Newcomen, Matthew (1610?–1669), vii. 416
Newcomen, Thomas (1663–1729), viii. 478; xiv. 258
Newcourt, Richard (d. 1716), *Repertorium Ecclesiasticum*, ix. 354, 537
Newdigate prize poem, xii. 138; xiii. 87; xiv. 149
Newdigate-Newdegate, lady, xiii. 552; *Gossip from a Muniment Room*, vii. 196
Newes come from Hell, iii. 492
Newes from Rome, iv. 534
New-fanglers, Address in verse to, iii. 98
Newfoundland, iv. 70; xiv. 289
Newgate Calendar, The, xiv. 228, 229, 544, 545
Newgate chronicle, xiii. 418
Newhaven, Scotland, xi. 233
Newhaven, in Reade's *Christie Johnstone*, xiii. 425
Newhouse, Captain, *The whole Art of Navigation*, iv. 459
Newington Green academy, x. 385, 386
Newlands, John Alexander Reina, xiv. 558
Newlin, Thomas (1688–1743), viii. 461
Newman, Francis William (1805–1897), xii. 461, 469; xiii. 175, 507; xiv. 593
Newman, John Henry (1801–1890), cardinal, iv. 45; x. 358, 369; xi. 81; xii. 178, 253 ff., 264, 265, 266 ff. (main entry), 272 ff., 276, 285, 287, 292, 299, 430, 453 ff., 459 ff., 468, *also see* Add.; xiii. 87, 148, 167, 507; xiv. 83, 118, 141, 417, 431, 462, 478, 507, 594
  Apologia pro vita sua, xii. 266 ff., xiii. 369
  Callista, xii. 277
  Development of Christian Doctrine, An Essay on the, xii. 269
  Dream of Gerontius, The, xii. 257, 268; xiii. 170, 171
  Grammar of Assent, A, xii. 269; xiv. 26
  Idea of a University, The, xiv. 418, 425
  'Lead, kindly Light,' xii. 269
  Lectures on the Prophetical Office of the Church, xii. 269
  Loss and Gain, xii. 277
  Pillar of Cloud, The ('Lead, kindly Light'), xiii. 170, 171, 176
  'Praise to the Holiest,' xii. 269
Newman, John Henry
  Scope and Nature of University Education, The, xii. 269
  Sermons for Mixed Congregations, xii. 268
  Thoughts on the Ministerial Commission, xii. 258
  Tract XC, xii. 260, 294
  Verses on various occasions, xiii. 170
Newman, Thomas (*fl.* 1578–1593), iv. 142
Newman, William, xiv. 236
Newmarket, vi. 480; viii. 208; x. 492
Newnes, Sir George, xiv. 534
Newport, Isle of Wight, vii. 177, 206, 447, 449
Newport, Mon. and Glos., ii. 74
Newport, Rhode island, ix. 281
Newport, Sir Richard, vii. 27
Newport Pagnell, ii. 61; vii. 167, 169
News, The, xiv. 197
News from Hell, or the Relation of a Vision, vii. 381
News of the World, The, xiv. 192
Newsletters, vii. 436 ff.
Newspaper society, the, xiv. 176
Newspapers: *Courant, or Weekly Newes from Foreign Parts*, iv. 394; *A Currant of Newes*, iv. 394; *Swedish Intelligencer*, iv. 398
Newspapers, classified lists of, xiv. 529 ff.
News-sheets, iv. 535
Newstead abbey, xii. 379
Newstead fort, Melrose, xii. 509
Newstead priory, xii. 31, 39
Newton, Alfred, x. 269; xiv. 298
Newton, Sir Charles Thomas (1816–1894), xii. 340, 498; *Essays in Art and Archaeology*, xii. 339
Newton, Sir Isaac (1642–1727), vii. 314, 396; viii. 332, 350, 352, 359 ff., 364, 478; ix. 115, 229, 283, 295, 298, 308, 476, 519, 524, 528; x. 134, 319, 373, 379, 384, 446, 447; xi. 194, 473; xiv. 261, 270, 555; *Letters to Bentley*, x. 466; *Optics*, ix. 297; x. 342; xiv. 283; *Principia*, viii. 361; ix. 331, 335; xiv. 257
Newton, John (1725–1807), x. 365, 521; xi. 80, 81, 83, 259, 401 ff.
Newton, Richard (1676–1753), ix. 569, 571, 574
Newton, Thomas (1542?–1607), iv. 5, 435, 436, 440, 446, 504; v. 90, 395; *Dyce-play and prophane Gaming*, vi. 395, 495
Newton, Thomas (1704–1782), bishop of Bristol, vii. 109
Newton, Wilts., viii. 83
Newton St Bridget (on Usk), Wales, vii. 37, 38
Newtonian school of mathematics, ix. 412, 413
New-Year's-Gift, in *The Masque of Christmas*, vi. 358
Niblung kings, the, in Morris's *Sigurd the Volsung*, xiii. 126
Nicaea, council of, xii. 278, 321

Nicaragua, XIV. 242
Niccolini, G., XII. 397
Niccols, Richard (1584–1616), editor of *A Mirror for Magistrates* (*q.v.*), III. 193, 197, 198; *Induction*, III. 197
Nice, VII. 99; X. 41, 42; XIII. 74
Nice Wanton, V. 110, 393, 412
Nichol, John (1833–1894), XI. 439, 440; XII. 397, 505; XIII. 472, 507; *Hannibal*, XIII. 194
Nichol, John Pringle (1804–1859), XIV. 555
Nicholas I, tsar of Russia, XIV. 294
Nicholas V, pope, II. 113, 114, 369; XIV. 100
Nicholas, A. N., VII. 449
Nicholas, Sir Edward (1593–1669), VII. 188, 363, 435, 436, 440
Nicholas, St, II. 127, 318; V. 8, 37, 38
Nicholas, Sir, in *The Weakest goeth to the Wall*, V. 316
Nicholas, Thomas (*fl.* 1560–1596), IV. 444, 448, 460
Nicholas, Thomas (1820–1879), XII. 512
Nicholas of Cusa, III. 416
Nicholas of Guildford (*fl.* 1250), I. 238
Nicholas de Lyra (1340), II. 62; *Postilla*, V. 42
Nicholas of Tusculum, II. 343–344
Nicholaus, *Antidotarium* of, II. 365
Nicholl, John (*fl.* 1607), IV. 460
Nicholls, Norton (1742?–1809), X. 133, 134
Nichols, John (1745–1826), IX. 140, 439, 441, 442, 453, 478, 487, 532; X. 184, 358, 454, 476, 486, 515, *also see* Add.; XII. 428, 512
Bibliotheca Topographica, XII. 345
History and Antiquities of Leicester, VIII. 462; XII. 345
Illustrations of the Literary History of the Eighteenth Century, XII. 345
Literary Anecdotes, X. 180, 244, 248, 473, 480, 483; XI. 321, 327, 332, 335, 337, 459, 467; XII. 345
Literary Illustrations, X. 250
Progresses of Elizabeth, V. 82, 256, 482
Progresses of King James I, V. 482; VI. 271
Nichols, John Bowyer (1779–1863), XII. 345, 512; XIV. 541
Nichols, John Gough (1806–1873), XII. 345, 512
Nicholson, George (1847–1908), XIV. 562
Nicholson, John ('Maps,' 1730–1796), XI. 338
Nicholson, Joseph Shield, XIII. 545
Nicholson, Reynold Alleyne, XIV. 537
Nicholson, William (1782?–1849), XI. 444; XII. 421; *Brownie of Blednock*, XI. 243
'Nick Frog' (Holland), XIV. 212
'Nickie Ben,' XI. 212
Nickleby, Kate (Dickens's), XIII. 317
Nickleby, Mrs (Dickens's), XIII. 314, 317
Nickleby, Nicholas (Dickens's), XIII. 317
Nickleby, Ralph (Dickens's), XIII. 317, 322
Nicklebys, the (Dickens's), XIII. 318
Nicodemus, The Gospel of, I. 133; II. 325, 326, 383; IV. 422; V. 15, 390
Nicolai, V. 295
Nicolas, Sir Nicholas Harris (1799–1848), II. 166; X. 491; XI. 437; XII. 303, 430; XIV. 52
Nicoll, John (1590–1667 or 1668), VII. 452; IX. 552
Nicoll, Robert (1814–1837), XI. 444; XIII. 507
Nicoll, Sir William Robertson, XI. 419; XII. 407, 418, 423, 424; XIII. 478, 481, 485, 537, 555 ff., 570; XIV. 528, 534
Nicolls, Mary Ellen, XIII. 440
Nicolls, Thomas (*fl.* 1550), IV. 3, 4, 440
Nicolson, William (1655–1727), *Historical Libraries*, IX. 356, 537
Nicopompus, in *Argenis*, IV. 258, 259
Nicuesa, IV. 68, 70
Nidd river, Yorks., VII. 180; XIII. 275
Niebuhr, Barthold Georg, XII. 280, 287, 305 ff., 310, 321, 474, 477, 478; XIV. 61, 119; *Griechische Heroengeschichten*, XII. 310; *History of Rome*, XII. 288, 301 ff.
Nield, Jonathan, XIII. 568
Nierembergius, Johan Euseb., VII. 405
Nietzsche, Friedrich Wilhelm, XIII. 21
Nieuport, battle of (1600), VII. 454
Nieuwentyt, Bernhard, *The Religious Philosopher*, X. 346
Niflheim, I. 63
Nigel, in Scott's *Fortunes of Nigel*, XII. 19
Niger, in *The Masque of Blacknesse*, VI. 342, 343
Niger, Ralph (*fl.* 1170), I. 450
Night, in *The Faerie Queene*, III. 234
Night, in *The Vision of the Twelve Goddesses*, VI. 337
Nightingale, in Fielding's *Tom Jones*, X. 32
Nightingale, Florence, XIII. 103, 365, 378; XIV. 182
Nightingale, ship, X. 203
Nigra, C., II. 417
Nikolaer, P., XIV. 490
Nile, river, X. 160; XIV. 191
Nimeguen, X. 222
Nimrod, X. 110
Nimrod, in Alfred's *Boethius*, I. 101
Nimrod, *pseud.* *See* Apperley, Charles James
Nine Nobles, II. 280
Nineteenth Century, The, XIII. 465; XIV. 172, 190, 534
Nineveh, XII. 339, 413, 497, 499; XIV. 192
Ninewells, Berwickshire, X. 323
Ninian, St, II. 103, 104, 127, 128
Ninus ('who built Nineveh'), II. 103
'Nipclose, Sir Nicholas,' *The Theatres*, XI. 282
Niphles, the, in *Club Law*, VI. 307 ff.
Nipper, Susan, in *Dombey and Son*, XIII. 325
Nisard, D., XII. 397
Nisbet, Alexander (1657–1725), IX. 355, 537

Nisbet, John, VIII. 355
Nisbet, Murdoch, II. 285, 479; III. 45
Nithhad, in *Deor*, I. 36
Nithsdale, XI. 243
Nithsdale Minstrel, XI. 444
Nivernais, duc de, X. 250
Nix, Richard (1447?–1535), bishop of Norwich, III. 42, 68
Nixon, Anthony (*fl.* 1602), IV. 460; *The Black Year*, VI. 46
Nixon, John, XIV. Add. 9
Nizolius, Marius, III. 424
Noah, II. 20, 79, 86, 427; VI. 84
Noah, in religious plays, III. 91, 318; V. 19, 44, 45, 47, 48, 124, 391
Noah's Ark (play), V. 391
Nob, VII. 67
Noble, John, XIV. 532, *also see* Add. 4, 5, 9
Noblenesse of the Asse, The, IV. 517
No-Body, and Some-Body: With the true Chronicle Historie of Elydure, VI. 92, 182, 432
Nobs, Dr Dove's horse, XI. 168
Nodier, Charles, V. 301; XII. 397
Noel, Baptist Wriothesley (1798–1873), XII. 472
Noel, Sir Edward, 1st baron Noel of Ridlington (1582–1643), IV. 265
Noel, Eric, XIII. 204
Noel, Henry (d. 1597), V. 72
Noel, Roden Berkeley Wriothesley (1834–1894), XII. 397; XIII. 194, 478, 485, 507
Boy, The, XIII. 203
Little Child's Monument, A, XIII. 183, 204
Livingstone in Africa, XIII. 204
Thalatta, XIII. 204
Vision of the Desert, A, XIII. 204
Water Nymph, The, XIII. 204
Noggs, Newman, in *Nicholas Nickleby*, XIII. 318
Nokes, James (d. 1692?), VIII. 177
Nolan, E., XIV. 209
Nollekens, Joseph (1737–1823), X. 473; XIV. 226
Nonconformist, The, XIV. 28
Nonconformist's Memorial, The, X. 519
Nonjurors, the, IV. 422
Noorden, C. Van, XIII. 534
Nora, in Thackeray's *Barry Lyndon*, XIII. 282
Norbury, Derbyshire, IV. 369
Norbury park, X. 260
Norcyn, David, II. 424
Nordeling, IV. 246
Norden, John (*fl.* 1600), IV. 495
Norden, John (1548–1625), III. 313, 330, 331, 531; VI. 463; *Speculum Britanniae*, III. 330; *The Surveyors Dialogue*, III. 331; IV. 512
Nördlingen, battle of, VII. 231
Nore, the, XI. 39
Norfolk, II. 134, 287, 304, 305; III. 95; VI. 290; VII. 21, 233, 241, 321; IX. 2, 241, 277, 353, 532; XI. 43, 47; XII. 153, 323, 346, 508, 520; XIV. 221, 290
Norfolk, dukes of. *See* Howard, Charles; Howard, Thomas; Mowbray, John
Norfolk Drollery, VII. 512
Norfolk gent his will and Testament..., The, IV. 393
Norgate, Kate, I. 446; XIV. 490
Norham castle, in Scott's *Marmion* XII. 10
Norland, lord, in Mrs Inchbald's *Every one has his Fault*, XI. 279
Norman, Robert (*fl.* 1590), IV. 460, 508
Norman carols, II. 376
Norman conquest, II. 396, 419; V. 1 ff., 6, 9, 11, 26, 39, 40, 251; VIII. 310, 384; IX. 355; XII. 261, 322; XIV. 52, 70, 72, 73, 101
Norman era, XI. 367
Norman *fabliaux*, IV. 353
Norman kings of England, XIV. 72
Norman law, VIII. 310, 311
Norman literature, I. 149 ff., 446
Norman-French language, XIV. 434
Normandy, V. 3, 4; VII. 451; IX. 532; XII. 508; XIV. 72
Normans, the, XII. 26, 316; XIV. 76
Normans in England, I. 136, 149, 151, 156; II. 421, 428; V. 3, 5, 26, 27
Norris, Edwin (1795–1872), XII. 352, 512
Norris, John (1657–1711), VII. 407; VIII. 347, 474; IX. 287; *An Essay towards the Theory of the Ideal or Intelligible World*, VIII. 348
Norris, John Pilkington, XII. 457
Norris, Mrs, in Jane Austen's *Mansfield Park*, XII. 239, 243
Norse language and literature, X. 129, 132, 451, 484, 489; XIV. 51, 434, *also see* Icelandic
North, Christopher, *pseud.* *See* Wilson, John
North, Sir Dudley (1641–1691), VIII. 475; IX. 238, 240, 494; *Discourses upon Trade*, VIII. 342
North, Dudley (1748–1829), XI. 141, 146
North, Francis, 4th earl of Guildford (1761–1817), IX. 198, 235, 238 ff., 494
North, Frederick, 2nd earl of Guildford (1732–1792), X. 306, 403, 404, 464; XI. 6, 10, 142; XII. 475; XIV. 214, 385, 607
North, George (*fl.* 1580), III. 553; IV. 444, 447
North, John (1645–1683), IX. 240, 494
North, Montagu, IX. 234
North, Roger (1653–1734), VII. 364; IX. 235, 238 ff., 494
Autobiography, IX. 238, 241
Discourse of Fish and Fish Ponds, IX. 241
Examen, IX. 233, 234, 238, 242
Life of Dr John North, IX. 238 ff.; XI. 329
Life of Francis North, Lord Guilford, IX. 198, 235, 238 ff.
Life of Sir Dudley North, IX. 238 ff.
Lives of the Norths, XI. 331

North, Roger
Reflections upon...Le Clerc's life of Mr John Locke, IX. 234
North, Sir Thomas (1535?–1601?), III. 320, 341, 345, 348, 424, 448, 551; IV. 439, 443, 445, 523; V. 100, 123, 196, 197, 199, 338; VI. 377, 495; *Dial of Princes, The* (trans. of *El Relox de Principes*), II. 340; III. 341, 345, 348; IV. 9; *Plutarch*, IV. 1, 3 ff., 7, 9 ff., 15; IX. 265
North and Gray, lord, IX. 239
North American Indians, XI. 5, 16, 31
North American Review, The, XIII. 91
North Berwick law, II. 275
North British Review, The, XI. 463; XII. 429, 456; XIII. 363; XIV. 118, 357
North Briton, The, X. 251, 390 ff., 522; XI. 33
North End, X. 12; XI. 356, 365
North Foreland, battle of, VIII. 11
North Petherton park, Somerset, II. 158
North Sea, the, I. 32
North Star, The, XIV. 193
North Walsham, Norfolk, XII. 323
North-West company, XIV. 358
Northallerton, II. 45
Northampton, II. 345; III. 380, 381, 548; X. 382, 384
Northampton, earls of. *See* Compton, Charles; Howard, Henry
Northampton, The copy of a letter written from, VII. 349
Northampton Mercury, The, XIV. 169
Northamptonshire, VIII. 5, 288; IX. 6, 532; X. 271, 365, 377, 505; XII. 507, 508
Northbrooke, John (*fl.* 1568–1579), V. 479; VI. 272, 378, 395; *A Treatise wherein Dicing, Dauncing...are reproved...*, VI. 386 ff., 461, 495
Northcote, James (1746–1831), IX. 162, 169; X. 473, 483; XI. 88, 472; XII. 172, 432
Northcote, James Spencer (1821–1907), XII. 512
Northcote, Sir Stafford (1818–1887), XIV. 491
Northern Echo, The, XIV. 193, 195
Northern Lass, The, IX. 363
Northleigh, John (1657–1705), VIII. 395
Northumberland, IV. 190; X. 490; XI. 469; XII. 507, 511; XIV. 100
Northumberland Household Book, X. 490
Northumberland, countess of. *See* Seymour, Elizabeth
Northumberland, dukes of. *See* Dudley, John; Percy, Sir Hugh
Northumberland, earls of. *See* Percy, Henry
Northumbria, I. 5, 14, 50, 62, 84, 89, 161, 305
Northumbria, dialect of, I. 132
Northumbrian coast, XII. 10
Northumbrian dialect, XIV. 434
Norton, near Daventry, III. 381
Norton, B., III. 528
Norton, Caroline Elizabeth Sarah (born Sheridan, afterwards lady Stirling-Maxwell) (1808–1877), XIII. 507; XIV. 309; *The Lady of La Garaye*, XIII. 177
Norton, Charles Eliot, XIII. 143, 467, 469, 470, 472, 551, 553; XIV. 152; *Letters*, XIII. 371, 386, 400
Norton, Fletcher (1716–1789), X. 525
Norton, John (d. 1612), IV. 400, 409, 411, 413
Norton, Robert (d. 1635), IV. 460
Norton, Thomas (*fl.* 1477), *Ordinall of Alchemy*, II. 211 ff.
Norton, Thomas (1532–1584), III. 46, 552; IV. 442; V. 66 ff., 75 ff.; VII. 306. See, also, *Gorboduc*
Norval, in Home's *Douglas*, X. 87
Norway, VI. 200; X. 222
Norwegian language, XIV. 458
Norwich, II. 57, 304, 305, 307; III. 167, 183, 367; IV. 361, 408, 409; V. 34, 46, 48, 132, 391; VI. 400; VII. 233, 239, 258, 280, 329, 330, 412, 450; X. 385; XI. 179, 428; XII. 87
Norwich, Horsham St Faith, IV. 127
Norwich, St Peter Mancroft church, VII. 234
Norwood, Richard (1590?–1675), IV. 460
Nostradamus, prognostication of, IV. 384
Nostrodamus, in *The Bugbears*, V. 115
Notable, Miss, in Swift's *Complete Collection of...Conversation*, IX. 106, 107
Notary, Julian (*fl.* 1496–1520), II. 326, 327
Notbrowne mayd upon the passyon of Cryste, The newe, II. 328; III. 491
Notch, in *The Masque of Augures*, VI. 331
Notes and Memorandums of the six days preceding the Death of a late Right Reverend, IX. 132
Notes and Queries, IX. 92, 377, 387; XII. 354, 370, 426, 428; XIII. 464
Notker of St Gall, I. 81, 99
'Notre Dame des Rochers,' X. 248
Nott, John (1751–1865), III. 170
Nottingham, II. 309; IV. 409; V. 35; VII. 226, 357, 439; X. 387; XI. 431; XIII. 449
Nottingham, earls of. *See* Finch, Daniel; Howard, Charles
Nottingham castle, IV. 181
Nottinghamshire, II. 299; IV. 365; IX. 540; XII. 497
Nottola, VI. 484
Nouronihar, in Beckford's *Vathek*, XI. 290, 291
Nouveau Dictionnaire historique, Le, V. 292
Nova Britannia, IV. 511
Nova Scotia, IV. 92; VII. 224; VIII. 187; XIV. 346, 347, 357
Nova Scotian, The, XIV. 346
Nova Solyma, IV. 260; VII. 129, 315, 421, 466, 476; IX. 385, 570
Novae Narrationes (1515, 1561), VIII. 465
Noval, theologian, X. 377
Novalis (Friedrich Ludwig von Hardenberg), XIII. 7, 9, 108, 192, 432, 468

Novella, VII. 345
Novelle, Italian, v. 127
Novello, Vincent (1781–1861), XII. 201
Novels, historical, II. 506
Novelty Fashion, Sir, in Cibber's *Love's Last Shift*, VIII. 160, 170, 176
Noverre, Jean George, *Lettres sur les Arts*, XI. 258
Now the fight's done, VIII. 96
Now ye Tories that glory, VIII. 96
Nowell, in *Every Man in His Humour*, VI. 248
Nowell, Alexander (1507?–1602), III. 552; *Catechism*, VII. 332
Noyes, Alfred, XII. 373; XIII. 493
Ntsikana's Hymn, XIV. 377
Nuce, Thomas (d. 1617), v. 395
Nugatores, v. 2
Nugent, Robert, earl Nugent (1702–1788), VII. Add.; x. 214, 456, 482
Numismatic society, XII. 347
Nun Appleton, Yorks., VII. 180, 182, 183
Nun in her Smock, XI. 328
Nuneham, IX. 162
Nuremberg Chronicon, IV. 427
Nürnberg, IV. 260; v. 25, 284; VII. 176
Nursery rhymes, XI. 475, 481
Nurture, in *The Passetyme of Pleasure*, II. 229
Nussey, Ellen, XIII. 403 ff., 408
Nut Brown Maid, The, II. 249, 320, 328, 407, 413, 429, 501; III. 280, 283, 491, 496; IV. 383; IX. 154
Nudd, father of Gwynn, I. 255
Nutt, Alfred Trübner (1856–1910), I. 253, 271, 272; XII. 518
Nuttall, R., IV. 437
Nye, Nathaniel (*fl.* 1648), IV. 460
Nye, Philip (1596?–1672), VIII. 63, 66
Nye, Stephen (1648?–1719), x. 377
Nym, in *Henry IV*, v. 187
Nymegen, peace of, VIII. 382
Nyren, John (1764–1837), XIV. 545

O., S. G. *See* Osborne, lord Sidney Godolphin
O. P. rioters, XIV. 440
'O for a bowl of fat Canary,' v. 125
O Lusty May with Flora quene, II. 283
O Willy was so blythe a Lad, IX. 364
'Oak and Brier' measure, III. 286
Oakeley, Frederick (1802–1880), XII. 259, 453, 460, 461
Oakham grammar school, VII. 317, 340
Oakly, Charles, in Colman's *Jealous Wife*, x. 89, 90
Oakly, Mr, in Colman's *Jealous Wife*, x. 89, 90
Oakly, Mrs, in Colman's *Jealous Wife*, x. 89
Oakum, in Smollett's *Roderick Random*, x. 37
Oaten, Edward Farley, XIV. 574
Oates, in Essex, VIII. 330 ff.
Oates, Titus (1649–1705), VIII. 38, 82, 95, 188, 266, 286; IX. 3, 265, 267, 493
Oates, The Melancholy Complaint of Dr Titus, VIII. 94
Obadiah, in Sterne's *Tristram Shandy*, x. 50
Obadiah, the prophet, VII. 382
Oberammergau, v. 18
Oberon, II. 338
Oberon, in *A Midsummer Night's Dream*, v. 183
Oberon, in *James IV*, v. 137
Oberon, in *Nimphidia*, IV. 193
Oblivion, act of, VII. 106
O'Brien, Charlotte Grace (1845–1909), XIV. 570
O'Brien, William (d. 1815), XI. 458; XIII. 245; *The Duel*, XI. 265
Observantines of the Franciscan Order, the, II. 251
Observator, The (L'Estrange's), VIII. 412; IX. 3, 4
Observator, The (Tutchin's), IX. 5
Observator Observed, The (1681), VIII. 412
Observer, The, XIV. 201, 228, 235
O'Callaghan, John Cornelius (1805–1883), XIV. 570
Occasional Conformity act, x. 373, 374
Occleve or Hoccleve, Thomas (1368?–1450?), II. 94, 142, 154, 159, 160, 164, 205 ff., 239, 253, 258, 266, 469; III. 168, 277, 280, 292, 311; IV. 158
  Ars Sciendi Mori, II. 207
  Complaint and *Dialogue*, II. 206, 207
  Complaint of the Virgin, II. 208
  De Regimine Principum, II. 206
  Emperor Jereslaus's Wife, The, II. 207
  Jonathas, II. 207
  Letter of Cupid, The, II. 162, 164, 208
  Male Règle, II. 206, 207, 505
  Mother of God, The, II. 208
  Sir John Oldcastle, II. 208
Occultism, VII. 508 ff.
Occurrences, An abstract of some speciall forreign, VII. 345
Oceaniae, in *The Masque of Blacknesse*, VI. 342
Oceanus, in *The Masque of Blacknesse*, VI. 342, 343
Ochiltree, Edie, in Scott's *Antiquary*, XII. 25, 350
Ochino, Bernardino (1487–1564), IV. 447; v. 104
Ockham, William of (d. 1349?), I. 200, 212, 455; II. 42, 52, 350, 355; III. 9; IV. 269, 272, 273; *Defensor*, II. 308; *Summa*, II. 363
Ockley, Simon (1678–1720), *Conquest of Syria* (*History of the Saracens*), x. 280, 281, 503
Ocland, Christopher (d. 1590), *Anglorum Praelia*, III. 428, 552
O'Clery, M., XIV. 570
O'Clery family, XIV. 309
O'Connell, Daniel (1775–1847), XIII. 353; XIV. 126 ff., 318, 325, 328, 329, 417, 510
O'Connor, T. P., XIII. 546, 547; XIV. 573
Octavia, in *The Civil Wars*, IV. 137

Octavian, I. 290, 470
Octavianus, III. 224
Octavio, marquis of Siena, in *The Fancies*, VI. 193
O'Curry, Eugene (1796–1862), XII. 518; XIV. 570; *Manners and Customs of the Irish*, XII. 360; *Manuscript Materials for Ancient Irish History*, XII. 360
O'Cutter, captain, in Colman's *Jealous Wife*, X. 90
Odcombe, IV. 89, 90
Odell, Jonathan, XIII. 240, 512
O'Dennis, II. 301
Odgers, Walter Blake, XIV. 536
'Odikle,' X. 130
Odin, I. 8; X. 222; XIII. 13, 126
Odo, St, I. 153
Odo of Cheriton (d. 1247), I. 366, 478
Odofredus, II. 363
O'Doherty, in *Noctes Ambrosianae*, XII. 160
O'Doherty, Sir Morgan, Maginn's, XIV. 313
O'Donnell, John Francis (1837–1874), XIV. 570; *Agents and Evictions*, XIV. 326; *Spinning Song, A*, XIV. 326
O'Donoghue, David James (1866–1917), XIV. 314, 567, 570
O'Donovan, Edmund (1844–1883?), XIV. 570
O'Donovan, John (1809–1861), XII. 518; XIV. 570; *Grammar of the Irish Language*, XII. 360
Odoric of Pordenone (1330), II. 80, 81, 86, 87
O'Dowds (Thackeray's), XIII. 286
O'Dymsy, in Barbour's *Bruce*, II. 106
Odyssey, the, I. 293; III. 293
Oecolampadius, Joannes, III. 413
Oedipus, V. 76; IX. 60
Oelsner, Hermann, XIII. 497
Oenone, in *The Araygnement of Paris*, V. 131
Oenophilus, in *Misogonus*, V. 110
O'er the Moor amang the Heather, IX. 374
O'er the Water to Charlie, IX. 376
Of a' the Airts, XI. 234
Offa, in *The Battle of Maldon*, I. 145; legend of, I. 218
Offa, in *Beowulf* and *Widsith*, I. 26, 34
Offa, laws of, I. 98
Offa of Mercia (d. 796), VIII. 310; XIV. 68
Offarum, Vitae Duorum, I. 34
Offering, in *The Masque of Christmas*, VI. 358
Officia Pastorum, V. 391
Officina Arbuteana, X. 245
O'Flaherty, in Cumberland's *West Indian*, XI. 257, 266
Og, in *The Second Part of Absalom and Achitophel*, VIII. 41, 42
Ogden, Rollo, XIV. 534
Ogham Inscriptions, XII. 516
Ogilby, John (1600–1676), VI. 197; VII. 487; IX. 68, 75
Ogilvie, James (*fl.* 1735), IX. 550
Ogilvy, captain, IX. 376
Ogilvy, David, lord Ogilvy (1725–1803), IX. 563
Ogir the Dane, II. 82
Ogle, Sir John (1569–1640), VII. 453
Ogleby, lord, in Colman's *Clandestine Marriage*, X. 90
Oglethorpe, Fanny, IX. 219
O'Grady, Standish Hayes (1846–1915), VII. 211; XII. Add. 5; XIV. 211, 305, *also see* Add. 3
O'Hagan, John (1822–1890), XIV. 570
O'Halloran, Sylvester (1728–1807), *Introduction to the...history and antiquities of Ireland*, X. 500, 503
O'Hanlon, John (1821–1905), XIV. 570
O'Hara, Kane (1714?–1782), X. 440; XIV. 570
Ohone, ohone, Fortune, my foe, VIII. 96
Ohthere (*fl.* 880), I. 94
Ohthere, in *Beowulf*, etc., I. 24, 25
O'Hussey, XIV. 318*b*
Oiseuse, dame, XIII. 210
Ojeda, IV. 68
O'Keeffe, Adelaide (1776–1855?), XI. 383, 483, 488
O'Keeffe, John (1747–1833), XI. 224, 257, 454, 458
Okehampton, X. 114
Okely, Francis (1719?–1794), IX. 328, 513, 518, 519
Okes, John, VII. 347
Olaf, I. 287
Olcon, in Drayton's *Eglogs*, IV. 173, 176
Olcott, Charles S., XIII. 553
Old English, X. 184, 223
Old English Ballads, X. 233
Old English charters, XII. 356
Old English Chronicle, IX. 355; XII. 349
Old English gospels, X. 223
Old English grammar, IX. 402
Old English history, XIV. 75
Old English language, XII. 326, 355
Old English literature, IV. 424; XIV. 52, 69, 440, 444, 449, 450, 453, 454
Old English poetry, X. 224; XIII. 151, 241, 242
Old English studies, IX. 355
Old lady, Scott's, II. 409, 414
Old Man's Lament, The, IX. 377
Old Smuggler, in Farquhar's *Constant Couple*, VIII. 175
Old Testament revision company, XII. 341
Old Tom of Bedlam, X. 233
Old Wives' Tale, I. 294
Oldbuck, Jonathan, in Scott's *Antiquary*, X. 231; XII. 25, 350
'Oldcastle, Humphry' (viscount Bolingbroke), IX. 221, 222
Oldcastle, Sir John (lord Cobham) (d. 1417), II. 47, 68, 208, 287; V. 187
Oldcastle, Sir John, IV. 394; V. 236, 319, 331 ff.
Oldcraft, Credulous, in *Wit At Severall Weapons*, V. 364
Olde, John (*fl.* 1545–1555), IV. 443
Olde Tenures (1525), VIII. 465

Oldenburg, Henry (1615?–1677), VIII. 247, 478
Oldfield, Anne (1683–1730), VIII. 176; X. 21
Oldfield, Joshua (1656–1729), X. 385
Oldfield, Laurel Cecil Francis, XIV. 536
Oldham, John (1653–1683), VIII. 82 ff. (main entry), 99, 100, 373, 395, 409, 412, *also see* Add.; IX. 473; X. 169
Careless Good Fellow, The, VIII. 88
Character of an Ugly Old Priest, The, VIII. 87
Dithyrambic, a Drunkard's Speech in a Masque, VIII. 84
Dream, The, VIII. 84
Garnet's Ghost, VIII. 85
Lamentation for Adonis, The, VIII. 86
Loyola's Will, VIII. 85
Passion of Byblis, The, VIII. 88
Poems and Translations, VIII. 86, 89
Prologue, VIII. 85
St Ignatius his Image, VIII. 85
Satyr address'd to a Friend that is about to leave the University, A, VIII. 88
Satyr against Vertue, VIII. 84
Satyr concerning Poetry, A, VIII. 88
Satyr upon a Woman, A, VIII. 85
Satyrs upon the Jesuits, VIII. 85
Sunday-Thought in Sickness, A, VIII. 88
Thirteenth Satyr of Juvenal, The, VIII. 88
To the Memory of Mr Charles Morwent, VIII. 84
Upon a Printer, VIII. 82
Upon the Works of Ben Jonson, VIII. 84
Oldisworth, William (1680–1734), IX. 183, 425
Oldmixon, John (1673–1742), VII. 444; VIII. 438; IX. 235, 237–238 (main entry), 437, 476, 494; X. 279
British Empire in America, IX. 237
Clarendon and Whitelocke compared, VII. 229
Critical History of England, IX. 204, 237, 238
Essay on Criticism, IX. 237
History, VIII. 168
History of...the Royal House of Stuart, IX. 238
Memoirs of the Press, IX. 238
Secret History of Europe, IX. 237
Oldrent, in *A Joviall Crew*, VI. 230
Oldwater (Oudewater), in Holland, VIII. 291
Oldys, William (1696–1761), VI. 51, 248; VIII. 137; IX. 534, 537, 538; *British Librarian*, IX. 357; *Dissertation on Pamphlets*, X. 166
Olearius, Adam, IV. 455
O'Leary, Arthur (1729–1802), XIV. 570
O'Leary, Ellen (1831–1889), XIV. 321, 571
O'Leary, John (1830–1907), XIV. 321, 571
Oley, Barnabas (1602–1686), VII. 27, 29, 156, 403; *Life of George Herbert*, VII. 154
Olif and Landres, I. 283
Olinda, in *Sicelides*, VI. 323
Oliphant, Dr Charles, IX. 560
Oliphant, Laurence (1829–1888), XIV. 164, 199, 522, 553
Altiora Peto, XIV. 165
Autobiography of a Joint-Stock Company, XIV. 165
Episodes in a Life of Adventure, XIV. 165
Piccadilly, XIV. 165
Russian Shores of the Black Sea, The, XIV. 165
Sympneumata, XIV. 165
Oliphant, Margaret Oliphant (1828–1897), XI. 456; XII. 380, 425; XIII. 557, 558, 565; XIV. 496, 521, 522
Autobiography, XIII. 431
Beleaguered City, A, XIII. 431
Chronicles of Carlingford, XIII. 430
Cuckoo in the Nest, The, XIII. 431
Kirsteen, XIII. 431
Literary History of England, XI. 307
Little Pilgrim in the Unseen, A, XIII. 431
Margaret Maitland, XIII. 431
Miss Marjoribanks, XIII. 430
Salem Chapel, XIII. 430, 431
Whiteladies, XIII. 431
Oliver, in *The London Prodigall*, V. 255
Oliver, D. E., XIII. 515
Oliver, Fielding's tutor, X. 20
Oliver, John Robert, XII. 512
Oliver, Pasfield, IX. 23
Oliver, uncle, in *The School for Scandal*, V. 254
Olives, mount of, V. 45
Olivia, in Mrs Cowley's *Bold Stroke for a Husband*, XI. 275
Olivia, in *Twelfth Night*, V. 194; VI. 305
Olivier, abbé, *Life and adventures of Signior Rozelli*, IX. 18
Olivier or Oliver, in *Sir Ferumbras* (Fierabras), I. 284, 302
Ollard, S. L., XII. 463; XIV. 592
Ollendorf series, XI. 373
Ollier, Charles (1788–1859), *Literary Miscellany*, XII. 74
Ollier, Edmund (1827–1886), XII. 436, 442
Ollier brothers, publishers, XII. 194
Ollyffe, John (1647–1717), X. 374
Olney, XI. 80, 81, 404
Olney Hymns, XI. 80, 402
Olofactus, in *Lingua*, VI. 315
Olot, in Spain, XIV. 293
Olwen, daughter of Yspaďaden Pen Kawr, I. 254
Olwen. See *Kulhwch and O.*
Olympus, VI. 329; X. 237; XII. 90
Olyver of Castylle and the fayre Helayne, The History of, II. 324, 325
Omar Khayyám, X. 144; XIII. 145, 146
Omnia-probate, in *Piers the Plowman*, II. 21
Omnium, duke of, Trollope's, XIII. 422
'Omnium, Jacob,' *pseud. See* Higgins, Matthew J.
Omond, Thomas Stewart, XII. 524; XIII. 249, 488, 512
Once a Week, XII. 398; XIII. 428, 440
O'Neil, Henry (1817–1881), XII. 512

O'Neill, Eliza, lady Becher (1791–1872), VIII. 184; XII. 171; XIII. 259; XIV. 319
O'Neill, Hugh, earl of Tyrone (1540?–1616), III. 244; XIV. 325
Onela, in *Beowulf*, I. 24, 26
Ongar, XII. 505
Ongentheow, in *Beowulf* and *Widsith*, I. 24 ff., 34
Onions, Charles Talbut, XIV. 611
Onslow, Arthur (1691–1768), IX. 209; X. 94, 244
Onslow, George, 1st earl of Onslow (1731–1814), X. 401
Ontario, XIV. 350
Onwhyn, Thomas (d. 1886), XII. 448
Oothoon, in Blake's *Visions of the Daughters of Albion*, XI. 190
Opalinsky, L., *Polonia Defensa contra Joan: Barclaium*, etc., IV. 254
Opdycke, J. B., XIV. 532
Ophelia, in *Hamlet*, V. 180, 200 ff.; VII. 8; VIII. 164
Opie, Amelia (1769–1853), XI. 344, 462; XII. 447
Opie, John (1761–1807), XI. 37, 360
Opinion, in *Time's Complaint*, VI. 320
Oporinus, IV. 380
Oppian, VII. 240
Oppression, in *Respublica*, V. 60
Oracle, The, XIV. 179
Oracle of Avignon, The, IX. 564
Orange, Frederick Henry, prince of, VII. 437
Orange, house of, VIII. 10
Orange, Mary, princess of, IX. 199
Orange, Maurice of Nassau, prince of, VII. 454
Orange, river, XIV. 372
Orange Free State, XIV. 375
Oranges and lemons, game of, V. 30
Orbilius, Pupillus, VIII. 159
Orbón, J. G., XIII. 466
Orc, Blake's, XI. 190, 194
Orchard, The, IV. 542
Ord, John Walker (1811–1853), XIII. 507
Ord, Mrs, XI. 346, 365
Ordella, in Fletcher's *Thierry and Theodoret*, VI. 122, 129; XII. 190
Order, in *Hymenaei*, VI. 346
Order of the Hospitalls of K. Henry the VIIIth and K. Edward the VIth, The, 1557, VIII. 451
Ordericus Vitalis (1075–1143?), I. 162, 163, 170, 451
Orders, the enclosed, XIV. 305
Orders and Fraternities, III. 484
Orders appointed...for setting roges and idle persons to worke, VI. 495
Orders of Callettes, or Drabbys, The XX, III. 87, 484
Orders of Fooles, The XX, III. 87, 484
Orders of Fooles, Twenty-five, III. 484
Orders of Knaves, The XXV, III. 87, 484; IV. 521
Ordlaf, in *Finnsburh*, I. 31
Ordovician rocks, XIV. 292
O'Reilly, John Boyle (1844–1890), XIV. 571, 573; *Amber Whale, The*, XIV. 322; *Songs from the Southern Seas*, XIV. 322
Oresme, N., IV. 512
Orestes, X. 108, 249
Orestes, in Kingsley's *Hypatia*, XIII. 363
Orestes and Pylades, I. 314
Orfeo, King, II. 414
Orfeo, Sir, I. 281, 288, 294, 295, 299, 300, 310, 311, 471
Orford, countess of. *See* Walpole, Margaret
Orford, earls of. *See* Walpole, George; Walpole, Horatio; Walpole, Sir Robert
Orgalus, in *Misogonus*, V. 110
Orgilio, in Johnson's *London*, X. 169
Orgilus, in *The Broken Heart*, VI. 191
Orgoglio, in *The Faerie Queene*, II. 234
Oriana, in *Amadis of Gaul*, VII. 75
Oriana, in Farquhar's *The Inconstant*, VIII. 169
Oriana, in *The Knight of Malta*, VI. 130
Oriana, in *The Satyr*, VI. 340
Oriana, in *The Wild-Goose Chase*, VI. 123
Oriental scholars, XII. 341 ff., 499 ff.
Oriental scholarship, 1600–1660, VII. 490
Orientius, XII. 337
Origen, III. 10; VII. 238, 505; VIII. 277; *Hexapla*, XII. 341, 501
Original Weekly Journal, The, IX. 433
Origo Mundi, V. 15
Orinda, the Matchless. *See* Philips, Katherine
Orinoco, river, XIV. 249
Orissa, XIV. 333
Orkborne, Dr, in Burney's *Camilla*, X. 65
Orkney, II. 115; IX. 552, 560
Orkney islands, XIV. 434
Orlando, III. 305
Orlando (Ariosto's), III. 230
Orleans, XI. 97
Orm or Ormin (*fl.* 1200?), I. 224, 225, 375, 376; II. 189; V. 6; *Ormulum*, I. 222 ff., 340, 375, 386 ff., 394, 398, 399, 458, 460; III. 440; IV. 37
Orme, Robert (1728–1801), X. 503; XIV. 97, 496, 579; *Historical Fragments of the Mogul Empire*, XIV. 334; *History of the Military Transactions...in Indostan*, X. 293; XIV. 333
Orme, William (1787–1830), XII. 523
Ormerod, George (1785–1873), XII. 512
Ormerod, Oliver (1580?–1626), IV. 521
Ormond, duke of, in *The Tatler*, IX. 34
Ormonde, duke of. *See* Butler, James
Ormonde, earl of, in *Secreta Secretorum*, II. 301
Ormont, lord (George Meredith's), XIII. 445
Ornsby, Robert (1820–1889), XII. 454, 460; XIV. 505
O'Rorke, J., XIII. 515
Orosius, Paulus, I. 66, 76, 81, 93 ff., 239, 436, 438, 440
O'Rourke, Edmund (Edmund Falconer, 1814–1879), XIV. 571
Orpheus, X. 114

Orpheus and Eurydice, I. 294, 311; II. 417
Orpheus and Eurydice, in Alfred's *Boethius*, I. 100
Orphic hymns, *Carmina*, III. 409, 416
Orr, Alexandra, XIII. 485
Orrery, earls of. *See* Boyle, Charles; Boyle, John; Boyle, Roger
Orsabrin, in *The Goblins*, VI. 239
Orseolo, in *The Humorous Courtier*, VI. 205
Orsin, in *Hudibras*, VIII. 76
Orsini, the, VI. 175
Orsini, Virginio, VI. 175
Orsino, in *Twelfth Night*, VI. 305; VII. 84
Ortelius, Abraham, IV. 73, 74
Orton, Job (1717–1783), X. 521
Osaka, IV. 100
Osbaldistone, Francis, in Scott's *Rob Roy*, XII. 17, 18, 26
Osbern (*fl.* 1090), monk of Canterbury, I. 153
Osbern of Gloucester (*fl.* 1148), II. 498
Osbert de Clare (*fl.* 1136), I. 449
Osborne, Charles E., XIV. 502
Osborne, Dorothy (lady Temple) (1627–1695), VI. 452; VIII. 371, 372, 380, 483; *Letters*, VIII. 15, 279
Osborne, Francis (1593–1659), VII. 446, 459; VIII. 379, 481; XI. 481; *A Miscellany of Sundry Essayes Paradoxes and Problematical Discourses, Letters and Characters*, VIII. 377; *Advice to a Son*, VII. 193; VIII. 377; IX. 397, 569
Osborne, George, in Thackeray's *Vanity Fair*, X. 34; XIII. 287, 289
Osborne, lady, XII. 285
Osborne, lord, in Jane Austen's *The Watsons*, XII. 234
Osborne, Mr, in Thackeray's *Vanity Fair*, XIII. 287, 288
Osborne, lord Sidney Godolphin (S. G. O.) (1808–1889), XIV. 181, 182
Osborne, Thomas (d. 1767), IX. 357; X 166; XI. 332, 337
Osbornes, the (Thackeray's), XIII. 286
Osbourne, Lloyd, XIV. 526
Oscar, X. 231
Oseas, in *A Looking Glasse for London*, V. 354
O'Shaughnessy, Arthur William Edgar (1844–1881), XIII. 140, 147, 496 (main entry)
Bisclavaret, XIII. 141
Chaitivel, XIII. 141
Disease of the Soul, The, XIII. 141
Epic of Women, An, XIII. 141
Fair Maid and the Sun, The, XIII. 141
Fountain of Tears, The, XIII. 141
Lays of France, XIII. 141
Love's Eternity, XIII. 141
Music and Moonlight, XIII. 141
'We are the music-makers,' XIII. 141
O'Shaughnessy, Eleanor W., XIII. 496
O'Shaunessy, in Egan's *Life in London*, XIV. 223
O'Shea, John Augustus (1839–1905), XIV. 571
Osiander, Andreas, III. 32
Oslaf (Ordlaf?), in *Beowulf*, I. 31
Osler, W., IV. 245
Osney, abbey of, and annals of, I. 178, 182, 257
Ospak, in Morris's *The Lovers of Gudrun*, XIII. 125
Osric, in *Hamlet*, VI. 170
Ossian, IX. 560; X. 55, 130, 137, 182, 222, 227 ff., 232, 234, 471, 472, 487 ff.; XI. 179, 181, 184, 187, 188, 206, 245; XII. 12, 40; XIII. 52, 151, 225 ff. *See, also, under* Macpherson
Ossianic poems, the, I. 275
Ossianic society, XII. 361; XIV. 305
Ossory, XI. 344; XIV. 246
Ossory, earl of. *See* Butler, Thomas
Ossory, lady. *See* Upper Ossory, countess of
Osteler, Thomasin, VI. 276
Ostend, fall of, VI. 170; VII. 454
Ostler, William (*fl.* 1601–1623), VI. 181, 276
O'Sullivan, Denis, XIV. 573
O'Sullivan-Beare, Philip (1590?–1660), XIV. Add. 3
Oswald, in Wordsworth's *Borderers*, XI. 99
Oswald, James (1715–1769), *An Appeal to Common Sense*, X. 348, 513, 514
Oswald, musician, X. 128
Oswald, St, king of Northumbria (605?–642), I. 82, 106, 120, 121, 148
Oswald, St, archbishop of York (d. 992), I. 113
Oswald, *Scots Airs*, IX. 361
Oswestry academy, X. 386
Oswin, Sir, in Mrs Inchbald's *To Marry or not to Marry*, XI. 279
Oswy, Oswin, king of Northumbria (612?–670), I. 12, 380
Otfried, Old High German poet, I. 118, 288
Othello (Shakespeare's), IV. 78; VIII. 164, 170; X. 73; XII. 171; XIV. 443
Othere, IV. 74
Otho, in Gray's *Agrippina*, X. 119
Otho, in *The Tragedy of Hoffman*, V. 327
Otho IV, I. 192
Otho, *Constitutions* of, II. 364
Otho de Granson, II. 187
O'Trigger, Sir Lucius, in Sheridan's *Rivals*, X. 90
Óttarr, I. 26
Ottawa, XIV. 351, 357
Otter, William (1768–1840), XI. 399; XIV. 247
Otterbourne, Thomas (*fl.* 1400), II. 498; IX. 535
Otterburn, II. 398, 408, 415
Ottery academy, X. 384
Ottery St Mary, III. 57; XII. 191; XIII. 276
Otto the Great, V. 6
Ottobon, *Constitutions* of, II. 364
Ottryngham, John, II. 366
Otuel, Sir, I. 302, 470
Otway, Caesar (1780–1842), XIV. 312, 315, 317, 571

Otway, Thomas (1652–1685), v. 292; viii. 17, 21, 181 ff. (main entry), 189, 191, 197, 409, 412, 438, 445; x. 67, 73, 86, 87; xii. 49
Alcibiades, viii. 181, 182, 184
Atheist, The, or The Second Part of the Souldier's Fortune, viii. 184
Beginning of a Pastoral on the Death of his late Majesty, The, viii. 44
Cheats of Scapin, The, viii. 182
Don Carlos, viii. 182
Friendship in Fashion, viii. 182
History and Fall of Caius Marius, The, viii. 182
Orphan, The, vi. 219; viii. 184; x. 74
Poet's Complaint to his Muse, The, viii. 94, 185
Souldier's Fortune, The, viii. 183
Titus and Berenice, viii. 181, 182
Venice Preserv'd, or a Plot Discover'd, viii. 94, 183 ff.
Windsor Castle, viii. 44, 185
Otway society, the, viii. 184
Oua, i. 87
Oudenarde, ix. 205
Oughtred, William (1575–1660), iv. 460
Ouida (Louise de la Ramée) (1839–1908), xiii. 562
Bimbi, xiii. 437
Dog of Flanders, A, xiii. 437
In Maremma, xiii. 436
Two Little Wooden Shoes, xiii. 436
Under Two Flags, xiii. 436
Oulton, Walley Chamberlain (1770?–1820?), x. 443; xi. 449
Oulton, Yorkshire, ix. 330
Oundle grammar school, vii. 331; viii. 2
Ouse, river, Yorkshire, vii. 180
Ouseley, Sir Gore (1770–1844), xii. 342, 502
Ouseley, Sir William (1767–1842), xii. 342, 502
Ousely valley, the, xiii. 428
Outlaw's Song of Traillebaston, ii. 503
Outram, George (1805–1856), xii. 421
Outram, Sir James (1803–1863), xiv. 496
Overbury, Sir Thomas (1581–1613), iii. 84, 95, 114, 487; iv. 103, 143, 338 ff., 345, 360, 521, 525; v. 479; vii. 384, 389, 437, 451, 453, 454; viii. 63, 357; xiv. 83; *A Perfect Wife*, iv. 265, 338, 414; *Characters*, iv. 102, 327, 338, 340; vi. 401, 495
Overdo, in *Bartholomew Fayre*, vi. 23
Overreach, Sir Giles, in Massinger's *A New Way to Pay Old Debts*, v. 352; vi. 160; xii. 171
Overton, John (1763–1838), xii. 472
Overton, John Henry (1835–1903), xiv. 496; *English Church in the Eighteenth Century, The* (with C. J. Abbey), xiv. 101; *William Law, Non-juror and Mystic*, ix. 309, 313, 324 ff.; xiv. 101
Ovey, John, viii. 105, 106
Ovid, i. 76, 197, 221; ii. 144, 150, 151, 176, 188, 259, 262, 316, 358, 360, 366;
Ovid
iii. 20, 86, 113, 181, 183, 187, 259, 347; iv. 16, 17, 19 ff., 24, 250, 349, 438, 469; v. 220, 221; vi. 18, 82, 87, 198, 300; vii. 51, 270, 370, 503; viii. 44, 51, 88, 372, 433, 444; ix. 46, 256, 258, 500, 502; x. 197, 218, 415; xi. 2, 425; xii. 337, 489, 490, 492; xiv. 171
Ad Macrum, v. 143
Ars Amandi, iv. 320; vi. 213
Metamorphoses, ii. 486; iv. 19, 20, 318, 414; vi. 207, 299, 313, 316; vii. 50; ix. 68, 160, 434, 435, 446, 478, 485, 559
Salmacis and Hermaphroditus, iv. 20
Tristia, iii. 183; iv. 20
Ovid, in *The Palice of Honour*, ii. 260
Ovid, in *The Poetaster*, vi. 44
Ovidius Exulans, ix. 259
Oviedo, John Gonsales de, iv. 70, 101; *Sumario de la natural y general Hystoria de las Indias* (*History of the West Indies*), iii. 453; iv. 69
Owayn, Sir, visit to Purgatory of, i. 339
Owein, in *Geraint*, i. 274
Owen, Hugh (d. 1618), iv. 262
Owen, James (1654–1706), ix. 571; x. 386
Owen, John (1580–1651), vii. 315, 324
Owen, John (1616–1683), iv. 242, 243, 261 ff., 502 ff.; viii. 111, 344, 345, 475; x. 377; *Epigrammata*, iv. 262
Owen, Sir Richard (1804–1892), xiv. 295, 299, 561 ff.
Owen, Robert (1771–1858), xiv. 403 ff., 478, 514, 602, 608
Owen, Robert Dale (1801–1877), xiv. 478, 505, 592, 602, 608
Owen, Sir Roger (1573–1617), iv. 265
Owen, Thomas, of Plas dû, iv. 262
Owen's Weekly Chronicle, xiv. 201
Owenson, Sydney. *See* Morgan, lady
Owl and the Nightingale, The, i. 219, 222, 223, 238 ff., 291, 361, 458, 460; ii. 217; vii. 112
Owles Almanacke, The, iv. 534
Owun, one of the scribes of the *Rushworth Gospels*, i. 132
Oxenedes. *See* John de
Oxenford, clerk of, in *The Canterbury Tales*, vii. 156
Oxenford, John (1812–1877), xiii. 263, 521; xiv. 236
Oxenham, John, in *Westward Ho!* xiii. 364
Oxenstierna, count, x. 223
Oxenstjerna, chancellor of Sweden, vii. 230, 231
Oxford, i. 89, 152, 180, 183 ff., 202, 222, 233, 337, 382; ii. 49, 50, 52, 55, 57, 58, 60, 65 ff., 69, 74, 102, 130, 185, 198, 204, 208, 224, 288, 294, 303, 305, 307, 308, 317, 331, 340 ff., 487, 488; iii. 5 ff., 9 ff., 13, 15, 19, 20, 28, 29, 33, 34, 39, 46, 48, 50, 51, 53, 67, 82, 94, 113, 167, 179, 185, 200, 321, 333, 344, 358, 418 ff., 427, 430, 436; iv. 9, 19, 51, 89, 120, 131, 136, 142, 190, 198, 200, 224,

Oxford
225, 228, 242 ff., 274, 297, 381, 398, 406 ff., 416, 427 ff., 432 ff., 548; v. 103, 109, 115, 118, 121, 132, 255, 256, 363 ff., 368; vi. 5, 29, 150, 198, 218, 285, 288, 293, 298, 312, 366, 387, 389, 397 ff., 404; vii. 35, 52, 87, 89, 97, 98, 101, 103, 104, 148, 151, 152, 157, 179, 190, 196, 200, 206, 207, 229, 246, 280, 288, 302, 303, 305, 308, 312, 316 ff., 319, 321, 336, 340, 345, 348, 357, 365, 412, 450, 454, 477, 517; viii. 4, 105, 108, 116, 118, 136, 189, 286, 304, 305, 330 ff., 363 ff., 370, 400; ix. 88, 92, 130, 170, 177, 182, 184, 188, 282, 290, 313, 324, 329, 330, 331, 334, 341, 342, 344 ff., 349, 355, 382, 383, 386, 387, 394, 395, 406, 410 ff., 533, 536, 538, 540, 541, 573, 574; x. 112, 114, 136, 159, 187, 198, 205, 238, 241, 268, 270, 294, 301, 309, 335, 356, 357, 362 ff., 378, 492; xi. 35, 40, 61, 62, 109, 118, 119, 158, 335, 357; xii. 59, 115, 138, 143, 157, 158, 187, 192, 256, 259 ff., 271, 273, 274, 277, 278, 285, 286, 288, 293 ff., 299, 304, 317, 318, 320, 327, 328, 333, 339 ff., 365; xiii. 23, 88, 89, 92, 93, 95, 96, 100, 102 ff., 120, 165 ff., 186, 196, 202, 203, 205, 209, 210, 228, 240, 280, 297, 317, 346, 350, 427, 435; xiv. 7, 24, 43, 45, 56, 69 ff., 73, 74, 76, 81, 86, 88, 90, 98, 99, 129, 149, 152, 154 ff., 191, 193, 205 ff., 215, 225, 263, 264, 295, 321, 383 ff., 409, 410, 414, 416, 417, 430 ff.
All Souls college, ii. 358; iii. 328, 423, 424; iv. 428; vii. 160, 162, 358; viii. 241, 348; ix. 294; x. 139, 275
Ashmolean museum, ix. 352; xiv. 285
Ashmolean society, xiv. 566
Ashmole's 'elaboratory,' ix. 413
Balliol college, ii. 44, 49, 50, 355; iv. 103, 427; viii. 244; ix. 539; x. 335; xi. 155; xii. 259, 260, 298, 333, 334; xiii. 87, 103, 129, 480, 483; xiv. 45
Bodleian library, iii. 201; iv. 56, 244, 248, 265, 430, 432, 433, 548; vii. 43, 64, 309; ix. 330, 342, 345, 349, 353, 357, 443, 530; x. 167, 191, 193, 281; xii. 334, 369, 503, 523; xiv. 96, 247
Botanic garden, xiv. 286
Brasenose college, iv. 428; vi. 38, 83, 295; vii. 42
Broadgates hall (Pembroke college), iii. 327, 424; vi. 111; vii. 143, 233
Canterbury hall, ii. 354, 355
Cardinal college (Christ Church), ii. 358; iii. 32
Christ Church, iii. 326, 327, 425, 434; iv. 81, 244, 250, 265; v. 70, 128; vi. 237, 286, 295, 299, 302, 303, 316 ff., 320, 323, 325, 326, 398; vii. 82, 341, 444, 457; viii. 181, 328, 329, 344; ix. 139, 147, 182, 256, 258, 264, 329, 332, 337, 345, 382, 391; x. 113, 117, 351 ff., 364; xi. 155, 322; xii. 327, 328, 333,

Oxford
339, 341, 354, 517; xiii. 93; xiv. 283. *See, also,* Cardinal college
Christ Church library, iii. 48
Christ Church meadows, xii. 158
Clarendon laboratory, xiv. 270
Clarendon press, xi. 341; xii. 328, 337
Corpus Christi college, iii. 19, 406, 415; iv. 235, 408, 422, 428; v. 103; vi. 303, 398, 399; vii. 16, 201, 310; viii. 125, 277; x. 139
Divinity school, iii. 320
'Drone Hall,' ix. 414
Durham (Trinity) college, i. 215; ii. 349, 362
Exeter college, ii. 73, 355; iv. 157, 278; vi. 188; vii. 86, 307, 309; viii. 291; xii. 260, 333, 334; xiii. 118
Folly bridge (Grand Pont), i. 209
Ford lectures, xiv. 81
Gloucester hall, ii. 349, 354; vii. 24
Hertford college, ix. 411, 571
Indian institute, xii. 343
Isis, vi. 93, 326, 327
Jesus college, vii. 37, 198; viii. 331, *also see* Add.
Jewry, i. 202
Law school, xiv. 416
Lincoln college, ii. 358; vii. 245, 317; x. 364, 365, 378; xii. 333; xiv. 109
Magdalen college, ii. 355, 358; iii. 327, 333, 420, 422, 425, 430; iv. 154, 429; vi. 294; viii. 277, 461; ix. 43, 381, 411, 412, 414; x. 300, 472; xii. 158, 260, 278, 327, 460
Magdalen college school, iii. 428, 432
Magdalen hall (now Hertford college), iv. 132; vi. 282; xii. 343
Marian foundations at, iii. 420
Merton college, i. 213, 332; ii. 163, 346, 353 ff., 363; iii. 426; iv. 427; vi. 294, 295, 300, 318; vii. 328, 329, 335; viii. 63; ix. 381, 411, 573; x. 241; xii. 234
Modern history school at, xiv. 416
Morisonian herbarium, xiv. 562
Natural Science school at, xiv. 416
New college, ii. 354, 356, 357; iii. 5, 187, 421; iv. 161, 163, 407, 408, 427; vi. 294; vii. 233, 326, 329; x. 109, 139, 270
Oriel college, ii. 288, 355; iii. 56, 325 422; iv. 427; xii. 107, 255 ff., 271, 274, 284 ff., 290, 292, 295, 334, 337, 458, 459, 464; xiii. 87, 103; xiv. 196, 418
Peckwater quadrangle, xi. 322
Pembroke college, ix. 412; x. 149, 158, 159, 268, 271, 276, 463, 472; xii. 520
Queen's college, ii. 73, 74, 326, 355, 363; iv. 161, 428; vi. 303; viii. 142; ix. 170, 483; xi. 58
Radcliffe observatory, xiv. 385
Romanes lecture, xiv. 34
Ruskin college, xiv. 409
St Alban hall, vi. 141
St Ebbe's, i. 202
St Edmund's hall, viii. 83; ix. 397

Oxford
St Edward's church, I. 202
St Frideswide, I. 191, 193; IV. 428
St Frideswide, cloister school of, II. 34
St John's college, III. 420 ff.; IV. 428; VI. 196, 316, 317, 318, 320, 326, *and see* Add. 2; VII. 62, 334; XIV. 384
St Mary hall, VII. 49; IX. 139
St Mary's church, II. 348; IV. 430; XII. 257, 259, 266, 268
St Mary's college, III. 3
Sheldonian press, IX. 330
Sheldonian theatre, XI. 341
Short's coffee-house in Cat Street, VII. 364
Trinity college, III. 420 ff., V. 114, 138; VII. 58, 150, 454; X. 238; XII. 133, 265
Union, the, XIII. 119
University college, II. 355; IV. 292; VIII. 353; IX. 129; X. 112
University press, IV. 410, 411; X. 223, 225; XI. 341, 469; XIII. 98. *See, also,* Clarendon press
Wadham college, VIII. 206, 215, 277, 364; IX. 386, 393; X. 478; XII. 330, 334
Worcester college, II. 354; VII. 342, 347, 435, 438; X. 460
Oxford, countess of. *See* Harley
Oxford, earl of, in *Death of Robert*, V. 324
Oxford, earl of, company of, V. 316
Oxford, earls of. *See* Harley, Edward; Harley, Robert; Vere, Aubrey de; Vere, Edward de; Vere, John de
Oxford, Franciscans of, I. 183 ff., 200 ff., 452 ff.; II. 349, 350; III. 48; IV. 419
Oxford, The Parliament dissolved at, VIII. 94
Oxford, The University of (Ackermann's), XIV. 222
Oxford and Cambridge Magazine, The, XIII. 112, 120, 121, 297, 358; XIV. 537
Oxford and Cambridge Miscellany Poems, IX. 485
Oxford and Cambridge Monthly Miscellany. See *Student, The*
Oxford college magazines, XIV. 539
Oxford Critic and University Magazine, The, XIV. 209, 537
Oxford English Dictionary, The, XIV. 438, 454, 455
Oxford Essays, XII. 294
Oxford Gazette, IX. 1
Oxford historical society, XII. 355
Oxford historical society's *Collectanea*, IX. 413
Oxford liberals, the, XII. 290, 292
Oxford Magazine, The, XIV. 208, 537
Oxford Magazine, Echoes from the, XIV. 208
Oxford movement, the, XII. 253 ff., 453 ff., *also see* Add.; XIV. 82
Oxford printers, IV. 547
Oxford Professorships:
Camden professorship of history, IX. 329; XII. 317, 328
Professorship of Chinese, XII. 343
Professorship of comparative philology, XII. 343
Oxford Professorships:
Professorship of ecclesiastical history, XII. 321
Professorship of Latin, XII. 337
Professorship of poetry, XII. 260, 265
Professorship of Sanskrit, XII. 343
Rawlinson professorship of Anglo-Saxon, XII. 344; XIV. 385
Regius professorship of Greek, XII. 328
Savilian professorships, VII. 288; IX. 386
Slade professorship of fine art, XIV. 152, 154, 155
Vinerian professorship of law, XI. 61
Oxford Sausage, The, X. 238
Oxford Spectator, The, XIV. 209, 537
Oxfordshire, VII. 96, 101, 150, 233; IX. 256, 258, 353; X. 385
'Oxonian Latin,' XIV. 410
Oxus, river, XIII. 92
Oxyrhynchus Logia, XII. 502
Ozell, John (d. 1743), IX. 418, 527; XI. 322
Ozoro, Esther, princess, XIV. 246

Pacata Hibernia, VII. 211, 436, 448
Pace, Richard (1482?–1590), III. 7, 49
Pacific ocean, the, IV. 68, 78, 86, 87; XIV. 241, 242, 244, 245, 358, 385
Pack, Major Richardson (1682–1728), VIII. 428
Packington, Warwickshire, X. 113
Packington's Pound, VIII. 96
Pacolet, in *The Tatler*, IX. 35
Pacquet, A, of Advice from Rome, VIII. 412; IX. 4
Padua, I. 213; III. 5, 7, 419, 423, 426, 431; V. 62; VI. 24, 176; VII. 233; VIII. 354, 361; X. 200; XII. 63; XIII. 61
Page, Anne, in *The Merry Wives of Windsor*, V. 189
Page, Gertrude, XIV. Add. 9
Page, John, II. 505
Page, William, XIII. 74
Page of Plymouth, V. 325
Paget, Francis Edward (1806–1882), XII. 277, 458, 461
Paget, Henry, son of 1st baron Paget, III. 183
Paget, John (1811–1898), *The New 'Examen,'* XIV. 65, 493
Paget, Nathan (1615–1679), VII. 107
Paget, Thomas, 3rd baron Paget (d. 1590), III. 183
Paget, William, 1st baron Paget (1505–1563), III. 183
Pagitt, Ephraim (1575?–1647), *Heresiography*, IX. 307
Pagnon, J., X. 485
Pagula, William de (d. 1350?), *Pupilla Oculi*, II. 498
Pailthorpe, F. W., XIII. 540
Pain, Barry, XIV. 537
Paine, Thomas (*fl.* 1642–1650), VII. 352
Paine, Thomas (1737–1809), X. 59, 308 508; XI. 46 ff., 189, 395, 400; XII. 279, 471; XIV. 121, 608
Age of Reason, The, XI. 48

Paine, Thomas
Common-Sense, XI. 47
Crisis, The, XI. 47
Rights of Man, The, XI. 47, 48, 276; XIV. 401
Painter, William (1540?–1594), *Palace of Pleasure, The*, III. 343, 490, 536; IV. 6, 7, 442, 447; V. 72, 73, 220, 221, 244; VI. 46, 49, 123, 137 ff., 150, 180, 182;
Rhoemo and Julietta, IV. 7
Paisley, IX. 566, 568; XI. 236, 237, 439, 440, 442 ff., *also see* Add.
Paisley, Black Book of, II. 128
Paisley Advertiser, The, XI. 237
Paita, XIV. 243
Pakington, Dorothy, lady (d. 1679), VII. 427
Palace Beautiful, in Bunyan's *Pilgrim's Progress*, VII. 173
Palaeographical society, XII. 356
Palaestrio, in *Miles Gloriosus*, V. 106
Palamon, in *The Knight's Tale*, II. 243 XIII. 123
Palamon, in *The Two Noble Kinsmen*, V. 256
Palamon and Arcite story, V. 256
Palamon and Arsett, V. 256
Palamon and Palaemon, I. 279, 286
Palaprat, VIII. 139
Pale, the English, in Ireland, II. 301, 303; XIV. 308
Paleario, Aonio, IV. 447
Palemon, in Thomson's *Autumn*, X. 104
Palermo, XIV. 73
Palermo, Michael Scot at, I. 199
Palestine, II. 79, 80, 123; IV. 68, *also see* Add.; XII. 320, 417, 478; XIV. 251, 253
Paley, Frederick Apthorp (1815–1888), XII. 331, 489
Paley, William (1743–1805), X. 344, 513; XI. 67, 73, 74; XII. 154, 279, 280, 419
Horae Paulinae, X. 346, 347
Natural Theology, X. 346, 347
Principles of Moral and Political Philosophy, X. 346
View of the Evidences of Christianity, X. 346, 347
Palgrave, Sir Francis (1788–1861), XIV. 52, 68, 71, 72, 496
Essay on the Original Authority of the King's Council, XIV. 67
History of England, XIV. 67
History of Normandy and of England, XIV. 67
History of the Anglo-Saxons, XIV. 67
Rise and Progress of the English Commonwealth, XIV. 67
Truth and Fictions of the Middle Ages: the Merchant and the Friar, XIV. 67
Palgrave, Francis Turner (1824–1897), VII. 180; XII. 115, 132, 372, 406; XIII. 189, 192, 489, 507; *Golden Treasury, The*, XIII. 192; *Visions of England*, XIII. 193
Palgrave, William Gifford (1826–1888), XIV. 553; *A year's journey through Central and Eastern Arabia*, XIV. 253
Palingenius, Marcellus, IV. 250, 447;
Zodiacus Vitae, III. 185
Palinode, in *The Shepheards Calender*, III. 226
Pall Mall Gazette, in *Pendennis*, XIII. 292
Pall Mall Gazette, The, XIV. 189, 194, 195, 530, 534
Palladian architecture, X. 110
Palladis Palatium, IV. 526
Palladius of Rome, IV. 371
Palladius on Husbondrie, II. 363, 502
Pallas, VII. 100; VIII. 76; IX. 115
Pallas, in *The Passetyme of Pleasure*, II. 226, 231
Pallas, Ireland, X. 195
Pallas, lady, in *The Garlande of Laurell*, III. 70
'Pallas the favourite of Agrippina,' IX. 225
Pallasmore, Ireland, X. 195
Palliser, Plantagenet (Trollope's), XIII. 423
Pallmall, Mr, in Jerrold's *Prisoner of War*, XIII. 269
Palmer, Arthur (1841–1897), XII. 338, 490, 494
Palmer, Edward Henry (1840–1882), XII. 342, 499
Palmer, Edwin, XII. 337
Palmer, Frank, XIV. 536
Palmer, George (1648), VII. 514
Palmer, George Herbert (of Harvard), VII. 29, 30
Palmer, Henry Spencer (1838–1893), XII. 514
Palmer, Herbert (1601–1647), VII. 426
Palmer, John (1742–1798), XI. 452, 454
Palmer, John (1742–1818), XIV. 168
Palmer, John (*fl.* 1826), XII. 341
Palmer, J. F., XIV. 561
Palmer, Mary (1716–1794), XI. 472
Palmer, Miss, niece of Sir Joshua Reynolds, XII. 132
Palmer, Roger, earl of Castlemaine (1634–1705), IV. 460
Palmer, Sir Roundell, 1st earl of Selborne (1812–1895), XII. 261; XIII. 507; XIV. 124, 511
Palmer, Samuel (d. 1724), X. 386, 475; *Vindication*, X. 374
Palmer, Samuel (d. 1732), IX. 538, 571, 572
Palmer, William (1803–1885), XII. 258, 461
Palmer, William (1811–1879), XII. 453, 461
Palmer, William Scott (Dowson, M. E.), XIV. 515
Palmerin d'Olivia, IV. 9, 447
Palmerin cycles, III. 359
Palmerin of England, XI. 422; XIII. 35
Palmers, the, in Jane Austen's *Sense and Sensibility*, XII. 236
Palmerston, viscount. *See* Temple, Henry John
Palotta, cardinal, VII. 35
Palsgrave, John (d. 1554), III. 469; V. 109;
Esclaircissement de la Langue Francoyse, III. 56, 555

Palsgrave's company, the, vi. 250
Paltock, Robert (1697–1767), x. 424
Pamela, in Richardson's novel, v. 245; x. 2, 4, 14, 15, 24
Pamela, in Sidney's *Arcadia*, iii. 352, 354
Pamela's Conduct in High Life, x. 6
Pammelia, Musicks Miscellanie, iv. 536
Pampa, the, xiv. 249
Pamphilus, in *Arcadia*, vi. 192
Pamphilus, in *The Jealous Lovers*, vi. 325
Pamphleteer, The, xi. 398; xiv. 121, 125, 512 ff.
Pamplona, viii. 126
Pan, ii. 226; vi. 368; vii. 370
Pan, in *The Penates*, vi. 341, 351
Panama, xiv. 243
Panape, in Drayton's *Eglogs*, iv. 173, 174
Pancake bell, the, in *The Shoemakers Holiday*, v. 357
Panchy, doctor, in Crowne's *City Politiques*, viii. 188
Pancks, in *Little Dorrit*, xiii. 331
Pandarus, ii. 173, 175
Pandolphus, in *Perfidus Hetruscus*, vi. 302
Pandora, in Drayton's *Idea*, iv. 172
Pandora, in *The Rival Friends*, vi. 325
Pandulfus, cardinal, v. 65, 151
Pangloss, in Colman's *Heir at Law*, xi. 280
Panizzi, Sir Anthony (1797–1879), xii. 368
Pannartz, printer, ii. 310
Panta river, or Blackwater, i. 41, 144
Pantagruel, ii. 258; ix. 264, 267, 271
Pantagrueline Prognostication, iv. 534
Panther, The, i. 428
Pantisocracy, xi. 118, 119
Pantomimes, etc., x. 440
Pantomimus, v. 24
Panton, George A., ii. 118, 450
Panurge, ix. 271, 272
Panurge, in *Pantagruel*, viii. 66
Paoli, Pascal (1725–1807), x. 190, 477, 479
Paolo and Francesca, i. 270, 363
Papal Falsehood, in *The Faerie Queene*, iii. 234
Papal States, xii. 36
Paper office, the, viii. 158
Papilia, in Pope's *Characters of Women*, ix. 82
Papillon, F. W., *Memoirs of Thomas Papillon*, ix. 240
Papillon, Thomas (1623–1702), ix. 240
Papineau, Louis Joseph (1786–1871), xiv. 348
Parable of the Three Jackdaws, viii. 99
Paracelsus (T. B. von Hohenheim, 1493–1541), iii. 113; iv. 278; vii. 235, 378, 396, 510; viii. 354; ix. 315; xiii. 55 ff.
Paracelsus (Browning's), xiii. 55 ff.
Paradin, Claude, *The Heroicall Devices of* (1591), vii. 405
Paradise, ii. 277
Paradyse of Daynty Devises, The, iii. 179, 512; iv. 113, 121
Parcae, the, in Alfred's *Boethius*, i. 100
Parcy Reed, i. 300
Pardoe, Julia S. H. (1806–1862), xiii. 565
Pardoner, in *Ane Pleasant Satyre*, iii. 124, 127
Pardoner (Chaucer's), vi. 160
Pardoner and Tapster, The, ii. 162, 164, 179
Pardonneur, d'un triacleur et d'une tavernière, Farce nouvelle d'un, v. 98
Paré, Ambrose, vii. 368, 505
Parganas, the, xiii. 276
Parian Chronicle, The, xii. 490
Paris, i. 152, 183 ff., 200; ii. 71, 92, 96, 125, 126, 198, 245, 251, 310, 315, 320, 329, 341 ff., 350, 356, 360, 367, 370, 371, 395; iii. 2 ff., 44, 97, 151, 153, 155, 157, 158, 167, 175, 208, 214, 418, 440; iv. 78, 81, 82, 127, 255, 256, 270, 293, 366, 368, 396, 402, 426, 429; v. 21, 25, 61, 101, 293, 301 ff.; vi. 146, 238, 269, 271, 390; vii. 22, 35, 45, 99, 183, 193, 205, 215, 268, 284 ff., 288, 296, 308, 312, 438, 484; viii. 111, 133, 136, 137, 198, 245, 246, 265, 282, 354, 371, 374, 379, 385; ix. 139, 149 ff., 213, 318; x. 38, 91, 118, 119, 213, 248, 250, 284, 303, 304, 307, 323, 324, 335, 395; xi. 1, 59, 60, 353, 354; xii. 103, 198, 365; xiii. 5, 58, 71, 82, 142, 277, 283, 381, 421; xiv. 66, 173, 183, 185, 190, 196, 217, 225, 235, 316, 328, 329, 342, 392
  Abbey of St Victor, i. 183; library, iii. 151
  Academy of, xi. 274
  Bastille, the, viii. 160; x. 38, 251; xi. 97, 189
  Bibliothèque Nationale, vii. 360
  British embassy, xiii. 278
  Cathedral school of Notre Dame, i. 183, 200
  Cemetery of the Innocents, iii. 87
  Collège Montaigu, ii. 370; iii. 2
  Collège de Navarre, iv. 276
  Collège Royal, iii. 158
  Hill and church of Ste Geneviève, i. 183, 184
  Hôtel de Carnavalet, x. 248
  Ile de la Cité, i. 183, 185
  Louvre, the, vii. 70; viii. 9; xii. 166
  Opéra-Comique, xi. 258
  Palais Royal, viii. 266
  Passy, xiii. 433
  Place Maubert, iii. 7
  Quartier Latin, i. 185
  Rue St Jacques, xi. 331
  Rue Vaugirard, viii. 134
  Scottish college, x. 295
  Sorbonne, the, i. 215; ii. 251; iii. 151
  Théâtre de la Foire, xi. 258
  Théâtre Français, v. 302
  University of, iv. 276; viii. 59
Paris, in *The Araygnement of Paris*, v. 131
Paris, in *The Roman Actor*, vi. 153, 155, 157, 159, 163
Paris, count, in *Romeo and Juliet*, v. 182
Paris, English scholars of, i. 152, 177, 183 ff., 233, 452 ff.

Paris, Gaston, I. 269, 283, 286, 290, 326; II. 398, 399, 417, 419
Paris, influence of, I. 149, 222
Paris, Matthew (d. 1259), I. 153, 160, 174, 178 ff., 179, 182, 183, 204, 214, 364, 450; II. 342, 488; III. 314; IV. 424; V. 38; XII. 515; *Historia Minor*, XII. 356, 517
Paris, Mrs, of Cambridge, XII. 200
Paris, peace of, X. 391; XI. 7
Paris, the judgment of, VI. 207
Paris, the judgment of, in *Reason and Sensuality*, II. 202
Paris and Vienne, II. 314, 315, 319, 332, 486
Parisian Greek press, XII. 522
Parisian salons, XI. 346, 351, 354, 364
Parisian scenery, XI. 258
Parisian stage, X. 79
Parisian typography, XII. 522
Park, Mungo (1771–1806), XIII. 467; XIV. 553
Park, Thomas (1759–1834), X. 452, 490
Parke, Gilbert, IX. 216
Parker, Charles Stuart, XIV. 505, 510, 606
Parker, Eric, XIV. 597
Parker, Gilbert, *Manifest Detection of Dice-Play*, III. 491; IV. 318
Parker, Henry (d. 1470), *Dives and Pauper*, II. 321, 323
Parker, Henry, 8th lord Morley (1476–1556), IV. 447
Parker, Henry (1604–1652), III. 114; IV. 310, 512
Parker, Henry Meredith (1796?–1868), XIV. 579; *Bole Ponjis*, XIV. 337; *The Draught of Immortality*, XIV. 336
Parker, Irene, *Dissenting Academies in England*, XIV. 51
Parker, John (*fl.* 1387), II. 61
Parker, John Henry (1806–1884), XII. 498
Parker, Martin (d. 1656?), II. 416; VII. 497, 499
Ballads, IV. 363
Mercurius Melancholicus, VII. 356
Robin Conscience, III. 491
When the King shall Enjoy his Own Again, VII. 352
Parker, Matthew (1504–1575), archbishop of Canterbury, I. 89, 90; III. 45, 46, 55, 470, 531; IV. 55, 397, 406, 423, 424, 426, 432, 545; V. 362, 482; VI. 397, 475; VII. 331; IX. 355, 357, 496; XIV. 486; *De Antiquitate Britannicae ecclesiae*, IV. 405
Parker, Sir Peter (1785–1814), XII. 389
Parker, Richard (1572–1629), IX. 538
Parker, Samuel (1640–1688), VII. 179, 184, 185, 303, 474; VIII. 98, 460; *Discourse of Ecclesiastical Polity*, VIII. 305, 475
Parker, Thomas, 1st earl of Macclesfield (1666?–1732), IX. 14, 16
Parker, William, 4th baron Monteagle (1575–1622), VII. 45
Parker society, VII. 306; XII. 355
Parkes, Bessie Rayner, XIV. 600
Parkes, Sir Henry (1815–1896), XIV. 364, 587; *Murmurs of the stream*, XIV. 362
Parkes, Joseph, *Memoirs of Sir Philip Francis*, X. 400, 401; XIV. 495
Parkes, William (*fl.* 1612), V. 479
Parkin, Charles (1689–1765), IX. 532
Parkin, Sir George Robert, XIV. 602
Parkinson, Anthony (1667–1728), IX. 538
Parkinson, John (1567–1650), IV. 542; XIII. 223; *Paradisi in sole Paradisus terrestris*, IV. 375; *Theatrum botanicum*, IV. 375
Parkyns, Sir William (1649?–1696), VIII. 163
Parlament of Byrdes, The, II. 501
Parlement of the Thre Ages, I. 333, 334; II. 37, 432, 434
Parley, Peter, *pseud.*, used by several writers, XI. 387, 481, 482
Parliament, the Good, II. 54
Parliament, use of English in, II. 70, 446
Parliament of Devils, The, II. 325, 502
Parliamentary Debates, XI. 49
Parliaments Letanie, The, VII. 383
Parma, XIII. 60
Parma, duke of, in *The Humorous Courtier*, VI. 205
Parmegiano, Il, X. 130
Parmeno, in *Celestina*, V. 99
Parmentier, F. J. A., XIII. 544
Parnaso Italiano, XIII. 224
Parnassus, III. 260; VI. 36, 310, 388; VII. 59; VIII. 372; IX. 102, 257; XIII. 210
Parnassus Biceps (1656), VII. 512
Parnassus trilogy, VI. 309 ff., 314, 315, 320, 327, 484; *The Pilgrimage*, VI. 310; *The Returne*, III. 270; IV. 139, 410, 533; V. 171, 221, 364; VI. 2, 39, 44, 309 ff., 322; *The Returne, Part II* (*Scourge of Simony*), VI. 313
Parnell, Charles Stewart (1846–1891), IX. 166; XIV. 183
Parnell, Henry Brooke, 1st lord Congleton (1776–1842), XIV. 513
Parnell, James (1637?–1656), VIII. 101, 416
Parnell, Thomas (1679–1718), VII. 198; IX. 75, 78, 131, 137, 166 ff. (main entry), 171, 444, 481, *also see* Add.; X. 482
Elegy to an old Beauty, IX. 167
Flies, The, IX. 167
Hermit, The, IX. 167
Homer's Battle of the Frogs and Mice, IX. 168
Hymn to Contentment, IX. 167
'Life, Writings and Learnings of Homer,' IX. 167, 168
Nightpiece on Death, IX. 167
Poem on Queen Anne's Peace, IX. 166
Poems on Several Occasions, IX. 77, 167
Parolles, in *All's Well that Ends Well*, V. 180; VI. 103
Parr, Samuel (1747–1825), IX. 526; X. 479; XI. 394; XII. 325 ff., 363, 490, 523; XIV. 602; *Memoirs*, XII. 325

Parrot or Perrot, Henry (*fl.* 1600–1626), III. 114; IV. 519, 522
Parrot, the, in *Speke, Parrot,* III. 76
Parry, John (d. 1782), X. 130
Parry, William (d. 1585), V. 345; in *If you know not me,* VI. 91
Parry, William (*fl.* 1823–1825), XII. 384, 397
Parry, Sir William Edward (1790–1855), XIV. 245, 553
Parsimonia, in *Psychomachia,* V. 60
Parson Hyberdyne's Sermon in praise of Thieves, III. 492
'Parson Lot' (Charles Kingsley), XII. 291
Parson of Kalenborowe, The (*Der Pfarrer von Kalenberg*), III. 82, 94, 488, 490
Parsons, in *Westward Ho!* XIII. 364
Parsons, Philip (1594–1653), VI. 475
Parsons or Persons, Robert (1546–1610), IV. 127, 306, 411, 495, 512; *Christian Directory,* IV. 237; *Christian Exercise,* IV. 410; *Conference about the Next Succession,* attributed to, VII. 352
Parsons, Robert (1647–1714), VIII. 213, 446
Parsons, Samuel (*fl.* 1732–1735), X. 384
Partenay, Romans of, I. 470
Parterick, Robertus, *alias* Robertus Langelye, II. 35
Parthenia, VI. 317, 485
Parthenopaeus, I. 286
Parthenopex de Blois, I. 286
Parthia, XII. 478
Particular Baptist fund, X. 387
Partington, Charles Frederick (d. 1857?), *The British Cyclopaedia,* XIV. 174
Partition treaty, IX. 112, 215
Partonope, I. 286, 470
Partridge, in Fielding's *Tom Jones,* IX. 405; X. 31, 39
Partridge, John (*fl.* 1566–1573), IV. 449
Partridge, John (1644–1715), IX. 94, 454, 461
Partridge, The, I. 428
Parzival, I. 269, 271, 280, 462. *See, also,* Wolfram von Eschenbach
Pascal, Blaise, III. 416; VII. 152; XII. 272; XIV. 483; *Lettres Provinciales,* VIII. 372; *The Mysterie of Semitism,* a translation of Pascal's *Lettres Provinciales,* VIII. 372; *Pensées,* VIII. 270, 373
Paschale, Lodovico, III. 262, 359
Paschasius Radbertus, I. 124
Pascoe, Charles Eyre, XIII. 544
Pascolato, M. P., XIII. 466
Pasiphaë, VI. 163
Pasor, Matthias (1599–1658), VII. 309
Pasqualigo, Luigi, *Il Fedele,* VI. 304, 472
Pasquier, *Les Recherches de la France,* VI. 35
Pasquill, III. 394, 395, 544
Pasquill, Pasquine of England, III. 394. *See, also, under* Marprelate
Pasquils Jests, IV. 532
Pasquils Palmodia, IV. 534
Pasquin, X. Add.
'Pasquin Pillar,' a, IV. 123
Passarowitz, peace of, IX. 244
Passe, C. de, IV. 542
Passerat, Jean, IV. 264; *Nihil,* VIII. 213
Passio Domini, V. 15, 16
Passion, Confrérie de la, V. 22
Passion of Christ, The. See Christ
Passion of the Fox, The, III. 482, 483
Passion of our Lord, The, I. 225, 226, 458
Passionate Morrice, The, IV. 526
Passionate Pilgrim, The, III. 266; IV. 119, 395
Passions of Martyrs, I. 75
Pastime of People, The, II. 328
Paston, Agnes, II. 305, 306
Paston, Anne, II. 308
Paston, Clement, II. 305
Paston, Edmund, II. 306
Paston, Elizabeth, II. 306
'Paston, George' (*i.e.* Emily Morse Symonds), XI. 429, 443, 457, 468; XII. 431, 451; XIV. 519, 520, 541; *Lady Mary Wortley Montagu,* IX. 244
Paston, John (1421–1466), II. 304 ff.
Paston, Sir John (1442–1479), II. 304 ff.
Paston, J., XIV. 541
Paston, Margaret, II. 304 ff.
Paston, Walter, II. 308
Paston, William (1378–1444), II. 304, 308, 359
Paston family, the, II. 304
Paston Letters, The, II. 286, 303, 429; V. 35; VII. 196; XIV. 82
Pastor Fidus, VI. 317, 485
Pastorals, VI. 487 ff.
Patenostre à l'Userier, La, III. 90, 487
Patent Rolls, the, VI. 280; XII. 355, 516
Pater, Walter Horatio (1839–1894), VII. 260, *also see* Add.; XI. 410, 417; XII. 271, 277, 438; XIII. 491; XIV. 462, 522, 523
  Appreciations, XIV. 158
  Child in the House, The, XIV. 159
  Imaginary Portraits, XIV. 158
  Marius the Epicurean, XIV. 158
  Plato and Platonism, XIV. 158
  Studies in the History of the Renaissance, IX. 39; XIV. 158
  Winckelmann, XIV. 158
Paterculus, Gaius Velleius, XII. 337
Patericke, Simon (d. 1613), IV. 8, 444
Paternoster, I. 220, 375, 376, 458
Paternoster, in *The Exeter Book,* I. 428
Paternoster, Kentish versions of the, I. 355
Pater Noster play, V. 51, 52
'Paternoster Row numbers,' XI. 325
Paterson, Alexander, XIV. 532
Paterson, Alice, XIV. 601
Paterson, Daniel (1739–1825), XIII. 223
Paterson, James (1805–1876), XI. 441; XIV. 536
Paterson, Ninian (*fl.* 1688), IX. 556; *Epigrammaton libri octo,* IV. 267
Paterson, Samuel (1728–1803), XI. 336; XII. 363, 523
Paterson, William (1755–1810), XIV. 553

Pathelin, Maître, II. 96; V. 19, 92, 101
Pathomachia or The Battell of Affections, VI. 323, 485
Patience, I. 320 ff., 333, 334, 472
Patience, in *Piers the Plowman*, II. 26 ff.
Patience, in *Tom Tyler*, V. 117
Patientia, in *Psychomachia*, V. 51
Patin, Guy, VII. 235
Patmore, Coventry Kersey Dighton (1823–1896), XII. 275, 421; XIII. 110, 189 ff., 208, 507; XIV. 238
  Angel in the House, The, XIII. 190, 191, 218, 247
  Odes, XIII. 218
  Unknown Eros, The, XIII. 190, 191
  Victories of Love, The, XIII. 190, 191
Patmore, Peter George (1786–1855), XII. 433; XIV. 523
Paton, George (1721–1807), X. 490
Paton, Waller Hugh (1828–1895), XI. 437
Paton, William Roger (1856–1921), XII. Add. 4
Patras, gulf of, XII. 38
Patrician, The, IX. 442
Patricius (Howell's), VII. 458
Patrick, St (373–463), I. 65, 68, 70, 339, 435; XII. 519; *Colloquy of St Patrick with Oisin, The*, XIV. 303
Patrick, Simon (1626–1707), VIII. 288, 292, 298, 301, 456, 457, 461
Patrick, Swift's servant, IX. 126
Patrick, Sir William Francis, XIV. 495, 496
Patrizzi, Francesco, III. 434, 438; V. 234
Patrum, Vitae Sanctorum, II. 323. *See, also*, Fathers
Patten, Robert (*fl.* 1717), IX. 565
Patten, William (*fl.* 1548–1580), III. 531
Patterne, Sir Willoughby (George Meredith's), XIII. 444 ff.
Pattison, Mark (1813–1884), VII. 101, 109, 114, 123, 127, 238, 310, 324; VIII. 352; XII. 254, 255, 292, 334, 460, 466, 469, *also see* Add. 1; XIV. 113, 432, 505, 594, 596, 602
  Essays, XIV. 109
  Essays and Reviews, IX. 280
  Isaac Casaubon, XII. 333; XIV. 109
  Memoirs, XIV. 109
  Milton, XIV. 109
  Scaliger, XII. 333
  Suggestions on academical organisation, XIV. 431
  'The Tendencies of Religious Thought,' XII. 295
Paues, Anna C., II. 59, 65
Paul, in Udall's *Diotrephes*, III. 378
Paul, father. *See* Sarpi
Paul, Lanfranc's kinsman, I. 153
Paul, Hamilton (1773–1854), XI. 436
Paul, Harry Gilbert, *John Dennis*, IX. 142
Paul, Herbert Woodfield, XIII. 478, 488, 503, 558, 568; XIV. 484, 487, 488, 493, 525; *Life of Froude*, XIII. 358
Paul, W. J., XIV. 573
Paul IV, III. 401
Paul, St, I. 72, 74, 115, 227; II. 129, 201, 227, 231, 234; III. 6, 10, 127, 415; IV. 224, 270; V. 50, 59; VI. 102; VII. 168; VIII. 291; IX. 28; XII. 285, 293, 477
Paul, St, tractate on the *Epistles* of, II. 365
Paul, St, Revelation or *Vision of*, I. 75, 86, 118, 227, 459, 460
Paulet, Sir Amyas (d. 1538), IV. 278
Pauli, Reinhold, I. 91, 102
Paulina, in Charlotte Brontë's *Villette*, XIII. 409
Paulina, in *Confessio Amantis*, II. 151
Paulina, in Markham's *Famous Whore*, IV. 376
Paulina, in *The Renegado*, VI. 155
Paulina, in *The Winter's Tale*, III. 356; V. 206
Pauline (Browning's), XIII. 53, 57
Pauline epistles, the, XII. 298
Paulinus, I. 75, 81
Paulinus of Périgueux, I. 76
Paulus Diaconus, I. 35; II. 364; VII. 503
Paulus Quaestor, I. 76
Pauper, in *Ane Pleasant Satyre*, III. 124, 126, 127, 128
Pausanias, III. 328; XII. 491
Pavia, IV. 429
Pavier, Thomas (*fl.* 1600–1608), IV. 394
Pavillard, Calvinist minister, X. 301
Pavillon, Nicholas, bishop of Aleth, VIII. 308
Pavy, duke of, in *Loves Sacrifice*, VI. 192
Pavy, Salathiel, VI. 9, 291
'Pavyllyon un [on] the Plas Parlos, the,' VI. 283
Pawson (tutor of John Hall), VII. 85
Pax, in the *Coventry Plays*, V. 21
Payn, James (1830–1898), XII. 426, 445, 451; XIII. 438, 565
Payne, Edward John (1844–1904), XI. 388; XIV. 496; *A History of the New World called America*, XIV. 98
Payne, G. A., XIII. 551
Payne, Henry, brother of Thos. Payne (1719–1779), XI. 333
Payne, John (d. 1787), X. 385, 469
Payne, Joseph (1808–1876), XIV. 608
Payne, Joseph Frank (1840–1910), XIV. 563
Payne, Roger (1739–1797), XI. 468
Payne, Thomas (*fl. c.* 1700), X. 385
Payne, Thomas (1719–1799), XI. 333 ff., 337, 468
Paynell, Thomas (*fl.* 1528–1568), III. 341; IV. 4, 439, 443, 445, 446, 447, 448
Pazzarello, in *The Young Admirall*, VI. 204
Peace, in Anglo-Norman plays, V. 21
Peace, in *The Castle of Perseverance*, V. 52
Peace, in *The Example of Virtue*, II. 228
Peace, in *The Passetyme of Pleasure*, II. 228
Peace, in *Piers the Plowman*, II. 10
Peace, Temple of, in *The Vision of the Twelve Goddesses*, VI. 337
Peacham, Henry (1576?–1643?), III. 114, 432; IV. 355, 520, 526, 533; V. 479; *Compleat Gentleman, The*, IV. 328, 543;

Peacham, Henry
vii. 263; ix. 396, 570; *Garden of Eloquence*, iii. 432, 553; *Minerva Britannia*, vii. 406, 479, *also see* Add.
Peacham, Henry (the elder), iv. 355, 525
Peachum, in Gay's *Beggar's Opera*, ix. 163
Peacock, George (1791–1858), viii. 361
xiv. 258, 555, 595
Peacock, Nathaniel, in Smollett's *History of an Atom*, x. 42
Peacock, Thomas Love (1785–1866), i. 275; iv. 137; ix. 183; xi. 285, 286, 307 ff. (main entry), 462, 489, *also see* Add.; xii. 60, 63, 255, 401, 404, 405, 412; xiii. 440, 442
Crotchet Castle, xi. 308
Four Ages of Poetry, The, xii. 74
Gryll Grange, xi. 285, 307, 308, 310
Headlong Hall, xi. 183, 308
Maid Marian, xi. 308
Melincourt, xi. 308, 309
Misfortunes of Elphin, The, i. 252; xi. 308, 309
Nightmare Abbey, xi. 308, 310
Peak, Godwin, in Gissing's *Born in Exile*, xiii. 459
Peak, the, Derbyshire, iii. 322; x. 131
Peake, R., iii. 553
Peaks, passes and glaciers, xiv. 254
Pearce, E. H., xiv. 597
Pearce, Zachary (1690–1774), ix. 527; x. 470
Pearch, George (*fl.* 1770–1775), ix. 190; x. 138, 465
Pearl, i. 148, 296, 320 ff., 326, 329, 332, 333, 378, 472; ii. 18, 133
Pearson, Charles Henry (1830–1894), ii. 35; xi. 456; xiv. 496
Pearson, John (1613–1686), vii. 152, 481; viii. 461; x. 357; *Exposition of the Creed*, vii. 323, 485; viii. 297, 300; ix. 329; *Vindiciae Epistolarum S. Ignatii*, ix. 329
Pearson, Karl, vii. 367; xiv. 470, 556, 560
Peasants' revolt, i. 371; ii. 47, 53, 63, 136, 143, 144; iii. 18
Peasenhall, x. 378
Peblis to the Play, ii. 244, 250, 270, 274, 471, 473; iii. 130; xi. 215
Pebody, Charles, xiv. 532
Peck, Francis (1692–1743), ix. 538
Peckard, G. P., vii. 154
Pecke, Samuel (*fl.* 1641–1655), vii. 347, 348, 497
A Continuation of Certain Speciall and Remarkable Passages, vii. 347
Diurnall Occurrences, vii. 347
Mercurius Candidus, vii. 347
Perfect Diurnall, A, vii. 347, 354, 360
Pecke, Thomas (*fl.* 1655–1664), iii. 470; iv. 503; vii. 355, 360, 361
Peckham, x. 201, 203
Peckham, John, archbishop of Canterbury (d. 1292), i. 210, 455
Peckover, Clem, in Gissing's *The Nether World*, xiii. 458
Pecksniff, Mercy, in *Martin Chuzzlewit*, xiii. 322
Pecksniffs, the, in *Martin Chuzzlewit*, xiii. 323
Pecksy, in Mrs Trimmer's *Robins*, xi. 379
Pecock, Reginald (1395?–1460?), bishop of Chichester, i. 286 ff., 296, 299, 301, 307, 471, 473, 480; iv. 226; xii. 134
Abbreviatio R. Pecock, ii. 288
Book of Faith, The, ii. 293
Donet, The, ii. 294
Filling of the Four Tables, The, ii. 291
Poor Men's Mirror, The, ii. 294
Repressor of overmuch blaming of the clergy, ii. 288, 289, 293, 294, 296; xii. 480
Pecunia, in *The Staple of Newes*, vi. 25
Pedante, in *Fedele and Fortunio*, v. 315
Pedantius, iv. 326; vi. 306, 327, 480
Pedantius, in Ascham's *Scholemaster*, iii. 434
Peden, Alexander (1626?–1686), ix. 549
Pedersen, Christiern, ii. 285
Pedlar, in Wordsworth's *Excursion*, xi. 106
Pedringano, in *The Spanish Tragedie*, v. 163
Pedro, Don, king of Spain, in *The King and the Subject*, vi. 147
Peebles, ii. 277
Peebles, Peter, in Scott's *Redgauntlet*, xii. 25
Peeke or Pike, Richard (*fl.* 1620–1626), vii. 453
Peel, Arthur W., xiv. 505
Peel, George, xiv. 505
Peel, Sir Robert (1788–1850), xi. 154, 415; xii. 154; xiii. 16, 24, 347, 348, 350, 353; xiv. 115, 127, 128 ff. (main entry), 134, 181, 186, 227, 412, 505, 510, 571
Peele, George (1558?–1597?), iii. 300; iv. 113 ff., 117, 121, 471, 473, 532; v. 85, 121–141 (main entry), 147, 182, 239, 255, 322, 327, 370, 416 ff., *also see* Add.; vi. 13, 249, 300, 303, 366; vii. 111; viii. 223
Arraignment of Paris, The, iv. 118; v. 128, 129; vi. 287, 337, 363, 365
Battell of Alcazar, The, v. 129, 239
Complaint of Oenone, xi. 179
Discursus Astraeae, v. 131
Edward I, v. 35, 129, 152, 153
'His golden locks time hath to silver turned,' iv. 113
Hunting of Cupid, The, iv. 118; v. 129
King David and Fair Bethsabe, v. 129, 131
Merrie Conceited Jests of George Peele, iv. 360; v. 132, 255
Old Wives Tale, The, v. 129 ff.; vii. 113
Turkish Mahomet, The, v. 129; x. 161
'Whenas the rye did reach to the chin,' v. 131
See, also, under *Sir Clyomon*
Peelites, xiv. 130, 187, 190, 198

Peers, Richard (1645–1690), IX. 345, 346
Peerson, Martin (1590?–1651?), IV. 465
Peet, W. Hubert, XI. 466; XIV. 531
Peg, in Arbuthnot's *History of John Bull*, IX. 135
Pegasus, XI. 166; XII. 101, 104
Pegge, Samuel (1704–1796), *Life of Grosseteste*, I. 204, 454
Peile, John (1838–1910), XII. 490
Peile, Thomas Williamson (1806–1882), XII. 490
Peirce, James (1674?–1726), X. 379
Peiresc, Nicolas Claude Fabri de, IV. 253, 257
Pekin, XIV. 248
Pelagius (*fl.* 400–418), I. 65
Pélerinage de l'homme, Le, II. 327
Pélerinaiges por aler en Iherusalem (*c.* 1231), II. 80
Pelham, Henry (1695?–1754), IX. 230, 243, 250; X. 388
Pelham, Henry (lord Lytton's), XIII. 417, 418
Pelham, Henry Francis (1846–1907), XII. 477; *History of the Roman Empire*, XII. 317; *Outlines of Roman History*, XII. 317
Pelham-Holles, Thomas, 1st duke of Newcastle (1693–1768), IV. 369; IX. 166; X. 35, 256, 388, 390
Pell, John (1611–1685), VII. 314
Pellegrini, M., *Fonti dell' Ingegno*, VII. 269
Pellew, George (1793–1866), XIV. 506
Pellico, Silvio, XII. 390
Pember, Robert (d. 1560), III. 432
Pemberton, Henry (1694–1771), VIII. 230; XI. 250
Pemberton, T. Edgar, XIII. 515, 544
Pembroke, countess of. *See* Herbert, Mary
Pembroke, earl of, in *John a Kent*, etc., V. 317
Pembroke, earls of. *See* Herbert, George Robert Charles; Herbert, Henry; Herbert, Philip; Herbert, William
Pembroke family, the, VI. 6, 143
Pembrokeshire, XII. 509
Penaunce, in *The Faerie Queene*, VI. 336
Pencrich, Richard, II. 70, 504
Pendarves, Mrs. *See* Delany, Mrs
Pendennis, Arthur (Thackeray's), XIII. 276, 290, 291, 293, 295, 297, 299
Pendennis, Helen (Thackeray's), XIII. 290, 291
Pendennis, major (Thackeray's), XIII. 291
Pendleton, John, XIV. 532
Pendragon, IX. 502
Penelope. *See* Rich, Penelope
Penelope, in *Confessio Amantis*, II. 152
Penelope, in *Gismond of Salerne*, V. 73
Penelope, in *Orchestra*, IV. 162
Penelope, in *Ulysses Redux*, VI. 303
Penelope to Ulysses, letter of, III. 181
Pengry, Moses, *Cooper's Hill latina redditum* (1676), VII. 487
Peniarth library, Welsh MS. in, I. 252
Penington, Isaac (1616–1679), VIII. 105, 106, 108, 109, 415, 416
Penington, Mary, wife of Isaac Penington, VIII. 109, 416
Peninsular war, the, XIV. 107, 122, 250, 459
Penitence, in *The Example of Virtue*, II. 227
Penitent Traytor, The, VII. 386
Penitentials, I. 87
Penlez, Bosavern, X. 33
Penn or Pen, Sir William (1621–1670), VIII. 107, 218
Penn, William (1644–1718), VIII. 105, 107, 111 ff., 268, 413, 414, 456; IX. 9, 406, 546; X. 377; XIV. 65, 509
Address to Protestants, VIII. 108
Christian Quaker, The, VIII. 111
Innocency with her Open Face, VIII. 111
More Fruits of Solitude, VIII. 113
No Cross No Crown, VIII. 107
Sandy Foundation Shaken, The, VIII. 107, 111
Some Fruits of Solitude, VIII. 107, 112
Pennant, Thomas (1726–1798), X. 270; XII. Add. 5; XIV. 246, 553; *British Zoology*, X. 269; *Tour in Scotland*, X. 182
Penne, George, XIV. 65
Pennecuick, Dr Alexander (1652–1722), *Description of Tweeddale*, IX. 370
Pennecuick, Alexander (d. 1730), IX. 370, 567
Britannia Triumphans, IX. 370
Elegy on Robert Forbes, IX. 370
Flowers from Parnassus, IX. 370
Merry Wives of Musselburgh, IX. 370
Presbyterian Pope, IX. 370
Rome's Legacy, IX. 370
Streams from Helicon, IX. 370
Truth's Travels, XI. 217
Pennell, Henry Cholmondeley (1837–1915), XIV. 545
Pennenden heath, XIV. 128
Pennethorne, John (1808–1888), XII. 340
Penniless Parliament of Threadbare Poets, The, IV. 345
Penniman, Josiah Harmar, VI. 4, 17, 23
Pennington, Montagu (1762–1849), *Memoirs of the Life of Mrs Elizabeth Carter*, X. 473; XI. 356, 473
Pennington, Sarah, lady, XIV. 600
Penniworth of Wit, II. 501
Pennsylvania, IV. 95; VIII. 107; XI. 47; XIV. 263, 350
Pennsylvania Magazine, XI. 47
Penny Cyclopaedia, The, XII. 487; XIV. 259, 409
'Penny Godlinesses,' XI. 334
Penny Illustrated Paper, The, XIV. 534
Penny Magazine, The, XIV. 409
'Penny Merriments,' XI. 334
Pennyboy, in *The Staple of Newes*, VI. 25
Penrith, II. 116; XI. 95, 414, 486; XII. 188
Penroodocke, Maister, V. 77
Penrose, Francis Cranmer (1817–1903), XII. 498; *Principles of Athenian Architecture*, XII. 340

Penry, John (1559–1593), III. 377 ff., 385, 390, 397
Aequity of an humble supplication, The, III. 377, 378, 538
An Exhortation, III. 378, *also see* Add.
A Supplication to the Parliament, III. 381
Defence of that which hath been written, III. Add.
Th'Appelation of John Penri, III. 381, 383
Penshurst, III. 351; VII. 54, 55; X. 500
Penthea, in *The Broken Heart,* VI. 191
Penthesilea, in *The Masque of Queens,* VI. 349
Penton, Stephen (1639–1706), IX. 405, 570; *Guardian's Instruction,* IX. 397; *New Instructions,* IX. 397
People, in *Res publica,* V. 60
People's Friend, The, XIII. 359
'People's Poet Laureate, The,' XIII. 150
Pepeling (Calais), III. 328
Pepwell, Henry (d. 1540), books printed by, II. 327
Pepys, John, father of Samuel, VIII. 253
Pepys, Sir Lucas (1742–1830), XI. 365
Pepys, Mrs, VIII. 256, 260
Pepys, Paulina, Samuel's sister, VIII. 259
Pepys, Samuel (1633–1703), II. 207; III. 97; IV. 460; V. 222; VI. 262; VII. 141, 214, 228, 362, 364; VIII. 22, 81, 107, 120, 124, 131, 136, 199, 200, 206, 215, 216, 218, 241 ff., 252 ff. (main entry), 262, 263, 301, 302, 320, 350, 355, 356, 358, 369, 385, 398, 399, 422, 424, 450; IX. 129, 244, 274, 275; XI. 319, 334; XIV. 283; *Diary,* VII. 184; VIII. 15; *Memoires of the Navy,* VIII. 258, 259
Pepys, Sir William Weller (1758–1825), XI. 363, 365, 473
Pepys Cockerell family, descendants of Samuel Pepys, VIII. 260
Pera, IX. 245
Peraldus, William, I. 355
Perceval, Arthur Philip (1799–1853), XII. 258, 453, 461
Perceval le Gallois, I. 271, 462, 471
Percies, the, in *Henry IV,* V. 187
Percius and Anthomiris (Perseus and Andromeda), V. 102
Percival, Sir John, IX. Add.
Percival, Thomas (1740–1804), XI. 489
Percy, in Hannah More's play, XI. 274
Percy, lady Elizabeth, afterwards duchess of Somerset (1667–1722), VIII. 380
Percy, Sir Henry, 1st earl of Northumberland (1342–1408), II. 55
Percy, Sir Henry, 6th earl of Northumberland (1502?–1537), III. 336, 337, 427; IV. 2
Percy, Sir Henry, 9th earl of Northumberland (1564–1632), VII. 435
Percy, Sir Hugh, 1st duke of Northumberland, of the third creation (1715–1786), X. 457
Percy, Thomas (1729–1811), bishop of Dromore, II. 494; X. 155, 170, 195, 201, 204, 215, 220, 273, 470, 480, 489, 496, *also see* Add.; XI. 333, 449
Complaint of Harold, X. 224
Dying Ode of Ragnar Lodbrog, X. 223
Five pieces of Runic Poetry, X. 222, 223, 225, 229; XIV. 51
Funeral Song of Hacon, X. 224
Incantation of Hervor, X. 223, 224, 229
Ransome of Egill, X. 224
Reliques of Ancient Poetry, II. 408, 410, 413, 494; IX. 188; X. 137, 202, 217, 225, 226, 232 ff.; XI. 360; XII. 4, 6, 133, 354; XIII. 225, 226
Percy, Thomas (1768–1808), X. 472, 489
Percy, William (1575–1648), III. 256, 264, 266; *Sonnets to the fairest Coelia,* III. 256, 266, 523
Percy anecdotes, the, XI. 472
Percy ballad, II. 398
Percy Folio MS., II. 40, 401, 408, 410, 414, 416, 428
Percy Memoir, X. 209
Percy papers, II. 409
Percy society, II. 199, 502; XII. 353, 355, 368, 369
Percyvelle, Sir (Perceval, Percevall, Percival), I. 267, 269, 271, 272, 284, 289, 294, 462. See, also, *Parzival*
Perdita, in *The Winter's Tale,* V. 34, 206, 217; XII. 87
Peredur, son of Evrawc, I. 253, 271
Peregrin (Howell's), VII. 458
Peregrinatio Religionis ergo, III. 12
'Peregrine of Odcombe,' X. 200
Perenna (Herrick's), VII. 6
Peres the Ploughmans Crede, II. 38, 39, 432, 434
Perfect, lady, in *Amends for Ladies,* VI. 223
Perfect Occurrences, VII. 354
Perfidious Britain, IX. 375
Perfidus Hetruscus, VI. 302, 486
Periander, VI. 474
Periander, tyrant of Corinth, VI. 321
Pericles, XII. 313
Pericles of Tyre, I. 135
Perin, VII. 316
Perin, Ales, in Stow's *Chronicle,* III. 314
Perindus, in *Sicelides,* VI. 323
Perkin, Sir William Henry, XIV. 558
Perkins, Jane G., XIII. 507
Perkins, John (d. 1545), *Profitable Book,* VIII. 315, 467
Perkins, Peter, *The Seaman's Tutor,* IV. 460
Perkins, Richard (*fl.* 1612), VI. 401
Perkins, William (1558–1602), IV. 235, 433, 494; VII. 373, 394, 395, 474; VIII. 277
Armilla aurea, and translation *A Golden Chaine,* VII. 280
Art of Prophesying, IV. 226, 491
Discovery of the damned Art of Witchcraft, IV. 535; VII. 372, 506
Whole Treatise of the Cases of Conscience, VII. 280

Perkins folio of Shakespeare, v. 278
Perkyn, John (*fl.* 1574), vi. 246
Perl mewn adfyd, iv. 411
Perlin, Étienne, iii. 478
Permo-Triassic strata, xiv. 292
Perne, Andrew (1519?–1589), iv. 141, 423, 432
Pernel Proudheart, in *Piers the Plowman*, ii. 12, 16
Pernet qui va au vin, Farce de, v. 98
Pérouse, J. F. G. de la (1741–1788), xiv. 553
Perowne, Thomas Thomason, xiv. 486
Perrault, Charles, viii. 163; ix. 390, 572; x. 220; xi. 380, 477, 485, 492; *Histoires ou Contes du Tems Passé*, xi. 374, 375; *Le Siècle de Louis le Grand*, ix. 391; *Parallèle des Anciens et des Modernes*, ix. 391
Perrin, Pierre, viii. 135; *Ariadne* (with Grabut), viii. 134
Perronet, Vincent (1693–1785), viii. 347, 475
Perrot, Thomas (*fl.* 1720–1733), x. 386
Perry, James (1756–1821), xii. 323; xiv. 170, 178, 184, 186, 187
Perry, John Tavenor, xii. 512
Perseus, xiii. 354
Perseus, in *Confessio Amantis*, ii. 147, 148
Perseus, in *The Masque of Queens*, vi. 349
Perseverance, in *The Example of Virtue*, ii. 228
Perseverance, in *The Passetyme of Pleasure*, ii. 225, 228
Perseveraunce, in *Magnyfycence*, iii. 77
Persia, ii. 71; iv. 84; vi. 238; x. 281, 503; xii. 342, 477; xiii. 55; xiv. 248
Persian language and literature, vii. 319; xii. 327, 342, 362; xiii. 145; xiv. 332, 334, 457, 458
Persians, in *The Royall Slave*, vi. 326
Persius, i. 76; iii. 20, 173; iv. 17, 206, 207, 264, 329, 345; vii. 311, 335; viii. 58, 61, 85; ix. 264, 269; xi. 393; xii. 222, 337, 482, 487, 489
Pertelote, in *Phyllyp Sparowe*, iii. 71
Perth, ix. 565 ff.; xi. 470
Perth, the Charterhouse, xiii. 115
Perth, duke and duchess of, ix. 563
Perthshire, x. 348; xiv. 436
Pertinax Surly, in *The Alchemist*, vi. 22
Pertz, Georg Heinrich, xiv. 92
Peru, iv. 86, 99; ix. 391
Perugia, chapter of, i. 212
Perugini, Mrs Kate, xiii. Add. 3
Peruvian speech, xiv. 457
Peshall, Sir John (1718–1778), ix. 346, 541
Pestalozzi, Johann Heinrich, ix. 389; xiv. 383, 390, 393, 404, 600, 602, 608
Pestilence, Treatise of the, ii. 319
Pet (seafarer), iv. 88
Peter, Gregory's deacon, i. 105
Peter, in Mrs Gaskell's *Cranford*, xiii. 378
Peter, in Swift's *Tale of a Tub*, ix. 100
Peter, Revelation of, i. 86
Peter, St, i. 118; ii. 275; iii. 400; iv. 264; v. 37, 50
Peter, St, shrine of, ii. 87
Peter, St, in *Lycidas*, vii. 114, 137
Peter, St, in *Piers the Plowman*, ii. 27
Peter, the wild boy (1712–1785), ix. 132
Peter de Alvernia, ii. 363
Peter de Bella Pertica (d. 1308), ii. 363
Peter of Blois (*fl.* 1160–1204), i. 173, 176, 187, 188, 450, 455
Peter de la Celle, i. 186
Peter Hispanus, *Summa*, ii. 363
Peter of Langtoft (d. 1307?), *Chronicle* of, i. 344, 350 ff., 358, 478; ii. 420; ix. 535
Peter of Peckham, ii. 507
Peter Pratefast, ii. 232
Peter de Riga, ii. 144
Peter the writer, i. 202
Peterborough, ix. 349, 534, 535; xii. 166, 329; xiv. 100, 101
Peterborough. *See* Benedict of
Peterborough, abbey of, i. 49, 398; iii. 95, 428; iv. 417, 418
Peterborough, earl of. *See* Mordaunt, Charles
Peterborough Chronicle, i. 109, 111 ff., 138, 386, 387, 397
Peterkin, Alexander (1780–1846), xi. 441
Peterloo affair, the, xii. 69; xiii. 14
Peters, Hugh (1598–1660), iv. 458; vii. 353, 355, 513; viii. 21, 319, 470; ix. 258
Peterson, Robert (*fl.* 1576–1606), iv. 442; *Il Galateo* (trans. of), iii. 341, 438, 550
Peterson, Sir William (1856–1921), xii. Add. 3
Petgoose, Dr, in Jerrold's *The Catspaw*, xiii. 269
Petit de Julleville, ii. 419
Petit-Dutaillis, C., *Studies and Notes supplementary to Stubb's Constitutional History*, xiv. 75, 499
Petition of Right, vii. 440
Petition to the King's most Excellent Majestie, A, vii. 388
Petowe, Henry (*fl.* 1598–1612), iv. 438
Petrarch, i. 216; ii. 184, 188; iii. 23, 62, 65, 68, 167 ff., 174, 176, 186, 188, 215, 218, 222, 226, 249 ff., 255, 257, 262, 263, 265, 268 ff., 272; iv. 124, 196, 197, 210, 213, 261, 322, 429, 447; v. 173, 230; vi. 364, 378; vii. 1, 2, 4, 7, 17, 18, 23; ix. 555; x. 158; xii. 217, 396, 410
    De Remediis utriusque Fortunae, ii. 367
    Epistles, ii. 366
    Passa la nave mia colma d' obblio, iii. 171
    Philologia, v. 101
    Sonnets to Laura, iii. 251
    Trionfi, xii. 76
    Una candida cerva, iii. 167
Petrarch, in Jonson's *Volpone*, vii. 274
Petrarchian rime form, xii. 91, 81
Petre, father (the Martin) in Dryden's *Fables*, viii. 48, 189
Petre, lord, ix. 70
Petre, M. D., xii. 470
Petrie, A., xiv. Add. 4

Petrie, George (1789–1866), XII. 512, 518; XIV. 317, 571
Ancient Music of Ireland, XIV. 328
Antiquities of Tara, XII. 351
Ecclesiastical Architecture of Ireland, XII. 351
Essay on Tara Hill, XIV. 312
Irish Military Architecture, XII. 351
Origin and uses of the Round Towers, XIV. 312
Round Towers of Ireland, XII. 351
Petrie, Henry (1768–1842), XII. 355, 356, 516, 518
Petrie, William Matthew Flinders, XII. 339
Petrograd, XI. 59; XII. 55; XIII. 55
Petronel Flush, Sir, in *Eastward Hoe*, VI. 48
Petronius, II. 178; IV. 256; VI. 32; VII. 164, 261, 503; IX. 255, 264, 266, 499
Petronius, in Cowper's *Progress of Error*, XI. 82
Petruchio, in *The Taming of the Shrew*, V. 181; X. 90
Petruchio, in *The Womans Prize*, VI. 135
Petrus Alphonsus, I. 479
Petrus Carmelianus, *The epitaph of the King of Scotland*, II. 330
Petrus Comestor, I. 154, 192, 226, 343
Petryonylla, The Life of St, II. 321, 486
Pettie, George (1548–1589), III. 343, 348, 432, 446, 447, 536; IV. 445; *The Petite Pallace of Pettie his Pleasure*, III. 343, 348; V. 123
Pettigrew, Thomas Joseph (1791–1865), XII. 523; *Life of Lord Nelson*, XII. 367
Pettitt, Henry (1848–1893), XIII. 267
Pettman, Rev. Charles, XIV. Add. 9
Pettus, Sir John (1613–1690), *Lovedays Letters Domestic and Forreine*, VII. 390
Petty, Sir William (1623–1687), VIII. 342, 473, 475, 478; *Political Arithmetic*, VIII. 343; *The Advice of W. P.*, IX. 389, 569; *Treatise of Taxes*, VIII. 343, 367
Petty, Sir William, 1st marquis of Lansdowne (1737–1805), XI. 59, 142; XIV. 214
Petty-Fitzmaurice, Sir Henry, 3rd marquis of Lansdowne (1780–1863), XII. 103; XIII. 87
Petulant, in Congreve's *Way of the World*, VIII. 153
Petyt, William (1636–1707), IX. 196, 356, 538; *Jus Parliamentarium*, IX. 357
Peutinger Table, I. 71
Pevensey, III. 95
Peyton, Kate, in Reade's *Griffith Gaunt*, XIII. 426
Peyton, Thomas (1595–1626), *The Glasse of Time*, VII. 406
Pfaffe Amis, III. 81
Pfannkuche, A., XIII. 464
Pfarrer von Kalenberg, Der, III. 82, 94, 490
Pfeiffer, Emily Jane (1827–1890), XIII. 179, 180, 508; XIV. 600
Phaedra, V. 74, 78; VI. 163
Phaedra, in Euripides' *Hippolytus*, VIII. 164
Phaedrus, III. 216; IX. 525, 561; X. 457
Phaedrus, Fables, XI. 479
Phaer, Thomas (1510?–1560), II. 213; III. 295, 302, 303, 448; IV. 17 ff.; *Of the Nature of Writts*, IV. 19; *Vergil*, IV. 19, 440
Phaëthon, in Sandys's *Ovid*, VII. 51
Phaëton, VI. 342
Phalaris, IX. 332 ff., 338, 391, 527, 572; XII. 324; *Epistles*, VIII. 385; IX. 93, 102, 115, 329, 524, 525
'Phalaris' (Junius), X. 409
Phalaris controversy, X. 352
Phantasma Radulphi, I. 332
Phant'sie, in *The Vision of Delight*, VI. 359
Pharamond, in Morris's *Love is Enough*, XIII. 125
Pharamond, in *The Spectator*, IX. 55
Pharaoh, VII. 370
Pharaoh, I. 428
Pharaoh, Sermon on the five wiles of, in *The Golden Legend*, II. 335
Pharetra, II. 366
Pharicles, in *Mamillia*, III. 350
Pharonnida (Chamberlayne's), VII. 75
Pharsalia, battle of, V. 171
Phelps, Samuel (1804–1878), VIII. 184, XIII. 69
Phelps, William (1776–1856), XII. 512
Phelps, W. L., XIII. 485
Phemis, in *The Masque of the Middle Temple*, VI. 355
Phenix, The, X. 166
Philadelphia, XI. 47, 49
Philadelphian society (1697–1703), IX. 308, 514, 515
Philador, in Greene's *Mourning Garment* III. 360
Philalethes (Henry Portsmouth), VII. 414
Philalethes (Robert Fellowes), XII. 466; *Eirenaeus Philoponos*, VII. 509
Philalethes, in Collier's *Essays*, IX. 211
Philammon, in Kingsley's *Hypatia*, XIII. 363
Philanagnostes Criticus, IX. 511
'Philander,' VII. 413
Philanglus (Howell's), VII. 458
Philanthropist, The, XII. 193
Philarete (Wither's), IV. 155
Philastrogus, *Lillies Ape Whipt* (1652), VII. 509
Philatus, in *The Glasse of Governement*, V. 113
Philautus, in Lyly's *Euphues*, IV. 523
Philautus, in Riche's *Don Simonides*, III. 349
Philautus, in *The Anatomy of Wit* and *Euphues and his England*, III. 345
Phileleutherus Anglicanus, X. 400
'Phileleutherus Lipsiensis,' IX. 336, 337, 525
Philemon, IX. 336, 525
Philemon and Baucis, VII. 252
Philenius, in *Club Law*, VI. 308, 309
Philibert, Vision of, II. 502

Philibert de Vienne, *The Philosopher of the Court*, III. 553; IV. 447
Philine, in Goethe's *Wilhelm Meister*, XIII. 346
Philip, in Mrs Gaskell's *Sylvia's Lovers*, XIII. 379
Philip, Alexander John, XIII. 544
Philip II, king of France, I. 307, 308
Philip II, king of Spain, X. 291, 505; III. 24, 196, 401, 431; IV. 71; V. 344; VI. 91; VII. 326; VIII. 125
Philip II, in Otway's *Don Carlos*, VIII. 182
Philip III (the Bold), king of France, I. 354
Philip III, king of Spain, X. 505
Philip V, king of Spain, IX. 228
Philip VI (of Valois), king of France, I. 357
Philip, James (*fl.* 1617), IX. 565
Philip or Phillip, John (*fl.* 1566), *The Plaie of Pacient Grissell*, V. 116, 117, 407
Philip, Rev. John, XIV. Add. 9
Philip of Macedon, III. 24
Philip of Spain, VIII. 125
Philippa of Hainault (1314?–1369), queen of England, I. 358
Philippe de Thaon, *Bestiary*, II. 419; *Li Cumpoz*, II. 420
Philippe le Bon, II. 313
Philipps, Fabian (1601?–1690), VII. 513
Philippus (Horace, *Epist.*), IX. 39
Philips, Ambrose (1675?–1749), VIII. 373; IX. 78, 86, 161, 165–166 (main entry), 181, 182, 190, 446, 481; XI. 144; XIII. 191
Andromaque, adapted by, VIII. 181
Collection of Old Ballads, IX. 166, 182
Distressed Mother, The, VIII. 181, 372; IX. 166, 183; X. 22, 69, 83, 86
Epistle to the Earl of Dorset, IX. 165
Pastorals, IX. 69, 77, 165
Philips, Claudy, musician, X. 464
Philips, James, VII. 88
Philips, John (1676–1709), IX. 181, 182, 486, 487; X. 109 ff.; 'Bacchanalian song,' IX. 182; *Cyder*, IX. 182; X. 96; *The Splendid Shilling*, IX. 169, 182, 256; X. 111, 147
Philips, John (*fl.* 1716), IX. 565
Philips, Katherine (b. Fowler, 'the Matchless Orinda') (1631–1664), IV. 260, 267; VII. 39, 413; VIII. 380; IX. 168, 473; XII. 124
'As men that are with visions graced,' VII. 88
'Come, my Lucasia, let us see,' VII. 88
'I did not love until this time,' VII. 88
'I have examined and do find,' VII. 88
Trans. of *Horatius* (Corneille's), VIII. 133
Trans. of *Pompée*, VIII. 180
Philips, Miles (*fl.* 1568–1582), IV. 73
Philisides, III. 352
Philistine war, in Cowley's *Davideis*, VII. 67
Philistines, the, IV. 31; XIII. 88, 91, 99, 101
Philistines, the, in *Samson Agonistes*, VII. 136
Philistus, IV. 122
Phillida, in *Galathea*, V. 126
Phillida flouts me, VIII. 96
Phillip, William, IV. 460
Phillippes, Henry, IV. 460
Phillips, Augustine (d. 1605), V. 219; VI. 248, 276
Phillips, Charles (1787–1859), XIV. 505
Phillips, Edward (1630–1696?), VII. 15, 96, 107, 117, 118, 120, 141, 265, 267; XI. 394
Phillips, John, nephew of Milton (1631–1706), VII. 96; IX. 264, 265, 267 ff., 272, 500; XI. 394
Don Quixote, IX. 268 ff., 275
Maronides, IX. 258
Present State of Europe, IX. 267
Trans. of *Pharamond and Almahide*, VIII. 371
Translations, IX. 268
Phillips, John (*fl.* 1841), XIV. 236
Phillips, Le Roy, XIII. 574
Phillips, Lionel, XIV. Add. 9
Phillips, Mrs Lionel, XIV. Add. 9
Phillips, Samuel (1814–1854), XIII. 565
Phillips, Stephen (1866–1915), XIII. 508, 522
Phillips, Sir T., IV. 512
Phillips, Watts (1825–1874), XIII. 522; XIV. 238
Camilla's Husband, XIII. 268
Dead Heart, The, XIII. 268
Lost in London, XIII. 268
Woman in Mauve, The, XIII. 268
Phillips of Bankside, mother, VI. 99
Phillis, in Mrs Gaskell's *Cousin Phillis*, XIII. 380
Phillis, in Steele's *Conscious Lovers*, IX. 64
Phillis, in *The Fayre Mayde of the Exchange*, VI. 100
Phillpotts, Henry (1778–1869), bishop of Exeter, XIV. 492, 514
Philo, VII. 264
Philobiblon society, the, XI. 416
Philobiblon Soc. Miscellanies, XII. 406
Philobone, in *The Court of Love*, II. 220, 221
Philoclea, in Sidney's *Arcadia*, III. 352
Philocles, in Dryden's *Secret Love*, VIII. 20
Philocosmia, in *De Eodem et Diverso*, I. 153
Philocosmus, in Daniel's *Musophilus*, IV. 88
Philodemus, XII. 340
Philogenet of Cambridge, in *The Court of Love*, II. 167, 218, 220, 221
Philogonus, in *Misogonus*, V. 110, 111
'Philo-Junius,' X. 404
Philological Museum, The, XII. 308
Philological society, XII. 344
Philomathes, VI. 320, 474
Philomathes, in *Fucus Histriomastix*, VI. 324
Philomedé, in Pope's *Characters of Women*, IX. 82
Philomela, VI. 319, 320, 474
Philomela, in *Confessio Amantis*, II. 151
Philomela, in Orosius, I. 95
Philomela, in *Progne*, VI. 300

Philomelus, in Thomson's *Castle of Indolence*, x. 107
Philomusus, in *The Glasse of Governement*, v. 113
Philomusus, in *The Pilgrimage to Parnassus*, vi. 310
Philomusus, in *The Returne from Pernassus*, vi. 311, 312
Philonices, in *Time's Complaint*, vi. 320
Philosarchus, in *The Glasse of Governement*, v. 113
Philosophia, in *De Eodem et Diverso*, i. 153
Philosophical or 'Invisible' college, viii. 364
Philosophical Transactions. *See* Royal society
Philosophy, land of, in *The Pilgrimage to Parnassus*, vi. 310
Philosophy, the beginnings of English, iv. 268 ff., 504 ff.
Philostratus, iv. 25; vi. 9; viii. 229; ix. 504
Philotas, in Daniel's *Philotas*, iv. 133, 135
Philotimus, in Collier's *Essays*, ix. 211
Philotimus, in *The Glasse of Governement*, v. 113
Philotus, iii. 122; v. 394; ix. 556
Philoxenus, in *Believe as you List*, vi. 148
Philpot, Thomas (*fl.* 1630–1660), vii. 361
Philpot, William Benjamin (1823–1889), xiii. 508
Phipps, Edmund (1808–1857), xii. 452; xiii. 554
Phiston, William (*fl.* 1571–1609), iv. 447
'Phiz,' *pseud. See* Browne, Hablot Knight
Phobetor, xiii. 330
Phoebades, or Virginian priests of the Sun, in Chapman's masque, vi. 355
Phoebe, in *As You Like It*, vi. 304
Phoebe, in *The Faerie Queene*, iii. 233
Phoebe, in *The Faithfull Shepheardesse*, vi. 368
Phoebe, in *Rosalynde*, iii. 358
Phoebus, iv. 122
Phoebus, Mr, in Disraeli's *Lothair*, xiii. 349
Phoenicia, xii. 316, 317, 478
Phoenix, i. 42, 52, 58, 59, 428, 430
Phoenix, the, in *Phyllyp Sparowe*, iii. 71
Phoenix Britannicus, x. 166
Phoenix Nest, The, iii. 523; iv. 109, 113, 116, 118, 159, 467
Photiades, Constantin, xiii. 570
Photius (codex Galeanus), xii. 325, 328, 491
Phraxanor, in Wells's *Joseph and his Brethren*, xii. 117
Phreas, John (d. 1465), ii. 499
Phronesis (Theology) in Wyclif's *Trialogus*, ii. 65
'Phylida was a fayer mayde,' iv. 119
Phyllida, iv. 122
Phyllis, xii. 133
Phyllis, in *Confessio Amantis*, ii. 151
Phyllis, in Owen's *Epigrammata*, iv. 265
Physicians, college of, viii. 361
Physicians, tracts from, iii. 493; vii. 511
Physiologus, Old English, i. 59, 60, 430. See, also, *Bestiaries*
Physiologus of Thetbaldus, i. 227. *See, also*, i. 60, 239
Picardy, ii. 251
Picart, Bernard, xiv. 212
Piccadilly, duke of, in Goldsmith's *Citizen of the World*, x. 206
Piccolomini, Allesandro, *Allesandro*, vi. 32
Pichot, Amédée, xi. 410; xii. 385, 397, 525
Picke, Samuel, *Festum Voluptatis*, 1639, vii. 413
'Pickel, colonel,' in *The Tatler*, ix. 34
Picken, Andrew (1788–1833), xiii. 565
Pickering, a Jesuit, viii. 266
Pickering, Edward (*fl.* 1662), viii. 358
Pickering, Sir Gilbert (1613–1668), viii. 2, 5
Pickering, Henry, grandfather of Dryden, viii. 2
Pickering or Pikering or Pickeryng, John, *Horestes*, v. 63 ff., 77, 396; vi 284
Pickering, William (*fl.* 1556–1571), iv. 390, 399, 546
Pickerings, the (Dryden's relatives), vii. 105
Pickersgill, Joshua, *The Three Brothers*, xii. 50
Pickle, Gamaliel, in Smollett's *Peregrine Pickle*, x. 38
Pickle, Mrs, in Smollett's *Peregrine Pickle*, x. 38
Pickle, Peregrine, x. 38
Picks, R., iii. 191
Pickwick, Samuel (Dickens's), ii. 177; xiii. 311, 322, 324
Picton, James Allanson (1832–1910), xii. 466; xiv. 478
Pictorial Times, The, xiv. 201
Pictorius, G., vii. 509
Picts, ii. 276
Picturesque Sketches of Rustic Scenery, xiv. 222
Piedmont, vii. 306; x. 119; xiii. 88
Pierce, G. A., xiii. 544
Pierce, Robert (1622–1710), viii. 358
Pierce, Thomas, vii. 474
Pierce Plowman. See *Peres* and *Piers*
Piero, in *Antonio and Mellida*, vi. 45
Pierre, in Otway's *Venice Preserv'd*, viii. 183
Pierre d'Ailly, *Imago Mundi*, i. 209
Pierre de la Seppade of Marseilles, version of *Paris and Vienne*, ii. 315
Pierrepont, Evelyn, 1st duke of Kingston (1665?–1726), ix. 243, 244
Pierrepont, William, 4th earl of Kingston, viii. 83
Piers, in *The Shepheards Calender*, iii. 225, 226
Piers of Fullham, ii. 501
Piers the Usurer, tale of, i. 341, 346

Piers Plowman, Vision of, I. 281, 291, 334, 348, 349, 352, 357, 360, 369, 371, 378; II. 1–42 (main entry), 72, 77, 192, 215, 233, 295, 351, 399, 422, 428, 432, 433, 435, 436; III. 181, 273, 274, 302, 303, 325, 448; IV. 37, 382, 414, 521; V. 4, 6, 13, 22, 35, 51; X. 120, 233; XII. 344, 354
Pigafetta, Antonio, IV. 69, 80
Pigeon, the, in Dryden's *Fables*, VIII. 48
Pigott, Mostyn T., XIV. 537
Pigott, Richard (1828?–1889), XIV. 183
Pigwiggen, in *Nimphidia*, IV. 193
Pike, G. Holden, XIV. 533
Pilate, I. 272; VII. 169
Pilate, in the religious plays, V. 16, 17, 19, 42, 44 ff.
Pilgrim Fathers, the, IV. 311, *also see* Add.; VII. 308
Pilgrimage of Grace, the, XIII. 366
Pilgrimage of the Soul, The, II. 314. *See, also*, II. 327, *and under* Lydgate *and* Deguileville
Pilgrims' Sea-voyage, The, II. 503
Pilkington, Francis (1560?–1625?), IV. 113
Pilkington, Gilbert (*fl.* 1350), I. 366
Pilkington, Letitia (1712–1750), XIV. 571
Pilkington, Mrs Mary (1766–1839), XI. 384, 482, 492
Biography for Boys, XI. 385
Biography for Girls, XI. 385
Marvellous Adventures, XI. 385
Moral Tales (trans.), XI. 385
Pilkington, Matthew (*fl.* 1729–1733), IX. 464, 466
Pillans, James (1778–1864), XIV. 404, 608
Pills to Purge Melancholy, II. 414
Pilon, Frederick (1750–1788), XI. 451
Pilot, The, XIV. 202
Pimlyco, or, Runne Red-cap, III. 482; IV. 362, 517, 532
Pinart, IV. 406
Pinch, Tom, in *Martin Chuzzlewit*, XIII. 323
Pindar, III. 259; IV. 30; VII. 64, 65; IX. 189, 487; X. 114, 127, 128, 458, 493; XII. 330, 482, 485, 489, *also see* Add.
Nemean ode, VII. 64
Olympian odes, VII. 64, 65
Paeans, XII. 340
Partheneia, XII. 340
Pindar, Sir Paul (1565?–1650), IV. 513
Pindar, Peter, *pseud. See* Wolcot, John
Pindaric odes, VIII. 44, 55, 84 ff., 94, 170, 233; XII. 128
'Pindarics,' XI. 248; XIII. 191, 198, 218, 227, 239
Pindarus, in Dryden's *Troilus and Cressida*, VIII. 29
Pine, John (1690–1756), XIV. 212
Pine, William, XI. 341
Pinero, Sir Arthur Wing, XIII. 514
Pinkerton, John (1758–1826), II. 113, 116, 269, 283; X. 312, 460, 490, 503, *also see* Add.; XII. 518; XIV. 553; *Walpoliana*, X. 246, 496
Pinkerton, Miss, XI. 379
Pinkie, battle of, II. 109; III. 147, 152
Pinkney, Miles (1599–1674), VII. 34, 35, 400
Pinner academy, X. 385
Pinwell, George John (1842–1875), XI. 489
Pinzon, Vincenzo, IV. 70
Piot, Lazarus, IV. 438
Piozzi, Gabriel, X. 187
Piozzi, Hester Lynch (Mrs Thrale) (1741–1821), VII. 176; X. 63, 65, 66, 158, 168, 170, 181, 186, 187, 267, 463, 471 ff., 484; XI. 350, 354, 364, 365; *Anecdotes of the late Samuel Johnson*, X. 189, 190
Pip, in *Great Expectations*, XIII. 333, 334, 339
Pipe, Hannah E., XIV. 600
Piper o' Dundee, The, IX. 378
Piper of Hamelin, The, III. 81
Pipes, Tom, in Smollett's *Peregrine Pickle*, X. 38
Pipkin, in *How a man may chuse*, etc., VI. 93
Pippa, Browning's, XIII. 59, 62, 81
Piraeicus, VIII. 66
Pirkheimer, Wilibald, III. 1, 22
Pisa, III. 49; V. 306; VII. 316; XII. 37, 70, 72, 75, 398
Pisa, palazzo Lanfranchi, XII. 36
Pisan, Christine de, VIII. 59
Pisano, in *The Traytor*, VI. 199
Piscator of Strassburg, IV. 276
Pistill of Susane. See *Swete Susane*
Pistol, Ancient, IV. 78; VI. 194; VIII. 127; XIV. 125; in *The Merry Wives of Windsor*, V. 187, 195, 203, 361
Pistorius, Hermann Andreas, X. 513
Pitcairn, Robert (1793–1855), XII. 517; XIV. 545
Pitcairne, Archibald (1652–1713), VIII. 409; IX. 559; *De Juramento illicito*, VIII. 97
Pithias, in *Damon and Pithias*, V. 119
Pits, John (1560–1616), IX. 538
Pitseus, John (1560–1616), V. 89, 406
Pitt, Christopher (1699–1748), IX. 486; X. 493; *The Art of Preaching*, X. 363; trans. of *The Æneid*, IX. 188; trans. of Vida's *Art of Poetry*, IX. 188, 189
Pitt, Humphrey, of Shifnal, X. 233
Pitt, Thomas (1653–1726), IX. 409, *also see* Add.
Pitt, Thomas, 1st lord Camelford (1737–1793), X. 250
Pitt, William, 1st earl of Chatham (1708–1778), VIII. 295; IX. 250, 409, 561; X. 102, 164, 190, 250, 256, 263, 272, 273, 388, 390 ff., 398, 399, 402, 403, 406, 408 ff., 476, 523, 526, 527; XI. 11, 12, 16, 51, 165, 351, *also see* Add.; XIII. 467; XIV. 63, 602
Pitt, William, the younger (1759–1806), VIII. 296; XI. 25, 29, 31, 33 ff., 39, 51, 52 ff. (main entry), 74, 118, 157, 392, 396; XII. 260; XIII. 467; XIV. 61, 91, 97, 119, 121, 122, 124, 128, 194, 214
Pitt-Rivers, Augustus Henry Lane F. St (1827–1900), XII. 512

Pittis, Wm (1674–1724), VIII. 405; IX. 15
Pitts, publisher, XIV. 227, 228
Pity, in *The Castle of Perseverance*, V. 52
Pity, in *The Court of Love*, II. 220
Pius II, II. 369; IV. 334
Pius IV, VIII. 296
Pius V, III. 401; IV. 302
Pius IX, XIV. 417
Pix, Mary, born Griffith (1666–1720?), VIII. 439
Pixérécourt, René C. Guilbert de, XIII. 264
Place, Francis (1771–1854), XIV. 408, 478, 602, 608
Placebo, in *Ane Pleasant Satyre*, III. 124, 126
Placidas, or *St Eustace*, V. 104
Placids, the, in Mrs Inchbald's *Every one has his Fault*, XI. 279
Plagiary, Sir Fretful, in Sheridan's *Critic*, XI. 272
Plague, the (1582), VI. 376, 383
Plague, the (1665), VII. 289, 512; VIII. 9, 253
Plain Man's Pathway to Heaven, The, VII. 168; XI. 369
Plan for a Prize Novel, A, XIII. 344
Planché, James Robinson (1796–1880), XII. 512; XIII. 270, 271, 273, 522; *History of British Costume*, XII. 348
Planché, Matilda Anne. *See* Mackarness
Planet, in *Jacke Drums Entertainment*, VI. 44
Plano Carpini, *Historia Mongolorum* of, II. 80
Plantagenet era, XI. 367
Plantagenets, the, IX. 222
Plantin, Christopher, III. 427; IV. 402, 403; IX. 167
Planudean anthology, the, VII. 14
Plarr, Victor Gustavus, XIII. 502
Plas Gwynant, Wales, XIV. 84
Plassey, XIV. 338
Plat or Platt, Sir Hugh (1552?–1611?), IV. 370, 513, 541 ff.
  Divers new sorts of soyle, etc., IV. 371
  Floraes Paradise, IV. 375
  Jewell House of Art and Nature, IV. 371
  New and admirable arte of setting corne, The, IV. 371
Plate fleet, the, IV. 200
Plato and Platonism, I. 99, 187, 213; II. 231; III. 3, 6, 173, 187, 214 ff., 219, 221, 222, 225, 234, 243, 245, 263, 299, 416, 420, 433, 434; IV. 73, 250, 270, 271, 285, 430, 439, 526; V. 209; VI. 21; VII. 7, 154, 277 ff., 302, 304; VIII. 24, 132, 273, 274, 276 ff., 282, 285, 287, 289, 291, 334, 348; IX. 46, 282, 300; XI. 70, 100; XII. 60, 67, 93, 284, 293, 475, 479, 480, 482, 484 ff., 489, 491, 492, 494, 495; *also see* Add.; XIII. 99; XIV. 23
  Axiochus, V. 5
  Euthydemus, XII. 327
  Gorgias, XII. 327, 330
  Phaedo, XII. 333, 335
  Phaedrus, III. 234; XII. 330
Plato
  Republic, The, III. 18, 214; X. 134; XII. 333
  Symposium, III. 214 ff.; XII. 62, 73
  Theaetetus, XII. 329
  Timaeus, III. 214; XII. 333
Platonic love, V. 379
Platonists, III. 9, 258
Platt, E. A., XIV. 598
Plattes, Gabriel (*fl.* 1638–1640), VII. 509
Plautus, III. 24, 53, 92; IV. 245; V. 101, 105 ff.; VI. 14 ff., 21, 22, 24, 26, 28, 303, 304, 306, 320; VIII. 17, 164, 165, 247; IX. 338, 526; X. 417; XI. 265; XII. 490, 492, 494
  Amphitruo, V. 107
  Aulularia, VI. 297; VIII. 123; XI. 277
  Menaechmi, IV. 4, 439; V. 102, 177, 220; VI. 300
  Miles Gloriosus, V. 102, 105, 162; VIII. 127; XII. 338
  Mostellaria, VI. 102
  Rudens, VI. 102
Playe of Playes and Pastimes, The, VI. 391
Players Petition to Parliament, The, VI. 407, 495
Playfair, John (1748–1819), XII. 144, 427; XIV. 292, 406, 409, 561, 563; *Illustrations of the Huttonian Theory of the Earth*, XIV. 291
Playford, John (1623–1686?), VII. 402; *Choice Ayres*, IX. 364; *Introduction to the Skill of Musicke*, IV. 144
Pleasance, queen, in *King Hart*, II. 262
Pleasand Ballatis, III. 142
Pleasant Battle between two Lap-dogs of the Utopian Court, A, VIII. 99
Pleasure, in Carew's *Coelum Britannicum*, VII. 19
Plegmund (d. 914), I. 92
Plegwin, Bede's letter to, I. 80
Pléiade, The, III. 227, 250, 258, 265; IV. 197; VII. 1; XIII. 211
Pleshy, Essex, XII. 510
Pleyel, Ignaz Joseph, XI. 226
Pliant, Dame, in *The Alchemist*, VI. 22
Pliny, the elder, I. 76, 80, 81, 191; II. 79 80, 363; III. 5, 20, 71, 109, 347, 420 IV. 1, 14, 15, 249, 439; VI. 9; VII. 261, 316; VIII. 66, 77; IX. 38, 534; XII. 336, 402, 487; *Epistolae*, IX. 349; *Natural History*, III. 347; V. 123, 126
Pliny, the younger, IV. 264, 439
Plomer, Henry R., XI. 466, 467, 469
Plot, Robert (1640–1696), IX. 413, 538; *Natural History of Oxfordshire*, IX. 352; *Natural History of Staffordshire*, IX. 352
Plotinus, VIII. 273, 277, 278, 282, 287 ff.; IX. 315, 323
Plouffe, Gédéon, XIV. 355
Plough Monday, V. 32
Ploughman's Tale, The, II. 36, 39, 162, 164, 215, 432, 434
Plow boys' performances, V. 32
Plowden, Edmund (1518–1585), *Law Reports*, VIII. 316, 467

Pluck, in *Nicholas Nickleby*, XIII. 317
Plume, captain, in Farquhar's *Recruiting Officer*, VIII. 171
Plume, Thomas (1630–1704), VII. 342
Plumers, the, XII. 182
Plumian professorship of astronomy, Cambridge, VII. 342; IX. 412, 413
Plummer, Charles, I. 79, 81, 83, 85, 93, 104, 112
Plummer, John (*fl.* 1444), VI. 281
Plumporridge, in *The Inner-Temple Masque*, VI. 70, 75
Plumpton Correspondence, II. 483, 500
Plunket, David, XIV. 126
Plunket, William Conyngham, 1st baron Plunket (1764–1854), XIV. 128, 510; *Life, Letters and Speeches*, XIV. 126
Plunkett, Henry Grattan ('Fusbos'), XIV. 236
Plutarch, III. 68, 92, 313, 346, 347, 429, 433; IV. 1, 3, 5, 10, 12, 15, 16, 23, 24, 342, 344, 439, 442, 527; V. 197, 221; VI. 19, 138, 406; VII. 392, 404; VIII. 31, 401; IX. 28, 265, 267, 337, 500; XI. 330, 351, 352; XII. 332, 335, 485, 487, 490, 497; XIV. 579
  De Educatione Puerorum, III. 346
  Life of Agis, VIII. 191
  Lives, X. 206, 481
  Moralia, IV. 6, 14, 249, 523; VII. 316
Pluto, I. 295; IV. 349
Pluto, in *The Devil and his Dame*, V. 329
Pluto, in *Friar Rush*, VI. 53
Pluto, in *The Merchant's Tale*, II. 184
Pluto, in *Troiane*, V. 69
Plutus, in *Love Restored*, VI. 351, 352, 355
Plutus, in *The Masque of the Middle Temple*, VI. 355
Plyant, lady, in Congreve's *Double-Dealer*, VIII. 148
Plyant, Sir Paul, in Congreve's *Double-Dealer*, VIII. 148, 149, 156
Plymouth, IV. 78, 200, 311, 350; VII. 449; VIII. 122; XI. 468; XIV. 122, 297
Plymouth, the Hoe, VI. 101
Plymouth Sound, X. 115
Plynlimmon, I. 250
Pneustis (Unbelief), in Wyclif's *Trialogus*, II. 65
Pocock, Isaac (1782–1835), XIII. 270, 522
  Magpie or the Maid? The, XIII. 265
  Miller and his Men, The, XIII. 264, 265
  Montrose; or, The Children of the Mist, XIII. 265
  Rob Roy Macgregor; or, Auld Lang Syne, XIII. 265
  Robber's Wife, The, XIII. 265
  Robinson Crusoe, XIII. 265
  Twenty Years Ago, XIII. 265
Pocock, Nicholas (1814–1897), IX. 196
Pococke, Edward, the elder (1604–1691), IX. 183, 529
Pococke, Edward, the younger (1648–1727), VII. 308, 319; IX. 529
Pococke, Richard (1704–1765), XIV. 246, 553
Podestà, the, in Crowne's *City Politiques*, VIII. 188
Podmore, Frank, XIV. 473, 478, 602
Poe, Edgar Allan, XIII. 121, 141, 438, 505; XIV. 318 *b*, 365; *Murders in the Rue Morgue, The*, XIII. 437
Poema Morale, I. 220, 227, 338, 376, 459, 460; X. 225
Poems on Affairs of State, VIII. 91, 410, 411, 445, 447
Poenitentia, in *The Castle of Perseverance*, V. 52
Poeta, in *Technogamia*, VI. 323
Poetical Amusements at a Villa near Bath, X. 278
Poetical Calendar (Fawkes and Woty's), X. 183
Poetical Magazine, The, XIV. 217, 218
Poetical Register, The, XI. 413
Poetry, land of, in *The Pilgrimage to Parnassus*, VI. 310
Poet's laureate, II. 506
Poggio, in *The Palice of Honour*, II. 260
Poggio Bracciolini, G. F., III. 93, 489; IV. 322
Poictiers, II. 336
Poins, in *Henry IV*, V. 189
Poiret, Pierre, IX. 307, 519 ff.
Poisson, Siméon Denis, XIV. 261
Poland, V. 308; VI. 303; VII. 200; XIV. 172
Poland, The Last Will and Testament of Anthony K. of, VIII. 93
Polar seas, the, XII. 248
Pole, in Meredith's *Sandra Belloni*, XIII. 445
Pole, David (d. 1568), IV. 428
Pole, Reginald (1500–1558), cardinal, archbishop of Canterbury, III. 7, 105, 420, 474; IV. 428
Pole, Thomas (1753–1829), XIV. 592
Pole, William de la, 1st duke of Suffolk (1396–1450), II. 288, 304, 424; IV. 182
Pole, William (1814–1890), XIV. 503
Polemia, in Arbuthnot's *History of John Bull*, IX. 134
Polemo-Middinia, X. 223
Polesworth. *See* Powlsworth
Poliarchus, in *Argemis*, IV. 258 ff.
Policy, in *The Passetyme of Pleasure*, II. 226
Polidori, G., XIII. 490, 496
Polidori, John William, XII. 247, 397
Polimanteia, V. 368, 369, 479
Polisarda, in *Palmerin of England*, VII. 75
Polish language, XIV. 458
Politian, VII. 315; X. 159
Political and social aspects of the later Elizabethan and earlier Stewart period, V. 476 ff.
Political Eclogues, XI. 34, 36, 40
Political Miscellanies, XI. 35
Political pamphlets, IV. 535
Political Register, X. 525
Political Science Quarterly, The, XIV. 80
Political Songs of England, I. 370
Political treatises and pamphlets in Jacobean times, VII. 455

Politick Would Be, Sir, in *Volpone*, vi. 21
Politicke perswasion, the Vice, in *Pacient Grissell*, v. 117
Politics, in *Confessio Amantis*, ii. 149
Politics and economics, early writings on, iv. 295 ff., 509 ff.
Politics for the People, xiii. 358
Poliziano, Angelo, iii. 5, 6, 20; iv. 69
Polla, in *Ignoramus*, vi. 322
Pollard, Alfred William, iv. 394; v. 18, 20, 92, *and see* Add. 3; vii. 11; xi. 467
Pollen, John Hungerford (1820–1902), xii. 462; *A Narrative of Five Years at St Saviour's, Leeds*, xii. 275
Pollexfen, Sir Hargrave, in Richardson's *Sir Charles Grandison*, x. 11
Pollitt, Charles, xiv. 532
Pollock, Sir Frederick, viii. 313; xiv. 80, 470, 494
Pollock, Sir F. and Maitland, F. W., *History of English Law*, i. 174, 181
Pollock, Walter Herries, xi. 448; xii. 447
Pollok, Robert (1798–1827), xi. 444; xii. 421; *The Course of Time*, xi. 244; xii. 129
Polly, in Dickens's *Mugby Junction*, xiii. 335
Polly, in Gay's *Beggar's Opera*, ix. 163; xi. 260
Polly, in *The Little Pretty Pocket Book*, xi. 376
'Polonaland,' v. 111
Polonia, prince (Thackeray's), xiii. 288
Polonius, in *Hamlet*, ii. 384; iii. 349; iv. 120; v. 172, 200 ff., 272, 278; vi. 161, 200; viii. 221, 377
Polter, R., iv. 460
Polwarth, ix. 364
Polwhele, Richard (1760–1838), x. 490; xii. 376
Polyander (Howell's), vii. 458
Polybius, iii. 432; iv. 259, 439; vii. 311, 488; ix. 528; x. 466; xii. 493
Polycarp, xii. 340
Polydore, in Otway's *Orphan*, viii. 183
Polynesian languages, xiv. 459
Polyphilus, in *The Rambler*, x. 172
Pomfret, countess of. *See* Fermor, Henrietta Louisa
Pomfret, John (1667–1702), viii. 444; ix. 167, 169, 170, 482; x. 183; *Choice, The*, ix. 170; *Poems on Several Occasions*, ix. 169
Pompeii, xii. 417, 497
Pompey, iv. 196
Pompey, in *Measure for Measure*, v. 190
Pompey the Little. *See* Coventry, Francis
Pompey's Ghost, xi. 234
Pompilia, in Browning's *The Ring and the Book*, xiii. 50, 66, 79
Pomponius Laetus, iii. 13
Pomponius Mela, iv. 439
Ponder, Nathanael, vii. 178
Ponet, John (1514?–1556), bishop of Winchester, iii. 473; iv. 447; v. 104
Ponsonby, William (1546?–1603), iv. 395, 397, 398
Ponsonby de Tomkyns, Mrs (Du Maurier's), xiii. 433
Pont-à-Mousson, iv. 253, 256
Pont-neuf, ii. 395
Ponthus, The History of King, ii. 325
Pontia, in Owen's *Epigrammata*, iv. 265
Pontifex, in Butler's *The Way of all Flesh*, xiii. 454
Pontine marshes, in Thackeray's *Ravenswing*, xiii. 281
Pontis, L. de, ix. 499
Ponto family, in Thackeray's *Book of Snobs*, xiii. 285
Pontoux, Claude de, iv. 24; *L'Idée*, iv. 178
Pontresina, xiii. 380
Pontus de Tyard, iii. 258, 263; *Les Erreurs Amoureuses*, iii. 258
Pool, John, *County Astrology* (1650), vii. 509
Poole, Austin Lane, x. Add.
Poole, John (1786?–1872), xiii. 522; *Lodgings for Single Gentlemen*, xiii. 270; *Paul Pry*, xiii. 270; *'Twixt the Cup and Lip*, xiii. 270
Poole, Joshua (*fl.* 1632–1646), viii. 238; xi. 249; *The English Parnassus*, vii. 466; viii. 238, 447
Poole, Matthew (1624–1679), vii. 323, 477; *Synopsis Criticorum Bibliorum*, vii. 322, 481
Poole, Reginald Lane, i. 420; xiv. 485, 500
Poole, Reginald Stuart (1832–1895), xii. 498
Poole, Stanley Lane, xi. 459; xiv. 252
Poole, Thomas (1765–1837), xi. 121, 405
Poor law, Elizabethan, v. 374, 375
Poor Man's Pittance, A, iii. 198
Poor priests (Wyclif's), ii. 56, 57, 59, 63, 66
Poor Tom. *See* Abraham man
Poore, Richard, bishop of Salisbury (d. 1237), i. 230
Pop upon Pope, A, ix. 85
Pope (actor) (d. 1604), iv. 360; vi. 248, 276
Pope, Alexander (1688–1744), iii. 78, 200, 452; iv. 21, 208, 280, 335; v. 209, 249, 268 ff., 274, 296; vi. 113; vii. 12, 20, 73, 269; viii. 39, 50, 51, 62, 77, 89, 143, 160, 177, 193 ff., 203, 229, 234, 235, 237, 284, 292, 370, 386, 427; ix. 17, 45, 66 ff. (main entry), 103, 123, 127, 129, 131, 133, 137, 138, 141 ff., 160, 161, 163 ff., 171, 174, 175, 177, 179 ff., 184, 185, 187 ff., 220, 228, 230, 247, 248, 250 ff., 258, 260, 340, 357, 369, 437, 442 ff., 452, 462, 466, 468 ff., 472, 474 ff., 480, 481, 483, 484, 497, 498, 509, *also see* Add.; x. 77, 80, 95, 102, 110, 113, 115, 119 ff., 126, 128, 138, 141, 145, 153, 169, 172, 174, 180, 184, 202, 208, 218, 219, 221, 227, 232, 238 ff., 242, 273, 277, 297, 299, 301, 319, 398, 447, 448, 457, 458, 461, 465 ff., 475, 493, *also see* Add.; xi. 36, 77, 79, 82, 86, 91, 142, 150, 175, 178, 201, 206 ff., 216,

Pope, Alexander
247, 254 ff., 320 ff., 330, 335, 356, 402, 410, 466, 467, 473; XII. 36, 40, 100, 145, 169, 177, 218, 363, 384, 397, 419, 438, 444; XIII. 27, 29, 43, 51, 70, 71, 239, 253, 512; XIV. 62, 108, 144, 200, 212, 249, 396, 399, 435, 436, 439, 447
Alcander Prince of Rhodes, IX. 68
Art of Sinking in Poetry (*Bathos*). See *Martinus Scriblerus* below
Augustus, To, XII. 42
Correspondence, XI. 328
Dialogues, IX. 87, 88
Dunciad, The, IV. 332; V. 270, 276; VII. 89; VIII. 40, 41; IX. 32, 77 ff., 82, 85, 88, 89, 131, 143, 144, 165, 188, 237, 251, 340, 409; X. 121, 163, 202; XI. 140, 212, 320, 328; XII. 41, 42
Elegy to the Memory of an Unfortunate Lady, IX. 70
Eloisa to Abelard, IX. 70, 71; X. 218
Epistle to a Young Lady, IX. 71
Epistle to Dr Arbuthnot, IX. 78, 86, 88, 133, 147, 171, 251; XII. 42, 73
Epistle to Mr Jervas, IX. 71
Epistle to Robert Earl of Oxford, IX. 74, 77
Epistles, IX. 81, 82, 86, 87
Essay on Criticism, VII. 69; IX. 70, 73, 77, 89
Essay on Man, IX. 73, 81 ff., 85, 89, 169, 295, 296; X. 185; XI. 140
Ethic Epistles, IX. 89
Fragment of a Satire, IX. 78
Full and True Account...Edmund Curll, IX. 78
Homer, V. 269; VIII. 158; IX. 72, 74 ff., 164, 167, 171; XI. 89, 90, 246, 320 ff.
Imitations of Horace, VII. 69; IX. 85 ff., 251
Letter to a Noble Lord, IX. 86, 251
Letter to H. Cromwell, XI. 250
Martinus Scriblerus...or the Art of Sinking in Poetry (*Bathos*), IX. 78, 171, 251, 271
Messiah, IX. 69; X. 159, 168
Moral Essays, IX. 81, 82
Narrative of Dr Robert Norris, IX. 77
Ode for Music on Saint Cecilia's Day, IX. 72
Ode on Solitude, IX. 68
Of False Taste, IX. 81
Of Taste, IX. 81
Of the Characters of Women, IX. 82
Of the Knowledge and Characters of Men, IX. 81
Of the Use of Riches, IX. 81
One Thousand Seven Hundred and Thirty-Eight, X. 168
Ovid's *Metamorphoses*, translation of, IX. 68
Pastorals, IX. 68, 69, 78
Prologue to the Satires, IX. 86
Rape of the Lock, The, IX. 70, 73, 241; X. 167; XIII. 263
Satires, VII. 89; IX. 86, 87
Selecta Poemata Italorum, IX. 76; X. 159

Pope, Alexander
Shakespeare, edited by, IX. 77; XI. 320
'Sober advice from Horace,' IX. 86
Song by a Person of Quality, XII. 101
Statius's *Thebais*, translation of, IX. 68
Temple of Fame, X. 219
Windsor Forest, IX. 69
Works (1717), IX. 74
Works in Prose, IX. 84
1740, IX. 88
Pope, Sir Thomas (1507?–1559), III. 51, 420, 424; X. 492
Pope, Walter (d. 1714), IX. 500; *The Catholic Ballad*, VIII. 97, 411
Popery, X. 301
Popes, The History of the, X. 499
Popham, Sir John (1531?–1607), VI. 188
Popish Courant, The (1678–1683), VIII. 412
Popish Plot, A Narrative of the, VIII. 97
'Poplicola,' X. 403
Poppaea, in Gray's *Agrippina*, X. 119
Popple, William (d. 1708), Locke's *Epistola de Tolerantia* trans. by, VIII. 331, 471
Porcher, Edwin A., XII. 339, 498
Porcupine, Peter, XI. 49
Porcupine, The, XI. 49
Pordage, in Oldham's *Thirteenth Satyr of Juvenal*, VIII. 89
Pordage, John (1607–1681), VII. 303, 474; IX. 307, 519
Pordage, Samuel (1633–1691?), VIII. 91, 403, 409; *Azaria and Hushai*, VIII. 92; *The Medal Revers'd*, VIII. 92
Porlock, in *Lorna Doone*, XIII. 434
Pornic, XIII. 77
Porphyro, in Keats's *Eve of St Agnes*, XII. 86, 87; XIII. 114
Porphyry, II. 363; VIII. 288
Porphyry, Commentary on, by William of Ockham, I. 212
Porrex, in *Gorboduc*, V. 67
Porritt, Edward, XIV. 532
Porrus (Porus), I. 307
Porson, Richard (1759–1808), IV. 263; IX. 526; XII. 323 ff. (main entry), 329 ff., 363, 481 ff., 486, 488, 490 ff.
Adversaria, XII. 329
Aristophanica, XII. 328
Letters to Mr Archdeacon Travis, X. 309, 317, 508; XII. 323
Miscellaneous Works, XII. 324
'Porson' type, XII. 324, 329
Porsoniana, XII. 408
Port, Sir John (d. 1557), VII. 331
Port Glasgow, XIII. 107
Port Royal, III. 424
Porte, the, IX. 244
Porten, Catharine, X. 300
Porteous mob, the, XII. 18
Porter, Anna Maria (1780–1832), XI. 305, 463
Porter, Charlotte, XIII. 479
Porter, Elizabeth, X. 160
Porter, Endymion (1587–1649), VI. 235; VII. 5, 12

Porter, Henry (*fl.* 1596–1599), v. 311, 312, 331, 475; vi. 12, 219; *The two angry Women of Abington*, v. 330
Porter, James (1753–1798), xi. 395
Porter, Jane (1776–1850), xi. 305, 464; *Scottish Chiefs*, xi. 306; *Thaddeus of Warsaw*, xi. 306
Porter, John, xiv. 541
Porter, Joseph, x. 385
Porter, P., *Tachmas, Prince of Persia*, viii. 190
Porter, Sir Robert Ker (1777–1842), xiv. 553
Porter and Jonson's *Hot Anger Soon Cold*, v. 331; vi. 12
Porteus, Beilby (1731–1808), x. 517
Portfolio of a Man of the World, ix. 191
Portia, in *The Merchant of Venice*, v. 169, 183, 197, 262, 379
Portiforiums, iii. 19
Portjafe, ii. 277
Portland, vii. 61
Portland, duchess of. *See* Harley, Margaret
Portland, earls of. *See* Bentinck, William
Porto Bello, x. 36; xiv. 201
Portraits, French, iv. 522, 523
Portsmouth, xii. 243; xiv. 225
Portsmouth, duchess of. *See* Kerouaille, Louise Renée de
Portsmouth academy, in O'Keeffe's *Wild Oats*, xi. 281
Portsmouth's Picture, On the duchess of, viii. 94
Portugal, ii. 276; vi. 169; viii. 271; x. 408, 500; xi. 72, 155; xii. 32, 488; xiv. 294
Portugal, prince of, in *The Spanish Tragedie*, v. 240
Portugal History, The (1677), viii. 451
Portuguese, the, xii. 13
Portuguese king, in *Believe as You List*, vi. 147
Portuguese language, xi. 355; xiv. 457, 458
Portuguese navy, the, xiv. 187
Portuguese songs, ii. 405
Portuguese writers, viii. 126
Portuus of Noblines, ii. 284
Pory, John (1570?–1635), iv. 445
Positive Atall, Sir, in Shadwell's *Sullen Lovers*, viii. 21
Possum, Peter, *pseud.* *See* Rowe, Richard
Post and Pair, in *The Masque of Christmas*, vi. 358
Post Boy, The, ix. 5; xi. 333
Poste, Edward (1823–1902), xii. 492
Postgate, John Percival, xii. 483
Posthast, in *Histrio-Mastix*, v. 322; vi. 43, 86
Posthumus, in *Cymbeline*, v. 206
Postman, The, xi. 333
Pote, Joseph (1703?–1787), xi. 341
Potez, H., xii. 525
Potion, in Smollett's *Roderick Random*, x. 36
Potiphar, xii. 117
Potpan, in *Romeo and Juliet*, v. 182
Potter, John (1674?–1747), ix. 527
Potter, Robert (1721–1804), x. 475, 476 xiii. 145
Potter's bar, xii. 186
Potts, R. A., xii. 400
Potts, Thomas (*fl.* 1612), iv. 535; vi. 104; vii. 374, 506; *Discoverie of Witches*, vi. 105
Poulton, Edward Bagnall, xiv. 560
Pounce, Peter, in Fielding's *Joseph Andrews*, x. 25
Pound, Ezra, xiii. Add. 2
Poundtext, Peter, in Scott's *Old Mortality*, xii. 27
Pourceaugnac, M. de (Molière's), vi. 160
Poussin, Nicholas, x. 106; xii. 173; xiii. 52
Pouts, captain, in *A Woman is a Weathercocke*, vi. 222
Poutsma, H., xiv. 611
Poverte, in *Magnyfycence*, iii. 77, 78
Poverty, in *Worke for Armorours*, vi. 56
Povey, Charles (1652?–1743), ix. 462; x. 411
Powell, Baden (1796–1860), xii. 295, 466, 469; xiv. 479
Powell, David (1552?–1598), i. 262; iii. 531
Powell, Frederick York (1850–1904), i. 369; ii. 39; xiv. 497
Powell, George (1658?–1714), viii. 177
Powell, Humphrey (*fl.* 1548–1556), iv. 414; *The Wyll of the Devyll*, iii. 86, 87
Powell, Mary, 1st wife of John Milton, vii. 101, 122
Powell, Mrs, actress (d. 1831), viii. 186
Powell, Stephen, xi. 342
Powell, Thomas (1572?–1635?), iv. 526; v. 479; vii. 39
Powell, William (*fl.* 1562–1563), iv. 384
Powell family, vii. 103
Power, in *Cooper's Hill*, vii. 60
Power, Cecil, *pseud.* *See* Allen, Grant
Power, John, xii. 523
Power, Lionel, xiv. 308
Power, Marguerite. *See* Blessington, countess of
Powers Key, in *The Bowge of Courte*, iii. 73
Powis, 1st baron, vii. 45
Powis, earl. *See* Herbert, Edward
Powis, lord, in *John a Kent*, v. 317
Powis castle, x. 115
Powlsworth (now Polesworth), iv. 169, 174, 186
Powys, prince of, i. 196
Poynter, Sir Edward John, xiii. 433
Poyntz, Sydnam (*fl.* 1645–1650), vii. 453
Poyser, Mrs, in *Adam Bede*, ix. 323
Poysers, the, in *Adam Bede*, xiii. 390, 392
Praagh, L. V., xiv. Add. 9
Practice of Piety, The, vii. 168
Praed, Winthrop Mackworth (1802–1839), x. 152; xi. 160; xii. 107, 108, 111–112 (main entry), 119 ff., 129, 130, 138, 421 xiii. 149, 161, 164, 230, 238, 253; xiv. 205, 206, 539
Arminius, xii. 111

Praed, Winthrop Mackworth
Gog, XII. 111
Goodnight to the Season, XII. 122
I enter thy garden of Roses, XII. 122
Josephine, XII. 111
Letter from Teignmouth, XII. 122
Letter of Advice, XII. 122; XIII. 239
Molly Mog, XII. 122
Red Fisherman, The, XII. 111, 112; XIII. 239
Tales, XII. 111
Time's Song, XII. 111, 112
Twenty Eight and Twenty Nine, XII. 122
Vicar, The, XII. 122
Prague, XII. 206; XIII. 162, 163
Praise, in *Mirour de l'Omme*, II. 142
Praise of Women, A, II. 162
Prat, in *The pardoner and the frere*, V. 97
Prat, D., IX. 511
Pratt, Ambrose, XIV. 535
Pratt, Charles, 1st earl Camden (1714–1794), X. 263
Pratt, Josiah (1768–1844), XII. 471
Pratt, Samuel Jackson (1749–1814), X. 265; XI. 395, 429
Praxapostolos, I. 77
Praxaspes, in *Cambises*, V. 65
Praxinoe, in *The Adoniazusae*, III. 226
Prayer, in *The Example of Virtue*, II. 227
Prayer, A, in *The Exeter Book*, I. 428
Prayer, Book of Common, III. 25, 28, 29, 31, 34, 445, 465, 475, 476; X. 362
Prayer Book, American, Scots and Irish, III. 34
Prayer-Book of 1552, VII. 325
Prayer to Our Lady, A, I. 232, 458
Prayer to the Virgin, A, I. 232, 458
Prayse of All Women, The, III. 90, 486
Preceptor, The, X. 170, 468
Preiddeu Annwvn, or *The Harrowings of Hell*, I. 251
Premierfait, Laurent du, III. 192
Prendergast, John Patrick (1808–1893), XIV. 497, 571; *History of the Cromwellian Settlement, The*, XIV. 96; *Ireland from the Restoration to the Revolution*, XIV. 96
Prendergast, Paul, *pseud.* *See* Leigh, Percival
Prentys, Richard (*fl.* 1403–1412), VI. 280
Pre-Raphaelite school of painting, XII. 154
Pre-Raphaelites, the, XIII. 8, 27, 110, 111, 113 ff., 121, 122, 139, 155, 156, 189, 196, 197, 207, 208, 211, 216, 218, 223; XIV. 139, 151, 363
Presbyterian histories, X. 519
Presbyterians, X. 522
Presbyterians, Satire against the, VII. 85
Prescott, William Hickling, X. 504; XII. 380, 524
Present State of Europe, IX. 267
Present State of the Republic of Letters, X. 176
Present State of the War, IX. 44
Press, The, XIII. 347, 353, 449; XIV. 181, 196, 198
Presse full of Pamphlets, A, 1642, VII. 502
Prester John, II. 79, 86, 87; IV. 70; X. 160
Prester John, The Letter of, II. 80
Preston, XI. 409
Preston, battle of, X. 358
Preston, John (1587–1628), IV. 433
Preston, Thomas (1537–1598), V. 396
'A geleflower gentle,' VI. 285
'A Lamentation from Rome,' VI. 285
Cambises, V. 63 ff.; VI. 284, 285, 298
Syr Clyomon and Clamydes, V. 129; VI. 284
Preston, *pseud.* of lord de Tabley, XIII. 205
Prestonpans, IX. 373
Prestwich, Edmund, *Hippolitus and Poems* (1651), VII. 413
Preti, Girolamo, VII. 87
Prevention of Cruelty to Animals Act, XIV. 445
Prévost, abbé, V. 289; XI. 465
Prévost, Antoine-François, X. 16; *L'Histoire de M. Cleveland*, X. 118; *Manon Lescaut*, X. 58, 118
Prevost, Sir George (1804–1893), XII. 454, 457, 463
Priam, in *Dido*, V. 145
Priamus, Sir, in *Morte Arthure*, II. 119
Priapus, VII. 360
Price, Bonamy, XIV. 596
Price, C., XIII. 504
Price, Fanny, in Jane Austen's *Mansfield Park*, XII. 235, 238, 239, 243
Price, John (1600–1676?), VII. 316, 489
Price, Laurence (*fl.* 1625–1680?), VII. 509
Price, Miss, maid of honour, VIII. 208
Price, Rees, X. 387
Price, Richard (1723–1791), X. 344, 345, 380, 513; XI. 20, 21, 71; XIV. 608
Additional Observations, X. 344
Appeal to the Public, X. 344
Discourse on the Love of our Country, X. 344
General Introduction, X. 344
Observations on Reversionary Payments, X. 344
Observations on the Nature of Civil Liberty, X. 344
Review of the Principal Questions in Morals, X. 344
Price, Richard (1790–1833), X. 492
Price, Sir Uvedale (1747–1829), XI. 472
Price, William, in Jane Austen's *Mansfield Park*, XII. 239
Prichard, Iltudus Thomas, XIV. 579; *The Chronicles of Budgepore*, XIV. 340
Prichard, James Cowles (1786–1848), XIV. 563
Pride, in *Confessio Amantis*, II. 147, 148
Pride, in *The Example of Virtue*, II. 227, 234
Pride, in *The Faerie Queene*, II. 236; III. 230, 234
Pride, in *Mirour de l'Omme*, II. 140
Pride, in *The Passetyme of Pleasure*, II. 231
Pride, in *Pathomachia*, VI. 324
Pride, in *Piers the Plowman*, II. 27, 28

Pride, colonel Thomas (d. 1658), XIV. 313
Pride, the swineherd in the *Mercuries*, VII. 356
Pride and Lowliness, A Debate between, III. 361
Pride of Life, The, V. 2, 52, 57, 391, 392
Prideaux, Edmund B. R., XIV. 592
Prideaux, Humphrey (1648–1724), IX. 495; X. 503; *LVIII Articles*, IX. 414
Prideaux, John (1578–1650), VII. 307
Prideaux, William Francis, XI. 416, 417, 488; XIII. 497; XIV. 526
Priest (translator), IV. 374
Priestis of Peblis, Thrie, II. 279
Priestley, Joseph (1733–1804), IX. 302; X. 346, 380, 384, 385, 513, 514; XI. 63, 64, 70, 390, 393, 399; XII. 165, 174, 183, 279; XIV. 23, 51, 258, 272 ff., 284, 385, 394, 398, 399, 402, 556, 558, 602, 608
Disquisitions relating to Matter and Spirit, X. 345
Doctrine of Philosophical Necessity, X. 345
Essay on the first principles of government, XIV. 400
Examination, An, X. 345, 348
Free Discussion, X. 345
History...of Electricity, X. 345
History of the Corruptions of Christianity, X. 309, 507
Miscellaneous Observations, XIV. 386, 395
Rudiments of English Grammar, XIV. 396
Priestley, Timothy (1734–1814), X. 385
Prillisk, county Tyrone, XIV. 314
Prima Pastorum, V. 17
Primaudaye, Peter de la, *French Academy*, III. 356, 437, 552
Primer or Office of the Blessed Virgin Mary, The, VIII. 54
Primerose, the Hon. Miss, X. 479
Primers, III. 28, 30, 31; IV. 384, 386, 495
Bishop Hilsey's, III. 30
Henry VIII's, III. 30
Marshall's, III. 30
Primitive Christianity Revived, VIII. 111
Primrose, Archibald Philip, 5th earl of Rosebery, X. Add.; XI. 390, 396, 438, 441; XIV. 507; *Chatham*, IX. 253
Primrose, David, VII. 308
Primrose, Dr, in *The Vicar of Wakefield*, X. 206, 209
Primrose, George, in *The Vicar of Wakefield*, X. 200, 201, 209
Primrose, James, VII. 511
Primrose, Moses, in *The Vicar of Wakefield*, X. 209
Primrose, Mrs, in *The Vicar of Wakefield*, X. 209
Primrose, Olivia, in *The Vicar of Wakefield*, X. 209
Primrose, Sophia, in *The Vicar of Wakefield*, X. 209
Prince (of Wales)'s company, the, VI. 261
Prince, John Critchley (1808–1866), XIII. 508
Pring, Martin (1580–1626?), IV. 94
Pringle, Thomas (1789–1834), XII. 421; XIV. 373 ff., *also see* Add. 5, 9
Afar in the Desert, XIV. 374
Bechuana Boy, The, XIV. 375
Captive of Camalu, The, XIV. 377
Ghona Widow's Lullaby, The, XIV. 376
Koranna, The, XIV. 377
Lion and Giraffe, The, XIV. 375
Lion Hunt, The, XIV. 375
Narrative of a Residence in South Africa, XIV. 373
Songs of the Emigrants, XIV. 374
Pringle-Pattison, Andrew Seth, XIII. 465; XIV. 469
Prinsep, James (1799–1840), XII. 512; *Benares illustrated*, XII. 352; *Essays on Indian Antiquities*, XII. 352, 353
Printers (1557–1625), IV. 546 ff.
Printing, Introduction of, into England, II. 310 ff., 483 ff.
Prior, Arthur, kinsman of Matthew Prior, IX. 146
Prior, George, father of Matthew Prior, IX. 146
Prior, Sir James (1790?–1869), X. 199 ff., 480, 483; XI. 390; *Life of Malone*, X. 159, 473
Prior, Matthew (1664–1721), III. 184; VIII. 48, 217, 218, 232, 444, 445; IX. 96, 141, 146 ff. (main entry), 162, 163, 165, 168, 169, 176, 182, 216, 217, 270, 461, 482, *also see* Add.; X. 96, 139, 202, 205, 214, 216, 369, *also see* Add.; XI. 88, 173, 174, 247, 248, 317, 327, 328; XII. 120, 223; XIII. 164; XIV. 205, 206, 211
Account of Examination before the Committee of Council, IX. 149
Advice to the Painter, IX. 148, 155
Alma: or the Progress of the Mind, IX. 152, 154
Answer to the Report of the Committee of Secrecy, IX. 149
Better Answer to Cloe Jealous, IX. 156
Carmen Seculare, IX. 149, 155
Cloe Hunting, IX. 156, 159
Dialogues of the Dead, IX. 153, 159, 160
Down-Hall, IX. 152, 155
English Ballad on the Taking of Namur, IX. 148, 155
English Padlock, IX. 155
Epistle to Fleetwood Shephard, IX. 148
Epistle to Lord ——, IX. 155
Erle Robert's Mice, IX. 151
Essay upon Learning, IX. 158, 159
Essay upon Opinion, IX. 159
Essays, IX. 153
Fable from Phaedrus, IX. 151
First and Second Hymns of Calliomachus, IX. 157
Georgics, The, IX. 157
Hans Carvel, IX. 155
Henry and Emma, IX. 153, 157
Hind and the Panther Transvers'd to the

Prior, Matthew
Story of the Country Mouse and the City Mouse (with Montagu), viii. 48, 404, 410, 411; ix. 147, 159
History of His Own Time, ix. 147, 217
Hymn to the Sun, ix. 148
Jinny the Just, ix. 156, 159
Journal at the Court of France, ix. 149
Journey to Copt-Hall, ix. 156
Letter to...Miss Margaret-Cavendish-Holles-Harley, ix. 153, 156
Letter to Monsieur Boileau Despréaux, ix. 155
'Noble lovely little Peggy,' xi. 347
Nut-brown Maid, The, ix. 152
Ode, An, ix. 147
Ode...to the Memory of...Colonel George Villiers, ix. 150
Ode Humbly Subscrib'd to the Queen, ix. 151
Ode presented to the King, ix. 148
Ode presented to the Queen, ix. 157
Orange, ix. 148
Picture of Seneca, ix. 147
Prelude to a Tale from Boccace, ix. 157
Satire on the Modern Translators, ix. 147
'Saunt'ring Jack and Idle Joan,' ix. 156
Secretary, The, ix. 148, 155
Seeing the Duke of Ormond's Picture, ix. 155
Session of the Poets, ix. 147, 155
Solomon on the Vanity of the World, ix. 143, 152, 154, 157
To a Child of Quality, ix. 156
To Cloe Weeping, ix. 156
To the Bishop of Rochester, ix. 148
To the Countess of Exeter, ix. 147, 149
To the King, ix. 148
Translation of an Epitaph upon Glanville, Bishop of Rochester, ix. 158
Two Riddles, ix. 151
Written in...Mezeray's History of France, ix. 150, 156
Prior, Melton, xiv. 534
Prior, Samuel, ix. 146
Prior park, Bath, x. 29
Priscian, i. 114, 118, 185, 210; ii. 360, 363, 366
Priscus, i. 20
Prison tracts, iv. 529; vii. 515
Prisoner, the, in *The Daunce and Song of Death*, iii. 87
Pritchard, Andrew (1804–1882), xiv. 298, 563
Pritchard, Hannah (1711–1768), xi. 261
Prithevi Raj, king of Delhi, xiv. 342
Private Wealth, in *Kynge Johan*, v. 65
Privy Malice, in *The Passetyme of Pleasure*, ii. 226, 234
Priwen or Pridwen, Arthur's ship, i. 248, 251
Proast, Jonas, viii. 475
Probationary Odes, x. 239; xi. 34, 36, 40
Probert, William (1790–1870), xiv. 201
'Probus,' xiv. 514
Probyn, John Webb, xiv. 513
Processus Talentorum, v. 19
Proclus, viii. 289
Procne, iii. 343
Procopius, i. 26
Procrustes, viii. 165
Procter, Adelaide Anne (1825–1864), xiii. 508, 542; *The Message*, xiii. 178
Procter, Bryan Waller (*pseud.* Barry Cornwall) (1787–1874), xi. Add.; xii. 115, 129–130 (main entry), 201, 407, 421, 433, 437, 438; xiii. 178, 469, 515; xiv. 200; *Sit down, sad soul*, xii. 130; *Song for Twilight*, xii. 130
Proctor, Ellen A., xiii. 496
Proctor, John, iii. 531
Proctor, Robert George Collier (1868–1903), xii. 523; *Bibliographical Essays*, xii. 369; *Index of Early Printed Books*, xii. 369; *The Printing of Greek in the Fifteenth Century*, xii. 369
Proctor, Thomas (*fl.* 1578–1584), iii. 190; *Pretie Pamphlets or Proctor's Precepts*, iii. 190
Prodigal Son, story of the, iii. 360
Prodigal Son, The, v. 108, 412
Prodigal Son, the Dutch Latin comedies of, iv. 320
Prodigal Son plays, v. 101, 109 ff., 410, 412
Prodromos, Theodore (Hilarion), iv. 249; v. 5
Prognostications, iv. 534
Progress of Man, The, xi. 41
Prologues and epilogues, collections of, x. 441
Prometheus, ii. 79
Prometheus, in *Mercury Vindicated*, vi. 358
Prometheus, in Shelley's poem, xii. 64 ff.
Prometheus, in *The Lords' Masque*, vi. 353
Promptorium Parvulorum. *See* Geoffrey the Grammarian
Promptorium Parvulorum sive Clericorum, xii. 519
Propertius, xii. 489, 490
Proserpine, vi. 313; xii. 339; xiii. 183
Proserpine, in *The Merchant's Tale*, ii. 184
Prosody of Old and Middle English before Chaucer, i. 372 ff., 480
Prosody from Chaucer to Spenser, iii. 273 ff., 525
Prosody of the 17th century, viii. 222 ff., 447 ff.
Prosody of the 18th century, xi. 446
Prosody of the 19th century, xiii. 225 ff., 511 ff.
Prosper, i. 75, 76
Prospero, in *The Rambler*, x. 172
Prospero, in *The Tempest*, v. 206, 207, 214; vii. 71; viii. 9; xii. 220
Pross, Miss, in *A Tale of Two Cities*, xiii. 332
Protagon (*i.e.* Henri IV), in *Euphormio*, iv. 256
Protasius, i. 75
Protesilaus, i. 279, 470
Protesilaus, in Wordsworth's *Laodamia*, xi. 107
Protestant drama, vi. 374

Protestant Post Boy, IX. 13, 432
Protestantism, VII. 304 ff.
Proteus, in *The Two Gentlemen of Verona*, III. 268; VI. 157; VIII. 126
Prothero, Sir George Walter, XII. 429, 520; XIV. 92, 497
Prothero, Rowland Edmund, V. 352; X. 299, 509; XII. 385, 386, 388, 397, 429, 470, 478
Proud Beauty, in *Robin Conscience*, III. 97
Proude Wyves Paternoster, The, III. 90, 97, 487
Proudies, the (Trollope's), XIII. 422, 424
Prout, father. *See* Mahony, Francis Sylvester
Prout, Samuel (1783–1852), *Sketches in Flanders and Germany*, XIV. 149
Prout, William (1785–1850), XIV. 558
Provençal legends, I. 115
Provençal poetry, X. 219; XIII. 211
Provençal version of Boethius, I. 99
Provence, V. 11, 49; X. 221
Proverbs, Old English, I. 363. *See, also, Hendyng* and *Alfred*
Prowse, William Jeffery ('Nicholas,' 1836–1870), XIII. 163, 508; *The City of Prague*, XIII. 162
Prudentia, in *The Tatler*, IX. 34
Prudentius, I. 75, 76; *Psychomachia*, I. 75; V. 51, 59
Prudentius, in *The Floating Island*, VI. 325
Prue, in Congreve's *Love for Love*, VIII. 150, 152, 161
Prusias, king of Bithynia, in *Believe as you List*, VI. 148
Prussia, X. 466; XIII. 19; XIV. 382, 383, 416, 419
Prussian army, the, XIII. 282
Prussian order of merit, XIII. 20
Prussian protestantism, XII. 260
Prussian *Realgymnasium*, XIV. 424
Pryme, George (1781–1868), XIV. 602
Prynne, William (1600–1669), IV. 306, 513, 518; VI. 204, 326, 387, 391, 401, 403, 406, 409, 495, 496; VII. 160, 197, 208, 352, 441, 446, 459, 498, 515; VIII. 67, 319, 469; IX. 348
  Animadversions on the Fourth Part of Coke's Institutes, VIII. 320
  Histrio-Mastix, V. 343, 372; VI. 40, 262, 391, 392, 403 ff.; VII. 145, 207, 313, 433
  Mr William Prynne, his defence of Stage-Playes or a Retraction of his former book, VI. 408
  The Republican and others Spurious good Old Cause briefly and truly anatomised, VII. 383
Pryor, Mrs, in Charlotte Brontë's *Shirley*, XIII. 409
Pryor, William, VII. 515
'Psalmanazar, George' (1679?–1763), IX. 498
Psalms, II. 14, 46, 318, 359, 502. *See, also, under* Bible
Psalms, Old English versions, I. 106, 147, 437, 438, 444; *Northern Psalter*, I. 341
Psalters, II. 318, 365
  Early English, I. 444
  Hampole's, II. 46, 47
  Old French, II. 420, 508
Psellus, in Lyly's *Euphues*, IV. 523
Pseudo-Kallisthenes, I. 135
Pseudo-Melito, I. 75
Psyche, XIII. 206; XIV. 311
Psyche, in Keats's *Ode to Psyche*, XII. 90
Psyche, in *Lingua*, VI. 314, 315
Psyche, in *Loves Maistresse*, VI. 103
Psyche et Filii ejus, VI. 486
Ptolemy and the Ptolemaic system, I. 213; II. 362, 366; III. 153, 156, 425; VIII. 282, 283, 350, 352; XIV. 579
Public Advertiser, The, X. 305, 400 ff., 479, 525; XI. 402
Public Ledger, X. 205, 208
Public Register, The, XI. 324
Public School Latin Primer, The, XIV. 413
Public Schools, principal (prior to 1650), VII. 492
Public Schools act (1868), XIV. 422
Public Schools commission, XIV. 421
Publick Oppression, in *Ane Pleasant Satyre*, III. 127, 128
Publius Cornelius, in *The Play of Lucrece*, V. 100
Publius Syrus, IX. 525; X. 471
Puca, the Irish, XIV. 307
Pucell, La Bel, in *The Passetyme of Pleasure*, II. 225, 226, 229, 232, 234
Puck, in *A Midsummer Night's Dream*, V. 160, 183; XIV. 307
Puck-Hairy, in *Love Restored*, VI. 370
Puck-Hairy, in *The Sad Shepherd*, VI. 371
Puckle, James (1667?–1724), IX. 479
Pudicitia, in *Psychomachia*, V. 51
Pueriles Confabulalunculae, VII. 315
Puff, in Sheridan's *Critic*, XI. 272
Pug, in *The Divell is an Asse*, VI. 24
Pugh, E. W., XIII. 544
Pughe, William Owen (1759–1835), XII. 518
Pugin, Augustus Charles (1762–1832), XII. 508; XIV. 222
Pugliano, Giovanni Pietro, IV. 149
Pui, the (a fourteenth century association), II. 428
Pulcheria, in *The Emperor of the East*, VI. 163
Pulci, Luigi, XII. 51, 52, 56; *Morgante Maggiore*, XII. 35
Pullen, Robert (d. 1147?), I. 185, 456; *Sententiarum Libri Octo*, II. 342
Pulling, F. S., XIV. 511
Pulpit, the English, from Fisher to Donne, IV. 224 ff., 490 ff.
Pulteney, David, IX. 220
Pulteney, Miss, IX. 165
Pulteney, William, earl of Bath (1684–1764), IX. 88, 162, 219, 220, 223, 224, 250 ff., 433, 491; X. 452; XI. 174, 248, 350, 352, 358; XIII. 239; *Seasonable Hints*, X. 389, 522

Pulton, Andrew (1654–1710), VIII. 305, 462
Pulton, Ferdinando (1536–1618), VIII. 46
Punch, X. 162; XIII. 162, 279, 282, 284, 294; XIV. 196, 235 ff., 548, 549
Punch and Judy, II. 385
Punch in London, XIV. 236
Punchinello, XIV. 236
Pundler, The, in *Lichtounis Dreme*, II. 278
Punic war, the second, XII. 303
Punic wars, the, IV. 62, 64
Puntarvolo, in Jonson's *Every Man out of his Humour*, X. 50
Punter, Mr, of St John's, Cambridge, VI. 397
Purcell, E. S., XII. 454, 458; *Life of Ambrose de Lisle*, XII. 276
Purcell, Francis, XIII. 555
Purcell, Henry (1658?–1695), VIII. 30, 395, 397, 428, 437; IX. 148; X. 433; *Dido and Aeneas*, VIII. 135; *Lilliburlero*, VIII. 96
Purcell, John, XIII. 142
Purchas, Samuel (1575?–1626), IV. 79, 85, 90 ff., 101, 103, 107, 460; XIV. 332, 333
  Hakluytus Posthumus, or Purchas his Pilgrimes, IV. 91, 92, 99, 398, 408
  Purchas his Pilgrim; Microcosmus or the Historie of Man, IV. 91
  Purchas his Pilgrimage, IV. 91
  Relation of a Voyage to Guiana...Performed by Robert Harcourt, The, IV. 97
Purfoote, Thomas, IV. 22, 384, 437
Purgatorio, The, X. 361
Purgatory of St Patrick, I. 191, 474
Puritan, The, IV. 360
Puritane Or The Widdow of Watling-streete, The, IV. 360; V. 236, 238, 254, 255, 442, 444; VI. 62
Puritane set forth in his lively Colours, A, VII. 384
Puritanism, VII. 158, 305, 370
Purley, XI. 400
Purnell, Thomas (1834–1889), XII. 435
Purser, Louis Claude, XII. 338
Pursuits of Literature, The, XII. 364
Purvey, John (1353?-1428?), II. 61; *Regimen Ecclesiae*, II. 61; translation of the Bible, II. 61, 62, 285, 442; III. 45; IV. 38
Purvis, David L., XIV. 553
Puschkin, XII. 395
Pusey, Edward Bouverie (1800–1882), XII. 253, 254, 261 ff. (main entry), 271 ff., 454, 457, 458, 462, *also see* Add.; XIII. 168
  Commentary on the Minor Prophets, XII. 341
  Entire Absolution of the Penitent: A Sermon, XII. 263
  Lectures on the Prophet Daniel, XII. 341
  Spiritual Letters, XII. 264
  Thoughts on the Benefits of the System of Fasting, XII. 258
Puseyite, a, XIV. 198
Puteanus, VII. 113
Putney, IX. 290, 308, 324 ff.; X. 299
Puttenham, George (d. 1590) or Richard (1520?–1601?), *Arte of English Poesie*, III. 180, 207, 269, 295, 302 ff., 450, 526; IV. 21, 23, 24, 52, 113, 114, 123; VII. 263, 271; XI. 248
Puysieu, de, IV. 257
Pwyll, prince of Dyved, I. 252
Pye, Henry James (1745–1813), XII. 133
  Aelfored, XII. 128, 422
  Commentary illustrating the Poetics of Aristotle, XII. 128
  Comments on the commentators of Shakespeare, XII. 128
  Summary of the duties of a J.P., XII. 128
Pyeboard, George, in *The Puritan*, IV. 360; V. 255
Pyke, in *Nicholas Nickleby*, XIII. 317
Pylades, I. 314; X. 249
Pym, in Browning's *Strafford*, XIII. 59, 67
Pym, Horace N., XIV. 502
Pym, John (1584–1643), V. 345; VII. 147, 441; IX. 258; XIV. 91
Pyne, William Henry (*pseud.* Ephraim Hardcastle, 1769–1843), XIV. 545; *Royal Residences*, XIV. 222; *Wine and Walnuts*, XIV. 222
Pynson, Richard (d. 1530), II. 161, 210, 319 ff., 326, 329 ff.; III. 56, 57, 59, *also see* Add.; IV. 400
Pyramus, in *A Midsummer Night's Dream*, V. 285; VI. 207, 316
Pyramus and Thisbe, in Sandys's *Ovid*, VII. 50
Pyrenees, the, XIII. 369; XIV. 251
Pyrenees, peace of the, IX. 226, 228
Pyrford, IV. 202
Pyrgopolinices, V. 105
Pyrocles, in Sidney's *Arcadia*, III. 352
Pyrrhus, II. 106
Pyrrye, C., *The prayse and disprayse of women*, III. 486
Pythagoras, VIII. 278, 282; IX. 515, 527
Pythagoras, in Sandys's translation of Ovid's *Metamorphoses*, VII. 5
Pythagorean doctrines, X. 103
Pythagorean numbers, VIII. 67
Pythagorism, VII. 376

'Q,' *pseud.* *See* Jerrold, Douglas William
'Quack Maurus' (Sir Rich. Blackmore), in Dryden's *Secular Masque*, VIII. 32
Quadragesms, VIII. 313
Quadratus, in *What You Will*, VI. 43
Quadrio, Francisco, V. 289
Quadripartitus, VIII. 310, 465
Quadrivium, the, II. 229, 230, 359, 362, 366; VII. 320
Quaker *Journals*, VIII. 103
Quaker literature, XII. 53
Quakers. *See* Society of Friends
Qualmsick, in *Pompey the Little*, IX. 408
'Quantification of the Predicate, the,' XIV 9
Quare of Ielusy, The, II. 91

Quaritch, Bernard (1819–1899), XII. 523; *General Catalogue*, XII. 368
Quarles, Francis (1592–1644), IV. 434; VII. 30, 45 ff. (main entry), 83, 153, 169, 176, 403, 513; VIII. Add.
Argalus and Parthenia, III. 355
Divine Fancies, VII. 46
Emblems, VII. 47; XIII. 52
Enchiridion, IV. 162
False World, thou ly'st, VII. 47
Feast for Wormes, A, VII. 46
World's a Theater, The, VII. 47
Quarll, Philip, XI. 373, 489
Quarterly Journal of Education, The, XIV. 409
Quarterly Journal of Microscopical Science, XIV. 289, 566
Quarterly Review, The, X. 270; XI. 40, 157, 162, 166, 393; XII. 141, 142, 149 ff. (main entry), 162, 163, 193, 194, 199, 288, 302, 364, 429; XIII. 230, 415, 467; XIV. 55, 82, 107, 115, 118, 141, 233, 314, 322, 403, 598, 600, 608
Quarterly reviewer (Keats's), VII. 75
Quater Brailes, the, III. 190
Quatre derniers choses, II. 312, 313
Quatrefoil of Love, The, II. 441
Quattuor novissimis, De, II. 313
Quebec, XIV. 360
Queen, The, XIV. 201
Queen Eleanor's Confession, II. 144
Queen of Portugal, ship, X. 35
'Queen of the Blues,' XI. 346
Queene, The, or the Excellency of her sex, VI. 449
Queene Elizabethe's Academy, XI. 368
Queen's company, the, V. 136; VI. 245 ff., 249, 262, 277
Queen's Crawley, in Thackeray's *Vanity Fair*, XIII. 286
Queen's university, Ireland, XIV. 417
Queensberry, duchess of. *See* Douglas, Catherine
Queensberry, duke of. *See* Douglas, Charles
Queensland, XIV. 368, 369
'Quene of Evene,' IV. 462, 463
Quentin Durward, II. 96
Querelle des femmes, VIII. 59
Querenghi, Antonio, IV. 259
Querolus, VI. 26
Quesnay, François, *Maximes générales*, X. 336; *Tableau économique*, X. 336
Questions concerning Liberty, Necessity, and Chance, The, VII. 288
Quevedo, IX. 277; *Visions*, IX. 3, 274, 418
Quha hes gud malt, and makis ill drynk, II. 279
Quhen Flora had ourfret the firth, II. 283
Quhy sowld nocht Allane honorit be? II. 279
Quia amore langueo, II. 426; III. 283
Quick, John (1748–1831), XI. 262
Quick, Robert Herbert (1831–1891), XIV. 602, 608
Quickly, Dame, XII. 438
Quickset, Sir Harry, in *The Tatler*, IX. 46, 50
Quicksilver, Francis, in *Eastward Hoe*, VI. 172
Quiggin, Edmund Crosby, XIV. 306, 307; 'Irish Influence on English Literature,' XIV. 307
Quignon, cardinal, III. 31
Quiller-Couch, Sir Arthur Thomas, XIII. 486, 497; XIV. 526
Quiller-Couch, Lillian Mary, IX. 574
Quillinan, Edward (1791–1851), XII. 422
Quilp, Daniel, in *The Old Curiosity Shop*, XIII. 319
Quilter, Harry, XIII. 568, 572, *also see* Add.
Quin, Edwin R. W. Wyndham, 3rd earl of Dunraven (1812–1871), XII. 509; XIV. 328, 568
Quin, James (1693–1766), X. 95, 96, 114, 264; XI. 258, 284, 454
Quinault, P., VIII. 17, 134
Quiney, Judith. *See* Shakespeare, Judith
Quiney, Thomas (*fl.* 1616), V. 219
Quinlan, M. A., XIII. 515
Quinte Essence, Book of, II. 427
Quintessence, queen, in Rabelais, IX. 106
Quintilian, II. 366; III. 23, 290, 294, 420, 434; IV. 348; VI. 9; VII. 261, 272; VIII. 58; XII. 220, 326, 487, *also see* Add.; XIV. 453
Quintus, in Owen's *Epigrammata*, IV. 265
Quintus Calaber, XIII. 478
Quintus Fabius, V. 123
Quintus Smyrnaeus, XII. 331
Quinze joyes de mariage, Les. *See* Sale, Antoine de la
Quiros, Pedro Fernandez de, IV. 101
Quisquilius, in *The Rambler*, X. 172
Quixote, Don, X. 41, 51, 52; XIV. 218
'Quixote in petticoats,' IX. 30
Quiz (*pseud.*), XIV. 545
Quod-bonum-est-tenete, in *Piers the Plowman*, II. 21

R. B. (? Richard Bower), *Apius and Virginia*, V. 63 ff., 396; VI. 284, 285
R. B. E., XIII. 466
R. C., *The Times Whistle*, IV. 333, 516, 520
R. C., *Mercurius Civicus*, VII. 349, 350; *The Weekly Intelligencer of the Commonwealth*, VII. 350; *The Kingdomes Weekly Intelligencer*, VII. 349, 353, 354
R. L. *See* Linche
'R. S., of the Inner Temple, Gentleman,' IV. 116, 467
R. S., *Foure-fould Meditation*, IV. 130
R. T., *The Opinion of Witchcraft Vindi cated*, VII. 395, 507
R. W. See under *Tancred and Gismund*
R. W. *See* Wilson, Robert
R. W. (1643), VII. 385
Rab (Dr John Brown's), XIV. 160
Rabanus of Mainz (Rabanus Maurus), I. 81; IV. 418
Rabbards, Ralph, II. 211
Rabbett, VII. 316

Rabelais, François, II. 94, 103, 257; III. 94, 151, 328, 453, 485; IV. 14, 246, 248, 321, 326, 533; VII. 256; VIII. 67 ff., 72, 77, 166, 372, 407; IX. 106, 263, 264, 270 ff.; X. 34, 50, 53; XI. 288; XII. 123, 168; *Gargantua*, IV. 8, 414; VIII. 59; IX. 267; *Pantagruel*, IV. 8, 353, 527; VIII. 59, 66, 385
Rabshakeh, in *Ezechias*, VI. 298
Raby, earl, in Hannah More's *Percy*, XI. 274
Raby, J. T., *Bi-centenary of the Birth of Johnson*, X. 161, 180
Racedown, Dorsetshire, XI. 99
Rachael, in Dickens's *Hard Times*, XIII. 329
Rachel, Elisa, XIII. 410
Racine, Jean, V. 202, 292, 293; VIII. 14, 27, 31, 133, 134, 376, 422, 435, 483; X. 86, 444; XII. 47, 381
  Achilles, VIII. 181
  Andromaque, VIII. 187, 373; IX. 166, 183; X. 69
  Athalie, VIII. 165
  Bajazet, X. 221
  Bérénice, VIII. 181, 182
  Britannicus, X. 118 ff.
  Iphigénie, X. 69, 221
  Mithridate, VIII. 22
  Phaedra and Hippolitus, VIII. 181
  Phèdre, IX. 103
Racine, Louis, V. 289
Radcliff, Ralph (1519?–1559), V. 103
Radcliffe, Alexander (*fl.* 1669–1696), IV. 18; VIII. 403; IX. 272, 500; *Ovid Travestie*, IX. 259; *The Ramble*, IX. 259, 263
Radcliffe, Ann (1764–1822), I. 279; XI. 286, 300 ff. (main entry), 304, 306, 464; XII. 58, 249; XIII. 420
  Castles of Athlin and Dunbayne, XI. 301
  Gaston de Blondeville, XI. 301
  Hazel Tree, The, XI. 301
  Italian, The, XI. 302, 303
  Letters, XI. 301
  Mysteries of Udolpho, XI. 300, 302, 303; XII. 235; XIII. 264
  Poems, XI. 301
  River Dove, The, XI. 301
  Romance of the Forest, XI. 302
  St Albans Abbey, XI. 301
  Sicilian Romance, XI. 301
Radcliffe, Elizabeth, daughter of the 3rd earl of Sussex, VI. 347
'Radcliffe, Dr John,' in *The Tatler*, IX. 34
Radcliffe, Nicholas (*fl.* 1368–1396), II. 442
Radcliffe, Richard, XIV. 595
Radford, D., XIII. 498
Radigund, in *The Faerie Queene*, III. 231, 236
Radirobanes, in *Argenis*, IV. 258, 259
Radley school, XIV. 414
Radnors, the, in Meredith's *One of Our Conquerors*, XIII. 443 ff., 448
Radway, X. 272
Radwinter, Essex, III. 321; V. 357
Rae J., *Life of Adam Smith*, X. 335
Rae, Peter (1671–1748), IX. 565
Rae, W. Fraser, XI. 266, 454, 456
Rae press at Kirkbride and Dumfries (1711–1720), XI. 470
Raeburn, Sir Henry (1756–1823), XI. 442
Raffaelle Sanzio. *See* Raphael
Raffles, Sir Thomas Stamford (1781–1826), XIV. 288, 563
Rafflesia, XIV. 288
Ragau, in *Jacob and Esau*, V. 112
Raglan, lord. *See* Somerset, lord Fitzroy James Henry
Ragley, near Alcester, VIII. 280; X. 271
Ragman Roll, II. 499, 501
Ragnar Lodbrok, X. 221, 222, 224, 227
Ragnell, in *Wedding of Sir Gawain*, I. 312
Rahab, in Blake's *Four Zoas*, XI. 196, 197
Rahere, V. 26
Raikes, Elizabeth, XIV. 599
Raikes, Jack (George Meredith's), XIII. 447
Raikes, Robert (1735–1811), XIV. 389
Raikes, Thomas (1777–1848), XIV. 505
Rainbow, the, in George Eliot's *Silas Marner*, XIII. 393
Raine, James (1791–1858), XII. 354, 512
Raine, John, XII. 354, 512
Rainham, Essex, X. 393
Rainolde, Richard, *Foundation of Rhetorike*, III. 432, 553
Rainolds or Reynolds, John (1549–1607), IV. 235, 236, 494; VI. 303, 319, 324, 472; VII. 309, 310, 317, 484, 489; *De Idolatria ecclesiae Romanae*, IV. 408; *Th'Overthrow of Stage-Playes*, VI. 398, 399, 496
Rainolds, William (1544?–1594), VII. 309, 485
Rainsford, lady Anne. *See* Goodere
Rainsford, Sir Henry, IV. 174
Rait, Robert Sangster, IX. Add.
Rajputana, XIV. 335
Ralegh, Sir Carew (1550?–1625?), IV. 55
Ralegh, Carew (1605–1666), VII. 447
Ralegh, Sir Walter (1552?–1618), III. 189, 212, 229, 233, 234, 272, 303; IV. 45, 51–65 (main entry), 67, 75, 78, 81, 85, 86, 88, 94, 103, 114, 117, 160, 164, 299, 450 ff.; V. 224, 338, 347; VI. 5; VII. 75, 190, 222, 271, 305, 306, 366, 440, 454; IX. 351, 537; X. 303; XII. 427
  Arts of Empire, The, IV. 55
  Breviary of the History of England, under William I (attributed to), IV. 55
  Cabinet Council, The, IV. 55, 64
  Cynthia, IV. 53
  Discourse on War in General, IV. 65
  Discovery of the large...Empire of Guiana, IV. 56
  History of the World, The, IV. 54, 58 ff.; VII. 433; IX. 146, 357
  Lie, The, IV. 54, 124
  Like Hermit Poor, IV. 54, 65
  Observations concerning the Royal Navy and Sea Service, IV. 58, 65
  Pilgrimage, The, IV. 54
  Prerogative of Parliaments, The, IV. 64
  Relation of the Cadiz Action, A, IV. 57

Ralegh, Sir Walter
Remains of Sir Walter Ralegh, The, IV. 65
Report...of the Fight about the Isles of the Açores this last summer, IV. 56
'Shepherd, what's love I pray thee tell,' IV. 109, 124
Steel Glass, In commendation of the, IV. 52
To-day a man, To-morrow none, IV. 65
Trade and Commerce, IV. 65
Vision upon this conceit of the Faery Queene, III. 272
War with Spain, A, IV. 65
Raleigh, Sir Walter (1861–1922), X. 418, 421; XI. 410, 433, 459, *also see* Add.; XII. 399, 405, 447; XIII. 491, 558; XIV. 526, 594; *Johnson on Shakespeare,* X. 181; *Six Essays on Johnson,* X. 184
Ralph, earl of Norwich, I. 141
Ralph, James (1705?–1762), X. 23; XI. 467; *The case of Authors by Profession,* X. 204
Ralph, Julian, XIV. 532
Ralph, in *Rauf Coilȝear,* II. 125 ff.
Ralph of Coggeshall (*fl.* 1207), I. 175, 449
Ralph of Diceto (d. 1202?), I. 159, 160, 173, 175, 188, 449
Ralpho, the squire, in *Hudibras,* VIII. 67, 70 ff., 76
Ram, William, *Rams little Dodeon,* IV. 374, 542
Ramah, in *Davideis,* VII. 66
Rámáyan of Válmíki, The, XII. 502
Rāmāyana, the, XII. 343, 502
Rambler, The, XIV. 118
Rambouillet, Hôtel de, VII. 391
Rambouillet, Mme de, IV. 338; IX. 37
Rameses II, XII. 487
Ramillies, IX. 151
Rampain, Zechariah, VII. 223
Ramsay, A., XIV. 613
Ramsay, Allan (1686–1758), I. 290; II. 95, 267, 269; IX. 361 ff., 366 ff. (main entry), 379, 438, 567; X. 110; XI. 144, 205, 209, 211, 212, 215 ff., 221, 228, 231, 338
Evergreen, The, II. 479; IX. 369, 567; X. 226; XI. 204, 217
Gentle Shepherd, The, IX. 161, 368; XI. 224, 237
Last Speech of a Wretched Miser, IX. 366, 367
Lochaber no more, IX. 368
Lucky Simpson's Last Advice, IX. 367
Monk and the Miller's Wife, The, IX. 367
My Peggy is a young thing, IX. 368
Scribblers lashed, IX. 369
Tea-Table Miscellany, IX. 360, 364, 368, 369, 371, 567; X. 233; XI. 206, 218
Vision, The, IX. 367; XI. 217
Ramsay, Andrew (1574–1659), IX. 556
Ramsay, Andrew Michael (1686–1743), *Vie de Turenne,* IX. 213
Ramsay, James Andrew Brown, marquis of Dalhousie (1812–1860), XIV. 575
Ramsay, John, scribe, II. 109, 110, 449
Ramsay, Sir John, viscount Haddington (1580?–1626), VI. 346
Ramsay, Robert (*fl.* 1630), VII. 5
Ramsay or Ramesey, William (*fl.* 1645–1676), VII. 509
Ramsay, William (1806–1865), XII. 492
Ramsden, J., XIII. 558
Ramsey, Edward Bannerman (1793–1872), XIV. 505
Ramsey, dame Mary, VII. 338
Ramsey school, Hunts., VII. 342
Ramus, Petrus, III. 416, 424; VII. 141, 276, 277; *Dialectica,* IV. 275, 276
Ramusio, Giovanni Battista (Ramutius), IV. 69, 101, 442
Rand, Benjamin, IX. Add.
Rand, Theodore H., XIV. 582
Randal, in Lillo's *Fatal Curiosity,* X. 78
Randal, Lord, I. 300
Randall, Jack, pugilist, XIV. 227
Randall (Randolph), Thomas (1605–1635), IV. 517, 520
Randolf, earl of Chester, rimes of, II. 399; V. 320
Randolf's Hall, in *Awntyrs of Arthure,* II. 122
Randolph, Robert, brother of Thomas Randolph (1605–1635), VI. 476
Randolph, Sir Thomas, 1st earl of Moray (d. 1332), in *Bruce,* II. 105
Randolph, Thomas (1523–1590), III. 187
Randolph, Thomas (1605–1635), VI. 28, 212, 475, 476; VII. 4, 38, 317, 489
Amyntas or the Impossible Dowry, VI. 234, 366, 371
Aristippus, or, The Joviall Philosopher, VI. 232, 233, 325, 372
Conceited Pedler, The, VI. 232, 325
Eglogue to Mr Johnson, An, VI. 232
Jealous Lovers, The, VI. 232, 325
Muses Looking-Glasse, The, VI. 233, 234, 371
Randolph, Thomas (1701–1783), X. 307, 507; XIV. 593
Random, Roderick, in Smollett's novel, X. 37, 204
Rands, William Brighty (1823–1882), XI. 489; XIV. 164, 523
Chaucer's England, XIV. 163
'Great, wide, beautiful, wonderful world,' XIV. 163
Henry Holbeach, XIV. 163
Lilliput Lectures, XIV. 163
Lilliput Legends, XIV. 163
Lilliput Levee, XIV. 163
Lilliput Revels, XIV. 163
Tangled Talk, XIV. 163
Ranger, in Hoadly's *Suspicious Husband,* X. 87
Ranke, Frederick Heinrich, VII. 176
Ranke, Leopold von, IX. 207, 208, 213; XIV. 100; *History of England,* IX. 206; X. 295, 503; *History of the Popes,* XIV. 63
Rankins, William (*fl.* 1587–1601), IV. 323, 516, 518, 519; V. 312; *Mirrour of Monsters,* VI. 395, 496

Ransome, Arthur, xiv. 528
Ransome, Cyril, xiii. 466
Ranulf de Glanville. *See* Glanville
Ranulph, earl of Chester. *See* Randolf
Raoul le Fevre, *Recuyell of the Histories of Troy*, ii. 230, 311 ff.
Raper, Robert William, xiv. 208
Raphael, in Kingsley's *Hypatia*, xiii. 363
Raphael (Milton's), vii. 101
Raphael Sanzio, ix. 59; x. 130; xii. 172; xiii. 111; xiv. 99
Rapids, the, in Morton's *Cure for the Heartache*, xi. 281
Rapin, René de (1621–1687), viii. 374, 375, 449; *Réflexions sur la poétique d'Aristote*, viii. 374
Rapin de Thoyras, Paul de (1661–1725), vii. 268; ix. 140, 495; x. 279; *Histoire d'Angleterre*, ix. 235, 236; x. 280
Rare Triumphs of Love and Fortune, v. 117, 162, 413
Rare Willie drowned in Yarrow, ix. 371
Rashdall, Hastings, xiv. 469, 480; *Universities of Europe*, i. 202
Rashleigh, in Scott's *Rob Roy*, xii. 21, 26
Rask, Rasmus Christian, *Anglo-Saxon Grammar*, xii. 344
Rasor, in Vanbrugh's *Provok'd Wife*, viii. 162
Raspe, Rudolf Eric (1737–1794), x. 424; *Baron Munchausen*, xi. 492
Rastall, William (1601), vi. 290
Rastell, Elizabeth, sister of Sir T. More, wife of John Rastell, lawyer and printer, iv. 198; v. 90
Rastell, Elizabeth (afterwards wife of John Heywood), iv. 198; v. 90
Rastell, John (d. 1536), ii. 327; iv. 70, 198, 354, 546; v. 57, 99, 100, 103, 253; viii. 467; *Interlude of the Nature of the Four Elements*, v. 57
Rastell, William (1508?–1565), iii. 40; v. 90, 92, 95; viii. 467
Ratcliffe, iv. 238
Rate, David, ii. 449
Rathbone, Hannah Mary (1798–1878), xiii. 565; *Diary of Lady Willoughby*, xiii. 434
Rathery, J. B., xii. 525
Rathmell academy, x. 386
Rathmill, Yorkshire, ix. 393
Rathmore, D. R. P., lord, xiv. 510
Ratis Raving, ii. 449, 498
Ratisbon, iii. 155; viii. 137
Ratramnus, i. 75, 117, 120, 124
Ratsey, Gamaliel, The Life and Death of, iv. 530
'Rattlesnake,' ship, xiv. 296
Rattlin, Jack, in Smollett's *Roderick Random*, x. 37
Rattray, Sylvester (*fl.* 1650–1666), xii. 521
Rauf Coilȝear, i. 291, 470; ii. 112, 125, 280, 451, 501
Raunce, John, vii. 509
Rausch, Danish tale of, iii. 94
Ravaillac, in *Friar Rush*, vi. 53
Ravaillac, Francis, iv. 363
Ravenna, ii. 364; xii. 34, 35, 48 ff., 324
Ravenscroft, Edward (*fl.* 1671–1697), viii. 168, 420
Careless Lovers, The, viii. 140
Italian Husband, The, viii. 194
King Edward and Alfreda, viii. 194
London Cuckolds, viii. 140
Mamamouchi, or the Citizen Turned Gentleman, viii. 140
Titus Andronicus, Ravenscroft's adaptation of, viii. 120, 140
Ravenscroft, Thomas (1592?–1635?), iv. 113, 465
Ravenswood, in Scott's *Bride of Lammermoor*, xii. 23
Ravis, Christian (1613–1677), vii. 309, 491
Ravis, Thomas (1560?–1609), vii. 316
Rawley, William (1588?–1667), iv. 278, 284
Rawlidge, Richard, vi. 496; *A Monster lately found out and discovered or the Scourging of Tipplers*, vi. 400, 403
Rawlins, John (*fl.* 1622), vii. 449
Rawlins, Thomas (1620?–1670), vi. 458; *The Rebellion*, viii. 129, 440
Rawlins, T. J., xiv. 542
Rawlinson, George (1812–1902), xii. 316, 334, 477, 478, 499; *The History of Herodotus*, xii. 317
Rawlinson, Sir Henry Creswicke (1810–1895), xii. 316, 317, 342, 477, 499
Rawlinson, Richard (1690–1755), ix. 342, 353, 355, 530, 531, 533, 535, 537, 538; x. 355; *Natural History of Surrey*, ix. 351
Rawnsley, Hardwicke Drummond, xiii. 479, 558
Rawnsley, Willingham Franklin, xiii. 478
Raworth, widow, vii. 361
Ray, James (*fl.* 1745), ix. 563, 565
Ray, John (1627–1705), vii. 479; viii. 478, 479; ix. 412; xiv. 282, 563, 565; *The Wisdom of God*, x. 346, 514
Rayleigh, lord. *See* Strutt, John William
Raymond, iv. 98
Raymond (Haji Mustapha), xiv. 335, 579
Raymund of Pennaforte, i. 355
Raymundus, in *Kynge Johan*, v. 66
Rayne, in Aberdeenshire, ii. 103
Rayner, Edward, x. 387
Rayner, J., of the Inner Temple (1658), iv. 511
Rayner, John, x. 387
Reach, Angus Bethune (1821–1856), xiv. 545
Read, Charles Anderson, xiv. 573
Read, Meredith, *Historic Studies*, x. 301
Reade, A. L., *Johnsonian Gleanings*, x. 157; *The Reades of Blackwood Hill*, x. 157
Reade, Charles (1814–1884), xiii. 267, 268, 425 ff., 432, 458, 459, 516, 522, 565, 566
Autobiography of a Thief, The, xiii. 427
Christie Johnstone, xiii. 425

Reade, Charles
Cloister and the Hearth, The, XIII. 426, 428; XIV. 255
Drink, XIII. 425
Foul Play, XIII. 425, 427
Gold, XIII. 425
Good Fight, A, XIII. 428
Griffith Gaunt, XIII. 425, 426
Hard Cash, XIII. 426, 427
Hero and a Martyr, A, XIII. 427
It is never too late to mend, XIII. 425, 427
Jack of all Trades, XIII. 427
Love me Little, Love me Long, XIII. 426
Masks and Faces, XIII. 425
Peg Woffington, XIII. 425
Put Yourself in his Place, XIII. 425, 427
Terrible Temptation, A, XIII. 426, 427
Wandering Heir, The, XIII. 426
Woman Hater, A, XIII. 427
Reade, John, XIV. 582
Reade, William Winwood (1838–1875), XIV. 479, 553; *African Sketch-Book,* XIV. 254
Reader, The, XIV. 200
Reading, II. 342; V. 116; IX. 563; XI. 376; XIII. 427, 430
Reading, John (1588–1667), VII. 514
Real Life in London, XIV. 225, 545
Real Presence, doctrine of the, I. 154
Real Presence and the Rule of Faith, A Poem on the, VIII. 47
Reardon, in Gissing's *New Grub Street,* XIII. 460
Reason, in *Complaint upon Love to Reason,* III. 187
Reason, in *The Goldyn Targe,* II. 253
Reason, in *Hymenaei,* VI. 346
Reason, in *Mirour de l'Omme,* II. 140, 141
Reason, in *Nature,* V. 54
Reason, in *Piers the Plowman,* II. 10, 26, 27
Reasons humbly offered by the Company... of Upholders, IX. 132
Rebecca, in *Jacob and Esau,* V. 112
'Rebel, A' (Defoe's), IX. 19
Recarede, king, I. 105
Recklessness, in *Piers the Plowman,* II. 25, 26
Reclus de Moiliens, the *Charité* of, II. 140; the *Miserere* of, II. 140
Record, The, XII. 258
Record commission, XII. 357; XIV. 52, 67
Record office, XIV. 67, 82
Recorde, Robert (1510?–1558), III. 107, 425, 493, 494; IV. 460; *The Castel of Knowledge,* III. 425, 553
Recorder, the, in *The Returne from Pernassus,* VI. 313, 314
Recreation, in *The Playe of Playes and Pastimes,* VI. 392
Rectitudines Singularum Personarum, VIII. 310, 465
Recueil des Historiens des Gaules, X. 282
Reculver, XII. 347
Red Barn murder, the, XIV. 228
Red Book of Hergest, I. 249, 252, 263, 461
Red Cross Knight, in *The Faerie Queene,* II. 234; III. 232; VII. 173
Red Horse, vale of, X. 112
Red house, Bexley Heath, XIII. 119
Red Indians, the, XIV. 459
Red Lion, the, in George Eliot's *Janet's Repentance,* XIII. 387
Red Riding Hood, XI. 375
Red sea, IV. 30
Redcap, in *Looke about you,* V. 321
Redding, Cyrus (1785–1870), XI. 289, 459 XII. 410; XIV. 534
Rede, Sir Robert (d. 1519), II. 360
Rede, William (d. 1385), IV. 427
Rede lecture, XIV. 81
Redesdale, lord. *See* Mitford, John Freeman
Redford, John (*fl.* 1535), V. 57, 392
Redhouse, Sir James William (1811–1892), XII. 342, 504
Redi, Francesco, XII. 443
Redman, William, bishop of Norwich (d. 1602), III. 432
Redmond, in *Britannia's Pastorals,* IV. 157
Redresse, in *Magnyfycence,* III. 77
Reed, Arthur William, V. Add. 2
Reed, Isaac (1742–1807), V. 275, 277; VI. 296; VIII. 423; IX. 497; X. 442; XI. 453
Reed, Joseph (1723–1787), X. 40, 440
Reede, in *Arden of Feversham,* V. 241
Rees, A., XIV. 599
Rees, Thomas Mardy, XIII. 503
Rees's *Cambro-British Saints,* I. 262
Reeve, Anne (Restoration actress), VIII. 9
Reeve, Clara (1729–1807), X. 47, 424; XI. 464
Champion of Virtue, X. 61; XI. 300
Charoba, X. 300
Old English Baron, X. 61 ff.; XI. 300
Progress of Romance, XI. 300
Reeve, Henry (1813–1895), XII. 153, 426, 427; XIV. 114, 171, 503
Reeve, John (1608–1658), X. 377
Reeve, L., XIV. 560
Reeve, Richard (1642–1693), IX. 345
Reeves, Mr, in Pepys's *Diary,* VIII. 350
Reeves, William (1815–1892), XII. 518; XIV. 328, 571; *Ecclesiastical Antiquities of Down and Connor,* XII. 361
Refined Courtier, III. 438
Reflector, The, XII. 192, 193, 434, 437, 442
Reform act, XI. 50
Reform bill, XI. 58; XIII. 24, 262, 342, 347, 348, 357, 384, 397; XIV. 57, 125, 129, 414, 427
Reformation, in *Respublica,* V. 60
Reformation, Scottish, and the stage, VI. 374
Reformation and Renascence in Scotland, III. 138 ff., 500 ff.
Reformation literature in England, III. 25 ff., 471 ff., *also see* Add.
Regales Aphorismi (1650), VIII. 470
Regan, in *King Lear,* V. 169
Regan, Morice (*fl.* 1171), *History of Ireland,* VII. 211, 448
Regeln für Schauspieler, XI. 284

Regensburg, XIV. 306
Reggio, X. 119, 224
'Regina' (K. Philips's), VII. 88
Reginald of St Augustine's, Canterbury, I. 191, 456
Reginella, in *The Goblins*, VI. 239
Regiomontanus. *See* Müller
Registrum Omnium Brevium (1531), VIII. 467
Regnard, Jean-François, *Le Retour Imprévu*, X. 22, 417
Regnault, Elias, XIII. 465
Regnault, François, IV. 402, 421
Regrets, in *The Court of Love*, II. 221
Regula placitandi (1691), VIII. 469
Regulus, XI. 273
Regulus, in Alfred's *Boethius* and *Orosius*, I. 95, 100
Rehearsal, The (Leslie's), IX. 5
Reid, John (1808–1841?), XII. 523
Reid, Stuart Johnson, XIV. 509
Reid, Thomas (1710–1796), IV. 294; X. 345, 347 ff., 512, 514; XI. 76, 400; XIV. 9, 10, 37, 49, 393, 474
Essays on the Active Powers of Man, X. 348
Essays on the Intellectual Powers of Man, X. 348
Inquiry into the Human Mind, X. 348
Works, XIV. 7, 11
Reid, T. D. (d. 1624), IV. 550
Reid, Sir Thomas Wemyss (1842–1905), XIII. 506, 558, 560; XIV. 199, 505, 509, 534; *Charlotte Brontë*, XIII. 379
Reidpath MS., II. 475
Reitz, Francis W., XIV. Add. 8, 9; *Africaanse Gedigte*, XIV. 373; *Ver in de Wildernis*, XIV. 375
Relation...of the isle of England (an Italian's), II. 500
Relation of the Ten grand, infamous Traytors, A, VII. 388
Relations, VII. 344 ff., 348
Religion, in Carew's *Coelum Britannicum*, VII. 19
Religious Tract society, X. 203; XI. 362
Reliquiae Antiquae, Wright and Halliwell, I. 362, 365
Remarks on the Academic, IX. 414
Rembrandt van Ryn, XI. 12; XII. 172, 173
Remedies against Discontentment...from the writings of auncient philosophers, IV. 343, 524
Remedy of Love, The, II. 162
Remembrance, dame, in *The Dreme*, III. 117, 118
Remembrancia, VI. 381, 491
Remonstrant clergy, VIII. 330
Remus, Uncle, XIV. 314
Renan, Ernest, I. 253, 274; XIII. 99 ff., 458; XIV. 502; 'The Poetry of the Celtic Races,' XIII. 100
Renard, G., XII. 525
Renascence, Englishmen and the Classical, III. 1 ff., 466 ff.
Renauard the fox, I. 366
Renaud de Beaujeu, I. 284
Renfrewshire, IX. 364, 370, 559; X. 500; XI. 237
Renfrewshire, Harp of, XI. 443
Rengifo, Spanish critic, VII. 265
Rennell, James (1742–1830), XIV. 334, 579
Rennie, John (1761–1821), XIV. 381
Renouard, A. A., IV. 263
Renouf, Sir Peter le Page (1822–1897), XII. 500
Renton, Richard, XIII. 485, 544; XIV. 502
Renuchio, in *Gismond of Salerne*, V. 75, 76
'Repentance,' ship, IV. 77
Repentance, in *The Faerie Queene*, III. 239
Repentance, in *Piers the Plowman*, II. 12, 23
Repington, Philip (d. 1424), II. 442
Reply of Friar Daw Topias, II. 40, 432, 435
Reports of cases, VIII. 319
Repository of Arts, Literature, etc., XIV. 216
Repository Tracts, XI. 362
Representative, The, XIII. 353
Reproch, in *The Faerie Queene*, III. 239
Repton school, VII. 331, 493
Requests, master of, III. 16
Reresby, Sir John (1634–1689), VIII. 264 ff., 451; *Memoirs*, VIII. 264, 265; *Travels*, VIII. 265
Resch, Wolfgang, dialogues, III. 81
'Resolution,' ship, XI. 145
Respublica, IV. 513; V. 59, 124, 392
Restless, Tom, in Johnson's *Idler*, X. 178
Restoration, the, IV. 107 140, 228, 315, 421, 425
Restoration comedy, VI. 214
Restoration pamphlets, XI. 470
Resurrection, V. 39
Retines, Robert de. *See* Robert the Englishman
Retinues of the Great People, A Song against the, I. 370
Retrospective Review, The, XII. 346, 430
'Retters,' Rethel or Retiers, near Reims, II. 156
Returne from Pernassus, The. *See* Parnassus trilogy
Return of the Knight of the Post from Hell..., The, IV. 352
Retz, cardinal de, VII. 436
Reuchlin, Johann, III. 113; VII. 264; *De arte cabbalistica*, IV. 275; *De verbe mirifico*, VII. 370; *Henno*, V. 101
Reunert, Theodore, XIV. Add. 9
Revels, Documents relating to the Office of the, V. 478
Revels, Master of the, VIII. 423
Revels Accounts, V. 122
Revenge, goddess of, in *Locrine*, V. 239
Revenge, in *Jeronimo*, V. 160
'Revenge,' the, lord Sandwich's battleship, VIII. 202
'Revenge,' the, Sir Richard Grenville's ship, IV. 56, 376
Reverdies, V. 34
Revesby in Lincolnshire, V. 32, 33
Revett, Nicholas (1720–1804), XII. 499

Review, The (Defoe's), IX. 1, 4, 5, 10, 11, 13, 14, 34, 432
Reviews and magazines in the early years of the 19th century, XII. 425 ff.
Revue des deux Mondes, La, IX. 71; XIII. 71, 75
Rex Fabarum, VI. 294
Rex Humanitas, in *Ane Pleasant Satyre*, III. 124
Reyher, A., *Les Masques Anglais*, VI. 334, 335, 487
Reynard the Fox, I. 366, 479; II. 245, 313, 314, 332, 486; III. 494; XI. 334
Reynolds, chancellor, X. 382
Reynolds (clerk to Essex), VII. 343
Reynolds, Edward (1599–1676), VII. 329
Reynolds, Edward, of Nottingham, X. 387
Reynolds, Frederick (1764–1841), XI. 428, 458; XIII. 522; *The Dramatist*, XI. 281
Reynolds, G. F., VI. 265, 266, 270
Reynolds, George William McArthur (1814–1879), XIII. 566; XIV. 545; *Pickwick Abroad*, XIII. 319
Reynolds, Henry (*fl.* 1627–1632), III. 305; IV. 138, 169; VI. 490; *Mythomystes*, VII. 264, 273, 466
Reynolds, John (1621–1650), IV. 526; *God's Revenge against Murder*, VI. 199
Reynolds, John (1667–1727), X. 386
Reynolds, John Hamilton (1796–1852), XII. 70, 82, 89, 418, 422
Reynolds, Sir Joshua (1723–1792), X. 85, 157, 181, 207, 213, 215, 262, 263, 265 ff. (main entry), 268, 348, 461, 462, 470, 472, 473, 483, 494, *also see* Add.; XI. 32, 143, 326, 350, 353, 360, 364, 472; XII. 132, 166, 172; *Discourses*, X. 265 ff.; XI. 200, 432
Reynolds, Myra, IX. 168
Reynolds's Weekly Newspaper, XIV. 192
Reysby, Nicholas, II. 480
Rhadamanth, in *Locrine*, V. 240
Rhadamanthus, XII. 136
Rhampsinitus's Treasure Chamber (Herodotus), IX. 39
Rhé, isle of, IV. 293; VII. 5
Rheged, Urien's lordship of, I. 249
Rheims, VI. 311; X. 119
Rheims, council of, I. 185
Rheims, English college at, IV. 274
Rhenanus, Beatus, III. 41
Rhetoric, in *The Passetyme of Pleasure*, II. 225, 231
Rhetorique, land of, in *The Pilgrimage to Parnassus*, VI. 310
Rhind, Alexander Henry (1833–1863), XII. 512; *Thebes, its Tombs and their Tenants*, XII. 351
Rhind lectures in archaeology, XII. 351
Rhine, the, V. 6; VII. 20; XI. 302; XII. 33, 418; XIII. 443; XIV. 221
Rhineland, the, XIV. 294
Rhinwallon and his sons, XII. 514
Rhodalind, in D'Avenant's *Gondibert*, VII. 71
Rhode, in *Solymannidae*, VI. 301
Rhode island (America), IX. 281, 282
Rhodes, island of (Mediterranean), II. 111; VIII. 117; XII. 339
Rhodes (prompter at Blackfriars), VI. 262
Rhodes, Cecil, XIV. Add. 8, 9
Rhodes, Hugh (*fl.* 1550–1555), *Boke of Nurture*, III. 341; XI. 368
Rhodes, John (*fl.* 1660), VIII. 118, 121
Rhodes, William Barnes (1772–1826), XIII. 523
Rhodes, W. E., XIV. 75
Rhonabwy, Dream of, I. 253
Rhone, the, II. 123
Rhuddlan, X. 115
Rhuys, life of Gildas by a monk of, I. 65
Rhyme of Sir Launcelot Bogle, The, in *The Bon Gaultier Ballads*, XIII. 161
Rhys, Ernest, XII. 399, 401; XIII. 485
Rhys, Sir John, I. 250 ff., 254, 255, 273, 463
Rhys ap Tewdwr, I. 256
Riah, in *Our Mutual Friend*, XIII. 336
Ribemont, in *Edward the Black Prince*, XI. 450
Ricardo, in *The Coxcombe*, VI. 120, 133
Ricardo, David (1772–1823), X. 335; XI. 75, 399; XIV. 2 ff., 21, 22, 186, 407, 479; *Principles of Political Economy and Taxation*, XIV. 2
Riccaltoun, Robert (1691–1769), *Winter*, X. 94
Riccoboni, Louis or Lewis, V. 289; X. 442
Rice, James (1843–1882), XIII. 560
Rich, Anthony (1804–1891), XII. 412
Rich, Barnabe (1540?–1620?), III. 536; IV. 4, 18, 436, 460, 526, 527, 528, 531, 535, 540; V. 220, 358, 479; IX. 556
  Apolonius and Silla, VI. 305
  Dialogue, between Mercury and an English Souldier, etc., V. 360
  Don Simonides, III. 349
  Farewell to the Military Profession, V. 316
  Honesty of this Age, The, IV. 317, 526; V. 349, 358, 360
  New Description of Ireland, VI. 173
Rich, Charles, 4th earl of Warwick, VIII. 268
Rich, St Edmund, of Abingdon or Pontigny (1170?–1240), I. 205, 339, 343, 456
Rich, Sir Henry, earl of Holland (1590–1649), VII. 224
Rich, Jeremiah (d. 1660?), VIII. 243
Rich, John (1682?–1761), IX. 163; X. 39, 70, 71, 85, 211; XI. 258, 282; XIII. 264; XIV. 213
Rich, Mary, countess of Warwick (1625–1678), VIII. 453
  Autobiography, VIII. 268, 269
  Diary, VIII. 269
  Occasional Meditations, VIII. 269
  Rules for a Holy Life, VIII. 269
Rich, Penelope, lady Rich (1562?–1607), III. 254; VII. 54
Rich, Richard (*fl.* 1609–1610), IV. 460

Rich, Sir Robert, 1st earl of Warwick, III. 254
Rich, Sir Robert, 2nd earl of Warwick (1587–1658), VII. 454; VIII. 269
Rich Cabnit furnished with a Varietie of exquisite Discriptions, The, VI. 401
Rich Closet of Physical Secrets, A (1652), VII. 512
Richard, in *Richard Casteler*, III. 369
Richard I, in *Histoire de la Guerre Sainte*, II. 420
Richard I, king of England, I. 174 ff., 199, 337; III. 325; VI. 97; IX. 535
Richard I, History of King, I. 175
Richard II, A Poem on the Deposition of, ed. T. Wright, II. 35
Richard II, king of England, I. 322; II. 3, 35 ff., 55, 71, 134, 137, 144, 145, 153, 154, 157, 158, 170, 346; III. 195, 196, 337; IV. 137, 169, 182; V. 44; VI. 280, 330; VII. 211; IX. 222, 233, 535; X. 284, 287
Richard II, pre-Shakespearean, V. 83
Richard III, king of England, III. 196, 282, 314, 334, 335; VII. 443; VIII. 123; X. 85, 131, 291, 505
Richard III, in Shakespeare's play, XII. 171
Richard III, Garrick as, XI. 257
Richard III, History of, III. 17, 334, 335, 531
Richard III, W. H. W. Betty as, XI. 283
Richard (Fitznigel), bishop of London, *Dialogus de Scaccario*, IV. 309
Richard, prior of Hexham (*fl.* 1138–1154), I. 161, 450; *Acts of King Stephen and the Battle of the Standard*, I. 161, 163, 167, 168, 449
Richard, Sir, in Robin Hood legends, II. 416
Richard, 3rd duke of York (1411–1460), II. 302
Richard Coeur de Lion, I. 287, 307 ff., 317, 318, 399, 470; II. 308, 325
Richard Coeur de Lion, in *Looke about you*, V. 320
Richard Coeur de Lion, in *Robert, Earle of Huntington*, V. 318, 319
Richard Duke of Yorke, The True Tragedie of, V. 135, 153, 184, 220, 237, 238, 260, 398, 433
Richard of Almaigne, X. 233
Richard of Armagh. *See* FitzRalph
Richard of Bury (1281–1345), I. 183, 213, 214, 456; II. 362; *Philobiblon*, IV. 411, 414, 415
Richard of Cirencester (d. 1401?), IX. 540; XII. 488
Richard de Conyngton (d. 1330), I. 453
Richard of Cornwall, brother of Henry III, I. 368
Richard of Devizes (*fl.* 1189–1192), I. 159, 163, 173, 176, 449; II. 342, 488
Richard of Dover, I. 188
Richard L'Evêque, I. 184
Richard of Middleton (d. 1308), VII. 505
Richard of St Victor (d. 1173?); *Benjamin*, II. 327, 498
Richard the Englishman (Richard of Wendover, d. 1252), II. 365
Richard the Redeless, II. 3, 36, 432 ff.
Richard the Third, The True Tragedy of, IV. 393; V. 153, 185, 398
Richardes, Thomas, V. 110
Richards, John Morgan, XIII. 562
Richards, Nathaniel (d. 1652), VII. 413; *Messallina*, VI. 266, 268, 458
Richardson, of Stratford, V. 168
Richardson, Sir Benjamin (1828–1896), IX. 138
Richardson, David Lester (1801–1865), XIV. 579; *Literary Chit-Chat*, XIV. 337; *Literary Leaves*, XIV. 337; *Literary Recreations*, XIV. 337
Richardson, Fanny, in Le Fanu's story, XIII. 415, 416
Richardson, Frederika, XIII. 555, 558
Richardson, John (1796–1852), XIV. 581, 583; *Canadian Brothers, The*, XIV. 360; *Wacousta*, XIV. 359; *War of* 1812, *The*, XIV. 359
Richardson, Jonathan (1665–1745), IX. 70, 443, 448; XII. 172
Richardson, Joseph (1755–1803), XI. 35, 36, 391
Richardson, Mary (d. of Samuel R.), X. 12, 61
Richardson, Robert (1850–1901), XIV. 369, 587
Richardson, Samuel (*fl.* 1643–1658), X. 520
Richardson, Samuel (1689–1761), I. 319; VI. 82; IX. 144, 248, 475; X. 1 ff. (main entry), 30, 31, 43, 46 ff., 58, 61, 63, 64, 171, 201, 411 ff., 458, *also see* Add.; XI. 327, 358, 365, 468, 474; XII. 168, 231 ff.; XIII. 340, 421
Clarissa Harlowe, VIII. 196; IX. 245; X. 2, 7 ff., 15 ff., 29, 48, 57, 252, 273; XI. 265, 277, 356
Collection of the Moral and Instructive Sentiments, X. 11
Meditations collected from the Sacred Books, X. 12
Pamela, VI. 99; IX. 400; X. 3 ff., 14 ff., 17 ff., 24 ff., 48, 79, 84, 89, 273; XI. 325; XII. 235
Sir Charles Grandison, X. 9, 10, 15 ff., 252, 273; XII. 238
Richardson, Thomas (? 1584), III. 191
Richardson, Thomas (1828–1831), XIII. 516
Richardson, Sir Thomas (1569–1635), VIII. 319
Richborough, XII. 347
Richelieu, Armand-Jean Duplessis duc de, cardinal, IV. 258, 260; VII. 446; VIII. 371, 383; IX. 228
Riches, in *Piers the Plowman*, II. 20
Richey, Alexander George (1830–1883), XIV. 497
Richmond, IX. 251; X. 95, 102, 395; XI. 259, 364; XIII. 281

Richmond, duke of. *See* Lennox, Charles
Richmond, Legh (1772–1827), xii. 472; *The Dairyman's Daughter*, xii. 281
Richmond, Yorkshire, ii. 49
Richmond churchyard, xii. 419
Richmond Examiner, The, xiv. 326
Richmond forest, vi. 239
Richmond gardens, xiv. 286
Richmond hill, x. 101, 104
Richmondshire, xii. 514
Richter, Helene, xiii. 553; xiv. 528
Richter, Jean Paul Friedrich, x. 422; xii. 445; xiii. 4, 7 ff., 447, 465, 468
Rickets, J., *Byrsa Basilica*, vi. 300, 476
Rickett, A. Compton, xiii. 493
Rickman, John, xi. 167, 169; xii. 188, 433
Ridd, John, in *Lorna Doone*, xiii. 434
Riddell, James (1823–1866), xii. 492
Riddell, Robert (d. 1794), ix. 368
Riddell ms., ii. 474
Riddles, Old English, i. 49, 51, 60, 61, 428, 430; runes in, i. 12; Latin, i. 78
Riddles, books of, iii. 488
Rideal, Charles F., xiii. 544
Rider, John (1562–1632), iii. 555; vii. 486
Riderhood, in *Our Mutual Friend*, xiii. 336
Ridgeley, Thomas (1667?–1734), x. 384
'Ridings,' v. 34
Ridley, Annie E., xiv. 599
Ridley, Glocester, x. 136
Ridley, Nicholas (1500?–1555), bishop of London, iii. 38, 179, 213, 419, 432, 473; iv. 232, 234
Ridolfi conspiracy, iii. 401
Ridpath, George (d. 1726), ix. 15, 550; *The Flying Post*, ix. 5, 434
Ridpath, George (1717?–1772), ix. 554
Rievaulx. *See* Ailred of
Rievaulx abbey, iv. 421
Rigaud, in *Little Dorrit*, xiii. 317, 331
Rigby, in Disraeli's *Coningsby*, xii. 155; xiii. 349, 350
Rigby, Elizabeth. *See* Eastlake, lady
Rigg, James Harrison, xiii. 548
Right of Succession, Poem on the, viii. 92
Righteousness, in Anglo-Norman plays, v. 21
Riguelme, Don Francisco, xii. 439
Rigveda, the, xii. 343, 503
Riley, Thomas, vi. 476
Riming Poem, i. 62, 374, 428
Rimini, Francesca, xii. 395
Rimmer, A., xiii. 544
Rinaldo (Tasso's), viii. 25
Ring of the Roy Robert, ii. 280
Ringsfield, Suffolk, vii. 33
Rintoul, Robert Stephen (1787–1858), xiv. 198, 534
Rio, A. F., xii. 440
Riot act, xiv. 387
Rip van Winkle, xiii. 266
Ripert-Monclar, count Amédée de, xiii. 55
Ripley, George (d. 1490?), ii. 469; *The Compound of Alchemy or the Twelve Gates*, and *Medulla Alchemiae*, ii. 211 ff.; *Vision*, ii. 212; *Scroll*, ii. 212
Risdon, Tristram (1580?–1640), *Survey of Devon*, ix. 353, 538
Rishanger, William (1250?–1312?), i. 181, 450
Ristori, Adelaide, v. 307; xiii. 514, 515
Ritchie, lady Anne Isabella (born Thackeray), xi. 491; xii. 447; xiii. 478, 485, 502, 529, 530, 549, 551, 558; xiv. 524, 605; *A Discourse on Modern Sibyls*, xiii. 377, 379
Ritchie, David George (1853–1903), xiv. 479
Ritchie, Leitch (1800?–1865), xii. 421, 451; xiv. Add. 5; *Schinderhannes*, xi. 304
Ritchie, William (1781–1831), xiv. 535
Ritson, Joseph (1752–1803), i. 361; ii. 205, 391; v. 277; vii. 443; ix. 567; x. 234, 239, 490, 492; xii. 516, 523
Bibliographia Poetica, ii. 198; xii. 363
Collection of all the Songs etc. on Robin Hood, xii. 364
Engleish Romanceës, x. 233
Northern Chorister, xi. 231
Observations on Warton's *History of English Poetry*, xii. 363
Select Collection of English Songs, xii. 364
Ritwise, John (? 1532), iii. 13; v. 102
Rivers, Alice, vii. 16
Rivers, earl of. *See* Woodville, Anthony
Rivers, Sir John, lord mayor of London, vii. 16
Rivers, Sir John (Charlotte Brontë's), xiii. 409
Rivière, Pierre, iii. 59
Rivière des Prairies, xiv. 355
Rivington, Charles (1688–1742), xi. 323
Rivington, Charles (1754–1831), xi. 327
Rivington, Francis (1745–1822), xi. 327
Rivington, Septimus, xiv. 598
Rivingtons, publishers, xi. 468
Rizzio, David, xiii. 133
Roach, Richard (1662–1730), ix. 307, 515, 575
Rob Roy (Robert Macgregor), in Scott's novel, xii. 18, 26
Robberds, J. W., xii. 380, 429
Robbers and Shefters, A ballett, iii. 492
Robene (Robin), in *Robene and Makyne*, ii. 249
Robert, duke, in *Thomas of Reading*, iii. 368
Robert, earl of Gloucester (d. 1147), i. 156, 166, 168, 169, 256, 258; v. 320
Robert, earl of Huntington, in *Looke about you*, v. 320
Robert, prior of Winchester, i. 176
Robert II, king of Scotland, ii. 102, 103, 117
Robert III, king of Scotland, ii. 280, 369
Robert of Artois, ii. 421

Robert of Avesbury (*fl.* 1350), II. 498; IX. 535
Robert of Cicylye, Kynge, V. 13, 49, 50
Robert of Cricklade (1157–1170), I. 191, 456
Robert of Gloucester (*fl.* 1260–1300), I. 336; II. 133; III. 440; IX. 535; *Chronicle*, I. 152, 170, 298, 335 ff., 347, 350, 377, 476; II. 194, 211; III. 279
Robert de Gretham (*fl.* 13th cent.), II. 508
Robert of Jumièges, archbishop of Canterbury (*fl.* 1037–1052), I. 111
Robert of Melun (d. 1167), I. 184, 456
Robert de Monte (1110?–1186), or Robert of Torigni, I. 168, 170, 172, 175, 256, 450
Robert of Sicily, I. 286, 465, 470
Robert the Bruce. *See* Bruce
Robert the Devil, I. 471; II. 501
Robert the Englishman, or Robert de Retines (*fl.* 1141–1143), I. 153
Robert the Robber, in *Piers the Plowman*, II. 12, 33
Roberto, in Greene's *Groatsworth of Wit*, III. 360
Roberts, Alexander, *A treatise of Witchcraft*, IV. 535; VII. 506
Roberts, C. T., XIV. Add. 9
Roberts, Daniel, *The Memoir of John Roberts*, VIII. 106, 416
Roberts, David (1757–1819), *The Military Adventures of Johnny Newcome*, XIV. 220, 545
Roberts, James (*fl.* 1564–1606), IV. 384, 394
Roberts, James, publisher, IX. 247; XI. 323
Roberts, Lewes or Lewis (1596–1640), IV. 513
Roberts, Robert Davies, XIV. 595
Roberts, William (1767–1849), XI. 475; XIV. 600
Robertson, Charles, XIV. 608
Robertson, Eben William (1815–1874), XII. 512
Robertson, Eric S., XI. 410
Robertson, Frederick William (1816–1853), XI. 411; XII. 290 ff., 469; XIII. 475; 'On the Glory of the Virgin Mother,' XII. 291
Robertson, George Croom (1842–1892), VII. 288; XII. 309, 476; XIV. 24, 473, 479
Robertson, James, X. 95
Robertson, James Logie, XII. 373, 409; XIII. 546
Robertson, John G., IX.
Robertson, John Mackinnon, VI. Add.; XIII. 472, 489
Robertson, Joseph (1810–1866), XII. 513, 518; XIV. 497; *Illustrations of the Topography of Aberdeen and Banff*, XII. 359
Robertson, T. (*fl.* 1520–1561), *Inventory of the Riches of the Cathedral of Sarum*, IV. 422
Robertson, Thomas William (1829–1871), XIII. 271 ff., 523
  Caste, XIII. 272
  David Garrick, XIII. 271
  M.P., XIII. 272
Robertson, Thomas William
  Ours, XIII. 272
  Play, XIII. 272
  School, XIII. 272
  Society, XIII. 271, 272
Robertson, William (d. 1686?), VII. 490
Robertson, William (1721–1793), X. 132, 281, 285, 287 ff. (main entry), 294, 297, 303, 307, 313, 315, 316, 324, 504, 505; XI. 76, 400; XII. 142, 300, 426; XIV. 102
  Disquisition concerning the Knowledge which the Ancients had of India, X. 288
  History of America, X. 288, 289
  History of Charles V, X. 287 ff.; XI. 326
  History of Scotland, X. 287 ff.; XIV. 50
Robertson, William Archibald Scott (1836–1897), XII. 513
Robespierre, Maximilien Marie Isidore, XI. 413; XIII. 12, 420
Robethon, Jean, IX. 236
Robethon, John (d. 1722), X. 295
Robin, in de la Halle's plays, V. 34
Robin, in Mrs Trimmer's *Robins*, XI. 379
Robin Conscience, The Booke in Meeter of, III. 81, 97, 491; IX. 51
Robin Good-fellow, IV. 353, 532, 533; V. 320
Robin Goodfellow, in *Love Restored*, VI. 351, 352, 357, 358, 370, 371
Robin Goodfellow, in *The Devil and his Dame*, V. 329
Robin Goodfellow, in *The Sad Shepherd*, VI. 11
Robin Hood, I. 218, 300, 369, 371; II. 110, 194, 309, 323, 399, 402, 411, 416, 417, 428, 502, 507; III. 68, 358; IV. 529; V. 32, 34, 35, 108, 317 ff., 324 ff.; VI. 238, 365; X. 490; XII. 3, 516
Robin Hood, IX. 166
Robin Hood, in *Looke about you*, V. 320
Robin Hood, in *Robert, Earle of Huntington*, V. 319, 323
Robin Hood, in *The Sad Shepherd*, VI. 11, 369 ff.
Robin Hood, True Tale of, II. 416. See, also, *Robyn*
Robin Hood and his Crew of Soldiers, V 35
Robin Hood and Little John, The Pastoral Comedy of, V. 318
Robin Hood and the Monk, II. 402, 408, 41
Robin Hood and the Potter, II. 408
Robin Hood's Death, II. 416
Robin's Courtship, IX. 364
Robins, Robert, *Whip for the Marshal's Court, A*, IV. 530
Robinson, Agnes Mary Francis, XIII. 481 484
Robinson, Benjamin (1666–1724), X. 386
Robinson, Clement (*fl.* 1566–1584), III 190, 191, 249, 524
Robinson, Elizabeth. *See* Montagu, Mr Elizabeth
Robinson, Emma, XIII. 566
Robinson, George (1737–1801), XI. 327

Robinson, Henry (1605?–1664?), IV. 310, 513; X. 372
Robinson, Henry Crabb (1775–1867), XI. 122, 133, 192, 197 ff., 411, 417, 423, 434; XII. 167, 201, 433, 441; XIV. 173, 178, 505; *Diary*, XIV. 113
Robinson, J., *The Birth of a Day* (1654), VII. 517
Robinson, James (*fl.* 1600), VI. 289, 290
Robinson, John, *Endoxa*, VII. 239
Robinson, John (1650–1723), bishop of London, IX. 249
Robinson, Sir John Richard, XIV. 532, 535, *also see* Add. 9
Robinson, Matthew, X. 262
Robinson, Matthew (1628–1694), XII. 488
Robinson, Mrs, widow of Rich. Burbage, VI. 276
Robinson, Nicholas (d. 1585), VI. 298
Robinson, Philip Stewart (1847–1902), XIV. 580; *In my Indian Garden*, XIV. 341
Robinson, Richard (*fl.* 1576–1600), 'Eupolemia,' IV. 391, 461, 545; *Harmony of King Davids Harp*, IV. 391
Robinson, Robert (1735–1790), X. 522
Robinson, Thomas, *New Citharen Lessons*, IV. 465
Robinson, Thomas (D.D.), IX. 527
Robinson, Mrs William, X. 261
Robinson des enfants, Le, XIII. 201
Rob's Jok cam to woo our Jenny, IX. 361
Robson, Mary, XI. 482
Roby, Henry John (1830–1915), XII. 492; XIV. 609
Elementary Latin Grammar, XII. 336
Essays on the Law of Cicero's Private Orations, XII. 337
Introduction to Justinian's Digest, XII. 337
Latin Grammar from Plautus to Suetonius, XII. 336
Roman Private Law, XII. 337
Robyn and Gandelyn, II. 408
Robyn Hode, The Gest of, II. 329, 402, 408, 416, 428
Robynson, Ralph (*fl.* 1551), VII. 298
Roca, Don Juan, in FitzGerald's *Painter of his own Dishonour*, XIII. 144
Rochdale, XII. 31, 519; XIV. 93
Roche, J., XIII. 465
Roche, James (1770–1853), XIV. 571
Roche, Regina Maria (1764?–1845), XI. 464; *Children of the Abbey*, XI. 299
Rochefort, XIV. 201
Rochefort, expedition to, X. 466
Rochefoucauld, XII. 432
Rochelle, III. 381, 382
Rochester, III. 95; IV. 421; VII. 82; VIII. 5; IX. 145, 538, 540; X. 352, 362; XIII. 335; XIV. 238
Rochester, in *Jane Eyre*, XIII. 407, 408
Rochester, bishop of, in *The merry jests of the widow Edith*, II. 327
Rochester, earls of. *See* Hyde, Lawrence; Wilmot, Henry; Wilmot, John
Rochow, F. E. von, XIV. 382
Rocke, Life of St, in *The Golden Legend*, II. 333
Rockingham, marquis of. *See* Watson-Wentworth, Charles
Rockingham ministry, the, X. 399
'Rod. Staf.,' V. 72
Rodamant, in *St Patrick for Ireland*, VI. 206
Roderick, Visigothic king, XII. 211
Roderigo, in *Othello*, V. 203
Rodes, Sir John, VII. Add.
Rodger, Alexander (1784–1846), XIII. 508
Rodger, M., XIV. 525
Rodney, George Brydges, 1st baron Rodney (1719–1792), XIV. 214, 245
Rodomont, III. 305
Roe, Sir John, IV. 206, 209, 216
Roe, Richard B., XIII. 240, 512
Roe, Sir Thomas (1581?–1644), IV. 90, 216; VII. 434, 437; X. 412; XIV. 332, 333, 580
Roe Head, XIII. 405
Roebuck, in Farquhar's *Love and a Bottle*, VIII. 70
Roebuck, John Arthur (1801–1879), XIV. 419
Roet, Sir Payn, II. 157
Roet or Rouet, Katharine (Swynford), II. 157
Roet or Rouet, Philippa, wife of Chaucer, II. 157
Roger, in *A Dialogue...against the fever Pestilence*, III. 109
Roger, in *The English Traveller*, VI. 94
Roger, count of Sicily, XII. 316
Roger, Mons., dancing-master, X. 440
Roger of Hoveden or Howden (d. 1201?), I. 160, 161, 172 ff., 178, 450; III. 314; IV. 68
Roger of Wendover (d. 1236), I. 159, 178, 179, 451; *Flores Historiarum*, I. 178, 179, 451; II. 318
Rogero, IV. 24
Rogero, the new, a tune, III. 190
Rogers, Arthur George Liddon, XIV. 497
Rogers, A. W., XIV. Add. 9
Rogers, Benjamin Bickley (1828–1919), XII. Add. 3
Rogers, Charles (1825–1890), X. 193, 478; XI. 441, 444; XII. 515
Rogers, Frederic, lord Blachford (1811–1889), *Letters*, XII. 277, 454
Rogers, F., *The Seven Deadly Sins in Literature*, IV. 321, 516
Rogers, Henry (1806–1877), XII. 427, 472, 473; 'The Religious Movement in Germany,' XII. 153
Rogers, James Edwin Thorold (1823–1890), XIV. 479, 497, 508, 509; *History of Agriculture and Prices, A*, XIV. 68; *Protests of the Lords*, XIV. 78
Rogers, John (1500?–1555), III. 44, 474; IV. 446
Rogers, John (1627–1665?), VII. 515; VIII. 319
Rogers, Mrs, X. 121, 126

Rogers, Samuel (1763–1855), IX. 170; XI. 148, 149, 291; XII. 36, 95 ff. (main entry), 101, 102, 124, 133, 139, 148, 150, 381, 382, 384, 408, 491; XIII. 230; XIV. 139, 403, 438
'Campagna of Rome, The,' XII. 98
Italy, XII. 96, 98
Jacqueline, XII. 96
Pleasures of Memory, The, XII. 41, 96, 97, 100
Table Talk, Porsoniana, XII. 325
Rogers, solicitor, X. 117
Rogers, Thomas (d. 1616), IV. 441, 495
Rogers, William (1819–1896), XIV. 609
Rogers, Woodes (d. 1732), XIV. 242, 553
Rogges, a Ballette, III. 492
Rogue pamphlets, IV. 529
Rogue pamphlets and burlesques, VII. 515
Rohan, house of, VIII. 35
Rohault, Jacques, *Traité de physique*, IX. 297
Rohilcand, XIV. 334
Rohilla Afghans, XIV. 334
Roi d'Angleterre et le Jongleur d'Ely, Le, V. 25
Rojas, Fernando de, *Celestina*, IV. 9, 447; V. 99, 100, 409; VIII. 125
Rokayle or Rokesle, Stacy de, II. 35
Roland, in *Rauf Coilȝear*, II. 126
Roland, tales and *Song* of, I. 281, 283, 291, 302, 470
Roland and Vernagu, I. 302, 465, 470
Rolfe, shoemaker, in the *Mercuries*, VII. 356
Rolland, John (*fl.* 1560), III. 499; *The Court of Venus*, III. 131; *The Sevin Sages*, III. 131
Rolle, Edward, X. 136
Rolle, Henry (1589?–1656), *Abridgment des plusiers Cases et Resolutions del Commun Ley*, VIII. 320, 469
Rolle, John (1750–1842), XI. 34
Rolle, Richard, of Hampole (1290?-1349), I. 364, 399; II. 43 ff., 49, 51, 58, 59, 62, 89, 91, 189, 299, 424, 425, 437 ff.; III. 31, 274, 275
Works by, or attributed to, Rolle:
Canticles, on the, II. 48
Ego dormio et cor meum vigilat, II. 47, 48
E.I.O. poem, II. 439
Lord's Prayer and Commandments, II. 48
Mending of Life (or the *Form of Living*), II. 46, 47
Mirror of St Edmund, The, II. 47
Pricke of Conscience, II. 48
Psalter (Rolle's versions and commentaries), II. 46, 47
Rolleston, George (1829–1881), XII. 513; XIV. 563; *Forms of Animal Life*, XIV. 300
Rolleston, Thomas William, XII. 401; XIV. 310, 330, 573
Rolliad, The, X. 239; XI. 34 ff., 39, 40, 42, 53, 391; XII. 120; XIII. 161
Rollington, Ralph, XIV. 532
Rollo, in *The Bloody Brother*, VI. 129, 138
Rollo, Norman duke, in *The Rolliad*, XI. 34
Rollock, Robert (1555?–1599), III. 553
Rolls series, the, XII. 336, 356; XIV. 74, 82
Rolt, Richard (1725?–1770), X. 468
Romagna, the, XII. 36
Romaine, William (1714–1795), X. 365; XII. 473
Roman alphabet in England, I. 426
Roman antiquities, IX. 352, 355, 538 ff., 552; XI. 286; XII. 346, 347, 350, 476, 510
Roman Breviary, I. 53; XII. 420
Roman Britain, XII. 507
Roman Caesars, in *The Roman Actor*, VI. 153
Roman catholic doctrine, XII. 261, 270
Roman catholicism, IX. 245; X. 42; XI. 167, 295; XIII. 44, 260, 366; XIV. 53, 55
Roman catholics, IX. 3, 4, 100, 101, 110; XII. 259, 260, 267, 271, 273, 275, 276; XIV. 212, 249, 314, 317, 329, 417
Roman catholics attacked, in *Loiola*, VI. 324
Roman conquest of Britain, XIV. 71
Roman empire, VIII. 286, 309, 378
Roman history, X. 319, 320
Roman history and life, Jonson's treatment of, VI. 19, 20
Roman jubilee of 1600, V. 161
Roman law, VIII. 309, 310, 312 ff., 317; X. 314; XI. 16; XII. 335; XIV. 80
Roman mythology, XIII. 271
Roman poets, IX. 68
Roman republic, the, IX. 561; X. 501
Roman ritual, in *Hymenaei*, VI. 345
Roman soldiers, in *Christus Redivivus*, VI. 295
Roman stage, VI. 373, 376, 390, 399
Roman studies, society for the promotion of, XII. 340
Roman tragedy, IX. 64; XI. 273
Roman wall, the, XII. 346, 508
Roman de Renart, Le, VIII. 59
Roman de la Rose. See *Rose*
Romance qualities in English verse, VIII. 223
Romances, I. 277 ff., 465 ff.; II. 194, 506
Romanello, III. 167
Romanes, George John (1848–1894), XIV. 479, 563
Romanes lecture, XIV. 34
Romanno, IX. 370
Romans, the, X. 232; XI. 273, 352, 362; XII. 249, 316
Romans, the, in *Believe as you List*, VI. 148
Romans, the, in *The Roman Actor*, VI. 152
Romany novels, XIV. 145, 146
Rombus, in *The May Lady*, VI. 336
Rome, I. 64, 71, 79, 149, 185, 196; II. 50, 55, 61, 66, 67, 71, 74, 75, 77, 79, 84, 119, 131, 238, 287, 288, 310, 345, 350; III. 5, 29, 32, 99, 154, 316, 329, 340, 365, 376, 400, 401; IV. 3, 127, 243, 254, 257, 264, 323, 424, 428, 429; V. 8, 16, 38, 58, 198, 312; VI. 8, 18 ff., 147 ff., 174, 311; VII. 10, 35, 99, 100, 180, 183,

Rome
206, 276, 297; VIII. 23, 221, 267, 291, 310, 388; IX. 73, 112, 159, 256, 274; X. 41, 104, 107, 169, 202, 231, 304, 313, 318, 319; XI. 273; XII. 50, 63, 67, 76, 92, 257, 273, 302, 340, 401; XIII. 72, 74, 77, 79, 104, 393, 435; XIV. 100, 108, 230
Capitol, the, IV. 13; X. 298, 304
English college, III. 422; IV. 127; V. 313
Temple of Jupiter, X. 304
Vatican library, IV. 429
Rome (state), XIV. 61, 68 ff., 79, 110, 175; history of, XII. 280, 301 ff., 322
Rome, church of, IV. 166, 262, 348, 352; V. 2, 10, 36, 40, 139, 209, 344, 366; VI. 3, 149, 150, 197, 324, 387; VII. 10, 142 ff., 208, 212, 217, 222, 223, 297, 304, 309 ff., 327, 378; VIII. 45 ff., 82, 86, 93, 111, 275, 294, 297, 302, 305, 306, 309, 310, 345; IX. 147, 195, 197; X. 293, 301, 373; XII. 259, 261, 262, 264, 269, 274, 276, 292, 299, 331; XIII. 178, 348, 361; XIV. 26, 54, 55, 110
Rome, court of, in *Mirour de l'Omme*, II. 141
Rome, St Paul at, XII. 477
Rome, street cries of, VI. 101
Rome and Keats, XII. 407
Rome for Canterbury or a true relation of the Birth and Life of William Laud, VII. 145
Romei of Ferrara, count Annibale, III. 437, 438; IV. 448; *Discorsi*, III. 438
Romelio, in *The Devils Law-case*, VI. 183
Romeo, in *Romeo and Juliet*, IV. 79; VII. 8; XII. 54
Romeo, W. H. W. Betty as, XI. 283
Romeus et Iulietta, VI. 486
Romford, Essex, VII. 46
Romford, Facey (Surtees's), XIV. 234
Romfrey, lord (George Meredith's), XIII. 446
Romillon, VI. 183
Romilly, John, 1st lord Romilly (1802–1874), XII. 356
Romilly, Sir Samuel (1757–1818), XI. 59; XIII. 418; XIV. 403, 479, 505, 511, 604
Romney, George (1734–1802), XI. 427
Romney, earl of. *See* Sidney, Henry
Romney, Kent, V. 90
Romola (George Eliot's), XIII. 383, 392, 395, 396
Romont, in *The Fatall Dowry*, VI. 223
Ronaldshay, II. 115
Roncesvalles, II. 112
Rondiel, in *Turnament of Totenham*, I. 366
Ronksley, William, XI. 482; *The Child's Week's Work*, XI. 371
Ronsard, Pierre de, III. 136, 250 ff., 257, 259, 262 ff., 266, 269, 296, 524; IV. 24, 196, 197, 210, 472; VI. 334; VIII. 385
Abrégé de l'art Poétique Français, III. 296
Amours, III. 259
Odes, III. 259
Sonnets, III. 259
Sonnets pour Hélène, III. 259
Röntgen rays, XIV. 270
Rood, legend of, I. 133, 341, 342. See, also, *Dream of the Rood* and Cross
Rood-Tree, Holy, V. 15, 389
Rookery, the, in *David Copperfield*, XIII. 327
Rooper, Thomas Godolphin (1847–1903), XIV. 609
Roper, Abel (1665–1726), IX. 461; XI. 471; *Post Boy*, IX. 5, 434
Roper, Mary, daughter of viscount Baltinglas, VII. 245
Roper, William (1496–1578), III. 470; V. 247; IX. 534
Roper, William John Duff, XIV. 597
Ros, Sir Richard, *La Belle Dame Sans Merci*, II. 161, 162, 164, 215, 216
Rosa, Salvator, X. 100, 106
Rosabella, in *Ignoramus*, VI. 322
Rosabelle, in Scott's *Lay of the Last Minstrel*, XII. 9
Rosalind, in *As You Like It*, I. 298; V. 169, 192, 193; VI. 123, 304
Rosalind, in Shelley's *Rosalind and Helen*, XII. 62
Rosalind (Spenser's), III. 214, 215, 217, 222, 224, 243
Rosaline, in *Love's Labour's Lost*, V. 178
Rosamond, in *The Civil Wars*, IV. 137
Rosamond's Pond, IX. 36
Rosamund, Fair, in *Looke about you*, V. 320
Rosamund, the Fair (d. 1176?), IV. 182; VII. 206
Roscellinus, I. 212
Roscius, VI. 250
Roscius, the English, XI. 282
Roscius, the young, XI. 452, 453. *See, also*, Betty, W. H. W.
Roscoe, Edward Stanley, XIV. 509
Roscoe, Elizabeth M., XIV. 521
Roscoe, Sir Henry E., XIV. 597
Roscoe, Robert, son of W. Roscoe, XI. 385
Roscoe, William (1753–1831), IX. 451; XI. 482; XIV. 505, 514
Butterfly's Ball, The, XI. 377, 385, 386, 476
Life of Leo X, XIV. 108
Life of Lorenzo de' Medici, XIV. 108
Memoirs of Benvenuto Cellini, XIV. 108
Roscoe, William Caldwell (1823–1859), XI. 420; XII. 408; XIII. 189, 508, 559
Roscommon, X. 196
Roscommon, earl of. *See* Dillon, Wentworth
Rose (George Meredith's), XIII. 446
Rose, poem by Hilarius, 191
Rose, F. Horace, XIV. Add. 9
Rose, George (1744–1818), XIV. 506
Rose, G. M., XIV. 581
Rose, Henry John (1800–1873), XIV. 593
Rose, Hugh James (1795–1838), XII. 254, 256, 272, 453, 454, 462
Rose, John Holland, XI. 396; XIII. 465
Rose, the Red, in *The Example of Virtue*, II. 227

Rose, Romaunt of the, or *Roman de la*, I. 280, 291, 321, 330; II. 150, 201, 202, 219, 222, 228, 230, 240, 244, 261, 280, 463; III. 170; V. 22; VIII. 59
Rose, Samuel (1767–1804), X. 480
Rose, the White, in *The Example of Virtue*, II. 227
Rose, William Stewart (1775–1843), XII. 422, *also see* Add.
Rose the Red and White Lily, II. 411
Rose-alley ambuscade, VIII. 35
Rosebury, earl of. *See* Primrose, Archibald Philip
Roseilli, in *Loves Sacrifice*, VI. 192
Rosemund, in *Confessio Amantis*, II. 151
Rosencrantz, in *Hamlet*, V. 201, 261
Roses, wars of the, I. 301; II. 228, 335, 358; III. 166, 211; IV. 137; VI. 90; VII. 194; XI. 280
Rosetta stone, XII. 491
Rosiall, in *The Court of Love*, II. 220, 221
Rosicrucianism, VII. 378
Rosicrucians, the, IV. 278
Rosier, James (1575–1635), IV. 461
Rosières, R., XII. 535
Rosimunda, in *The Bugbears*, V. 115
Rosin, Will, in *The Tatler*, IX. 41
Rosinante, in *Don Quixote*, VIII. 67; IX. 268
Rosiphelee, in *Confessio Amantis*, II. 151, 219
Roslyn, Guy, XIII. 552
Ross, Alexander (1591–1654), VII. 238, 239, 407, 466, 474, 511, 512; VIII. 408
Ross, Alexander (1699–1784), IX. 374, 567
Bridal O't, The, IX. 372
Helenore, or the Fortunate Shepherdess, II. 110; IX. 372
Rock and the Wee Pickle Tow, The, IX. 372
Wooed and Married and a', IX. 372
Ross, Sir James Clark (1800–1862), XIV. 245, 296, 553, 563
Ross, John. *See* Rous
Ross, John, printer, IV. 413
Ross, Sir John (1777–1856), XIV. 245, 554
Ross, J. H., XIV. 586
Ross, Robert E., XIII. 524; XIV. 527, 528
Rossaline, in *Antonio and Mellida*, VI. 48
Rossall school, XIV. 414
Rosset, François de, VI. 33, 174, 176
Rosseter, Philip (1575?–1623), IV. 113, 142, 143, 465
Rossetti, Christina Georgina (1830–1894), IX. 178; X. 369; XI. 482; XII. 119, 276, 277; XIII. 111, 137, 138 ff. (main entry), 147, 148, 175, 178, 181, 252, 496 (main entry)
Ballad of Boding, A, XIII. 140
Birthday, A, XIII. 139
Brandons Both, XIII. 140
Christmas Carol, A, XIII. 140
Dream Land, XIII. 138
End, An, XIII. 138
German-French Campaign, The, XIII. 140
Goblin Market, XIII. 138, 139
Rossetti, Christina Georgina
Later Life, XIII. 138
Martyr's Song, XIII. 139
Maude Clare, XIII. 140
Monna Innominata, XIII. 138
New Poems, XIII. 138
Oh roses for the flush of youth, XIII. 138
Old and New Year Ditties, XIII. 140
'Passing away,' XIII. 140
Pause of Thought, A, XIII. 138
Prince's Progress, The, XIII. 138
Sleep at Sea, XII. 128
Testimony, A, XIII. 138
Rossetti, Dante Gabriel (1828–1882), X. 220; XI. 305, 416, 431; XII. 87, 92, 119, 154, 275; XIII. 52, 54, 72, 110 ff. (main entry), 119, 120, 122, 129, 132, 133, 137, 140, 147, 166, 185, 187, 205, 207, 219, 221, 223, 252, 440, 442, 448, 474, 490 ff. (main entry), 496, *also see* Add. 2; XIV. 462
Ave, XIII. 112
Ballads and Sonnets, XIII. 112
Blessed Damozel, The, XIII. 111 ff., 116, 138
Bride's Prelude, The, XIII. 114
Burden of Nineveh, The, XIII. 112, 138
Card-Dealer, The, XIII. 115
Dante and his Circle, XIII. 112
Dante at Verona, XIII. 118
Early Italian Poets, The, XIII. 112
Eden Bower, XIII. 115
Hand and Soul, XIII. 111
House of Life, The, XIII. 112, 117
Jenny, XIII. 116
King's Tragedy, The, II. 472; XIII. 112, 114
Last Confession, The, XIII. 116
Love's Nocturn, XIII. 116
My Sister's Sleep, XIII. 111, 113, 138
Pax Vobis (*World's Worth*), XIII. 112
Poems (1870), XIII. 112, 211
Rose Mary, XIII. 112, 115
Sister Helen, XIII. 115
Song of the Bower, The, XIII. 117
Staff and Scrip, The, XIII. 112, 116
Stream's Secret, The, XIII. 116
Troy Town, XIII. 115
White Ship, The, XIII. 112, 114, 116
Wood-spurge, XIII. 179
World's Worth, XIII. 112
Rossetti, Elizabeth Eleanor (born Siddal), XIII. 112
Rossetti, Maria Francesca, XIII. 118
Rossetti, William Michael (1829–1919), XI. 406, 412, 431, 433, 441; XII. 381, 384, 397, 399 ff., 404, 405, 407, 409, 410, 418; XIII. 72, 110, 138, 490, 491, 495, 496, 499, 561, *also see* Add. 2
Rossi, V. 307
Rosslyn, earls of. *See* Erskine, Francis; Wedderburn, Alexander
Ross-shire, XIV. 294
Rostand, Edmond, *Chantecler*, VIII. 47
Rostgaard, Frederik, *Deliciae Quorundam Poetarum Danorum*, IV. 267

Roswall and Lilian, I. 291, 470
Roswitha. *See* Hrotsvitha
Rot amongst the Bishops, VII. 145
Rota, The Censure of the, VII. 389
Rota club, VII. 362, 389
Rotha, river, XIII. 94
Rotheram, Thomas (1423–1500), IV. 432
Rotherham, Caleb (1694–1752), X. 386
Rotherham school, III. 428; V. 80
Rotherhithe, VII. 308, 318
Rothes, lady, wife of Benet Langton, XI. 365
Rothesay, duke of. *See* Stewart, David
Rothwell, X. 371
Rothwell, John, bookseller, XI. 338
Rotrou, Jean de, VIII. 13
Rotterdam, VII. 308; VIII. 282; IX. 246
Rotterdam, in *The Unfortunate Traveller*, III. 363
Rotuli de oblatis et finibus, XII. 355
Rotuli Normanniae, XII. 355
Rouen, II. 335, 352, 505; IV. 142, 402, 427; VII. 22, 308; IX. 256, 270; XIV. 73
Rouen academy, XI. 274
Rougham, IX. 241
Rougon-Macquart family, Zola's, XIII. 457
'Round Robin,' III. 80
Round Table, the, I. 235, 251, 255, 260, 264, 266, 267, 286, 327, 336; II. 116, 122, 123; XII. 354
Roundway Down, battle of, VII. 350
Rous or Ross, John (1411?–1491), II. 498; *Historia Regum Angliae*, V. 31; IX. 349, 534
Rous, John (1584–1644), *Diary* of, VII. 224, 225, 453
Rous or Rouse, John, Bodley's librarian (1574–1652), IV. 251; VII. 132, 135, 453
Rouse, William Henry Denham, XIII. 486; XIV. 598
Rousseau, Jean-Jacques, IV. 260; V. 292; VIII. 141; IX. 399, 401; X. 18, 57 ff., 134, 155, 190, 323, 324, 458; XI. 19, 27, 32, 71, 73, 79, 87, 93, 292, 295, 296, 305, 382; XII. 44, 76, 164, 168, 177, 178, 397, 525; XIII. 13, 341, 417; XIV. 248, 405
Discourse, X. 57, 59
Émile, X. 59, 135; XIV. 382, 391 ff., 395, 421
La Nouvelle Héloise, X. 17, 19, 60; XIV. 382
Le contrat social, XI. 139
Letter to Philopolis, X. 57
Rêveries, X. 60
Routh, Edward John (1831–1907), XIV. 265, 556
Routh, Martin Joseph (1755–1854), IX. 209; XII. 260, 327, 462; *Reliquiae Sacrae*, XII. 278, 327
Rover, in O'Keeffe's *Wild Oats*, XI. 281
Rovers, The, XI. 41
Row, Charles Adolphus, XIV. 417, 596
Row, John (1568–1646), IX. 550; XII. 515
Row, John (1598?–1672?), IX. 558
Rowallane, the House of, IX. 556
Rowbotham, John Frederick, XIV. 598
Rowcroft, Charles, XIV. 369, 587
Rowe, Nicholas (1674–1718), V. 166, 222, 267 ff., 271; VI. 3, 248; VIII. 193, 195 ff., 440, 445; IX. 75, 144, 476; X. 69, 82, 86, *also see* Add.
Ambitious Stepmother, The, VIII. 195
Biter, The, VIII. 196
Fair Penitent, The, VI. 165; VIII. 195, 197; X. 68, 73
Lucan, trans. of, VIII. 197
Lutrin, trans. of Boileau's, VIII. 197
Rowley, Satyr on Old, VIII. 97
Royal Convert, The, VIII. 196
Shakespeare, XI. 319, 320
Tamerlane, VIII. 195
Tragedy of Jane Shore, The, VI. 90; VIII. 196; X. 68, 74
Tragedy of Lady Jane Grey, The, VIII. 181, 196; XI. 322
Ulysses, VIII. 196
Rowe, Richard, *pseud.* Peter Possum (1828–1879), XIV. 362, 587
Rowe, Thomas (1657–1705), X. 385
Rowland (*i.e.* Michael Drayton), IV. 172, 173, 175
Rowland, David (*fl.* 1569–1586), trans. of *Lazarillo de Tormes*, III. 536; IV. 9, 446; VIII. 127
Rowland, William, VII. 509
Rowlands, *alias* Verstegen, Richard (*fl.* 1565–1620), VII. 353; *Restitution of Decayed Intelligence*, III. 81
Rowlands, Samuel (1570?–1630?), III. 114, 482; IV. 323, 334, 357 ff., 363, 516, 517, 519, 526, 529, 530; V. 371, 479; VII. 395, 407; IX. 32, 51; XII. 376
Betraying of Christ, The, IV. 357
God save the King, IV. 351
Greenes Ghost haunting Coniecatchers, IV. 358
Letting of Humours Blood in the Head-Vaine, The, IV. 333, 357, 360
Looke to it for Ile Stabbe ye, IV. 358
Melancholy Knight, The, IV. 359
Terrible Battell betweene the two consumers of the whole world, A, IV. 358
Tis merrie when Gossips meete, IV. 341, 357
Tis mery when Knaves mete, IV. 517
Rowlandson, Thomas (1756–1827), X. 479; XIV. 215 ff., 221 ff., 225, 232, 235, 540, 541, 543
Rowley, in Sheridan's *School for Scandal*, XI. 271
Rowley, Alexander, VII. 490
'Rowley, Old,' VIII. 207
Rowley, Samuel (d. 1633?), V. 312, 475, 476; VI. 215
Bristow Tragedy, The, VI. 96
Joshua, V. 333
Noble Souldier, The, VI. 215
When you see me, You know me, V. 333, 334, 344, 362
Rowley, Thomas (*pseud.*, *see* Chatterton), X. 236; XI. 390

Rowley, William (1585?–1642?), IV. 532, 533; V. 236, 249 ff., 333, 349, 366, 370; VI. 58–80 (main entry), 104, 116, 132, 138 ff., 145, 184, 185, 190, 424, 427, 445, 455; VIII. 132
Alls Lost by Lust, VI. 59, 68, 71; VIII. 129
Birth of Merlin, The. See *Birth*
Match at Midnight, A, VI. 68
New Wonder, A Woman never vext, A, VI. 68, 70, 72
Search for Money, A; or, the Lamentable Complaint for the Loss of the Wandering Knight, Monsieur L'Argent, VI. 59
Shoo-maker a Gentleman, A, III. 371; VI. 68, 70
Witch of Edmonton, The, VI. 58, 69, 76, 96, 190
Rowley, William and J. Fletcher, *The Maid in the Mill*, VIII. 128, 129
Rowley, William and T. Middleton, *The Spanish Gipsie*, VIII. 129
Rowley poems, the, X. 234, 236, 237, 241, 485, 486, 492
Rowllis Cursing, Sir John, II. 269, 280
Rowntree, John Wilhelm, XIV. 592
Rowton heath, battle of, VII. 6, 39
Roxana, in Lee's *Rival Queens*, VIII. 261
Roxburgh, duke of. *See* Ker, John
Roxburgh, earl of. *See* Ker, Robert
Roxburghe Ballads, VIII. 411; IX. 361, 378; XII. 368
Roxburghe club, II. 503; XII. 357, 365, 393
Roxburghshire, X. 93; XII. 511
Roxolana, in D'Avenant's *Siege of Rhodes*, VIII. 261
Roy, J. A., XIV. 571
Roy, Ram Mohan, XIV. 336, 341, 580
Roy, Richmond (Meredith's), XIII. 441
Roy, William (*fl.* 1527–1531), III. 40, 80, 473; translation of *Dialogus inter patrem christianum et filium contumacem*, III. 80; *Rede me and be not wrothe*, III. 80, 105, 481
Royal academy, X. 265, 266; XI. 181; XIII. 449
Royal Archaeological institute, XII. 349
Royal Asiatic society, XII. 352
Royal Botanic society, XIV. 288
Royal Dublin society, XIV. 288
Royal Historical and Archaeological association of Ireland, XII. 351
Royal Horticultural society, XIV. 287
Royal Irish academy, XII. 351, 352
Royal Lancasterian institute, XIV. 403
Royal society, VII. 222, 234, 270, 302, 303, 305, 478; VIII. 8, 61, 62, 247, 248, 277, 291, 329, 354 ff., 358, 359, 361, 364 ff., 368, 369; IX. 27, 32, 130, 213, 352, 358, 387, 389, 412, 413, 573; X. 466; XI. 334; XII. 319; XIV. 266, 280, 283, 284, 286, 287, 460, 461; *Philosophical Transactions*, IX. 139, 358, 538; *Proceedings*, XIV. 264
Royal society of Antiquaries of Ireland, XII. 352
Royal society of Painters in Water Colours, XIV. 221
Roydon, Matthew (*fl.* 1580–1622), IV. 471
Roydon, Owen, III. 190; IV. 471
Rubens, Peter Paul, V. 331; XI. 12; XIV. Add. 3
Rubini, Giovanni Battista, X. 199
Rudd, Anthony (1549?–1615), IV. 199
Rudd, Mrs, X. 190
Rudd, Thomas (1584?–1656), IV. 456
Ruddiman, Thomas (1674–1757), IX. 493, 561, 562, 566; X. 193, 498; XI. 342, 470; XII. 350, 508
Ruddiman, Walter, printer, IX. 567
Ruddiman's Magazine, XI. 234, 235
Ruddiman's Weekly, IX. 562
Rudge, Barnaby (Dickens's), XIII. 317, 320
Rudolf II, emperor, in *Euphormio*, IV. 256
Rudyerd or Ruddier, Sir Benjamin (1572–1658), *Le Prince d'Amour*, IV. 209; VII. 512
Rueda, Lope de, *Comedia de los Engaños*, VIII. 126
Rufa, in Pope's *Characters of Women*, IX. 82
Ruff, in *Cambises*, V. 64
Ruffhead, Owen (1723–1769), IX. 447; X. 390, 522
Ruffians Rant, The, XI. 232
Ruffio (Hall's), IV. 330
Rufina, St, I. 74
Rufinus, I. 66, 75, 117
Rugbeian, The, XIV. 539
Rugby school, VII. 326, 336, 493; IX. 408; XII. 288, 302, 304, 328, 474; XIII. 86, 87, 102, 103, 370; XIV. 386, 413, 414, 422
Rugge, Thomas (d. 1672), *Diurnall*, the, VIII. 241
Ruggieri (Boccaccio's), VI. 304
Ruggiero, in *Orlando Furioso*, III. 231, 236
Ruggle, George (1575–1622), *Ignoramus*, IV. 410, 518; VI. 314, 322, 323, 327, 476
Ruhnken, David, XII. 325
Ruin, The, I. 1, 4, 39, 423, 428
Rule, Britannia, IX. 186
Rule, Gilbert (1629?–1701), IX. 547
Rümelin, Gustav, V. 209, 305
Rumford, in *Club Law*, VI. 309
Rumford, count von. *See* Thompson, Sir Benjamin
Rump: or an exact collection of the choycest Poems and Songs relating to the Late Times, VII. 1, 385, 512
Rump parliament, VI. 408; VII. 161, 355 ff., 360 ff., 383; VIII. 74, 75, 79
Runcie, John, XIV. Add. 5
Runciman, James (1852–1891), XIV. 535
Runes, I. 7, 424. *See, also,* Add. to third impression
Runic monuments, XII. 513
Runic ode, X. 224
Runic Poem, I. 62
Runic poems, X. 489
Runnymede, VII. 60

Rupert, prince (1619–1682), VII. 178, 227, 383, 438, 512, 513; VIII. 202, 358, 359; XIV. 459
'Rupert of debate,' the, XIV. 129
Rusconi, Carlo, V. 306
Rushe, Anthony (1537–1577), V. 102
Rushton, Northants., VIII. 46
Rushworth, John (1612?–1690), I. 132; VII. 351, 355 ff., 434, 435, 440; IX. 193; *Collections of Private Passages of State*, VII. 187, 350; *London Poet, The*, VII. 187, 350; *Perfect Diurnall of the Armies*, VII. 355
Rushworth, Mr, in Jane Austen's *Mansfield Park*, XII. 239, 241
Rushworth Gospels, I. 132
Ruskin, John (1819–1900), I. 217; IV. 45; VII. 25, 126; IX. 321; XI. 28, 386, 387, 482, 485, 491, *also see* Add.; XII. 173, 177, 178, 372, 438, *also see* Add. 1; XIII. 8, 110, 120, 128, 451, 458; XIV. 139, 148 ff. (main entry), 157, 158, 408, 416, 462, 515, 523, 524, *also see* Add. 3
Academy Notes, XIV. 151
Aratra Pentelici, XIV. 155
Arrows of the Chace, XIV. 154
Art of England, The, XIV. 156
Cestus of Aglaia, The, XIV. 154
Crown of Wild Olive, The, XIV. 154, 415, 416
Elements of English Prosody, XIII. 248, 512
Enquiries on the causes of the Colour of the Water of the Rhine, XIV. 150
Ethics of the Dust, The, XIV. 154
Facts and Considerations on the Strata of Mont Blanc, XIV. 150
Fors Clavigera, XIV. 148, 154, 155
Joy for Ever, A, XIV. 152
Lectures in Landscape, XIV. 155
Lectures on Architecture and Painting, XIV. 152
Lectures on Art, XIV. 155
Modern Painters, XIV. 138, 148 ff., 155, 157
Mornings in Florence, XIV. 155
Munera Pulveris, XIV. 138, 152
Note on the Peforration of a Leaden Pipe by Rats, XIV. 150
Notes on the Construction of Sheepfolds, XIV. 151
On the Old Road, XII. Add.; XIV. 149
Pleasures of England, The, XIV. 156
Poetry of Architecture, The, XIV. 149, 150
Political Economy of Art, The, XIV. 152, 153
Praeterita, XIV. 148, 150, 156, 157
Pre-Raphaelitism, XIV. 151
Queen of the Air, The, XIV. 154
Relation between Michael Angelo and Tintoret, The, XIV. 155
St Mark's Rest, XIV. 155
Salsette and Elephanta, XIV. 149
Sesame and Lilies, XIV. 154
Seven Lamps of Architecture, The, XIV. 150, 151, 153
Ruskin, John
Stones of Venice, The, XIV. 150, 151, 415
Time and Tide, XIV. 154
Two Paths, The, XIV. 152
Unto this Last, XIV. 148, 152 ff.
Ruskin, John, and Scott's MSS., XII. 372
Ruskin college, XIV. 409
Rusport, lady, in Cumberland's *West Indian*, XI. 264
Russel, Alexander (1814–1876), XIV. 203, 204, 535
Russell, Alexander (1715?–1768), X. 466
Russell, Arthur, of Killowen, XIV. 329
Russell, Charles, 1st baron Russell (1832–1900), XIV. 329
Russell, Sir Edward R., XIII. 515; XIV. 535
Russell, E. S., XIII. 573
Russell, Francis, 5th duke of Bedford (1765–1805), X. 246; XI. 29, 30, 389
Russell, George, XIV. Add. 9
Russell, George William Erskine, *Collections and Recollections*, XIV. 296, 537; *Matthew Arnold*, XIII. 87, 88, 488; *Sydney Smith*, XIV. 203
Russell, John, 1st earl of Bedford (1486?–1555), III. 167
Russell, John, 4th duke of Bedford (1710–1771), X. 29, 404
Russell, lord John, 1st earl Russell (1792–1878), XI. 396; XII. 319, 412; XIII. 350; XIV. 107, 116, 121, 126, 198, 417, 502, 506, 511, 604; 'Earls Grey and Spencer,' XII. 153; *Life of William Lord Russell*, IX. 199
Russell, Lucy, countess of Bedford (d. 1627), IV. 15, 175, 176, 197, 202, 203, 205, 211, 216, 265; VI. 9, 337
Russell, Matthew (1834–1912), XIV. 329, 571
Russell, R., contributor to *The Grub Street Journal*, XI. 466
Russell, Rachel, lady (1636–1723), VIII. 272, 452; *Letters*, VIII. 272, 452; IX. 201; X. 500
Russell, Robert, XIV. Add. 9
Russell, Robert C., XIV. 373
Russell, Thomas (1762–1788), X. 456
Russell, William, lord Russell (1639–1683), VIII. 272, 452; IX. 199, 203, 239, 490; X. 351, 500
Russell, William (1741–1793), X. 504; *History of Modern Europe*, X. 294
Russell, William Clark (1844–1911), XIII. 566
Russell, Sir William Howard, XIV. 173, 178, 182, 190, 535
Russell, Wriothesley, 2nd duke of Bedford (1680–1711), VIII. 272
Russell, house of, XI. 30
Russell's Farewell, VIII. 96
Russet, in Colman's *Jealous Wife*, X. 89
Russia, V. 308; X. 466; XI. 58, 72, 358; XII. 46, 55; XIII. 55; XIV. 132, 137, 173, 294

Russia and Landor, xii. 440
Russian language, xiv. 434, 457, 458
Russo-Turkish war, xiv. 179
Rust, George (d. 1676), viii. 290, 456
Rusticus, in *Horestes*, v. 64
Rusticus ad Academicos, viii. 111
Ruth, iv. 43; x. 104
Ruth, in Biblical comedies, v. 101
Ruth, in Crabbe's *Tales of the Hall*, xiii. 380
Rutherford, Mark (William Hale White) (d. 1914), xi. 412; xiii. 438–439, 567; *Autobiography*, xiii. 431; *The Revolution in Tanner's Lane*, xiii. 438
Rutherford, Samuel (1600–1661), vii. 483; ix. 544, 545
Rutherford, William Gunion (1853–1907), xii. 492; *The New Phrynichus*, xii. 334
Rutherforth, Thomas (1712–1771), viii. 473
Ruthven, x. 230
Ruthven, William, 1st earl of Gowrie (1541?–1584), xiv. 486
Ruthwell Cross, the, Dumfriesshire, i. 12, 56, 57, 425; ii. 88
Rutland, vii. 340; ix. 541
Rutland, duchess of. *See* Manners, Catherine
Rutland, duke of. *See* Manners, Charles
Rutland, earl of. *See* Manners, Roger
Rutt, John Towill, xiv. 608
Rutter, Joseph (*fl.* 1635), viii. 13; *Shepherd's Holiday, The*, vi. 366, 491; version of the *Cid* by, viii. 180
Ruysbroek, Johannes, ix. 314, 318
Ruyter, admiral de, viii. 11
Ryan, Richard (1796–1849), xiv. 571
Rycaut, Sir Paul (1628–1700), ix. 247, 495
Rydal mount, xi. 109, 409
Ryder, Dudley, 1st earl of Harrowby (1762–1847), xiv. 115, 510
Rye, Sussex, vi. 110
Rye, Walter, xii. 520
Rye house plot, viii. 44, 90; ix. 199, 202, 239, 364
Ryland, John Collett (1723–1792), x. 522
Ryland, Jonathan Edwards (1798–1866), xiv. 518
Ryland, William Wynne (1732–1783), xiv. 216
Rylands, Mrs John, xii. 365
Ryle, John Charles (1816–1900), xii. 471, 473
Ryley, J. Horton, xiv. 576
Rymenhild, princess, in *Horn*, i. 304, 306
Rymer, Thomas (1641–1713), v. 222; vi. 21, 129, 441; vii. 268; viii. 164, 167, 194, 213, 374 ff., 410, 433, 441; ix. 122, 473; x. 219, 220; xi. 286
Edgar, or the English Monarch, viii. 195, 441; ix. 140
Foedera, viii. 195; ix. 141, 356, 495; x. 280; xii. 355, 516
Reflections on Aristotle's Treatise of Poesie, ix. 140
Short View of Tragedy, A, vii. 275; viii. 163, 195, 221, 375; ix. 140
Rymer, Thomas
Tragedies of the Last Age, The, viii. 195, 375
Tragedies of the Last Age considered. ix. 140
Ryswick, peace of, viii. 90; ix. 149, 205, 214
Ryves, Bruno (1596–1677), *Mercurius Rusticus*, vii. 351

S., J. K. *See* Stephen, James Kenneth
S., Mr, vi. 296, 297
S. B., vii. 250
S. G. O. *See* Osborne, lord Sidney Godolphin
S. R., *The Noble Souldier*, v. 333
S. S., *pseud.*, xi. 378, 430
'Sa Singularité' (duchess of Queensberry), ix. 162
Saadi, x. 144
Sabellian heresy, i. 224
Sabellianism, x. 377
Sabie, Francis (*fl.* 1587–1596), iv. 471, 472
Sabina, in Kingsley's *Two Years Ago*, xiii. 365
Sabine, Joseph (1770–1837), xiv. 287, 288, 563
Sabine women, vi. 392
'Sabinus,' in Pope's *Epistles*, ix. 81
Sablé, Mme de, xiii. 552
Sabren, in *Locrine*, v. 239
Sabrina, in Geoffrey of Monmouth, i. 171
Sabrinae Corolla, xii. 329
Sacharissa (Dorothy, countess of Sunderland), viii. 267, 380. *See, also*, Sunderland
Sacharissa (Waller's), vii. 54 ff.
Sacheverell, Henry (1674?–1724), ix. 11, 13, 95, 130, 139, 234, 394, 473, 478, 490, 571; x. 353, 374, 390; xiv. 212
Sachs, Hans, *Goodly disputation*, iii. 80
Sachs, Julius von, xiv. 283
Sack-full of News, The, iii. 95, 488
Sackville, Charles, 6th earl of Dorset (lord Buckhurst) (1638–1706), vii. 180; viii. 49, 91, 133, 136, 198 ff., 203 ff., 212, 214 ff., 410, 411, 444, 445; ix. 146, 148, 169, 278; x. 226; *To all you Ladies now at Land*, viii. 217; *To Mr Edward Howard*, viii. 217; version of *Pompée*, viii. 180
Sackville, Sir Edward, 4th earl of Dorset (1591–1652), vii. 222, 235
Sackville, lord George. *See* Germain, George Sackville
Sackville, Richard, 5th earl of Dorset (1622–1677), viii. 13
Sackville, Thomas, 1st earl of Dorset and lord Buckhurst (1536–1608), ii. 220; iii. 192, 193, 197, 199 ff., 228, 283, 285, 287, 517; iv. 145, 193, 265; v. 66, 67, 69, 78, 227; viii. 222; *Induction*, ii. 228; iii. 192, 193, 200, 201, 228. See, also, *Gorboduc*
Sacrament, songs based on the, ii. 387
Sacred Books of the East, xii. 343

Sacrifice of Abraham, The, v. 390, 391
Sacro Monte, at Varallo-Sesia, xiii. 450
Sad Circumspeccyon, in *Magnyfycence*, iii. 77
Sadducees, vii. 303, 370
Sadler, John (d. 1595?), iv. 440
Sadler, John (1615–1674), vi. 477; vii. 509
Sadler, Sir M. E., xiv. 592, 596
Sadler, Sir Ralph (1507–1587), xii. 376; *Life, Letters and State Papers*, xii. 16
Sadler, Thomas (1822–1891), xiv. 505
Sadlier, Mary Ann, xiv. 581
Sadoleto, Jacopo, bishop of Carpentras, iii. 420
Saeferth (Sigeferth?), in *Widsith*, i. 34
Saemund, x. 487
Saenger, S., xiv. 478
Saewulf of Malmesbury, iv. 68
Saffron Walden, iii. 213; v. 372
Saffron Walden academy, x. 385
Saga library, xiii. 127
Sage, John, bishop (1652–1711), iv. 151; ix. 547, 561
Sagittarius, bishop of Embrun, i. 67
Sahara, the, xiv. 167
St Albani, Chronica Monasterii, i. 449, 451
St Albans, i. 153, 159, 174, 178, 179, 181, 182, 193, 214; ii. 80, 81, 302, 317, 318; iv. 409, 426; v. 7, 38; vi. 196; xi. 80; xii. 182
St Albans, library at, iii. 48
St Albans, duke of. *See* Beauclerk, Charles
St Albans, earl of. *See* Jermyn, Henry
St Albans, The Book of, ii. 318, 323, 420; iv. 364, 370, 375, 543
St Albans' grammar school, vi. 197; vii. 330
St Aldegonde, in Disraeli's *Lothair*, xiii. 350
St Andrews, ii. 126, 129, 250, 259, 273, 285, 367, 368 ff.; iii. 122, 140, 142, 149, 151, 157, 424, 426; vii. 448; ix. 129, 359, 378, 542, 545, 566; x. 295; xi. 243; xii. 359; xiv. 40, 209, 210, 297, 424, 432
  St Leonard's college, ii. 369, 370
  St Mary's college, ii. 369, 370
  St Salvator's college, ii. 369; x. 291
  United college, xii. 259
St Andrews College Echoes, The, xiv. 209
St Andrews University Magazine, The, xiv. 538
St Angelo, x. 314
St Anne, v. 48, 56
St Asaph, ii. 288; ix. 196, 329, 350, 541; xi. 364, 399
St Barbe, in Disraeli's *Endymion*, xiii. 351
St Bartholomew, massacre of, iii. 402; iv. 276; v. 341; vii. 191, 304; viii. 87; xiv. 54, 118
St Bertin's monastery in Flanders, i. 89
St Brice's day, massacre of, v. 31
St Catharine's convent, mount Sinai, xii. 341
Saint Chaumont, marchioness de, sister of Gramont, viii. 263
St David's, i. 89, 194, 196; viii. 305; ix. 540
St David's, see of, xii. 308
St Domingo, v. 361
Saynt Dyryk, v. 97
St Edmund's. *See* Bury St Edmunds
St Edmundsbury. *See* Bury St Edmunds
Saint-Évremond, Charles de Marguetel de Saint-Denis de (1613?–1703), vi. 273; viii. 30, 135, 174, 199, 212, 376, 377, 402, 424, 445, 481; ix. 499
St Gall or St Gallen, v. 36, 37; Bede's *Death Song* at, i. 61
St-Gelais, Mellin de, v. 62
St Gelais, Octavien, bishop of Angoulême, iii. 153, 502
St George, guild of, xiv. 153 ff.
St Germain, court of, viii. 267; x. 295
Saint-German, Christopher (1460?–1540), *Doctor and Student*, viii. 315, 467
St Gluvias, Cornwall, x. 193
St Helena, xiii. 276
St Hubert's abbey in the Ardennes, i. 82
St Ives, vii. 54
St James's Chronicle, x. 479; xi. 402
St James's Gazette, ix. 445; xiv. 189, 195
St Jean de Luz, xiii. 456
St John, Charles George William (1809–1856), xiv. 545
St John, Henrietta, ix. 217
St John, Henry, 1st viscount Bolingbroke (1678–1751), v. 288; viii. 410, 411; ix. 14, 15, 81, 83, 85, 89, 95 ff., 112, 124, 131, 150 ff., 161, 166, 185, 192, 207, 216 ff. (main entry), 252, 288, 433, 434, 444, 445, 467, 472, 478, 483, 487, 504, 509, 547; x. 272, 279, 301, 386, 482, 521; xi. 2 ff., 9, 12, 26; xii. 426; xiii. 346, 419
  Case of Dunkirk consider'd, ix. 224
  Craftsman Extraordinary, ix. 221
  Dissertation upon Parties, ix. 224, 225
  Final Answer, A, ix. 223
  First Vision of Camelick, ix. 221
  Idea of a Patriot King, ix. 230, 231
  Letter on the Spirit of Patriotism, ix. 229, 230
  Letter on the True Use of Retirement, ix. 228, 233
  Letter to Sir William Wyndham, ix. 218, 219, 223
  Letters and Correspondence, ix. 216
  Letters on the Study...of History, ix. 226 ff.
  Occasional Writer, The, ix. 223, 491
  Of the State of Parties at the Accession of George I, ix. 231
  Philosophical Works, ix. 295
  Plan of a General History of Europe, ix. 228
  Reflections on Exile, ix. 218
  Remarks upon the History of England, ix. 221, 223
  Some Reflections on the Present State of the Nation, ix. 231
St John, Henry. *See* Oldcastle, Humphry
St John, knights of (Hospitallers), i. 189; ii. 111; iii. 13; vii. 333

St John, Percy Bolingbroke (1821–1889), XI. 387, 489
St John's day, VIII. 54
St Kilda, X. 102
St Leonards, lord. *See* Sugden, Edward Burtenshaw
St Lo, George (1682?–1729), IV. 102, 461
Saint-Martin, Louis Claude de (1743–1803), IX. 328, 521
St Mary Charlcombe, X. 22
St Michael's mount, IV. 200
St Michael's mount, in Arthurian legend, I. 256, 260
St Michel, Elizabeth, wife of Samuel Pepys, VIII. 253
'Saynt Modwin,' V. 97
'Saynt Myghell,' in *The Four P.P.*, V. 97
St Neot, X. 510
St Ogg's, in *The Mill on the Floss*, XIII. 392
St Omer, IX. 213; college at, III. 422; IV. 402; VII. 45; VIII. 266
St Osyth, VII. 373
St Patrick's Purgatory. *See* Staunton, W.
St Petersburg. *See* Petrograd
St Pierre, Eustace de, in Colman's *Siege of Paris*, XI. 257
Saint-Pierre, Jacques Henri Bernardin de, *Paul et Virginie*, XI. 280
St Pierre, Martinique, XIV. 165
St Prassede, church of, XIII. 69
St Praxed's, the bishop of (Browning's), XIII. 63
Saint-Preux, in Rousseau's *La Nouvelle Héloïse*, X. 17; XII. 60
Saint-Réal, Abbé de, *Don Carlos*, VIII. 182, 439; *La Conjuration des Espagnols contre la république de Venise en* 1618, VIII. 183
St Scholastica's day, II. 345, 346
St Serf, in Wyntoun, II. 131
St Serf's priory, Lochleven, II. 129
St Serfe, Sir Thomas, *Taruzo's Wiles, or the Coffee House*, VIII. 131, 189, 422
Saint-Simon, Louis de Rouvroy, duc de, IX. 250; X. 66; XIII. 22, 442, 447; *Memoirs*, III. 147
St Stephen, Life of, in *The Golden Legend*, II. 314
St Stephen and Herod, II. 408
'Saint Sunday,' V. 97
St Thomas, play on, V. 56
Saint Thomas de l'Enfer, rue de, in *Sartor Resartus*, XIII. 6
St Ursula, Guiscard and Sigismund, The Life of, II. 486
Sainte-Beuve, Charles Augustin, III. 147; IX. 61; X. 255, 317; XI. 87, 404; XII. 211, 524, 525; XIII. 99
Sainte Maria Virgine, I. 220
Ste Marie, near Pornic, XIII. 77
Saints, Legends of the, I. 298; III. 92
Saints, Lives of the, I. 120 ff., 128, 151, 229, 286, 298; III. 19. *See, also, under* Barbour, Bokenam, Lydgate
Saintsbury, George, II. 233; V. 20, 21; VIII. 8, 30, 42, 54; IX. 158; X. 413, 418, 421, *also see* Add.; XI. 183, 393, 419, 423, 429, 434, 443, 446, 459, 463, 492, *also see* Add.; XII. 376, 381, 410, 412, 413, 418, 421, 425, 426, 433, 441, 444 ff., 449, 453, 524, *also see* Add.; XIII. 27, 472, 478, 485, 488, 495, 498, 509, 530, 544, 553, 559, 567, 568, 570, *also see* Add. 3; XIV. 493, 509, 516, 524, 528, 570; *History of Criticism*, XI. 353; *History of English Prosody, A*, I. 289, 338, 350; II. 424; IX. 157; XIII. 32, 512
Sakuntala, XII. 502, 503
Sala, George Augustus Henry (1828–1896), XII. 435; XIII. 532, 541; XIV. 191, 192, 535
Saladin, I. 307; II. 87; VII. 159
Salamenes, in Byron's *Sardanapalus*, XII. 49
Salamis, XIII. 135
Salanio, in *The Merchant of Venice*, IV. 79
Saldar, countess de (Meredith's), XIII. 441
Sale, Antoine de la, *Les Quinze Joyes de Mariage*, III. 89, 90, 485; IV. 8, 526; VIII. 59
Sale, George (1697?–1736), IX. 529
Sale of Authors, The, X. 131
Salem, grand jury of, XI. 12
Salernitano, Masuccio, VI. 102
Salerno, Salernum, Salerne, III. 109; V. 76; VI. 304
Salesbury or Salisbury, William (1520?–1600?), *A Dictionary of Englishe and Welshe*, III. 461, 555
Salisbury, IV. 190, 228, 274, 409, 421; VI. 141; VII. 29, 244, 245, 277, 333; VIII. 245, 319, 360; IX. 200, 221, 287, 294, 538; X. 22, 207, 209, 346, 470; XI. 424; XII. 192; XIII. 424
Salisbury. *See* John of
Salisbury, countess of (Drayton's), IV. 182
Salisbury, countess of, in *Edward IV*, V. 244, 245
Salisbury, earl of. *See* Cecil, Sir Robert
Salisbury, marquis of. *See* Gascoyne-Cecil, Robert A. T.
Salisbury breviary, IV. 427
Salisbury cathedral inventory, V. 37
Salisbury plain, V. 251; IX. 269
Salisbury Postman, The, XIV. 169
Salisbury theatre, XI. 451
Salle, Eusèbe de, XII. 385
Sallust, I. 76; II. 366; III. 20, 164, 290, 291, 416, 429, 431; IV. 439; VI. 86; VII. 131; IX. 340, 528; XII. 306, 476; *Catiline*, IV. 4; *Jugurtha*, IV. 4
Sally in our Alley, II. 272
Salmacis and Hermaphroditus, in Sandys's trans. of Ovid, VII. 50
Salmasius or Saumaise, Claude de, III. 157; VII. 125, 131, 307, 422; *Defensio Regia*, VII. 104; *Plinianae Exercitationes*, VII. 316
Salmon, David, XIV. 592, 602
Salmon, George (1819–1904), XIV. 263, 556

Salmon, Nathaniel (1675–1742), IX. 355, 538
Sal-Nitro, de, VIII. 354
Salomon and Marcolf, I. 218
Salomon and Saturn, Dialogue of, I. 11, 62, 76, 432
Salonius, bishop of Gap, I. 67
Salt, Henry (1780–1827), XIV. 247
Salt, Henry Stephens, XII. 445; XIII. 478, 489, 570
Salt, Samuel (d. 1792), XII. 180, 181, 183, 189, 191
Salter, Samuel (d. 1778), VIII. 457
Salter, Thomas (*fl.* 1580), IV. 518
Salterne, George, *Tomumbeius*, VI. 301, 477
Saltire, lord, in Henry Kingsley's *Ravenshoe*, XIII. 433
Saltmarsh, John (d. 1647), VII. 246, 352, 426, 494, 499
Saltonstall, Wye (*fl.* 1630–1640), III. 114, 487; IV. 461, 521, 522; VII. 485; *Picturae loquentes or Pictures drawn forth in characters*, IV. 341
Saltrey. *See* Henry of
Salutati, Coluccio, V. 61
Salutation and Conception, The, V. 21
Salutation tavern, in Arbuthnot's *History of John Bull*, IX. 135
Salvian, *De Gubernatione Dei*, VI. 390
Salvin, Osbert (1835–1898), XIV. 297, 563
Salvini, Tommaso, V. 307; XIII. 515
Salzmann, Auguste, XII. 339
Salzmann, C. G., XI. 395
Samarah, XI. 289
Samaria, woman of, III. 88
Samaritan, in *Piers the Plowman*, II. 24, 27
Samaritan language, VII. 319
Samber, Robert, XI. 374, 492
Sambourne, Edwin Linley (1844–1910), XIV. 239
Sampson, dominie, in Scott's *Guy Mannering*, XII. 25
Sampson, Elizabeth. *See* Inchbald, Mrs
Sampson, George, XII. 405; XIV. 528
Sampson, John, XI. 184, 431 ff.
Sampson, Thomas (1517?–1589), III. 45
Sampson, William (1590?–1636?), *The true tragedy of Herod and Antipater*, IV. 377, 539; VI. 456
Sampson Legend, Sir, in *Love for Love*, VIII. 151, 164
Samson, I. 74; VIII. 164
Samson, abbot, of Bury (1135–1211), I. 176; II. 342; XIII. 15, 16
Samson, in *Samson Agonistes*, VII. 121, 122, 136
Samson de Nanteuil, II. 508
Samuel, II. 106; XII. 321
Samuel, son of Beulan, I. 70
San Domingo, XI. 114
San Francisco, VIII. 112
San Juan de Ulloa, IV. 73
Sanazzaro or Sannazaro or Sannazarius, Jacopo, III. 219, 262, 300, 351, 352, *also see* Add.; IV. 261, IX. 69; *Arcadia*, III. 219, 351; VI. 364
Sanazzaro, in *The Great Duke of Florence*, VI. 156
Sancho, in *The Spanish Gipsie*, VI. 77
Sancho Panza, in *Don Quixote*, VIII. 70; X. 41, 51
Sancroft, William (1617–1693), archbishop of Canterbury, IV. 55, 426; VII. 159; VIII. 99, 298, 461, 463; X. 355; *Fur Praedestinatus*, VIII. 306
Sand, George (Mme Dudevant), XIII. 71, 272, 283
Sandars, Nicholas, *De Origine ac Progressu Schismatis Anglicani*, IX. 196, 198
Sandells, of Stratford, V. 168
Sanders, Lloyd C., XI. 456; XIV. 510
Sanderson, John (d. 1602), *Institutionum Dialecticarum libri quatuor*, IV. 274, 508
Sanderson, Robert (1587–1663), IX. 513; VII. 149, 150, 157, 252, 426, 463, 474; VIII. 293; *De juramenti promissorii obligatione*, VII. 280; *De obligatione conscientiae*, VIII. 280
Sanderson, Robert (1660–1741), IX. 495; X. 280
Sanderson, Sir T. H., XIV. 509
Sanderson, William, seaman, III. 327
Sanderson, Sir William (*c.* 1586–1676), VII. 447, 454, 518
Sandford, Sir Francis (1824–1893), XIII. 88
Sandford, Harry, in *Sandford and Merton*, XI. 382
Sandford or Sanford, James (*fl.* 1567), IV. 436; VI. 377; VII. 517
Sandham, Elizabeth, XI. 383, 489
Sandle bridge, Cheshire, XIII. 372
Sandon, Essex, II. 208
Sandoval, Prudencio de, *History of Charles V*, IX. 278, 501
Sandown castle, VII. 227
Sandwich, earls of. *See* Montagu, Edward; Montagu, John
Sandwich islands, XIV. 245
Sandys, Edwin (1516?–1588), archbishop of York, III. 189; IV. 235, 299, 494, 513; VII. 49
Sandys, Sir Edwin (1561–1629), III. 406; IV. 235; *Europae Speculum*, III. 548
Sandys, George (1578–1644), IV. 439, 461; VI. 102; VII. 16, 49 ff. (main entry), 56 ff., 409; VIII. 229; IX. 67
  Aeneid, trans. of 1st book, VII. 52
  Christ's Passion, VII. 52
  Ovid, VII. 53, 67
  Paraphrase of songs in Old and New Testaments, VII. 52
  Paraphrase upon the Psalms of David, VII. 52, 67
  Paraphrases, VII. 86
  Paraphrases of Job, Ecclesiastes, Lamentations of Jeremiah, etc., VII. 52
  Relation of a Journey, IV. 89, 401
  Song of Solomon, VII. 52
Sandys, Sir John Edwin (1844–1921), XII. 482, 485, 489; *Classical Scholarship*, 206

Sangster, Charles (1822–1893), XIV. 350, 357, 582
Sannie Beyers, XIV. 377
Sanny Briggs, IX. 365
Sansfoy, in *The Faerie Queene*, III. 234
Sanskrit language and literature, XII. 318, 327, 343, 352, 362; XIV. 97, 416
Sanskrit scholars, XIV. 334, 335, 337
Sansovino, F., IV. 448
Santa Maria Maggiore, XIII. 69
Santander, VII. 53
Santon Downham, Suffolk, VII. 224
Santorio, VI. 175
Santos, Brazil, Jesuit college (library) at, III. 359
Sapience, in *Ane Pleasant Satyre*, III. 125
Sapience, in *The Example of Virtue*, II. 228
Sapience, in *The Palice of Honour*, II. 260
Sapience (Wisdom), in *The Passetyme of Pleasure*, II. 228
Sapientia Salomonis, play, VI. 486
Sapless, Miss, in Morton's *Way to get Married*, XI. 281
Sappho, IV. 30; XI. 232, 426; XII. 329
'Sappho,' in Pope's *Imitations of Horace*, IX. 85, 251
Saracen, princess, in *The Golden Legend*, II. 334
Saracenic wars, VII. 367
Saracens, in romance, I. 282, 293, 302, 304 ff., 317
Saracens, the, II. 350, 366; IV. 68; X. 281; XI. 25
Saravia, Adrian (1531–1613), III. 409; VII. 309, 317
Sarcastic, Mr, in Peacock's novel, XI. 309
Sardanapalus, in Byron's drama, XII. 49
Sardego, in *The City Witt*, VI. 225, 229
Sardinia, IV. 259
Sardinian legation, X. 301
Sardou, Victorien, XIII. 266, 272, 525
Sargent, E., XII. 409
Sargent, John Young (1829–1915), XII. 493
Sarmiento, IV. 78
Sarpedon, IX. 70, 74
Sarpi, Paolo (father Paul), IV. 448; VII. 190, 308; X. 164, 460, 464; *History of the Council of Trent*, IX. 197
Sarrazin, Gabriel, V. 161; XIII. 485, 491, 495
Sarsnet, Mrs, in Holcroft's *Deserted Daughter*, XI. 277
Sarto, Andrea del, X. 119
Sarum, dean of. *See* Bridges, John
Sarum Missal, II. 315; III. *also see* Add.; IV. 421, 427
Sarum Ordinale, II. 315
Sarum play, V. 37
Sarum Use, the, II. 377; IV. 427
Sassanian or New Persian Empire, the, XII. 478
Satan, IV. 167; VII. 370, 373, 375, 397, 503, 509; XI. 106, 193, 196, 197, 199, 305; XIV. 306
Satan, in Dryden's *The State of Innocence*, VIII. 28
Satan, in *Genesis B*, I. 46, 47
Satan, in *Mary Magdalene*, V. 20
Satan, in Milton's *Paradise Lost*, I. 47; VII. 118, 119, 136; IX. 60, 339; XII. 48, 85, 398
Satan, in *The Devill is an Asse*, VI. 24
Satan, Old English, I. 428
Satire, in *The Muses Looking-Glasse*, VI. 233
Satire, political and ecclesiastical, VIII 408 ff.
Satire against Satirists, The, VI. 88
Satyre against Separatists, A, VII. 408
Satire Ménippée, III. 388, 398; IV. 449
Satires, Satyres, IV. 518, 519
Satires on political characters (Civil War) VII. 512
Saturday papers, in *The Spectator*, IX. 59
Saturday Review, The, XII. 306, 471, 475; XIV. 71, 76, 85, 110, 146, 180, 194, 198, 199, 531, 533 ff.
Saturn, II. 276
Saturn, in Alfred's *Boethius*, I. 100
Saturn, in Keats's *Hyperion*, XII. 85
Saturn, in *The Four Ages*, VI. 92, 93
Saturn, in *The Testament of Cresseid*, II. 248
Saturnalia, V. 8; VI. 319, 474; X. 226
Saturn's rings, VIII. 350
Saul, II. 10, 151; VII. 67, 296, 395
Saul, in Cowley's *Davideis*, VII. 66
Saumur (in Anjou), VIII. 265
Sauncepere, lady, in *The Bowge of Courte*, III. 73
Saunders, Charles, *Tamerlane the Great* (1681), VIII. 401
Saunders, Sir Edmund (d. 1683), VIII. 469
Saunders, Sir Edward (d. 1576), III. 189
Saunders, Julius, X. 385
Saunders, Montagu, XIII. 537
Saunders, 'Silenus,' IX. 240
Saurin, Bernard-Joseph, *Béverlei*, X. 68, 81
Savage, Eliza Mary Ann, XIII. 454
Savage, Henry (1604?–1672), IX. 539
Savage, John (1673–1747), IX. 499
Savage, Marmion W. (1803–1872), XIV. 323, 571; *Bachelor of the Albany, The*, XIV. 324; *Falcon Family, The*, XIV. 324; *Reuben Medlicott*, XIV. 324
Savage, Richard (d. 1743), IX. 449, 486, *also see* Add.; X. 95, 165, 274, 454, 460, 464, 465; XI. 246; XII. 424
Author to be Let, The, XI. 330
Bastard, The, IX. 186, 187
Volunteer Laureat, IX. 187
Wanderer, The, IX. 186
Savage, Samuel Morton (1721–1791), X. 384
Savage family, Warwickshire, XII. 441
Savannah, X. 368
Savery, Thomas (1650?–1715), IV. 461, XIV. 258

Savigny, Friedrich Karl von, xiv. 79; *Geschichte des römischen Rechts im Mittelalter*, xiv. 80
Savile, in *The Scornful Ladie*, vi. 133
Savile, Sir George, marquis of Halifax (1633–1695), viii. 268, 370, 387 ff., 481, *also see* Add.; ix. 190, 201, 490
A Lady's Gift: Advice to a Daughter, viii. 388; xi. 371
Anatomy of an Equivalent, viii. 388
Character of a Trimmer, The, viii. 387, 388
Character of King Charles the Second, viii. 387, 388
Letter to a Dissenter, viii. 387; ix. 4, 418
Miscellanies, viii. 387
Savile, Sir Henry (1549–1622), i. 213; iii. 421, 424 ff., 428; iv. 4, 265, 411, 440; vii. 205, 312, 314, 316, 328, 329, 443, 483, 485, 487; viii. 360
Savile, Henry (1642–1687), viii. 200, 210, 212, 452
Savile family, vii. 87
Savilian professor of astronomy, ix. 386
Savilian professorships at Oxford, vii. 288
Saville or Savile, captain Henry, iv. 461
Saviolo, Vincentio (*fl.* 1595), iii. 553; v. 479
Savonarola, Girolamo, iii. 8, 17; vii. 376; xii. 440, 477
Savonarola, in *Romola*, xiii. 394, 395
Savonarola, Don Jeremy, *pseud. See* Mahony, Francis Sylvester, xiv. 316
Savory, Hester, xii. 194
Savoy, xiii. 74
Savoy, Charles Emmanuel, duke of, vii. 306
Savoy, house of, iii. 402
Savoy alps, the, xiii. 83
Savoy and Shelley, xii. 403
Savoy conference, iii. 34; viii. 7, 273, 285, 294; ix. 383
Saw ye my Father, ix. 374
Sawbridge, John (1732?–1795), x. 503
Sawle, Rose, lady Graves, xii. 441
Sawles Warde, i. 227, 228, 355, 459
Sawney will ne'er be my love again, viii. 96
Sawtrey, William (d. 1401), ii. 422
Sawyer, Bob, in *Pickwick Papers*, x. 41
Sawyer, Edmund (d. 1759), x. 504
Sawyer, Elizabeth (d. 1621), vi. 190
Sawyer, mother, in *The Witch of Edmonton*, vi. 54
Saxe Coburg, house of, xii. 232
Saxo Grammaticus, i. 8, 9, 25, 27, 28, 34, 37; v. 159, 221
Saxon, Old, paraphrase of Bible, i. 46
Saxon drummer, in *The Rolliad*, xi. 34
Saxon language, xiii. 29
Saxon poems, x. 237
Saxons, the, xii. 26; xiv. 68, 76
Saxony, vii. 231, 453
Saxony, Eastphalian, v. 6
Say, Samuel (1676–1743), xi. 250
Say, Sir William, iii. 3
Sayce, Archibald Henry, xiv. 533
Sayer, James (1748–1823), *A Nightmare*, xiv. 214; 'Elijah's Mantle,' xiv. 214
Sayers, Frank (1763–1817), xi. 160, 161, 172, 177 ff., 428; xiii. 227, 512
Cyclops, xi. 179
Dramatic Sketches, xi. 179
Moina, xi. 179
Starno, xi. 179
To Night, xi. 179
Sayers, Tom (1826–1865), xiv. 183, 231
Sayes court, Deptford, viii. 245, 246, 354, 365
Sayings of the Fathers, xii. 341
Sayle, Charles Edward, xii. 518
Say-well, in *Piers the Plowman*, ii. 19
Scaccario, Dialogus de. See Fitz-Neale
Scales, lord. *See* Woodville, Antony
Scaliger, Julius Caesar and Joseph Justus, iii. 301, 305, 424, 426; iv. 22, 255, 259 ff., 322, 500, 519; vi. 9, 37, 225; vii. 261, 263, 268, 272, 307, 310, 320, 477; viii. 321; ix. 170; xiv. 109
Scaliger, Julius Caesar, *Poetices libri septem*, ix. 60
Scaliger, Joseph Justus, *Censura Euphormionis*, iv. 260
'Scallogrim,' x. 224
Scamperdale, lord (Surtees's), xiv. 234
Scandal, in Congreve's *Love for Love*, viii. 152
Scandaroon, vii. 449
Scandinavia, v. 283, 307; xiii. 123; xiv. 293
Scandinavian gods, the, xiii. 271
Scandinavian legend, x. 221, 490. *See, also*, Norse *and* Icelandic
Scandinavian poetry, x. 132, 228, 487
Scandinavian studies, x. 222, 484
Scarborough, ii. 424
Scarborough, Sir Charles (1616–1694), vii. 320
Scarborough, earl of. *See* Lumley, Richard
Scardassale, Tomasso, xii. 55
Scarron, Paul, viii. 67, 69, 183, 407; ix. 256, 257, 259, 500, 502; x. 482
City Romance, viii. 170
Don Japhet d'Arménie, viii. 372
Les trois Dorothées, viii. 372
Nouvelles tragi-comiques, viii. 372
Roman Comique, viii. 372; x. 26
Typhon, ix. 268
Virgile Travesti, viii. 65; ix. 256, 257
Scarth, Harry Mengden (1814–1890), xii. 513
Scattercash, lord, xiv. 232
Sceldwea, in *Beowulf*, i. 28
Scenici, v. 24
Schaarschmidt, C., *Joh. Saresberiensis*, i. 184
Scharf, Sir George (1820–1895), x. 254
Schaub, lady, x. 126
Schaub, Sir Luke (d. 1758), x. 126
Schaw, Quintyne, ii. 268; *Advyce to a Courtier*, ii. 266
Schedoni, in Mrs Radcliffe's *Italian*, xi. 302, 304

Scheidt, Caspar, III. 82
Schelling, Felix E., v. 129; vi. 4, 7, 8, 11, 17, 23, 90, 305, 363; xiii. 515
Schelling, Friedrich Wilhelm Joseph von (1775–1854), ix. 328, 522; xi. 137; xiv. 9, 11, 16; *System des transzendentalen Idealismus*, xi. 136
'Schembertlaufen,' v. 25
Scheppig, Richard, xiv. 481
Schepss, Georg, i. 101
Scherer, Edmond, vii. 138; xiii. *also see* Add. 3
Schevill, Rudolph, viii. 125, 126, 128
Schiavonetti, Luigi (1765–1810), x. 453
Schick, John, ii. 237
Schiedam, ii. 327
Schildburg, witticisms on, iii. 95
Schilders, Richard, iii. Add.; iv. 402
Schiller, Johann Christoph Friedrich von, v. 300, 303, 465; viii. 182, 439; x. 504; xi. 42, 138, 414; xii. 4, 7, 90, 168, 254, 436, 526; xiii. 4, 22, 277, 465, 468
Das Ideal und das Leben, xi. 130
Das Reich der Schatten, xi. 130
Der Pilgrim, vii. 177
Die Räuber, xi. 303, 414
Die Sehnsucht, vii. 177
Horen, v. 299
Robbers, The, xiii. 418
Wallenstein, xiii. 260
Schipper, Jakob, i. 96
Schism, the Great, i. 371
Schism act, ix. 394; x. 373, 374
Schisme, A Treatise of, iv. 381
Schlegel, August Wilhelm and Johann Elias, v. 209, 222, 290, 299, 300, 303, 304, 307
Schlegel, August Wilhelm von, xi. 135, 448; xii. 169, 527; xiii. 3, 4, 8
Schlegel, Caroline, v. 299
Schlegel, Friedrich, v. 304; ix. 328; xii. 343
Schlegel, Johann Heinrich, x. 448
Schlegel, Karl Wilhelm Friedrich von, ix. 522
Schleich, ii. 320
Schleiermacher, Friedrich Daniel Ernst, *A Critical Essay on the Gospel of St Luke*, xii. 280, 288, 289, 308, 470
Schlettstadt, iii. 13
Schlosser, F. C., ix. 226; x. 302
Schmidt, Alexander, v. 305; xiii. 466
Schmidt, Erich, x. 18
Schmidt, K., xiii. 465
Schmitz, Leonhard, xii. 478
Schofield, W. H., Pref. x, i. 61
Scholars and scholarship, 1600–1660, vii. 476 ff.
Scholastica, i. 74
Scholefield, James (1789–1853), xii. 329, 473, 482, 491
Schole-howse of Women, The, iii. 486; iv. 318, 340, 523
Schomberg, Frederick Hermann, duke of (1615–1690), viii. 202
Schomburgh, Sir Robert (1804–1865), iv. 57
School plays, v. 410
Schoole of Slovenrie, The (trans. of Dedekind's *Grobianus*), iii. 82; iv. 528
Schooling, John Holt, xiv. 549
Schoolmen, vii. 482, 483
Schools, public, to the time of Colet, 341 ff., 487 ff.
Schopenhauer, Arthur, ix. 522; xiii. 457
Schort Memoriale of the Scottis corniklis for addicioun, The, ii. 285, 479
Schott, Peter, of Strassburg, iii. 14
Schreiner, Olive, xiv. Add. 9
Schröder, F. L., v. 298, 299, 307
Schröer, Arnold, i. 114; vi. 155
Schück, Henrik, v. 308
Schulenburg, Countess Ehrengard Melusina von der, duchess of Kendal (1667–1743), ix. 115
Schulpforte, iv. 260
Schulze-Gävernitz, G. von, xiii. 545
Schwellenberg, Mrs, x. 260
Schwenckfeld, Caspar von, ix. 315
Schwenter, Daniel, v. 285
Sciarrha, in *The Traytor*, vi. 199
Science, in Tudor moralities, v. 57
Scientific periodicals, xiv. 565, 566
Scilly isles, vii. 214; x. 466
Scintilla, or a light broken into darke warehouses, iv. 407, 545
Scioppius, Gaspar, iv. 260; vii. 311
Scipio, i. 95; iv. 62
Scipio, C. (*pseud.*), xii. 427
Scipio Africanus, v. 123
Sclater, William Lutley, xiv. Add. 9
Scobell, Henry (d. 1660), viii. 469; *Severall Proceedings in Parliament*, vii. 354
Scoble, John, xiv. Add. 9
Scogan, Henry (1361?–1407), ii. 159, 161, 162, 164, 187, 498
Scogan, John (*fl.* 1480?), ii. 498; iii. 92, 94. See, also, *Skoggan, Geystes of*
Scogin's Jests, xi. 334
Scolimorrhodia (*i.e.* England), in *Euphormio*, iv. 256
Scoloker, Anthony (*fl.* 1548), iv. 448
Scop, the, i. 3, 58; v. 26, 27
Scoresby, William (1789–1857), xiv. 554
Scornfu' Nansie, ix. 360
'Scorpion, The' (J. G. Lockhart), xii. 154, 158
Scot, John (*fl.* 1552–1571), iv. 412
Scot, Michael (1175?–1234?), i. 153, 199, 456
Scot, Reginald (1538?–1599), iii. 495; v. 479; vii. 366, 370, 371, 374, 395, 396, 506; viii. 357; *Discoverie of Witchcraft*, iii. 112 ff.; iv. 326, 530, 534; *Perfite platforme of a hoppe-garden, A*, iv. 542
Scot, Robert, xi. 331
Scot, Thomas (*fl.* 1605), iv. 520
Scot or Scott, Thomas (d. 1660), vii. 361; viii. 470
Scot of Scotstarvet, Sir John (1585–1670), iv. 261; ix. 550

Scot the Minotaur, in the *Mercuries*, VII. 356
Scota, Pharaoh's daughter, in *The Orygynale Cronykil*, II. 130
Scotch Drink, II. 278
Scotch jig, IX. 362
Scotch Presbyterian Eloquence, IX. 548
Scotch Wooing of Willy and Nanny, IX. 363
Scotia, dame, in *The Complaynt of Scotland*, III. 153
Scotichronicon, II. 128, 451
Scotish Feilde, I. 292; II. 40, 432, 435
Scotists, theological school of, I. 211
Scotland, v. 35, 171, 262; VI. 5, 169, 238, 361, 371; VII. 206 ff., 253 ff., 358, 435, 438; VIII. 47, 111, 356; IX. 4, 11 ff., 19, 130, 192, 194, 202, 203, 214, 215, 259, 301, 352, 359, 361 ff., 519; X. 42, 43, 55, 131, 132, 154, 182, 192, 226, 227, 231, 281, 282, 291, 321, 324; XI. 209, 211, 217, 232, 235, 240, 241, 315; XII. 1, 6, 12, 18, 30, 129, 142, 143, 156, 161, 167, 251, 337, 344, 349 ff., 357 ff., 370; XIII. 2, 115; XIV. 94, 95, 103, 159, 185, 204, 209, 255, 291, 327, 357, 374, 434, 437
  Church of, IV. 305; XI. 244; XII. 478
  Court of exchequer, XII. 350
  Free church, XII. 296
Scots, VII. 200, 214, 231, 308, 363, 458
Scots, lowland, XII. 24
Scots, The Tragedie of the King of, VI. 286
Scots Acts, The, XII. 357
Scots (Middle) anthologies, II. 267 ff., 478 ff.
Scots dialect, XIII. 233
'Scots Gentleman in the Swedish Service,' *i.e.* Defoe, IX. 19
Scots Magazine, IX. 562; X. 191, 192, 477, 479; XI. 232, 242, 243
Scots Minstrelsie, IX. 567; XI. 444
Scots Nightingale, IX. 372
Scots novels, XIII. 431
Scots Observer, The, XIV. 199
Scots papers, the (1646), VII. 347
Scots Spy, IX. 562
Scotsman, The, XIV. 176, 192, 203, 204, 531 ff., 535
Scotsmen, X. 148, 281, 282, 285, 289, 393, 396; XIV. 243, 345, 368
Scott, Alexander (1525?–1584?), II. 269, 281; III. 132, 134, 135, 136, 499, *also see* Add.; IX. 361, 365; XI. 203
  Derisioun and Scorne of Wantoun Wemen, III. 135
  Justing and Debait, The, III. 135; XI. 215
  Lament of the Master of Erskine, III. 134, 135
  Lo Quhat it is to Lufe, III. 135
  New Yeir Gift to Queen Mary, III. 134, 135
  Of May, III. 134
  Oppressit Hairt Indure, III. 135
  Up Helsum Hairt, III. 135
  When his Wife Left Him, IX. 360
Scott, Alexander John (1805–1866), XII. 466
Scott, Charles W. H., 4th duke of Buccleuch (1772–1819), XI. 239
Scott, Clement, XIII. 515, 525; XIV. 192, 535
Scott, D. C., XIV. 350
Scott, Henry, 3rd duke of Buccleuch (1746–1812), X. 335
Scott, Hew (1791–1872), *Fasti Ecclesiae Scoticanae*, XII. 359, 518
Scott, Hugh Stowell (*pseud.* Henry Seton Merriman, 1862–1903), XIII. 566
Scott, H. Spencer, XIV. 537
Scott, James, duke of Monmouth (1649–1685), VII. 364; VIII. 30, 36, 37, 90, 92, 99; IX. 6, 159, 160, 214; XIII. 434
Scott, James, of Heckmondwike academy, X. 385
Scott, James (1733–1814), X. 401, 525
Scott, James R. A., XIII. 485
Scott, John (*fl.* 1654–1696), VIII. 257
Scott, John (1730–1783), X. 474
Scott, John (1783–1821), XII. 161, 163
Scott, John, 1st earl of Eldon (1751–1838), XI. 158; XII. 62; XIV. 406, 509
Scott, Martha, X. 393
Scott, Michael (1175?–1234?), XI. 131
Scott, Michael (1789–1835), XII. 451; *Tom Cringle's Log*, XIV. 255
Scott, Robert (1811–1887), XII. 333, 487
Scott, Robert Falcon (1868–1912), XIV. 554; *Journal of Last Expedition*, XIV. 246
Scott, Sir Robert Forsyth, IV. 275; *Admissions to the College of St John*, X. 393
Scott, Temple, XIII. 491, 555
Scott, Thomas (1580?–1626), IV. 452
Scott, Thomas (*fl.* 1695), VIII. 441
Scott, Thomas (1747–1821), IX. 313; XII. 281, 461, 473
Scott, Walter (1614?–1694), IX. 552
Scott, Sir Walter (1771–1832), I. 199, 279, 283, 287; II. 87, 107, 186, 250, 409 ff., 414; III. 148, 366; IV. 45; VI. 58, 132, 226; VII. 231; VIII. 4, 5, 20, 42, 44, 54, 167, 261, 441, 451; IX. 12, 150, 154, 453; X. 26, 27, 41, 50, 55, 56, 58, 62, 93, 133, 137, 158, 190, 217, 232, 234, 236, 238 ff., 424, 451, 476, 489 ff.; XI. 27, 109, 117, 131, 145, 149, 150, 154, 158, 162, 170, 219, 220, 231, 236, 240, 241, 285, 286, 295 ff., 300 ff., 304, 305, 307, 309, 382, 405, 410, 416, 423, 441, 442, 444, 459, 464, 465; XII. 1 ff. (main entry), 34, 45, 46, 51, 57, 62, 95, 101, 102, 112, 120, 122, 125, 126, 128, 131, 133, 138, 144, 147, 150, 155, 157, 161 ff., 168, 170, 205, 212, 213, 223, 230, 237, 241, 245, 249 ff., 254, 255, 266, 300, 303, 357, 358, 367, 370, 372 ff. (main entry), 384, 385, 394, 397, 412, 422, 429, 430, 447, 451, 513, 517, *also see* Add.; XIII. 9, 15, 25, 63, 137, 160, 171, 226, 228, 230, 259, 263, 292, 295, 303, 306, 307, 312, 320, 338, 340, 379, 434, 457, 469; XIV. 50,

Scott, Sir Walter
94, 96, 156, 170, 223, 228, 278, 334, 341, 346, 373, 375, 399, 450, 491
Abbot, The, XII. 26, 29
Albert Graeme, XII. 7, 9
Allan a Dale, XII. 14
Anne of Geierstein, XIV. 106
Antiquary, The, XII. 29, 151, 350; XIII. 265
Apology for Tales of Terror, XII. 5
Black Dwarf, The, XII. 156
Bonnie Dundee, XII. 14; XIII. 234, 235
Border Antiquities, XII. 16
Bridal of Triermain, The, XII. 13
Bride of Lammermoor, The, XII. 22
Brignal Banks, XII. 14
County Guy, XII. 14
Donald Caird, XII. 14
Doom of Devorgoil, The, XII. 13
Eve of St John, The, XII. 7
Fortunes of Nigel, The, VIII. 174; XII. 18, 372
Gray Brother, The, XII. 7
Guy Mannering, XII. 18, 21, 151; XIV. 255
Hail to the Chief, XII. 12
Halidon Hill, XII. 13
Harold the Dauntless, XII. 13
Heart of Midlothian, The, XII. 17, 18; XIII. 380
Ivanhoe, X. 63, 220, 227; XII. 26, 378, 379; XIV. 107
Kenilworth, XII. 372
Kinmont Willie, II. 415, 417; XII. 6
Lady of the Lake, The, XII. 11, 12, 377
Lay of the Last Minstrel, XI. 127, 131; XII. 7 ff., 14, 146, 381; XIII. 233
Legend of Montrose, The, XII. 29, 372
Life of (Lockhart's), XIV. 106
Life of Dryden, VIII. 124
Life of Napoleon, XII. 16, 372, 378, 379; XIV. 106
Lord of the Isles, II. 108; XII. 13
Love Wakes and Weeps, XII. 14
Macduff's Cross, XII. 13
Macgregor's Gathering, XII. 14
Marmion, XII. 9 ff., 42, 149, 365, 372
Minstrelsy of the Scottish Border, IX. 373, 375; XI. 242; XII. 6, 7, 364, 372, 378, 380
Old Mortality, XII. 18, 21, 22, 27; XIII. 265
One Volume More, XII. 364
Otterbourne, XII. 6
Peveril of the Peak, XIII. 265
Pibroch of Donald Dhu, The, XII. 14
Poetical Works, XII. 364
Prefatory Memoir to Sterne, XII. 366
Proud Maisie, XII. 14; XIII. 234
Quentin Durward, X. 44; XII. 26; XIII. 419
Rebecca's Hymn, XII. 14
Redgauntlet, XII. 18, 21, 26, 29
Rest, Warrior, Rest, XII. 12, 14
Rob Roy, XII. 17, 29
Rokeby, XII. 12, 13, 105

Scott, Sir Walter
Sun upon the Weirdlaw Hill, The, XII. 14
Swift's *Works*, XII. 372
Tales of a Grandfather, XII. 16
Tales of my Landlord, XII. 151, 380
Talisman, The, X. 227
Tragedy of Auchindrane, The, XII. 13
Vision of Don Roderick, The, XII. 13
Waken Lords and Ladies Gay, XII. 14
Wandering Willie's Tale, XII. 22, 29
Waverley, VII. 86, 88; XI. 301; XII. 26, 151, 372; XIII. 239
Waverley novels, XI. 293; XII. 251; XIV. 163
Weary Lot, A, XII. 14
When Israel of the Lord Beloved, XII. 14
Woodstock, XII. 372; XIII. 265
Young Lochinvar, XII. 14; XIII. 234, 235
Works edited by, XII. 16
Scott, Sir W., Sheriff Court at Selkirk, XII. Add.
Scott, Wm (1813–1872), XII. 454; XIV. 198
Scott, Wm Bell (1811–1890), XII. 384, 399, 405, 450; XIII. 110, 156, 186, 187, 508;
Sphinx, The, XIII. 187
Scott of Amwell, VIII. 230
Scottish antiquities, XII. 25, 351
Scottish ballads, XII. 125, 358
Scottish bar, X. 191; XII. 143; XIV. 7, 112
Scottish book-clubs, XII. 355, 357, 359
Scottish booktrade, XI. 342
Scottish Calvinism, XIII. 18
Scottish campaigns of 1639 and 1640, VII. 22, 24, 194
Scottish-Canadians, XIV. 345
Scottish Chaucerians, I. 297; II. 239 ff., 471 ff.
Scottish church, X. 356
Scottish dialect, IX. 361; X. 174; XI. 204, 238; XII. 125; XIV. 209, 447, 457
Scottish dialect, in *The Sad Shepherd*, VI. 371
Scottish divines, XII. 284
Scottish drama, X. 87
Scottish education, XIV. 405 ff.
Scottish historians, XIV. 94 ff.
Scottish Historical Review, The, XII. 358
Scottish history, X. 295; XIV. 101
Scottish humour, XIV. 209
Scottish king, in *Eastward Hoe*, VI. 30
Scottish language, the, II. 88 ff., 446; VII. 455
Scottish literature, the earliest, II. 100 ff., 447 ff.
Scottish literature from 1603–1786, IX. Add.
Scottish Minstrel, The, XI. 233
Scottish moors, XIII. 10
Scottish music, X. 232
Scottish novels, XII. 25 ff., 30
Scottish parliament, IV. 306; X. 36
Scottish Pasquils, VIII. 411
Scottish peasants, XI. 206; XII. 414; XIII. 2, 16
Scottish people, VIII. 69, 121, 298, 299
Scottish philosophers, X. 345, 347

Scottish philosophy, xiv. 6 ff., 41, 48, 209
Scottish poems, xiv. 377
Scottish poetry, x. 226, 233; xii. 14, 45, 358
Scottish popular music, ix. 361 ff.
Scottish popular poetry, ix. 359 ff., 565 ff.
Scottish press, iv. 412, 547
Scottish prose literature, ix. 215
Scottish pulpit, xiv. 119
Scottish Registers, The, xiv. 95
Scottish school of rhetoric, xiv. 398, 399, 428
Scottish schools commission, xiv. 421
Scottish State Papers in Jacobean times, vii. 435
Scottish Text society, xii. 344, 359
Scottish theology, xii. 296
Scottish universities, ii. 487, 489; x. 182; xiii. 2; xiv. 410, 411, 424
Scottish university periodicals, xiv. 239
Scottish verse, xi. 203 ff.
Scottish writers, x. 285, 290 ff.
Scotts of Eskdale, the, xii. 9
Scotus or Erigena, Joannes (*fl.* 850), i. 154, 434; iii. 214; iv. 269 ff.; *De Divisione Naturae*, iv. 270; trans. of pseudo-Dionysian writings, iv. 270
Scougal, Henry (1650–1678), ix. 547
Scourge, The, xiv. 221, 223
Scourge of Simony, The. See Parnassus trilogy
Scrag, Sir Gosling, in Smollett's *Peregrine Pickle*, x. 39
Scrape, Ezekiel, viii. 122
Scratch, lord, in Reynolds's *Dramatist*, xi. 281
Scribes, i. 17
Scriblerus, xiii. 452
Scriblerus, Martinus. See *Memoirs of Martinus Scriblerus*
Scriblerus club, ix. 103, 131, 166, 167, 281
'Scriblerus Secundus' (Henry Fielding), x. 21
Scriptores Rerum Anglicanarum, x. 312
Scriptoria, i. 18, 153, 426
Scriptural chronology, ix. 227
Scripture, in *Piers the Plowman*, ii. 20, 21, 25
Scripture paraphrases (metrical), xi. 244
Scriven, Yorks., vii. 224
Scrivener, Frederick Henry Ambrose (1813–1891), xii. 340, 501
Scrocca, in *Sicelides*, vi. 323
Scroggs, The Lord Chief Justice, his Speech in the King's Bench, viii. 90
Scroop, Adrian (1601–1660), viii. 470
Scroop, Sir Car or Carr (1649–1680), viii. 213
Scroope-Grosvenor suit, ii. 156, 158
Scrope, George Julius Poulett (1797–1876), xiv. 292, 563
Scrope, Richard le (1350?–1405), ii. 422, 423
Scrope, William (1772–1852), xiv. 545
Scroupe, Jane, in *Phyllyp Sparowe*, iii. 71
'Scrub,' x. 201
Scruple, in Wilson's *Cheats*, viii. 122
Scruton, William, xiii. 559
Scudamore, James, *Homer à la Mode*, ix. 258, 500
Scudéry, Georges de, ix. 500; *Ibrahim*, viii. 22, 193
Scudéry, Madeleine de, iv. 327; vi. 239; vii. 222, 391; viii. 132, 186, 434
Almahide, viii. 22, 371; ix. 268
Clélie, iv. 523; viii. 22, 371, 372
Ibrahim, ou L'illustre Bassa, viii. 20, 193, 371
Le Grand Cyrus, iv. 523; viii. 15, 20, 22, 119, 194, 371; x. 14
Scudmore, in *A Woman is a Weathercocke*, vi. 221
Scully, William Charles, xiv. 589, *also see* Add. 5, 10
Scyld, in *Beowulf*, i. 2, 22, 25, 28
Scylla, iii. 343
Scylla, in Keats's *Endymion*, xii. 82
Scythia, ii. 130
Sea and travel, the literature of the, iv. 66 ff., 453 ff.
Seafarer, i. 1, 2, 38, 42, 54, 275, 423, 428
Seafaringe Men, in Hope of Good Fortune, In Prais of, iv. 97
Seagrim, Molly, in Fielding's *Tom Jones* x. 31
Seagull, capt., in *Eastward Hoe*, vi. 47, 48, 355
Seaman, Lazarus (d. 1675), xi. 336
Seaman, Owen, xiii. 500; xiv. 548
Search, Edward. *See* Tucker, Abraham
'Searle, J.,' xii. 416
Searle, Laurence, iv. 141
Sebastian, in *The Tempest*, v. 194, 206
Sebastian story, the, vi. 149
Seccombe, Thomas (1866–1924), xi. 448; xiii. 573; xiv. 537
Sechnall, Hymn of St, i. 65
Secker, Thomas (1693–1768), x. 386, 517; xi. 355 ff.; *Lectures on the Church Catechism*, x. 362; *Memoirs*, ix. 393, 394, 574
Second and Third Blast of retrait from plaies and theatres, A, vi. 390, 392, 496. See, also, *Third Blast, The*
Second collection of tracts proving...the only true God, x. 378
Second Maiden's Tragedy, The, vi. 178
Second Merchant's Tale, The. See *Beryn, The Tale of*
Secreta Secretorum, ii. 149, 301, 483
Secularist, The, xiii. 108
Secunda, St, i. 74
Secunda Pastorum, v. 15, 18, 19
Secundus, Johannes, vii. 83, 489
Security, bill of, ix. 215
Sedaine, Michel-Jean, x. 79; *Le philosophe sans le savoir*, x. 68; xi. 265
Sedan, xiii. 445
Sedbergh school, iii. 427; vii. 329, 330, 493
Seddon, John (1725–1770), x. 385

Sedgefield, Durham, XI. 244
Sedgwick, Adam (1785–1873), XIV. 289, 291, 292, 294, 295, 563, 593, 595; XIV. 300
Sedgwick, Joseph (*fl.* 1653), IX. 571
Sedgwick, William (1610?–1669?), VII. 509
Sedition, in *Kynge Johan*, V. 65
Sedley, Amelia, in *Vanity Fair*, XIII. 286 ff., 290, 296
Sedley, Catharine, countess of Dorchester (1657–1717), VIII. 216
Sedley, Sir Charles (1639?–1701), VII. 180; VIII. 133, 136, 142, 143, 198 ff., 215, 217, 420, 423, 444, 446; IX. 169, 174
  Antony and Cleopatra, VIII. 139, 216
  Beauty the Conqueror, VIII. 139
  Bellamira, or the Mistress, VIII. 139
  Grumbler, The, VIII. 139
  Happy Pair, The, VIII. 216
  Mulberry Garden, VIII. 134, 137, 139, 143, 216
  'Not Celia that I juster am,' VIII. 216
  'Phyllis is my only Joy,' VIII. 216
  Tyrant King of Crete, VIII. 139, 216
  Vergil's *Eclogues*, VIII. 216
Sedley, Jos, in *Vanity Fair*, XIII. 286
Sedley family, in *Vanity Fair*, XIII. 286, 288
Sedulius, copy at Antwerp, I. 72, 76
Seebohm, Frederic (1833–1912), XII. 513; XIV. 78, 497; *English Village Community, The*, XII. 348; XIV. 79; *Oxford Reformers of* 1498, *The*, XIV. 79; *Tribal System of Wales, The*, XII. 348
Seeley, Sir John Robert (1834–1895), XII. 469, 493; XIV. 90 ff., 197, 426, 479, 497, 594, 606, 609
  Ecce Homo, XII. 154, 297; XIV. 91
  Essays on a liberal education, XIV. 432
  Expansion of England, The, XIV. 61 ff.
  Growth of British Policy, The, XIV. 93
  Lectures and Essays, XIV. 91
  Life and Times of Stein, The, XIV. 92
  Natural Religion, XIII. 452
Seeley, Robert Benton (1789–1886), XII. 473
See-well, in *Piers the Plowman*, II. 19
Segar, Sir William (d. 1633), IV. 543; *Honor Military and Civill*, IV. 401
Segismundo, in Calderon's *La Vida es Sueño*, XIII. 144, 145
Seine, river, XIV. 185, 221
Selborne, X. 270, 271
Selbourne, earl of. *See* Palmer, Sir Roundell
Selden, Camille, XIII. 559
Selden, John (1584–1654), III. 97; IV. 49, 55, 190, 299, 425, 432, 434, 461; V. 371, 479; VI. 6, 376; VII. 148, 315, 318 ff., 442, 475, 484, 485, 496; VIII. 62, 309, 469; IX. 355; XIV. 309
  De Dis Syris, VII. 281, 318
  De jure naturali et gentium juxta disciplinam Hebraeorum, VII. 281
  Fleta, edition of, VIII. 318, 465
  Fortescue's *De Laudibus*, edition of, VIII. 318
Selden, John
  Historia Placitorum Coronae, VIII. 320
  History of the Common Law of England, VIII. 320
  History of Tithes, VII. 281; VIII. 322
  Jani Anglorum Facies Altera, VIII. 318
  Mare Clausum, VII. 281, 307; VIII. 318
  Marmora Arundeliana, VII. 316, 489
  Table-Talk, VII. 392; VIII. 60, 321 ff.; X. 472
  Titles of Honour, IV. 408, 513
  Works, VIII. 322
Selden society, XII. 355; XIV. 80, 81
'Select Society,' the, X. 281, 288, 290
Selena, in Drayton's *Eglogs*, IV. 173, 175, 176
Selim, in Lyttelton's *Persian Letters*, X. 114
Selimus, V. 85 ff., 134, 238, 398, 418
Sélincourt, Ernest de, XI. 408, *also see* Add.; XII. 405 ff.
Selio and Olimpio (*Caelo and Olympo*?), VI. 93
Selkirk, Alexander (1676–1721), IX. 19; XIV. 243, 554
Selkirkshire, XII. 5
Sell, Henry, XIV. 532
Sell's *Dictionary of the World's Press*, XIV. 174
Sellar, William Young (1825–1890), XII. 493; *Roman Poets of the Republic*, XII. 337
Seller, John (*fl.* 1700), IV. 461
Selling. *See* Tilly, William
'Selma,' X. 130, 227, 229
Selvaggia, XIII. 118
Selwyn, George Augustus (1719–1791), X. 88, 494; XIII. 364
Selwyn, Thomas Kynaston, XIV. 597
Selwyn, William, XIV. 589, 595, *also see* Add. 5
Selymus, in *Solymannidae*, VI. 301
Semans sacred safetye..., *The*, IV. 399
Semitic peoples, XII. 296
Semitic religions, VII. 318
Semly academy, X. 387
Sempill, Francis (1616?–1682), *The Banishment of Povertie*, IX. 365
Sempill, Sir James (1566–1625), IX. 545
Sempill, Robert (1530?–1595), II. 280; III. 122, 132, 149, 150, 505; IV. 412
  Ballat on Margret Fleming, II. 280
  Defence of Crissell Sandelandis, II. 280
  Life of the Tulchene Bischope of St Andrews, III. 132
  Legend of a Lymaris Lyfe, III. 150
  Sege of the Castel of Edinburgh, III. 150
Sempill, Robert (1595?–1665?), IX. 364, 365, 372; *Life...of Habbie Simson*, IX. 365; XI. 211
Sempills of Beltrees, the, IX. 556
Semple, John, IX. 549
Sempringham, I. 344. *See, also*, Gilbert of
Sempronio, in *Celestina*, V. 99
Sempronius, in Addison's *Cato*, IX. 64
Semur, XIII. 431

Sénancour, Étienne Pivert de, XIII. 93, 94; *Obermann*, XI. 288
Sencer, in *The Wise-woman Of Hogsdon*, VI. 83
Sendall, Walter J., XIV. 537
Seneca, L. Annaeus, I. 76, 99, 100, 213, 355; II. 363, 366; III. 173, 189, 198, 430; IV. 2, 4 ff., 23, 333, 348, 349, 439, 440, 523, 525; V. 61 ff., 66, 70 ff., 76, 78 ff., 84, 88, 118, 149, 152, 157, 158, 162, 163, 238 ff., 248, 288, 324, 334, 394 ff.; VI. 9, 20, 296, 299 ff., 311, 319, 327, 366; VII. 261, 272, 304, 390; VIII. 13, 133, 188, 378, 447; IX. 28, 41, 55, 57, 233, 265, 418; XII. 49
Agamemnon, V. 75, 78, 79; VI. 178
Consolatio ad Helviam, IX. 218
Hecuba, VI. 295
Hercules Furens, IV. 249; V. 75, 78
Hercules Oetaeus, V. 75, 78
Medea, V. 75, 78; VI. 295
Morals, IX. 273, 275
Octavia, V. 61, 63, 75, 79; VI. 301
Oedipus, V. 75, 78, 80, 85; VI. 295
Phaedra, V. 75
Tenne Tragedies, V. 80, 162, *and see* Add. 2
Thebais, V. 68, 78, 80
Thyestes, III. 198; V. 75, 76, 78, 79; VI. 46, 178, 301
Troas (=*Troades*), V. 80; VI. 295
Seneca, in Gray's *Agrippina*, X. 119
Senior, Nassau William (1790–1864), XIV. 480, 506
Conversations, XIV. 116
Correspondence and Conversations of A. de Tocqueville, XIV. 116
'European and American State Confederacies,' XII. 153
Journals kept in France and Italy, XIV. 116
Journals...relating to Ireland, XIV. 116
Senlac, XIV. 72
Sennacherib, IV. 30; XII. 499
Sense, in *Complaint upon Love to Reason*, III. 187
Sense of the House, The, VII. 385
Sensual Appetite, in *The Nature of the Four Elements*, V. 57
Sensualitie, in *Ane Pleasant Satyre*, III. 124 ff.
Sensuality, in *Nature*, V. 54
Sensuality, in *The Example of Virtue*, II. 227
Sententiae Pueriles, XI. 367
Sentry, captain, in *The Spectator*, IX. 51
Sephestia, in *Menaphon*, III. 356, 357
Septem contra Christum, XII. 294
Septennial act, IX. 224
Septuagint. See under Bible
Serafina, in FitzGerald's *The Painter of his own Dishonour*, XIII. 144
Serafino dell' Aquila, III. 187, 253
Serbia, XIV. 191
'Serena,' X. 299
Seres, William (d. 1579?), IV. 384, 386, 397
Sergeant, Emily Frances Adeline (1851–1904), XIII. 566
Sergeant, John (1622–1707), VIII. 475; *Solid Philosophy*, VIII. 346
Sergius I, II. 347
Serlio, Sebastian, III. 553
Serre, de la, VII. 391
Serres, Jean de, IV. 448; VI. 33, 138
Serres, Olivier de, IV. 312
Sertorius, in Robert Landor's *Fawn of Sertorius*, XII. 230
Servatius, Michael, prior, III. 3
Servetus, Michael, III. 400
Serving-man's Comfort, The, V. 351, 353, 374
Servius, IV. 264
Servus, in *Saturnalia*, VI. 319
Sesostris, X. 301
Set at Maw, The, VI. 98
Seth, I. 134; II. 20
Seth, James, XIV. 467
Seth's wife, VII. 255
Seton, George, 5th baron Seton (1530?–1585), XII. 27
Seton, George, 5th earl of Winton (d. 1749), IX. 247
Seton, Henry, in Scott's *Abbot*, XII. 27
Seton, Mary, in Scott's *Abbot*, XII. 27
Setoun, Christopher, in *Bruce*, II. 105
Setter, the pimp, in Congreve's *Old Bachelor*, VIII. 147
Settle, Elkanah (1648–1724), VIII. 4, 21, 271, 409, 441
Absalom Senior, VIII. 26, 41, 92
Cambyses, VIII. 192
City Rambler, The, XI. 322
Empress of Morocco, The, VIII. 192, 193, 401, 403
Female Prelate, The, VIII. 193
Ibrahim, VIII. 193
Love and Revenge, VIII. 193
Seven Champions of Christendom, V. 32. 34; X. 220
Seven Dayes of the Weeke, The, VI. 319, 320, 474
Seven deadly sins, V. 42, 52, 313
Seven Deadly Sins, in Lydgate, II. 201. *See, also*, Dunbar *and* Vices
Seven Deadly Sins, in *The Faerie Queene*, III. 237; VI. 335
Seven Sages of Rome, Romance of the, I. 286, 308, 309, 470; II. 150, 177, 308; IV. 361
Seven Sins (Byrhtferth's), I. 131
Severall Proceedings, VII. 353
Severn, Joseph (1793–1879), XII. 92, 407
Severn, river, IV. 190; X. 112
Severn, river, Layamon and, I. 234, 265
Severus, Alexander, VI. 299
Sévigné, Madame de, II. 395; IX. 245; X. 248, 273; XIII. 376
Seville, III. 422; IV. 69, 71
Seward, Albert Charles, XI. 426; XIV. 559
Seward, Anna (1747–1809), X. 479, 491, *also see* Add.; XI. 459; XII. 124, 376, 422
Seward, Thomas (1708–1790), X. 136

Seward, William (1747–1799), x. 473
Sewell, Anna (1820–1878), xi. 489
Sewell, Eleanor L., xiii. 566
Sewell, Elizabeth Missing (1815–1906), xii. 462; xiii. 566; xiv. 600
Sewell, G. A., ix. 436
Sewell, John, xi. 335
Sewell, William (1804–1874), xii. 462; xiv. 596, 598, 609
Sexburga, ii. 210
Sexby, Edward (d. 1658), vii. 460
Sexton, Alexander Humboldt, xiv. 592
Sextus Placidus, English version of *Medicina de quadrupedibus*, i. 136
Seymour, Edward, 1st earl of Hertford and duke of Somerset (1506?–1552), iii. 26, 152, 175, 418, 419, 431; vii. 325, 326
Seymour, Elizabeth, countess of Northumberland, x. 209, 470, 482
Seymour, Laura, xiii. 425
Seymour, Robert (1800?–1836), xiii. 311; xiv. 232, 235
Seymour, Thomas, baron Seymour of Sudeley (1508?–1549), iv. 230, 231
Seymour, William, 2nd duke of Somerset (1588–1660), ix. 202
Seymour-Conway, Francis, earl and 1st marquis of Hertford (1719–1794), x. 118, 249, 274, 495
Seymour-Conway, Francis Charles, 3rd marquis of Hertford (1777–1842), xiv. 115
Seynt Albons, Bellum apud, ii. 302
Seyssel, Claude de, iv. 3
Seyton, Catherine, in Scott's *Abbot*, xii. 22, 27
Sforza, in *The Duke of Millaine*, vi. 155, 158, 159, 163
Shackleton, Elizabeth, xiv. 323
Shackleton, Mary. *See* Leadbeater, Mary
Shackleton, Richard (1728–1792), xi. 1, 2; xiv. 323
Shadow, in *Henry IV*, v. 360
Shadow of Night, The, vi. 30
Shadwell, Charles (d. 1726), *Fair Quaker of Deal*, viii. 168
Shadwell, Lionel Lancelot, xiv. 602
Shadwell, Thomas (1642?–1692), v. 291; vii. 183; viii. 6, 21, 28, 40, 41, 49, 91, 92, 133, 168, 173, 193, 214, 215, 398, 401, 403, 404, 409, 410, 430, 441; ix. 79
Bury Fair, viii. 174
Epsom Wells, viii. 174
Humorists, The, iv. 333
Libertine, The, viii. 174
Medal of John Bayes, The, viii. 2, 3, 5, 40, 92
Miser, The, viii. 134, 174
Scowrers, The, ix. 362
Squire of Alsatia, The, viii. 174
Sullen Lovers, viii. 134, 173, 174
Tempest, The, viii. 120, 398
Timon of Athens, adaptation of, viii. 120, 174
Tory Poets, The, viii. 40
True Widow, A, viii. 40, 401
Snaen, Margaret Josephine, xiv. 600
Shaftesbury, vii. 74; x. 20
Shaftesbury, earl of. *See* Cooper, Anthony Ashley
Shaftesbury academy, x. 387
Shaftesbury's Farewell, viii. 92
Shafton, Sir Piercie, ii. 218
Shah, B. B., xiv. 575
Shairp, John Campbell (1819–1885), xi. 411, 417, 441; xii. 259, 381, 457, 466; xiii. 473, 504; xiv. 525
Shakebag, in *Arden of Feversham*, v. 200, 240
Shakerley, Jeremy (*fl.* 1651), vii. 509
Shakespeare, Hamnet, v. 169, 175, 219
Shakespeare, John, v. 167, 172, 219
Shakespeare, Judith, v. 169, 172, 175, 219
Shakespeare, Richard, v. 167
Shakespeare, Susanna, v. 168, 219
Shakespeare, William (1564–1616), i. 1, 7, 152, 274, 276, 296, 298, 316; ii. 104, 173, 176, 266, 391, 412, 415; iii. 24, 54, 62, 107, 156, 188, 198, 200, 212, 244, 247, 252, 253, 259, 260, 263 ff., 268, 271, 283, 284, 300, 302, 305, 320, 323, 327, 335, 351, 356, 362, 371, 374, 385, 455, 460, 465, *also see* Add.; iv. 3, 6, 7, 10, 43 ff., 49, 50, 55, 77 ff., 88, 115, 117, 129, 132, 137, 168, 183, 193, 195 ff., 199, 243, 248, 266, 300, 349, 390, 392 ff., 472, 473, 544, 545, *also see* Add.; v. 56, 63, 83, 91, 100, 119, 120, 126 ff., 131, 135 ff., 145 ff., 153, 155 ff., 165–308 (main entry), 309 ff., 314, 315, 319, 322, 323, 324, 326, 327, 328, 330 ff., 336, 346 ff., 370 ff., 380; vi. 1 ff., 13, 20, 28 ff., 39, 42, 43, 51, 52, 55, 57, 62, 69, 70, 77, 85, 95 ff., 106, 108 ff., 113, 118, 119, 123, 125 ff., 139, 140, 143, 151 ff., 157, 165, 167, 180, 185, 188, 193, 195, 196, 206, 211, 218, 256, 276, 278, 290, 291, 311 ff., 316, 330, 336, 359, 365, 370, 373, 381, 394, 399, 405, 409, 437; vii. 3, 7, 8, 16, 73, 95, 101, 111 112, 116, 133 ff., 140, 146, 153, 161, 163, 164, 176, 221, 259, 272, 275, 366, 387, *also see* Add.; viii. 13, 17, 27 ff., 119 ff., 125, 127 ff., 150, 155, 157, 163, 164, 176, 181, 185, 191, 196, 197, 202, 205, 214, 219, 221 ff., 230, 231, 233, 237, 377, 411; ix. 42, 77, 80, 118, 140, 142, 144, 145, 188, 296, 351, 362, 363, 396, 447 ff., 474 ff., 479, 509; x. 1, 13, 27, 31, 50, 68, 69, 82, 85 ff., 120, 127, 143, 145, 146, 148, 167, 177, 179, 180, 184, 186, 202, 227, 234, 236, 445, 452, 454, 460, 462, 469, 474, 490, 505; xi. 10, 13, 133 ff., 181 ff., 206, 255, 260, 282, 284, 290, 291, 319, 320, 322, 327, 354, 414 ff., 447, 450, 451, 453, 457, 472, 474, *also see* Add.; xii. 23, 24, 30, 40, 49, 68, 70, 83, 88, 91, 93, 98, 106, 108, 111, 120, 168, 169, 171, 177, 186, 189 ff., 196, 211, 218, 243, 268, 280, 331, 347, 369, 394, 396, 398, 404, 407, 409, 422, 432, 434, 440, 476, 490, 524; xiii 13,

Shakespeare, William
39, 43, 63, 64, 82, 101, 117, 129, 136, 144, 198, 210, 230, 231, 233, 242, 244, 253, 257, 261, 303, 304, 312, 317, 382, 390, 407, 411, 495, *also see* Add. 2 XIV. 106, 142, 147, 157, 307, 308, 339, 358, 434, 435, 442, 446 ff.
Bibliography, V. 397, 426 ff.
Boydell's edition, XIV. 215
Folios:
First Folio, IV. 394, 395; VI. 6, 248
Perkins Folio, the, XII. 368
Second Folio, IV. 394
Plays and poems:
All's Well that Ends Well, V. 174, 177, 180, 181, 190, 212, 220, 265; VI. 103
Antony and Cleopatra, V. 177, 196, 198–199 (main entry), 204, 217, 221, 291; VIII. 28, 216; X. 433
As You Like It, I. 298; III. 349, 385; IV. 79; V. 126, 127, 139, 171, 177, 183, 188, 191 ff. (main entry), 220, 300, 318, 369; VI. 28, 213, 305, 365, 367; VIII. 224; XIV. 443
Comedy of Errors, The, IV. 4, 79; V. 174, 175, 177, 179, 180, 183, 188, 191, 215, 219, 220, 283, 320; VI. 14, 215
Coriolanus, V. 196 ff. (main entry), 202, 221, 265, 266, 278, 374; VIII. 443; XI. 274
Cymbeline, V. 138, 189, 195, 203 ff. (main entry), 215, 221, 265, 290, 298; VI. 110, 121, 200, 236; VIII. 226, 428; X. 433
Hamlet, I. 16; III. 179, 349, 456; IV. 44, 336, 394; V. 76, 79, 81, 145, 157 ff., 169, 177, 179, 193, 198 ff. (main entry) 202, 203, 210, 214, 216, 221, 248, 260 ff., 265, 267, 273, 274, 278, 283, 288, 290, 294, 295, 298 ff., 304, 307, 327, 333, 340, 349, 356; VI. 34, 45, 46, 49, 121, 155, 162, 170, 177, 178, 186, 190, 200, 209, 217, 220, 248, 266, 268, 272 ff., 302, 312, 325, *also see* Add.; VIII. 116 121, 152, 224; IX. 268; X. 77, 81, 83, 141; XI. 135, 258; XII. 170; XIII. 66, 67; XIV. 447
Henry IV, IV. 393; V. 161, 174, 184, 187, 189, 194, 220, 260 ff., 264, 298, 300, 356; VI. 49; VIII. 116, 120
Henry V, II. 77; III. 349; IV. 188, 192, 393; V. 152, 189, 194, 195, 220, 243, 249, 260, 261, 263, 300, 346; VI. 2, 222, 253; IX. 187; X. 121
Henry VI, V. 129, 147, 153, 175, 184 ff. (main entry), 220, 221, 237, 248, 260, 263, 275, 280, 290, 300; VI. 247; VII. 110; VIII. 188
Henry VIII, V. 195, 221, 261, 333, 344, 346; VI. 116, 128, 137, 231
Julius Caesar, V. 196–197 (main entry), 199, 221, 265, 268, 284, 287, 288, 290, 294, 296, 300; VI. 19, 49, 127; IX. 142; X. 81; XI. 353, 413
King John, V. 147, 161, 174, 184, 185 (main entry), 220, 294, 300, 356; VIII. 426

Shakespeare, William
Plays and poems:
King Lear, III. 102, 355, 448, 517; IV. 394, 534; V. 179, 196, 199, 203, 204 (main entry), 214, 221, 260 ff., 266, 272, 273, 279, 283, 294, 295, 298, 306, 310, 333; VI. 153, 158, 186, 190, 200, 209, 248; VII. 128; VIII. 120, 443; X. 81, 91, 429; XI. 258, 283, 450; XII. 94, 170
Lover's Complaint, A, V. 223, 224, 233
Love's Labour's Lost, IV. 119, 366, 394, 434; V. 126, 174, 175, 177 ff. (main entry), 182, 215, 220, 224, 233, 260, 264, 315, 356; VI. 214, 335; VIII. 126, 425
Love's Labour's Won. See *All's Well that Ends Well*
Lucrece, XI. 181
Macbeth, IV. 206; V. 169, 179, 199, 201, 203 (main entry), 213, 221, 241, 265, 268, 288, 290, 294, 298, 300, 315, 333; VI. 49, 76, 98, 158, 192, 217, 315, 318, 349; X. 77, 81, 141, 460; XI. 261, 282, 283, 352, 450; XII. 94; XIII. 30
Measure for Measure, V. 119, 188, 190–191 (main entry), 212, 220, 245, 265, 298, 397; VI. 99, 110, 236; VIII. 120; XIV. 443
Merchant of Venice, The, IV. 79, 394; V. 174, 175, 181, 183 (main entry), 216, 220, 260, 278, 283, 298, 300, 301; VI. 300; VIII. 194; XIV. 441, 449
Merry Wives of Windsor, The, III. 181; V. 169, 187, 189 (main entry), 220, 252, 260, 263, 284, 291, 298, 308, 348, 369; VI. 95; VIII. 116, 436
Midsummer Night's Dream, A, III. 349; IV. 394, 533; V. 174, 181 ff. (main entry), 188, 192, 203, 216, 220, 260, 265, 272, 277, 283, 285, 298, 300, 317; VI. 207, 213, 285, 367; VIII. 120; X. 432, 433; XIII. 30
Much Ado about Nothing, IV. 393; V. 126, 127, 191 (main entry), 192, 207, 220, 260, 284, 285, 298, 358; VIII. 224; XIII. 262; XIV. 440
Othello, III. 188; V. 177, 199, 202–203 (main entry), 204, 206, 221, 260, 261, 264, 266, 277, 284, 288, 290, 294, 295, 298, 301, 302, 304; VI. 186, 192, 248; VIII. 120, 375; X. 73, 81; XI. 352; XII. 170; XIII. 30, 67, 412
Passionate Pilgrim, The, V. 148, 221, 223, 224, 233
Pericles, II. 152; III. 456; V. 178, 188 (main entry), 190, 221, 236, 237, 260; VI. 2, 110; X. 78, 436
Phoenix and the Turtle, The, V. 221, 224, 233
Poems, V. 221, 260, 275
Rape of Lucrece, The, III. 198; IV. 394; V. 166, 170, 219, 221, 223, 227 (main entry), 228, 233, 259; VI. 312
Richard II, IV. 78, 393; V. 145, 153, 174, 175, 184 (main entry), 185, 220, 260, 262, 298, 300, 324, 326, 346, 371, 374; VI. 36, 49; VIII. 443

Shakespeare, William
Plays and poems:
Richard III, III. 88, 458; IV. 393; V. 79, 174, 175, 184 ff. (main entry), 213, 220, 260, 261, 269, 271, 279, 281, 290, 291, 295, 297, 300; VI. 46, 129, 248, 301; VII. 265; VIII. 123, 426; XII. 150
Roman plays, V. 100, 196, 197, 199, 221; VI. 182
Romeo and Juliet, II. 391; III. 268, 271, 359; IV. 79, 393, 434; V. 77, 174, 175, 181, 182 (main entry), 185, 216, 221, 242, 244, 260 ff., 265, 268, 269, 279, 283, 294, 296, 298, 299, 301, 322, 374; VI. 93, 221 ff., 248, 300, 311, 335; VIII. 120, 151, 182; X. 432; XI. 133, 260
Sonnets, IV. 392, 394, 407; V. 166, 170, 172, 174, 176, 219, 221, 223 ff., 228–233 (main entry); VI. 30; XI. 181; XIII. 450; XIV. 304
Sonnets to Sundry Notes of Music, IV. 119; V. 224
Taming of the Shrew, The, III. 454; V. 115, 147, 181 (main entry), 220, 283, 285; VI. 97, 138; VIII. 126, 140; X. 433; XIV. 443. See, also, under *Taming of a Shrew*
Tempest, The, III. 178; IV. 21, 78, 79; V. 172, 178, 188, 192, 203 ff., 206–207 (main entry), 215, 220, 285, 298, 299, 300; VI. 23, 24, 110, 239; VIII. 9, 120, 126, 135, 224, 226, 430; X. 433; XI. 274; XII. 191, 516
Timon of Athens, V. 196 (main entry), 198, 221, 265, 291, 308; VIII. 120, 174; XI. 265
Titus Andronicus, IV. 393; V. 75, 139, 147, 152, 163, 164, 174, 175, 177, 178–179 (main entry), 182, 184, 185, 188, 191, 194, 195, 204, 218, 221, 260, 283, 322; VI. 23; VIII. 140, 420
Troilus and Cressida, IV. 298; V. 195–196 (main entry), 221, 260, 261, 263, 264; VI. 30, 44, 207; VIII. 29; XI. 319
Twelfth Night, IV. 78; V. 138, 191, 192, 193–194 (main entry), 220, 300; VI. 204, 305; VII. 84; VIII. 126
Two Gentlemen of Verona, III. 268; V. 126, 174, 177, 180 (main entry), 182, 220; VIII. 126
Two Noble Kinsmen, The, VIII. 120
Venetian Comedy, The, i.e. *The Merchant of Venice*, V. 175
Venus and Adonis, IV. 128, 165, 180, 195, 222, 328, 394, 413; V. 166, 169, 170, 219, 221, 223, 225 ff. (main entry), 233, 259; VI. 86, 198, 311, 312; XI. 181
Winter's Tale, The, III. 356; V. 138, 189, 194, 204 ff. (main entry), 215, 217, 220, 374; VI. 23, 24, 110, 236, 350; VIII. 226; X. 85, 429, 433; XI. 414
Songs by:
'Full fathom five,' XII. 191
'Hark, hark, the lark,' V. 126
'In me thou see'st,' XII. 92
?'On a day (alack the day!),' IV. 119
Shakespeare, 'Chandos' portrait of, VIII. 50
Shakespeare and Fletcher, *History of Cardenio, The*, VIII. 127
Shakespeare and the continent, V. 85, 209, 287 ff., 305, 306, 456 ff.
Shakespeare festival at Stratford, X. 192
Shakespeare society, V. 247; XII. 355, 368, 369, 504
Shakespearean scholars, XII. 344
Shaking of the Sheets, The, III. 87, 484
Shallow, Justice (Shakespeare's), V. 187, 189, 350
Shallow Mannerly, Sir, in Crowne's *The Country Wit*, VIII. 188
Shalott, Lady of (Tennyson's), XIII. 37
Shame, in *The Faerie Queene*, III. 239
Shan van Vocht, The, XIV. 311
Shandon, captain, in Thackeray's *Pendennis*, IV. 252; XII. 159; XIII. 292; XIV. 177, 194
Shandy, Tristram, in Sterne's novel, XIV. 345
Shandy, Walter, in Sterne's novel, X. 50
Shandy family, in Sterne's novel, X. 49
Shankes, John (d. 1636), VI. 276, 277
Sharp, Amy, XIII. 498
Sharp, Becky (Thackeray's), V. 213; XIII. 276, 286 ff., 290, 296
Sharp, Elizabeth Amelia, XIII. 476
Sharp, Granville (1735–1813), XII. 473
Sharp, James (1613–1679), archbishop of St Andrews, VIII. 91; XII. 22
Sharp, John (1645–1714), archbishop of York, IX. 394
Sharp, John (*fl.* 1756), X. 131
Sharp, Robert Farquharson, XIII. 515
Sharp, William ('Fiona Macleod,' 1855–1905), XII. 373, 404, 407; XIII. 216, 485, 491, 498, 504, 508, 559, *also see* Add. 3
Sharpe, Charles Kirkpatrick (1781?–1851), II. 409; XI. 444; XII. 150, 430, 518
Sharpe, Gregory (1713–1771), IX. 529
Sharpe, Lewis (*fl.* 1640), VI. 458
Sharpe, Roger (*fl.* 1610), IV. 520
Sharpe, William, engraver, XII. 323
Sharper, in Congreve's *Old Bachelor*, VIII. 147
Sharpham, Edward (*fl.* 1607), IV. 350, 529; VI. 458; *Cupid's Whirligig*, VI. 218; *The Fleire*, VI. 218
Sharpham park, X. 20
Shaw, Cuthbert (1739–1771), X. 471
Shaw, Stebbing (1762–1802), XII. 513
Shaw, William (1749–1831), X. 471, 472, 489; XIV. 592, 609
Shaw, William A., XIV. 484, 487, 489, 499, 501
Shawcross, J., XI. 415; XII. 527
Shawe, Isabella. *See* Thackeray, Isabella
Shaylor, J., *The Fascination of Books*, XI. 378
Sheafe, Streatfield, and Evans, X. 375
Sheale, Richard, II. 415
Sheane, Hubert, XIV. Add. 7
Sheares, William, VI. 38

Sheath and Knife, II. 412
Sheavyn, Miss Phoebe, V. 370, 371
Sheba, queen of, X. 160
Shebbeare, John (1709–1788), X. 40, 41, 523, 525; *Letters to the people of England*, X. 389
Shebden hall, Upper, near Halifax, Yorks., VII. 233
Sheehan, John (1812–1882), XIV. 571
Sheen, VIII. 386; IX. 70
Sheeres, Sir Henry (d. 1710), VIII. 402; IX. 267, 528
Sheffield, VII. 353; X. 386; XI. 340, 469; XII. 136; XIII. 156
Sheffield, earl of. *See* Holroyd, John Baker
Sheffield, John, 3rd earl of Mulgrave, afterwards 1st duke of Buckingham and Normanby (1648–1721), VIII. 50, 202, 204, 211, 219 ff., 396, 443, 444, 481; IX. 70, 152, *also see* Add.
Essay on Poetry, VIII. 205, 219, 375, 409, 446
Essay on Satire, VIII. 35, 212, 219
Ode on Love, VIII. 219
Temple of Death, VIII. 219
Vision, The, VIII. 219
Sheffield Daily Telegraph, The, XIV. 531, 532, 534
Sheffield Iris, The, XIV. 203
Sheffield place, Sussex, X. 312
Sheffield university, XIV. 432
Sheil, Richard Lalor (1791–1851), XIII. 257 ff., 261, 523; XIV. 127, 135, 316, 326, 511, 571
Adelaide; or The Emigrants, XIII. 258
Apostate, The, XIII. 258; XIV. 319
Bellamira; or, The Fall of Tunis, XIII. 258, 259
Evadne; or, The Statue, XIII. 259; XIV. 319
Huguenot, The, XIII. 259
Montoni, XIII. 259
Sketches of the Irish Bar, XIV. 319
Shelburne, earl of. *See* Petty, William
Sheldon, Gilbert (1598–1677), archbishop of Canterbury, VII. 117, 150, 151, 153, 426; VIII. 3, 298, 302, 305
Sheldon, Ralph (1623–1684), IX. 348
Shelford, Robert, *Discourses*, VII. 33, 153, 426
Shelley, lady Jane, XII. 404
Shelley, Mrs (Harriet Westbrook), XII. 59, 62
Shelley, Mrs (Mary Wollstonecraft Godwin), XII. 35, 37, 59, 61, 62, 64, 71, 76, 399 ff., 403, 404, 451, 452
Frankenstein, XII. 247, 248
Last Man, The, XII. 248
Lodore, XII. 248
Valperga, XII. 248
Shelley, Percy Bysshe (1792–1822), I. 370; IV. 153; VII. 76, 77, 109; VIII. 237; XI. 44, 46, 102, 112, 117, 150, 158, 308, 405, 410, 414, 416, 422, 463; XII. 33 ff., 37, 39, 44, 56, 57 ff. (main entry), 79, 89, 91, 92, 94, 106, 107, 112, 113, 115, 119, 120, 126, 136, 138, 139, 157, 162,
Shelley, Percy Bysshe
174, 179, 180, 199, 205, 219, 222, 247, 248, 392 ff., 397, 399 ff. (main entry), 405, 407, 445, 521, 527, *also see* Add.; XIII. 23 ff., 27, 44, 52, 56, 57, 69, 108, 109, 129, 130, 137, 138, 184, 204, 230, 239, 250, 442, 481, 489; XIV. 198, 363, 373, 453
Adonais, IV. 152; VII. 114; XII. 71, 73 ff., 78, 87, 93; XIII. 236
Alastor, XI. 202; XII. 58, 59, 70, 71; XIII. 236, 237
Apollo, Hymn of, XII. 72
Arethusa, XII. 72
Aziola, XII. 75
Castlereagh Administration, Lines written during the, XII. 40
Cenci, The, XII. 61, 68 ff., 213
Certain Letters of Percy Bysshe Shelley, XIII. 75
Charles I, XII. 75
Christianity, On, XII. 60
Cloud, The, XII. 71, 72, 75
Cosimo and Fiordispina, XII. 71
Daemon of the World, The, XII. 59
Defence of Poetry, The, XII. 74, 75, 78
Edward Williams, Lines to, XII. 75
Epipsychidion, IX. 169; XII. 73, 74
Euganean Hills, Lines written among the, XII. 63
Future State, On a, XII. 60
Hellas, XII. 75
Intellectual Beauty, Hymn to, XII. 59, 60
Julian and Maddalo, XII. 34, 62, 63
Laon and Cythna, XII. 61
Liberty, To, XII. 72
Life, On, XII. 60
Lord Chancellor, To the, XII. 62
Love, On, XII. 60
Maria Gisborne, Letter to, XII. 62, 73
Masque of Anarchy, The, XII. 69
Medusa, XII. 58
Mercury, Hymn to, XII. 71
Metaphysics, On, XII. 60
Mont Blanc, XII. 60
Morals, On, XII. 60
Naples, To, XII. 72
Napoleon's death, Lines on, XII. 75
Orpheus, XII. 71
Pan, Hymn of, XII. 72
Peter Bell the Third, XII. 70
Prince Athanase, XII. 61
Prometheus Unbound, XI. 202; XII. 58, 65 ff., 70
Queen Mab, XI. 180; XII. 59, 60; XIII. 53, 227, 236, 237
Revolt of Islam, The, III. 246; XI. 202; XII. 59, 61; XIII. 130, 236
Rosalind and Helen, XII. 62
St Irvyne, XI. 299; XII. 59
Sensitive Plant, The, XII. 70, 71
Skylark, To a, XII. 70, 72, 77
Stanzas written in dejection, near Naples, XII. 63
Swellfoot the Tyrant, XII. 70
Tasso, XII. 64

Shelley, Percy Bysshe
Translation of Plato's *Symposium*, XII. 73
Triumph of Life, The, XII. 58, 76
Vision of the Sea, A, XII. 71
West Wind, Ode to the, VII. 181; XII. 72; XIV. 351
When the lamp is shattered, XII. 75
William Shelley, To, XII. 62
Witch of Atlas, The, XII. 71
Zastrozzi, XI. 299; XII. 59
Shelley society, XII. 400 ff.
Shelton, Thomas (1601–1650?), *Tachygraphy*, VIII. 243
Shelton, Thomas (*fl.* 1612–1620), IV. 395, 443; IX. 269; *Don Quixote*, VIII. 127, 128; IX. 278
Shenstone, William (1714–1763), III. 184; IX. 217, 412, 574; X. 112, 113, 135 ff., 149 ff. (main entry), 153, 156, 271 ff., 369, 456, 496, 497; XI. 206, 248, 251, 252, 255; XII. 132; XIII. 227, 232, 239
Dying Kid, The, X. 151
Economy, X. 150
Elegies, X. 151
'Here in cool grot,' X. 151
Jemmy Dawson, X. 151
Judgment of Hercules, X. 150
Levites, X. 151
Love and Honour, X. 150
Miscellaneous Poems, X. 151
Moral Pieces, X. 150
Ode to Memory, X. 151
'Odes, Songs, Ballads, etc.,' X. 151
Pastoral, X. 151
Progress of Taste, The, X. 150
Ruined Abbey, The, X. 150
Rural Elegance, X. 274
Schoolmistress, The, IX. 191, 405; X. 105, 136, 151; XI. 247, 323
Song of Valentine's Day, X. 151
Shepheard, Henry, XIII. 559
Shepherd, Luke (*fl.* 1548), *John Bon and Mast Parson*, III. 81, 481
Shepherd, Miss, in *David Copperfield*, XIII. 327
Shepherd, Richard Herne (1842–1895), VII. 251; XI. 412, 414, 417, 433; XII. 35, 399, 401, 412, 431, 435; XIII. 464, 493, 503, 532, 541, 542
Shepherd of Hermas, I. 75
'Shepherd Tony,' III. 302; IV. 117 ff. *See, also*, Munday, Anthony
Shepherds, Play of the, V. 19. See, also, under *Secunda Pastorum* and *Officia Pastorum*
Shepherds of the Scottish border, II. 396
Shepherdson, William, XIV. 532
Sheppard, Sir Fleetwood (1634–1698), VIII. 215, 410, 411, 433, 444, 447; IX. 473; *King James's Declaration*, VIII. 94
Sheppard, Jack (1702–1724), IX. 23
Sheppard, John (1785–1879), XIV. 518
Sheppard, John George, XIV. 609
Sheppard, Samuel (*fl.* 1646–1652), VII. 274, 347, 350, 351, 356 ff., 413, 466, 497, 498
Mercurius Dogmaticus, VII. 357
Mercurius Mastix, VII. 357
Mercurius Pragmaticus, VII. 356, 357, 360
Mercurius Pragmaticus Reviv'd, VII. 357
Mercurius Scommaticus, VII. 357
Phreneticus, VII. 357
Royall Diurnall, The, VII. 357
Socratic Session, The, VII. 274, 466
Weepers, The, VII. 357, 359
Sheppard, William (d. 1675?), VIII. 469
Shepperton church, in George Eliot's *Amos Barton*, XIII. 387
Sherborne, III. 167
Sherborne school, VII. 330
Sherbrooke, viscount. *See* Lowe, Robert
Sherburne, Sir Edward (1618–1702), VII. 87, 413; VIII. 447; 'Chloris! on thine eyes I gaze,' VII. 87; 'Love once love ever,' VII. 87; *The Vow*, VII. 87
Sheridan, Alice, XIV. 309
Sheridan, Caroline E. S. *See* Norton, Caroline E. S.
Sheridan, Mrs Frances (1724–1766), X. 438; XIV. 309; *Journey to Bath*, XI. 454
Sheridan, Helen Selina, countess of Dufferin (1807–1867), XIII. 177, 499
Sheridan, Richard Brinsley (1751–1816), IV. 361; V. 127, 254; VIII. 137, 139, 153; X. 88, 90, 92, 263, 265, 438; XI. 51, 54 ff., 251, 261, 262, 265, 266 ff. (main entry), 282, 396, 414, 452, 454, 457; XII. 49, 390, 411, 412, 443; XIII. 269; XIV. 107, 120, 121, 186, 214, 309, 498
Critic, The, VIII. 26, 402; X. 83, 87; XI. 271, 272
Duenna, The, X. 71; XI. 267, 269
'Here's to the maiden,' VI. 238
Ode to Scandal, XI. 271
Pizarro, XII. 526
Rivals, The, X. 89; XI. 266, 267, 269
St Patrick's Day, XI. 267
School for Scandal, The, X. 91; XI. 268 ff., 273, 275, 276
Trip to Scarborough, A, XI. 268
Sheridan, Thomas (1719–1788), IX. 453, 464, 467; XI. 250, 255; XIV. 309, 400, 609; *British Education*, XIV. 391, 397 ff.
Sheridan, Tom (1775–1817), XIV. 309
Sheriff, Laurence (d. 1567), VII. 336
Sheriff Hales academy, X. 386
Sheriffmuir, IX. 373
Sherlock, Thomas (1678–1761), IX. 293, 503, 508; X. 360, 517; *Letter...on...the late Earthquake*, X. 358; *Remarks*, X. 357; *Trial of the Witnesses of the Resurrection*, IX. 294; X. 358
Sherlock, William (1641?–1707), VIII. 347, 461, 462, 475; X. 358; *Defence of Dr Sherlock's notion of a Trinity in Unity*, X. 378; *Practical Discourse concerning a Future Judgment*, VIII. 304; *Vindication of the Trinity*, X. 378, 379

Sherman, John (d. 1671), *Commonplaces*, VIII. 278, 279; *A Greek in the Temple*, VIII. 278
Sherman, Stuart Pratt, VI. 190 ff., 194
Sherrard, William, XIV. 286
Sherry or Shirrye, Richard (*fl.* 1550), IV. 442; *Treatise of Schemes and Tropes*, III. 432, 553
Sherwen, John (1749–1826), X. 486
Sherwood, Mrs Mary Martha (1775–1851), XI. 369, 380, 479, 482; XIV. 335, 580
Fairchild Family, XI. 381
Henry Milner, XI. 381
Infant's Progress, XI. 381
Little Henry and his Bearer, XI. 381; XIV. 336
Susan Grey, XI. 381
Sherwood forest, IV. 190; V. 318; VI. 11, 365
Shetland, II. 413, 414, 417; IX. 552
Shetland dance, V. 32
Shetland islands, XIV. 434
Sheva, in Cumberland's *Jew*, XI. 282
Shewell, head of Coventry academy, X. 385
Shields, Alexander (1660?–1700), IX. 547
Shiels, Robert (d. 1753), *Lives of the Poets*, X. 184
Shifnal, IX. 256; X. 233
Shilleto, Richard (1809–1876), XII. 312, 330, 493
Shiloh, oracle of, in Cowley's *Davideis*, VII. 67
Shimei, in Dryden's *Absalom*, VIII. 39
Ship money fleet, the, IV. 107
Ship of Fools, The, prose version, II. 324, 325
Shipley, Sir Arthur Everett, XII. 508
Shipley, Orley, *Dryden as a Hymnodist*, VIII. 54
Shippen, William, XII. 174
Shipton-Moyne, near Tetbury, Gloucestershire, VIII. 82
Shipton-under-Wychwood, II. 35
Shipwrights' play, the, V. 391
Shirley, *pseud.* *See* Skelton, Sir John
Shirley (Charlotte Brontë's), XIII. 409
Shirley, Henry (d. 1627), VIII. 442; *The Martyr'd Souldier*, VI. 458
Shirley, James (1596–1666), V. 344, 366; VI. 27, 132, 135, 140, 188–209 (main entry), 211, 234, 421, 449 ff., *also see* Add.; VII. 3, 489; VIII. 124; IX. 318; XII. 190; XIII., *also see* Add. 2
Arcadia, III. 355; VI. 205
Ball, The, V. 350; VI. 32, 202
Beauties, The, VI. 204
Bird in a Cage, The, VI. 204
Brothers, The, VI. 203
Cardinall, The, VI. 200, 209; VIII. 121
Changes: or, Love in a Maze, VI. 201
Constant Maid, The, VI. 197, 203
Contention for Honour and Riches, A, VI. 206
Contention of Ajax and Ulysses for the Armor of Achilles, The, VI. 198, 207
Coronation, The, VI. 132, 140, 204, 205
Shirley, James
Court Secret, The, VI. 197, 206
Cupid and Death, VI. 207
Doubtfull Heir, The, VI. 197, 205
Dukes Mistris, The, VI. 200
Echo, or the Infortunate Lovers, VI. 198
Example, The, VI. 202, 208
Gamester, The, V. 352; VI. 202; X. 86, 433
Gentleman of Venice, The, VI. 197, 200, 205, 206
'Glories of our blood and state, the,' VI. 198
Grateful Servant, The, VI. 144, 203
Hide Parke, VI. 202
Honoria and Mammon, VI. 206
Humorous Courtier, The, VI. 205, 208
Imposture, The, VI. 205
Lady of Pleasure, The, VI. 202
Latin grammars, VI. 198
Love Tricks, VI. 201
Loves Crueltie, VI. 199, 208
Maides Revenge, The, VI. 199
Narcissus, or The Self-lover, VI. 198
Opportunitie, The, VI. 204, 208; VIII. 129
Polititian, The, VI. 197, 200
Rosania, or Love's Victory, VI. 205
Royall Master, The, VI. 197, 205, 208; XIII. 401
St Patrick for Ireland, VI. 197, 206
Sisters, The, VI. 206
Traytor, The, VI. 199, 200, 208; XIII. 259
Triumph of Beauty, The, VI. 207
Triumph of Peace, The, VI. 197, 207, 363
Wedding, The, VI. 201, 208
Wittie Faire One, The, VI. 201
Young Admirall, The, VI. 204, 208; VIII. 129
Shirley, John (1366?–1456), II. 161, 166, 170
Shirley, John, *Lord Jeffrey's Life*, XI. 330
Shirley, William (*fl.* 1739–1780), *Edward the Black Prince*, XI. 449
Shirreff, Emily Anne Eliza (1814–1897), XIV. 430, 600, 609
Shirrye, Richard. *See* Sherry
Shirwood, William (*fl.* 1260), I. 456
Shore, Jane (d. 1527?), IV. 182
Shore, Jane, in *Edward IV*, VI. 90, 91
Shore, Jane, in *The History of K. Richard III*, III. 335
Shore, Jane, The tragedy of, VIII. 196
Shore, John, 1st baron Teignmouth (1751–1834), XIV. 602
Shore, Louisa (1824–1895), XIII. 509
Shore, master, in chronicle play, VI. 98
Shore, mistress, in Praed's *Red Fisherman*, XII. 112
Shore, William Teignmouth, XIII. 544
Short, Ames, X. 387
Short, John, X. 385
Short, Peter, printer, IV. 546
Short parliament, the, VII. 54, 224, 285
Short Treatise against Stage-Playes, A, VI. 403, 497
Shorter, Clement King, XIII. 464, 503, 555, 556, 559, 569; XIV. 516

Shorter catechism, the, XIV. 405
Short-hand, X. 469
Shorthouse, Joseph Henry (1834–1903), XI. 411; XIII. 566, *also see* Add. 3; *John Inglesant*, XII. 277; XIII. 434, 435
Shortreed, Robert, XII. 4
Shotover Papers, The, XIV. 207
Shower, John (1657–1715), X. 385
Shrapnel, doctor (George Meredith's), XIII. 446
Shrewsbury, II. 2; III. 182; IV. 408; V. 39, 171, 391; VI. 252; VII. 326, 337; VIII. 171
Shrewsbury, duchess of, IX. 125
Shrewsbury, duke of. *See* Talbot, Charles
Shrewsbury, earls of. *See* Talbot, George; Talbot, Sir John
Shrewsbury, lady, in Gramont's *Memoirs*, VIII. 264
Shrewsbury academy, X. 386
Shrewsbury Chronicle, The, XII. 174
Shrewsbury school, III. 424, 425, 428, 429; IV. 159; V. 103; VII. 336, 493; IX. 165, 408; XII. 328, 329, 331, 333, 335, 336, 339; XIII. 449; XIV. 386, 413, 422
Shrimp, in *John a Kent*, V. 317
Shropshire, IV. 120; VI. 37; VII. 27, 78, 330, 337; VIII. 142, 274; XI. 120; XII. 166, 346, 509, 520; XIII. 142; XIV. 233
Shuckburgh, Evelyn Shirley (1843–1906), XII. 493
Shute, bishop of Durham, XIV. 492
Shuter, Edward (1728?–1776), X. 212
Shutte, R. N., XIV. 514
Shuttlewood, John (1632–1689), X. 387
Shylock, in Shakespeare's *Merchant of Venice*, V. 145, 181, 183, 366; VI. 69; XII. 171
Shylock, Macklin as, X. 85; XI. 257
Sibbald, James (1745–1803), XI. 446
Sibbald, Sir Robert (1641–1712), IX. 552; X. 193
Sibbes, Richard (1577–1635), VII. 426
Siberch, John (*fl.* 1521–1522), IV. 409, 547
Sible Hedingham, II. 208
Sibly, Ebenezer (d. 1800), VII. 511
Sibthorp, Richard Waldo (1792–1879), XII. 454
Sic Perrell in Paramouris lyis, II. 280
Sichaeus, in *Didone*, V. 76
Sichel, Edith, XIV. 515
Sichel, Walter, IX. 231; X. 422; *Bolingbroke and his Times*, IX. 98, 132, 217, 218, 220, 232; *Life of Sheridan*, XI. 272, 456
Sicily, IV. 258, 259; V. 206; VI. 156; VII. 75, 99; IX. 280; XII. 316, 475; XIV. 73, 292, 293
Sicily, Athenian expedition to, IV. 62
Siculus, Diodorus, IV. 408, 436
Sidanen, in *John a Kent and John a Cumber*, V. 317, 475
Siddal, Elizabeth Eleanor. *See* Rossetti, Elizabeth Eleanor
Siddons, Mrs Sarah (1755–1831), VIII. 184, 191, 196; X. 88; XI. 260, 261, 454, 461; XII. 171, 409
Sidgwick, Frank, II. 408
Sidgwick, Henry (1838–1900), XII. 469; XIV. 36 ff., 425, 426, 473, 480, 602, 606; *Methods of Ethics, The*, XI. 66; XIV. 37, 38
Sidley, Sir William, IV. 265
Sidmonton, IX. 168
Sidmouth, XIII. 70
Sidmouth, viscount. *See* Addington, Henry
Sidney, in Kelly's *False Delicacy*, XI. 263
Sidney, Algernon (1622–1683), II. 163; VIII. 267, 452; IX. 240; X. 290
Sidney, Dorothy. *See* Spencer, Dorothy
Sidney, Sir Henry (1529–1586), III. 429; IV. 72, 391
Sidney, Henry, earl of Romney (1641–1704), VIII. 167, 251, 268; IX. 495; *Diary* of, VIII. 267, 453
Sidney, lord Henry, in Disraeli's *Coningsby*, XIII. 350
Sidney, lady Mary, IV. 7
Sidney, Sir Philip (1554–1586), III. 175, 188 ff., 199, 212, 219, 220, 227, 236, 240 ff., 247, 253 ff., 257, 259, 261, 264, 265, 267, 285, 299 ff., 312, 340, 342, 349, 351 ff., 357, 364, 425, 429, 432, 437, 446, 524, 527, 535, 553, *also see* Add.; IV. 10, 18, 81, 108, 113, 116 ff., 121, 124, 125, 145, 149, 150, 152, 158 ff., 172, 179, 196, 210, 264 ff., 275, 391, 434, 447; V. 66, 173, 222, 226, 341, 347, 349; VI. 2, 14, 113, 196, 272, 302, 364 ff., 392, 497; VII. 25, 26, 114, 140, 154, 259, 306, 337, *also see* Add.; IX. 35, 69; X. 174, 222; XII. 493; XIV. 460
Apologie for Poetrie (*Defence of Poesie*), II. 154, 415; III. 199, 219, 255, 259, 299; V. 63, 70, 117, 130, 337; VI. 15, 267, 303, 388; VII. 261, 263, 271
Arcadia, III. 188, 265, 351, 353, 354, 358; IV. 265, 398, 401, 414; V. 254, 338; VI. 137, 180, 191, 192, 205, 212, 213; VII. 263, 265; X. 221; XI. 179
Astrophel and Stella, III. 253, 254, 256, 265; IV. 117, 133, 142, 177, 222
De Mornay, trans. of, IV. 21
Excellent sonnet of a nymph, An, IV. 118
May Lady, or The Lady of the May, The, IV. 117; VI. 336, 369
Sonnets, IV. 392
Sidney, Philip, 3rd earl of Leicester (lord Lisle) (1619–1698), II. 163; VIII. 51, 267
Sidney, Robert, 2nd earl of Leicester (1595–1677), VII. 54
Sidney, Sir Robert, IV. 154
Sidney, Thomasine, VII. 86
Sidney or Sydney, house of, VII. 54; IX. 496
Sidney Letters (Sydney Papers), VII. 436, VIII. 267, 453; X. 500
Sidonia, in Disraeli's *Coningsby*, XIII. 346, 349, 351, 360
Sidonius Apollinaris, I. 76; XIV. 303
Sidrophel, in *Hudibras*, VIII. 61, 72, 73
Siege of London, The, VI. 90

Siegen, Ludwig von, VIII. 359
Siena, VIII. 126
Sievers, Eduard, ix, I. 46, 55, 60, 101, 372
Sigebert, II. 341
Sigeferth, in *Finnsburh*, I. 31
Sigemund, in *Beowulf*, I. 23, 26
Sigeric, I. 121
Sigeric, archbishop of Canterbury, I. 116
Sigerson, George [Eironach], XIV. 303, 573
Sigewulf, I. 121
Sigferth or Sigweard, I. 126, 127
Sigmund, in Morris's *Sigurd the Volsung*, XIII. 126
Signs of Death, I. 227, 458
Signy, in Morris's *Sigurd the Volsung*, XIII. 126
Sigrdrífumál, I. 62
Sigrim the wolf, I. 366
Sigurd, in Morris's *Sigurd the Volsung*, XIII. 126
Sikes, Bill, in *Oliver Twist*, XIII. 316
Sikes, George, VII. 447
Sikes, Thomas, XII. 256
Silburn, Percy Arthur Baxter, XIV. Add. 10
Silchester, XII. 513
Silence, in *Henry IV*, V. 189, 194
Silenus, III. 389
Silexedra, in *Euphues and his England*, III. 345, 350
Silia, in Pope's *Characters of Women*, IX. 82
Silius Italicus, IV. 249, 414; IX. 44, 182
Sillery, IV. 259
Silurian system, XIV. 292, 294
Silva, Juan de, IV. 448
Silvanus, VI. 304, 486
Silver, Henry, XIV. 238, 239
Silvester, pope, V. 16
Silvestre, J. B., *Universal Palaeography*, XII. 356, 517
Silvestre, P., VIII. 481
Silvia, in Congreve's *Old Bachelor*, VIII. 147
Silvia, in Farquhar's *Recruiting Officer*, VIII. 169, 171
Silvius, in *As You Like It*, VI. 304
Simancas, XIV. 85
Simancas, archives of, X. 289
Simcox, Edith, XIV. 480
Simcox, George Augustus (1841–1905), XII. 493; XIII. 207, 509
Simcox, William Henry (1843–1889), XII. 493
Simeon, Charles (1759–1836), XII. 281, 473
Simeon, Sir John (1756–1824), IV. 209
Simeon, Joseph (1594–1671), VI. 477
Simeon of Durham (*fl.* 1130), I. 90, 148, 160 ff., 174, 449
Simeon Stylites, St, XIV. 305
Simeon Stlyites (Tennyson's), XIII. 29
Simiane, Madame de, X. 248
Simmias of Rhodes, IV. 123
Simmons, Bartholomew (1804–1850), *Flight to Cyprus, The*, XIV. 327; *Napoleon's last look*, XIV. 327
Simmons, Nevill (*fl.* 1692), XI. 340
Simmons, Samuel (*fl.* 1667), VII. 116, 117; XI. 315
Simnel, Lambert (*fl.* 1487–1525), VII. 203
Simon, abbot of St Albans, I. 178
Simon, H., XIV. 478
Simon, Richard, *Histoire Critique du Vieux Testament*, VIII. 42
Simon Magus, VII. 370
Simon de Meopham. *See* Meopham
Simon de Montfort. *See* Montfort
Simon of Swynsett, V. 66
Simon of Tournay, I. 456
Simon and Jude, SS., I. 354
Simond, L., XII. 525
Simonides, IX. 54
Simon's Town, XIV. 254
Simony, in *Negromansir*, III. 77
Simony, in *Piers the Plowman*, II. 7, 8
Simple, Sir Gervase, in *Changes*, VI. 202
Simplicity, in *The World tost at Tennis*, VI. 75
Simpson, Harold, XIII. 515
Simpson, Sir James Young (1811–1870), XII. 513; *Archaeological Essays*, XII. 350
Simpson, John Palgrave (1807–1887), XIII. 521; *A Scrap of Paper*, XIII. 525
Simpson, Joseph, X. 464
Simpson, Mrs Mary Charlotte Muir, XIV. 506
Simpson, Richard (1820–1876), V. 247, 248, 344; XIV. 118, 506
Simpson, Selwyn George, XIII. 499
Simpson, Thomas (1710–1761), XIV. 257
Simrock, Karl, V. 305
Simson, Archibald. *See* Symson
Simson, Habbie, IX. 364, 365
Simson, Patrick (1556–1618), IX. 550
Sin, in *Mirour de l'Omme*, II. 140, 141
Sinai, mount, II. 13, 79; VII. 170; XII. 341, 478
Sinclair, Catherine (1800–1864), XI. 482; *Holiday House*, XI. 386
Sinclair, George (d. 1696), IX. 560
Sinclair, James (d. 1762), X. 323
Sinclair, John (1683–1750), IX. 565
Sinclair, Sir John (1754–1835), X. 488; XIV. 514
Sinclair, May, XIII. 555 ff., 573, *also see* Add. 1
Sinclair, William, bishop of Dunkeld (d. 1337), II. 110
Sinfiotli, in Morris's *Sigurd the Volsung*, XIII. 126
Sing, Cheyte, XI. 20
Singer, Samuel Weller (1783–1858), V. 277; VI. 95; VII. 74, 77; IX. 67
Singleton, Hugh (*fl.* 1579), IV. 398
Singleton, Mrs Mary Montgomerie (afterwards lady Currie, *pseud.* Violet Fane, 1843–1905), XIII. 180, 504
Singleton, Thomas, IX. 392
Sinker, Robert (1838–1913), XII. 370, 523
Sinners Beware, I. 226, 227, 458
Sinon, in *The Palice of Honour*, II. 260, 261
Sion college, London, IV. 418
Sion nunnery, Chudleigh, IV. 418

Sir Bevis, IV. 529
Sir Clyomon...and Sir Clamydes, V. 414, 417
Sir Edmundbury Godfrey's Ghost, VIII. 92
Sir Eglamore, VIII. 96
Sir Gawayne, XII. 517
Sir Patrick Spens, X. 233
Sir Tristrem, XII. 7. *See also* Tristram, Sir
Siriz, Dame, V. 25, 55
Sisamnes, in *Cambises*, V. 65
Sisley, Clement, IV. 141
Sisley, Thomas, IV. 141
Sivagi, Maratha chieftain, XIV. 338
Siward, abbot of Abingdon, I. 110
Six Articles, the, IV. 299
Six Yeomen of the West, The, III. 371
Sixille, or Six Hills, priory of, near Market Rasen, I. 344
Sixtus IV, pope, II. 348
Sixtus V, pope, IV. 429; VI. 174, 175
Sixtus V, in *The White Divel*, VI. 176
Skaldskaparmál, I. 27
Skeat, Walter William (1835–1912), I. ix, 298; II. 1 ff., 5, 8, 13, 22, 23, 26, 28, 30, 34 ff., 36, 38 ff., 166, 194, 216, 236, 241; VI. 339; XII. 505; XIII. 249; XIV. 611; *Etymological Dictionary of the English Language*, XII. 344
Skelton, John (1460?–1529), II. 154, 210, 221, 223, 250, 257, 258, 316, 321, 328, 330, 331; III. 27, 52, 60 ff., 67–79 (main entry), 184, 185, 279, 302, 480, 481, 486, *also see* Add.; IV. 322, 361, 517, 521; V. 319; VIII. 65
Against the Scottes, III. 70
Against venomous tongues, III. 72
Apollo that Whirrlyd up his chare, III. 72
Bowge of Court, The, II. 323; III. 62, 73, 74, 78, 109; VII. 174
Colyn Clout, III. 69, 74 ff., 78
De bono ordine, III. 77
Edward the Forth, Of the death of, III. 70
Enterlude of Godly Queene Hester, III. 77
Eulogium pro suorum temporum conditione, III. 70
Garlande of Laurell, The, III. 67, 69, 70, 77
Garnesche, poems against, III. 68, 72, 73
Hymns on the battle of the Spurs, conquest of Terouenne, and victory of Flodden, III. 70
In Bedel, III. 72
Lawde and Prayse made for our Sovereigne Lord the Kyng, A, III. 70
Magnyfycence, III. 62, 77, 78; V. 54, 57, 60, 392
Mannes Lyfe the Peregrynacioun, Of, III. 67
Merie Tales of Master Skelton, III. 93, 94, 487; IV. 327
Nacyoun of Folys, III. 61
Negromansir, III. 77, 80
New Gramer in Englysshe compylyd, The, III. 67
Northumberlande, Upon the doulourus dethe of the Erle of, III. 70
Skelton, John
Phyllyp Sparowe, III. 68, 71 ff., 75
Prince Arturis Creacyoun, III. 70
Replycacion agaynst certayne yong scolers abjured of late, III. 69
Robin Hood, a pageant of, III. 68
Speculum principis, III. 67
Speke, Parrot, III. 67, 75, 76
Three Fooles, The Boke of, III. 61
Tunnyng of Elynour Rummyng, The, III. 73, 88; IV. 362
Ware the Hauke, III. 72
Why come ye nat to courte, III. 76, 77
Skelton, Sir John (*pseud.* Shirley, 1831–1897), XIII. 559; XIV. 506, 525; *John Dryden, In Defence*, VIII. 45; *Nugae Criticae*, XIV. 161; *Table Talk of Shirley, The*, XIV. 161
Skelton, John Henry, *My Book, or, The Anatomy of Conduct*, XIII. 278
Skelton, Matthew, X. 362
Skelton, Philip (1707–1787), IX. 465; XIV. 571
Skene or Skeyne, Gilbert (1522?–1599), III. 108, 494
Skene, James (1775–1864), XII. 26, 381
Skene, William Forbes (1809–1892), XII. 518; XIV. 497; *Celtic Scotland*, XIV. 95; *Four Ancient Books of Wales*, I. 247, 249
Skewton, Mrs, in *Dombey and Son*, XIII. 325
Skiddaw, XII. 188
Skimpole, Harold, in Dickens's *Bleak House*, IX. 81; XII. 205; XIII. 328
Skink, in *Looke about you*, V. 320
Skinner, Cyriack, VII. 108
Skinner, David, VII. 141
Skinner, John (1721–1807), IX. 567; XI. 226
Ewie wi' the Crookit Horn, IX. 372
Old Age, IX. 372
Tullochgorum, IX. 372
Tune your Fiddle, IX. 372
Skinner, Vincent, IV. 447
Skinnerswell, V. 44
Skiöldr and *Skiöldunga Saga*, I. 25, 27, 32
Skipsey, Joseph (1832–1903), XIII. 509
Skipton school, VII. 330
Skirving, Adam (1719–1803), IX. 373
Skoggan, IV. 360
Skoggan, The Geystes of, III. 91, 93, 94, 104, 487, 488
Skoloker, Anthony, III. 80
Skot, John (or Scott, or Scot) (*fl.* 1530), II. 328
Skrine, Huntley, XIV. 602
'Skroddler' (William Mason), X. 136
Skye, XII. 13; XIII. 209
Slade, Matthew (1569–1628?), VII. 308
Slade professor of fine art at Oxford, XIV. 152, 154, 155
Sladen, Douglas Brooke Wheelton, XIV 584, 586
Slander, in *The Faerie Queene*, II. 234
Slang, Jack, X. 199
Slater, Francis Carey, XIV. Add. 5

Slater, John Herbert, xiii. 532
Slater, Samuel (d. 1704), x. 522
Slaughden quay, xi. 141
Slearys, the, in Dickens's *Hard Times*, xiii. 329
Sleeman, Sir William Henry (1788–1856), xiv. 338, 554
Sleidanus, Johannes, iv. 448
Sleigh, Dr, x. 201
Slender, in *The Merry Wives of Windsor*, iii. 181; v. 189, 194
Slick, Sam, *pseud. See* Haliburton, Thomas Chandler
Slingsby, Sir Henry (1602–1658), vii. 453; xii. 376; *Civil War Memoirs*, xii. 16; *Diary*, vii. 224
Slingsby, Jonathan Freke, *pseud. See* Waller, John Francis
Slipslop, Mrs, in Fielding's *Joseph Andrews*, x. 25; xi. 266
Sloane, Sir Hans (1660–1753), ix. 139, 443; xiv. 285, 563, 566
Slop, Dr, in *Tristram Shandy*, x. 50
Slope, Obadiah (Trollope's), xiii. 422
Sloperton, xii. 103
Sloss, Duncan J., xi. 188
Sloth, in *Confessio Amantis*, ii. 147
Sloth, in Dunbar's *Sevin Deidlie Synnis*, ii. 255
Sloth, in *Piers the Plowman*, ii. 12, 16, 23, 28, 33
Slough of Despond, in Bunyan's *Pilgrim's Progress*, vii. 178
Slowboy, Tilly, in Dickens's *The Cricket on the Hearth*, xiii. 324
Sludge, Mr (Browning's), xiii. 63, 72, 73
Sluys, battle of, i. 357, 359
Sly, in *The Malcontent*, vi. 170
Slye (actor), vi. 248, 276
Smaland, i. 94
Small, John (1828–1886), xii. 517
Small, Roscoe Addison, vi. 3, 4, 17
Small *v.* Attwood, xiv. 124
Smalridge, George (1663–1719), ix. 153; x. 352, 353, 517
Smaragdus, i. 117
Smart, Christopher (1722–1771), x. 60, 123, 138, 153–154 (main entry), 156, 177, 457; *Hannah*, x. 207; *Song to David*, x. 153, 154
Smart, lady, in Swift's *Complete Collection of...Conversation*, ix. 106
Smart, Thomas Burnett, xiii. 486, 488
Smeaton, Oliphant, xiii. 466
Smectymnuus, viii. 72
Smedley, Francis Edward (1818–1864), xiv. 216, 545; *Frank Fairleigh*, xiv. 234; *Harry Coverdale's Courtship*, xiv. 234; *Lewis Arundel*, xiv. 234
Smedley, Jonathan (*fl.* 1689–1729), ix. 448
Smedley, Menella Bute, xiii. 177, 509
Smeeton, George (*fl.* 1800–1828), xiv. 231
Smelfungus, in Sterne's *Sentimental Journey*, x. 42
Smellie, William (1740–1795), xi. 440, 470; *Philosophy of Natural History*, xi. 327
Smelt, Jacob, in *The Weakest goeth to the Wall*, v. 316
Smelt, Leonard (1719?–1800), xi. 365
Smetham, James (1821–1889), xiv. 525
Smethwick, John (*fl.* 1623), iv. 394, 395
Smiglesius, Martin, x. 198
Smike, in *Nicholas Nickleby*, xiii. 318, 320, 321
Smiles, Samuel (1812–1904), xii. 430, 450; xiv. 506, 613
Smirdis, in *Cambises*, v. 65
Smith, in Buckingham's *Rehearsal*, ix. 147
Smith, Adam (1723–1790), iv. 312; viii. 343; x. 158, 173, 285, 321, 324, 334, 335 ff. (main entry), 511, 512; xi. 76, 400; xii. 142, 426, 427; xiv. 2, 3, 21, 22, 153, 387; *Theory of Moral Sentiments*, x. 335, 337; *Wealth of Nations, The*, viii. 367; x. 335 ff., 340; xi. 71; xiv. 381, 400, 401
Smith, Albert, xiv. 545
Smith, Albert Richard (1816–1860), xiv. 236, 546
Smith, Alexander (1830–1867), xi. 437; xiii. 156 ff., 509; xiv. 525
Barbara, xiii. 159
City Poems, xiii. 158
Dreamthorp, xiii. 158; xiv. 160
Edwin of Deira, xiii. 158
Life Drama, A, xii. 114; xiii. 158 ff.
On the Writing of Essays, xiv. 160
Summer in Skye, A, xiii. 158; xiv. 160
Smith, Alfred Charles (b. 1822), xii. 513
Smith, Arthur Lionel, *Frederick William Maitland*, xiv. 79, 494
Smith, Blanche. *See* Clough
Smith, Charles, xiv. 555
Smith, Charles Eastlake, xiv. 523
Smith, Charles Roach (1807–1890), xii. 513; 'Antiquarian Notes' (*Gentleman's Mag.*), xii. 346; *Retrospections*, xii. 347
Smith, Charlotte (1749–1806), xi. 465; xiii. 239; *The Old Manor House*, xi. 299
Smith, Edmund (or 'Rag') (1672–1710), ix. 181 ff., 487; *Phaedra and Hippolitus*, viii. 181; ix. 183
Smith, Edward, vii. 444
Smith, Edward, xiv. 558
Smith, Miss Egerton, xiii. 83
Smith, Francis (*fl.* 1661), viii. 10
Smith, Gamaliel (*see* Bentham, Jeremy), xi. 398
Smith, George (*c.* 1643), vii. 498; *Scotish Dove*, vii. 350
Smith, George, editor of Bede (1693–1756), x. 498
Smith, George (1824–1901), xiv. 194, 534
Smith, George (1840–1876), xii. 499; xiv. 192; *Chaldaean Genesis*, xii. 342
Smith, George Charles Moore, iv. 350; vi. 295, 297, 307, 308, 324, 458; xiii. 559
Smith, George Gregory, iii. 304; xi. Add.
Smith, Goldwin (1823–1910), xii. 447; xiii. 350; xiv. 90 ff., 343, 344, 497, 506
Empire, The, xiv. 90

Smith, Goldwin
Irish History and Irish Character, xiv. 90
Lectures on Modern History, xiv. 90
On the Foundations of the American Colonies, xiv. 90
Three English Statesmen, xiv. 91
Smith, Harriet, in Jane Austen's *Emma*, xii. 240
Smith, Harry B., xiii. 542
Smith, Henry (1550?–1591), iv. 237, 494; vii. 427
Smith, Henry John Stephen (1826–1883), xiv. 262, 264, 556
Smith, Horatio ('Horace') (1779–1849), xii. 422; *Rejected Addresses*, xi. 151; xii. 120; xiv. 238
Smith, James, Massinger's patron, vi. 144
Smith, James (1605–1667), vii. 413, 512; viii. 232, 408; *Musarum Deliciae*, vii. 512
Smith, James (1775–1839), xii. 422; *Rejected Addresses*, xi. 151; xii. 120; xiv. 200, 238
Smith, James, of Hawthorn, Virginia, *Junius Unveiled*, x. 305
Smith, James Cruickshank, xiii. 559
Smith, Sir James Edward (1759–1828), xiv. 287, 564
Smith, James Elimalet (1801–1857), xii. 473; xiv. 535
Smith, John (d. 1612), iii. 422
Smith, captain John (1580–1631), iv. 104, 311, 461, 513; *General History of Virginia*, iv. 95, 401; *Map and description of Virginia*, iv. 411; *Sea Grammar*, iv. 95, 105
Smith, John (1618–1652), viii. 288 ff., 301, 456, 457; *Select Discourses*, viii. 288
Smith, John, *The Mysterie of Rhetorique Unvail'd* (1657), vii. 466
Smith, John (*fl.* 1673–1680), x. 377; *Designed End to the Socinian Controversy*, x. 379
Smith, John (1747–1807), xii. 518
Smith, John (*fl.* 1819), viii. 242, 243
Smith, John, M.D., xiii. 487
Smith, John Christopher (1712–1795), x. 426, 432, 433
Smith, John Pye (1774–1851), xii. 469
Smith, John Russell (1810–1894), xii. 523
Smith, John Thomas (1766–1833), x. 473; xi. 434; xii. 513; *A Book for a Rainy Day*, xiv. 226, 546
Smith, Joseph, xii. 523
Smith, Joseph T., xiv. 563
Smith, Logan Pearsall, xiv. 611
Smith, Lucy Toulmin (1838–1911), xii. 518
Smith, Miles (d. 1624), vii. 317, 482
Smith, Miss M. Steele, Pref. ix.
Smith, Mr, in Burney's *Evelina*, x. 65
Smith, Mrs, in Jane Austen's *Persuasion*, xii. 240
Smith, Nowell C., xi. 408
Smith, Ralph, xi. 332
Smith, Reginald Bosworth (1839–1908), xii. 316, 478
Smith, Reginald J., xii. 426
Smith, Richard, iv. 399
Smith, Robert, *Strange Lamentable and Tragical Histories*, iv. 449
Smith, Robert Archibald (1780–1829), xi. 233, 236, 444, 445
Smith, Robert Harvey, xiv. 538
Smith, Sir Robert Murdoch (1835–1900), xii. 339, 498
Smith, Robert Payne (1819–1895), xii. 341, 503
Smith, Samuel, xi. 334
Smith, Sydney (1771–1845), xi. 343, 461, 483; xii. 143, 144, 146, 281, 426, 427, *also see* Add. 2; xiv. 139, 203, 394, 403, 405, 409, 410, 506
Smith, Thomas (1638–1710), ix. 349, 530
Smith, Sir Thomas (1513–1577), iii. 331, 418, 419, 423, 425, 432, 433, 553, 556; iv. 70, 513; vii. 191; viii. 467; ix. 496; *Discourse on the Commonwealth of England*, iii. 331, 531; iv. 297
Smith, Sir Thomas (1558?–1625), iv. 461
Smith, Sir Thomas (d. 1644), vii. 454
Smith, Thomas, university librarian, Cambridge, iv. 228
Smith, Walter (*fl.* 1525), *The merry jests of the widow Edith*, ii. 327, 486; iii. 88, 89, 487
Smith, Walter Chalmers (1824–1908), xiii. 509
Smith, Wentworth (*fl.* 1601–1623), v. 312, 319, 371; vi. 89, 100, 168; *The Hector of Germanie*, v. 331. See, also, *Lady Jane*
Smith, William (*fl.* 1596), iii. 256, 264, 266; iv. 117; *Chloris*, iii. 256, 266, 524; iv. 121, 472
Smith, William (Rouge Dragon) (1550?–1618), iii. 324
Smith, William (1756–1835), xi. 157, 421
Smith, William (1769–1839), xiv. 291, 564
Smith, Sir William (1813–1893), xii. 429, 478, 493
Dictionary of Christian Antiquities, xii. 335
Dictionary of Christian Biography, xii. 317, 335
Dictionary of Greek and Roman Antiquities, xii. 335
Dictionary of Greek and Roman Biography, xii. 317, 335
Dictionary of Greek and Roman Geography, xii. 317, 335
Dictionary of the Bible, xii. 317, 335
Latin Dictionary, xii. 335
Smith, William, *History of Canada*, xiv. 358, 583
Smith, William Anderson, xiv. 535
Smith, William Henry (1808–1872), xii. 469, 470; xiv. 480
Smith, William James, *Grenville Papers*, x. 410

Smith, William Robertson (1846–1894), XII. 342, 470; *Old Testament in the Jewish Church, The*, XII. 296; *Prophets of Israel, The*, XII. 296
Smith and Dame, II. 501
Smith and Elder, publishers, X. 204; XIII. 415
Smith-Hill house, X. 196
Smollett, Elizabeth (d. 1763), X. 41
Smollett, Sir James (1648–1731), X. 36
Smollett, Lydia, X. 47
Smollett, Tobias George (1721–1771), VI. 24, 28; VIII. 162; IX. 236, 245; X. 20, 21, 29, 35 ff. (main entry), 50, 56, 65, 204, 205, 395, 397, 418 ff., 431, 504, 522, *also see* Add.; XI. 264, 330; XII. 2, 30, 231, 245, 246, 250, 251; XIII. 305, 308, 309, 314; XIV. 215, 223, 225, 554
Advice, X. 36
Briton, The, X. 390
Burlesque Ode on the Loss of a Grandmother, X. 36
Don Quixote (trans.), X. 40
Ferdinand Count Fathom, X. 39, 40
'Habbakuk Hilding, Justice and Chapman,' X. 34, 39
History of an Atom, X. 40, 42
History of England, X. 40, 202, 293, 502; XI. 449; XIV. 50
Humphrey Clinker, X. 36, 39, 42, 43; XIII. 279; XIV. 255
Letters from France and Italy, IX. 247
Memoirs of a Lady of Quality, X. 39
Ode to Independence, X. 43
Peregrine Pickle, IX. 245, 405, 409, 410; X. 34, 37 ff., 43; XI. 449
Present State of the Nations, X. 41
Regicide, The, X. 36, 37, 39
Reprisal, The, X. 40; XI. 449
Reproof, The, X. 36
Roderick Random, IX. 245; X. 34, 36 ff., 43, 45, 48; XI. 262, 449
Sir Launcelot Greaves, X. 40, 41
Tears of Scotland, X. 36
Travels through France and Italy, X. 42, 43; XIV. 213
Universal History, X. 41
Smug, in *The Merry Devill*, V. 252
Smug of Lemnos, in *Mercury Vindicated*, VI. 357
Smyrna, XIV. 251
Smyth, Nicolas, IV. 436
Smyth, Richard, *A Confutation of the true and Catholic Doctrine*, III. 33
Smyth, William (1765–1849), XIV. 109, 498; *Lectures on the French Revolution*, XIV. 110
Smythe, A. J., XIII. 515
Smythe, George A. F. P. S., 7th viscount Strangford (1818–1857), XIV. 196; *Historic Doubts*, IX. 224, 231
Smythe, James Moore, IX. 449
Smythe, Sir John, IV. 461
Smythe, Robert, XIV. 597
Smythe exhibition, X. 198
Snap, Miss Laetitia, in Fielding's *Jonathan Wild*, X. 28
Snape, Andrew (1675–1742), IX. 510
'Snark' (Lewis Carroll's), XIII. 167
'Snawdoun' (=Stirling), III. 120
Sneakup, Pyannet, in *The City Witt*, VI. 229
Sneer, in Sheridan's *Critic*, XI. 272
Sneerwell, lady, in Sheridan's *School for Scandal*, XI. 270
Snell, F. J., XIII. 560
Snelling, Thomas, VI. 477
Sneyd, Honora. *See* Edgeworth, Honora
Snitterfield, X. 112
Snob, Mr, *pseud.* of W. M. Thackeray, XIII. 278, 284, 285
Snob, The, XIII. 277; XIV. 207
Snodgrass, Augustus, in *The Pickwick Papers*, XIII. 313
Snowden, Jane, in Gissing's *The Nether World*, XIII. 458
Snowdon, X. 115
Snuff, in *Cambises*, V. 64
Soames, Sir William, trans. of *Art Poétique*, VIII. 373; X. 169
Soane, George (1790–1860), XI. 491
'Soaping Club,' X. 191
Sober, Mr, in Johnson's *Idler*, X. 178
Sobieski, John III, king of Poland, VIII. 94
Sobry, Mlle A., XIII. 545
Social [and political] aspects of the later Elizabethan and earlier Stewart period, V. 476 ff.
Social satire in Middle English, I. 360 ff.
Social tracts of Elizabethan England, IV. 515
Socialism, XII. 290
Society for Promoting Christian Knowledge, IX. 407, 573
Society for the Diffusion of Useful Knowledge, XII. 307
Society for the Encouragement of Learning, XI. 325
Society for the Suppression of Vice, XI. 380
Society islands, XIV. 244
Society of Antiquaries of London, XII. 345, 347, 506, 510
Society of Antiquaries of Scotland, IX. 372; XII. 349
Society of Friends, VII. 169; IX. 307; X. 519
Society of Friends, the early, VIII. 412
Socinian heresies, the, VII. 21
Socinianism, X. 373, 377 ff.; XII. 287
Socinians, VIII. 275, 291
Socinus, VII. 150
Socrates, II. 313; III. 216, 420; V. 93; IX. 524, 529; XII. 309, 313, 442, 475
Sodom and Gomorrah, in *Cleanness*, I. 323
'Sodom of Italy,' in *The Unfortunate Traveller*, III. 364
Sodomy, in *The Three Laws*, V. 58
Sodor and Man, bishopric of, X. 359
Sohrab, in Arnold's poem, XIII. 92
Soirées de Médan, XIII. 456
Sol, in Welsh tradition, I. 255
Solace, in *Ane Pleasant Satyre*, III. 124, 126

Solander, Daniel Charles (1736–1782), XIV. 289
Solebay, battle of, VII. 56; VIII. 11, 24
Solempne, Anthony de, IV. 409
Solihull, X. 112
Solinus, Julius, I. 76, 81; IV. 448
Solitary, in Wordsworth's *Excursion*, XI. 106
Solitary Plot, Sir, in *The Example*, VI. 202
Solleysel, IV. 369
Solomon, in *New Atlantis*, VII. 299, 303
Solomon, in *The Palice of Honour*, II. 260
Solomon, king, I. 62, 63, 134, 205, 349; II. 21, 129, 207, 319, 370; IX. 337; XI. 235, 290
Solomon, The Wisdom of (15th century tract), II. 284
Solomon and Marcolphus, Dialogue or communing between the wise king, II. 319, 486
Solomon's house, in *New Atlantis*, IX. 388
Solomon's Song, II. 395
Solomons, Ikey, junior, *pseud.* of W. M. Thackeray, XIII. 279
Solorzano, A. del Castillo, IX. 418
Solway Moss, battle of, III. 147
Solyman II, sultan, in *Solymannidae*, VI. 301
Solyman the magnificent, in D'Avenant's *Siege of Rhodes*, VIII. 117
Solymannidae, VI. 301, 486
Some, Robert (1542–1609), III. 390, *also see* Add.
Some wiser than Some, VII. 386
Somer and Wynter, Debate and Stryfe Betweene, II. 501
'Somer is comen with love to toune,' II. 501
Somers, Sir George (1554–1610), IV. 78; V. 220
Somers, John, lord Somers (1651–1716), VIII. 445; IX. 8, 94, 101, 112, 113, 150; X. 295, 373
Somers' Tracts, VII. 456; VIII. 10, 411; IX. 217, 435, 539; X. 499; XII. 16, 376
Somersby, Lincolnshire, XII. 39; XIII. 23
Somerset, IV. 190; X. 393; XI. 99, 101, 155; XII. 509, 512
Somerset, lord Charles, XIV. 373
Somerset, dukes of. *See* Seymour, Edward; Seymour, William
Somerset, earl of. *See* Carr, Robert
Somerset, Edward (1557), *The Pore estate to be holden for best*, III. 179
Somerset, Edward, 4th earl of Worcester (1553–1628), IV. 143, 203, 259
Somerset, Edward, 2nd marquis of Worcester (1601–1667), VII. 392; VIII. 479; *Century of Inventions*, VIII. 359
Somerset, Elizabeth, duchess of. *See* Percy, lady Elizabeth
Somerset, lord Fitzroy James Henry, 1st baron (1788–1855), XIV. 94, 173
Somerset, Frances, duchess of (lady Hertford, d. 1754), X. 94, 271 ff.
Somerset, Frances (Devereux), duchess of (d. 1674), IV. 421
Somerset, Henry, 1st marquis of Worcester, VIII. 470, 471
Somerset, Henry Charles, 6th duke of Beaufort (1766–1835), XIV. 232
Somervile, William (1675–1742), X. 109 ff., 271, 273, 449, 497
  Chace, The, X. 109 ff.; XIV. 232
  Epistle to Mr Thomson, X. 110
  Hobbinol, X. 111
  Occasional Poems, X. 109
  Rural Sports, X. 111
Somerville, Elizabeth, XI. 489
Somerville, James (1632–1690), *Memorie of the Somervilles*, XII. 376
Somerville, Mary (1780–1872), XIV. 556
Somerville, Thomas (1741–1830), XIV. 498
Somme des Vices et des Virtus, or *Li Livres roiaux des Vices et des Vertus*, or *Somme le Roi*, I. 354
Sommer or Somer, Sir Henry (*fl.* 1407–1413), II. 208
Sommers, Will, in *When you see me, etc.*, V. 333
Somner, William (1598–1669), VII. 481; IX. 539; *Canterbury*, IX. 353; *Dictionarium*, IX. 355
Somnus, in *Lingua*, VI. 315
Somnus, in *The Vision of the Twelve Goddesses*, VI. 337
'Son of the Marshes, A.' *See* Jordan, Denham
Sonare, III. 249
Song to the Virgin, A, I. 232, 458
Song-Books and Miscellanies, IV. 109 ff., 462 ff.
Song writers, IV. 468
Songer, Ralph, IV. 432
Songes and Sonnettes. See under *Tottel's Miscellany*
Songs of Divers Noblemen and Gentlemen, IV. 142
'Songs of Selma,' X. 130
Sonnenthal, V. 306
Soothness, in *Piers the Plowman*, II. 8
Soowthern. *See* Southern
Sophia, in Cumberland's *Brothers*, XI. 264
Sophia, Charlotte, queen of Prussia, IX. 290
Sophia, Dorothea, X. 499
Sophia, electress of Hanover, IX. 200, 290, 490; XIV. 111
Sophister, The, VI. 481
Sophistici Elenchi, I. 206
Sophocles, III. 430, 433; IV. 4; V. 289, 295 ff.; VI. 295, 298; VII. 489; VIII. 30, 149; IX. 477; XII. 68, 328, 332, 333, 338, 340, 403, 480, 482, 483, 485 ff., 491, 494, 495; XIII. 90, 257, 497
  Ajax, Latin version of, VI. 300
  Electra, V. 75
  Oedipus, V. 295; IX. 142; XI. 283; XII. 327, 329; XIII. 145
  Oedipus Coloneus, XII. 327
  Philoctetes, X. 79

Sophonisba, in *The Wonder of Women*, vi. 49
Sophonisba, or Hannibal's Overthrow, viii. 185
Sophora tree, xiv. 286
Sophron, xii. 329
Sopwell nunnery, near St Albans, ii. 318
Sorastanus, duke of Tuscany, in *Perfidus Hetruscus*, vi. 302
Sorbière, Samuel de, xi. 331
Sorby, Henry Clifton (1826–1908), xiv. 293, 564
Sorcery, in *Confessio Amantis*, ii. 149
Sordido, in *Every Man out of his Humour*, iv. 358; v. 354; vi. 40
Sorel, Charles, *Remarques sur le Berger extravagant*, iv. 260, 523; *Le Berger Extravagant*, viii. 372
Sorley, Charles Hamilton (1895–1915), xiii. 509, *also see* Add. 2
Sorrel, Hetty, in *Adam Bede*, xiii. 390, 391
Sorrow, in Sackville's *Induction*, iii. 200
Sorrow for another's joy, in *Confessio Amantis*, ii. 147
Sorrowes Joy, iv. 165
Sosia, Amphitryon's servant, v. 107
Sotheby, Samuel (1771–1842), xi. 336
Sotheby, William (1757–1833), xii. 128, 422
Sotherton, in Jane Austen's *Mansfield Park*, xii. 241
Soties, v. 22, 91
Soto, in *The Spanish Gipsie*, vi. 77
Soto, Andrew de, iv. 94
Soudan, the, xiv. 191
Souhaits des hommes, et les souhaiz et beautés des dames, Les, iii. 89
Soul, the, in *Mirour de l'Omme*, ii. 140
Soul and Body Addresses, i. 61, 129, 227, 428, 458, 459
Souldiers Catechism, The, vii. 382
Soulsby, Lucy Helen Muriel, xiv. 599
Sound, the, viii. 254
Sourton down, vii. 348
Souter, Alexander, xii. 488
Souter, Johnie, in Burns's *Tam o' Shanter*, xi. 219
South, Esquire, in Arbuthnot's *History of John Bull*, ix. 134, 135
South, Robert (1634–1716), vii. 246, 247; viii. 303, 370, 461, 462; ix. 32, 147, 387; *Animadversions upon Dr Sherlock's Vindication*, viii. 304; x. 378; *Sermons*, viii. 304
South Africa, xiv. 372 ff., 457
South African Magazine, The, xiv. 588
South African Philosophical society, xiv. Add. 4
South Cadbury, Somerset, x. 393
South Eastern railway, xiii. 334
South English Legendary, The, xiv. 306
South Sea, the, xiv. 242, 243
South Sea Bubble, ix. 21, 105, 162, 220; xiv. 212
South Sea company, x. 272, 299
South Sea islands, x. 228
Southampton, iv. 190; x. 132; xii. 232, 519; xiii. 276
Southampton, Arthur at, in Wace's *Brut*, i. 237
Southampton, earl of. *See* Wriothesley, Henry
Southampton, Minot's poem on the battle of, i. 357, 359
Southcott, Joanna (1750–1814), xi. 163; xiii. 153
Southdean, x. 93
Southern, Henry (1799–1853), xii. 430
Southern or Soowthern, John (*fl.* 1584), iv. 24, 25; *Pandora*, iv. 472
Southerne or Southern, Thomas (1660–1746), viii. 181, 195, 400, 401, 442
Disappointment, The, viii. 189, 191
Fatal Marriage, The, viii. 191, 192
Fate of Capua, The, viii. 191
Isabella, x. 118, 433
Loyal Brother, The, viii. 34, 190
Maids Last Prayer, The, viii. 191
Money the Mistress, viii. 191
Oroonoko, or the Royal Slave, viii. 191, 192; x. 118
Sir Anthony Love, viii. 191
Spartan Dame, The, viii. 190, 191; xi. 317
Wives' Excuse, The, viii. 55, 191, 396
Works, viii. 190
Southesk, earl of (d. 1905), xiv. 584
Southey, Mrs Caroline Anne (born Bowles, 1786–1854), xi. 156, 421, 422; xii. 124, 127, 401, 414; *The Mariner's Hymn*, xii. 128
Southey, Charles Cuthbert, xi. 422; xii. 219
Southey, Mrs Edith (born Fricker), xi. 155, 156
Southey, Herbert, xi. 156
Southey, Isabel, xi. 156
Southey, Sir Richard, xiv. Add. 11
Southey, Robert (1794–1843), iii. 78, 536; iv. 89, 252, 267; viii. 244; ix. 170, 178; x. 217, 221, 364, 367, 368, 485, 486, 518; xi. 40, 118, 119, 122, 124, 126, 149, 153 ff. (main entry), 172, 173, 176 ff., 201, 202, 250, 254, 294, 309, 341, 393, 401, 411, 413, 415 ff., 420, 468, 490, *also see* Add.; xii. 42, 59, 95, 96, 98, 101, 107, 111, 113, 120, 122, 124, 133, 135, 136, 138, 150, 154, 158, 164, 167, 179, 182, 186, 205, 208, 210, 214 ff., 219, 268, 303, 364, 401, 415, 424, 429, 441, 527; xiii. 52, 157, 225 ff., 230, 233, 239, 244 ff., 306; xiv. 184, 312, 387, 403, 462, 506, 592, 601
All for Love, xi. 166
Amadis, xi. 162
Ballads, xi. 159, 160
Battle of Blenheim, xi. 160
Bishop Hatto, xi. 160
Book of the Church, The, xi. 167; xiv. 55
Botany Bay Eclogues, xi. 159
Chronicle of the Cid, xi. 162
Colloquies, xi. 167; xii. 215, 230

Southey, Robert
'Come, for ye know me!' XI. 161
Commonplace Books, XI. 163
Cross Roads, The, XI. 160
Curse of Kehama, The, XI. 162, 164; XIII. 232
Doctor, The, XI. 163, 168, 169
Essays Moral and Political, XI. 167
Expedition of Orsua, XI. 163
Fall of Robespierre, XI. 161
History of Brazil, XI. 162
History of Portugal, XI. 162
History of the Peninsular War, XI. 167; XIV. 107
Holly-Tree, XI. 159
Inchcape Rock, XI. 160
Joan of Arc, XI. 158, 159, 161, 413
Lay of the Laureate, XI. 166
Letters, XI. 156, 159, 170
Letters from Spain and Portugal, XI. 161, 163
Letters of Espriella, XI. 162
Life of John Wesley, IX. 328; XI. 167
Life of Nelson, XI. 162 ff., 167
Lives of the Admirals, XI. 167
Madoc, XI. 159, 161, 162, 173
Metrical Tales, XI. 161
Minor Poems, XI. 161
My days among the Dead are passed, XI. 159
Ode to Horror, XI. 158
Old Woman of Berkeley, The, XI. 160; XII. 111, 123
Oliver Newman, XI. 166
Omniana, XI. 162, 163; XIII. 164
Palmerin, XI. 162
Poet's Pilgrimage to Waterloo, XI. 166
Queen Orraca, XI. 160
Roderick, XI. 159, 166
Sappho, XI. 158
Specimens of Later English Poetry, XII. 132
Story of the Three Bears, XI. 168
Tale of Paraguay, XI. 166
Thalaba, XI. 160, 161, 164, 180; XII. 145; XIII. 227, 232, 236
Vindiciae Ecclesiae Anglicanae, XI. 167
Vision of Judgment, A, XI. 166; XII. 36, 53, 54, 199; XIII. 240, 244
Wat Tyler, XI. 157 ff., 161
Well of St Keyne, XI. 160
Southland, T., *Love à la Mode* (1663), VIII. 422
Southover, VIII. 244
Southward, John, XIV. 536
Southwark, II. 233
Southwark, priory of St Mary Overes, II. 135
Southwark, St Saviour's church, II. 135, 137
Southwell, III. 428, 478
Southwell, Robert (1561?–1595), III. 177; IV. 127 ff., 139, 140, 218, 237, 477, 495, 496
Burning Babe, The, IV. 130
Maeoniae, IV. 130
Southwell, Robert
New Heaven, New Warre, IV. 130
New Prince, New Pompe, IV. 130
Saint Peters Complaint, IV. 128 ff.
Southwell, Sir Robert (d. 1599), III. 183
Southwell, Sir Robert (1635–1702), IX. 92; X. 500
Southwell's *Notes and Illustrations on the Bible*, XI. 326
'Southwerke,' in *Colin Blowbol's Testament*, III. 86
Sovereign of the Seas, The, VI. 84
Sowden, Mr, IX. 246
Sowdone of Babylone, I. 471
Spa, IV. 202
Spademan, John, X. 385
Spagnoletto school, IX. 252
Spain, I. 153; II. 310, 340; V. 99, 123, 132, 304, 306, 337, 341, 347, 356, 359, 365; VI. 79, 103, 147, 150, 248, 364, 396; VII. 53, 180, 191, 194, 197, 198, 200, 215, 219, 222, 274, 306, 367, 455; VIII. 65, 271, 329; IX. 6, 7, 23, 221, 231, 256, 265, 268, 277; X. 182, 306, 391, 404; XI. 27, 72, 280; XII. 32, 42, 149, 488; XIII. 2, 40, 107, 258, 396; XIV. 102 ff., 122, 180, 241, 250, 251, 293
Spain and Byron, XII. 393
Spalatro, VII. 309
Spalding, John (*fl.* 1650), *History of Scotland*, IX. 550; XII. 359
Spalding, Robert (*fl.* 1592–1607), VII. 317
Spalding, William (1809–1859), V. 258; XIV. 480, 525
Spalding club, XII. 359
Spalding school, IX. 330
Spaniards, the, VII. 64, 210; X. 288; XIV. 125, 242, 245, 250
Spanish affairs, IX. 215; X. 291
Spanish ambassador at the English court, VI. 148
Spanish American colonies, XIV. 122
Spanish armada, the, VII. 282; XIV. 84, 97
'Spanish Armada, The,' in Sheridan's *Critic*, XI. 272
Spanish bull-fight, XII. 43
Spanish coast, the, XIV. 73
Spanish drama and English, V. 1, 303
Spanish fleets, VII. 446
Spanish influences, VII. 165, 260; VIII. 14, 17, 23, 124 ff., 424, 425
Spanish language and literature, VII. 142, 265; VIII. 162, 308, 311, 353, 354; IX. 4, 277, 403, 413; X. 40, 72, 233; XI. 359; XII. 13, 157, 272, 308; XIII. 143, 144; XIV. 251, 385, 434, 457 ff.
Spanish Main, the, XIV. 241
Spanish mysticism, VII. 155
Spanish navy, the, XIV. 187, 201
Spanish plays, VI. 124
Spanish politics, VIII. 384
Spanish prince, the, in *Mucedorus*, V. 253
Spanish romances, V. 254; VI. 239, 365
Spanish sources, VI. 123, 132, 136, 204, 205, 208; VIII. 144
Spanish succession, the, IX. 11, 228, 231

Spanish succession, war of the, XIV. 89
Spanish (Peninsular) war, the, XI. 103
Spanish wines, V. 358
Spanus, in Robert Landor's *Fawn of Sertorius*, XII. 230
Spare your good, III. 491
Sparling, H. Halliday, XIV. 573
Sparrow, John (1615–1665?), IX. 515, 517
Sparrowe, Thomas (*fl.* 1629–1633), VI. 478
Sparsit, Mrs, in Dickens's *Hard Times*, XIII. 330
Sparta, youths of, III. 22
Speaker, The, XIV. 199, 534
Spectacle de la Nature, XI. 382
Spectacle of Lovers, II. 326
Spectacula, Roman, VI. 373
Spectacula theatralia, in Rome, V. 38
Spectakle of Luf or *Delectatioun of Wemen*, II. 284, 479
Spectator (Mr Addison's), XIII. 445
Spectator, The, V. 286, 290; VIII. 378; IX. 18, 32, 33, 35, 41, 48 ff. (main entry), 69, 144, 165, 171, 181, 220, 412, 436, 438, 439, 441, 444, 448, 455, 474, 492; X. 26, 56, 69, 90, 171, 172; XI. 146, 280, 317; XII. 140, 193, 223, 231; XIII. 284; XIV. 213, 441, 442, 444, 446, 461
Spectator, The (founded 1828), XIV. 141, 172, 194, 198, 199, 530, 534
Spectator, The (1862), XIII. 440
Speculum Christiani, II. 319, 426, 503
Speculum Ecclesiae, I. 206
Speculum Stultorum, II. 144
Spedding, James (1808–1881), IV. 280; V. 248; VII. 203; XI. 463; XIII. 24, 142, 246, 479; XIV. 506; *Evenings with a Reviewer*, XIV. 63; *Life and Letters of Bacon*, XIV. 63; *Studies in English History* (with J. Gairdner), XIV. 82, 83
Speech of a Fife Laird, IX. 366
Speeches, in Jacobean times, VII. 439 ff.
Speed, John (1552?–1629?), III. 313, 323, 325, 335, 336, 532; IV. 159, 461; VII. 203, 442; IX. 352; *Historie of Great Britaine*, III. 325; IV. 58
Speed, Miss, X. 126
Speed, Samuel (1631–1682), *Prison Pietie*, VII. 45
Speght, Thomas (*fl.* 1598), II. 162, 217; III. 449; X. 236
Speke, John Hanning (1827–1864), XIV. 554; *Journal of the discovery of the source of the Nile*, XIV. 253
Spelman, Sir Henry (1564?–1641), III. 323; VII. 442; VIII. 318, 469; IX. 344, 355, 539, 540; *Glossarium Archaiologicum*, IX. 356
Spelman, Sir John (1594–1643), IX. 534
Spence, Catherine Helen, XIV. 587; *Clara Morison*, XIV. 369
Spence, F., VIII. 481
Spence, Joseph (1699–1768), VIII. 370; IX. 67, 68, 73, 77, 131, 141, 188, 448, 451, 485; X. 119, 244; XI. 323, 467; *Anecdotes*, VIII. 322; X. 174; *Essay on Pope's Odyssey*, IX. 77
Spencer, in *The Fair Maid of the West*, VI. 101
Spencer, Dorothy (born Sidney), countess of Sunderland (1617–1684), VII. 54; VIII. 251, 267, 268, 453
Spencer, Edm. (translator), IV. 439
Spencer, Gabriel (d. 1598), VI. 3
Spencer, George, 5th duke of Marlborough (1766–1840), XII. 365
Spencer, George John, 2nd earl Spencer (1758–1834), XII. 365, 366
Spencer, Henry, 1st earl of Sunderland (1620–1643), VII. 55
Spencer, Henry le. *See* Despenser, Henry le
Spencer, Herbert (1820–1903), IX. 401; XII. 275; XIII. 385; XIV. 28 ff., 33, 38, 43, 199, 393, 478, 480, 609
Autobiography, XIV. 28
Classification of the Sciences, The, XIV. 28
Data of Ethics, The, XIV. 30, 35
Descriptive Sociology, XIV. 28
'Development Hypothesis, The,' XIV. 28
Education, XIV. 28, 395, 396, 421
Factors of Organic Evolution, XIV. 28
First Principles, XIV. 28
'Genesis of Science, The,' XIV. 28
Man versus *The State, The*, XIV. 28
Principles of Biology, XIV. 28
Principles of Ethics, XIV. 28
Principles of Psychology, XIV. 28, 30
Principles of Sociology, XIV. 28, 30
'Programme of a System of Synthetic Philosophy,' XIV. 28
'Progress: its law and cause,' XIV. 28
'Proper Sphere of Government, The,' XIV. 28
Social Statics, XIV. 28, 31
Study of Sociology, The, XIV. 28
Spencer, Sir John (*fl.* 1595), III. 213
Spencer or Spenser, John (1559–1614), VII. 316
Spencer, John (1630–1693), VII. 490
Spencer, John Charles, viscount Althorp and 3rd earl Spencer (1782–1845), XIV. 115, 125, 180
Spencer, Sir Robert (*fl.* 1603), VI. 339, 340
Spencer, Robert, 2nd earl of Sunderland (1640–1702), VIII. 268; IX. 183, 213, 442, 483
Spencer, William, VII. 483
Spencer, William Robert (1769–1834), VII. 84; XII. 131, 422
Spencer family, of Althorp, III. 213
Spens, Sir Patrick, I. 300; II. 395, 413
Spense, *Bellum grammaticale*, IX. 551
Spenser, Edmund (1552?–1599), I. 170; II. 163, 165, 184, 213, 220, 233 ff., 332, 337; III. 66, 168, 185, 188, 199, 200, 211–246 (main entry), 247, 250 ff., 254, 256 ff., 264, 271, 272, 273, 283 ff., 293, 294, 302, 303, 305, 320, 327, 409, 425, 435, 448, 455, 519 ff., 524, 527, *also see* Add.; IV. 17, 25, 47, 77, 88, 109, 117, 121, 124, 125, 131, 135, 138, 139, 149,

Spenser, Edmund
150, 158, 165, 167, 173, 180, 183, 208, 211, 248, 266, 330, 360, 390, 434, 513, 516, 525; v. 18, 156, 171, 183, 225 ff., 234, 327, 368; vi. 2, 11, 103, 113, 196, 311, 312, 329, 336, 366, 388; vii. 2, 10, 26, 46, 49, 62, 70, 73, 76, 110, 135, 176, 210, 272, 274; viii. 40, 48, 51, 88, 219, 222, 228, 230, 233, 239, 284, 384; ix. 68, 69, 143, 158, 165, 184, 188, 189, 338, 396, 477, 479, 483; x. 105 ff., 132, 174, 184, 221, 224, 227, 238, 239, 397; xi. 157, 179, 182, 206, 247, 252, 255, 425; xii. 3, 86, 93, 168, 177, 208, 221, 272, 392, 440, 455; xiii. 38, 233, 235, 238, 512; xiv. 113, 307, 487
Amoretti, iii. 215, 243, 256, 257
Astrophel, iii. 240; iv. 118
Colin Clout's Come Home Again, iii. 183, 213, 214, 242, 243; iv. 53, 134
Complaints, iii. 241, 250; v. 85 ff., 136
Discourse of Civil Life, vii. 211, 448
Dreames, iii. 229
Dying Pelican, The, iii. 229
Epithalamion, iii. 228, 243; vii. 209; xii. 79
Faerie Queene, The, i. 284; ii. 228, 233, 234; iii. 199, 213, 218, 228 ff. (main entry), 242 ff., 271, 286, 409, 448; iv. 53, 54, 67, 76, 120, 222, 321, 398; v. 83, 87, 239, 338; vi. 330, 335, 365; vii. 173, 209, 253, 449; viii. 65, 279; x. 235, 240, 241, 492; xii. 44, 61, 79, 87; xiv. 308
Hymnes in honour of Love and Beautie, iii. 215 ff., 221, 243
Mutabilitie, vii. 209
Nine Comedies, iii. 229
Prosopopoia or Mother Hubberd's Tale, iii. 241, 246, 286; viii. 36, 226
Prothalamion, iii. 228, 243
Ruines of Time, The, iii. 250; v. 85
Ruins of Rome, The, iii. 250; v. 86, 238
Shepheards Calender, The, ii. 213; iii. 66, 214, 218 ff. (main entry), 225, 226, 228, 230, 238, 242 ff., 284, 286, 300, 302 ff., 442, 448; iv. 118, 171, 196, 398; v. 157, 225, 338; vi. 305, 364, 365; vii. 13; ix. 161
Tears of the Muses, The, iii. 241, 396; vii. 112
Veue of the Present State of Ireland, vii. 209 ff., 448
Visions of Bellay, The, iii. 250, 251
Visions of Petrarch, The, iii. 250
Spenser society, the, iv. 156
Spenserian stanza, x. 155; xi. 241, 247, 250; xii. 11, 44, 74, 100, 138; xiii. 229, 234 ff.; xiv. 311
Spenserians, iv. 149 ff., 223
Speranza, in *The Faerie Queene*, vi. 335
Spes (Hope), in *Piers the Plowman*, ii. 27
Spezia, bay of, xii. 37, 75, 76
Sphere, The, xiv. 201
Spice islands, the, iv. 67, 72, 73, 76, 98
Spickernell, Thomas (*fl.* 1594), iv. 362
Spielmann, Marion Harry, xiii. 530, 555, 559; xiv. 236, 532, 549; *The History of Punch*, xiv. 236, 532, 549
Spigott, in *Times Complaint*, vi. 320
Spilman or Spelman, Thomas, iv. 124
Spinagros, Sir, in *Golagros and Gawane*, ii. 123
Spingarn, Joel Elias, vi. 9; ix. 60, 61
Spinola, v. 361
Spinoza, Baruch (or Benedict), ix. 291, 298; xi. 100; xii. 60, 402; xiii. 18, 98, 439; xiv. 8, 41, 47, 469, 477; *Ethics*, xiii. 383; *Tractatus Theologico-Politicus*, xiii. 383
Spira, Vindelin de, iv. 421
Spirit of Men, The, i. 428
Spiritual Sangis, iii. 142
Spiritualitie, in *Ane Pleasant Satyre*, iii 125, 126, 127, 128
Spithead, xiv. 243
Splügen pass, the, xiii. 83
Sponge (Mr Surtees's), xiv. 234
Sport, in *The Tears of the Muses*, iii. 241
Sporting Magazine, The, xiv. 232
Sporting periodicals, xiv. 547
Sportive Wit (1656), vii. 512
'Sporus,' in Pope's *Epistle*, ix. 251, 252
Spottiswoode, John (1565–1637), iii. 165; *History of the Church and State of Scotland*, vii. 208, 448; xii. 359
Spottiswoode society, xii. 358, 359
Spoyle of Antwerp, The, v. 344
Spragge, Sir Edward (d. 1673), viii. 202
Spraggon, Jack (Surtees's), xiv. 234
Sprat, Thomas (1635–1713), vii. 257, 264; viii. 5, 25, 26, 91, 365, 369, 378, 394, 402, 410; ix. 32, 148, 158, 495; *History of the Royal Society*, viii. 379, 480; ix. 387, 412, 573; xiv. 460; *Life of Cowley*, x. 184; *True Account of that Horrid Conspiracy*, ix. 239
Spratt, Albert William (1842–1920), xii. Add. 3
Spratt, Thomas Abel Brimage (1811–1888), xii. 339, 498
Sprenger, Jacob, vii. 368, 375, 377, 394, 505
Sprigg, Joshua (1618–1684), vii. 450
Spring, Tom, xiv. 231
Springer, the, in Emily Brontë's *Wuthering Heights*, xiii. 411
Springett, Mrs (born Mary Proude, afterwards wife of Isaac Penington), viii. 109
Springlove, in *A Joviall Crew*, vi. 230
Springly, Tom, in *The Tatler*, ix. 36
Sprott, Thomas (*fl.* 1270?), ix. 535
Spur, Mercurius, x. 471
Spurcock, Sir Launcelot, in *The London Prodigall*, v. 255
Spurgeon, Charles Haddon (1834–1892), xii. 473
Spurs, battle of, iii. 70
Spurstow, William (1605?–1666), vii. 416
Spy, The (Hogg's), xi. 239
'Square-Cap' (Cleiveland's), vii. 97

Squeerses, the, in *Nicholas Nickleby*, XIII. 319, 321, 325
Squeezum, justice, in Fielding's *Coffee-House Politician*, X. 21, 29
Squire of Low Degree, I. 288, 315, 471
'Squirrel,' the (ship), IV. 74
Staal Delaunay, Madame de, X. 135
Stabat Mater, II. 383
Stables, William Gordon (1840–1910), XIII. 566
Stacions of Rome, The, II. 503
Staël, Madame de, V. 301; XII. 282; XIII. 468; *De l'Allemagne*, XIII. 3, 4
Stael, Peter, IX. 412
Stafford, East Gate street, VII. 250
Stafford, Edward, 3rd duke of Buckingham (1478–1521), II. 358
Stafford, Sir Edward, ambassador (d. 1605), IV. 79
Stafford, George, III. 27, 37
Stafford, Henry, 2nd duke of Buckingham (1454?–1483), III. 193
Stafford, Henry, 1st lord Stafford (1501–1563), III. 194
Stafford, John, archbishop of Canterbury (d. 1453), II. 288
Stafford, the Hon. John, *The Spartan Dame* (1719), VIII. 442
Stafford, Thomas, lieutenant, VII. 211
Stafford, W., *A Briefe Conceipt of English Policy*, V. 355, 363, 479
Stafford family, the, III. 188; IV. 132
Staffordshire, VIII. 146; IX. 533, 538; XI. 374; XII. 509, 513; XIII. 390
Staffordshire Advertiser, The, XIV. 529, 532
Stage-Players Complaint, The, VI. 406, 497
Stage-Playes, A Short Treatise against, VI. 497
Stage-Playes, An Ordinance...for The Utter Suppression and abolishing of, VI. 495
Stagyrite, the. *See* Aristotle
Stählin, K., V. 341
Staines, in Greene's *Tu Quoque*, VI. 219
Stair, earls of. *See* Dalrymple, Sir John
Stair, viscount. *See* Dalrymple, James
Stallard, Dr, IV. 382
Stallybrass, J. S., I. 420, 424
Stamboul, XIV. 247
Stamford, II. 345; IX. 308
Stamford News, The, XIV. 202
Stamp act, XI. 5, 7, 10
Stanbridge, John (1463–1510), II. 498
Standard, colonel, in Farquhar's *The Constant Couple*, VIII. 170
Standard, The, XIV. 180, 188, 189, 196
Standish, Arthur (*fl.* 1611), IV. 541
Stanford (Lincoln, Rutland and Northamptonshire), IX. 538
Stanford, Sir Charles Villiers (1852–1924), X. 130; XIII. 474
Stanford, Sir Wm (1509–1558), VIII. 467
Stanhope, Arthur Charles (d. 1770), X. 494; XIV. 391
Stanhope, Charles, 3rd earl Stanhope (1753–1816), XI. 390
Stanhope, Sir Edward (1546?–1608), IV. 427
Stanhope, Eugenia, X. 258, 494
Stanhope, lady Hester Lucy (1776–1839), IX. 244; XIV. 506
Stanhope, James, 1st earl of Stanhope (1673–1721), IX. 17, 483, 486
Stanhope, Leicester Fitzgerald Charles, 5th earl of Harrington (1784–1862), XII. 384
Stanhope, Philip, X. 257, 258, 494
Stanhope, Philip Dormer, 4th earl of Chesterfield (1694–1773), IV. 103; VIII. 388; IX. 152, 190, 246, 250, 252, 254, 485; X. 164, 167, 173, 176, 188, 207, 255 ff. (main entry), 369, 460, 463, 475, 477, 494, *also see* Add.; XI. 82, 173, 248, 260, 323; XIII. 321; XIV. 605
  Letters, VIII. 389; IX. 133, 471, 498; XI. 278, 371
  Letters to his Godson, X. 257 ff.
  Letters to his Son, X. 255, 257, 258; XIV. 390, 391
  Letters to A. C. Stanhope, XIV. 391
  'The Duty, Utility and Means of Pleasing,' X. 258
Stanhope, Philip, 5th earl of Chesterfield (1755–1815), X. 257; XIV. 391
Stanhope, Philip Henry, 5th earl Stanhope (1805–1875), IX. 498; XI. 396; XIV. 498
  History of England, XIV. 89
  History of the War of the Succession in Spain, XIV. 89
  Life of the Younger Pitt, XIV. 90
  Miscellanies, XIV. 89
  Reign of Queen Anne, The, XIV. 90
Stanley, Alice, countess dowager of Derby, lady Strange (born Spencer), VII. 112, 113
Stanley, Arthur Penrhyn (1815–1881), IV. 35; XII. 153, 264, 283, 288, 295, 319, 320–321 (main entry), 464, 467, 468, 470, 474, 477, 478, *also see* Add.; XIII. 96, 473, 541; XIV. 506, 601
  Epistles of St Paul to the Corinthians, XII. 292
  Lectures on the Church of Scotland, XII. 321
  Lectures on the Jewish Church, XII. 294; XIII. 98
  Life of Arnold, XII. 320; XIII. 370; XIV. 413
  Memorials of Canterbury, XII. 321
  Memorials of Westminster Abbey, XII. 321
  Oxford lectures, XII. 321
  Sinai and Palestine, XII. 321
Stanley, Edward, 3rd earl of Derby (1508–1572), VII. 83
Stanley, Edward G. G. S., 14th earl of Derby (1799–1869), XII. 334; XIII. 175, 509; XIV. 74, 90, 125, 129, 182, 197
  Iliad (trans.), XIV. 130

Stanley, Edward H. S., 15th earl of Derby (1826–1893), xiv. 509
Stanley, Ferdinando, lord Strange, 5th earl of Derby (d. 1594), vi. 247, 249
Stanley, Henry, 4th earl of Derby (1531–1593), iii. 382; xii. 518
Stanley, Sir Henry Morton (1841–1904), xiv. 192, 554
Stanley, Maria Josepha, lady (d. 1863), x. 299, 302
Stanley, Owen, xiv. 296, 564
Stanley, Thomas (1625–1678), iv. 125; vi. 197; vii. 4, 85, 87, 88, 94, 413, 475, 489; xii. 324, 328
Basia, vii. 83
Blush, The, vii. 84
Celia, To, vii. 84
'Chide, chide no more,' vii. 84
Clarissa, To, vii. 84
Cupido Cruci Affixus, vii. 83
History of Philosophy, vii. 83, 281
Kiss, The, vii. 84
Pervigilium, vii. 83
'Tell me no more,' vii. 83
Venus Vigils, trans. of, vii. 489
Stanley, Venetia, ix. 351
Stanley, William, 9th earl of Derby (1656–1702), x. 358
Stanley family, the, ii. 40
Stanley of Alderley, Henrietta Maria, lady (d. 1895), xiv. 430
Stanley's remedy, or the way to reform wandring beggars, etc., iv. 513
Stanley's catalogue of Parker mss. at Corpus, iv. 426
Stanmore, Gordon Arthur Hamilton, lord (1829–1912), xiv. 508, 510
Stannard, Henrietta E. V. (*pseud.* John Strange Winter, 1856–1911), xiii. 566
Stans Puer ad Mensam, ii. 502
Stansby, William, iv. 400
Stanyhurst, Richard (1547–1618), ii. 265; iii. 295, 307, 318, 319, 448, 527; x. 293; *Description of Ireland*, iii. 319; xiv. 308; trans. of *Vergil*, iv. 17 ff., 23, 399, 440
Stapfer, Paul, x. 422
Stapleton, Augustus Granville (1800–1880), xiv. 506, 508
Stapleton, Thomas (1535–1598), iii. 415, 470
Stapylton, Sir Robert (d. 1669), vii. 487, 489; viii. 421; *Hero and Leander*, viii. 123; *The Slighted Maid*, viii. 123; *The Stepmother*, viii. 123
Star, The, xiv. 194
Star, The (1888), xiv. 195
Star Chamber, the, iii. 76, 375, 378; iv. 279, 379, 380 ff., 386, 387, 411; v. 371, 372; vi. 290, 404; vii. 343, 345, 346, 441, 456; viii. 315; x. 287; xi. 311, 312
Starcatherus, i. 25
Starkey, John (*fl.* 1671), vii. 120; xi. 339
Starkey, Thomas (*fl.* 1499?–1538), iii. 478, 496; *Dialogue between Cardinal Pole and Thomas Lupset*, iv. 300, 573
Starkie, Thomas, xiv. 536
Starlight, captain, xiv. 370
State of Grace, the carvel of the, in *The Palice of Honour*, ii. 261
State papers and other public documents in Jacobean times, vii. 433
State papers of the Earl of Clarendon, x. 294
State papers for 1616, vi. 402
State Poems (1697), viii. 410
Stately, lord, in Crowne's *The English Frier*, viii. 188
Statham, E. Reginald, xiv. Add. 10
Statham, Nicholas (*fl.* 1467), viii. 314, 466
Statilia, in *The Bond-Man*, vi. 155
Stationers' company, iii. 96, 375, 378, 445; iv. 59, 63, 378 ff., 431; v. 260, 371; x. 12; xi. 312, 313, 467
Stationers' registers, iii. 79, 81, 396; iv. 9, 544 ff.; xi. 314; xii. 357, 368, 515
Statius, i. 170; ii. 150, 366; iv. 250; vii. 487; ix. 44, 527; xii. 306; *Silvae*, ix. 341; *Thebais*, iv. 253; ix. 68, 446
Statuta Ecclesiae Scoticanae, xii. 359
Statutes of the Realm (1235–1713), viii. 466
Staubach, the, xii. 47
Staunton, Howard (1810–1874), v. 279
Staunton, W., *St Patrick's Purgatory*, iv. 353, 527
Stavordale, lord, xiv. 503
Stead, J. J., xiii. 559
Stead, William Thomas (1849–1912), xiv. 193, 195, 535
Stearne, John, *A Confirmation and Discovery of Witch-Craft*, vii. 376, 507
Stebbing, William, xiv. 496
Stedman, Edmund Clarence, xiii. 485, 491
Steele, Anne (1717–1778), x. 522
Steele, Joshua (1700–1791), xi. 250, 251 (main entry), 256; xiii. 240
Steele, Sir Richard (1672–1729), vi. 82; vii. 244; viii. 145, 175, 390; ix. 5, 26 ff. (main entry), 75, 94, 109, 114, 118, 124, 142, 144, 161, 165, 171, 172, 248, 271, 436, 438 ff., 446, 456, 462, 569; x. 26, 67 ff., 80, 92, 205, *also see* Add.; xi. 261, 280, 320; xii. 177; xiii. 312, 429; xiv. 169, 197, 441, 446, 448, 461
Apology for Himself and his Writings, ix. 29
Christian Hero, The, ix. 28, 30, 33, 42
Conscious Lovers, The, ix. 57, 64
Drummer, The, ix. 43
Fishpool, The, ix. 439
Funeral, or Grief-à-la-mode, ix. 30
Lover, The, ix. 437, 439, 441
Lying Lover, The, viii. 131; ix. 30; xi. 322
Miscellanies, viii. 158
Miscellany, ix. 169
Old Whig, The, ix. 439, 442
Plebeian, The, ix. 439, 442
Reader, The, ix. 439, 442
Spinster, The, ix. 439
Tea-Table, The, ix. 442
Tender Husband, The, ix. 30, 33; x. 70

Steele, Sir Richard
Town Talk, The, IX. 439, 442
See, also, *Spectator, The*, and *Tatler, The*
Steele sisters, the, in Jane Austen's *Sense and Sensibility*, XII. 237, 240, 243
Steere, W., IX. 435
Steerforth, James, in *David Copperfield*, XIII. 327
Steevens, George (1736–1800), III. 252; V. 275 ff.; IX. 477; X. 263, 462, 471, 490, *also see* Add.; XI. 333; XII. 365; *Shakespeare*, XI. 320
Steevens, George Warrington (1869–1900), XIV. 193, 208, 535
Steill, David, dean, II. 280; III. 132
Attributed to: *The Ring of the Roy Robert*, II. 132; *Absent*, II. 132; *The Lantern of Lufe*, II. 132
Stein, III. 2
Stein, Sir Aurel (b. 1862), XII. Add. 5
Stella (lady Rich), alluded to in *Fame's Memorial* and *The Broken Heart*, V. 347; VI. 191, 196
Stella (Sidney's), III. 254; IV. 196; VI. 113
Stella (Swift's). *See* Johnson, Esther
Stella (Waller's), VII. 54
Stella, To, X. 168
Stelliana (Venetia Stanley), in Digby's *Memoirs*, VII. 222
Stelvio pass, in George Meredith's novel, XIII. 447
Stendhal (Marie Henri Beyle), V. 301; XIII. 447; XIV. 138
Stengesius, G., VII. 368, 505
Stenhouse, William (1773?–1827), IX. 361; XI. 444, 446
Stennett, Joseph (1663–1713), X. 387, 522
Stephano, in *Damon and Pithias*, V. 118
Stephano, in *The Tempest*, V. 206
Stephen, in Dickens's *Hard Times*, XIII. 329
Stephen, king of England, I. 111, 161, 166, 168, 171, 172, 364, 369; II. 350; XIV. 72
Stephen, Caroline Emelia, XII. 427
Stephen, Sir James (1789–1859), X. 300; XII. 153, 282, 427, 471; XIII. 471; XIV. 507; *Essays in Ecclesiastical Biography*, XIV. 109, 120; *Lectures on the History of France*, XIV. 109, 110
Stephen, Sir James Fitzjames (1829–1894), XIV. 194, 198, 481, 498, 507; *Liberty, Equality, Fraternity*, XIV. 21; *The Story of Nuncomar*, XIV. 110
Stephen, James Kenneth (1859–1892), XIII. 162, 509; XIV. 205 ff., 337, 537; *Lapsus Calami*, XIII. 166; XIV. 206, 208
Stephen, Sir Leslie (1832–1904), VIII. 245; IX. 253; X. 409, 411, 413, 422, 445, *also see* Add.; XI. 394, 395, 397, 411, 417, 419, 423, 439; XII. 131, 381, 404, 426, 431, 433, 441, 445, 464, 468, 486, 524; XIII. 97, 100, 180, 360, 407, 473, 478, 485, 488, 510, 553, 559, 567; XIV. 56, 65, 81, 103, 111, 143–144 (main entry), 467, 470, 472, 481, 486, 488, 493, 494, 498, 509, 515, 524 ff., 561, 595
Stephen, Sir Leslie
Agnostic's Apology, An, XIV. 144
English Utilitarians, The, XIV. 35, 144
Essays on Free Thinking and Plain Speaking, XIV. 143
History of English Thought in the 18th century, IX. 310, 321, 324; X. 296; XIV. 35, 144
Hours in a Library, XII. 148; XIII. 379; XIV. 143
Johnson, XIV. 144
Life of Sir James Fitzjames Stephen, XIV. 110
Playground of Europe, The, XIV. 143, 248, 254
Science of Ethics, The, XIV. 35
Sketches from Cambridge, XIV. 143
Studies of a Biographer, XIV. 144
Stephen de Haselfield, II. 351
Stephens, Alexander (1757–1821), X. 524
Stephens, Catherine, countess of Essex, XII. 171
Stephens, Frederick George, XIII. 110, 491
Stephens, French family of, printers and scholars, VII. 307, 477
Stephens, George (1813–1895), I. 425; XII. 513
Stephens, James Brunton (1835–1902), XIV. 369, 587; *Convict Once*, XIV. 368; *To a Black Gin*, XIV. 368; *Universally Respected*, XIV. 368
Stephens, Jeremiah (1591–1665), IX. 539
Stephens, John (*fl.* 1615), III. 487; VI. 497; VII. 379; *Satyrical essayes, characters and others*, IV. 340 ff., 345, 518, 521, 524
Stephens, John (d. 1726), IX. 277, 343, 501, 539; *Pablo de Segovia*, IX. 278; *Spanish Libertines*, IX. 278
Stephens, Robert (1665–1732), IX. 529
Stephens, Thomas, VII. 487
Stephens, Thomas (1549?–1619), XIV. 322
Stephens, William Richard Wood (1839–1902), XII. 457; XIV. 488, 507; *History of the English Church*, vol. II, XIV. 101; *Life and Letters of E. A. Freeman*, XIV. 67, 71
Stephens, Winifred, XIII. 566
Stephenson, B. C. and Scott, Clement, *Diplomacy*, XIII. 525
Stephenson, George (1781–1848), XIV. 381
Stepmothers Tragedy, The, V. 325
Stepney, George (1663–1707), VIII. 410, 411, 447; IX. 174, 176, 487; XIV. 180
Sterling, John (1806–1844), XI. 441; XII. 288, 425, 467; XIII. 18, 24, 473, 552; XIV. 180
Sterling, Joseph, X. 491
Sterne, Laurence (1713–1768), IV. 248, 264; IX. 127, 128; X. 15, 39, 43, 46 ff. (main entry), 56 ff., 352, 369, 421, *also see* Add.; XI. 174, 289, 296, 347, 429; XII. 56, 124, 177, 250; XIII. 7, 319, 326, 420, 421, 428; XIV. 142, 146, 217, 223, 554; *Sentimental Journey*, X. 42, 47; XIV. 240, 246; *Tristram Shandy*, IV.

Sterne, Laurence
252; IX. 136, 137; X. 44, 47 ff., 252; XI. 206, 260, 341; XIII. 295; XIV. 216
Sternhold, Thomas (d. 1549), III. 46; *Psalms*, VIII. 41
Stesichorus, XII. 329
Stettin, duke of, VI. 291, 292
Steuart, Archibald Francis, X. 295
Steuart, Sir James (1712–1780), *Inquiry into the Principles of Political Economy*, X. 337, 338, 514
Stevens, B., XIV. 584; *The Golden Treasury of Australian Verse*, XIV. 365
Stevens, George Alexander (1710–1784), XI. 472
Stevens, John (d. 1726), IX. 533
Stevens, William Bagshaw (1756–1800), X. 491
Stevenson, Elizabeth. *See* Gaskell, Elizabeth Cleghorn
Stevenson, Francis Seymour, I. 204
Stevenson, John (1798–1827?), XIII. 378
Stevenson, Sir John Andrew (1760?–1833), XII. 410, 411
Stevenson, John Hall (1718–1785), X. 47; XI. 172 ff., 428; XII. 120
Crazy Tales, XI. 174, 175
Fables for Grown Gentlemen, XI. 174
Makarony Tales, XI. 174
Pastoral Cordial, XI. 174
Pastoral Puke, XI. 174
Stevenson, Joseph (1806–1895), XII. 356; XIV. 499
Stevenson, Matthew (*fl.* 1654–1685), *Norfolk Drollery* (1673), VII. 512
Stevenson, Mrs Margaret Isabella, XIV. 526
Stevenson, Robert Alan Mowbray (1847–1900), XIV. 525, *also see* Add. 3
Stevenson, Robert Louis (1850–1894), I. 367; VI. 230; VIII. 112; XI. 387, 441; XII. 30, 168, 176, 178, 179, 381, 433; XIII. 214, 441, 509, 523; XIV. 161 ff., 211, 462, 525, 526, 538, 554
A Child's Garden of Verses, XIII. 215
Across the Plains, XIV. 162
Amateur Emigrant, The, XIV. 162
Beach of Falesa, The, XIV. 162
Beau Austin (with W. E. Henley), XIV. 163
Black Arrow, The, XIV. 162, 443
Catriona, XIV. 162
Christmas Sermon, A, XIV. 162
'College Magazine, A,' XIV. 210
Familiar Studies, XIV. 162
In the South Seas, XIV. 162
Inland Voyage, An, XIV. 162, 240
Kidnapped, XIV. 162
Markheim, XIV. 162
Master of Ballantrae, The, XIV. 162
Memories and Portraits, XIV. 162, 210
New Arabian Nights, The, XIV. 162
'Old Scotch Gardener, An,' XIV. 210
Ordered South, XIV. 161
Pavilion on the Links, The, XIV. 162
St Ives, XIV. 163
Silverado Squatters, The, XIV. 162
Stevenson, Robert Louis
Thrawn Janet, XIV. 162
Travels with a Donkey, XIV. 162
Treasure Island, XIV. 162, 255
Virginibus Puerisque, XIV. 162
Weir of Hermiston, XIV. 163
Stevenson, William (*fl.* 1546–1560), VI. 296, 297, 478
Stevenson, William (1772–1829), XIII. 372
Stevenson, William Henry, I. 90
Steventon, Hampshire, XII. 231
Steward, Augustine, IV. 141
Steward, Richard (1593?–1651), VII. 147, 160, 426, 428
Stewards, manor house, near Romford, VII. 46
Stewart, in Blind Harry's *Wallace*, II. 112
Stewart, Alexander (1493?–1513), II. 369
Stewart, Arabella, IV. 265
Stewart, David, duke of Rothsay (1378?–1402), III. 120
Stewart, Dugald (1753–1828), IX. 301; XI. 75, 76, 221, 222, 400; XII. 4, 427; XIV. 16
Elements of the Philosophy of the Human Mind, XI. 76
Life of Adam Smith, X. 335, 504, 511, 512, 514
Life of Robertson, X. 289
Outlines of Moral Philosophy, XI. 76
Philosophical Essays, XI. 76
Philosophy of the Active and Moral Powers, XI. 76
Progress of...Philosophy, XI. 76
Stewart, Esmé, 1st duke of Lennox (1542?–1583), X. 288
Stewart, Henry, earl of Darnley (1545–1567), III. 131, 164; XIII. 133
Stewart, Henry B. M. C. (1725–1807), cardinal of York, II. 77
Stewart, Hugh Fraser, XII. 488
Stewart, lord James, earl of Mar and Moray (1531?–1570), III. 159
Stewart, Sir James (d. 1713), IX. 546, 547
Stewart, James, XIV. Add. 10
Stewart, John, duke of Albany (1481–1536), III. 70
Stewart, Matthew, 4th or 12th earl of Lennox (1516–1571), III. 164
Stewart, prince James Francis Edward, the Old Pretender, VIII. 44
Stewart, Robert, viscount Castlereagh (1769–1822), XII. 69, 392; XIV. 121, 122, 508
Stewart, royal family of, IV. 104, 274, 304, 307, 311, 312, 315; VIII. 2, 6, 8, 38, 258, 261, 301, 303, 309, 312, 321, 349 ff., 358, 361; X. 351, 352, 355, 500
Stewart, T. B. Phillips (1864–1892), XIV. 357, 582
Stewart of Baldines, *Ane Abbregement of Roland Furious*, III. 137
Stewart cause, the, XIV. 96
Stewart dramatists, VIII. 366; XII. 198
Stewart period, X. 40, 286, 355, 397 XIV. 86, 114, 281, 284
Stewart princesses, XIV. 111

Stewarte, III. 131; *Flyting betwix the Sowtar and the Tailyour*, III. 131; *For to declare the hie Magnificence of Ladies*, III. 131
Stewarte, W. or Stewarte of Lorne?, *This Hinder Nycht*, III. 131; IV. 322
Stewarton, Ayrshire, II. 126
Steyne, lord (Thackeray's), XIII. 286 ff., 291
Stiefel, A. L., VI. 32, 124, 140, 204, 205, 208
Stiggins (Dickens's), VI. 28
Still, John, bishop of Bath and Wells (d. 1608), VI. 296
Stilling, Johann Heinrich (Jung-Stilling), VII. 177; IX. 328
Stillingfleet, Benjamin (1702–1771), X. 135; XI. 344, 345
Stillingfleet, Edward (1635–1699), bishop of Worcester, VIII. 46 ff., 292, 298, 302, 332, 346, 370, 402, 462, 471, 475; IX. 195, 196, 199, 330, 335; X. 373, 377; XI. 416; XII. 259
Irenicum, VIII. 300
Origines Britannicae, VIII. 300
Origines Sacrae, VIII. 300
Vindication of the Doctrine of the Trinity, VIII. 46, 331
Stillingfleet, James, IX. 313, 330
Stinstra, John, X. 19
Stipes, in *The Rival Friends*, VI. 324
Stirling, III. 120, 122; IV. 163; VII. 455; IX. 552; XI. 373, 440, 469
Stirling, Amelia Hutchison, XIV. 481
Stirling, earl of. *See* Alexander, Sir William
Stirling, James Hutchison (1820–1909), XIII. 478; XIV. 474, 481; *Secret of Hegel, The*, XIV. 42; *Sir W. Hamilton: being the Philosophy of Perception*, XIV. 7; *Text book to Kant*, XIV. 42
Stirling-Maxwell, lady. *See* Norton, Caroline E. S.
Stirry, Thos., VII. Add.
Stobaeus, Johannes, III. 416; XII. 328, 484
Stock, Thomas (*fl.* 1780), XIV. 389
Stockbridge, IX. 456
Stockdale, John (1749?–1814), X. 463; XIV. 121
Stockdale, Percival (1736–1811), X. 446, 463, 473; XIV. 609; *Memoirs*, X. 183
Stockenstrom, Sir Andries, XIV. Add. 10
Stocker, Thomas (*fl.* 1569–1592), *Diodorus Siculus*, IV. 4, 436, 439
Stockholm, V. 283
Stockport, XI. 375
Stockton, III. 95; XI. 486
Stockwell, in Cumberland's *West Indian*, XI. 264
Stockwood, John (d. 1610), VI. 386, 497
Stodart-Walker, A., XIV. 595
Stoddard, Richard Henry, XIII. 532
Stoddart, Anna M., XIV. 516, 600
Stoddart, Sir John (1773–1856), XIV. 178, 179
Stoddart, Sarah. *See* Hazlitt, Sarah
Stoddart, Thomas Tod (1810–1880), XIII. 509
Stoics, the, VII. 376; IX. 55, 63
Stoicus Vapulans, VI. 486
Stoke Newington, VIII. 199; IX. 6, 21, 24
Stoke Newington academy, X. 386
Stoke Pogis, X. 121, 123, 126
Stokes, Sir George Gabriel (1819–1903), XIV. 265 ff., 557
Stokes, Margaret McNair (1832–1900), XII. 518; XIV. Add. 3; *Early Christian Architecture in Ireland*, XIV. 328
Stokes, Whitley (1830–1909), V. 16; XII. 518; XIV. 305, *also see* Add. 3; *Thesaurus Palaeo-Hibernicus*, XII. 361
Stokes, William (1804–1878), *The Life of George Petrie*, XIV. 312, 328, *also see* Add. 3
Stoll, Elmer Edgar, VI. 169
Stone, Edmund (d. 1768), VIII. 476
Stone, William Johnson, XIII. 246, 247, 511
Stonehenge, III. 106, 322; VII. 443; IX. 354, 532, 536, 540; XII. 192
Stonehewer, Richard (1728?–1809), X. 133
Stonor park, IV. 412
Stonyhurst, XIV. 249
Stopes, Mrs Charlotte Carmichael, VI. 286
Storer, James Sargant (1771–1853), XI. 404
Storer, Thomas (1571–1604), IX. 472
Stork, Charles Wharton, VI. 170
Storm of wind, the great (15 January 1362), II. 12
Storr, Francis, XIV. 602
Storr, Vernon Faithfull, *Development of English Theology*, XIII. 384
Story, Robert Herbert (1835–1907), XII. 423; XIV. 507
Story, William Wetmore, XIII. 74
Story of the St Alb-n's Ghost, IX. 130
Stothard, Thomas (1755–1834), XI. 377; XII. 408
Stoughton, Dr, VIII. 281
Stoughton, John (1807–1897), XII. 464, 473
Stourbridge, X. 159
Stourbridge and Bromsgrove academy, X. 387
Stout, George Frederick, XIV. 469
Stow, IX. 235
Stow, David (1793–1864), XIV. 602
Stow, George William, XIV. Add. 10
Stow, John (1525?–1605), II. 162, 164, 217; III. 111, 314, 318, 321, 323 ff., 332, 335, 532, 553; IV. 389; V. 83, 371; VI. 254, 282, 463; VII. 203; IX. 352; XII. 349
Annals, I. 336; III. 438; IV. 381
Brief Chronicle, IV. 389
Chronicles of England, III. 314 ff., 324; V. 242
Summarie of Englyshe Chronicles, III. 324
Survey of the Cities of London and Westminster, III. 330; IV. 389; V. 321, 479; IX. 353; XII. 354
Stowe, X. 101 ff., 126
Stowe, Harriet Beecher, XI. 492; XII. 393, 398; *Uncle Tom's Cabin*, XIII. 427

Stowe, John (scribe of *Jack Napes*), II. 424
Stowe, William Henry (1825–1855), XIV. 535
Stowey. *See* Nether Stowey
Strabo, III. 109, 420; VII. 311
Strachan, John, XII. 519; *Thesaurus Palaeo-Hibernicus*, XII. 361
Strachan, Lionel Richard Mortimer, XIII. 499
Strachey, J. St Leo, XII. 426
Strada, *Prolusiones*, VI. 190
Stradling, Sir John (1563–1637), VII. 407, 487; *Epigrammata*, IV. 360
Strafford, earls of. *See* Wentworth, Thomas
Strafford's Letters and Despatches, The Earl of, VII. 194, 435
Strahan, George (1744–1824), X. 462, 472
Strahan, James Andrew, XIV. 536
Strahan, William (1715–1785), X. 294, 511; XI. 326
Strange, in *A Woman is a Weathercocke*, VI. 222
Strange, Ferdinando. *See* Stanley, Ferdinando
Strange, lady. *See* Stanley, Alice
Strange Metamorphosis of Man, A, IV. 522
Strange Predictions, VII. 394
Strangeness, in *The Passetyme of Pleasure*, II. 234
Strange's men, lord, V. 161; VI. 254, 255
Strangford, 7th viscount. *See* Smythe, George A. F. P. S.
Strap, in Smollett's *Roderick Random*, X. 37 ff.
Straparola, Gian Francesco, IV. 6
Strassburg, II. 329; III. 80, 333, 431, 434; VII. 304; IX. 412
Strassburg. *See* Gottfried von
Stratford, John de, archbishop of Canterbury (d. 1348), II. 352
Stratford-atte-Bowe, VIII. 313
Stratford de Redcliffe, viscount. *See* Canning, Stratford
Stratford-on-Avon, IV. 394; V. 165 ff., 171, 222, 374; VI. 141, 247; VII. 278; X. 112, 192, 271, 385; XI. 451; XII. 369
Stratford-on-Avon, New Place, V. 166, 170, 219; VI. 278
Strathclyde, II. 88, 99
Strathmore, earl of. *See* Lyon, John
Stratonice, in *The Tatler*, IX. 38
Straunge Newes out of Affrick, VI. 388
Straus, Ralph, XI. 468
Strauss, David Friedrich, XII. 467; XIII. 469, 553; *Life of Jesus*, XII. 292; XIII. 383
Straw, Jack, I. 369
Straw, Sir John, in Barnabe Googe's *Eclogues*, III. 186
Strawberry hill, VII. 204; X. 244, 245, 495, 496; XI. 341, 363
Strawberry hill press, X. 127, 244, 245, 253, 254, 496; XI. 469
Streamer, court jester, in *Beware the Cat*, III. 494
Strean, Annesley, X. 195, 483
Streater, John (*fl.* 1650–1670), VII. 358; *A Politick Commentary on the life of Caius July Caesar*, VII. 358; *Observations, Historical Political and Philosophical*, VII. 358; *Secret Reasons of State*, VII. 358
Streatfeild, Richard Alexander, XIII. 571, 572, *also see* Add. 1
Streatfield, Miss, X. 65
Streatham, X. 186, 189; XI. 364
Streatham Letters, XI. 365
Street, George Edmund (1824–1881), XIII. 119
Street, George Slythe, XII. 398
Street, Peter, a carpenter, VI. 258
Street, Sir Thomas (1626–1696), VII. 365
Street ballads, IV. 535
Strength, in *The Pride of Life*, V. 52
Strensham, in Worcestershire, VIII. 60
Streoneshalh. *See* Whitby
Strickland, Agnes (1796–1874), XI. 482; XIV. 507; *Lives of the Queens of England*, XIV. 111; *Lives of the Queens of Scotland*, XIV. 111; *The Moss House*, XI. 384
Strickland, Elizabeth (1794–1875), XIV. 111, 507
Strickland, Hugh Edwin (1811–1853), XIV. 563
Strickland, Mr (*fl.* 1572), III. 402
Stritch, A. R., XIV. 573
Strode, Ralph (*fl.* 1350–1400), I. 332, 333; II. 54, 135, 443
Strode, William (1599?–1645), VII. 160, 426; *The Floating Island*, VI. 325, 327, 478
Strong, Chevalier, in *Pendennis*, XIII. 291
Strong, Dr, in *David Copperfield*, XIII. 327
Strong, Isobel, XIV. 526
Strong, James, *Joanereidos* (1645), VII. 513
Strong, Sandford Arthur (1863–1904), XII. 499
Strowd, Tom, in *The Blind Beggar*, V. 373
Strozza, Ercole, III. 253
Struldbrugs, in *Gulliver's Travels*, IX. 105
Strumbo, in *Locrine*, V. 239
Struther, William (*fl.* 1633), IX. 545
Struthers, John (1776–1853), XII. 423
Strutt, John William, 1st baron Rayleigh, XIV. 269
Strutt, Joseph (1749–1802), XII. 376, 412, 519; XIV. 499, 546; *Sports and Pastimes*, XIV. 230
'Strutt, Lord,' in Arbuthnot's *History of John Bull*, IX. 134
'Strutt, The Lord' (Charles of Spain), XIV. 212
Struwelpeter, the English, XI. 491
Strype, John (1643–1737), V. 482; IX. 209–210 (main entry), 212, 354, 496, 539
Annals of the Reformation, IX. 210
Ecclesiastical Memorials, IX. 210
Life of Edmund Grindal, IX. 210
Life of John Aylmer, IX. 210
Life of John Whitgift, IX. 210
Life of Matthew Parker, IX. 210

Strype, John
Life of Sir John Cheke, IX. 210
Life of Sir Thomas Smith, IX. 210
Memorials of Thomas Cranmer, IX. 210
Stuart, lord Bernard (1623?–1646), VII. 6
Stuart, Daniel (1766–1846), XI. 405, 416; XIV. 179, 183, 184, 187, 194
Stuart, Elena, XIII. 553
Stuart, Gilbert (1742–1786), X. 502, 505
Stuart, James (1713–1788), XII. 499
Stuart, James (1775–1849), XIV. 188
Stuart, James (1843–1913), XIV. 432, 602, *also see* Add. 10
Stuart, James, of Dunearn, XI. 236
Stuart, John, 3rd earl of Bute (1713–1792), VI. 7; IX. 245, 497, 498; X. 41, 131, 390 ff., 394, 396, 399, 401, 523; XI. 174, 348; XIV. 213
Stuart, John (1813–1877), XII. 513; *The Book of Deer*, XII. 350; *The Sculptured Stones of Scotland*, XII. 350
Stuart, J. A. Erskine, XIII. 559
Stuart, lady Louisa, IX. 246; XI. 348, 349
Stuart, Peter (*fl.* 1788–1805), XIV. 179, 184
Stuart, Robert (1812–1848), XII. 513; *Caledonia Romana*, XII. 350
Stuart-Wortley, John, 2nd baron Wharncliffe (1801–1855), IX. 248
Stub, Edmund (*fl.* 1611–1631), VI. 478
Stubber, in *Blurt Master-Constable*, V. 362
Stubbs, Charles William, XIII. 548, *also see* Add. 2
Stubbs, Stubbes or Stubbe, Henry, the younger (1632–1676), VII. 317, 475, 489, *also see* Add.; *The* Plus Ultra *reduced to a Non Plus*, VIII. 291
Stubbs, John (1543?–1591), V. 341
Stubbs, John William, *History of the University of Dublin*, X. 198
Stubbs or Stubbes, Philip (*fl.* 1583–1591), VI. 387, 393 ff., 401, 409, 462, 497; *The Anatomy of Abuses*, III. 362; V. 352, 357, 359, 371, 479; VI. 376, 386, 393, 394
Stubbs, Robert, in Thackeray's *The Fatal Boots*, XIII. 280, 282
Stubbs, William (1825–1901), bishop of Oxford, I. 157, 160, 161, 172, 173, 175; VIII. 306; XII. 271, 273; XIV. 57, 69, 74 ff. (main entry), 101, 143, 499
Appendices to the *Report of the Commission on Ecclesiastical Courts*, XIV. 75
Constitutional History of England, The, XIV. 75
Councils and Ecclesiastical Documents, XIV. 75
Registrum Sacrum Anglicanum, XIV. 74
Rolls series, edited by, XIV. 74
Select Charters, XIV. 75
Stubs, John, VIII. 414
Student, The (1751), X. 175, 466
Student, The (Edinburgh), XIV. 209, 210
Studioso, in *The Returne from Pernassus*, V. 360; VI. 311, 312
Studioso, in *Time's Complaint*, VI. 320
Studiosus, in *The Pilgrimage to Parnassus*, VI. 310
Studious Desire, in *The Nature of the Four Elements*, V. 57
Studley, John (1545?–1590?), IV. 440; V. 395
Study, Wit's wife, in *Piers the Plowman*, II. 19, 20
Study to be Quiet, VII. 515
Stukeley, Captaine Thomas, V. 399
Stukeley, William (1687–1765), IX. 352, 358, 540; *Itinerarium Curiosum*, IX. 352; *Stonehenge*, IX. 354
Stukely, Thomas (1525?–1578), VII. 75
Stumps, Bill (Dickens's), XIV. 444
Stupido, in *The Pilgrimage to Parnassus*, VI. 310
Sturgion, John (*fl.* 1657), X. 520
Sturm, John, III. 429, 430, 432, 434, 554
Sturm und Drang, V. 297 ff., 463 ff.
Sturmy, Samuel, IV. 462
Sturt, Henry, XIV. 469
Sturt, John (1658–1730), VII. 402
Stuttgart, VII. 309
Stymmelius, Christopher, V. 101, 413
Styria, XIII. 432
Styx, river, XI. 352
Suard, Jean Baptiste Antoine, X. 422; XI. 354
Subiaco, printing press at, II. 310
Subscription controversy, X. 377
Subtle, in *The Alchemist*, V. 369; VI. 22
Successio, IX. 68
Suckdry, in Wilson's *Projectors*, VIII. 123
Suckling, Alfred Inigo (1796–1856), XII. 513
Suckling, Sir John (1609–1642), III. 172; IV. 168, 187; V. 222; VI. 11, 212, 239, 458; VII. 2, 4, 7, 15, 20 ff. (main entry), 25, 57, 273, 399, 466; X. 115; XI. 318
A Session of the Poets, VII. 16, 22, 153, 263, 274
Aglaura, VI. 238; VII. 22; VIII. 226
An Account of Religion by Reason, VII. 21, 22
Ballad of a Wedding, VII. 23
Brennoralt, or The Discontented Colonell, VI. 238; VII. 22
Fragmenta Aurea, VII. 22
Goblins, The, VI. 238, 239; VII. 22
Letter to Mr Henry Jermyn, VII. 21
'O, for some honest lover's ghost,' VII. 23
'O, that I were all soul, that I might prove,' VII. 21
'Out upon it! I have loved,' VII. 23
The Sad One, VII. 22
''Tis now since I sat down before that foolish fort, a heart,' VII. 21
'Why so pale and wan, fond lover?' VI. 238; VII. 23
Suckling, Sir John, father of the poet, VII. 21
Sudbury, Simon of, archbishop of Canterbury (d. 1381), II. 55, 56
Sudbury, Suffolk, VII. 223; IX. 217
Suddard, S. J. Mary (1888–1909), VI. Add.; IX. Add.; XI. 411; XII. 404, 407; XIII. 491, 566; XIV. 528

Suddene (Isle of Man), in *Horn*, I. 304
Sue, Eugène, *Mystères de Paris*, XIII. 427
Sue, Marie J. E., XIII. 559
Suetonius, III. 10; IV. 4, 14, 15, 342, 417, 440; VI. 154; VII. 370, 392, 503; VIII. 378; XII. 206
Suez canal, XIV. 195
Sufferance, in *Piers the Plowman*, II. 20
Suffolk, II. 134, 156, 197, 214, 224; III. 337; VII. 33, 223; X. 294; XI. 140; XII. 198, 256, 331, 508, 513, 520; XIII. 142; XIV. 221
Suffolk, countess of. *See* Howard, Henrietta
Suffolk, dukes of. *See* Brandon, Charles; Pole, William de la
Suffolk, earl of. *See* Howard, Thomas
Sugden, Edward Burtenshaw. baron St Leonards (1781–1875), XIV. 501, 514
Suidas, IX. 336; XII. 328, 484, 490, 491, 494
Sulby academy, X. 387
Suliotes, XII. 39
Sulky, in Holcroft's *Road to Ruin*, XI. 277
Sullivan, Alexander Martin (1830–1884), XIV. 571
Sullivan, Sir Edward (1822–1885), XIV. 538
Sullivan, Timothy Daniel (1827–1914), XIV. 571
God Save Ireland, XIV. 321
Madness of King Conchobar, The, XIV. 321
Michael Dwyer, XIV. 321
Siege of Dunboy, The, XIV. 321
Soldier's Wake, A, XIV. 321
Song from the Backwoods, XIV. 321
Story of Blanaid, The, XIV. 321
Sullivan, William Francis (1756–1830), XI. 490
Sully, Maximilien de Béthune, duc de, IV. 312; IX. 231; *Mémoires*, X. 135, 467
Sulpicius Severus, I. 75
Sulpitius, III. 13, 20
Sumatra, XI. 278
'Sumer is i-cumen in,' I. 360; II. 393; IV. 462, 463; V. 29
Summa Ostiensis, II. 364
Summer, in folk-plays, V. 31
Summerly, Felix, *pseud.* *See* Cole, Sir Henry
Summers, Life and Death of Will, III. 488
Summerson, Esther, in *Bleak House*, XIII. 328
Sumner, Charles Richard (1790–1874), VII. 129, 141
Sumner, John Bird (1780–1862), XII. 473
Sumner, Robert Carey (1729–1771), XIV. 386
Sun, The, XIV. 194
Sun rises Bright in France, IX. 377
Sunatorrek, I. 9
Sunchildism, in Butler's *Erewhon Revisited*, XIII. 453
Sunday newspapers, XIV. 192, 201
'Sunday observance, letter sent from heaven on,' I. 134
Sunday schools, XIII. 51; XIV. 382, 389
Sunday Schools' Union, XIV. 389
Sunderland, countess of. *See* Spencer, Dorothy
Sunderland, earls of. *See* Spencer, Henry; Spencer, Robert
Sundridge, Kent, VI. 112
Sunninghill, near Windsor, VII. 16
'Sunshine,' the (ship), IV. 76
Superbia, in *Psychomachia*, V. 51
Superstition, in *A True Inventory*, VII. 382
Supplantation, in *Confessio Amantis*, II. 148
Supporters of the Bill of Rights, The, X. 401
Surat, IV. 90, 99
Surface, Charles, in Sheridan's *School for Scandal*, V. 254; X. 90; XI. 269 ff.
Surface, Joseph, in Sheridan's *School for Scandal*, VIII. 148; X. 75; XI. 270, 271
Surflet, Richard, IV. 538, 541
Surinam, VIII. 140
Surly, in Crowne's *Sir Courtly Nice*, VIII. 189
Surmy's *Mariner's Magazine*, IX. 106
Surrey, II. 353; III. 385; IV. 156, 190; VI. 247, 282; VII. 277; VIII. 242, 244; IX. 531, 539; XI. 183; XII. 507, 508, 511; XIII. 275; XIV. 294
'Surrey, Another Freeholder of,' X. 401
Surrey, countess of, in *The Garden of Laurell*, III. 70
Surrey, earls of. *See* Howard, Henry; Howard, Thomas
Surrey archaeological collections, XII. 507
Surtees, Robert (1779–1834), IX. 377; XII. 6, 513; *History of Durham*, XII. 354
Surtees, Robert Smith (1803–1864), XIV. 216, 546, 547
Ask Mamma, XIV. 234
Handley Cross, X. 111; XIV. 234
Hawbuck Grange, XIV. 234
Jorrocks' Jaunts, XIV. 234
Mr Facey Romford's Hounds, XIV. 234
Mr Sponge's Sporting Tour, XIV. 234
Surtees society, XII. 354
Susan, in Meredith's *Earth and a Wedded Woman*, XIII. 443
Susan, in *The Witch of Edmonton*, VI. 54
Susanna, in Biblical comedies, V. 101
Susanna, in *Ralph Roister Doister*, V. 106
Susanna, The Story of, II. 120, 121
Susanna and the elders, III. 350
Susannah, in Sterne's *Tristram Shandy*, X. 50
Susenbrotus, VI. 486
Susenbrotus, *Epitome Troporum*, III. 429
Suso, Heinrich, IX. 314
Suspirius, in *The Rambler*, X. 172
Sussex, IV. 190; V. 135; VI. 110; VII. 22, 232; VIII. 244, 298; X. 312, 378; XII. 507, 511, 523; XIV. 221, 294
Sussex, duke of. *See* Augustus Frederick
Sussex, lord, in Glover's *Boadicea*, XI. 258
Sussex archaeological collections, XII. 507
Susy Pye, in *Young Beichan*, II. 411

Sutcliffe, Matthew (1550?–1629), III. 538; IV. 491; VII. 309, 310, 484; *An Answere to a certaine libel supplicatorie*, III. 391; *An Answere unto a certaine calumnious letter*, III. 390, 391
Sutherland, Alexander (1852–1902), XIV. 584, 587; *Victoria and its Metropolis*, XIV. 371
Sutherlandshire, VII. 231
Sutton, Christopher (1565?–1629), IV. 496
Sutton, Henry Septimus (1825–1901), XIII. 509
Sutton, Ned, IX. 191
Sutton, Oliver, bishop of Lincoln (d. 1299), II. 348
Sutton, Thomas (1532–1611), VII. 332, 338
Sutton, Thomas (1585–1623), VI. 224, 402
Sutton, Yorkshire, X. 47
Sutton Vallamore, Kent, VII. 361
Svears, the, I. 25
Svend Aagesen, I. 34
Swabia, V. 305
Swadlin, Thomas (1600–1670), VII. 509
Swain, Charles (1801–1874), XII. 423
Swainson, Charles Anthony (1820–1887), XII. 478
Swainson, William (1789–1855), XII. 523
Swalle, Abel, XI. 319
Swallow, Hereward's mare, in *Deeds of Hereward*, I. 364
Swallow, in *Time's Complaint*, VI. 320
Swallow, tale of, in Henryson's *Fables*, II. 246
Swan, the, in *Mum, Sothsegger*, II. 36
Swan, John, M.D., X. 467
Swan, privateer, XIV. 242
Swarthmore MSS., VIII. 412
Swavesey, Cambridgeshire, X. 280
Sweden, V. 307, 308; VII. 200, 345; VIII. 137, 267; X. 193, 500
Swedenborg, Emanuel, XI. 432; *Memorable Relations*, XI. 188
Swedenborgianism, XI. 181; XIII. 46, 47
Swedes, the, in *Beowulf*, I. 24, 25
Swedish government, the, XIV. 287
Swedish language, XIV. 458
Sweet, Henry (1845–1912), XII. 505; XIII. 248; XIV. 611; *New English Grammar*, XIV. 444
Sweet Trinity, II. 414
Sweet William's Ghost, II. 414
'Sweete violets (Loves paradice) that spred,' IV. 117
Swete Susane, Epistill of, II. 112, 116, 120, 121, 272, 450; III. 278
Sweyn, king of England and Denmark (d. 1014), I. 127
Sweynheym, printer, II. 310
Swift, Deane (1707–1783), IX. 124, 467
Swift, Godwin, IX. 91, 92
Swift, Jonathan, the elder, IX. 91
Swift, Jonathan, dean of St Patrick's (1667?–1745), III. 82, 417; IV. 45, 49, 251; VII. 167, 176; VIII. 146, 158, 160, 232, 234, 292, 302, 305, 380 ff., 386; IX. 17, 23, 25, 34, 35, 45, 46, 67, 75, 78 ff., 84, 85, 87, 91 ff. (main entry), 129 ff., 133, 136, 139, 144, 151, 152, 157, 158, 160, 163 ff., 172, 184, 186, 202, 208, 209, 217, 220, 250, 326, 327, 340, 390, 401 ff., 440 ff., 445 ff., 452 ff., 469, 470, 472, 481, 569, 572, *also see* Add.; X. 14, 20, 27, 140, 185, 198, 202, 214, 316, *also see* Add.; XI. 16, 18, 27, 30, 81, 173, 187, 247, 261, 286, 314, 320, 330, 332, 343, 449, 466; XII. 20, 55, 56, 120, 164, 168, 175, 177, 376, 444; XIII. 295, 312, 453; XIV. 168, 197, 212, 215, 309, 313, 398, 448, 451, 455, 461, 518, 572
Advantages proposed by repealing the Sacramental Test, IX. 110
Answer to The Story of the injured lady, IX. 116
Argument against abolishing Christianity, IX. 108
Battle of the Books, IX. 93, 100, 102, 333, 392
Baucis and Philemon, IX. 94, 119
Beasts Confession to the Priest, IX. 122
Cadenus and Vanessa, IX. 97, 98, 120; XIII. 254
Character of Mrs Johnson, IX. 99
Complete collection of...Conversation, IX. 99, 106
Conduct of the Allies, IX. 95, 115, 131
Dennis's Invitation to Steele, IX. 121
Description of a City Shower, IX. 119, 161
Description of the Morning, IX. 119, 161
Directions to Servants, IX. 99, 107
Discourse on the Dissensions in Athens and Rome, IX. 94, 112
Drapier's Letters, IX. 98, 115, 457, 459, 463 ff.
Epistle to Mr Gay, IX. 121
Essay on Modern Education, IX. 398
Examination of certain Abuses in Dublin, IX. 117
Fable of Midias, IX. 121
Grand Question debated, IX. 119
Gulliver's Travels, IX. 98, 103 ff., 132, 137, 458, 464, 466, 471; X. 43, 84; XI. 373; XIII. 452; XIV. 169, 255, 444
Hints towards an Essay on Conversation, IX. 106
Humours of the Age, IX. 465
Importance of the Guardian considered, IX. 114
Inquiry into the behaviour of the Queen's last Ministry, IX. 113
Journal of a Modern Lady, The, IX. 121; XIII. 426
Journal to Stella, IX. 42, 95, 124 ff., 130, 236, 438
Lady's Dressing Room, IX. 121
Last Judgment, IX. 121
Legion Club, IX. 99, 121
Letter concerning the Sacramental Test, IX. 110
Letter of Advice to a young Poet, IX. 118
Letter to a very young Lady, IX. 118

Swift, Jonathan
Letter to a Young Gentleman, IX. 111
Letter to Mr Harding the printer, IX. 115
'Letter to the Athenian Society,' IX. 92
Letter to the Lord High Treasurer, A, XIV. 396
Letter to the October Club, IX. 96
Letter to the shopkeepers...concerning the brass half-pence, IX. 115
Letter to the whole people of Ireland, IX. 116
May the Cook-maid's Letter, IX. 107
Memoirs relating to...the Queen's Ministry, IX. 113
Modest Proposal, IX. 99, 117
Mr C-ns's Discourse on Free Thinking, put into plain English, IX. 111
On Mrs Biddy Floyd, IX. 119
On Poetry, IX. 99, 122
On the Death of Dr Swift, IX. 123
On the Education of Ladies, IX. 398, 401, 402
On the present miserable state of Ireland, IX. 117
Petition of Mrs Frances Harris, IX. 94, 107
Polite Conversation, VIII. 176
Predictions for the ensuing year...Isaac Bickerstaff, IX. 94, 454, 461
Preface to the B—p of S-r-m's Introduction, IX. 110
Progress of Beauty, IX. 121
Progress of Marriage, IX. 121
Project for the advancement of Religion, IX. 109
Proposal for correcting...the English Tongue, IX. 118; XIV. 462
Proposal for the universal use of Irish manufacture, IX. 98, 114
Public Spirit of the Whigs, IX. 114, 440
Reasons...for repealing the Sacramental Test, IX. 110
Sentiments of a Church of England Man, IX. 108, 109
Serious and useful Scheme, IX. 117
Sermons, IX. 112
Short character of Thomas Earl of Wharton, IX. 113
Short view of the state of Ireland, IX. 116
Some advice...to the members of the October Club, IX. 113
Some free thoughts upon the present state of affairs, IX. 113
Some Observations upon...the Report...relating to Wood's halfpence, IX. 116
Some Remarks on the Barrier Treaty, IX. 95, 113
Story of an injured lady, IX. 116
Strephon and Chloe, IX. 121
Swearers Bank, The, IX. 116
Tale of a Tub, A, III. 398; IX. 94, 100, 101, 135, 308, 382, 392, 396; X. 353; XIII. 9
Traulus, IX. 121
Virtues of Sid Hamet the Magician's Rod, IX. 95, 121

Swift, Jonathan
W-ds-r Prophecy, The, IX. 96, 121
Works, XII. 16, 372
See, also, Wagstaff, Simon
Swift, Thomas, IX. 91
Swift, W., XII. 440
Swinburne, Algernon Charles (1837–1909), IV. 186, 209; V. 154; VI. 8, 9, 62, 71, 77, 79, 173, 367; VII. 1, 144, 262, *also see* Add.; X. 152; XI. 411, 412, 420, 434, 441; XII. 117, 130, 154, 208, 209, 218, 219, 268, 275, 398, 400, 404, 407, 424, 438, 441, 442, *also see* Add.; XIII. 82, 90, 105, 116, 117, 129 ff. (main entry), 138, 147, 191, 193, 207, 209, 214, 219 ff., 245, 252, 426, 432, 438, 440, 442, 448, 478, 488, 490, 491, 493 ff. (main entry), 506, 512, 544, 559, *also see* Add. 2, 3; XIV. 206, 365, 367, 453, 462
Adieux à Marie Stuart, XIII. 135
Anactoria, XIII. 131
Artemis, hymn to, XIII. 130
Astrophel, XIII. 135, 137
Atalanta in Calydon, XIII. 130, 131, 133, 205; XIV. 442, 444
Athens, an ode, XIII. 135
Ave atque Vale, XIII. 133
Birthday Ode, XIII. 134
Bothwell, XIII. 133, 135
By the North Sea, XIII. 134
Century of Roundels, A, XIII. 135, 137
Channel Passage, A, XIII. 136
Chastelard, XIII. 130, 133, 135
Christmas Carol, A, XIII. 132
Dark Month, A, XIII. 135
Dirae, XIII. 133
Dolores, XIII. 131, 132, 141, 253
Erechtheus, VII. 122; XIII. 133, 136
Essays and Studies, XIII. 136
Faustine, XIII. 131, 132
Forsaken Garden, A, XIII. 133
Heptalogia, XIII. 134
Hertha, XIII. 132
Ilicet, XIII. 131, 132
Itylus, XIII. 132
Jacobite's Lament, The, XIII. 136
Laus Veneris, XIII. 131, 132, 141, 146, 253
Leper, The, XIII. 131, 141
Litany, A, XIII. 132
Locrine, XIII. 135
Marino Faliero, XIII. 134, 135
Mary Stuart, XIII. 133, 135
Masque of Queen Bersabe, The, X. 217; XIII. 132
Match, A, XIII. 132
Midsummer Holiday, A, XIII. 135
Miscellanies, XIII. 136
Poems and Ballads, XIII. 27, 130 ff., 136, 137, 141, 211
Proserpine, III. 184
Queen Mother and Rosamund, The, XIII. 129
Quia Multum Amavit, XIII. 132
Rosamund Queen of the Lombards, XIII. 136

Swinburne, Algernon Charles
Sisters, The, XIII. 136
Song for the Centenary of Walter Savage Landor, XIII. 134
Song of Italy, A, XIII. 132
Songs before Sunrise, XIII. 132
Songs of the Springtides, XIII. 134
Studies in Song, XIII. 134
Study of Shakespeare, A, XIII. 136
Super Flumina Babylonis, XIII. 132
'Three damsels in the queen's chamber,' XIII. 140
Tristram of Lyonesse, I. 273; XIII. 134, 135, 137, 253
Triumph of Time, The, XIII. 131, 132, 253
Swinburne, Henry (1560?–1623), VIII. 467
Swinburne, Sir John, XIII. 129
Swineshead, Richard (*fl.* 1350), II. 498
Swinhoe, Gilbert, *Unhappy Fair Irene*, X. 161
Swinnerton, Frank, XIII. 573; XIV. 527
Swinnerton, Sir John, VI. 220
Swiss confederation, the, XIV. 71, 73
Swiss education, XIV. 419, 423
Swiss Family Robinson, The, XI. 492
Swiss liberty, X. 303
Swithun, St (d. 862), I. 116, 120, 121, 131
Switzerland, II. 310; VII. 306; X. 134, 200, 201, 205, 366; XII. 33 ff., 41, 44, 59, 60, 247, 311, 315, 420; XIII. 88, 96; XIV. 151, 294
Switzerland and Byron, XII. 395
Switzerland and Shelley, XII. 403
Swiveller, Dick, in *The Old Curiosity Shop*, XIII. 320
Swoboda, V. 97
Swynderby, William (the hermit preacher of Lincoln), II. 61
Sybant, A., V. 285
Sybilla, in *The Lords' Masque*, VI. 354
Sybilla, in *The Vision of the Twelve Goddesses*, VI. 338, 339
Sydenham, XII. 102
Sydenham, Thomas (1624–1689), VIII. 363, 472, 479; X. 164, 465, 467; XII. 355
Sydenham society, XII. 355
Sydney. *See* Sidney
Sydney, Australia, XII. 330; XIV. 361 ff.
Sydney Gazette, The, XIV. 362
Sydney Mail, The, XIV. 370
Sydney Papers. See Sidney
Syke, Henry, IX. 335
Sykes, Frank W., XIV. Add. 10
Sykes, Sir Mark Masterman (1771–1823), XII. 365
Sylla's ghost, in Ben Jonson's *Catiline*, VIII. 85
Sylli, in *The Maid of Honour*, VI. 152, 153
Sylvanus (Mantuan's), III. 225
Sylvester, James Joseph (1814–1897), XIV. 262, 263, 557; *The Laws of Verse*, XIII. 248
Sylvester, Joshua (1563–1618), IV. 23, 124, 131, 185, 331, 434, 443, 475, 531; VI. 9; VII. 407; trans. of *Du Bartas*, VII. 118
Sylvester, St, I. 74, 75
Sylvia, in Drayton's *Eglogs*, IV. 173
Sylvius, Aeneas, III. 62, 65, 179; *Tractatus de curialium miseriis*, III. 65
Sylvius, lady, VIII. 251
Sym and his Brudir, II. 273; XI. 215
Sym Sadle-gander, II. 232
Syme, David, XIV. 535
Symes, John Elliotson, V. 353
Symmachus, IX. 330
Symmes (Marprelate printer), III. 382
Symmons, Edward, VII. 513
Symon, 'the Anker of London Wall' (*fl.* 1512–1529), IV. 496
Symon, James David, XIV. 532, 538
Symonds, John Addington (1840–1893), V. 149; VI. 13; XI. 411; XII. 404; XIII. 207, 500, 504, 507, 509; XIV. 108, 527
Blank Verse, XIII. 248
Le jeune homme caressant sa Chimère, XIII. 208
Renaissance in Italy, The, XIII. 208; XIV. 157
Shakespeare's Predecessors in the English Drama, XIV. 158
Symonds, William (1566–1616?), IV. 513
Symons, Arthur, XI. 412, 415, 423, 434; XII. 132, 404, 406, 415, 442, 445, *also see* Add.; XIII. 485, 493, 496, 499, 500, 502, 503, 508, 557, 570, *also see* Add. 2; XIV. 518, 521, 523, 527, 528
Symphosius, 5th cent. Latin poet, I. 60, 76
Symposium, The, XIV. 208
Symson, Archibald (1564?–1628), VII. 485; IX. 545
Synge, Edward, bishop of Elphin, X. 199
Synge, John Millington (1871–1909), XIV. 571
Aran Islands, The, XIV. 330
Deirdre of the Sorrows, XIV. 330
In Kerry, XIV. 330
In Wicklow, West Kerry and Connemara, XIV. 330
Playboy of the Western World, The, XIV. 329, 330
Riders to the Sea, The, XIV. 330
Tinker's Wedding, The, XIV. 330
Well of the Saints, The, XIV. 330
Synge, M. B., XIV. 551
Syntax, Dr (William Combe's), XIV. 217 ff., 221
Syon monastery, Isleworth, IV. 418
Syphax, in Addison's *Cato*, IX. 63
Syracusans, in *The Bond-Man*, VI. 161, 163
Syracuse, V. 118, 119; VI. 155, 225; VII. 199; X. 135; XIII. 81
Syria, X. 503; XIV. 246, 252
Syriac language and literature, VII. 318, 319; VIII. 364; IX. 393; XII. 341, 342

T. C., *Morall Discourses and Essayes*, VII. 386
T. D. (? Deloney), *Canaan's Calamitie*, VI. 51
T. F., *Newes from the North*, VI. 387, 495
T. T., *pseud.* of W. M. Thackeray, XIII. 278

T. T. *See* Thorpe, Thomas
T. T., *A Myrror for Martinists*, III. 397
Ta Fhairshon, in *The Bon Gaultier Ballads*, XIII. 161
Taal. *See* Cape-Dutch
Tabachetti, artist, XIII. 450
Tabarin, IX. 257
Tabernaemontanus, *Eicones plantarum*, IV. 375
Tablet, The, XIV. 326
Tacitus, Cornelius, I. 143, 187, 188; III. 20, 329, 338, 426, 429; IV. 30, 342, 345, 421, 440; V. 33; VI. 225, 235; VII. 131, 263, 370, 487, 503; IX. 254, 274; X. 120, 197; XI. 2, 426; XII. 306, 475, 483, 493, *also see* Add.; XIV. 59, 98; *Agricola*, IV. 4; XI. 165; *Annals*, III. 426; IV. 5; *Description of Germany*, IV. 5; *Histories*, IV. 4
Tactus, in *Lingua*, VI. 314, 315
Tadpole, in Disraeli's *Sybil*, XIII. 349
Taffy, in Du Maurier's *Trilby*, XIII. 433
Taillefer, V. 26
Tailor, Robert (*fl.* 1614), *The Hogge hath lost his Pearle*, VI. 219, 220, 459; VIII. 182
Taine, Hippolyte Adolphe, I. viii; II. 190; IV. 247; VIII. 19, 33; XIII. 456, 473, 544; *Histoire de la Littérature Anglaise*, X. 316, 483
Tait, A. (*c.* 1796), XI. 441
Tait, Archibald Campbell (1811–1882), XII. 260
Tait, Peter Guthrie (1831–1901), XIV. 263, 267, 555, 557
Tait's Edinburgh Magazine, XII. 430
Talbot, Catherine (1721–1770), X. 171; XI. 352, 356 ff., 473, 475
Talbot, Charles, duke of Shrewsbury (1660–1718), IX. 87, 151, 216
Talbot, Sir Charles, baron (1685–1737), X. 94, 95
Talbot, George, 6th earl of Shrewsbury (1528?–1590), III. 188
Talbot, George (*c.* 1635), VII. 45
Talbot, Sir John, 1st earl of Shrewsbury (1338?–1453), II. 303
Talbot, William Talbot, 1st earl, XI. 29
Talbott, James, IX. 571
Tales, An Alphabet of, II. 503
Tales in Middle English, I. 360
Talfourd, Sir Thomas Noon (1795–1854), IX. 475; XII. 201, 211, 432, 434, 435, 438; XIII. 483, 516, 523; XIV. 323; *Ion*, XII. 113; XIII. 58
Talgol, the butcher, in *Hudibras*, VIII. 68
Taliesin (*fl.* 550), I. 248, 249, 255, 268, 462
Taliesin, The Book of, I. 247, 251, 252
Talkative, in Bunyan's *Pilgrim's Progress*, VII. 173
Tallents, Francis (1619–1708), X. 386
Talleyrand-Périgord, Charles Maurice de, prince of Benevento, XIV. 115
Tallis, Thomas (1510?–1585), IV. 384
Tallwch (father of Tristram), I. 273
Tallyho, Bob, in *Real Life in London*, XIV. 227
Talma, François Joseph, V. 294, 307; XII. 198
Talmud, the, VIII. 291
Tam, in *Lichtounis Dreme*, II. 278
Tam Lin, II. 413
Tam o' Shanter, XI. 219
Tamerlane, VII. 164
Tamil language, XII. 362
Taming of a Shrew, The (ballad), III. 91, 487
Taming of a Shrew, The (anon. play), IV. 394; V. 115, 118, 147, 162, 181, 403, 438; VI. 170; VIII. 126
Tamlane, I. 295, 300
Tamworth, IV. 169
Tamworth manifesto, the, XII. 154
Tamyra, countess of Montsorry, in *Bussy d'Ambois*, VI. 33
Tancred, in *Gismond of Salerne*, V. 75, 76
Tancred (Disraeli's), XIII. 348
Tancred and Gismund. V. 87, 138, 397, 399
Tandler, Tobias, VII. 396. 505, 511
Tanfield, Elizabeth, VII. 150
Tanganyika, lake, XIV. 192
Tangent, in Morton's *Way to get Married*, XI. 281
Tangier, VIII. 202, 219, 257
Tannahill, Robert (1774–1810), XI. 237, 445
  Bonnie Wood of Craigielea, XI. 236
  Braes o' Balquither, XI. 236
  Gloomy Winter's noo Awa', XI. 236
  Jessie the Flower of Dunblane, XI. 236
  Lass of Arrinteenie, XI. 236
  Loudon's bonnie Woods and Braes, XI. 236
  Poems and Songs, XI. 236
  Rob Roryson's Bonnet, XI. 236
Tanner, John (*fl.* 1744), IX. 350
Tanner, Thomas (1674–1735), IX. 342, 350 (main entry), 351, 353, 354, 540, 541; *Bibliotheca Britannico-Hibernica*, IX. 350, 356; *Notitia Monastica*, IX. 350, 356, 358
Tantalus, in Orosius, I. 95
Tantalus, in *Thyestes*, V. 76, 78
Taoist classics, XII. 343
Taper, in Disraeli's *Sybil*, XIII. 349
Tapley, Mark, in *Martin Chuzzlewit*, XIII. 323
Tappertit, Sim, in *Barnaby Rudge*, XIII. 321
Tara hill, Ireland, XII. 512; XIV. 127
Tarant, prince of, in *A Very Woman*, VI. 156
Tarlton, Richard (d. 1588), III. 92, 201, 384, 387; IV. 353, 360, 527, 531, 533, 535; V. 313, 329; VI. 217, 232, 273, 397, 467; VII. 383; *Jigge of a horse loade of Fooles*, VI. 391; *The Seven Deadly Sins*, VI. 249
Tarn Wadling, near Hesket, in Cumberland, II. 116, 122
Tarpeia, VIII. 5
Tarquin, in *The Rape of Lucrece*, VI. 101
Tarquin and Tullia, VIII. 92

Tarrarantantara, etc., VI. 307
Tarrent, Dorset, I. 230
Tars, King of, I. 471
Tartaglia, N., IV. 448
Tartars, the, XI. 17
Tartarus, VI. 329; XII. 217
Tartary, II. 80; V. 144; XIV. 248
Tartufe (Molière's), XIII. 446
Tasker, William (1740–1800), XI. 429
Tasmania, XIV. 325
Tasso, Torquato, III. 230, 257, 261, 262, 432; IV. 23, 131, 448, 543; VI. 366, 371; VII. 70, 74, 78, 83, 263, 265, 268; VIII. 25, 194, 219; IX. 185, 338; X. 234, 241; XI. 157; XII. 50, 64, 423, 442
  Amintà, III. 261; IV. 131; VI. 137, 317, 318, 365, 490; VII. 264
  Gerusalemme Liberata, III. 230; VI. 98
  Jerusalem Delivered, X. 127, 435
  Padre di Famiglia, V. 157
Tassoni, Alessandro, *Secchia Rapita*, IX. 70
Taste Vin, in *Le Testament de Taste Vin*, III. 85
Tate, Nahum (1652–1715), VIII. 196, 394, 401, 410, 411, 443
  Brutus of Alba, XI. 319
  Cuckold's Haven, or An Alderman No Conjuror, VI. 47, 48
  Island Princesse, The, VIII. 120
  King Lear, adaptation of, VIII. 41, 120; XI. 258
  Psalms, VIII. 41
Tatham, Frederick, XIII. 197
Tatham, John (*fl.* 1632–1664), VIII. 421
  Distracted State, The, VIII. 121
  Love Crowns the End, VIII. 121
  Rump, The, VIII. 121, 122, 142
  Scotch Figgaries, The, VIII. 121
Tatler, The, VIII. 140, 158, 175, 390; IX. 18, 32, 33 ff. (main entry), 63, 94, 109, 118, 119, 125, 144, 161, 165, 404, 412, 437 ff., 441, 485, 569; XI. 317, 373; XII. 140, 193; XIII. 318; XIV. 461, 462
Tatler in Cambridge, The, XIV. 208, 537
Tatlock, J. S. P., II. 174, 464
Tattle, in Congreve's *Love for Love*, VIII. 152, 156
Tatton, R. G., XIV. 609
Tattycoram, in *Little Dorrit*, XIII. 331
Tatwin (d. 734), I. 78, 435
Taubman, Matthew (d. 1690?), VIII. 97, 410
Tauler, Johann, IX. 314, 315, 519
Taunton, IV. 132
Taunton academy, X. 386
Taunton commission (Endowed schools), XIV. 421, 422, 429, 430
Tautphoeus, baroness von. *See* Montgomery, Jemima
Taverner, Richard (1505?–1575), IV. 444
Tavernier, Jean Baptiste, XIV. 333; *Voyages in the East*, IX. 268
Tavie, Welshman, in *Club Law*, VI. 308, 309
Tavistock, IV. 157, 194, 409
Tawny-coat, in *If you know not me*, VI. 92
Taxarum omnium beneficiorum Angliae, Liber, II. 364
Taxes, Song against the King's, II. 421
Tay, firth of, IX. 552
Tay, river, X. 274
Tayis Bank, II. 281
Taylor, Abraham (*fl.* 1727–1740), X. 384
Taylor, Alfred E., XIII. 567
Taylor, Mrs Ann, of Ongar (1757–1830), XI. 384, 482
Taylor, Ann, afterwards Mrs Gilbert (1782–1866), XI. 384, 483; *My Mother*, XI. 383
Taylor, Ann and Jane, XI. 483; *Hymns for Infant Minds*, XI. 383; *Original Poems*, XI. 383; *Rhymes for the Nursery*, XI. 383
Taylor, Charles (1840–1908), XII. 341, 501
Taylor, E. J., IX. 519
Taylor, Francis (*fl.* 1654), VII. 322, 490
Taylor, Helen, XIV. 486
Taylor, Henry (1711–1785), *Thoughts on... the Grand Apostacy*, X. 309, 507
Taylor, Sir Henry (1800–1886), XI. 411; XII. 107, 112–113 (main entry), 211, 423; XIII. 467; XIV. 507
  Edwin the Fair, XII. 112, 113
  Isaac Comnenus, XII. 112
  Minor Poems, XII. 113
  Philip van Artevelde, XII. 112, 113; XIII. 177, 194
  'Quoth tongue of neither maid nor wife,' XII. 113
  St Clement's Eve, XII. 112
Taylor, Isaac (1759–1829), XI. 384, 483
Taylor, Isaac (1787–1865), XII. 470; XIV 481, 609
Taylor, Isaac (1829–1901), XII. 505
Taylor, James W., XII. 513
Taylor, Jane (1783–1824), XI. 384, 483; *Twinkle, Twinkle, Little Star*, XI. 383
Taylor, Jefferys (1792–1853), XI. 384, 483
Taylor, Jeremy (1613–1667), VII. 130, 144, 146, 148, 150, 162 ff. (main entry), 213, 426, 427, 475; VIII. 250, 293, 294, 297, 303, 368 ff., 377, 386, 456; IX. 62; X. 360, 364, 366; XI. 2; XII. 169, 176, 193, 253, 277, 283; XIV. 460
  Ductor Dubitantium, VII. 163, 280
  Golden Grove, The, VII. 163
  Great Exemplar, The, VII. 165
  Holy Dying, VII. 163 ff.
  Holy Living, VII. 163, 165
  Liberty of Prophesying, The, VII. 165; VIII. 344; X. 372
  Marriage Ring, The, VII. 163
  Sacred order and offices of Episcopacy, The, VII. 165
  'The House of Feasting,' IV. 247
  Worthy Communicant, The, VII. 163, 165
Taylor, John, the 'water-poet' (1580–1653), III. 288; IV. 361, 517, 518, 520, 532, 533, 534, 545, 546; V. 144, 148; VI. 261; VII. 387, 494, 498, 499, 514, 515
  All the Workes of J. T., IV. 392
  John Taylor's Wit and Mirth, IV. 360

Taylor, John
Kicksey Winsey, or A Lerry Come-Twang, A, IV. 392
Pennyles Pilgrimage, The, IV. 392
Taylor, John, LL.D. (1694–1761), X. 385, 409, 463; *Defence of the Common rights of Christians*, X. 380; *Scripture doctrine of Original Sin*, X. 380
Taylor, John (1704–1766), IX. 341, 528
Taylor, John (1757–1832), X. 480
Taylor, John (1781–1864), X. 527; XII. 195, 203
Taylor, John Edward (1791–1844), XIV. 535
Taylor, Joseph (1586?–1653?), VI. 248, 276, 277
Taylor, Joseph, XI. 483
Taylor, Mary, XIII. 404, 405
Taylor, Nathaniel, X. 385
Taylor, Philip Meadows (1808–1876), XIII. 566; XIV. 580
Confessions of a Thug, XIII. 432; XIV. 338
Ralph Darnell, XIV. 338
Seeta, XIV. 338
Tara, XIV. 338
Tippoo Sultan, XIV. 338
Taylor, Robert (1784–1844), XIV. 482
Taylor, Robert, bookseller (*c.* 1763), XI. 315
Taylor, S. A., XIV. 541
Taylor, Thomas (*c.* 1704), VIII. 476
Taylor, Thomas (1758–1835), XIV. 482
Taylor, Tom (1817–1880), XII. 407; XIII. 264, 268, 516, 522, 524; XIV. 196, 238, 519, 548
Anne Boleyn, XIII. 267
Arkwright's Wife, XIII. 267
Fool's Revenge, The, XIII. 267
Jeanne Darc, XIII. 267
Lady Clancarty, XIII. 267
Plot and Passion, XIII. 267
Still Waters Run Deep, XIII. 267
Ticket-of-Leave Man, The, XIII. 267
'Twixt Axe and Crown, XIII. 267
Taylor, William, of Norwich (1765–1836), X. 484; XI. 179, 423, 428; XII. 4, 97, 380, 429; XIII. 169, 244, 468
Taylor, William, publisher (d. 1724), IX. 19; XI. 323
Taylor, William Cooke (1809–1849), XIV. 571
Taylor, quack oculist, in Foote's drama, X. 88
Taylor family, the, XI. 384, 483
Tayster. *See* John de
Tea, X. 467
Teachum, Mrs, in Sarah Fielding's *Governess*, XI. 380
'Teachwell, Mrs,' XI. 379
Teazle, lady, in Sheridan's *School for Scandal*, X. 90; XI. 269 ff.; XII. 171
Teazle, Sir Peter, in Sheridan's *School for Scandal*, XI. 269, 270
Techmessa, in *The Jealous Lovers*, VI. 325
Techne, in *The Queenes Arcadia*, VI. 317
Teddington, VII. 42; XIV. 283
Tediousness, in Tudor moralities, V. 57
Tedman, Mr, in Fanny Burney's *Wanderer*, X. 65
Tedworth, the drummer of, IX. 436
Tees, river, XIII. 136, 149
Tegner, XII. 395
Teignmouth, lord, XIV. 577
Teixeira, Antony, IX. 501
Telegonus, in *Confessio Amantis*, II. 149
Telemachus, V. 108; X. 134
Telesius, III. 416
Telfer, Jamie, of the Fair Dodhead, XII. 3
Tellus, in *Endimion*, V. 341
Telugu language, XII. 362
Temperance, the house of, in *The Faerie Queene*, VI. 335
Temperley, Harold William Vazielle, XIV. 508
Tempesti, VI. 174, 176
Templars, the, I. 189
Temple, the, in the Cross legend, I. 134
Temple, the (Palestine), V. 15, 49
Temple, Dorothy, lady, IX. 92, 93; X. 410. *See* Osborne, Dorothy
Temple, earl. *See* Grenville, Richard Temple
Temple, Frederick (1821–1902), archbishop of Canterbury, XIV. 602, 609, 610; 'The Education of the World,' XII. 295
Temple, Henry John, 3rd viscount Palmerston (1784–1865), XIII. 422; XIV. 124, 129, 132, 171, 172, 182, 184, 185, 187, 420, 505, 508; *Civis Romanus* speech, XIV. 126
Temple, Sir Richard (1634–1697), VIII. 476
Temple, Sir Richard, viscount Cobham (1669?–1749), VIII. 428; IX. 445; X. 103
Temple, Sir William (1555–1627), IV. 274 ff., 509; VII. 343; *Admonitio*, IV. 276
Temple, Sir William (1628–1699), VII. 266 ff.; VIII. 267, 268, 342, 379–386 (main entry), 482; IX. 47, 91 ff., 102, 103, 170, 332 ff., 390, 454 ff., 524, 572; X. 221, 224, 238, 484; XIV. 51, 63
An Essay upon the Advancement of Trade in Ireland, VIII. 384
An Essay upon the present State and Settlement of Ireland, VIII. 384
An Introduction to the History of England, VIII. 384
Essay on Ancient and Modern Learning, VIII. 385; IX. 391, 392
Essay upon the Original and Nature of Government, VIII. 384
Letters, VIII. 380, 381
Memoirs, VIII. 380 ff.
Miscellanea, VIII. 384
Observations upon the United Provinces of the Netherlands, VIII. 383
Of Heroic Virtue, X. 222
Of Poetry, X. 222
Survey of the Constitution and Interests of the Empire..., A, VIII. 384
Upon Conversation, VIII. 386

Temple, Sir William
Upon Health and Long Life, VIII. 385, 386
Upon Poetry, V. 286; VIII. 385, 386
Upon Popular Discontents, VIII. 386
Upon the Cure of the Gout, VIII. 385, 386
Upon the different conditions of life and fortune, VIII. 386
Upon the Gardens of Epicurus or Of Gardening, VIII. 385, 386
Temple, William Johnson (1739–1796), X. 193, 478
'Temple of the Muses,' XI. 337
Temple revels, Middle, VIII. 244
Temple's Gallicisms, VIII. 383
Templum Chrystallinum, II. 225
Temporalitie, in *Ane Pleasant Satyre*, III. 126, 127, 128
Temptation, in *Mirour de l'Omme*, II. 140
Ten Brink, Bernhard, I. viii, 102, 143, 420; II. 28; III. 75; V. 20, 39
Tençons, V. 27
Teneriffe, IX. 180
Tenison, Thomas (1636–1715), archbishop of Canterbury, VIII. 250, 305, 307, 431, 462; IX. 195; X. 353; *Baconiana*, VIII. 402; *The Creed of Mr Hobbes Examined*, VII. 301, 475
Tennant, William (1784–1848), XI. 445
Anster Fair, XI. 243
Cardinal Bethune, XI. 243
Dingin doon O The Cathedral, XI. 243
John Baliol, XI. 243
Tangier's Giant, XI. 243
Thane of Fife, XI. 243
Tennent, Sir James Emerson (1804–1869), XIV. 197, 554
Tenniel, Sir John (1820–1914), XI. 477, 491; XII. 411; XIV. 235, 239, 549
Tennyson, Alfred, 1st lord Tennyson (1809–1892), I. 247, 266, 269, 284, 373; II. 176, 182, 400; IV. 47, 112; VII. 137; IX. 73; X. 143, 152, 220; XI. 77, 111, 158, 159, 409; XII. 39, 63, 106, 113, 118, 126, 139, 154, 219, 271, 438, 483; XIII. 23 ff. (main entry), 69. 71, 72, 85, 120, 131, 140, 143, 147, 148, 152, 153, 155, 157 ff., 176, 179, 184, 188, 192, 194, 195, 200, 214, 216, 219, 221, 228, 230, 231, 240, 241, 243, 244, 246, 250 ff., 277, 297, 421, 442, 463, 473 ff. (main entry), *also see* Add. 3; XIV. 15, 148, 238, 255, 306, 321, 349, 378 ff., 443, 456, 493, 515, 517
A Dream of Fair Women, VI. 338
Akbar's Dream, and Other Poems, XIII. 39
Aylmer's Field, XIII. 40
Balin and Balan, XIII. 35, 36
Ballad of the Fleet, A, XIII. 39
Ballads and other Poems, XIII. 39
Becket, XIII. 39
Brook, The, XIII. 34, 36
'By night we linger'd on the lawn,' XIII. 33
Tennyson, Alfred
'Calm is the morn without a sound,' XIII. 33
Charge of the Heavy Brigade, The, XIII. 40, 42
Charge of the Light Brigade, The, XIII. 186
Claribel, XIII. 26, 27, 44
Columbus, XIII. 40
'Come into the garden, Maud,' XIII. 35
Coming of Arthur, The, XIII. 35
Crossing the Bar, XIII. 44
Cup, The, XIV. 380
Daisy, The, XIII. 42
'Dark house, by which once more I stand,' XIII. 33
Death of Œnone, The, XIII. 39
Defence of Lucknow, The, XIII. 40
Demeter, XII. 332; XIII. 41
Demeter and other Poems, XIII. 39
Despair, XIII. 40, 42
Dora, XIII. 29, 39
Dream of Fair Women, A, XIII. 25, 26
Dying Swan, The, XIII. 26, 250
Elaine, XIII. 35
Enid and Nimuë, XIII. 35
Enoch Arden, XI. 148; XIII. 38, 39, 379
Flight, The, XIII. 42
Four Idylls of the King, XIII. 35
Gardener's Daughter, The, XIII. 34, 40
Gareth and Lynette, XIII. 35, 37
Geraint and Enid, XIII. 35
Grandmother, The, XIII. 39, 40
Guinevere, XIII. 35
Harold, XIII. 39
Helen's Tower, XIII. 177
'Hollyhock' song, the, XIII. 244
Holy Grail, The, XIII. 35, 37
'I cannot see the features right,' XIII. 33
'I have led her home,' XIII. 35
Idylls of the King, XIII. 27, 29, 31, 35 ff., 41, 201, 448
In Memoriam, VII. 42, 52; VIII. 229; XII. 116, 330; XIII. 10, 27, 32 ff., 37, 183; XIV. 380
In the Children's Hospital, XIII. 40
Lady of Shalott, The, XIII. 25, 26, 29; XIV. 442
Last Tournament, The, XIII. 35, 37
Locksley Hall, XIII. 30, 34, 161; XIV. 374
Locksley Hall, Sixty Years After, XIII. 39, 40, 42
Lotos Eaters, The, XIII. 25 ff., 29
Love and Duty, XIII. 30
'Love thou thy land,' XIII. 30
Lucretius, XIII. 39 ff.
Mariana, XIII. 26
Maud, XI. 151; XIII. 34, 72, 161
Maud, and Other Poems, XIII. 34, 42
Miller's Daughter, The, XIII. 25, 40, 190
Morte d'Arthur, XIII. 29, 30, 35
Nimuë (Vivien), XIII. 35
Northern Farmer, The, XIII. 39
'Now sleeps the crimson petal,' XIII. 31
'O that 'twere possible,' XIII. 35

Tennyson, Alfred
Ode on the Death of the Duke of Wellington, XIII. 34
Œnone, XIII. 25, 26, 28, 29, 41
'Of old sat Freedom,' XIII. 30
'Oh yet we trust that somehow good,' XIII. 33
'Old Yew, which graspest at the stones,' XIII. 33
Palace of Art, The, VII. 253; XIII. 25, 26, 28, 30
Passing of Arthur, The, XIII. 35
Pelleas and Ettarre, XIII. 35
Poems (1830), XIV. 139
Poems, Chiefly Lyrical (1830), XIII. 25
Poems (1833), XIII. 25
Poems, 2 vols. (1842), XII. 101; XIII. 25
Poems, by Two Brothers, XIII. 25
Princess, The, XIII. 30, 31, 251; XIV. 430
Queen Mary, XIII. 39
Recollections of the Arabian Nights, XIII. 26
Revenge, The, XIII. 39, 40, 42; XIV. 84
Rivulet, The, XIV. 380
Rizpah, XIII. 40
'Sad Hesper o'er the buried sun,' XIII. 33
St Simeon Stylites, XIII. 41
St Telemachus, XIII. 40, 41
Sir John Oldcastle, XIII. 40
Sisters, The, XIII. 42
Spinster's Sweet-Arts, The, XIII. 40
'Spirit haunts the year's last hours, A,' XIII. 26
'Splendour falls, the,' XIII. 31
'Sweet and low,' XIII. 31
'Tears, idle tears,' XIII. 31, 42
Tiresias, XIII. 40, 41, 142
Tiresias and Other Poems, XIII. 39
Tithonus, XIII. 29, 41
To Virgil, XIII. 42
'To-night the winds begin to rise,' XIII. 33
True and the False, The, XIII. 35
Two Voices, The, XIII. 30, 40
Ulysses, XIII. 29, 30, 32; XIV. 241
'Unwatch'd, the garden bough shall sway,' XIII. 33
Vastness, XIII. 30, 41
Village Wife, The, XIII. 39, 40
Vision of Sin, The, VIII. 237; XIII. 26, 27, 30, 32, 253
Voyage of Maeldune, The, XII. 361; XIII. 42, 251; XIV. 328
'We fell out,' XIII. 31
'When on my bed the moonlight falls,' XIII. 33
'Witch-elms that counterchange the floor,' XIII. 33
'With trembling fingers did we weave,' XIII. 33
Wreck, The, XIII. 42
'You ask me, why,' XIII. 30
Tennyson, Charles. *See* Turner, Charles Tennyson
Tennyson, Frederick (1807–1898), XIII. 23, 45 ff., 78, 473, 479
Daphne, and other Poems, XIII. 46
Days and Hours, XIII. 46
Isles of Greece, The, XIII. 46
Poems of the Day and Year, XIII. 46
Psyche, XIII. 47
River of Life, XIII. 47
Tennyson, Hallam, 2nd lord Tennyson, XIII. 473–474, 478, 479
'Tenth Muse,' the, XIII. 175
Tercer (America), V. 139
Terence, II. 331, 359, 360; III. 20, 24, 53, 429, 430; IV. 4, 235, 245, 320, 414, 417, 428, 440; V. 6, 104, 105, 116; VI. 14, 15, 32, 297; VII. 487; VIII. 155, 247, 442; IX. 46, 58, 270, 274, 338, 418, 525, 526; X. 91, 429; XI. 266, 426; XII. 494
Adelphi, VI. 48; X. 90; XI. 265
Andria, V. 101, 103, 104, 115, 411; IX. 64
Eunuchus, V. 104, 105; VI. 300; VIII. 139
Heautontimoroumenos, V. 102, 104
Hecyra, II. 321
Phormio, V. 102
Terens in English, V. 103, 411
Terentia, IX. 218
Terentian, I. 120
Teresa, St, VII. 34, 35, 37, 143; XIII. 356, 398
Tereus, in *Confessio Amantis*, II. 151
Tereus, in *Philomela*, VI. 320
Tereus, in *Progne*, VI. 299
Tereus and Procne, III. 343
Terilo, William, IV. 534; *Satire on Brazen Head*, I. 210
Term Catalogues, The, IV. 404; VIII. 182, 188; XI. 339; XII. 357
Ternate, XIV. 298
Terni, cataract of, XII. 44
Terouenne, siege of, II. 338; III. 70
Terra, in *Lingua*, VI. 315
Terriss, William (1847–1897), XIII. 515
Terry, Charles Sanford, *Catalogue of publications of Scottish Historical Societies*, XII. 358, 519
Terry, Edward (1590–1660), IV. 462; *Relation of a Voyage to the Easterne India*, XIV. 333
Terry, Ellen, XIII. 513, 515
Tertullian, III. 9, 416; VII. 34, 505, 510; XII. 488
Tervey, tykes of, II. 275
Tesauro, E., *Cannocchiale Aristotelico*, VII. 269
Tessa, in *Romola*, XIII. 395
Tessaranactus (*i.e.* James I), in *Euphormio*, IV. 256
Test, The, X. 389, 390, 522
Test act, the, X. 374; XIII. 24
Testament, New, II. 290, 292, 300, 430; III. 7, 13, 27, 42 ff., 127, 233, 448; IV. 27, 28, 34, 47; VII. 173, 304, 316, 317, 326
Beza's Latin version, III. 45
Genevan, of William Whittingham, III. 44

Testament, New
Greek text of, VIII. 277
Irish version of, IV. 414
Luther's preface to, III. 45
Purvey's version, III. 45
Scots, of Murdoch Nisbet, III. 45
Tindale's, II. 330; III. 42, 43; VII. 432
Wycliffite, II. 285, 430; III. 45
Testament, Old, II. 230, 292, 335; III. 43 ff., 234; IV. 27, 28, 30, 46, 49, 170; VII. 324; VIII. 37
Tindale's, III. 44
Wycliffite, II. 430
Testament de Taste Vin, Le, III. 85, 483
Testament of the Hawthorne, The, III. 86, 483
Testaments (English, Latin and French), III. 482 ff.
Testaments, mock, IV. 357, 521
Testimony, in Crowne's *Sir Courtly Nice*, VIII. 189
Tetbury, Gloucestershire, VIII. 82, 83
Tetterbys, the, in Dickens's *The Haunted Man*, XIII. 324
Teufelsdröckh (Carlyle's), XIII. 3, 6, 9
Teutonic languages, X. 223
Teutonic law, VIII. 310
Teutonic tribes, X. 313
Tewkesbury, II. 297; IX. 394
Tewkesbury academy, X. 386
Texte, Joseph, X. 16, 413, 458; XII. 407, 525, 527
Textor, J. Ravisius, V. 107 ff., 407, 410; VI. 87; Latin *Dialogi*, V. 101; *Juvenis, Pater, Uxor*, V. 108, 109; *Thersites*, V. 108, 109
Thackeray, Amelia (born Webb), XIII. 276
Thackeray, Anne (born Becher), XIII. 276
Thackeray, Isabella (born Shawe), XIII. 278, 280
Thackeray, Richmond, XIII. 275, 276
Thackeray, Thomas, XIII. 275
Thackeray, William, bookseller, XI. 335
Thackeray, William Makepeace (1811–1863), I. 287; II. 176; V. 179, 212, 231; VII. 199; IX. 40, 127, 133, 190; X. 45, 120, 154, 422; XI. 306, 307, 385, 387, 423, 476, 483; XII. 21, 24, 109, 121 ff., 125, 128, 131, 178, 250, 252, 426, 430, 431; XIII. 142, 154, 162, 170, 177, 178, 189, 199, 275 ff. (main entry), 307, 344, 352, 386, 388, 406, 421, 422, 425, 433, 442, 457, 525 ff., 554, *also see* Add. 2; XIV. 142, 148, 152, 171, 177, 187, 194, 205, 224, 235 ff., 539, 540, 549
Amours of Mr Deuceace, The, XIII. 279
Ballads of Policeman X, The, XIII. 294
Barbazure, XIII. 284
Barry Lyndon, The Luck of, X. 44; XIII. 281, 284, 292, 300, 414
Bedford Row Conspiracy, The, XII. 431
Book of Snobs, The, XI. 297; XIII. 281, 284
Catherine, XIII. 279, 280, 282, 418
Christmas Books, XIII. 292, 294
Comic Tales and Sketches, XIII. 281

Thackeray, William Makepeace
Denis Duval, X. 39; XIII. 300
Diary of Fitz-Jeames de la Pluche, XIV. 237
Dr Birch and his Young Friends, XIII. 294
English Humourists of the Eighteenth Century, The, X. 53, 418, 484; XIII. 294
Esmond, Henry, The History of, XIII. 277, 286, 292, 293, 297, 298, 300, 407
Fatal Boots, The, XIII. 280, 282
Fêtes of July, The, XIII. 283
Fitz-Boodle, Confessions of, XIII. 281
Flore et Zéphyr, XIII. 278
Four Georges, The, XII. 431; XIII. 295
George de Barnwell, XIII. 280, 418
Great Hoggarty Diamond, The, XIII. 281, 288
Irish Sketch Book, The, XIII. 282 ff., 414
Jeames's Diary, XIII. 284, 526
Kickleburys on the Rhine, The, XIII. 294
Legend of the Rhine, A, XIII. 284, 294
Lords and Liveries, XII. 246
Lovel the Widower, XIII. 299
Major Gahagan, XIII. 279, 281
Men's Wives, XIII. 281
Miss Tickletoby's Lectures on English History, XIII. 284; XIV. 237
Mr Punch's Prize Novelists, XIII. 284; XIV. 237
Mrs Perkins's Ball, XIII. 292, 294
Newcomes, The, IV. 113; V. 213; XIII. 120, 277, 278, 295 ff., 299, 300
Notes of a Journey from Cornhill to Grand Cairo, XIII. 284
Novels by Eminent Hands, XII. 246
Our Street, XIII. 292
Paris Sketch Book, The, XIII. 281, 282; XIV. 196
Pendennis, IV. 252; X. 44; XII. 159; XIII. 276, 290 ff., 294, 391; XIV. 440
Philip, The Adventures of, XIII. 280, 288, 299, 300
Professor, The, XIII. 310
Ravenswing, The, XIII. 281
Rebecca and Rowena, XIII. 284, 294
Rose and the Ring, XIII. 294
Roundabout Papers, X. 204; XIII. 299
Scaramouch, XIII. 351
Second Funeral of Napoleon, The, XIII. 283
Shabby Genteel Story, A, XIII. 280, 299
Snobs of England, The, XIII. 284; XIV. 237
Timbuctoo, XIII. 277; XIV. 207
Vanity Fair, V. 213; XIII. 281, 284 ff., 292, 294; XIV. 255
Virginians, The, XIII. 297 ff.
Yellowplush Papers, The, IX. 57; XII. 431; XIII. 278, 281
Thackeray, William Makepeace, grandfather of the novelist, XIII. 275
Thaise, in *Confessio Amantis*, II. 152
Thalaba, XIII. 357
Thalander, in *Sicelides*, VI. 323
Thalia, in *The Tears of the Muses*, III. 2

Thame, VII. 104
Thames, river, IX. 187; X. 102; XI. 362; XII. 265; XIII. 93, 120; XIV. 221
Thamesis (Thames), in *The Masque of Beauty*, VI. 344
Thanet, isle of, IX. 536
Thaon, P. de (*fl.* 1120), I. 226, 227
Tharmas, in Blake's *Vala*, XI. 195
Thaxted, Essex, IV. 91
Theagenes (Digby), in his *Memoirs*, VII. 222
Theal, G. McCall, XIV. Add. 10
Thealma and Clearchus, VII. 251
Theatre, The, IX. 144, 439, 442
Theatre, the Elizabethan, VI. 241–278, 459 ff. *See, also, under* specific names below:
Blackfriars, VI. 170, 243, 248, 255, 257 ff., 262, 270, 273, 276 ff., 289 ff., 312, 404
Cockpit, VI. 262, 272
Curtain, VI. 247, 253 ff., 378, 384 ff.
Fortune, VI. 250, 253, 255, 256, 258, 259, 261, 268, 269, 272, 292, 398
Globe, VI. 69, 247, 248, 253, 255 ff., 261, 267, 269, 270, 272, 275 ff.
Golding (now Golden) lane, VI. 258
Hope, VI. 260, 261, 264, 267, 275, 402
Newington Butts, VI. 247, 254, 255
Phoenix, VI. 262
Red Bull, VI. 262, 266, 272
Rose, Southwark, VI. 83, 247, 250, 254, 255, 257, 259, 261
Salisbury court, VI. 232, 233, 262
Swan, VI. 259 ff., 263 ff., 267, 268, 273
Theater, VI. 243, 246, 247, 249, 251 ff., 257, 378, 384 ff., 391
Theatre Royal, Drury lane, VI. 33, 261
Whitefriars, VI. 140, 262
Theatre for Worldlings, A, III. 213, 250
Theatre Regulation act, XIII. 257
Theatres, A Second and Third Blast of retrait from plaies and, VI. 390, 392, 496
Theatres, closing of the, VI. 210, 229, 234, 238
Theatres, war of the, VI. 4, 39
Theatrical histories, dictionaries and general records, X. 442 ff.
Theatrical pamphlets, Georgian era, XI. 449 ff.
Thebes, subject of the wars of, I. 279, 285, 286, 307
Thebes, The Siege of, II. 308
Thebes, Cambridge university so called by Dryden, VIII. 4
Thecla, I. 74
Thegan's *Life of Ludwig the Pious*, I. 90
Thel, in Blake's *Book of Thel*, XI. 186
Theloall, S., *Le Digest des Briefes Originals* (1579), VIII. 467
Thelwall, John (1764–1834), XI. 119; XIII. 240, 512; XIV. 610
Themech, IV. 215
Themistocles, IX. 524; XII. 363
Thenot, in *The Faithfull Shepheardesse*, VI. 368
Theobald, archbishop of Canterbury (d. 1161), I. 185; II. 341
Theobald, Lewis (1688–1744), V. 270 ff.; VIII. 177; IX. 77 ff., 84, 86, 89, 143, 145, 168; X. 440; XI. 322; *Richard II*, XI. 316; *Shakespeare*, XI. 320; *Shakespeare Restored*, IX. 79, 448, 449
Theobaldus Stampensis (d. 1161), II. 341
Theocrine, in *The Unnaturall Combat*, VI. 159
Theocritus, III. 62, 218, 219, 221, 222, 224 ff., 300; IV. 121, 411, 440; VI. 364; VII. 9, 83, 87; VIII. 44; IX. 69, 372, 526; X. 492; XI. 143, 426; XII. 330, 331, 486, 489, 495; XIII. 34, 45; *The Adoniazusae*, III. 226
Theodberht, I. 26
Theodore, in Walpole's *Castle of Otranto*, X. 61
Theodore (602?–690), archbishop of Canterbury, I. 5, 71 ff., 77, 82, 87
Theodoric of Chartres, I. 185
Theodoric the great, XII. 322, 476
Theodorus Prodromus, IV. 259
Theodosius, VII. 395; XII. 476
Theodosius, in *The Emperour of the East*, VI. 158
Theodotion, IX. 330
Theodric I, I. 26
Theodric, in *Deor*, I. 36, 37
Theodric, Ostrogothic king, I. 20, 21, 34, 36, 37, 99
Theognis, XI. 392; XII. 484
Theological Falsehood, in *The Faerie Queene*, III. 234
Theological learning (1600–1660), VII. 484
Theologus, in *A Dialogue...against the fever Pestilence*, III. 109
Theology, in *Piers the Plowman*, II. 8
Theophanius, count, I. 105
Theophilus, *De Urinis*, II. 365
Theophilus, the legendary, VII. 503
Theophrastians, III. 91, 487
Theophrastus, III. 416; IV. 323, 335 ff., 339, 341 ff., 436, 521; VII. 379, 384, 386; IX. 46; *Characters*, VIII. 63; XII. 332, 485
Theophrastus Such (George Eliot's), XIII. 402
There'll Never be Peace till Samie comes Hame, IX. 377
There's nae luck aboot the Hoose, IX. 373
Therry, Sir Roger (1800–1874), XI. 392
Thersites, III. 280; V. 410
Thersites, in Dryden's *Troilus and Cressida*, VIII. 29
Thersites, in Shakespeare's *Troilus and Cressida*, VI. 44
Theseus, XIII. 354
Theseus, in Alfred's *Orosius*, I. 95
Theseus, in *A Midsummer Night's Dream*, V. 183; VI. 213, 214
Theseus, in *Palamon and Arcyte*, VI. 299
Theseus, in *The Two Noble Kinsmen*, V. 256
Thespis, V. 176
Thetbaldus, I. 227

Thetford, Norfolk, VIII. 257
Thetford, St Mary's priory, VI. 281
Thetis, in *Iliad*, VI. 347
Thierry, J. N. A., XIV. 77; *Norman Conquest*, XIV. 107
Thims, Gregory, VII. 498
Third Blast, The, VI. 378, 391, 392, 395
Third collection of Tracts, X. 378
Thirlestane keep, III. 132
Thirlwall, Connop (1797–1875), XII. 280, 288, 302, 303, 307 ff. (main entry), 318, 470, 478; XIV. 593; *History of Greece*, XII. 308; *Letters to a Friend*, XII. 309; 'On the Irony of Sophocles,' XII. 308
Thirsk, the Three Tuns, XIV. 203
Thirty years' war, VII. 50, 437, 453; XIV. 459
Thirty-Nine Articles, the, XIV. 383
'This is the Time' (refrain), VIII. 96
Thisbe, in *A Midsummer Night's Dream*, V. 285; VI. 207, 316
Thom, M., III. 189
Thom, William (1798?–1848), XI. 445
Thomalin, in *The Shepheards Calender*, III. 222
Thomas (*c.* 1170), I. 273, 310, 316
Thomas, in *Piers the Plowman*, II. 12
Thomas, Acts of, I. 75
Thomas, C. H., XIV. Add. 10
Thomas, Edward (1813–1886), XII. 352, 512, 513; *Ancient Indian Weights*, XII. 353
Thomas, Edward, XIII. 495; XIV. 516, 521, 523
Thomas, Frederick Moy, XIV. 535
Thomas, Lord Cromwell, V. 236, 238, 246, 247, 332, 442, 444
Thomas, Mrs, IX. 84
Thomas, St (apostle), I. 74, 75, 120, 232
Thomas, St, *English Song on*, I. 117
Thomas, St E. Hake, XIV. 527
Thomas, Samuel (1627–1693), X. 386
Thomas, Thomas, Cambridge printer (1553–1588), III. 427; IV. 409, 410; VII. 486, 487
Thomas, W. Moy, IX. 244, 248
Thomas, William (d. 1554), III. 554; *A Historye of Italye*, III. 105
Thomas, William (1670–1738), IX. 533, 540
Thomas, William Luson (1830–1900), XIV. 535
Thomas à Becket, Thomas of Canterbury. *See* Becket
Thomas à Kempis. *See* Kempis
Thomas Aquinas, St. *See* Aquinas
Thomas de Bungay (*fl.* 1290), I. 210, 456; II. 350
Thomas de Eccleston (*fl.* 1250), I. 203, 453
Thomas de Hales (*fl.* 1250), I. 233; *Luve Ron*, I. 233
Thomas of Accon, St, VII. 332
Thomas of Burton (*fl.* 1397), II. 498
Thomas of Ely (*fl.* 1175), I. 449
Thomas of Erceldoune (True Thomas) (*fl.* 1220?–1297?), I. 316, 356, 471; II. 100
Thomas of Woodstock, duke of Gloucester (1355–1397), II. 158
Thomas of Woodstock, V. 399
Thomas the Rimer, IV. 363
Thomas Rymer, II. 413
Thomas Saga, I. 191
Thomason, George (d. 1666), IV. 425; XI. 468, 470; collection of tracts of the times (1641–1660), VII. 346, 422, 491, 494, 499, 500, 502
Thompson, in *Cocke Lorell's bote*, III. 84
Thompson, A. Hamilton, *Military Architecture during the Middle Ages*, XII. 349
Thompson, Sir Benjamin, count von Rumford (1753–1814), XIV. 259, 556
Thompson, Benjamin (1776?–1816), XI. 260
Thompson, D'Arcy Wentworth, XIV. 610
Thompson, David (1796–1868), XIV. 359
Thompson, Edward (1738?–1786), VII. 184; X. 525
Thompson, Francis (1859–1907), XII. 404, 441; XIII. 140, 216 ff., 223, 510, *also see* Add. 2
Absence, XIII. 219
Hound of Heaven, The, XIII. 218
Inconstant, The, XIII. 218
Penelope, XIII. 219
Thompson, Henry (1797–1878), XI. 475
Thompson, Henry Yates, XIV. 195
Thompson, Sir John, 1st baron Haversham (1647–1710), IX. 12, 421, 422
Thompson, John S., XIV. 536
Thompson, John Vaughan (1779–1847), XIV. 296, 564
Thompson, Joseph, XIV. 386, 592, 597
Thompson, Nathaniel (*fl.* 1685), VIII. 98, 410, 411
Thompson, Thomas Perronet (1783–1869), XIV. 514
Thompson, William (1712?–1766?), XI. 172, 429
Thompson, William Hepworth (1810–1886), XII. 330, 331, 494; XIII. 142; XIV. 469
Thoms, William John (1803–1885), XI. 467; XII. 519; *Anecdotes and Traditions*, XII. 354
Thomson, Anstruther, XIV. 541
Thomson, Sir Charles Wyville (1830–1882), XIV. 296, 297, 564
Thomson, Clara Linklater, X. 412, 413; XIII. 553
Thomson, David (1817–1880), XII. 513
Thomson, David Croal, XIII. 541
Thomson, George (1757–1851), XI. 207, 230, 232, 435, 439, 445; XII. 373; *Irish Airs*, XI. 236; *Scottish Airs*, XI. 226, 227, 231, 236; XII. 372; *Welsh Airs*, XI. 235
Thomson, I., *Pyramus and Thisbie*, III. 191
Thomson, James (1700–1748), VI. 49; VII. 137; IX. 69, 181, 186, 254, 486; X. 73, 93 ff. (main entry), 112 ff., 147, 149, 152, 183, 230, 274, 369, 446 ff., 454, 460; XI. 86, 144, 206 ff., 216, 242,

Thomson, James
244, 314; XII. 131, 132, 136, 177, 504; XIII. 35, 235, *also see* Add. 2
Agamemnon, X. 108
Alfred, X. 107 ff., 433, 437
Autumn, X. 94, 99 ff., 103, 104
Britannia, X. 94, 104
Castle of Indolence, The, III. 246; X. 95, 98, 100, 103, 105 ff., 114, 148, 235; XI. 247; XII. 100
Coriolanus, X. 96, 108, 114
Edward and Eleonora, X. 108
Hymn, A, X. 103
Liberty, X. 94, 95, 104, 105, 128
Poem sacred to the Memory of Sir Isaac Newton, X. 94
Return from the Fox-Chace, X. 101
Rule, Britannia, X. 109
Seasons, The, X. 93 ff., 109, 110, 112, 125, 145, 148; XI. 247, 315; XIII. 372
Sophonisba, X. 94, 108
Spring, X. 94, 96, 98 ff., 128, 273
Summer, X. 94, 96, 99 ff., 103, 104
Tancred and Sigismunda, X. 108
Winter, X. 94, 96, 99 ff.
Thomson, James, 'B.V.' (1834–1882), XI. 434; XIII. 106 ff., 147, 187, 193, 489 (main entry), 570
City of Dreadful Night, The, XIII. 106 ff.
Insomnia, XIII. 109
Sunday at Hampstead, XIII. 109
Sunday up the River, XIII. 109
To Our Ladies of Death, XIII. 109
Vane's Story, and other Poems, XIII. 109
Weddah and Om-el-Bonain, XIII. 109
Thomson, John, XII. 144
Thomson, John Arthur, XIV. 481
Thomson, J. Charles, XII. 434; XIII. 476, 493, 532
Thomson, Sir Joseph John, XIV. 269
Thomson, Richard (d. 1613), VII. 316
Thomson, Thomas (1768–1852), XII. 357 ff., 518
Thomson, Thomas Napier (1798–1869), XI. 443
Thomson, William (*fl.* 1725), *Orpheus Caledonius*, IX. 361, 567; X. 233
Thomson, William (1746–1817), X. 291, 505
Thomson, William (1819–1890), *An Outline of the Laws of Thought*, XIV. 9, 482
Thomson, Sir William, lord Kelvin (1824–1907), XIV. 265 ff., 556, 557
Thomson, William Roger, XIII. 544; XIV. Add. 5
Thopas, Sir (Chaucer's), IV. 359
Thopas, Sir, in Lyly's *Endimion*, VIII. 127
Thor, X. 237
Thor, children of, III. 84
Thor, myths of, I. 297
Thorbiorga, in Taylor's *Edwin the Fair*, XII. 113
Thoreau, Henry David, XII. 166, 176
Thoresby, Ralph (1658–1725), IX. 540; XI. 340; XII. 514, 516: *Leeds*, IX. 353, 540
Thorgerðr, daughter of Egill Skallagrimsson, I. 9
Thorie or Thorius, John (*fl.* 1586–1593), IV. 253, 448
Thorius, Raphael (d. 1625), IV. 531
Thorn, A. E., XIV. 521
Thornberry, Job, in Colman's *John Bull*, XI. 280
Thornborough, John (1551–1641), VII. 145
Thornbury, George Walter (1828–1876), XIII. 189, 510
Thorndike, Ashley Horace, VI. 121; VIII. 181
Thorndike, Herbert (1598–1672), VIII. 462; *Epilogue to the Tragedy of the Church of England*, VIII. 294; *The Reformation of the Church of England*, VIII. 294; trans. of *Veni Creator*, VIII. 295
Thorne, J., XIV. 613
Thorne, Robert (d. 1527), IV. 87
Thorne, William (*fl.* 1397), II. 498
Thorneganus (or Byrhtferth), I. 131
Thornes, the, in Trollope's novels, XIII. 422
Thorney abbey, II. 289
Thornhill, squire, in *The Vicar of Wakefield*, X. 209
Thornley, George, VII. 489
Thornton, in Mrs Gaskell's *North and South*, XIII. 378, 381
Thornton, in Lytton's *Pelham*, XIII. 418
Thornton, Bonnell (1724–1768), X. 429, 455, 461; XIV. 594; *The Connoisseur*, XI. 448
Thornton, Henry (1760–1815), XII. 281, 473
Thornton, Percy Melville, XIV. 597
Thornton, Robert de (*fl.* 1440), IV. 422
Thornton, Robert John (1768?–1837), XI. 432
Thornton, William Thomas (1813–1880), XIV. 22, 482
Thornton-le-Dale, near Pickering, II. 44
Thornton-le-Street, II. 44
Thoroton, Robert (1623–1678), *Antiquities of Nottinghamshire*, IX. 353, 540
Thorowgood, in Lillo's *George Barnwell*, X. 74, 75
Thorowgood, G., VII. 514
Thorpe, Benjamin (1782–1870), I. 116, 117; XII. 344, 505; XIV. 52, 69, 499; *Yule-tide Stories*, XII. 368
Thorpe, Isabella, in Jane Austen's *Northanger Abbey*, XI. 299, 300; XII. 236
Thorpe, John (1682–1750), IX. 540
Thorpe, Thomas (1570?–1635?), IV. 394, 395; V. 223 ff. (T. T.), 225
Thorpe, Thomas Edward, XIV. 557
Thorpe, William (d. 1407?), II. 69
Thorpe, Examination of William, II. 300
Thorpes, the, in Jane Austen's *Northanger Abbey*, XII. 236
Thorstein, the Red, I. 287

Thou, Jacques Auguste de (Thuanus), III. 163, 326; *Historiae sui temporis*, VI. 33; IX. 204, 206
Though Fortune cannot favor, III. 190
Thought, in *Piers the Plowman*, II. 19
Thoyras, Rapin de, X. 502
Thracian Wonder, III. 357
Thrale, Mrs. *See* Piozzi, Hester Lynch
Thrales, the, X. 181, 182
Thrasher, justice, in Fielding's *Amelia*, X. 21, 29
Three Children, the, I. 74
Three Fates, the, in *Filostrato e Panfila*, V. 62
Three Kings' Sons, II. 483, 503
Three Mile Cross, near Reading, XIII. 430
Three Ravens, The, II. 412
Three Speeches, VII. 381
Three Systers of Mantua, The, V. 116
Thring, Edward (1821–1887), XIV. 425, 602, 610; *Theory and Practice of Teaching*, XIV. 426
Throckmorton, Job (1545–1601), III. 380, 381, 382, 383, 390, 391, 538, 539, 542
Throsby, John (1740–1803), IX. 540
Thrum, Sir George, in Thackeray's *The Ravenswing*, XIII. 281
Thrush and the Nightingale, The, I. 362, 465; II. 500
Thrytho, in *Beowulf*, I. 23
Thuanus. *See* Thou
Thucydides, III. 429, 432; IV. 3, 4, 43, 440; VII. 218, 283; IX. 340, 528; X. 135; XII. 303, 330, 333, 338, 474, 482, 483, 485, 486, 492, 493, 495, *also see* Add.; XIV. 59, 85, 98
Thule, I. 26, 100, 216; II. 84
Thumb, Tom, XI. 373, 375
Thunder, Harry, in O'Keeffe's *Wild Oats*, XI. 281
Thunder and Lightning, in *The Rehearsal*, VIII. 34
'Thunderer, The' (*The Times*), XIV. 180
Thurgarton, Nottinghamshire, II. 299
Thurland, Sir Edward (1606–1683), VIII. 83
Thurloe, John (1616–1668), VII. 188; *Collection of the State Papers of*, VII. 187, 435, 452
Thurloe Papers, X. 294
Thurlow, Edward, 1st lord Thurlow (1731–1806), X. 306; XI. 78, 142, 143, 254
Thurnall, Tom, in Kingsley's *Two Years Ago*, XIII. 365
Thurneysen, I. 246
Thurston, king, in *Horn*, I. 287
Thurtell, John (1794–1824), XIII. 418; XIV. 201, 228, 230
Thyer, Robert (1709–1781), VIII. 60, 62
Thylde (a seaman), IV. 68
Thynne, Francis (1545?–1608), III. 114; IV. 519
Thynne, lady Isabella, VII. 55
Thynne, Thomas, 3rd viscount Weymouth and 1st marquis of Bath (1734–1796), X. 306
Thynne, Thomas, 2nd marquis of Bath, XI. 148
Thynne, William (d. 1546), II. 161, 162, 164, 169, 217, 218; III. 291, 311
Thynnes, the, IX. 168
Thyrsis, in Milton's *Arcades*, VII. 113
Thyrza, in Gissing's novel, XIII. 459, 461
Tibbe, daughter of Rondill the refe, in *The Turnament of Totenham*, I. 366
Tibbs, Mrs, in *A Citizen of the World*, V. 181
Tiberius, in *Sejanus*, VI. 20
Tiberius, emperor of Rome, IX. 234; X. 320; XII. 306
Tibet Talkapace, II. 232
Tibullus, III. 113; VIII. 215; XII. 492
Tichborne, Chidiock, IV. 129
Tichmarsh, Northants., VIII. 2
Tickell, Richard (1751–1793), X. 438; XI. 35, 391
Tickell, Thomas (1686–1740), IX. 165, 170 ff., 181, 435 ff., 440, 444, 483; X. 137, 458
Colin and Lucy, IX. 173
Epistle from a Lady in England, IX. 173
Fragment of a Poem on Hunting, IX. 173
Iliad, The, IX. 75, 171, 173
Kensington Gardens, IX. 173
On Queen Caroline's rebuilding of the Lodgings...at Queen's College, IX. 172
Oxford, IX. 173
Part of the Fourth Book of Lucan, IX. 173
Poem to...the Lord Privy Seal on the Prospect of Peace, IX. 171, 172
Royal Progress, The, IX. 172
To Mr Addison, IX. 170, 173
To Sir Godfrey Kneller, IX. 173
To the Earl of Warwick on the Death of Mr Addison, IX. 171
Tickler, Timothy, in *Noctes Ambrosianae*, XII. 160
Tieck, Dorothea, V. 303
Tieck, Johann Ludwig, V. 85, 222, 299, 303 ff.; XIII. 4, 192, 465
Tierney, George (1761–1830), XIV. 121, 511
Tierra del Fuego, XIV. 243
Tighe, Mary (born Blackford) (1772–1810), XII. 423; XIV. 571; *Psyche*, XIV. 311
Tigris, river, IV. 90
Tilbury. *See* Gervase of
Tilbury, IX. 7
Tiler, Margaret, IV. 442
Tilghman, Richard, X. 409
Tillbrook, Samuel, XIII. 241, 247, 512
Tillemont, Louis S. le N. de, X. 292, 308, 499; *Histoire des Empereurs*, X. 314; *Mémoires Ecclésiastiques*, X. 314
Tilley, Arthur Augustus, VIII. 63
Tillotson, John (1630–1694), archbishop of Canterbury, VII. 176; VIII. 272, 292, 296, 297, 303, 304, 370, 389, 458, 459, 461, 462; IX. 195, 196, 289, 293; X. 353, 354, 359, 360, 379, 498; XII. 259; *The Wisdom of being religious*, VIII. 369
Tilly, count J. T. von, VII. 21

Tilly, William, of Selling or Celling (d. 1494), III. 5, 52
Tillyard, Alfred Isaac, XIV. 594
Tilney, Edmund (d. 1610), III. 536; VI. 249, 384
Tilney, Henry, in Jane Austen's *Northanger Abbey*, XII. 234, 236
Timaeus, J. J. C., X. 446
Time, in *The Passetyme of Pleasure*, II. 226
Time's Complaint, VI. 320, 474
Times, Song on the, I. 370
Times, The, XI. 155, 467; XII. 171, 273, 315; XIII. 11, 20, 69, 278, 347, 467; XIV. 118, 151, 165, 170 ff., 177 ff., 187 ff., 198, 201, 410, 536
Times of India, The, XIV. 339
Times Whistle, The. *See* R. C.
Timme, Thomas, IV. 448, 518
Timoclia at the sege of Thebes by Alexander, V. 102
Timoleon of Corinth, in *The Bond-Man*, VI. 163
Timon, play, VI. 487
Timon (Shakespeare's), XIII. 242
Timon's villa, in Pope's *Epistles*, IX. 81
Timor mortis conturbat me, II. 257
'Timotheus,' VIII. 55
Timothy, in *Sir Courtly Nice*, VIII. 189
Timothy Thinbeard, in *If you know not me*, VI. 84
Timperley, Charles H. (1794–1846?), XI. 467
Timur (Tamerlane), XI. 18
Tina, in George Eliot's *Mr Gilfil's Love Story*, XIII. 387
Tinchebray, battle of, I. 157
Tincker of Turney, The, IV. 362
Tindal, Matthew (1657–1733), IX. 288, 293 ff., 302, 309, 508, 512; X. 521; *Christianity as Old as the Creation*, IX. 293, 311
Tindal, Nicholas (1688–1774), *Continuation of Mr Rapin de Thoyras's History*, IX. 235, 236, 495
'Tindal, William,' X. 475
Tindale or Tyndale, William (d. 1536), I. 211; II. 330; III. 13, 26, 27, 39 ff. (main entry), 441, 462, 472; IV. 38, 39, 40 ff., 46, 380
Articles whereof John Frith died, III. 41
New Testament, XII. 521
Obedience of a Christian Man, The, III. 39
Parable of the Wicked Mammon, The, III. 39
Practice of Prelates, The, III. 41
Revelation of Anti-Christ, The, III. 39
Sum of Scripture, The, III. 39
Tintagol or Tintagel, the castle of, I. 259, 273
Tintern abbey, X. 134
Tintoretto, XIII. 397
Tipperary, IX. 166; XIV. 321, 326
Tiptoft, John, earl of Worcester (1427?–1470), II. 286, 499
Tiresias, III. 173
Tiresias, in *Narcissus*, VI. 316
Tiriel, in Blake's poem, XI. 187
Tirzah, in Blake's *Four Zoas*, XI. 196, 197
Tisbury, Wiltshire, IV. 161
Titania, XI. 374
Titania, in *A Midsummer Night's Dream*, V. 183
Titania, in *Nimphidia*, IV. 193
Titania, in *The Whore of Babylon*, VI. 53
'Titanic,' ship, XIV. 195
Titans, the, in Keats's *Hyperion*, XII. 85
Titchburne, Robert, VII. 513
Titere Tu, in Wilson's *Cheats*, VIII. 122
Titian, XII. 172, 173; XIV. 171
Titinillus. *See* Tutivillus
Titmarsh, Michael Angelo, *pseud.* of W. M. Thackeray, XIII. 278, 281, 284, 294, 422
Titmarsh, Samuel, in Thackeray's *Great Hoggarty Diamond*, XIII. 281
Tito, in *Romola*, XIII. 395, 396
Titus, in school plays, V. 103
Titus, emperor of Rome, X. 303; XII. 249
Titus, Silius (1623?–1704), VII. 460; VIII. 410
Titus and Gesippus, II. 326
Titus and Vespasian, I. 333, 334, 471; V. 221
Tityrus (Vergil's), III. 223
Tiverton academy, X. 387
Tivoli, XII. 419
Tixall, IV. 184
Tixall Poetry, VII. 86
To pass the Place, III. 491
Tobacco, in *The Queenes Arcadia*, VI. 318
Tobacco, king of Trinidado, in *Lingua*, VI. 315
Tobacco in England, An Advice how to plant, IV. 531
Tobacco pamphlets, IV. 530
Tobacconist, The, VI. 28
Tobin, John (1770–1804), XI. 458; *The Honeymoon*, XI. 454
Toby, Abel's Kinsman, IX. 442, 462
Toby, uncle, in Sterne's *Tristram Shandy*, X. 25, 50 ff.
Tocqueville, Alexis C. H. Clérel de, XI. 26; XII. 475
Tod, James (1782–1835), XII. 513; XIV. 580; *Annals and Antiquities of Rajasthan*, XIV. 335; *Antiquities of Rajpootana*, XII. 352
Todd, Alpheus (1821–1884), XIV. 359, 584
Todd, Henry John (1763–1845), X. 239, 461
Todd, James Henthorn (1805–1869), XII. 360, 519; XIV. 571; *St Patrick, Apostle of Ireland*, XII. 361; *Life of St Patrick*, XIV. 328
'Todgers's,' in *Martin Chuzzlewit*, XIII. 323, 423
Todhunter, Isaac (1820–1884), XIV. 555, 565, 610
Todhunter, John (1839–1916), XII. 400, 404; XIII. 510; XIV. 211, *also see* Add. 3
Todlen Butt and Todlen Ben, IX. 360

Toft Trees, Norfolk, vi. 290
Tofte, Robert (d. 1620), iii. 209, 256, 264, 266; iv. 442
Ariostos Satyres, iv. 377, 520, 540
Blazon of Jealousie, The, iii. 209
Laura, iii. 257, 266, 524
Pastoralls of Julietta, iv. 377
Tokens, The Fifteen, ii. 329
Toland, John (1670–1722), viii. 332, 410; ix. 17, 282, 289 ff., 294, 295, 300, 427, 508
Amyntor, ix. 291, 297
Christianity not mysterious, viii. 331; ix. 289 ff.
Letters to Serena, ix. 290, 291
Life of Milton, ix. 291
Nazarenus, ix. 291
Pantheisticon, ix. 292
Toledo, xiii. 452
Toledo, scholars at, i. 153, 199; ii. 365; iv. 69
Toleration act, x. 373, 376, 378, 380, 382
Toller, Thomas Northcote, xiv. 611
Tolomei, vii. 265
Tolosa, ix. 269
Tolous, Erl of, i. 471
Tolstoy, Leo, count, v. 208; xii. 250
Tom, in *King Lear*, v. 263
Tom, in Steele's *Conscious Lovers*, ix. 64
Tom, Corinthian (Egan's), xiv. 223, 224, 226, 227, 230
Tom a Lincoln, xi. 334
Tom of all Trades, v. 364
Tom of Bedlam, vi. 297
Tom Drum, in *Master Peachey and his men*, iii. 369, 372
Tom Potts, ii. 411
Tom Tel-Troths Message and his pens Complaint, iv. 352; v. 363
Tom Tell-Trothe's New-yeares Gift, iv. 353, 526, 527; v. 355, 479
Tom Thynne's Ghost, viii. 92
Tom Tosspot, ii. 232
Tom Tyler and his Wife, v. 117, 118, 410
Tomkin, the Tinker, in *Piers the Plowman*, ii. 16
Tomkins, Thomas (d. 1656), iv. 465
Tomkis or Tomkys, Thomas (*fl.* 1604–1615), vi. 315, 479; viii. 400; x. 433; *Albumazar*, iv. 410; vi. 314, 322, 323; viii. 366; *Lingua*, vi. 314, 322, 323, 327
Tomkyn, in *Turnament of Totenham*, i. 366
Tomkyns or Tomkins, Thomas (1637?–1675), vii. 117, 120
Tomline, Sir George Pretyman (1750–1827), xiv. 507
Tomlins, Frederick Guest (1804–1867), xiv. 236
Tomlinson, in Lytton's *Paul Clifford*, xiii. 418
Tomlyn (Marprelate printer), iii. 382
Tommy, in *The Little Pretty Pocket Book*, xi. 376
'Tommy Lucretius,' x. 122
Tommy Thumb's Pretty Song Book, xi. 375
Tompson, Charles, jun., xiv. 587; *Wild Notes*, xiv. 362
Tomson, Rosamund. *See* Watson, Rosamund Marriott
Tomy Lin, xi. 231
Tonbridge school, iii. 428; vii. 330
Tone, Theobald Wolfe (1763–1798), xiv. 514, 571
Tong, William (1662–1727), x. 385
Tongue, Cornelius, xiv. 541
Tongue, Israel (1621–1680), 'Apocalyptical Expositions,' viii. 286
Tonna, Charlotte Elizabeth, *The Maiden City*, xiv. 321
Tönnies, F., vii. 288
Tonson, Jacob (d. 1735), xi. 320
Tonson, Jacob (1656?–1736), vii. 117, 141; viii. 44, 49, 213, 392, 394, *also see* Add.; ix. 68, 77, 162, 350; xi. 318 ff., 327, 332, 334; *Miscellany*, ix. 68, 74, 119, 165, 446; xi. 319, 320
Tonson, Jacob (d. 1767), x. 180; xi. 320, 323
Toogood, C. G., xiv. 490
Tooke, John Horne (1736–1812), x. 402, 524; xi. 400; xii. 494; *Diversions of Purley, The*, x. 401, 405; xii. 326
Tooke, Thomas (1774–1858), xiv. 482
Tooke, William (1777–1863), x. 524
Toole, John L., xiii. 515
Tooley or Toolie, Nicholas, vi. 139
Toomevara (Charlotte Eccles's), xiv. 325
Tooting, ix. 7
Toots, in *Dombey and Son*, xiii. 325
Top Book of All, xi. 375, 386, 490
Topcliffe, Richard (1532–1604), iv. 128
Topham, captain, xiv. 214
Toplady, Augustus Montagu (1740–1778), x. 365, 517; *An old Fox tarred and feathered*, x. 367; *Historic Proof*, x. 367; 'Rock of Ages,' x. 367
Topsell, Edward (d. 1638?), viii. 479; *Historie of Fourefooted Beastes*, iv. 374; *The Historie of Serpents*, iv. 374; *Theater of Insects*, iv. 374
Torchbearers' dance, the, in *The Lords' Masque*, vi. 354
Torcy, Jean-Baptiste Colbert, marquis de, ix. 152, 216
Torfaeus, Thermodus, x. 225
Torfrida, in Kingsley's *Hereward the Wake*, xiii. 366
Tories, xiii. 14, 24
Tories Confession, viii. 97
Tories' Triumph, viii. 97
Torigni, Robert de. *See* Robert de Monte
Tor-lutha, x. 229
Toronto, xiv. 343, 349, 358
Trinity college, xiv. 350
University of, xii. 351
Torquatus (*i.e.* Ben Jonson), vi. 39
Torquemada, Antonio de, iv. 448
Torquil, in Byron's *The Island*, xii. 46
Torrens, Henry Whitelock (1806–1852), xiv. 337, 580
Torrens, Robert (1780–1864), xiv. 194, 482

Torrens, William Torrens McCullagh (1813–1894), XIV. 510, 511, 513, 571; *Life of Melbourne*, XIV. 326
Torrent of Portugal, I. 316, 472; II. 182
Torrigiano, Pietro, IV. 227
Toscar, X. 229
Tosier, captain John, IV. 462
Total Rout, A, VII. 382
Totila, king of the Goths in Italy, XIII. 461
Totnes, X. 352
Totnes, earl of. *See* Carew, Sir George
Tottel, Richard (d. 1594), II. 198; III. 166, 180, 181, 194, 248; IV. 384, 396, 546; *Tottel's Miscellany*, III. 134 ff., 166, 170, 173, 174, 179 ff., 185 ff., 248, 283, 509, 524; IV. 110, 168, 170, 387, 397, 546; VII. 1
Tottenham, XII. 417
Touchstone, in *As You Like It*, V. 190, 192, 193, 214; XIII. 64
Touchstone, in *Eastward Hoe*, VI. 48
Touchwood, lady, in Congreve's *Double-Dealer*, VIII. 148, 149
Touchwood, lord, in Congreve's *Double-Dealer*, VIII. 148
Toulmin, Joshua (1740–1815), IX. 494; X. 518, 520
Toulouse, X. 335; XIII. 88
Toulouse, Dominicans at, I. 200
Toup, Jonathan (1713–1785), XII. 494; *Emendations on Suidas*, XII. 324, 490
Tour of Dr Syntax through London, The, XIV. 219
Touraine, IX. 226
Tourguénieff, Ivan S., XIII. 195
Touris, William, *The Contemplacyon of sinners*, II. 323
Tournay, in *The Unfortunate Traveller*, III. 363
Tournay, John, VII. 33
Tournay, siege of, Laurence Minot on, I. 357, 359
Tournehem, III. 3
Tourneur, Cyril (1575?–1626), V. 327, 376; VI. 116, 128, 166–187, 444, 459, *also see* Add.; XII. 116
Atheist's Tragedie, The, VI. 137, 166, 167, 179
Funeral Poem, A (on Sir Francis Vere), VI. 166
Griefe on the Death of Prince Henry, A, VI. 166
Nobleman, The, VI. 166
Revengers Tragoedie, The, VI. 166, 167, 178, 179
Transformed Metamorphosis, The, VI. 166
Tours, VIII. 245
Tout, Thomas Frederick, XIV. 485, 497
Tovey, Duncan Crookes (1842–1912), X. 103, 451; XIII. 488, 508; XIV. 507
Towgood, Matthew (*fl.* 1710–1746), X. 385, 387
Towgood, Michaijah (1700–1792), X. 374, 384, 387; *The Dissenting Gentleman's Answer*, X. 375
Towneley MSS., IX. 565
Towneley plays, III. 91; V. 13, 15, 18, 20, 40, 47, 389, 390
Townley, in Sheridan's *Trip to Scarborough*, XI. 268
Townley, James (1714–1778), X. 432, 438; *False Concord*, X. 90; *High Life below Stairs*, X. 88
Townley Gallery, XII. 509
Townsend, Joseph (1739–1816), XI. 400; *Dissertation on the Poor Laws*, XI. 74
Townsend, Meredith White (1831–1911), XIV. 198, 535
Townshend or Townsend, Aurelian (*fl.* 1601–1643), VII. 16, 20, 413, *also see* Add.
Townshend, Charles, 2nd viscount Townshend (1674–1738), IX. 16, 17, 163, 219
Townshend, Charles (1725–1767), X. 399, 523; XI. 10, 12
Townshend, Chauncey Hare (1798–1868), XIII. 542
Townshend, Hayward (*fl.* 1601), VII. 440
Townshend, lord John, XI. 35
Towton, battle of, II. 306
Towton, battlefield of, V. 171
Towwouse, Mrs, in Fielding's *Joseph Andrews*, X. 26
Tox, Miss, in *Dombey and Son*, XIII. 325
Toynbee, Arnold (1852–1883), XIV. 592
Toynbee, Paget, XII. 415, 525
Toynbee, Mrs Paget, X. 247, 248, 250, 251, 284, 495, *also see* Add.; XI. 282
Tozer, in Mrs Oliphant's *Salem Chapel*, XIII. 431
Tozer, Henry Fanshawe (1829–1916), XII. 475, *also see* Add. 4
Trabb's boy, in *Great Expectations*, XIII. 334
Tracts, collections of, in Jacobean times, VII. 455
Tracts for the Times, XII. 256, 257, 276, 455 ff.; XIII. 358
Tracy, Antoine L. C. Destutt, comte de, XIV. 6, 8
Trade books, XI. 325
Trade catalogues, early, IV. 548
Trade and Plantations commission, IX. 406
Tradescant, John (d. 1637?), XIV. 285
Tradescant, John (1608–1662), XIV. 285, 564
Trafton, A., XIII. 559
Tragedus, in *Lingua*, VI. 315
Tragedy, in *A Warning for Faire Women*, V. 326
Tragedy, in *The Muses Looking-Glasse*, VI. 233
Tragedy, early English, V. 394
Traherne, Philip (d. 1723), VII. 404
Traherne, Thomas (1637?–1674), VII. 15, 42 ff. (main entry), 144, 153, 155, 157, 163, 403, 404, 427, *also see* Add.; XI. 384
Centuries of Meditations, VII. 43, 143
Christian Ethics, VII. 43
News, VII. 44
Poems, VII. 43

Traherne, Thomas
Roman Forgeries, VII. 43
Serious and patheticall Contemplation of the Mercies of God, A, VII. 43
Silence, VII. 44
Thoughts, poems on, VII. 44
Ways of Wisdom, The, VII. 44
Wonder, VII. 44
Traill, Catharine Parr (1802–1899), XIV. 581; *Lost in the Backwoods* (*The Canadian Crusoes*), XIV. 360
Traill, Henry Duff (1842–1900), I. ix; X. 422; XI. 417; XIII. 464, 473, 478, 510, 544, 545, 547, *also see* Add. 2; XIV. 511, 527
Age of Despair, The, XIII. 166
Ballad of Baloonatics Craniocracs, The, XIII. 166
Enfant Terrible, An, XIII. 166
Laputa Outdone, XIII. 166
New Fiction, The, XIV. 146
New Lucian, The, XIV. 146
Number Twenty, XIV. 146
Recaptured Rhymes, XIII. 166
Saturday Songs, XIII. 166; XIV. 146
Social England, editor of, I. 363
Trajan, emperor of Rome, II. 76; XII. 303
Tranent Muir, IX. 373
Tranquillus, in *The Tatler*, IX. 39
Transit, Robert, *pseud.* *See* Cruikshank, Isaac Robert
Transition English, I. 217 ff., 335 ff., 458 ff., 474 ff.
Transition English song collections, II. 372 ff., 490 ff.
Translators, IV. 1 ff., 435 ff.
Transome, Harold, in *Felix Holt*, XIII. 397
Transubstantiation, VIII. 296
Trant, Olive, IX. 219
Traperon, William, IV. 446
Trapezuntius, III. 50
Trapp, Joseph (1679–1747), IX. 181, 184, 487, 510, 512, 519
Trappola, in *The Bugbears*, V. 115
Trautmann, M., I. 60, 118
Travailes of The three English Brothers, The, IV. 533
Traveller, The, XIV. 194
Travers, Walter (1548?–1635), III. 405, 406, 413, 426; IV. 236
Travis, George (1741–1797), X. 310; XII. 490; *Letters to Gibbon*, X. 309, 508; XII. 323
Treasury of South African Poetry and Verse, The, XIV. 377
Treatise of a Gallant, IX. 51
Trebizond, II. 79
Treble, H. R., XIV. 528
Tregarva, in Kingsley's *Yeast*, XIII. 360, 361
Tregelles, Samuel Prideaux (1813–1875), XII. 340, 501
Trelawney, Edward John (1792–1881), XII. 38, 76, 398, 404, 452; XIV. 527; *Recollections of...Shelley and Byron*, XII. 37
Trelawny, Sir Jonathan (1650–1721), bishop of Winchester, IX. 151; X. 352
Tremebundus or Tremulus (Charles Lamb), XII. 200
Tremellius, John Immanuel (1510–1580), III. 422
Tremor, Sir Luke, in Mrs Inchbald's *Such Things Are*, XI. 278
Trench, Miss Maria (1828?–1917), XII. Add. 2
Trench, Melesina (1768–1827), XII. 452
Trench, Richard Chenevix (1807–1886), VII. 41; XI. 407; XII. 271 ff., 452, 463; XIII. 24, 167, 173, 510; XIV. 611; *Lord! many times I am aweary quite*, XIII. 174; *Sacred Latin Poetry*, XIII. 172
Trench, W. F., III. 193, 194
Trent, in Fielding's *Amelia*, X. 33
Trent, council of, III. 30, 400; VII. 190; X. 460; XII. 260; XIV. 100
Trent, Mr, in *The Old Curiosity Shop*, XIII. 319
Trent, river, IV. 190
Trentals of St Gregory, I. 312
Tresham (Browning's), XIII. 67
Trevecca, X. 366
Trevelyan, George Macaulay, II. 38; XIII. 568; *The life of John Bright*, XIV. 133, 508
Trevelyan, Sir George Otto, XI. 396; XII. 427; XIV. 60, 493, 537
Treveris, Peter (*fl.* 1527), IV. 374
Treves, V. 39; XIV. 303
Treves, Sir Frederick, XIII. 485
Treveth. *See* Trivet
Trevisa, John (1326–1412), II. 59, 70 ff., 85, 188, 189, 287, 295, 300, 313, 323, 333, 444; III. 441
Trevithick, Richard (1771–1833), XIV. 258
Trevor, Sir John (1637–1717), VIII. 482
Trévoux, Mémoires de, V. 291
Trial of Treasure, The, V. 60, 393
Triamour, Sir, I. 316, 465, 471
Tribulation, in *The Alchemist*, VI. 22, 23
Tribulation, The Twelve profits of, II. 323
Tribune, The, XIV. 202
Trier, IV. 429
Trieste, XIV. 313
Trifler, The, XIV. 387
Trim, corporal, in Sterne's *Tristram Shandy*, X. 50, 51, 53, 55
Trim, Ireland, IX. 93
Trimmer, Mrs Sarah (1741–1810), XI. 372, 374, 383, 476, 483; XIV. 592, 602, 610
Comparative view of the New Plan of Education, A, XIV. 402, 403
Fabulous Histories (*The History of the Robins*), XI. 378 ff.
Familiar Introduction to the Knowledge of Nature, XI. 382
Guardian of Education, XI. 380
Oeconomy of Charity, The, XIV. 390
Reflections upon...charity schools, XIV. 389
Trincalo, in *Albumazar*, VI. 323
Trinculo, in *The Tempest*, V. 206

Trinidad, IV. 61
Trinitarianism, X. 379
Trinity, the, XII. 283
Trinity, the, in *The foure P.P.*, V. 97
Trinity, Pageant of the Holy, V. 9
Trinity in Unity, dogma of, III. 243
Trinket, lord, in Colman's *Jealous Wife*, X. 89, 90
Trinket, Mrs (Etherege's), VIII. 138
'Trip, Tommy,' XI. 377
Triple alliance of 1668, VIII. 381; IX. 228
Tripoli, XI. 72
Tripolis, in Syria, IV. 84
Trismegist, VIII. 282
Trissino, III. 290, *also see* Add.; VII. 265; *Sofonisba*, V. 62
Tristram, Sir, in Arthurian legend, I. 236, 261, 267, 270, 272 ff., 282, 283, 290, 297 ff., 309, 310, 313, 316, 462, 471; II. 100, 336, 337; III. 68
Tristram and Iseult, II. 174
Tristrem, Sir, II. 272
Trithemius, Johannes, III. 112; *Antiphonus Maleficiorum*, III. 112
Trivet or Treveth, Nicholas (1258–1328?), I. 181, 450; II. 150; V. 61
Trivium, the, II. 229, 230, 359, 363, 366; VI. 310; VII. 320
Troad, the, XIV. 252
Troilus, I. 306
Troilus, in *Confessio Amantis*, II. 148
Troilus, in Dryden's *Troilus and Cressida*, VIII. 29
Troilus, in Henryson's *Testament of Cresseid*, II. 248
Troilus and Cressida, III. 181, 190
Trojan horse, the, VIII. 73; XI. 252
Trojan war, the, IV. 136
Trokelowe, John of (*fl.* 1330), I. 181
Trollope, Sir Andrew (d. 1461), II. 303
Trollope, Anthony (1815–1882), XI. 149; XII. 245; XIII. 386, 421 ff. (main entry), 427, 432, 530, 544, 566; XIV. 194, 554
Autobiography, XIII. 421, 424
Barchester novels, XIII. 430
Barchester Towers, XIII. 422
Doctor Thorne, XIII. 422
Duke's Children, The, XIII. 423
Framley Parsonage, XIII. 422
Kellys and the O'Kellys, The, XIII. 421
Last Chronicles of Barset, The, XIII. 422
Macdermots of Ballycloran, The, XIII. 421
Orley Farm, XIII. 423
Phineas Finn, XIII. 423
Small House at Allington, The, XIII. 422, 423
Three Clerks, The, XIII. 421
Vendée, La, XIII. 421
Vicar of Bullhampton, The, XIII. 423
Warden, The, XIII. 332, 422
Way We Live Now, The, XIII. 423
Trollope, Frances (1780–1863), XII. 245, 452; XIII. 322, 421; *The Vicar of Wrexhill*, XII. 246; *The Widow Barnaby*, XII. 246
Trollope, Thomas Adolphus (1810–1892), XII. 245; XIII. 567; XIV. 598
Trombet, Anthony, III. 50
Tropes, V. 11
'Trot, John' (viscount Bolingbroke), IX. 221
Trot of Turriff, the, VII. 254
Trotte, Nicholas (*fl.* 1588), V. 77
Trotter, Mrs A. F., XIV. Add. 10
Trotter, John Bernard (1775–1818), XII. 439
Trotton, Sussex, VIII. 181
Trotwood, Miss Betsey, in *David Copperfield*, XIII. 327
Troubadours, Provençal, V. 26
Trouvères, V. 3, 21, 26, 27
Trowbridge, Wiltshire, XI. 148, 149
Trowbridge academy, X. 387
Trowle, in *The Play of the Shepherds*, V. 19
Troy, V. 69, 227; VIII. 23; XII. 338, 497
Troy, in *The Four Ages*, VI. 92
Troy, Gest Hystoriale of the Destruction of, I. 306, 333, 472; II. 118, 202, 450
Troy, legends of, I. 148, 195, 234, 258, 279, 285, 306, 342; II. 172, 301
Troy, plains of, XIII. 353
Troy Book, I. 291, 333, 334
Troy-books, V. 196, 221
Troye, VI. 93
Troylous and Pandor, VI. 283
Trudge, in Colman's *Inkle and Yarico*, XI. 279
True and impartial Narrative of the Dissenters' New Plot, A, VIII. 99
'True Blue Poet, the,' VIII. 40
True description of the Pot-Companion Poet, A, VII. 387
True Inventory of the goods and chattels of Superstition, A, VII. 382
True Loyalist, IX. 376
True Patriot, The, X. 28, 29, 417
True Presbyterian without Disguise, The (1680), VII. 409
True Relation, in *The Palice of Honour*, II. 261
Trueman, in Lillo's *George Barnwell*, X. 74, 75
Trulla, in *Hudibras*, VIII. 68, 69
Trulliber, parson, in Fielding's *Joseph Andrews*, X. 20, 26
Trumbull, Thomas, in Scott's *Redgauntlet*, XII. 21
Trumbull, Sir William (1639–1716), IX. 68, 74, 149
Trumpet Club, in *The Tatler*, IX. 50
Trunnion, commodore, in Smollett's *Peregrine Pickle*, X. 38, 41, 43, 50
Trunnion, Grizzle, in Smollett's *Peregrine Pickle*, X. 38
Truscott, S. J., XIV. Add. 10
Truso, in Ohthere's voyage, I. 94
Trussell, John (d. 1642), *Touchstone of Tradition*, VII. 444
Truth, XIV. 190, 200
Truth, in Anglo-Norman plays, V. 21

Truth, in Carew's *Coelum Britannicum*, vii. 19
Truth, in *Horestes*, v. 64, 65
Truth, in Medwall's interlude, v. 54
Truth, in *Piers the Plowman*, ii. 2 ff., 12, 13, 15
Truth, in *The Passetyme of Pleasure*, ii. 229, 235
Truth, in *Two Lamentable Tragedies*, v. 326
Truth, ffaythfulnesse and Mercye, v. 102
Truth Flatters Not, vii. 381
Tryall of Chevalry, The, vi. 459
Tryan, in George Eliot's *Janet's Repentance*, xiii. 388
Tryce, John, vi. 287
Tryman, Mrs, in *The City Witt*, vi. 229
Tryon, Thomas (1634–1703), ix. 307, 515
Tschudi, Ægidius, x. 304
Tuam, xiv. 329
Tubbe, Henry, vii. Add.
Tubney academy, x. 387
Tucca, in *Satiro-Mastix*, vi. 42, 44, 272
Tucca, in *The Poetaster*, v. 315; viii. 127
Tuck, friar, v. 35, 318
Tuck, friar, in Scott's *Ivanhoe*, xii. 18
Tucker, Abraham (1705–1774), x. 346, 514; xi. 250; xii. 431; xiii. 244; *Freewill, Foreknowledge and Fate*, x. 343; *Light of Nature pursued*, x. 343; *Man in Quest of Himself*, x. 343
Tucker, Herbert, xiv. Add. 5
Tucker, Josiah (1712–1799), xi. 73; xiv. 593
Tucker, Miss, in Jerrold's *Time Works Wonders*, xiii. 269
Tucker, R., xiv. 556
Tucker, Thomas (*fl.* 1607), vi. 319 ff.
Tuckney, Anthony (1599–1670), viii. 274 ff., 291, 457; *Eight Letters*, viii. 276
Tuckwell, William, xiv. 596
Tudor, Charley (Trollope's), xiii. 423
Tudor, Jasper, Duke of Bedford, The Epitaph of, ii. 321
Tudor, Owen (d. 1461), iv. 182; viii. 22
Tudor period, x. 40, 283, 284; xi. 367; xiv. 86
Tudor princesses, xiv. 111
Tudors, the, iv. 135; viii. 132, 312, 315, 356; xiv. 75
Tuer, Andrew White (1838–1900), xi. 476; xiv. 610
Tuffley, Mary, wife of Defoe, ix. 6
Tufnell, Henry (1805–1854), xii. 301
Tufthunt, Tom, in Thackeray's *A Shabby Genteel Story*, xiii. 299
Tuftons, the, ix. 168
Tuke, Sir Brian (d. 1545), ii. 161
Tuke, Sir Samuel (d. 1674), vii. 518; *Adventures of Five Hours*, viii. 16, 130, 131, 421, 423
Tulkinghorn, Mr, in *Bleak House*, xiii. 329
Tulliver, Mr and Mrs, in *The Mill on the Floss*, xiii. 392
Tulliver, Maggie, in *The Mill on the Floss*, xiii. 382, 392, 393
Tulliver, Tom, in *The Mill on the Floss*, xiii. 382
Tulloch, John (1823–1886), xii. 286, 464; xiv. 483
Tulloch, William Weir, xiv. 516
Tullus Aufidius, in *Coriolanus*, v. 198
Tully, in *The Palice of Honour*, ii. 261. *See, also*, Cicero
Tully's *Offices*, ix. 274
Tuman-bey, in *Tomumbeius*, vi. 301
Tunbridge school, xiv. 388
Tunbridge Wells, viii. 159, 262; x. 207; xi. 347
Tundale, The Vision of, xiv. 306
Tungland, flying friar of, ii. 255
Tunis, ix. 245
Tunstall, Cuthbert (1474–1559), iii. 7, 40, 42
Tupper, Martin Farquhar (1810–1889), xiii. 147, 201, 510; *Crock of Gold, The*, xiii. 149; *Proverbial Philosophy*, xiii. 148 ff.
Turbervil, Henry (d. 1678), *Manual of Controversies*, viii. 47
Turbervile, George (1540?–1610), iii. 177, 186, 187, 190, 201, 204, 209, 283 ff., 510; iv. 389, 446, 541; viii. 224, 225
Booke of faulconrie, iv. 373
Epitaphs, Epigrams, and Sonets, iii. 187, 524
Green that you wish me wear, The, iii. 187
Heroical Epistles of...Ovid, trans., iii. 187; iv. 19, 439
Lover, The, iii. 187
Noble arte of venerie or hunting, iv. 374
Pretie epigram of a scholer, iii. 187
Rayling Rout of Sycophants, To the, iii. 187
Tragical Tales, iv. 7, 442
Translations of Mancinus's *A Plaine Path to Perfect Vertue*, Mantuan's *Eclogues*, iii. 187
'Turbulent, Mr,' x. 254
Turenne, Henri de la Tour d'Auvergne, vicomte de, vii. 452; viii. 202
Turgenev, Ivan, *The Jew*, ix. 39
Turgesius, Norwegian conqueror of Ireland, in *Albion's England*, iv. 136
Turgis, or Clarges, Miss, wife of Giles Dury, vii. 363
Turgot (d. 1115), i. 451
Turgot, Anne-R.-J., *Réflexions*, x. 336
Turin, iv. 277; x. 323
Turk, A (Defoe), ix. 19
Turk, Milton Haight, *Legal Code of Alfred*, i. 97
Turk, the Great, v. 97
Turkestan, ii. 79; ix. 248
Turkey, iv. 89, 325; vii. 200, 201; viii. 137, 308; ix. 247, 248; xii. 42; xiv. 135, 179, 182
Turkey company, the, iv. 98; ix. 240
Turkish captain, in *A Challenge for Beautie*, vi. 103
Turkish knight, the, in the mummers' play, v. 33

Turkish language and literature, IX. 245; XII. 342; XIV. 458
Turkish Spy, IX. 19
Turks, in *The Renegado*, VI. 155
Turks, the, II. 330; VII. 442, 449, 453; VIII. 286; IX. 6; XII. 38, 45
Türlin, H. von dem, I. 269
Turnament of Totenham, I. 366, 480; II. 501
Turnbull, Arthur, XI. 416
Turnbull, William (d. 1454), II. 369
Turnebus, Adrian, III. 424; VII. 307
Turner, C. L., *Original Records*, X. 384
Turner, Charles Tennyson (1808–1879), XII. 119; XIII. 23, 45 ff., 473, 478, 479
  Buoy-Bell, The, XIII. 46
  Lattice at Sunrise, The, XIII. 46
  Letty's Globe, XIII. 46
  Ocean, The, XIII. 46
  Sonnets, Old and New, XIII. 46
Turner, Daniel (1710–1798), X. 475; *Cautionary Stories* (*The Daisy, The Cowslip*), XI. 384, 476, 483
Turner, Henry Gyles, XIV. 584
Turner, Joseph Horsfall, XIII. 557, 559
Turner, Joseph Mallord William (1775–1851), II. 336; XII. 173, 346, 372, 382, 408, 409, 411; XIV. 150, 151, 154, 516, 523, 524
Turner, Mr, and Hannah More, XI. 360
Turner, Robert (*fl.* 1640–1664), VII. 509
Turner, Sharon (1768–1847), XIV. 51, 67, 499; *History of England*, XIV. 52; *History of the Anglo-Saxons*, XII. 344
Turner, Thomas, VII. 515
Turner, W. (?), VI. 483
Turner, Whitely, XIII. 559
Turner, William, dean of Wells (d. 1568), III. 81, 474; IV. 542; VIII. 479
  Endightment against Mother Messe, III. 81
  Examination of the Mass, III. 81
  Hunting of the Fox, The, III. 81
  Hunting of the Wolf, The, III. 81
  New herball, IV. 374, 403
Turner, William (1761–1859), XIII. 372
Turnop, in *John a Kent*, V. 317
Turnus (Vergil's), III. 305
Turton, Thomas (1780–1864), bishop of Ely, XII. 325, 478, 481, 491; XIV. 593, 599
Tuscany, II. 119
Tusculum. *See* Nicholas of
Tusser, Thomas (1524?–1580), III. 183 ff., 281, 285, 510; IV. 371, 407, 513; V. 480; VIII. 223, 231; XII. 416
  Conditions of Husbandrie, The, III. 184
  Five Hundreth pointes of good husbandry, III. 183; IV. 370, 375
  Hundreth good pointes of husbandrie, A, III. 183; IV. 370
  Hundreth good poynts of huswifery, III. 183
  Ladder to Thrift, The, III. 184
  Things Thriftie, III. 184
Tutchin, John (1661?–1707), VIII. 411; IX. 8; *The Observator*, IX. 5
Tutin, John Ramsden, XI. 406, 411
Tutivillus, the merry devil, V. 44, 47, 52, 56
Tuvill, David, IV. 524; *Essayes morall and theologicall*, IV. 345; *Essayes politicke and morall*, IV. 345
Twa Corbies, The, II. 412
Twain, Mark, *The Prince and the Pauper*, III. 104
'Twas within a Furlong of Edinburgh Town, IX. 363
Tweddell, George Markham, XII. 415
Tweddell, John (1769–1799), XI. 429
Tweed, river, II. 88, 90, 100; IV. 303, 304; VII. 208; X. 110; XII. 11
Twelfth Day Gift, XI. 376
Twelfth Night feast, VII. 12
Twells, Leonard (d. 1740), IX. 529
Twelve Tables, the, III. 113
Twemlow, in *Our Mutual Friend*, XIII. 337
Twickenham, VII. 21; IX. 77, 78, 163, 246, 250, 448; X. 360
Twineall, in Mrs Inchbald's *Such Things Are*, XI. 278
Twining, Thomas (1735–1804), XII. 494
Twiss, Horace (1787–1849), XIV. 509
Twisse, William (1578?–1646), VII. 482, 484
Twist, Oliver (Dickens's), XIII. 316
'Twitcher, Jemmy,' X. 397
Two Noble Kinsmen, The, V. 236, 238, 255 ff., 442, 444
Twrch Trwyth (Nennius's *porcus Troit*), I. 247, 254
Twyford, in Motteux's *Rabelais*, IX. 272
Twyn, John, IX. 2; XI. 313
Twyne, Brian (1579?–1644), VII. 247; IX. 346, 347, 540
Twyne, Lawrence (*fl.* 1576), IV. 449
Twyne, Thomas (1543–1613), III. 448; IV. 436, 440, 445, 447; *Phisicke against Fortune*, VI. 378, 390, 498
Twysden, Sir Roger (1597–1672), IX. 344, 540
Twysdens, the, IX. 168
Tyb, in *Johan Johan*, V. 98
Tydd St Giles, X. 377
Tyerman, Luke, X. 518
Tyers, Thomas (1726–1787), IX. 438; X. 471
Tyke, in Morton's *School of Reform*, XI. 281
Tyler, Josiah, XIV. Add. 10
Tyler, Miss, XI. 155
Tyler, Wat, I. 369; II. 346
Tyll Howleglas. See *Howleglass*
Tymme, Thomas (d. 1620), IV. 442
Tynan, Katharine. *See* Hinkson, Katharine Tynan
Tyndale, William. *See* Tindale
Tyndall, John (1820–1893), XIV. 261, 554, 557
Tyndarus, in *The Jealous Lovers*, VI. 325
Tyne, river, XII. 10
Typhon, IX. 502
Typographical Antiquities, II. 319
Týr (Old Norse alphabet), I. 10

Tyre, in *King Alisaunder*, I. 307
Tyrol, XI. 27; XII. 369; XIV. 294
Tyrold, Sir Hugh, in Burney's *Camilla*, X. 65
Tyrone, county, XIV. 314
Tyrone, earl of. *See* O'Neill, Hugh
Tyros Roving Megge, IV. 519
Tyrrell, Elizabeth, lady, IV. 434
Tyrrell, George (1861–1909), XII. 461, 470; *Nova et Vetera*, XII. 299
Tyrrell, James (1642–1718), VII. 475; IX. 233, 506
Tyrrell, Robert Yelverton (1844–1914), XII. 338, 494; XIV. 211, 538, 573
Tyrrell family, II. 81
'Tyrtaeus of the United Irishmen,' XIV. 310
Tyrwhit, W., IV. 525
Tyrwhitt, Thomas (1730–1786), II. 22, 160, 163 ff., 198, 207, 215, 217; V. 277; X. 241, 485, 491; XI. 250, 251, 255, 333; XII. 494; *Essay on the Language...of Chaucer*, X. 241; *Introductory Discourse to the Canterbury Tales*, X. 241
Tysilio's *Brut*, I. 235, 263
Tyssot de Patot, S., IX. 428
Tytan, in *The Golden Age*, VI. 93
Tytler, Alexander Fraser, lord Woodhouselee (1747–1813), X. 510; XIV. 94; *Roman History*, XII. 301
Tytler, James (1747?–1805), XIV. 535; *Bonnie Brucket Lassie*, XI. 235; *I hae laid a Herring in Saut*, XI. 235
Tytler, Patrick Fraser (1791–1849), XIV. 499; *History of Scotland*, XIV. 94, 95
Tytler, William (1711–1792), II. 241; XIV. 94; *Inquiry as to the Evidence...against Mary Queen of Scots*, X. 288, 465, 505
Tyton, Francis (*fl.* 1649–1669), XI. 316

Uath Mac Denomain, giant in *Fled Bricrend*, I. 327
Ubaldini, cardinal, IV. 259
Ubbe, in *Havelok*, I. 304
Udall or Uvedale, John (1560?–1592), III. 183, 376 ff., 383 ff., 389 ff., 397, 539, 552; IV. 494; *Demonstration of Discipline, A*, III. 380, 384; *Dialogue concerning the strife of our Church, A*, III. 376; *Diotrephes*, III. 377, 378, 380, 381, 389
Udall, Nicholas (1505–1556), IV. 440, 443, 444; V. 102, 103 ff. (main entry), 111, 407; VII. 327, 328; *Ezechias*, V. 70; VI. 298, 479; *Floures for Latine Spekynge*, V. 104; *Ralph Roister Doister*, III. 448; IV. 115; V. 104 ff., 108, 111, 113, 117, 119; VI. 14
Ueberweg, F., *History of Philosophy*, I. 211
Uffenbach, Z. Conrad von, IX. 574; XII. 488
Uganda, XIV. 254
Ugolino, count (Dante's), V. 324; XII. 396
Ugolino, *Philogena*, V. 101
Ulfilas, bishop of the West Goths (b. 311?), I. 7
Ulloa, A. de, XIV. 552
Ulrici, Hermann, V. 305
Ulster, VII. 211, 212; IX. 301
Ulstermen, XIV. 310
Ulysses, III. 181, 293; IX. 60, 256, 259; XIII. 450
Ulysses, in *Confessio Amantis*, II. 149
Ulysses, in *The Four Ages*, VI. 92
Ulysses, in *Thersites*, V. 108
Ulysses, in *Troilus and Cressida*, IV. 298 V. 167, 196
Ulysses (Tennyson's), XIII. 29
Una, in *The Faerie Queene*, II. 234; III. 232, 234, 236, 237; XII. 87
Underdowne, Thomas (*fl.* 1566–1587), *Aethiopian Historie*, IV. 3, 19, 436; *Ovid*, IV. 19, 438, 439
Underhill, Cave (1634–1710?), VIII. 151
Underhill, George Frederick, IX. 164
Underhill, Thomas (*fl.* 1650–1665), XI. 316
Underwood (actor), VI. 277
Underwood (pamphleteer), VII. 356
'Unicorn,' the (ship), IV. 107
Uniformity, Act of (1662), VII. 321
Uniformity, acts of, XIV. 402
Unitarian histories, X. 519
United Irishman, The, XIV. 325
United Provinces, or Dutch republic, VIII. 384
United States of America, XI. 47 ff., 72; XIII. 88, 295; XIV. 49, 66, 72, 143, 293, 318, 321, 324, 344, 346, 434
United States of America, ballads in, II. 396
United States Catalog, XII. 520
Unity (a house), in *Piers the Plowman*, II. 27, 28
Universal Chronicle, or Weekly Gazette, X. 178, 461, 467
Universal Laughter, IX. 567
Universal Review, The, XIII. 450, *also see* Add. 1
Universal Spectator, The, IX. 433
Universal Visiter, The, X. 177, 183, 466
Universities, Act of Incorporation, III. 421
Universities, Reports on, XIV. 602, 603
Universities, schools and scholarship in the 16th century, English, III. 418 ff., 549 ff.
Universities and Public Schools to the time of Colet, II. 341 ff., 487 ff.
University dramas, V. 394; VI. 232, 293–327, 468 ff.
University Maga, The (Edinburgh), XIV. 210
University tutorial classes, XIV. 409
University wits, V. 121–141 (main entry), 181, 186, 414 ff.
Unnion and Valentine, in *The Tatler*, IX. 34
Unthrifts, Ballad against, III. 87, 474
Unwin, Mary (1724–1796), XI. 80, 81, 83, 85, 88, 90, 404
Unwin, Morley (d. 1767), XI. 80

Unwin, William Cawthorne (1745?–1786), xi. 91
Upcott, William (1779–1845), viii. 242; xii. 507
'Upheaving of Ælfred, The,' x. 219
Upper Ossory, Anne, countess of (d. 1804), x. 247 ff., 255, 495
Uppingham school, vii. 340; xiv. 426
Upplönd (Norway and Sweden), i. 26
Upsala, x. 135
Upton, John (1707–1760), v. 273; ix. 479; *Critical Observations on Shakespeare*, ix. 145; editions of Epictetus and Spenser's *Faerie Queene*, ix. 145
Upton, Nicholas (1400?–1457), ii. 318; *De officio militari*, iv. 376
Ural mountains, xiv. 294
Urania, xii. 74, 114
Urania, in *Cupid's Revenge*, vi. 128
Uranus, planet, xiv. 264
Urbain, Charles, iv. 500
Urban IV, v. 12
Urban V, ii. 49
Urban VI, ii. 56
Urban, Erich, *Owenus und die deutschen Epigrammatiker des XVII Jahrhunderts*, iv. 267
'Urban, Sylvanus,' x. 162; xii. 428
Urbino, vi. 48, 204
Ureisun of ure Louerde, On, i. 233, 459
Urfé, Honoré d', x. 14; *Astrée*, viii. 14
Uriah, i. 93
Urian, in Arthurian legend, i. 259
Urie, Robert, xi. 341
Urien, lord of Rheged, i. 249
Urizen (Blake's), xi. 190, 193 ff.
Urquhart, Alexander (*fl.* 1660), vii. 254
Urquhart, David (1805–1877), xiv. 137, 512, 514
Urquhart, John (1808–1827), xii. 523
Urquhart, Sir Thomas (1611–1660), i. 69; ii. 103; iv. 8; vii. 232, 237, 253 ff., 464; viii. 59, 372, 385; ix. 271
Ekskubalauron, vii. 255, 258
Epigrams, vii. 255
Gargantua, vii. 256
Logopandecteision, vii. 255, 258
Pantagruel, vii. 256
Pantochronocanon, vii. 255
Rabelais, translation of, vii. 254, 255, 258
Trissotetras, vii. 255
Urquhart, Sir Thomas, senior, vii. 253
Urry, John (1666–1715), ii. 162; *Chaucer*, xi. 322
Ursa Major, constellation of, viii. 68
Ursely, Mistress, in *The Rival Friends*, vi. 324
Urson, John, in *The Masque of Augures*, vi. 362
Ursula, in Layamon, i. 237
Ursula, the pig woman, in *Bartholomew Fayre*, vi. 23
Urthona, in Blake's *Vala*, xi. 195
Ury, viii. 111
'Usagers,' the, x. 356
Useful Knowledge, society for the Diffusion of, xiv. 409
Usener, H., ii. 407
Ushant, iv. 79
Ushaw college, xiv. 53
Usher, House of, in *Little Dorrit*, xiii. 331
Usk, Thomas (d. 1388), *The Testament of Love*, i. 394; ii. 159, 162, 164, 166, 469
Usk, river, vii. 37, 38
Ussher, James (1581–1656), archbishop of Armagh, iv. 239, 305, 433, 434, 513; vii. 32, 33, 46, 105, 124, 139, 148, 153, 308, 312, 315 ff., 427, 477, 483, 485, 489; viii. 268; ix. 233, 530; xiv. 308, 572; *A Body of Divinitie*, vii. 149; *Annales Veteris et Novi Testamenti*, xiv. 309; Greek works, vii. 316
Usuard, i. 81
Usuria, in Arbuthnot's *History of John Bull*, ix. 134
Usurped Power, in *Kynge Johan*, v. 65
Usury, tracts on, iv. 509 ff., 518
Uter Pendragon, v. 251
Uther, in Arthurian legend, i. 259, 315
Uther Pendragon, in *The Birth of Merlin*, v. 250
Utilitarian society (Mill's), xiv. 14
Utopia, iv. 73, 245; vii. 378; xiii. 361
Utrecht, ii. 310; vi. 260; ix. 331, 335, 336; x. 191
Utrecht, congress of, ix. 135
Utrecht, peace of, ix. 69, 171, 218, 226, 228
Utrecht Psalter, xii. 516
Uttoxeter, xi. 340

'V,' *pseud. See* Clive, Caroline Archer
Vaal, river, xiv. 372
Vacarius, ii. 34, 350
Vafþrúðnismál, i. 62
Vagabond literature, iii. 492
Vagatorum, Liber, iii. 102, 104, 492
Vaillant, J., viii. 466
Vain Glory, in *Mirour de l'Omme*, ii. 140
Vain Glory, in *The Example of Virtue*, ii. 227
Vala, in Blake's poems, xi. 196, 199
Valckenaer, Lodewyk Kaspar, xii. 325
Valdés, Francisco de, iv. 448
Valdes, Juan de, *A Hundred and Ten Divine Considerations*, vii. 155
Valence (Browning's), xiii. 64, 67
Valens, emperor of the eastern Roman empire, xii. 322
Valentine, in *Wit without Money*, vi. 123
Valentine, in Congreve's *Love for Love*, viii. 151, 152, 158, 164, 168
Valentine and Orson, ix. 35
Valentine and Orson, translation, ii. 324
Valentine and Orson, lost play, v. 319
Valentinian, emperor of Rome, xii. 322
Valerio, in *The Dukes Mistris*, vi. 200
Valerius, in *The Rape of Lucrece*, vi. 101
Valerius, Epistle of, to Rufinus, i. 177, 189
Valerius Maximus, ii. 129, 150, 366
Valhalla, x. 222

Valiant Welshman, The, VI. 138, 459
Valkyries, I. 40
Valla, in *The Palice of Honour*, II. 260
Valla, Filelfo, IV. 322
Valla, Laurentius, III. 6, 20, 179, 470; IV. 3; *Elegantiae*, III. 429
Valladolid, III. 422; VI. 103
Vallance, Aymer, XIII. 491, 493
Vallans, William (*fl.* 1578–1590), III. 511
Valley of the Shadow of Death, in Bunyan's *Pilgrim's Progress*, VII. 178
Vallombrosa, VIII. 23; XIII. 352
Valpy, Abraham John, XIV. 512
Valuation of gold and silver, II. 330
Vanbrugh, Giles, father of Sir J. V., VIII. 160
Vanbrugh, Sir John (1664–1726), VIII. 133, 146, 157, 159 ff. (main entry), 171, 175, 176, 396, 423, 427, 431; X. 67, 92, 211; XI. 257; XII. 443
  Confederacy, The, translation of d'Ancourt's *Les Bourgeoises à la Mode*, VIII. 162, 168
  Journey to London, A, VIII. 162
  Pilgrim, The, VIII. 120, 396
  Provok'd Wife, The, VIII. 161, 162
  Relapse or Virtue in Danger, The, VIII. 160, 163, 164, 166
  Relapse, The, XI. 268, 455
Vancouver, George (1758–1798), XIV. 244, 245, 554
Vandals, the, XIV. 302
Vandermast (Greene's), V. 136
Van Doren, C., XI. 463
Van Dyck, Sir Anthony, VII. 55
Van Dyke, Henry D., XIII. 478
Vane, Anne (1705–1736), IX. 251
Vane, Sir Henry, the elder (1589–1655), VII. 219
Vane, Sir Henry, the younger (1613–1662), VII. 115, 219, 359, 442, 447, 513
Vane, Sir Walter, VIII. 329
Vanessa. *See* Vanhomrigh, Hester
Van Helmont, J. B., VII. 394, 396
Vanhomrigh, Hester (Swift's Vanessa), IX. 97, 98, 120, 126
Vanity Fair, XIV. 340
Van Lier, XI. 403
Van Mildert, William (1765–1836), X. 359
Van Pape Jans landendes, II. 330
Vansittart, Nicholas, 1st lord Bexley (1766–1821), XIV. 512
Van Wilder, Philip, VI. 282
Vapid, in Reynolds's *Dramatist*, XI. 281
Varallo-Sesia, XIII. 450
Varchi, Benedetto, *Lezzioni*, IX. 61
Vardens, the, in *Barnaby Rudge*, XIII. 320
Varennes, XIII. 12
Varian, Ralph (*i.e.*Duncathail), XIV. 573
Varillas, Antoine, IX. 197, 478, 488; *Histoire de l'Hérésie*, VIII. 46
Varina (Miss Jane Waring), IX. 92
Variorum Dunciad, The, IX. 132
Varnhagen von Ense, Karl August, XIII. 7
Varro, Marcus Terentius, II. 129; IV. 264, 371; VIII. 11
Varronian form of satire, VIII. 36
Vasquez, Francisco, IV. 448
Vathek, in Beckford's novel, XI. 290, 291
Vatican, the, XIII. 74
Vatican decrees, the, XIV. 118
Vaughan, Charles Edwyn, XII. 404, 524; XIII. 473, 490, 491, 493
Vaughan, Henry (1622–1695), I. 232; VII. 15, 26, 37 ff. (main entry), 45, 142, 404, *also see* Add.; XI. 185; XIII. 139, 174, 191, 195
  Amoret, poems to, VII. 38, 40
  Authoris de se Emblema, VII. 47
  Burial of an Infant, The, VII. 41
  Charnel House, VII. 38
  Childhood, VII. 41
  Christ's Nativity, VII. 41
  Corruption, VII. 30, 41
  Dawning, The, VII. 41
  Eagle, The, VII. 40
  Elizabeth, Epitaph on the little lady, VII. 39
  'I saw Eternity the other night,' VII. 41
  Mount of Olives, The, VII. 39, 41
  Olor Iscanus, VII. 38, 42
  Peace, VII. 41
  Pious Thoughts and Ejaculations, VII. 42
  Poems, with the tenth Satyre of Juvenal Englished, VII. 38
  Rainbow, The, VII. 41
  Retirement, The, VII. 42
  Retreat, The, VII. 41
  Rhapsodis, on the Globe tavern, VII. 38
  Silex Scintillans, VII. 37 ff., 47
  Thalia Rediviva, VII. 41
  They are all gone into the world of light, VII. 41
  'To his retired friend, an Invitation to Brecknock,' VII. 39
  True Christmas, The, VII. 42
  World, The, VII. 41
Vaughan, Richard (1550?–1607), IV. 265
Vaughan, Richard, 2nd earl of Carbery (1600?–1686), VIII. 60
Vaughan, Robert (1795–1868), XIV. 507
Vaughan, Robert Alfred (1823–1857), XII. 427, 470
Vaughan, Thomas (1622–1666), VIII. 455; 'Eugenius Philalethes,' VII. 37, 42, 378, 405, 511
Vaughan, Thomas (*fl.* 1772–1820), XI. 281, 458
Vaughan, Thomas (*c.* 1831), XIV. 596
Vaughan, William (1577–1641), III. 306; IV. 462
Vautor, Thomas (*fl.* 1619), IV. 465
Vautrollier, Thomas (d. 1587?), IV. 400, 413
Vaux, F. B., XI. 490
Vaux, Sir Nicholas, 1st baron Vaux of Harrowden (d. 1523), III. 57
Vaux, Thomas, 2nd baron Vaux of Harrowden (1510–1556), III. 179, 189, 508; IV. 466; *Thassault of Cupid upon the fort*, III. 179; *The aged Lover renounceth love*, III. 179; *When I look back*, III. 179

Vaux, William Sandys Wright (1818–1885), XII. 513
Vavasour, in Disraeli's *Tancred*, XIII. 350
Vavasour, Elsley, in Kingsley's *Two Years Ago*, XIII. 160, 361, 365
Veal, Edward (1632?–1708), x. 385
Veale, captain, in Fielding's *Voyage to Lisbon*, x. 35
Vedas, the, XII. 502
Vega, Lope de, VIII. 128, 130, 144; *Don Lope de Cardona*, VIII. 129; *Mayor Imposibile*, VIII. 189
Vega, Luis Gutierres de la, IV. 448
Vegetius, Flavius, II. 366; IV. 440
Veitch, John (1829–1894), XI. 446; XIV. 474, 483
Veitch, William (1640–1722), XIV. 493, 507
Veitch, William (1794–1885), XII. 494
Veitia Linage, Joseph de, *The Spanish Rule of Trade to the West Indies*, IX. 278, 501
Veldener, John, of Louvain, II. 311
Veley, Margaret (1843–1887), XIII. 510
Japanese Fan, A, XIII. 181
Marriage of Shadows and other Poems, A, XIII. 180
Michaelmas Daisies, XIII. 181
Unknown Land, The, XIII. 181
Velleius Paterculus, IV. 348
Velvet-Breeches, in *A Quip for an Upstart Courtier*, III. 361
Venables, George Stovin (1810–1888), XIII. 185, 316; XIV. 535
Venantius Fortunatus, I. 8, 76
Venedotian code of laws of Wales, I. 249
Veneering, in *Our Mutual Friend*, XIII. 336, 337
Vener, lake, I. 26
Venerie de Twety, II. 318
Venetian, in *Hymenaeus*, VI. 304
Venetian, the, in *The Fyrste Boke of the Introduction of Knowledge*, III. 105
Venetian ambassador's chaplain's account of Jonson's *Pleasure Reconciled*, VI. 360
Venezuela, XI. 72
Venice, II. 79; III. 5, 167; IV. 63, 68, 69, 90, 163, 216, 250, 256, 322, 353; V. 71; VI. 148, 157, 174; VII. 16, 100, 192, 197, 198, 200, 208, 437, 442, 449; IX. 150, 245; X. 119, 274, 496; XII. 33 ff., 49, 52, 63, 365, 396; XIII. 61, 104, 135, 397, 402; XIV. 216, 368
Venice, republic of, XI. 114
Venice, Rezzonico palace, XIII. 84
Venn, Henry (1725–1797), IX. 313; X. 365; XII. 473
Venn, John (1759–1813), XII. 281
Venn, John (1834–1923), VII. 320; XII. 471
Venn, Thomas, captain, IV. 462
Venning, Ralph (1621?–1674), VII. 316
Ventum, Harriet, XI. 490
Venus, II. 219, 261, 392, 393; III. 17; IV. 196; VII. 370; VIII. 70; IX. 153
Venus, in *Confessio Amantis*, II. 135, 146, 148, 149, 150
Venus, in *Reason and Sensuality*, II. 202
Venus, in *The Golden Targe*, II. 253
Venus, in *The Hue and Cry after Cupid*, VI. 346, 347
Venus, in *The Kingis Quair*, II. 242
Venus, in *The Masque of Christmas*, VI. 358, 359
Venus, in *The Palice of Honour*, II. 260, 261
Venus, in *The Passetyme of Pleasure*, II. 225, 229
Venus, in *The Temple of Glass*, II. 203
Venus, in *The Testament of Cresseid*, II. 248
Venus, in *Troiane*, V. 69
Venustulus, in *The Rambler*, X. 172
Verard, Antoine, books published by, II. 328, 329; III. 56
Verbruggen, John (*fl.* 1688–1707?), VIII. 191
Vercelli Book, The, I. 12, 53, 54, 56, 61, 430
Verden, IX. 231
Vere, Aubrey de, 20th earl of Oxford (1626–1703), IX. 150
Vere, Edward de, 17th earl of Oxford (1550–1604), III. 351, 508; IV. 113, 117, 466; *If women would be fair*, III. 189; 'What cunning can expresse,' IV. 116
Vere, Sir Francis (1560–1609), VI. 166; VII. 453
Vere, Sir Horace, baron Vere of Tilbury (1565–1635), VII. 453
Vere, John de, 13th earl of Oxford (1443–1513), in the *Paston Letters*, II. 305
Verelst, Harry (d. 1785), XIV. 334, 580
Verges, in *Much Ado about Nothing*, V. 191, 362
Vergil, I. 68, 71 ff., 75, 76, 192, 209, 227, 258, 330; II. 97, 175, 231, 240, 258, 259, 261 ff., 275, 308, 331, 339, 360, 486; III. 19, 20, 24, 62, 65, 113, 119, 157, 178, 200, 218, 219, 221, 223, 224, 226, 230, 234, 264, 300, 304, 305, 347, 416; IV. 16 ff., 21 ff., 121, 138, 169, 250, 252, 264, 329, 414, 440, 516, 527; VI. 197, 225; VII. 59, 68, 138, 263, 267, 268, 271, 334, 366, 503; VIII. 10, 44, 65, 69, 372, 375, 446; IX. 43 ff., 59, 69, 256, 338, 359, 372, 434, 435, 473, 486, 487, 500, 502, 561; X. 102, 114, 117, 305, 475, 493, 509; XI. 2, 426, 433; XII. 67, 76, 326, 329, 337, 422, 476, 482, 484, 486, 489, 490, 493, 495, *also see* Add.; XIII. 45, 123, 173, 175, 312, 380; XIV. 135, 303, 374
Aeneid, I. 258, 284, 285; II. 175, 316; III. 178, 185, 304; VI. 298, 303; VII. 52, 61, 66, 86, 117, 133, 300, 451; VIII. 9, 50, 67, 70, 77; IX. 188, 257, 258; X. 231; XI. 34; XIII. 125, 126
Bucolics, III. 62
Eclogues, VI. 364; VIII. 216; the second, III. 264; IV. 120
Georgics, VI. 235, 364; VIII. 50, 216; X. 96, 104, 196
O fortunatos nimium, X. 111
Vergil, in *The Palice of Honour*, II 260

Vergil, in *The Poetaster*, VI. 18, 42, 44
Vergil, Polydore (1470?–1555?), III. 314, 532; VII. 203; *History*, II. 260
Verinus, Michael, IV. 267
Veritas, in the *Coventry Plays*, V. 21
Veritas, in *Time's Complaint*, VI. 320
Veritas (=Christ), in Wyclif's *Dialogus*, II. 65
Veritie, in *Ane Pleasant Satyre*, III. 125, 126
Vermigli. *See* Martyr, Peter
Vernagu, I. 302
Verneuil, John (1583?–1647), VII. 309
Verney, Sir Edmund (1590–1642), VII. 194, 195
Verney, Sir Edmund, the younger (1616–1649), VII. 196
Verney, Edward, VII. 194
Verney, Francis, VI. 479
Verney, Mary, VII. 194
Verney, Sir Ralph (1613–1696), VII. 195, 196, 440
Verney, Ralph, 2nd earl Verney (1712?–1791), XI. 5, 6
Verney, Tom, VII. 196
Verney Family, Letters, Papers and Memoirs of the, VII. 194, 195, 439
Vernon, Diana, in Scott's *Rob Roy*, XII. 17, 22, 26
Vernon, Edward, admiral (1684–1757), X. 36; XIV. 201, 243
Vernon, lady Susan, in Jane Austen's *Lady Susan*, XII. 233
Vernon MS., I. 475
Vernon MS., poems of, III. 274
Verona, VII. 9
Verona, congress of, XII. 38
Verrall, Arthur Woolgar (1851–1912), XII. 332, 333, 494; XIV. 208
Verres, Gaius, XI. 17
Verrier, Paul, XIII. 513
Versailles, VIII. 132; IX. 153; XI. 21, 189; XII. 185
Verses addressed to the Imitator of Horace, IX. 85, 251
Verstegen, Richard. *See* Rowlands, Richard
Vertewis of the Mess, The, II. 284
Vertot, Aubert de, X. 319
Vertue, George (1684–1756), X. 253; XIV. 214
Vertues, the, in *The Muses Looking-Glasse*, VI. 233
Verulam, in *The Ruines of Time*, III. 241
Vesalius, Andreas, III. 421; VIII. 349
Vesey, Agmondesham, X. 261, 264; XI. 344 ff.
Vesey, Mrs Elizabeth (1715–1791), X. 261, 264; XI. 344 ff., 348, 362 ff., 473
Vesey, Sir Thomas (1668?–1730), XI. 344
Vesey-Neroni, signora (Trollope's), XIII. 422
Vespasian, emperor, IV. 14; XIV. 309
Vespucci, Americo, III. 18
Vestiarian controversy, III. 34
Vesuvius, XIII. 460; XIV. 247
'Veteran' (Junius), X. 405
Veterano, in *The Antiquary*, VI. 239
Vetusta Monumenta, XII. 506
Vholes, Mr, in *Bleak House*, XIII. 329
Vicars, John (1580?–1652), IV. 266, 502; VIII. 67
Vicars, Thomas (*fl.* 1607–1641), *The Madnesse of Astrologers*, IV. 535; VII. 509
Vicary, Thomas (d. 1561), III. 107, 494
Viccars, John (1604–1660), *Against William Li-Lie*, VII. 509
Vice, the, in *Horestes*, V. 64, 65
Vice, the, in *Jacke Jugeler*, V. 107
Vice, the, in *Looke about you*, V. 320
Vice, the, in stage plays, VI. 285, 297
Vice, the, Mery-reporte, in *The Play of the Wether*, V. 94
Vice, the, of the moralities, V. 56, 106, 113
Vice Ambidexter, in *Cambises*, V. 64
Vicentine hills, XIV. 293
Vicenza, III. 6
Vicenza, olympic academy at, V. 62
Vices, in *Mirour de l'Omme*, II. 140 ff.
Vices, the, in *Pathomachia*, VI. 324
Vices and Virtues, I. 228, 459
Vices et des Vertus, Li Livres roiaux des, I. 354
Vices et des Vertus, Somme des, II. 139, 315
Viciis, Summa seu Tractatus de, I. 355
Vickers, Robert, XIV. 595
Victor, Benjamin (d. 1778), X. 442, 443; XI. 449
Victoria, Australia, XIV. 319
Victoria, in *Fedele and Fortunio*, V. 315
Victoria, a Latin comedy, IV. 477
Victoria, lake, XIV. 192
Victoria, queen of Great Britain, VIII. 358; XI. 386; XII. 292, 311; XIII. 342, 487; XIV. 111, 170
Victoria, St, I. 75
Victoria County Histories, XII. 346
Victorian age, the, X. 142; XIII. 1, 22, 23, 85, 98, 137, 386, 451; XIV. 47, 65, 138, 159
Victorian drama, XIV. 173
Victorian humour, XI. 281
Victorian liberals, XIII. 16
Victorian literature, XIII. 243, 244
Victorian novels, XIII. 384, 391, 408, 409, 423, 444, 456
Victorian writers, XII. 95, 106, 177
Victory, The, VIII. 202
Vida, Marco Girolamo (*c.* 1489–1566), III. 290, 292; IV. 261; IX. 70; *Art oj Poetry*, IX. 188, 189, 486
Vida's Game of Chess, X. 480
Vidocq, Eugène François, *Mémoires*, XIII. 437
Vie de Seint Auban, XII. 515
Vienna, IV. 163; V. 283, 298, 299, 306; VII. 453; VIII. 330; IX. 6, 244; X. 323; XI. 274; XIV. 247
Vienna, congress of, XII. 39
Vietor, I. 57
Views of Cottages and Farmhouses in England and Wales, XIV. 222

Vigani, John Francis (1650?–1712), IX. 335, 412
Vígfússon, Gúdbrandr (1828–1889), XIV. 497
Vigny, Alfred de, V. 302; X. 486; XII. 398
Vigo, X. 291
Vigors, Nicholas Aylward (1785–1840), XIV. 288
Viking club, XII. 355
Viljoen, Ben J., XIV. Add. 10
Vilkina Saga, I. 32, 35
Villafranca, XIII. 73
Village, The (1783), X. 471
Village festivals, V. 24
Village Politics, XI. 362
Villanegas, Matilda de, in Lewis's *The Monk*, XI. 303
Villanus, in *Fucus Histriomastix*, VI. 324
'Villario,' in Pope's *Epistles*, IX. 81
Villemain, A. F., XII. 398
Villeroy, in Southerne's *Fatal Marriage*, VIII. 191, 192
Villiers, Barbara, countess of Castlemaine, duchess of Cleveland (1641–1709), VIII. 16, 143, 263, 264
Villiers, C. P., XIV. 513
Villiers, Edward, 1st earl of Jersey (1656–1711), IX. 149, 150
Villiers, Frederick, XIV. 535
Villiers, George, 1st duke of Buckingham (1592–1628), II. 118, 279, 282, 293; V. 288, 289, 347; VI. 149, 360; VII. 5, 17, 187, 198, 205, 219, 222, 306, 381, 434, 438, 439, 440, 451
Villiers, George, 2nd duke of Buckingham (1628–1687), VII. 63; VIII. Add.; IX. 203, 222, 476; VIII. 91, 97, 175, 208, 215, 369, 373, 376, 380, 403, 410, 411; *Advice to a Painter*, VIII. 92; *Poetical Reflections, etc., by a Person of Quality*, VIII. 39, 408; *The Rehearsal*, VII. 63; VIII. 17, 20, 21, 25, 26, 34, 48, 118, 402; IX. 147, 161; XI. 272
Villiers, George W. F., 4th earl of Clarendon (1800–1870), XIV. 131, 509
Villon, François, II. 205, 251, 257, 258, 401; XIII. 133, 211; *Ballade des Dames du temps jadis*, XIII. 118; *Le Grant et le petit Testament*, III. 85, 483
Vilvain, Robert (1575?–1663), VII. 517
Vilvorde, III. 43
Vincent, Mrs (*fl.* 1760), XI. 260
Vincent, Mrs, in Mrs Oliphant's *Salem Chapel*, XIII. 431
Vincent, Thomas (*fl.* 1627–1648), VI. 479
Vincent, Thomas (1634–1678), X. 386
Vincent, William (1739–1815), XI. 157; XII. 495; XIV. 598
Vincent de Beauvais, *Speculum* of, II. 80
Vincentio Saviolo his Practise, III. 344
Vindication of Mr Weld, A, VII. 506
Vinegar family, in *The Champion*, X. 23
Vines, Sydney Howard, XIV. 562
Vinet, Alexandre Rodolphe, XII. 283
Vinogradoff, Sir Paul, XIV. 494; *Villainage in England*, XIV. 51, 68
Vint, Mercy, in Reade's *Griffith Gaunt*, XIII. 425, 426
Vintners, The retayling, IV. 513
Viola, in *The Coxcombe*, VI. 120, 123, 133
Viola, in *Twelfth Night*, V. 126, 169, 193; VI. 126, 305; VIII. 145
Violante, in *The Gamester*, VI. 202
Violante, in *The Spanish Curate*, VI. 139
Violante, in *The Triumph of Love*, VI. 120
Violetta, in Cumberland's *Brothers*, XI. 264
Viret, P., IV. 448
Virgilius, The Lyfe of, II. 329, 486
Virgilius Restauratus, IX. 138
Virgin cult, I. 220, 223, 231, 232, 362. *See, also, under* Mary
Virgin Mary. *See* Mary, the Blessed Virgin
Virgin Mary, in *Mirour de l'Omme*, II. 141
Virgin Mary, Hymn to, in *Speculum Christiani*, II. 319
Virginia, in *Appius and Virginia*, VI. 182
Virginia, in *Confessio Amantis*, II. 152
Virginia, colony and state of, II. 396; III. 327; IV. 75, 81, 94 ff., 104, 513; V. 347; VI. 48, 355; VII. 50, 52, 70, 453; VIII. 142; X. 270; XI. 12
Virginia company, the, IV. 311; VII. 153
Virginian princes and priests, in Chapman's *Masque*, VI. 355
Virginius, in *Appius and Virginia*, VI. 182
Virginius, in Knowles's drama, XIII. 261
Virgins Complaint for the Losse of their sweethearts, The, VII. 386
Virginus, in Hall's *Virgidemiarum*, IV. 331
'Virro,' in Pope's *Epistles*, IX. 81
Virtue, in *The Example of Virtue*, II. 227
Virtues, in *Pathomachia*, VI. 324
Virtues, the seven, in *Mirour de l'Omme*, II. 141
Viry, comtesse de, X. 126
Vischer, cartographer (*fl.* 1610), *View of London*, VI. 260, 261
Vischer, Friedrich Theodor, V. 305
Visconti, Bernabo, II. 158
Vishnu Purana, The, XII. 503
Visions of Tundale, The, II. 504
'Visto,' in Pope's *Epistles*, IX. 81
Vistula, in Ohthere, I. 94
Vistula, the, in *Widsith*, I. 35
Visus, in *Lingua*, VI. 315
Vita de Do-best, in *Piers the Plowman*, II. 40
Vitalian, pope, I. 380
Vitelli, in *The Renegado*, VI. 155, 157
Vitelli, Cornelio, III. 5, 6
Vitellius, IV. 14
Vitruvius, IV. 416
Vitry, de, in *Thierry and Theodoret*, VI. 138
Vitry, Jacques de, III. 489
Vittoria, in Webster's *The White Divel*, VI. 175, 176, 185, 186; XII. 68
Vittoria (George Meredith's), XIII. 445, 446
Vives, Johannes Ludovicus (1492–1540), III. 429, 436, 470; IV. 9, 448; VII. 482, 486; *De Institutione Christianae Feminae*, VIII. 125
Vivian, I. 238

Vivian, in Lytton's *The Caxtons*, XIII. 420
Viviani, Emilia, XII. 73, 74
Vizetelly, Henry (1820–1894), XIV. 535
Vogan, Thomas Stuart Lyle, XII. 473
Vogler, Abt (Browning's), XIII. 78
Voigt, Johan Carel, XIV. Add. 10
Voiture, Vincent, VIII. 376, 385; IX. 444, 473; *Letters of Affaires, Love and Courtship*, VII. 390, 391; VIII. 372
Volksdrama, German, V. 295
Volney, XII. 403
Volpone, in Ben Jonson's play, X. 50; XII. 68
Volscians, in *Coriolanus*, V. 198
Völsunga Saga, I. 23, 35; XIII. 125, 126
Voltaire, F. M. Arouet de, II. 191; V. 209, 288 ff., 296, 301, 302, 306, 307, 459 ff.; VII. 119; VIII. 35, 159, 261, 428; IX. 49, 153, 226, 295, 529; X. 41, 68, 69, 71, 79, 83, 86 ff., 134, 135, 190, 202, 204, 210, 279, 285, 287, 288, 303, 308, 420, 431, 434, 439, 469, 481; XI. 263, 265, 290, 291, 295, 296, 307, 309, 353, 474; XII. 177, 206, 208; XIII. 9, 52, 339, 453, 468
Almida, X. 86
Alzira, X. 82
Appel à toutes les Nations de l'Europe, V. 292, 293
Brutus, V. 288; X. 82
Candide, IV. 359; X. 49
Écossaise, L', X. 86, 429
Ériphyle, V. 288
Essai sur les Mœurs, XIV. 102
Histoire de Charles XII, X. 283
Indiscret, L', X. 86
Irène, V. 292
La Henriade, XI. 79
La Loi Naturelle, IX. 83
Letter to the Academy, XI. 354
Lettres Anglaises, X. 169
Lettres philosophiques, V. 287, 288, 294
Mahomet, V. 288; X. 81; XI. 253
Merope, X. 82, 86
Mort de César, V. 288 ff.
Nanine, X. 17, 411
Orestes, X. 86
Sémiramis, V. 288; X. 86; XI. 352
Tancred, XI. 352
Zaïre, V. 288; X. 81, 82, 118; XI. 352
Zobeide, X. 86
Volumen Britanniae, or the *Book of Britain*, I. 70 ff.
Volumnia, in *Coriolanus*, V. 198
Völundarkviða, Old Norse poem, I. 36
Volunteer movement, the, XIV. 239
Volusene, Florence (1504?–1547?), III. 470
Vondel, J. van den, VII. 423; *Lucifer*, VII. 118
Vopiscus, VI. 139
Voragine, Jacobus a (1230–1298), I. 55, 134, 343; V. 15
Vörösmarty, Michael, V. 308
Vorstius, Conrad, VII. 308
Vortigen, I. 71
Vortipor of Pembrokeshire, I. 67
Vosges, mountains, I. 33
Voss, Johann Heinrich, V. 303
Vossius, Gerardus Johannes, VII. 307
Vossius, Isaac, VII. 307, 309
Votes of Parliament, XI. 333
Vox and the Wolf, I. 366
Vox Populi, Vox Dei, III. 492
Voyage of Domingo Gonsalez, by F. Godwin, IX. 106
Voyages, burlesque and wagering, IV. 533
Vrihat-Katha, III. 494
Vril, in Lytton's *The Coming Race*, XIII. 420
Vulcan, in *The Hue and Cry after Cupid*, VI. 347
Vulcan, in *Love's Maistresse*, VI. 84
Vulcan, in *Mercury Vindicated*, VI. 357, 358
Vulcan, in *Thersites*, V. 108
Vulcan (Herrick's), VII. 13
Vulgar Errors in Practice Censured, IV. 251
Vulgate, the. *See under* Bible
Vulliamy, Mary. *See* Meredith, Mary

W. G., VIII. 9
W. H. (? William Hunnis), IV. 121
W. H. (of Shakespeare's sonnets), V. 172, 174, 225, 232
W. M., *The Man in the Moon*, IV. 337, 342, 521
W. R., IV. 2
W. R. (possibly Ralegh), III. 189
W. S., V. 238, 247, 255; VI. 62
Wace (*fl.* 1170), I. 170, 232, 234, 235 ff., 256, 263 ff., 336, 337, 343, 350, 447, 462; II. 420
Wace, Henry, XII. 317
Waddell, Peter Hately (1817–1891), XI. 437
Wadding, Luke (1588–1657), XIV. 308, 572
Waddington, Samuel, XIII. 207, 489, 510
Wade, I. 218
Wade, George (1673–1748), IX. 373
Wade, Miss, in *Little Dorrit*, XIII. 331
Wade, Thomas (1805–1875), XII. 107, 423; *Jew of Arragon, The*, XII. 119; *Mundi et Cordis...Poems and Sonnets*, XII. 119
Wade, Sir Thomas Francis (1818–1895), XII. 343, 500
Wadeson, Anthony (*fl.* 1600), *Humorous Earle of Gloster*, VIII. 126
Wadford. *See* Wodeford, William of
Wadham, Edward, *English Versification*, XIII. 247, 513
Wadington. *See* William of
Wadmore, F., XIV. 541
Wadsworth, head of Attercliffe academy, X. 386
Waes of Scotland, The, IX. 377
Wafer, Lionel (1660?–1705?), IV. 462
Wag, The, XIV. 235
Wag, Tom, in *Pendennis*, XIV. 440
Wager, Lewis (*fl.* 1566), V. 393; VI. 378, 409; *Life and Repentance of Marie Magdalene*, VI. 378, 499
'Wager,' ship, XIV. 243, 244

Wager, William (*fl.* 1566), *The longer thou livest, the more fool thou art*, v. 60, 393
Wagner, P. A., xiv. Add. 10
Wagner, Wilhelm Richard, *Lohengrin*, x. 227; *Tannhäuser*, x. 227
Wagstaff, Simon, *pseud.* of Jonathan Swift, ix. 106, 460
Wagstaff, Théophile, *pseud.* of W. M. Thackeray, xiii. 278
Wagstaffe, John (1633–1677), vii. 396; *The Question of Witchcraft debated*, vii. 395, 507
Wagstaffe, Thomas (1645–1712), x. 517; *Vindication*, x. 355; *Defence of the Vindication*, x. 355
Wagstaffe, Thomas (1692–1770), x. 355
Wagstaffe, William (1685–1725), ix. 443, 470
Wahabees, the, xiv. 253
Wainewright, Latham, xiv. 594
Wainewright, Thomas Griffiths (1794–1852), xiii. 418
Waitz, Georg, xiv. 68
Wake, Sir Isaac (1580?–1632), vi. 469
Wake, William (1657–1737), ix. 407, 509; x. 353, 354
Wakefield, v. 373; xiii. 455
Wakefield, Edward Gibbon (1796–1862), xiv. 483, 512, 514, 587, 588
Wakefield, Gilbert (1756–1801), ix. 73, 75, 443, 447, 450; x. 385; xii. 470, 495; xiv. 602; 'Diatribe,' xii. 326
Wakefield, Henry, bishop of Worcester (*fl.* 1375–1395), ii. 61
Wakefield, Mrs Priscilla (1751–1832), xi. 378, 484; xiv. 600
Instinct Displayed, xi. 383
Introduction to Botany, xi. 383
Juvenile Anecdotes, xi. 383
Leisure Hours, xi. 383
Mental Improvement, xi. 383
Wakefield, Robert (d. 1537), iii. 53
Wakefield grammar school, ix. 330
Wakefield Plays, v. 18, 46 ff.
Wakem, Philip, in *The Mill on the Floss*, xiii. 392
Wakeman, William F., xii. 513
Waking Vision, The, viii. 92
Walbrook, Herbert Mackinnon, xiii. 515
Walcheren expedition the, xiv. 115
Walcott, Mackenzie Edward Charles (1821–1880), xii. 348, 513, 520; *History of the Cathedrals...of Scotland*, xii. 349; *Traditions and Customs of Cathedrals*, xii. 349
Waldby, John, brother of R. Waldby, ii. 443
Waldby, Robert, archbishop of York (d. 1398), ii. 443
Waldef, i.e. *Waltheof*, i. 287, 472
Waldegrave, James, 2nd earl Waldegrave (1715–1763), *Memoirs*, ix. 253, 254, 498
Waldegrave, Maria, countess, afterwards duchess of Gloucester, vii. 204
Waldegrave, Robert (1554?–1604), iii. 110, 376, 378 ff., 385, 387 ff., *also see* Add.;
Waldegrave, Robert iv. 363; vi. 393; *The Four Great Lyers*, iii. 110
Waldegrave, Samuel (1817–1869), xii. 473
Waldegrave, Timothy, x. 385
Walden, Thomas de (Netter) (d. 1430), ii. 443
Waldens, the, of Edmonton, xii. 201
Waldenses, the, xiv. 79
Waldershare, in Disraeli's *Endymion*, xiii. 350
Waldhere, i. 30, 32, 33, 35, 36, 41, 277, 423
Wales, v. 27, 323, 361; vi. 310, 361; vii. 37, 42, 78, 113, 143, 197, 321; viii. 60, 106; ix. 350, 352; x. 115, 182, 277, 394; xi. 12; xii. 166, 344, 349; xiii. 372; xiv. 79, 84, 215, 292, 294, 307, 434
Wales, church of, xii. 266
Wales, Joan of Kent, princess of, ii. 56
Wales, prince of, ix. 104
Wales, prince of, in *Edward III*, v. 244
Wales, The Four Ancient Books of, i. 462; xii. 518
Wales, university of, xiv. 433
Walesby, F. P., x. 478
Walewski, count, xiv. 185
Walford, Edward, xiv. 612
Walford, L. B., xiii. Add. 3
Walgainus = Gawain, in Arthurian legend, i. 269
Walhalla, i. 63
Walker, Alexander, xiv. 533
Walker, Anthony, Εὕρηκα Εὕρηκα, *The Virtuous Woman Found*, viii. 269; *A true Account of the Author of a Book called* Εἰκὼν Βασιλική, viii. 269
Walker, A. Stoddart, xiv. 516
Walker, Clement (d. 1651), vii. 450; viii. 407
Walker, Sir Edward (1612–1677), vii. 206, 447
Walker, Ferdinand, iv. 448
Walker, George, *Anglo-Tyrannus* (1650), vii. 514
Walker, Henry, vii. 351 ff. (main entry), 358, 360, 365, 494, 498 ff., 517
Collection of passages...by one who was groom of his chamber, A, vii. 356
Collections of Notes at the Kings Tryall, vii. 355
Declaration called out of the Journals of both Houses of Parliament, A, vii. 355
Heads of a Diarie, vii. 355
History of the Life Reigne and Death of the late King Charles, vii. 353
King's Last Farewell to the World, The, vii. 353
Mad Designe, The, vii. 356
Mercurius Morbicus, vii. 355
Packets of Letters, vii. 355
Perfect Occurrences of Every Dayes Journall, vii. 352, 353
Prelates Pride, The, vii. 352
Serious Observations lately made touching his Majesty, vii. 356
Severall Proceedings, vii. 355

Walker, Henry
Terrible outcry against the loytering exalted Prelats, A, VII. 352
The true manner of the crowning of Charles the Second King of Scotland, VII. 356
To your tents O Israel, VII. 352
'Τραγήματα' *Sweetmeats*, VII. 355
Tuesdaies Journall, VII. 355
Two letters from Liverpool, VII. 354
Wren and the Finch, The, VII. 352
Walker, captain Howard, in Thackeray's *The Ravenswing*, XIII. 281
Walker, Hugh, XI. 221, 441; XII. 453; XIII. 485, 488, 544, 559, 568, *also see* Add. 2; XIV. 528; *The Literature of the Victorian Era*, XIII. 50
Walker, Mrs Hugh, XIII. 498, 568; XIV. 528
Walker, John (1674–1747), VII. 478; VIII. 407
Walker, John (1692?–1741), IX. 528
Walker, John (1732–1807), XIII. 240
Walker, Josiah, XI. 436, 441
Walker, Obadiah (1616–1699), VIII. 305; IX. 488, 569; *Oxford Theses relating to the English Reformation*, IX. 197
Walker, Patrick (d. 1745), IX. 549
Walker, Richard (1679–1764), XIV. 286
Walker, Robert (1798–1854), XIV. 596
Walker, Sidney (1795–1846), XIII. 245
Walker, W., IX. 318
Walker, William (brother of Henry Walker), VII. 353
'Walking Morte,' the, in *A Caveat or Warening for Commen Corsetors*, III. 104
Walkington, Thomas (d. 1621), III. 91; IV. 519
Walkley, Arthur Bingham, XIII. 515
Wallace, Alfred Russel (1823–1913), XI. 75; XIV. 35, 250, 298, 299, 554, 564
Wallace, Charles Wallace, VI. 256, 257, 270 ff., 275, 278
Wallace, James (d. 1688), IX. 560
Wallace, James (*fl.* 1684–1724), IX. 554
Wallace, Robert (1697–1771), IX. 562; *Various prospects of Mankind*, XI. 74
Wallace, Sir William (1272?–1305), II. 101, 103, 105, 108 ff., 280; VI. 453; XIV. 95
Wallace, William, editor of Mackintosh's *History of the Revolution*, XIV. 59
Wallace, William (1844–1897), XIV. 483; *Hegel's Philosophy of Mind*, XIV. 45; *Lectures and Essays*, XIV. 45; *Logic of Hegel, The*, XIV. 45
Wallace, William, editor of Burns, XI. 438, 439, 442
Wallace. See Harry, Blind
Wallace Craigie, near Dundee, XII. 350
Wallas, Graham, XIV. 478, 602
Wallensis, John (*fl.* 1283), I. 456
Wallensis, Thomas (d. 1255), II. 318
Wallensis, Thomas (d. 1350?), I. 456
Waller, Alfred Rayney (1867–1922), IX. 155; X. 44; XII. 167, 431; XIII. 515; XIV. 518, 519; *The Writings of Matthew Prior*, IX. 147, 148, 153, 155, 157, 158
Waller, Edmund (1606–1687), IV. 183; VI. 437; VII. 4, 48, 49, 53 ff. (main entry), 64, 67 ff., 73, 180, 183, 268, 270, 409 ff.; VIII. 5, 18, 81, 120, 133, 227, 228, 234 ff., 267, 369, 371, 376, 381, 394, 408, 410, 411, 444, 446; IX. 67 ff., 73, 157, 158; X. 226, 432, 475; XI. 246; XII. 132; XIV. 436
Aeneid, trans., VII. 86
Battle of the Summer Islands, The, VII. 55, 56
Behold the brand of beauty tossed, VII. 55, 58
Divine Poems, VII. 55
Go, lovely Rose! VII. 55, 58
Instructions to a Painter, VII. 56
Maides Tragedy, The, version of, VIII. 120
Of the Danger His Majesty [Being Prince] Escaped in the Road at St Andere, VII. 53
Of the Last Verses in the Book, VII. 56
Of the Misreport of her being Painted, VII. 55
On the Statue of King Charles I at Charing Cross, VII. 56
Panegyric to my Lord Protector, VII. 56
Pompée, version of, by Waller and lord Buckhurst, VIII. 180
Puerperium, VII. 58
Saraband, VIII. 231
To a Very Young Lady, VII. 55
To Amoret, VII. 58
Upon a Late Storm, and of the Death of His Highness ensuing in the same, VII. 56; VIII. 5
Waller, John Francis (1810–1894), XIV. 572; *Kitty Neil*, XIV. 326; *Song of the Glass, The*, XIV. 326; *Spinning Wheel Song, The*, XIV. 326
Waller, lady, wife of Sir Wm Waller, VII. 350
Waller, R., *Life of Hooke*, XIV. 283
Waller, Sir William (1597?–1668), VII. 349, 350
Wallerston, VII. 453
Walley, Henry, VII. 346; *Heads of Chiefe Passages in Parliament*, VII. 350; *The Kingdomes Weekly Account of Heads*, VII. 350; *The True Informer*, VII. 350
Walley, John (*fl.* 1557), IV. 397
Wallin, head of Bristol academy, X. 387
Wallington, Nehemiah (1598–1658), *Historical Notices*, VII. 223, 454
Wallis, F., XIV. 521
Wallis, G., XIII. 545
Wallis, John (1616–1703), VII. 288, 289, 308, 475, 489; VIII. 360, 479; IX. 386, 411, 412; XIV. 281
Arithmetica Infinitorum, VIII. 359
Doctrine of the Blessed Trinity, X. 378
English Grammar, XIII. 244
Truth tried, VII. 279
Wallis, Samuel (1728–1795), XIV. 244
Walpole, George, 3rd earl of Orford (1730–1791), X. 245, 246

Walpole, Horace, 1st baron Walpole (1678–1757), IX. 223; X. 495
Walpole, Horatio (Horace), 4th earl of Orford (1717–1797), IV. 89, 293; V. 276, 292, 478; VII. 176, 204, 443; VIII. 262, 451; IX. 143, 190, 246, 248, 250 ff., 354; X. 47, 60 ff., 87, 116, 118, 119, 123, 126, 127, 135, 136, 215, 237, 242 ff. (main entry), 256, 259, 260, 262, 268, 272, 285, 316, 362, 399, 400, 425, 450, 484 ff., 505, 523, *also see* Add.; XI. 91, 145, 154, 173 ff., 258 ff., 262, 273, 282, 341, 346, 350, 351, 356, 358, 364, 365, 429, 449, 465, 469; XII. 345; XIII. 52, 321; XIV. 62, 284
Ædes Walpolianae, X. 253
Anecdotes of Painting, X. 135, 253, 254
Castle of Otranto, The, X. 60, 61, 227, 234, 254; XI. 300; XII. 3
Catalogue of the Royal and Noble Authors, X. 184, 253
Correspondence, X. 253
Description of the Villa, X. 245
Essay on Gardening, X. 250
Historic Doubts on Richard III, IX. 131, 135, 250, 254, 291, 305
Last Journals, X. 295
Letters, X. 284, 291, 292; XI. 354, 363
Letters to George Montagu, X. 247
Letters to Mann, X. 251
Memoirs, IX. 253
Miscellaneous Antiquities, X. 131
Miscellaneous Letters, X. 247
Mysterious Mother, The, X. 254, 255
Private Correspondence, X. 247
Short Notes of My Life, X. 252, 291
Works, X. 247
Walpole, Margaret, countess of Orford, wife of 2nd earl (d. 1781), X. 246
Walpole, Sir Robert, 1st earl of Orford (1676–1745), IX. 81, 87, 115, 117, 121, 163, 165, 219 ff., 229, 230, 232, 243, 251, 252, 254, 281, 426, 433; X. 71, 84, 94, 114, 116, 243, 246, 249, 252, 256, 299, 358, 389, 428; XI. 174; XIV. 63, 128, 212
Walpole, Robert, 2nd earl of Orford (d. 1751), X. 246
Walpole, Sir Spencer (1839–1907), XIV. 499, 506; *History of England*, XIV. 93
Walpole, Hon. Thomas, 2nd son of the 1st lord Walpole of Wolterton, X. 495
Walpurgis night, VII. 368
Walsh, Benjamin Dann, XIV. 595
Walsh, Edward (1805–1850), XIV. 305, 321, 572
Walsh, John Henry, *pseud.* Stonehenge (1810–1888), XIV. 547
Walsh, Shelford, XIII. 519
Walsh, William (1663–1708), VIII. 157, 402, 411, 445, 447; IX. 68, 69, 174 ff., 487; XI. 250
Antidote, The, IX. 176
'Caelia, too late you would repent,' IX. 175
Despairing Lover, The, IX. 175
Walsh, William
Jealousy, IX. 175
Walsh, archbishop William John, XIV. 592
Walsh, William Shepherd, XIII. 568
Walsingham, Edward (*fl.* 1643–1659), VII. 454
Walsingham, Sir Francis (1530?–1590), IV. 80, 82, 382; V. 85, 345, 482; VI. 244, 249, 272, 383, 384, 392, 400; VII. 191
Walsingham, John (d. 1340?), I. 456; *The Reply of Friar Daw Thopas*, II. 40
Walsingham, Mrs, XI. 348
Walsingham, The Foundation of the Chapel of, II. 321, 486
Walsingham, Thomas (d. 1422?), II. 38, 499; *Historia Anglicana*, II. 47
Walter, archdeacon of Oxford, I. 168, 257
Walter, friend of Henry of Huntingdon, I. 167
Walter, Hubert (d. 1205), I. 173, 181; *Tractatus de Legibus et Consuetudinibus Regni Angliae*, VIII. 311
Walter, John (1739–1812), XIV. 177, 178
Walter, John (1776–1847), XIV. 174, 178 ff., 183
Walter, John (1818–1894), XIV. 183, 535
Walter, Richard (1716?–1785), XIV. 243, 554
Walter, Sir, in *A Chart Mayd in Cheapeside*, VI. 74
Walter, the steward, grandson of Banquo, II. 104
Walter, William (*fl.* 1520), books translated by, II. 325, 326; *The History of Titus and Gesippus*, II. 326; *The History of Guystarde and Sygysmonde*, II. 325; *The Spectacle of Lovers*, II. 326; III. 486
Walter de Bardes, IV. 309, 509
Walter de Bibelsworth (*fl.* 1270), II. 507
Walter de Merton (d. 1277), II. 351 ff., 355
Walter of Evesham (*fl.* 1320), I. 456
Walter of Hemingburgh (*fl.* 1300), I. 181, 450
Walter of Henley, II. 499; *Book of Husbandry*, IV. 307, 364, 369, 514, 541
Walters, John C., XIII. 537, 544
Waltham, IV. 238; XII. 186
Walthamstow, XIII. 118
Waltharius, I. 32, 33
Waltheof (d. 1076), II. 399
Walton (pirate), in *Fortune by Land and Sea*, VI. 104
Walton, Anne, VII. 250
Walton, Brian (1600?–1661), VII. 318, 319, 478, 481; *Polyglot Bible*, VII. 481; VIII. 294; list of contributors to *Polyglot Bible*, VII. 481
Walton, Christopher (1809–1877), IX. 309, 318, 328, 511, 513 ff.
Walton, Sir Edgar H., XIV. Add. 10
Walton, Izaak (1593–1683), III. 405, 406, 415; IV. 119, 124, 125, 163, 198, 199, 201, 236, 246, 373, 374, 422; VII. 27 ff., 76, 77, 82, 149, 156, 232, 250 ff. (main entry), 256 ff., 390, 402, 403, 463; VIII. 293, 295; IX. 277

Walton, Izaak
Compleat Angler, The, VII. 81, 250, 251, 253; XI. 318
Life of Donne, VII. 250
Life of Geo. Herbert, VII. 26, 29
Lives, VII. 250 ff.; X. 193
Reliquiae Wottonianae, VII. 250
Walton, James, father of Izaak Walton, VII. 250
Walton, John (*fl.* 1410), II. 499
Wanderer, in Wordsworth's *Excursion*, XI. 106
Wanderer, The, I. 4, 37, 38, 275, 372, 424, 428
Wandering Jew, The, IV. 342
Wanley, Humfrey (1672–1726), I. 45, 129, 428; IX. 356, 358, 541; XI. 336, 337, 467
Wanstead, IV. 132; VI. 336
Wantage, I. 107
Wantonness, in *Ane Pleasant Satyre*, III. 124 ff.
Wapull, George, *The Tide tarries no man*, V. 60, 393; VI. 284
Warbeck, Perkin (1474–1499), VII. 203
Warburton, Bartholomew Eliott George (1810–1852), XIV. 527, 554; *The Crescent and the Cross*, XIV. 251
Warburton, John (1682–1759), V. 146; IX. 540
Warburton, Rowland Eyles Egerton (1804–1891), X. 119; XIII. 510
Warburton, William (1698–1779), bishop of Gloucester, V. 271 ff., 278, 296; VII. 89; VIII. 295; IX. 82, 83, 86 ff., 145, 296, 297, 327, 443, 444, 447, 449, 475, 476, 509, 510, 512; X. 167, 180, 276, 305, 396, 465, 524
Alliance between Church and State, IX. 296; X. 375
'Aristarchus on the Hero of the Poem,' IX. 89
Divine Legation of Moses, IX. 296, 341
Remarks on Hume's *Natural History of Religion*, IX. 296
Shakespeare, IX. 144; XI. 320
View of Lord Bolingbroke's Philosophy, IX. 296
Warburton's cook, VI. 36, 165, 195
Ward, Sir Adolphus William (1837–1924), V. 82, 134, 254, 368; VI. 27, 283; VIII. 124, 373; IX. 30, 326; X. 80, 350, 445; XIII. 532, 549, 551; XIV. 515; *George Crabbe*, XI. 140, 141, 418, 420
Ward, Artemus (*pseud.*), XIV. 346
Ward, Edward (1667–1731), IX. 256, 258 ff., 268, 501, 502
Hudibras Redivivus, IX. 260, 261
London Spy, IX. 262, 263
Republican Procession, IX. 261
Vulgus Britannicus, IX. 260, 261
Wine and Wisdom, IX. 262
Ward, Harry Leigh Douglas (1825–1906), XII. 519; *Catalogue of Romances*, I. 191, 270
Ward, Harry Marshall (1854–1906), XIV. 564
Ward, Henry Snowden, XIII. 544
Ward, Mrs Humphry (Mary Augusta), XIII. 556, *also see* Add. 3; XIV. 533
Ward, James, of Nottingham, XIII. 499
Ward, Jem (1800–1885), XIV. 231
Ward, John (*fl.* 1613), IV. 465
Ward, John (1679?–1758), IX. 530
Ward, John William, 1st earl of Dudley (1781–1833), XIV. 126
Ward, Richard (*fl.* 1710), VIII. 279, 280, 456
Ward, Robert, *Fucus Histriomastix*, VI. 324, 327, 472, 480
Ward, Robert Plumer (1765–1846), XII. 452; XIII. 554; *Tremaine*, XIII. 350
Ward, Roger (*fl.* 1582), IV. 386, 408
Ward, Samuel, of Ratcliffe (*fl.* 1570), IV. 238
Ward, Samuel (1577–1640), VII. 318
Ward, Seth (1617–1689), bishop of Salisbury, VII. 288, 475, 517; VIII. 360, 364, 479; XIV. 281; *Vindiciae Academiarum*, IX. 386, 387, 500, 571
Ward, Thomas Humphry, XIII. 487, 488; *English Poets*, XIII. 100
Ward, Wilfrid Philip (1856–1916), XII. Add. 2; XIII. 501; XIV. 483, 507; *Life of Newman*, XII. 257, 426, 453, 456, 460, 463
Ward, William George (1812–1882), XII. 259, 271, 275, 463; XIII. 104; XIV. 483, 507, 513; *Essays on the Philosophy of Theism*, XIV. 26; *The Ideal of a Christian Church*, XII. 261, 276
Warden, Master, in *Three Speeches*, VII. 381
Wardlaw, Elizabeth, lady (1677–1727), XI. 231; *Gilderoy*, IX. 364; *Hardyknute*, II. 417; IX. 364; X. 226
Wardlaw, Henry (d. 1440), II. 367 ff.
Wardlaw, Walter (d. 1390), II. 128
Wardour, Isabella, in Scott's *Antiquary*, XII. 22
Wardour street work, XIII. 187
Ware, Christopher, the elder (1625?–1690), VII. 478, 489, 492; IX. 569
Ware, Hertfordshire, VI. 172; XII. 182
Ware, Sir James (1594–1666), VII. 481; X. 293; XII. 349; XIV. 308, *also see* Add. 3; *History of Ireland*, IV. 414
Ware, James Redding, XIV. 611
Warham, William (1450?–1532), archbishop of Canterbury, III. 9, 32, 49; VII. 326
Waring (Browning's), XIII. 186
Waring, Edward John, XII. 523
Waring, Jane (Swift's 'Varina'), IX. 92
Waring, Susan M., XIII. 559
Warinus, I. 170
Warkworth, John (d. 1500), II. 302, 482; *Chronicle*, IV. 423
Warne, Charles (1802–1887), XII. 513
Warner, Sir George Frederick, V. 248
Warner, George Townsend, XIV. 597
Warner, John (1736–1800), XIII. 245; *Metronariston*, XIII. 240, 513

Warner, John, *The Gaine of Losse* (1645), VII. 517
Warner, Mary Amelia (1804–1854), VIII. 184
Warner, Rebecca, X. 463
Warner, Richard, XII. 382
Warner, William (1558?–1609), III. 349; V. 83; *Albion's England*, III. 198, 199, 357; IV. 88, 136, 477; *Menaechmi*, IV. 4, 439; *Pan his Syrinx*, III. 350, 536
Warning for Faire Women, A, V. 81, 163, 325, 326, 398, 476; VI. 96
Warr, George Charles Winter (1845–1901), XII. 495
Warrack, Grace, II. 300, 482
Warre, Edmond, XIV. 597
Warren, Mrs Anne, XII. 452
Warren, George, *Impartial Description of Surinam* (1667), IV. 462
Warren, Hardick, VII. 509
Warren, John Byrne Leicester, 3rd lord De Tabley (1835–1895), XIII. 194, 203, 205, 206, 501; XIV. 502; *Philoctetes*, XIII. 205; *Soldier's Fortune, The*, XIII. 205
Warren, Matthew (1642–1706), X. 386
Warren, Mrs, in Holcroft's *Road to Ruin*, XI. 277
Warren, Samuel (1807–1877), XII. 452
Warren, Sir Thomas Herbert, XIII. 474, 478
Warricombe, Sidwell (Gissing's), XIII. 461
Warrington, XI. 469
Warrington, George, in *Pendennis*, XIII. 292
Warrington academy, X. 385; XIV. 51, 272, 385, 399
Warringtons, the, in *The Virginians*, XIII. 297, 298
Wars of Cyrus King of Persia, V. 398; VI. 288
Warsaw, V. 283
Warschewiczki, Stanislaus, IV. 3
Warter, John Wood (1806–1878), XI. 422; XII. 219
Warton, George, almanack maker, VII. 509
Warton, Joseph (1722–1800), IX. 443 ff., 450; X. 125, 164, 224, 238, 239, 240–241 (main entry), 473, 492, 493; *Essay on Pope*, X. 240, 466
Warton, Thomas, the elder (1688?–1745), VII. 265; X. 223, 226 ff., 492; XI. 133
Warton, Thomas, the younger (1728–1790), I. viii, 361, 377; II. 203, 205, 211, 225, 319; III. 51, 77, 157, 174, 187, 192, 193, 252; V. 71, 78, 143, 253; VI. 283, 294, 295; VII. 265; IX. 69, 73, 82, 144, 479, 574; X. 137, 184, 186, 224, 233, 238 ff. (main entry), 485, 486, 492; XI. 34, 133; XII. 133; XIV. 594, 595
History of English Poetry, X. 239; XII. 363
Pleasures of Melancholy, X. 125
Poems, X. 239
Progress of Discontent, IX. 191
Triumph of Isis, X. 136
Verses on Sir Joshua Reynolds's painted window, X. 239
Warwick, IV. 190; VIII. 291
Warwick, countesses of. *See* Rich, Mary; Rich, Penelope
Warwick, earl of, in *Henry V*, V. 262
Warwick, earls of. *See* Rich, Charles; Rich, Robert
Warwick castle, VIII. 110
Warwick school, IV. 266
Warwick's company, earl of, VI. 249
Warwickshire, II. 315; IV. 200; V. 56, 187; VII. 196; IX. 533; X. 112, 113, 271 ff., 275, 276, 278, 385; XII. 326, 441, 442; XIII. 382; XIV. 231
Warwickshire Coterie, the, X. 496
'Washer of the Ford, the,' XIV. 320
Washington, George, XI. 190
Washington, George, in *The Virginians*, XIII. 297
Waspe, in *Bartholomew Fayre*, VI. 23
Wasse, Joseph (1672–1738), IX. 340, 528
Wassel, in *The Masque of Christmas*, VI 358
Wastell, Simon (d. 1632), VII. 83
Waster, in *Piers the Plowman*, II. 14
Wastoure. See *Wynnere*
Wat, in *Piers the Plowman*, II. 12, 16
Wat, in shepherd carols, II. 378
Waterfield, William, XIV. 339, 580
Waterford, X. 257
Waterhouse, Edward (1619–1670), VIII. 466, 469; IX. 571; *An Humble Apologie for Learning*, VII. 392, 509, 517
Waterland, Daniel (1683–1740), IX. 509; X. 354, 358, 359, 516, 517; *Advice to a Young Student*, IX. 411; *Review of the Doctrine of the Eucharist*, X. 360; *Vindication of Christ's Divinity*, X. 359
Waterloo, battle of, XII. 43, 381; XIV. 66, 227
Watermen, company of, VI. 259
Watermeyer, Egidius Benedictus (1824–1867), XIV. Add. 10; *After a Storm*, XIV. 378
Waterson, Simon, IV. 398
Waterton, Charles (1782–1865), XIV. 554; *Wanderings in South America*, XIV. 249
Watkin, William Thompson (1836–1888), XII. 514; *Roman Cheshire*, XII. 347; *Roman Lancashire*, XII. 347
Watkins, John (*fl.* 1792–1831), XI. 456
Watkins, John, of Whitby, XII. 416
Watkins, Richard, IV. 384
Watling street, I. 178
Watreman, W., translator of Boehme, IV. 442
Wats, Edmond, IV. 409
Watson, Scots poet, II. 279
Watson, Christopher (d. 1581), IV. 439
Watson, David (1710–1756), IX. 528
Watson, Emma, in Jane Austen's *The Watsons*, XII. 234
Watson, Henry, apprentice to Wynkyn de Worde, books translated by:
Church of Evil Men and Women, The, II. 324

Watson, Henry
History of Olyver of Castylle and the fayre Helayne, The, II. 324
Ship of Fools, The, II. 324; III. 59
Valentine and Orson, II. 324
Watson, James (d. 1722), XI. 342, 470; *Choice Collection of...Scots Poems*, IX. 366, 367, 556, 567; X. 226; XI. 204, 217
Watson, James (1739?–1790), XIV. 216
Watson, John, XIV. 478
Watson, John (d. 1530), III. 61
Watson, John Selby (1804–1884), XII. 491, 492; *Life of Porson*, X. 317
Watson, Joshua (1771–1855), XII. 256, 454
Watson, Richard (1612–1685), VII. 188
Watson, Richard (1737–1816), bishop of Llandaff, X. 508; XI. 98, 400; XII. 279, 280; XIV. 602; *Apology for Christianity*, X. 307, 308; *Apology for the Bible*, X. 308
Watson, Richard (1781–1833), XI. 483
Watson, Robert (1730?–1781), X. 505; *History of Philip II*, X. 291; *History of Philip III*, X. 291
Watson, Robert Addison, XIII. 488
Watson, Rosamund Marriott (born Tomson) (d. 1911), XIII. 510
Watson, Seth B., XI. 415
Watson, Thomas (1513–1584), V. 394; VI. 490; *Absalom*, VI. 296, 480
Watson, Thomas (1557?–1592), III. 252, 253, 256, 257, 292, 294, 524; IV. 114, 117, 121, 171, 181, 465, 472; *Amyntas*, IV. 131; ΕΚΑΤΟΜΠΑΘΙΑ, or *The Passionate Centurie of Love*, III. 252; IV. 118, 123, 196; *Tears of Fancie, or Love Disdained, The*, III. 253
Watson, Sir William, XII. 408; XIII. 570
Watson-Wentworth, Charles, 2nd marquis of Rockingham (1730–1782), XI. 5, 7, 52; XIV. 214
Watt, James (1736–1819), XIV. 258, 381
Watt, Lauchlan Maclean, IX. Add.; XIV. 525
Watt, Robert (1774–1819), XI. 467; XII. 521, 523; *Bibliotheca Britannica*, XII. 370; *Catalogue of Medical Books*, XII. 370
Watt, William, XI. 445; *Kate Dalrymple*, XI. 243; *Tinkler's Waddin*, XI. 243
Watt of Harden, XII. 3
Watteau, Antoine, VIII. 156; XIII. 52
Watton, John, II. 319, 503
Watts, Alaric Alexander (1797–1864), XII. 423; XIII. 510; *Lyrics of the Heart*, XIII. 207
Watts, George Frederick, XIII. 474
Watts, Isaac (1674–1748), IX. 177 ff., 393, 487; X. 156, 183, 274, 374, 381, 385, 475, 521, 522; XI. 373, 383, 477, 479; XIII. 244
Divine and Moral Songs, XI. 184, 372
Divine Songs for Children, IX. 178
Elegy on Mr Thomas Gouge, IX. 178
Essay on Civil Power, X. 375
Watts, Isaac
Horae Lyricae, IX. 178
Humble attempt, X. 375
'Hush! my dear, lie still and slumber,' XI. 186
Sapphics, XI. 179
Sluggard, The, XI. 375
'When the fierce north wind,' IX. 179
Watts, John (1818–1887), XIV. 610
Watts, William (1590?–1649), VII. 345
Watts Dunton, Walter Theodore (1832–1914), IV. 35; X. 236; XI. 476; XII. 406, *also see* Add.; XIII. 137, 194, 491, 495, 510, 544, 555; XIV. 527; *Aylwin*, XIII. 207; XIV. 145; *Coming of Love, The*, XIV. 145; *Renascence of Wonder in Poetry, The*, XIV. 144
Waugh, Arthur, XIII. 478, 485, 486, 508, 533, 573
Waugh, Edwin (1817–1890), XIII. 511
Waurin, *Chroniques et istoires*, I. 236
Waverley, in Surrey, monastery and annals of, I. 178, 193, 337
Waverley, Edward, in Scott's novel, XII. 18, 22, 151
Way, Albert (1805–1874), XII. 519
Way, Arthur S., XIII. 478
Wayland, John, III. 194
Waymouth, George (*fl.* 1605), IV. 99
Waynflete, William (1395?–1486), bishop of Winchester, II. 355, 357, 359, 489; VII. 327
Waynour (Guinevere), in *Morte Arthure*, II. 118
Waynright, James, VII. 438
Wayte, William (1829–1898), XII. 495
Weakest goeth to the Wall, The, V. 316, 476
Weale, John (1791–1862), XII. 523
Weale, William Henry James, XII. 523
Wealhtheow, in *Beowulf*, I. 22, 23, 24
Wealth and Health, V. 60, 393
Weare, William (d. 1823), XIV. 201, 228, 230
Wearing of the Green, The, XIV. 311
Wearmouth, monastery of, I. 5, 71, 72, 78, 80, 83 ff., 89; IV. 418
Weathercock, in *The London Prodigall*, V. 255
Weaver, John (1673–1760), X. 440; *The Loves of Mars and Venus*, X. 70
Webb, Alfred John (1834–1908), XIV. 572
Webb, Daniel (1719?–1798), XI. 250
Webb, John (1611–1672), IX. 540
Webb, Philip, XIII. 119
Webb, Richmond, grandfather of W. M. Thackeray, XIII. 276
Webb, Thomas Ebenezer (1821–1903), XIV. 572
Webbe, George, VII. 487
Webbe, Joseph (*fl.* 1612–1633), IV. 435
Webbe, William (*fl.* 1586–1591), III. 206, 295, 301 ff., 527; IV. 19, 21; V. 131; *A Discourse of English Poetrie*, III. 301; V. 72
Webber, Byron, XIV. 541

Weber, Henry William (1783–1818), xi. 472; xii. 358, 375, 517, 519
Weber, Immanuel, *De Nigello Wirekero*, i. 192
Weber, Wilhelm Eduard, xiv. 268
Webster, Augusta (1837–1894), xiii. 180, 511
Webster, Benjamin Nottingham (1797–1882), xiii. 268, 515, 516, 524
Webster, James (1658?–1720), ix. 547
Webster, John (1580?–1625?), iv. 6; v. 163, 222, 311, 319, 327, 376; vi. 45, 46, 49, 55, 61, 69, 96, 166–187 (main entry), 195, 200, 401, 423, 424, 444 ff.; vii. 466; viii. 436; xii. 68, 116; xiii. 198, 411
  Appius and Virginia, vi. 168, 182, 445, *also see* Add.
  Cure for a Cuckold, A, vi. 69, 182, 184, 185, 445, 447
  Devil's Law-case, The, v. 364; vi. 168, 182 ff., 445, 447
  Dutchesse of Malfy, The, iii. 355; v. 368; vi. 173, 175, 179 ff., 200, 445, 447, *also see* Add.
  Guise, The, vi. 182
  Monumental Column, A, vi. 185, 446
  Monuments of Honor, vi. 168, 185
  Murther of the Sonne upon the Mother, A Late, vi. 182, 195
  Thracian Wonder, The, vi. 69, 185, 445, 447
  White Divel, The (*Vittoria Corombona*), vi. 173 ff., 177, 179 ff., 186, 445, 446; viii. 443; xii. 191
Webster, John (1610–1682), vii. 496, 510, 517; ix. 384, 571; *Academiarum Examen*, vii. 392; ix. 386; *Displaying of supposed Witchcraft, The*, vii. 396, 397, 507; ix. 62
Webster, Noah, xiv. 611
Webster, Richard, iii. 197
Weckherlin, Georg Rudolph (1584–1653), vii. 309
Wedderburn, Alexander, 1st earl of Rosslyn (1733–1805), xii. 142, 426
Wedderburn, Alexander Dundas O., xiv. 524
Wedderburn, David (1580–1646), ix. 558
Wedderburn, James (1495?–1553), iii. 141, 153
Wedderburn, John (1500?–1556), iii. 141, 153
Wedderburn, Robert (1510?–1557?), iii. 141, 153
Wedding of Sir Gawain. See *Gawain*
Wedgwood, Hensleigh (1803–1891), xii. 506
Wedgwood, Josiah (1730–1795), xi. 121
Wedgwood, Julia, xiii. 471
Wednesday Journal, ix. 433
Weekes, John, vii. 9
Weekly Discoverer Stripp'd Naked, The (1681), viii. 412
Weekly Dispatch, The, xiv. 192
Weekly Journal, ix. 433
Weekly Magazine, ix. 562
Weekly Pacquet of Advice from Rome (Care's), ix. 4
Weekly Post, The, vii. 355
Weekly Register, The, xii. 463
Weekly Times, The, xiv. 192
Weelkes, Thomas (*fl.* 1602), iv. 113, 465
Weever, John (1576–1632), iv. 334, 517, 519; v. 253; vii. 407; ix. 350, 540
Wegener, R., vi. 266, 268
Wegg, Silas, in *Our Mutual Friend*, xiii. 336
Weier, Johann, iii. 112; *De Praestigiis Demonum et Incantationibus ac Beneficiis*, iii. 112
Weierstrass, Karl, xiv. 264
Weigel, Valentin, vii. 509; ix. 315
Weimar, v. 300, 306; vii. 177; xi. 259; xii. 38, 158, 302; xiii. 277, 385
Weir, Arthur (1864–1902), xiv. 357, 582
Weir, William (1802–1858), xiv. 535
Weisse, Christian, v. 285, 297, 298
Weissel, Josefine, xiii. 489
Weland Saga, i. 12, 100, 218
Weland Saga, in *Deor*, i. 36
Welbeck Papers, ix. 99
Welby, Thomas Earle, xiii. 495
Welcum to May, ii. 282
Weldon, Walter Frank Raphael (1860–1906), xiv. 564
Wellbred, in *Every Man in His Humour*, vi. 43
Welldon, Sir Anthony (d. 1649?), vii. 454, 518
Weller, Matilda, xiii. 107
Weller, Sam, in *The Pickwick Papers*, xiii. 314, 322, 387
Wellerisms (Dickens's), xiii. 319
Wellesley, Sir Arthur. *See* Wellington, duke of
Wellesley, Richard Colley Wellesley, marquis (1760–1842), xi. 392; xiv. 128, 511
Wellington, Arthur Wellesley, 1st duke of (1769–1852), xi. 167; xii. 97, 154; xiv. 115, 122, 127, 128, 136, 180, 187, 294, 411, 459, 511; *Despatches*, xiv. 107
Wellington college, xii. 333
Wells, Charles Jeremiah (1799?–1879), xii. 107, 424; xiii. 495; *Joseph and his Brethren*, xii. 117
Wells, dean of (William Graham), ix. 96
Wells, Herbert George, xiii. 456, 573
Wells, J. T., xiii. 465
Wells, Somerset, i. 213; iv. 422
Wells, William Charles (1757–1817), xiv. 298, 564
Wellsman, W., xiv. 532
Wellwood. *See* Welwood
Welsh, Charles, xi. 376, 468, 476, 478, 479, 482, 483; *A Bookseller of the Last Century, John Newbery*, x. 210, 482, 484; xi. 377
Welsh, Jane. *See* Carlyle, Jane Welsh
Welsh, the, xiv. 303
Welsh, the, in Jonson's *For the Honour of Wales*, vi. 371

Welsh academy system, x. 387
Welsh bards, x. 487
Welsh character, xiv. 307
Welsh education, xiv. 433
Welsh language, xii. 308; xiv. 458
Welsh literature, xiii. 199; xiv. 304, 306, 307
Welsh mountains, x. 101
Welsh question, the, ii. 423
Welsh Tudor court, xiv. 307
Welshpool, viii. 106
Welsted, Leonard (1688–1747), ix. 78, 86, 188, 449, 487
Welton, James, xiv. 592
Welwood or Wellwood, James (1652–1727), vii. 447; viii. 440
Welwood, John, ix. 549
Welwood, William (*fl.* 1577–1622), iv. 462
Welwyn, x. 139
Wem, Shropshire, xii. 165, 166
Wemmick, in *Great Expectations*, xiii. 334
Wemys, Schir Johne of, in *Wyntoun*, ii. 130
Wenck, F. A. W., x. 304, 507
Wendland, i. 94
Wendoll, in *A Woman Kilde with Kindnesse*, vi. 83
Wendover, xi. 5
Wendover. *See* Roger of
Wenley, Robert Marks, xiv. 483
Wenlock, Sir John, baron Wenlock (d. 1471), ii. 303
Wentworth, captain, in Jane Austen's *Persuasion*, xii. 240, 242
Wentworth, Charles (1789–1864), xiv. 531
Wentworth, Sir Charles (1810–1869), xiv. 531
Wentworth, Peter (1592–1675), ix. 130
Wentworth, Thos. (1568?–1628), viii. 470
Wentworth, Sir Thomas, 1st earl of Strafford (1593–1641), iv. 311; vii. 140, 148, 187, 197, 206, 219, 223, 224, 435, 439, 441, 512; viii. 220; xiii. 58, 59; *Letters and Despatches*, vii. 194, 435
Wentworth, Thomas, 3rd earl of Strafford (1672–1739), ix. 151, 216
Wentworth, William Charles (1793–1872), xiv. 588; *Australasia*, xiv. 362; *Description of New South Wales, A*, xiv. 371
Werferth, i. 93, 105
Wermueller, Otto, iv. 411
Werner, Friedrich L. Z., x. 80; xiii. 468
Werther, x. 134, 227, 229
Wertherism, xiii. 417
Werwolf, the, in *William of Palerne*, i. 316
Wesel, ix. 235
Wesley, Charles (1707–1788), ix. 313, 324, 325; x. 364, 365, 369, 517, 518
Wesley, John (1703–1791), iv. 229; ix. 313, 324 ff., 513; x. 1, 59, 350, 363 ff., 423, 517, 518; xi. 79, 422; xii. 259, 278; xiv. 389; *Journals*, ix. 327, 571; x. 368, 369
Wesley, Samuel, the elder (1662–1735), ix. 393, 572; x. 374, 385, 386; *Letter from a country divine*, ix. 394
Wesleyans, ix. 308, 328
Wesleys, the, xi. 259
Wessels, J. W., xiv. Add. 10
Wessex, xiii. 320
Wessex, West Saxons, law of, viii. 310, 311
Wessex under Alfred, i. 88, 89
West, Sir Edward (1782–1828), xiv. 483; *Essay on the Application of Capital to Land*, xiv. 3
West, Gilbert (1703–1756), ix. 145, 479, 487; x. 114, 448; *Abuse of Travelling*, ix. 189; *Education*, ix. 189; *The Institution of the Order of the Garter*, x. 433
West, H. E., xiii. 566
West, John and West, Alice, *The severall notorious and lewd cousonages of*, iv. 530
West, Rebecca, xiii. Add. 3
West, Richard (*fl.* 1606–1619), iv. 520
West, Richard (1716–1742), ix. 189; x. 117, 118, 120 ff., 124, 132, 243, 251
West, William (*fl.* 1568–1594), viii. 467
West Cowes, xiii. 72
West Hythe, Kent, ii. 61
West Indian planter, xiii. 70
West Indies, iv. 92; vii. 453; viii. 191; ix. 260; x. 36, 392; xi. 264; xii. 420; xiii. 355, 369; xiv. 86, 251, 323, 434
West Saxon Gospels, i. 132, 133
Westbrook, Harriet. *See* Shelley, Mrs
Westbrooks, the, xii. 62
Westbury, near Bristol, xi. 159, 161
Westbury, lord. *See* Bethell, Richard
Westbury, William, vii. 327
Westbury-on-Trym, ii. 49, 74
Westcote, Thomas (*fl.* 1624–1636), *Devonshire*, iv. 308, 514
Westcott, Brooke Foss (1825–1901), bishop of Durham, iv. 41; xii. 298, 340, 467, 470; xiii. 496
Westeraes, Sweden, ii. 319
Western, A., xiii. 513
Western, Mrs, in Fielding's *Tom Jones*, x. 22
Western, squire, in Fielding's *Tom Jones*, viii. 161; x. 22, 89, 206; xiv. 231
Western, Sophia, in Fielding's *Tom Jones*, x. 28, 33, 34, 89
Western isles of Scotland, x. 231, 462, 475
Westernesse (Wirral?), in *Horn*, i. 304
Westgarth, William (1815–1889), xiv. 588
Australia Felix, xiv. 371
Half-a-century of Australian Progress, xiv. 371
Personal Recollections, xiv. 371
Victoria and the Australian Goldmines, xiv. 371
Victoria, late Australia Felix, xiv. 371
Westmacott, Charles Molloy (*pseud.* Bernard Blackmantle), xiv. 547; *English Spy, The*, xiv. 225; *Points of Misery*, xiv. 225
Westmeath, x. 196
Westminster, in *Piers the Plowman*, ii. 8, 32

Westminster, III. 19, 69; IV. 128, 422, 544; V. 9, 350, 366; VI. 3, 261, 327; VII. 62, 160, 207, 333; VIII. 5, 255, 295, 301, 370. *See, also, under* London
Westminster, King street, III. 244
Westminster, St Margaret's church, III. 69
Westminster abbey, II. 158, 317; VI. 6, 113; VII. 250; VIII. 21, 55, 61
Caxton's press at, II. 310 ff.
Poet's corner, IV. 195
St Benedict's chapel, II. 158
Westminster Abbey (Ackermann's), XIV. 222
Westminster assembly, IV. 382, 434; VII. 312, 319, 340; VIII. 323; X. 373
Westminster Drolleries (1671, 1672, 1674), VII. 512; VIII. 116, 423
Westminster and Foreign Quarterly Review, The, XII. 430
Westminster gate-house, IV. 65
Westminster Gazette, The, XIV. 195
Westminster hall, III. 61; VI. 332; VII 62, 347; VIII. 317
Westminster Magazine, X. 92
Westminster Quibbles (1672), VII. 512
Westminster Review, The, XI. 60, 61; XII. 152, 307, 310, 318, 351, 430; XIII. 384, 385, 465; XIV. 84, 158
Westminster school, III. 321, 327, 425, 427 ff.; IV. 80, 164; V. 102, 104, 105, 122; VI. 3, 232, 237, 246, 288, 325; VII. 27, 62, 82, 317, 326, 328, 333, 334, 338, 341, 361; VIII. 2, 50, 185, 328, 344
Westminster scrutiny, XI. 53
Westmoreland (the Greyhound), in *Mum, Sothsegger*, II. 36
Westmorland, IV. 190; VII. 440; VIII. 101; X. 386; XI. 103, 109, 111; XIV. 221
Westmorland, earl of, in *Henry V*, V. 262
Westmorland, earl of. *See* Fane, Mildmay
Westmorland Gazette, The, XII. 445; XIV. 203
Weston, Elizabeth Jane (1582-1612), VII. 487
Weston, Jessie Laidlay, I. 270, 328, *also see* Add.
Weston, Mrs, IX. 71
Weston, Richard, 1st earl of Portland (1577–1635), VI. 148, 149; VII. 219
Weston, Rev. Stephen (1747–1830), XII. 490, 491
Weston, Thomas (1737–1776), XI. 257
Westôn Favell, X. 365
Weston Underwood, XI. 88, 404
Westport, Wilts., VII. 282
Westropp, Hodder M. (d. 1884), XII. 514
Westward for Smelts, IV. 361, 523, 531, 532
Westwood, John Obadiah (1805–1893), XII. 514
Westwood, Thomas (1814?–1888), XII. 201; XIII. 511; *Quest of the Sancgreall, The*, XIII. 188; *Springlets*, XIII. 188
Wetherald, Ethelwyn, XIV. 349
Wever, R., *Lusty Juventus*, V. 59, 392
Wexford, XIV. 315
Wey, William (1407?–1476), II. 499
Weymouth, 3rd viscount. *See* Thynne Thomas
Wha wadna fecht for Charlie, IX. 378
Whachum, in *Hudibras*, VIII. 72, 73
Whale, The, I. 428
Whalley, Peter (1722–1791), IX. 532; X. 505
Whalley, Thomas Sedgwick (1746–1828), XI. 429
Wharfe river, VII. 180
Wharncliffe, lord. *See* Stuart-Wortley, John
Wharton, Anne (1632?–1685), VIII. 444
Wharton, duke of, in Pope's *Epistles*, IX. 81
Wharton, Sir George (1617–1681), VII. 501; *Mercurius Elencticus*, VII. 357
Wharton, Henry (1664–1695), II. 73; VII. 483; VIII. 306, 463; IX. 489
Wharton, Philip, 4th lord Wharton (1613–1696), VIII. 97
Wharton, Thomas, 1st marquis of Wharton (1648–1715), VIII. 96; IX. 45, 94, 95, 455, 487; X. 117, 122, 123, 127, 131, 133, 135; XI. 30
Wharton, William, *A New Song of the Times*, VIII. 97
Wharton, William James Lloyd, XIV. 551
'What bird so sings yet so dos wayl?' V. 125
What is Love? XIV. 304
Whateley, Anne. *See* Hathwey, Anne
Whateley, Thomas (d. 1772), X. 399, 523; XI. 389
Whately, Richard (1787–1863), XI. 415; XII. 242, 243, 285 ff., 292, 447, 470, 471; XIV. 116, 483, 610
Elements of Logic, XIV. 16
Historic Doubts relative to Napoleon Buonaparte, XII. 285
Letters on the Church, XII. 285
Rhetoric, XIV. 428
Whatley, Stephen (*fl.* 1725–1732), IX. 495
Wheatley, Henry Benjamin, VI. 260; VIII. Add.; XI. 396, 467, 469; XIV. 508
Wheatley, Oxon., VII. 104
Wheatstone, Sir Charles (1802–1875), XIV. 261, 557
Wheeler, George, *Journey into Greece* (1682), IV. 462
Wheeler, Harold Felix Baker, XIV. 541
Wheeler, James Talboys (1824–1897), XIV. 338, 339, 580
Wheeler, John (*fl.* 1601–1608), IV. 310, 514
Wheeler, mistress Elizabeth, in Herrick's *Hesperides*, VII. 13
Wheeler, Stephen, XII. 206, 439
Wheelock or Wheloc, Abraham (1593–1653), I. 112; VII. 319, 320, 483, 485
Whelpdale, in Gissing's *New Grub Street*, XIII. 455
Whetham, William Cecil Dampier, XIV. 555
Whethamstede, John (d. 1465), IX. 535

Whetstone, George (1544?–1587?), III. 189, 299, 343, 519, 536; IV. 443; V. 63, 120, 190, 220, 397, 403, 408, 409; VI. 499
Life of Sir Nicholas Bacon, XII. 357, 515
Mirour for Magestrates, VI. 395, 403, 499
Promos and Cassandra, III. 299, 527; V. 117, 119, 120
Rich his Farewell to the Militarie Profession, III. 343
Rock of Regard, The, III. 343
Touchstone for the Time, VI. 395
Whewell, William (1794–1866), VIII. 351; XIV. 207, 258, 483, 557, 565, 593, 594; *History of the Inductive Sciences*, XIV. 17, 259, 289; *On the principles of English university education*, XIV. 412; *Thoughts on the Study of Mathematics*, XIV. 412
Whibley, Charles, XI. 396; XII. 444; XIII. 489, 499, 530, 546, 547; XIV. 537
'Which nobody can deny,' VIII. 95, 97
Whichcote or Whitchcote, Benjamin (1609–1683), VII. 279; VIII. 273 ff., 280, 288, 290, 291, 297, 457; IX. 300; *Aphorisms*, VIII. 276, 277, 281; *Sermons*, VIII. 277
Whig Examiner, IX. 151, 437, 439
Whigs of Fife, The, IX. 378
Whipping of the Satyre, The (1601), IV. 517
Whirler, Jack, in Johnson's *Idler*, X. 178
Whistle Binkie, XI. 445
'Whistlecraft,' VII. 79
Whistlecraft, Mr (J. H. Frere), XII. 52
Whistler, Anthony (1714–1754), IX. 412; X. 271 ff., 496; *The Shuttlecock*, X. 272
Whistler, James McNeill, XIII. 433, 495
Whiston, William (1667–1752), IX. 509; X. 377
Historical Preface, X. 379
Josephus, IX. 295
Primitive Christianity, X. 379
Primitive Christianity Revived, IX. 295
Whitaker, Jeremiah (1599–1654), VII. 317
Whitaker, John (1735–1808), X. 510
Course of Hannibal over the Alps, X. 320
Genuine History of the Britons, X. 320
Gibbon's History...reviewed, X. 310, 508
History of Manchester, X. 310, 320
Whitaker, Joseph (1820–1895), XIV. 532
Whitaker, L., IV. 90
Whitaker, Thomas Dunham (1759–1821), XII. 345, 514; *History of Richmondshire*, XII. 346
Whitaker, William (1548–1595), III. 422; IV. 275; VII. 309, 316
Whitbourne, Sir Richard (*fl.* 1579–1627), IV. 462
Whitbread, Samuel (1758–1815), XIV. 120, 406, 511
Whitbread's brewery, XI. 38
Whitby, I. 42, 96; XI. 429; XII. 10; XIII. 380
Whitchurch, X. 272, 387
Whitchurch, Edward (d. 1561), III. 194, 195; IV. 396
Whitchurch, James Wadham, XIV. 610
Whitchurch, T., III. 44
Whitchurch school, VII. 330
White, Blanco. *See* White, Joseph Blanco
White, Edward (*fl.* 1594–1603), IV. 384, 393
White, Gertrude, in Black's *Macleod of Dare*, XIII. 432
White, Gilbert (1720–1793), X. 269 ff., 496, *also see* Add.; XIII. 429; XIV. 166; *Natural History of Selborne*, X. 269; *Naturalist's Calendar*, X. 270
White, Gleeson, XI. 476
White, Henry Kirke (1785–1806), XI. 172, 422; XII. 424; *Oft in danger, oft in woe*, XII. 136; *The Star of Bethlehem*, XII. 136
White, James (1775–1820), XII. 438; *The Falstaff Letters*, XII. 183, 185
White, John, *Three Letters to a Gentleman*, X. 375
White, Joseph (1745–1814), Bampton lectures, X. 309, 508
White, Joseph Blanco (1775–1841), XII. 471; XIII. 46
White, R. (1645–1703), VII. 402
White, Richard Grant, V. 279
White, Robert, printer, VII. 361
White, Robert (1802–1874), XI. 444
White, Sir Thomas (1492–1567), III. 420; VII. 332, 334
White, Thomas (1550?–1624), VI. 376, 386, 499
White, Thomas (1593–1676), VII. 475; *Sciri, sive sceptices et scepticorum a jure disputationis exclusio*, VII. 302
White, Thomas (*fl.* 1700), XI. 484; *A Little Book for Little Children*, XI. 369, 370
White, Thomas Pilkington, XII. 514
White, W. (*fl.* 1599), V. 158
White, Walter (1811–1893), XIV. 554
White, William Hale. *See* Rutherford, Mark
White Book of Rhyðerch, The, I. 252
White Canons, II. 349
White Cock and Hen, of St Domingo, III. 106
White Harts, the, in *Mum, Sothsegger*, II. 36
White sea, the, I. 94
Whitefield, George (1714–1770), IV. 229; X. 88, 276, 363 ff., 518, 522; XI. 79
Whitefoord, Caleb (1734–1810), X. 482
Whitefoot, John, VII. 461
Whitefriars, his eminence of, in Scott's *Fortunes of Nigel*, XII. 21
Whitehall, John, VII. 476
Whitehall Evening Post, IX. 21, 433
Whitehaven, IX. 91
Whitehead, Charles (1804–1862), XII. 107 424; XIII. 418
As yonder Lamp in my Vacated Room, XII. 119
Cavalier, The, XII. 119
Jack Ketch, XII. 119
Richard Savage, XII. 119
Solitary, The, XII. 118

Whitehead, George (1636?–1723), VIII. 416
Whitehead, John (1740?–1804), x. 518
Whitehead, Paul (1710–1774), x. 525; XII. 118; XIV. 547; *The Gymnasiad*, XIV. 230
Whitehead, William (1715–1785), x. 438; XI. 34; XII. 118; *Creusa, Queen of Athens*, x. 86; *Roman Father*, x. 86; *School for Lovers*, x. 86
Whitehorne, Peter (*fl.* 1550–1563), IV. 3, 7, 446, 462
Whitelocke, Bulstrode (1605–1675), VI. 408; VII. 447, 454, 460; VIII. 117
Journal of his Swedish Embassy, VII. 230
Memorials of the English Affairs, VII. 229, 230; VIII. 323
Monarchy asserted to be the best, most Ancient and legall form of Government, VII. 231
Notes upon the King's Writt, VII. 230
White's Chocolate house, IX. 33
Whiteway, Mrs, IX. 100
Whitfield, Henry, IX. 313
Whitford or Whytford, Richard (*fl.* 1495–1555?), III. 470; IV. 496
Whitford, Vernon (George Meredith's), XIII. 447
Whitgift, John (1530–1604), archbishop of Canterbury, III. 213, 375 ff., 380, 385, 390, 392, 397, 406, 413, 422, 424, 548; IV. 275, 382, 411, 494, 519, 545; v. 365, 482; VI. 384; IX. 496
Whithorn, Galloway, II. 127, 128
Whithorne, Thomas (*fl.* 1590), IV. 112, 465
Whiting, Lilian, XIII. 485
Whiting, Nathaniel, *Albino and Bellama*, VII. 80, 413
Whiting, Richard (d. 1539), III. 49
Whitley, William Thomas, x. 519
Whitlock, John (1625–1709), x. 387
Whitman, Walt, IV. 50, 246; x. 148, 368; XI. 409; XII. 404; XIII. 108, 151, 337, 489; XIV. 208
Whitney, Geoffrey (1548?–1601), VII. 479
Whitsun plays, v. 13, 34, 48
Whittaker, Edmund Taylor, XIV. 555
Whittaker, Thomas, XIV. 479; *Catalogue of Bentham's MSS.*, XI. 397
Whittaker, William Joseph, XIV. 80
Whittemore, T., XIII. Add. 2
Whitten, Wilfred, XIV. 546
Whittier, John G., VIII. 113
Whittingham, William (1524?–1579), III. 44, 45, 46
Whittington, Richard (d. 1423), II. 288
Whittington, Robert (*fl.* 1520), III. 341, 555; IV. 435, 436; Tully's *Offices*, IV. 5; *The Forme and Rule of Honest lyvinge*, IV. 5, 439; *The Remedyes against all casuall Chances*, IV. 5, 440
Whittlesea or Whittlesey or Whittlesay, William, archbishop of Canterbury (d. 1374), II. 365
Whitty, Edward Michael (1827–1860), XIV. 199
Who liveth so merry in all this land? III. 484
Whole Duty of Man, The, VII. 148, 427
Whymper, Edward (1840–1911), XIV. 255, 554
Whyte, E. A. and S., x. 480
Whyte, Samuel (1733–1811), XIV. 572
Whyte-Melville, George John (1821–1878), XIII. 434, 564; XIV. 366
Wibourne, Nathaniel, *Machiavellus*, VI. 305, 480
'Wickedshifts' (lord Brougham), XIV. 116
Wickens, William (d. 1699), x. 386
Wicket, The, III. 25
Wicket-gate, the, in Bunyan's *Pilgrim's Progress*, VII. 173
Wickfields, the, in *David Copperfield*, XIII. 327
Wickham, Edward Charles (1834–1910), XII. 495
Wickhambrook, Suffolk, XI. 140
Wickham Brook academy, x. 387
Wickins, Nathan, VII. 515
Wicklow, XIV. 329
Wicksteed, Clara Mabel, XIII. 545
Wiclif. *See* Wyclif
Wicquefort, A. de, *L'Ambassadeur et ses Fonctions*, VII. 191
Widdowes, Giles (1588?–1645), *The Lawless Kneeless Schismatical Puritan*, VII. 160, 427
Widford, Hertfordshire, XII. 182, 186
Widia (Wudga), in *Waldhere*, I. 36
Widsith, I. 1, 3, 19 ff., 31, 34, 36, 37, 424, 428, *also see* Add.; v. 26
Wieland, Christopher Martin, v. 296 ff., 301, 304, 307; VII. 177; x. 19, 422; XII. 422; *Clementina della Poretta*, x. 18
Wier, Johann, VII. 366, 371, 396; VIII. 357; *De Praestigiis demonum*, VII. 370, 506
Wife of Auchtermychty, The, IX. 361
Wife of Bath, VII. 382
Wife of Usher's Well, I. 300; II. 414
Wife's Complaint, The, I. 38, 39, 424, 428
Wiggin, Kate D., XIII. 544
Wiggington, Giles (*fl.* 1569–1592), III. 397
Wight, isle of, IV. 190; x. 252; XII. 188, 509; XIII. 129
Wight, John (*fl.* 1585), IV. 410, 411
Wight, John, editor of *Morning Post*, XIV. 188
Wight, O. W., XII. 371
Wight, Willie, of Aikwood, XII. 3
Wightman, Frances Lucy, wife of Matt. Arnold, XIII. 87
Wiglaf, in *Beowulf*, I. 1, 24, 25
Wigstons, the, III. 382, 383
Wihenoe, the Breton, I. 257
Wil Bagnal's Ghost, III. 99
Wil and Wit, I. 228, 459
Wilberforce, Henry William (1807–1873), XII. 274, 463
Wilberforce, Robert Isaac (1802–1857), XII. 454, 455, 463, 473; XIV. 507; *The Doctrine of the Incarnation*, XII. 274
Wilberforce, Samuel (1805–1873), bishop of Oxford, VIII. 250; XI. 490; XII. 473

Wilberforce, William (1759–1833), x. 262, 269; xi. 52, 259, 405; xii. 282, 473; xiv. 120, 177, 373, 403, 507, 514; *A Practical View of Christianity*, xii. 281
Wilbye, John (*fl.* 1598–1614), iv. 113, 465
Wilcock, William (*fl.* 1480), ii. 318
Wilcox, Thomas (1549?–1608), iii. 403; iv. 518
Wild, Jonathan, in Fielding's *Jonathan Wild*, x. 27, 39
Wild, Mrs Jonathan, in Fielding's *Jonathan Wild*, x. 28
Wild, Robert (1609–1679), viii. 409, 411
Wildair, Sir Harry (Farquhar's), viii. 170, 172
Wilde, George (1610–1665), vi. 326, 480; *Love's Hospitale*, vi. 326
Wilde, Jane Francisca, lady (*pseud.* 'Speranza,' 1826–1896), xiv. 318, 572
Wilde, Oscar F. O'F. W. (1856–1900), xiii. 524; xiv. 158, 211, 329, 527, 528, *also see* Add. 3; *Ballad of Reading Gaol, The*, xiv. 159; *De Profundis*, xiv. 159
Wilde, Sir William Robert Wills (1815–1876), xii. 351, 514; xiv. 572
Wilder, Theaker, x. 198
Wilderspin, Samuel (1792?–1866), xiv. 405, 610
Wilfer family, in *Our Mutual Friend*, xiii. 337
Wilford, John (*fl.* 1723–1742), *Monthly Catalogue*, xi. 339, 471
Wilfrid, St, bishop of York (634–709), i. 16, 82, 85
Wilkes, John (1727–1797), vi. 7; x. 190, 296, 390 ff. (main entry), 399, 401, 402, 404, 405, 452, 474, 522 ff., *also see* Add.; xi. 8; xii. 54; *Essay on Woman*, x. 397; *The North Briton*, vii. 200; x. 251
Wilkes, T., viii. 429
Wilkes, William, vi. 38
Wilkie, Sir David (1785–1841), xii. 177; xiv. 545
Wilkie, William (1721–1772), ix. 557
Wilkin, Simon (1790–1862), vii. 235
Wilkins, Augustus Samuel (1843–1905), xii. 337, 495
Wilkins, Sir Charles (1749?–1836), xii. 343, 503
Wilkins, David (1685–1745), viii. 322, 469; *Concilia*, ix. 350, 356, 540
Wilkins, George (*fl.* 1607), iv. 527, 532; *The Miseries of Inforst Mariage*, v. 242; vi. 69, 97; viii. 142; *The Travailes of The three English Brothers*, vi. 69, 455
Wilkins, Henry Musgrave (*c.* 1822–1887), xii. 495
Wilkins, John (1614–1672), vii. 466, 517; viii. 273, 277, 297, 364, 463, 476; ix. 386, 571; *Ecclesiastes or the Gift of Preaching*, viii. 369
Wilkins, William Glyde, xiii. 532, 544
Wilkins, William Henry (1860–1905), xiv. 500
Wilkinson, Charles Allix, xiv. 597
Wilkinson, J., *Select Views in Cumberland*, xi. 408
Wilkinson, James John Garth (1812–1899), xi. 433
Wilkinson, Sir John Gardner (1797–1875), xii. 317, 477, 500; xiv. 554; *Manners and Customs of the Ancient Egyptians*, xii. 342
Wilkinson, Tate (1739–1803), x. 430, 446; xi. 449, 454
Wilkinson, Thomas, a friend of Wordsworth, xi. 409
Wilkinson, William Clever, xiii. 498
Wilks, Mark (1760–1831), xiv. 580; *Historical Sketches of the South of India*, xiv. 335
Wilks, Robert (1665?–1732), viii. 170, 172, 173; x. 21
Will (Anima), in *Piers the Plowman*, ii. 27
Will, in *Damon and Pithias*, v. 119
'Will,' in Shakespeare's sonnets, v. 229
Will Stewart and John, ii. 410
'Will ye go to the coals in the morning?' ix. 373
Willem, a Fleming, i. 366
Willes or Willey, Richard (*fl.* 1558–1573), iv. 75, 456
Willet, Andrew (1562–1621), vii. 406
Willet, John, in *Barnaby Rudge*, xiii. 321
Willett, B. W., xiii. 555
William, in *Piers the Plowman*, ii. 12
William, duke of Gloucester (1689–1700), ix. 200, 236
William I (the Conqueror), king of England, i. 111, 141, 149, 150, 155, 256, 396; ii. 342; iii. 338; v. 252; viii. 310, 384; ix. 343; x. 110, 467; xii. 31; xiii. 366; xiv. 72
William II, king of England, i. 162, 189; xiv. 111
William III, king of Great Britain, viii. 49, 92, 93, 99, 122, 195, 201, 215, 220, 261, 264, 267, 268, 294, 300, 305, 306, 307, 380, 382, 452; ix. 7, 8, 92, 148, 155, 175, 180, 200, 202, 203, 208, 213, 228, 233, 235, 258, 271; x. 295, 356, 373, 389, 502; xiv. 64, 65, 212
William IV, king of Great Britain, xi. 141
William Augustus, duke of Cumberland (1721–1765), ix. 162, 563
William de Kilkenny, ii. 352
William de Mandagoto, ii. 364
William de la Mare (*fl.* 1284), i. 210, 456
William de Monte Lauduns (*c.* 1346), ii. 364
William de Shareshull (*fl.* 1360), ii. 37
William of Auvergne, i. 207
William of Boldensele (*c.* 1336), ii. 80
William of Champeaux, i. 183
William of Drogheda (d. 1245?), ii. 499
William of Durham (d. 1249), ii. 352
William of Heytesbury, *Sophismata*, ii. 363

William of Malmesbury (d. 1143?), I. 5, 72, 90, 91, 96, 97, 101, 105, 106, 155, 157, 159, 162, 164, 168, 171, 172, 218, 243, 250, 256, 257, 262, 269, 337, 450, 451, 460; II. 396, 398, 399, 412; III. 368; XII. 355, 516
William of Newburgh (1136–1198), I. 68, 160, 161, 168, 169, 171 ff., 245, 257, 450, 451; IX. 534
William of Ockham. *See* Ockham
William of Palerne, I. 281, 286, 292, 316, 357, 378, 472
William of Ramsey (*fl.* 1219), II. 499
William of Shoreham, I. 353 ff., 476; III. 274
William of Tyre, The continuation of (1261), II. 80
William of Wadington, *Manuel des Pechiez*, I. 204, 344 ff., 348, 349; II. 139, 150, 420; V. 41
William of Worcester (1415–1482?), II. 308; IV. 68
William of Wychwood, II. 35
William of Wykeham. *See* Wykeham
William Rufus, in *Satiro-Mastix*, VI. 44
William the Clerk, II. 509
William the trouvère, II. 507
Williams, Alfred M., XIV. 573, 610
Williams, Anna (1706–1783), X. 187, 458, 470, 479; XI. 350; *Miscellanies*, X. 168
Williams, Caleb, in Godwin's novel, XI. 46, 293
Williams, Sir Charles Hanbury (1708–1759), XI. 172 ff., 429; XII. 120; *Works*, XI. 173
Williams, Daniel (1643?–1716), IX. 503; X. 387; *Defence*, X. 387; *Gospel Truth*, X. 377; *Peace with Truth*, X. 377
Williams, David (1738–1816), XIV. 610
Williams, Edward (*fl.* 1560), *Virgo Triumphans; or Virginia Really and truly valued*, IV. 96, 462
Williams, Edward Ellerker (1793–1822), XII. 76, 383, 398
Williams, Gardner F., XIV. Add. 10
Williams, George (1814–1878), XII. 514
Williams, Helen Maria (1762–1827), XI. 177, 430; XII. 124
Williams, Isaac (1802–1865), XII. 258, 261, 265–266 (main entry), 424, 454, 455, 463; XIII. 167, 511; *Autobiography*, XII. 266; *On reserve in communicating religious knowledge*, XII. 260; *The Cathedral*, XII. 266; XIII. 171
Williams, Jane, friend of Shelley, XII. 73, 75, 76
Williams, John (1582–1650), archbishop of York, IV. 265, 266, 306, 422, 426; VII. 62, 154, 219, 333, 491
Williams, John (1761–1818), XI. 472
Williams, John (Ab Ithel) (1811–1862), XII. 514
Williams, J. B., XIV. 535
Williams, Mary, XIII. 544
Williams, Oliver, VII. 362, 363, 496, 501; *An Extract Accompt*, VII. 361
Williams, Oliver
Occurrences from Foreign parts, VII. 361
Politicus, VII. 361
Publick Intelligencer, VII. 361
Williams, Richard D'Alton (1822–1862), XIV. Add. 3; *The Munster War Song*, XIV. 318
Williams, Sir Roger (1540?–1595), IV. 462
Williams, Rowland (1817–1870), XII. 295, 466, 471, 478; *Psalms and Litanies*, XII. 296
Williams, R. A., XIII. 513
Williams, Sarah or 'Sadie' (d. 1868), XIII. 180, 511
Williams, T., *The Excellency and Praeheminence of the Law of England* (1680), VIII. 470
Williams, William, *Occult Physick* (1660), VII. 510
Williams, W. S., XIII. 407, 414
Williams, Zachariah (1673?–1755), X. 468; *Account of an Attempt to ascertain the Longitude at Sea*, X. 176, 468
Williams murders, the, XII. 227
Williams's library, Dr, IX. 307, 511, 514, 520; X. 520
Williamson, Alexander William (1824–1904), XIV. 272, 277, 558
Williamson, Sir Joseph (1633–1701), VII. 363, 364; IX. 212, 213, 496
Williamson, Peter (1730–1799), IX. 562
Williamson, Richard, XIV. 598
Williamson, William Crawford (1816–1895), XIV. 290, 565
Willibald (700?–786), I. 435
Willie, in *The Shepheards Calender*, III. 222
Willie and Earl Richard's daughter, II. 411
Willie's gane to Melville Castle, IX. 374
Willie's Lyke-Wake, II. 411
Willikin, in *Ane Pleasant Satyre*, III. 127
Willing, James, XIII. 556
Willingham, lady Maria, in Mrs Gore's *Mothers and Daughters*, XII. 246
Willington, James (*i.e.* Oliver Goldsmith), X. 203
Willis, Browne (1682–1760), IX. 358, 540; *History of the Mitred Abbies*, IX. 354; *Survey of the cathedrals*, IX. 354
Willis, N. P., XII. 382
Willis, Richard (1664–1734), IX. 572
Willis, Robert (1800–1875), XII. 514; *Architectural History of Cambridge*, XII. 348
Willis, Thomas (1621–1675), VIII. 479; XIV. 281
Willison, John (1680–1750), IX. 549
Willmott, Robert Aris (1809–1863), (?) *Conversations at Cambridge* (1836), XI. 417
Willobie his Avisa, IV. 472
Willoughby, Francis, 5th baron of Parham (1613?–1666), VII. 453
Willoughby, Sir Henry (*fl.* 1616–1621), IV. 165
Willoughby, Sir Hugh (d. 1554), I. 94; IV. 69, 71, 72, 84, 88

Will's coffee-house, IX. 33, 122, 256, 271, 348
Wills, James (1790–1868), XIV. 312, 572
Wills, William Gorman (1828–1891), XIII. 524, 556; XIV. 572; *Charles I*, XIII. 268; *Marie Stuart*, XIII. 268
Wills, William Henry (1810–1880), XIII. 542; XIV. 236
Wills, William John (1834–1861), XIV. 364
Wills, W. R., XIV. 588
Willughby, Francis (1635–1672), VIII. 479; XIV. 565; *History of Fishes*, XIV. 282; *History of Insects*, XIV. 282; *Ornithology*, XIV. 282
Wilmington, earl. *See* Compton, Spencer
Wilmot, Hon. Alexander, XIV. 588, *also see* Add. 4, 11
Wilmot, Henry, 1st earl of Rochester (1612?–1658), VIII. 206
Wilmot, John, 2nd earl of Rochester (1647–1680), IV. 197, 214, 222, 224; VII. 180, 358; VIII. 4, 25, 28, 35, 83, 86, 91, 174, 188, 193, 199, 200 ff., 206–215 (main entry), 219, 300, 373, 379, 409 ff., 423, 444 ff., 459, 461, *also see* Add.; IX. 18, 174, 198, 445, 489; X. 169
Commons' Petition to the King (1679), VIII. 94
Dispute, The, VIII. 93
Epistolary Essay, An, VIII. 209
History of Insipids, The, VIII. 94
Maim'd Debauchee, The, VIII. 215
Nothing, VIII. 213
On the Young Statesmen, VIII. 94
Satire against Mankind, A, VIII. 214
Session of the Poets, VIII. 136
Valentinian, VIII. 220
Wilmot, Robert (*fl.* 1568–1608), V. 72, 73, 76
Wilmot, in Lillo's *Fatal Curiosity*, X. 77, 78
Wilson, Alexander (1766–1813), XI. 237, 445; *Watty and Meg*, XI. 236
Wilson, Alexander (d. 1852), XIII. 511
Wilson, Andrew (1831–1881), XIV. 554
Wilson, Arthur (1595–1652), IV. 64; VII. 447, 454
Wilson, Arthur, *History of King James I*, IX. 233
Wilson, Caroline (1787–1846), XII. 473
Wilson, Charles, *Memories of Congreve* (1730), VIII. 428
Wilson, Charles Robert (1863–1904), XIV. 338, 339, 580
Wilson, Sir Charles William (1836–1905), XII. 514
Wilson, Daniel (1778–1858), XII. 473
Wilson, Sir Daniel (1816–1892), XII. 514; *Archaeology and Prehistoric Annals of Scotland*, XII. 351; *Prehistoric Man*, XII. 351
Wilson, David Alec, XIII. 471
Wilson, David Mackay, XIV. Add. 11
Wilson, Fred. J. F., XIV. 536
Wilson, Henry Bristow (1803–1888), XII. 466, 471; XIV. 598; *The Communion of Saints*, XII. 284; 'The National Church,' XII. 295
Wilson, Horace Hayman (1786–1860), XII. 343, 503; XIV. 97, 337, 495, 500, 580; *Ariana Antiqua*, XII. 352, 353
Wilson, James Maurice, XIV. 426, 597, 606
Wilson, John (1627?–1696), VIII. 421
A New Anatomie, VII. 384
Andronicus Comnenus, VIII. 124
Belphegor, VIII. 123
Cheats, The, VIII. 122
Projectors, The, VIII. 123
Trans. of *The Praise of Folly*, III. Add.
Wilson, John (1720–1789), IX. 557
Wilson, John (1774–1855), XII. 173
Wilson, John, 'Christopher North' (1785–1854), XI. 244, 411, 437, 440, 442; XII. 156 ff., 425, 445, *also see* Add.; XIII. 25, 26, 108, 148, 187, 479; XIV. 232; *City of the Plague, The*, XII. 158; *Isle of Palms, The*, XII. 158; *Noctes Ambrosianae*, XI. 239; XII. 159, 160; XIV. 313
Wilson, John, of Kilmarnock, XI. 342
Wilson, John Dover, IV. 320; V. 114; *Martin Marprelate and Shakespeare's Fluellen*, III. Add.
Wilson, J. G., XIII. Add. 2
Wilson, John Mackay (1804–1835), XII. 452, 453; *Tales of the Borders*, XIV. 203
Wilson, John Matthias (1813–1881), XIV. 472
Wilson, Mr, in Fielding's *Joseph Andrews*, IX. 408; X. 30
Wilson, Robert, the elder (d. 1600), V. 312, 320, 370; VI. 15, 246; *The Three Ladies of London*, V. 314, 366, 393; *The Three Lords and Three Ladies of London*, V. 314; VI. 249
Wilson, Robert, the younger (1579–1610), V. 236, 312, 313, 319, 323, 331
Wilson, Robert Arthur (1820?–1875), XIV. 572
Wilson, Samuel, IV. 462
'Wilson, Rev. T.,' XI. 481
Wilson, Sir Thomas (1560?–1629), IV. 447
Wilson, Thomas (1525?–1581), III. 21, 23, 24, 290 ff., 431, 432, 446, 447, 470, 527, 554; IV. 1, 436, 438; VII. 476, 479
Arte of Rhetorique, II. 162; III. 23, 431, 432
Discourse uppon usurye, IV. 313, 514, 518
The Rule of Reason, conteining the arte of logique, V. 105, 408; VII. 276
Three Orations of Demosthenes, III. 24
Wilson, Thomas (1663–1755), bishop of Sodor and Man, IX. 572; X. 351, 358, 518; XII. 268; *Maxims*, X. 359; *Parochialia*, X. 359; *Sacra Privata*, X. 359
Wilson, Walter (1781–1847), X. 519; XII. 201
Wilson, William (1801–1860), XII. 424; XIV. 592

Wilton, III. 351; IV. 124, 132; VII. 61; XII. 192
Wilton, Ralph de, in Scott's *Marmion*, XII. 11
Wiltshire, IV. 314; VI. 281; VII. 29, 74, 282; IX. 187, 351, 531; XI. 148, 178; XII. 345, 508, 510, 513
Wiltshire, earls of. *See* Boleyn, Sir Thomas; Butler, James
Wily Beguiled (1606), V. 129; VI. 300
Wimble, Will, in *The Spectator*, IX. 53; X. 199
Wimborne, IV. 421; IX. 146
Wimpole, IX. 152, 153; XI. 347
Winch, Sir Humphrey (1555?–1625), VIII. 470
Winchcomb, John, in *Jack of Newbury*, III. 368
Winchelsea, sea fight off, II. 120
Winchester, VII. 250, 444; IX. 151, 221, 534; X. 109, 132, 139, 224, 238, 355, 492; XII. 231, 327, 348, 517; XIV. 73, 101
Winchester, annals of, I. 178
Winchester, library of, IV. 422
Winchester, monastery and school of, I. 113, 114, 116, 118, 125
Winchester, Elhanan, XII. 471
Winchester Chronicle, I. 104, 109, 112. See, also, under *Chronicle*
Winchester college, II. 355 ff., 359, 489; III. 187, 418, 427 ff.; IV. 161, 163, 242, 261, 262, 265; V. 103; VII. 233, 241, 326, 328, 329, 331, 334, 493; VIII. 181
Winchester diocese, VII. 326, 327
Winchester downs, X. 303
Winchester school, IX. 188, 300, 405, 408 ff., 573; XIV. 386, 387, 406, 422
Winchilsea, countess of. *See* Finch, Anne
Winchilsea, earl of. *See* Finch, Heneage
Wind Blaws Cauld, IX. 362
Windele, John (1801–1865), XII. 519
Windermere, lake, XII. 158
Windham, Joseph (1739–1810), X. 260, 261
Windham, William (1750–1810), X. 473; XI. 388, 389; XIV. 120, 507, 511
Windisch, Wilhelm O. E., XIV. 307
Windsor, I. 369; II. 357; IV. 191, 420; V. 116, 348; VI. 274; VII. 16, 59, 60, 98, 254, 307, 309, 327, 459; VIII. 97, 321, 358; IX. 193; X. 111, 224, 238, 260, 360; XI. 38; XII. 59
Windsor, Maidens' tower, III. 178
Windsor, Nova Scotia, XIV. 346
Windsor, St George's chapel, II. 158; VI. 288
Windsor castle, XII. 345
Windsor forest, IX. 67; XIII. 355
Wine-god, the, in Hawes's *A Joyful Meditation*, etc., II. 226
Winestead, in Holderness, VII. 178
Wing, Vincent (1619–1668), VII. 509
Wingate, David (1828–1892), XIII. 511
Wingate, Edmund (1596–1656), VIII. 465, 470
Wingfield, Anthony (1550?–1615?), VI. 306, 327, 480
Wingfield, Henry, III. 81; *Contra Expugnatores Missae* (six dialogues), III. 81
Wingfield, Lewis Strange (1842–1891), XIV. 554, 572; *Lady Grizel*, XIV. 328; *My Lords of Strogue*, XIV. 328; *Slippery Ground*, XIV. 328
Winkle, Nathaniel, in *The Pickwick Papers*, XIII. 314
Winkworth, Catherine (1827–1878), XIII. 511; XIV. 600
Winkworth, Susanna (1820–1884), XIV. 600
Winstanley, Gerrard (*fl.* 1648–1652), IX. 307
Winstanley, Lilian, XII. 405
Winstanley, William (1628?–1698), VII. 15, 25, 91, 92
Winteney, nuns of, I. 230, 458, 459
Winter, in folk-plays, V. 31
Winter, John Strange, *pseud.* *See* Stannard, Henrietta E. V.
Winter, R., V. 71
Winter Dreame, A, VII. 386
Winter Evening Entertainments, XI. 370
Winterslow, Wiltshire, XII. 167, 192, 432
Winterton, Ralph (1600–1636), VII. 489
Winthrop, Dolly, in George Eliot's *Silas Marner*, XIII. 393
Winthrop, John (1588–1649), VII. 353
Winton, earl of. *See* Seton, George
Winwood, Sir Ralph (1563?–1617), V. 480; VII. 438; X. 504
Winworth, lord, in Kelly's *False Delicacy*, XI. 263
Winzet, Ninian (1518–1592), III. 505; IV. 412; *Certain Tractatis for Reformation*, II. 285; III. 154
Wireker, Nigel (*fl.* 1190), I. 173, 176, 192, 455; III. 102
Wirgman, Augustus Theodore, XIV. Add. 11
Wirksworth, XIII. 389
Wirral, I. 304
Wirtenberg, Journals of two dukes of, V. 479
Wisbech, X. 377
Wisbech school, VII. 330
Wisconsin, V. 85
Wisdom, in Carew's *Coelum Britannicum*, VII. 19
Wisdom, in *The Example of Virtue*, II. 227, 228, 230
Wisdom, in *The Passetyme of Pleasure*, II. 228
Wisdom, in *Piers the Plowman*, II. 10
Wisdom, who is Christ, V. 392
Wisdome of Doctor Dodypoll, The, VI. 459
Wise, Andrew, IV. 393
Wise, Thomas J., XI. 412, 414, 419; XII. 400, 401, 406, 407, 418, 423, 424, *also see* Add.; XIII. 474, 476, 478, 481 ff., 485, 486, 493, 495, 555, 569, 570, *also see* Add. 2; XIV. 528, *also see* Add. 3

Wiseman, Nicholas Patrick Stephen (1802–1865), XII. 259, 260, 264, 274–5 (main entry), 352, 461, 463; XIV. 54; *Fabiola, or the Church of the Catacombs*, XII. 275, 277; 'High Church Claims,' XII. 275
Wiseman, Sir Robert, *The Law of Laws* (1686), VIII. 470
Wiseman of West Chester, The, V. 316
Wishart, George (1513–1546), III. 147
Wishart, George (1599–1671), bishop of Edinburgh, IX. 550
Wishfort, lady, in Congreve's *Way of the World*, VIII. 153
Wissembourg, battle of, XIV. 328
Wit, in *Piers the Plowman*, II. 10, 19, 20
Wit, in Tudor moralities, V. 57
Wit and Drollery (1656), VII. 512
Wit Restor'd (1658), VII. 413, 512
Witch being overtaken, A most certain true and strange discovery of a, VII. 375
Witch controversy, IV. 534; V. 377; VII. 366 ff.
Witch controversy, post-classical sources, 503 ff.
Witch of Edmonton, The, IV. 535
Witchcraft, V. 482
Witchcraft, illustrations of, III. 495
Witchcraft literature of Scotland, XII. 519
Witches, VI. 104
Withals, John (*fl.* 1556), III. 555
Witham, Essex, III. 183
Witham, Henry Thomas Moire, XIV. 290, 565
Wither or Withers, George (1588–1667), IV. 121, 150, 154 ff. (main entry), 166, 333, 434, 479, 482 ff., 518, 520, 534; V. 371; VII. 30, 72, 112, 180, 351, 406, 466, 502; VIII. 67, 227; XII. 434, 438
  Abuses Stript and Whipt, or Satiricall Poems, IV. 155; VI. 401, 499; VII. 433
  Faire Virtue, the Mistress of Phil'Arete, IV. 155
  Fidelia, IV. 155
  Great Assises holden in Parnassus, VII. 274
  Haleluiah, IV. 156
  Hymnes and Songs of the Church, IV. 155, 395
  Motto, IV. 155
  Nuptial Poems, IV. 154
  Rocking Hymn, A, IV. 156
  Scholars Purgatory, The, IV. 156, 396, 546
  Shepherd's Hunting, The, IV. 155
Witherow, Thomas (1824–1890), XIV. 572
Withers, Hartley, XIV. 515
Witherspoon, John (1723–1794), IX. 549
Withies, The, II. 408
Wititterlys, the, in *Nicholas Nickleby*, XIII. 317
Witness, The, XIV. 160, 203
Wits, or Sport upon Sport, The (1672), VII. 512; VIII. 116
Wits Commonwealth, IV. 348, 526
Wits Theatre of the Little World, IV. 526
Wits Treasury (1655), VII. 512
Wittenberg, III. 418; VI. 374; VIII. 29
Wittenberg, in *The Unfortunate Traveller*, III. 363
Wittie, Robert, VII. 511
Wittol, in Congreve's *Old Bachelor*, VIII. 147
Witts Recreations, VII. 7, 401, 402, 411, 413
Witwoud, in Congreve's *Way of the World*, VIII. 153
Wode, Thomas, III. 131
Wodeford or Wadford, William of (*fl.* 1381–1390), II. 54, 443
Woden, I. 40, 218; V. 35
Wodrow, Robert (1679–1734), VII. 452; IX. 369, 554; *History of the Sufferings of the Church of Scotland*, XII. 359
Wodrow society, XII. 359
Woeful Treaty, The, IX. 502
Woerth, battle of, XIV. 328
Woffington, Margaret, X. 87
Wohunge of ure Louerde, The, I. 233, 459
Wokey, Somerset, III. 57
Wolcot, John, 'Peter Pindar' (1738–1819), VI. 102; X. 479; XI. 391, 393, 439; XII. 7, 120
  Bozzy and Piozzi, XI. 38
  Instructions to a celebrated Laureat, XI. 38
  Ode upon Ode, XI. 37
  The Lousiad, XI. 37
Wolf, Friedrich August, XII. 28, 300; *Prolegomena ad Homerum*, XII. 301
Wolf, L., XIII. 545
Wolfe, Charles (1791–1823), XII. 424; *Remains*, XII. 138; *The Burial of Sir John Moore*, XII. 122, 138; *To Mary*, XII. 138
Wolfe, Jer., IV. 437
Wolfe, John (d. 1601), IV. 386; IX. 362
Wolfe, lieut.-gen., in *The Virginians*, XIII. 297
Wolfe, Reyner or Reginald (d. 1573), III. 318, 319; IV. 400
Wolfenbüttel, IV. 429
Wolfram, Beddoes's *Dirge* for, XII. 116
Wolfram von Eschenbach, I. 268, 269, 271, 289, 294
Wollaston, Sir John (d. 1596), VII. 354
Wollaston, William (1660–1724), IX. 294, 505, 509; *Religion of Nature Delineated*, IX. 299
Wollaston, William Hyde (1766–1828), XIV. 557, 558
Wollstonecraft, Mary. *See* Godwin, Mrs Mary Wollstonecraft
Wolseley, Sir Charles (1630?–1714), VIII. 210
Wolseley, Garnet Joseph Wolseley, viscount (1833–1913), XIV. 507; *Life of Marlborough*, XIV. 89
Wolseley, Robert (1649–1697), VIII. 163
Wolsey, in *Henry VIII*, V. 195
Wolsey, in *When you see me, You know me*, V. 333

Wolsey, Thomas (1475?–1530), cardinal, II. 358; III. 7, 26, 28, 37, 41, 52, 53, 57, 69, 75, 76 ff., 80, 197, 316, 317, 368, 429; IV. 227, 314, 428; V. 58, 102; VI. 256, 298; VII. 4; VIII. 65; X. 169; XIV. 100, 487
Wolston, near Coventry, III. 382
Wolter, Charlotte, V. 306
Wolverhampton, viscount. *See* Fowler, Sir H. H.
Wolzogen, E. L. von, XIII. 561
Woman, A Song on, I. 362
Woman Loved not Loving, the, in Heywood's *Love*, V. 93
Woman of Samaria, I. 225, 226, 458
Women, controversy on, VII. 513
Women, satires on, Medieval, English and French, III. 88 ff., 485 ff.
Wonderful News from the North, VII. 375
Wonders of Creation, The, I. 428
Wonders of the East, I. 135
Wood, Adam, VII. 513
Wood, Anthony à (1632–1695), I. 199; II. 224; III. 51, 176, 199, 318, 328, 330, 419; IV. 19, 51, 198, 244, 247, 251, 427; V. 256; VI. 29, 38, 50, 196, 197, 294; VII. 15, 16, 23, 24, 38, 42, 43, 84, 160, 317, 345, 359, 363 ff., *also see* Add.; VIII. 39, 292, 301, 360; IX. 267, 341, 342, 344 ff. (main entry), 381 ff., 391, 411, 413, 530, 535, 538, 541, 573
Antiquities of the City of Oxford, IX. 346, 354
Athenae Oxonienses, IX. 345, 347, 350, 351, 353, 356
Fasti, IX. 342, 344, 345
Historia...Universitatis Oxoniensis, IX. 346 ff.; XI. 341
Life and Times (*Autobiography*), IX. 341, 345, 348
Wood, Butler, XIII. 554, *also see* Add. 3
Wood, Charles W., XIII. 567
Wood, Mrs Henry (1814–1887), XIII. 430, 567
Wood, John Turtle (d. *c.* 1888), XII. 514
Wood, Lucky, IX. 366
Wood, Mary Anne Everett. *See* Green, Mary Anne Everett
Wood, Robert (1717?–1771), XIV. 554
Wood, Robin à, V. 35
Wood, T. M., XIII. 562
Wood, William (1671–1730), IX. 98, 115, 123, 457, 459, 463
Woo'd and Married and a', XI. 231
Woodberry, George Edward, XII. 399, 400, 405; XIII. 495
Woodbridge, Suffolk, XI. 140; XII. 198; XIII. 142, 143
Woodcock, captain, VII. 105
Woodcock, Catherine (d. 1658), VII. 105
Woodes, Nathaniel, V. 393
Woodfall, George (1767–1844), XIV. 535
Woodfall, Henry Sampson (1739–1805), X. 400, 401, 407, 408, 525, 526; XIV. 186, 535
Woodfall, William (1746–1803), XIV. 186, 535
Woodford, Samuel (1636–1700), VII. 109; VIII. 238, 447
Woodford Bridge, Essex, X. 386
Woodhouse, Emma, in Jane Austen's *Emma*, XII. 239, 243
Woodhouse, James (1735–1820), XII. 424
Woodhouse, John (*fl.* 1676), X. 386
Woodhouse, Mr, in Jane Austen's *Emma*, XII. 240
Woodhouse, Peter (*fl.* 1605), IV. 519
Woodhouse, Robert (1773–1827), XIV. 258
Woodhouselee, lord. *See* Tytler, A. F.
Woodlarke, Robert (d. 1479), II. 358
Woodroffe, Thomas (*fl.* 1678), VIII. 269
Woods, Benjamin (d. 1596), IV. 98
Woods, Julian Edmund Tenison (1832–1889), XIV. 588; *A History of the Discovery and Exploration of Australia*, XIV. 371
Woodside, David, XIV. 470
Woodstock, II. 159; VI. 299, 323
Woodville or Wodville or Wydville, Anthony, baron Scales and 2nd earl Rivers (1442?–1483), II. 303, 499
Books translated by: *Cordyale, or the Four last things*, II. 313; *Dictes and Sayings of the Philosophers*, II. 313, 427; III. 289, 290; *Moral Proverbs of Christine de Pisan, The*, II. 313
Woodville, Elizabeth (1437?–1492), II. 358
Woodward, Account of the sickness and death of Dr, IX. 132
Woodward, George Moutard (1760?–1809), XI. 453
Woodward, Henry (1714–1777), X. 212; XI. 257
Woodward, Joan (married Edward Alleyn), VI. 250
Woodward, John (1665–1728), VIII. 479; IX. 129, 132, 467, 470; XIV. 284, 291, 565
Woodward, Josiah, IX. 523
Woodward family, the, IV. 216
Wooing of Robin and Joan, IX. 364
Wooler, Miss, XIII. 405
Wooley, Francis, IV. 202
Wooll, John, *Memoirs of Warton*, X. 164, 493
Woolman, John (1720–1772), VIII. 14; X. 520
Woolner, Thomas (1825–1892), XIII. 38, 110, 511; *My Beautiful Lady*, XIII. 111, 189; *Of my Lady in Death*, XIII. 111
Woolnoth, *The Coffee Scuffle*, VII. 516
Woolsey, Mr, in Thackeray's *The Ravenswing*, XIII. 281
Woolston, Thomas (1670–1733), IX. 288, 509; X. 358; *Discourses*, IX. 294
Woolwich, II. 158; VII. 23; XIV. 415
Wootton, IX. 243
Wootton, John (1668?–1765), IX. 162
Worcester, II. 2, 49, 57; IV. 409, 418; V. 168; VI. 241; VII. 45, 254, 255; VIII. 60; IX. 194, 196, 329, 330, 530, 540; XI. 344; XIII. 430; XIV. 100

Worcester. *See* Florence of
Worcester, annals of, I. 178
Worcester, battle of, VII. 225, 250, 254; VIII. 206, 246
Worcester, earls of. *See* Somerset, Edward; Tiptoft, John
Worcester, marquises of. *See* Somerset, Edward; Somerset, Henry
Worcester, or Botoner, William (1415–1482?), II. 499
Worcester copy of *Pastoral Care*, I. 93
Worcester or Evesham Chronicle, I. 109 ff. See, also, under *Chronicle*
Worcester's company, earl of, VI. 97, 100, 250, 254
Worcestershire, IV. 547; VI. 316; X. 113, 149; XII. 350
Word to the Wise, play, X. 465
Worde, Wynkyn de (d. 1534?), II. 224, 300, 311, 312, 315, 319, 322 ff., 329, 393, 428; III. 56, 95, 98, 482, 483, 486, 489, 491; IV. 226, 227, 369, 400, 427
Wordsworth, Anne (born Cookson), XI. 95
Wordsworth, Charles, XIV. 598
Wordsworth, Christopher (1774–1846), XII. 329; XIV. 508, 593
Wordsworth, Christopher (1807–1885), bishop of Lincoln, XI. 95, 411; XII. 340, 495; *Scholae Academicae*, IX. 411, 573, 574
Wordsworth, Dorothy (1804–1847), XI. 95, 99, 102, 103, 409 ff., 416, 442; XII. 193, 194
Wordsworth, John, brother of the poet, XI. 95, 103, 105
Wordsworth, John (1843–1911), XII. 496
Wordsworth, Mary, XI. 103
Wordsworth, William (1770–1850), I. 170, 246, 358; II. 208; III. 221, 297; IV. 45, 49, 132, 136, 195; VII. 42, 115, 137, 181, 185, *also see* Add.; IX. 69, 168, 169, 277, 450; X. 125, 133, 145, 186, 217, 234; XI. 26 ff., 31, 77, 83, 86, 93 ff. (main entry), 117, 120 ff., 126, 129, 131, 135, 149, 150, 152, 162, 198, 201, 202, 248, 309, 341, 405, 413, 416, 417, 420, 432, 442, *also see* Add.; XII. 39, 44, 57 ff., 61, 63, 77, 81, 93, 94, 100, 101, 106, 107, 110, 112 ff., 118, 119, 126, 139, 147, 158, 162, 166, 170, 174, 176, 177, 179, 181, 188, 192, 200, 201, 205, 208, 213, 214, 218, 219, 255, 266, 392, 397, 402, 403, 407, 433, 524, 527; XIII. 7, 9, 23 ff., 29, 34, 38, 43, 44, 46, 49, 50, 52, 57, 63, 69, 71, 91, 93, 94, 97, 136, 158, 168, 169, 171, 173, 186, 188, 191 ff., 195, 196, 198, 200, 219, 228, 230, 232, 236, 250, 258, 429, 431, 442; XIV. 15, 184, 187, 255, 278, 327, 346, 350, 363, 373, 399, 404
  Affliction of Margaret, XI. 110
  Apology for the French Revolution, XI. 24
  Borderers, The, XI. 98, 100; XIII. 418
  Cintra, tract on, XI. Add.
  Composed after a journey across the Hambleton hills, X. 102
Wordsworth, William
  Composed upon an Evening, XI. 108
  Convention of Cintra, XI. 27, 103
  Descriptive Sketches, XI. 97
  Ecclesiastical Sonnets, XI. 108
  Essay, X. 97
  Evening Walk, An, XI. 97
  Excursion, The, III. 178; IV. 137, 191; XI. 85, 99, 100, 102, 103, 105, 106, 113, 116; XII. 59, 79, 146, 193; XIV. 382, 395, 403
  Extempore Effusion on the Death of James Hogg, XII. 95
  Fountain, The, XI. 110
  Goody Blake, XI. 101
  Green Linnet, The, XI. 110
  Guilt or Sorrow, XI. 98
  Incidents on Salisbury Plain, XI. 98, 100
  Laodamia, XI. 107, 116; XIII. 90
  Leech-Gatherer, XI. 104
  Lucy, XI. 110, 113
  Lyrical Ballads, XI. 86, 101, 123, 150, 151; XII. 40, 42
  Michael, XI. 105, 113, 116
  Nutting, XI. 112
  Ode on Intimations of Immortality, III. 221; VII. 41; XI. 102; XII. 84; XIII. 230
  Ode to Duty, XI. 104, 105
  Peter Bell, X. 129; XI. 132; XII. 70
  Prelude, The, XI. 85, 95 ff., 100, 102, 104, 113, 116, 123; XII. 83; XIV. 351, 394, 395, 403
  Recluse, The, XI. 100 ff.
  River Duddon, XI. 108
  Ruined Cottage, The, XI. 99, 105, 109, 116
  Simon Lee, XI. 101, 114
  Skating-scene, XI. 112
  Story of Margaret, XI. 99
  There was a Boy, XI. 111
  Thorn, The, XI. 132
  Tintern Abbey, X. 102; XI. 85, 101, 113; XII. 80; XIV. 351
  Two April Mornings, XI. 110
  Venetian Republic, On the extinction of the, XII. 46
  White Doe of Rylstone, XI. 106
  Yew-trees, XI. 110
Wordsworth, William, Jnr, XI. 405
Wordsworth society, XI. 406
Wordsworths, the, XII. 445
Work for Chimney-sweepers, IV. 530
Worke for Cutlers, VI. 487
Workers' Educational association, XIV. 409
Working Men's association, XIII. 357
Working Men's college, XIV. 408, 409
Working Parson, A (Charles Kingsley), XIII. 358
Works of the Learned, IX. 83, 136
Work-well, in *Piers the Plowman*, II. 19
World, The, X. 171, 173, 253; XI. 324; XIV. 200, 231
World, the, in *Mirour de l'Omme*, II. 140

World, the (Mydlerd, a mirror called), in *Piers the Plowman*, II. 25
World and the Child, The, II. 233; V. 54, 392
World Displayed, The, XIV. 554
World in Miniature, The, XIV. 221
'World is full of care..., The,' VII. 460
Worldly Shame, in *Nice Wanton*, V. 110
Worldly Wiseman, in Bunyan's *Pilgrim's Progress*, VII. 173
Wormius, Olaus, X. 223, 238; *Literatura Runica*, X. 224
Worms, I. 33; II. 330; III. 7, 42
Worrall, John, *Bibliotheca Legum* (1736), VIII. Add.
Worseley, Ralph (*fl.* 1553), VI. 481
Worsfold, William Basil, XIII. 488
Worsley, Philip Stanhope (1835–1866), XII. 334, 482; XIII. 175, 511
Worth, Richard Nicholls (1837–1896), XII. 514
Worthies, the Nine, in *The Parlement of the Thre Ages*, II. 37
Worthington, John (1618–1671), VII. 310, 477, 478, 490; VIII. 273, 281, 285, 286, 288, 455, 457, 458
Worthy, in Vanbrugh's *Relapse*, XI. 268
Wortley, Anne, IX. 248
Wortley, lady Emmeline Stuart (1806–1855), XIII. 511
Wortley, Sir Francis (1591–1652), VII. 495, 499; *A Loyall Song*, VII. 388
Wotton, Surrey, VIII. 242, 244, 245, 354
Wotton, Sir Henry (1568–1639), III. 425, 426, 428, 554; IV. 119, 124, 163, 198 ff., 215, 216, 218, 265, 297, 484; V. 482; VI. 219, 256, 269; VII. 99, 113, 188, 191, 205, 250, 252, 308, 343, 437, 442, 463; IX. 167, 170, 187; XIV. 178
  Characters of Essex and Buckingham, VII. 192
  Courtlie Controversie of Cupid's Cautels, V. 161
  History of Venice, VII. 192
  'How happy is he born and taught,' IV. 126
  Life and Death of Essex, VII. 192
  Panegyrick of King Charles (in Latin), VII. 192, 513
  Reliquiae Wottonianae, IV. 164; VII. 192
  Some Observations by Way of Parallel, VII. 192
  State of Christendom, The, VII. 192
  Tancredo, IV. 164
  'You meaner beauties,' IV. 163
Wotton, Henry, *Essay on the Education of Children* (1672), IX. 382, 569
Wotton, John, IV. 117; *Damaetas' Jig in praise of his love*, IV. 119; 'Jolly Shepherd,' IV. 119
Wotton, Thomas, IV. 406
Wotton, William (1666–1727), IX. 93, 103, 332, 382, 465, 524, 530, 572; *Reflections*, IX. 391
Wotton-under-edge, VIII. 83
Woty, William (1731?–1791), X. 183, 469; XI. 172, 426, 431
Would Be, lady, in *Volpone*, VI. 9; VII. 274
Wowing of Jok and Jynny, The, II. 273, 274
Wrage, E., XIII. 570
Wragge, captain, in Wilkie Collins's *No Name*, XIII. 437
Wrath, in *Piers the Plowman*, II. 12, 23
Wratislaw, Albert Henry, XIV. 598
Wratislaw, Theodore, XIII. 495
Wraxall, Sir Frederick Charles Lascelles, 3rd baronet (1828–1865), XIII. 567
Wraxall, Sir Nathaniel William, 1st baronet (1751–1831), XI. 396; XIV. 508
Wrayburne, Eugene, in *Our Mutual Friend*, XIII. 336
Wreittoun, John, IV. 413
Wrekin, the, IV. 190; VIII. 171
Wren, Sir Christopher (1632–1723), IV. 427; V. 481; VIII. 250, 364; IX. 331; XIV. 281
Wren, Matthew (1629–1672), VII. 476
Wrenn, Christopher, VI. 481
Wrest, Beds., VIII. 60
Wretchedness of this World, Of the, III. 181
Wright, Abraham (1611–1690), *Five Sermons*, VII. 160, 427
Wright, Edward (1558?–1615), IV. 462
Wright, James (1643–1713), *Historia Histrionica*, VI. 408, 499; VIII. 115, 424; *History of Rutland*, IX. 353, 533, 541
Wright, John (*fl.* 1609), IV. 394
Wright, John (1805–1843?), XII. 424
Wright, John Martin Frederick, XIV. 595
Wright, Joseph, *Country Conversations* (1694), VIII. 163, 434
Wright, Leonard (*fl.* 1591), *Friendly Admonition to Martin Marprelate*, III. 397, 539
Wright, Thomas (1810–1877), I. viii, 351, 361; II. 35 ff., 39, 40, 47, 166, 420 ff., 424, 426; III. 91; XII. 347, 353, 365, 514; XIII. 366; XIV. 523, 541
  Anecdota Literaria, XII. 354
  Biographia Literaria of the Anglo-Saxon period, XII. 354
  Early English Poetry, XII. 354
  Original Letters, XII. 354
  The Glory of God's Revenge against Murther and Adultery, VIII. 194
Wright, William (1830–1889), XII. 342, 499
Wright, William, D.D., XIII. 559
Wright, William Aldis (1831–1914), I. 337; V. 280; XII. 331, 341, 493, 502; XIII. 497
Wright's Chaste Wife, The, II. 504
Wrington, Somerset, VIII. 328
Wriothesley, Charles (1508?–1562), III. 478, 532
Wriothesley, Henry, 3rd earl of Southampton (1573–1624), IV. 390; V. 169, 171, 174, 223, 225, 229, 346, 347, 370; VI. 272; VII. 447
Wrong, in *Piers the Plowman*, II. 4, 32
Wroth, lady Mary (*fl.* 1621), *Urania*, III. 355
Wroth, Sir Thomas (1584–1672), IV. 520

Wroxeter, XII. 347
Wudga, in *Widsith*, I. 35
Wulff, Peter, V. 307
Wulfgeat, Aelfric's English letter to, I. 126
Wulfmaer, I. 144
Wulfsige, I. 124, 127
Wulfstan, archbishop of York (d. 1023), I. 5, 124, 125, 127, 128 ff., 134, 145
Wulfstan, St (1012?–1095), bishop of Worcester, I. 164
Wulfstan, voyage of, I. 94
Wulfstan of Winchester (*fl.* 1000), I. 125, 441, 442
Wülker, R., I. ix, 50, 102, 106
Wünn, A., XIII. 546
Würzburg, VII. 20
Wyatt, Alfred John, I. Add.; XIII. 127, 492
Wyatt, Sir Francis (1575?–1644), VII. 50
Wyatt, Sir Thomas (1503?–1542), II. 213, 218, 389; III. 23, 24, 166 ff., 201, 210, 212, 227, 247 ff., 281 ff., 285, 287, 297, 298, 302, 303, 447, 511, *also see* Add.; IV. 24, 25, 108, 110, 116, 118, 196, 197, 329; VII. 1; VIII. 222; X. 131; XIII. 253
Comparison of love to a streame, III. 172
Complaint upon Love to Reason, III. 187
Courtiers life, Of the, III. 173
Forget not yet the tried intent, III. 172
Furious goone, The, III. 187
Galley charged with forgetfulnesse, My, III. 171
How by a kisse he found both his life and death, III. 172
How oft have I, III. 169
How to use the court and him selfe therin, III. 173
Love called Anna, Of his, III. 168
Love, Fortune, and my minde, III. 170
Love to Skorn, My, III. 171
Lover compareth his hart to the overcharged gonne, The, III. 172
Lover professeth himself constant, The, III. 173
Madame, withouten many wordes, III. 172
Meane and sure estate, Of the, III. 173
Psalm 37, III. 174
Some Fowles there be, III. 169
Though I myself be bridled of my mind, III. 168
Unstable dream, III. 170
Was never file, III. 169
What should I say! III. 172
Whoso list to hunt, III. 167
Wiat, being in prison, to Brian, III. 173
Yet was I never of your love agreved, III. 171
Wyche, Sir Peter (d. 1643), VIII. 369
Wycherley, William (1640?–1716), VIII. 133, 142 ff. (main entry), 165, 214, 215, 386, 421, 423, 427; IX. 68, 84, 443, 473; X. 67, 89, 425, 433; XI. 319; XII. 443
Country Wife, The, VIII. 134, 144, 145, 168; XI. 268
Gentleman Dancing-master, The, VIII. 131, 144
Love in a Wood, VIII. 143, 144
Wycherley, William
Plain Dealer, The, VIII. 134, 143, 145, 422; XI. 269
Wychwood, XIII. 93
Wyclif, John (1320?–1384), I. 204, 211, 213, 332, 367, 371, 400; II. 41, 43 ff., 73, 74, 77, 85, 285, 287, 299, 351, 355, 358, 439 ff.; III. 25, 39, 69, 105, 441, 442; IV. 38, 39, 46, 273, 428; V. 51; VI. 374; XII. 517
Cruciata, II. 56
De Benedicat Incarnacione, II. 53, 64, 66
De Civili Dominio, II. 49, 54
De Composicione Hominis, II. 53
De Ecclesia, II. 54
De Ente Predicamentali, II. 53
De Logica, II. 53
De Materia et Forma, II. 53
De Veritate Sacrae Scripturae, II. 56, 58, 59
Determinatio, II. 54
Dialogus, II. 65
Opus Evangelicum, II. 61, 65
Trialogus, II. 65, 66
Wyclif society, II. 49; XII. 355, 504
Wycliffe-on-Tees, II. 49
Wycliffite versions, *Old Testament*, II. 300, 335, 430, 431, 440
Wye, river, VIII. 140; IX. 258; X. 134, 277; XII. 414
Wyer, Robert (*fl.* 1529–1556), IV. 546
Wyeth, Joseph (1663–1731), VIII. 415
Wyf of Auchtirmuchty, The, II. 273; XI. 243
Wygar, the smith, maker of Arthur's corslet, in Layamon, I. 236, 265
Wykeham, William of (1324–1404), bishop of Winchester, II. 355 ff., 506; VII. 326
Wykehamist, The, XIV. 539
Wykes, Thomas, of Osney (*fl.* 1258–1293), I. 182, 451
Wyl Bucke his testament, III. 482, 483
Wyld, Henry Cecil, XIV. 611
Wylie, James Hamilton (1844–1914), XIV. 500; *History of the Reign of Henry V*, XIV. 83
Wylie, William Howie, XIII. 473
Wylie Beguylie, VI. 300
Wylie Wife of the Hie Toun Hie, The, II. 413
Wylkin, John, IV. 435
Wylkinson, John, IV. 5
Wyll of the Devyll, The, III. 86, 484; VII. 382
Wyman, Charles William Henry, XIV. 535
Wymond, in *Rauf Coilȝear*, II. 125, 126
Wyndham, George, XIII. Add. 2
Wyndham, Henry Penruddocke (1736–1819), IX. 254, 497
Wyndham, Henry Saxe, XIII. 515
Wyndham, Sir William, 3rd baronet (1687–1740), IX. 252
Wynken, in Drayton's *Idea*, IV. 172
Wynn, Charles Watkin Williams (1775–1850), XI. 154, 170; XIII. 226, 227, 232
Wynne, Arnold, XIII. 515

Wynne, John (1667–1743), viii. 331, 476
Wynne, Luttrell, viii. 241
Wynne, Sir Richard (d. 1649), vii. 455
Wynnere and Wastoure, i. 333, 334; ii. 35 ff., 432, 434
Wynnstay, x. 115
Wyntoun, Andrew of (1350?–1420?), ii. 103, 104, 117, 121, 122, 129–132 (main entry), 452; *Orygynale Cronykil*, i. 333; ii. 91, 115, 239, 280, 452; xii. 517
Wyrd, i. 41
Wyrley, William (1565–1618), iv. 376, 543
Wyse, Henry T., xiv. 536
Wyse, Sir Thomas (1791–1862), xiv. 610
Wyss, J D., *The Swiss Family Robinson*, xi. 492
Wytfliet, iv. 101

Xanthian marbles, xii. 339
Xenophon, iii. 426, 429; iv. 5, 259, 440, 441, 543; ix. 204, 529; xi. 358; xii. 313, 332, 339, 484, 485; *Cyropaedia*, iii. 426; iv. 4; vii. 316
Xylander Gulielmus, iv. 249
Xystus, Betuleius, vi. 486

Yagoube, xiv. 248
Yahoos, in *Gulliver's Travels*, ix. 105
Yalden, Thomas (1670–1737), ix. 174, 176, 188, 487; x. 183; *Hymn to Darkness*, ix. 176
Yarico, in Colman's *Inkle and Yarico*, xi. 280
Yarington, Robert (*fl.* 1601), v. 325, 476; vi. 96; *Two Lamentable Tragedies*, v. 324 ff., 328, 332; vi. 96
Yarmouth, iii. 363; iv. 327; vi. 241; vii. 91; xii. 362
Yarranton, Andrew (1616–1684?), iv. 462
Yarrow, ii. 284; ix. 371; xi. 239, 445
Yarrow ballads, ix. 364
Yates, Edmund Hodgson (1831–1894), xiii. 301, 567; xiv. 200, 535
Yates, James (*fl.* 1582), iv. 472
Yates, James (1789–1871), xii. 515; xiv. 610; *Textrinum Antiquum*, xii. 348
Yates, Mary Ann (1728–1787), x. 264
Yates, Mr, in Jane Austen's *Mansfield Park*, xii. 239
Yates, Richard (1706?–1796), xi. 257
Yates, William Walsh, xiii. 557, 559
Yaxley, John, vi. 307
Ydgrunites, in Butler's *Erewhon*, xiii. 452
Ye Jacobites by Name, ix. 376
Ye Mariners of England, ii. 226
Year Books, viii. 313, 314, 316, 317, 320, 466
Year Books of Edward II, xiv. 81
Yeats, Jack Butler, xiii. 573, *and see* Add. 1
Yeats, William Butler, xi. 433, 434; xii. 405; xiv. 329, 573
Yeddo, iv. 100
Yedingham, ii. 45, 48
Yeldham, Walter (*pseud.* Aliph Cheem), xiv. 580; *Lays of Ind*, xiv. 340
Yellowplush, Charles James, *pseud.* of W. M. Thackeray, xiii. 278 ff., 284
Yelverton, Sir Christopher (1535?–1612), v. 70, 77
Yeo, H., xiv. 532
Ylmandun (Ilmington), i. 126
Yloop, M. (? Pooly), iii. 189
Ynglinga Saga, i. 3, 25, 94
Ynglingatal, i. 25, 26
Yong or Young, Bartholomew (*fl.* 1577–1598), iv. 7, 9, 117, 121, 122, 441, 445, 447, 472
Yonge, Charlotte Mary (1823–1901), xi. 387, 475, 476, 484, 491; xii. 451; xiii. 567; *Heir of Redclyffe, The*, xii. 277; xiii. 120, 435; *Lances of Lynwood*, xiii. 434; *Little Duke, The*, xii. 277
Yonge, James (*fl.* 1423), ii. 301
Yonge, Nicholas (d. 1619), *Musica Transalpina*, iv. 113, 114
Yonge, Philip, bishop of Norwich, xi. 143
Yonge, Walter (1581?–1649), vii. 455
'Yonge Harton' = Haughton, v. 328
Yorick, xiv. 327
Yorick, in *Hamlet*, iii. 456
Yorick, in Sterne's *Tristram Shandy*, x. 50
York, i. 59, 79, 84, 86, 111, 127, 129; ii. 49, 72, 325, 399, 422, 423; iii. 28; iv. 310, 408, 409; vii. 49, 197, 453; ix. 386, 532, 565; x. 47, 360, 362, 421, 425, 450; xi. 312, 341, 347, 351, 366, 373, 469; xii. 510; xiv. 9, 288
York, the Ainsty of, vii. 180
York, Anne Hyde, duchess of (1637–1671), viii. 46, 402
York, cardinal of. *See* Stewart, H. B. M. C.
York, duke of, company of players of, viii. 119, 182
York, duke of, in *Henry VI*, v. 186
York, Edward, 2nd duke of (1373?–1415), *The Master of Game*, ii. 286, 479; iv. 541
York, house of, ii. 297, 298
York, James, duke of. *See* James II
York, school of, i. 5, 84, 87
York Herald, The, xiv. 203
York *Manuale* (1390), ii. 325; (1509), iii. 442
York Mercury, The, xiv. 169
York minster library, iv. 421
York Plays, v. 13, 15, 18, 20, 42, 45 ff., 51, 52, 56, 389, 390, 391
York press, xi. 468
York printers, iv. 547
Yorke, Philip, 1st earl of Hardwicke (1690–1764), ix. 209; x. 295
Yorke, Philip, 2nd earl of Hardwicke (1720–1790), x. 295, 502; *Miscellaneous State Papers*, x. 295
Yorkshire, i. 344, 357; ii. 88, 396, 420; iv. 190; v. 242, 243; vii. 178, 180, 224,

Yorkshire
227, 233, 246, 373; VIII. 220, 271; IX. 91, 140, 330, 393; X. 47, 101, 131, 262, 385, 386; XII. 12, 246, 281, 507, 516; XIII. 275; XIV. 185, 233, 249
Yorkshire dales, XI. 168
Yorkshire dialect, XII. 415
Yorkshire Library, the, XII. 519
Yorkshire Tragedy, A, IV. 394; V. 236, 238, 242, 243, 332, 442, 444; VI. 95; X. 73
Yorkshire United college, X. 385
Youghal, II. 303; IV. 60; VIII. 146
Youll, Henry (*fl.* 1608), IV. 465
Young, Arthur (1741–1820), XI. 400; XIV. 554, 565
Annals of Agriculture, XI. 72, 397
Political Arithmetic, XI. 73
Tour in Ireland, XI. 73
Travels in France, XI. 73
War in North America, The, XI. 72
Young, A. B., XI. 462
Young, Bartholomew (*fl.* 1577–1598), VI. 365; *Amorous Fiammetta* (trans. from Boccaccio), IV. 7
Young, Edward (1683–1765), V. 297; IX. 82, 188, 190, 250, 254, 439, 449, 460, 481; X. 1, 138 ff. (main entry), 156, 183, 458, *also see* Add.; XI. 140, 250, 251; XIII. 552
Brothers, The, X. 140
Busiris, X. 73, 83, 139
Complaint (The), or Night Thoughts. See *Night Thoughts*
Imperium Pelagi, X. 140, 141
Job, X. 139, 142
Last Day, The, X. 142
Letters to Tickell, X. 139
Night Thoughts, VIII. 380; X. 124, 141 ff., 147; XI. 323
Ocean, X. 140, 141
Resignation, X. 140, 142
Revenge, The, X. 73, 139
Universal Passion, The, X. 139, 140, 142
Young, Elizabeth, X. 95
Young, George (1777–1848), XI. 429
Young, James (1811–1883), XII. 519
Young, John (1534?–1605), bishop of Rochester, III. 214
Young, John (1750?–1820), X. 475; *A Criticism on the Elegy written in a Country Churchyard*, X. 188
Young, Patrick (1584–1652), VII. 316, 482, 483, 485, 489; IX. 530
Young, Sir Peter (1544–1628), IX. 530
Young, Richard, *A short and sure way to Grace*, XI. 334; *The Seduced Soul reduced*, XI. 334
Young, Robert (*fl.* 1663), IX. 547
Young, Thomas (1587–1655), VII. 96, 98, 416
Young, Thomas (1773–1829), XIV. 259, 557
Young, William, X. 25
Young, William Thomas, XII. Add. 2
Young Beichan, II. 411
Young England' movement, IX. 231
Young Hunting, II. 412
Young Ireland party, XIV. 311, 317, 320, 321, 324, 357
Young Lochinvar, II. 411
Young Man's Calling, XI. 369
Younge, Richard (*fl.* 1637–1671), VII. 514
Younger, John (1785–1860), XII. 424
Younger, W., *A brief View, etc.*, VII. 355
Youth, in *Confessio Amantis*, II. 148
Youth, in Henryson, II. 249
Youth, in Lydgate's *Pilgrimage*, II. 201
Youth, in *Piers the Plowman*, II. 22
Youth (renamed Virtue), in *The Example of Virtue*, II. 227, 234
Youth, in *The Parlement of the Thre Ages*, II. 37
Youth (interlude), V. 54, 393
Ypocras, daughter of, II. 79
Ypotis, Meditations of Chylde, I. 286, 472; II. 308
Ysopet, VIII. 59
Yspadaden Pen Kawr, I. 254
Ystorya Brenhined y Brytanyeit, I. 263
Yucatan, XIV. 241
Yule, XIV. 574
Yule, Alfred, in Gissing's *New Grub Street*, XIII. 460
Yuletide carols, II. 379
Yuste, X. 289
Yver, Jacques, *Le Printemps d'Iver*, V. 161, 252
Ywain and Gawain, and *Sir Ywain*, I. 279, 280, 282, 284, 288, 312, 468

Zabeta, III. 207
Zacher, J., 425
Zadkiel, VII. 511
Zama, XII. 303
Zampini-Salazar, F., XIII. 485
Zanga, in Young's *The Revenge*, X. 73
Zanoni (lord Lytton's), XIII. 419
Zanzibar, IV. 85
Zara, in Congreve's *Mourning Bride*, VIII. 152
Zárate, Augustin de, IV. 448
Zarina, in Byron's *Sardanapalus*, XII. 49
Zaripha, in *The Travailes of The three English Brothers*, VI. 69
Zeal, in *The Playe of Playes and Pastimes*, VI. 391
Zeal-of-the-land Busy, in *Bartholomew Fayre*, VI. 23, 28; VIII. 147
Zechariah, V. 48
Zedlitz, K. A. von, XIV. 382
Zelauto (Munday's), III. 349
Zelmane, in Sidney's *Arcadia*, III. 352
Zelotypus, VI. 487
Zend language, XII. 343
Zenocia, in *The Custome of the Countrey*, VI. 131
Zenocrate, in *Tamburlaine*, V. 150
Zepheria, III. 256, 266, 524
Zerbst, V. 48
Zermat, U., I. 443
Zetha, in *Jacob and Esau*, V. 111
Zeuner, R., I. 444
Zeuss, J. C., I. 34, 421

Ziegler, H., I. 429
Zimmer, Heinrich, I. 65, 68, 70, 269, 464; XIV. 302; *Nennius Vindicatus*, I. 246, 464
Zimmermann, O., I. 439
Zimri (Buckingham), in Dryden's *Absalom*, VIII. 39, 41
Zinzendorf, Nicolaus Ludwig, count von, X. 350, 364
Zipangu, IV. 86
Zittau, V. 285
Zoas, the, in Blake's *Vala*, XI. 195
Zoilus, IX. 481
Zoilus, in *Wisdom of Solomon Paraphrased*, VI. 59
Zola, Émile, XI. 152; XII. 55; XIII. 427; *L'Assommoir*, XIII. 425, 522; *Thérèse Raquin*, XIII. 456
Zoological Journal, The, XIV. 565
Zoological Miscellany, The, XIV. 565
Zoological society of London, XIV. 287
Zoologist, The, XIV. 289, 566
Zosimus, IX. 337
Zouch, Henry (1725?–1795), X. 252, 495
Zouche, lord. *See* Curzon, Robert
Zouche, Richard (1590–1661), VI. 481; VIII. 317, 470
Zozimus, XIV. 327
Zulkais, in Beckford's *Episodes*, XI. 292
Zupitza, J., I. ix, I. 426, 429, 432, 442, 445
Zurich, III. 44, 53; IV. 402
Zurich letters, the, III. 415
Zutphen, battle of, III. 351
Zwingli, Huldreich (1484–1531), II. 69; III. 37, 39, 413; IV. 448; VII. 306